Professional VB.NET

Fred Barwell
Richard Blair
Richard Case
Jonathan Crossland
Bill Forgey
Whitney Hankison
Billy S. Hollis
Rockford Lhotka
Tim McCarthy
Jan D. Narkiewicz
Jonathan Pinnock
Rama Ramachandran
Matthew Reynolds
John Roth
Bill Sempf
Bill Sheldon
Scott Short

D1066954

Wrox Press Ltd. ®

Professional VB.NET

wrox

Published by Wrox Press Ltd,
Arden House, 1102 Warwick Road, Acocks Green,
Birmingham, B27 6BH, UK
Printed in the United States
ISBN 1861004974

Trademark Acknowledgements

Wrox has endeavored to provide trademark information about all the companies and products mentioned in this book by the appropriate use of capitals. However, Wrox cannot guarantee the accuracy of this information.

Credits

Authors
Fred Barwell
Richard Blair
Richard Case
Jonathan Crossland
Bill Forgey
Whitney Hankison
Billy S. Hollis
Rockford Lhotka
Tim McCarthy
Jan D. Narkiewicz
Jonathan Pinnock
Rama Ramachandran
Matthew Reynolds
John Roth
Bill Sempf
Bill Sheldon
Scott Short

Technical Architect
Kate Hall

Technical Editors
Victoria Blackburn
Paul Jeffcoat
Gareth Oakley

Author Agents
Sarah Bowers
Avril Corbin
Laura Jones

Project Administrator
Rob Hesketh

Category Managers
Bruce Lawson
Sonia Mullineux

Production Manager
Simon Hardware

Technical Reviewers
Nick Apostolopoulos
Martin Beaulieu
Maxime Bombardier
Billy Cravens
Robin Dewson
David Espinosa
Damien Foggon
Hope Hatfield
Mark Horner
Wilfried Jansoone
Kenneth Lo
Ron Miller
Paul Morris
Gerry O'Brien
Dale Onyon
Troy Proudfoot
Scott Robertson
Sean M. Schade
Larry Schoeneman
Brian Sherwin
Adwait Ullal
Konstantinos Vlassis
Helmut Watson
Thearon Willis
Jonathan Winer
Donald Xie

Production Coordinator
Pip Wonson

Illustrations
Paul Grove

Index
Michael Brinkman
Andrew Criddle

Proof Reader
Keith Westmoreland

Cover
Dawn Chellingworth

About the Authors

Fred Barwell

Fred is an MCSD and a graduate from the University of Waterloo with a Bachelor of Mathematics, Honors Computer Science and Information Systems degree. He has been developing software professionally for over 10 years, primarily with Visual Basic and SQL Server. Fred currently runs his own consulting business, working as a software architect. His experience includes small to large scale, multi-national client server applications, with more recent work involving web site development using the Microsoft DNA model. Fred was recently contracted by Microsoft to aid in the development of a .NET WinForms application to demonstrate many of the new features of the .NET Framework. When not at his computer, he is usually tending to his aquarium or playing baseball. Fred would like to thank Alex Lisitsky, Hao Quach, Ed Musters, Craig McQueen, and Gord Schmidt for their support, and also Mark Boulter from Microsoft for his time and assistance. You can contact Fred at fbarwell@hotmail.com.

Richard Blair

Rich, who has degrees in English and Drama, drifted into the computer industry when he realized he just wasn't that good of a waiter (*the maitre d'hotel never liked me anyway*). So now, he may not be a programmer, but he could play one on TV. He has presented at the 2000 Wrox Developer's conferences with Richard Anderson, and was grateful for the chance to finally justify his education. Rich is currently a consultant specializing in web applications.

> *I would like to thank my Kathy and Graehme for putting up with my late nights. I would also like to thank all of the people at Wrox; they are without a doubt in my mind some of the greatest people to work with.*

Richard Case

Richard is a Financial Analyst Programmer with Financial Objects PLC based in Covent Garden, London, England, where he works on the company's advanced banking software. Richard is also a Microsoft Certified Solutions Developer. He has been using Visual Basic since version 3 and is looking forward to using it for many years to come. Richard can be reached at richard@vbdotnet.co.uk.

> *I'd like to thank Kate, my soon to be wife, for putting up with me while I have been writing the book and the support she has given me. I would also like to thank everyone at Wrox Press for giving me the opportunity to contribute to the book and being so helpful. And last, but not least, I would like to thank my parents for their encouragement throughout my life.*

Jonathan Crossland

Jonathan Crossland is co-author of *Professional Windows DNA* and a Systems Component Architect for Makoot Ltd in the UK. First acting as a promoter for the company and now MD, Jonathan spends a great number of hours with his team, promoting web services. Although occupying various roles in this new company, including marketing and management, Jonathan prefers the designing and architecting of innovative ideas and therefore cannot wait for the company to grow.

Jonathan has worked in the industry for just over 7 years, and works with VB.NET, C#, XML, VB6, and other related technologies.

You can contact him at jonathanc@makoot.com or find a job on his web site www.makoot.com.

Bill Forgey

Bill has several years of consulting experience in software design and development. He has created many applications using ASP, Delphi, Pascal, Visual C++, and Visual Basic. He specializes in n-tier architecture using SQL, ADO, and COM development.

Currently, he is the Technical Lead at a large bank introducing project methodology, new technologies, and training to different development teams throughout the bank. He lives in Sacramento, California and can be contacted via e-mail at bforgey@vbcentral.net.

Thanks goes out to a great team of editors and reviewers at Wrox Press. Finally, special thanks to Sarah Bowers and Kate Hall for making it all possible.

Whitney Hankison

Whitney is a Financial Systems Analyst with the County of Santa Barbara in California. She specializes in VB programming and System Architecture/Network Configuration. She has been working in the computer field since 1984 and holds MCP certifications in NT Server and Workstation. Whitney can be reached at whankison@earthlink.net.

I'd like to thank Wrox Press for the opportunity to write and being wonderful people to work with. I'd also like to thank all of my friends and family who have been so patient with my work load and schedule. I also thank God for His continual help and guidance.

Billy S. Hollis

Billy Hollis first learned BASIC over 25 years ago, and is co-author of the first book ever published on Visual Basic.NET, *VB.NET Programming with the Public Beta*, from Wrox Press. He is a frequent speaker at conferences, including Comdex and the Visual Basic Insiders Technical Summit (VBITS), often on the topics of software design and specification, object-based development in Visual Basic, and Microsoft.NET.

Billy is MSDN Regional Director of Developer Relations in Nashville, Tennessee for Microsoft, and has hosted Developer Days in Nashville for the last three years. He has his own consulting company in Nashville that focuses on training, consultation, and software development for the Microsoft.NET platform.

I need to thank several folks at Microsoft who have provided me with the opportunity to learn more about VB.NET, including Jennifer Ritzinger, Mike Iem, and many others. Thanks also to Tim Landgrave, Ken Spencer, and Keith Pleas for getting me involved in early training and writing projects on .NET. And finally, my family has been supportive as always as I've squeezed in the time to write for this book, often at their expense. Those of us in the software industry love this time of intense innovation, but I'm sure Cindy, Ansel, and Dyson will be happier when things get back to the normal pace of change.

Rockford Lhotka

Rockford Lhotka is co-author of *VB.NET Programming with the Public Beta*, author of *Professional Visual Basic 6 Distributed Objects* and *Visual Basic 6 Business Objects* and is a columnist for Visual Basic Programmers Journal and MSDN Online. He speaks at several major conferences around the world. Rockford is the Principal Technology Evangelist for Magenic Technologies, one of the nation's premiere Microsoft Certified Solution Providers dedicated to solving today's most challenging business problems using 100% Microsoft tools and technology.

Tim McCarthy

Tim McCarthy is a Principal Engineer at InterKnowlogy (www.interknowlogy.com), where he architects and builds highly scalable n-tier web applications utilizing the latest Microsoft technologies. He is a regular speaker at Microsoft Developer Days. Tim is also an instructor at the University of California, San Diego, where he teaches Microsoft developer courses.

Tim's hobbies include spending time with his wife, Miriam, his daughter, Jasmine, and his three step kids, Angie, BD, and Chris. He also loves to workout, drink beer, and lives for Notre Dame football and basketball.

Jan D. Narkiewicz

Jan D. Narkiewicz is Chief Technical Officer at Software Pronto, Inc (jann@softwarepronto.com). Jan began his career as a Microsoft developer thanks to basketball star, Michael Jordan. In the early 90s Jan noticed that no matter what happened during a game, Michael Jordan's team won. Similarly, no matter what happened in technology, Microsoft always won (then again this strategy is ten years old and may need some revamping). Clearly there was a bandwagon to be jumped upon. Over the years Jan managed to work on an e-mail system that resided on 17 million desktops, helped automate factories that make blue jeans you have in your closet (trust me you own this brand) and kept the skies over the Emirate of Abu Dhabi safe from enemy aircraft. All this was achieved using technology such as COM/DCOM, COM+, C++, VB, C#, ADO, SQL Server, Oracle, DB2, ASP.NET, ADO.NET, Java, Linux, and XML. In his spare time, Jan is Academic Coordinator for the Windows curriculum at U.C. Berkeley Extension, teaches at U.C. Santa Cruz Extension, writes for ASPToday, and occasionally plays some football (a.k.a. soccer).

Jonathan Pinnock

Jonathan Pinnock started programming in Pal III assembler on his school's PDP 8/e, with a massive 4K of memory, back in the days before Moore's Law reached the statute books. These days he spends most of his time developing and extending the increasingly successful PlatformOne product set that his company, JPA, markets to the financial services community. JPA's home page is www.jpassoc.co.uk.

He seems to spend the rest of his time writing for Wrox, although he occasionally surfaces to say, "remember me?" to his wife and two children.

My heartfelt thanks go to Gail, who first suggested getting into writing, and now suffers the consequences on a fairly regular basis, and to Mark and Rachel, who just suffer the consequences.

Rama Ramachandran

Rama Ramachandran is Vice President, Technology with Imperium, a Microsoft Gold Certified Partner for e-commerce. He is a Microsoft Certified Solution Developer and Site-Builder, and designs and develops web and e-commerce applications using .NET, ASP/+, COM, Visual Basic, SQL Server, and Windows 2000. Rama co-authored *Introducing.Net*, *Professional ASP Data Access*, and *Professional Visual InterDev 6 Programming* (all from Wrox) as well as four books on Visual Basic from Que Publishing.

Rama is also the ASP Pro at Devx.com where he answers ASP related questions. He teaches Visual Basic and Web Development at Fairfield University as well as at the University of Connecticut. He lives in Stamford, Conn., with his wife Beena and their sons Ashish and Amit. Reach Rama at ramabeena@hotmail.com.

This book is dedicated to my wife Beena and our children – Ashish and Amit. They make my life whole. I'm great at writing about technology, but get tongue-tied trying to say how much I love and care about the three of you. I am grateful to our prayer-answering God for your laughing, mischievous, adoring lives. Thanks for being there, Beens. I love you.

Matthew Reynolds

After working with Wrox Press on a number of projects since 1999, Matthew is now an in-house author for Wrox Press writing about and working with virtually all aspects of Microsoft.NET. He's also a regular contributor to Wrox's ASPToday, C#Today and Web Services Architect. He lives and works in North London and can be reached on matthewr@wrox.com.

For Fanjeev Sarin.

Thanks very much to the following in their support and assistance in writing this book: Len, Edward, Darren, Alex, Jo, Tim, Clare, Martin, Niahm, Tom, Ollie, Amir, Gretchen, Ben, Brandon, Denise, Rob, Waggy, Mark, Elaine, James, Zoe, Faye, and Sarah. And, also thanks to my new friends at Wrox, which include Rob, Charlotte, Laura, Karli, Dom S, Dom L, Ian, Kate, Joy, Pete, Helen, Vickie, John, Dave, Adam, Craig, Jake, Julian, and Paul.

John Roth

John began his career like so many in the industry as "that guy who knows the computer stuff", the one who could whip up a macro as fast as Julia Childs could tuck into a soufflé. Eventually, realizing that he could actually make a living having fun, John started his own company (John Roth Consulting) and he hasn't looked back in the ten years since.

He considers himself fortunate to have been able to fill the role of Senior Developer and Web Developer at Compaq, to teach both students and other instructors at institutions like the University of British Columbia and Douglas College, and to work with many other wonderful clients, big and small. Great people, cool technologies... ask John and he'll tell you, "life really doesn't suck!"

John can be reached by e-mail at john.roth@ispeakgeek.com. He's working on putting a site there he swears! Maybe after he finishes his next book ... yeah, right!

I'd like to dedicate my part of this book to my partner, my best friend, and the love of my life. Andrea, you have no idea how much you mean to me ...

Bill Sempf

Bill Sempf is an experienced Internet strategist with a ten-year track record of using technology to help organizations accomplish specific business objectives. He is completely obsessed with the belief that Web Services are the "next big thing", and he is usually right about stuff like that.

A Microsoft Certified Professional, Certified Internet Business Strategist, and member of the International Webmaster's Association, Bill has built nearly one hundred dynamic webs for startups and Fortune 50 companies alike. He would like to thank his wife Gabrielle for putting up with all of these projects, and ones to follow. Bill can be reached at bill@sempf.net.

Bill Sheldon

Bill is a software developer and aspiring author originally from Baltimore, Maryland. Holding a degree in Computer Science from the Illinois Institute of Technology (IIT), he has managed to work as a software developer since his departure from the U.S. Navy, following the Gulf War. He has held his Microsoft Certified Solution Developer (MCSD) certification for several years, and is currently employed as a Principal Engineer with InterKnowlogy. As a software engineer, Bill designs software solutions and develops business components for extranets, intranets, and the Internet.

He and his wife live in Southern California where they enjoy beautiful weather and a short commute to the office.

This book is dedicated to my loving and wonderful wife Tracie. For putting up with long nights and lost weekends as I dug through software and typed. She is the one who is always there to keep my head on straight and life in some semblance of order. Thanks for putting up with me, Love Always.

And to my parents. There are so many things. Thank you both for the sacrifices made for all of your kids. Thank you for always being there and encouraging us to strive for what interested us, and reminding us we could do anything we set our minds to.

To my Mother, for the late nights spent finishing school papers that I waited until the last minute complete ... A habit I've completely outgrown, well maybe not completely ...

To my Father, for the weekends and nights spent supporting my involvement in scouting, for teaching me to take care of myself and supporting me unconditionally in pursuing my future ... hopefully you'll be able to read more of these in the years to come.

Scott Short

Scott Short is currently a Senior Consultant with Microsoft Consulting Services. He works with a variety of hi-tech companies helping them develop scalable, available, and maintainable e-business applications. Scott has also contributed to other Wrox Press books including *Introducing .NET* and *Professional Windows DNA*. When not working with the latest beta software, authoring books, or presenting at developer conferences, Scott enjoys spending time in the Colorado Rocky Mountains skiing, backpacking, hiking, and rock climbing with his incredibly supportive wife, Suzanne.

I would like to dedicate my contributions to this book to our newest member of the family, my son Colin Patrick Short.

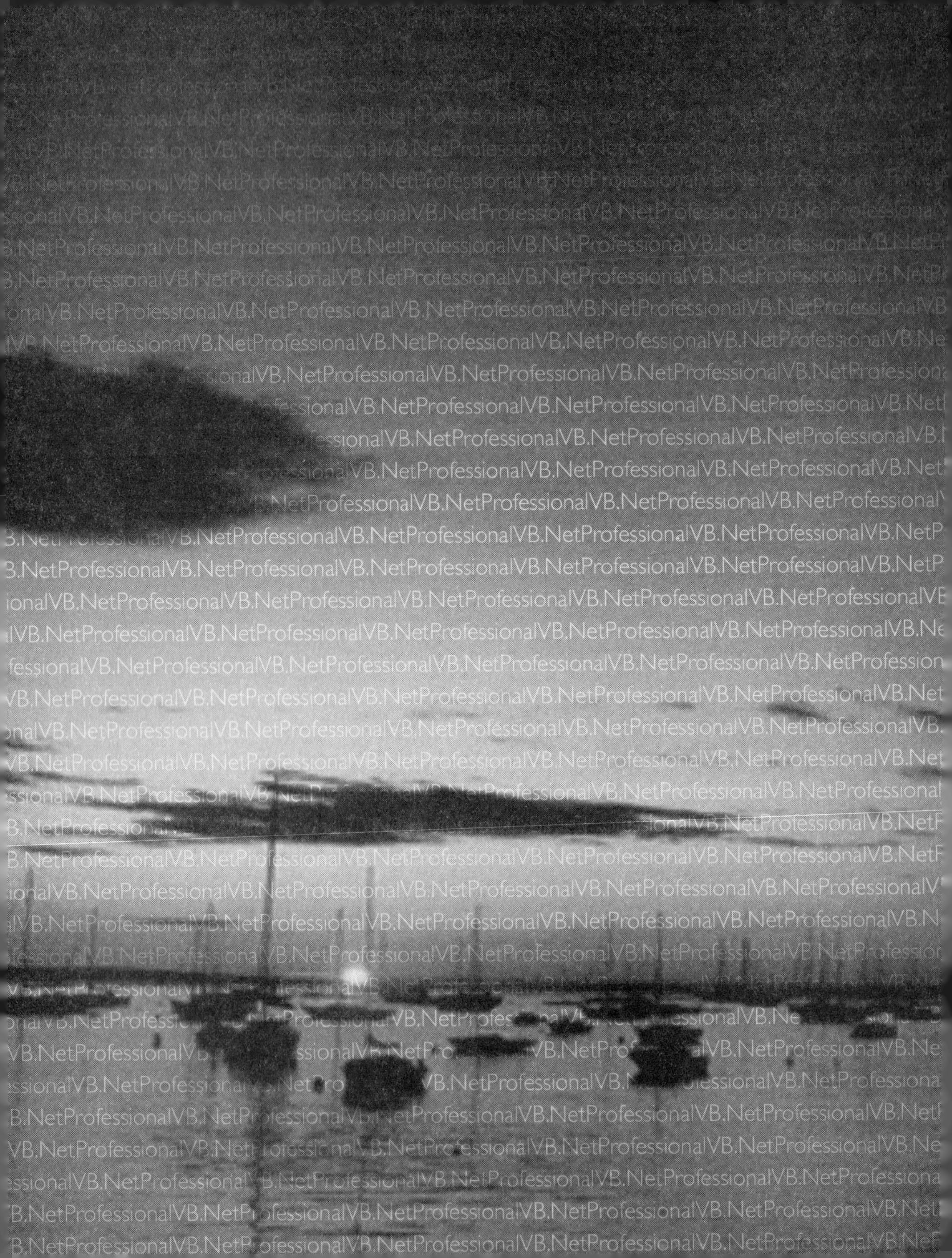
VB.NetProfessional

Table of Contents

Table of Contents

Table of Contents

Table of Contents

Table of Contents

Table of Contents

Table of Contents

Table of Contents

Table of Contents

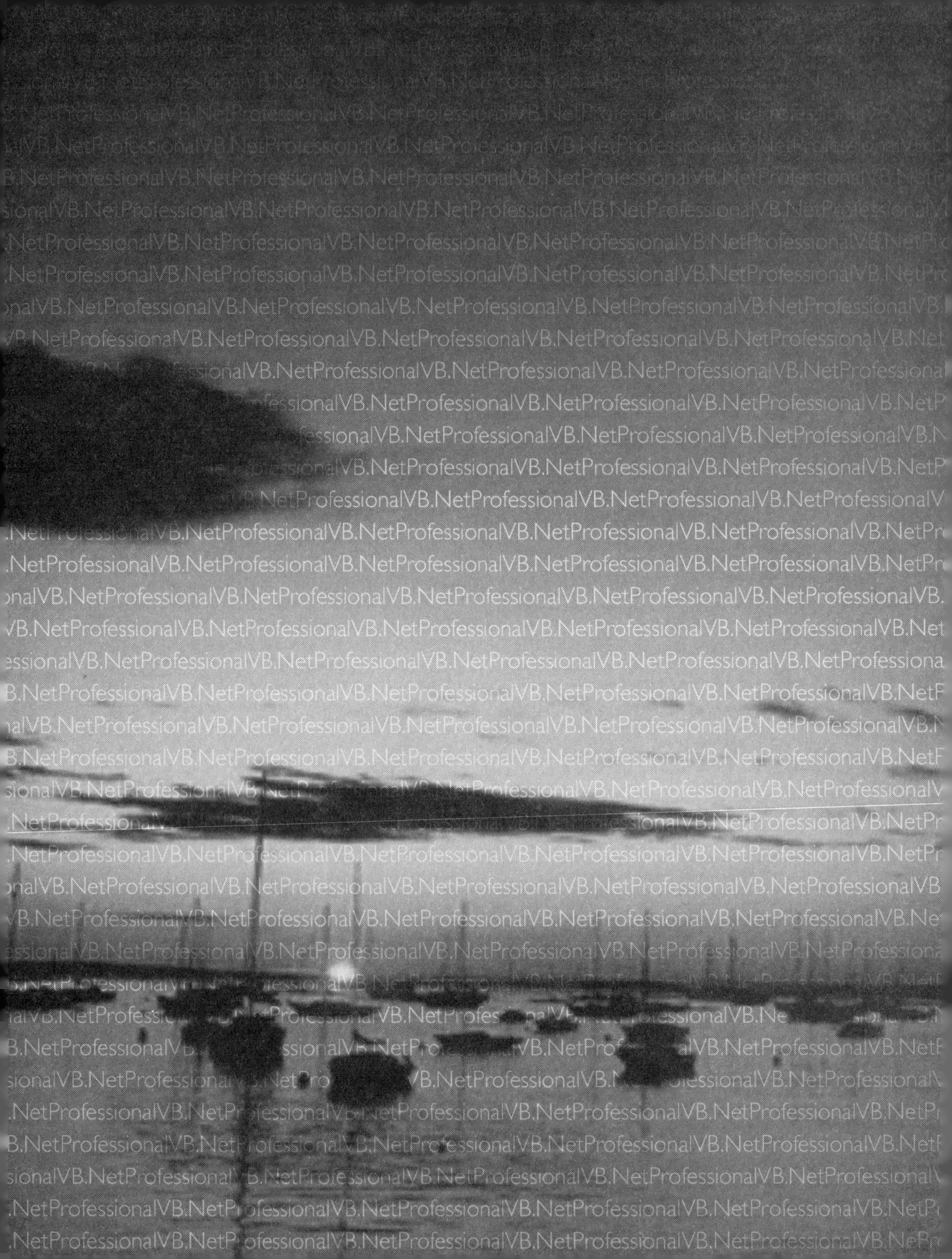
VB.NetProfessional

Introduction

.NET is designed to provide a new environment within which you can develop almost any application to run on Windows, and possibly in the future on other platforms, with VB.NET likely to be the most popular development tool for use with this framework. VB.NET is a .NET compliant language and as such has, except for legacy reasons, almost identical technical functionality as the new language C# and .NET compliant C++. Using VB.NET, a dynamic Web page, a component of a distributed application, a database access component, or a classic Windows desktop application can be developed.

In order to incorporate VB into the .NET Framework, a number of new features have been added to create VB.NET. For the most part, the changes are so extensive that VB.NET could be viewed as a new language rather than just an upgrade. However, these changes were necessary to give developers the features that they have been asking for: true OOP, easier deployment, better interoperability, and a cohesive environment to develop both traditional and Web applications.

In this book, we cover this initial release of VB.NET virtually from start to finish: we begin by looking at the .NET Framework, and end by looking at best practices for creating and deploying Windows and Web Services and the security involved. In between, we look at everything from database access to integration with other technologies such as XML, along with investigating the new features in detail. You will see that VB.NET has emerged as a powerful, yet still easy to use language that will allow you to target the desktop just as easily as the Internet.

Who Is this Book for?

As VB.NET is still under development, this book is primarily aimed at experienced Visual Basic developers. Particularly, it is for those who need to make the transition to VB.NET and want more detailed and up-to-date information than was available in *VB.NET Programming with the Public Beta*. Although the .NET Framework provides a new and powerful way to program for the Internet, this book is not for Web developers, who should instead refer to *Professional ASP.NET*.

What You Need to Use this Book

In order to use this book to the full, you will need either the full product release of the Enterprise or Professional edition of VS.NET or Beta 2. A few chapters require additional software; for example, you will also need SQL Server in order to work through the examples in Chapters 17 and 18. In addition, you will need MSMQ to work with queued transactions in Chapter 17, which is provided along with Windows 2000 Server and Windows 2000 Professional.

What Does this Book Cover?

Chapter 1 begins with attempting to explain the importance of .NET, and just how much it changes application development. To gain an understanding of why we need .NET, what's wrong with current development technologies, including COM and the DNA architectural model will be looked at first followed by how .NET corrects the drawbacks in these technologies will be investigated including the Common Language Runtime (CLR).

Chapter 2 turns to a brief overview of the changes made to Visual Basic because of .NET. It starts with the IDE and then carries on to data and application types, object capabilities, error handling, and other syntax and additional changes.

With Chapter 3, we now turn to our first look at VB.NET. This chapter will only provide a brief practical introduction to creating a VB.NET application, as the topics covered here will be looked at in much more detail in later chapters.

Chapter 4 focuses on the Integrated Development Environment (IDE). The different windows and menu choices that can be manipulated in the IDE will be examined and described. In that context, it will be necessary to look at Windows Forms, Web Forms, and several other technologies that are covered in considerably more detail in other chapters.

Chapter 5 examines the core of the .NET platform, the Common Language Runtime (CLR). The CLR is responsible for managing the execution of code compiled for the .NET platform – covering in particular, versioning and deployment, memory management, cross-language integration, Meta Data, and the IL disassembler.

Chapter 6 will introduce many of the types used in Visual Basic, in particular, the base `Object` class. The main goal of this chapter is to get you familiar with value and reference types and to help those with a background in VB6 understand some of the key differences in how variables are defined in VB.NET.

Namespaces are the subject of Chapter 7. This chapter introduces namespaces and their hierarchical structure. An explanation of namespaces and some common ones are given. In addition, it looks into creating new namespaces, and importing and aliasing namespaces within projects.

Chapter 8 looks at Windows Forms and will concentrate primarily on forms and built-in controls. What is new and what has been changed from previous versions of Visual Basic will be discussed, along with the `System.Windows.Forms` namespace. All of the enhancements to Windows Forms which are now available in VB.NET, and how developers can take advantage of these when either updating existing applications or indeed writing new ones, are included in this chapter.

Chapter 9 covers how error handling works in VB.NET by discussing the CLR exception handler in detail and the new `Try...Catch...Finally` structure. In addition, error handling between managed and unmanaged code, error and trace logging, and how we can use these methods to obtain feedback on how our program is working, will be looked at.

In Chapter 10, we will look at creating Windows controls. In particular, we will discuss how to inherit from another control, build a composite control, and write controls from scratch based on the `Control` class.

Chapter 11 explores the creation and use of classes and objects in VB.NET. This chapter will define objects, classes, instances, encapsulation, abstraction, polymorphism, and inheritance.

Chapter 12 examines inheritance and how it can be used within VB.NET. We will explain the syntax that supports inheritance within VB.NET, creating simple and abstract base classes, how to create the base classes from which other classes can be derived (as well as creating those derived classes), as well as subclassing.

Chapter 13 looks at object-oriented programming in depth, and fully defines the features listed and explores how we can use these concepts. Four major object-oriented concepts (abstraction, encapsulation, polymorphism, inheritance) will be explained, as well as how these concepts can be applied in our design and development to create effective object-oriented applications.

Chapter 14 focuses on assemblies and their use within the CLR. The structure of an assembly, what it contains, and the information it contains will be examined. In addition, the manifest of the assembly and its role in deployment will be looked at.

In Chapter 15, we will learn about threading and see how the various objects in the .NET Framework enable any consumer of it to develop multithreaded applications. We will examine how threads can be created, how they relate to processes, and the differences between multitasking and multithreading.

Chapter 16 discusses COM and .NET component interoperability, and what tools Microsoft has provided to help link the two technologies together. A legacy basic COM object will be run from a VB.NET program as well as running some VB.NET code in the guise of a COM object.

Chapter 17 explores the .NET Component Services, in particular, transaction processing and queued components. Included here is the `RegSvcs` tool, used to register components with Component Services.

Chapter 18 focuses on what you will need to know about the ADO.NET object model in order to be able to build flexible, fast, and scalable data access objects and applications. The evolution of ADO into ADO.NET will be explored and the main objects in ADO.NET that you need to quickly get up and running in order to build data access into your .NET applications will be explained.

Chapter 19 presents the features of the .NET Framework that facilitate the generation and manipulation of XML. This chapter will describe the .NET Framework's XML related namespaces and a subset of the classes exposed by these namespaces will be examined in detail. This chapter will also touch on a set of technologies that utilize XML, specifically ADO.NET and SQL Server.

Chapter 20 explores Web Forms and how you can benefit from their use. Using progressively more complex examples, this chapter explains how you are provided with the power of Rapid Application Development for developing Web applications.

Chapter 21 encompasses an entirely new form of Visual Basic control development, custom Web controls. It looks at the various forms of custom Web control development that are available in the .NET Framework. The basic structure of web user and sub-classed controls will be examined, along with a look at composite and templated controls, and some best practices for control design.

Chapter 22 looks at how to create and consume Web Services using VB.NET. The abstract classes provided by the CLR to set up and work with Web Services will be discussed, as well as some of the technologies supporting Web Services, before covering security in Web Services. Finally, some of the disadvantages to using any distributed architecture and the future with Web Services will be examined.

Chapter 23 examines how VB.NET is used in the production of Windows Services. The creation, installation, running, and debugging of Windows Services will be looked at. Included within this section will be an example of a remoting service and the use of the `InstallUtil.exe` utility.

In Chapter 24, we will look at what Visual Studio.NET and the CLR have to offer us in the way of deployment. This chapter will give an understanding and basic knowledge of the deployment options available.

Chapter 25 examines the additional tools and functionality with regards to security provided by .NET. `Caspol.Exe` and `Permview.exe` will be discussed and how they assist in establishing and maintaining security policies. The `System.Security.Permissions` namespace will be looked at and how it relates to managing permissions. Finally, three types of security – role-based, code access-based, and identity-based – will be examined and we'll see how they relate and how they can be used in the permissions processing sections of code.

Conventions

We have used a number of different styles of text and layout in the book to help differentiate between the different kinds of information. Here are examples of the styles we use and an explanation of what they mean:

Bullets appear indented, with each new bullet marked as follows:

- **Important Words** are in a bold type font
- Words that appear on the screen in menus like the File or Window are in a similar font to the one that you see on screen
- Keys that you press on the keyboard, like *Ctrl* and *Enter*, are in italics
- If you see something like `Object`, you'll know that it's a filename, object name, or function name

Code in a gray box shows new, important, pertinent code:

```
Dim objMyClass as New MyClass("Hello World")

Debug.WriteLine(objMyClass.ToString)
```

Sometimes you'll see code in a mixture of styles, like this:

```
Dim objVar as Object

objVar = Me

CType(objVar, Form).Text = "New Dialog Title Text"
```

The code with a white background is code we've already looked at and that we don't wish to examine further.

Advice, hints, and background information come in an italicized, indented font like this.

> **Important pieces of information come in boxes like this.**

Customer Support

We've tried to make this book as accurate and useful as possible, but what really matters is what the book actually does for you. Please let us know your views, either by returning the reply card at the back of the book, or by writing to us at feedback@wrox.com. Please be sure to mention the book title in your message.

Source Code

The source code for this book is available for download at http://www.wrox.com.

Errata

We've made every effort to ensure there are no errors in this book. However, to err is human, and we recognize the need to keep you informed of errors as they're spotted and corrected. Errata sheets are available for all our books, at http://www.wrox.com. If you find an error that hasn't already been reported, please let us know.

E-mail Support

If you wish to directly query a problem in the book with an expert who knows the book in detail, then e-mail support@wrox.com with the title of the book and the last four numbers of the ISBN in the subject field of the e-mail. A typical e-mail should include the following things:

- ❑ The **name**, **last four digits of the ISBN**, and **page number** of the problem in the Subject field.
- ❑ Your **name**, **contact info**, and the **problem** in the body of the message.

We *won't* send you junk mail. We need the details to save your time and ours. When you send an e-mail, it will go through the following chain of support:

❑ Customer Support – Your message is delivered to our customer support staff who are the first people to read it. They have files on the most frequently asked questions and will answer anything general immediately. They answer general questions about the book and the Web site.

❑ Editorial – Deeper queries are forwarded to the technical editor responsible for that book. He/she has experience with the programming language or particular product and are able to answer detailed technical questions on the subject. Once an issue has been resolved, the editor can post the errata to the web site.

❑ The Authors – Finally, in the unlikely event that the editor can't answer your problem, they will forward the request to the author. We try to protect authors from any distractions from writing. However, we are quite happy to forward specific requests to them. All Wrox authors help with the support on their books. They'll mail the customer and the editor with their response, and again all readers should benefit.

P2P.WROX.COM

For author and peer support, join the VB.NET mailing lists. Our unique system provides **programmer to programmer™ support** on mailing lists, forums, and newsgroups – all *in addition* to our one-to-one e-mail system. Be confident that your query is not just being examined by a support professional, but by the many Wrox authors and other industry experts present on our mailing lists. At p2p.wrox.com, you'll find a number of different lists aimed at Visual Basic programmers that will support you, not only while you read this book, but also as you develop your own applications.

Why this System Offers the Best Support

You can choose to join the mailing lists or you can receive them as a weekly digest. If you don't have the time or facility to receive the mailing list, then you can search our online archives. Junk and spam mails are deleted, and your own e-mail address is protected by the unique Lyris system. Any queries about joining or leaving lists, or the lists in general should be sent to listsupport@p2p.wrox.com.

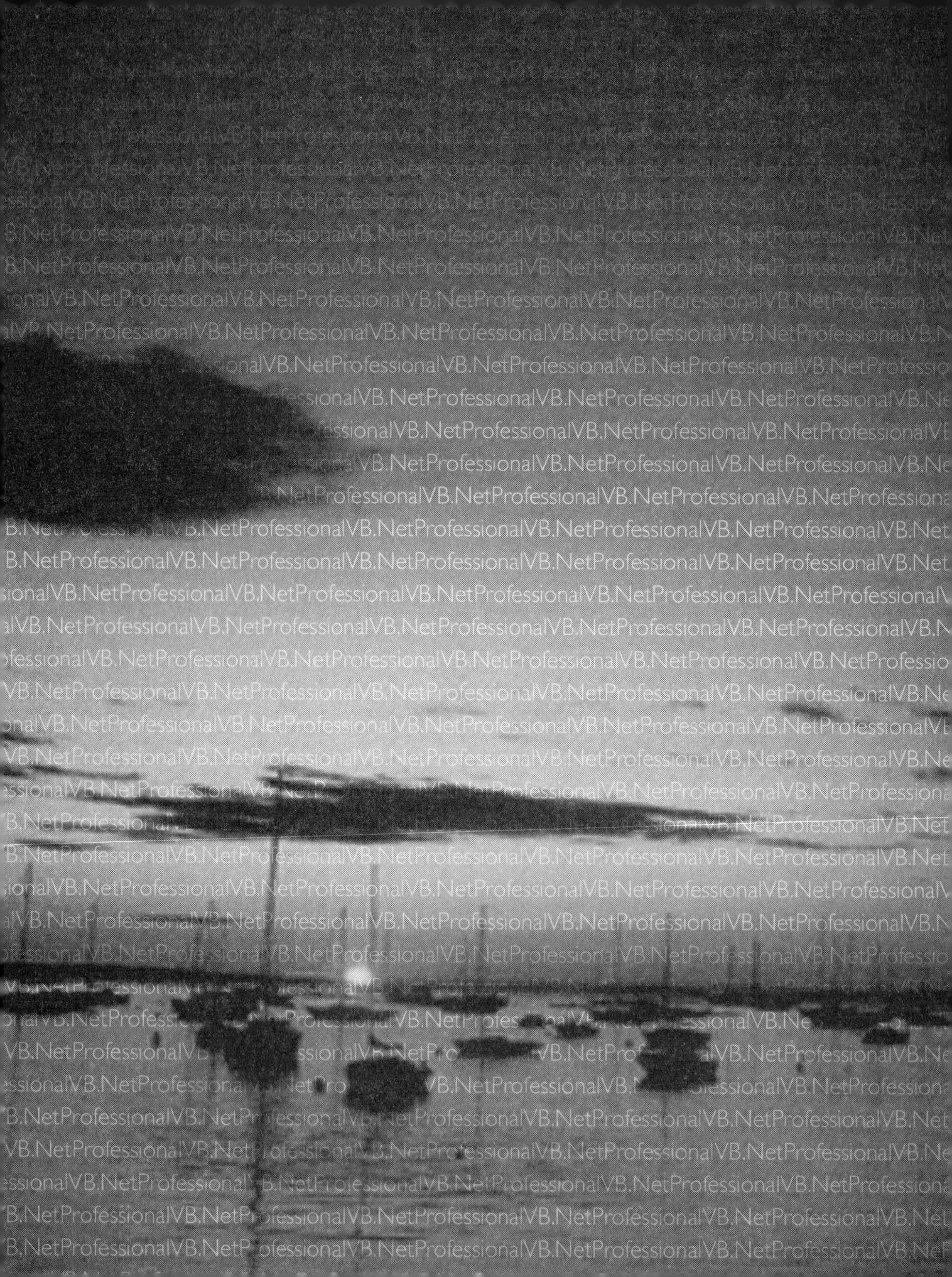
VB.NetProfessional

Why Do We Need Microsoft.NET?

Every new generation of software development comes about because of limitations in the previous generation. As new hardware and networking technologies become available, we find that our previous tools do not provide ideal vehicles for developing software that works with these new technologies.

The latest major technological change to drive the need for a new generation of development platforms is the widespread commercial acceptance of the Internet. In only about seven or eight years, the Internet has gone from being a curiosity to a common source of connectivity for the majority of businesses.

We've been developing Internet-enabled software for several years now, but the tools we've had to use all have an ad-hoc nature to them. Internet interfaces were bolted on to operating systems and other technologies that had been developed before the Internet became a force. Microsoft Windows is based on 1980s technologies, and COM was implemented in the early nineties. Work on Unix began way back in 1970! Java was originally developed for consumer electronics devices, and later adapted as an Internet tool.

Now for the first time, a complete software development platform, **Microsoft.NET**, has been designed from the ground up with the Internet in mind, although .NET is not exclusively for Internet development. Many of the innovations contained in this platform are driven by limitations in our current tools and technologies. Therefore, to understand why .NET is important and what its benefits are, it is helpful to first understand the drawbacks to our current tools and the limitations we face as software developers in a world dominated by the Internet.

We will discuss these drawbacks in the context of the Microsoft platform. However, it's important to note that almost all the drawbacks described below for current Microsoft tools and technologies apply in one form or another to all platforms currently available for Internet development, and many of them have unique drawbacks of their own. Tools and technologies for developing Internet software all suffer from a relative lack of maturity compared to equivalent tools for, say, client-server software. This is primarily due to the short span of time that the Internet has been important to business-oriented software development.

To gain our understanding of why we need .NET, we'll first look at what's wrong with our current set of development technologies, including COM and the DNA architectural model, and then examine how .NET corrects the drawbacks in these technologies.

What's Wrong with What We Have Now?

Microsoft began its Internet development efforts in 1995. Until that time, its focus for several years had been on moving desktop and server operating systems to 32-bit, GUI-based technologies.

Once Microsoft realized the importance of the Internet, it made a dramatic shift. The company became refocused on marrying its Windows platform to the Internet. It succeeded in making Windows a serious platform for the development of Internet applications. According to a survey in late 1999, about half of the top fifty e-commerce Internet sites were based on Microsoft COM architectures. By the turn of the century, COM/COM+ and Visual Studio 6 had become arguably the best available choice for Internet development.

Nevertheless, there were areas in which Microsoft technologies were less than ideal for Internet development. It had been necessary for Microsoft to make some compromises to quickly produce Internet-based tools and technologies. The most glaring example was Active Server Pages. Creating user interfaces with interpreted script and limited visual elements was a real step back from the form-based user interfaces produced in Visual Basic and other tools. And while Active Server Pages were simple in concept and very accessible to new developers, they did not encourage structured or object-oriented development, so many applications were written with a vast amount of interpreted script, leading to problems with debugging and maintenance.

Visual Basic and other languages have continued to be used in Internet applications on Microsoft platforms, but mostly as components that worked through Active Server Pages. Before Microsoft.NET, Microsoft tools have clearly lacked the level of integration and ease-of-use for web development that would be ideal. The few attempts that were made to place a web interface on traditional languages, such as WebClasses in VB, were compromise attempts and never gained wide acceptance. The end result has been that developing a large Internet application has required the use of a large set of tools and technologies that are at best loosely integrated.

The DNA Programming Model

In the late 1990s, Microsoft attempted to bring some order to the chaos with its concept of **Windows DNA applications**. DNA paints a broad picture of standard three-tier development based on COM, with Active Server Pages (as well as Win32 clients) in the presentation layer, business objects in a middle layer, and a relational data store and engine in the bottom layer. Here is a typical diagram of a generic Windows DNA application:

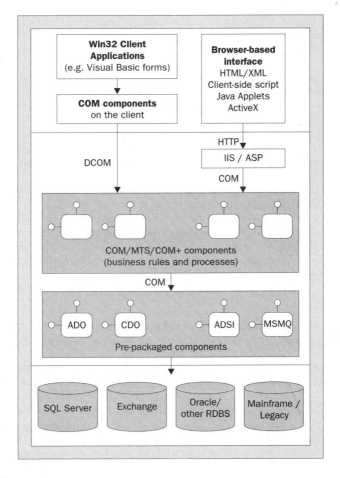

Presentation Tier

In Windows DNA, there are two major choices for user interfaces – Win32 clients and browser-based clients.

Win32 clients, most often produced with a visual development tool such as Visual Basic, are often the simplest to create, and offer a rich user interface. The drawback is that such client software is difficult to deploy and maintain, requiring an install on every client and a change to every client when an upgrade is needed.

Besides the logistical difficulties of getting the software to the clients and maintaining/updating it, there is another serious issue. DLL conflicts on the client are frequent because of variations in the version of the operating system and other software installed on the client. We discuss these problems in more detail below in the section titled *DLL Hell*.

Browser-based clients are somewhat more difficult to create, and offer a more limited user interface with fewer controls and less control over layout of the screen and the handling of screen events. However, they are far easier to deploy. All the client needs is a compatible browser and an Internet or intranet connection.

Browser-based clients can use technologies such as client-side script or Java applets to make the user interface richer and more functional. These options work for most modern browsers. Applying these technologies adds additional development time, and they do not address all user interface issues.

There are some "in-between" options. If clients are restricted to certain browsers, Dynamic HTML (DHTML) can be used to add further functionality to the interface. If clients are restricted to Internet Explorer, ActiveX controls can be used to make an interface close to that available in a Win32 client. However, ActiveX controls add deployment issues of their own. Visual Basic can be used for ActiveX controls, but then deploying the controls requires lots of supporting Visual Basic DLLs on the client. ActiveX controls are typically written in C++ instead to make the install as lightweight as possible. This adds to development time and requires a higher level of development expertise.

One important factor that is often overlooked in the DNA model is that there may be a need to implement both Win32-based and Internet-based user interfaces. Alternatively, there may be a need to have different levels of user interfaces, say one for novice or occasional users and one for advanced users. This is quite practical as long as the design of the system keeps the user interface layer as thin as possible. Normally, it should only contain logic to manage the user interface and to basic validation of user data. Especially for web interfaces, validation of data in the client layer is important to minimize round trips to the server.

Middle Tier

The middle tier in a DNA application should encapsulate as much of the business processing as possible. Besides rules needed to validate data on the client, most business rules should be in this layer.

The middle tier often breaks down into multiple sub-tiers. One tier may handle the interface to the client, another handles the business rules, and another the interface to the data repositories.

Visual Basic is the most common language used to write middle-tier components. This is a more sophisticated type of development than for typical forms-based Visual Basic programs, requiring a higher level of expertise in COM and object-oriented programming concepts. It is also important to understand how to create components that scale well, which often means developing components that are implemented using Microsoft Transaction Server on Windows NT or COM+ Services on Windows 2000. Such components typically use stateless designs, which can look very different from the stateful designs often used in client-based components.

Understanding the nuances of COM is important in constructing a middle tier because the components in this layer must work together. Versioning all the components properly so that they understand each other's interfaces can be a challenge.

Components in the middle tier may talk to a variety of protocols and components to communicate data to the data tier. The diagram shows examples such as HTTP, ADO (ActiveX Data Objects), ADSI (Active Directory Service Interfaces), and CDO (Collaboration Data Objects), but that list is by no means exhaustive.

Data Tier

Most business applications must store information for long-term use. The nature of the storage mechanism varies with the installation. Usually a relational database management system (RDBMS) is required, with the most common options being Microsoft SQL Server and Oracle. If the information is more based around documents and messages, a messaging data store such as Exchange may be required. Moreover, many installations still depend on legacy mainframe systems.

Besides holding the data, the data tier may also have logic to process, retrieve, and validate data. Stored procedures, written in some variation of the SQL language, can be used in RDBMS databases to do this.

Issues with the DNA Model

The concept behind DNA is reasonably sound, but actually making it work has many challenges. For example, there are many possible locations for programming logic in a DNA application. Some of them are:

- Visual Basic code in forms
- Visual Basic used in components on the client
- Visual Basic used in components on the server
- VBScript or JavaScript for server-side scripting in Active Server Pages
- VBScript or JavaScript for client-side scripting
- HTML, DHTML, CSS (Cascading Style Sheets)
- XML, XSL
- C++ in ActiveX components
- Stored procedures (Transact-SQL in SQL Server or PL-SQL in Oracle)

With this many options, inexperienced developers have a lot of opportunity for inappropriate choices, such as putting logic on the client that belongs on the server, or creating VBScript for formatting when Cascading Style Sheets might work better. Designing and constructing a complex DNA-based application calls for a high level of expertise with a number of different technologies.

Limitations of COM

DNA applications are based on communicating within and between tiers using **COM** (**Component Object Model**) interfaces. Active Server Pages, for example, must use COM components for any logic not implemented in script. Even Visual Basic 6 forms-based interfaces are COM-based underneath (though VB hides the details). The middle tier typically requires COM components on the server. And the technologies used to communicate with the data tier, such as ADO and CDO, are COM-based.

While COM is a viable platform for enterprise-level Internet applications today, it also has limitations of its own for Internet development. Let's cover some of the major ones.

DLL Hell

COM-based applications are subject to major deployment and configuration issues. Small changes in COM interfaces can accidentally render entire applications inoperable.

This problem, in which small problems cascade through an entire component-based tier, is often referred to as **DLL Hell**, and experienced COM developers will attest to the appropriateness of the term. Getting a large set of DLLs to a compatible state of versioning requires a highly sophisticated skill level and a well-controlled deployment process.

Other Deployment Issues

While DLL Hell is most common in the middle tier, there are also deployment issues in the client tier that are caused by COM. Any forms-based interface will depend on a host of COM components to function. Some of them are from the tool (such as Visual Basic) used to create the interface, and others may be custom-written DLLs that must be installed locally on the client.

All of the COM-based components require registration of their class IDs on the local client machine. These GUID-based identifiers must be placed in the local client's Windows Registry. This is typically done by a complex installation program. Getting all necessary components registered and properly versioned on the client is a variant of DLL Hell, and this makes deploying client applications to large numbers of desktop machines quite expensive. This has driven many application designers to use browser-based interfaces whenever possible to avoid deployment costs, even though the browser user interface is not as flexible.

Lack of Interoperability with Other Platforms

COM works well on pure Microsoft platforms. But COM does not provide the ability to activate components or interoperate with them if they are on other platforms such as Unix. As Microsoft applications become more enterprise-level, this becomes a significant problem. Large organizations often have a variety of operating platforms, and need more interoperability.

Lack of Built-In Inheritance

Software development technologies have moved steadily toward object-oriented concepts. There are a number of reasons for this, but one of the most important is to gain more reuse of software functionality.

One of the most important ways functionality can be reused is for a software component to be *inherited* by another component, and then extended with new functionality. Chapter 12 covers this issue in detail, so we won't go into it very deeply here. However, it is important to note that the capability for inheritance is critical to the ability to develop complex application frameworks, and to understand that COM does *not* support inheritance natively.

Inheritance has been possible on Microsoft platforms at the source language level, using languages such as C++ and Delphi. However, since inheritance is not built into the basic structure of COM, many languages (such as Visual Basic 6) don't support it, and there was no capability on Microsoft platforms before Microsoft.NET to allow languages to inherit from components written in another language.

Limitations of VB6 for DNA Application Development

Visual Basic 6 is easily the most popular language for developing applications with the DNA model. As noted above, it can be used in two major roles – forms-based VB clients and COM components (either on the client or the server).

There are other options, of course, including C++, J++, and various third-party languages such as Delphi and Perl, but the number of VB developers outnumbers them all put together.

That does not mean VB6 is without limitations for such development; some of the most serious ones include:

- ❑ No capability for multithreading
- ❑ Lack of implementation inheritance and other object-oriented features

❑   Poor error-handling ability

❑   Poor integration with other languages such as C++

❑   No effective user interface for Internet-based applications

Lack of multithreading implies, for example, that VB6 can't be used to write an NT-type service. There are also situations in which the apartment threading used by components created in VB6 limits performance.

VB6's limited object-oriented features, particularly the lack of inheritance, make it unsuitable for development of object-based frameworks. Because of this, VB6 developers are at a disadvantage for some types of development, especially on large, complex applications, compared to C++ or Java developers.

VB6's archaic error handling becomes especially annoying in a multi-tier environment. It's difficult in Visual Basic to track and pass errors through a stack of component interfaces.

Integration of multiple languages in a COM application is a challenge. VB6's implementation of COM, although easy to use, causes problems with such integration. Class parameters (object interfaces) in VB6 are "variant compliant", forcing C++ developers who want to integrate with VB to convert parameters to types less appropriate for their purposes. These varying data structures and interface conventions must be resolved before components in Visual Basic can be integrated into a multiple language project. Besides necessitating extra code, these conversions may also mean a performance hit.

But perhaps the biggest drawback to using Visual Basic became apparent when many developers moved to the Internet. While VB6 forms for a Win32 client were state-of-the-art, for applications with a browser interface Visual Basic 6 was relegated mostly to use in components.

Microsoft tried to address this problem in Visual Basic 6 with WebClasses and DHTML Pages. Neither caught on. WebClasses offered an obscure programming model, and limited control over visual layout. DHTML Pages in Visual Basic 6 must send a (usually large) DLL to the client, and so need a high-bandwidth connection to be practical, limiting their use mostly to intranet applications. DHTML Pages are also restricted to Internet Explorer.

All of these limitations needed to be addressed, but Microsoft decided to look beyond just Visual Basic and solve these problems on a more global level. All of these limitations are solved in Visual Basic.NET through the use of technology in the .NET Framework.

Additional Limitations in DNA-Based Internet Development

There are a few additional areas in which current Microsoft tools and technologies fall short of the ideal for Internet application development.

Different Programming Models for Internet Development vs. Other Types of Development

With DNA-based software development, creating software that is accessed by a user locally is done very differently from development for the Internet. The starkest example of this is the typical use of Visual Basic forms for client-server user interfaces versus the use of Active Server Pages for Internet user interfaces. Even though both situations involve designing and implementing GUI-based user interfaces, the tools and programming techniques used are quite different.

Having very different programming models for these similar types of development causes several problems:

❑ Developers have to learn multiple programming models.

❑ Code developed for one type of interface cannot typically be used for the other type of interface.

❑ It is uncommon to have both local and web-based user interfaces, even though this could facilitate a better user experience for local users. It is usually too expensive to implement two completely different interface tiers.

No Automatic State Management for Internet Sessions

Developers using Visual Basic 6 forms and local components are accustomed to making the user interface more convenient by creating user interfaces that "remember" things for the user. In computer science terms, we say that the VB forms interface maintains **state**. If a piece of information is placed in a text box, it stays there until it is explicitly changed or removed by the developer or user.

Active Server Pages, however, have no such capability. Every time a page is rendered, the programmer must make sure that all the visual controls have their information loaded. It is the programmer's responsibility to manage the state in the user interface, and to transfer state information between pages.

This causes developers to have to write a lot of code for Internet user interfaces that is not relevant to the business problem being solved. In addition, if an Internet application is going to run on a group of web servers (often called a web farm), then considerable additional work is necessary to design a state management system that is independent of a particular server.

Weak User Interfaces over the Web

It is possible to produce fairly sophisticated user interfaces for the Web by using Dynamic HTML and writing a lot of JavaScript. However, most web-based applications actually offer fairly primitive user interfaces because it takes too much time and expertise to write a sophisticated one. (Including a lot of nice graphics does not make a user interface sophisticated – it just makes it pretty.)

Those of us who cut our teeth on producing state-of-the-art interactive user interfaces in VB during the mid-1990s have never been satisfied with the compromises necessary for web interfaces. Better user interfaces on the web would be an enormous boost for user productivity, but today's tools are simply unable to deliver in that area.

Disadvantages of the Windows API – The Need to Abstract the Operating System

A final area in which limitations should be discussed is Windows itself. Even though Microsoft finally achieved very high levels of reliability and stability with Windows 2000, the underlying Application Programming Interface (API) is still based on the original API for Windows 1.0, released in 1985.

Today's applications need to use the API for a variety of purposes. Visual Basic developers are familiar with the need to use the API to monitor Windows messages, manipulate controls, read and write INI files, and a variety of other tasks.

This is some of the fussiest programming Visual Basic developers ever have to do. The Windows API is hard to program to for a variety of reasons. It is not object-based, which means learning complex calls to functions with long lists of arguments. The naming scheme for the functions is inconsistent. Furthermore, since the whole API is written in C++, getting calling conventions right on data types such as strings is very messy.

There is a larger issue as well. As hardware platforms proliferate, it is no longer enough for software just to run on desktop clients and servers. There are handheld and wireless devices of various kinds, kiosks, and other types of systems, many of which run on different processors and do not use standard Windows as an operating system. Any software written with calls to the Windows API cannot be portable to any of these systems without major changes.

The trend towards portable software began with standardization of languages in the 1960s, but has never reached an ideal state. Today the need is more pressing than ever and the only way software produced with Microsoft tools can become more portable is to abstract away the Windows API, so that application software does not write directly to it. This opens the possibility for an equivalent layer of abstraction on other platforms that could allow Microsoft-based software to run on them.

The Solution – Microsoft.NET

Microsoft realized a few years ago that, while it was possible to write good Internet applications with Windows-based technologies, it was highly desirable to find ways to develop applications faster and make it far easier to deploy them. Other platforms (such as Unix) and other development environments (such as WebSphere) were continuing to raise the bar for developing Internet applications, making it essential that Microsoft address the limitations of the DNA programming model.

After keeping their efforts under wraps for a couple of years, Microsoft introduced their Microsoft.NET initiative at the Professional Developers Conference (PDC) in Orlando, Florida in July 2000. Most of us who got that initial exposure to Microsoft.NET sensed that this was a turning point in the world of software for Microsoft platforms.

Microsoft's .NET initiative is broad-based and very ambitious. It includes the **.NET Framework**, which encompasses the languages and execution platform, plus extensive class libraries providing rich built-in functionality. Besides the core .NET Framework, the .NET initiative includes protocols (such as the **Simple Object Access Protocol**, commonly known as **SOAP**) to provide a new level of integration of software over the Internet, and a set of pre-built web-based services called **Hailstorm**.

How important is .NET to Microsoft? Their executives have stated publicly that 80% of Microsoft's R&D resources in 2001 are being spent on .NET. It is expected that, eventually, most Microsoft products will be ported to the .NET platform.

General Goals of .NET

Many of the goals Microsoft had in mind when designing .NET reflect the limitations we previously discussed for development with previous tools and technologies. These goals include:

Creation of Highly Distributed Applications

The trend in business applications for decades has been towards a more highly distributed model. The Internet carries that trend forward. Many applications in the next generation will need to have some of their elements distributed among various organizations. This contrasts with today's dominant model in which all the elements of an application (except possibly a browser-based client) are located solely within an organization.

Simplified Software Development

Today's Internet-enabled software is too costly to produce and requires too much expertise on the part of the developer. Developers need to be able to concentrate on the business logic in their applications, and to stop writing logic for state management, scalability, etc. Writing software for the Internet should not require expertise in a long list of Internet-specific technologies.

A related goal is to have development for the Internet look very much like development for other types of software. A component accessed over the local network or over the Internet should be manipulated with code very much like that for a component accessed on the local machine. The software platform should be able to take care of the details in transmitting information to and from the component.

User interface development also needs to be as similar as possible for the Internet compared to local access. While using local, platform-specific interfaces will always offer more flexibility than a browser-based interface, Microsoft.NET aims to make those two types of interfaces as similar in development philosophy as possible.

Better User Interfaces over the Web

A consequence of the previous goal is to make Web-based user interfaces richer and more flexible than they are now, bringing them as close as possible to the richness of local, forms-based interfaces.

Simplified Deployment

The problems of DLL Hell, and the need for large installs of forms-based applications, are just two examples of current deployment issues. Microsoft.NET aims to make deployment as simple as it was for DOS – just copy a compiled module over to a system and run it. No registration, no GUIDs, no required installation procedure.

Support for a Variety of Languages

While the idea of one grand, unifying language sounds good in theory, in the real world, different types of developers need different tools. Microsoft.NET is designed with the philosophy of supporting a multitude of languages, from Microsoft and others, and allowing the development community to evolve languages that best fit various development needs.

An Extendable Platform for the Future

A new platform needs the capability to adapt to changing conditions through extensions and variations. .NET aims to be more extendable and flexible than any current software development platform.

Future Portability of Compiled Applications

With current operating systems being based on 1970s and 1980s designs, it's not a bold prediction that operating systems will make major changes and perhaps entirely new ones will be introduced in the next decade. Investments in software development need to be carried forward to those platforms. The goal of .NET is to allow applications to move from current platforms to future platforms with a simple copy, and no recompilation.

The Structure of Microsoft.NET

These are ambitious goals. To understand how they are accomplished, it is important to look at the general structure of Microsoft.NET.

One way to look at .NET is to see how it fits into the rest of the computing world. Here is a diagram of the major layers of .NET, showing how they sit on top of an operating system, and provide various ways to interface to the outside world:

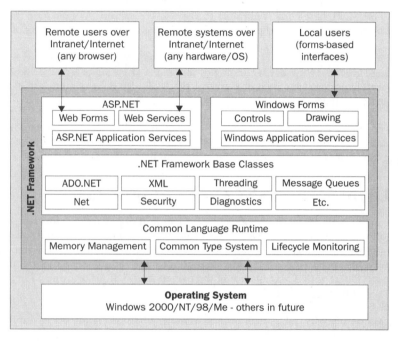

The first point of this diagram is that .NET is a framework that covers all the layers of software development above the operating system. It provides the richest level of integration among presentation technologies, component technologies, and data technologies ever seen on a Microsoft, or perhaps any, platform. Secondly, the entire architecture has been created to make it as easy to develop Internet applications, as it is to develop for the desktop.

Starting at the bottom of the diagram, the .NET Framework sits on top of the operating system, and interfaces to it. .NET "wraps" the operating system, insulating software developed with .NET from most operating system specifics such as file handling and memory allocation. This prepares for a possible future in which the software developed for .NET is portable to a wide variety of hardware and operating system foundations. (The initial version of Visual Studio.NET supports all versions of Windows 2000 plus Windows NT4, Windows 98, and Windows Millennium Edition, but not Windows 95.)

The .NET Framework itself starts with the execution engine, memory management, and component loading, and goes all the way up to multiple ways of rendering user and program interfaces. In between, there are layers that provide just about any system-level capability that a developer would need.

(MSIL)
source → byte code → binary code

The Foundation – The Common Language Runtime

At the base is the **Common Language Runtime**, often abbreviated to **CLR**. This is the heart of the .NET Framework. The core of the CLR is an execution engine that loads, executes, and manages code that has been compiled into an intermediate byte-code format called **Microsoft Intermediate Language** (**MSIL** and occasionally referred to as just **IL**). This code is not interpreted – it is compiled to native binary code before execution by just-in-time compilers built into the CLR.

That means there are two levels of compilers in .NET. The language compiler takes the source code and creates MSIL. This MSIL byte code is portable to any .NET platform. At execution time, this code is then compiled by the just-in-time compilers into binary code for the machine being used for execution.

The CLR also supports and enforces a common system of data types and a standard interface convention. These are two of the key technologies that make cross-language inheritance possible. In addition to allocation and management of memory, the CLR also does reference tracking for objects, and handles garbage collection.

Chapter 5 will cover the capabilities of the CLR in detail, including its ability to handle compiled code from multiple languages and to allow cross-language interoperability. *Do not skip that chapter!* Understanding the CLR is an important step in understanding .NET as a whole.

The Next Layer – The .NET Class Framework

The next layer up in the framework provides the services and object models for data, input/output, security, and so forth. It is called the **.NET Class Framework**, sometimes referred to as the **.NET base classes**. For example, the next generation of ADO, called **ADO.NET**, resides here (though regular ADO is also available in Microsoft.NET to provide compatibility for older code). Also included is the core functionality to do things with XML, including the parsers and XSL transformer. There is a list below of additional functionality in the .NET Class Framework.

You might be wondering why .NET includes functionality that is, in many cases, duplication of existing class libraries. There are several good reasons:

- ❑ The .NET Class Framework libraries are implemented in the .NET Framework, making them easier to integrate with .NET-developed programs.

- ❑ The .NET Class Framework brings together most of the system class libraries needed into one location, which increases consistency and convenience.

- ❑ The class libraries in the .NET Class Framework are much easier to extend than older class libraries.

- ❑ Having the libraries as part of the .NET Framework simplifies deployment of .NET applications. Once the .NET Framework is on a system, individual applications don't need to install base class libraries for functions like data access.

What is in the .NET Class Framework?

The .NET Class Framework contains literally hundreds of classes and interfaces. Here are just some of the functions of various libraries in the .NET Class Framework:

- ❑ Data access and manipulation

❑ Creation and management of threads

❑ Interfaces from .NET to the outside world – Windows Forms, Web Forms, Web Services, and console applications

❑ Definition, management, and enforcement of application security

❑ Application configuration

❑ Working with Directory Services, Event Logs, Processes, Message Queues, and Timers

❑ Sending and receiving data with a variety of network protocols

❑ Accessing Meta Data information stored in assemblies, which are the execution units of .NET (think of them as DLLs and EXEs)

Much functionality that a programmer might think of as being part of a language has been moved to the .NET Framework Classes. For example, the Visual Basic keyword Sqr for extracting a square root is no longer available in .NET. It has been replaced by the System.Math.Sqrt method in the Framework Classes.

It's important to emphasize that all languages based on the .NET Framework have these Framework Classes available. That means that COBOL, for example, can use the same function mentioned above for getting a square root. This makes such base functionality widely available and highly consistent across languages. All calls to Sqrt look essentially the same (allowing for syntactical differences among languages) and access the same underlying code. Here are examples in Visual Basic.NET and C#:

```
' Example using Sqrt in Visual Basic.NET
Dim dblNumber As Double = 200
Dim dblSquareRoot As Double
dblSquareRoot = System.Math.Sqrt(dblNumber)
Label1.Text = Cstr(dblSquareRoot)

' Same example in C#
Double dblNumber = 200;
Double dblSquareRoot;
dblSquareRoot = System.Math.Sqrt(dblNumber);
label1.Text = Double.ToString(dblSquareRoot);
```

In Chapter 7, we will look at the topic of **namespaces**, which are the logical groupings of the classes in the .NET Framework. It will also discuss some of the important namespaces and the classes they contain.

User and Program Interfaces

In a sense, this top layer is an extension of the .NET Framework Classes layer immediately underneath it. It comprises user and program interfaces that allow .NET to work with the outside world.

These interfacing technologies are all highly innovative:

❑ **Windows Forms** are a language-independent forms engine that brings the drag-and-drop design features of Visual Basic to all .NET-enabled languages, and also enables developers to develop forms-based interfaces with little or no access to the Win32 API. They are discussed in Chapters 8 and 10.

❑ **Web Forms** brings drag-and-drop design and an event-driven architecture to Web-based interfaces, implementing a programming model that is much like standard VB6 forms-based development. User interfaces created with Web Forms also have built-in browser independence and state management. Chapters 20 and 21 discuss various elements of Web Forms.

❑ **Web Services** are perhaps the most important of the three. Web Services allow remote components, possibly running on completely different operating systems, to be invoked and used. This capability for communications and interoperability with remote components over the Internet serves as the mechanism by which highly-distributed applications can be built, going far beyond what is feasible with existing technologies like DCOM. Chapter 22 goes in depth on Web Services.

XML as the .NET "Meta-language"

Much of the underlying integration of .NET is accomplished with XML. For example, Web Services depend completely on XML for interfacing with remote objects. Not only that, but the information about execution modules, called **assemblies**, can be exported as XML.

ADO.NET, the successor to ADO, is heavily dependent on XML for remote representation of data. Essentially, when ADO.NET creates what it calls a **DataSet** (a more complex successor to a recordset), the data is converted to XML for manipulation by ADO.NET. Then the changes to that XML are posted back to the datastore by ADO.NET when remote manipulation is finished. (Chapters 18 and 19 discuss ADO.NET and its use with XML in more detail.)

With XML as an "entry point" into so many areas of .NET, future integration opportunities are multiplied. Using XML to expose interfaces to .NET functions allows developers to tie components and functions together in new, unexpected ways. XML can be the glue that ties pieces together in ways that were never anticipated, both to Microsoft and non-Microsoft platforms.

How Microsoft.NET Attains Its Goals

Now that we've had a short introduction to the structure of .NET, we can better understand how it meets the goals Microsoft set out for it.

Simplified Software Development

There are several ways that Microsoft.NET simplifies the development of business application software:

Pre-Written Functionality

The Framework Base Classes make it unnecessary to write system-level code. These classes furnish a wide array of functionality, and can be extended via inheritance if additional functionality is needed. It is no longer necessary to start over from scratch if a particular pre-built component does not do exactly what is needed.

Transparent Integration of Internet Technologies

In Microsoft.NET, the protocols and mechanisms for accessing Internet resources are built into the platform in such a way that the developer does not need to handle the details. Web Services, for example, are created by merely marking a function as a `<WebMethod>`. Creation of simple web interfaces with Web Forms does not require an extensive knowledge of HTML, or how to handle information from an HTTP post operation. The controls used in Web Forms automatically emit JavaScript (if the browser in use can run it) to handle data validation on the client. (If the browser doesn't support JavaScript, the data validation is transparently run on the server.)

This integration of web technologies reduces the expertise barriers to web development. While it is still very helpful to know a lot about HTML, Dynamic HTML, and so forth, traditional VB developers will find the transition to developing web software much easier with VB.NET than with Active Server Pages.

Unified Programming Models for All Types of Development

We've already mentioned how Web Services are just regular functions with a `<WebMethod>` attribute attached. That means they are created just like local routines. Also, consuming a Web Service is very much like using local components. Once the Web Service's location is referenced, Web Service classes are instantiated the same way as local classes, and their interface looks like a typical object interface. Web Services even have IntelliSense in the development environment, just like local components.

Likewise, developing user interfaces in Windows Forms is very similar to developing them in Web Forms. There are commonly used controls, such as labels and text boxes, in both, with similar sets of properties and methods. Not everything can be the same, because the disconnected model for Web Forms means it is impractical to have as many events as in Windows Forms. (The mouse-moving events are mostly missing from Web Forms, for example.) However, the amount of commonality makes it easy to transition between the two types of development, and easier for traditional VB developers to start using Web Forms.

Highly Distributed Systems

The vision of Microsoft.NET is globally distributed systems, using XML as the universal glue to allow functions running on different computers across an organization or across the world to come together in a single application. In this vision, systems from servers to wireless palmtops, with everything in between, will share the same general platform, with versions of .NET available for all of them, and with each of them able to integrate transparently with the others.

Web Services are the mechanism for reaching this vision. In Web Services, software functionality becomes exposed as a service that doesn't care what the consumer of the service is (unless there are security considerations). Web Services allow developers to build applications by combining local and remote resources for an overall integrated and distributed solution.

The remote components that become integrated into local applications may come from a variety of sources. Manufacturers may expose a Web Service that tells their customers when products will be ready. Retail sites can expose their latest items on sale through a Web Service. In addition, Microsoft is jump-starting the availability of Web Services with its Hailstorm initiative.

It is hard to over-emphasize the potential importance of Web Services. Consider, for example, the potential for Web Services to replace packaged software. A commercial software company could produce a Web Service that, for instance, calculates sales tax for every jurisdiction in the nation. A subscription to that Web Service could be sold to any company needing to calculate sales tax. The customer company then has no need to deploy the sales tax calculator because is it just called on the Web. The company producing the sales tax calculator can dynamically update it to include new rates and rules for various jurisdictions, and their customers using the Web Service don't have to do anything to get these updates.

There are endless other possibilities. Stock tickers, weather information, current financial rates, shipping status information, and a host of other types of information could be exposed as a Web Service, ready for integration into any application that needs it.

Better User Interfaces over the Web

Web Forms are a giant step towards much richer web-based user interfaces. Their built-in intelligence allows rich, browser-independent screens to be developed quickly, and to be easily integrated with compiled code.

But Web Forms are just the first step. Microsoft has announced an initiative for the future called the **Universal Canvas** that should begin to overcome some of the inherent limitations of HTML for user interfaces. (Search the MSDN web site for "Universal Canvas" if you want to know more.)

Simplified Deployment

Executable modules in .NET are self-describing. Once the CLR knows where a module resides, it can find out everything else it needs to know to run the module, such as the module's object interface and security requirements, from the module itself. That means a module can just be copied to a new system and immediately executed.

Also, the CLR is capable of loading multiple versions of a single DLL, allowing them to execute side-by-side. Each executable module identifies the particular DLL it needs, and the CLR runs it against that one. Versioning difficulties should be dramatically reduced with .NET.

This is a huge leap from today's complex deployment. While advanced applications will still need an installation program to accomplish tasks such as setting up database connections and other configuration information, install programs will be much simpler than today. Simple applications will not need an installation program at all.

Support for a Variety of Languages

The CLR executes binary code in MSIL, and that code looks the same regardless of the original source language. All .NET-enabled languages use the same data types and the same interfacing conventions. This makes is possible for all .NET languages to interoperate transparently. One language can call another easily, and languages can even inherit classes written in another language and extend them. No current platform has anywhere near this level of language interoperability.

The net effect is that language choice becomes mostly a matter of taste. .NET-enabled languages will typically have the same performance characteristics, the same overall functionality, and will interoperate with other languages the same.

One of the most important aspects of meeting this goal is that Visual Basic becomes a first-class language. It has almost exactly the same capabilities as C#. It gets inheritance, structured error handling, and the other advanced features. Coupled with the large number of developers who know Visual Basic, and the advantages of VB such as good readability, VB.NET should set the stage for Visual Basic to continue to be the most popular programming language in the world, and to simultaneously interoperate with a variety of other languages.

Extendability of the Platform

The completely object-based approach of .NET is designed to allow base functionality to be extended through inheritance (unlike COM), and the platform's functionality is appropriately partitioned to allow various parts (such as the just-in-time compilers discussed in the next chapter) to be replaced as new versions are needed.

It is likely that, in the future, new ways of interfacing to the outside world will be added to the current trio of Windows Form, Web Forms, and Web Services (such as the Universal Canvas mentioned earlier). The architecture of .NET makes this quite practical.

Future Portability

By abstracting away as much platform-specific access as possible, .NET allows the future possibility of moving software to other hardware and operating system platforms. The main elements of .NET have been submitted to standards bodies, with the intent of standardizing the implementation of .NET on different systems. The ultimate goal is that compiled code produced on one implementation of .NET (such as Windows) could be moved to another implementation of .NET on a different operating system merely by copying the compiled code over and running it.

The Role of COM

When the .NET Framework was first introduced, some uninformed journalists interpreted it as the death of COM. That is completely incorrect. COM is not going anywhere for a while. In fact, Windows will not boot without COM.

.NET integrates very well with COM-based software. Any COM component can be treated as a .NET component by other .NET components. The .NET Framework wraps COM components and exposes an interface that .NET components can work with. This is absolutely essential to the quick acceptance of .NET, because it makes .NET interoperable with a tremendous amount of older COM-based software.

Going in the other direction, the .NET Framework can expose .NET components with a COM interface. This allows older COM components to use .NET-based components as if they were developed using COM. (Chapter 16 discusses COM interoperability in more detail.)

No Internal Use of COM

It is important, however, to understand that native .NET components do not interface using COM. The CLR implements a new way for components to interface, one that is not COM-based. Use of COM is only necessary when interfacing to COM components produced by non-.NET tools.

Over a long span of time, the fact that .NET does not use COM internally may lead to the decline of COM. But that is for the very long term. For any immediate purposes, COM is definitely important.

The Role of DNA

Earlier in the chapter, we discussed the limitations of the current DNA programming model. These limitations are mostly inherent in the technologies used to implement DNA today, not in the overall structure or philosophy. There is nothing fundamentally wrong with the tiered approach to development specified by the DNA model. It was specifically developed to deal with the challenges in design and development of complex applications. Many of these design issues, such as the need to encapsulate business rules, or to provide for multiple user interface access points to a system, do not go away with .NET.

Applications developed in the .NET Framework will still, in many cases, use a DNA model to design the appropriate tiers. However, the tiers will be a lot easier to produce in .NET. The presentation tier will benefit from the new interface technologies, especially Web Forms for Internet development. The middle tier will require far less COM-related headaches to develop and implement. And richer, more distributed middle tier designs will be possible by using Web Services.

The architectural skills that experienced developers have learned in the DNA world are definitely still important and valuable in the .NET world.

Additional Benefits

In addition to the advantages conferred by meeting the goals we discussed previously, .NET offers a number of additional benefits. These include:

- ❑ Faster development (less to do, the system handles more).
- ❑ More reuse because of inheritance.
- ❑ Higher scalability – many capabilities to help applications scale are built into .NET.
- ❑ Easier to build sophisticated development tools – debuggers and profilers can target the Common Language Runtime, and thus become accessible to all .NET-enabled languages.
- ❑ Fewer bugs – whole classes of bugs should be unknown in .NET. With the CLR handling memory management, memory leaks should be a thing of the past, for example.
- ❑ Potentially better performance – Microsoft's heavy investment in system level code for memory management, garbage collection, and the like have yielded an architecture that should meet or exceed performance of typical COM-based applications today.

Impact on Visual Basic

We previously covered the limitations of Visual Basic in today's DNA programming model. To recap, they were:

- ❑ No capability for multithreading
- ❑ Lack of implementation inheritance and other object features
- ❑ Poor error-handling ability

- ❑   Poor integration with other languages such as C++
- ❑   No effective user interface for Internet-based applications

Since VB.NET is built on top of the .NET framework, all of these shortcomings have been eliminated. Visual Basic basically piggybacks on the stuff that was going to be implemented anyway for C++, C#, and third-party .NET languages.

In fact, VB gets the most extensive changes of any existing language in the Visual Studio suite. These changes pull VB in line with other languages in terms of data types, calling conventions, error handling, and, most importantly, object-orientation. These changes will be covered in detail throughout the book.

Microsoft includes a migration tool in Visual Studio.NET, and it can assist in porting VB6 projects to .NET, but it will not do everything required. There will be some areas, including unsupported, obsolete syntax such as GOSUB, where the tool merely places a note that indicates something needs to be done.

Avoiding Confusion – the Role of the .NET Enterprise Servers

Microsoft released several products early in 2001, which they describe as being part of the .NET Enterprise Server family. Products in the .NET Enterprise Server family include

- ❑   SQL Server 2000 (discussed in *Professional SQL Server 2000 Programming* from Wrox Press, ISBN 1861004486)
- ❑   Commerce Server 2000 (discussed in *Professional Commerce Server 2000* from Wrox Press, ISBN 1861004648)
- ❑   BizTalk Server (discussed in *Professional BizTalk* from Wrox Press, ISBN 1861003293)
- ❑   Exchange 2000
- ❑   Host Integration Server (the successor to SNA Server)
- ❑   Internet Security and Administration (ISA) Server (the successor to Proxy Server)

Some of the marketing literature for these products emphasizes that they are part of Microsoft's .NET strategy. However, it is important that you understand the difference between these products and the .NET Framework upon which Visual Basic.NET is based. The .NET Enterprise Servers are *not* based on the .NET Framework. Most of them are successors to previous server-based products, and they use the same COM/COM+ technologies as their predecessors.

These .NET Enterprise Servers still have a major role to play in future software development projects. When actual .NET Framework projects are developed, most will depend on the technologies in the .NET Enterprise Servers for functions like data storage and messaging. However, the first actual product based on the .NET Framework is Visual Studio.NET, which contains Visual Basic.NET.

Summary

This chapter has attempted to explain the importance of .NET, and just how much it changes application development. Understanding these concepts is essential to using VB.NET in the most effective manner.

It is possible to use VB.NET merely to write the same kinds of software as were written in VB6, only faster and more cleanly. However, this would be failing to use much of the value of VB.NET. The real opportunites are in doing entirely new types of applications such as Web Services, and in creating application frameworks that promote reuse of code. The rest of the book explains the concepts and technologies you'll need to do that.

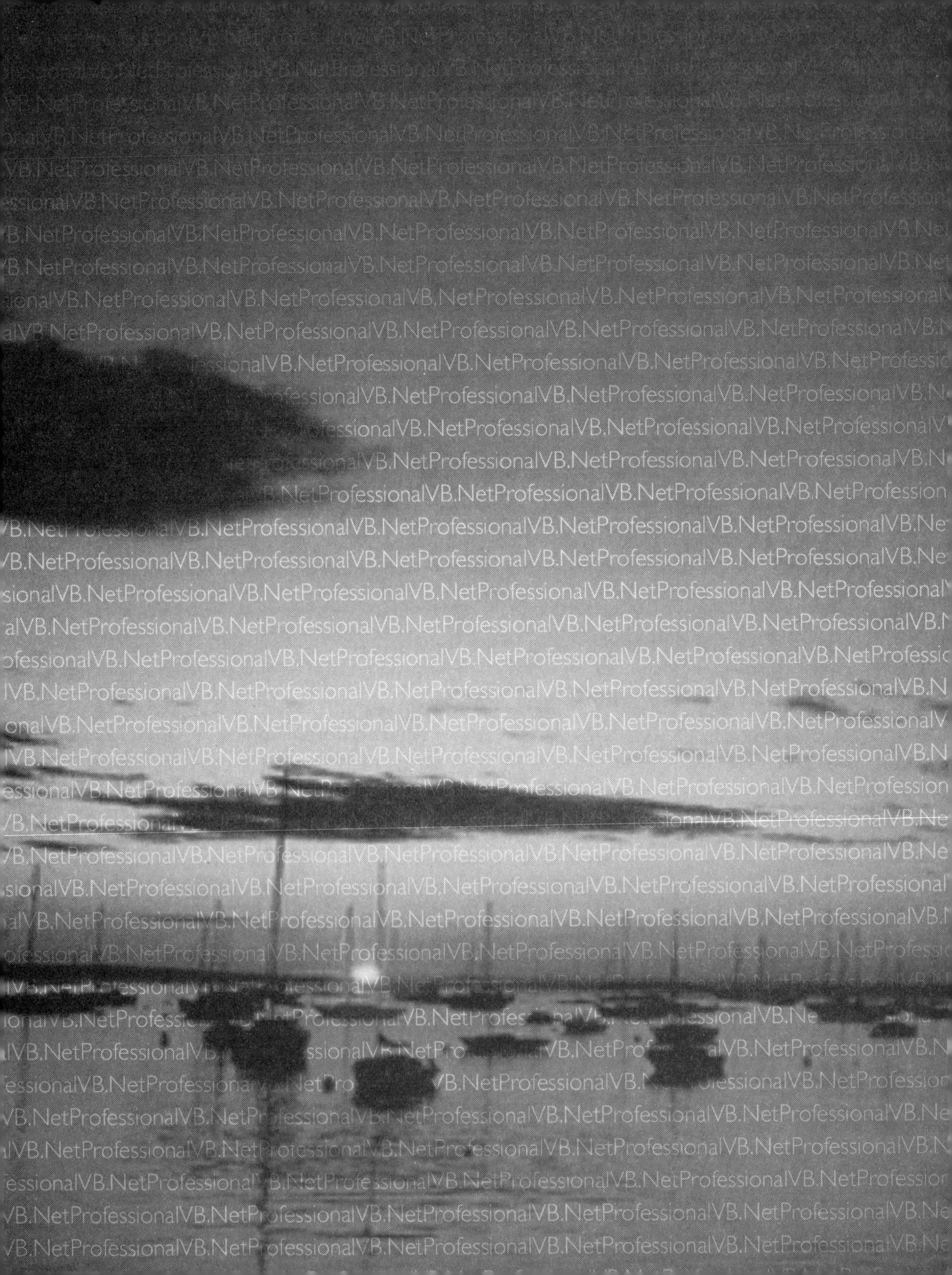
VB.NetProfessional

An Overview of New Features in VB.NET

VB.NET – it may be one small step for IT, but it's a giant leap forward for VB developers! VB.NET is not your regular new version of VB that added and modified technical features to core technology. VB.NET breaks the mold! It is virtually a new programming language, based around new core technology – the .NET paradigm. The technical changes are so extensive that VB developers will be able to compete with C#, C++, and Java developers!

Visual Basic revolutionized the Windows programming world, by making it relatively easy to create applications. This had a number of effects: programmers could now rapidly prototype or develop complete systems and non-programmers could now more easily retrain as programmers. With Visual Basic, some of the complexities of developing Windows-based applications were hidden behind an easy-to-use development environment.

From versions 1 to 3, VB had come a long way – but it was still not technically equal to the likes of C++, for example, a lot of functionality still required an intimate knowledge of the Windows API, a responsibility VB was designed to avoid.

When version 4.0 hit the streets in 1996, another minor revolution began. VB4 was completely rewritten – previous versions were written in assembler, while VB4 was written in C++. VB programmers could now write 32bit applications, they could create their own DLLs, and they could create other applications that referenced those DLLs and those created by others. Programmers could also begin to use some object-oriented features such as classes and encapsulation. VB was getting much better, but version 4 was less than the most stable development platform.

In 1997, Microsoft released version 5. This version went a long way to stabilize version 4's problems. It also did away with 16 bit compilations altogether. Quickly on the heels of version 5, came version 6. Although this version continued to stabilize the development platform, it did not bring the object-oriented features of Visual Basic to the same levels as Java, C++, or Delphi.

Object-oriented language developers (C++, Smalltalk, etc.) snigger behind the back of VB for its lack of inheritance. There is also the problem that VB hides too much from the programmer. It is impossible, for example, to write free-threaded applications and therefore Windows Services with VB. Although a whole industry has developed to create tools to extend Visual Basic and add the ability to write Windows Services, up until VB.NET it has never been possible to do these things with Visual Basic alone.

It's taken three versions (VB4, VB5, and VB6), and five years to get here, but now VB.NET provides its loyal community of developers with the object-oriented technology that we have been waiting anxiously to get our hands on. VB.NET is a .NET compliant language and as such has, except for legacy reasons, almost identical technical functionality as the new language C# and .NET compliant C++. We are now talking full object-orientation – including full inheritance (sub-classing), parameterized constructors, and overloading. We also have new technologies such as web forms and web services!

We've already discussed (in the previous chapter) how the root of all these changes is the .NET Framework and the Common Language Runtime (CLR) – so let's turn our attention in this chapter to a brief overview of the changes made to Visual Basic as a result, starting with the IDE.

New IDE Features

When you install Visual Studio.NET, the first thing you will notice is there is just one Visual Studio element in the Start menu. There are not separate entries for VB, VC++, or C#. This is the first physical hint of the CLR at work. All of the Visual Studio languages share the same IDE because they can now all work together.

> Because the .NET languages are tied to the .NET Framework, and the .NET Framework is actually a separate installation for Windows, there is actually no need to use Visual Studio.NET to develop applications. You could just use your favorite text editor to create the source files and use the compilers provided by the framework. However, this would make code management and debugging much more difficult.

You will notice that VB, C++, and C# projects can be created in VisualStudio.NET. You will also notice that the VB project types are a bit different from previously. Since VB.NET takes advantage of the .NET Framework, there is no longer any reason to create ActiveX EXEs or DLLs, because COM is not used in the .NET Framework. However, we can still create DLLs by using a Class Library or Web Service project. These types of project will be discussed at length in Chapters 11 – 13 and 22, respectively.

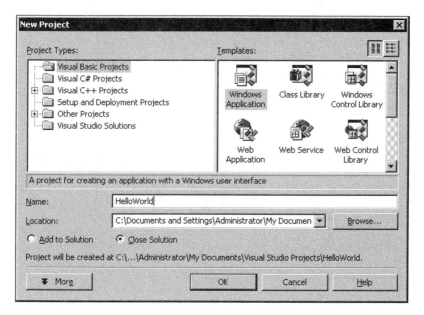

Although most VB developers will notice the changes to the IDE first, there is nothing that will not make us feel at home. In fact, most of the changes will actually improve productivity and ease of use. The Solution Explorer and Class View help us navigate our projects better. The Task List allows us to track things to be done. While the collapsible code regions in the code window can lessen distractions from surrounding code, letting us focus on the problems at hand.

The new IDE will be explained fully in Chapter 4 but there are some differences worth noting here.

The Toolbox

The Toolbox is similar to that in VB6. Controls are grouped together on tabs that can be added or removed as the situation warrants. Controls are used in the same way: we select a control by clicking on it, and then draw it on our form.

The Solution Explorer

The Solution Explorer provides a way to see what exactly is contained in your current solution. VB.NET allows you to group various projects into one solution, much the same way as groups worked in VB6. The Solution Explorer window gives us a file-level view of what is happening in our solution. One really nice feature is the References list, which provides a quick view of all of the objects that your solution references.

The Class View

The Class View allows us to see all of the classes of the current solution, along with their properties and methods:

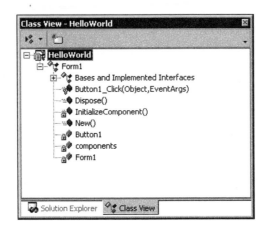

The Properties Window

The Properties window allows properties to be grouped by category, including (but not limited to): Appearance, Behavior, Design, and Layout. Each of these categories can be collapsed to save screen real estate allowing you to concentrate on just the features you need.

The Code Window

The code window will probably seem the most alien to you. This isn't because the code window is that much different, but because of the syntactical changes to VB.NET over VB6:

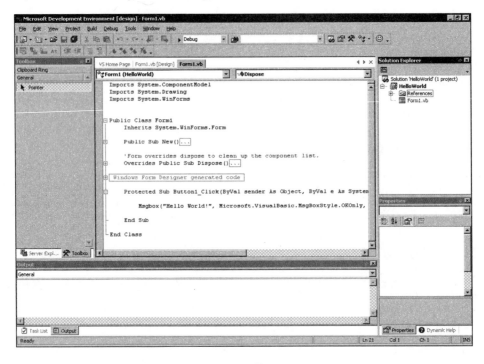

It is now possible to collapse each function or subroutine to just its declaration line. For large source files, this can be a tremendous help in focusing attention on just one function, sub, or class. The other statements at the top are the `Imports` statements at the top of the file. These allow us to use the functions within the imported libraries as native code without reference.

Changes in Data Types

In order for VB.NET to truly take advantage of all the benefits of the .NET Framework some fundamental changes were required. These changes are very evident in how VB.NET handles data types. The goal was for all of the Visual Studio languages to share common types and thereby aid compatibility. And to this end, VB.NET sees the most changes.

Chapters 5 and 6 will explain all of these changes in detail, but we will look at some of the types that will cause most of your VB6 applications to either break or give odd results.

Boolean

One of the things most programmers had trouble dealing with when coming from another language was the numerical value for `True`. In VB6 and VB.NET, the value of `True` is -1.

When interacting with other .NET languages the Boolean value will be cast to the appropriate numerical value. That is, in VB.NET `True = -1`, in C# `True <> 0`.

> However, in any version of Visual Basic you should always use the Boolean values of **True** or **False**. Not only does it make your code easier to read, you avoid any problems if future updates change the numerical value.

Integer

The underlying storage of integers was changed in VB.NET to bring it into line with other languages. The following chart explains the differences:

Integer Type	Visual Basic 6	Visual Basic.NET	CLR type
8 bit integer	Byte	Byte	System.Byte
16 bit integer	Integer	Short	System.Int16
32 bit integer	Long	Integer	System.Int32
64 bit integer	n/a	Long	System.Int64

These changes have the biggest impact when calling Windows API functions. For many of us who use API functions it has become automatic to convert when writing the declaration statement. Whenever a function prototype called for an integer we learned to write the declaration with a long data type. With VB.NET, this is no longer necessary:

```
Private Declare Function GetFileSize Lib "kernel32" (ByVal hFile As Long, _
lpFileSizeHigh As Long) as Long
```

and becomes instead:

```
Private Declare Function GetFileSize Lib "kernel32" (ByVal hFile As Integer, _
lpFileSizeHigh As Integer) as Integer
```

Strings

Another change that may affect calling API functions is how VB.NET handles strings. There is now no such thing as a fixed length string. This really isn't too much of a problem, but if you are counting on the size of a string to be of a certain length, you will have to create it differently:

In VB6 we would write:

```
Dim strFixed as String*100
```

While in VB.NET:

```
Dim strFixed as String
strFixed = New String(CChar(" "), 100)
```

The other important thing to note here is that in VB.NET strings are objects. Hence, why the New keyword is used to create the string of 100 spaces.

Variant

VB.NET has done away with the variant data type. It has been combined with the Object type. The reason for this lies in the new object-oriented nature of VB.NET. Since, everything is now an object in .NET.

Application Types

There are eight application types: Windows Application, Class Library, Windows Control Library, Web Application, Web Service, Web Control Library, Console Application, and Windows Service. Each of these types is focused on a particular type of application, although there is now a lot less of a difference between traditional desktop applications and those that function over the Internet, because Microsoft has designed the .NET Framework with Web applications in mind.

Let's look at some of these types of applications.

Windows Application

A **Windows Application** is the new way to present a GUI for Win32 applications and makes use of the new **Windows Forms**. Since .NET is now part of the Visual Basic name it is easy to get the idea that standard desktop applications are not considered very important, and might have received little attention in the language. This would be a false premise.

All of the Visual Studio languages use Windows Forms as the basis of building desktop windows applications. When we select a project type of Windows Application, we are directing the creation of a standard Win32 application. The added benefit of this model in VB.NET is that creating applications that have both a Win32 interface and a Web interface is much easier. This is because all .NET components have a consistent interface model. For example, the new .NET version of ASP (called ASP.NET) is now strongly typed and does not require everything to be a variant. Therefore, middle tier components can be accessed in exactly the same way from ASP.NET as they are from the desktop.

In Chapter 8, we will delve into Windows Forms in more detail; we will see that Windows Forms are classes and that they must be instantiated before they are shown (just as with any other class):

Web Applications

Web Applications are actually part of ASP.NET and instead of having Windows Forms as the user interface they make use of **Web Forms** – allowing us to easily build a Web interface just as we would a desktop interface. The main concept with Web Forms is the split between display code and logic code. This improves ASP, where it is possible to intermix application logic and display code and hence write confusing code.

This improvement is made by dividing a given Web Form into two parts: an HTML template that controls the UI display and a component that handles all the application logic. Controls on a Web Form actually run on the server, but are displayed in the client browser. This requires that the server has a lot of intelligence, and in a sense, this is what the .NET Framework is all about. Because the server handles the actual implementation "behind-the-scenes", Web Applications can look and behave a lot more like Win32 applications.

In addition, since the UI code is completely separated, supporting different browsers is less of a burden. The browser is only responsible for displaying a control; the server takes care of the execution. Therefore, you will see only plain "vanilla" HTML at the client-side, limiting issues with cross-browser functionality. Chapter 20 of this book will help get you up to speed with Web Forms, but other aspects of Web Forms and ASP.NET can be found in *Professional ASP.NET* (ISBN: 1861004885, Wrox Press).

Web Services

Web Services are where the capabilities of VB.NET really bring the VB developer into a new era. Depending on your age, you may remember the days when an application ran on one computer and one computer only. All aspects of the application were contained within that one system. Then came the days when those applications might access a remote database. Programmers could focus on developing the core business functionality of the application without having to first develop the low level foundations. With the advent of DCOM, programmers could create a business process that ran across the network splitting the workload. However, if you have ever had the task of creating this functionality, you will be much relieved at the new simplicity.

Web Services correct many of the problems involved with creating distributed systems. They allow us to expose our components to any consumer over the Internet. We could have a Web Service that provides some information, such as mortgage rates in our region. A developer for a real estate company on the other side of the country could subscribe to this service, and similar services across the country, and include the information in his application. This developer would not have to concern himself with how the information is gathered, tracked, and entered into the system. He can just include the functionality in his application.

As with Web Applications, Web Services rely on ASP.NET to handle the Web interface. The communication is handled using the **SOAP (Simple Object Access Protocol)** standard, which in turn relies on XML. Web Services and SOAP will be discussed in Chapter 22.

New Object Capabilities

Almost everything is an object in VB.NET. (Well except for the primitive data types, which we will look at more closely in Chapter 5, and any legacy code accessed via the `Microsoft.VisualBasic.Compatibility.VB6` namespace.) The benefit of this is that VB.NET is now a true OO language. There has been a lot of clamor for true object-oriented languages in Visual Basic. However, for most VB programmers that do not also use other object-oriented languages, these features may seem overrated. It should be noted that without proper object-oriented design it is very possible to get into trouble with OOP. So, what are the parts of an OO language? Let's take a look at the four main concepts:

❑   **Polymorphism**: We have had polymorphism since VB4. Polymorphism allows us to take a defined interface for a class and implement different functionality for the methods. In VB 4 – 6 this was accomplished with the `Implements` keyword followed by the name of the interface definition ProgID. In this way an interface that defined an animal class, could be modified so that the `Eat` method would have the desired effect whether the *implementation* defined a cat or a hippopotamus.

❑   **Encapsulation**: Again, this has been around since version 4.0. Encapsulation allows us to hide our algorithms from other developers and only expose an interface to the functionality. For example, we could create an `Encryption` method. We would not want other users to know what encryption algorithms are used, so we could just expose the `Encryption` method and return the encrypted result. The same thing is true whenever you call a Windows API; the actual implementation is hidden away.

❑   **Abstraction**: This is actually a pretty basic concept to programming in general, and it has also been around since VB 4.0 officially. Because OOP allows programmers to combine data with the methods that act on the data, abstraction is rather important. Function libraries provide a similar role in non-OOP languages. From the animal analogy above, a cat or hippopotamus are implementations of the animal abstraction.

❑   **Inheritance**: This is the new feature to VB.NET that brings it officially into the OOP world. Since VB4, programmers have had something called **interface inheritance**. This was rather limiting. In previous versions of Visual Basic, we could implement an interface, but then we would have to write all the code to actually give the new class its functionality. If we created another class that implemented the same interface, we would have to again write all the code to implement the methods.

VB.NET now gives us full **implementation inheritance** and **visual inheritance**, also known as **subclassing**. This means we can create a class with some general functionality, and extend it using inheritance, by using the `Inherits` keyword, without having to rewrite the base functionality. For example, we could create a base class called `Animal` and give it a `Walk` method. We could then create a class called `Cat` that inherits from `Animal`. By default, this new `Cat` class could `Walk`. We do not have to write any new code. The `Cat` class will just use the `Walk` method from the `Animal` class.

In Chapters 11 – 13 of this book, we will give you the background you need to take full advantage of VB.NET's new OOP features.

Structured Error Handling

One of the most unpleasant features in previous versions of Visual Basic was its error handling. The older versions relied on global error handlers: `On Error GoTo` and `On Error Resume Next`. Many programmers have had difficulty tracking down the precise location of errors due to this mechanism's "all or nothing" approach. When an error occurs the code immediately jumps to the handler, and if none is found, it cascades up the call stack.

VB.NET gives us a more structured approach and brings it inline with other languages such as C++, and Java. This new block structure allows us to nest our error handling code and increase readability, maintainability, and controllability.

Try...Throw...Catch...Finally

This new error handling structure known as **exception handling**, will seem a bit odd to most VB developers at first, but its power will soon convince you that it is a definite improvement. The basic structure looks like:

```
Try
    Some statement(s)
    [Throw New Exception(…)]
Catch
    Some statement(s)
[Catch]
Finally
    Some statement(s)
End Try
```

What this structure allows us to do is test our code and if there are problems, catch the error. Every `Try` block must have either a `Catch` or a `Finally` block, or both. If not, a syntax error will be generated.

Chapter 9 will cover error handling in depth.

Syntactical Incompatibilities

When moving from previous versions of Visual Basic to VB.NET it is important to note that you will have to change your code. Some of the incompatibilities result from the data type changes that we have already briefly looked at. Other problems result from changes to the Visual Basic language, itself. A migration tool is included with VB.NET, but it cannot convert all of your code. For many applications, it may not be feasible to make all the necessary modification required. For more up-to-date information, please refer to Microsoft's site at http://msdn.microsoft.com/library/techart/vb6tovbdotnet.htm, but some examples include:

Properties

Properties are no longer created as separate declarations for `Get` and `Set/Let`. This is best illustrated with a brief example:

VB6:

```
Dim mstrName as String

Property Get Name() as String
   Name = mstrName
End Property

Property Let Name(strNameIn as String)
   mstrName = strNameIn
End Property
```

VB.NET:

```
Dim mstrName as String

Property Name() as String
   Get
       Name = mstrName
   End Get
   Set(byVal sName as String)
       mstrName = Value
   End Set
End Property
```

Notice that the new way is actually a bit more intuitive, by combining the Get and Set in to one property declaration.

User-Defined Types

VB.NET does away with the keyword Type and replaces it with the keyword Structure:

```
Public Structure udtMyNewStruct 'Structure replaces Type
   Dim arMyArray() as String
   Public Sub Initialize()
       ReDim arMyArray(10)
   End Sub
   Dim FullName as String
End Structure
...
udtMyNewStruct.Initialize()
udtMyNewStruct.arMyArray(0) = "New Value"
udtMyNewStruct.FullName = "Balthasar Keach"
```

It is important to notice the inclusion of the Initialize subroutine. Fixed-length strings, arrays, and anything requiring the New keyword, all require initialization to be used in a structure. The Initialize method must be called prior to setting any values for the structure. Structures are based on the System.ValueType namespace, rather than System.Object.

Scoping

VB.NET now supports **block-level scoping** of variables. If your programs declare all of the variables at the beginning of the function or subroutine, this will not be a problem. However, the following VB6 code presents a problem when moving to VB.NET:

```
For x = 1 to 10
    Dim strValue as string
    If x = 5 Then
        strValue = "the value is 5"
    End If
Next x
strResult = strValue
```

Because `strValue` is declared within the `For...Next` loop, the statement outside the loop actually refers to a different variable.

ByVal

By default, all parameters are passed *by value* in VB.NET. This is a crucial difference over VB6, where the default was *by reference*. Therefore, if you are counting on modifying parameters in your routines you must make sure to define the parameters using the `ByRef` keyword. Objects are still passed by reference.

GoSub and Return

`GoSub` has been part of the basic language since the beginning. In the early days it was the only way to segment program logic into discrete units of work. Microsoft carried this construct forward through VB6, even though its use was, for the most part, discouraged. The `GoSub/Return` construct was kept probably because of the way Visual Basic implemented error handling, with `On Error Goto...Resume`. However, because we now have the new `Try...Catch...Finally` structure approach to error handling, `GoSub` has been removed from the language completely. `Return` is now used to pass back results from functions, as we will see shortly.

Additional Changes

Besides syntactical changes that might cause your existing code to break, VB.NET has introduced some other changes that you should be aware of.

Parentheses and SubRoutines

In previous versions of Visual Basic, only functions required the use of parentheses around the parameter list. In VB.NET all function or subroutine calls require parentheses around the parameter list, even if it is empty:

```
x = foo(a, b, c)
x = foobar()

'Calling a sub with no parameters
'Note the parentheses are required
```

```
otherFoo()

'Calling a sub with parameters
otherFoobar(a, b, c)
```

Set is Gone

Because everything is an object in VB.NET, there is no longer any reason to differentiate between a simple variable assignment and an object assignment, so Set is no longer used as an assignment operator. This makes the language much simpler.

You are not penalized if you still type:

```
Set oMyObject = New oSomeObject
```

but the VB.NET IDE will just quietly correct the line to:

```
oMyObject = New(oSomeObject)
```

Return

One of the complaints from VB developers coming from other languages was the way VB handled return values. For example, take the following VB6 function:

```
Public Function getCurrentRate(iLoanType as Integer) as Double
    Dim decRate as Decimal
    'Lookup code here
    getCurrentRate = decRate
End Function
```

At a quick glance, it is difficult to see where the actual rate is passed back to the calling routine. In VB.NET this becomes a lot more intuitive:

```
Public Function getCurrentRate(iLoanType as Integer) as Double
    Dim decRate as Decimal
    'Lookup code here
    Return decRate
End Function
```

It is now very clear what is getting returned to the calling routine.

DefType

The DefType statement was used to default variables whose names began with defined letters to be of a specified type. For example, DefInt A-G would default all variable names beginning with the letters A through G to be integers. Not only did this practice make the code difficult to read, but it also aided the introduction of strange runtime bugs resulting from implicit casting. The DefType statement has been removed from VB.NET, since VB.NET now relies on explicit casting when setting values. For example:

```
Dim i as integer
Dim x as string
i= 42
x = i.ToString()   'x now equals "42"
```

Summary

The .NET Framework affects everyone developing applications on a Windows platform. Visual Basic developers, unfortunately, have to bear the weight of most of these changes. For the most part, the changes are so extensive that VB.NET could be viewed as a new language rather than just an upgrade. However, these changes were necessary to give developers the features that they have been asking for: true OOP, easier deployment, better interoperability, and a cohesive environment to develop both traditional and Web applications. VB.NET has empowered the VB development community with a language that raises them to the same technical level as C#, C++, and Java developers. To do this there had to be extensive change to the language – but once you get used to it, you will be excited by the programming opportunities that it opens up!

The rest of this book focuses on the topics introduced here in far greater detail, and will help you come to grips with the changes, as well as help you exploit them to build robust applications. You will see that VB.NET has emerged as a powerful, yet still easy to use, language that will allow you to target the desktop just as easily as the Internet.

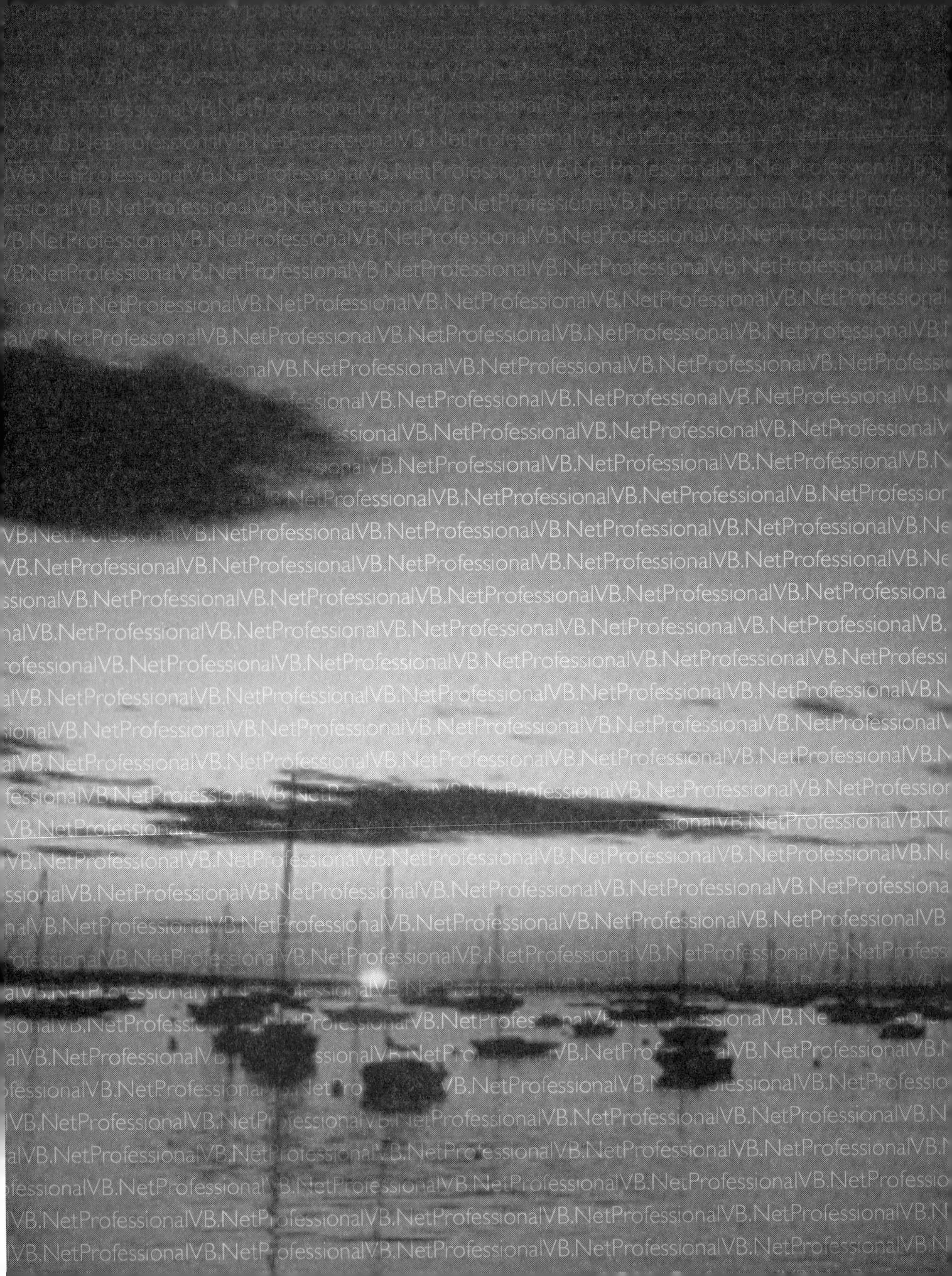
VB.NetProfessional

3

A First Look at a VB.NET Program

The first two chapters have introduced .NET and explained why it is an important and necessary step in the evolution of programming on the Windows platform. In this chapter, we are going to look practically at how these changes affect us, as developers, when creating applications. We will start by walking through the creation of a simple Hello World Windows application. We will then build up this application throughout the course of the chapter, dissecting the code at each stage to explain the changes that have been made. We will cover many topics, including:

- ❑ Project types
- ❑ Generated code
- ❑ Code regions
- ❑ Imports statements and namespaces
- ❑ Forms as classes
- ❑ Class constructors
- ❑ Setting of form properties
- ❑ Adding controls

> **This chapter will only provide a brief practical introduction to creating a VB.NET application, as we will look at all of the subjects covered here in much more detail in later chapters. If you have used VB.NET before (perhaps you've read *VB.NET Programming with the Public Beta*, ISBN 1861004915 or *Beginning VB.NET*, ISBN 1861004966), both by Wrox Press Ltd, please feel free to skip this chapter.**

Creating the Sample Application

Let's begin by starting Visual Studio.NET. There have been some big changes to the IDE since VB6, the full details of which will be covered in the next chapter. For now, we just need to create a new project by either selecting New Project from the Visual Studio.NET start page, or by selecting New | Project from the File menu. The New Project dialog box will appear.

The New Project Dialog

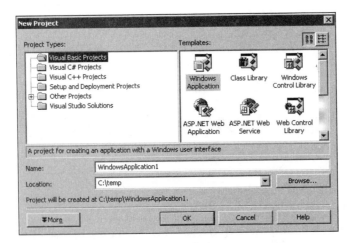

As this figure shows, all of the available project types in Visual Studio.NET are accessed through one dialog box. There is no longer one IDE for Visual Basic and a different one for Visual C++. All of the .NET languages (except Visual FoxPro) share one common IDE.

This dialog box is split into two sections. The first section, which is the file tree view on the left of the dialog box, represents the different project types that can be created. The second section is the list view on the right of the dialog box, which displays all of the project templates that can be created for the selected project type.

The Project Template

The different types of project templates that can be created for Visual Basic are listed in the following table:

Template	Description
Windows Application	A WinForms-based project (equivalent to a VB6 Standard EXE project).
Class Library	A project to create a library of classes for use in another application (similar to a VB6 ActiveX DLL project).
Windows Control Library	A project to create a control for use in Windows applications (similar to a VB6 ActiveX Control project).

Table continued on following page

Template	Description
ASP.Net Web Application	A project where the user interface is created using web pages and resides on a web server. This project type is equivalent to a Visual InterDev project in the previous version of Visual Studio.
ASP.NET Web Service	A project that creates a set of methods that is exposed to other applications over the Web. Chapter 22 covers Web Services in detail.
Web Control Library	A project to create a control that can be used in web applications (similar to a VB6 ActiveX Control project).
Console Application	A project that creates a command line application.
Windows Service	A project that will create a Windows service.
Empty Project	An empty project will be created with no files other than the project file.
Empty Web Project	An empty project will be created on the web server.
New Project In Existing Folder	Provides a wizard so that you can create a project in an existing folder.

Since we are creating a Windows application, select Windows Application as the template for the project and give the project the name of HelloWorld. Then click OK.

The Solution Explorer

When the selected project template is created, a number of files will be automatically added to the project for us. The number and type of files added will depend on the project template selected. In our case, two code files (Form1.vb and AssemblyInfo.vb) have been added to the project, which you can see in the Solution Explorer:

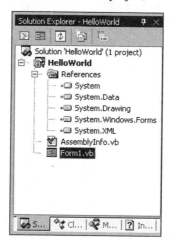

The Solution Explorer shows all of the projects that make up the solution. A **solution** can be thought of as a collection of projects that provide a solution to a problem.

Users of VB6 may find it useful to think of a solution as being similar to a VB6 project group, although solutions can contain projects from each of the .NET languages.

As you can see from the screenshot above, a solution called HelloWorld has been created for us that contains one project (also called HelloWorld). The Solution Explorer also shows us visually what references a project contains and allows us to remove a specific reference and add new ones. A reference in VB.NET allows us to access the functionality of external objects. We are able to reference type libraries (such as COM libraries and other projects created in VB6), other .NET components, and Web Services. Notice that, when VB.NET created the project for the template we selected, it added a selection of references that are needed for this project template, listed under the References node.

The Default Namespaces of a Windows Application

The references added to our project are detailed in the table below and relate directly to namespaces:

Reference	Description
System	The `System` namespace is often referred to as the root namespace as it provides functionality that all applications will use. All the base data types (`String`, `Object`, etc.) are contained within the classes of the `System` namespace, along with classes that represent the garbage collector, attributes, and exceptions. It also acts as the parent namespace for a large number of child namespaces, some of which are included in the remaining of the table.
System.Data	The `System.Data` namespace consists of classes that are used to implement the functionality of ADO.NET, which is used for data access. This namespace will be covered in more detail in Chapter 18.
System.Drawing	The `System.Drawing` namespace provides access to the GDI+ graphics functionality. GDI+ is an updated version of the old *Graphics Device Interface (GDI)* functions provided by the Windows API.
System.Windows.Forms	The `System.Windows.Forms` namespace provides a set of classes that can be used to create traditional Windows-based applications. This namespace will be covered in detail in Chapter 8.
System.XML	The `System.XML` namespace contains classes that can be used for processing XML. The XML processing provided is standards based and will be covered in Chapter 19.

Alongside the References node, you will see all of the files that make up the project. In our case, we have two (Form1.vb and AssemblyInfo.vb). Note that there is only one file extension for VB source files (.vb). We no longer have one extension for a class module and a different one for a form – all of the differences are held within the source files themselves.

We will start by looking at the Form1.vb file produced for us, as it contains the code that represents the main window of our application. Then towards the end of the chapter we will briefly discuss the AssemblyInfo.vb file that has also been created for us.

The form is visible on the screen by default but, if you have closed it, you can easily reopen it again by right-clicking on Form1.vb in the Solution Explorer and selecting View Designer from the popup menu.

The Properties Window

The Properties window should also be visible. If not, you can access it through the View menu or by pressing the *F4* key.

The Properties window is just like that in VB6. It is used to set the properties of the currently selected item – for example, a project file or a control on a form.

> Note that, in VB.NET, we no longer have a `Caption` property. All items that had a `Caption` property in VB6 now have a `Text` property instead.

Change the Text property of Form1 to Hello World:

Therefore, to set the caption of a Button control (the new name for Command Buttons), we would now use the Text property, rather than the Caption property, like so:

```
btnCancel.Text = "&Cancel"
```

We have now created the example project that we are going to examine and build upon in the remainder of the chapter. Users of VB6 may be forgiven for wondering what has changed. It is only when we look at the code that we can fully appreciate how forms in VB.NET work and how they differ from previous versions of VB.

Analysis of the HelloWorld Example

Now bring up the code window for the form by right-clicking on the form or the Solution Explorer and selecting View Code from the popup menu.

Tabs vs. MDI Interface

You will probably have noticed the tabs that are visible below the toolbar:

In previous versions of the VB IDE, we accessed child windows using an MDI interface. This is still available in Visual Studio.NET but the default is to use the new tabbed arrangement of child windows. This means that, for every child window open, there will be a corresponding tab that you can use to select the child window that you would like to work with. Child windows can include:

❑   Project files (both in code and designer mode)

❑   MSDN Help

❑   The Visual Studio.NET start page

You can change the arrangement that is used between the tabbed and MDI interface by using the Options dialog box (accessible via Tools | Options). You can also force the development environment to use the MDI interface as opposed to the tabbed interface by using the command line option /mdi.

To do this, open a command line window and navigate to the directory that contains the development environment executable, devenv.exe. This is likely to be in C:\Program Files\Microsoft Visual Studio.Net\Common7\IDE. Then enter Devenv /mdi on the command line and press *Enter*.

Likewise, to force the development environment to use the tabbed interface, use the command line option /mditabs.

Forms as Classes

Let's start with the first two lines of code; these start the declaration for our form:

```
Public Class Form1
    Inherits System.Windows.Forms.Form
```

The first line declares a new class called Form1. In VB.NET, we can declare classes in any code file, not just in a class module (.cls) file as was the case in VB6. We can also declare any number of classes in a code file, which can lead to confusion.

The second line specifies that the class derives from the Form class contained in the System.Windows.Forms namespace.

Therefore, we can deduce from these two lines of code that forms in VB.NET are classes. Specifically, forms are now classes that directly or indirectly derive from the System.Windows.Forms.Form class. This class is used to create dialog boxes and windows for traditional Windows-based applications.

We can also deduce from the Inherits keyword that the VB language has been improved to provide better object-oriented features, which will be covered in Chapters 11 – 13.

Because the class is declared with a name of `Form1`, our form will be called `Form1`. We can rename the file that contains the class but this does not change the actual name of the class – you must remember to change the `Public Class` *FormName* line as well in order to reflect the new name.

One of the very neat outcomes of forms being implemented as classes is that you can now derive one form from another form. This technique is called **visual inheritance**.

Windows Forms will be covered in much more detail in Chapter 8.

Code Regions

Now we'll turn our attention to the `Windows Form Designer generated code` line. To the left of this box, you will notice a small box with a plus (+) sign inside it:

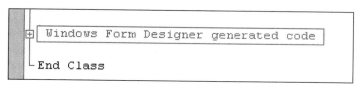

This is a new feature of VB.NET called a **code region**. As the name suggests, a code region is a section of code that is grouped together into a region. If you click on the plus sign, you will be able to see the following code:

```
#Region " Windows Form Designer generated code "

  Public Sub New()
    MyBase.New()

    'This call is required by the Windows Form Designer.
    InitializeComponent()

    'Add any initialization after the InitializeComponent() call

  End Sub

  'Form overrides dispose to clean up the component list.
  Protected Overloads Overrides Sub Dispose(ByVal disposing As Boolean)
    If disposing Then
      If Not (components Is Nothing) Then
        components.Dispose()
      End If
    End If
    MyBase.Dispose(disposing)
  End Sub

  'Required by the Windows Form Designer
  Private components As System.ComponentModel.Container

  'NOTE: The following procedure is required by the Windows Form Designer
  'It can be modified using the Windows Form Designer.
  'Do not modify it using the code editor.
  <System.Diagnostics.DebuggerStepThrough()> Private Sub _
```

```
        InitializeComponent()
    '
    'Form1
    '
    Me.AutoScaleBaseSize = New System.Drawing.Size(5, 13)
    Me.ClientSize = New System.Drawing.Size(292, 273)
    Me.Name = "Form1"
    Me.Text = "Hello World"

  End Sub


#End Region
```

When you create a VB project using the Windows Application template, a code region is automatically added to the form class for you. The `Windows Form Designer generated code` region is automatically created and maintained by VS.NET (it is required to set up the layout of the form) and altering it can produce unwanted results.

Clicking on the minus sign (–) in the box will collapse this code region and hide it again. Code regions are useful because they allow you to organize specific areas of code and hide them when you don't wish to see them, providing more screen real estate for the bits of code that you are concentrating on.

We can also create our own code regions by using the `#Region` and `#End Region` declarations. For example, if we wanted to create a new code region called `Data Access Code`, we would add the following to the source code:

```
#Region "Data Access Code"
'Include any data access code within the region tags
#End Region
```

We can also use this method to collapse and hide the contents of a whole class, if desired.

Let's step through the code in the `Windows Form Designer generated code` region.

The Constructor

The **constructor** procedure is one of the many new object-oriented features of VB.NET and it will be covered in detail in Chapter 11. This procedure is called before any other code in the class, which means that it is the ideal place to perform any initialization tasks.

The constructor in VB.NET replaces the `Class_Initialize` function in VB6. All code that would have been placed in `Class_Initialize` in previous versions of VB should now be placed in a class constructor.

In VB.NET, a constructor is added to a class by adding a procedure called New:

```
Public Sub New()
   MyBase.New()

   'This call is required by the Windows Form Designer.
   InitializeComponent()

   'Add any initialization after the InitializeComponent() call

End Sub
```

When you create a constructor in VB.NET, the first line contained in the procedure must either call another constructor in the same class or the constructor of the base class. This will ensure that all of the objects in the inheritance hierarchy are correctly initialized. We can use the `MyBase` keyword to access the immediate base class of the class that contains the keyword. In our program, the `MyBase` keyword is used to invoke the base class's (`System.Windows.Forms.Form`) constructor.

Notice also, that the form designer has automatically added a call to `InitializeComponent` in the constructor. We will cover this procedure later in the chapter.

After the call to `InitializeComponent`, we can add any other initialization code that we need to run before the window is shown to the user. If we needed to get any configuration information out of a database, for example, this is where we would add that code.

The Destructor

We can also create a class **destructor** – which replaces the `Class_Terminate` event in VB6 – by adding a sub-procedure called `Finalize` to our class.

VB.NET uses a garbage collector to destroy objects, rather than a reference counting mechanism. This means that, although an object may no longer be referenced by any other object, it will continue to exist until the garbage collector destroys it. Generally, it is not possible to know exactly when this garbage collection will take place and in which order the objects will be garbage collected. The `Finalize` method is called just before the garbage collection occurs but, since we won't know when this will happen, this method should not be used to contain any code that needs to be run within a specific period after an object goes out of scope. This is called **non-deterministic finalization**.

Overriding Procedures

As we discussed earlier, the `Form` class in `System.Windows.Forms` is used to create windows and the `Dispose` method, as the comment informs us, is called to clean up all of the components on the form:

```
'Form overrides dispose to clean up the component list.
Protected Overloads Overrides Sub Dispose(ByVal disposing As Boolean)
    If disposing Then
        If Not (components Is Nothing) Then
            components.Dispose()
        End If
    End If
    MyBase.Dispose(disposing)
End Sub
```

However, the `System.Windows.Forms.Form` class is actually derived from another class, called `ContainerControl`. The `System.Windows.Forms.Form` class inherits all the methods of the `ContainerControl` class, but the `ContainerControl`'s `Dispose` method is altered in `System.Windows.Forms.Form` because VS.NET has **overridden** the original by using the `Overrides` keyword.

When we have one of more procedures or properties in a class with the same name (but with different properties), we say that the procedure or method has been **overloaded**. VS.NET has automatically added the `Overloads` keyword, since the `Dispose` method has been overloaded as well.

Don't worry if all this sounds a little confusing right now; inheritance, the `Overrides` keyword, and the `Overloads` keyword will be covered in detail in Chapter 12.

The `Dispose` procedure has one argument called `disposing`. This argument is used to indicate whether we should dispose of unmanaged resources only (`disposing = False`) or managed and unmanaged resources (`disposing = True`). As VB.NET lives in the managed world only, a check is made to ensure that `disposing` is equal to `True`:

```
If disposing Then
```

Then a simple check follows to see if a variable called `components` of type `System.ComponentModel.Container` has been instantiated. The `System.ComponentModel.Container` class is used to track and hold a number of components, which can be visual and non-visual. If `components` has been instantiated, its `Dispose` method will be, releasing any resources held by it:

```
If Not (components Is Nothing) Then
    components.Dispose()
End If
```

When we override a procedure of a base class and we are adding functionality, it is advisable to call the base class's version of the procedure. This helps to make sure that the base class is in the correct state:

```
MyBase.Dispose(disposing)
```

Variable Declaration

The next line of code is the declaration of a variable of type `System.ComponentModel.Container`:

```
'Required by the Windows Form Designer
Private components As System.ComponentModel.Container
```

Variables are declared in pretty much the same way as they were in VB6 by using the `Public`, `Private`, `Static`, and `Dim` keywords. However, the keywords `Protected` and `Friend` have been introduced with VB.NET.

A variable that is declared as `Protected` is visible within the class it is declared in or any class that is derived from the class in which it is declared.

The `Friend` keyword existed in VB6 for use with class methods and properties but it could not be used to declare variables. If you declare a property with the `Friend` keyword in VB.NET it will be accessible from anywhere within the same assembly and not accessible from outside the assembly.

Attributes

Before we talk about the contents of the `InitializeComponent` procedure, we will take some time to discuss its declaration:

```
<System.Diagnostics.DebuggerStepThrough()> Private Sub _
        InitializeComponent()
```

The `<System.Diagnostics.DebuggerStepThrough()>` section before the `Private` keyword will more than likely be new to you, and is known as an **attribute**. Attributes are used as a mechanism by which we can supply additional information about:

❑   Assemblies

❑   Modules

❑   Classes

❑   Methods

❑   Properties

❑   Variables

The additional information supplied by the attribute can be used by the application in which it's defined, the compiler, or any other external application. There are a large number of built in attributes contained within the .NET framework, although we are not limited to these and can define our own.

Attributes are added to your code using **attribute blocks**, which begin with < and end with >. The actual attributes appear within the attribute block. In the above example we only have one attribute – `System.Diagnostics.DebuggerStepThrough()`, but we can include more than one attribute in a block by separating them with commas.

The actual attribute contained within an attribute block can have the following parts:

❑   **Attribute modifier** (optional). This allows us to apply the attribute to a particular code file (a module) or the whole assembly. An attribute modifier appears before the name of the attribute followed by a colon. If an attribute block has a modifier then it must appear at the top of the file containing it after any `Imports` statements (discussed later). We discuss the use of attribute modifiers later in this chapter.

   If an attribute does not contain any modifiers then it applies to the element where it was declared. In the case of the `System.Diagnostics.DebuggerStepThrough` attribute, it was declared within the method declaration, and therefore the attribute applies to the method.

❑   **Attribute name** (mandatory). This is the name of the attribute, which is the class name that implements the attribute. All attributes' class names end with the word `Attribute`, but when declaring an attribute in a block we can leave off the ending `Attribute` text from the class name – in other words, the above attribute could also be written as:
   `<System.Diagnostics.DebuggerStepThroughAttribute()>`

❑   **Attribute parameters** (optional). The last part of the attribute declaration is to include any parameters that are needed. In the case of the above attribute, there are no parameters, but as you will see later in the chapter there are a number of attributes that take parameters. If an attribute does not have any attributes then you must use empty brackets.

The `System.Diagnostics.DebuggerStepThrough()` attribute included in the declaration of the `InitizializeComponent` method is used to inform the debugger not to step through this method when the application is being debugged. If you try to Step Into this method from where it is called, the debugger will in fact step over the method. This can be very useful to stop the developer from stepping through any code that was auto-generated and tempting them to change it.

Form Properties Set in Code

As mentioned earlier, VB.NET has added a sub to the code called `InitializeComponent`. As the name suggests, this handles the initialization of the components that are contained on the form. The comment that is added before the procedure warns us that the form designer modifies the code contained in the procedure and that we should not modify the code directly:

```
'NOTE: The following procedure is required by the Windows Form Designer
'It can be modified using the Windows Form Designer.
'Do not modify it using the code editor.
<System.Diagnostics.DebuggerStepThrough()> Private Sub _
        InitializeComponent()
    '
    'Form1
    '
    Me.AutoScaleBaseSize = New System.Drawing.Size(5, 13)
    Me.ClientSize = New System.Drawing.Size(292, 273)
    Me.Name = "Form1"
    Me.Text = "Hello World"

End Sub
```

The four lines of the `InitializeComponent` procedure are assigning values to properties of our `Form1` class. All properties of the form and controls are now set directly in code. When you change the value of a property of the form or a control – through the Properties window – that is different from the default value, an entry will be added to `InitializeComponent` that will assign the entered value to the property. In the case of our application, we set the `Text` property of the form to `"Hello World"`, which caused the following line of code to be added automatically (and the text to appear in the title bar of the form):

```
Me.Text = "Hello World"
```

In previous versions of VB, the properties that were changed from the default values were stored in a region of the form file (.frm) that could not be edited directly though VB.

The other three properties of the form class that are being set in the `InitializeComponent` sub have been summarized in the table below:

Property	Description
AutoScaleBase Size	This property is used to store the size of the font used to layout your form at design time. At runtime, the font that is actually rendered is compared to this property and the form is automatically scaled accordingly. This helps to ensure the form looks the same at runtime as it did at design time.
ClientSize	This property is used to set the area within a form in which controls can be placed (the client area). It is the size of the form minus the size of the title bar and form borders. The property is of type System.Drawing.Size.
Name	This property is used to set the textual name of the form. By default the property is set to an empty string.

You will have probably also noticed that the code is accessing the properties of the form using the Me keyword. The Me keyword is special in that it acts as a variable that refers to the instance of the class in which it's used. This isn't entirely necessary but people argue that it aids in the understanding of the code.

The AssemblyInfo.vb File

Now that we have taken a look at the code produced for us in `Form1.vb` we are going to move on and take a brief look at the other file produced for us: `AssemblyInfo.vb`. A complete listing of the file is included below:

```
Imports System.Reflection
Imports System.Runtime.InteropServices

' General Information about an assembly is controlled through
' the following set of attributes. Change these attribute values
' to modify the information associated with an assembly.

' Review the values of the assembly attributes

<Assembly: AssemblyTitle("")>
<Assembly: AssemblyDescription("")>
<Assembly: AssemblyCompany("")>
<Assembly: AssemblyProduct("")>
<Assembly: AssemblyCopyright("")>
<Assembly: AssemblyTrademark("")>
<Assembly: CLSCompliant(True)>

'The following GUID is for the ID of the typelib if this project
'is exposed to COM
<Assembly: Guid("6CCAA661-F174-454C-948E-D3E25426484C")>

' Version information for an assembly consists of the following
' four values:
'
'       Major Version
'       Minor Version
'       Build Number
'       Revision
'
' You can specify all the values or you can default the Build
' and Revision Numbers by using the '*' as shown below:

<Assembly: AssemblyVersion("1.0.*")>
```

The `AssemblyInfo.vb` file is added to the project to provide a centralized place where we can set information about and properties of the resulting assembly. The information and properties of the assembly are set using a number of attributes that we will cover later on in this section.

Namespaces and the Imports Keyword

If you look at the Solution Explorer, you will see that we have a reference to the **System.Drawing** component.

The `System.Drawing` component provides access to GDI+ graphics functionality, an updated version of the old Graphics Device Interface functions provided by the Windows API.

By adding a reference to a component like this, we can use its functionality in our program. As an example, here's a line of code that uses the full reference for the `System.Drawing` component's `Color` structure:

```
Dim CarColor As System.Drawing.Color
```

Here, the `Color` structure is in the `System.Drawing` **namespace**. A namespace is used to organize classes, structures, and other types into a single meaningful hierarchy. As well as providing a way to organize classes and other types, namespaces reduce name collision.

You can omit the full namespace prefix if you import the namespace into your code by using the `Imports` statement. The top two lines of the generated code in the `AssemblyInfo.vb` file are `Imports` statements:

```
Imports System.Reflection
Imports System.Runtime.InteropServices
```

`Imports` statements must be used at the beginning of a code file before any other code. In our code, the `System.Reflection` namespace is imported, so we can use the `AssemblyTitle` attribute in our code by simply using the following:

```
<Assembly: AssemblyTitle("")>
```

as opposed to:

```
<Assembly: System.Reflection.AssemblyTitle("")>
```

As you can see, this significantly reduces the amount of code that we have to type, but we must beware the consequences of not using the full namespace declaration. The single biggest consequence is that, if you import two namespaces that both contain a type which has the same name, and you try to declare a variable of this type without using the full namespace declaration, the compiler won't know which version to use. Imagine that, as well as importing the `System.Drawing` namespace, we import a `WroxColor` namespace that also contains a `Color` structure. If we refer to the `Color` object subsequently in our code without specifying its full namespace, we will see an error like the following:

```
Protected Sub Button1_Click(ByVal sender As Object, ByVal e As System.EventArgs)
    Dim objColor As Color
End Sub
                              The name 'Color' is ambiguous, imported from the namespaces or types
                              'WroxColor, System.Drawing'.
Class
```

The program will not run until this ambiguity is clarified by referencing the `Color` structure's full namespace.

You can view the namespaces that are available to your application by using the Object Browser, which can be accessed by using the *Ctrl-Alt-J* key combination or through the View | Other Windows menu option:

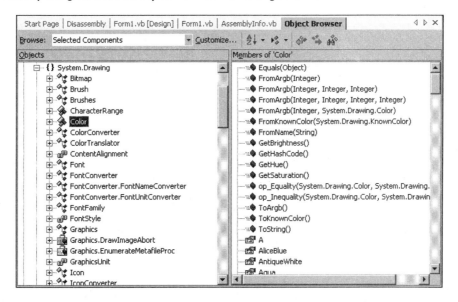

The Object Browser is split into two panes. The pane to the left lists all of the namespaces that are available to your application. The namespaces listed will depend on the references that you have included in your project. You can expand the namespace nodes to reveal the classes, structures, and other types that are contained within the namespace. If you select a class or other type from the left-pane, all of its members will be listed in the right-pane.

Namespaces can also be nested inside other namespaces. Nesting helps to organize classes into a more logical structure, which cuts down confusion and aids the developer. For example, in the `System.Drawing` namespace, the `Drawing` namespace is a child of (is nested within) the `System` namespace. A parent namespace can be used across multiple components.

Namespaces will be examined more thoroughly in Chapter 7.

Assembly Attributes

The remaining lines of code within the `AssemblyInfo.vb` file are attribute blocks. The attribute blocks are used to set information about the resulting assembly. All the attribute blocks within this file have the **assembly modifier** (`Assembly:`). For example:

```
<Assembly: AssemblyTitle("")>
```

The assembly modifier is used to make the attribute defined apply to the entire assembly. The attributes set within this file all provide information that is contained within the assembly Meta Data. The attributes contained within the file are summarized in the following table:

Attribute	Description
AssemblyCompany	This attribute is used to set the name of the company that produced the assembly. The company name set here will appear within the version resource of the resulting compiled file. This can be seen by right-clicking the file within Windows Explorer and selecting Properties and then looking on the Version tab.
AssemblyCopyright	This attribute is used to set the copyright information of the produced assembly. The copyright information also appears within the version resource of the resulting compiled file.
Assembly Description	This attribute is used to provide a textual description of the assembly.
AssemblyProduct	This attribute is used to set the product name of the resulting assembly. The product name will appear within the version resource of the resulting compiled file.
AssemblyTitle	This attribute is used to set the name of the assembly. The title will appear within the resource information of the compiled file as the Description.
AssemblyTrademark	This attribute is used to assign any trademark information to the assembly. This information also appears within the version resource for the compiled file.
AssemblyVersion	This attribute is used to set the version number of the assembly. This is a very important attribute as the version number plays a huge role in helping to avoid DLL hell when deploying applications (and assemblies). Assembly version numbers will be covered in more detail in Chapter 14.
CLSCompliant	This attribute is used to indicate whether the assembly is compliant with the Common Language System. The CLS is a subset of the Common Language Runtime. More information about writing CLS compliant code can be found in MSDN.
Guid	If your assembly is to be exposed as a traditional COM object (see the Project Properties window) then the ID entered using this attribute will become the ID of the resulting type library.

Enhancing the Sample Application

We are now going to enhance our application and examine the new code that is added for us. Before we start, make sure that the form is visible in design mode (View | Designer).

Accessing the Toolbox

Before we start enhancing our application, we also need to know how to access the **toolbox**. There are two ways to access the toolbox if it is not currently visible. The first is to select Toolbox from the View menu, and the second is to access the toolbox from the vertical bar that runs along the left side of VS.NET. If you look at the bar now, you will notice that there is a tab with the text Toolbox. If you move your mouse over the tab, the toolbox will slide into view from the left:

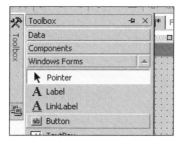

Both of these two options will display the toolbox. If you haven't set up the toolbox to be permanently visible, it will slide out of the way and disappear whenever focus is moved away from it. This is a new feature of the IDE that has been added to help maximize the available screen real estate by hiding windows that are no longer being used. If you do not like this feature and you would like the toolbox to be permanently visible, all you need to do is click the push-pin icon on the title bar of the toolbox so it looks like the one in the figure below:

The functionality of the toolbox has been greatly increased in VB.NET and this will be covered in detail in Chapter 4.

Adding Controls

Now that you know how to access the toolbox, add a button control to the form and set its Text property to "Click Me" and its Name property to btnClickMe. Your form should look similar to the following figure:

Adding an Event Handler

A button that doesn't do anything when it is clicked is no use at all. So let's add some code to respond to the button being clicked. In the event handler, add the following code to the `Click` event of `btnClickMe`:

```
System.Windows.Forms.MessageBox.Show("Hello World", _
                            "Chapter 3 Example", _
                            MessageBoxButtons.OK, _
                            MessageBoxIcon.Information)
```

You may have noticed from this code that you now must use parentheses when calling procedures, even if you are not interested in the return value. In previous versions of VB, the above line of code could have been written as:

```
MsgBox "Hello World!"
```

> **When calling a procedure that lacks parameters in VB.NET, you must use empty parentheses.**

Code Listing

We can now examine the code changes that have been made to our application. A complete listing has been included below:

```
Public Class Form1
    Inherits System.Windows.Forms.Form

#Region " Windows Form Designer generated code "

    Public Sub New()
        MyBase.New()

        'This call is required by the Windows Form Designer.
        InitializeComponent()

        'Add any initialization after the InitializeComponent() call

    End Sub

    'Form overrides dispose to clean up the component list.
    Protected Overloads Overrides Sub Dispose(ByVal disposing As Boolean)
        If disposing Then
            If Not (components Is Nothing) Then
                components.Dispose()
            End If
        End If
        MyBase.Dispose(disposing)
    End Sub
    Friend WithEvents btnClickMe As System.Windows.Forms.Button
```

```
'Required by the Windows Form Designer
Private components As System.ComponentModel.Container

'NOTE: The following procedure is required by the Windows Form Designer
'It can be modified using the Windows Form Designer.
'Do not modify it using the code editor.
<System.Diagnostics.DebuggerStepThrough()> Private Sub _
        InitializeComponent()
    Me.btnClickMe = New System.Windows.Forms.Button()
    Me.SuspendLayout()
    '
    'btnClickMe
    '
    Me.btnClickMe.Location = New System.Drawing.Point(96, 112)
    Me.btnClickMe.Name = "btnClickMe"
    Me.btnClickMe.TabIndex = 0
    Me.btnClickMe.Text = "Click Me"
    '
    'Form1
    '
    Me.AutoScaleBaseSize = New System.Drawing.Size(5, 13)
    Me.ClientSize = New System.Drawing.Size(292, 273)
    Me.Controls.AddRange(New System.Windows.Forms.Control() {Me.btnClickMe})
    Me.Name = "Form1"
    Me.Text = "Hello World"
    Me.ResumeLayout(False)

End Sub

#End Region

    Private Sub btnClickMe_Click(ByVal sender As System.Object, ByVal e As
System.EventArgs) Handles btnClickMe.Click
        System.Windows.Forms.MessageBox.Show("Hello World", _
                                "Chapter 4 Example", _
                                MessageBoxButtons.OK, _
                                MessageBoxIcon.Information)

    End Sub
End Class
```

Code Changes

The first change that has been made to our code is the addition of a new variable to represent our new button:

```
Friend WithEvents btnClickMe As System.Windows.Forms.Button
```

When you add any type of control to the form, a new variable will be added to the form class. Controls are now represented by variables and, just as form properties are set in code, so form controls are added in code. The Button class in the System.Windows.Forms namespace implements the button control on the toolbox. You will find that all of the controls that can be added to a form from the toolbox will have a class that implements the functionality of the control, and the classes are usually contained in the System.Windows.Forms namespace. The WithEvents keyword has been used when declaring the new variable so that we can respond to the events of the button.

The majority of the code additions that have occurred are in the `InitializeComponent` procedure. As mentioned earlier, this procedure is used to set up the form and any controls contained on the form. It follows then that, when we add a control to the form, additional code will be added to the `InitializeComponent` procedure to set up this new control. In the case of our example application, eight lines of code have been added to help set up and add our button control. The first addition to the procedure is a line that creates a new instance of the `Button` class and assigns it to the new variable that we talked about above:

```
Me.btnClickMe = New System.Windows.Forms.Button()
```

When a new instance of the form is created, we will need to create a new instance of the button that is contained on the form. Before we actually add the new button to the form we need to stop the layout engine of the form from working. This is accomplished by using the next line of code added for us:

```
Me.SuspendLayout()
```

The next four lines of code that have been added are setting properties of the button through code. The `Location` property of the `Button` class sets the location of the top left corner of the button within the form:

```
btnClickMe.Location = New System.Drawing.Point(80, 16)
```

The location of a control is expressed in terms of a `Point` structure, which is basically an (x, y) coordinate pair.

The next property of the button that is set through code is the `Name` property:

```
Me.btnClickMe.Name = "btnClickMe"
```

The `Name` property acts in exactly the same way as it did for the form – it provides a way to set the textual name of the button. The `Name` property has no effect on how the button is displayed on the form.

The next two lines of code assign values to the `TabIndex` and `Text` properties of the button:

```
Me.btnClickMe.TabIndex = 0
Me.btnClickMe.Text = "Click Me"
```

The `TabIndex` property of the button is used to set the order in which the control will be selected when the user cycles through the controls on the form using the *Tab* key. The higher the number, the later the control will get focus. Each control should have a unique number for its `TabIndex` property. As shown earlier, the `Text` property of a button can be used to set the text that appears on the button.

Once the properties of the button have been set there needs to be a way to add the button to the form. This is accomplished with the next line of code added for us:

```
Me.Controls.AddRange(New System.Windows.Forms.Control() {Me.btnClickMe})
```

This line of code adds our new button to the collection of child controls for the form. The `System.Windows.Forms.Form` class (from which our `Form1` class is derived) has a property called `Controls` that keeps track of all of the child controls of the form. Whenever we add a control to a form, code similar to that discussed above will be added to the form automatically for us.

The final code change to the `InitializeComponent` sub turns the layout logic of the form back on, so that our new button will be correctly added to the form:

```
Me.ResumeLayout(False)
```

We have now covered the majority of the code changes. The only change that needs to be explained is the event handler we added for the button. Event handlers have a similar naming convention to that of previous versions of VB, the control name followed by an underscore and then the event name and any parameters. In our example, we added an event handler for the `Click` event of the button. Event handlers can be added by using the drop-down lists at the top of the code window:

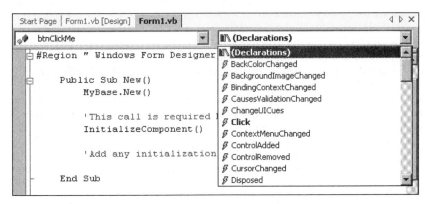

The left drop-down box lists all of the available class names for which we can add event handlers. The right drop-down box lists all the events for the selected object. This is exactly the same as in previous versions of VB, although it has been enhanced to allow you to handle the events of the classes that you have overridden. The overridden object is represented in the list of objects by the text (Overrides).

We have now covered all of the additions that have been made to our code as the result of adding a button to the form. The code is very simple and very intuitive to read, and represents a huge change from previous versions of VB.

Stepping through the Hello World Example

Having created the sample Hello World application, we are going to look at how to build the application. We will first take a look at build configurations.

Build Configurations

In previous versions of VB, your project only had one set of properties. There was no way to have one set of properties for a debug build and one for a release build – you had to manually change all the properties as required before you built the application. This has now been changed with the introduction of build configurations, which let you have one set of project properties for a debug build and one set for a release build. You are not limited to the two default build configurations (debug and release), as you can create as many different configurations as you want. The properties that can be set for a project have been split into two groups: those that are independent of build configuration and which apply to all build configurations, and those that apply to the active build configuration only. For instance, the Project Name and Project

`Location` properties are the same irrespective of what build configuration is active, whereas the code optimization options can be different depending on the active build configuration. This isn't a new concept and has been available to Visual C++ developers for some time, but it is the first time it has been introduced into VB.

What does this mean to us? Well, it enables us to turn off optimization when we are developing our application and create symbolic debug information that will help if we encounter any errors. But, once we are ready to ship the application and we are happy that the application is stable, we can switch to a release build which will be optimized, smaller in size, and quicker.

You can access the project properties dialog box by right-clicking the project in the Solution Explorer and choosing **Properties** from the pop-up menu, or by selecting **Properties** from the **Project** menu.

Either of these two methods will display the Property Pages for your project. To the left of the dialog box, you can see two folders that represent the two groups of project properties mentioned earlier. Each of the folders contains a number of sections that logically group properties together further. The first is called **Common Properties** and this is where you will change the properties that are independent of build configuration and can be thought of as global. The second folder is called **Configuration Properties** and this contains a number of sections where you can change properties that are dependent on the active build configuration. When you select a section from the **Configuration Properties** folder, the configuration drop-down box becomes enabled. This drop-down allows you to select the build configuration that you would like to set the properties of. The current active configuration will be listed as **Active,** with the configuration name in brackets. There is a second drop-down box labeled **Platform**. This enables you to select the target platform for the project.

When you create a new project in VB, two build configuration options will be created for you: **Debug** and **Release**. This is probably sufficient in the majority of cases but, occasionally, you may want to create a new build configuration. This is easily done and you can even use an existing configuration as the template for the new one. You can add and delete build configurations by using the Configuration Manager, available by clicking the **Configuration Manager** button at the top right side of the project properties dialog box:

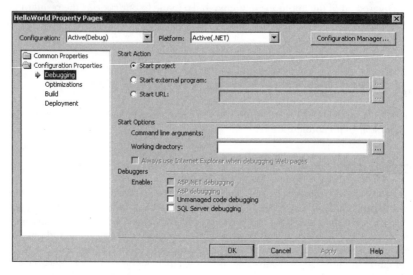

If you have more than one project in the current solution, you can choose which projects are included in a particular build configuration. You assign projects to build configurations through the Configuration Manager.

To change the currently active build configuration, you use the drop-box to the right of the run button on the toolbar to select the configuration that you would like to use. The drop-down contains the following options:

❑   Debug

❑   Release

❑   Configuration Manager...

The last option provides a way into the Configuration Manager, giving a simple two-click method for changing configurations:

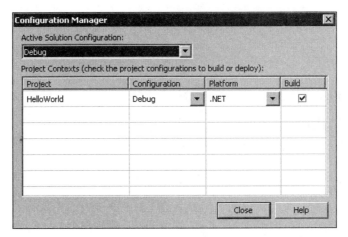

The Configuration Manager will contain an entry in the grid for each project that is in the current solution. You can include/exclude a project from the build of the selected build configuration (shown in the combo-box at the top of the window) by using the checkbox in the column of the grid labeled Build. If the checkbox is selected then the project will be built. You can also select which configuration and target platform of the project you would like to use in this particular build configuration using the combo-boxes in the respective columns

Building Our Application

We are now going to build our application using the Debug build configuration, so make sure it is the active build configuration. We have a whole Build menu devoted to building our project/solution.

The menu has a few options that are summarized below:

Menu Item	Description
Build	Will use the currently active build configuration to build the project.
Rebuild	Will clean all intermediate files (object files etc.) and the output directory before building the project using the active build configuration.
Batch Build	Will allow you to build multiple versions of the project using one or more of the build configurations in one go.
Configuration Manager	Will show the dialog box to allow edit, add, and delete build configurations.

If you have more than one project in your solution, the menu will have a few more options that will allow you to either build all of the projects in the solution or to build the currently selected project only:

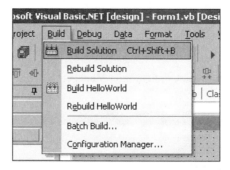

Select Build from the menu. The example project will now be built. You can keep track of what is happening by looking in the Output window:

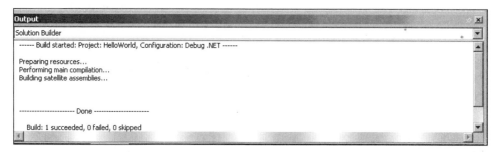

When the project has been built successfully, the Output window will look something like the figure above. You can now look in the output directory, specified in the project properties, to find the executable that has been created.

If the build was unsuccessful you will also be informed of this by having an item added to the Task List window (usually found along the bottom of the main VS.NET window) for each error encountered:

The task will include the reason for the error and where the error occurred. By double-clicking the error task you will be taken directly to the location of the error. Once all the errors have been fixed you can attempt to build the application as described above.

Running Our Application

Clicking on the Start button, or selecting Debug | Start or pressing *F5*, produces the following:

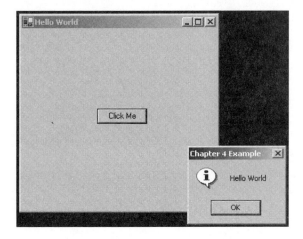

Summary

We are now at the end of our brief practical introduction to VB.NET and its differences with VB6. This chapter, although fairly short, has introduced quite a few topics:

- ❑ How to create projects and the different project templates available
- ❑ Code regions and how the form designer uses them to hide code that it doesn't want the developer to change
- ❑ Namespaces and how to import them into our applications
- ❑ Forms are classes, and the properties of forms are set in code
- ❑ New object-oriented features of VB
- ❑ Build configurations and how to build and run a project

Although we have touched upon some of the changes to the IDE, the next chapter is going to look at VS.NET in depth so that you will soon feel at home using it.

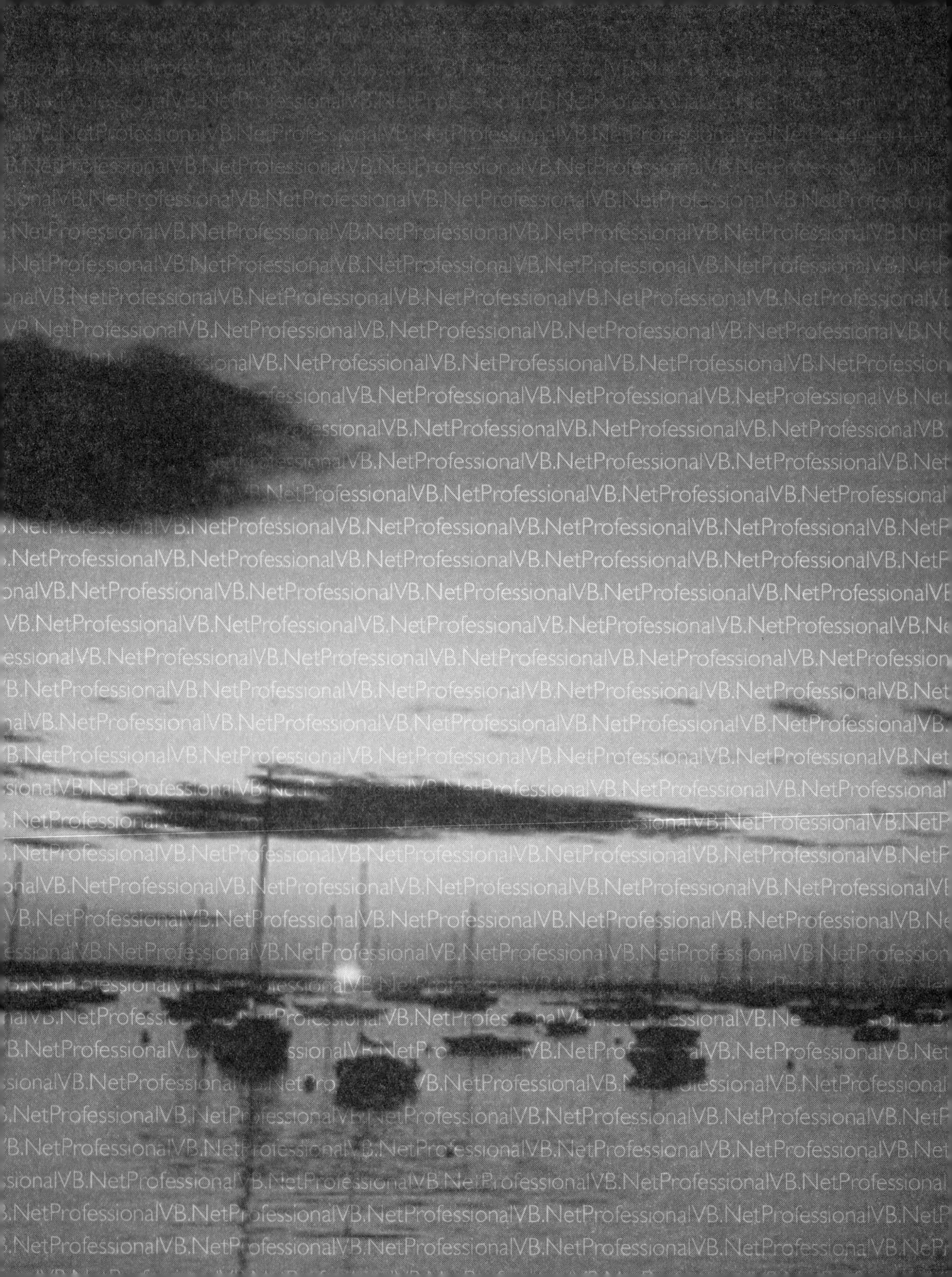
VB.NetProfessional

Visual Studio.NET Integrated Development Environment

Previous chapters have given an overview of the conceptual foundation of Microsoft.NET and VB.NET in particular. Most of the rest of the book will look in depth at the features of the language and how to program in it. First, however, it is helpful to look a bit more closely at what a developer sees when they sit down to actually write Microsoft.NET systems – the Visual Studio.NET Integrated Development Environment (IDE).

The focus here is to see the different windows and menu choices that can be manipulated in the IDE. In that context, it will be necessary to look at Windows Forms, Web Forms, and several other technologies that are covered in considerably more detail in other chapters. As that happens, references will point you to the chapters that contain more information.

The topics to be covered in this chapter include:

❑   The Start Page

❑   "Profiles" to arrange the IDE in different configurations

❑   How the IDE looks when working on a Windows Form

❑   How the IDE varies for other types of project

❑   The various windows available in the IDE and what you can use them for

❑   The menu options in the IDE and how the menus have changed from previous versions

❑   Macros

❑   Debugging

The Visual Studio.NET IDE

Overall, Visual Studio.NET will look familiar to users of previous Visual Studio versions. In many respects, it combines the best of the various IDEs which were previously used in Microsoft development tools. It has a general look and feel similar to the Visual Basic 6 IDE, but takes, for example, the Solution Explorer window from the Project Explorer in Visual Interdev.

In Visual Studio.NET, exactly the same IDE is used for all Visual Studio languages and the IDE is specifically designed to manage projects using more than one language at a time. The languages used in, and managed by, the Visual Studio.NET IDE can be extended beyond Microsoft languages to a long list of third-party languages that are being brought into the .NET Framework, such as COBOL and Eiffel.

To satisfy such a wide variety of developers, who may be coming from a host of previous languages (and other development environments), there are a lot of options and configurable features that can allow the IDE to be customized to the needs of a particular developer, as we will show in the following pages.

Solutions Versus Projects

One key difference to understand before examining the IDE is the distinction between a **project** and a **solution**. In previous versions of Visual Basic, an entire program was considered to be a "project", and would generate a single EXE or DLL file.

Visual Interdev changed the focus to that of a "solution", which encompassed many elements beyond just those that go into an EXE or DLL. For example, images (amongst other file types) could often be considered part of a solution in Visual Interdev.

Visual Studio.NET has adopted this solution-based view of the current work. A solution may contain more than one project, and may also have images, XML files, and other elements which are part of the programming effort. A solution can generate more than one EXE or DLL, and some elements do not get compiled at all.

One important feature of the IDE is that it can handle multiple languages. Each project is in a particular language, and different projects may be in different languages. Classes in one project can be called from another project, making it possible to get inter-language interoperability and cross-language debugging during the code development phase.

For a particular solution, one project is designated as the Startup Project, like the way that a project can have a Startup Form. This Startup Project is normally the first one loaded, or created, but can be changed with an option on the Project menu (discussed later in the chapter).

A Tour of the Visual Studio.NET IDE

When Visual Studio.NET is first installed and run, a window similar to that shown below is displayed:

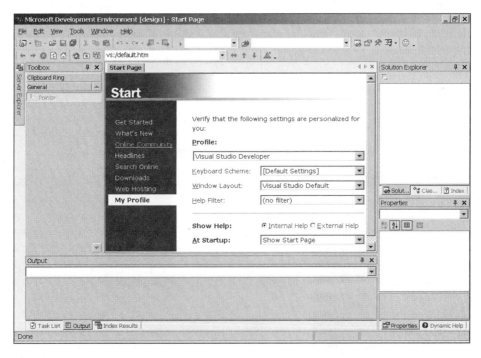

This is the Visual Studio Start Page, which, at first startup, will have the My Profile option selected on the left of the Start Page so as to allow the new user to select an appropriate profile to adapt the environment to their needs.

Profiles

Visual Studio.NET provides the developer with several options to choose from, in order to make the environment simulate an expected layout from earlier versions. By choosing a profile, several aspects of the IDE are customized at once, such as the position of the code window and properties windows, and what windows take precedence in the environment. For example, if the Visual Basic Developer profile is selected, the Toolbox by default is always on the screen. For other profiles, such as Visual Studio Developer, the Toolbox becomes a tab on the left side of the screen, in a similar way to the Server Explorer tab, and must be selected by hovering the mouse pointer over it, which causes the Toolbox to "slide out". (If the screen is set to such a profile, it can be changed to make the Toolbox show all the time, by clicking on the pushpin in the upper right corner of the Toolbox when it is pulled out. This will cause it to stay on the screen.)

The examples in this section mostly use the layout from the Visual Basic Developer profile. When other profiles are used, this will be mentioned.

Selecting Help Options

Answering a long-standing gripe about Visual Studio 6, the help system can be filtered to offer language help for just one language. As seen in the Start Page screenshot above, there is a Help Filter dropdown box. When Visual Studio.NET is installed, it is set to (no filter). Most Visual Basic developers will want to set this option to Visual Basic Documentation. Other languages are also available in the drop down. (If you take the defaults during installation, then accessing help requires insertion of the Visual Studio disks, but there is an option at installation time to install the help files to your system so that the disks are not needed.) The user also has the choice of showing the help inside the IDE (as a tabbed window in the same area that code is shown), or completely outside the IDE as a separate window that can be positioned and manipulated.

The Start Page

Once a profile is selected, the startup screen for Visual Studio.NET looks as shown below:

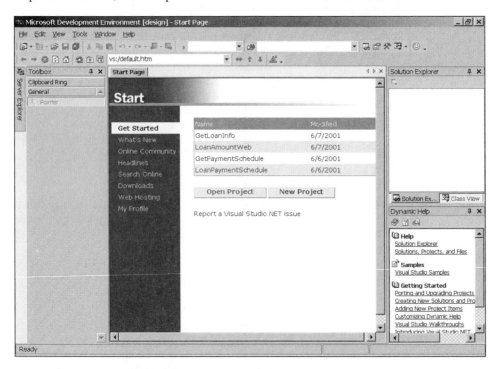

This Start Page lists the projects worked on most recently, together with options to open an existing project or create a new project.

A Place for News and Information

Notice that there are several categories to the left of the Start Page window, such as What's New and Headlines. Some of this content comes from the Web, and some comes from XML files in one of the Visual Studio directories or the Visual Studio help files. The What's New section is a particularly good source of valuable information on changes in Visual Studio.NET, taken from the help files.

Headlines is from the MSDN web site and gives Microsoft a place to communicate new information on Visual Studio to users – information regarding the availability of service packs, for instance. It requires a connection to the Internet. Other sections that need Internet connectivity include Online Community, Downloads, and Web Hosting. Online Community furnishes links to web sites and newsgroups that you may find helpful. Downloads takes you to a web site that holds a variety of pre-written code that you can use for samples. Web Hosting gives links to services that may be helpful for web-related development, including a place where you can host Web Services.

Creating a New Project

If the Create New Project option is selected from the Start Page (or if File | New | Project is selected from the pull down menus) then the dialog depicted in the figure below appears:

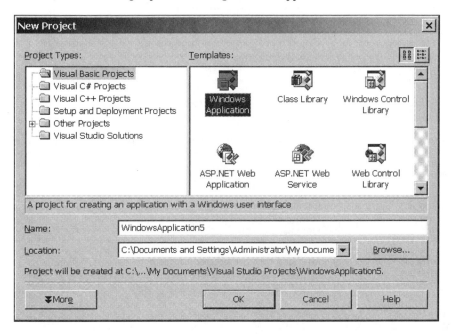

This style of option dialog is becoming popular with Microsoft, promoting a common look and feel, as seen in Windows Explorer. Rather than using tabbed dialogs, a tree structure is displayed in the left window, and the contents of the right window vary to reflect the currently selected option in the tree.

Note the types of projects that can be selected. Several of them are new, such as the web-based ones (ASP.NET Web Application, ASP.NET Web Service, and Web Control Library). Many are discussed in other chapters of this book. As the scroll bar on the right indicates, there are more options than are displayed on the above screen. Here is the complete set of Visual Basic project types that are available when Visual Studio.NET is installed, with brief descriptions of their purpose:

Type of Project	Purpose	Where covered in this book
Windows Application	Forms-based local application in Windows Forms, much like a typical VB6 forms program.	Chapter 8
Class Library	Project to contain a set of related classes for use by other programs. Compiles to a DLL-based component.	See Chapter 14 for more on components in Visual Basic.NET
Windows Control Library	Project to create one or more Windows Forms controls. This replaces the User Control type of project in VB6.	Chapter 10
ASP.NET Web Application	Create a browser-based application with Web Forms.	Chapter 20
ASP.NET Web Service	Create a Web Service.	Chapter 22
Web Control Library	Create a server control to be placed on Web Forms.	Chapter 21
Console Application	Create an application with a character-based user interface. There is no corresponding capability in VB6, though it is possible in Visual C++ 6.	Used in several chapters throughout the book.
Windows Service	Create a program that will run as a Windows Service (also known as an NT Service). This is a terminate-and-stay-resident application with no user interface that is intended for long-running use and typically performs some sort of system level task.	Chapter 23
Empty Project	Create a project with no pre-written code at all. All code will be written from scratch. The only thing that gets created is an empty folder for the project.	
Empty Web Project	Create an empty project as above, but create it with a virtual root directory off of the web server.	
New Project in Existing Folder	Create an empty project, but place it in an existing project folder.	

Some projects are language-dependent, and the generated modules to start the project are created in the appropriate language. This means, for example, that many of the same types of project covered above are also present in the Visual C# Projects folder.

Other folders contain projects that span multiple languages. Some of these are in the Setup and Deployment Projects folder, which is discussed briefly later in this chapter. The Other Projects folder contains a couple of additional project types – Database Projects, which allows work on database elements such as stored procedures and triggers, and Extensibility Projects, which allows construction of add-ins to the Visual Studio environment.

Note that this screen varies depending on your installation options. If you did not install C++, for example, then the Visual C++ Projects folder will not appear.

To show some more sample screens, we will select the Windows Application option under Visual Basic Projects. The following screens will basically be the new version of the equivalent screens for developing a forms-based project in Visual Basic 6.

Working on a Windows Form

The first screen for a new Visual Basic Windows Forms project looks as shown below:

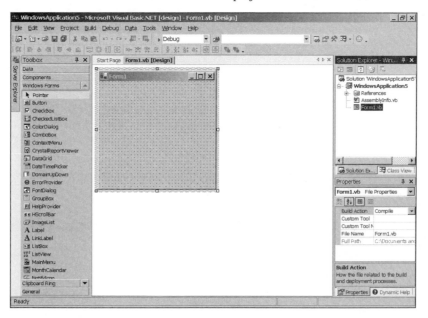

This looks generally familiar to a VB6 developer and the interface also works the same way as in VB6, using drag-and-drop from the Toolbox onto the form surface to layout the form.

Tabbed Windows

One of the first things that you notice about the interface is the prevalence of tabs at various locations to change the content of windows. Just below the toolbars is one set of tabs currently containing Start Page and Form1.vb [Design]. This set of tabs is at the top of the window that VB6 developers expect to contain form layouts and code. This window now handles additional displays besides forms and code. It allows selection of the Start Page, for example. And it no longer uses a Multiple Document Interface
 (MDI) arrangement for the windows. It now only shows one item, namely the one whose tab is selected. In the screen above, only two tabs are present, but more tabs appear here as code windows and additional forms are created. (The old MDI child arrangement can still be set by going to the Tools | Options dialog and checking MDI environment.)

The Toolbox

The Toolbox is a little different from VB6. Instead of the icon-only grid of available controls, a linear list is presented, with each control having both an icon and a description. This is another example of a Visual Interdev-influenced feature in Visual Studio.NET. In addition, the Toolbox continues the tab-based metaphor because pressing a tab causes different controls to appear in the Toolbox. There are several more tabs than in earlier versions of Visual Basic, many of them featuring non-visual components. It should be noted that the tabs shown at any particular time vary with the type of project being worked on.

The list of controls on the Windows Forms tab in the Toolbox is similar to that available in VB6 when doing form design. There are controls such as labels, text boxes, and so forth. One of the most notable controls is the `MainMenu` control, which places a standard Windows drop-down menu on the form. Another control, called a `ContextMenu` control, provides pop-up windows. These controls give the developer a far superior way to manipulate menus in Windows Forms than was available in VB6. More details on these differences are covered in the chapter on Windows Forms later in the book.

It is possible to customize the Toolbox by selecting the Tools | Customize Toolbox option. This then shows a tabbed dialog with various options for controlling the Toolbox. Some of the capability that was formerly in the Project | Components and Project | References dialogs in Visual Basic 6 has been moved to this new dialog in Visual Studio.NET.

The Component Tray

There is one change that is quite noticeable from previous versions of Visual Basic. In VB6 and before, all controls that were dragged onto a form were shown on the form, even if they were invisible at run-time. The most common such control was a `Timer`. In VB.NET, such controls do not appear on the form. If a `Timer` is dragged on to a Windows Form, the screen looks something like this:

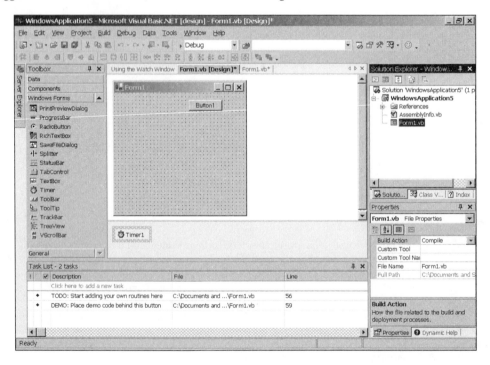

Notice that the `Timer` control appears in a pane just below the form design surface. This pane is called the **component tray**, and it is needed because there are many more controls and components available in Visual Basic.NET that do not have a visible manifestation on the form. We will see an example later in this chapter – a performance counter component.

The Solution Explorer

The Solution Explorer will be familiar to Visual Interdev users. Since the VS.NET IDE is oriented around solutions rather than projects, the Solution Explorer is a replacement for the Project Explorer in Visual Basic 6, and looks generally similar. However, because a solution is more complex than a project, it holds many project elements besides code and forms. We'll see an example from a Web Forms project later in this chapter.

The Solution Explorer is used, like the Project Explorer in VB6, to display various elements in the solution. Another common use of the Solution Explorer is to change the properties of programming elements. Right-clicking on an item in the Solution Explorer gives a context-sensitive menu of useful options, the bottom one being Properties for any element that has properties to manipulate.

Just below the Solution Explorer is another set of tabs. The Class View tab will be familiar to C++ users, and is similar to the Object Browser window in VB6. It allows an alternative way to look at the class structure of the elements in a project. If it is selected for the project above, it looks as follows:

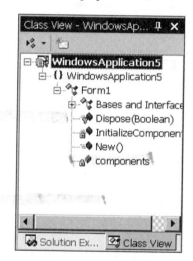

The Class View allows exploration of the base class for a given class, as well as the class members (properties and methods). The icons next to the members give information such as whether the member is private (in that case it has a padlock icon). The Class View is useful in some instances where the Object Browser would have been used in VB6. (The Object Browser is still available in Visual Studio.NET, and is accessed through View | Other Windows | Object Browser.)

The Properties Window and Dynamic Help

The Properties window itself is not much changed from Visual Studio 6. However, the Dynamic Help tab below the Properties window is new. Dynamic Help makes a guess at what you might be interested in looking at, based on what you have done recently. The following figure shows a sample screen using Dynamic Help:

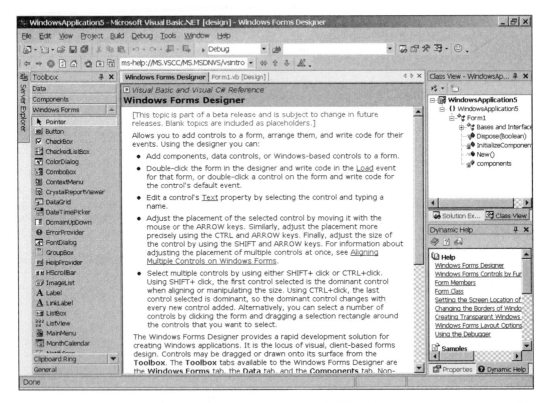

The options in the Dynamic Help window are categorized into three areas. The top category, entitled Help, gives the best guesses on features that the environment thinks you might be trying to use. Just below that is a section called Samples, and it points to a help page that lists a variety of sample applications that you can examine. Below that is a category called Getting Started, and this contains a variety of help options on introductory material.

One of the options in the Getting Started category is Visual Studio Walkthroughs. These are step-by-step guides on how to do the basics for the different types of project that can be created in Visual Studio.NET.

The New Code Window

One of the biggest and most useful enhancements in the Visual Studio.NET IDE is the new code window. The following figure is a sample screen showing the code from the form (Form1) that was inserted automatically when the Windows Forms project was created:

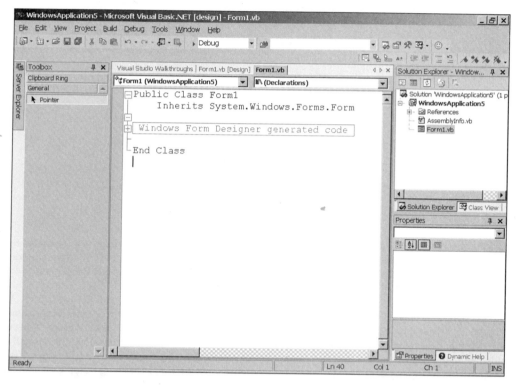

This code editor window looks mostly familiar, except for the gray line on the left with the plus and minus signs. This line is the visual indication that the code inside routines in Visual Studio.NET can either be visible or hidden on the screen, a feature known as **Outlining**.

Notice that there is a minus sign next to every routine (sub or function). This makes it easy to hide or show code on a routine-by-routine basis. If code for a routine is hidden, the routine declaration is still shown, and has a plus sign next to it to indicate that the body code is hidden.

This Outlining feature should be very useful when a developer is working on two or three key routines in a module, and wishes to avoid scrolling through many screens of code that are not important to the current task.

There is another option to show or hide larger regions of code. The #Region directive is used for this within the IDE, though it has no effect on the actual application. A region of code is demarcated by the #Region directive at the top and the #End Region directive at the end. The #Region directive that begins a region should include a description, and it will appear next to a plus sign used to show the code when the code is minimized. For example, in the last screenshot, there is a code section labeled Windows Form Designer generated code. It is hidden because normally there is no need for the developer to see or manipulate this code. But, if the plus sign is clicked, it comes into view. The following figure shows what the code window looks like after the plus sign is clicked:

The outlining enhancement to show and hide sections of code was probably inspired by the fact that the Visual Studio.NET designers generate a lot of code when a project is first begun. Items that were hidden in Visual Studio 6 (such as the logic which sets initial form properties) are actually inside the generated code in Visual Studio.NET.

In most respects, seeing all of these functions in code is an improvement because it is easier for the developer to understand what is going on, and possibly to manipulate the process in limited, special cases. However, since designer-generated code does not generally need to be manipulated by the developer, it is usually hidden and out of the way. As a nice side benefit of this, developers can hide their own code when it is not relevant to the task at hand. Outlining can be turned off by selecting Edit | Outlining | Stop Outlining from the Visual Studio menu.

That menu also contains some other useful functions. If you would like to temporarily hide a section of code, highlight it, and select Edit | Outlining | Hide Selection. The selected code will be hidden and replaced with an ellipsis with a plus sign next to it. Clicking the plus sign brings the code back into display. There are also options for toggling outlining on and off, and for making a block of code display only the routine definitions.

One additional capability of the text editor that is quite useful is line numbering. Go to Tools | Options, open the Text Editor folder, and then select the All Languages folder. Checking the Line numbers checkbox will cause the editor to number all lines, giving you an easy way to reference particular lines unambiguously.

The Task List

There are a number of optional windows that can be used in Visual Studio.NET. One that is sure to be popular is the **Task List**. First seen in Visual Interdev, the Task List is a great productivity tool to track pending changes and additions in code. It's also a good way for the Visual Studio.NET environment to communicate information that the developer needs to know, such as errors in the current code. Visual Basic developers will be happy to know that the Task List can show all current syntax errors in the code, so it's not necessary to do a "Run With Full Compile" and then look at errors one at a time. When the Task List is displayed, it usually appears just below the window that holds code and forms.

The Task List is displayed with the Show Tasks option on the View menu. There are several options available. The following screenshot shows this menu selected, illustrating the various options for showing tasks:

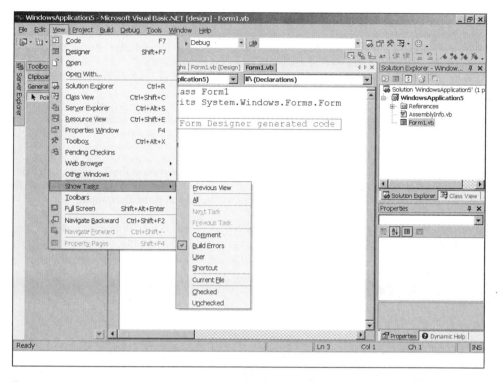

The Comment option is for tasks embedded into code comments. This is done by creating a comment with the apostrophe, and then starting the comment with "TODO:". This can be followed with any text desired. Such a comment will show up in the Task List if either the Comment option or the All option is selected.

In addition to using the TODO: token, a user can create their own comment tokens in the options for Visual Studio, via the Tools I Options I Environment I Task List menu.

The following figure shows a Task List with the All view options selected, and with a couple of items displayed. In this case, a new token called DEMO has been added, and one of the tasks is indicated with that token:

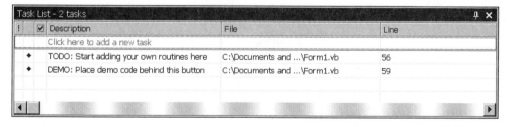

Besides helping developers track these tasks, embedding the tasks in code brings another benefit. Clicking on a task in the Task List causes the code editor to jump right to the location of the task without hunting through code for it.

Another view of the Task List that is useful is **Build Errors**. This view summarizes all of the things that prevent a clean build of the code and, as with tasks embedded in comments, clicking on a build error task takes the code editor to the location of the error. It's not necessary to explicitly choose **Build** for these errors to display – the environment automatically checks code continuously and inserts build errors in the list. As with other tasks, build errors are also included if the Task List is set to **View All Tasks**.

The user also has the option of simply typing tasks into the list. These are shown when the **View | Show Tasks | User** option for filtering the Task List is selected, or when all tasks are displayed.

The Command Window

Another window that can be displayed in the same location on the screen as the Task List, by clicking on its tab, is the **Command Window**. It is shown by selecting the menu option **View | Other Windows | Command Window**. When the window is displayed, a ">" prompt will be displayed to allow input.

The Command Window can be used to access Visual Studio menu options and commands by typing them in instead of selecting them in the menu structure. For example, if the Command Window is displayed, and the command `File.AddNewProject` is typed in, the Command Window would look like this:

If *Enter* is now pressed, the dialog box to add a new project will appear. Note that IntelliSense is available to help enter commands in the Command Window.

The Command Window also has an **Immediate** mode in which expressions can be evaluated. This mode is accessed by typing **Immed** at the ">" prompt. In this mode, the window title changes to indicate that the Immediate mode is active.

> **In this mode, the window behaves very much like the Immediate window in Visual Basic 6.**

While a program is running, you can type in arithmetic expressions for evaluation, change the content of variables, and do other debugging functions. The mode can be changed back to Command mode by typing >cmd while in the Immediate mode.

Other Debug-Related Windows

Once a program is running, various other windows become available for display in the same general area as the Task List and the Command Window. Most are available from the **View | Other Windows** menu. The windows include:

Output

The compile process puts progress messages in this window, and your program can also place messages in it using the `Console` object. That is, the line:

```
Console.WriteLine("This is printed in the Output Window")
```

will cause the string This is printed in the Output Window to appear as the last line in the Output Window. (Note that the `Console` object can have its output routed to various places, and can even be used to write character-based applications. By default, it sends output to the Output window.)

Anything written to the Output window is only shown while running a program from the environment. During execution of the compiled module, no Output window is present, so nothing can be written to it.

Call Stack

This lists the procedures that are currently calling other procedures and waiting for their return. This was accessed in Visual Basic 6 with a menu option on the View menu.

Breakpoints

This is an enhanced breakpoint handler in which breakpoints can be defined and monitored. It is improved from the breakpoint handler in VB6, for example, by having a continuous monitor on the number of times that a breakpoint has been reached. This is useful for debugging problems that only occur after a certain number of iterations of a routine. (Note that breakpoints are saved when a solution is saved by the IDE.)

Locals

This window is used to monitor the value of all variables that are currently in scope. As in VB6, even arrays can be examined, via a tree-control interface.

Autos

This displays variables used in the statement currently being executed and the statement just before it. These variables are identified and listed for you automatically, hence the window name.

Watch Windows

There are four of these, called Watch 1 to Watch 4, and each can hold a set of variables or expressions for which you want to monitor the value. Variables can also have their values changed with Watch windows. Values can be displayed in regular form or in hexadecimal. Variables can be added to Watch windows by right-clicking on the variable in the code editor, and then selecting Add Watch.
Note that the Locals, Autos, and Watch windows only automatically appear when a program is being run in the environment. Managing these windows is done with the Debug | Windows sub-menu.

Undocking Windows

Even though the windows discussed above are **docked** when they are first displayed, most of them can be **undocked** (the exception is the window used for design surfaces and code editing). Using the mouse, you can click and drag the title bar for the Task List, the Properties window, and several others out into the main window, making the windows free-floating. The following figure shows a sample screen with the Task List and the Properties window undocked and free-floating:

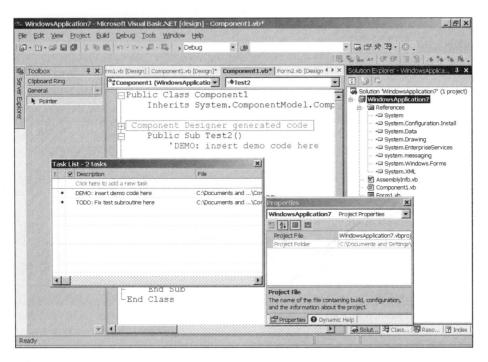

These windows can be dragged completely outside of the main windows for the Visual Studio.NET IDE. Also note that, when the Properties window was made free-floating, it brought the tabs below it along, so that the Dynamic Help window has become free-floating also. This is a characteristic common to all of the tabbed groups of windows that can be either docked or free-floating.

To put the windows back into docked position, you just drag them there, but it takes practice to get them exactly where you want them. Keep repositioning the mouse pointer until the dragged outline changes into the position that you want.

In some cases, you may not be able to easily make the windows dock in the exact same position that they came from. The easiest way to place all the windows back in default positions is to restore a profile on the Start Page. If the Start Page is not currently displayed, it can be brought up with Help | Show Start Page.

AutoHide

Most of the windows discussed above, plus the Server Explorer discussed below, have an icon in their upper right hand corner that shows a "push-pin" whenever they are in a docked state. This icon turns the AutoHide feature on and off.

When the push-pin is vertical, AutoHide is off. The window displays in its normal position. When the push-pin is horizontal, AutoHide is on, and the window will retract when it is not being used. In the retracted state, it is represented by a tab along the edge of the screen where it would normally appear.

Typically, you will want to turn on AutoHide for windows such as the Toolbox when they are not being actively used. This allows more screen real estate to be used for display of code and other windows that you are using.

The Server Explorer

As development has become more server-centric, developers have a greater need to discover and manipulate services on the network. The Server Explorer is a new feature in Visual Studio.NET that makes this easier.

Visual Interdev made a start in this direction with a **Server Object** section in the Interdev Toolbox. The Server Explorer is more sophisticated. It allows, for example, exploration and alteration of SQL Server database structures that would have previously been done with the SQL Enterprise Manager.

The Server Explorer is a pullout tab on the left side of the IDE. When it is extended, the window looks as follows:

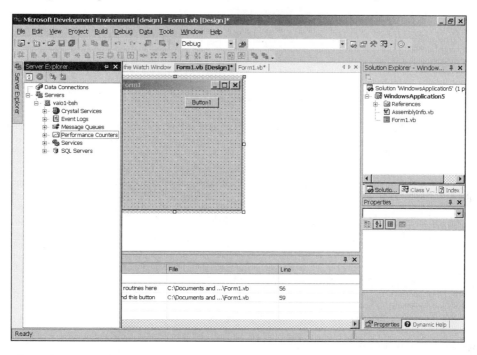

Notice the wide variety of server resources that are available for inspection, or for use in the project. The Server Explorer makes it unnecessary for a developer to go to an outside resource to find, for example, what message queues are available. The **Add Server** option allows a new server to be selected and inspected. The Server Explorer even provides the ability to stop and restart services on the server.

The Server Explorer subsumes much of the functionality in the Data View in Visual Studio 6. However, it is far more powerful and easier to use.

As an example of the Server Explorer's capabilities, the following figure shows the screen that appears when you right-click on the **Data Connections** option in the Server Explorer, and then choose the **Add Connection** option. The resulting screen brings together all the information needed to establish a connection to a server database in a tabbed dialog. Some elements of this dialog are similar to other screens that have been used in the past, such as the **ODBC Connection** dialog in the **Control Panel**. However, this screen is more accessible to the developer:

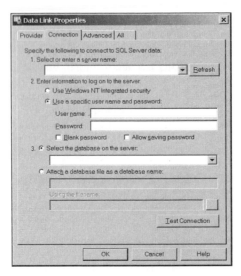

Here's another example of the power of the Server Explorer. If you are running on any version of Windows 2000, you can easily add performance monitoring to your application. This allows your application to implement what are called "performance counters", which track a number and display how the number changes in the Windows Performance Monitor (which is accessed in the example below). All this is done by merely dragging and dropping a performance counter from the Server Explorer into your application, and incrementing the counter in your code as desired. The following steps describe the process:

1. Start a new **Windows Application** project, and on the blank form that is created with the project, drag a `Button` from the Toolbox onto the form.

2. In the Server Explorer window, right-click on **Performance Counters**, and select **Create New Category**. The resulting dialog will look like this:

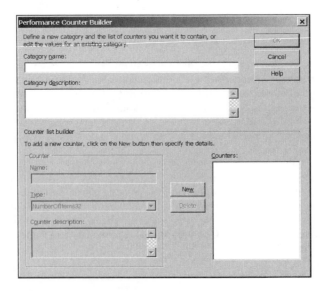

3. In the Category name menu, enter Test Counters, and in the Counter list builder section of the dialog, press the New button. You can then enter MyCounter in the Name field for the counter and press the OK button.

4. Expand the Performance Counters section of the Server Explorer if necessary, and scroll down to the Test Counters category that you just created, where the MyCounter performance counter will be shown. Now click on MyCounter and drag and drop it on to the form. Notice that a new control named PerformanceCounter1 has been added to the form in the tray just under the visible design surface of the form.

5. Click on PerformanceCounter1 and, in the Properties window, change its `ReadOnly` property to `False`.

6. Double-click the button on the form to get to its click event routine, and enter the following code:

```
PerformanceCounter1.Increment()
```

7. Start the program running by selecting Debug | Start.

8. Open your Control Panel and select the Administrative Tools | Performance menu. Now right-click on the right side of the screen and select Add Counters to bring up the following dialog:

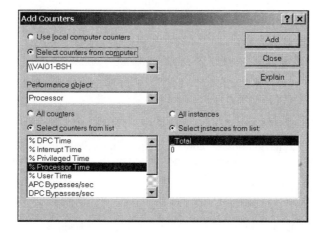

9. In the Performance Object drop-down, select the Test Counters category. The MyCounter counter will be highlighted. Press the Add button. Then press the Close button.

10. Arrange the windows on the screen so that you can see both the performance monitor screen and your form with the single button. Now start pressing the button. Note that your counter goes up on the graph every time you do so.

This task would have been enormously more difficult in previous versions of Visual Basic.

Differences When Doing Other Types of Project

The above examples have all used sample screens from a Windows Forms project. There are a few differences when doing other types of project and developing other parts of a project, such as a component.

Web Forms

When creating a Web Application project, the biggest difference is that the design surface for a Web Form is actually a web page editor. It looks a lot like a Visual Basic form design surface, but completely different types of controls appear in the Toolbox. The following figure shows a typical start screen for a Web Application project:

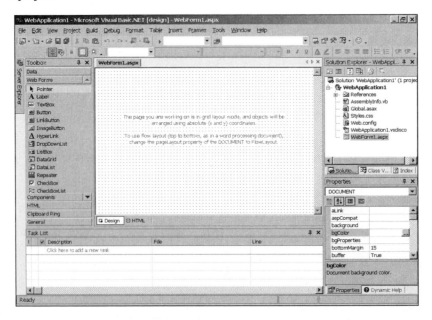

One obvious change is that the Solution Explorer contains a lot more elements. Two options (discussed next) also ensure that the user knows how controls are positioned on the Web Forms design surface.

The Web Page Editor

Two tabs in the lower left portion of the screen, labeled Design and HTML, give different views of the web page being designed. The Design view is a WYSIWYG display that is almost a cross between the typical form layout view in Windows Forms and a web page editor such as FrontPage. The HTML view shows the actual HTML that is used behind the page to create and position the controls that are being placed on the design surface. Either view can be used to modify the web page layout.

This design surface is inspired by a similar construct in Visual Interdev. However, the design mode for Web Application projects is far more powerful than the visual designer included in Interdev. The advent of server-side web controls makes Web Forms much closer to the drag-and-drop design experience of VB forms.

The Toolbox for Web Forms contains different controls to those used for Windows Forms, because it contains the server-side web controls specifically designed for Web Applications. These server-side controls are discussed in more detail in Chapter 20.

Layout of Web Forms

There are two quite different ways of laying out Web Forms. Both involve selecting controls in the Toolbox and placing them on the design surface. They differ in where the controls end up on the design surface and the way that controls are positioned in the underlying HTML. These two methods are called **Grid Layout** and **Flow Layout**. Grid Layout is the default. Which of these is applied to a given Web Form is determined by the `PageLayout` property of the form.

In Grid Layout, the controls are actually placed on a grid on the design surface. This gives them fixed positions and allows for a WYSIWYG style display that is conceptually similar to Windows Forms and forms in previous versions of Visual Basic.

In Flow Layout, the design surface is similar to a word processing document. The user can insert text and paragraph marks, and the result is translated into HTML. When a control is dropped onto the design surface, it is placed in the text where the cursor is currently positioned.

The differences between these layout techniques show up most dramatically in the underlying HTML template. In Web Forms, any control that is placed on the design surface has code generated for it in the underlying HTML template. For example, placing a button on the Web Form in Flow Layout mode will cause the following code to be inserted into the HTML template:

```
<asp:Button id=Button1 runat="server" Text="Button"></asp:Button>
```

This declaration for the control includes no positioning information at all. The control is merely rendered in the Web Form at whatever point it is encountered when running the form.

If a button is dropped in Grid Layout form, however, the inserted code is more complex. It looks something like this (although it is all on one line in the HTML view of the form):

```
<asp:Button id="Button1" style="Z-INDEX: 101; LEFT: 211px; POSITION: absolute;
TOP: 79px" runat="server" Text="Button"></asp:Button>
```

The positioning information in the HTML above causes the control to be rendered in the position in which it was dropped on the form. The ASP.NET runtime engine takes care of reading this positioning information and emitting HTML that will position the control properly.

The Component Designer

Visual modules are not the only ones with designers in Visual Studio.NET. Components have a designer also. The following figure shows the design surface and the Toolbox for the Component Designer. (The Component Designer is accessed by selecting Project | Add Component and then selecting the Component Class template):

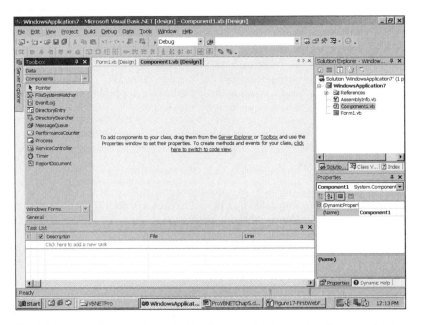

As with the visual designers, elements from the Toolbox can be dragged and dropped onto the design surface. Once that happens, they receive a default name and have logic automatically generated to integrate them into the component. This design surface works a lot like the tray that appears below visible Windows Forms and holds non-visible controls and components.

The Toolbox shown above illustrates that many areas of pre-defined functionality are available to components in Visual Basic.NET. Once these functional pieces are dragged onto the design surface, their properties become available in the Properties window, and their events become available in the code window. This makes it much easier to integrate, for example, a message queue, which can then hold messages from one program or system until another program or system is ready to process the message. Very little explicit coding is required in Visual Studio.NET to integrate a message queue with a process because the designer takes care of setting the message queue to typical defaults and writing the instantiation code for the queue. The following figure shows the property box for a message queue that was dragged onto the design surface:

The designer also adds the code to instantiate the message queue. You can see it if you go to the code window for the component, and then press the plus sign next to the region that says **Component Designer Generated Code**. Close to the top of this code, this line appears:

```
Friend WithEvents MessageQueue1 As System.Messaging.MessageQueue
```

Later, in the InitializeComponent sub, this line appears:

```
Me.MessageQueue1 = New System.Messaging.MessageQueue()
```

This fits the model used by the IDE, in which the designer writes as much code as possible and hides it from you so you don't normally have to worry about it. Components such as `MessageQueue1` above are treated very much like controls that are placed on a form. They are instantiated and managed automatically, and all you need to do is manipulate their properties, methods, and events.

Toolbars in Visual Studio.NET

There is a long list of toolbars available in Visual Studio.NET, and each developer should spend some time exploring them to find the most useful combination. The following figure shows the screen that allows the user to select the toolbars that will be displayed in the environment:

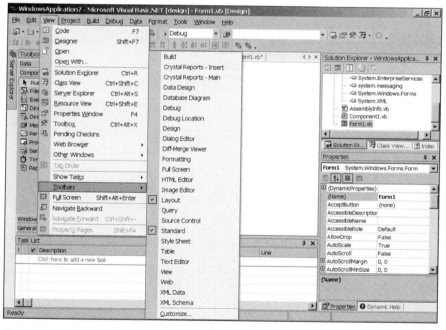

This is a lot of toolbars! In addition to choosing which toolbars to be displayed, the user can, as in Visual Studio 6, manipulate the buttons that are included on each toolbar, create their own toolbars, and dock or float each one as desired.

As in previous versions of Visual Studio, the toolbars are dynamic and can change position and buttons based on the current project type. For example, the toolbars change slightly for a Web Application project, and many of them disappear when you are working on a component.

Debug Versus Release Configurations

One toolbar element that is new is a drop-down box on the Standard toolbar that can be used to select the configuration of the solution (extended project) that you are working on. The choices are Debug and Release, or we can create a configuration of our own with the Configuration Manager. The default is normally Debug and, if you look at the previous figure, you'll see the drop-down just below the Tools menu option on the top menu bar.

Your solution automatically has Debug and Release configurations set up when it is created. The Debug configuration is normally what you use when you work on a project. In this configuration, the program is compiled with full symbolic debug information, and contains no optimization. Then, when the program is ready for release, it can be switched to the Release configuration, and a compile will be done with optimization and without debug symbols.

Other configurations can also be created with the Configuration Manager. A given configuration can include information on what components in the solution to build or not to build, and the target platforms for which a build is being created. You can create as many configurations as you like, and have different ones for different development tasks. For example, you can have one configuration that only builds a specific component (leaving the rest of the solution untouched), and you would select that configuration when you wanted to work specifically on that component. If a solution contained several components, a configuration could be created to work on each one individually.

The Menu Structure of Visual Studio.NET

The menus in Visual Studio.NET during normal development are similar to those in Visual Studio 6. There are fewer top-level items, and more layered menus.

In the following run down of the menus, the most important new features and differences from previous versions of VB will be highlighted.

File Menu

The File menu is similar to that in Visual Basic 6, with a few changes. For example, the File menu has new submenus for Recent Files and Recent Projects. Also, the option to compile a program is no longer on the File Menu – it has been moved to the new Build menu (see below).

Other new options on the File Menu include the Add New Item and Add Existing Item options. Add New Item displays a dialog that includes a wide variety of programming elements that can be added to the current project, such as a form, a class, an XML file, an XML schema, and so forth. (These elements can also be added from the Project menu, which has specific options for some of them as well as the Add New Item option.)

Edit Menu

The Edit menu is also similar to the one in Visual Basic 6 but, when code is being edited, the menu has new submenus at the bottom for Advanced, Outlining, and IntelliSense. The Advanced option allows editing functions such as making a block commented or uncommented, and making a selection of text upper case or lower case. The IntelliSense sub menu has options for:

❑   Forcing an IntelliSense window to display immediately with members (properties and methods) listed

❑   An immediate display of the parameters for a member, sub, or function

❑   An immediate display of the help string associated with a member

❑   Forcing completion (during code editing) of the first matching word in the IntelliSense list

View Menu

The View menu is now particularly rich, and is shown opened up in the previous screenshot. There are many, many options for windows and dialogs that can be displayed. This menu should be one of the first areas of deeper investigation, for a developer just getting started with the Visual Studio.NET environment.

This menu is accessed often to display and hide various windows to shift the programmer's view during different phases of development. For example, during early phases, the Toolbox might be appropriate to show all the time but, during debugging, it's just in the way. The much enlarged set of possible windows means that it will be more necessary than with previous versions to show different windows at different times.

Project Menu

The Project menu is used to add various programming elements, such as forms and classes, to a project. It is perhaps the one most similar to its VB6 counterpart, but it does have two new important options:

❑   The Add Web Reference option is used to point to a Web Service. More details on using Web Services are available in Chapter 22.

❑   The Set as Startup Project option is a new menu option. It makes the current project the one that the solution starts up with. (In VB6, this was done by right-clicking on the project in the Project Explorer and, in fact, that still works in the Solution Explorer in VS.NET.)

Build Menu

The Build menu will be familiar to C++ users, but is a change from Visual Basic 6. It takes on the Make MyFileName.exe option on the Visual Basic 6 File menu, but also has some additional options, including batch building and the Configuration Manager.

Debug Menu

The old Run menu in Visual Basic 6 has been folded into the Debug menu in Visual Studio.NET. The ability to run a program like in VB6 is on the Debug menu under the option Start Without Debugging.

There are also a couple of new options:

❑   Processes – gives access to the Processes dialog box. Access to different processes lets you debug multiple programs at the same time in a single solution by attaching debugging to any active process. It has a Help button that describes what you can do in detail.

❑ Exceptions – error-handling in the .NET Framework depends on the concept of an **exception**. This is a class that holds information about errors, similar in concept to the Err object in VB6, but much more sophisticated. There are many different types of exception. This menu option gives a dialog that lets you determine what happens when a particular type of exception is thrown. Exceptions have default behaviors when they are thrown, but this dialog lets you override the default behavior. For example, you can set a particular type of exception to always cause debugging in the environment to become active, or you can set an exception type to be ignored if you need to get past it during testing.

Tools Menu

The Tools menu in Visual Studio.NET has some new options added in comparison to its Visual Basic 6 equivalent. Significantly, the Add Procedure option has been removed. This option is not needed as much because the editor automatically sets up procedures in the editor when you begin working on one. For example, if you type Public Property MyProperty() As Integer and hit the *Enter* key, you will get the following code automatically generated for you:

```
Public Property MyProperty() As Integer
    Get

    End Get
    Set(ByVal Value As Integer)

    End Set
End Property
```

New capabilities on the Tools menu include options to connect to a database or server, to generate a Globally Unique ID (GUID), and to start add-ins such as Spy++. The Tools menu also gives access to the new macro capabilities, including a macro development environment that is discussed in more detail later in the chapter.

Window Menu

The Window menu offers some new options for arranging windows in the environment. You can even add new groups of windows, as well as set the active window to be docked, hidden, or floating.

Help Menu

The Help menu includes the traditional help options, such as Contents and Index, plus a number of new help options, including:

❑ Edit Filters – change the filters being applied to the help searches. Filters allow help to be restricted, for example, to a particular language.

❑ Show Start Page – bring back the Start Page into the window used for form design surfaces and code editing.

❑ Check For Updates – check on the Web for applicable updates to Visual Studio.NET.

Other Changes from VB6

The Query and Diagram menus from Visual Basic 6 are missing from the top level. Their functions are folded into the View menu. Note that these options are only available on the menu while connected to a data source – otherwise they are grayed out.

Macros in Visual Studio

C++ developers have long had one feature that many Visual Basic developers craved – **macros**. In Visual Studio.NET, macros become part of the environment and are available to any language. However, as in the Microsoft Office suite, macros can only be written with Visual Basic syntax.

Macro options are accessible from the Tools menu. The following figure shows a screen with the Macros menu open:

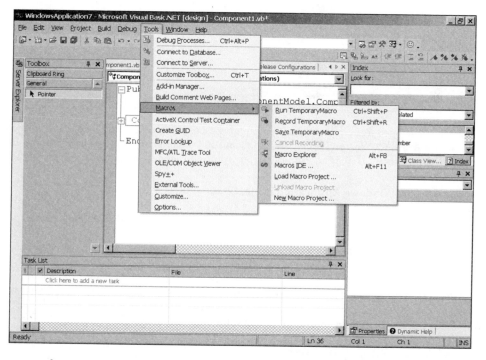

The concept of macros will be familiar to advanced word processing and spreadsheet users. The idea is to record a series of keystrokes and/or menu actions, and then play them back by pressing a certain keystroke combination.

For example, suppose one particular function call with a complex set of arguments is constantly being called on in code, and the function call usually looks about the same except for minor variations in the arguments. The keystrokes to code the function call could be recorded and played back as necessary, which would insert code to call the function that could then be modified as necessary.

Macros can be far more complex than this, containing logic as well as keystrokes. Microsoft Word users are familiar with the idea of recording macros into Visual Basic code, to allow for editing and customization of macros. The macro capabilities of Visual Studio.NET are so comprehensive that macros have their own Integrated Development Environment as shown below:

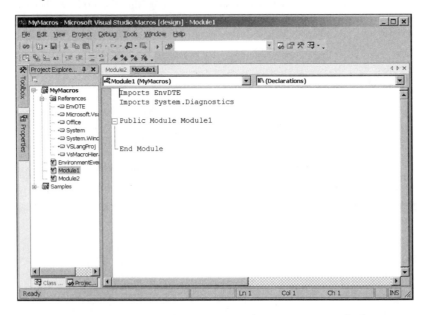

Macros can be developed from scratch in this environment, but more commonly they are recorded using the Record Temporary Macro option on the Macros menu, and then renamed and modified in the above development environment. Here is an example of recording and modifying a macro:

1. Start a new Windows Application project.

2. In the new project, add a button to the Form1 that was created with the project.

3. Double-click the button to get to its click event routine.

4. Select Tools | Macros | Record Temporary Macro. A small toolbar will appear on top of the IDE with buttons to control recording of the macro (Pause, Stop, and Cancel).

5. Press the *Enter* key and then type in the following line of code:

```
Console.Writeline ("Macro test").
```

6. Press the *Enter* key again.

7. In the small toolbar, press the Stop button.

8. Select Tools | Macro | Save Temporary Macro. The Macro Explorer will appear (in the location normally occupied by the Solution Explorer), and the new macro will be in it. You can name the macro anything you like.

9. Right-click the macro and select Edit to get to the macro editor. You will see code something like this in your macro:

```
DTE.ActiveDocument.Selection.NewLine()
DTE.ActiveDocument.Selection.Text = "Console.WriteLine (""A macro test"")"
DTE.ActiveDocument.Selection.NewLine()
```

The code that appears in step 9 can vary based on how you typed in the line. If you made a mistake and backspaced, for example, those actions will have their own corresponding lines of code.

The code in a macro recorded this way is just standard VB.NET code, and it can be modified as desired. However, there are some restrictions on what you can do inside the macro IDE. For example, you cannot refer to the namespace for setting up database connections.

To run a macro, you can just double-click it in the Macro Explorer, or select Tools | Macros | Run Macro. You can also assign a keystroke to a macro in the Keyboard dialog in the Tools | Options | Environment folder.

No doubt there will be much exchanging of useful macros over the Internet once Visual Studio.NET developers start creating them. Of course, the ILOVEYOU virus taught us that script viruses can be dangerous, so we'll need to be careful.

The New Deployment Tools

The Package and Deployment Wizard in Visual Basic 6 has been replaced with a much more comprehensive set of tools in Visual Studio.NET, which, of course, works with all of the Visual Studio.NET languages. To access the new tools, select the File | Add Project | New Project option. On the New Project dialog, select the Setup and Deployment Projects option on the left side:

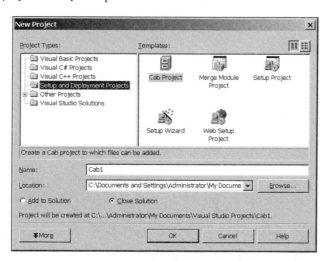

The Setup Wizard option is closest to the VB6 Package and Deployment Wizard, and the Setup Project option is a bare-bones alternative for creating a setup program. The other options offer new capabilities, including the ability to set up a web-based project (Web Setup Project). The Cab Project assists with the creation and management of Windows cabinet (Cab) files, which can hold compressed files for deployment.

The Merge Module Project option is used to package files or components that will be shared between multiple applications. They create a merge module (.msm) file that includes all files, resources, registry entries, and setup logic for a component. This .msm file can then be merged into other deployment projects.

Chapter 24 contains more information on deployment in .NET.

Visual Editors for XML, XSD Schemas, and XSLT files

Visual Studio.NET uses XML and related technologies throughout – as a data store, as a formatting mechanism, and as glue to tie together functional areas. So it's no surprise that Visual Studio.NET includes editors for web-related files, such as XML, XSLT, and, of course, HTML files.

These editors can all be accessed through the Project | Add New Item option, which displays the dialog box shown below for creating new items with various formats. The editors are also used if XML, XSLT, or HTML files are brought into the project with Project | Add Existing Item:

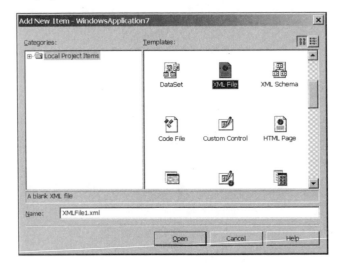

The editors are similar to XML and HTML editors that have been around for a while. They do auto-generation of closing XML tags, for example. While there are commercial editors that probably have more features, the advantage of these editors is their complete integration into the Visual Studio.NET environment. More details regarding the use of XML in VB.NET can be found in Chapter 19.

Debugging Across Projects and Processes

A major innovation in Visual Studio.NET is the most comprehensive debugger ever seen in a Microsoft environment. Using the technologies inherent in the .NET Framework, the debugger can:

❑   Move transparently from language to language in a single project

❑   Debug into and through components that are imported into a project

❑   Track execution from one process to another

❑   Carry debugging into stored procedures

The debugging screens look a lot like those that Visual Studio developers are accustomed to. The difference is mostly the increased reach of the debugger into areas where it could not go before.

Extended IntelliSense

IntelliSense has been a popular feature of Microsoft tools and applications since it was first introduced. Visual Studio.NET includes some new IntelliSense features that take the concept even further.

For example, if you type `Exit` and a space, IntelliSense will display a list of keywords in a drop-down which could follow `Exit`. Other keywords that have dropdowns to present available options include `Goto`, `Implements`, `Option`, and `Declare`. IntelliSense also displays more tooltip information in the environment than before. Not only that, but IntelliSense *also* includes a feature to help the developer match up pairs of parentheses, braces, and brackets.

Summary

For the first time, all Microsoft languages have been brought into one development environment, and it is a powerful one. While being generally familiar to users of previous versions of Visual Basic, the IDE offers many new features that should boost programmer productivity.

The IDE is also very customizable. Various windows can be used or hidden, and can assume varying positions. A new user should expect to spend some time experimenting with different layouts to see which works best. It is also worth some effort to explore the various menu options, to be aware of all of the tools at your disposal.

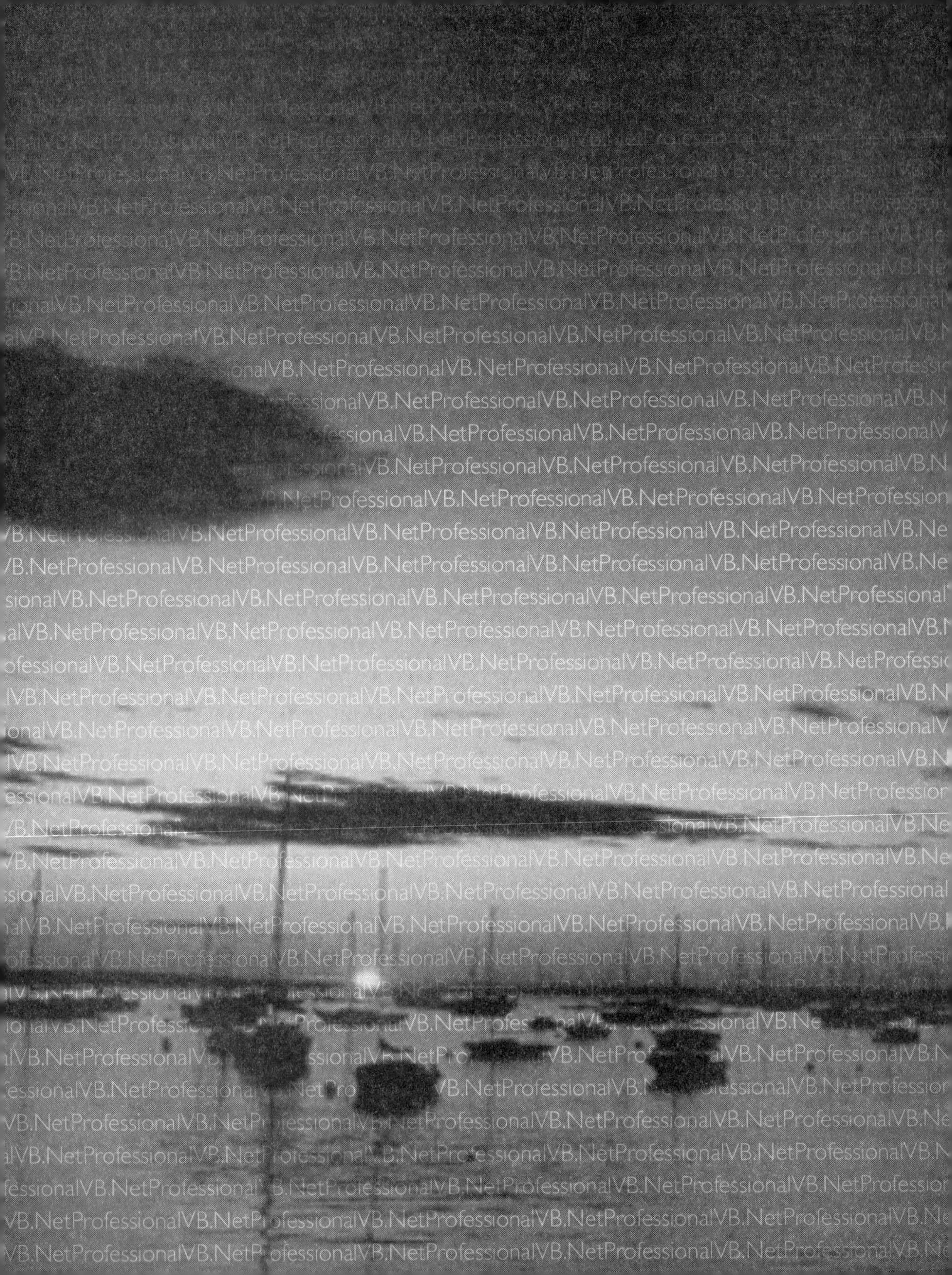
VB.NetProfessional

The Common Language Runtime

At the core of the .NET platform is the **Common Language Runtime (CLR)**. In a lot of ways the CLR can be viewed as a better VB runtime. The CLR is responsible for managing the execution of code compiled for the .NET platform. One of the VB runtime's primary goals was to manage the execution of code compiled with previous versions of VB. For example, both the CLR and the VB runtime manage allocating and freeing memory on behalf of the application. In this chapter we will talk about many of the features provided by the VB runtime that have been enhanced by the CLR.

The architects of .NET realized that there is quite a bit of base functionality that is needed across all procedural languages. Many languages ship with their own runtime to provide base functionality like memory management. Instead of each language shipping with its own runtime, wouldn't it be better if all languages could leverage one common runtime? This is exactly what the CLR provides.

Functionality exposed by the CLR can be made available to all .NET languages. For example, VB developers have been asking for better support for more advanced features for quite some time. These include operator overloading, implementation inheritance, threading, the ability to marshal objects, and many more. However building these features into a language is not trivial. The CLR supports these advanced features and many more. Since VB.NET is built on top of the .NET platform, many of the shortcomings of previous versions of VB have been eliminated.

In this chapter we will cover some of the more significant features provided to .NET applications by the CLR. These include:

❑ **Versioning and deployment**. The CLR provides a more simple and robust way to handle managing different versions of code. .NET has simplified the deployment requirements for applications as well.

❑ **Memory management**. The Garbage Collector (GC) is responsible for collecting objects no longer referenced by the application.

❑ **Cross-language integration**. The CLR enables managed code (code that is compiled to run under the control of the CLR) written in one language to seamlessly integrate with code written in another language. This includes cross-language inheritance, exception handling, marshaling of data, and debugging.

❑ **Meta Data**. Much of the magic performed by the CLR can only be accomplished because .NET applications expose rich Meta Data. This Meta Data contains information about the types an application exposes, its dependencies on other .NET applications, the memory layout for objects, etc.

Before we explore the major features of the CLR, let's look at the major components that make up a .NET application.

An Overview of a .NET Application

A .NET application is composed of three primary entities: assemblies, modules, and types. An **assembly** is the primary unit of deployment of a .NET application. **Modules** are the individual files that make up an assembly. **Types** are the basic unit of encapsulating data and behavior behind an interface composed of public fields, properties, and methods. Let's take a look at a diagram of a .NET application:

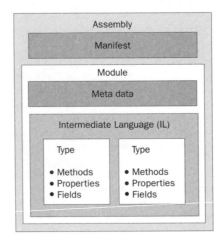

Let's briefly talk about each of the entities represented in the diagram.

Assemblies

An **assembly** is the primary unit of deployment for .NET applications. An assembly is composed of a manifest and one or more modules (described later) and/or files like HTML, XML, video clips, and images.

The **manifest** contains:

❑ Information about the identity of the assembly. The identity information stored in the manifest includes its textual name and version number. If the assembly is public, the manifest will also contain the assembly's public key. The public key is used to help ensure types exposed by the assembly reside within a unique namespace and may also be used to identify the source of the assembly.

❑ A declarative security request describing the assembly's security requirements, as the assembly is responsible for declaring the security it requires. Requests for permissions fall into three categories: required, optional, and denied. The identity information may be used as evidence for determining whether or not to approve the security requests.

❑ A list of other assemblies that the assembly depends on. The CLR uses this information to locate an appropriate version of the required assemblies at runtime. The list of dependencies also includes the exact version number of each assembly at the time the assembly was created.

❑ A list of all types and resources exposed by the assembly. If any of the resources exposed by the assembly are localized, the manifest will also contain the default culture (language, currency, date/time format, etc.) the application will target. The CLR uses this information to locate specific resources and types within the assembly.

The manifest can be stored in a separate file or in one of the modules.

Modules

A **module** is either a DLL or an EXE Windows PE (Portable Executable) file. It contains **Intermediate Language** (**IL**), associated Meta Data, and may optionally contain the assembly's manifest. If the module does contain the assembly's manifest, it is the one and only module that contains the manifest for the assembly – there can only be one manifest per assembly. By default, the VB.NET compiler will create a single module assembly where the module contains the assembly's manifest.

IL is a platform independent way of representing managed code within a module. Before managed code can be executed, the CLR is responsible for compiling the associated IL into native machine code. The CLR provides multiple compilers for this purpose. The install-time compiler will compile all IL associated with an assembly when it is installed on the system. The JIT (just-in-time) compiler will compile the IL on a method-by-method basis the first time the method is called by the application. By default your assembly will be processed by the JIT compiler.

The Meta Data associated with the IL provides additional information relating to the types declared in IL. The Meta Data contained within the module is used extensively by the CLR. For example, if a client and an object reside within two different processes, the CLR will use the type's Meta Data to marshal data between the client and the object.

Types

A **type** is a template used to describe the encapsulation of data and an associated set of behaviors. Unlike COM, which is scoped at the machine level, types are scoped at the assembly level. In *The Common Type System* section later in this chapter, we will learn about the two kinds of types: reference and value types. Reference types can be loosely thought of as classes, whereas value types can be loosely thought of as structures (which have replaced the VB6 user-defined types).

A type has properties, methods, and fields. Fields are variables that are scoped to the type. For example, a Person class may declare a field called Name to hold the person's full name. Methods define particular behaviors exhibited by the type. Properties look like fields to the client but can have code behind them that usually performs some sort of data validation. For example, a Dog data type can expose a property to set its sex. Code could be placed behind the property to only allow it to be set to either "male" or "female".

Versioning and Deployment

.NET offers VB.NET developers a major improvement over the versioning and deployment offered by COM and previous versions of VB. Components and their clients are often installed at different times by different vendors. For example, a VB application may rely on a third party grid control to display data to the user. Runtime support for versioning is crucial for ensuring that an incompatible version of the grid control does not cause problems for the VB application. Furthermore, deployment of applications written in previous versions of VB was problematic.

Better Support for Versioning

In previous versions of VB, managing the version of your components was challenging. VB developers have the ability to set the version number of the component. However, this version number is not used by the runtime. COM components are often referenced by their ProgID. Recall that ProgIDs are developer friendly strings that are used to identify the component, like `Word.Application`. ProgIDs can be fully qualified with the targeted version of the component, like `Word.Application.9`. However, VB does not provide any support for appending the version number on the end of the ProgID.

The versioning support is provided by the CLR for all components loaded in the **Global Assembly Cache** (**GAC**). The GAC is used to store assemblies intended to be used by multiple applications. Two features that the CLR provides for assemblies installed within the GAC are side-by-side versioning and automatic QFEs (hotfixes). **Side-by-side versioning** means that multiple versions of the same component can be stored in the GAC simultaneously. **Automatic QFE** support means that if a new version of the component that is compatible with the old version is available in the GAC, the CLR will load the updated component. The version number maintained by the developer who created the referenced assembly drives this behavior.

As mentioned in the previous section titled *An Overview of a .NET Application*, the assembly's manifest contains the version numbers of assemblies referenced by the application. The CLR uses this list to locate a compatible version of the referenced assembly at runtime. The version number of an assembly takes the following form:

`Major.Minor.Revision.Build`

Changes to the major and minor version numbers of the assembly signal that the assembly is no longer compatible with previous versions. The CLR will not use versions of the assembly that have a different major or minor number unless you explicitly tell it to do so. If an assembly was originally compiled against a referenced assembly with the version number of `3.4.1.9`, the CLR will not load an assembly stored in the GAC unless it has a major and minor number of `3.4`.

Incrementing the revision and build numbers indicates that the new version is compatible with the previous version. Therefore, if a new assembly that has an incremented revision and/or build number is loaded into the GAC, the CLR can load the new assembly for clients that were compiled against a previous version.

Versioning is discussed in more detail in Chapter 14, Assemblies.

Better Deployment

Applications written using previous versions of VB were often complicated to deploy. Components referenced by the application needed to be installed and registered, the correct version of the VB runtime needed to be available, etc. The Component Deployment tool helped by allowing the VB developer to easily create complex installation packages. However, applications would no longer work properly due to dependent components inadvertently replaced by non-compatible versions.

Since the CLR uses a defined set of search rules for locating local assemblies referenced by a .NET application, components do not need to be registered. This also allows the CLR to support side-by-side execution of different versions of the same component. For example, one application could be using a newer version of ADO.NET without adversely affecting another application that relied on a previous version. Furthermore, once the CLR becomes a part of the operating system, there will be no need to distribute the runtime used by the application. In summary, a .NET application can be effectively distributed using the following command:

```
xcopy \\server\appDirectory "c:\Program Files\appDirectory" /E /O /I
```

The command will copy all of the files from the \\server\appDirectory to the c:\Program Files\appDirectory including all of its subdirectories. It will also transfer the file's ACLs as well.

Deployment is discussed in much more detail in Chapter 24.

Memory Management

VB developers have long enjoyed the benefits of the VB runtime's memory management features. Therefore one of the most touted benefits of the CLR will be old hat for VB developers, automatic memory management. In this section we will take a look at the memory management features from the perspective of what was provided by the VB runtime. Specifically, we will look at some of the shortcomings of the VB runtime's memory management and then we'll see how the CLR Garbage Collector (GC) solves these problems.

Better Garbage Collection

The VB runtime has provided automatic garbage collection for some time now. The VB6 runtime automatically releases references to objects once they are no longer referenced by the application. Once all of the references are released on a VB object, the underlying plumbing will automatically release the object from memory. For example, say we had a method that used the Scripting.FileSystem object to write an entry to a log file. Let's take a look at the following VB6 code:

```
' Requires a reference to Microsoft Scripting Runtime (scrrun.dll)
Sub WriteToLog(strLogEntry As String)
   Dim objFSO As Scripting.FileSystemObject
   Dim objTS As Scripting.TextStream

   objTS = objFSO.OpenTextFile("c:\temp\AppLog.log", _
           ForAppending)
   Call objTS.WriteLine(Date & vbTab & strLogEntry)
End Sub
```

In `WriteToLog` we create two objects, a `FileSystemObject` and a `TextStream`. We then use these objects to create an entry in the log file. Once we exit from the Sub, the VB runtime will unreference the objects resulting in both of them getting deactivated. This would also be true if the function dynamically created an array.

As we all know there are situations where objects that are no longer referenced by the application will not get properly cleaned up. Let's take a look at one of the leading causes of this, cyclical references.

Cyclical References

One of the most common situations where the VB runtime is unable to ensure that objects no longer referenced by the application are deactivated is when a VB application contains a cyclical reference. An example of a cyclical reference is when object A holds a reference to object B and object B holds a reference to object A.

The reason why cyclical references are problematic is because the VB runtime relies on COM's reference counting mechanism to determine whether an object can be deactivated. Recall that each COM object is responsible for maintaining its own reference count and is responsible for destroying itself once the reference count reaches zero. The client(s) of the object is responsible for updating the reference count appropriately by calling the `AddRef` and `Release` methods on the object's `IUnknown` interface.

Problems occur if the client does not properly maintain the COM object's reference count. For example, the object will never get deactivated if a client forgets to call `Release` when the object is no longer referenced (and no other clients call `Release` one too many times). Fortunately, the VB6 runtime takes care of updating the reference count for us.

Unfortunately, the object's reference count is an invalid indicator of whether or not the object is still being used by the application. Recall from the previous example that objects A and B hold a reference to each other. Say our application invalidates its references to objects A and B by setting their associated variables equal to `Nothing`. Even though both objects A and B are no longer referenced by the application, the VB runtime cannot ensure that the objects get deactivated. The reason is that A and B still reference each other. Let's take a look at an example (this is VB6 code again):

```
' Class:    CCyclicalRef

' Reference to another object.
Dim m_objRef As Object

Public Sub Initialize(objRef As Object)
    Set m_objRef = objRef
End Sub

Private Sub Class_Terminate()
    Call MsgBox("Terminating.")
    Set m_objRef = Nothing
End Sub
```

The `CCyclicalRef` class implements an `Initialize` method that accepts a reference to another object and saves it as a member variable. The following code demonstrates using the `CCyclicalRef` class to create a cyclical reference:

```
Dim objA As New CCyclicalRef
Dim objB As New CCyclicalRef

Call objA.Initialize(objB)
Call objB.Initialize(objA)

Set objA = Nothing
Set objB = Nothing
```

We first create two instances of CCyclicalRef: objA and objB. Both objects now have a reference count of one. Then we call the Initialize method on each object passing it a reference to the other. Now each of the object's reference counts are equal to two, one held by the application and one held by the other object. Next we explicitly set objA and objA to Nothing. This decrements each object's reference count by one. Unfortunately, since the reference count for both instances of CCyclicalRef is now one, the objects will not be released from memory until the application is terminated. As we will see, the CLR Garbage Collector solves the cyclical references problem.

The CLR Garbage Collector

The **Garbage Collector** (GC) is responsible for collecting objects no longer referenced by the application. The approach the GC takes to accomplish this task is quite different from the reference count approach used by the VB runtime. Objects are responsible for deactivating themselves as soon as their reference count reaches zero. Therefore an object is generally released from memory once the last reference has been set to Nothing.

The GC may automatically be invoked by the CLR or the application may explicitly invoke the GC by calling GC.Collect. Since objects will not be released from memory until the GC is invoked and setting an object reference to Nothing does not invoke the GC, a period of time often elapses between when the object is no longer referenced by the application and when the GC collects it.

As long as all references to the object are either implicitly or explicitly released by the application, the GC will take care of freeing the memory allocated to the object. Unlike COM objects, managed objects are not responsible for maintaining their reference count nor are they responsible for destroying themselves. Instead the GC is responsible for cleaning up objects that are no longer referenced by the application. Periodically the GC will determine which objects need to be cleaned up through a process of elimination. The GC accomplishes this by leveraging the information the CLR maintains about the running application.

The GC obtains a list of objects that are directly referenced by the application. Then for each of these "root" objects, it discovers all of the objects that are referenced either directly or indirectly by the "root" object. Once the GC has identified all objects directly and indirectly referenced by the application, the GC is free to clean up all remaining objects.

Because the GC goes through a process of elimination when locating objects that are no longer referenced by the application, the GC will in fact clean up objects containing cyclical references. This is a huge improvement over the VB runtime's garbage collection implementation.

Finalize

The GC calls the Object.Finalize method immediately before it collects an object that is no longer referenced by the application. Reference types are able to override the Finalize method to perform any necessary cleanup. However, developers must be careful not to treat the Finalize method as if it were a destructor.

Class_Terminate in prior versions of VB does not have a functional equivalent in .NET. Since the GC has ultimate control over the lifetime of a managed object, there will more than likely be a delay between the time the object is no longer referenced by the application and when the GC collects it. Because of this, expensive resources that are released in the Finalize method may stay open longer than need be.

Another issue with relying on the Finalize method to perform necessary cleanup is that the GC will usually be triggered by low memory situations. Execution of the object's Finalize method will more than likely incur performance penalties because of this. Therefore the code path in the Finalize method should be as short and quick as possible.

All cleanup activities should be placed in the Finalize method. However, to ensure that resources are released in a timely fashion, objects that require timely cleanup should implement either a Dispose or a Close method. This method should be called by the client application just before setting the reference to Nothing. Let's take a look at an example:

```
Module Module1

    Class DemoDispose
        Private m_disposed As Boolean = False

        Public Sub Dispose()
            If (Not m_disposed) Then
                ' Call cleanup code in Finalize.
                Finalize()

                ' Record that object has been disposed.
                m_disposed = True

                ' Finalize does not need to be called.
                GC.SuppressFinalize(this)
            End If
        End Sub

        Protected Overrides Sub Finalize()
            ' Perform cleanup here ...
        End Sub
    End Class

End Module
```

The DemoDispose class overrides the Finalize method and implements code to perform any necessary cleanup. In this class, we are assuming that the cleanup code contained within the Finalize method should only be run once. We ensure that the Dispose method will only call Finalize once by checking the value of the private m_disposed property before calling Finalize and then setting it to True once Finalize has been called. We then call GC.SuppressFinalize to ensure that the GC does not call Finalize when the object is collected.

The example above implements all of the object's cleanup code in the Finalize method to ensure that the object will be cleaned up properly before the GC collects it. The Finalize method serves as a safety net in case the Dispose or Close methods were not called before the GC collects the object.

Faster Memory Allocation for Objects

Whenever a VB program creates an object, some memory is allocated for that object, and the memory is allocated in a region of virtual memory reserved for the program called the **heap**. The CLR introduces the concept of a **managed heap**. Managed objects are allocated on the managed heap and the CLR is responsible for controlling access to these objects in a type-safe manner.

One of the advantages of the managed heap is that memory allocations are very efficient. Typically when unmanaged code allocates memory on the unmanaged heap, it scans through some sort of data structure looking for a free chunk of memory that is large enough to accommodate the allocation. The managed heap maintains a reference to the end of the most recent heap allocation. When a new object needs to be created on the heap, the CLR allocates memory on the top of memory that has previously been allocated and then increments the reference to the end of heap allocations accordingly. Let's take a look at an example:

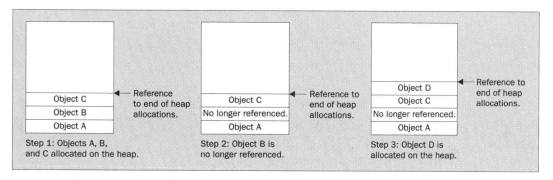

First, the CLR allocated memory for objects A, B, and C on the managed heap. Next the reference to object B was released by the application. Finally, memory for object D was allocated directly above the previously allocated memory (object C) and the reference to the end of the heap allocations was incremented accordingly.

You may be asking, "Sure, allocations are fast, but what about memory fragmentation?" For example, the previous figure showed that object B is no longer referenced. However, memory for object D was allocated directly above object C even if object D could have been squeezed between object A and C. Worse yet, after numerous allocations, there may not be sufficient memory on top of the managed heap to accommodate future requests. This is where the GC comes to the rescue.

If the CLR is unable to allocate memory on the managed heap, the GC is invoked. Recall that the GC is responsible for collecting objects that are no longer referenced by the application. Once all of the objects have been collected, the GC is responsible for compacting the heap. This basically squeezes out all of the spaces between the remaining objects.

GC Optimizations

The GC supports the concept of **generations**. The primary purpose of generations is to improve the performance of the GC. Garbage collection is an expensive operation. In general, it is more efficient to perform garbage collection over a portion of the objects as opposed to the entire set of objects allocated within the application.

The theory behind generations is that objects that have been recently created tend to have a higher probability of being garbage collected than objects that have been living on the system for quite some time. Think of this in terms of a mall parking lot where cars represent objects created by the CLR.

People have different shopping patterns when they visit the mall. Some people will spend a good portion of their day in the mall where others will only stop long enough to pick up an item or two. If we apply the theory behind generations to trying to find an empty space to park our car, we will have a higher probability of finding a space where cars have recently parked. In other words, we are looking for a space that was occupied by the person that just needed to quickly pick up an item or two. The longer a car has been parked in the parking lot, the higher the probability that they are an all day shopper and the lower the probability their parking space will be freed up any time soon.

Generations provide a means for the GC to identify recently created objects versus long-lived objects. An object's generation is basically a counter indicating how many times it has successfully avoided garbage collection. In version 1.0 of the .NET Framework, an object's generation counter starts at zero and can have a maximum value of two. Let's take a look at an example that demonstrates this:

```
Module Module1

    Public Sub Main()
        Dim myObject As Object = New Object()
        Dim i As Integer

        For i = 0 To 3
            Console.WriteLine(String.Format("Generation = {0}", _
                    GC.GetGeneration(myObject)))
            GC.Collect()
            GC.WaitForPendingFinalizers()
        Next i
    End Sub

End Module
```

The code above creates an object and then iterates through a loop four times. For each loop, we display the current generation count for our object and then call the GC. The `GC.WaitForPendingFinalizers` method blocks until the GC has completed.

```
Generation = 0
Generation = 1
Generation = 2
Generation = 2
```

Each time the GC was run, the generation counter was incremented for myObject to a maximum of 2.

Recall that each time the GC is run, the managed heap is compacted and the reference to the end of the most recent memory allocation is updated. After compaction, objects of the same generation will be grouped together. Generation two objects will be grouped at the bottom of the managed heap and generation one objects will be grouped next. Since new generation zero objects are placed on top of the existing allocations, they will be grouped together as well.

So why is this significant? Recall that recently allocated objects have a higher probability of having shorter lives (shoppers running in for an item or two). Since objects on the managed heap are ordered according to generations, the GC can opt to collect newer objects. Obviously running the GC over a portion of the heap would be quicker than running it over the entire managed heap.

When invoking the GC with the `Collect` method, you can call an overloaded version of the `Collect` method that accepts a generation number. The GC will then collect all objects no longer referenced by the application that belong to the specified generation or belong to a younger generation. The `Collect` method without any parameters collects objects no longer referenced by the application that belong to all generations.

Another optimization is that a reference to an object may implicitly go out of scope and therefore be collected by the GC. Let's take a look that the following program:

```
Imports System
Imports System.Threading

Module Module1

    Public Class Demo
        Public Sub New ()
            Debug.WriteLine("Demo.New was called on thread with hash code " _
                & Thread.CurrentThread.GetHashCode())

        End Sub

        Protected Overrides Sub Finalize()
            Debug.WriteLine("Demo.Finalize was called.")
        End Sub
    End Class

    Public Sub Main()
        ' Create new object.
        Dim myObject As Demo = New Demo()

        ' Force garbage collection.
        ' Since myObject is no longer referenced,
        ' it will be collected by the GC.
        GC.Collect()
        GC.WaitForPendingFinalizers()

        Debug.WriteLine("Application terminating.")
    End Sub

End Module
```

When the code is compiled and executed, the application produces the following output:

```
Demo.New was called on thread with hash code 2
Demo.Finalize was called.
Application terminating.
```

myObject's `Finalize` method was called before the application terminated even though the reference to myObject was not explicitly released. Since myObject was never used by the application, it implicitly went out of scope as soon as it was created.

Cross-Language Integration

In previous versions of VB, interoperating with code written in other languages was challenging. If you wanted to use functionality developed in other languages you were pretty much limited to two options, COM interfaces or DLLs with exported C functions. If you wanted to programmatically expose functionality written in VB, you were limited to creating COM interfaces.

Since VB.NET is built on top of the CLR, it is able to interoperate with code written in other .NET languages. You are even able to derive from a class written in another language. In order to support this type of functionality, the CLR relies on a common way of representing types and rich Meta Data used to describe these types.

The Common Type System

Each programming language seems to bring its own island of data types with it. For example, VB represents strings using the BSTR struct (the internal representation of the String data type), C++ offers char and wchar data types, and MFC offers the CString class. The C++ int data type is a 32-bit value where the VB Integer data type, prior to VB.NET, is a 16-bit value. Obviously passing parameters between applications written using different languages can be challenging.

To help resolve this problem, C has become the lowest common denominator for interfacing between programs written in multiple languages. An exported function written in C that exposes simple C data types can be consumed by VB, JAVA, Delphi, and a variety of other programming languages. In fact, the Windows API is exposed as a set of C functions.

Unfortunately in order to access a C interface, you must explicitly map C data types to the language's native data types. For example, a VB developer would use the following statement to map to the GetUserNameA Win32 function (note that GetUserNameA is the ANSI version of the GetUserName function):

```
' Map GetUserName to the GetUserNameA exported function
' exported by advapi32.dll.
'    BOOL GetUserName(
'        LPTSTR lpBuffer,  // name buffer
'        LPDWORD nSize     // size of name buffer
'    );
Public Declare Function GetUserName Lib "advapi32.dll" Alias "GetUserNameA" _
ByVal strBuffer As String, nSize As Long) As Long
```

Notice that we explicitly mapped the lpBuffer C character array data type to the strBuffer VB String parameter. This is not only very cumbersome, but also very error prone. If we accidentally mapped a variable declared as Long to the lpBuffer the application would not generate any compilation errors. However, calling the function at runtime would more than likely result in an access violation.

COM provided a more refined method of interoperating between languages. VB introduced a de facto common type system for all languages that supported COM – variant compatible data types. However, variant data types are very cumbersome to work with for non-VB developers. The underlying C data structures that make up the variant data types like BSTRs and SAFEARRAYs are more complicated than they need to be.

Wouldn't it be nice if there were a set of common data types that is used across all programming languages? That's exactly what the **Common Type System** (**CTS**) provides. The CTS provides every language running on top of the .NET platform with a base set of types and mechanisms for extending those types.

Every type supported by the CTS is derived from System.Object. Therefore, every type supports the following methods:

Boolean Equals(*Object*)	Used to test equality with another object. Reference types should return True if the *Object* parameter references the same object. Value types should return True if the *Object* parameter has the same value. (Reference and value types will be discussed later in this section.)
Int32 GetHashCode()	Generates a number corresponding to the value of an object. If two objects of the same type are equal, then they must return the same hash code. The sorting algorithms implemented in System.Collections use this value extensively.
Type GetType()	Gets a Type object that can be used access Meta Data associated with the type and as a starting point for navigating the object hierarchy exposed by the Reflection API. (The Reflection API will be discussed later in this chapter.)
String ToString()	The default implementation returns the fully qualified name of the class of the object. This method is often overridden to output data that is more meaningful to the type. For example, all base types return their value as a string.

Reference and Value Types

Types supported by the CTS fall into two categories, value types and reference types. An instance of a reference type is an object like an ADO.NET DataSet object or an IO.File object. An instance of a value type is a primitive variable like a DateTime, Boolean, or Double.

The core value types supported by the .NET platform reside within the root of the System namespace. These types are often referred to as the .NET "primitive types". They include:

- ❑ Boolean
- ❑ Byte
- ❑ Char
- ❑ DateTime
- ❑ Decimal
- ❑ Double
- ❑ Guid
- ❑ Int16
- ❑ Int32

- ❑ Int64
- ❑ Sbyte
- ❑ Single
- ❑ TimeSpan

These types will be described in detail in Chapter 6.

Note that there are types that represent unsigned integers UInt16, UInt32, UInt64, but they are not CLS compliant and therefore may not be portable to other platforms. The VB.NET compiler allows the developer to use keywords that serve as aliases to the types defined above. The keywords allow the developer to use a more natural syntax when declaring variables for holding primitive types. For example, the following declarations are equivalent:

```
Dim y as Long;
' ... may seem more natural than ...
Dim x as New System.Int32
```

The primary difference between reference and value types is how instances of the two categories of types are treated by the CLR. One difference is that the GC collects instances of reference types that are no longer referenced by the application. Instances of value types are automatically cleaned up when the variable goes out of scope. Let's take a look at an example:

```
Sub Test()
    Dim myInteger as Integer
    Dim myObject as Object
End Sub
' myInteger is automatically cleaned up when the Sub ends.
' But myObject is not cleaned up until the GC is run.
```

Another difference in the behavior of value types versus reference types is when one variable is set equal to another or passed as a parameter to a method call. When a variable of a *reference* type (A) is set equal to another variable of the same type (B), variable A is assigned a reference to B. Both variables reference the same object. When a variable of a *value* type (A) is set equal to another variable of the same type (B), variable A receives a copy of the contents of B. Each variable will have its own independent copy of the data. Let's take a look at a scenario that demonstrates why we need both reference and value types.

It would be very inconvenient and error prone if the Decimal type behaved like a reference type. Say we are writing an e-commerce application and need to display a confirmation screen that includes a subtotal and the total amount purchased including tax and shipping. To accomplish this, we create two reference variables called subtotal and total of our special decimal reference type. Our application would first calculate the subtotal. It would then calculate the total by setting it equal to the subtotal, and then add tax and shipping to it. Our code would look something like this:

```
' Use a decimal reference type.
Dim total as DecimalRef = new DecimalRef()
Dim subtotal as DecimalRef = new DecimalRef()

' Calculate subtotal.

' Set total equal to subtotal and apply tax and shipping.
```

```
total = subtotal
total = total + tax + shipping
' Oops ...
' We just applied tax and shipping to subtotal as well.
```

If `total` and `subtotal` are reference variables, then `subtotal` would always have tax and shipping applied to it as well since `total` and `subtotal` would reference the same object. Instead, we would have to do something like this:

```
total = subtotal.Clone()
total = tax + shipping
```

The `total` variable is set to a clone of `subtotal` instead of a reference to `subtotal`. The syntax above is not very natural. I think you would agree that we would like to use the previous syntax with one exception. We would like to set `total` equal to the *value* of `subtotal`, as opposed to its *reference* without calling the `Clone` method on `subtotal`. This is where value types come in.

Value types are derived from `System.ValueType`. Instances of types that derive from `System.ValueType` are copied by value and not by reference. As we will see, VB.NET provides a very natural syntax for working with value types.

```
' Use a decimal reference type.
Dim total as Double
Dim subtotal as Double

' Calculate subtotal.

' Set total equal to the value of subtotal and then apply tax and shipping.
total = subtotal
total = total + tax + shipping
' We correctly applied tax and shipping only to total.
```

Yet another difference between the behaviors of value types versus reference types is how equality is determined. Two variables of a given reference type are determined to be equal if both variables refer to the same object. Two variables of a given value type are determined to be equal if the **state** of the two variables are equal.

The final difference between value types and reference types is how instances of a type are initialized. When a variable is declared as a reference type, the variable is initialized with a default value of `Null`. The variable will not reference an object until explicitly done so by the application. In contrast, a variable declared as containing a value type will always reference a valid object. We'll see an example of this in the next section.

Custom Types

A custom type is a set of data and related behavior that is defined by the developer. Previous versions of VB allowed the developer to create types. However, there were several limitations. For example, a class could not be created that derived implementation from another class, a UDT could not contain behavior in the form of methods, and a class could not contain overloaded methods (methods of the same name but which accept different parameters). In this section we will discuss how VB.NET allows the developer to define custom reference and value types that have less limitations than previous versions of VB.

Reference types can be defined in VB.NET by declaring classes. Let's look at the following code used to create and then test the behavior of a custom reference type:

```
Module Module1

    Public Class Test
        Public myString As String
        Public myInteger As Integer
    End Class

End Module
```

We first define a custom reference type called `Test`. For the sake of simplicity, the class contains two public fields, one of type `String` and one of type `Integer`. In general, it is better to expose properties as apposed to fields. We will discuss properties later in the chapter. Next we will write a simple console application to test the behavior of our new reference type:

```
Public Sub Main()
    ' Notice that the declarations are NOT equivalent.
    ' - x references an object of type Test.
    ' - y can reference an object of type Test,
    '   but y does not reference an object yet.
    Dim x As Test = New Test()
    Dim y As Test

    x.myInteger = 4
    x.myString = "Test"

    ' Reference to x is assigned to y.
    y = x
```

In `Main`, we first declare two reference variables of type `Test`. Notice that since `y` is not initialized with the new operator, it does not reference an object and has an initial value of `Nothing`. This is quite different for value types since variables declared as an instance of a value type can never be equal to `Nothing`.

Next, we initialize the `myInteger` and `myString` fields of the object referenced by x. We then set `y` equal to the newly initialized object:

```
    y.myInteger = 1
    y.myString = "Changed"

    Console.WriteLine(String.Format( _
        "x:  myInt = {0} and myString = {1}", _
        x.myInteger, x.myString))
    Console.WriteLine(String.Format( _
        "y:  myInt = {0} and myString = {1}", _
        y.myInteger, y.myString))
End Sub

End Module
```

Finally, we modify the fields of the object referenced by `y` and then write the value of the fields of the object referenced by x and y. Let's take a look at the output of the program:

```
x:  myInt = 1 and myString = Changed
y:  myInt = 1 and myString = Changed
```

Since both x and y reference the same object, the output of x reflects the changes made to y. Hopefully this demo did not reveal anything that was surprising. However, there are times where you do not want this behavior.

Let's take a look at a modified version of the previous program. This time we will implement and use a value type by declaring a structure:

```
Module Module1

    Public Structure Test
        Public myString As String
        Public myInteger As Integer
    End Structure
```

We declare a structure instead of a class this time. Declaring Test as a Structure signals the VB.NET compiler to have Test derive from System.ValueType and therefore a value type.

```
    Public Sub Main()
        ' Notice that both declarations are equivalent.
        ' Both x and y are instances of type test.
        Dim x As New Test()
        Dim y As Test

        x.myInteger = 4
        x.myString = "Test"

        ' Reference to x is assigned to y.
        y = x
```

We initialize x and then set y equal to x. Since x and y are both instances of value types, y is set equal to the *value* of x.

```
        y.myInteger = 1
        y.myString = "Changed"

        Console.WriteLine(String.Format( _
            "x:  myInt = {0} and myString = {1}", _
            x.myInteger, x.myString))
        Console.WriteLine(String.Format( _
            "y:  myInt = {0} and myString = {1}", _
            y.myInteger, y.myString))
    End Sub

End Module
```

We then change the fields in y and finally write the value of the fields in both x and y to the console. Let's take a look at the output of the program:

```
x:  myInt = 4 and myString = Test
y:  myInt = 1 and myString = Changed
```

Notice that when we changed the value of the fields in y it did not affect x. This is exactly the behavior we require for primitive types.

Previous versions of VB allowed the creation of primitive data types by defining user-defined types (UDTs). One serious drawback of UDTs is that you cannot associate behavior with the data type. For example, say we wanted to create a type that represents a US phone number between 000-000-0000 and 999-999-9999. We could create a VB UDT to represent the phone number:

```
Type PHONE
    iAreaCode   As Integer
    iPrefix     As Integer
    iSuffix     As Integer
End Type
```

However, you cannot associate any behavior with the UDT to ensure that the data type contains a valid phone number. VB.NET allows developers to create custom value types that have behavior associated with it such as validating a phone number. Let's take a look at an example:

```
Module Module1

    Sub Main()
        Dim PhoneNumber As PhoneNumber

        PhoneNumber.AreaCode = "3a3"
        PhoneNumber.Prefix = "555"
        PhoneNumber.Suffix = "1212"

        Console.Write(PhoneNumber.PhoneNumber)
    End Sub

    Public Structure PhoneNumber
        Private _AreaCode As String
        Private _Prefix As String
        Private _Suffix As String

        Public Property AreaCode() As String
            Get
                AreaCode = _AreaCode
            End Get
            Set(ByVal Value As String)
                Validate(Value, 3)
                _AreaCode = Value
            End Set
        End Property

        Public Property Prefix() As String
            Get
                Prefix = _Prefix
            End Get
            Set(ByVal Value As String)
                Validate(Value, 3)
                _Prefix = Value
            End Set
        End Property
```

```
        Public Property Suffix() As String
            Get
                Suffix = _Suffix
            End Get
            Set(ByVal Value As String)
                Validate(Value, 4)
                _Suffix = Value
            End Set
        End Property

        Public ReadOnly Property PhoneNumber() As String
            Get
                PhoneNumber = String.Format("({0}) {1}-{2}", _
                _AreaCode, _Prefix, _Suffix)
            End Get
        End Property

        Private Sub Validate(ByVal Value As String, ByVal Length As Integer)
            If (Value.Length <> Length Or Not IsNumeric(Value)) Then
                MsgBox("The property must contain {0} numbers.")
            End If
        End Sub
    End Structure
End Module
```

The PhoneNumber value type contains three private fields of type String to hold the area code, prefix, and suffix. Instead of allowing users of this type to directly modify the fields, we expose properties. The major advantage properties have over fields is the ability to invoke behavior when a property is read or set. This behavior is defined in the form of Get and Set accessors.

We defined four properties: AreaCode, Prefix, Suffix, and PhoneNumber. AreaCode, Prefix, and Suffix provide validation to ensure that they are not passed invalid data. All three of these properties call the Validate method to perform the necessary validation.

PhoneNumber is a read-only property that returns a formatted string containing the phone number. Since the private fields may not have been initialized, we must check to see if they contain a Null value. If a field contains a Null value, we initialize it to all zeros.

There is another aspect with respect to value types that developers should be aware of. Recall that all value types derive from System.ValueType. System.ValueType overrides Object.Equals and Object.GetHashCode. The implementation of both methods uses the Reflection API. (Don't take my word for it. In a later section we will fire up the IL Disassembler and see for ourselves!) Since there is a cost involved with using the Reflection API to navigate the internals of the object, consider overriding these methods with a more direct and efficient method of determining an appropriate hash code and whether or not the value of two types are equal.

Boxing and Unboxing Value Types

There are some cases where it makes sense to treat an instance of a value type as if it were an instance of a reference types. An example of this is when a value type is passed ByRef as a parameter of a method. This is where the concept of **boxing** becomes important.

Boxing occurs when an instance of a value type is converted to a reference type. An instance of a value type can be converted either to `System.Object` or to any other interface type implemented by the value type. Let's take a look at an example. How many boxing operations occur in the following code?

```
Option Strict Off

Module Module1

    Public Function Add(ByVal x As Object, ByVal y As Object) As Object
        Add = x + y
    End Function

    Public Sub Main()
        Dim x As Integer = 2
        Dim y As Integer = 3
        Dim sum As Integer

        sum = Add(x, y)

        Console.WriteLine("{0} + {1} = {2}", x, y, sum)
    End Sub

End Module
```

Six boxing operations occur in `Main`. Both x and y are boxed before they are passed to `Add`. Then x, y, and sum are boxed before they are passed to `WriteLine`. In addition, the implementation of `Add` indirectly calls the VB helper function, `ObjType.AddObj` in the `Microsoft.VisualBasic.Helpers` namespace where yet another boxing operation occurs on the sum of the two numbers returned by the `Add` method.

This implicit type conversion behavior is very similar to the overhead associated with the `Variant` data type in previous versions of VB. Therefore the practice of avoiding excessive use of the `Variant` data type carries over to .NET and the `Object` data type. By having `Add` accept and return parameters of type `Integer` instead of `Object`, we can reduce the number of boxing operations down to three (those required by `Console.WriteLine`). In addition, having a strongly typed interface will also ensure that the caller only passes numeric values (32 bit integers).

The exception to this rule is if you pass a value parameter multiple times to a method that accepts a reference parameter. In this case it is advantageous to box the value parameter once before passing it multiple times to methods that accept reference parameters. Let's take a look at an example:

```
' Declare an instance of a value type.
Dim s as String

' Four implicit boxing operations.
Console.WriteLine("{0}, {1}, {2}, {3}", s, s, s, s)

' One intentional implicit boxing operation.
Dim o as Object = s
Console.WriteLine("{0}, {1}, {2}, {3}", o, o, o, o)
```

Since the most compatible overloaded method for `Console.WriteLine` accepts a string and four `System.Object` parameters, the first call to `Console.WriteLine` will implicitly box s four separate times. No boxing is performed on the second call to `Console.WriteLine` since we intentionally box s to `System.Object` once and then passed the boxed version four times to `Console.WriteLine`.

Unboxing involves the conversion of an instance of a reference type back to its original value type. Unfortunately, VB.NET does not support the ability to explicitly unbox values. VB relies on the helper functions in the `Microsoft.VisualBasic.Helpers` namespace. For example in our `Add` example, `IntegerType.FromObject` is called to unbox the return parameter of type `Object` back to an `Integer`. These helper functions are considerably less efficient than C#'s support for explicit unboxing. This is all the more reason to carefully use variables that are declared as `Object`.

Meta Data

Meta Data is information that enables components to be self-describing. Meta Data is used to describe many aspects of a .NET component including classes, methods and fields, and the assembly itself. Meta Data is used by the CLR to facilitate all sorts of things like validating an assembly before it is executed and performing garbage collection while managed code is being executed. VB developers have used Meta Data for years while developing and using components within their applications.

VB developers use Meta Data to instruct the VB runtime on how to behave. For example, VB developers can set the "Unattended Execution" property in the project properties dialog box. This property determines whether unhandled exceptions are shown on the screen in a message box or are written to the NT Event Log.

COM components referenced within VB applications have accompanying type libraries containing Meta Data about the components, their methods, and properties. The VB developer could use the Object Browser to view this information. The information contained within the type library is also what is used to drive IntelliSense.

Additional Meta Data can be associated with your component by installing it within COM+. Meta Data stored in COM+ is used to declare the support its component needs at runtime such as transactional support, serialization support, and object pooling.

Better Support for Meta Data

.NET refines the use of Meta Data within your VB.NET applications in three significant ways:

- ❑ .NET consolidates the Meta Data associated with a component.

- ❑ Since a .NET component does not have to be registered, installing and upgrading the component is easier and less problematic.

- ❑ .NET makes a much clearer distinction between attributes that should only be set at compile time versus those that can be modified at runtime.

Let's look at each of these points separately.

Prior to .NET, Meta Data associated with a VB component was scattered in multiple locations and in multiple formats. Meta Data instructing the VB runtime how to behave such as the "Unattended Execution" property is compiled into the VB generated executable. Basic COM attributes, like the required threading model, are stored in the registry. Whereas COM+ attributes, like the transactional support required, are stored in the COM+ catalog. In contrast, all attributes associated with VB.NET components are represented in one format and consolidated in one location, within the files that make up the assembly.

Since much of the COM and COM+ component's Meta Data is stored separately from the executable, installing and upgrading components can be problematic. First, COM/COM+ components must be registered to update the registry/COM+ catalog before they can be used. Second, the COM/COM+ component executable can be upgraded without upgrading its associated Meta Data.

The process of installing and upgrading a .NET component is greatly simplified. Since all Meta Data associated with a .NET component must reside within the file that contains the component itself, no registration is required. Once a new component is copied onto the application's directory, it can be immediately used. Upgrading the component becomes much less problematic since the component and its associated Meta Data cannot get out of sync.

Another problem with COM+ is that attributes that should only be set at compile time may be reconfigured at runtime. For example, COM+ can provide serialization support for "neutral" components. A component that does not require serialization must be designed to accommodate multiple requests from multiple clients simultaneously. Hopefully it is self evident that the developer knows at compile time whether or not a component requires support for serialization from the runtime. However, under COM+, the attribute describing whether or not client requests should be serialized can be altered at runtime.

.NET makes a much better distinction between attributes that should be set at compile time versus ones that should be set at runtime. For example, whether a .NET component is serializable is determined at compile time. This setting cannot be overridden at runtime.

Attributes

Attributes are used to decorate entities such as assemblies, classes, methods, and properties with additional information. Attributes can be used for a variety of purposes. For example, the attribute can be informational only, used to request a certain behavior at runtime, or even invoke a particular behavior from another application. Let's take a look at an example:

```
Module Module1

    <Serializable()> Public Class Demo
        <Obsolete("Use Method2 instead.")> Public Sub Method1()
            ' Old implementation ...
        End Sub

        Public Sub Method2()
            ' New implementation ...
        End Sub
    End Class


    Public Sub Main()
```

```
        Dim d As Demo = New Demo()

        d.Method1() ' Will generate a compiler warning.
    End Sub

End Module
```

By decorating the Demo type with the Serializable attribute, the base class library will provide serialization support for instances of the Demo type. For example, you can use the ResourceWriter type to stream an instance of the Demo type to disk. An attribute was also associated with Method1 for the purpose of marking the method obsolete. VB.NET will display an IntelliSense warning if Method1 is referenced within the application:

'Public Sub Method1()' is obsolete: 'Use Method2 instead.'

VB.NET allows the developer to use a shorthand notation for the name of the attribute. For example, the fully qualified name of the Obsolete attribute is System.ObsoleteAttribute. VB.NET allows developers to drop the Attribute from the end of the name. A less natural, yet equally valid way of declaring an attribute would be:

```
' VB.NET Equivalent:
Public Sub <System.ObsoleteAttribute("Use Method2 instead.")> Method1()
End Sub
```

There are many times where you would want to associate multiple attributes with an entity. The following is an example of declaring multiple attributes for a class:

```
Module Module1

    <Serializable(), Obsolete("No longer used.")> Public Class Test
        ' Implementation ...
    End Class


    Public Sub Main()
        Dim t As Test = New Test()

        t.Method1() ' Will generate a compiler warning.
    End Sub

End Module
```

The Reflection API

The .NET Framework provides the Reflection API for accessing all Meta Data associated with managed code. Developers can use the Reflection API to examine Meta Data associated with an assembly and its types, even the currently executing assembly.

The Assembly class in the System.Reflection namespace can be used to access the Meta Data in an assembly. The LoadFrom method can be used to load an assembly and the GetExecutingAssembly method can be used to access the currently executing assembly. You can then use the GetTypes method to obtain the collection of types defined in the assembly.

You can also access the Meta Data of a type directly from an instance of that type. Since every object derives from System.Object, every object supports the GetType method. The GetType method returns a Type object that can be used to access the Meta Data associated with the type.

The Type object exposes countless methods and properties for obtaining the Meta Data associated with a type. For example, you can obtain a collection of properties, methods, fields, and events exposed by the type by calling the GetMembers method. You can also obtain the Type object for the object's base type by calling the DeclaringType method.

IL Disassembler

One of the more handy tools that ships with the .NET SDK is the **IL Disassembler** (ildasm.exe). It can be used to navigate the Meta Data within a module such as the types the module exposes and its properties and methods. The IL Disassembler can also be used to display the IL contained within a module.

Let's use the IL Disassembler to prove a previously made statement that the implementation of System.ValueType's Equals and GetHashCode methods use the Reflection API. The IL Disassembler that ships with the .NET Framework SDK can be found in your Microsoft.Net\FrameworkSDK\Bin directory. Once the IL Disassembler has been launched, select File and then Open. Open mscorlib.dll (which will be located in Framework directory). Once mscorlib.dll has been loaded, expand the System folder, then the ValueType folder, and finally double-click on the Equals method. A window similar to the one below should be displayed:

```
ValueType::Equals : bool(class System.Object)                          _ □ ×
.method public hidebysig virtual instance bool
        Equals(class System.Object obj) il managed
{
  // Code size       136 (0x88)
  .maxstack  3
  .locals (class System.RuntimeType V_0,
           class System.RuntimeType V_1,
           class System.Object V_2,
           class System.Object V_3,
           class System.Object V_4,
           class System.Reflection.FieldInfo[] V_5,
           int32 V_6)
  IL_0000:  ldarg.1
  IL_0001:  brtrue.s    IL_000e
  IL_0003:  ldstr       "obj"
  IL_0008:  newobj      instance void System.ArgumentNullException::.ctor(clas
  IL_000d:  throw
  IL_000e:  ldarg.0
  IL_000f:  call        instance class System.Type System.Object::GetType()
  IL_0014:  castclass   System.RuntimeType
  IL_0019:  stloc.0
  IL_001a:  ldarg.1
  IL_001b:  call        instance class System.Type System.Object::GetType()
  IL_0020:  castclass   System.RuntimeType
  IL_0025:  stloc.1
  IL_0026:  ldloc.1
  IL_0027:  ldloc.0
```

The screenshot above shows the IL for the Equals method. Notice that the Reflection API is used to navigate through the instance of the value type's fields to determine whether or not the values of the two objects being compared are equal.

As we have demonstrated, the IL Disassembler is a useful tool for learning about the implementation details of a particular module.

Summary

In many ways the CLR can be thought of as an improved version of the VB runtime. In this chapter, we introduced the CLR and compared and contrasted it with the VB runtime.

We discussed the memory management features of the CLR and how they compare to the VB runtime. We discussed how the CLR eliminates the circular reference problem that has plagued VB developers. We then discussed how the CLR more efficiently allocates memory for objects than its VB runtime counterpart. Next we discussed the `Finalize` method and why it should not be treated like the `Class_Terminate` method. Specifically:

❑ Whenever possible, do not implement the `Finalize` method in your class. `Finalize` is often called in low memory situations. In addition, classes that implement a `Finalize` method pay a performance penalty.

❑ If the `Finalize` method is used to perform necessary cleanup, make the code path for the `Finalize` method as short and quick as possible.

❑ There is no way to accurately predict when an object no longer referenced by the application will be collected by the GC unless the GC is invoked explicitly.

❑ If you implement the `Finalize` method, implement either a `Dispose` or a `Close` method that can be called by the client when the object is no longer needed.

❑ The order in which the GC collects objects on the managed heap is indeterminate. The `Finalize` method should not call methods on other objects referenced by the object being collected.

We also discussed why it is important to provide a common runtime and type system that can be targeted by multiple languages. We discussed the two kinds of types supported by the CLR, reference types and value types. We learned about the differences between these two types and how each type is treated by the CLR. Specifically:

❑ All types derive from `System.Object`.

❑ Collecting an instance of an unboxed value type (primitive type) when it goes out of scope is more efficient and usually more timely than collecting an instance of a reference type (object).

❑ When a variable declared as `Object` is set equal to a value type or a value type parameter is declared as `ByRef`, the value type is converted to a reference type via a process called "boxing".

❑ For better performance, explicitly "box" an instance of a value type before passing it multiple times to methods that accept `System.Object` or `ByRef` parameters.

❑ For better performance, value types should override `Object.Equals` and `Object.GetHashCode` with a more efficient implementation than the one provided by `System.ValueType`.

Next, we talked in depth about how the CLR offers better support for Meta Data. We discussed how Meta Data is used to make types "self describing". We looked at examples where Meta Data is used by the CLR and the .NET Class Library. Then we learned how to extend Meta Data by creating our own attributes. Then we briefly discussed the Reflection API.

Finally, we reviewed the IL Disassembler utility (`ildasm.exe`). The IL Disassembler is used to display the IL contained within a module. We used the IL Disassembler to verify a statement made earlier in the chapter that the implementation of the `Equals` and `GetHashCode` methods overridden by `System.ValueType` does in fact use the Reflection API.

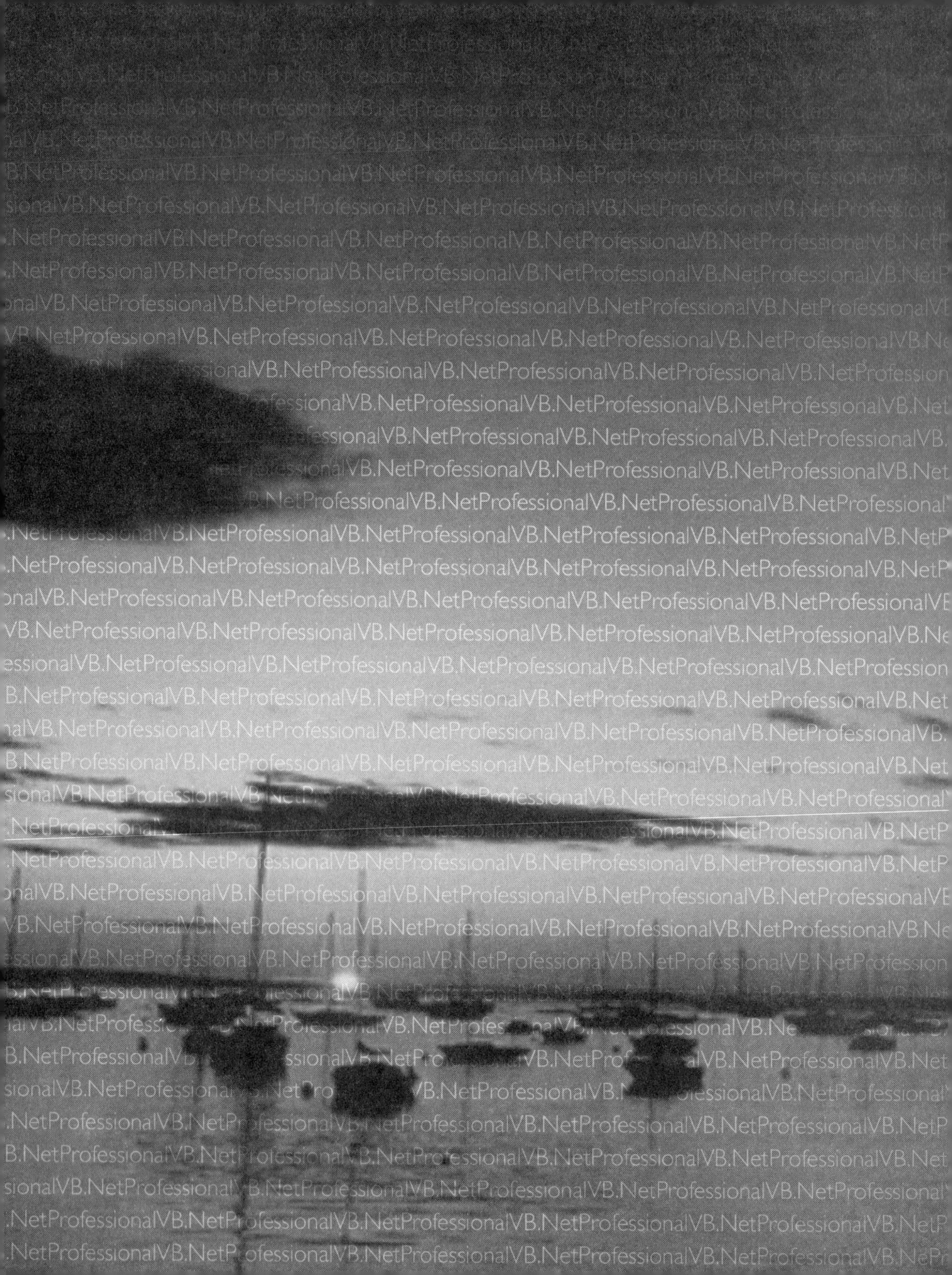
VB.NetProfessional

6

Variables and Types

This chapter will introduce many of the base types used in Visual Basic. Under .NET all objects share a logical inheritance from the base `Object` class. The advantage of this common heritage is the ability to rely on certain common functions of every variable. However, this logical inheritance does not require a common physical implementation for all variables. Experienced developers generally look at integers, characters, and simple types as being the basic building blocks of any language. In .NET the structure is the common underlying implementation of types such as `Integer`, `Long`, `Character`, and even `Byte`. These types are then extended with classes that provide more advanced capabilities. The generic `Object` class definition is the implementation basis for all objects; strings and collections made up of both types of objects in VB.NET. One of the most important things to remember is that .NET has only two major variable types, value and reference.

The main goal of this chapter is to familiarize with these types and to help those with a background in VB6 understand some of the key differences in how variables are defined in VB.NET. We'll begin by looking at value types, followed by a clear definition of a logical grouping called primitive types. We will go on to look at classes, how as reference types they work and how some of the basic classes are used. In short, we will consider all of the following:

❑   Value types (structures)

❑   Primitive types

❑   Reference types (classes)

❑   `Option Strict` and `Option Explicit`

❑   Explicit conversions

❑   Parameter passing `ByVal` and `ByRef`

❑   Boxing

❑   Retired keywords and functions

In this chapter we will look at different ways of categorizing types but in the end whether it is primitives, arrays or even interfaces we are talking about, the types are always based on one of these two basic types.

Value types are what Visual Basic developers would often refer to as data types. They represent simple data storage located on the stack, a more detailed definition of how value types work on the stack is covered later in this chapter.

Reference types are based classes and gain implementation inheritance from their parent classes. The two type families are treated differently within assignment statements, and their memory management is handled differently, and it is important to understand how these differences impact the software you will write in VB.NET. Understanding the foundations of how data is manipulated in the .NET framework will enable you to build more reliable and better performing applications

Value Types (Structures)

The value type consists of variables where the actual data is stored on the **stack**. Value types aren't as versatile as reference types, but they do provide better performance in most circumstances. There are also differences in behavior from reference types that you need to account for when programming with each type. In this section, we'll examine how the behavior between value and reference types differs when a simple assignment occurs. In both cases, the data associated with the original variable, is assigned to the target variable. In the case of a value type, this means that the actual data value is copied. However, in the case of a reference type this means that only the reference is copied.

> First, let's look at the basic difference between the stack and the heap. The stack is a comparatively small memory area where processes and threads store numeric data. For example integers and decimals value both have a fixed number of bytes regardless of the actual value held by a variable of these types. Another important example is an address, because an address is actually a reference to a location on the heap. Of course translating this address takes time, but the heap is not as structured as the stack. The heap is where dynamically sized variable types are stored. Unlike a Character value which is always 2 bytes, a string could vary anywhere from 2 bytes to close to all of the memory available in your system.

Of course that is the reason they are stored separately, because when a process needs to retrieve a variable it has to search the stack, looking for the variable specified. Not that this is a linear search, but even with complex algorithms, if the stack included large variable size items such as strings, this would take a long time. By only storing a reference to these potentially large variably sized data values on the stack the program as a whole runs much quicker since the process can quickly locate the data associated with a variable. However, this difference in how data is stored also has the potential to change the behavior of variables.

A good way to illustrate this is using a value type and reference type for examples. We'll use a comparison between the System.Drawing.Point, a value type, and the System.Text.StringBuilder object (a reference type) for our test. The Point structure is used as part of the .NET graphics library that is part of the System.Drawing namespace. The StringBuilder class is part of the System.Text namespace and is used to improve performance when editing strings. First let's look at using the Point structure:

```
Dim ptX As New Point(10, 20)
Dim ptY As Point

ptY = ptX
ptX.X = 200

Debug.WriteLine( ptY.ToString())
```

The output from this operation will be {X=10,Y=20}, the reason for this is that once we have copied the Point ptX into ptY, the value has copied the data into the locations on the stack that are associated with ptY. When ptX is changed, only the memory locations on the stack associated with ptX are updated thus causing these two items to differ. This is no different from if we had declared ptY as an integer. After first setting it to another variable, we would expect it to be independent of changes to the value we used to create it. However, this is not the case when we look at reference types:

```
Dim objX as New System.Text.StringBuilder("Hello World")
Dim objY as System.Text.StringBuilder

objY = objX
objX.Replace("World", "Test")

Debug.WriteLine(objY.ToString())
```

In this case, although objX was modified the output of the string will in fact be "Hello Test" (when objY is written). The reason for this is that when objY is assigned the value of objX all that is transferred is those values that are on the stack. In the case of an object, this is a reference to the memory location where the actual data is located. Thus, when the data in that memory location is changed, the data associated with every object that holds a reference to that memory is changed. This is normally referred to as a **shallow copy** and while it is possible to change this default behavior, it normally requires additional programming. Of course, to every rule, there is an exception, and as we'll discuss later in this chapter the primitive string class has been implemented so as to create deep copies by default.

Of course, the difference between value types and reference types goes beyond just how they react when copied. Other features that are provided by objects will be examined further later in this chapter. This section is going to look at some of the most commonly used value types and provide a better understanding of how .NET works with these types.

Boolean

We considered titling this section "Three Values for True-False" because the VB.NET Boolean value has been implemented such that it actually has three values, two of them for True. The reason for these two True values is backward compatibility. In short, the problem is that under VB6 Boolean True equated to a −1, in contrast to every other major language that we know of where Boolean True defaults to an integer 1. Within .NET, True equates to a 1, so to avoid developers having to examine every Boolean expression to ensure valid return values, a solution that supports −1 within Visual Basic, but exposes the .NET standard of 1 to the rest of the world, has been developed.

Of course reaching this compromise solution involved making some decisions, which taken independently are rather inconsistent and add significant complexity to a simple True / False evaluation. When used in a Boolean expression, a True Boolean value equates to a −1. However, if this value is converted to any other format, it immediately equates to 1. The best way to illustrate how VB.NET works is with a simple code snippet. This snippet, however, follows poor programming practice in that it does reference Boolean values as integers, and in particular does so with implicit conversions:

```
Dim blnTrue as Boolean = True
Dim blnOne as Boolean = 1
Dim blnNegOne as Boolean = -1
Dim blnFalse as Boolean = False

' The condition below works based on the implicit conversion of
' the Boolean even though the variable is assigned a value of 1
' above...

If blnOne = -1 Then
   Debug.WriteLine(blnTrue)
   Debug.WriteLine(blnOne.ToString)
   Debug.WriteLine(Convert.ToString(Convert.ToInt32(blnNegOne)))
End If

' Let's explicitly convert to another integer type, and test
' the result.
' In this case the condition will fail. It is possible to use
' an implicit conversion and the result will NOT be the same.
' It is important to note that the output of the last debug line
' above clearly shows how converting blnNetOne to an integer
' results in a positive one regardless of what was originally
' assigned.

If Convert.ToInt16(blnNegOne) = 1 Then
   Debug.WriteLine(blnFalse)
   Debug.WriteLine(Convert.ToString(Convert.ToInt32(blnFalse)))
End If
```

The code above will not work if you are using `Option Strict`, but it is a good illustration of what we should expect if we are casting implicitly vs. explicitly. The output from this code snippet, with each value on a separate line in the Visual Studio Output window, is:

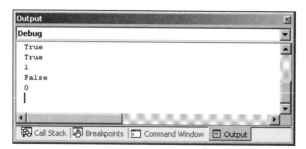

This snippet illustrates several different features of the VB.NET Boolean logic. The first point to note is that there are constant values `True` and `False` that should always be used in place of any integer values. This is the truly correct way of determining a Boolean value. However, in the snippet, the conditional expressions specifically avoid doing this. The first conditional illustrates that, regardless of how a Boolean in VB is initialized, if the casting is done implicitly between an integer and Boolean value it evaluates `True` as −1 and not 1.

The second conditional statement uses an explicit casting to make the Boolean an integer value. In this case, the value of 1 equates to `True`, even though we initialized this Boolean value with a −1. That is because under .NET the value of `True` is 1 and the code used to do an explicit conversion is part of .NET. It is also a good illustration of the risk of relying on implicitly converted values. If at some point the default value associated with `True` were to change, the code above would act differently.

The difference between the explicit and implicit conversion is subtle, and you should take two steps to avoid having a problem. The first is to always use the `True` Boolean values of `True` and `False` in your code. The second is that if you are in any doubt as to how the return value from a function will be handled, assign it to a Boolean variable and then use that local variable in conditional expressions.

To illustrate this further let's look at a theoretical class. We're not going to provide an implementation of `MyCSharpClass`, instead just accept that it has a single method `TestTrue()` which doesn't accept any parameters. As will be discussed in Chapter 7, we've referenced this class and can create an instance of `MyCSharpClass` using a complete reference. So now that we have created an instance of this, C# implementation calls to `TestTrue()` method are made:

```
Dim objMyClass as New MyCSharpClass()

If objMyClass.TestTrue() = 1 Then
  Debug.WriteLine("CSharp uses a 1 for true but does it" & _
  " implicitly convert to a 1 in VB?")
End If

If objMyClass.TestTrue() = True Then
  Debug.WriteLine("CSharp True always converts to Visual Basic True.")
End If
```

The key point made here is that the first conditional in the above sample is unclear. Will it ever work? The answer it turns out is "No", because even in runtime from a different language the Visual Basic compiler will ensure that the value `true` converts to an integer -1. However, the second condition is not only clear but also not open to future modifications of the Visual Basic language definition. To create reusable code it is always better to avoid implicit conversions. In the case of Booleans, if the code needs to check for an integer value, explicitly evaluate the Boolean, and create an appropriate integer, your code will be far more maintainable and prone to fewer unexpected results.

Integer

In VB6 there were two types of integer values. The `Integer` type was limited to a maximum of 32767 and the `Long` type supported a maximum of 2147483647. Under .NET a new integer type was added. The `Short` replaces the old `Integer` value from VB6. The `Integer` has been promoted to support the range previously supported by the `Long` type, and the `Long` type is bigger then ever. However, it is important to note that each of these types also has two additional alternative types. In total there are nine integer types that VB.NET supports, which are:

Type	Memory Allocation	Min Value	Max Value
Short	2 Bytes	-32768	32767
Int16	2 Bytes	-32768	32767
UInt16	2 Bytes	0	65535
Integer	4 Bytes	-2147483648	2147483647
Int32	4 Bytes	-2147483648	2147483647
UInt32	4 Bytes	0	4294967295

Table continued on following page

Type	Memory Allocation	Min Value	Max Value
Long	8 Bytes	-9223372036854775808	9223372036854775807
Int64	8 Bytes	-9223372036854775808	9223372036854775807
UInt64	8Bytes	0	18446744073709551615

Short

A Short value is limited to the maximum value that could be stored in two bytes. This means there are sixteen bits and that the value must range between –32768 and 32767. This limitation may or may not be based on the amount of memory physically associated with the value. It is a definition of what must occur in .NET. This is important, because there is no guarantee that the implementation will actually use less memory then using an Integer value. It is possible that the operating system will allocate the same memory used for an Integer type and just limit the possible values, in order to optimize memory or processing. It should be noted that the Short (or Int16) value type can be used to map SQL smallint values.

Integer

The Integer type is defined as having the maximum value that could be stored in four bytes. It is not defined as a four-byte implementation, but a value that can be safely stored and transported in four bytes. This gives the Integer and Int32 value types a range from –2147483648 to 2147483647. For almost all normal functions this range will be more than adequate to handle most tasks. The main reason you would use an Int32 in place of an Integer value has to do with future portability and interfaces. The Integer value in VB 6 was limited to a two-byte value. If knowing that in the future as the language changes, your 32 bit integer values continue to have that limitation, which might be important for certain interfaces; the solution is to use the Int32 value type. Finally, keep in mind that the new sizing of the Integer value type matches the size of an int value in SQL Server so that you can align the column type of a table with the variable type in your program.

Long

The Long type is aligned with the Int64 value. These numbers have an eight-byte range meaning they can go from -9223372036854775808 to 9223372036854775807. When working with SQL remember that the Long value type now matches the bigint type. Let's face it, this is a big range, but if you need to either add or multiply together Integer values then you will often need a large value that can contain the result. It is common when doing math operations on one type of integer to use a larger type to capture the result if there is a chance that the result could exceed the limit of the types being manipulated.

Unsigned Types

Another way to have additional space available is to use one of the unsigned types. The unsigned types provide a useful buffer that will hold a result that might exceed an operation by a small amount, but that isn't the main reason they exist. The UInt16 happens to have the same characteristics as the Character type, while the UInt32 has the same characteristics as a system memory pointer. These types are used when interfacing with software that expects these values, and are the underlying implementation for other value types.

Explicit Casting

Most of the integer types allow for limited implicit conversions. In particular, it is possible to assign the value of a smaller type into a larger type. The reverse, however, will result in a compilation error since the compiler doesn't have any safe way of handling the assignment when the larger value is outside the range of the smaller value. The good news is that this means that comparison operations where the smaller version can be safely promoted from `Small` to `Integer` or `Long` can be safely carried out using different signed types.

When explicitly casting, from a larger type, `Long`, to a smaller type, `Integer` or `Short`, be sure to first verify that the value is within the appropriate range. While the compiler will allow you to cast from `Long` to `Short`, if a value is out of range at runtime your program will throw an exception. Let's look at a simple example of how we can convert between different integer types with `Option Strict ON`:

```
Dim shrShort As Short
Dim shrUInt16 As UInt16
Dim shrInt16 As Int16
Dim intInteger As Integer
Dim intUInt32 As UInt32
Dim intInt32 As Int32
Dim lngLong As Long
Dim lngInt64 As Int64

shrShort = 0
shrUInt16 = Convert.ToUInt16(shrShort)
shrInt16 = shrShort
intInteger = shrShort
intUInt32 = Convert.ToUInt32(shrShort)
intInt32 = shrShort
lngInt64 = shrShort

lngLong = lngLong.MaxValue
If lngLong > Short.MaxValue Then
  shrShort = Convert.ToInt16(lngLong)
End If
intInteger = CInt(lngLong)
```

The preceding snippet provides some excellent examples of what might not be intuitive behavior. The first thing to note is that we can't implicitly cast from `Short` to `UInt16`, or any of the other unsigned types for that matter. That is because with `Option Strict` the compiler will not allow an implicit conversion that might result in a value out of range or loss of data. In this case, if the variable `shrShort` contained a –1 then the value wouldn't be in the allowable range for an unsigned type.

The second item illustrated in the code above is the shared function `MaxValue`. All of the integer and decimal types have this method. As the name indicates it returns the maximum value for the specified type. There is a matching `MinValue` method for getting the minimum value. As shared methods, the methods can be called on either an instance of the class (`LngLong.MaxValue`) or by referencing the class (`Short.MaxValue`).

One item that isn't apparent in the code above is the fact that when possible all conversions should be avoided. If you look at the definition for the `Convert."methodname"` functions you will see that each has been overloaded to accept various types. However, if you look at the definition of the `CInt` function that most VB6 programmers are familiar with, it is defined to accept a parameter of type `Object`. This is important because, as will be mentioned later in this chapter, this involves **boxing** the value type. Boxing is important because when a value type is boxed there is a performance implication.

Finally, although the code above will compile, it will not execute. That is because the final statement does not check to ensure that the value being assigned to the intInteger value is within the maximum for an Integer type. Unlike the preceding conditional to ensure that only values within the appropriate range are assigned to the short value, the assignment to intInteger will throw a runtime error with a value out of bounds.

Decimal

Similarly to the integer types there are different implementations of value types to support real numbers. However, unlike the integer types there are only three implementations. The Single and Double types work the same way in VB.NET as in VB6. The difference is that the Currency type that was a specialized version of the Double type has become obsolete and the new Decimal value type has been added.

Type	Memory Allocation	Negative Range	Positive Range
Single	4 Bytes	-3.402823E38 to -1.401298E-45	1.401298E-45 to 3.402823E38
Double	8 Bytes	-1.79769313486231E308 to -4.94065645841247E-324	4.94065645841247E-324 to 1.79769313486232E308
Currency	Obsolete	-	-
Decimal	16 Bytes	-79228162514264337593543950335 to 0.0000000000000000000000000001	0.00000000000000000000000000001 to 79228162514264337593543950335

Single

The Single type contains four bytes of data and its precision can range anywhere from 1.401298E-45 to 3.402823E38 for positive values. In addition, it has a range from – 3.402823E38 to – 1.401298E-45 for negative values.

You might wonder how a value that is stored as four bytes, in the same way as an Integer value type, can have a number that is so much larger than even the Long type. The difference has to do with how the numbers are stored and more importantly the second part of the definition for a real number. That is the level of precision. You'll notice there are six digits after the decimal in this definition. When a real number starts to get very large or very small it will round the associated value to the closest number.

For example, while it is possible to represent a Long with the value of 9223372036854775807, the Single type rounds this value to 9.223372E18. At first glance this might seem like a reasonable action, but the thing to keep in mind is that this isn't a reversible action. There are various code examples that talk about how, when working with very small numbers, this loss of precision can result in minor errors. The code below shows how it can result in very large errors:

```
Dim lngMax as Long = Long.MaxValue - 2000000
Dim sngRnd as Single

Debug.WriteLine lngMax.ToString()
sngRnd = Convert.ToSingle(lngMax)
Debug.WriteLine sngRnd.ToString()
sngRnd -= 2000000
Debug.WriteLine sngRnd.ToString()
lngMax = Convert.ToInt64(sngRnd)
Debug.WriteLine lngMax.ToString()
```

This code might appear simple enough and as you can tell we are working at reducing the total by 400,000 but the results are probably not what you expect:

```
9223372036854775807
9.223372E18
9.223372E18
-9223372036854775807
```

That's right, the two million does not cause a difference in the value since it was below the precision level for a number this size. In attempting to return to an integer value, we find that the conversion reverses the sign and makes this the largest (or smallest) negative number that can be stored in a 64 bit integer.

Double

Of course, the behavior of the preceding example changes dramatically if we replace the value type of `Single` with `Double`. A `Double` uses an eight-byte area to store values and as a result has both a greater precision and range. The range for a `Double` is from 4.94065645841247E-324 to 1.79769313486232E308 for positive values. Negative values have a similar range from -1.79769313486231E308 to -4.94065645841247E-324. Again you'll note that the scientific notation indicates that the largest value would be 1 followed by 308 zeros. You'll also note that the precision has increased allowing for a number to contain 15 digits before rounding begins.

This greater level of precision makes the `Double` value type a much more reliable variable when conducting math operations. It is possible to represent most operations with complete accuracy with this value. It should be noted, however, that the `Double` wasn't the only eight-byte decimal value in VB6. One of the variable types, which has become obsolete, is the `Currency` type. The `Currency` type was a specialized version of the `Double`, which was designed to support numbers using nineteen available digits. While this was certainly better precision than the 15-digit precision available, it really pales in comparison to the new 28 digit `Decimal` type.

Decimal

The `Decimal` type is new with VB.NET and is really a hybrid of a twelve-byte integer value combined with two additional 16-bit values to control the location of the decimal point and sign of the overall value. All told a `Decimal` value will consume sixteen bytes. The maximum value that can be stored is 79228162514264337593543950335. This value can then be manipulated, by adjusting where the decimal place is located. For example, the maximum value while accounting for four decimal places is 7922816251426433759354395.0335. This is because a `Decimal` isn't stored as a traditional number. As noted a `decimal` is a 12-byte integer value, and then the location of the decimal in relation to the available 28 digits is stored. The `Decimal` does not inherently round numbers the way that a double does.

As a result the closest precision to zero that a decimal supports is 0.00000000000000000000000000001. This value is pretty small but we haven't discussed negative values. Just as with the location of the decimal point the decimal has a separate value to indicate if the possible value is positive or negative. As a result the positive and negative ranges are exactly the same, regardless of the number of decimal places. What this means is that as you require a larger number of decimal places you reduce the maximum size of the value. In many ways, this trade off makes logical sense since after all how often are you going to want fifteen digits on either side of the decimal point? Measurements that involve great decimal accuracy seldom occur with very large values.

Char and Byte

The default character set under VB.NET is the Unicode character. As a result when you declare a variable to be of type Char you are creating a two-byte value, since by default all characters in the Unicode character set require two bytes. In order to declare a character value we have two possibilities. The first uses a constant string that is followed by the special character, c. Placing a c following a literal string informs the compiler that the value should be treated as a character. Of course you can only create single characters one at a time, as shown with the two methods for creating character values in VB.NET:

```
Dim chrLtrA as Char = "a"c
Dim chrAscA as Char = ChrW(97)
```

While having everything in VB.NET support Unicode is great, there is a drawback if you need to work with ASCII. If you wanted to transform your characters into a string for use as part of an ASCII interface it requires the runtime library to check each value. In part to support bypassing this checking, VB.NET supports the Byte value type. A variable declared as a Byte is just that, a value between 0 and 255 that matches exactly the range of the old ASCII character set. One circumstance where you will want to use a Byte array is if you are working to interface with older systems that still use ASCII. When using a Byte array, the underlying runtime library knows that there is no conversion from Unicode needed for the associated characters and as a result the interface will operate significantly faster.

As with other primitive types, it is possible to assign a constant value. However, under VB.NET the Byte value type expects a numeric value. In order to assign the letter "a" to a Byte requires some level of manipulation. The snippet below shows how to carry out the assignment of a single character as part of the declaration of Byte, and uses the explicit conversion of these types:

```
Dim bytLtrA as Byte = Microsoft.VisualBasic.Asc ("a")
Dim bytAscA as Byte = 97
```

DateTime

The Visual Basic Date keyword has always supported a structure of both date and time. Under VB.NET the Date structure continues to operate as it did in VB 6. However, unlike VB6 the Date structure is implemented as part of the .NET framework's DateTime structure. You can in fact declare your date values as being associated with either type. However, if you want to get a better idea of the available methods of the date class the place to look is in the help for the DateTime structure type.

.NET provides a new static value that can be used to initialize a Date value. VB6 programmers are undoubtedly familiar with the Now() function that initializes a Date value with the local date and time. This function has not been changed, but now the functions Today() and UtcNow() have been added. These functions can be used to initialize a date object with the current local date or date and time based on the Universal Coordinated Time, also known as Greenwich Mean Time, respectively.

```
Dim dteNow as Date = Now()
Dim dteToday as Date = Today()
Dim dteGMT as DateTime = DateTime.UtcNow()
```

Primitive Types

While standard definitions vary between languages, it is fair to say that every development language has a group of elements such as integers and strings that are termed **primitive types**. The basic concept is that values such as 123 and "Hello World" are the basic values to any system. The types that deal with these values are often different from other system data types. Good examples of this are C++ and Java where there are for example primitive integer, decimal, and string values (to name a few). These types differ from the other types that are tied to class definitions. These languages are object oriented but they have an entire set of primitives that fall outside the object realm.

On the other hand there are also a few languages such as, Small Talk where an attempt has been made to implement all of the primitive types as objects. However, attempting to implement primitives as true objects has a distinct disadvantage, in that creating objects takes additional system resources. The result is that the runtime code created by such languages tends to have performance issues.

The following table describes the primitive types currently supported by .NET.

Type	Base Implementation	Default	Comments
Boolean	Value (structure) type	False	Can be True or False
Byte	Value (structure) type	0	A single byte of data
Short or Int16	Value (structure) type	0	Two-byte integer
Char	Value (structure) type	ChrW(0)	Two-byte Unicode character
Integer or Int32	Value (structure) type	0	Four-byte integer
Long or Int64	Value (structure) type	0	Eight-byte integer
Single	Value (structure) type	0	Four-byte floating point value
Double	Value (structure) type	0	Eight-byte floating point value
Decimal	Value (structure) type	0	Sixteen-byte floating point value
Date or DateTime	Value (structure) type	01/01/0001 12:00:00 AM	Eight-byte representation of a date, a time, or a date and time
String	Reference (class) type	Null	Unicode

VB.NET has taken an alternative route to primitives. The first thing to realize is that VB.NET did not create special rules to handle primitive types. The definition of a primitive in VB.NET isn't based on how it is stored or implemented, for example value types vs. reference types. In VB.NET primitives have sets of additional attributes that other variables do not have. These three capabilities make up the complete definition of a primitive:

❑ Allows for the assignment of an initial static value

❑ Is a reserved word

❑ Can be used to define constant values

```
Const intX as Integer = 15
Dim strY as String
Dim intZ as Integer

strY = "Hello World"
intZ = 21
```

As the code snippet above shows, it is possible to assign static values such as numbers and strings into the primitive types. The sample above demonstrates not only the `Integer` primitive that is also a value type, but also the `String` primitive that is a reference type. Note that if you are working in Visual Studio .NET, you will see that these variable names all change from the default text color to indicate their reserved status.

You'll notice that instead of the typical `Dim` statement that is used to define the type of a variable, that the first statement uses the reserved word `Const`. A `Const` is a value that you assign in the source code at design-time, but which isn't modifiable at runtime. The ability for a type to be used as a constant, as noted above, is one of the three requirements for the classification of that type as a primitive.

In examining the different primitive types, the `String` stands out. As will be discussed later in this chapter, in VB.NET the `String` is a type of class. As a class it is a reference type, and thus stored on the heap. On the other hand, types like integers are structures and stored on the stack. It is important to realize that the classification of a type as a primitive has nothing to do with its classification as a value type or reference type, or where the data associated with that data type is eventually stored.

As a quick reminder, the stack and heap refer to areas within a computer's memory. The stack is a comparatively small memory area where certain values with only a limited number of bytes are stored, while the heap is a larger memory area.

In the case of types such as `Integers`, the actual value associated with this variable is kept on the stack so that the computer can access this data quickly. However, things that are dynamic or require significant amounts of memory are stored in the heap. Things on the heap are referenced by keeping a pointer to the value on the stack, and thus the alternative name of **reference**. Thus, while the storage location does impact the underlying base that a variable has it does not impact its status as a primitive type.

Reference Types (Classes)

We have spent quite a bit of time looking at value types. However, a lot of the power of VB.NET is harnessed in objects. An object is defined by its class, while the class definition describes what data, methods, and other attributes an instance of that class will support. When your code instantiates an object from a class, the object created is a **reference type**. There are literally thousands of reference type objects provided by Microsoft as the core of the .NET Common Runtime Library.

Earlier in this chapter we discussed how one difference between value types and reference types was where they were stored. However, that is not the only difference. Classes, as we will tend to refer to reference types, have several other differences from structures. In looking beyond just the differences, a class can have private and protected methods, the ability to receive events, constants, and can extend a base class by a capability known as inheritance. Additionally classes can be used to define how an operator such as = or + works when that object is involved in the equation. This book contains three full chapters (11, 12, and 13) to go into details on all of these capabilities.

This section is going to look at some of the base objects that are used throughout the system. The `Object` class is the base class for every object in the system. More importantly, this class replaces the `Variant` type that was the default in VB6. The `String` class is one of the primitives mentioned earlier in this chapter. As the only reference type that is categorized as a primitive, and one of the most commonly used classes in most VB development, understanding this class and some of the minor changes it has experienced is important. The section looks at how to determine if a variable has been declared but not yet instantiated, and finally looks into the array structure and some of the classes that have been provided to implement additional capabilities based on that class.

Overview of Objects

Before we get to some specific objects, however, let's have a basic overview of objects in case you aren't familiar with programming in an object-oriented environment. Objects are a way of associating the value or values stored in a variable with a set of behaviors. For example, when we think of a `String` we think of a set of characters. These characters are the value or property of the `String` object. There are certain behaviors that can be associated with a `String`. These behaviors include the ability to replace characters, or to change the case of the characters. Implementation of behaviors is done by an object's methods. This is a change from traditional programming in that it moves away from data being acted on by system functions. Instead, the code that manipulates data is associated with the data that will be manipulated.

Each object definition, or class, is a self-contained definition of the data and implementation of the methods to alter that data. This is an oversimplification but is the basis on which objects are defined. The next layer of complexity we can add to this is inheritance. Inheritance is where you can take an existing object and create a specialized version of this object. In theory, this specialization could require a complete new implementation, such as when working with COM. However, in .NET you can actually inherit the implementation.

Under .NET every object can implement inheritance. This can be done explicitly, by specifying a parent in the class definition, or implicitly. The `Object` class defines and implements the baseline methods of an object in .NET. These methods include `Equals`, `GetHashCode`, `GetType`, and `ToString`. Because every object in .NET inherits from the base `Object` class it is always possible to call these methods. However, this does not mean that a class can't override these methods, and some such as `ToString` are specifically designed to be overridden.

As will be discussed in detail in Chapter 13, overriding a function involves creating a method with the same name and parameters as the method on the base class. Now when a variable is defined based on that class, a call to the overridden method will automatically execute on the new class not the base class. A variable based on a class, is called an instance. To actually get a valid instance, the new method on the class is normally called, which results in an instance. Some classes such as the Object class are never instantiated directly, meaning that while you can define a variable of type Object, you can't assign it a New Object(). Such classes are called abstract, in that they allow the assignment of classes that are derived based on their definition, but do not actually exist.

As the next section will examine, the ability to assign any object to a variable described as type Object can be very powerful. Of course this isn't a new discovery, it was well known even before Visual Basic 6, what is new is that VB.NET will now allow you to truly create classes based on inheritance. However, we are starting to get beyond the scope of this chapter which is oriented toward working with existing data types.

Instance Methods

When a variable is created as an instance of a class it is possible to call the methods associated with that class. However, not all methods are created equal, there are actually two ways that an object can implement methods.

The first, which most programmers are quite familiar with, involves methods that are available when an instance of an object has been created. These are called **instance methods** and generally require some element associated with the object to exist. The ToString() method is a good example of an instance method. It requires an instance of an object to exist and importantly, if that instance has overridden the base ToString() method, the instance's version of that method will be called. This is true even if the instance is currently referenced in a variable defined as type Object for example.

Static Methods

The second type of method is called a **static method** (also known as a **shared method**). Static methods are similar to static variables. They don't draw on instance data and as a result you can specify the type of object and static method you desire. It is important to understand that when a static method is called the method on the class specified will be used. These methods do not look for an inherited version as instance methods do, and even if a method with the same name and parameters exists, the method that is on the referenced object will be used.

A good example of a static method is the Equals method on the base Object class. Checking to see if two objects have the same data is more involved than, say, checking two value types. To get around this it is possible for an object to define a method that will be called when the equality operator is used. You will see more on this in Chapter 13, but, for now, such an action is referred to as **operator overload**. It is not necessary for objects to carry out this overload, and if they don't then a way is needed to be able to test for equality.

```
Dim objStrOne As New System.Text.StringBuilder("Hello")
Dim objStrTwo As System.Text.StringBuilder = objStrOne

'The conditional below will not compile
'If objStrOne = objStrTwo Then

If Object.Equals (objStrOne, objStrTwo) Then
  Debug.WriteLine("The data referenced by these objects is the same.")
End If
```

The code snippet above demonstrates how for a class such as `StringBuilder` the equality operator has not been overloaded. However, since like other objects, the `StringBuilder` class ultimately inherits from the `Object` class, we can use a static method on the `Object` class to determine if the two instances are the same. Having this implemented as a static method means it can be referenced without needing to create or reference an actual instance. Since we are starting to discuss `Object` methods it's probably appropriate to discuss the `Object` class.

Object

The `Object` "class" in VB.NET is the great exception. For consistency, we have chosen to group it with the classes, but in reality `Object` is the basis for both value and reference types. This definition as the parent of everything helps VB.NET support the runtime specification of classes. At its core, every variable is an object and can be treated as such, but, underneath the covers, the `Object` class is implemented as a reference type. In fact later in this chapter, the fact that value types are in fact converted to reference types when used in object variables is discussed.

The lines below can work equally well in VB6 and VB.NET:

```
Dim varObj
Dim objVar
```

The reason we say "can work", is that under VB.NET a project must be defined using the `Option Strict` `Off` setting. However, these lines have a subtle difference in VB.NET. This section will discuss how these lines create objects in VB.NET. Unlike VB6, where these were `Variant` memory locations, in VB.NET each one of these is a reference to an instance of the `Object` class.·

The `Object` class is the basis of every type. In VB6 there was a construct called a `Variant`. The `Variant` type was defined as a data type with the type information embedded within it. The `Variant` had the ability to support all of the different data types that existed in Visual Basic 6. A `Variant` was implemented to provide a reference to a memory area on the heap. The definition didn't define any specific ways of accessing this data area. Although at a much lower level this memory area contained separate chunks of data that would minimally describe the data area associated with a given `Variant`, this wasn't exposed to VB developers.

The VB6 runtime environment managed interpreting `Variants` for VB programmers. This was in some ways good, because those programmers could set up a situation where they knew what the contents of the variant should be and then just program as if that is what was there. If the contents of the memory area in fact were an object of the appropriate type then the call to a method on that object would succeed. While this was simple to do, it left VB6 programs open to some unusual runtime errors that are generally harder to track and debug. VB.NET replaces the memory location associated with a `Variant` with a reference type of an `Object`. On the other hand, when interfacing with ASP pages or other scripted code, `Variants` were a requirement due to the way that these loosely typed languages worked.

Interestingly enough when you are not using `Option Strict`, the behavior of VB6 `Variants` and VB.NET `Objects` is almost identical. Since the `Object` class is the basis of all types, you can assign any variable to an `Object`. Reference types will maintain their current reference and implementation but will be generically handled while value types will be packaged into a box and placed into the memory location associated with the `Object`. The first thing to recognize about the new `Object` is that it supports all of the capabilities that were available from the `Variant` type.

However, the `Object` class goes beyond the VB6 variant type in that it supports methods. We briefly looked at one of the static methods associated with the `Object` class just prior to the start of this section. There are other instance methods that are available, for example `ToString`. This method will, if implemented, return a string representation of an instance. Since the `Object` class defines it, it can be called on any object.

```
Dim objMyClass as New MyClass("Hello World")

Debug.WriteLine(objMyClass.ToString)
```

Which brings up the question of how does the `Object` class know how to convert custom classes to `Strings`? The answer to this question is that it doesn't. For this method to actually return the data of an instance in `String` format a class must override this function with a version that does this. Otherwise when this code is run the default version of this function defined at the `Object` level will return the name of the current class as its string representation.

Finally it needs to be noted that the `Object` class continues to fill the role of the `Variant` class even when `Object Strict` is enabled. The declaration is more explicit, however – anything that can be done with `Object Strict` disabled can be done with it enabled. The difference is that with `Option Strict` you must explicitly define the type of object whose property or method you wish to access if you don't want to only access those methods available from the base `Object` class:

```
Dim objVar as Object

objVar = Me

CType(objVar, Form).Text = "New Dialog Title Text"
```

The snippet above shows a generic object being created under the `Object Strict` syntax. It is then assigned a copy of the current instance of a VB.NET form. The name `Me` is reserved in VB and its use will be described further in the next chapter. Once it has been assigned, if we want to access the `Text` property of this class we need to cast it as something other than a base `Object`. The `CType` command covered later in this chapter accepts the object we are interested in as its first parameter and the class to which we are casting this object as its second parameter. In this case the current form instance is of type `Form`, and by casting this we can reference the `Text` property of the current form.

This may seem difficult, but later in this chapter when we talk about explicit casting and `Option Strict` we'll show how we can modify the preceding sample to make it more generic while still maintaining the explicit declaration. This should give you a solid basis for how the `Object` class as the basis for all classes in .NET will play an important role in all of your VB.NET development.

String

Another class that will play a large role in your development projects is the `String` class. Those familiar with VB6 are going to find that having `Strings` defined as a class is more powerful then the VB6 data type of `String` with which they are familiar. However, as part of that transition there have been some changes to `Strings`. Additionally, the `String` class is special within .NET because it is the one primitive type that is not a value type. In order to make `Strings` compatible with some of the underlying behavior it has some interesting characteristics.

Shared Methods	Description
Empty	This is actually a property. It can be used when an empty String is required. It can be used for comparison or initialization of a String.
Compare	Compares two objects of type String.
CompareOrdinal	Compares two Strings, without considering the local national language or culture.
Concat	Concatenates one or more Strings.
Copy	Creates a new String with the same value as an instance provided.
Equals	Determines whether two Strings have the same value.
Equality operator (=)	An overloaded version of the equality operator that compares two Strings.
Inequality operator (op_Inequality)	A method that accepts two parameter Strings for comparison. The method returns True if the Strings are not equal.

The subset of String object methods above is shared, which as noted earlier means that the methods are not specific to any String. The next table lists instance methods, called based on a specific String variable. The methods on the String class replace the functions that Visual Basic 6 had as part of the language for string manipulation. The table below lists only a subset of the instance methods on the String class:

Instance Methods	Description
Chars	Gets the character at a specified position in the String.
CompareTo	Compares the String with a specified object.
CopyTo	Accepts the start position in the current String, as well as the target String, the start position in the target String and the number of characters to copy. Copies the characters from the current String to the passed-in target.
EndsWith	Determines whether the end of the String matches a passed-in String.
Equals	Compares the String with a String passed in. Overloaded versions of this function automatically convert Integers and other types to Strings for comparison.
GetEnumerator	Returns an object that can iterate through the characters in the String.
IndexOf	Returns the index of the first occurrence of a passed-in String.
IndexOfAny	Returns the index of the first occurrence of any character from a passed-in array of characters in the current String.
Insert	Inserts into the String a passed-in String at the index position specified.
LastIndexOf	Returns the index of the last occurrence of a passed-in String.

Table continued on following page

Instance Methods	Description
LastIndexOfAny	Returns the index of the last occurrence of any character from a passed-in array of characters in the current `String`.
Length	Gets the number of characters in the `String`.
PadLeft	Right-aligns the characters in the `String`, padding on the left with spaces or a specified character based on a parameterized total length.
PadRight	Left-aligns the characters in the `String`, padding on the left with spaces or a specified character based on a parameterized total length.
Remove	Deletes the specified number of characters starting from the chosen index.
Replace	Replaces all occurrences of a passed in `String`, with a different `String`.
Split	Accepts a `String` to be used as a delimiter. This function then breaks the `String` into an array of `Strings` on the delimiter. The array of `Strings` is returned.
StartsWith	Determines whether the beginning of the `String` matches the String passed-in.
Substring	Retrieves a substring from the `String`, based on start position and optionally the number of characters to retrieve.
ToCharArray	Returns the characters that make up the `String` to an array of characters.
ToLower	Returns a copy of the `String` in lowercase.
ToUpper	Returns a copy of the `String` in uppercase.
Trim	Removes all copies of a character or array of characters from both the beginning and end of the `String`. Removes spaces if no character is specified.
TrimEnd	Removes all copies of a character or array of characters from the end of the `String`. Removes spaces if no character is specified.
TrimStart	Removes all copies of a character or array of characters from the start of the `String`. Removes spaces if no character is specified.

The String() Function

Let's look at one of the changes from VB6. The `String()` function which allows for the creation of a `String` with a set length and populated with a specific character no longer exists in VB.NET. This is because as an object the `String` class has a constructor. More accurately, the `String` class has several different constructors:

```
Dim strConstant as String = "ABC"
Dim strRepeat as New String("A"c, 20)
```

You'll notice that the second example of constructing a new string actually does so by imitating the capability of the VB6 `String()` function. However, this function, as well as other `String` creation functions, has now been encapsulated in the `String` class. Not only have creation functions been encapsulated, but also other string specific functions, such as character and substring searching, case changes, and others are now available from the class to which they apply. This change alone will save new VB programmers hours of time trying to find a function to return the first few characters of a string.

The SubString Method

Although not documented as removed, the `Left`, `Right`, and `Mid` functions are at least deprecated in VB.NET. This is largely due to the fact that the .NET `String` class has a method called `SubString`. This single method replaces the three functions that VB6 programmers are accustomed to using to create substrings. There are two versions of this; the first accepts a starting position and the number of characters to retrieve, while the second accepts simply the starting location:

```
Dim strMyString as String = "Hello World"

Debug.WriteLine(strMystring.SubString(0,5))
Debug.WriteLine(strMyString.SubString(6))
```

The PadLeft and PadRight Methods

Another change related to the `String` class is the removal of the `LSet` and `RSet` statements. These functions have been replaced by the `PadLeft` and `PadRight` methods. These methods allow you to justify a `String` so that it is left or right justified. As with `SubString`, the `PadLeft` and `PadRight` methods have been overloaded. The first version of these methods requires only a maximum length of the `String`, and then uses spaces to pad the `String`. The other version requires two parameters, the length of the returned `String`, and the character that should be used to pad the original `String`:

```
Dim strMyString as String = "Hello World"

Debug.WriteLine(strMyString.PadLeft(30))
Debug.WriteLine(strMyString.PadLeft(20,"."c))
```

The String as an Immutable Class

The VB.NET `String` class isn't entirely different from the `String` type that VB programmers have used for years. The majority of `String` behaviors remain unchanged, and the majority of functions are still available as methods. However, in order to support the default behavior that people associate with the `String` primitive, the `String` class isn't declared the same way many other classes are. `Strings` in .NET do not allow editing of their data. When a portion of a `String` is changed or copied, the operating system allocates a new memory location and copies the resulting `String` to this new location. This ensures that when a `String` is copied to a second variable, the new variable references its own copy.

To support this behavior in .NET, the `String` class is defined as an **immutable class**. What this means is that each time a change is made to the data associated with a `String`, a new instance is created, and the original referenced memory is released for garbage collection. This is an expensive operation, but the result is that the `String` class behaves as people expect a primitive type to behave. Additionally, when a copy of a `String` is made, the `String` class forces a new version of the data into the referenced memory. This ensures that each instance of a `String` will reference only its own memory:

```
Dim strMyString as String
Dim intLoop as Integer

For intLoop = 1 to 1000
   strMyString = strMyString & "A very long string"
Next
Debug.WriteLine(strMyString)
```

The code shown above does not perform well. This is not very different from the type of logic that is used to traverse a recordset and build a table of results to a query. Each time the assignment operation to `strMyString` occurs the system will allocate a new memory buffer based on the size of the new string, and copy both the current value of `strMyString` and the new text which is to be appended. The system then frees the previous memory that must be reclaimed by the garbage collect. As this loop continues that memory allocation requires a larger and larger chunk of memory. The result is that operations such as this can take a long time. However, VB.NET offers an alternative:

```
Dim objMyStrBldr as New System.Text.StringBuilder()
Dim intLoop as Integer

For intLoop = 1 to 1000
   ObjMyStrBldr.Append("A very Long string")
Next
Debug.WriteLine(objMyStrBldr.ToString())
```

The code above although it works with strings does not use the `String` class. This is because as part of VB.NET a new class called the `StringBuilder` performs better on strings that will be edited repeatedly. This class does not store a string in the conventional manner. Instead a string is stored as an array of characters, and editing or appending more characters does not involve allocating new memory for the entire string. Since the preceding code snippet does not need to reallocate the memory used for the entire string each time another set of characters is appended it performs significantly faster. In the end, an instance of the `String` class is never explicitly needed because the `StringBuilder` class implements the `ToString` method to roll up all of the characters into a string. While the concept of the `StringBuilder` class isn't new, the fact that it is now available as part of the VB.NET implementation means developers no longer need to roll their own versions of string memory managers.

DBNull

One of the changes in VB.NET is that the `IsNull` and `IsEmpty` functions that were common in VB6 have become obsolete. As a result, VB.NET provides an alternative way of determining if a variable has not been initialized, `IsDBNull()`. The `IsDBNull` method accepts an object as its parameter and returns a Boolean indicating if the variable has been initialized. In addition to this method, VB.NET has access to the `DBNull` class. The class is part of the `System` namespace and in order to use it you declare a local variable with the `DBNull` type. This variable is then used with an `is` comparison operator to determine if a given variable has been initialized:

```
Dim sysNull as System.DBNull
Dim strMyString as String

If strMyString is sysNull Then
   StrMyString = "Initialize my String"
End If
```

```
If Not IsDBNull(strMyString) Then
    Debug.WriteLine strMyString
End If
```

In the snippet above the strMyString variable is declared but not yet initialized. The first conditional is evaluated to True and as a result the string is initialized. The second conditional then ensures that the declared variable has been initialized. Since this was accomplished in the preceding code, a line is written to the Output window. In both cases, the sysNull value is used not to verify the type of the object, but to verify that it has not yet been instantiated with a value.

Array

Initially when VB.NET was announced, there were to be a lot of significant changes to arrays from the way they worked in VB6. A major reason for these changes involved getting rid of the Variant_Array structure. This structure introduced with COM, was hidden from most VB programmers, but was ever present. It was necessary because VB defined arrays in a unique way. The variant array has been removed from not only VB but from every .NET language. The reason it was removed is that under .NET, arrays are handled the same way, where they always start at 0 and have a defined number of elements. However, the way that an array is declared in VB.NET still varies slightly from other .NET languages.

When VB.NET was announced it was said that arrays would always begin at 0 and that they would be defined based on the number of elements in the array. However, in VB6 the Option Base statement allowed arrays to be declared as starting at 1 or any other specified value, and this meant that they were defined based on their upper limit. The Option Base This = statement resulted in a problem when converting existing code. To resolve this issue the engineers at Microsoft developed a compromise. All arrays in .NET will begin at 0, however, in VB.NET when an array is declared the definition is based on the upper limit of the array, not the number of elements.

The result is that while some of the more esoteric declarations that were available in VB6, such as Dim intMyArr(15 to 30) are no longer supported, the majority of capabilities remain unchanged. It is still possible to declare an array with multiple indices. Specifically we can declare any single type as an array. The basic Array class is never explicitly declared for a variable's type. The System.Array class that serves as the base for all arrays is defined such that it cannot be created, but must be inherited. As a result, to create an Integer array a set of parentheses is added to the declaration of our variable. These parentheses indicate that the system should create an array of the type specified. These parentheses may be empty or may contain the size of the array. An array can be defined as having a single dimension using a single number, or as having multiple dimensions. Let's examine some simple examples to demonstrate different ways of creating arrays:

```
Dim arrMyIntArray1(20) as Integer
Dim arrMyIntArray2() as Integer = {1, 2, 3, 4}
Dim arrMyIntArray3(4,2) as Integer
Dim arrMyIntArray4( , ) as Integer = _
    { {1, 2, 3, 4},{5, 6, 7, 8},{9, 10, 11, 12},{13, 14 , 15 , 16} }
Dim arrMyIntArray5() as Integer
```

The samples above demonstrate five different ways to declare an array of Integers.

In the first case we define an array of Integers that spans from arrMyIntArray1(0) to arrMyIntArray1(20). This is a 21-element array, because all arrays start at 0 and end with the value defined in the declaration as the upper bound.

The UBound Function

The declaration of arrMyIntArray2 actually defined an array that spans from arrMyIntArray2(0) to arrMyIntArray1(3). This is because when we declare an array by specifying the set of values it still starts at 0. However, in this case we are not specifying the upper bound; if we wish to verify the upper bound, we can use the UBound function:

```
Debug.Writeline CStr(UBound(ArrMyIntArray2))
```

The UBound function is available in VB.NET as is its companion LBound. This function computes the upper bound for a given array. In theory, the LBound function does the same thing for the lower bound, but since all arrays in VB.NET are 0-based, it doesn't have much value anymore.

Multi-Dimensional Arrays

The declaration of arrMyIntArray3 is a multi-dimensional array. This declaration creates an array with 15 elements ranging from arrMyIntArray3(0,0) through arrMyIntArray3(2,1) to arrMyIntArray3(4,2). As with all elements of an array, when it is created without specific values the values of each of these elements is created with the default value for that type. This case also demonstrates that the size of the different dimensions can vary. It is also possible to nest deeper than two levels, but this should be done with care as such code is difficult to maintain.

The fourth declaration, arrMyIntArray4(,) is created with values. The values are mapped based on the outer set being the first dimension and the inner values being associated with the next inner dimension. To better illustrate this statement, the value of arrMyIntArray4(0,1) is 2 while the value of arrMyIntArray4(2,3) is 12. The code snippet below illustrates this using a set of nested loops to traverse this array. Additionally, it provides an example of calling the UBound function with a second parameter to specify that we are interested in the upper bound for the second dimensions of the array:

```
Dim intLoop1 as Integer
Dim intLoop2 as Integer
For intLoop1 = 0 to UBound(arrMyIntArray4)
  For intLoop2 = 0 to UBound(arrMyIntArray4, 2)
    Debug.WriteLine arrMyIntArray4(intLoop1, intLoop2).ToString
  Next
Next
```

The ReDim Statement

The final declaration arrMyIntArray5() is an array which has not yet been instantiated. If an attempt were made to assign a value into this array, it would trigger an exception. The solution to this is to use the ReDim keyword. ReDim was part of VB6, however, it has changed slightly in VB.NET. The first change is that you must first Dim an instance of the variable: you cannot use the ReDim statement as the initial declaration of a variable. The second change is that you cannot change the number of dimensions in an array. An array with three dimensions cannot grow an additional dimension or be reduced to only two dimensions.

```
Dim arrMyIntArray5() as Integer

' The statement below would compile but would cause a runtime exception.
'arrMyIntArray5(0) = 1

ReDim arrMyIntArray5(2)
ReDim arrMyIntArray3(5,4)
ReDim Preserve arrMyIntArray4(UBound(arrMyIntArray4),2)
```

The statements in the code snippet above illustrate the different facets of the ReDim command. The ReDim of arrMyIntArray5 instantiates values so that it can store data. Because this array was declared, but not initialized, it is not possible to use it to hold data until it has been allocated with actual data elements.

The second statement is redimensioning the arrMyIntArray3 variable defined earlier. Note that it is changing the size of both the first and second dimension. While it is not possible to change the number of dimensions in an array it is possible to resize any of an array's dimensions. This capability is required for declarations such as Dim arrMyIntArray6(, , ,) As Integer to be legal.

The Preserve Keyword

The last item in the code snippet illustrates an additional keyword associated with redimensioning. The Preserve keyword indicates that the data that is stored in the array prior to redimensioning it should be transferred to the newly created array. If this keyword is not used then the data that was stored in an array is lost. Additionally, this statement actually reduces the second dimension of the array. While this is a perfectly legal statement it should be noted that this means that even though we have asked to preserve the data, the data values 4, 8, 12, 16 that were assigned in the original definition of this array will be discarded. These are lost because they were assigned in the highest index of the second array. Since arrMyIntArray4(1,3) is no longer valid, the value of 8 which resided at this location has been lost.

Arrays continue to be very powerful in VB.NET. The ability to create almost any class as part of an array and to change the size of arrays on the fly will handle most of what needs to be done. However, the basic array class is just that, basic. While it provides a powerful framework it does not provide a lot of other features that would allow for more robust logic to be built into the array. To accomplish more advanced features such as sorting and dynamic allocation the base Array class has been inherited by the classes that make up the Collections namespace.

Collections

The Collections namespace is part of the System namespace and provides a series of classes that implement advanced array features. While being able to make an array of existing types is powerful, sometimes more power is needed in the array itself. The ability to inherently sort or dynamically add dissimilar objects in an array is provided by the classes of the Collections namespace:

Class	Description
ArrayList	Implements an array whose size increases automatically as elements are added.
BitArray	Manages an array of Booleans that are stored as bit values.
Hashtable	Implements a collection of values organized by key. Sorting is done based on a hash of the key.

Table continued on following page

Class	Description
Queue	Implements a first-in, first-out collection.
SortedList	Implements a collection of values with associated keys. The values are sorted by key, and are accessible by key or index.
Stack	Implements a last-in-first-out collection.

The preceding table contains some of the collection objects that are available as part of the System.Collections namespace. Each of these collections is based around storing a collection of objects. This means that in addition to the special capabilities each provides it also provides one capability not found in the base Array class. Since everything in .NET is based on the Object class, it is possible to have these collections contain elements that are different, and as all objects inherit from Object, these classes will be storing simply a collection of objects. However, it is possible that the actual objects being stored might be very different. Let's look at an example:

```
Dim objMyArrList As New Collections.ArrayList()
Dim objItem As Object
Dim intLine As Integer = 1
Dim strHello As String = "Hello"
Dim objWorld As new StringBuilder("World")

' Add an integer value to the array list.
  objMyArrList.Add(intLine)

' Add an instance of a string object
  objMyArrList.Add(strHello)

' Add a single character cast as a character
  objMyArrList.Add(" "c)

' Add an object that isn't a primitive type
  objMyArrList.Add(objWorld)

' To balance the string, insert a break between the line
' and the string "Hello", by inserting a string constant
  objMyArrList.Insert(1, ". ")

For Each objItem In objMyArrList

   ' Output the values...
   Debug.Write(objItem.ToString())
Next
```

The preceding code snippet is an example of implementing the new ArrayList collection class. The collection classes, as this example shows, are more versatile than any similar structures that Visual Basic 6 ever had. In this case, a new instance of an ArrayList is created, along with some related variables to support the demonstration. The code then shows four different types of variable being inserted into the same ArrayList. You'll notice that the code then inserts another value into the middle of the list. Note that at no time has the size of the array been declared nor has a redefinition of the array size been required.

Part of the reason for this is that the Add and Insert methods on the ArrayList class are defined to accept a parameter of type Object. This means that the ArrayList object can literally accept any value in .NET. This comes at a slight performance cost for those variables that are value types. This cost is explained later in this chapter in the discussion of boxing. However, the point of this snippet is to show the power of just one of the new collection classes.

The System.Collections.Specialized Namespace

In addition to the classes above that are part of the `System.Collections` namespace, VB.NET has additional classes available as part of the `System.Collections.Specialized` namespace. These classes tend to be oriented around a specific problem. For example the `ListDictionary` class is designed to take advantage of the fact that while a hash table is very good at storing and retrieving a large number of items, it can be costly when there are only a few items. Thus to get the most performance it is possible to use a collection that will provide better performance when only a small number of items is expected. Similarly the `StringCollection` and `StringDictionary` classes are defined so that when working with strings the time spent interpreting the type of object is reduced and overall performance is improved.

Class	Description
ListDictionary	A singly linked list that allows a small number of elements to be accessed faster than other collection implementations. This collection should not be used for a large number of elements.
StringCollection	Implements a collection of strings.
StringDictionary	Implements a hash table, but the key is strongly typed as a string rather than as a base object.

Option Strict and Option Explicit

When discussing a variety of the topics in this chapter the words `Option Strict` have been mentioned. `Option Strict` is one of three options that can be assigned globally to a project. These options are interpreted at compile time. `Option Explicit` was part of VB6 and has not been changed. This option still ensures that all variables have been declared prior to use, and is a great way to catch spelling errors between your declared variables and the code you are writing. However, the settings for `Option Compare` and `Option Strict` also impact the performance of the project once it has been compiled.

To edit these settings start by right-clicking the project in the Solution Explorer and selecting the **Properties** menu item to open the project's Property Pages. The left side of the dialog contains a tree section that will default to **Common Properties**. By selecting the **Build** node the display will look similar to the figure shown:

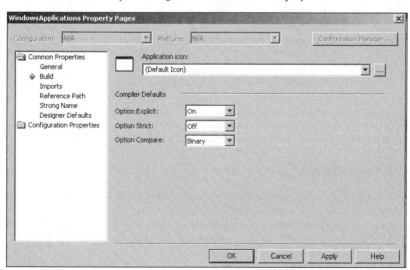

This screen allows you to toggle the settings associated with each option. The Option Explicit and Option Strict settings can be turned on or off, while the Option Compare allows for selection between Binary or Text. It should be noted that it is possible to change the settings of these options in the source files of your project. While this ability allows you to adapt if for some reason you need to include a class or module that isn't up to the same standards as the rest of your project, in general this should be avoided. In brief, here is what each option does:

❑ Option Strict – When turned on this option requires that the compiler be able to determine the type of each variable. Additionally if an assignment between two variables requires a type conversion, for example from Integer to Boolean, the conversion between the two types must be expressed explicitly.

❑ Option Explicit – When turned on this option ensures that any variable name is declared. Of course, if you are using Option Strict, then this setting does not matter since the compiler would not recognize the type of an undeclared variable. There is to my knowledge no good reason to ever turn this option off.

❑ Option Compare – This option determines whether strings should be compared as binary strings or if the array of characters should be compared as text.

It is probably not a big surprise that the setting for comparing text can impact performance. Doing a text comparison implies that the binary values which are stored to represent a string must be converted prior to comparing them. The advantage of a text-based comparison, however, is that the character "A" is equal to "a" because the comparison is case-insensitive. This allows for comparisons that don't require an explicit case conversion of the compared strings. In most cases, however, since this conversion still occurs it is better to use binary comparison and explicitly convert case as required.

Most experienced developers will say without fail that using Option Strict and being forced to recognize when type conversions are occurring is a good thing. Certainly, when you are developing software that will be deployed in a production environment anything that can be done which will help prevent runtime errors is a good thing. However, Option Strict can slow the development of a program because you are forced to explicitly define each conversion that needs to occur. If you are developing a prototype or demo component that has a limited life you might find this option limiting.

If that were the end of the argument, then many developers would simply turn the option off, as it currently defaults, and forget about it. However, Option Strict has a runtime benefit. When type conversions are explicitly identified, the system does them faster. Implicit conversions require the runtime system to first identify the types involved in a conversion and then obtain the correct handler.

Another advantage of Option Strict is that you will see where every implicit conversion might have occurred. Perhaps you did not realize that some of the assignment operations you were doing involved type conversion. Setting your project for explicit conversions means that you may change certain variable types in order to avoid conversions and thus reduce the number of conversions in your project. This means you get not only conversions that run faster but also hopefully a smaller number of conversions. The recommendation is that you should always keep Option Strict enabled and use explicit conversions.

Explicit Conversions

Having told you to always do explicit conversions, what tools are available to support these conversions? VB.NET has a plethora of ways to convert values. Some of them are being brought forward and updated based on familiar ways from VB6. Others such as the ToString method can be an inherent part of every class in .NET. Of course as mentioned earlier, just because the ToString method is a part of every class, thanks to inheritance, doesn't mean it will be implemented for every class.

The next set of conversion methods to look at, is based on the conversions supported by VB6. As the preceding wording indicates, this list isn't an exact match of the list from VB6, but most of these should be familiar to VB6 developers. The following are all twelve of these functions that, coincide with the primitive data types described at the start of this chapter:

CBool()	CByte()	CChar()	CDate()
CDbl()	CDec()	CInt()	CLng()
CObj()	CShort()	CSng()	CStr()

Each of these functions has been designed to accept the input of the other primitive data types (as appropriate) to convert that item to the type indicated by the function name. Thus, the CStr class is used to convert Integers and Dates and other primitive types to Strings. The disadvantage of these functions is that they have been designed to support any object. This means that if a primitive type is used, the function automatically boxes the parameter prior to getting the new value. As noted later in this chapter, boxing can result in a performance loss. Finally, although these are available as functions within the VB language, as with everything in .NET these functions are actually implemented in a class. Because the class uses a series of type-specific overloaded functions for the implementation of conversion, the conversions run faster when the members of the Convert class are called explicitly.

```
Dim intMyShort = 200
Convert.ToInt32(intMyShort)
Convert.ToDateTime("9/9/2001")
```

The classes that are part of the System.Convert namespace implement not only the conversion methods listed above but other common conversions as well. These additional methods include standard conversions for things like unsigned integers and pointers.

All of the preceding type conversions are great for value types and the limited number of classes to which they apply. However, these implementations are oriented around a limited set of known types. It is not possible to convert a custom class to an Integer using these classes. More importantly, there should be no reason to have such a conversion. Instead, a class will provide a method that returns the appropriate type and no type conversion will be required. However, as was discussed in talking about the Object class earlier in this chapter, when Option Strict has been enabled you need to cast an object to an appropriate type in order to be able to access the properties and members of that class.

The CType Function

The CType function accepts two parameters. The first parameter is the object which is having its type cast. The second parameter is the name of the object to which it is being cast. There are some limits on the second parameter. The first limitation is that it can't be a variable containing the name of the casting target. Casting occurs at compile time, any form of dynamic name selection would need to occur at runtime. If you really need runtime casting then you need to turn off Option Strict and pay the performance and maintenance price of having object types evaluated by the runtime environment.

However, for most development projects it is possible to effectively cast objects as part of the development process. This is because the VB.NET class structure is based on object hierarchies. Let's review the example shown earlier in this chapter where we cast an object to allow access to the Text property of our Form object. However, this time instead of casting this as a Form object we are going to cast it as a different object:

```
Dim objVar as Object

objVar = Me

CType( objVar, Control).Text = "New Dialog Title Text"
```

This time the code snippet casts the base object as a `Control` instead of as a `Form`. However, not only does the code compile but it also works without error. The reason is that as with all objects a `Form` inherits its base definition from the `Object` class. However, it does not inherit from `Form` directly; instead the `Form` class inherits from the `ContainerControl` class, which inherits from the `ScrollableControl` class that, in turn, inherits from the `Control` class. Since the `Text` property is available as part of this class we can cast the base object as this class and at runtime the `Text` property of the form will be updated with the correct text.

This is an important feature because it means that even though we have enabled `Option Strict` and obtained the performance benefit of not needing to determine variable type and capabilities at runtime, several dozen different classes could actually use this code. Each class would function as expected, and would perform better than if we had turned off `Option Strict`.

Most developers have little or no trouble understanding this concept for classes provided as part of the development environment. For some reason, however, they don't keep this concept in mind when developing custom classes. Some developers will explain how they need runtime evaluation of an object in a method call because both the `Employee` and `Employer` class would use this method. While both the `Employee` and `Employer` class have a `Name` property, they are different objects with different properties and methods. The developers will then go on to explain how, since these were defined as different objects, it wasn't possible to put the name of either of these classes as the appropriate type for the object in the current function.

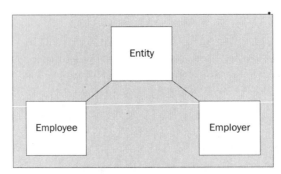

The answer of course is to have both of these custom classes inherit from a common base class that defines the `Name` property, as shown above. Using a base class that just holds the items in common between objects has several advantages. It reduces maintenance, since in many cases, shared properties and methods are the same, and helps show common processes across an organization. The key, however, is that by enforcing `Option Strict` you can actually force the developers on a project to think about inheritance and how it can help solve your business problem.

Parameter Passing

When an object's methods or an assembly's procedures and functions are called, we often want to provide input for the data to be operated on by the code. VB.NET has changed the way that methods, procedures, and functions are called and how those parameters are passed. The first change actually makes writing such calls more consistent. Under VB6 the parameter list for a procedure call didn't require parentheses. On the other hand, a call to a `function` did require parentheses around the parameter list.

> In VB.NET, the parentheses are always required and the **Call** keyword is obsolete.

Another change in VB.NET is the way parameters with default values are handled. As with VB6 it is possible to define a method, procedure, or function that provides default values for the last parameter(s). This way it is possible to call a function such as `PadRight` passing either a single parameter defining the length of the string and using a default of space for the padding character, or with two parameters, the first still defining the length of the string, but the second now replacing the default of space with a dash.

```
Public Function PadRight(ByVal intSize as Integer, _
      Optional ByVal chrPad as Char = " "c)
End Function
```

To use default parameters it is necessary to make them the last parameters in the function declaration, and VB.NET requires that every `Optional` parameter have a default value. It is not acceptable to just declare a parameter and assign it the `Optional` keyword. In VB.NET the `Optional` keyword must be accompanied by a value that will be assigned if the parameter is not passed in.

Finally the most important change associated with to parameters in VB.NET relates to how the system handles parameters. In VB6 the default was that parameters were passed **by reference**. Passing a parameter by reference means that if changes are made to the value of a variable passed to a method, function, or procedure call, these changes are to the actual variable and therefore available to the calling routine.

Passing a parameter by reference sometimes results in unexpected changes being made to a parameter's value. It is partly due to this that parameters default to passing **by value** in VB.NET. The advantage of passing by value is that regardless of what a function might do to a variable while it is running, when the function completes, the calling code still has the original value. Making this the default results in safer code, however, in theory with a performance cost.

We say "in theory" because VB.NET does not use the common implementation of passing parameters by reference. Passing by value means that if you have a string consisting of ten thousand lines of text, and pass it `By Value`, the entire set of data is copied to another location in memory. This has the potential to significantly impact performance. In most languages, the solution to this is to accept the risk that the routine you are calling might modify this data and pass it by reference.

The common implementation for passing by reference has less to do with the fact that the function or procedure being called might modify the data, than it does to what is passed to the function. As discussed earlier in this chapter, objects are reference types. As such, they maintain a reference to where the actual data is stored on the stack. Normally what occurs when an object is passed by reference is that this memory pointer from the stack is passed to the function or procedure. As a result of only passing a pointer to the referenced data, the function or procedure has access to the original data. The advantage, however, is that instead of needing to copy the ten thousand lines of text in our example only a handful of bytes used to reference the location of this text need to be copied.

However, VB.NET does not follow this model. When an object's property is passed by reference to a function or procedure the data is copied. Not only is the data copied but, since by definition variables passed by reference allow for the return of changes, the data is copied back. That's right, while most implementations avoid copying the data when a variable is passed by reference VB.NET actually passes it twice. A potentially very large performance hit on a function call that passes data by reference.

Thus under VB.NET the decision to pass something by reference not only involves the possibility of unexpected changes to the original value, but also requires significantly more system resources. The `ByRef` option in VB.NET will use more system resources as the parameter data is copied in for use by the function and then copied back to its original location. On the other hand, the new default of `ByVal` only copies the data once. When considering how to pass parameters this should be kept in mind and the ability to return data as part of a function (as opposed to using a `ByRef` parameter) should be considered.

Boxing

Normally when a conversion, implicit or explicit, occurs the original value is read from its current memory location and then the new value is assigned. For example to convert a `Short` to a `Long`, the system reads the two bytes of `Short` data, and writes them to the appropriate bytes for the `Long` variable. However, under VB.NET if a value type needs to be managed as an object then the system will perform an intermediate step. This intermediate step involves taking the value that is on the stack and copying it to the heap, a process referred to as **boxing**. As noted earlier, the `Object` class is implemented as a reference type. Therefore, the system needs to convert value types into reference types for them to be objects. This doesn't cause any problems or require any special programming, however, it has a performance impact.

> Note that boxing is not a value type; in fact boxing isn't something you declare.

In a situation where you are copying the data for a single value type this is not a significant cost. However, if you are processing an array of literally thousands of values the time spent moving between a value type and a temporary reference type can add up.

To date boxing has been addressed as a C# issue, however, the reality is that it is a .NET issue and impacts VB.NET as much as any other language used within the .Net Framework. There are ways to limit the amount of boxing that occurs. One method that has been shown to work well is to create a class based on the value type you need to work with. On first thought this seems counter intuitive because it costs more to create a class. The key, however, is how often you reuse the data that is contained in the class. By repeatedly using this object to interact with other objects, you will save on the creation of a temporary boxed object.

There are two important areas to examine with examples to better understand boxing. The first involves the use of arrays. When an array is created, the portion of the class which tracks the element of the array is created as a reference object, but each of the elements of the array is created directly. Thus an array of integers consists of the array object and a set of integer value types. When you update one of these values with another integer value there is no boxing involved:

```
Dim arrInt(20) as Integer
Dim intMyValue as Integer = 1

arrInt(0) = 0
arrInt(1) = intMyValue
```

Neither of the above assignments of an integer value into the integer array that was defined previously requires boxing. In each case, the array object identifies which value on the stack needs to be referenced and the value is assigned to that value type. The point here is that just because we have referenced an object doesn't mean we are going to box a value. The boxing only occurs when the values being assigned are being transitioned from a value to reference type:

```
Dim objStrBldr as New System.Text.StringBuilder()
Dim objSortedList as New System.Collections.SortedList()
Dim intCount as Integer

For intCount = 1 to 100
  objStrBldr.Append(intCount)
  objSortedList.Add(intCount, intCount)
Next
```

This code snippet illustrates two separate calls to object interfaces. One of these calls requires boxing of the value intCount, while the other does not. As you can tell there is nothing in the code to indicate which call is which. The answer is that the StringBuilder's Append method has been overridden to include a version that accepts an Integer, while the Add method of the SortedList collection expects two objects. While the Integer values can be recognized by the system as objects, doing so requires the runtime library to box up these values so that they can be added to the sorted list.

The key to boxing isn't that you are working with objects as part of an action, but that you are passing a value to a parameter that expects an object, or are taking an object and converting it to a value type. However, one time that boxing does not occur is when you call a method on a value type. There is no conversion to an object, so if you need to assign the intCount to a string using the intCount.ToString method, you will not be boxing the integer value as part of the assignment of the string. On the other hand, you are explicitly creating a new object so the cost is similar. The only difference would be in our example where the Add method boxes the intCount value twice; converting this value to an object before making that call would save on the creation of one of these boxes.

Retired Keywords and Functions

During the course of this chapter we have covered several changes from VB6 that are part of VB.NET. They include the removal of the Currency type, String function, Rset, and Lset functions. Other functions such as Left, Right, and Mid have been discussed as becoming obsolete although they may still be supported. Functions such as IsEmpty and IsNull have been replaced with new versions. We have also mentioned that the ability to use the Option Based setting for declaring the start of an array has been removed.

VB.NET has removed an array of keywords many of which most VB6 programmers will never miss. For example the DefType statement has been removed. This statement was a throwback to Fortran allowing a developer to indicate for example that all variables starting with the letters I, J, K, L, M, N would be integers. Most programmers have probably never used this function and it really isn't the type of function that has a logical replacement in VB.NET.

Another pair of keywords that is no longer available is the GoTo and GoSub functions. The GoTo command essentially allowed a function that was executing to transfer the executing thread to a different function without maintaining itself in the call stack. It is another function that has been known as obsolete for several years, and VB.NET is finally cleaning it up.

One of the real advantages of VB.NET is the way that it is removing some of the more esoteric and obsolete functions that have survived in Visual Basic. The list below contains the majority of such functions. As with others that have already been discussed, some have been replaced, for example the math functions are now part of the System.Math library, while others such as IsObject really don't have much more meaning than LBound in the context of .NET, where everything is an object and the lower bound of all arrays is 0.

Elements of VB6 that have been removed as part of VB.NET
As Any
Atn function
Calendar property
Circle statement
Currency
Date function and statement
Date$ function
Debug.Assert method
Debug.Print method
DefType
DoEvents function
Empty
Eqv operator
GoSub statement
Imp operator
Initialize event
Instancing property
IsEmpty function
IsMissing function
IsNull function
IsObject function
Let statement
Line statement
LSet
MsgBox function
Now function
Null keyword

Elements of VB6 that have been removed as part of VB.NET
`On ... GoSub`
`On ... GoTo`
`Option Base`
Option Private Module
`Property Get`, `Property Let`, and `Property Set`
`PSet` method
`Rnd` function
`Round` function
`RSet`
`Scale` method
`Set` statement
`Sgn` function
`Sqr` function
`String` function
`Terminate` event
`Time` function and statement
`Time$` function
`Timer` function
`Type` statement
`Variant` data type
`VarType` function
`Wend` keyword

One last retired concept from Visual Basic 6.0 is the User Defined Type (UDT). Retired is probably too strong a word, but the UDT has been removed from the Visual Basic vocabulary. Instead, the ability to create a user defined set of variables as a type has been replaced with the ability to create custom structures and custom classes in VB.NET. The UDT by that name is now gone and in its place are two new more powerful constructs in structures and classes.

The important thing to remember about VB.NET is that it isn't Visual Basic 7. It is version 1 of an entirely new language based on the .NET Framework. This new language keeps many of the syntax and coding standards of Visual Basic, but it really is a whole new language.

Summary

This chapter has really looked at many of the basic building blocks of VB.NET. The items which are part of this chapter are used throughout project development and understanding something about how they work will help you to write more stable and better performing software. There are five specific points to take note of, whether you are an experienced VB6 programmer or a programmer learning VB.NET without prior VB experience:

- ❏ Beware of array sizes, all arrays start at 0 and are defined not by size but by the highest index
- ❏ Remember to use the `StringBuilder` class for string manipulation
- ❏ Use `Option Strict`, it's not just about style it's about performance
- ❏ Beware of parameters that are passed `ByValue` so changes are not returned
- ❏ Take advantage of the new collection classes

While this chapter covered many other items such as how the new `Decimal` type works and how boxing works, these five items are really the most important. Whether you are creating a new library of functions or a new user interface, these five items will consistently turn up in some form. While .NET provides a tremendous amount of power, this chapter has hopefully provided information on places where that power comes at a significant performance cost.

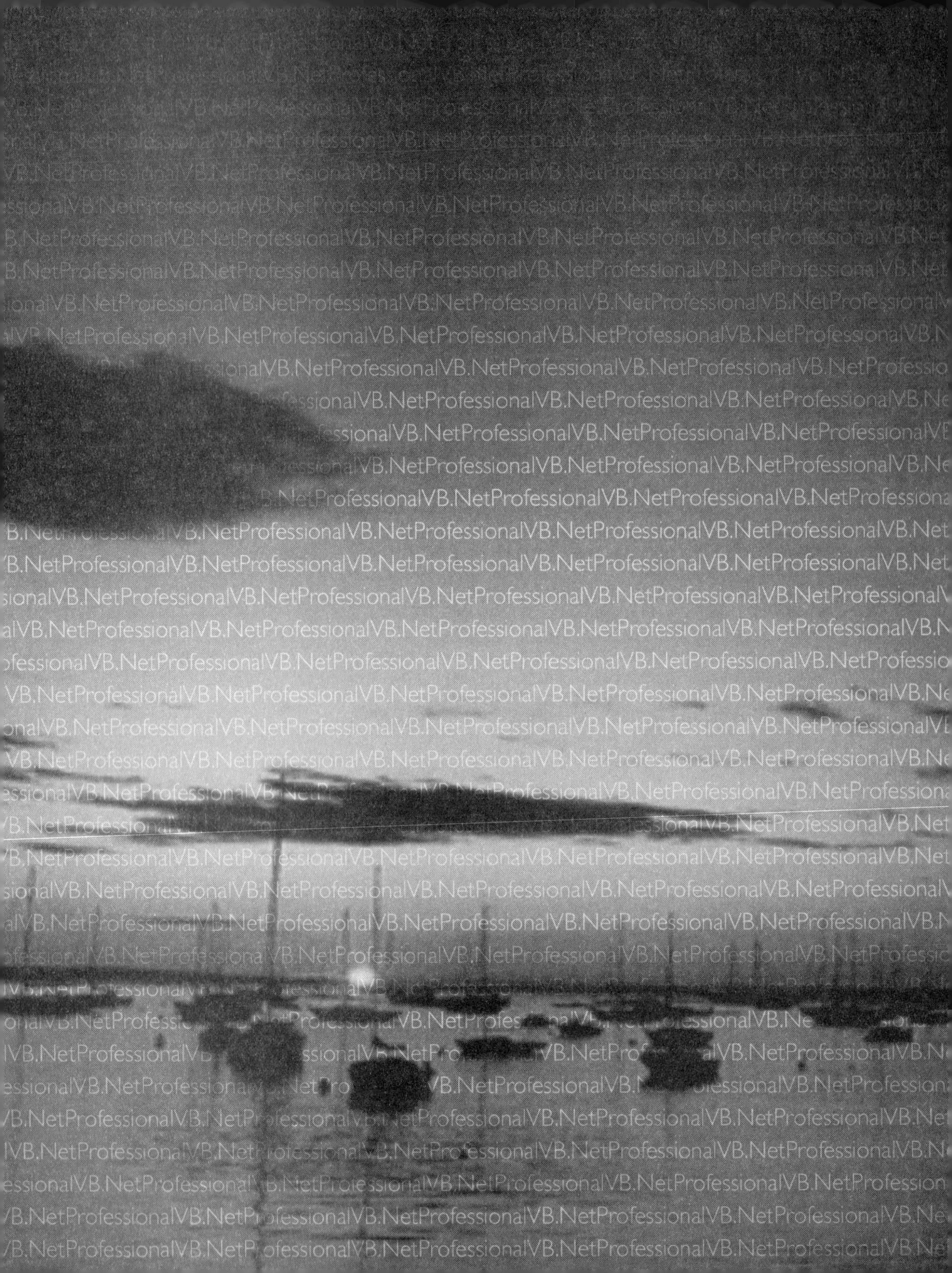
VB.NetProfessional

7

Namespaces

Namespaces encapsulate the very building blocks of .NET. As noted in Chapter 6, even basic variable types such as strings and arrays are associated with a namespace. However, if namespaces were only used to manage the basic building blocks of the language, they probably wouldn't merit coverage in their own chapter. Namespaces provide the infrastructure that organizes and simplifies object references across the entire .NET Framework. Namespaces apply not only within Visual Basic but also across the entire Common Language Runtime (CLR) environment.

One thing that namespaces are not related to is inheritance. Namespaces are related to the identification of classes, not the parent class or class hierarchy. Although namespaces are organized as a hierarchical structure, this hierarchy is not based on inheritance, but rather on logical groupings of functionally related objects. For example, the `System.IO` namespace contains classes, structures, interfaces, etc. related to working with input and output streams and file system tools. While all of the objects in this namespace do eventually inherit from the `Object` base class, they do not necessarily inherit from the same or even related classes within the object model. The `System.IO` namespace represents a logical grouping of classes based on the function of working with file streams.

For those familiar with COM, the concept of namespaces is the logical extension of programmatic identifier (ProgID) values. For example, the `Scripting.FileSystemObject` functionality tends to be encompassed in the `System.IO` namespace, though this is not a one-to-one mapping. However, namespaces aren't just about a change in name, but the logical extension of the COM naming structure to expand its ease of use and extensibility.

The use of namespaces will be a shift in paradigm, but one that you should have little problem adapting to by the end of this chapter. The primary topic areas in this chapter are:

- ❑ An introduction to the concept of namespaces
- ❑ A review of some of the default project global namespaces
- ❑ Using namespaces and the `Imports` statement
- ❑ How the compiler searches for class references
- ❑ Aliasing a namespace
- ❑ Creating your own namespace

What is a Namespace

A namespace is a combination of a naming convention and an assembly, which organizes collections of objects and prevents ambiguity in object references. A namespace may be and often is implemented across several physical assemblies but, from the reference side, it is the namespace that ties these assemblies together. A namespace consists of not only objects but child namespaces too, for example, the `IO` child namespace of the `System` namespace.

Namespaces provide identification beyond the component name. With a namespace, it is possible to put a more meaningful title – `System`, for example – followed by a grouping – `Text`, for example – to group together a collection of classes that contain similar functions. For example, the `System.Text` namespace contains a powerful class called `StringBuilder`. To reference this class, we can use the fully qualified namespace reference of `System.Text.StringBuilder`.

As noted in the introduction of this chapter, the structure of a namespace is not a reflection of the physical inheritance of classes that make up a namespace. For example, the `System.Text` namespace contains another child namespace called `RegularExpressions`. This namespace contains several classes, but these classes do not inherit or otherwise reference the classes that make up the `System.Text` namespace. Let's use a couple of diagrams to better illustrate this separation.

The following diagram shows how the `System` namespace contains the `Text` child namespace, which also has a child namespace called `RegularExpressions`.

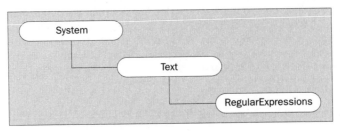

Both of these child namespaces – `Text` and `RegularExpressions` – contain a number of objects, shown here in the inheritance model for these classes:

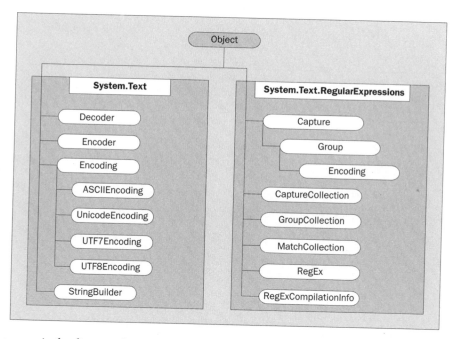

As you can see in the diagram above, while some of the classes in each namespace do inherit from each other, and while all of the classes eventually inherit from the generic Object, the classes in System.Text.RegularExpressions do not inherit from the classes in System.Text.

You might be wondering at this point what all the fuss is about. To emphasize the usefulness of namespaces, we can draw another good example from this diagram. The complete reference to the Encoder class is System.Drawing.Imaging.Encoder. At least, that's one reference, and it's not the same as the System.Text.Encoder class shown in the preceding diagram. Being able to clearly identify classes with the same name, but involving very different functions, is yet another advantage of .NET's use of namespaces.

Experienced COM developers may note that, unlike a ProgID that is a one level relationship between the project assembly and class, a single namespace can use child namespaces to extend the meaningful description of a class. The System namespace, imported by default as part of every project, contains not only the default Object class, but also many other classes that are used as the basis for every .NET language. Let's list a subset of some of the top-level namespaces and their child namespaces. This list does not include any classes or other components associated with these namespaces.

Parent	Child	Sub-Child	Sub-Sub-Child	Sub-Sub-Sub-Child
Microsoft	Csharp			
System	VisualBasic	Compatibility	VB6	
		CompilerServices		
		Helpers		
	Win32			

Table continued on following page

Parent	Child	Sub-Child	Sub-Sub-Child	Sub-Sub-Sub-Child
Microsoft System (continued)	CodeDom	Compiler		
	Collections	Specialized Collections		
	Component Model	Design	Serialization	
	Configuration	Assemblies		
	Data	Common		
		OleDb		
	Diagnostics	SQLClient		
		SQLTypes		
		SymbolStore		
	Drawing	Design		
		Drawing2D		
	IO	Imaging		
		Internal		
		Printing		
		Text		
		IsolatedStorage		
	Net	Configuration		
		Sockets		
	Reflection	Cache		
		Emit		
	Resources			
	Runtime	CompilerServices	CSharp	
		InteropServices	Expando	
	Security	Remoting	Activation	
		Remoting	Channels	
		Serialization	Contexts	
			Lifetime	
			Messaging	

Parent	Child	Sub-Child	Sub-Sub-Child	Sub-Sub-Sub-Child
Microsoft	Security	Security	Meta Data	
System	(continued)	(continued)		
(continued)				
			Proxies	
			Services	
			Formatters	Binary
			X509 Certificates	
		Cryptography		
		Permissions		
	Text	Policy		
		Principal		
		Util		
		RegularExpressions		
	Threading			
	Timers		Component Model	Com2 Interop
	Windows	Forms	Design	
			PropertyGrid Internal	
	XML	Schema		
		Serialization		
		XPath		
		XSL		

The preceding list contains namespaces only. Most of these namespaces contain several classes and, as you can tell, this means there are literally thousands of classes available. However, what if a class you need isn't available in your project? The problem may be with the references in your project. For example, in the above list, under Microsoft.VisualBasic, you see the namespace Compatibility. By default, this isn't part of your assembly and using it requires adding a **reference** to your project assembly. The concept of referencing a namespace is very similar to the ability to reference a COM object in VB6.

While the concept and implementation of namespaces enhance the old structure, the COM components previously installed on your system are still available.

In fact, with all this talk about referencing, it's probably a good idea to look at an example of adding an additional namespace to a project. Before we do that, we need to know a little bit about how a namespace is implemented.

Namespaces are implemented in .NET assemblies. The System namespace is implemented in an assembly provided with Visual Studio called System.dll. By referencing this assembly, the project gains the ability to reference all of the child namespaces of System that happen to be implemented in this assembly. Using the preceding table, the project can import and use the System.Text namespace because its implementation is in the System.dll assembly. However, although it is listed above, the project cannot import or use the System.Data namespace unless it references the assembly that implements this child of the System namespace, System.Data.dll.

Let's create a sample project so that we can examine the role that namespaces play within it. Using VS.NET, create a new VB.NET Windows Application project called **Namespace_Sampler**. We are going to create a simple form that will retrieve some of the .NET related settings from the registry.

The Microsoft.VisualBasic.Compatability.VB6 library isn't part of VB projects by default. To gain access to the classes in this namespace, we need to add it to our project. Open the **Add Reference** dialog by right-clicking on the **References** node in the **Solution Explorer**. This dialog has three tabs, each containing elements that can be referenced from your project. The first tab contains .NET assemblies that have been provided by Microsoft. The second tab contains all of those familiar COM components from Visual Basic 6. Finally, the third tab contains the custom .NET assemblies created by you. It is possible to browse your system for other component files if the one that you are looking for isn't listed.

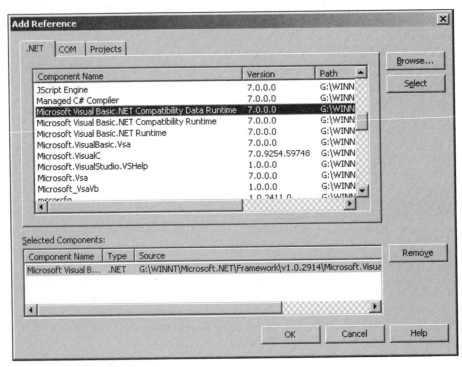

As you can see in the preceding screenshot, the available .NET namespaces are listed by a component name. This is not the same as the namespace name. Selecting the Microsoft Visual Basic.NET Compatibility Data Runtime component will add the desired `Microsoft.VisualBasic.Compatibility.VB6` namespace. Although the lower window doesn't have enough space to fully display the path, the file name for this namespace is `Microsoft.VisualBasic.Compatibility.dll`. Highlighted in the screenshot is a new compatibility library for data access, `Microsoft.VisualBasic.Compatibility.Data.dll`, which contains the second half of the compatibility library.

This implementation, while a bit surprising at first, is very powerful. Firstly, it shows the extensibility of namespaces – the single `Microsoft.VisualBasic.Compatibilty.VB6` namespace is implemented in two separate assemblies. Secondly, it allows us to include only the classes that we need – in this case, those that are related to the VB6 environment or to database tools, or both types.

Namespace_Sampler Namespaces and References

Highlighting their importance to every project, references (including namespaces) are no longer hidden from view, available only after opening a dialog box. As shown in the Namespace_Sampler Solution Explorer window, every new project comes with a set of referenced namespaces:

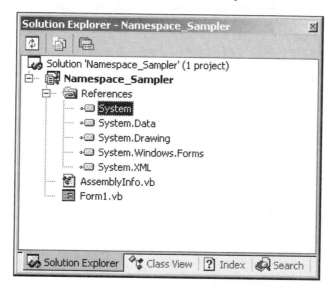

The list of default references changes based on the type of project. For example, if the Namespace_Sampler project was a VB.NET Web Application, the list of references would change appropriately – the reference to the `System.Windows.Forms` namespace assembly would be replaced by references to the `System.Web` and `System.Web.Services` namespace assemblies. A better way of referring to the references might be as references to components. Just as, behind each ProgID, there was a DLL or EXE that implemented the actual class, each namespace has, at its core, a DLL or EXE that implements it. Note that this is not necessarily a one-to-one relationship. What references provide in relation to namespaces is the ability to import and use all of the namespaces, with their component structures, classes, and interfaces in a referenced assembly. Just as with the `Compatibility` namespace discussed earlier, importing the `System` namespace does not mean that you necessarily have access to every class potentially defined under it. While you do gain the ability to import any of the related namespaces that are part of the referenced assembly, if a portion of the namespace is defined in an assembly not imported, then you won't see a reference to those components in Visual Studio.

> Note that there are four categories of reference. In addition to referencing a namespace's assembly, you can continue to reference legacy COM components. Additionally, it is possible to reference the new Web Services described in Chapter 22. Finally, other projects in the current workspace can be referenced as part of a project.

For example, both System.Text and System.Data are children of the System namespace. However, while the System.Text classes are defined as part of the default System.dll that implements the System namespace, the System.Data classes are not. As a result, in order to be able to import and use the System.Data classes, a separate reference is added to the System.Data.dll that implements the System.Data classes. Unfortunately, there is currently no documentation listing where a namespace is actually implemented. So, while the implementation of namespaces allows for dynamic additions, the ability to find these additions is currently limited.

Later in this chapter, when we look at implementing a custom namespace, we'll see how the ability to separate the implementation of different parts of the same namespace across separate component files is a very powerful concept for extending a custom namespace.

In addition to making the namespaces available, references play a second important role in your project. One of the advantages of .NET is using services and components built on the CLR that allow you to avoid DLL conflicts. The various problems that can occur related to DLL versioning, commonly referred to as DLL "hell", involve two types of conflict. The first situation occurs when you have a component that requires a minimum DLL version and an older version of the same DLL causes your product to break. The alternative situation is when you require an older version of a DLL and a new version is incompatible. In either case, the result is that a shared file, outside of your control, creates a system-wide dependency that impacts upon your software. As part of .NET, it is possible – but not required – to indicate that a DLL should be shipped as part of your project to avoid an external dependency.

In order to indicate that a referenced component should be included locally, you can select it in the Solution Explorer and then examine the properties associated with that reference. One editable property is called Copy Local. For those assemblies that are part of a Visual Studio installation, this value defaults to False. However, for custom references, this property will default to True to indicate that the referenced DLL should be included as part of the assembly. Changing this property to True changes the path associated with the assembly. Instead of using the path to the referenced file's location on the system, the project creates a subdirectory based on the reference name and places the files required for the implementation of the reference in this subdirectory.

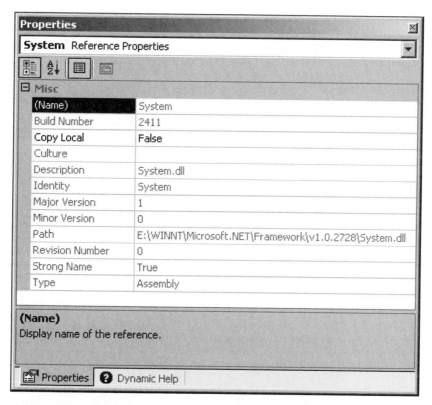

The benefit of this is that, in theory, even if another version of the DLL is later placed on the system, your project's assembly will continue to function. This protection from a conflicting version comes at a price, however. Future updates to the namespace assembly to fix flaws will be in the system version but not in the private version that is part of your project's assembly. To resolve this, Microsoft's solution is to place new versions in directories based on their version information. If you examine the path information for all of the Visual Studio references, you will see that it includes a version number. As new versions of these DLLs are released, they will be installed in a separate directory. This method allows for both an escape from DLL hell, by keeping new versions from stomping on old versions, but also allows for old versions to be easily located for maintenance updates. For this reason, in many cases, it is better to leave alone the default behavior of Visual Studio to only copy custom components locally, until your organization implements a directory structure with version information similar to that of Microsoft.

Common Namespaces

The generated list of references shown in the Solution Explorer for the newly created Namespace_Sampler project includes most but not all of the namespaces that are part of your Windows Application project. For example, one important namespace not displayed as a reference is `Microsoft.VisualBasic` and the accompanying `Microsoft.VisualBasic.dll`. Every VB project includes the namespace `Microsoft.VisualBasic`. This namespace is part of the Visual Studio project templates for Visual Basic and is, in short, what makes Visual Basic.NET different from C# or any other .NET language. The implicit inclusion of this namespace is the reason that you can call `IsDBNull` and other methods of Visual Basic directly. The only difference in the default namespaces that are included with VB.NET and C# Windows Application projects is that the former use `Microsoft.VisualBasic` and the latter use `Microsoft.Csharp`.

In order to see all of the namespaces that are imported automatically, such as the
`Microsoft.VisualBasic` namespace, right-click on the project name in the Solution Explorer and select
Properties from the context menu. This will open the project properties dialog. Select the Imports node that
is under the Common Properties node and you will see `Microsoft.VisualBasic` at the top of the list:

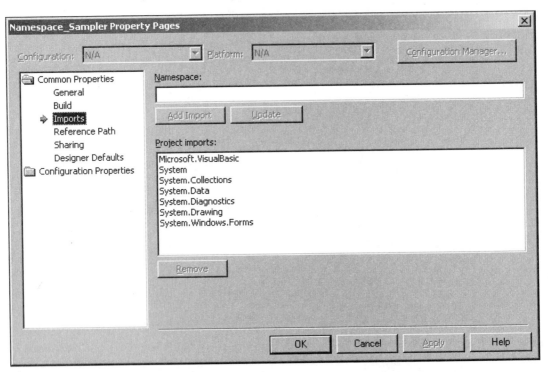

When looking at the project's global list of imports, you can see that, in addition to the
`Microsoft.VisualBasic` namespace, the `System.Collections` and `System.Diagnostics`
namespaces are also imported into the project. Unlike the other namespaces in the list, these namespaces are
not listed as references. That is because the implementation of the `System.Collections` and
`System.Diagnostics` namespaces is part of the referenced `System.dll`. Similarly to
`Microsoft.VisuaBasic`, importing these namespaces allows references to the associated classes, such that
a fully qualified path is not required. Since these namespaces contain commonly used classes, it is worthwhile
to always include them at the project level.

This leads into the question, "Just what makes up each of these namespaces?" As noted earlier, the
`Microsoft.VisualBasic` namespace provides the basic functions and methods that interface a Visual
Basic assembly with the .NET runtime. The `System` namespace provides the basic classes that make up
every .NET language. It contains classes such as `Array`, `Integer`, `Long`, and `String`. As noted in
Chapter 6, these basic types are shared across all .NET language implementations – not just the design of
the interfaces but also the actual implementation of the types that make up the `System` namespace the
same. The ability to have true reuse of the same implementation across different .NET language
implementations is one key advantage of .NET. While more detailed information is available on all of the
namespaces, the following listing brings together brief descriptions of some of the namespaces commonly
used in Visual Basic projects.

❑ System.Collections – Contains the classes that support various feature rich object collections. Included automatically, it has classes for arrays, lists, dictionaries, queues, hash tables, etc.

❑ System.Data – Included in all Visual Basic projects; contains the classes to support the core features of ADO.NET.

❑ System.Diagnostics – Included in all Visual Basic projects, this namespace includes the debugging classes. The Trace and Debug classes provide the primary capabilities but the namespace contains dozens of classes to support debugging.

❑ System.Drawing – Simple drawing classes to support Windows Application projects.

❑ System.Windows.Forms – The classes to create Windows Forms in Windows Application projects. This namespace contains the form elements.

❑ System.Web.UI.HTMLControls – Included in Web Application projects, this namespace contains classes to automatically generate standard HTML controls that support all browsers.

❑ System.Web.UI.WebControls – Included in Web Application projects to create server-based Web controls. These controls, while not based on standard HTML, support advanced features such as validation.

❑ System.EnterpriseServices – Not included automatically, the System.EnterpriseServices implementation must be referenced to make it available. This namespace contains the classes that interface .NET assemblies with COM+.

❑ Microsoft.VisualBasic.Compatibility.VB6 – Not included automatically. The Microsoft.VisualBasic.Compatibility.dll and Microsoft.VisualBasic.Compatibility.Data.dll implementations must be referenced to make them available.

❑ Microsoft.Win32 –Provides classes to manage system events and the Windows registry. While not included automatically, this namespace is implemented as part of the CLR and so is available to all projects.

Of course, to really make use of the classes and other objects in the above listing, you really need more detailed information. In addition to resources such as Visual Studio's help files, the best source of information is the **Object Browser**. It is available by selecting **View | Other Windows | Object Browser**.

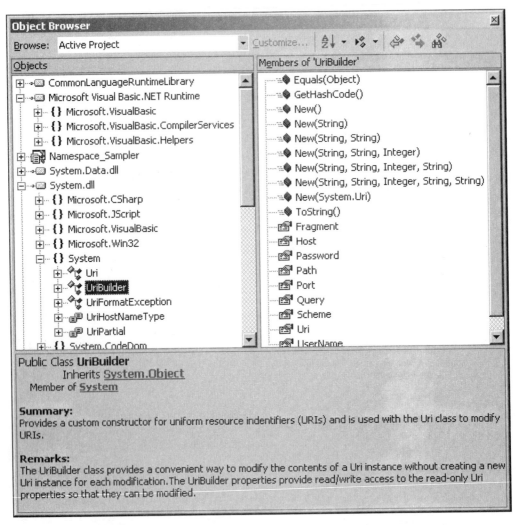

The **Object Browser** displays each of the referenced assemblies and allows you to drill down into the various namespaces. The previous screenshot illustrates how the `System.dll` implements a number of namespaces, including some that are part of the `System` namespace. By drilling down into a namespace, it is possible to see some of the classes available. By further selecting a class, the browser shows not only the methods and properties associated with the selected class but also a brief outline of what that class does.

Using the **Object Browser** is an excellent way to gain insight, not only into which classes and interfaces are available via the different assemblies included in your project, but also into how they work. As you can guess, the ability to actually see not only which classes are available but what and how to use them is important in being able to work efficiently. To effectively work in the .NET CLR environment requires finding the right class for the task.

Importing and Aliasing Namespaces

Not all namespaces should be imported at the global level. Although we have looked at namespaces that are included at this level, it is much better to import namespaces only in the module where they will be used. Importing a namespace at the module level does not change setting the reference, but does mean that you don't add it into the list of imports on the project's property page. Similar to variables used in a project, it is possible to define a namespace at the module level. The advantage of this is similar to the use of local variables in that it helps to prevent different namespaces from interfering with each other. As this section will show, it is possible for two different namespaces to contain classes or even child namespaces with the same name.

Importing Namespaces

The development environment and compiler need a way to prioritize the order in which namespaces should be checked when a class is referenced. It is always possible to unequivocally specify a class by stating its complete namespace path. Using `System.Text.StringBuilder` is an example of doing this. However, if every reference to every class needed its full namespace declaration, that would make VB.NET and every other .NET language difficult to program in. After all, who would want to type `System.Collections.ArrayList` each time they wanted an instance of the `ArrayList` class. If you review the global references, you'll see the `System.Collections` namespace. Thus, you can just type `ArrayList` whenever you need an instance of this class.

In theory, another way to reference the `StringBuilder` class is to use `Text.StringBuilder` but, with all namespaces imported globally, there is a problem with this. The problem is caused by what is known as **namespace crowding**. Because there is a second namespace, `System.Drawing`, which has a child called `Text`, the compiler doesn't have a clear location for the `Text` namespace and therefore cannot resolve the `StringBuilder` class. The solution to this problem is to make it so that only a single version of the `Text` child namespace is found locally. Then the compiler will use this namespace regardless of the global availability of the `System.Drawing.Text` namespace.

To explain, let's first return to the Namespace_Sampler project. Create a simple user interface consisting of a button, a text box, and a couple of labels. After placing the controls on the form, there are a few minor changes in the property windows for the various controls. Change the text of the form to "Namespace_Sampler". Change the name of the button to `btnStart` and the button's text to Read Settings. Rename the text box as `txtInstallRoot`, remove the default text, and change the enabled property to False. Finally, change the text of the labels to match the ".NET Installation Directory:" and ".NET SDK Installation Directory:" label text:

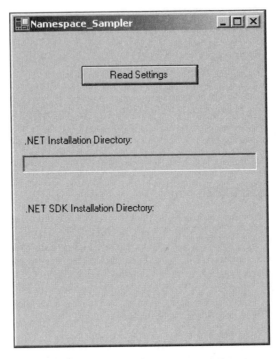

The final step in editing the form is to create a `Click` event handler for the button by double-clicking the button. This `btnStart_Click` event handler is where we will add some custom code. The code will open the registry subkey associated with the .NET Framework and copy the installation directory to the text property of the `txtInstallRoot` control. The function will then use the same registry key and copy the value for the .NET SDK installation path to a string builder object. The string builder object, used with some simple Graphic Device Interface objects, draws the path of the SDK directory on the form.

The `Imports` statements shown are located before the declaration of the `Form1` class in the code module for the **Namespace_Sampler** form. They specify to the compiler those namespaces that the code will use:

```
Imports Microsoft.Win32
Imports System
Imports SysDraw = System.Drawing

Public Class Form1
    Inherits System.Windows.Forms.Form

    Windows Form Designer generated code

    Private Sub btnStart_Click(ByVal sender As System.Object, ByVal e As
System.EventArgs) Handles btnStart.Click

    End Sub
End Class
```

Each `Imports` statement illustrates a different facet of importing namespaces. The first, `Imports Microsoft.Win32`, is a namespace that is not imported at the global level. Looking at the reference list, you may not see the Microsoft assembly referenced directly. However, opening the Object Browser reveals that this namespace is actually included as part of the `System.dll`. This namespace includes the registry access classes that the Namespace_Sampler project uses to retrieve .NET installation information. While this class provides access to capabilities that are part of the Windows API, keep in mind that, as part of the Common Runtime Library, the namespace has to provide classes that are managed code. How the underlying implementation actually interfaces, either to the Windows API or directly to resources such as the registry, is hidden.

You may recognize the second imported namespace, `Imports System`, as a repeat from the global import list. The reason it is called out specifically within this module is to resolve the namespace crowding issue mentioned earlier. Because the `System` namespace is referenced at the module level, it is possible to access the `StringBuilder` class using only the `Text.StringBuilder` reference. To demonstrate the namespace crowding problem, temporarily comment out this import statement from the module and check your Task List for errors.

As noted earlier, the `StringBuilder` references become ambiguous because both `System.Text` and `System.Drawing.Text` are valid namespaces at the global level. As a result, the compiler has no way to distinguish which `Text` child-namespace is being referenced. Without any clear indication, the compiler flags `Text.StringBuilder` declarations in the command handler. However, using the `Imports System` declaration in the module tells the compiler that, before checking namespaces imported at the global level, it should attempt to match incomplete references at the module level. Since the `System` namespace is declared at this level, while `System.Drawing` (for the moment) is not, there is no ambiguity as to which child-namespace `Text.StringBuilder` belongs to.

This demonstrates how the compiler looks at each possible declaration:

- ❑ First, see if the item is a complete reference such as `System.Text.StringBuilder`.

- ❑ If the declaration does not match a complete reference, then the compiler looks to see if the declaration is from a child-namespace of one of the module level imports.

- ❑ Finally, if a match has not been found, the compiler looks at the global level imports to see if the declaration can be associated with a namespace imported for the entire assembly.

While the preceding logical progression of moving from a full declaration through module to global level imports does resolve the majority of issues, it does not handle all possibilities. Specifically, if we imported `System.Drawing` at the module level, the **namespace collision** would return. This is where the third import statement in `form1.vb` becomes important. This import statement uses an **alias**.

Aliasing Namespaces

Aliasing has two benefits in .NET. The first is that aliasing allows a long namespace such as `System.EnterpriseServices` to be replaced with a shorthand name such as `COMPlus`. The second is that it adds a way to prevent ambiguity of child namespaces at the module level.

As noted earlier, the `System` and `System.Drawing` namespaces both contain a child-namespace of `Text`. Since we will be using a number of classes from the `System.Drawing` namespace, it follows that this namespace should be imported into the form's module. However, were this namespace imported along with the `System` namespace, the compiler would once again find references to the `Text` child-namespace to be ambiguous. However, by aliasing the `System.Drawing` namespace to `SysDraw`, the compiler knows that it should only check the `System.Drawing` namespace when a declaration begins with that alias. The result is that, although multiple namespaces with the same child-namespace are now available at the module level, the compiler knows that one (or more) of them should only be checked at this level when they are explicitly referenced.

Let's add some code to `btnStart_Click`:

```
Private Sub btnStart_Click(ByVal sender As System.Object, ByVal e As
System.EventArgs) Handles btnStart.Click

    Dim objRegKey As RegistryKey
    Dim txtBldr As Text.StringBuilder
    Dim bshBlue As SysDraw.Brush
    Dim fntTimesNR As SysDraw.Font
    Dim grpGraph As SysDraw.Graphics

    ObjRegKey = Registry.LocalMachine.OpenSubKey( _
            "Software\microsoft\.NETFramework", True)

    txtBldr = New Text.StringBuilder()

    bshBlue = New SysDraw.SolidBrush(System.Drawing.Color.Blue)
    fntTimesNR = New SysDraw.Font("Times New Roman", 10, FontStyle.Regular)
    grpGraph = Me.CreateGraphics

    txtInstallRoot.Text = Convert.ToString( _
            objRegKey.GetValue("InstallRoot"))

    txtBldr.Insert(0, objRegKey.GetValue("sdkInstallRoot"))
    grpGraph.DrawString(txtBldr.ToString, fntTimesNR, _
                    bshBlue, 8, 224)

End Sub
```

Now let's walk through this code.

```
Dim objRegKey As RegistryKey
...
ObjRegKey = Registry.LocalMachine.OpenSubKey( _
        "Software\microsoft\.NETFramework", True)
```

These lines declare and then instantiate the variables for the `btnStart_Click` procedure. It is possible to declare and instantiate variables on a single line but, for readability, the two steps have been separated. The first item created is the `RegistryKey` object. Unlike some objects created using a public new method, registry keys are assigned from the framework's `Registry` object. As such, instead of instantiating a new key, one of the base keys (`CurrentUser`, `LocalMachine`, `ClassesRoot`, `Users`, `PerformanceData`, `CurrentConfig`, or `DynamicData`) is assigned to an instance of a `RegistryKey`. This assignment has been combined with opening a subkey from that registry hive. Once a subkey has been opened, the methods associated with the `RegistryKey` object provide a simple interface to retrieve and update the values stored under that key.

```
Dim txtBldr As Text.StringBuilder
...
txtBldr = New Text.StringBuilder()
```

The next object created is of the `StringBuilder` class. This class is something of an overkill for what the **Namespace_Sampler** application needs. However, using it demonstrates an easily recognizable conflict within the namespace hierarchy. It is also an excellent class for when a program needs to conduct a great deal of string manipulation.

There have been several solutions proposed in the past to resolve the performance issue that has long plagued string manipulation. As noted in articles, such as the Microsoft Knowledge Base article Q170964, the act of concatenating strings and manipulating the characters that make up a typical system string can take a lot of time. In short, the problem is that, if you have allocated the memory for a 2KB string and then need to add 200 more characters, you are going to need to allocate another buffer, larger than the first, and then copy all of the data into it. This isn't a new problem and many programmers have been working around it in both Visual Basic and other languages.

With .NET, Microsoft has, at last, provided a native class that will allow you to optimize string-handling functions. Looking closer at the `StringBuilder` *class shows that it is optimized to improve the performance of manipulating a large string or the repeated modification of a small string.*

```
Dim bshBlue As SysDraw.Brush
Dim fntTimesNR As SysDraw.Font
Dim grpGraph As SysDraw.Graphics
...
bshBlue = New SysDraw.SolidBrush(System.Drawing.Color.Blue)
fntTimesNR = New SysDraw.Font("Times New Roman", 10, FontStyle.Regular)
grpGraph = Me.CreateGraphics
```

The preceding code creates GDI objects used by the Namespace_Sampler project. As noted, they are declared based on an aliased namespace. One item in particular to note is that the declaration of the `bshBlue` object is using an **abstract base class**. Abstract base classes define a set of common methods and properties that other classes will support when derived from the base class. In this case, the abstract `Brush` class defines a set of common capabilities that are implemented in classes such as `HatchBrush`, `TextureBrush`, or `SolidBrush`. These classes often have different new methods but expose the same basic brush capabilities.

After the `Brush` has been instantiated, the function creates an instance of a `Font` object that will format the text. A `Graphics` object will use the `Font` object along with the `Brush` object to output the string from the registry. Unlike the `Brush` and `Font` instances that are newly created, the `Graphics` object is obtained from the form. As in Visual Basic 6, the `Me` reference represents the current instance of an object. It is used because the graphics need to act within the context of a class that has a user interface. In this case, that class is the form where the `Graphics` object will display a string. The CLR has been set up to force the relationship between a GDI object and the instance on which the GDI object will act via the `CreateGraphics` method.

```
txtInstallRoot.Text = Convert.ToString( _
          objRegKey.GetValue("InstallRoot"))
```

Once all of the variables have been declared and the appropriate objects instantiated, the code does the actual work of displaying the .NET registry information. The first step is to retrieve the Installation Root of the .NET framework. The .NET Framework is the Common Runtime Library that contains the assemblies associated with system imports. However, you'll notice that the call to actually get the `InstallRoot` from the registry is encapsulated by an explicit conversion. Another way to make this explicit call for an efficient translation is to take advantage of the returned object's native `ToString` method. Instead of preceding the call, which is in many ways more difficult to read, the code might be considered more readable if written in the following manner:

```
txtInstallRoot.Text = objRegKey.GetValue("InstallRoot").ToString
```

As noted in Chapter 6, although it is possible to allow these conversions to be handled implicitly, it is better to make such conversions explicit. The GetValue function is defined to return an object, which can then be manipulated by the calling function to account for the different types of registry values. Even if the registry value is not a string, it needs to be converted to a string value since the intention is to assign it to the Text property of the text box.

```
txtBldr.Insert(0, objRegKey.GetValue("sdkInstallRoot"))
grpGraph.DrawString(txtBldr.ToString, fntTimesNR, _
                    bshBlue, 8, 224)
```

The last step, shown above, is to retrieve the second registry value associated with the installation directory of the .NET SDK. In this case, the call does not need to be wrapped with a call to explicitly cast the return value because the Insert function of the StringBuilder class has been overloaded to accept an Object as the second parameter. Overloading is explained in detail in Chapter 12 but, in short, a method is overloaded when a class contains several copies of the method, each having the same name but a different parameter list. The Insert function expects an index to indicate where the string is being inserted, because the StringBuilder is implemented as an array of characters. This would, for example, allow you to load the lines of a text file from disk into the StringBuilder object, edit the content, and then output the result back into the file. For additional efficiency, before starting the in-memory editing, you could determine the file size and make a call to the StringBuilder's Capacity method to allocate memory before assigning the various strings.

The GDI DrawString function is somewhat a duck out of water in this module. Ideally, GDI functions live in a class' Paint method, triggered by the Paint event. It may seem unusual that items that we generate on screen need to be placed in relation to a particular event, such as Paint. However, the difference between controls and custom graphics is that the control class implements its own handler for the Paint event. That way, when the system fires the event indicating that the screen area needs to be redrawn, the event is passed to the control that can put the appropriate information back on the screen. Our example is fine for illustrating how the Graphics class works, however. To be more robust, we should save the text value in our txtBldr class and repeat the logic to paint the desired information in a Paint event handler.

Up until now, we have taken advantage of classes and namespaces provided as part of the system to create a simple Windows application. We have touched on a number of areas that might be of interest but we haven't talked much about how to really extend the environment. The ability to create custom classes that can be reused is something that every Visual Basic 6 programmer is familiar with in the context of COM.

Creating a Namespace

Every assembly created in .NET is part of some root namespace. By default, this logic actually mirrors COM in that assemblies are assigned a namespace that matches the project name. However, unlike COM, in .NET it is possible to change this default behavior. In this way, just as Microsoft has packaged the system level and common runtime language classes using well-defined names, it is possible for us to create our own namespaces. Of course, it's also possible to create projects that match existing namespaces and extend those namespaces, but that is very poor programming practice.

Creating an assembly in a custom namespace can be done at one of two levels. However, unless you want the same name for each assembly that will be used in a large namespace, you will normally reset the root namespace for the assembly. This is done through the assembly's project pages, reached by right-clicking on the assembly name in the Solution Explorer window.

The next step is optional but, depending on whether you want to create a class at the top level or at a child level, you can add a `Namespace` command to your code. There is a trick to being able to create top level namespaces, or multiple namespaces within the modules that make up an assembly. Instead of replacing the default namespace with another name, delete the default namespace and only define the namespaces in the modules using the `Namespace` command.

The `Namespace` command is accompanied by an `End Namespace` command. This `End Namespace` command must be placed after the `End Class` tag for any classes that will be part of the namespace:

```
Namespace MyMetaNamespace
    Class MyClass1
        'Code
    End Class
End Namespace
```

Of course, the example above is a little simple. The `Namespace` command can also be nested. Using nested `Namespace` commands is how child namespaces are defined. The same rules apply – each `Namespace` must be paired with an `End Namespace` and must fully encompass all of the classes that are part of that namespace.

The following code demonstrates the structure used to create a `MyMetaNamespace` namespace, which also has a child namespace called `MyMetaNamespace.MyChildNamespace`:

```
Namespace MyMetaNamespace
    Class MyClass1
        'Code
    End Class
    Namespace MyChildNamespace
        Class MyClass2
            'Code
        End Class
    End Namespace
End Namespace
```

Of course, the best way to demonstrate creating custom namespaces is with a project-based example.

IKLibrary Project

This time, we will create a new class library project that we will place in the custom namespace, `IK`. In order to make this as independent as possible, the new project will be created as a separate solution. Eventually, we will import this namespace into our original Namespace_Sampler project to extend its capabilities. In order to keep this new version separate, the download library will contain the Namespace_Sampler project created in the previous sections and a separate Namespace_Sampler_Ext project that will be integrated with the new classes. Additionally, after we have looked at this basic class library, we will take a quick look at a Web Service. It will also be placed in the `IK` namespace, but it will have some specific advantages and, in particular, a gotcha when we go to add it to the Namespace_Sampler_Ext project.

Select Save All and then File | New | Blank Solution. Create a new Visual Basic Class Library project called IKLibrary. Right-click on the IKLibrary project in the Solution Explorer to display the IKLibrary Property Pages. Earlier in this chapter, this dialog was used to examine the global imports for a project. Now, clicking on General in the Common Properties node, we can see some of the top-level project properties:

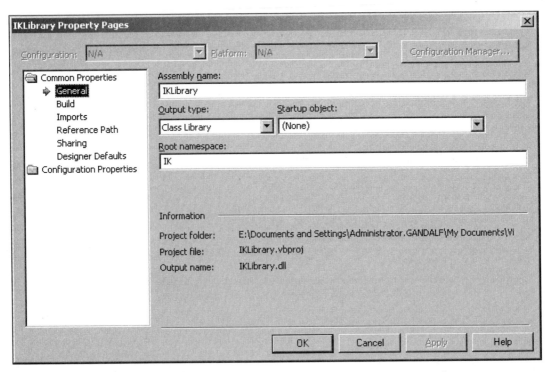

Change the **Root namespace** to our `IK` namespace. It is possible to define an assembly as being associated with any custom namespace since, as was mentioned earlier, it is possible for a namespace to be implemented in multiple files.

The `IKLibrary` assembly will contain a single class which will get the list of .NET assemblies that are installed at the root level of a selected web site. This class would be simple to expand to gain additional information about .NET assemblies installed within other assemblies or other folders on the site. However, the ability to traverse and identify those assemblies at the root level will provide a sufficient example of using the IIS Metabase's ADSI interface from .NET. In order to tell the difference between a .NET assembly and a traditional ASP application, the class will look to see if the application's home directory contains a `Web.config` file. Such a file is part of all .NET web assemblies, both traditional Web Applications and Web Services. The `Web.config` file contains several important settings associated with the web applications, such as how sessions should be managed, and security and database information. If this file is not present then, for the purposes of this demonstration, the code will assume that the folder in question is not associated with .NET.

Add the following to `Class1.vb`:

```
Imports System
Imports FSO = System.IO

Namespace Metabase
Public Class Class1
        Public Function GetAssemblyList(ByVal lngInstance As Long) As _
                ArrayList
            Dim objMetabase As Object
            Dim objKey As Object
```

```
            Dim strName As String
            Dim strPath As String
            Dim strAppPath As String
            GetAssemblyList = New ArrayList()

            objMetabase = GetObject("IIS://localhost/W3SVC/" & _
                            lngInstance & "/root")

            strPath = objMetabase.Path
            For Each objKey In objMetabase
                strName = objKey.Name
                Try
                    strAppPath = objKey.Path
                Catch
                    strAppPath = strPath & "\" & strName
                End Try
                If FSO.File.Exists(strAppPath & "\Web.config") Then
                    GetAssemblyList.Add(strAppPath)
                End If
            Next objKey

        End Function
    End Class
End Namespace
```

Now let's walk through this code. The statements start by importing a couple of namespaces:

```
Imports System
Imports FSO = System.IO

Namespace Metabase
```

The first, System, we have seen before, but the second, System.IO, we haven't yet discussed. This namespace encapsulates the File System Object functions and is aliased as the FSO namespace accordingly. The other item is the declaration of another namespace, IIS Metabase, at the top of the module.

You might be wondering why we used the IKLibrary Property Pages – the preceding screenshot – to set a namespace for the project. The difference is that, declared in this fashion, we are creating a child namespace to the root namespace defined for the project. This is the same concept that is working for things such as System.Text or System.IO. In each of these, there is a set of classes that have been encapsulated with a starting and ending Namespace keyword to indicate the child namespace with which the classes are associated. This is where the power of descriptive namespaces begins to take effect. Not only can we nest classes within the Namespace declaration but we can nest additional namespaces, as with System.Drawing.Text. Thus, the ability to describe the functions of the classes that are grouped under a given namespace is practically limitless yet, at the same time, these long names can be quickly pared down to a short alias for ease of use and readability. The structure that defines a namespace should be unique and should help the developer referencing it to know what to expect in the classes that it contains.

On to the next chunk of code on our walkthrough:

```
Public Class Class1
    Public Function GetAssemblyList(ByVal lngInstance As Long) As _
        ArrayList
        Dim objMetabase As Object
```

```
Dim objKey As Object
Dim strName As String
Dim strPath As String
Dim strAppPath As String
GetAssemblyList = New ArrayList()
```

The code above declares a typical class, in this case the default Class1. This is a very simple class in that it only contains a single custom function. The function GetAssemblyList was added to this class and will implement the code to retrieve an ArrayList containing the list of .NET assemblies found on the selected web site. In order to support this, there are several variables declared and, importantly, the return value is initialized. This is important because, as you might expect, based on the syntax of the function declaration, the return value has not actually been instantiated. Attempting to assign elements to the return value without explicitly instantiating an actual ArrayList object to hold the elements will result in an error.

The Metabase

The next statements are the first calls to the IIS Metabase LDAP interface:

```
objMetabase = GetObject("IIS://localhost/W3SVC/" & _
                        lngInstance & "/root")
```

The Metabase, for those of you unfamiliar with it, contains settings similar to the system registry. However, the settings in the Metabase are specific to IIS and are based on the Lightweight Directory Access Protocol (LDAP). The LDAP protocol is an industry standard specification that defines the basic types of operations and reference methods for common information stores such as Active Directory. As a result, the interfaces to retrieve data from the IIS Metabase and Active Directory, or even things such as WMI, are all similar. In each case, the reference starts with a request to get an object.

The string to connect starts with "IIS://" to define the type of LDAP object that we are requesting. Other types, such as Active Directory and WMI, use "ADSI://" and "WMI://" respectively. The next part, "localhost", defines the machine. This is not a NetBIOS, DNS, or TCP/IP name. The operating system recognizes the name localhost as referring to the local machine and does not attempt to resolve this name externally. It is possible to use LDAP to access directories on other machines. Of course, for remote access to work, the account executing the code must have permission at the administrator level (in the case of the IIS Metabase) in order to access the data. The next part is the "W3SVC" key name, which represents the World Wide Web Service portion of IIS. If we were interested in settings related to SMTP or FTP, we would replace this string with the appropriate key name.

The next level is the instance ID for the site of interest. Each web site that is created on IIS is assigned a unique identifier. This number is assigned when the site is created and is not editable. The default web site has a value of 1 for the instance ID, the next site – normally the administration site – is assigned a value of 2, and so forth. Finally, the string includes the key name of "root". Each web site has a root directory where the IIS Metabase stores the information related to the web site's applications and folders. This structure is shown in the Web Management Console and it is possible to programmatically traverse this structure and read information related to each folder.

```
strPath = objMetabase.Path
```

Reading the structure starts by getting the path for the root directory. When you type the code above into VS.NET, you'll see that, although it doesn't match any available value in the IntelliSense lookup options, the .NET compiler accepts it. That is as long as you have turned `Option Strict` off. Although previous chapters have recommended using `Option Strict On` whenever possible, this is one of those cases where it isn't possible. While the compiler recognizes that the `objMetabase` variable has been assigned an LDAP object that resides outside of the CLR definitions, it isn't happy that it can't associate a .NET type with this object. The `Path` value in the IIS Metabase is defined as a string defining the physical path on the local file system for the currently selected object. For the root of a web site this value is always defined, so we will rely on its presence and assign it to a local variable for use later in this class.

The interesting thing to note is that, while we have defined a simple object from the .NET framework to hold this instance of an LDAP object, we are essentially calling methods and functions that exist outside of the CLR. The syntax to open the Metabase is the same syntax used in Visual Basic 6 or Windows Script Host, and the underlying object returned also remains the same.

```
For Each objKey In objMetabase
    strName = objKey.Name
    Try
        strAppPath = objKey.Path
    Catch
        strAppPath = strPath & "\" & strName
    End Try
    If FSO.File.Exists(strAppPath & "\Web.config") Then
        GetAssemblyList.Add(strAppPath)
    End If
Next objKey


    End Function
  End Class
End Namespace
```

The code above completes the `IKLibrary` class. The code starts by using the Visual Basic `For Each` command structure to loop through each of the keys that are stored in the collection that is part of the underlying object. Each of these keys can be one of a limited set of types that includes files, folders, and virtual directories. You'll notice that applications weren't mentioned; this is because, to IIS, web applications are a specialized form of virtual directory. Even though the folder associated with a web application might be located as a sub folder on the root directory, for the application to have separate security and threading from the root directory, it is necessary to define it in the Metabase as a virtual directory.

It is common to have a sparse data structure under LDAP. Not every directory that is part of a web site will have an entry in the Metabase. Only those directories that have had the default values or some IIS related setting modified, even if the modification is removed, will have an entry in the IIS Metabase. Thus, if .NET didn't define each project as having special characteristics in the Metabase, there wouldn't be an entry for the ASP.NET assemblies.

The next step is that, like the path for the root directory, each web resource must have a name. As a result, we can safely get this name and assign it into a local variable. However, just as not every directory has a mandatory entry, not all properties are mandatory. Consequently, the code uses a `Try...Catch` block for error handling before accessing the IIS Metabase `Path` property. Error handling is covered in detail in Chapter 9, but a simple handler is needed here because of the sparse nature of the Metabase. When you attempt to access a property that is not defined on a key, an error is thrown. The specific error is beyond the scope of this chapter, but the fact that it has been thrown indicates that the value requested is not defined for the current object. The handler just accepts that the property wasn't available and implements default logic, before continuing with the execution of the program.

A custom path is defined whenever IIS cannot append the resource name to the root path. Thus, if a custom path is defined for a resource, it is the path where that specific resource lives on the disk. Otherwise, we can use the root path and append the resource name to get the path for this resource. At this point, if we wanted we could populate the assembly array with this information and return the path for each resource on a web site which has information in the IIS Metabase.

However, the goal is to provide a list of .NET related assemblies that are defined at the root level for the specified web site. One thing that is unique about .NET assemblies is that they include a Web.config file, which contains settings related to the assembly. In many ways, this is another smaller version of some of the settings associated with the IIS Metabase, but the Web.config file contains settings which have no meaning for traditional ASP applications.

For the purposes of IKLibrary, all that is required is that we determine if this file resides in the folder associated with that resource. The File class, defined as part of the IO namespace, is a static (shared) class that provides the static Exists method to solve this question. Similarly to the registry class, you do not instantiate instances of this class. To work with files in .NET, you create Stream objects that are part of the System.IO namespace and then associate them with files opened using the open method on the static file object.

However, in this case we don't need to open the files. A simple check on the Exists method indicates if the current resource has an associated Web.config file, making it a .NET related application. One great thing about the Exists method is that we don't even need to be checking a valid path for the Web.config file. The method was designed to not throw an error regardless of why the string that it was passed didn't evaluate as a valid file. This final check complete, the path information of the selected resource is added to the ArrayList collection.

Now that we have stepped through creating a Metabase namespace within our parent IK namespace, let's create a second namespace. This one will be a second child in the IK namespace called IKRegistry. Again, IK is appended to this name order to prevent any clash with the Microsoft.Win32.Registry namespace. It will contain a single class called NetClass with a single method, GetNetVersion. This method will open the registry, read the version information associated with the .NET Framework, and return this value as a string.

```
Namespace IKRegistry
    Public Class NetClass
        Public Function GetNetVersion() As String
            Dim objRegKey As Microsoft.Win32.RegistryKey

            objRegKey = Microsoft.Win32.Registry.LocalMachine.OpenSubKey( _
                "Software\microsoft\.NETFramework", True)

            GetNetVersion = objRegKey.GetValue("Version").ToString
        End Function
    End Class
End Namespace
```

The code shown above uses the same registry classes that were discussed earlier in this chapter. Instead of getting the installation paths, the version of the .NET framework in use on the system is retrieved. Just as with the library class, the function returns the desired value.

The next step is to make use of the IKLibrary assembly in the Namespace_Sampler_Ext project. First, add the custom assembly as a project reference for the Namespace_Sampler_Ext assembly. Right-clicking on the Reference node in the Solution Explorer will open the Add Reference window. In this case, our goal isn't to add a predefined namespace, so we will hit the Browse button on the Add Reference screen. By default, the file selection dialog will open to our current project directory. Browse to the Bin directory located in the project directory for the IKLibrary project. Select the IKLibary.dll file, click Open, and then OK.

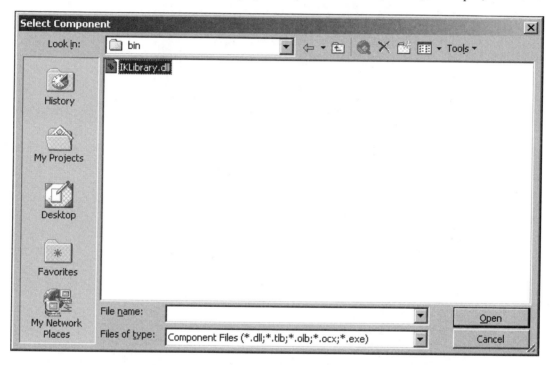

This brings us to two possible issues.

The first issue has appeared with the release of Beta 2 of VS.NET and appears to be a bug. In the past, after including this class, we would modify the properties for the reference to indicate that we do not want a local copy. In this way, as changes are made in development, we can simply recompile the calling assembly and test the new version of the IK namespace implementation. However, with the release of Beta 2, changing the Copy Local property to False results in a runtime error when you enter the module that references the new assembly. The result is that, after each change to the referenced IKLibrary implementation, the Namespace_Sampler_Ext project has to remove and then add the IKLibrary reference for the change to take effect. Hopefully, this issue will be resolved by RTM.

The second issue does not occur in our example. The .NET compiler will not allow you to add a reference to your assembly if the targeted implementation includes a reference, which isn't also referenced in your assembly. The good news is that the compiler will help. If, after adding a reference, that reference doesn't appear in the IntelliSense list generated by VS.NET, go ahead and type the reference to a class from that reference. The compiler will flag it with one of its Microsoft Word-like spelling or grammar error underlines. By then clicking on the underlined text, the compiler will tell you which other assemblies need to be referenced in the project in order to use the class in question.

Modify your form by adding a `ListBox` named `lstAssemblies`, a `Label`, and by moving the controls around, until the form looks as close as possible to the following screenshot:

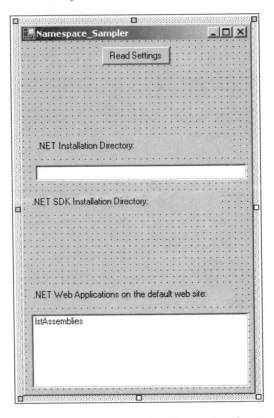

The final step is to edit the `btn_Start_Click` event handler to take advantage of our new object:

```
    Private Sub btnStart_Click(ByVal sender As System.Object, ByVal e As
System.EventArgs) Handles btnStart.Click
        Dim objRegKey As RegistryKey
        Dim txtBldr As Text.StringBuilder
        Dim bshBlue As SysDraw.Brush
        Dim fntTimesNR As SysDraw.Font
        Dim grpGraph As SysDraw.Graphics
        Dim objIKLib As New IK.Metabase.Class1()
        Dim colAssmb As New ArrayList()
        Dim objItem As Object
        Dim objIKLib2 As New IK.IKRegistry.NetClass()

        objRegKey = Registry.LocalMachine.OpenSubKey( _
                "Software\microsoft\.NETFramework", True)

        txtBldr = New Text.StringBuilder()

        bshBlue = New SysDraw.SolidBrush(System.Drawing.Color.Blue)
        fntTimesNR = New SysDraw.Font("Times New Roman", 10, _
                FontStyle.Regular)
```

```
grpGraph = Me.CreateGraphics

txtInstallRoot.Text = Convert.ToString( _
        objRegKey.GetValue("InstallRoot"))

txtBldr.Insert(0, objRegKey.GetValue("sdkInstallRoot"))
grpGraph.DrawString(txtBldr.ToString, fntTimesNR, _
                bshBlue, 8, 224)

' Prevent re-painting the ListBox while adding items.
lstAssemblies.Items.Clear()
lstAssemblies.BeginUpdate()
' Loop through the collection returned and add each assembly name.
colAssmb = objIKLib.GetAssemblyList(1)

For Each objItem In colAssmb
    lstAssemblies.Items.Add(objItem.ToString())
Next objItem
' Tell the control the update is complete so it will repaint.
lstAssemblies.EndUpdate()

'Get the version of the .NET Assembly.
fntTimesNR = New SysDraw.Font("Times New Roman", 14, FontStyle.Bold)
grpGraph.DrawString(objIKLib2.GetNetVersion(), fntTimesNR, _
                bshBlue, 105, 70)

        End Sub
```

Let's now examine this code.

```
Dim objIKLib As New IK.Metabase.Class1()
Dim colAssmb As New ArrayList()
Dim objItem As Object
```

Without reviewing all of the code described in previous sections, three new local variables have been added to the btnStart_Click event handler. The first variable is an instance of our new IKLibrary class.

You'll also notice that, in this case, we have declared and instantiated both the custom class and the local ArrayList class that will hold the return result from our custom class. Because we will loop through the results stored in this array list to populate the ListBox, we need a way to keep the results locally as each item is passed to the objItem variable for processing.

```
' Prevent re-painting the ListBox while adding items.
lstAssemblies.Items.Clear()
lstAssemblies.BeginUpdate()
' Loop through the collection returned and add each assembly name.
colAssmb = objIKLib.GetAssemblyList(1)

For Each objItem In colAssmb
    lstAssemblies.Items.Add(objItem.ToString())
Next objItem
' Tell the control the update is complete so it will repaint.
lstAssemblies.EndUpdate()
```

The code above is used to populate the lstAssemblies ListBox. As shown later in this section, the ListBox is populated with the path to each .NET assembly when the btnStart button is clicked. In order for this to function properly, the ListBox is first cleared of any contents from a previous click. Next, a performance enhancement associated with the ListBox class is used. The BeginUpdate() method on the ListBox class tells the control that, instead of updating its display as each item is added, we expect to add several items and it should hold all display updates until the new items have all been added.

The code then makes the call to GetAssemblyList, passing the instance ID of 1. This tells the library class to retrieve the list of .NET assemblies installed in the root directory of the default web site. The collection is then assigned to the colAssmb defined earlier, and the Visual Basic For Each structure is used to retrieve each object from the collection. Then, using the native ToString conversion that is part of the object class, the strings are added to the Items list of the ListBox.

Once the updates to the ListBox are done, the companion function to BeginUpdate, EndUpdate, is called to indicate to the control that it should repaint all of the new information to the user display. While this completes the incorporation of a custom namespace, before we examine the updated interface it's important to note that, in time, the thought of creating a library class may seem as obsolete as using a .bas module.

```
'Get the version of the .NET Assembly.
fntTimesNR = New SysDraw.Font("Times New Roman", 14, FontStyle.Bold)
grpGraph.DrawString(objIKLib2.GetNetVersion(), fntTimesNR, _
                    bshBlue, 105, 70)

    End Sub
```

The code above is added to paint the version information in the upper portion of the display window. Notice how the call to the GetNetVersion function is directly embedded in the DrawString function. The result when the new project is run is shown here:

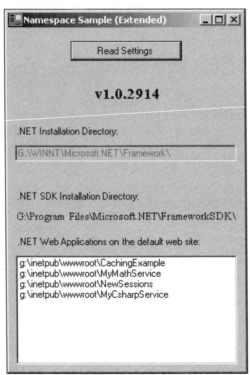

Summary

The introduction of namespaces with .NET provides a powerful tool that helps to abstract the logical capabilities from their physical implementation. While there are differences in the syntax of referencing objects from a namespace, as opposed to referencing the same object from a COM style component implementation, overall there are several similarities. This chapter has introduced namespaces and their hierarchical structure, and has demonstrated:

- ❑ That namespace hierarchies are not related to class hierarchies
- ❑ Reviewing and adding the references with a Visual Basic Assembly
- ❑ Importing and aliasing namespaces at the module level
- ❑ Creating your own custom namespaces

Namespaces play an important role in enterprise software development. By allowing you to separate the implementation of related functional objects, while retaining the ability to still group these objects, you improve the overall maintainability of your code. Everyone who has ever worked on a large project has been put in the situation where a fix to a component is delayed because of the potential impact on other components in the same project. Regardless of the logical separation of components in the same project, those who watched the development process worried about testing. With totally separate implementations for related components, it is not only possible to alleviate this concern, but it is easier than ever before for a team of developers to work on different parts of the same project.

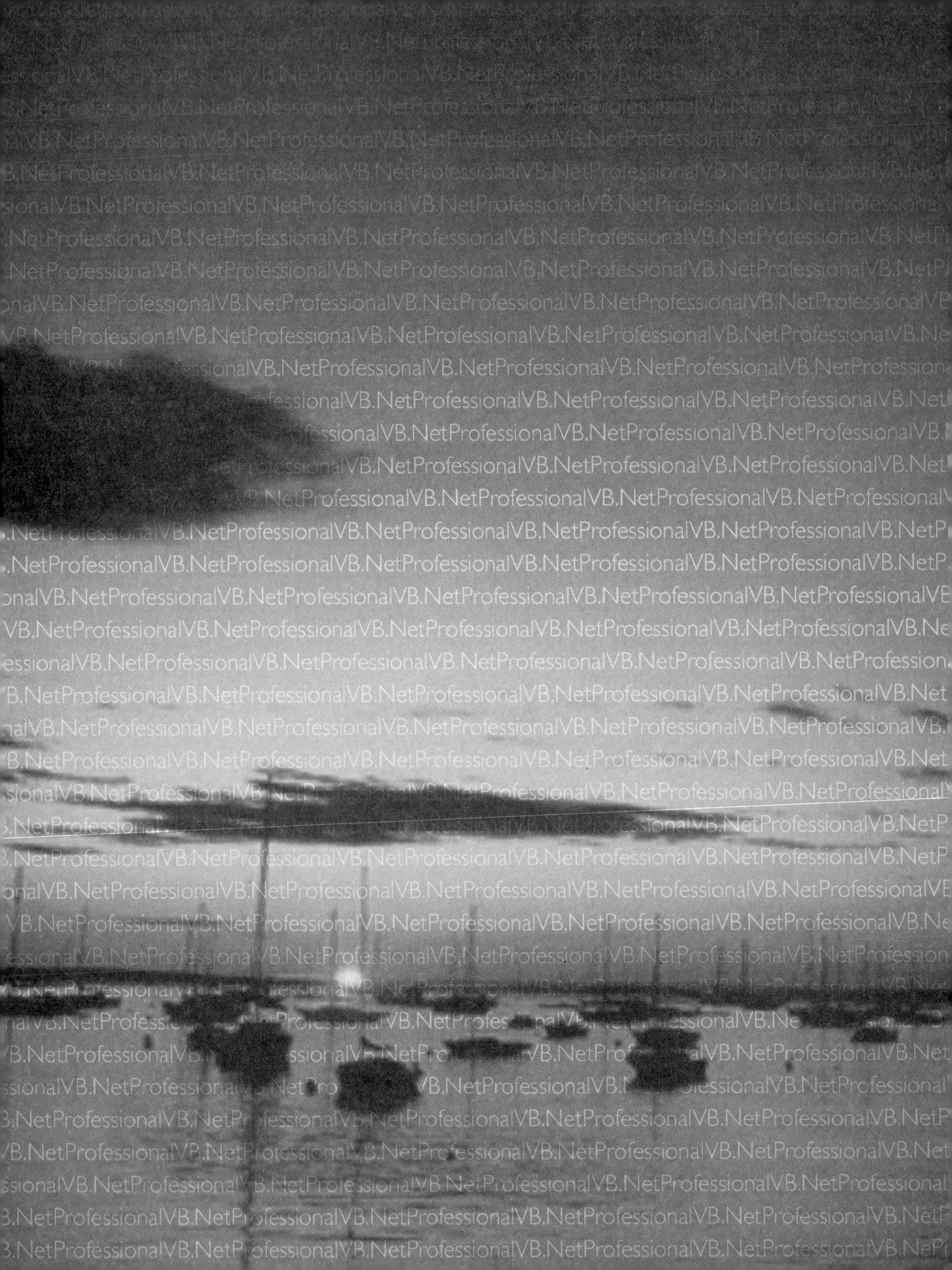
VB.NetProfessional

Windows Forms

Windows Forms (sometimes abbreviated to WinForms) is the part of the .NET framework you use to create applications for the Win32 client just as you would with previous versions of Visual Basic. It is quickly obvious when you start developing a Windows application that the Microsoft development team made some fabulous improvements over the Visual Basic of old. Yes, some of your familiar controls have been retired, but no functionality has been lost. Believe us – you'll love the new world!

This chapter will concentrate primarily on forms and built-in controls. We'll discuss what is new and what has been changed from previous versions of Visual Basic. We'll talk a bit about the System.Windows.Forms namespace as well.

> **It is important to note here that while this chapter assumes you'll be writing a Windows application using Visual Studio.NET it is possible to write a .NET windows application using nothing more than a text editor, and still take full advantage of everything Windows Forms has to offer.**

The System.Windows.Forms Namespace

A Visual Basic 6 standard EXE application begins with the immediate ability to create forms and controls built in from the start. Every VB6 application comes complete with all the user interface capability even if it's never used. For instance, you may want a VB6 application that has no user interface whatsoever, yet VB6 still compiles in all the code for it as part of the VB runtime. Visual Basic .NET, however, now allows you to pick and choose the assemblies you need, in order to minimize the unnecessary bulk of your finished application. It's possible, therefore, to create a VB application not only with no user interface, but also no user interface *code* compiled into the application. If you've flipped to this chapter, however, you're obviously not interested in an application without a user interface, so we'd better introduce the pieces you'll need in order to add forms and controls to your program.

In order to create an application that has a user interface, you need to reference the `System.Windows.Forms.dll` assembly, thus gaining access to the `System.Windows.Forms` namespace. This namespace is the source for all the rich capability you need for a windows application, from menus to message boxes.

> Note that when you create a new VB.NET application, you are presented with a list of possible application types. Your choice in this menu determines what assemblies will be pre-selected for you. Selecting the Windows Application type, for example, automatically gives you a reference to the `System.Windows.Forms.dll` namespace.

For a quick browse of what's in the `System.Windows.Forms` namespace, create a new windows application, and then use the Object Browser. Expand the System.Windows.Forms.dll/System.Windows.Forms tree and you'll see all the types defined within. The following figure shows the Object Browser expanded to the Form type:

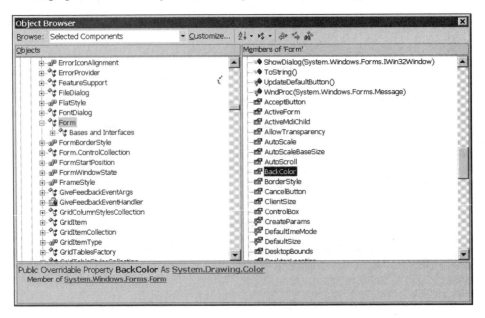

If you scroll through the namespace, you'll notice all sorts of familiar controls such as the CheckBox and Button.

> *A detail worth noting is that the* `System.Windows.Forms` *namespace makes frequent use of another namespace,* `System.Drawing`*. The* `System.Drawing` *namespace contains all the information about fonts, colors, pens, printing, etc, and is a useful namespace if you want to start drawing your own controls.*

Forms as Classes

Before we explore forms in VB.NET, let's step back to Visual Basic 6 for a moment. If you pay close attention to forms in Visual Basic 6, you will probably notice that a form and a class are essentially the same thing, with forms having the added feature of a user interface. Visual Basic has always done a tremendous job of hiding the complexities of setting a form up for you. When people make the realization that a form is really just a class, they start to wonder where and how Visual Basic defines and instantiates the form variable. They start questioning how it became possible to simply start using the variable Form1 in code, without ever actually declaring it using coding such as:

```
Public WithEvents Form1 As New Form1
```

For example, if you want to use a class called Class1, you must first declare a variable, and then instantiate the object by using coding such as:

```
Dim objMyClass As Class1
Set objMyClass = New Class1
```

When you start using a form, however, you magically get a variable already defined and instantiated for you. Visual Basic has always hidden the line Public WithEvents Form1 As New Form1 from you. (VB experts are always aware of this hidden assignment and often choose not to use it in order to more precisely control the lifetime of their forms.)

In VB.NET, all forms are now true classes, and it's abundantly obvious. There are no more secrets going on behind the scenes. All the properties are defined directly in code, instead of via a special series of settings in the .frm file. When you make a change to your form using the design window, you will see it appear in the code itself.

> Pay very special attention to the fact that you no longer get a 'free of charge' variable set up for you. A form called Form1 is now a class name, *and only a class name*. If you want to use it throughout your application, you'll need to set up your own object variable to reference it.

What is a Form in .NET?

Now that VB supports inheritance, forms take part in an inheritance structure that provides all the functionality you expect. You can also see where all that ability comes from. Forms in .NET are classes in the truest sense of the word.

In VB6, forms were saved as proprietary .frm files. (They were clearly objects that could be created and destroyed, but you never really saw their code as such.) By contrast, in VB.NET forms are saved in .vb files like any class. It's the functionality they inherit that makes a class a *form*, as opposed to just any class.

If you view the object hierarchy of a form, you can see that it's really a subclass seven levels removed from the Object class. The following tree shows the superclasses of the Form class with a brief description of what the Form class inherits from each.

Class Hierarchy	Description
Object	The highest superclass from which all .NET objects inherit.
MarshalByRefObject	Provides code dealing with the lifetime management of objects.
Component	Provides the base implementation of the IComponent interface, and allows for object sharing between applications.
Control	The base class for all components with a visual interface.
ScrollableControl	Provides auto-scrolling ability.
ContainerControl	Allows a component to contain other controls.
Form	The main window for an application.

Forms at Design Time

Non-UI Controls No Longer Sit on Your Form

A very nice change to VB.NET is the design time placement of controls that have no immediate user interface. The Timer control in VB6, for instance, would be sited directly on your form as a small icon. In VB.NET, these controls are placed in their own special 'tray' beneath the form in the design window.

A simple form with a Timer control appears as follows:

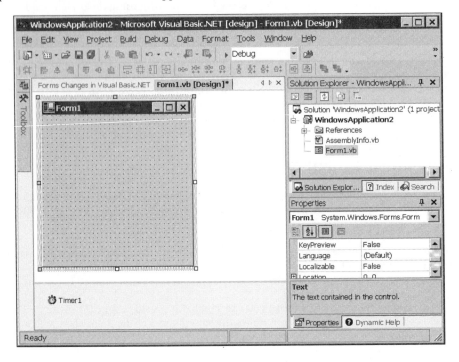

The Design Time Grid

The design time grid is the series of small dots that appear on a form in the designer. In VB6 this grid was set globally. In VB.NET, each form can uniquely manage how the grid affects its controls using the following properties:

- ❑ ShowGrid: Toggles the display of the grid

- ❑ SnapToGrid: Determines if child controls will align and size to the grid when they are dragged and dropped

- ❑ GridSize: Sets the distance, in pixels, between the dots of the grid

To change the default values of these setting, open the Tools | Options *screen and select the* Windows Forms Designer *section.*

Setting the Startup Form

To define which form will be loaded first when your application runs, you need to open the Properties window for the project and set the Startup object setting. Do this using the Project | Properties menu. You can also invoke the window by right-clicking the project name in the Solution Explorer, and selecting Properties from the context menu.

Note: If the Properties *menu item doesn't appear under your* Project *menu, open the Solution Explorer (Ctrl-Alt-L), and highlight the project name, then try again.*

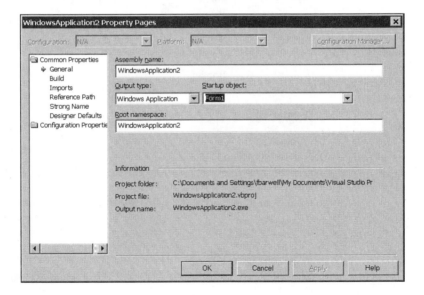

Form Borders

Changing the FormBorderStyle property of a form affects the way it can be manipulated by the user. The following table outlines the differences between the different FormBorderStyle settings, and the effect these settings have on other properties of the form:

FormBorderStyle Setting	Appearance	Effect of Other Form Properties
None	No border User cannot resize form	HelpButton: no effect MaximizeBox: no effect MinimizeBox: no effect SizeGripStyle: no effect
FixedSingle	Single 3D border User cannot resize form	HelpButton: toggles help button in toolbar (only if maximize and minimize buttons are disabled) MaximizeBox: enables/disables MinimizeBox: enables/disables SizeGripStyle: no effect
Fixed3D	3D border User cannot resize form	HelpButton: toggles help button in toolbar (only if maximize and minimize buttons are disabled) MaximizeBox: enables/disables MinimizeBox: enables/disables SizeGripStyle: no effect
FixedDialog	Dialog box style border User cannot resize form	HelpButton: toggles help button in toolbar (only if maximize and minimize buttons are disabled) MaximizeBox: enables/disables MinimizeBox: enables/disables SizeGripStyle: no effect
Sizeable	Same as FixedSingle in appearance User can resize form	HelpButton: toggles help button in toolbar (only if maximize and minimize buttons are disabled) MaximizeBox: enables/disables MinimizeBox: enables/disables SizeGripStyle: toggles display of handle in bottom right corner

FormBorderStyle Setting	Appearance	Effect of Other Form Properties
FixedToolWindow	Single border Use cannot resize form Form1 [x]	HelpButton: no effect MaximizeBox: no effect MinimizeBox: no effect SizeGripStyle: no effect
SizeableToolWindow	Single border User can resize form Form1 [x]	ControlBox: toggles X button in upper right corner HelpButton: no effect MaximizeBox: no effect MinimizeBox: no effect SizeGripStyle: toggles display of handle in bottom right corner

Always on Top

Some applications have the ability to remain visible at all times, even when they do not have the focus. To accomplish this 'Always on Top' effect in Visual Basic 6, you needed to resort to an API call. In Visual Basic.NET, forms have been given a new property called TopMost. Set it to True to have a form overlay others even when it is inactive.

Startup Location

Often you'll want a form to be centered on the screen when it first appears. VB.NET does this automatically for you when you set the StartPosition property. Here are the settings and their meanings:

StartPosition Value	Effect
Manual	Show the form positioned at the values defined by the form's Location property.
CenterScreen	Show the form centered on the screen.
WindowsDefaultLocation	Show the form at the windows default location.
WindowsDefaultBounds	Show the form at the windows default location, with the windows default bounding size.
CenterParent	Show the form centered in its owner.

Form Opacity (Transparency)

A fun new property to Windows Forms is the Opacity property of any rich control such as a form. The opacity measures how opaque or transparent a form is. A value of 0% makes the form fully transparent. A value of 100% makes the form fully visible. Any value between 0 and 100 makes the form partially visible as if it was a ghost.

We're not sure how practical this property will be in a business application, but it makes for some nice UI glitz. The following block of code shows how to fade a form out and back in when the user clicks a button named Button1. You may have to adjust the Step value of the array depending on the performance of your computer:

```
Private Sub Button1_Click(ByVal sender As System.Object, _
                          ByVal e As System.EventArgs) _
                          Handles Button1.Click
    Dim i As Double

    For i = -1 To 1 Step 0.005
        ' Note - opacity is a value from 0.0 to 1.0 in code
        Me.Opacity = System.Math.Abs(i)
    Next i
End Sub
```

Visual Inheritance

By inheriting from System.Windows.Forms.Form, any class representing a form automatically gets all the properties, methods, and events that a form based on Windows Forms is supposed to have. However, a class does not have to inherit directly from the System.Windows.Forms.Form class in order to become a Windows Form. It can become a form by inheriting from another form, which itself inherits from System.Windows.Forms.Form. In this way controls originally placed on one form can be directly inherited by a second form. Not only is the design of the original form inherited, but also any code associated with these controls (for example processing logic behind an **Add New** button). This means that it is possible to create a base form with processing logic required in a number of forms, and then create other forms which inherit the base controls and functionality.

The Inheritance Picker tool is provided in VB.NET to aid this process. It should be noted at this point, however, that a form must be compiled into either an .EXE or .DLL file before it can be used by the Inheritance Picker. Once that is done, the addition of a form that inherits from another form in the project can be performed via the **Project | Add Inherited Form**.

MDI Forms

Multiple Document Interface (MDI) forms are able to contain other forms. An MDI application consists of a parent MDI form and multiple children MDI forms. The child forms are kept contained within the parent and move when the parent moves.

To set up an MDI application you need a form that will act as the MDI parent. First, create a new windows application, and set the IsMDIContainer property of Form1 to True. Next, add a new form to your project, and name it ChildForm.

To open a form as a child within your parent, you need to set its `MDIParent` property to the parent form. Use the following code in `Form1` to display the child form within it:

```
Private WithEvents ChildForm1 As ChildForm
Private WithEvents ChildForm2 As ChildForm

Private Sub ParentForm_Load(ByVal sender As System.Object, _
                            ByVal e As System.EventArgs) _
                            Handles MyBase.Load
    ChildForm1 = New ChildForm()
    ChildForm1.MdiParent = Me
    ChildForm1.Show()

    ChildForm2 = New ChildForm()
    ChildForm2.MdiParent = Me
    ChildForm2.Show()
End Sub
```

Windows Menu

To provide a menu item that will list the available child windows that are owned by the parent, add a new `MainMenu` control to `Form1`. (See the section on menus for further details on this.) Create a menu item (usually called **Windows**) and set its `MDIList` property to `True`. This property will cause the list of child windows to automatically appear as menu items beneath the **Windows** menu, automatically switch between child windows when the user selects an item, and automatically update itself when child windows are added and removed from the parent.

Arranging Child Windows

MDI parent forms have a method called `LayoutMDI` that will automatically arrange child forms in the familiar cascade or tile layout. Add a menu item to your Windows menu called **Tile Vertical** and insert the following code into your form to handle it:

```
Me.LayoutMDI(System.Windows.Forms.MDILayout.TileVertical)
```

When you're done, your application will look like the image on the left. Selecting **Tile Vertical** from the menu will yield the result on the right:

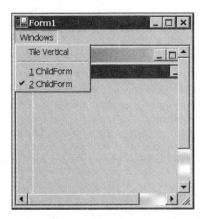 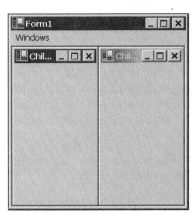

Your code should look something like this:

```
Public Class Form1
    Inherits System.Windows.Forms.Form

Windows Form Designer generated code

    Private WithEvents ChildForm1 As ChildForm
    Private WithEvents ChildForm2 As ChildForm

    Private Sub Form1_Load(ByVal sender As System.Object, _
                      ByVal e As System.EventArgs) _
                      Handles MyBase.Load
      ChildForm1 = New ChildForm()
      ChildForm1.MdiParent = Me
      ChildForm1.Show()

      ChildForm2 = New ChildForm()
      ChildForm2.MdiParent = Me
      ChildForm2.Show()
    End Sub

    Private Sub MenuItem2_Click(ByVal sender As System.Object, _
                      ByVal e As System.EventArgs) _
                      Handles MenuItem2.Click
      Me.LayoutMdi(System.Windows.Forms.MdiLayout.TileVertical)
    End Sub
End Class
```

Setting Limits on the Form Size

In previous versions of Visual Basic, to prevent a user from shrinking or expanding a form beyond a certain limit, you needed to check the size of the form in the Resize event, and essentially reset the height and width of the form only after it had exceeded the limits. This resulted in a terrible flickering effect. VB.NET now has MaximumSize and MinimumSize properties on the form to handle this for you. Simply set them to the sizes you desire. Use 0, 0 for no limit.

Scrollable Forms

Many users will ask that you place what seem to be countless fields on a single form. No amount of reorganizing and reducing spaces between the fields seem to help. While you could split the data entry into multiple screens, it is often done with regret. (Imagine what web surfing would be like if you couldn't scroll a web page.)

Forms in VB.NET are based on a class called ScrollableControl. This base class will give you, with no programming on your part, scroll bars to pull controls into view that are off the edge of your forms.

The scrollable control class on which a form is based automatically gives a form scrollbars when it is sized smaller than the child controls sited on it. To enable this feature, set the AutoScroll property of your form to True. When you run your program, resize the form to make it smaller than the controls require and presto – instant scrolling.

> Note: You cannot have both **Autoscroll** and **IsMdiContainer** both set to **True** at the same time.

Forms at Runtime

Form Lifetime

The lifecycle of a form is like all objects. It is created, and later destroyed. Since forms have a visual component, they use system resources such as handles. These are created and destroyed at interim stages within the lifetime of the form. Forms can be created and will hold state as a class, but will not appear until they are activated. Likewise, closing a form doesn't destroy its state.

The following table summarizes the states of a form's existence, how you get the form to that state, the events that occur when the form enters a state, and a brief description of each:

Code	Events Fired	Description
MyForm = New Form1	None	The form's New() method will get called (as will InitializeComponent)
MyForm.Show() or MyForm.ShowDialog()	HandleCreated	Use Show() for modeless display
		Use ShowDialog() for modal display
	Load	
	VisibleChanged	The HandleCreated event only fires the first time the form is shown, or after it has previously been closed
	Activated	
MyForm.Activate()	Activated	A form can be activated when it is visible but does not have the focus
MyForm.Hide()	Deactivate	Hides the form (sets the Visible property to False)
	VisibleChanged	
MyForm.Close()	Deactivate	Closes the form and calls Dispose to releases the windows resources
	Closing	During the Closing event, you can set the CancelEventArgs.Cancel property to True to abort the close
	Closed	
	VisibleChanged	
	HandleDestroyed	Also called when the user closes the form using the control box or X button
	Disposed	The Deactivate event will only fire if the form is currently active
		Note: There is no longer an Unload event. Use the Closing or Closed event instead

Table continued on following page

Code	Events Fired	Description
MyForm.Dispose()	None	Use the Close() method to finish using your form
MyForm = Nothing	None	Releasing the reference to the form flags it for garbage collection. The garbage collector will call the form's Finalize() method

Controls

As expected, VB.NET introduces controls and features to make meeting your deliverables and requirements easier. Some controls have been renamed, others have been replaced, but nothing has been lost. This section will cover the features that all controls use (such as docking), and then address each of the standard controls available to you, as well as the important changes from previous versions of VB of which to be aware.

Design Features Common to All Controls

Control Tab Order

A wonderful new feature of the design environment is a tool that allows you to set the tab order of the controls on a form simply by clicking on them in sequence. To activate the feature, open a form in the designer, and select the View | Tab Order menu item. This will show a small number in the upper left corner of each control on your form representing the tab index of that control.

To set the values simply click on each control in the sequence you want the tab flow to operate. The following screenshot shows a simple form with the tab order feature enabled:

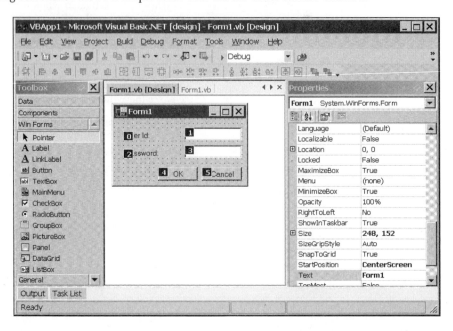

In VB.NET it is possible to have two or more controls with the same tab index value. At runtime, VB will break the tie by using the z-order of the controls. The control that is highest in the z-order will receive the focus first. The z-order can be changed by right-clicking the control and selecting **Bring to Front**.

Control Arrays

Control arrays, as you understood them in previous versions of VB, are gone in VB.NET. However, you now have a better way to do it. There were two good reasons why you wanted to use them:

❑ To have a single method handle the events of multiple controls

❑ To dynamically add new controls to your form at runtime.

In order to make all this work, VB.NET now allows you to totally customize, *at runtime*, the methods that handle the events of your controls.

The first thing to notice is that you can no longer assign the same name to multiple controls on your form. Furthermore, the `Index` property is gone from the standard set of control properties.

To get the control array effect, you need to connect a single method to multiple control events. Then, since you are without the `Index` property, your handler will need a way to determine what control fired the event. To do this, simply use the `Sender` parameter.

A simple example is helpful to see how to set this up. First, create a new windows application, and add two buttons to the form as follows:

Double click **Button1**, to switch over to the code that handles the `Button1.Click` event. In order to make this method respond to the `Button2.Click` event as well, simply add the `Button2.Click` event handler to the end of the `Handles` list, and then add some simple code to display a message box indicating what button triggered the event:

```
' Note the change in the method name from Button1_Click. Since
' two objects are hooked up, it's a good idea to avoid having the
' method specifically named to a single object.
Private Sub Button_Click(ByVal sender As System.Object, _
                         ByVal e As System.EventArgs) _
        Handles Button1.Click, Button2.Click
    Dim buttonClicked As Button

    buttonClicked = CType(sender, Button)

    ' Tell the world what button was clicked
    MessageBox.Show("You clicked """ & buttonClicked.Text & """")
End Sub
```

Run the program and click on the two buttons. Each one will trigger the event and display a message box.

Next, we'll enhance the program to add a third button dynamically at runtime. First, add another button to your form that will trigger the addition of Button3 as follows:

Call your new button addNewButton and add the following code to handle its Click event:

```
Private Sub addNewButton_Click(ByVal sender As System.Object, _
                               ByVal e As System.EventArgs) _
                               Handles addNewButton.Click

    Dim newButton As Button

    ' Create the new control
    newButton = New Button()

    ' Set it up on the form
    newButton.Location = New System.Drawing.Point(200, 152)
    newButton.Size = New System.Drawing.Size(80, 32)
    newButton.Text = "Button3"

    ' Add it to the form's controls collection
    Me.Controls.Add(newButton)

    ' Hook up the event handler
    AddHandler newButton.Click, AddressOf Me.Button_Click
End Sub
```

When the addNewButton button is clicked, the code creates a new button, sets its size and position, and then does two essential things. Firstly, it adds it to the form's controls collection, and secondly, it connects the click event to the method that will handle it.

With this done, run the program and click the addNewButton button. Button3 will appear. Then, simply click Button3 to prove that the click event is being handled. You should get the following result:

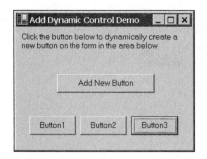

Automatic Resizing and Positioning Controls

Raise your hand if you've written a program and thought of having your controls automatically resize and move around the form when the user resizes it? Keep your hand up if you never bothered to make it happen because of the amount of programming in the form's `Resize` event that it was going to require and your time simply wasn't a luxury. Chances are most of those who read this will have their hand in the air.

There have been some third party controls that you can purchase to address this issue – and some did a pretty good job of it actually (some not so good). VB.NET offers this feature built in, and is probably the first feature that makes people say "Oh wow, finally!" when they start playing around with the form designer.

If you've tried resizing and moving controls at runtime, you'll quickly come to realize that it's not as simple as it seems. Some controls need to move, some need to stretch, some need to do both. VB.NET covers these needs by way of `Docking`, and `Anchoring`.

Docking

Docking refers to gluing a control to the edge of a parent control. If the parent control moves or is stretched, the docked control will do the same. A perfect example of a docked control is a menu bar or a status bar, docked top and bottom of a form respectively. Docking is similar to the `Align` property of controls such as the VB6 status bar.

To work through an example, create a new windows application, and place a label on a form. We've set the background color to white, placed a solid border around, it and set its `TextAlign` to `MiddleCenter` in order to have something that looks like this:

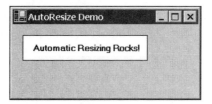

It would be great to glue this label to the top of the form. To do this, view the `Dock` property of the label. If you pull it down you'll see a small graphic like this:

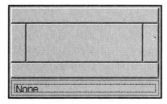

Simply click the top section of the graphic to tell the label to stick to the top of the form. The other sections give you other effects. (A status bar would use the bottom section, for example). When you run your program, and stretch the window sideways, you'll get the following effect:

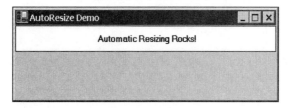

> **If you attempt to dock multiple controls to the same edge, VB.NET must decide how to break the tie. Precedence is given to controls in reverse z-order. In other words, the control that is furthest back in the z-order will be the first control that is next to the edge. If you dock two controls to the same edge and want to switch them, right-click the control you want docked *first* and select Send To Back.**

If you want a gap between the edge of your form and the docked controls, set the `DockPadding` property of the parent control. You can set a different value for each of the four directions (`Left`, `Right`, `Top`, `Bottom`). You can also set all four properties to the same value using the `All` setting.

Anchoring

Anchoring is similar to docking, except you can specifically define the distance each edge of your control will maintain from the edges of a parent.

To get the effect, add a button to the program started above as follows:

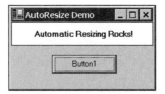

Dropping down the `Anchor` property of the button gives you this graphic:

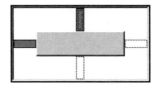

The four rectangles surrounding the center box allow you to toggle the anchor settings of the control. The above graphic shows the default anchor setting of `TopLeft` for all controls.

When the setting is on (dark gray), the edge of your control will maintain its starting distance from the edge of the parent as the parent is resized. The following series of images show some of the different combinations and the effects they have:

Setting	Effect
`Top`	Button maintains its distance from the top, and moves to stay proportionately from the left and right.

Setting	Effect
Top, Right	Button maintains the same distance from the top and right
Top, Right, Bottom	Button maintains its distance from the top, right, and bottom edges. It must stretch its height to do this:
Right, Bottom	
Top, Bottom, Left, Right	

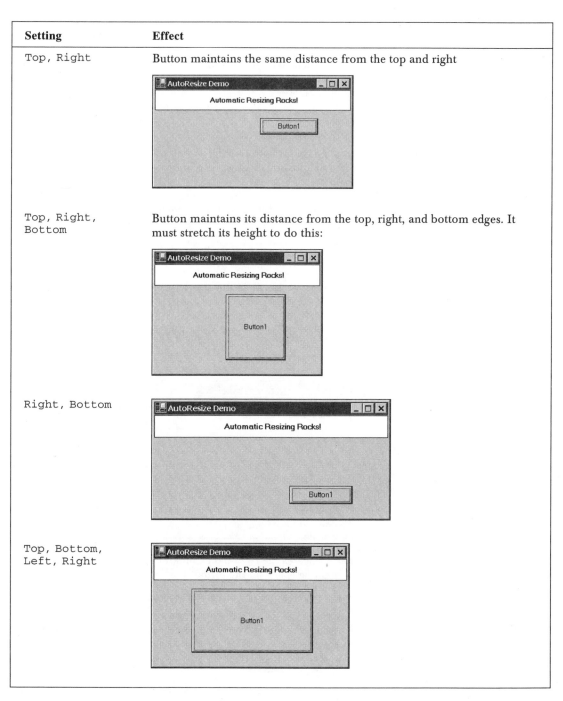

The above examples give you the basic idea of how to make anchoring and docking work. Once you get the hang of it, you can make fantastic use of nested panel controls to resize your form in almost limitless ways.

> Note that you should set the `Anchor` properties of your controls *after* you have designed the entire form since the anchoring effect occurs at design time as well. It can be very frustrating at design time when you need to adjust the size of your form but don't want the controls to move around.

The Splitter Control

The splitter control is a great new tool that helps with resizing as well. A splitter lets a user decide the width (or height) of sections that make up a form. Windows Explorer uses a splitter to divide the folder tree view and folder content windows.

Placing a splitter on your form at design time is a bit tricky if you're new to the feature. To save yourself some frustration, follow this basic sequence of steps:

❑   Create a new application and place one panel on the form that will act as the left half of the form, and set its `Dock` property to `Left`

❑   Place the splitter control on the form – it will automatically dock. Be sure the splitter is sited on the form itself, and not within the panel. Place a button in the panel, and set the button's `Anchor` property to `Top, Left, Right`

❑   Your form should now look something like this (we've made the splitter extra fat and turned on the borders so you can see it):

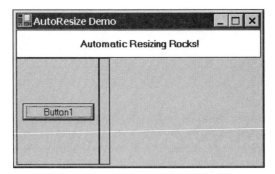

❑   Next, add another panel that will act as the right panel, and set its dock property to `Fill`. This tells it to take up the remaining space on the form

❑   Add a button to the right panel, and, as with the first, set its `Anchor` property to `Top, Left, Right`

When you run the form, the splitter will automatically operate and adjust the sizes of the two panels, and in turn, the sizes of the two buttons:

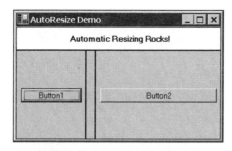

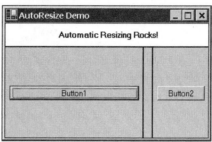

It's a good idea to change the back color of the splitter to a bright color like red at design time. This will make it easier to see and select. At runtime, change the color to something less vibrant.

Validating Data Entry and the Error Provider

Validating Controls

Most controls that you place on a form require that their content be validated in some way. A text box might require a numeric value only, or simply require that the user provide any value and not leave it blank.

VB.NET gives you some new features that make this task significantly easier than it was in previous versions. Most especially is the addition of the ErrorProvider control.

To illustrate the use of this control, create a new Windows application project and place on it two text boxes that will hold a user name and password as follows:

In the next few pages, we'll add code that will simply verify that the user has filled in both textboxes before proceeding.

The Validating Event

The `Validating` event fires when your control begins its validation. It is here that you need to place your code that will validate your control. Place the following code in the `Validating` events of your two textboxes:

```
        Private Sub userNameTextbox_Validating(ByVal sender As Object, _
                    ByVal e As System.ComponentModel.CancelEventArgs) _
                    Handles userNameTextbox.Validating
            If userNameTextbox.Text = "" Then
                MessageBox.Show("User name cannot be blank")
            End If
        End Sub

        Private Sub passwordTextbox_Validating(ByVal sender As Object, _
                    ByVal e As System.ComponentModel.CancelEventArgs) _
                    Handles passwordTextbox.Validating
            If userNameTextbox.Text = "" Then
                MessageBox.Show("Password cannot be blank")
            End If
        End Sub
```

Run the program and tab between the controls without entering any text to get the error message. It is simple, and perhaps too effective. Imagine the effect on a large form with dozens of textboxes that is designed to handle high-speed data entry. The users will probably hate this design if they're interrupted with a message box on every mistake. This is addressed in the next few sections.

The Validated Event

The `Validated` event is fired once the validation of your control has finished running the validating events.

The CausesValidation Property

The `CausesValidation` property determines if the control will participate in the validation strategy on the form. In effect, a control with a `CausesValidation` setting of `True` (it is `True` by default) will have two effects:

❑ The control will have its `Validating`/`Validated` events fired when appropriate

❑ The control will trigger the `Validating`/`Validated` events for other controls

It is important to understand that the validation events fire for a control, *not when the focus is lost*, but when the focus shifts to a control that has a `CausesValidation` value of `True`.

To see this effect, set the `CausesValidation` property of the password textbox in your application to `False` (be sure to leave it `True` for the username and OK button). When you run the program, tab off the username textbox and again to the OK button. Notice that it isn't until you hit the OK button that the validating event of the username textbox fires. Also, notice that the validating event of the password field *never* fires.

Ultimately, if you determine that the control is not valid, you need to decide how to act. The simplest solution is to set the focus to the control and display an error message indicating what is wrong, but users often hate this interruption, especially if they're entering a screen full of data. The solution to this dilemma is the `ErrorProvider` control, which we'll add to our application next.

The Error Provider

How many times has a user approached you with the following requirement: show me graphically all the fields that are wrong, and what is wrong with them, but don't interrupt the data entry process until I reach the end of the form and try to press the OK button.

While this desired behavior is definitely a valid request, it often leads to some rather interesting challenges. For instance, what if half the fields are wrong? How do you display a single message box for a dozen errors? Nobody will read a single gigantic message listing all the errors. You can try displaying only the first error, but then the user will fix it, only to get another one.

You then might attempt to highlight the invalid fields. Text boxes are easy – just set the background color to red perhaps. But what about list boxes? Setting the background color on such a large control would look horrible. And what about controls that have no background color? How do you indicate an error for those?

VB.NET addresses this problem with the `ErrorProvider` control. Adding this control to a form allows you to set an error message for each control on your form that can be shown in a tooltip when the field is not valid. To indicate which fields are invalid, the `ErrorProvider` control will automatically display a small icon next to each control. Placing the mouse over this icon will invoke the tooltip.

Back in the application, set the `CausesValidation` property back to `True` for the password field, and then add an `ErrorProvider` control to your form. (The error provider control has no specific user interface, so it will be added to the section beneath your form.)

To hook it up to your fields, use the `SetError` method. Change the code in the `Validating` events of the two textboxes as follows:

```
    Private Sub userNameTextbox_Validating(ByVal sender As Object, _
            ByVal e As System.ComponentModel.CancelEventArgs) _
            Handles userNameTextbox.Validating
    If userNameTextbox.Text = "" Then
        ErrorProvider1.SetError(userNameTextbox, _
                            "User Name cannot be blank")
    Else
        ErrorProvider1.SetError(userNameTextbox, "")
    End If
End Sub

    Private Sub passwordTextbox_Validating(ByVal sender As Object, _
            ByVal e As System.ComponentModel.CancelEventArgs) _
            Handles passwordTextbox.Validating
    If passwordTextbox.Text = "" Then
        ErrorProvider1.SetError(passwordTextbox, _
                            "Password cannot be blank")
    Else
        ErrorProvider1.SetError(passwordTextbox, "")
    End If
End Sub
```

Run the application and tab through the fields. Position the mouse over the error icon of the password field and you should see the following result:

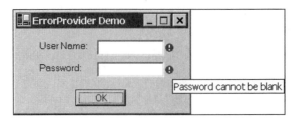

The properties of the error provider allow you to change things such as the icon used, and where the icon will appear in relation to the field that has the error. For instance, you might want the icon to show up beneath a field instead. You can also have multiple error providers on your form. Often you may only want to warn a user that something doesn't look quite right. A second error provider with a yellow icon could be used to provide this feature.

Menus

Designing menus in VB.NET is yet another area that has been completely redesigned. A menu is now a control that you add to your form like any other control.

The menu designer is extremely intuitive – the menu appears on your form just as it would at runtime, and you simply fill in the menu items you need.

Main Menus

Main menus are the standard menus you see that remain docked at the top of a form. Create a new Windows application and add a textbox to your form. Set its MultiLine property to True and stretch it out. This example will create a trivial text editor to demonstrate the use of menus.

Next, add a MainMenu control to your form. The menu designer will activate and you simply type your menu items and use the properties window to set the parameters.

Create the following File and Edit menu items. To set the properties of the individual menu items, simply click to select them and the properties window will show you the specific properties for that item:

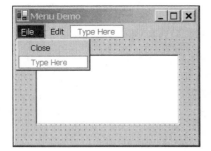 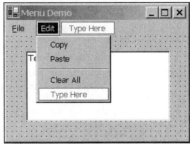

To create the separator in the Edit menu, enter a hyphen as the text of a menu item.

The following code runs the menus of our sample app so far:

```
Private Sub copyMenuItem_Click(ByVal sender As System.Object, _
                              ByVal e As System.EventArgs) _
                              Handles copyMenuItem.Click
    ' Copy the selected text to the Clipboard.
    TextBox1.Copy()
End Sub

Private Sub pasteMenuItem_Click(ByVal sender As System.Object, _
                              ByVal e As System.EventArgs) _
                              Handles pasteMenuItem.Click
    ' Paste the the Clipboard text into TextBox1
    TextBox1.Paste()
End Sub

Private Sub closeMenuItem_Click(ByVal sender As System.Object, _
                              ByVal e As System.EventArgs) _
                              Handles closeMenuItem.Click

    Me.Close()
End Sub

Private Sub clearAllMenuItem_Click(ByVal sender As System.Object, _
                              ByVal e As System.EventArgs) _
                              Handles clearAllMenuItem.Click

    TextBox1.Text = ""
End Sub
```

Context Menus

Next, we'll add a simple context menu that will allow the user to change the color of the textbox. Context menus appear as small pop up menus when the user right-clicks on a form or control.

When you add a context menu to the form, it is edited in the same way a main menu is – at the top of the form. At design time, this positioning is only done to give you a place to edit the menu. At runtime, the context menu will appear in a specific location on the form, which we'll see in the code example that follows.

Double click the ContextMenu control in the toolbox to add a new context menu to the form. Set up the context menu as follows:

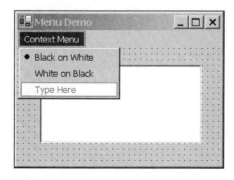

To create the "radio button" indicators beside a menu item requires two properties to be set. The Checked property tells VB that the menu item will display a checkmark, while the RadioCheck property will tell VB that the checkmark should be displayed as a dot.

Note that it is a standard to use radio checks when the selections are mutually exclusive, and checkmarks when more than one item can be chosen at the same time. VB.NET will not prevent you from having two menu items with a radio check next to them at the same time. It is up to you to manage this in code.

To hook up the context menu to appear when the user right-clicks the text box, simply set the ContextMenu property of the text box to the context menu you added to the form – that's all there is to it.

When you run the application and right-click on the textbox, you will have the following result:

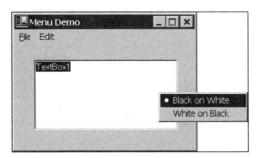

The following code can be used when you select the items in the context menu. Note the change of the Checked property. VB will not do this for you even though it is a very common standard that radio buttons are mutually exclusive:

```
Private Sub blackOnWhiteMenuItem_Click(ByVal sender As System.Object, _
                                ByVal e As System.EventArgs) _
            Handles blackOnWhiteMenuItem.Click
    TextBox1.ForeColor = System.Drawing.Color.Black
    TextBox1.BackColor = System.Drawing.Color.White

    ' toggle the radio check
    blackOnWhiteMenuItem.Checked = True
    whiteOnBlackMenuItem.Checked = False
End Sub

Private Sub whiteOnBlackMenuItem_Click(ByVal sender As System.Object, _
                                ByVal e As System.EventArgs) _
            Handles whiteOnBlackMenuItem.Click
    TextBox1.ForeColor = System.Drawing.Color.White
    TextBox1.BackColor = System.Drawing.Color.Black

    ' toggle the radio check
    blackOnWhiteMenuItem.Checked = False
    whiteOnBlackMenuItem.Checked = True
End Sub
```

Run the application, right-click the textbox and select the White on Black option. If you open the context menu again, you'll see that the radio check has been changed:

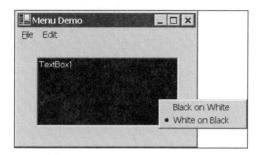

Dynamically Manipulating Menus at Runtime

Menus can be adjusted at runtime using code. Context menus for instance may need to change depending on the state of your form.

The following code shows how to add a new menu item to the context menu, and also how to clear the menu items. Although simple, it can be expanded for more advanced uses. For instance, you may want to store a list of recently accessed files in the registry. When your application loads, you could read this list back, and insert a menu item into the file menu for each item, and use the same event handler for each:

```
' Add a new menu item at the top of ContextMenu1
Private Sub AddMenuItemExample()
    Dim newMenuItem As MenuItem

    ' Create the new menu item
    newMenuItem = New MenuItem("New Menu Item!")

    ' Set up the event that will handle it's click event
    AddHandler newMenuItem.Click, AddressOf Me.NewMenuItem_Click

    ' Add it to the menu
    ContextMenu1.MenuItems.Add(0, newMenuItem)
End Sub

' This method is here to handle the click event of a new menu item that
' is added dynamically at runtime
Private Sub NewMenuItem_Click(ByVal sender As System.Object, _
                              ByVal e As System.EventArgs)
    MessageBox.Show("New menu item clicked!")
End Sub

' Remove all the menu items from ContextMenu1
Private Sub ClearMenuExample()
    ContextMenu1.MenuItems.Clear()
End Sub
```

Duplicating Menus

Another task that you can perform with menus at runtime is cloning. You may, for instance, want to have a context menu duplicate the functionality of the Edit menu in a `MainMenu` control. To accomplish this, use the `CloneMenu()` method. The following example will replace the context menu of the textbox in the application above with the same edit menu from `MainMenu1`:

```
Private Sub CloneMenuExample()
    Dim newContextMenu As ContextMenu

    newContextMenu = New ContextMenu()
    newContextMenu.MenuItems.Add(editMenuItem.CloneMenu())

    TextBox1.ContextMenu = newContextMenu
End Sub
```

> Note: Since `CloneMenu()` clones the object in its entirety, all the event handlers will be cloned as well. You don't need to copy the event handler connections for all the menu items in the cloned menu.

To switch back, simply reassign `ContextMenu1` to the `ContextMenu` property of the textbox as follows:

```
TextBox1.ContextMenu = ContextMenu1
```

Toolbars

The Toolbar control has definitely undergone some big improvements. It now hosts a collection of `ToolBarButton` objects, each with its own set of properties and behaviors. In VB6, you could try using a `ToolBar` control for limited functionality, or perhaps the `CoolBar` control, but neither were really as clean as the new version in VB.NET.

As with previous examples so far, create a new windows application to begin a simple demonstration on how to use the ToolBar control. Add a ToolBar control to your form and then expand the `Buttons` property to invoke the collection designer. ToolBars, as you might expect, host a collection of `ToolBarButton` objects. For now, simply add three buttons to your toolbar. You'll have the following result:

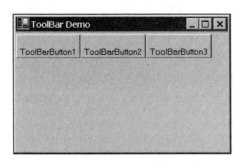

Next, we'll make the first button simply close the application, the second will act as a separator, and the third will be a drop-down that will invoke a context menu control. To do this reopen the Toolbar Button collection designer and make the following changes:

❑ Change the Text property of the first button to Close

❑ Change the Style property of the second button to Separator

❑ Change the Text property of the third button to Background Color, and the Style property to DropDownButton

When you're done, your form will appear as follows:

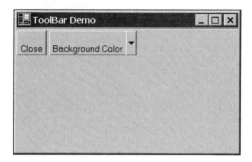

To capture the Click event of the Close button, add the following code to your form. Note the approach used to identify which button was clicked:

```
Private Sub ToolBar1_ButtonClick(ByVal sender As System.Object, _
                                 ByVal e As
System.Windows.Forms.ToolBarButtonClickEventArgs) _
                                 Handles ToolBar1.ButtonClick
    Select Case ToolBar1.Buttons.IndexOf(e.Button)
        Case 0  ' Close button
            Me.Close()
            ' Add more cases to handle other buttons. For this example we
            ' only need one condition
    End Select
End Sub
```

When you run your application and click the Close button, your application will exit.

Next, we'll set up the drop-down button. Add a context menu to the form (see above section) and design it to contain two items – gray and white. If you like, assign radio checks to each as was done in the context menu sample above. In the form's Load event, add the following code:

```
Private Sub Form1_Load(ByVal sender As System.Object, _
                       ByVal e As System.EventArgs) Handles MyBase.Load
    ToolBarButton3.DropDownMenu = ContextMenu1
End Sub
```

That's all there is to it. You can, of course add code similar to that shown above to handle the events of the context menu. Run the application and click the drop-down toolbar button:

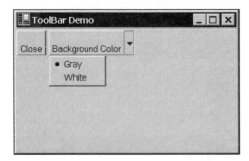

The toolbar buttons provide many other useful features to make them much nicer than the simple example shown above – images can be assigned to the buttons, the text can be aligned to the right instead of below, and the buttons themselves can appear flat if you prefer.

While the new toolbar is certainly a big improvement over the old version, there are still a few features that it lacks. One in particular is a combo box. A workaround you can try would involve placing a combo box on a panel, and docking the panel to the top of the form.

DataGrid

The DataGrid control has been significantly upgraded from its predecessor. Its use is primarily tied to the `DataSet` object but it can be bound to virtually anything from an array to a collection. You can even hook it up to a set of list box items if you really want to. If you become familiar with the new data objects, you'll very naturally start using the DataGrid. In essence, the DataGrid is a front-end user interface to the data objects in .NET. It is incredibly easy to use once you understand how the objects interact.

For this section, we'll create a simple grid and hook it up to a custom DataSet. The many properties of the grid are pretty self explanatory such as the appearance and colors of the columns, so we won't go into that. The intent of this sample is to give you a simple grid that is up and running. Ultimately, the DataGrid is the mother control of all the data binding ability in .NET. Be aware, however, that the topic of data binding is beyond the scope of this chapter. For more details on the DataSet object, see Chapter 18.

To begin, create a new Windows application and place a DataGrid on the form. Set the `CaptionText` property to something like `"Employees"`. (When complete the grid will show a few people and an ID for each.)

We'll fill the DataGrid's data programmatically using a custom function named `SetupData()` that we'll call from the `Load` event of the form as follows:

```
Private Sub Form1_Load(ByVal sender As Object, _
                       ByVal e As System.EventArgs) _
                       Handles MyBase.Load
    SetupData()
End Sub
```

```
Private Sub SetupData()
    Dim EmployeeData As DataSet
    Dim EmployeeTable As DataTable
Dim IdColumn As DataColumn
    Dim NameColumn As DataColumn
```

```
Dim Row As DataRow

' Make the DataSet
EmployeeData = New DataSet("EmployeeData")

' Make a table
EmployeeTable = New DataTable("Employee")

' Make a column for the table
IdColumn = New DataColumn("ID")
IdColumn.AutoIncrement = True
IdColumn.DataType = Type.GetType("System.Int32")
EmployeeTable.Columns.Add(IdColumn) ' add column to table

' Make a second column
NameColumn = New DataColumn("Name")
NameColumn.DefaultValue = "<Name>"
NameColumn.DataType = Type.GetType("System.String")
EmployeeTable.Columns.Add(NameColumn) ' add column to table

' Add three rows of data
Row = EmployeeTable.NewRow
Row("Name") = "John"
EmployeeTable.Rows.Add(Row)

Row = EmployeeTable.NewRow
Row("Name") = "Julie"
EmployeeTable.Rows.Add(Row)

Row = EmployeeTable.NewRow
Row("Name") = "Bill"
EmployeeTable.Rows.Add(Row)

' Add the table to the DataSet
EmployeeData.Tables.Add(EmployeeTable)

' Connect the DataSet/table to the DataGrid
DataGrid1.SetDataBinding(EmployeeData, "Employee")
End Sub
```

When you run the application, the DataGrid will fill with three rows of data: one for John, Julie, and Bill. Note that we really didn't have to do anything special for the DataGrid itself, save the final call to SetDataBinding. This method connected the DataGrid to the EmployeeData DataSet and the DataGrid took care of the rest. When you run the application, you'll get the following result:

Note that the fourth entry automatically fills in the ID column since we set its AutoIncrement property to True, and the Name column has the default value of <Name>. This was all defined in the DataSet – we did nothing with the DataGrid itself.

The DataGrid will automatically manipulate the DataSet to which it is bound, so if your users add more information to the DataSet, you can easily extract it. Add another button to the form and place the following code in its Click event:

```
Private Sub btnOutput_Click(ByVal sender As System.Object, _
                            ByVal e As System.EventArgs) _
                            Handles OutputButton.Click
    Dim EmployeeDataSet As DataSet
    Dim row As DataRow
    Dim i As Integer

    EmployeeDataSet = DataGrid1.DataSource
    For i = 0 To EmployeeDataSet.Tables("Employee").Rows.Count() - 1
        row = EmployeeDataSet.Tables("Employee").Rows(i)
        Debug.WriteLine(row.Item("id") & ", " & row.Item("Name"))
    Next
End Sub
```

Run the application, add a few rows of data, and click on the new button. The Output window will display the contents of the grid:

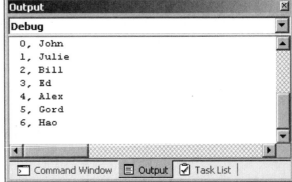

Common Dialogs

VB.NET provides you with seven common dialog controls. Each is a control that will open a predefined form that is identical to the one used by the operating system. The sections below outline the use and basic properties of each control that customize its use.

OpenFileDialog, SaveFileDialog Control

These two controls will open the standard dialog control that allows a user to select files on the system. They are virtually identical except for the buttons and labels that appear on the actual dialog box when it is shown to the user. Each prompts the user for a file on the system, by allowing the user to browse the files and folders available.

Use the following properties to set up the dialogs:

Property	Comments
InitialDirectory	Defines the initial location that will be displayed when the dialog box opens.
	For example:
	`OpenFileDialog1.InitialDirectory = "C:\Program Files"`
Filter	String that defines the 'Files of type' list. Separate items using the pipe character. Items are entered in pairs with the first of each pair being the description of the file type, and the second half as the file wildcard.
	For example:
	`OpenFileDialog1.Filter = "All Files|*.*|Text Files|*.txt|Rich Text Files|*.rtf"`
FilterIndex	Integer that specifies the default filter item to use when the dialog box opens.
	For example, with the above filter used, default to text files as follows:
	`OpenFileDialog1.FilterIndex = 2`
RestoreDirectory	Boolean value that, if True, will force the system's default directory to be restored to its location as it was when the dialog box was first opened. This is False by default.
Filename	Holds the full name of the file that the user selected, including the path.
ShowDialog()	Display the dialog.

The following code will open the standard dialog box asking the user to select a file that currently exists on the system, and simply displays the choice in a message box upon return:

```
OpenFileDialog1.InitialDirectory = "C:\"
OpenFileDialog1.Filter = "Text files|*.txt|All files|*.*"
OpenFileDialog1.FilterIndex = 1
OpenFileDialog1.RestoreDirectory = True

OpenFileDialog1.ShowDialog()

MessageBox.Show("You selected """ & OpenFileDialog1.FileName & """")
```

ColorDialog Control

As the name obviously implies, this control gives the users a dialog box from which they can select a color. Use the following properties to set up the dialogs:

Property	Comments
Color	The System.Drawing.Color that the user selected. You can also use this to set the initial color selected when the user opens the dialog.
AllowFullOpen	Boolean value that, if True, will allow the user to select any color. If False, the user is restricted to the set of default colors.
ShowDialog()	Display the dialog.

The coding for this property looks something like this:

```
ColorDialog1.Color = TextBox1.BackColor

ColorDialog1.AllowFullOpen = True
ColorDialog1.ShowDialog()

TextBox1.BackColor = ColorDialog1.Color
```

FontDialog Control

This control will display the standard dialog box allowing a user to select a font. Use the following properties to set up the dialogs:

Property	Comments
Font	The System.Drawing.Font that the user selected. Also used to set the intial font.
ShowEffects	Boolean value that, if True, will make the dialog box display the text effects options of underline and strikeout.
ShowColor	Boolean value that, if True, will make the dialog box display the combo box of the font colors. The ShowEffects property must be True for this to have an effect.
FixedPitchOnly	Boolean value that, if True, will limit the list of font choices to only those that have a fixed pitch (such as courier, or lucida console).
ShowDialog()	Display the dialog.

The coding syntax for these properties looks like this:

```
FontDialog1.Font = TextBox1.Font

FontDialog1.ShowColor = True
FontDialog1.ShowEffects = True
FontDialog1.FixedPitchOnly = False
FontDialog1.ShowDialog()

TextBox1.Font = FontDialog1.Font
```

Printer Dialog Controls

There are three more common dialog controls, namely PrintDialog, PrintPreviewDialog, and PageSetupDialog that can all be used to control the output of a file to the printer. You can use these in conjunction with the PrintDocument component to run and control print jobs.

Drag and Drop

Implementing a drag and drop operation in .NET is accomplished using a short sequence of events. Typically it begins in a MouseDown event of one control, and always ends with the DragDrop event of another.

To demonstrate the process, we'll begin with a new windows application. Add two listboxes to your form and add three items to the first using the Items property designer. This application will allow you to drag the items from one listbox into the other.

The first step in making drag and drop work is specifying whether or not a control will accept a drop. By default, all controls will reject such an act and not respond to any attempt by the user to drop something onto them. In our case, set the AllowDrop property of the second listbox (the one without the items added) to True.

The next item of business is to invoke the drag and drop operation. This is typically (although you're not restricted to it) done in the MouseDown event of the control containing the data you want to drag. This is done using the DoDragDrop method. The DoDragDrop method defines the data that will be dragged, and the type of dragging that will be allowed. In our situation, we'll drag the text of the selected listbox item, and we'll permit both a move and a copy of the data to occur.

Switch over to the code window of your form and add the following code to the MouseDown event of ListBox1:

```
Private Sub ListBox1_MouseDown(ByVal sender As Object, _
                    ByVal e As System.Windows.Forms.MouseEventArgs) _
                    Handles ListBox1.MouseDown
    Dim DragDropResult As DragDropEffects

    If e.Button = MouseButtons.Left Then
        DragDropResult = ListBox1.DoDragDrop( _
                        ListBox1.Items(ListBox1.SelectedIndex), _
                        DragDropEffects.Move Or DragDropEffects.Copy)
        ' Leave some room here to check the result of the operation


    End If
End Sub
```

You'll notice the comment above about leaving room to check the result of the operation. We'll fill that in shortly. For now, calling the DoDragDrop method has got us started.

The next step involves the recipient of the data – in our case, ListBox2. There are two events here that will be important to monitor – the DragEnter and DragDrop event.

As can be predicted by the name, the DragEnter event will occur when the user first moves over the recipient control. The DragEnter event has a parameter of type DragEventArgs that contains an Effect property and a KeyState property.

The Effect property allows you to set the display of the drop icon for the user to indicate if a move or a copy will occur when the mouse button is released. The KeyState property allows you to determine the state of the *Ctrl*, *Alt*, and *Shift* keys. It is a Windows standard that when both a move or a copy can occur, a user is to indicate the copy action by holding down the *Ctrl* key. Therefore, in this event we will check the KeyState property and use it to determine how to set the Effect property.

Add the following code to the DragEnter event of ListBox2:

```
Private Sub ListBox2_DragEnter(ByVal sender As Object, _
                            ByVal e As DragEventArgs) _
                            Handles ListBox2.DragOver
    If e.KeyState = 9 Then ' Control key
        e.Effect = DragDropEffects.Copy
    Else
        e.Effect = DragDropEffects.Move
    End If
End Sub
```

Note that you can also use the DragOver event if you want, but it will fire continuously as the mouse moves over the target control. In this situation, you only need to trap the initial entry of the mouse into the control.

The final step in the operation occurs when the user lets go of the mouse button to drop the data in its destination. This is captured by the DragDrop event. The parameter contains a property holding the data that is being dragged. It's now a simple process of placing it into the recipient control as follows:

```
Private Sub ListBox2_DragDrop(ByVal sender As Object, _
                ByVal e As System.Windows.Forms.DragEventArgs) _
                Handles ListBox2.DragDrop
    ListBox2.Items.Add(e.Data.GetData(DataFormats.Text))
End Sub
```

One last step – we can't forget to manipulate ListBox1 if the drag and drop was a move. Here's where we'll fill in the hole we left in the MouseDown event of ListBox1. Once the DragDrop has occurred, the initial call that invoked the procedure will return a result indicating what ultimately happened. Go back to the ListBox1_MouseDown event and enhance it to remove the item from the listbox if it was moved (and not simply copied):

```
Private Sub ListBox1_MouseDown(ByVal sender As Object, _
                ByVal e As System.Windows.Forms.MouseEventArgs) _
                Handles ListBox1.MouseDown
    Dim DragDropResult As DragDropEffects

    If e.Button = MouseButtons.Left Then
        DragDropResult = ListBox1.DoDragDrop( _
                        ListBox1.Items(ListBox1.SelectedIndex), _
                        DragDropEffects.Move Or DragDropEffects.Copy)
        If DragDropResult = DragDropEffects.Move Then
            ListBox1.Items.RemoveAt(ListBox1.SelectedIndex)
        End If
    End If
End Sub
```

When you're done, run your application and drag the items from Listbox1 into Listbox2. Try a copy by holding down the control key when you do it. The following screenshot shows the result after Item1 has been moved, and Item3 has been copied a few times:

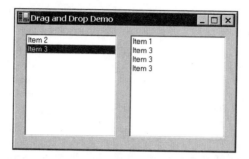

Summary of Standard Windows.Forms Controls

VB.NET of course contains most of the controls which you are accustomed to using in previous versions. The following few pages list out the basic controls that are generally quite intuitive and didn't warrant a full example to explain them. Where appropriate, the important differences from previous versions of VB are stated.

Button

❑ Formerly known as CommandButton

❑ Now uses the Text property instead of Caption

❑ Can now display both an icon and text simultaneously. The image is set using the Image property (instead of Picture). The image position can be set using the ImageAlign property (left, right, center, etc.)

❑ Text on the button can be aligned using the TextAlign property

❑ Can now have different appearances using the FlatStyle property

❑ No longer has the Default and Cancel properties. These are now managed by the form itself using the AcceptButton and CancelButton properties

CheckBox

❑ Now uses the Text property instead of Caption

❑ Can now appear as a toggle button using the Appearance property

❑ Check box and text can now be positioned within the defined area using the CheckAlign and TextAlign properties

❑ Uses the CheckState property instead of Value

❑ Has a FlatStyle property controlling the appearance of the check box

CheckedListBox

❑ A listbox that has checkboxes beside each item (see ListBox)

ComboBox
- ❑ As with the new ListBox control, can now hold a collection of objects instead of an array of strings (see ListBox)
- ❑ Now has a MaxDropDownItems property that specifies how many items to display when the list opens

DataGrid
- ❑ See previous section

DateTimePicker
- ❑ Formerly known as a DTPicker

DomainUpDown - New!
- ❑ A simple one line version of a listbox
- ❑ Can hold a collection of objects, and will display the ToString() result of an item in the collection
- ❑ Can wrap around the list to give a continuous scrolling effect using the Wrap property

GroupBox
- ❑ Formerly known as a Frame

HelpProvider – New!
- ❑ Allows quick and easy help configuration. Adding a HelpProvider control to your form puts extra properties in your other controls where you can set various help properties of the controls such as help text that will appear when the user presses *F1*, and links into compiled (.chm) help files or HTML help files

HScrollBar
- ❑ Unchanged

ImageList
- ❑ Same as previous versions, but with an improved window for managing the images within the list. The MaskColor property is now TransparentColor

Label
- ❑ Essentially the same as previous versions
- ❑ Caption is now Text
- ❑ Can now display an image and text
- ❑ The TextAlign property is especially useful. The text of a label beside a text box in VB6 would always be a few pixels higher than the text in the text box. Now by setting the label's TextAlign property so that the vertical alignment is Middle, this problem is solved.
- ❑ Can now specify if a mnemonic should be interpreted (if UseMnemonic is True, the first ampersand in the Text property will indicate to underline the following character and have it react to the *Alt* key shortcut, placing the focus on the next control in the tab order that can hold focus such as a textbox)

LinkLabel – New!
- ❑ Identical to a label, but behaves like a hyperlink with extra properties such as LinkBehavior (for example, HoverUnderline), LinkColor, and ActiveLinkColor

ListBox

❑ A listbox can now hold a collection of objects instead of an array of strings. Use the `DisplayMember` property to specify what property of the objects to display in the list, and the `ValueMember` property to specify what property of the objects to use as the values of the list items. (This is similar to the `ItemData` array from previous versions.) For example, the combo box can store a collection of, say, employee objects, and display to the user the `Name` property of each, as well as retrieve the `EmployeeId` as the value of the item currently selected

❑ Can no longer be set to display checkboxes using a `Style` property. Use the `CheckedListBox` control instead

ListView

❑ Same functionality as the VB6 version but with an improved property editor that allows you to define the list view item collection *and* its subitems at design time.

❑ Subitems can have their own font display properties

❑ New `HeaderStyle` property instead of `HideColumnHeaders`

MainMenu

❑ See previous section

MonthCalendar

❑ Formerly known as `MonthView`

NotifyIcon – New!

❑ Great new control that gives you an icon in the system tray

❑ Tooltip of the icon is set by the `Text` property of the control

❑ Popup menus are set using a `ContextMenu` control (see section on Menus earlier in chapter)

NumericUpDown – New!

❑ A single line text box that displays a number and up/down buttons that increment/decrement the number when clicked

Panel – New!

❑ The panel control is essentially nothing more than a container for other controls. You can use it to group controls together for resizing needs (see the section on the Splitter Control), or simply to easily make visible, or invisible, many controls at once simply by showing or hiding the panel on which they are all sited

PictureBox

❑ `Image` property defines the graphic to display instead of `Picture`

❑ Use the `SizeMode` property to auto stretch, or center the picture

ProgressBar

❑ Now has a `Step()` method that automatically increments the value of the progress bar by the amount defined in the `Step` property

RadioButton

❑ Formerly known as `OptionButton`

❑ Use `Checked` property to specify value (formerly `Value`)

❑ Use `CheckAlign` and `TextAlign` to specify where the radio button and text appear in relation to the area of the control

RichTextBox
- ❑ Essentially the same control as before with a few new properties such as `ZoomFactor`, `WordWrap`, `DetectURLs`, and `AutoWordSelection`
- ❑ Use the `Lines()` array to get or set specific individual lines of text of the control

Splitter
- ❑ See previous section

StatusBar
- ❑ Has a `Panels` collection and a `ShowPanels` property. If `False`, the status bar will display only the `Text` property. This would be equivalent to setting the VB6 status bar control `Style` property to `sbrSimple`
- ❑ The StatusBar control docks to the bottom of the parent control by default. (See section on docking.) You could change this if you want (although we're not sure how intuitive a floating status bar would be)

TabControl
- ❑ Formerly known as the `TabStrip` control
- ❑ Now has a `TabPages` collection of `TabPage` objects. A `TabPage` object is a subclass of the Panel control specialized for use in the `TabControl`
- ❑ Uses the `Appearance` property to display the tabs as buttons if desired (formerly the `Style` property of the `TabStrip` control)

TextBox
- ❑ Now has a `CharacterCasing` property that can automatically adjust the text entered into upper, or lower-case
- ❑ `ReadOnly` property now used to prevent the text from being edited. This used to be the `Locked` property

  Note: The `Locked` property now determines if the control can be moved or resized

- ❑ Now has `Cut`, `Copy`, `Paste`, `Undo`, and `ClearUndo` methods

Timer
- ❑ Essentially unchanged from previous versions
- ❑ The timer is now *disabled* by default
- ❑ You cannot set the interval to zero to disable it

ToolBar
- ❑ See previous section

ToolTip – New!
- ❑ Adding a tooltip control creates a new property for the various controls on your form. For instance, if your tooltip control is called `ToolTip1`, and you have a textbox on your form, the textbox will have a new property called `Tooltip on Tooltip1`. If you assign some text to this property, the textbox will automatically display it as its tooltip. You can have multiple tooltip controls on your form if you wish, but assigning text to both of them for the same control will give you two overlapping tooltips on the screen – something to obviously avoid

TrackBar
- ❑ Formerly known as the Slider control, essentially unchanged

TreeView
- ❑ Same functionality as in VB6 but with a new **Node Tree Editor** that allows you to visually design the tree

VScrollBar
- ❑ Unchanged

Retired Controls

Some controls have also been 'retired'. The following list outlines the controls from VB6 that you won't find in VB.Net, and how to reproduce their functionality:

Spinner
- ❑ Use the `DomainUpDown` or `NumericUpDown` control

Line and Shape
- ❑ VB.NET has no line or shape control, nor any immediate equivalent. A 'cheap' way of reproducing a horizontal or vertical line is to use a label control. Set its background color to that of the line you want, and then either the `Size.Height` or `Size.Width` value to 1
- ❑ Diagonal lines and shapes must be drawn using GDI+ graphics methods

DirListBox, FileListBox, DriveListBox

- ❑ You would typically use these controls to create a file system browser similar to Windows Explorer. VB.NET has no equivalent controls. You can use the `OpenFileDialog` and `SaveFileDialog` (see previous section) to accomplish your needs in most circumstances.

Image
- ❑ Use the `PictureBox` control

Using ActiveX Controls

While VB.NET is optimized to use Windows Forms controls, you can certainly place an ActiveX control on your form and use it as well.

To do this, right-click on your toolbox and select Customize Toolbox. The first tab will display all the COM controls registered on your system. Simply select the controls you wish to use and they will be added to your toolbox, from where you can add them to your form. When you add an ActiveX control to the toolbox, VB.NET essentially wraps the functionality in order to make it work in the .NET framework. Keep in mind that adding an ActiveX control to your application can add significantly to the size of the compiled application. ActiveX controls must also be registered on the system which is a big step backward in comparison to .NET's "xcopy deployment" strategy.

Other Handy Programming Tips

Switch the Focus to a Control
- ❑ Use the `.Focus()` method. To set the focus to `TextBox1`, for example, use the following code:

```
TextBox1.Focus()
```

Change the Cursor

❏   To switch the cursor to an hourglass, for example, use the `Cursor` object as follows:

```
Cursor.Current = Cursors.WaitCursor ' hourglass
Cursor.Current = Cursors.Default ' pointer
```

Quickly Determine the Container Control or Parent Form

❏   With the use of group boxes and panels, controls are often contained many times removed from the ultimate form. You can now use the `FindForm` method to immediately get a reference to the form. Use the `GetContainerControl` method to access the immediate parent of a control.

Traversing the Tab Order

❏   Use the `GetNextControl` method of any control to get a reference to the next control on the form in the tab order.

Convert Client Coordinates to Screen Coordinates (and back)

❏   Want to know where a control is in screen coordinates? Use the `PointToScreen` method. Convert back using the `PointToClient` method.

Change the Z-Order of Controls at Runtime

❏   Controls now have both `BringToFront` and `SendToBack` methods.

Where is the Mouse Pointer?

❏   The control class now exposes a `MousePosition` property that returns the location of the mouse in screen coordinates.

Managing Child Controls

❏   Container controls such as a group box or panel can use the `HasChildren` property and `Controls` property to determine the existence of, and direct references to, child controls respectively.

Maximize, Minimize, Restore a Form

❏   Use the form's `WindowState` property.

Summary

The new features and improvements to Windows Forms in VS.NET mean that countless tasks required by virtually every application that used to be awkward are now simple and elegant. It would seem that the Windows Forms team at Microsoft just never let up when it comes to improving the tools. This chapter has run through all of the significant enhancements to Windows Forms which are now available in VB.NET, and how developers can take advantage of these when either updating existing applications or indeed writing new ones. Using these tools should prove both enjoyable and productive – happy coding!

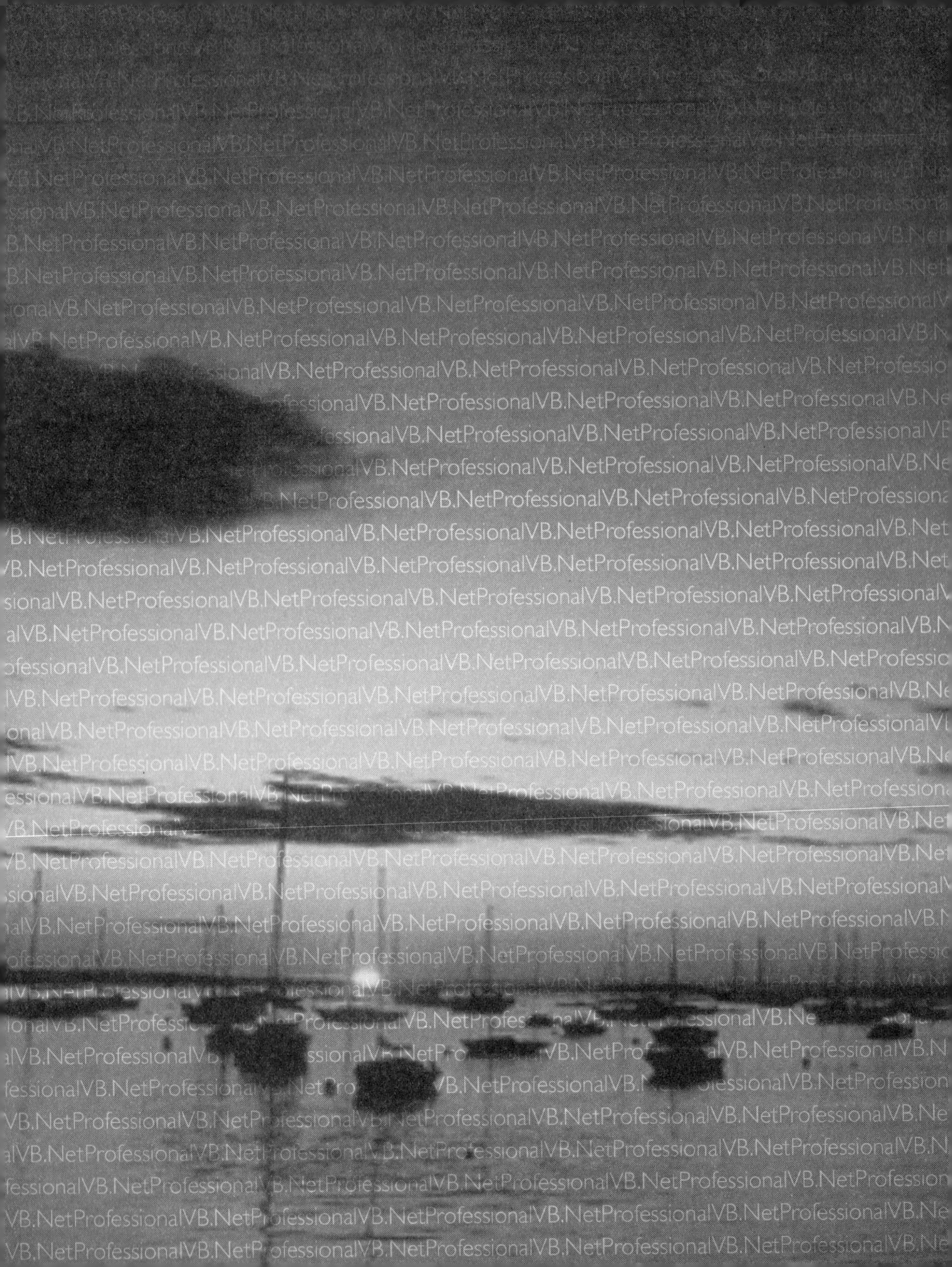
VB.NetProfessional

9

Error Handling

Error handling is an important topic in any programming language. If a program lets errors through the users will be confused and the program will not produce the results that were originally intended.

In this chapter, we will cover how error handling works in VB.NET by discussing the CLR exception handler in detail and the programming methods that are most efficient in catching errors. We will begin by discussing error handling in general. Next, we will discuss the Try...Catch...Finally structure, the Exit Try statement, and nested Try structures, and the exception handler's methods and properties. We will then go on to discuss error handling between managed and unmanaged code, and how VB.NET assists us in that area. We will finish up with talking about error and trace logging and how we can use these methods to obtain feedback on how our program is working.

The CLR Exception Handler

The error handling techniques within Visual Basic have, in the past, been very much left up to developers. Left to our own devices, we came up with many very effective methods of handling exceptions and ensuring our users could report any errors to us effectively, however, there was lack of built-in VB routines to handle this. The CLR has provided us with an Exception object, which inherits from the System.Exception class in VB.NET. This Exception object provides developers with a standard exception handling mechanism, which has a long track record of success in the C++ development environment.

All exceptions in VB.NET inherit from System.Exception. The Exception object is extended through many namespaces in the runtime environment. Below is a table of some of the most common namespaces and the classes that extend the exception functionality:

Namespace	Class
System	ApplicationException
	SystemException
	VB6Exception
System.Data	InvalidConstraintException
System.IO	IOException
System.Runtime.InteropServices	COMException
System.Web.Services.Protocols	SoapException
System.XML	XmlException

The System namespace holds many of the Exception classes that happen on a routine basis in our applications. Below is a table of some of the Exception classes that exist within the System namespace and their descriptions:

Class	Description
ApplicationException	Occurs when a non-fatal application error occurs
ArgumentNullException	Occurs when a Null argument is passed and cannot be accepted as Null
DivideByZeroException	Occurs when a 0 is used as a divisor in an arithmetic routine
MissingFieldException	Occurs in an attempt to access a non-existent field
MissingMemberException	Indicates a DLL versioning problem
OutofMemoryException	Occurs when there is not enough memory to continue
OverflowException	Occurs in an arithmetic overflow situation
SystemException	Occurs when a recoverable exception occurs
Vb6Exception	Occurs when an exception occurs with a function within the VB6 compatibility library

Standardizing Error Handling

Standardizing error handling within our VB applications is an important consideration when writing code. If the error handling code isn't standardized, errors could happen outside our error handling structures and bring our application to an abrupt, ungraceful stop. Indeed, the whole idea behind error handling is to gracefully handle unexpected events so that the user of our application can report the error and continue without losing data.

The concept behind error handling begins with the ability to accurately trap the error. In the .NET application architecture the error may not only not be part of the set of modules in the current VB project, but originate in a module on another entirely separate machine. Our aim should be to cover any code that could raise an error and handle any errors in a uniform manner. Programmers still have to make decisions as to how to present the errors to a user (with message boxes, application log generation or any other approach), the outcome being consistency.

Still included in VB.NET are our VB6 On Error statements available with the Err object. The On Error statement requires a section of code that executes the GoTo statement, which goes to a label that contains error handling code, which should informally handle our exception and present it to the user. Your goal should be to standardize this error handling code within your modules as well as determining how to standardize the way errors are handled in your Try...Catch...Finally blocks of code.

The On Error Statement

When thinking about the concept of global error handling it is important to differentiate between the use of the On Error statement in VB and the new Try...Catch...Finally model available in .NET.

In situations where there is a system error during a call to a DLL, the On Error statement is the only way the error will trapped. In this case, the error can be caught by checking the Err object and its properties for the details of the error.

The On Error statement is the recommended approach for error trapping from a global perspective because without it any runtime exception is fatal in our application. The traditional On Error statement still has a solid place in our programming environment because we want to prevent these fatal errors in situations where the Try...Catch...Finally block would be cumbersome to use.

> Note that the **On Error** statement cannot be used when a **Try...Catch...Finally** block is already present in a procedure.

Most readers will be familiar with the On Error statement, but if you've not programmed with versions of VB prior to VB.NET here's an example:

```
Sub CustomErrorExample()
    On Error Goto ErrorHandler
    Dim intX As Integer
    Dim intY As Integer
    Dim intZ As Integer
    intY = 0
    intX = 5
    ' Cause a "Divide by Zero"
    intZ = intX / intY
    MessageBox.Show(Str(intZ))

    Exit Sub

ErrorHandler:
    UnhandledExceptionHandler()
End Sub
```

In our example above we force a divide-by-zero error to occur by initializing our divisor variable to be zero and then using it in a division problem, but this approach would work well for any other system error that may be thrown while this procedure is running.

We start our code by setting up our On Error statement that refers to the ErrorHandler label at the bottom of our procedure:

```
On Error Goto ErrorHandler
```

Then when our divide-by-zero error occurs, the code after the `ErrorHandler` label is executed. In this case, we have referred to another subroutine within the same class. Here we have standardized the manner in which we will handle exceptions caught by our `On Error` statement. Any code that needs to be in the error handler to trap and handle any specific errors we would want to treat would be placed in this subroutine. The standard error handler just shows a simple message box so that the user can report the error to the programmer:

```
Sub UnhandledExceptionHandler()
    MessageBox.Show("Unhandled Error:" & Err.Description)
End Sub
```

In addition to familiar properties such as `Description`, the `Err` object now has a `GetException` method that returns an `Exception` object, which we'll be looking at shortly.

The Exception Handler

In this section, we will be going over examples that illustrate the exception handler, its structures, properties, and methods. We'll start by looking at the `Try...Catch...Finally` block structure and how we can include `Exit Try` statements and create nested `Try` structures. We'll then go into detail about the properties and methods within the `Exception` object by looking at examples that utilize them.

Try...Catch...Finally

The exception handler for VB.NET uses the `Try...Catch...Finally` blocks found in the past only in the C++ language. Under this model a `Try...Catch...Finally` block of code surrounds the code where an exception might occur. The simple `Try` statement comes before the block of code, the `Catch` block of code is where we specify what types of errors to look for, and the `Finally` block of code is always executed and contains cleanup routines for exception situations. Since the `Catch` block is specific to the type of error we want to catch, we will often use multiple `Catch` blocks in our `Try...Catch...Finally` structure.

For our examples below, we need an `Imports System.Windows.Forms` statement in the class declaration section so that we can use the `Messagebox.Show` method. Let's look at a very simple piece of code that will cause a divide-by-zero error to occur:

```
Sub HandlerExample()
    Dim intX As Integer
    Dim intY As Integer
    Dim intZ As Integer

    intY = 0
    intX = 5

    ' First Required Error Statement.
    Try
        ' Cause a "Divide by Zero"
        intZ = intX / intY
    ' Catch the error.
    Catch objA As System.OverflowException
```

```
         Messagebox.Show("Caught the divide by zero error")
    Catch
         Messagebox.Show("Caught any other errors")
    ' Finally section always gets processed after a try
    Finally
         Messagebox.Show(Str(intZ))
    ' End of try loop
    End Try

End Sub
```

Note how we have surrounded all the code that has potential to cause an error within our
Try...Catch...Finally block. In our example we have two Catch statements. The first one demonstrates
catching a specific error, that of an overflow caused by a divide-by-zero condition, and allowing us to use the
properties of the Exception object by populating the variable objA with it:

```
Catch objA As System.OverflowException
     Messagebox.Show("Caught the divide by zero error")
```

The message box displayed when this code is run will look like
the following:

The other statement that we include catches any other errors that occur in our Try block (this code block will
be skipped over as we don't have any other errors in our code):

```
Catch
     Messagebox.Show("Caught any other errors")
```

> When we have a specific Catch statement, it is a good idea to also have a second statement
> to catch any other errors. Then, if an error passes the first Catch, the second will
> certainly catch it.

After catching the error the Finally block executes and displays a message box
with the value of intZ in our code, which in this case is 0 because the integer was
initialized to that and the division problem didn't complete due to our divide-by-
zero error:

Finally blocks are optional, however, they are always executed if present. There is usually cleanup code
that needs to go at the end of our Try blocks, and it fits nicely into our Finally portion of the structure.

The Exit Try Statement

The Exit Try statement will break out of the Try or Catch block and continue at the Finally block under a given circumstance. Let's look at an example of the use of an Exit Try statement. In our example below, we are going to exit a Catch block if the value of intY is 0 because we know that our overflow error was caused by a divide-by-zero error:

```
Sub HandlerExample2()
    Dim intX As Integer
    Dim intY As Integer
    Dim intZ As Integer

    intY = 0
    intX = 5

    Try
        ' Cause a "Divide by Zero"
        intZ = intX / intY
    ' Catch the error.
    Catch objA As System.OverflowException
        MessageBox.Show("Caught the divide by zero error")
        If intY = 0 Then
            Exit Try
        Else
            MessageBox.Show("Error not divide by 0")
        End If
    Catch
        MessageBox.Show("Caught any other errors")
    Finally
        MessageBox.Show(Str(intZ))
    End Try
End Sub
```

In our first Catch block we have inserted an If block, so that we can exit the block given a certain condition (in this case that the overflow exception was caused by the value of intY being 0). The Exit Try goes immediately to the Finally block and completes the processing there:

```
        If intY = 0 Then
            Exit Try
        Else
            MessageBox.Show("Error not divide by 0")
        End If
```

Now if the overflow exception is caused by something other than a divide-by-zero we'll get a message box displaying Error not divide by zero.

Nested Try Structures

Errors can occur within the Catch portion of the Try structures, and cause further exceptions to occur. The ability to nest Try structures is available so that we can use a second Try structure to cover exceptions that could occur in code executing within the Catch portion of the initial try structure.

In our following example, we will use the new Throw method to raise a custom error. It's often helpful to be able to throw our own more general exceptions both to make it easier for users to report an error, and also to be able to handle similar exceptions in a standard way:

```
Sub HandlerExample3()
    Dim intX As Integer
    Dim intY As Integer
    Dim intZ As Integer

    intY = 0
    intX = 5

    ' First Required Error Statement.
    Try
        ' Cause a "Divide by Zero"
        intZ = intX / intY
    ' Catch the error.
    Catch objA As System.OverflowException
        Messagebox.Show(objA.Message)

        Try
            Throw (New Exception("0 as divisor"))
        Catch objB As Exception
            Messagebox.Show(objB.Message)
        End Try

    Catch
        Messagebox.Show("Caught any other errors")
    Finally
        Messagebox.Show(Str(intZ))
    End Try
End Sub
```

First, note now that the `Message` property of our `objA` exception object is displaying our divide-by-zero error:

```
Messagebox.Show(objA.Message)
```

This will result in a message box that looks like this:

Next, a nested `Try` structure catches another error within our `Catch` block, which is deliberately raised by the `Throw` method. The `Throw` method requires a type of exception to be thrown, here we have just specified a generic `Exception` object with a `Message` property of `"0 as divisor"`:

```
Try
    Throw (New Exception("0 as divisor"))
Catch objB As Exception
    Messagebox.Show(objB.Message)
End Try
```

The resulting message box would look like this, the reason for our exception is now much more obvious to the end user:

> Note that the nested **Try** structure does not have a **Finally** statement. At a bare minimum, the **Try...Catch...Finally** structure requires a **Try** and an **End Try**, with either a **Catch** or a **Finally** block; otherwise, we'll get a syntax error.

The Exception's Properties and Methods

The Exception class has properties that relate to each portion of the exception. In this section, we will discuss by way of example the properties and methods of the object and how they are used. We'll start with tables of the properties and methods, and descriptions of each. We'll then continue with examples of the properties and methods, and how each can be used within our Try...Catch...Finally structures.

Below is a table of the properties of the Exception class:

Property	Description
HelpLink	A string indicating the link to the help for this exception
InnerException	Returns the exception object reference to an inner (nested) exception
Message	A string that contains the error
Source	A string containing the name of an object that generated the error
StackTrace	A read-only property that holds the stack trace as a text string
TargetSite	A read-only string property that holds the method that threw the exception

Below is a table of the methods of the Exception class:

Method	Description
Equals	Determines if one exception object is equal to another
GetBaseException	Returns the first exception in the chain
GetHashCode	Similar to a hash table, serves as a hash function
GetObjectData	Used to hold the data in the Exception object when serializing it
GetType	Gets the type of the object which caused the exception
ToString	Returns the error string, which might include as much information as the error message, the inner exceptions, and stack trace, depending on the error

The `Message` property has been used in our previous examples of the `Try...Catch...Finally` block, so let's look at some examples of how the other properties and methods listed above can be used.

InnerException and TargetSite

The `InnerException` property is used to store an exception trail. This comes in handy when multiple exceptions occur. It's quite common for an exception to occur that sets up circumstances whereby further exceptions are raised. As exceptions occur in a sequence, we can choose to **stack** our exceptions for later reference by use of the `InnerException` property of our `Exception` object. As each exception joins the stack, the previous `Exception` object becomes the inner exception in the stack.

We'll be extending our previous code sample, but this time we'll be adding a reference to an `InnerException` object to the exception we are generating with the `Throw` method:

```
Sub HandlerExample4()
    Dim intX As Integer
    Dim intY As Integer
    Dim intZ As Integer

    intY = 0
    intX = 5

    ' First Required Error Statement.
    Try
        ' Cause a "Divide by Zero"
        intZ = intX / intY
    ' Catch the error.
    Catch objA As System.OverflowException

        Try
            Throw (New Exception("0 as divisor", objA))
        Catch objB As Exception
          Messagebox.Show(objB.Message)
          Messagebox.Show(objB.InnerException.Message)
          Messagebox.Show(objB.TargetSite.Name)
        End Try

    Catch
        Messagebox.Show("Caught any other errors")
    Finally
        Messagebox.Show(Str(intZ))
    End Try
End Sub
```

As before, we catch the divide-by-zero error in the following statement, which stores our exception in `objA` so that we can reference its properties later:

```
    Catch objA As System.OverflowException
```

We throw a new exception with a more general message (`"0 as divisor"`) that is easier to interpret and build up our stack by appending `objA` as the `InnerException` object at the end of our `New Exception` statement:

```
        Throw (New Exception("0 as divisor", objA))
```

We catch our newly thrown exception in another `Catch` statement. Note that it does not catch any specific type of error:

```
Catch objB As Exception
```

We then display three message boxes:

```
Messagebox.Show(objB.Message)
Messagebox.Show(objB.InnerException.Message)
Messagebox.Show(objB.TargetSite.Name)
```

The message box that is produced by our custom error, which is held in the `objB` variable, looks like this:

The `InnerException` property is holding the exception object that was generated first. The `Message` property of the `InnerException` looks like this:

The `TargetSite` property gives us the name of the method that threw our exception. This information comes in handy when troubleshooting and thus could be integrated into the error message so that the end user could report the method name back to us in case of an error. In our example, we have displayed the value of this property in a message box for illustration – the currently executing method is `HandlerExample4` as shown:

Source and StackTrace

The `Source` and `StackTrace` properties provide the user with information regarding where the error occurred. This supplemental information can be invaluable for the user to pass on to the troubleshooter and help get errors resolved more quickly. The example below uses these two properties and shows the feedback when the error occurs:

```
Sub HandlerExample5()
    Dim intX As Integer
    Dim intY As Integer
    Dim intZ As Integer
```

```
        intY = 0
        intX = 5

        ' First Required Error Statement.
        Try
            ' Cause a "Divide by Zero"
            intZ = intX / intY
        ' Catch the error.
        Catch objA As System.OverflowException
            objA.Source = "HandlerExample5"
            Messagebox.Show("Error Occurred at :" & _
                objA.Source & objA.StackTrace)
        Finally
            Messagebox.Show(Str(intZ))
        End Try
    End Sub
```

The output from our message box statement is very detailed and gives the entire path and line number where our error occurred as shown:

Error Occurred at :HandlerExample5   at WindowsApplication11.Form1.HandlerExample5() in C:\Documents and Settings\kateh\My Documents\Visual Studio Projects\WindowsApplication11\Form1.vb:line 70

OK

GetBaseException, GetHashCode, and Equals

The GetBaseException method comes in very handy when deep in a set of thrown exceptions. This method returns the originating exception, which makes debugging easier and helps keep the troubleshooting process on track by sorting through information that can be misleading.

The GetHashCode method allows a programmer to generate a unique number for assignment to an object. An object will always return the same result to the GetHashCode method, and so can be used in comparing to see if two reference type objects are the same.

The Equals method will evaluate whether one exception is identical to another.

Below are examples of each of these methods:

```
Sub HandlerExample6()
    Dim intX As Integer
    Dim intY As Integer
    Dim intZ As Integer

    intY = 0
    intX = 5

    ' First Required Error Statement.
    Try
        ' Cause a "Divide by Zero"
```

```
        intZ = intX / intY
    ' Catch the error.
    Catch objA As System.OverflowException

        Try
            Throw (New Exception("0 as divisor", objA))
            Catch objB As Exception
                Messagebox.Show(str(objB.GetHashCode))

            If objA.Equals(objB.InnerException) Then
                Messagebox.Show("Exceptions the same")
            End If

            Try
                Throw (New Exception("New error", objB))
            Catch objC As Exception
                Messagebox.Show(objC.GetBaseException.Message)
            End Try
        End Try

    Finally
        Messagebox.Show(Str(intZ))
    End Try
End Sub
```

In the code where we have used `GetHashCode`, the system generates a hash code and returns it, so that we can display it in a message box that looks like this:

The hash code generated will vary on different computers and at different instances of the object. Hashcode generation is truly unique for each computer and instance of an object on each computer.

We can also evaluate whether `objA` is the same as the `InnerException` object of another exception, in this case `objB`:

```
        If objA.Equals(objB.InnerException) Then
            Messagebox.Show("Exceptions the same")
        End If
```

The two exception objects are evaluated to be the same:

The InnerException property provides the information that the GetBaseException method needs; therefore, as our example executes the Throw statements, they set up the InnerException property. The purpose of the GetBaseException method is to provide the properties of the initial exception in the chain that was produced. Hence, objC.GetBaseException.Message returns the Message property of the original OverflowException message even though we've thrown multiple errors since the original error occurred:

```
Messagebox.Show(objC.GetBaseException.Message)
```

To put it another way, the code traverses back to the exception caught as objA, and displays the same message as the objA.Message property would, that being:

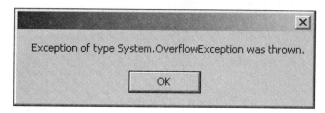

GetType and ToString

The GetType and ToString methods return more valuable information about the error message and how and when it was generated. The GetType method returns additional information about the type of error that occurred. The GetType method inherits from the Object class and has many of the Object class's properties and methods. The GetType method can return such things as the full name of the exception type, the base class of the exception type, whether the exception type is public or is an interface, and even what namespace the exception type belongs to. In the following example, we have illustrated two properties of the GetType method, those being FullName and BaseType.FullName:

```
Sub HandlerExample7()
    Dim intX As Integer
    Dim intY As Integer
    Dim intZ As Integer

    intY = 0
    intX = 5

    ' First Required Error Statement.
    Try
        ' Cause a "Divide by Zero"
        intZ = intX / intY
    ' Catch the error.
    Catch objA As System.OverflowException
        Messagebox.Show(objA.GetType.FullName)
        Messagebox.Show(objA.GetType.BaseType.FullName)
        Messagebox.Show(objA.ToString)
    Finally
        Messagebox.Show(Str(intZ))
    End Try
End Sub
```

The first message box that we show contains the full name of our error and is displayed by the code:

```
Messagebox.Show(objA.GetType.FullName)
```

The message box itself looks like:

Our second message box is displayed by the following code:

```
Messagebox.Show(objA.GetType.BaseType.FullName)
```

The message that shows the `BaseType.FullName` looks like this:

The `ToString` method returns a combination of the `GetType.Fullname` method, the `Message` property and the `StackTrace` property of the current exception. In our code, the message box that displays the `ToString` method is:

```
Messagebox.Show(objA.ToString)
```

The message box displayed looks like this:

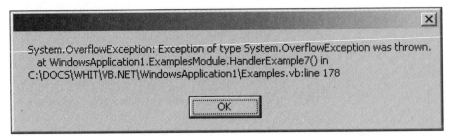

HelpLink

The `HelpLink` property sets the help link for a specific `Exception` object to a string. The example below shows the syntax for the `HelpLink` property:

```
Sub HandlerExample8()
    Dim intX As Integer
    Dim intY As Integer
    Dim intZ As Integer

    intY = 0
```

```
        intX = 5

        ' First Required Error Statement.
        Try
            ' Cause a "Divide by Zero"
            intZ = intX / intY
        ' Catch the error.
        Catch objA As System.OverflowException
            objA.HelpLink = ("file:///C:/test/help.html")
            Messagebox.Show(objA.HelpLink)
        Finally
            Messagebox.Show(Str(intZ))
        End Try
    End Sub
```

This results in the following screenshot:

Error Handling between Managed and Unmanaged Code

The ability to trace the stack of calls in an application all the way back to the originating module and location of the module becomes a very important factor if you have interoperability between new VB.NET code and old VB6 code. This ability to trace the stack of calls can help us in determining our next action, based on what kind of error the application got and where it happened.

If an OLEDB error happened in a module running as a COM object on another machine while doing interactions with database data, we may want to react to the problem differently from if we got that same type of error on a local machine. In addition, as errors pass through layers of code, some errors will generate other errors, perhaps misleading us as to what the original error actually was. That is why it is so important to be able to trap the location of the error, as well as accurately being able to identify the error. We accomplish this in VB.NET by using stack-tracing properties provided in the runtime environment.

In VB.NET the error handling between managed and unmanaged code is now handled through the automatic population of an Exception object that carries through to the front-end application. We can use the properties and methods of the Exception object that we have already discussed to find out the information we need to proceed appropriately.

Our example of error handling will use an unmanaged VB6 component on the back-end that generates a divide-by-zero error. The purpose of our unmanaged component is to perform an arithmetic operation on data to derive an answer and pass the answer back to the front-end application. The VB6 DLL is called VBNet.dll and needs to be included as a reference in the VB.NET application on the front-end. The VB6 DLL has a class called Unmanaged, which has a function called CauseError. The DLL will pass the overflow error back through to the front-end application where there is code to display it accordingly.

We'll look now at the function we exposed within the VB6 DLL. The class is named Unmanaged, with the function named CauseError:

```
Function CauseError() As Integer
    Dim iResult As Integer
    Dim iDividor As Integer
    Dim iDivisor As Integer

    iDivisor = 5
    iDivisor = 0

    iResult = iDividor / iDivisor

    CauseError = iResult

End Function
```

Now, as we can see in our code, it is set up to do a simple math problem, and we have forced a divide-by-zero error to occur and go untrapped back to the calling application:

```
iDivisor = 5
iDivisor = 0

iResult = iDividor / iDivisor
```

The line of code that generates the error causes an `Exception` object to be passed back to the front-end application, where it will be handled and alert the user to do extra work to resolve our problem. The fact that an exception has been thrown takes us out of the `CauseError` function and populates an `Exception` object to return to the front-end application.

Now let's look at our front-end code; the `ComponentExample` subroutine in a **VB.NET** project calls our `CauseError` function and determines what to do based on whether the `Exception` object is populated:

```
Sub ComponentExample()
    Dim objX As New VBNet.Unmanaged()
    Dim intY As Integer

    Try
        intY = objX.CauseError
        MessageBox.Show("The answer is: " & intY)
    Catch a As System.Exception
        MessageBox.Show("Caught Error:" & _
            a.Message & " " & a.Source)
    End Try

    objX = Nothing
End Sub
```

If you don't have VB6, you can find VBNet.dll in the source code downloadable from the Wrox web site.

We first instantiate an instance of our unmanaged component:

```
Dim objX As New VBNet.Unmanaged()
```

We then call our component returning the numeric result to a variable so that we can deal with it later:

```
intY = objX.CauseError
```

When the component returns the error, we display properties of the `Exception` object in a message box:

```
Catch a As System.Exception
    MessageBox.Show("Caught Error:" & _
        a.Message & " " & a.Source)
```

Our message box looks like this:

Error Logging

Error logging is important in many applications as an alternative way to decipher what exactly is going on when errors occur. It is common for end-users of the applications to not remember what the error said exactly and so we can trap specific errors in a log for ease of finding in such situations that we don't want to re-create the error in order to get the specific error message.

While error logging is very important, we only want to use it to trap specific levels of errors, as it carries overhead and can reduce the performance of our application. In general, the overhead it carries is writing the events to the log on a hard disk, which is an extra step in our application that isn't always necessary. The impact to our program will vary, as the hard disk speed varies on each system that the program is running on. We want to only log errors that will be critical to our application integrity, for instance an error that would cause the data that the application is working with to become invalid.

There are two main approaches to error logging:

❑   Many programmers use a trace file based approach, which would write any information in a free-form style to a simple text file located in a strategic location.

❑   We can also take advantage of the event log that is available on NT and Windows 2000 based machines. VB.NET now provides a component that can be used to write and read from the system, application, and security logs on any given machine.

The type of logging you choose depends on the categories of errors you wish to trap and the types of machine you will run your application on. If you choose to write to the event log, you need to categorize the errors and write them in the appropriate log file. Resource-, hardware-, and system-level errors would best fit into the system event log. Data access errors would fit best into the application event log. Permission errors would best fit into the security event log. Since the event log only is available on NT or Windows 2000 machines, the trace file method of logging would be a good choice if the need is to support other client machines.

The Event Log

The **event log** is available on NT and Windows 2000 based machines. There are three logs on these machines, these being the system, application, and security logs.

The event logging operations, while available since VB6, have greatly been enhanced through an event log component that allows a programmer both read and write capabilities with all of the available logs on a machine. The `EventLog` component is part of the `System.Diagnostics` namespace and is accessed through adding the namespace as a reference to the VB.NET project. The component is what provides us with functionality such as adding and removing custom event logs, reading and writing from the standard Windows event logs and creating customized event log entries.

> *In contrast, Visual Basic versions 5.0 and 6.0 exposed only three methods and properties of the `App` object by which event logging can be enabled, which were the `LogMode` property, the `LogPath` property, and the `LogEvent` method. The `LogMode` and `LogPath` properties returned information about how and where logging happened, and the `LogEvent` method wrote an event to the application log.*

Event logs can get full, as they have a limited amount of space, so we only want to write critical information to our event logs. We can customize each of our system event log's properties by changing the log size and determining how the system will handle events that occur when the log is full. We can configure the log to overwrite when it is full, or overwrite all events older than a given number of days. It is important to remember that the event log that is written to is based on where the code is running from, so that if there are many tiers we can locate the proper event log information to research the error further.

There are five types of event log entries we can make. These five types are separated into event type entries and audit type entries.

Event type entries are:

- **Information** – added when events such as a service starting or stopping occurs
- **Warning** – occurs when a non-critical event occurs that might cause future problems, such as disk space getting low
- **Error** – should be logged when something occurs that will prevent normal processing, such as a startup service not being able to start

Audit type entries will usually go into the security log and can be either:

- **Success audit** – for example, a success audit might be a successful login through an application to a SQL Server
- **Failure audit** – a failure audit might come in handy if a user doesn't have access to create an output file on a certain file system

If we don't specify the type of event log entry an information type entry is generated.

Each entry in an event log has a `Source` property. The `Source` property is required, and is a programmer-defined string that is assigned to an event that helps categorize the events in a log. A new `Source` must be defined prior to being used in an entry in an event log. The `SourceExists` method is used to determine if a particular source already exists on the given computer. We recommend that you use a string that is easily sorted based on where the error originated such as the component name, or a programmer-defined grouping for the source. For instance, packaged software often uses the software name as the Source in the application log. As shown in the following screenshot, this helps group errors that occur by any given software package:

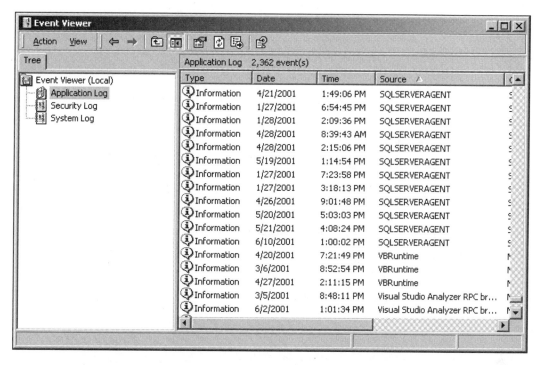

The `EventLog` object model is based on the `System.Diagnostics` namespace. Therefore, in order to use the `EventLog` component, you need to include an `Imports System.Diagnostics` statement in the declarations section of your code.

> Note that certain security rights must be obtained in order to manipulate event logs. Ordinary programs can read all of the event logs and write to the application event log. Special privileges, on the administrator level, are required to perform tasks such as clearing and deleting event logs.

The most common events, methods, and properties are listed and described in the following tables:

Event	Description
EntryWritten	Generated when an event is written to a log

Methods	Description
CreateEventSource	Creates an event source in the specified log
DeleteEventSource	Deletes an event source and associated entries
WriteEntry	Writes a string to a specified log
Exists	This can be used to determine if a specific event log exists

Table continued on following page

Methods	Description
SourceExists	Used to determine if a specific source exists in a log
GetEventLogs	Retrieves a list of all event logs on a particular computer
Delete	Deletes an entire event log – *use this method with care*

Properties	Description
Source	Specifies the source of the entry to be written.
Log	Used to specify a log to write to. The three logs are system, application, and security. The system log is the default if not specified.

Below is an example that illustrates some of the methods and properties listed above:

```
Sub LoggingExample1()

    Dim objLog As New EventLog()
    Dim objLogEntryType As EventLogEntryType

    Try
        Throw (New EntryPointNotFoundException())
    Catch objA As System.EntryPointNotFoundException
        If Not objLog.SourceExists("Example") Then
            objLog.CreateEventSource("Example", "System")
        End If
        objLog.Source = "Example"
        objLog.Log = "System"
        objLogEntryType = EventLogEntryType.Information
        objLog.WriteEntry("Error: " & objA.Message, objLogEntryType)
    End Try

End Sub
```

We have declared two variables – one to instantiate our log and the other to hold our entry's type information. Note that we need to check for the existence of a source prior to creating it. These two lines of code accomplish this:

```
If Not objLog.SourceExists("Example") Then
    objLog.CreateEventSource("Example", "System")
```

Once we have verified or created our source, we can then set the `Source` property of the `EventLog` object, set the `Log` property to specify which log we want to write to, and `EventLogEntryType` to `Information` (other choices are `Warning`, `Error`, `SuccessAudit`, and `FailureAudit`). If we attempt to write to a source that does not exist in a specific log, we will get an error. After we have set these three properties of our `EventLog` object, we then can write our entry. In our example, we concatenated the word `Error` with the actual exception's `Message` property to form our string to write to our log:

```
objLog.Source = "Example"
objLog.Log = "System"
objLogEntryType = EventLogEntryType.Information
objLog.WriteEntry("Error: " & objA.Message, objLogEntryType)
```

The following is the copy of the event log that was generated from our example:

Event Type:	Information
Event Source:	Example
Event Category:	None
Event ID:	0
Date:	6/2/2001
Time:	9:42:54 AM
User:	N/A
Computer:	Computer01
Description:	The description for Event ID (0) in Source (Example) cannot be found. The local computer may not have the necessary registry information or message DLL files to display messages from a remote computer. The following information is part of the event: Error: Attempt to load the class failed.

Writing to Trace Files

As an alternative on platforms that don't support event logging, or if we can't get direct access to the event log, we can write our debugging and error information to trace files. A **trace file** is a text-based file that we generate in our program to track detailed information about an error condition. Trace files are also a good way to supplement our event logging on Windows NT and Windows 2000 machines if we wish to track detailed information that would potentially fill our event log.

A more detailed explanation of the variety of trace tools and uses in debugging follows in the *Measuring Performance via the Trace Class* section of this chapter, but we will cover some of the techniques for using the StreamWriter interface in our development of a trace file in this section.

The concepts involved in writing to text files include setting up **streamwriters** and **debug listeners**. The StreamWriter interface is handled through the System.IO namespace and allows us to interface to the files in the file system on a given machine. The Debug class interfaces with these output objects through listener objects. The job of any listener object is to collect, store up, and send the stored output to text files, logs, and the Output window. In our example, we will use the TextWriterTraceListener interface.

As we will see, the StreamWriter object opens an output path to a text file, and by binding the StreamWriter object to a listener object we can direct debug output to a text file.

TraceListeners are output targets and can be a TextWriter class, an EventLog class, or route output to the default Output window (which is DefaultTraceListener). The TextWriterTraceListener accommodates the WriteLine method of a Debug interface by providing an output object that stores up information to be flushed to the output stream, which we setup by the StreamWriter interface.

Following is a table of commonly used methods from the `StreamWriter` object:

Method	Description
Close	Closes the `StreamWriter`.
Flush	Flushes all the content of the `StreamWriter` to the output file designated upon creation of the `StreamWriter`.
Write	Writes byte output to the stream. Optional parameters allow designation of where in the stream (offset).
WriteLine	Writes characters followed by a line terminator to the current stream object.

Below is a table of the methods associated with the `Debug` object, which provides the output mechanism for our text file example to follow:

Method	Description
Assert	Checks a condition and displays a message if `False`
Close	Executes a flush on the output buffer and closes all listeners
Fail	Emits an error message in the form of an Abort/Retry/Ignore message box
Flush	Flushes the output buffer and writes it to the listeners
Write	Writes bytes to the output buffer
WriteLine	Writes characters followed by a line terminator to the output buffer
WriteIf	Writes bytes to the output buffer given a specific condition is `True`
WriteLineIF	Writes characters followed by a line terminator to the output buffer if a specific condition is `True`

Below is an example of how we can open an existing file (called `mytext.txt`) for output and assign it to the `Listeners` object of the `Debug` object so it can catch our `Debug.WriteLine` statements:

```
Sub LoggingExample2()
    Dim objWriter As New _
        IO.StreamWriter(File.Open("c:\mytext.txt", FileMode.Open))
    Debug.Listeners.Add(New TextWriterTraceListener(objWriter))
    Try
        Throw (New EntryPointNotFoundException())
    Catch objA As System.EntryPointNotFoundException
        Debug.WriteLine(objA.Message)
        objWriter.Flush()
        objWriter.Close()
        objWriter = Nothing
    End Try
End Sub
```

Looking in detail at our code above, we first create a `StreamWriter` that is assigned to a file in our local file system:

```
Dim objWriter As New _
        IO.StreamWriter(File.Open("c:\mytext.txt",FileMode.Open))
```

We then assign our `StreamWriter` to a debug listener by using the `Add` method:

```
Debug.Listeners.Add(New TextWriterTraceListener (objWriter))
```

In our example above, we force an error condition and catch it, writing the `Message` property of the `Exception` object (which is `Entry point was not found.`) to the debug buffer through the `WriteLine` method:

```
Debug.WriteLine(objA.Message)
```

We finally flush the listener buffer to the output file and free our resources.

```
objWriter.Flush()
objWriter.Close()
objWriter = Nothing
```

Debugging and Measuring Performance

The .NET Framework has enhanced the capabilities we have to debug and measure the performance of our applications.

The debug capabilities have been expanded not only by the use of the `Debug` object as we illustrated earlier, but also with some system events that we can generate. Debugging our application will always go beyond the development stage, as we can never anticipate 100% of what our users will do while using our applications.

We discussed and illustrated in the previous logging and trace file examples, how we can use the `Debug` statements in the Visual Studio.NET environment to develop output to event logs and files. In this section, we'll expand that capability by coupling it with the use of the `Trace` class. We can now trace the performance of our application via the use of this class. It is important that an application has the ability to have its performance measured so that we can make improvements as our application environment changes, as it always will over time.

The major difference between what we have seen using our `Debug` statements and using tracing techniques is in their respective purpose. The `Debug` class is primarily used to write information to log files after an error has occurred or in order to be able to track information about variables during program execution. The use of the `Trace` class and tracing techniques described in this section allows us to see how well a piece of code or an entire application is performing. The two classes have many of the same properties and methods, and both even use listener objects to accomplish output. The biggest difference is that `Trace` class statements are compiled into release versions of code while `Debug` statements are not.

The topic of debugging and measuring performance brings up the subject of **instrumentation**. Instrumentation is a widely used term, which simply means that an application has a built-in ability to give the programmer feedback on what's going on within it as it runs. It is important to build these features into our programs, but at the same time, we must consider the overhead of doing the instrumentation constantly. This consideration brings up two points – first, that we must strategically place our instrumentation and second, that we should use conditional compilation statements and trace switches to trigger our instrumentation activity.

Conditional compilation statements have been around for quite a while, and come in quite handy when we want to run code only if certain conditions are met. Basically, a piece of code that is included in a conditional compilation section is surrounded by an #If ... #End If block. If the condition within the #If is met then the code is executed, otherwise it is skipped. There are two ways of setting up conditions to be tested in our #IF statements: #CONST directives and trace switches:

❑ A #Const directive is simply setting up a constant in the code with a #CONST statement. For instance, if we wanted to test for whether the version of code we had was the English version we would include a #CONST EnglishVersion at the top of our code and then we could use an #If EnglishVersion within our code.

❑ Trace switches are objects we set up in our code that allow us to check a condition and generate our tracing output based on that condition. Our examples in this section will illustrate the use of trace switches and conditional compilation tests further.

Measuring Performance via the Trace Class

The trace tools in the Visual Studio.NET Framework evolve around the Trace class, which provides properties and methods that help us trace the execution of our code. By default, tracing is enabled in VB.NET, so not unlike our previous debug discussion, all we have to do is setup the output and utilize its capabilities.

We can specify the detail level we want to perform for our tracing output by configuring trace switches. Trace switches can be either BooleanSwitch or TraceSwitch. BooleanSwitch has a value of either 0 or 1, and is used to determine if tracing is off or on respectively; while TraceSwitch allows us to specify a level of tracing based on five enumerated values. We can manage a BooleanSwitch or TraceSwitch as an environment variable. Once a switch is established, we can create and initialize it in code and use it with either trace or debug.

A TraceSwitch can have five enumerated levels that can be read as 0-4 or checked with four properties provided in the switch class interface. The four properties return a Boolean value based on whether the switch is set to a certain level or higher. The five enumerated levels for TraceSwitch are:

Level	Description
0	None
1	Only error messages
2	Warning and error messages
3	Information, warning, and error messages
4	Verbose, information, warning, and error messages

The four properties are `TraceError`, `TraceWarning`, `TraceInfo`, and `TraceVerbose`. For example, if our switch was set at number 2 and we asked for the `TraceError` or `TraceWarning` properties they would return `True`, while the `TraceInformation` and `TraceVerbose` properties would return `False`.

An environment variable is either managed via the command line or under **My computer | Properties | Advanced** within the **Environment Variables** button.

Within the **Environment Variables** button, you add a new **User** variable, giving it the SwitchName and Value for that switch.

From the command line, type:

```
Set _Switch_MySwitch = 0
```

The value on the left of the equals is the name of the switch, and the value on the right of the equals is either 0 or 1 for a `BooleanSwitch` or 0 – 4 for a `TraceSwitch`. Note that there is a space between the word Set and the leading underscore of _Switch. Once you have typed the above line, if you follow that by the plain SET command at the command line it will show your new switch as an environment variable as shown in the following screen shot:

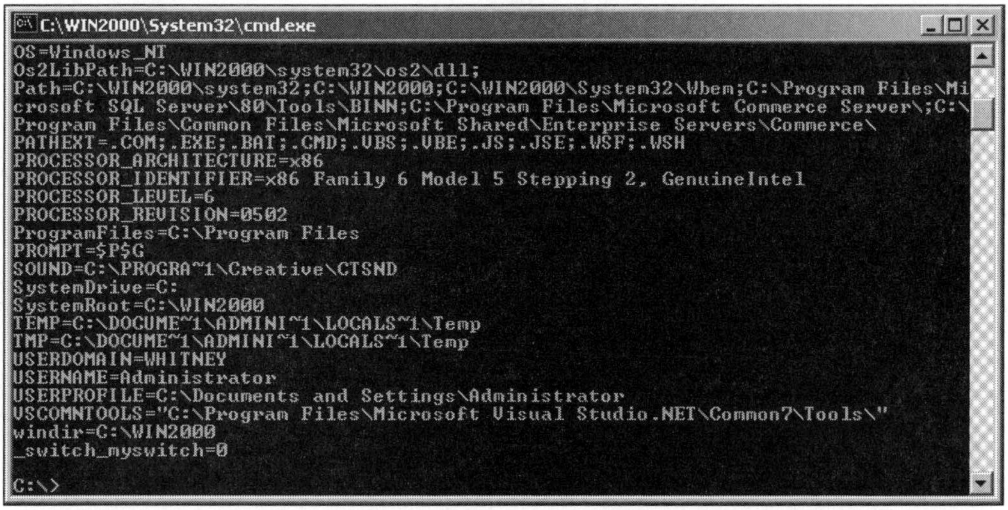

For the example that follows, we have the output directed to the default Output window:

```
Sub TraceExample1()
    Dim objTraceSwitch As TraceSwitch
    objTraceSwitch = New TraceSwitch("ExampleSwitch", "Test Trace Switch")
    objTraceSwitch.Level = TraceLevel.Error
    Try
        Throw (New EntryPointNotFoundException())
    Catch objA As System.EntryPointNotFoundException
        Trace.WriteLineIf(objTraceSwitch.TraceVerbose, _
            "First Trace " & objA.Source)
        Trace.WriteLineIf(objTraceSwitch.TraceError, _
            "Second Trace " & objA.Message)
    End Try
End Sub
```

We begin by assigning our switch to an existing registry entry and set its level:

```
objTraceSwitch = New TraceSwitch("ExampleSwitch", "Test Trace Switch")
objTraceSwitch.Level = TraceLevel.Error
```

After we throw our exception, we first cause our trace output listener to catch the Source property of our Exception object based on whether the value of our switch is TraceVerbose or better:

```
Trace.WriteLineIf(objTraceSwitch.TraceVerbose, _
    "First Trace " & objA.Source)
```

Since the tracing level is set to Error the above line is skipped and we continue by writing a trace to the Output window to include the message information if the level is set to Error:

```
Trace.WriteLineIf(objTraceSwitch.TraceError, _
    "Second Trace " & objA.Message)
```

As we can see in our Output window shown, we successfully wrote only the second trace line based on the level being Error on our trace switch:

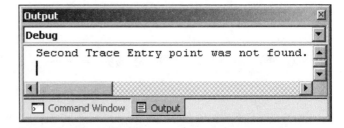

The other thing we want the ability to do is to determine the performance of our application. Overall, our application might appear to be working fine, but it is always a good thing to be able to measure the performance of our application so that environment changes or degradation over time can be counteracted. The basic concept here is to use conditional compilation so that we can turn on and off our performance-measuring code:

```
Sub TraceExample2()
    Dim connInfo As New Connection()
    Dim rstInfo As New Recordset()
    #Const bTrace = 1
    Dim objWriter As New _
        IO.StreamWriter(File.Open("c:\mytext.txt", FileMode.OpenOrCreate))
    connInfo.ConnectionString = "Provider = sqloledb.1" & _
        ";Persist Security Info = False;" & "Initial Catalog = Northwind;" & _
        "DataSource = LocalServer"
    connInfo.Open(connInfo.ConnectionString, "sa")
    Trace.Listeners.Add(New TextWriterTraceListener(objWriter))

    #If bTrace Then
        Trace.WriteLine("Begun db query at " & now())
    #End If

    rstInfo.Open("SELECT CompanyName, OrderID, " & _
        "OrderDate FROM Orders AS a LEFT JOIN Customers" & _
        " AS b ON a.CustomerID = b.CustomerID WHERE " & _
        "a.CustomerID = 'Chops'", connInfo, _
```

```
        CursorTypeEnum.adOpenForwardOnly, _
        LockTypeEnum.adLockBatchOptimistic)

    #If bTrace Then
        Trace.WriteLine("Ended db query at " & now())
    #End If

    Trace.Listeners.Clear()
    objWriter.Close()
    rstInfo.Close()
    connInfo.Close()
    rstInfo = Nothing
    connInfo = Nothing

End Sub
```

This subroutine uses ADO, so be sure to add a reference to an ADO library and an `Imports ADODB`
statement in the declarations section of the module.

In this simple example we are trying to measure the performance of a database query using a conditional
constant defined as `bTrace` by the following code:

```
#Const bTrace = 1
```

We establish our database connection strings, then right before we execute our query we write to a log file
based on whether we are in tracing mode or not:

```
#If bTrace Then
    Trace.WriteLine("Begun db query at " & now())
#End If
```

Again, after our query returns we'll write to our log only if we are in tracing mode:

```
#If bTrace Then
    Trace.WriteLine("Ended db query at" & now())
#End If
```

It is always important to remember that tracing will potentially slow the application down, so we want to use
this functionality only when troubleshooting and not let it run all the time.

Summary

In this chapter we reviewed the exception handler provided with the CLR and went over the methods it gives us to handle exceptions through the Try...Catch...Finally model. We discussed:

- ❑ Nested Try structures
- ❑ The Exit Try statement
- ❑ Properties and methods of the Exception object including: Message, StackTrace, Source, InnerException, HelpLink
- ❑ Handling Exception objects as returned from unmanaged code
- ❑ Error logging to event logs and trace files
- ❑ Instrumentation and measuring performance
- ❑ Tracing techniques

We used several examples in each section to illustrate the use of each method, property, and technique. It is most important to note from this chapter that error handling within VB.NET has been standardized and that the process has changed significantly from previously with VB6. As we work through these improvements, the sophistication and completeness provided by the CLR will increase the ability to lower overall critical messages that appear in applications.

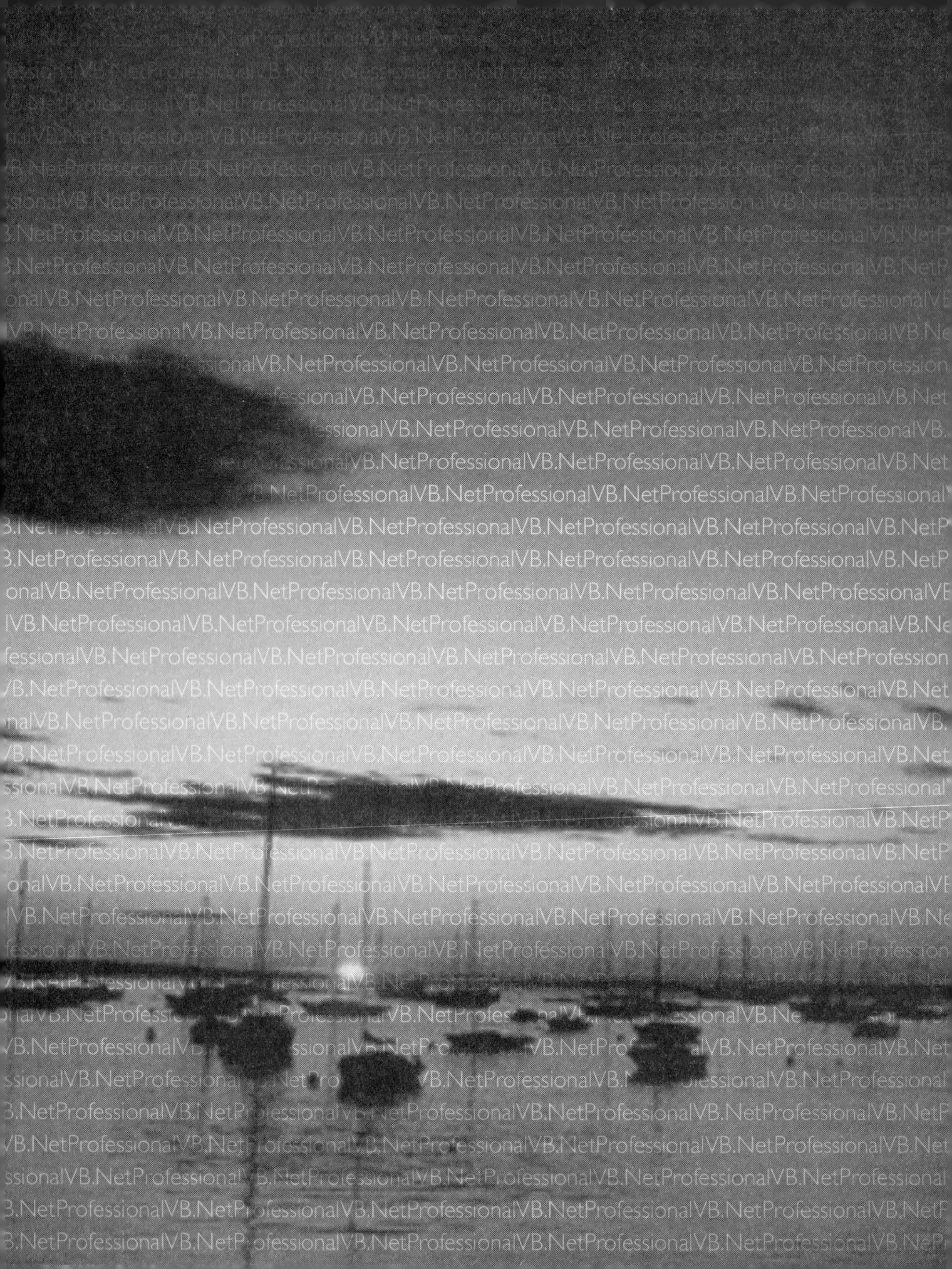

10

Creating Windows Controls

In comparison to VB6, the new options for deployment of form-based interfaces in the .NET Framework mean that user interfaces created with Windows Forms are less costly to install and support. Not only that but Windows Forms also possess greatly enhanced functionality, in comparison to that available to us in VB6, enabling us to design better interfaces and facilitate better user experiences.

Windows Forms interfaces are based on using controls. As with a form, a control is simply a special type of .NET class. It inherits (either directly or indirectly) from a base class called `Control` that ensures the availability of functionality common to all controls. Each control can then render its own functionality or, indeed, (when permitted) override functionality that it inherits.

In this chapter we will look at the nature of Windows Forms interfaces, and the three main techniques available to developers in creating user interfaces, namely:

- ❏ Inherit from another control
- ❏ Build a composite control
- ❏ Write from scratch based on the `Control` class

We will then go on to look in more detail at the base `Control` and `UserControl` classes, and consider a number of examples in order to illustrate how these can be used in developing custom Windows Forms controls.

Sources of Controls

There are four primary sources of controls for use on Windows Forms interfaces:

❑ Controls packaged with the .NET Framework (called **built-in controls** for the rest of the chapter)

❑ Existing ActiveX controls that are imported into Windows Forms

❑ Third-party .NET-based controls from a software vendor

❑ Custom controls created specifically for a particular purpose by the developer (maybe you!)

Built-In Controls

The set of controls that comes with the .NET Framework is comparable to the set offered with previous versions of Visual Basic, with some changes and additions. Chapter 8 on Windows Forms covered the basics of using these controls.

Many Windows Forms interfaces can be built completely with built-in controls. The stability and fast implementation of built-in controls make them attractive for a wide variety of purposes.

Existing ActiveX Controls

It is relatively straightforward to use existing ActiveX controls in Windows Forms. They can be referenced in the same way as .NET controls, and a wrapper for them will be automatically created.

However, performance considerations suggest that ActiveX controls should only be used when it is impractical to find or create an appropriate .NET equivalent.

Third-Party Controls

If the set of built-in controls proves insufficient for the needs of a particular application, another option is to acquire more visual controls from a commercial software vendor. Such "third-party" controls have been available in previous versions of Visual Basic for many years, and continue to be an option for Visual Basic.NET (without the need for any amendments). Controls from reputable vendors are often as robust as built-in controls, typically more feature-rich than built-in controls, and are available in a wide variety.

Custom Controls

When neither built-in controls nor third-party controls are sufficient to meet the developer's needs, the next option is creation of custom controls. This option was also possible in previous versions of Visual Basic by developing what were known as ActiveX controls (UserControls). However, custom controls in Visual Basic.NET have two main advantages over VB6 UserControls: simpler development and more flexibility.

Three Ways to Develop Custom Controls in .NET

There are three basic techniques for creation of custom Windows Forms controls in .NET, corresponding to three different starting points. This range of options gives the developer the flexibility to choose a technique that allows an appropriate balance between simplicity and flexibility.

Inherit From Another Control

The simplest technique starts with a complete Windows Forms control that is already developed. A new class is created that inherits the existing control. (See Chapter 12 for a complete discussion of inheritance in .NET classes.) This new class immediately has all the functionality of the base class from which it inherits. New logic can be added to create additional functionality in this new class or, indeed, to override functionality from the parent (when permitted).

Most of the built-in Windows Forms controls can be used as the base class for such an inherited control. (There are a few that cannot be inherited from, such as the `NotifyIcon` control, and the `ProgressBar`.) Third-party controls may also be candidates for extension into new custom controls through inheritance.

Here are some examples of scenarios in which it might make sense to extend an existing Windows Forms control:

- ❏ A textbox with built-in validation for specific types of information
- ❏ A self-loading listbox, combo box, or data grid
- ❏ A picture control that chooses a new image at random from a directory each time it appears on a form
- ❏ A menu control that varies its options based on the current user
- ❏ A `NumericUpDown` control that generates a special event when it reaches 80% of its maximum allowed value

The more times such functionality is needed, the more sense it makes to package it in a custom control. If a textbox that needs special validation or editing will only be used in one place, it probably does not make sense to create an inherited control. In that case, simply adding some logic in the form where the control is used to handle the control's events, and manipulating the control's properties and methods is probably sufficient. But, if such functionality is needed in many locations in an application, packaging the functionality in an inherited control can centralize the logic and facilitate reuse, thereby removing maintenance headaches.

Build a Composite Control

In some cases, a single existing control does not furnish the needed functionality, but a combination of two or more existing controls does. Here are some typical examples:

- ❏ A set of textboxes to hold a name, address, and phone number, with the combined information formatted in a particular way
- ❏ A set of buttons with related logic that are always used together
- ❏ A set of option buttons with a single property exposed as the chosen option
- ❏ A data grid together with buttons that alter its appearance or behavior in specific ways

As with inherited controls, composite controls are only appropriate for situations that require the same functionality in multiple places. If the functionality is only needed once, then simply placing the relevant controls on the form and including appropriate logic in the form itself is usually better.

Composite controls are the closest relative to VB6 UserControls and, because of that, they are sometimes referred to as "UserControls". In fact, the base class used to create composite controls is the UserControl class in .NET.

Write a Control from Scratch Based on Control Class

If a control needs to have special functionality not related to any existing control, then it can be written from scratch to draw its own interface and implement its own logic. This option requires more work from the developer, but allows the flexibility to do just about anything that is possible in form design within .NET.

For this case, it is necessary to inherit from the Control class, which gives basic functionality such as properties for colors and size. With this basic functionality already built in, the main tasks to be performed to get a custom control working are to add on any specific properties and methods needed for this control, to write the rendering logic that will paint the control to the screen, and to handle mouse and keyboard input to the control.

The Base Classes for Control Creation

There are two classes that are used in different circumstances as a starting point to create a control. It is helpful to understand something about the structure of these classes to see when use of each is appropriate.

It is important to note that the classes being discussed in this chapter are all in the System.Windows.Forms namespace. There are similarly named classes for some of these in the System.Web.UI namespace (which is used for Web Forms), but these classes should not be confused with anything discussed in this chapter.

The Control Class

The Control class is contained within the System.Windows.Forms namespace and contains the basic functionality to define a rectangle on the screen, provide a handle for it, and process routine operating system messages. This gives the class the ability to perform such functions as handling user input through the keyboard and mouse. The Control class serves as the base class for any component that needs a visual representation on a Win32-type graphical interface. Besides custom controls that are inherited from the Control class, the Form class also ultimately derives from the Control class. (The class hierarchy that connects these classes is shown shortly in *The UserControl Class* topic.)

In addition to these low-level capabilities, the Control class also includes such visually related properties as Font, ForeColor, BackColor, and BackGroundImage. Many of these will be familiar to Visual Basic developers because they are also members of the standard VB form. The Control class has additional properties that are used to manage layout of the control, such as docking and anchoring.

The Control class does not contain any logic to do any painting on the screen and, while it does offer access to the keyboard and mouse, it does not contain any actual input processing logic. The developer of a custom control based on the Control class must provide all of these capabilities.

The complete list of members of the Control class is too long to list here, but it is available in the help files for Visual Studio.NET. Here are some of the most important members of the Control class from the perspective of a VB developer:

Properties	Description
AllowDrop	If set to True then this control will allow drag and drop operations and events to be used.
Anchor	Determines which edges of the control are anchored to the container's edges.
BackColor, Font, ForeColor	Visual properties which are the same as corresponding properties in Visual Basic 6 and earlier.
CanFocus	A read-only property that indicates whether the control can receive focus.
CausesValidation	A new property of forms and controls that indicates whether entering the control causes validation on the control itself or on controls contained by this control that require validation.
Controls	A collection of child controls which this control contains.
Dock	Controls to which edge of the container this control is docked.
Enabled	Property indicating whether the control is currently enabled.
Handle	The HWND handle that this control is bound to.
Location, Size	Properties that relate to the size and position of the control.
Visible	Property that indicates whether the control is currently visible on the screen.

Methods	Description
BringToFront	Brings this control to the front of the zorder.
DoDragDrop	Begins a drag and drop operation.
Focus	Attempts to set focus to this control.
Hide	Hides the control by setting the visible property to False.
Refresh	Forces the control to repaint itself, and to force a repaint on any of its child controls.

Table continued on following page

Methods	Description
Show	Makes the control display by setting the visible property to True.
Update	Forces the control to paint any currently invalid areas.
WndProc	A very important method that allows access to Windows messages. Since this is implemented in the Control class, all Windows Forms classes can have easy access to Windows messages.

Events	Description
Click, DoubleClick, GotFocus, KeyDown, KeyPress, KeyUp, MouseDown, MouseEnter, MouseMove, MouseUp, Resize	Same as corresponding events in Visual Basic 6 and earlier.
DragDrop, DragEnter, DragLeave, DragOver	Events relating to drag and drop operations.
Leave	Occurs when the control is left (focus is lost).
MouseHover	New mouse event to determine when the mouse cursor has hovered over the control.
Paint	Occurs when the control is forced to repaint itself to the screen.
PropertyChanged	Occurs when a property of the control has changed.

Many of these members, and the ones summarized for the other classes in the hierarchy below, will be discussed in detail in some of the sections that follow in this chapter. Examples will be shown to illustrate usage, especially for capabilities that are new.

All controls ultimately derive from the Control class. As we shall see later, some types of custom controls derive from it directly.

The UserControl Class

The built-in functionality of the Control class is a great starting point for controls that will be built from scratch, with their own display and keyboard handling logic. However, there is no capability in the Control class to make it into a container. A custom control derived from the Control class cannot contain multiple controls – it can only manage a rectangular window that represents a single control.

That means that composite controls cannot use the Control class as a starting point. Composite controls combine two or more existing controls, so the starting point must be a container.

The class that meets this need is the UserControl class. Since it ultimately derives from the Control class, it has all of the properties and methods listed above for the Control class.

However, the UserControl class does not derive directly from the Control class. It derives from the ContainerControl class, which, in turn, derives from the ScrollableControl class. The class hierarchy looks like this:

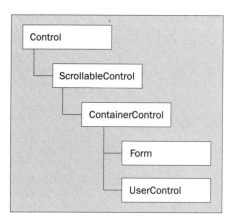

As the name suggests, the ScrollableControl class adds support for scrolling the client area of the control's window. Almost all the members implemented by this class relate to scrolling. They include AutoScroll, which turns scrolling on or off, and controlling properties such as AutoScrollPosition, which gets or sets the position within the scrollable area.

The ContainerControl class derives from ScrollableControl and adds the ability to support and manage child controls. It manages the focus and the ability to tab from control to control. It includes properties such as ActiveControl to point to the control with the focus, and Validate, which validates the last unvalidated control (the most recently changed control that has not had its validation event fired).

Neither ScrollableControl nor ContainerControl are usually inherited from directly. Instead, they add functionality that is needed by their more commonly used child classes, the Form class and the UserControl class.

The UserControl class can contain other child controls, but the interface of UserControl does not automatically expose these child controls in any way. Instead, the interface of UserControl is designed to present a single, unified interface to outside clients such as forms or container controls. Any object interface that is needed to access the child controls must be specifically implemented in your custom control, and the example below demonstrates this.

The external interface of the UserControl class consists exclusively of members inherited from other classes, though it does overload many of these members to gain functionality suitable for its role as a base class for composite controls.

Inheriting from Another Control

Now that we have some background on the options for creating custom controls, we are ready to look in depth at the procedures used for their development. First, we will look at creating a custom control by inheriting from an existing control and extending it with new functionality.

We will start by describing the general steps needed to create a custom control via inheritance, and then illustrate this with two examples. It is important to understand that many of the techniques described for working with a control created through inheritance also apply to the other ways that a control can be created. Whether inheriting from the `Control` class, the `UserControl` class, or from an existing control, a control is a .NET class. Creating properties, methods, and events, and coordinating these members with the Visual Studio designers, is done in a similar fashion regardless of the starting point.

Overview of the Process

Here are the general steps involved in the creation of a custom control via inheritance:

1. In a new Windows Control Library project, the class that is created will inherit from the `System.Windows.Forms.UserControl` namespace. The line that specifies the inherited class must be changed to inherit from the control that is being used as the starting point.

2. The class file then gets new logic added as necessary to add new functionality, before the project is compiled with a `Build` operation in order to create a `DLL` containing the new control's code.

3. The control is now ready to be used. It can be placed in the Windows Forms toolbox with the **Customize Toolbox** option in Visual Studio. From that point forward, it can be dragged onto forms like any other control.

Example 1 – A Numeric-Only Textbox

As our first example, we will create a textbox that only allows the user to put in a numeric entry. The starting point will be a normal Windows Forms textbox that allows entry of any character. The new, inherited control will have additional logic to restrict input to those characters appropriate for numeric entry.

The basic requirements for the control are to:

❑   Allow digits

❑   Allow entry of one decimal point only

❑   Allow a minus sign, but only at the first position in the textbox

❑   Throw away (or ignore) all other characters entered by the user

Step-By-Step Process to Create the Control

1. Start a new Windows Control Library project in Visual Studio.NET (under the category of Visual Basic projects). Give it the name **NumericTextbox**, rename the resulting project module `NumericTextbox.vb` (by default it will be named `UserControl1.vb`), and bring up the code window for this class.

2. The first two lines of the class will look like this:

```
Public Class UserControl1
    Inherits System.Windows.Forms.UserControl
```

As we need to inherit from a text box, these lines should be changed so as to read:

```
Public Class NumericTextBox
    Inherits System.Windows.Forms.TextBox
```

3. Next, we need to add the code for our new functionality. In our case, this is just one extra event routine which excludes the keys that we don't want to handle. To do that, place an event routine for the KeyPress event in the code. This is accomplished by opening the left-hand drop-down box in the code window and selecting the option **Base Class Events**, before selecting the **KeyPress** event in the right-hand drop-down box of the code window. Here is a sample screen showing the KeyPress event about to be selected:

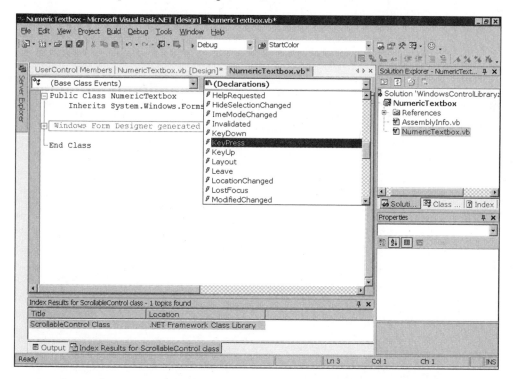

This action will cause the following code for an empty KeyPress event to be generated (the code below has line continuation characters added to facilitate readability):

```
Private Sub NumericTextbox_KeyPress(ByVal sender As Object, _
            ByVal e As System.Windows.Forms.KeyPressEventArgs) _
            Handles MyBase.KeyPress

End Sub
```

4. The following code should be added to the `KeyPress` event to monitor keystrokes from the user:

```
Private Sub NumericTextbox_KeyPress(ByVal sender As Object, _
                ByVal e As System.Windows.Forms.KeyPressEventArgs) _
                Handles MyBase.KeyPress

    Dim KeyAscii As Integer
    KeyAscii = Asc(e.KeyChar)

    Select Case KeyAscii

        Case 48 To 57, 8, 13        ' these are the digits 0-9, backspace,
                                    ' and carriage return
            ' we're OK on these, don't do anything

        Case 45                     ' minus sign

            ' The number can only have one minus sign, so
            ' if we already have one, throw this one away
            If InStr(Me.Text, "-") <> 0 Then
                KeyAscii = 0
            End If

            ' if the insertion point is not sitting at zero
            ' (which is the beginning of the field), throw away the minus
            ' sign (because it's not valid except in first position)
            If Me.SelectionStart <> 0 Then
                KeyAscii = 0
            End If

        Case 46                     ' this is a period (decimal point)

            ' if we already have a period, throw it away
            If InStr(Me.Text, ".") <> 0 Then
                KeyAscii = 0
            End If

        Case Else
            ' provide no handling for the other keys
            KeyAscii = 0

    End Select

    ' If we want to throw the keystroke away, then set the event
    ' as already handled. Otherwise, let the keystroke be handled normally.
    If KeyAscii = 0 Then
        e.Handled = True
    Else
        e.Handled = False
    End If

End Sub
```

5. Build the project to create a `DLL` containing the `NumericTextbox` control.

6. Create a new Windows Application project to test the control. Name the new project anything you like. Now right-click on the Windows Forms tab in the Toolbox, and select Customize Toolbox, and then click the tab for .NET Framework Components. Hit the Browse button and navigate to the directory containing your NumericTextbox project, in order to select the NumericTextbox.dll file (found in the /bin subdirectory). Return to the Customize Toolbox dialog, check the box, and click the OK button.

7. Scroll to the bottom of the controls on the Windows Forms tab. The NumericTextbox control should be there.

8. Drag a NumericTextbox control onto the form as you would a normal TextBox. Start the project. Test the NumericTextbox to check that it only accepts numeric input.

Changing Logic in a Custom Control

Since you created a new Windows Application project to test the NumericTextbox, you should be aware that, when you accessed NumericTextbox.dll, the new project made a copy of it in its own directory. This is necessary to run the application (see Chapter 24 on deployment in .NET to see why this is the case).

If you change the logic in the NumericTextbox control and then build a new version of it, that new version will not be automatically supplied to the Windows Application project used to test the control. It will be necessary to remove the control from the toolbox (via Customize Toolbox) and then refer to the changed version of the control.

This caution applies to controls created via any of the techniques presented later in the chapter.

Debugging a Custom Control

Since the process described in the previous section is fairly clumsy, it is easier to test new controls by adding a new Windows Application to the same project that is being used to create the control. Then, when new versions of the control are built, the Windows Application in the project automatically uses the new version. This is the recommended technique to use during development of any type of custom control, and we will use it for the remaining examples in the chapter.

However, note that there is one additional step needed if a new Windows Application is added to a solution to test a custom control. The Windows Application project must be set as the startup project in the solution properties (this can be done by right-clicking on the project name in the Solution Explorer window and selecting Set as Startup Project). Otherwise, the default startup is the control project, and you will receive an error message if you try to execute the solution with the control still designated as the startup project.

Adding Additional Logic to a Custom Control

While the first example above is completely functional and can be useful, most custom controls are not this simple. Typically, a custom control has more complex logic to add capability to the base control.

Besides handling base class events, as in the first example above, custom controls can have new logic added via any of the following:

❏   Overriding of properties and methods in the base class

❑　Creation of new properties and methods in the child control class

❑　Defining new events that the child control class will generate for handling in a Windows Form that contains the control

If you are unfamiliar with object syntax in VB.NET, it may be helpful to read Chapter 11 to understand the syntax used in each of these cases before reading the rest of this chapter. The discussion below does not define overriding, for example, or discuss the syntax of class properties.

Overriding a property or method in the base class is used when the functionality in that property or method is not sufficient for the new class. In the overriding logic, it is often necessary to call the original property or method in the base class using the MyBase keyword.

Further details on the MyBase keyword can be found in Chapter 12.

More commonly, however, a custom control needs to have properties, methods, and events that the base control does not possess. The following section discusses defining custom properties and methods for an inherited control and, after the next example, the process for defining a custom event is covered.

Creating a Property for a Custom Control

Creating a property for a custom control is just like creating a property for any other class.

Once a property is created for a control, it automatically shows up in the Properties window for the control. However, there are some additional capabilities that you can use to make the property work better with the designers and windows in Visual Studio.NET.

Setting Default Values and Creating Attributes for a Property

Properties typically need a **default value**, that is, a value the property will take on automatically when a control is instantiated. As you might expect, you can use your own internal logic in a control to set a default value for a property. Typically this means creating a module-level variable or constant initialized to the default value. Alternatively, you can initialize the default value in the constructor for the control. These techniques work fine, and are especially useful if the default value is different for different instantiations of the control, as in the case where the default Text property for a button is the name of the button.

If all instantiations of your control will have the same default value for a particular property, there is another technique for creating the default value that is often preferable. This involves using an attribute. There are various attributes that can be assigned in meta data to classes, properties, and methods. The one for creating a default value is called, appropriately enough, DefaultValue. It will be used in the next example to assign a default value to a property. However, here is a code snippet that shows a DefaultValue attribute being set:

```
<DefaultValue(100)> _
Public Property MyProperty() As Integer
    Get
        Return mnMyProperty
    End Get
    Set(ByVal Value As Integer)
        mnMyProperty = Value
    End Set
End Property
```

In this case, the default value for `MyProperty` is set to 100. Including this line will cause the value of 100 to show up in the **Properties** window for a control as soon as it is dragged onto a form. Note also the use of the `mnMyProperty` module level variable that contains the value of the property.

`DefaultValue` is not the only attribute that is useful for properties. The `Description` attribute is also one that should be used with most properties. It contains a text description of the property that shows up in the **Properties** windows when a property is selected. To include a `Description` attribute, the declaration of the property above would look like this:

```
<DefaultValue(100), _
Description("This is a description for my property")> _
Public Property MyProperty() As Integer
```

Attributes reside in namespaces, just as components do. To use one, it is necessary to refer to the appropriate namespace. The attributes above are available by referring to the `System.ComponentModel` namespace with the following line at the top of the class's code:

```
Imports System.ComponentModel
```

If you start to use an attribute and get a build error, the most likely reason (assuming that your syntax for the attribute is correct) is that the namespace for the attribute is not yet referred to in your project.

> *To add a new namespace to a project, simply click on the* **References** *|* **Add Reference** *menu in the* **Solution Explorer** *window.*

Once a property has an attribute, the attribute can be fetched in code. First, you need a reference to the attributes collection for the property, and then you can get to the individual attribute. Here is example code to fetch the `DefaultValue` attribute property for `MyProperty`:

```
Dim attributes As AttributeCollection = _
    TypeDescriptor.GetProperties(Me)("MyProperty").Attributes

' Now need a reference to the DefaultValue attribute, which is
' in the collection we just referenced above.
Dim myAttribute As DefaultValueAttribute = _
    CType(attributes(GetType(DefaultValueAttribute)), DefaultValueAttribute)
```

Making Your Properties Work Well with the Designer

There are two main ways that properties of classes interact with the Visual Studio environment. Firstly, properties are displayed in the **Properties** window, and they can be edited there. Secondly, the visual designers in VS.NET create code in form modules to set the properties of the controls contained on the form. (You can see this code when you expand the section of a form's code labeled `Windows Forms Designer generated code`.)

Serializing a Property in Code

However, the visual designers do *not* insert code to set *all* the properties of every control. Some controls have dozens of properties, and setting them all would require many lines of code. So the designers only generate code to set those properties that need a value other than their default value. That is, if you edit a property in the **Properties** window, and you set it to a value other than the default, the designer will generate code for that property. If the property is left with its default value, the designer will not generate code for it.

Generating code to set a property is called **serializing** the property. Designers check to see if a property needs to be serialized by using a method on the control containing the property. The method returns a Boolean value indicating whether a property needs to be serialized (`True` if it does, `False` if it does not).

If a property is named `MyProperty`, then the method to check serialization is called `ShouldSerializeMyProperty`. It would typically look something like this:

```
Public Function ShouldSerializeMyProperty() As Boolean
    If mnMyProperty = mnMyPropertysDefaultValue Then
        Return False
    Else
        Return True
    End If
End Function
```

If a property in a custom control does not have a related `ShouldSerialize...` method, then the property is always serialized. Code for setting the property's value will always be included by the designer in the generated code for a form. For that reason, it's a good idea to always include such a method for every new property created for a control.

Note that the above code example shows the default value of the property being held in a module level variable. The default value can also be held in and called from a `DefaultValue` attribute, as discussed in the previous topic.

Providing a Reset Method for a Control Property

It is also possible to relate a method to reset the property's value to the default to a property in a control. As an example of this, in the case of a property named `MyProperty`, the reset method is named `ResetMyProperty`. It typically looks something like this:

```
Public Sub ResetMyProperty()
    mnMyProperty = mnMyPropertysDefaultValue
End Sub
```

As with the `ShouldSerialize...` method, the default property value can be called from an attribute if one has been included with the property declaration.

Defining a Custom Event for the Inherited Control

Most developers are familiar with adding properties and methods to classes, but adding an event is less common. If you want to read more about adding an event to a class, Chapter 12 takes up this topic. However, as a brief overview, the basic three steps involved in creating an event for a custom control are:

❑ Declare the event in the control. The event can have any arguments that are appropriate, but they cannot have named arguments, optional arguments, or arguments that are `ParamArrays`. Here is code for declaring a generic event:

```
Public Event MyEvent(ByVal MyFirstArgument As Integer, _
                     ByVal MySecondArgument As String)
```

❑   Elsewhere in the control's code, implement code to raise the event. The location and circumstances of this code vary depending on the nature of the event, but a typical line that raises the event above looks like this:

```
RaiseEvent MyEvent(nValueForMyFirstArgument, sValueForMySecondArgument)
```

Often this code will be in a method that raises the event. This allows the raising of the event to be done in a uniform fashion. If the event will be raised from several places in your control, doing it with a method is preferred. If the event will only be raised in one place, the code to do it can just be placed in that location.

❑   The form that contains the control can now handle the event. The process for doing that is the same as handling an event for a built-in control.

The following example creates a custom property and a custom event in a control.

Example 2 – A Checked ListBox that Limits the Number of Selected Items

Our next example inherits the built-in CheckedListBox control, and extends its functionality. If you are not familiar with this control, it works just like a normal ListBox control, except that selected items are indicated with a check in a checkbox at the front of the item rather than highlighting the item.

To extend the functionality of this control, we will create a property called MaxItemsSelected. This property will hold a maximum value for the number of items that a user can select. The event that fires when a user checks on an item is then monitored to see if the maximum has already been reached.

If selection of another item would exceed the maximum number, the selection is prevented, and an event is fired to let the consumer form know that the user has tried to exceed the maximum limit. The code that handles the event in the form can then do whatever is appropriate. In our case, we are just putting up a message box to tell the user that no more items can be selected.

We will place DefaultValue and Description attributes on our MaxItemsSelected property to assist in the designer. We will also implement methods for ShouldSerializeMaxItemsSelected and ResetMaxItemsSelected.

Here is the step-by-step construction of our example:

1.   Start a new Windows Control Library project in Visual Studio.NET. Give it the name LimitedCheckedListBox and name the resulting project module LimitedCheckedListBox.vb, before bringing up the code window for this class.

2.   Ensure that the following line is in the declarations at the top of the class (before the line declaring the class):

```
Imports System.ComponentModel
```

This allows us to utilize the attributes that we require from the System.ComponentModel namespace. The class declaration needs to be altered so that it reads as follows:

```
Public Class LimitedCheckedListBox
    Inherits System.Windows.Forms.CheckedListBox
```

3. We are ready to begin adding our own code. First, we need to implement the
`MaxSelectedItems` property. We need a module level variable to hold the property's
value, so insert this line just under the two lines in step 2:

```
Private  mnMaxSelectedItems As Integer = 4
```

4. Now create the code for the property itself. Insert the following code into the class just
above the line that says `End Class`:

```
<DefaultValue(4), _
 Description("The maximum number of items allowed to be checked")> _
Public Property MaxSelectedItems() As Integer
    Get
        Return mnMaxSelectedItems
    End Get
    Set(ByVal Value As Integer)
        mnMaxSelectedItems = Value
    End Set
End Property
```

This code sets the default value of the `MaxSelectedItems` property to 4, and sets a
description for the property to be shown in the **Properties** window when the property is
selected there.

5. Now we need to declare the event that will be fired when a user selects too many items.
The event will be named `MaxItemsExceeded`. We will include arguments in our event to
indicate the maximum that was exceeded (this is just for illustration – that number could
be fetched from the control's properties). Just under the code for step 3, insert the
following line:

```
Public Event MaxItemsExceeded(ByVal MaxAllowed As Integer)
```

6. Next, we need to insert code into the event routine that fires when the user clicks on an
item. For the `CheckedTextBox` base class, this is called the `ItemCheck` property. Open
the left-hand drop-down in the code window and select the option **Base Class Events**.
Then select the **ItemCheck** event in the right-hand drop-down of the code window. The
following code will be inserted to handle the `ItemCheck` event (line continuation
characters have been added to make it easier to read the generated code):

```
Private Sub LimitedCheckedListBox_ItemCheck(ByVal sender As Object, _
        ByVal e As System.Windows.Forms.ItemCheckEventArgs) _
        Handles MyBase.ItemCheck

End Sub
```

7. The following code should be added to the `ItemCheck` event to monitor it for too
many items:

```
Private Sub LimitedCheckedListBox_ItemCheck(ByVal sender As Object, _
```

```
                 ByVal e As System.Windows.Forms.ItemCheckEventArgs) _
                 Handles MyBase.ItemCheck
```

```
' Check to see if we are over the limit and that the user is
' trying to check an item rather than uncheck an item.
If (Me.CheckedItems.Count >= mnMaxSelectedItems) _
     And (e.NewValue = CheckState.Checked) Then

     ' If we have exceeded the maximum, fire an event to indicate that
     ' and change the state of the latest item to unchecked.
     RaiseEvent MaxItemsExceeded(mnMaxSelectedItems)
     e.NewValue = CheckState.Unchecked
End If
```

```
End Sub
```

8. Now create code to deal with serialization and resetting of the MaxSelectedItems property. Insert this code just above the End Class line:

```
Public Function ShouldSerializeMaxSelectedItems() As Boolean

     If mnMaxSelectedItems = DefaultMaxSelectedItems() Then
          Return False
     Else
          Return True
     End If
End Function

Public Sub ResetMaxSelectedItems()
     mnMaxSelectedItems = DefaultMaxSelectedItems()
End Sub

Private Function DefaultMaxSelectedItems() As Integer
     ' Get default for MaxSelectedItems.
     ' First need a reference to the attributes collection
     ' for the property.
     Dim attributes As AttributeCollection = _
          TypeDescriptor.GetProperties(Me)("MaxItemsSelected").Attributes

     ' Now need a reference to the DefaultValue attribute, which is
     ' in the collection we just referenced above.
     Dim myAttribute As DefaultValueAttribute = _
          CType(attributes(GetType(DefaultValueAttribute)), DefaultValueAttribute)

     ' Finally, return the default value
     Return myAttribute.Value

End Function
```

Notice that we are getting the default value for the property from the attributes collection. We have constructed a function to hold the logic that does that. If you expect this function to be called a lot, you might want to use a static variable in the function so that the process of getting the default from the attributes collection is only done once. In that case, the function would look like this:

```
Private Function DefaultMaxSelectedItems() As Integer

    Static nHoldDefault As Integer
    If nHoldDefault <> 0 Then
        Return nHoldDefault
    End If

    ' Get default for MaxSelectedItems.
    ' First need a reference to the attributes collection
    ' for the property.
    Dim attributes As AttributeCollection = _
        TypeDescriptor.GetProperties(Me)("MaxItemsSelected").Attributes

    ' Now need a reference to the DefaultValue attribute, which is
    ' in the collection we just referenced above.
    Dim myAttribute As DefaultValueAttribute = _
        CType(attributes(GetType(DefaultValueAttribute)), DefaultValueAttribute)

    ' Finally, set the default value to a variable to use
    nHoldDefault = myAttribute.Value
    Return nHoldDefault

End Function
```

9. Build the project to create a DLL containing the LimitedCheckedListBox control.

10. Add a new Windows Application project to the solution (using the File | Add Project | New Project menu) to test the control. Name the new project anything you like. Right-click on the solution (not the project, but the solution!) in the Solution Explorer, and select Properties. In the dialog box that comes up, change the drop-down under Single Startup Project to select your new Windows Application project.

11. In the new Windows Forms project, right-click on the Windows Forms tab in the Toolbox, and select Customize Toolbox. In the dialog box that appears, click the tab for .NET Framework Components, and browse to select the LimitedCheckedListBox.dll file. Return to the Customize Toolbox dialog, check the box and click the OK button.

12. Scroll to the bottom of the controls on the Windows Forms tab. The LimitedCheckedListBox control should be there.

13. The Windows Application will have a Form1 that was created automatically. Drag a LimitedCheckedListBox control onto Form1, just as you would a normal listbox. Change the CheckOnClick event for the LimitedCheckedListBox to True (to make testing easier). Note that this property was inherited from the base CheckedListBox control.

14. In the Items property of the LimitedCheckedListBox, click the button to add some items. Insert the following list of colors: Red, Blue, Green, Black, Yellow, White, Brown. At this point, your Windows Application Project should have a Form1 that looks something like this:

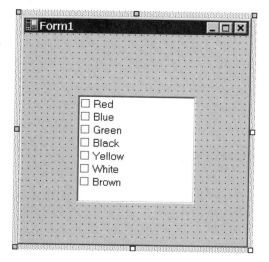

15. Bring up the code window for `Form1`. In the left-hand drop-down above the code window, select **CheckedListBox1** to get to its events. Then, in the right-hand drop-down, select the **MaxItemsExceeded** event. The empty event will look like this:

```
Private Sub LimitedCheckedListBox1_MaxItemsExceeded(ByVal MaxAllowed _
    As Integer) Handles LimitedCheckedListBox1.MaxItemsExceeded

End Sub
```

16. Now insert code to handle the event. The simplest way is to just put up a message box telling the user about going over the limit. Here is code for that:

```
MsgBox("You are attempting to select more than " _
    & CStr(MaxAllowed) _
    & " items. You must uncheck some other item before checking this one.")
```

17. Now start the Windows Application project. Check and uncheck various items in the listbox to see that the control works as it is supposed to. You should get a message box whenever you attempt to check more than four items. (Four items is the default maximum, and we have not changed it.) If you uncheck some items, then you can check items again until the maximum is once again exceeded. When finished, close the form to stop execution.

18. Look at the code in the `Windows Form Designer generated code` region and examine the properties for `LimitedCheckedListBox1`. Note that there is no line of code that sets `MaxSelectedItems`.

19. Go back to the design mode for `Form1` and highlight `LimitedCheckedListBox1`. In the Properties window, change the `MaxSelectedItems` property to 3.

20. Now, return to the code window and look again at the code that declares the properties for `LimitedCheckedListBox1`. Note that there is now a line of code that sets `MaxSelectedItems` to the value of 3.

21. Go back to the design mode for Form1 and highlight LimitedCheckedListBox1. In the Properties window, right-click the MaxSelectedItems property. In the pop-up menu, select Reset. The property will change back to a value of 4, and the line of code that sets the property that you looked at in the step just above will be gone.

These last few steps showed that the `ShouldSerializeMaxSelectedItems` and the `ResetMaxSelectedItems` methods are working as they should.

A Composite UserControl

As we discussed at the beginning of the chapter, sometimes inheriting an existing control is not sufficient to get the functionality you need. The next step up in complexity and flexibility is to combine more than one existing control to become a new control. This is similar to the process of creating a `UserControl` in VB6, but it is easier to do in Visual Basic.NET.

The main steps in the process of creating a `UserControl` are:

❑ Start a new Windows Control Library project, and assign names to the project and the class representing the control.

❑ The project will contain a design surface that looks a lot like a form. Drag controls onto this surface just as you would a form. Write logic loading and manipulating the controls as necessary, very much like you would with a form. It is usually particularly important to create resize logic that will reposition and resize the controls on your `UserControl` when it is resized on the form containing it.

❑ Create properties of the `UserControl` to expose functionality to a form that will use it. This typically means creating a property to load information into and get information out of the control. Sometimes properties to handle cosmetic elements are also necessary.

❑ Build the control and refer to it in a Windows Application exactly as we did for the inherited controls discussed earlier.

Note a key difference between this type of development and inheriting a control as we did in the examples above. A `UserControl` will not by default expose the properties of the controls it contains. It will expose the *properties* of the `UserControl` class plus any custom properties that we give it. If we want properties for contained controls to be exposed, we must explicitly create logic to expose them.

Example of a Composite UserControl

To demonstrate the process of creating a composite `UserControl`, we will build one that looks like this:

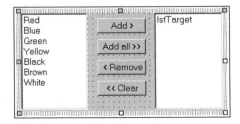

This type of layout is common on wizards and in other user interfaces that require selection from a long list of items. The control has one listbox holding a list of items that can be chosen (on the left side), and another listbox containing the items chosen so far (on the right side). Buttons allow items to be moved back and forth.

Loading this control means loading items into the left listbox, which we call `lstSource` and refer to as the source listbox. Getting selected items back out will involve exposing the items that are selected in the right listbox, named `lstTarget` and referred to in our discussion as the target listbox.

The buttons in the middle that transfer elements back and forth will be called `btnAdd`, `btnAddAll`, `btnRemove`, and `btnClear`, from top to bottom respectively.

There are lots of ways to handle this kind of interface element in detail. A production-level version would have the following characteristics:

❑ Buttons would gray out (disable) when they are not appropriate. For example, `btnAdd` would not be enabled unless an item is selected in `lstSource`.

❑ Items that have been transferred from `lstSource` to `lstTarget` would not be shown in `lstSource`. If they are removed from `lstTarget`, they should show in `lstSource` again.

❑ Items can be dragged and dropped between the two listboxes.

❑ Items can be selected and moved with a single double-click.

Such a production-type version contains too much code to discuss in this chapter. For our example, we are making the following allowances:

❑ Buttons do not gray out when they should be unavailable.

❑ Items transferred from `lstSource` will not disappear from the list. It will be possible to add duplicate items to `lstTarget`.

❑ Drag-and-drop is not supported.

❑ No double-clicking is supported.

Adding code to correct these deficiencies in a production application is straightforward and involves no techniques that are not familiar to an experienced VB developer. Some of the object models that need to be manipulated (especially the properties and methods of the listboxes) are different from earlier versions, but the overall conceptual process is not. Even drag and drop is done just as it would be in a form in VB6.

This leaves us with the following general tasks to make the control work:

❑ Create a `UserControl` project

❑ Add the listboxes and buttons to the `UserControl` design surface

❑ Add logic to resize the controls when the `UserControl` changes size

❑ Add logic to transfer elements back and forth between the listboxes when buttons are pressed. Note that more than one item may be selected for an operation so several items may need to be transferred when a button is pressed.

❑ Expose properties to allow the control to be loaded and selected items to be fetched by the form that contains the control

How Does Resize Work?

The steps above are fairly straightforward. Even the resize logic is made easy by using the built-in capabilities of Windows Forms controls. The listboxes can be docked to the sides to help manage their resizing. Then only their width needs to be managed. The buttons need to have an area set aside for them and then to be properly positioned within the area. But the sum total of this logic is far less than would be required with a similar control in VB6 (I know – I wrote one just like this in VB6 and getting the resize logic right was one of the more tedious aspects).

Setting a Minimum Size for Controls

Since we need the buttons to always be visible, this `UserControl` needs to have a minimum size. To take care of that, we will add logic in our `Resize` event to prevent the width and height of the control from dropping below certain minimums.

Exposing Properties of Sub-Controls

Most of our controls contained in our composite control do not need to expose their interfaces to the form that will be using the composite control. The buttons, for example, are completely private to the `UserControl` – none of their properties or methods needs to be exposed.

The easiest way to load up the control is to expose the appropriate properties of the source listbox. Similarly, the easiest way to allow access to the selected items is to expose the appropriate properties of the target listbox. In this way the UserControl will expose a limited number of their properties.

As an example, we have also implemented a `Clear` method that clears both listboxes simultaneously. This allows the control to be flushed and reused by a form that consumes it.

Stepping Through the Example

Here is the step-by-step procedure to build our composite `UserControl`:

1. Start a new Windows Control Library project. Name it **SelectComboControl**.

2. In the class file that is generated, change the name of the class to **SelectCombo**, and change the name of the associated VB module to **SelectCombo.vb**.

3. Go to the design surface for the control. Drag two listboxes and four buttons onto the control and arrange them so that they look something like this:

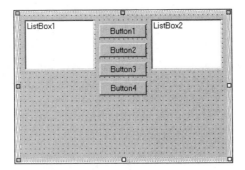

4. Change the names and properties of these controls as follows:

Original name of control	New name of control	Properties to set for control
Listbox1	lstSource	Dock = Left
Listbox2	lstTarget	Dock = Right
Button1	btnAdd	Text = "Add >"
		Size = 80,24 (80 twips wide by 24 twips high)
Button2	btnAddAll	Text = "Add All >>"
		Size = 80,24 (80 twips wide by 24 twips high)
Button3	btnRemove	Text = "< Remove"
		Size = 80,24 (80 twips wide by 24 twips high)
Button4	btnClear	Text = "<< Clear"
		Size = 80,24 (80 twips wide by 24 twips high)

5. Set up variables to hold the minimum size for the control and the size of the area for the buttons. That code should go just under the class declaration lines, and should look like this:

```
' Make the width of the area for the buttons 100 twips
Dim mnButtonAreaWidth As Integer = 100

' Set minimum height and width for the control
Dim mnMinControlWidth As Integer = 200
Dim mnMinControlHeight As Integer = 200
```

6. Set up resize logic to arrange these controls when the composite control is resized. Go to the code window for the class. Get an empty Resize event by selecting **Base Class Events** in the left-hand drop-down, and then **Resize** in the right-hand box. Place this code in the Resize event:

```
Private Sub SelectCombo_Resize(ByVal sender As Object, ByVal e As
System.EventArgs) Handles MyBase.Resize

    ' Check for minimum width and height.
    ' Throw exception if new width or height too small
    Dim sError As String
    SError = "Attempted to make SelectCombo user control too small."

    If MyBase.Size.Width < mnMinControlWidth Then
        Dim eComboException As New ApplicationException(sError)
        eComboException.Source = Me.ToString
    End If
    If MyBase.Size.Height < mnMinControlHeight Then
        Dim eComboException As New ApplicationException(sError)
        eComboException.Source = Me.ToString
```

```
    End If

    'Set source and target list boxes to appropriate width. Note that
    'docking the list boxes makes their height the right size automatically.
    Dim nListboxWidth As Integer
    nListboxWidth = CInt(0.5 * (Me.Size.Width - mnButtonAreaWidth))
    lstSource.Size = New Size(nListboxWidth, lstSource.Size.Height)
    lstTarget.Size = New Size(nListboxWidth, lstSource.Size.Height)

    'Now position the buttons between the list boxes.
    Dim nLeftButtonPosition As Integer
    nLeftButtonPosition = nListboxWidth + _
            ((mnButtonAreaWidth - btnAdd.Size.Width) \ 2)
    btnAdd.Location = New Point(nLeftButtonPosition, btnAdd.Location.Y)
    btnAddAll.Location = New Point(nLeftButtonPosition, btnAddAll.Location.Y)
    btnRemove.Location = New Point(nLeftButtonPosition, btnRemove.Location.Y)
    btnClear.Location = New Point(nLeftButtonPosition, btnClear.Location.Y)

End Sub
```

7. Put logic in the class to transfer items back and forth between the listboxes and clear the target listbox when `btnClear` is pressed. This logic is surprisingly short because it involves manipulating the collections of items in the listboxes. Here are the click events for each of the buttons:

```
    Private Sub btnAdd_Click(ByVal sender As Object, ByVal e As System.EventArgs)
Handles btnAdd.Click
    Dim objItem As Object
    For Each objItem In lstSource.SelectedItems
        lstTarget.Items.Add(objItem)
    Next objItem
End Sub

    Private Sub btnAddAll_Click(ByVal sender As Object, ByVal e As
System.EventArgs) Handles btnAddAll.Click
    Dim objItem As Object
    For Each objItem In lstSource.Items
        lstTarget.Items.Add(objItem)
    Next objItem
End Sub

Private Sub btnClear_Click(ByVal sender As Object, ByVal e As System.EventArgs)
Handles btnClear.Click
    lstTarget.Items.Clear()
End Sub

Private Sub btnRemove_Click(ByVal sender As Object, ByVal e As System.EventArgs)
Handles btnRemove.Click

    ' Have to go through the collection in reverse
    ' because we are removing items.
    Dim nIndex As Integer
    For nIndex = lstTarget.SelectedItems.Count - 1 To 0 Step -1
        lstTarget.Items.Remove(lstTarget.SelectedItems(nIndex))
    Next nIndex
End Sub
```

In each case, it is easier (less typing for you) to create the event with the drop-downs at the top of the code editor, and then put the necessary logic in the event. Note that the logic in the `Click` event for `btnRemove` has one oddity to take into account the fact that items are being removed from the collection. We must go through the collection in reverse because if we remove items, the looping enumeration is then messed up and a runtime error will be generated.

8. Create the public properties and methods of the composite control. In our case, we need the following members:

Member	Purpose
`Clear` method	Clears both listboxes of their items
`Add` method	Adds an item to the source listbox
`AvailableItem` property	An indexed property to read the items in the source listbox
`AvailableCount` property	Exposes the number of items in the source listbox
`SelectedItem` property	An indexed property to read the items in the target listbox
`SelectedCount` property	Exposes the number of items available in the target listbox

The code for these properties and methods is as follows:

```
Public ReadOnly Property SelectedItem(ByVal iIndex As Integer) As Object
    Get
        Return lstTarget.Items(iIndex)
    End Get
End Property

Public ReadOnly Property SelectedCount() As Integer
    Get
        Return lstTarget.Items.Count
    End Get
End Property

Public ReadOnly Property AvailableCount() As Integer
    Get
        Return lstSource.Items.Count
    End Get
End Property

Public Sub Add(ByVal objItem As Object)
    lstSource.Items.Add(objItem)
End Sub

Public ReadOnly Property AvailableItem(ByVal iIndex As Integer) As Object
    Get
        Return lstSource.Items(iIndex)
    End Get
End Property

Public Sub Clear()
```

```
        lstSource.Items.Clear()
        lstTarget.Items.Clear()

    End Sub
```

9. Build the control. Then create a Windows Application project to test it in. As in previous examples, it will be necessary to refer to the control using Customize Toolbox. Then it can be dragged from the toolbox, have items added, be resized, etc. When the project is run, the buttons can be used to transfer items back and forth between the listboxes, and the items in the target listbox can be read with the SelectedItem property.

Keep in mind that you can also use the techniques for inherited controls in composite controls too. You can create custom events, apply attributes to properties, and create ShouldSerialize and Reset methods to make properties work better with the designer. (That wasn't necessary here because most of our properties were ReadOnly.)

Building a Control from Scratch

The last technique to discuss is to derive a control from the Control class. Such a control gets a fair amount of base functionality from the Control class. We saw a partial list of properties and methods of the Control class earlier in the chapter. These properties arrange for the control to automatically have visual elements such as background and foreground colors, fonts, window size, etc.

However, such a control does not automatically use any of that information to actually display anything. A control derived from the Control class must implement its own logic for painting the control's visual representation. In all but the most trivial examples, such a control also needs to implement its own properties and methods to gain the functionality it needs.

The techniques above for default values, ShouldSerialize and Reset methods, etc, all work fine with controls created from the Control class, so we will not go over that capability again. Instead, we will concentrate on the capability that is very different in the Control class – the logic to paint the control to the screen.

Painting a Custom Control with GDI+

The base functionality used to paint visual elements for a custom control is in the part of .NET called GDI+. A complete explanation of GDI+ is too complex for this chapter, but here is an overview of some of the main concepts needed:

GDI+

GDI+ is the new version of the old GDI (Graphics Device Interface) functions provided by the Windows API. GDI+ provides a new API for graphics functions, which then takes advantage of the Windows graphics library.

GDI+ functions are in the System.Drawing namespace. Some of the classes and members in this namespace will look familiar to developers who have used the Win32 GDI functions. Classes are available for such items as pens, brushes, and rectangles. Naturally, the System.Drawing namespace makes these capabilities much easier to use than the equivalent API functions.

The `System.Drawing` namespace enables you to manipulate bitmaps and indeed utilize various structures for dealing with graphics such as `Point`, `Size`, `Color`, and `Rectangle`. In addition to this there are a number of classes available to developers, which include:

- `Cursors` class, containing the various cursors that you would need to set in your application, such as an hourglass or an insertion `I-beam` cursor
- `Font` class, including capabilities like font rotation
- `Graphics` class, containing methods to perform routine drawing constructs, including lines, curves, ellipses, etc.
- `Icon` class
- The `Pen` and `Brush` classes

System.Drawing Namespace

The `System.Drawing` namespace includes many classes and it also includes some subsidiary namespaces. We will be using one of those in our example – `System.Drawing.Text`. First, let's look at important classes in `System.Drawing`.

System.Drawing.Graphics Class

Many of the important drawing functions are members of the `System.Drawing.Graphics` class. Methods like `DrawArc`, `DrawEllipse`, and `DrawIcon` have self-evident actions. There are over forty methods that provide drawing related functions in the class.

Many drawing members require one or more points as arguments. A point is a structure in the `System.Drawing` namespace. It has X and Y values for horizontal and vertical positions, respectively. When a variable number of points are needed, an array of points may be used as an argument. The next example below uses points.

One odd thing about the `System.Drawing.Graphics` class that you should know is that it cannot be directly instantiated. That is, you can't just enter code like this to get an instance of the `Graphics` class:

```
Dim grfGraphics As New System.Drawing.Graphics()
```

That's because the constructor (`Sub New`) for the class is private. It is only supposed to be manipulated by objects that can set the `Graphics` class up for themselves. There are several ways to instantiate a `Graphics` class, but the one most commonly used in the creation of Windows controls is to get a reference to a graphics object for a window out of the arguments in a `Paint` event. That technique is used in our example further down. For now, to understand the capabilities of GDI+ a little better, let's do a quick example on a standard Windows Form.

Using GDI+ Capabilities in a Windows Form

Here is an example of a form that uses the `System.Drawing.Graphics` class to draw some graphic elements on the form surface. The example code runs in the `Paint` event for the form, and draws an ellipse, an icon (which it gets from the form itself), and two triangles, one in outline and one filled.

Start a Windows Application project in Visual Basic.NET. On the `Form1` that is automatically created for the project, place the following code in the `Paint` event for the form:

```
Dim grfGraphics As System.Drawing.Graphics
grfGraphics = e.Graphics

' Need a pen for the drawing. We'll make it violet.
Dim penDrawingPen As New _
    System.Drawing.Pen(System.Drawing.Color.BlueViolet)

' Draw an ellipse and an icon on the form
grfGraphics.DrawEllipse(penDrawingPen, 30, 150, 30, 60)
grfGraphics.DrawIcon(Me.Icon, 90, 20)

' Draw a triangle on the form.
' First have to define an array of points.
Dim pntPoint(3) As System.Drawing.Point

pntPoint(0).X = 150
pntPoint(0).Y = 150

pntPoint(1).X = 150
pntPoint(1).Y = 200

pntPoint(2).X = 50
pntPoint(2).Y = 120

grfGraphics.DrawPolygon(penDrawingPen, pntPoint)

' Do a filled triangle.
' First need a brush to specify how it is filled.
Dim bshBrush As System.Drawing.Brush
bshBrush = New SolidBrush(Color.Blue)

' Now relocate the points for the triangle.
' We'll just move it 100 twips to the right.
pntPoint(0).X += 100

pntPoint(1).X += 100

pntPoint(2).X += 100


grfGraphics.FillPolygon(bshBrush, pntPoint)
```

Then start the program and, when it comes up, the form will look something like this:

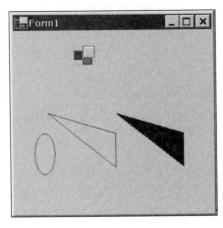

As you can see, the graphics functions are not difficult to use. The hardest part is figuring out how to initialize the objects needed, such as the graphics object itself, and the necessary brushes and pens.

For an example, we will create a custom control that functions as a label, but allows the text to be rendered at any angle.

First, start a new project in Visual Basic.NET of the Windows Control Library type. The created module will have a class in it named `Control1`. Rename the default class to `TextRotator` and change the `Inherits` statement like so:

```
Public Class TextRotator
    Inherits System.Windows.Forms.Control
```

Our `TextRotator` control needs to know the angle to rotate the text. So we need a module-level variable and a property procedure to support a `RotationAngle` property. First of all, place a declaration right under the line that causes the class to inherit the `System. Windows.Forms.Control` class.

```
Inherits System.Windows.Forms.Control
Private msngRotationAngle As Single = 0
```

Then insert the following property procedure in the class to create the `RotationAngle` property:

```
Public Property RotationAngle() As Single
Get
    Return msngRotationAngle
End Get
Set(ByVal Value As Single)
    If (msngRotationAngle >= -180) And (msngRotationAngle <= 180) Then
        msngRotationAngle = Value
        Me.Invalidate() ' Forces a repaint of the window
        ' This is a method of the Control class
    Else
        ' Should raise an error here
    End If
End Set
End Property
```

Now, place code to handle the `Paint` event, that is, to draw the text when the control repaints. We will use some code similar to that in the section on drawing with the GDI+ (above). To provide a place for this code, we override the `OnPaint` method of the `Control` base class:

```
Protected Overrides Sub OnPaint(ByVal e As
System.Windows.Forms.PaintEventArgs)
    ' First let the base UserControl take care of painting.
    MyBase.OnPaint(e)

    ' Declare a brush, a font, and a graphics
    ' object to use.
    Dim bshBrush As Brush
    Dim fntFont As Font

    ' We can get the graphic object directly from
```

```
        ' the PaintEventArgs parameter of the event.
        Dim grfGraphics As Graphics = e.Graphics

        ' Fix up the brush and the font.
        bshBrush = New SolidBrush(Me.ForeColor)
        fntFont = Me.Font

        ' Need to see how far to shift the drawing of the text
        ' so that it becomes visible. This calculation can be very
        ' complex, but we will simplify it for the example by making
        ' the starting point the center of the window for the control.
        ' (Code below assumes Option Strict is Off).
        Dim ShiftHorizontal As Single
        Dim ShiftVertical As Single
        ShiftHorizontal = Me.Size.Width * 0.5
        ShiftVertical = Me.Size.Height * 0.5

        ' Now draw some rotated text.
        grfGraphics.RotateTransform(RotationAngle)
        grfGraphics.DrawString(Me.Text, fntFont, bshBrush, ShiftHorizontal,
    ShiftVertical)
        grfGraphics.ResetTransform()

    End Sub
```

We also need to repaint the control when the text is changed in it, so we need to place code in the OnTextChanged event of the base class. Get an empty OnTextChanged event and place the following code in it:

```
    Private Sub TextRotator_TextChanged(ByVal sender As Object, _
            ByVal e As System.EventArgs) Handles MyBase.TextChanged
        Me.Invalidate()
    End Sub
```

The Invalidate method of the control forces a complete redraw of the control. As we discuss below, ideally this type of logic should be placed in all of the events that affect the rendering of the control, such as a font change event.

Now build the control library by selecting Build from the Build menu. This will create a DLL in the /bin directory where the control library solution is saved.

Then, start a new Windows Application project and right-click on the Windows Forms tab in the Toolbox. In the Customize Toolbox dialog, first make sure that the .NET Components tab is selected, and then use the Browse button to point to the deployed DLL for the control library. The Toolbox should now contain the TextRotator control.

Drag the TextRotator control onto the form in the Windows Application project. Notice that its property window includes a RotationAngle property. Set that to 20, for 20 degrees. Set the Text property to anything you like. When you run the project, the TextRotator control will display the string in its Text property at a 20 degree angle. Here's a sample screen:

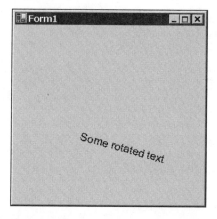

This control can now be manipulated in code just like any other control.

A Full Implementation of this Control

For simplicity, we have left off many things that should be done for a production level control. You'll note that the `RotationAngle` property notes a place to declare an error if the rotation angle is out of bounds. Also, there are many events that should force a repaint of the control. We included one of those above (the `TextChanged` event), but there are a number of others, such as the `FontChanged` event.

The painting logic needs additional refinement also. Getting all the GDI+ positioning and painting logic correct is very fussy programming.

This need to take care of details means that doing a control this way takes more work than the earlier techniques. On a more positive note, however, this technique offers the ultimate in flexibility, and is sometimes required to get the functionality that a custom control needs.

Summary

This chapter has discussed the creation of custom controls in Visual Basic.NET, illustrating how much easier it is to do this in comparison with previous versions of Visual Basic. The advent of full inheritance capabilities in VB.NET means that it is a lot easier for developers to utilize functionality simply by inheriting from the namespaces built into the .NET Framework. It is probably best to start by overriding these existing controls in order to learn the basics of creating properties and coordinating them with the designer, building controls and testing them, etc. These techniques can then be extended by the creation of composite controls, as we have illustrated with worked examples within this chapter.

If necessary, you can go on to create controls from scratch based on the `Control` class, but be aware that this takes a fair amount of work in comparison to the other two options.

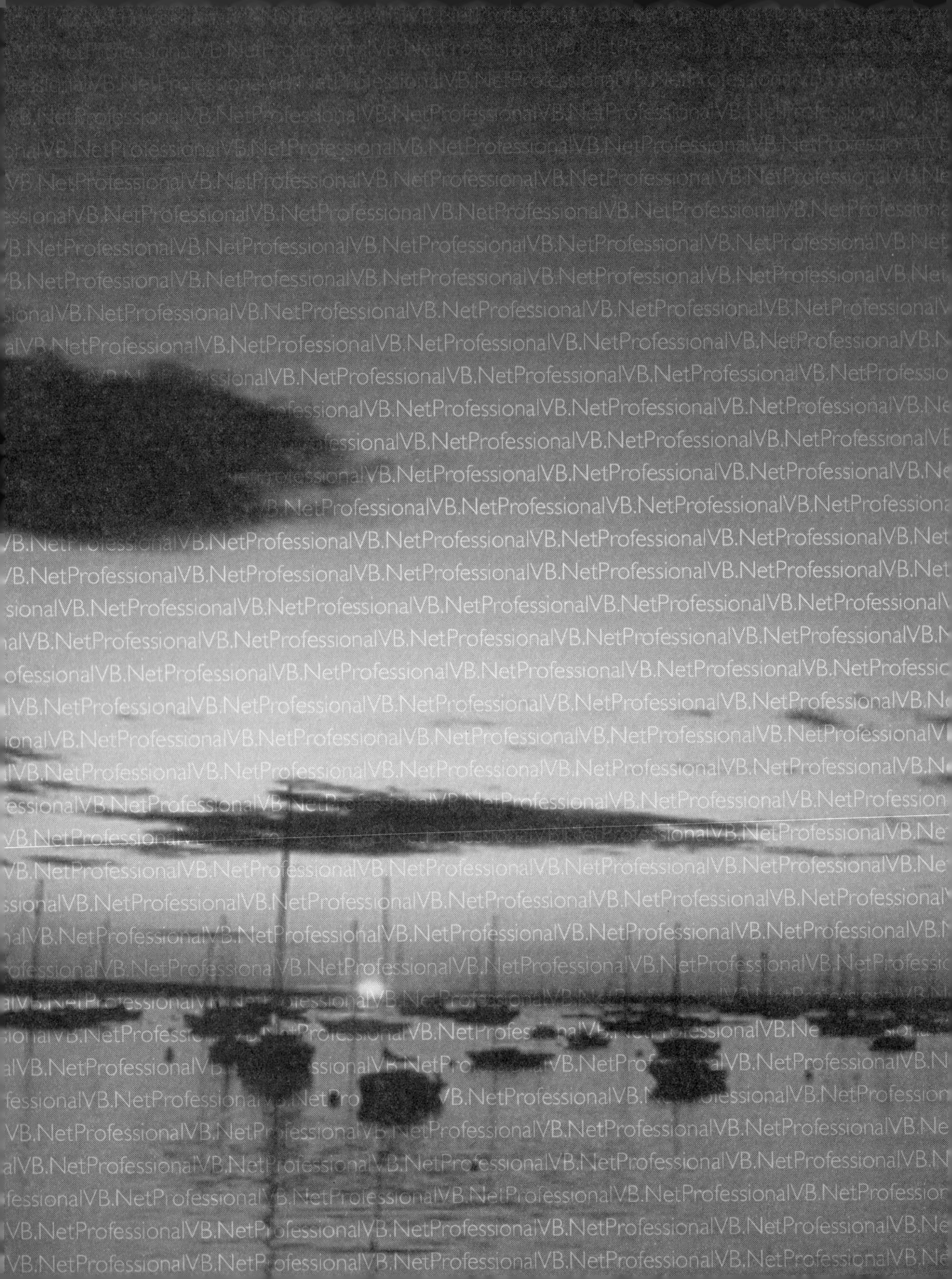
VB.NetProfessional

11

Object Syntax Introduction

Visual Basic has had powerful object-oriented capabilities since the introduction of version 4.0. VB.NET carries that tradition forward. VB.NET simplifies some of the syntax and greatly enhances these capabilities, and now supports the four major defining concepts required for a language to be fully object-oriented:

❑ **Abstraction**. VB has supported abstraction since VB4. Abstraction is merely the ability of a language to create "black box" code – to take a concept and create an abstract representation of that concept within a program. A `Customer` object, for instance, is an abstract representation of a real-world customer. A `Recordset` object is an abstract representation of a set of data.

❑ **Encapsulation**. This has also been with us since version 4.0. It's the concept of a separation between interface and implementation. The idea is that we can create an interface (`Public` methods in a class) and, as long as that interface remains consistent, the application can interact with our objects. This remains true even if we entirely rewrite the code within a given method – thus the interface is independent of the implementation.

Encapsulation allows us to hide the internal implementation details of a class. For example, the algorithm we use to compute Pi might be proprietary. We can expose a simple API to the end user, but we hide all of the logic used by our algorithm by encapsulating it within our class.

❑ **Polymorphism**. Likewise, polymorphism was introduced with VB4. Polymorphism is reflected in the ability to write one routine that can operate on objects from more than one class – treating different objects from different classes in exactly the same way. For instance, if both `Customer` and `Vendor` objects have a `Name` property, and we can write a routine that calls the `Name` property regardless of whether we're using a `Customer` or `Vendor` object, then we have polymorphism.

❑ VB, in fact, supports polymorphism in two ways – through late binding (much like Smalltalk, a classic example of a true OBJECT-ORIENTED language) and through the implementation of multiple interfaces. This flexibility is very powerful and is preserved within VB.NET.

❑ **Inheritance**. VB.NET is the first version of VB that supports inheritance. Inheritance is the idea that a class can gain the pre-existing interface and behaviors of an existing class. This is done by inheriting these behaviors from the existing class through a process known as subclassing. With the introduction of full inheritance, VB is now a fully OBJECT-ORIENTED language by any reasonable definition.

We'll discuss these concepts in detail in Chapter 13, using this chapter and Chapter 12 to focus on the syntax that enables us to utilize these concepts.

Additionally, because VB.NET is a component-based language, we have some other capabilities that are closely related to traditional concepts of object-orientation:

❑ **Multiple interfaces**. Each class in VB.NET defines a primary (or default) interface through its Public methods, properties and events. Classes can also implement other, secondary interfaces in addition to this primary interface. An object based on this class then has multiple interfaces, and a client application can choose by which interface it will interact with the object.

❑ **Assembly (component) level scoping**. Not only can we define our classes and methods to be Public (available to anyone), Protected (available through inheritance) and Private (only available locally), but we can also define them as Friend – meaning they are only available within the current assembly or component. This is not a traditional object-oriented concept, but is very powerful when designing component-based applications.

In this chapter we'll explore the creation and use of classes and objects in VB.NET. In Chapter 12, we'll examine inheritance and how it can be used within VB.NET. In Chapter 13, we'll explore object-oriented programming in depth, fully defining the features listed and exploring how we can use these concepts.

Before we get too deep into code, however, it is important that we spend a little time familiarizing ourselves with basic object-oriented terms and concepts.

Object-Oriented Terminology

To start with, let's take a look at the word *object* itself, along with the related *class* and *instance* terms. Then we'll move on to discuss the four terms that define the major functionality in the object-oriented world – encapsulation, abstraction, polymorphism, and inheritance.

Objects, Classes, and Instances

An **object** is a code-based abstraction of a real-world entity or relationship. For instance, we might have a Customer object that represents a real-world customer – such as customer number 123 – or we might have a File object that represents c:\config.sys on our computer's hard drive.

A closely related term is **class**. A class is the code that defines our object, and all objects are created based on a class. A class is an abstraction of a real-world concept, and it provides the basis from which we create instances of specific objects. For example, in order to have a Customer object representing customer number 123, we must first have a Customer class that contains all of the code (methods, properties, events, variables, etc.) necessary to create Customer objects. Based on that class, we can create any number of objects – each one an **instance** of the class. The following diagram illustrates this:

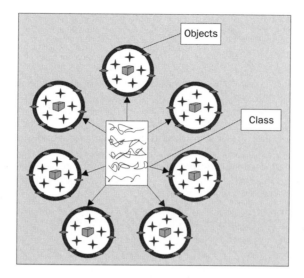

In this diagram, we can see that we have a single class that contains our program code. Based on that class, we are able to create multiple objects. Each object is identical to the others – except that it may contain different data.

Continuing with the `Customer` example, we may create many instances of `Customer` objects based on the same `Customer` class. All of the `Customer` objects are identical in terms of what they can do and the code they contain, but each one contains its own unique data. This means that each object represents a different physical customer:

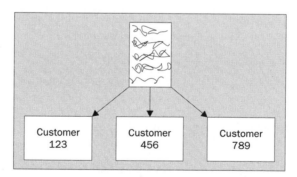

As illustrated in the diagram, we have a single `Customer` class. We have three instances of that class – each one an object containing a different set of customer data – thus representing three different real-world customers within our application.

Composition of an Object

In the computer, an object consists of some data (state information) and behavior (a set of routines). Our programs use an interface to get access to an object's data and behavior. We can represent the object as something like the following diagram:

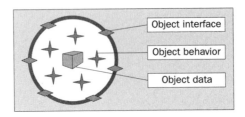

In this diagram, we can see that the object's data and behaviors are contained within the object, so a client application can treat the object like a black box accessible only through its interface. This is a key object-oriented concept called **encapsulation**. The idea is that any programs that make use of this object won't have direct access to the behaviors or data – but rather those programs must make use of our object's interface.

Let's walk through each of the three elements in the diagram in detail.

Interface

The interface itself is defined as a set of methods (Sub and Function routines), properties (Property routines), events, and attributes (variables) that are declared Public in scope.

> *The word* attribute *is overloaded in the world of .NET. .NET refers to attributes as coding constructs that we can use to control compilation, the IDE, etc. – things such as <WebMethod()>. In object-oriented circles, however, the term* attribute *refers to the module level variables within a class.*

We can also have Private methods and properties in our code. While these methods can be called by code *within* our object, they are not part of the interface and cannot be called by programs written to use our object. Another option is to use the Friend keyword, which defines the scope to be our current project, meaning that any code within our project can call the method, but no code outside of our project (that is, from a different .NET assembly) can call the method.

> *To complicate things a bit, we can also declare methods and properties as* Protected, *which are available to classes that inherit from our class. We'll discuss* Protected *in Chapter 12 along with inheritance.*

For example, we might have the following code in a class:

```
Public Function CalculateValue() As Integer

End Function
```

Since this method is declared with the Public keyword, it is part of our interface and, thus, can be called by client applications that are using our object. We might also have a method such as:

```
Private Sub DoSomething()

End Sub
```

This method is declared as being Private and, so, it is not part of our interface. This method can only be called by code *within* our class – not by any code outside of our class, such as the code in a program that is using one of our objects.

On the other hand, we can do something like this:

```
Public Function CalculateValue() As Integer
   DoSomething()
End Function
```

In this case, we're calling the `Private` method from within a `Public` method. While code using our objects can't directly call a `Private` method, we will frequently use `Private` methods to help structure the code in our class to make it more maintainable and easier to read.

Finally, we can use the `Friend` keyword:

```
Friend Sub DoSomething()

End Sub
```

In this case, the `DoSomething` method can be called by code within our class, or from other classes or modules within our current VB.NET project. Code from outside our project will not have access to the method.

The `Friend` scope is very similar to the `Public` scope, in that it makes methods available for use by code outside of our object itself. However, unlike `Public`, the `Friend` keyword restricts access to code within our *current* VB.NET project – preventing code in other .NET assemblies from calling the method.

> *This is very unlike the C++* friend *keyword, which implements a form of tight coupling between objects and which is generally regarded as a bad thing to do. Instead, this is the same* Friend *keyword that VB has had for many years and which was later adopted by Java to provide component-level scoping in that language as well.*

Implementation or Behavior

The code *inside* of a method is called the **implementation**. Sometimes it is also called **behavior** since it is this code that actually makes the object do useful work.

For instance, we may have an `Age` property as part of our object's interface. Within that method, we may have some code (perhaps written by an inexperienced developer, since it is just returning a non-calculated value):

```
Private mintAge As Integer

Public ReadOnly Property Age() As Integer
   Get
      Return mintAge
   End Get
End Sub
```

In this case, the code is returning a value directly out of a variable, rather than doing something better like calculating the value based on a birth date. However, this kind of code is often written in applications, and it seems to work fine for a while.

The key concept here is to understand that client applications can use our object even if we change the implementation – *as long as we don't change the interface*. As long as our method name and its parameter list and return data type remain unchanged, we can change the implementation all we want.

The code necessary to call our `Age` property would look something like this:

```
theAge = MyObject.Age()
```

The result of running this code is that we get the `Age` value returned for our use. While our client application will work fine, we'll soon discover that hard coding the age into the application is a problem and so, at some point, we'll want to improve this code. Fortunately, we can change our implementation *without changing the client code*:

```
Private mdtBirthDate As Date

Public ReadOnly Property Age() As Integer
  Get
    Return DateDiff(DateInterval.Year, mdtBirthDate, Now())
  End Get
End Sub
```

We've changed the *implementation* behind the interface – effectively changing how it behaves – without changing the interface itself. Now, when our client application is run, we'll find that the `Age` value returned is accurate over time where, with the previous implementation, it was not.

It is important to keep in mind that encapsulation is a syntactic tool – it allows our code to continue to run without change. However, it is not *semantic* – meaning that, just because our code continues to run, doesn't mean it continues to do what we actually wanted it to do.

In this example, our client code may have been written to overcome the initial limitations of the implementation in some way, and thus might not only rely on being able to retrieve the `Age` value, but the client code might be counting on the result of that call being a fixed value over time.

While our update to the implementation won't stop the client program from running, it may very well prevent the client program from running *correctly*.

Member or Instance Variables

The third key part of an object is its data, or **state**. In fact, it might be argued that the *only* important part of an object is its data. After all, every instance of a class is absolutely identical in terms of its interface and its implementation – the only thing that can vary at all is the data contained within that particular object.

Member variables are those declared so that they are available to all code within our class. Typically member variables are `Private` in scope – available only to the code in our class itself. They are also sometimes referred to as **instance variables** or as **attributes**.

> *In VB.NET, the term* attribute *is overloaded. We can have .NET attributes in our code, such as* `<Description()>` *or* `<WebMethod()>`. *These are different from the object-oriented definition of attribute, which refers to instance variables contained within a class.*

We shouldn't confuse instance variables with *properties*. In VB, a `Property` is a type of method that is geared around retrieving and setting values, while an instance variable is a variable within the class that may *hold* the value exposed by a `Property`.

For instance, we might have a class that has instance variables:

```
Public Class TheClass
    Private mstrName As String
    Private mdtBirthDate As Date
End Class
```

Each instance of the class – each object – will have its own set of these variables in which to store data. Because these variables are declared with the `Private` keyword, they are only available to code within each specific object.

While member variables *can* be declared as `Public` in scope, this makes them available to any code using our objects in a manner we can't control. Such a choice directly breaks the concept of encapsulation, since code outside our object can directly change data values without following any rules that might otherwise be set in our object's code.

If we want to make the value of an instance variable available to code outside of our object, we should use a `Property` method to make this happen:

```
Public Class TheClass
    Private mstrName As String
    Private mdtBirthDate As Date

    Public ReadOnly Property Name() As String
      Get
         Return mstrName
      End Get
    End Property
End Class
```

Since the `Name` property is a method, we are not directly exposing our internal variables to client code – and so we preserve encapsulation of our data. At the same time, through this mechanism we are able to safely provide access to our data as needed.

Member variables can also be declared with `Friend` scope – which means they are available to all code in our project. Like declaring them as `Public`, this breaks encapsulation and is strongly discouraged.

Now that we have a grasp on some of the basic object-oriented terminology, we are ready to explore the creation of classes and objects. First, let's see how VB allows us to interact with objects, and then we'll dive into the actual process of authoring those objects.

Working with Objects

By this point in the book, we've already interacted with and used countless objects – though we may not have given it much thought at the time.

In the .NET environment, and within VB in particular, we use objects all the time without even thinking about it. Every control on a form – and, in fact, every form – is an object. When we open a file or interact with a database we are using objects to do that work.

In this section of the chapter, we'll explore the use of objects in some detail. We'll see how to create them, how to indicate that we're done using them, and how to interact with them from our code.

Object Declaration and Instantiation

Objects are created using the New keyword – indicating that we want a new instance of a particular class. There are a number of variations on how or where we can use the New keyword in our code. Each one provides different advantages in terms of code readability or flexibility.

> *Unlike previous versions of VB, VB.NET doesn't use the* CreateObject *statement for object creation.* CreateObject *was an outgrowth of VB's relationship with COM and, since VB.NET doesn't use COM, it has no use for* CreateObject. *We can access COM objects through an interoperability mechanism but, even in that case, we would not call* CreateObject *as we may have done in the past.*

The most obvious way to create an object is to declare an object variable and then create an instance of the object:

```
Dim obj As TheClass

obj = New TheClass()
```

The result of this code is that we have a new instance of TheClass ready for our use. To interact with this new object, we will use the obj variable that we declared. The obj variable contains a reference to the object – a concept we'll explore more later.

We can shorten this by combining the declaration of the variable with the creation of the instance:

```
Dim obj As New TheClass()
```

> *In previous versions of VB this was a very poor thing to do, as it had both negative performance and maintainability effects. However, in VB.NET, there is no difference between our first example and this one, other than that our code is shorter.*

This code both declares the variable obj as data type TheClass and also creates an instance of the class – immediately creating an object that we can use from our code.

Another variation on this theme is:

```
Dim obj As TheClass = New TheClass()
```

Again, this both declares a variable of data type TheClass and creates an instance of the class for our use.

This third syntax provides a great deal of flexibility while remaining compact. Though it is a single line of code, it separates the declaration of the variable's data type from the creation of the object.

Such flexibility is very useful when working with inheritance or with multiple interfaces. We might declare the variable to be of one type – say an interface – and instantiate the object based on a class that implements that interface. We'll cover interfaces in detail in Chapter 12 but as an example here, let's create an interface named ITheInterface:

```
Public Interface ITheInterface
   Sub DoSomething()
End Interface
```

Our class can then implement that interface, meaning that our class now has its own native interface and also has a secondary interface – ITheInterface:

```
Public Class TheClass
   Implements ITheInterface

   Public Sub DoSomething() Implements ITheInterface.DoSomething
      ' implementation goes here
   End Sub
End Class
```

We can now create an instance of TheClass, but reference it via the secondary interface by declaring the variable to be of type ITheInterface:

```
Dim obj As ITheInterface = New TheClass()
```

We can also do this using two separate lines of code:

```
Dim obj As ITheInterface
obj = New TheClass()
```

Either technique works fine and achieves the same result, which is that we have a new object of type TheClass, being accessed via its secondary interface. We'll discuss multiple interfaces in more detail in Chapter 12.

So far we've been declaring a variable for our new objects. However, sometimes we may simply need to pass an object as a parameter to a method – in which case we can create an instance of the object right in the call to that method:

```
DoSomething(New TheClass())
```

This calls the DoSomething method, passing a new instance of TheClass as a parameter.

This can be even more complex. Perhaps, instead of needing an object reference, our method needs an Integer. We can provide that Integer value from a method on our object:

```
Public Class TheClass
   Public Function GetValue() As Integer
      Return 42
   End Function
End Class
```

We can then instantiate the object and call the method all in one shot, thus passing the value returned from the method as a parameter:

```
DoSomething(New TheClass().GetValue())
```

Obviously, we need to carefully weigh the readability of such code against its compactness – at some point, having more compact code can detract from readability rather than enhancing it.

Notice that nowhere do we use the Set *statement when working with objects. In VB6, any time we worked with an object reference we had to use the* Set *command – differentiating objects from any other data type in the language.*

In VB.NET, objects are not treated differently from any other data type, and so we can use direct assignment for objects just like we do with Integer *or* String *data types. The* Set *command is no longer valid in VB.NET.*

Object References

Typically, when we work with an object we are using a *reference* to that object. On the other hand, when we are working with simple data types such as Integer, we are working with the actual value rather than a reference. Let's explore these concepts and see how they work and interact.

Object References

When we create a new object using the New keyword, we store a reference to that object in a variable. For instance:

```
Dim obj As New TheClass()
```

This code creates a new instance of TheClass. We gain access to this new object via the obj variable. This variable holds a reference to the object. We might then do something like this:

```
Dim another As TheClass

another = obj
```

Now we have a second variable, another, which *also* has a reference to that same object. We can use either variable interchangeably, since they both reference the exact same object. The following diagram illustrates this:

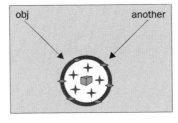

The thing we need to remember is that the variable we have is *not* the object itself but, rather, is just a reference or pointer to the object itself.

Simple Data Types

The rules are different for simple or elementary data types. These include:

- ❏ Boolean
- ❏ Byte
- ❏ Char
- ❏ Date
- ❏ Decimal
- ❏ Double
- ❏ Integer
- ❏ Long
- ❏ Short
- ❏ Single

For these simple data types, the variable really *contains* the value:

```
Dim int1 As Integer = 5
```

Now we have a variable, int1, which contains the value 5. We can then write code similar to our object code above:

```
Dim int2 As Integer

int2 = int1
```

The result is that we have another variable, int2, which also has the value of 5. However, each of these variables maintains its own separate value – they don't both point to the same thing. This means we can change the value of one variable without impacting the value of the other:

```
int1 = 10
```

At this point our variables have values as shown in the diagram:

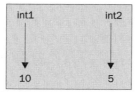

This is one of the most fundamental differences between objects and simple data types.

Treating Simple Values as Objects

Though simple data types are treated differently from objects in that a variable holds the actual value rather than a reference to the value, we can also treat these values as though they were objects in some ways.

This is a key concept in the .NET platform – *everything* is ultimately an object, even simple data types.

To understand this better, we can take a look at the way a simple `Integer` variable works. We are familiar with declaring and using an `Integer` variable:

```
Dim int1 As Integer = 42

int1 += 10
```

However, we can also call methods on the variable, since `int1` not only contains an `Integer` value, but also provides an object representation of that value. For instance, we can call its `GetType` method to find the underlying data type of the object:

```
MsgBox(int1.GetType())
```

The result of this code is a message box displaying the text **System.Int32** – which is the underlying .NET data type of a VB `Integer`.

In fact, variables that contain simple data types typically have a number of methods that provide services related to that data type. The `Integer` variable, for instance, also has `MaxValue` and `MinValue` properties that indicate the maximum and minimum allowed value for the data type.

Dereferencing Objects

When we are done working with an object, we can indicate that we're through with it by dereferencing the object.

To dereference an object, we need to simply set our object reference to `Nothing`:

```
Dim obj As TheClass

obj = New TheClass()
obj = Nothing
```

This code has no impact on our object itself. In fact, the object may remain blissfully unaware that it has been dereferenced for some time.

Once any and all variables that reference an object are set to `Nothing`, the .NET runtime can tell that we no longer need that object. At some point, the runtime will destroy the object and reclaim the memory and resources consumed by the object.

Between the time that we dereference the object and the time that .NET gets around to actually destroying it, the object simply sits in memory – unaware that it has been dereferenced. Right before .NET does destroy the object, the framework will call the `Finalize` method on the object. We'll discuss the `Finalize` method in more detail later in the chapter when we discuss the details of an object's life cycle. As part of that discussion, we'll explore more fully how .NET destroys our objects by using what is known as garbage collection.

Early vs. Late Binding

One of the strengths of Visual Basic has long been that we had access to both early and late binding when interacting with objects.

Early binding means that our code directly interacts with the object, by directly calling its methods. Since the VB compiler knows the object's data type ahead of time, it can directly compile code to invoke the methods on the object. Early binding also allows the IDE to use IntelliSense to aid our development efforts; it allows the compiler to ensure that we are referencing methods that do exist and that we are providing the proper parameter values.

> *In previous versions of VB, early binding was also known as vtable binding. The vtable was an artifact of COM, providing a list of the addresses for all the methods on an object's interface. In .NET, things are simpler and there is no real vtable. Instead, the compiler is able to generate code to directly invoke the methods on an object. From a VB coding perspective this makes no difference, but it is quite a change behind the scenes.*

Late binding means that our code interacts with an object dynamically at runtime. This provides a great deal of flexibility since our code literally doesn't care what type of object it is interacting with as long as the object supports the methods we want to call. Because the type of the object isn't known by the IDE or compiler, neither IntelliSense nor compile-time syntax checking is possible but, in exchange, we get unprecedented flexibility.

If we enable strict type checking by using `Option Strict On` at the top of our code modules, then the IDE and compiler will enforce early binding behavior. By default, `Option Strict` is turned off and so we have easy access to the use of late binding within our code.

Implementing Late Binding

Late binding occurs when the compiler can't determine the type of object that we'll be calling. This level of ambiguity is achieved through the use of the `Object` data type. A variable of data type `Object` can hold virtually any value – including a reference to any type of object. Thus, code such as the following could be run against any object that implements a `DoSomething` method that accepts no parameters:

```
Option Strict Off

Module LateBind
  Public Sub DoWork(ByVal obj As Object)
    obj.DoSomething()
  End Sub
End Module
```

If the object passed into this routine *does not* have a `DoSomething` method that accepts no parameters, then a runtime error will result. Thus, it is recommended that any code that uses late binding always provides error trapping:

```
Option Strict Off

Module LateBind
  Public Sub DoWork(ByVal obj As Object)
    Try
```

```
        obj.DoSomething()
    Catch ex As Exception When Err.Number = 438
        ' do something appropriate given failure to call the method
    End Try
  End Sub
End Module
```

Here, we've put the call to the DoSomething method in a Try block. If it works then the code in the Catch block is ignored but, in the case of a failure, the code in the Catch block is run. We would need to write code in the Catch block to handle the case that the object did not support the DoSomething method call. This Catch block, in fact, only catches error number 438, which is the error indicating that the method doesn't exist on the object.

While late binding is flexible, it can be error prone and it is slower than early bound code. To make a late bound method call, the .NET runtime must dynamically determine if the target object actually has a method that matches the one we're calling, and then it must invoke that method on our behalf. This takes more time and effort than an early bound call where the compiler knows ahead of time that the method exists and can compile our code to make the call directly. With a late bound call, the compiler has to generate code to make the call dynamically at runtime.

Use of the CType Function

Whether we are using late binding or not, it can be useful to pass object references around using the Object data type – converting them to an appropriate type when we need to interact with them. This is particularly useful when working with objects that use inheritance or implement multiple interfaces – concepts that we'll discuss in Chapter 12.

This is done using the CType function – allowing us to use a variable of type Object to make an *early bound* method call:

```
Module LateBind
  Public Sub DoWork(obj As Object)
    Dim local As TheClass

    local = CType(obj, TheClass)
    local.DoSomething()
  End Sub
End Module
```

Here, we've declared a variable of type TheClass, which is an early bound data type that we want to use. The parameter we're accepting, though, is of the generic Object data type, and so we use the CType() method to gain an early bound reference to the object. If the object isn't of type TheClass, the call to CType() will fail with a trappable error.

Once we have a reference to the object, we can call methods by using the early bound variable, local.

> *Since all the method calls with CType() are early bound, this code will work even if we override the default and set Option Strict On.*

This code can be shortened to avoid the use of the intermediate variable. Instead, we can simply call methods directly from the data type:

```
Module LateBind
  Public Sub DoWork(obj As Object)
    CType(obj, TheClass).DoSomething()
  End Sub
End Module
```

Even though the variable we're working with is of type `Object` and, thus, any calls to it will be late bound, we are using the `CType` method to temporarily convert the variable into a +specific type – in this case, the type `TheClass`.

> Again, if the object passed as a parameter is not of type **TheClass**, we will get a trappable error, so it is always wise to wrap this code in a **Try...Catch** block, as we discussed for late binding.

The `CType` function can be very useful when working with objects that implement multiple interfaces, since we can reference a single object variable through the appropriate type as needed. For instance, as we discussed earlier, if we have an object of type `TheClass` that also implements `ITheInterface`, we can use that interface with the following code:

```
Dim obj As TheClass

obj = New TheClass
CType(obj, ITheInterface).DoSomething()
```

In this way, we can make early bound calls to other interfaces on an object without needing to declare a new variable of the interface type. We'll discuss multiple interfaces in detail in Chapter 12.

Creating Classes

Using objects is fairly straightforward and intuitive. It is the kind of thing that even the most novice programmers pick up and accept rapidly. *Creating* classes and objects is a bit more complex and interesting, however, and that is what we'll cover through the rest of the chapter.

Creating Basic Classes

As we discussed earlier, objects are merely instances of a specific template – called a class. The class contains the code that defines the behavior of its objects, as well as defining the instance variables that will contain the object's individual data.

Classes are created using the `Class` keyword, and include definitions (declaration) and implementations (code) for the variables, methods, properties, and events that make up the class. Each object created based on this class will have the same methods, properties, and events, and will have its own set of data defined by the variables in our class.

The Class Keyword

If we wanted to create a class that represents a person – a `Person` class – we could use the `Class` keyword like so:

```
Public Class Person
    ' implementation code goes here
End Class
```

As we know, VB.NET projects are composed of a set of files with the .vb extension. Each file can contain multiple classes. This means that, within a single file, we could have something like this:

```
Public Class Adult
    ' implementation code goes here
End Class

Public Class Senior
    ' implementation code goes here
End Class

Public Class Child
    ' implementation code goes here
End Class
```

The most common approach is to have a single class per file. This is because the VS.NET Solution Explorer and the code-editing environment are tailored to make it easy to navigate from file to file to find our code. For instance, if we create a single class file with all these classes, the Solution Explorer simply shows a single entry:

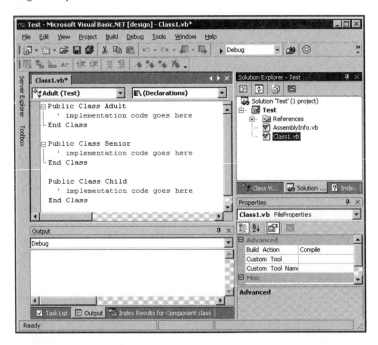

However, the VS.NET IDE does provide the Class View window. If we do decide to put multiple classes in each physical .vb file, we can make use of the Class View window to quickly and efficiently navigate through our code – jumping from class to class without having to manually locate those classes in specific code files:

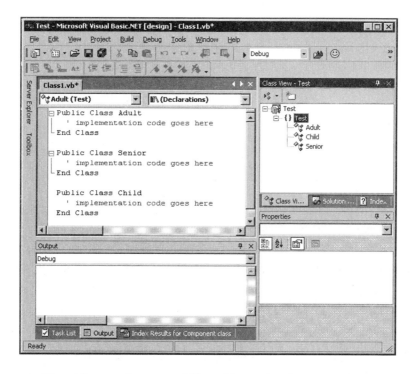

Of course, the Class View window is incredibly useful even if we keep to one class per file, since it still provides us with a class-based view of our entire application.

In this chapter, we'll stick with one class per file, as it is the most common approach. Open the VS.NET IDE and create a new Windows Application project. Name it Chapter11Demo.

Choose the Project | Add Class menu option to add a new class module to the project. We'll be presented with the standard Add New Item dialog.

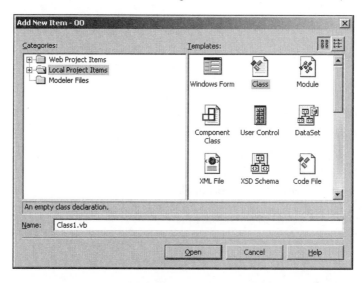

Change the name to `Person.vb` and click **Open**. The result will be the following code that defines our `Person` class:

```
Public Class Person

End Class
```

It is worth noting that *all* VB.NET source files end in a `.vb` extension, regardless of which type of VB source file we choose (form, class, module, etc.) when we are adding the file to our project. In fact, any forms, classes, components, or controls that we add to our project are actually class modules – they are just specific types of class that provide the appropriate behaviors. Typically, these behaviors come from another class via *inheritance*, which we'll discuss in Chapter 12.

> *The exception is the* `Module`, *which is a special construct that allows us to include code within our application that is not directly contained within any class. As with previous versions of Visual Basic, methods placed in a Module can be called directly from any code within our project.*

With our `Person` class created, we're ready to start adding code to declare our interface, implement our behaviors, and to declare our instance variables.

Member Variables

Member or instance variables are variables declared in our class that will be available to each individual object when our application is run. Each object gets its own set of data – basically each object gets its own copy of the variables.

At the beginning of the chapter, we discussed how a class is simply a template from which we create specific objects. Variables that we define within our class are also simply templates – and each object gets its own copy of those variables in which to store its data.

Declaring member variables is as easy as declaring variables within the `Class` block structure. Add the following code to our `Person` class:

```
Public Class Person
    Private mstrName As String
    Private mdtBirthDate As Date

End Class
```

We can control the scope of our variables by using the following keywords:

❑   `Private` – available only to code within our class

❑   `Friend` – available only to code within our project/component

❑   `Protected` – available only to classes that inherit from our class – discussed in detail in Chapter 12

❑   `Public` – available to code outside our class

Typically, member variables are declared using the `Private` keyword – making them available only to code within each instance of our class. Choosing any other option should be done with great care, as all the other options allow code *outside* our class to directly interact with the variable – meaning that the value could be changed and our code would never know that a change took place.

One common exception to making variables Private *is the use of the* Protected *keyword, as we'll discuss in Chapters 12 and 13.*

Methods

Objects typically need to provide services (or functions) that we can call when working with the object. Using their own data, or data passed as parameters to the method, they manipulate information to yield a result or to perform a service.

Methods declared as Public, Friend, or Protected in scope define the interface of our class. Methods that are Private in scope are only available to the code within the class itself, and can be used to provide structure and organization to our code. As we discussed earlier, the actual code within each method is called *implementation*, while the declaration of the method itself is what defines our interface.

Methods are simply routines that we code within the class to implement the services that we want to provide to the users of our object. Some methods return values or provide information back to the calling code. These are called **interrogative methods**. Others, called **imperative methods**, just perform a service and return nothing to the calling code.

In Visual Basic, methods are implemented using Sub (for imperative methods) or Function (for interrogative methods) routines within the class module that defines our object. Sub routines may accept parameters, but they don't return any result value when they are complete. Function routines can also accept parameters, and they always generate a result value that can be used by the calling code.

Another way to return values from either a Sub *or* Function *is by using* ByRef *parameters. When a parameter is declared using the* ByRef *keyword (as opposed to the default* ByVal *keyword), any changes to the value* within *our method are passed back to the calling code. Such value changes are known as* **side effects** *of a method. In both procedural and object-oriented design, this technique is frowned upon and should be avoided when possible, since it can make code difficult to read and understand.*

A method declared with the Sub keyword is merely one that returns no value. Add the following code to our Person class:

```
Public Sub Walk()
    ' implementation code goes here
End Sub
```

The Walk method would presumably contain some code that performed some useful work when called, but has no result value to return when it is complete.

To use this method, we might write code such as:

```
Dim myPerson As New Person()

myPerson.Walk()
```

Once we've created an instance of the Person class, we can simply invoke the Walk method.

Methods that Return Values

If we have a method that does generate some value that should be returned, we need to use the `Function` keyword.

```
Public Function Age() As Integer
   Return DateDiff(DateInterval.Year, mdtBirthDate, Now())
End Function
```

Notice that we need to indicate the data type of the return value when we declare a `Function`. In this example, we are returning the calculated age as a result of the method. We can return any value of the appropriate data type by using the `Return` keyword.

We can also return the value without using the `Return` keyword, by setting the value of the function name itself:

```
Public Function Age() As Integer
   Age = DateDiff(DateInterval.Year, mdtBirthDate, Now())
End Function
```

This is functionally equivalent to the previous code. Either way, we can use this method with code similar to the following:

```
Dim myPerson As New Person()
Dim intAge As Integer

intAge = myPerson.Age()
```

The `Age` method returns an `Integer` data value that we can use in our program as required – in this case we're just storing it into a variable.

Indicating Method Scope

Adding the appropriate keyword in front of the method declaration indicates the scope:

```
Public Sub Walk()
```

This indicates that `Walk` is a `Public` method and is thus available to code outside our class and even outside our current project. Any application that references our assembly can make use of this method. By being `Public`, this method becomes part of our object's interface.

On the other hand, we might choose to restrict the method somewhat:

```
Friend Sub Walk()
```

By declaring the method with the `Friend` keyword, we are indicating that it should be part of our object's interface *only for code inside our project* – any other applications or projects that make use of our assembly will not be able to call the `Walk` method.

```
Private Function Age() As Integer
```

The `Private` keyword indicates that a method is only available to the code within our particular class. `Private` methods are very useful to help us organize complex code within each class. Sometimes our methods will contain very lengthy and complex code. In order to make this code more understandable, we may choose to break it up into several smaller routines, having our main method call these routines in the proper order. Additionally, we may use these routines from several places within our class and so, by making them separate methods, we enable reuse of the code. These sub-routines should never be called by code outside our object – and so we make them `Private`.

There is also a `Protected` scope, which we'll discuss in Chapter 12 when we cover inheritance.

Method Parameters

We will often want to pass information into a method as we call it. This information is provided via parameters to the method. For instance, in our `Person` class, perhaps we want our `Walk` method to track the distance the person walks over time. In such a case, the `Walk` method would need to know how far the person is to walk each time the method is called. Add the following code to our Person class:

```
Public Class Person
   Private mstrName As String
   Private mdtBirthDate As Date
   Private mintTotalDistance As Integer

   Public Sub Walk(ByVal Distance As Integer)
     mintTotalDistance += Distance
   End Sub

   Public Function Age() As Integer
      Return DateDiff(DateInterval.Year, mdtBirthDate, Now())
   End Function
End Class
```

With this implementation, a `Person` object will sum up all of the distances that are walked over time. Each time the `Walk` method is called, the calling code must pass an `Integer` value indicating the distance to be walked. Our code to call this method would be similar to the following:

```
Dim myPerson As New Person()

myPerson.Walk(12)
```

The parameter is accepted using the `ByVal` keyword. This indicates that the parameter value is a *copy* of the original value. This is the default way VB.NET accepts all parameters. Typically, this is desirable because it means that we can work with the parameter inside our code – including changing its value – with no risk of accidentally changing the original value back in the calling code.

If we do want to be able to change the value in the calling code, we can change the declaration to pass the parameter by reference by using the `ByRef` qualifier:

```
Public Sub Walk(ByRef Distance As Integer)
```

In this case, we'll get a reference (or pointer) back to the original value rather than receiving a copy. This means that any change we make to the `Distance` parameter will be reflected back in the calling code – very similar to the way object references work, as we discussed earlier in the chapter.

> Using this technique can be dangerous, since it is not explicitly clear to the caller of
> our method that the value will change. Such unintended side effects can be incredibly
> hard to debug and should be avoided.

Properties

The .NET environment provides for a specialized type of method called a **property**. A property is a
method specifically designed for setting and retrieving data values. For instance, we declared a variable
in our `Person` class to contain a name, so our `Person` class may include code to allow that name to be
set and retrieved. This could be done using regular methods:

```
Public Sub SetName(ByVal Name As String)
   mstrName = Name
End Sub

Public Function GetName() As String
   Return mstrName
End Function
```

Using methods like these, we would write code to interact with our object such as:

```
Dim myPerson As New Person()

myPerson.SetName("Jones")
MsgBox(myPerson.GetName())
```

While this is perfectly acceptable, it is not as nice as it could be through the use of a property. A
`Property` style method consolidates the setting and retrieving of a value into a single structure, and
also makes the code within our class smoother overall. We can rewrite these two methods into a single
property. Add the following code to the `Person` class:

```
Public Property Name() As String
   Get
      Return mstrName
   End Get
   Set(ByVal Value As String)
      mstrName = Value
   End Set
End Property
```

By using a property method instead, we can make our client code much more readable:

```
Dim myPerson As New Person()

myPerson.Name = "Jones"
MsgBox(myPerson.Name)
```

The `Property` method is declared with both a scope and a data type:

```
Public Property Name() As String
```

In this example, we've declared the property as `Public` in scope, but it can be declared using the same scope options as any other method – `Public`, `Friend`, `Private`, or `Protected`.

As with other methods, a `Public` property is accessible to any code outside our class, while `Friend` is available outside our class, but only to code within our VB project. `Protected` properties are available through inheritance, as we'll discuss in Chapter 12, and `Private` properties are only available to code within our class.

The return data type of this property is `String`. A property can return virtually any data type as appropriate for the nature of the value. In this regard, a property is very similar to a method declared using the `Function` keyword.

Though a `Property` method is a single structure, it is divided into two parts – a getter and a setter.

The getter is contained within a `Get...End Get` block and is responsible for returning the value of the property on demand:

```
Get
   Return mstrName
End Get
```

Though the code in this example is very simple, it could be more complex – perhaps calculating the value to be returned or applying other business logic to change the value as it is returned.

Likewise, the code to change the value is contained within a `Set...End Set` block:

```
Set(ByVal Value As String)
   mstrName = Value
End Set
```

The `Set` statement accepts a single parameter value that stores the new value. Our code in the block can then use this value to set the property's value as appropriate. The data type of this parameter must match the data type of the property itself. By having the parameter declared in this manner, we can change the variable name used for the parameter value if needed.

By default, the parameter is named `Value`. However, if we dislike the name `Value`, we can change the parameter name to something else, for example:

```
Set(ByVal NewName As String)
   mstrName = NewName
End Set
```

In many cases, we may apply business rules or other logic within this routine to ensure that the new value is appropriate before we actually update the data within our object.

Parameterized Properties

The `Name` property we created is an example of a single-value property. We can also create property arrays or parameterized properties. These properties reflect a range, or array, of values. As an example, a person will often have several phone numbers. We might implement a `PhoneNumber` property as a parameterized property – storing not only phone numbers, but also a description of each number. To retrieve a specific phone number we'd write code such as:

```
Dim myPerson As New Person()
Dim strHomePhone As String

strHomePhone = myPerson.Phone("home")
```

Or, to add or change a specific phone number, we'd write:

```
myPerson.Phone("work") = "555-9876"
```

Not only are we retrieving and updating a phone number property, but also we're updating some specific phone number. This implies a couple of things. First off, we're no longer able to use a simple variable to hold the phone number, since we are now storing a list of numbers and their associated names. Secondly, we've effectively added a parameter to our property – we're actually passing the name of the phone number as a parameter on each property call.

To store the list of phone numbers we can use the Hashtable class. The Hashtable is very similar to the standard VB Collection object, but it is more powerful – allowing us to test for the existence of an existing element. Add the following declaration to the Person class:

```
Public Class Person
   Private mstrName As String
   Private mdtBirthDate As Date
   Private mintTotalDistance As Integer
   Private colPhones As New Hashtable()
```

We can implement the Phone property by adding the following code to our Person class:

```
Public Property Phone(ByVal Location As String) As String
  Get
    Return colPhones.Item(Location)
  End Get
  Set(ByVal Value As String)
    If colPhones.ContainsKey(Location) Then
      colPhones.Item(Location) = Value
    Else
      colPhones.Add(Location, Value)
    End If
  End Set
End Property
```

The declaration of the Property method itself is a bit different from what we've seen:

```
Public Property Phone(ByVal Location As String) As String
```

In particular, we've added a parameter, Location, to the property itself. This parameter will act as the index into our list of phone numbers and must be provided both when setting or retrieving phone number values.

Since the Location parameter is declared at the Property level, it is available to all code within the property – including to both the Get and Set blocks.

Within our `Get` block, we use the `Location` parameter to select the appropriate phone number to return from the `Hashtable`:

```
Get
   Return colPhones.Item(Location)
End Get
```

With this code, if there is no value stored matching the `Location`, we'll get a trappable runtime error.

Similarly, in the `Set` block, we use the `Location` to update or add the appropriate element in the `Hashtable`. In this case, we're using the `ContainsKey` method of `Hashtable` to determine whether the phone number already exists in the list. If it does, we'll simply update the value in the list – otherwise, we'll add a new element to the list for the value:

```
Set(ByVal Value As String)
   If colPhones.ContainsKey(Location) Then
      colPhones.Item(Location) = Value
   Else
      colPhones.Add(Location, Value)
   End If
End Set
```

In this way, we're able to add or update a specific phone number entry based on the parameter passed by the calling code.

ReadOnly Properties

There are times when we may want a property to be readonly – such that it can't be changed. In our `Person` class, for instance, we may have a read-write property for `BirthDate`, but just a readonly property for `Age`. In such a case, the `BirthDate` property is a normal property, as follows:

```
Public Property BirthDate() As Date
  Get
    Return mdtBirthDate
  End Get
  Set(ByVal Value As Date)
    mdtBirthDate = Value
  End Set
End Property
```

The `Age` value, on the other hand, is a derived value based on `BirthDate`. This is not a value that should ever be directly altered and, thus, is a perfect candidate for readonly status.

We already have an `Age` method – implemented as a `Function`. Remove that code from the `Person` class, as we'll be replacing it with a `Property` routine instead.

The difference between a Function routine and a ReadOnly Property is quite subtle. Both return a value to the calling code and, either way, our object is running a subroutine defined by our class module to return the value.

The difference is less a programmatic than a design choice. We could create all our objects without any Property *routines at all, just using methods for all interactions with the object. However,* Property *routines are obviously attributes of the object, while a* Function *might be an attribute or a method. By carefully implementing all attributes as* ReadOnly Property *routines, and any interrogative methods as* Function *routines, we will create more readable and understandable code.*

To make a property readonly, we use the ReadOnly keyword and only implement the Get block:

```
Public ReadOnly Property Age() As Integer
  Get
    Return DateDiff(DateInterval.Year, mdtBirthDate, Now())
  End Get
End Property
```

Since the property is readonly, we'll get a syntax error if we attempt to implement a Set block.

WriteOnly Properties

As with readonly properties, there are times when a property should be writeonly – where the value can be changed, but not retrieved.

Many people have allergies, so perhaps our Person object should have some understanding of the ambient allergens in the area. This is not a property that should be read from the Person object since allergens come from the environment rather than from the person, but it is data that the Person object needs in order to function properly. Add the following variable declaration to our class:

```
Public Class Person
  Private mstrName As String
  Private mdtBirthDate As Date
  Private mintTotalDistance As Integer
  Private colPhones As New Hashtable()
  Private mintAllergens As Integer
```

We can implement an AmbientAllergens property as follows:

```
Public WriteOnly Property AmbientAllergens() As Integer
  Set(ByVal Value As Integer)
    mintAllergens = Value
  End Set
End Property
```

To create a writeonly property, we use the WriteOnly keyword and only implement a Set block in our code. Since the property is writeonly, we'll get a syntax error if we attempt to implement a Get block.

The Default Property

Objects can implement a default property if desired. A default property can be used to simplify the use of our object at times, by making it appear as if our object has a native value. A good example of this behavior is the Collection object, which has a default property called Item that returns the value of a specific item, allowing us to write code similar to:

```
    Dim colData As New Collection()

    Return colData(Index)
```

Default properties *must be* parameterized properties. A property without a parameter cannot be marked as the default.

This is a change from previous versions of VB, where any property could be marked as the default.

Our Person class has a parameterized property – the Phone property we built earlier. We can make this the default property by using the Default keyword:

```
Default Public Property Phone(ByVal Location As String) As String
  Get
    Return colPhones.Item(Location)
  End Get
  Set(ByVal Value As String)
    If colPhones.ContainsKey(Location) Then
      colPhones.Item(Location) = Value
    Else
      colPhones.Add(Location, Value)
    End If
  End Set
End Property
```

Prior to this change, we would need code such as the following to use the Phone property:

```
Dim myPerson As New Person()

MyPerson.Phone("home") = "555-1234"
```

But now, with the property marked as Default, we can simplify our code:

```
myPerson("home") = "555-1234"
```

By picking appropriate default properties, we can potentially make the use of our objects more intuitive.

Events

Both methods and properties allow us to write code that interacts with our objects by invoking specific functionality as needed. It is often useful for our objects to provide notification as certain activities occur during processing. We see examples of this all the time with controls, where a button indicates it was clicked via a Click event, or a textbox indicates its contents have changed via the TextChanged event.

Our objects can raise events of their own – providing a powerful and easily implemented mechanism by which objects can notify our client code of important activities or events. In VB.NET, events are provided using the standard .NET mechanism of **delegates**. We'll discuss delegates after we explore how to work with events in VB.

Handling Events

We are all used to seeing code in a form to handle the `Click` event of a button – code such as:

```
Private Sub button1_Click (ByVal sender As System.Object, _
    ByVal e As System.EventArgs) Handles button1.Click

End Sub
```

Typically we just write our code in this routine without paying a lot of attention to the code created by the VS.NET IDE. However, let's take a second look at that code, since there are a couple of important things to note here.

First off, notice the use of the `Handles` keyword. This keyword specifically indicates that this method will be handling the `Click` event from the `button1` control. Of course, a control is just an object – so what we're indicating here is that this method will be handling the `Click` event from the `button1` *object*.

Also notice that the method accepts two parameters. The Button control class defines these parameters. It turns out that *any* method that accepts two parameters with these data types can be used to handle the `Click` event. For instance, we could create a new method to handle the event:

```
Private Sub MyClickMethod(ByVal s As System.Object, _
    ByVal args As System.EventArgs) Handles button1.Click

End Sub
```

Even though we've changed the method name, and the names of the parameters, we are still accepting parameters of the same *data types* and we still have the `Handles` clause to indicate that this method will handle the event.

Handling Multiple Events

The `Handles` keyword offers even more flexibility. Not only can the method name be anything we choose, but a single method can handle multiple events if we desire. Again, the only requirement is that the method and all the events being raised must have the same parameter list.

> *As an aside, this explains why all the standard events raised by the .NET system class library have exactly two parameters – the sender and an* EventArgs *object. By being so generic, it is possible to write very generic and powerful event handlers than can accept virtually any event raised by the class library.*

One common scenario where this is useful is where we have multiple instances of an object that raises events, such as two buttons on a form:

```
Private Sub MyClickMethod(ByVal sender As System.Object, _
    ByVal e As System.EventArgs) _
    Handles button1.Click, button2.Click

End Sub
```

Notice that we've modified the `Handles` clause to have a comma-separated list of events to handle. Either event will cause our method to run, giving us a central location to handle these events.

The WithEvents Keyword

We should be familiar with handling events as we just discussed, since this type of code is typical in both Windows Forms and Web Forms. What we don't normally see with controls on forms is how the control itself is declared. This is because the control declaration is contained in the hidden region of code that is created and maintained by the VS.NET IDE on our behalf.

On a form with a button control, however, if we look in the hidden code region we'll see that the button is declared using the `WithEvents` keyword:

```
Friend WithEvents button1 As System.Windows.Forms.Button
```

It is this keyword that tells VB that we want to handle any events raised by the object within our code.

The `WithEvents` keyword makes any events from an object available for our use, while the `Handles` keyword is used to link specific events to our methods so we can receive and handle them. This is true not only for controls on forms, but also for any objects that we create.

The `WithEvents` keyword cannot be used to declare a variable of a type that doesn't raise events. In other words, if the `Button` class didn't contain code to raise events, we'd get a syntax error when we attempted to declare the variable using the `WithEvents` keyword.

The compiler can tell which classes will and won't raise events by examining their interface. Any class that will be raising an event will have that event declared as part of its interface. In VB.NET, this means that we will have used the `Event` keyword to declare at least one event as part of the interface for our class.

Raising Events

Our objects can raise events just like a control, and the code using our object can receive these events by using the `WithEvents` and `Handles` keywords. Before we can raise an event from our object, however, we need to declare the event within our class by using the `Event` keyword.

In our `Person` class, for instance, we may want to raise an event any time the `Walk` method is called. If we call this event `Walked`, we can add the following declaration to our `Person` class:

```
Public Class Person
    Private mstrName As String
    Private mdtBirthDate As Date
    Private mintTotalDistance As Integer
    Private colPhones As New Hashtable()
    Private mintAllergens As Integer

    Public Event Walked()
```

Our events can also have parameters – values that are provided to the code receiving the event. A typical button's `Click` event receives two parameters, for instance. In our `Walked` method, perhaps we want to also indicate the distance that was walked. We can do this by changing the event declaration:

```
    Public Event Walked(ByVal Distance As Integer)
```

Now that our event is declared, we can raise that event within our code where appropriate. In this case, we'll raise it within the `Walk` method – so any time that a `Person` object is instructed to walk, it will fire an event indicating the distance walked. Make the following change to the `Walk` method:

```
Public Sub Walk(ByVal Distance As Integer)
   mintTotalDistance += Distance
   RaiseEvent Walked(Distance)
End Sub
```

The `RaiseEvent` keyword is used to raise the actual event. Since our event requires a parameter, that value is passed within parentheses and will be delivered to any recipient that handles the event.

In fact, the `RaiseEvent` statement will cause the event to be delivered to all code that has our object declared using the `WithEvents` keyword with a `Handles` clause for this event, or any code that has used the `AddHandler` method.

If more than one method will be receiving the event, the event will be delivered to each recipient one at a time. The order of delivery is not defined – meaning that we can't predict the order in which the recipients will receive the event – but the event will be delivered to all handlers. Note that this is a serial, synchronous process. The event is delivered to one handler at a time, and it is not delivered to the next handler until the current handler is complete. Once we call the `RaiseEvent` method, the event will be delivered to all listeners one after another until it is complete – there is no way for us to intervene and stop the process in the middle.

Receiving Events with WithEvents

Now that we've implemented an event within our `Person` class, we can write client code to declare an object using the `WithEvents` keyword. For instance, in our project's Form1 code module, we can write the following:

```
Public Class Form1
   Inherits System.Windows.Forms.Form

   Private WithEvents mobjPerson As Person
```

By declaring the variable `WithEvents`, we are indicating that we want to receive any events raised by this object.

We can also choose to declare the variable without the `WithEvents` keyword, though, in that case, we would not receive events from the object as described here. Instead we would use the `AddHandler` method, which we'll discuss after we cover the use of `WithEvents`.

We can then create an instance of the object, as the form is created, by adding the following code:

```
Private Sub Form1_Load(ByVal sender As System.Object, _
   ByVal e As System.EventArgs) Handles MyBase.Load

mobjPerson = New Person()

End Sub
```

At this point, we've declared the object variable using `WithEvents`, and have created an instance of the `Person` class so we actually have an object with which to work. We can now proceed to write a method to handle the `Walked` event from the object by adding the following code to the form. We can name this method anything we like – it is the `Handles` clause that is important as it links the event from the object directly to this method, so it is invoked when the event is raised:

```
Private Sub OnWalk(ByVal Distance As Integer) Handles mobjPerson.Walked
   MsgBox("Person walked " & Distance)
End Sub
```

We're using the `Handles` keyword to indicate which event should be handled by this method. We're also receiving an `Integer` parameter. If the parameter list of our method doesn't match the list for the event, we'll get a compiler error indicating the mismatch.

Finally, we need to call the `Walk` method on our `Person` object. Add a button to the form and write the following code for its `Click` event:

```
Private Sub button1_Click(ByVal sender As System.Object, _
      ByVal e As System.EventArgs) Handles button1.Click

   mobjPerson.Walk(42)

End Sub
```

When the button is clicked, we'll simply call the `Walk` method, passing an `Integer` value. This will cause the code in our class to be run – including the `RaiseEvent` statement. The result will be an event firing back into our form, since we declared the `mobjPerson` variable using the `WithEvents` keyword. Our `OnWalk` method will be run to handle the event, since it has the `Handles` clause linking it to the event.

The following diagram illustrates the flow of control:

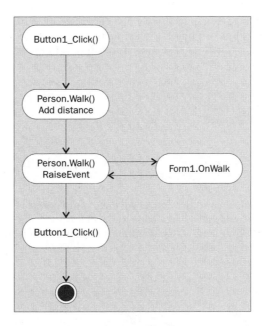

The diagram illustrates how the code in the button's click event calls the `Walk` method, causing it to add to the total distance walked and then to raise its event. The `RaiseEvent` causes the `OnWalk` method in the form to be invoked and, once it is done, control returns to the `Walk` method in the object. Since we have no code in the `Walk` method after we call `RaiseEvent`, the control returns to the `Click` event back in the form, and then we're all done.

Receiving Events with AddHandler

Now that we've seen how to receive and handle events using the `WithEvents` and `Handles` keywords, let's take a look at an alternative approach. We can use the `AddHandler` method to dynamically add event handlers through our code.

`WithEvents` and the `Handles` clause require that we declare both the object variable and event handler as we build our code, effectively creating a linkage that is compiled right into our code. `AddHandler`, on the other hand, creates this linkage at runtime, which can provide us with more flexibility. Before we get too deep into that, however, let's see how `AddHandler` works.

In Form1, we can change the way our code interacts with the `Person` object – first eliminating the `WithEvents` keyword:

```
Private mobjPerson As Person
```

and then also eliminating the `Handles` clause:

```
Private Sub OnWalk(ByVal Distance As Integer)
  MsgBox("Person walked " & Distance)
End Sub
```

With these changes, we've eliminated all event handling for our object and so our form will no longer receive the event, even though the `Person` object raises it.

Now we can change the code to dynamically add an event handler at runtime by using the `AddHandler` method. This method simply links an object's event to a method that should be called to handle that event. Any time after we've created our object, we can call `AddHandler` to set up the linkage:

```
Private Sub Form1_Load(ByVal sender As System.Object, _
    ByVal e As System.EventArgs) Handles MyBase.Load
  mobjPerson = New Person()
  AddHandler mobjPerson.Walked, AddressOf OnWalk
End Sub
```

This single line of code does the same thing as our earlier use of `WithEvents` and the `Handles` clause – causing the `OnWalk` method to be invoked when the `Walked` event is raised from our `Person` object.

However, this linkage is done at runtime, and so we have more control over the process than we have otherwise. For instance, we could have extra code to decide *which* event handler to link up. Suppose we have another possible method to handle the event in the case that a message box is not desirable. Add this code to Form1:

```
Private Sub LogOnWalk(ByVal Distance As Integer)
  System.Diagnostics.Debug.WriteLine("Person walked " & Distance)
End Sub
```

Rather than popping up a message box, this version of the handler logs the event to the Output window in the IDE.

Now we can enhance our `AddHandler` code to decide which handler should be used – dynamically at runtime:

```
   Private Sub Form1_Load(ByVal sender As System.Object, _
      ByVal e As System.EventArgs) Handles MyBase.Load
    mobjPerson = New Person()
    If Command() = "nodisplay" Then
      AddHandler mobjPerson.Walked, AddressOf LogOnWalk
    Else
      AddHandler mobjPerson.Walked, AddressOf OnWalk
    End If
   End Sub
```

If the word `nodisplay` is on the command line when our application is run, the new version of the event handler will be used – otherwise we'll continue to use the message box handler.

Constructor Methods

In VB.NET, classes can implement a special method that is always invoked *as* an object is created. This method is called the **constructor**, and it is always named `New`. We've seen this used before – most notably in a regular Windows form, where the `New` method is used to hold any initialization code for the form.

The constructor method is an ideal location for such initialization code, since it is always run before any other methods are ever invoked – and it is only ever run once for an object. Of course, we can create many objects based on a class – and the constructor method will be run for each object that is created.

> *The constructor method of a VB.NET class is similar to the `Class_Initialize` event in previous versions of Visual Basic – but is far more powerful since, in VB.NET, we can accept parameter values as input to the method.*

We can implement a constructor in our classes as well – using it to initialize our objects as needed. This is as easy as implementing a `Public` method named `New`. Add the following to our `Person` class:

```
   Public Sub New()
     Phone("home") = "555-1234"
     Phone("work") = "555-5678"
   End Sub
```

In this example, we're simply using the constructor method to initialize the home and work phone numbers for any new `Person` object that is created.

Parameterized Constructors

We can also use constructors to allow parameters to be passed to our object as it is being created. This is done by simply adding parameters to the `New` method. For example, we can change the `Person` class as follows:

```
   Public Sub New(ByVal Name As String, ByVal BirthDate As Date)
     mstrName = Name
     mdtBirthDate = BirthDate

     Phone("home") = "555-1234"
     Phone("work") = "555-5678"
   End Sub
```

With this change, any time a `Person` object is created, we'll be provided with values for both the name and birth date. This changes how we can create a new `Person` object, however. Where we used to have code such as:

```
Dim myPerson As New Person()
```

Now we will have code such as:

```
Dim myPerson As New Person("Peter", "1/1/1960")
```

In fact, since our constructor expects these values, they are mandatory – any code wishing to create an instance of our `Person` class *must* provide these values. Fortunately, there are alternatives in the form of optional parameters and method overloading (which allows us to create multiple versions of the same method – each accepting a different parameter list – something we'll discuss later in the chapter).

Constructors with Optional Parameters

In many cases, we may want our constructor to accept parameter values for initializing new objects – but we also want to have the ability to create objects without providing those values. This is possible through method overloading, which we'll discuss later, or through the use of optional parameters.

Optional parameters on a constructor method follow the same rules as optional parameters for any other `Sub` routine – they must be the last parameters in the parameter list and we must provide default values for the optional parameters.

For instance, we can change our `Person` class as shown:

```
Public Sub New(Optional ByVal Name As String = "", _
    Optional ByVal BirthDate As Date = #1/1/1900#)
  mstrName = Name
  mdtBirthDate = BirthDate

  Phone("home") = "555-1234"
  Phone("work") = "555-5678"
End Sub
```

Here we've changed both the `Name` and `BirthDate` parameters to be optional, and we are providing default values for both of them. Now we have the option of creating a new `Person` object with or without the parameter values:

```
Dim myPerson As New Person("Peter", "1/1/1960")
```

or

```
Dim myPerson As New Person()
```

If we don't provide the parameter values then the default values of an empty `String` and `1/1/1900` will be used and our code will work just fine.

Termination and Cleanup

In the .NET environment, an object is destroyed and the memory and resources it consumes are reclaimed when there are no references remaining for the object.

As we discussed earlier in the chapter, when we are using objects, our variables actually hold a reference or pointer to the object itself. If we have code such as:

```
Dim myPerson As New Person()
```

we know that the myPerson variable is just a reference to the Person object we created. If we also have code like this:

```
Dim anotherPerson As Person
anotherPerson = myPerson
```

we know that the anotherPerson variable is also a reference to *the same object*. This means that this specific Person object is being referenced by two variables.

When there are *no* variables left referencing an object, it can be terminated by the .NET runtime environment. In particular, it is terminated and reclaimed by a mechanism called garbage collection, which we'll discuss shortly.

> **Unlike COM (and thus VB6), the .NET runtime does not use reference counting to determine when an object should be terminated. Instead, it uses a scheme known as garbage collection to terminate objects. This means that, in VB.NET, we do not have deterministic finalization, so it is not possible to predict exactly when an object will be destroyed.**

Before we get to garbage collection, however, let's review how we can eliminate references to an object.

We can explicitly remove a reference by setting our variable equal to Nothing, with code such as:

```
myPerson = Nothing
```

> *There are two schools of thought as to whether we should still explicitly set variables to Nothing even when they fall out of scope. On the one hand, we can save writing extra lines of code by allowing the variable to automatically be destroyed but, on the other hand, we can explicitly show our intent to destroy the object by setting it to Nothing manually.*

We can also remove a reference to an object by changing the variable to reference a different object. Since a variable can only point to one object at a time, it follows naturally that changing a variable to point at another object must cause it to no longer point to the first one. This means we can have code such as:

```
myPerson = New Person()
```

which causes the variable to point to a brand new object – thus releasing this reference to the prior object.

These are examples of *explicit* dereferencing. VB.NET also provides facilities for *implicit* dereferencing of objects when a variable goes out of scope. For instance, if we have a variable declared within a method, when that method completes the variable will be automatically destroyed – thus dereferencing any object to which it may have pointed. In fact, any time a variable referencing an object goes out of scope, the reference to that object is automatically eliminated.

This is illustrated by the following code:

```
Private Sub DoSomething()
   Dim myPerson As Person

   myPerson = New Person()
End Sub
```

Even though we didn't explicitly set the value of myPerson to Nothing, we know that the myPerson variable will be destroyed when the method is complete since it will fall out of scope. This process implicitly removes the reference to the Person object created within the routine.

Of course, another scenario where objects become dereferenced is when the application itself completes and is terminated. At that point, all variables are destroyed and so, by definition, all object references go away as well.

Now that we understand how object references come and go, let's discuss garbage collection and the termination of VB.NET objects in more detail.

Garbage Collection

In .NET, objects are destroyed through a garbage collection mechanism. At certain times (based on specific rules), a task will run through all of our objects looking for those that no longer have any references. Those objects are then terminated; the garbage is collected.

> *The .NET garbage collection mechanism is a very complex bit of software, and the details of its inner workings are beyond the scope of this book.*

This means that we can't tell exactly when an object will really be finally destroyed. Just because we eliminate all references to an object doesn't mean it will be terminated immediately. It will just hang out in memory until the garbage collection process gets around to locating and destroying it. This is called **nondeterministic finalization**.

In some environments, such as COM, objects are destroyed in a deterministic fashion – meaning that we can tell *exactly* when the object will be terminated. In COM this is implemented through a reference counting mechanism, where each object keeps track of the number of references that are pointing at the object at any point in time. When that number reaches zero, the object knows that it can immediately destroy itself.

The major benefit of garbage collection is that it eliminates the circular reference issues found with reference counting. If two objects have references to each other, and no other code has any references to either object, the garbage collector will discover and terminate them, whereas, in a reference counting environment, these objects would sit in memory forever.

Garbage collection provides a potential performance benefit. Rather than expending the effort to destroy objects as they are dereferenced, with garbage collection this destruction process typically occurs when the application is otherwise idle – often decreasing the impact on the user. However, garbage collection may also occur when the application is active, in the case that the system starts running low on resources.

We can trigger the garbage collection process manually through code:

```
System.GC.Collect()
```

This process takes time, however, so it is not the sort of thing that should be done in a typical application.

Technically, we can call this method each time we set an object variable to Nothing – thus causing that object to be destroyed almost immediately. However, what we'd be doing is causing the garbage collector to scan all the objects in our application just to destroy one single object. This is very expensive in terms of performance.

It is far better to design our applications in such a way that it is acceptable for our objects to sit in memory for a time before they are finally terminated. This way we can allow the garbage collector to run from time to time based on its own rules – possibly collecting many dereferenced objects at a time, which is far more efficient and will have less impact on our application's performance.

To accomplish this goal, we need to design our objects such that they don't maintain expensive resources in instance variables. Things like database connections, open files on disk, or large chunks of memory (such as an image) are examples of expensive resources. If we rely on the destruction of the object to release this type of resource, we might be keeping that resource tied up for a lot longer than we expected.

Since the object isn't destroyed when we set it to Nothing, that means that the expensive resource isn't released then either. One solution to this is provided by the IDisposable interface, which we'll discuss shortly.

The Finalize Method

The question then becomes how to write code so our objects can perform any required cleanup processing before they are terminated. There are two points in time when we may want to do this cleanup – immediately when the last reference to the object is released, and right before the object is finally destroyed by the garbage collection mechanism.

There is no automatic way to handle cleanup as the last reference to an object is released. Implementing the IDisposable interface, which we'll discuss shortly, provides one possible solution.

However, the garbage collection mechanism does provide a mechanism by which we can run code immediately before our object is terminated. As an object is being terminated, the garbage collection code will call the object's Finalize method – allowing us to take care of any final cleanup that might be required:

```
Protected Overrides Sub Finalize()
  ' clean up code goes here
  MyBase.Finalize()
End Sub
```

This code uses both the Protected scope and Overrides keyword – concepts that we'll discuss later as we cover inheritance. For now, it is sufficient to know that these keywords are required as we create the Finalize method in our own classes.

Notice that we not only write our own cleanup code here (as indicated by the comment), but we also call MyBase.Finalize(), which causes our base class code to do any cleanup it requires as well. The MyBase keyword is discussed thoroughly in Chapter 12 when we cover inheritance – for now it is enough to know that this line of code should always be included in our Finalize method to ensure complete cleanup before our object is terminated.

It is also critical to remember that this method may be called long after the object is dereferenced by the last bit of client code (perhaps even minutes later).

The IDisposable Interface

In some cases the Finalize behavior is not acceptable. If we have an object that is using some expensive or limited resource – such as a database connection, a file handle, or a system lock – we might need to ensure that the resource is freed as soon as the object is no longer in use.

To accomplish this, we can implement a method to be called by the client code to force our object to clean up and release its resources. This is not a perfect solution, but it is workable. The thing to remember is that this method is not called automatically by the .NET runtime environment, but instead must be called directly by the code using the object.

The .NET framework provides the IDisposable interface that formalizes the declaration of this cleanup method. We'll discuss creating and working with multiple interfaces in detail later so, for now, we'll just focus on the implementation of the Dispose method from a cleanup perspective.

Any class that derives from System.ComponentModel.Component automatically gains the IDisposable interface. This includes all of the forms and controls that are used in a Windows Forms UI, as well as various other classes within the .NET framework. For most of our custom classes, however, we'll need to implement the interface ourselves.

We can implement it in our Person class by adding the following code to the top of the class:

```
Public Class Person
  Implements IDisposable
```

This interface defines a single method – Dispose – that we need to implement in our class. It is implemented by adding the following code to the class:

```
Private Sub Dispose() Implements IDisposable.Dispose
  colPhones = Nothing
End Sub
```

In this case, we're using this method to release our reference to the HashTable object that the colPhones variable points to. While not strictly necessary, this illustrates how our code can release other objects when the Dispose method is called.

It is up to our client code to call this method at the appropriate time to ensure that cleanup occurs. Typically, we'll want to call the method immediately prior to releasing the reference to our object.

This is not always as easy as it might sound. In particular, an object may be referenced by more than one variable and just because we're dereferencing the object from *one* variable doesn't mean it has been dereferenced by *all* the other variables. If we call the Dispose method while other references remain – our object may become unusable and may cause errors when invoked via those other references. There is no easy solution to this problem – so careful design is required in the case that we choose to use the IDispose interface.

In our application's **Form1** code, we use the OnLoad method of the form to create an instance of the Person object. In the form's OnClosed method, we may want to make sure we clean up by disposing of the Person object. To do this, add the following code to the form:

```
Private Sub Form1_Closed(ByVal sender As Object, _
    ByVal e As System.EventArgs) Handles MyBase.Closed

  CType(mobjPerson, IDisposable).Dispose()
  mobjPerson = Nothing

End Sub
```

The OnClosed method runs as the form is being closed, and so it is an appropriate place to do cleanup work.

Before we can dereference the Person object, however, we can now call its Dispose method. Since this method is part of a secondary interface (something we'll discuss more later), we need to use the CType() method to access that specific interface in order to call the method:

```
CType(mobjPerson(), IDisposable).Dispose()
```

CType() allows us to indicate the specific interface by which we want to access the object – in this case the IDisposable interface. Once we're using that interface, we can call the Dispose method to cause the object to do any cleanup before we release our reference:

```
mobjPerson() = Nothing
```

Once we've released the reference, we know that the garbage collection mechanism will eventually find and terminate the object – thus running its Finalize method. In the meantime, however, we've forced the object to do any cleanup immediately, so its resources are not consumed during the time between our release of the reference and the garbage collection terminating the object.

Advanced Concepts

So far we've seen how to work with objects, how to create classes with methods, properties, and events, and how to use constructors. We've also discussed how objects are destroyed within the .NET environment and how we can hook into that process to do any cleanup required by our objects.

Now let's move on to discuss some more complex topics and variations on what we've discussed so far. First, we'll cover some advanced variations in terms of the methods we can implement in our classes, including an exploration of the underlying technology behind events.

From there we'll move on to delegates, the difference between components and classes, and .NET attributes as they pertain to classes and methods.

Advanced Methods

So far, the methods we've worked with have been quite straightforward. They've either been Sub or Function routines. We've also discussed Property routines, which are a specialized type of method.

Now let's take a look at some advanced concepts that provide us with a great deal more power and capability as we work with methods.

Overloading Methods

Methods often accept parameter values. Our Person object's Walk method, for instance, accepts an Integer parameter:

```
Public Sub Walk(ByVal Distance As Integer)
  mintTotalDistance += Distance
  RaiseEvent Walked(Distance)
End Sub
```

Sometimes we may not want to require the parameter. To solve this issue we can use the Optional keyword to make the parameter optional:

```
Public Sub Walk(Optional ByVal Distance As Integer = 0)
  mintTotalDistance += Distance
  RaiseEvent Walked(Distance)
End Sub
```

This doesn't provide us with a lot of flexibility, however, since the optional parameter or parameters must always be the last ones in the list. Additionally, all this allows us to do is choose to pass or not to pass the parameter – suppose we want to do something fancier such as allow different data types, or even entirely different lists of parameters?

Method **overloading** provides exactly those capabilities. By overloading methods, we can create several methods of the *same name*, with each one accepting a different set of parameters or parameters of different data types.

As a simple example, instead of using the Optional keyword in our Walk method, we could use overloading. We'll keep our original Walk method, but add the Overloads keyword to indicate that it will no longer be unique. Change the code in our Person class to:

```
Public Overloads Sub Walk(ByVal Distance As Integer)
  mintTotalDistance += Distance
  RaiseEvent Walked(Distance)
End Sub
```

Then we can create another method – a method with the same name, but with a different parameter list (in this case no parameters). Add this code to the class, without removing or changing the existing Walk method:

```
Public Overloads Sub Walk()
  RaiseEvent Walked(0)
End Sub
```

Now we have the option of calling our `Walk` method in a couple of different ways. We can call it with a parameter:

```
objPerson.Walk(42)
```

or without a parameter:

```
objPerson.Walk()
```

We can have any number of `Walk` methods in our class by using the `Overloads` keyword – as long as each individual `Walk` method has a different **method signature**.

Method Signatures

All methods have a signature, which is defined by the method name and the data types of its parameters.

```
Public Function CalculateValue() As Integer

End Sub
```

In this example, the signature is `CalculateValue()`.

If we add a parameter to the method, the signature will change. For instance, we could change the method to accept a `Double`:

```
Public Function CalculateValue(ByVal Value As Double) As Integer
```

then the signature of the method is `CalculateValue(Double)`.

Notice that, in VB.NET, the return value is not part of the signature. We can't overload a `Function` routine by just having its return value's data type vary. It is the data types in the parameter list that must vary to utilize overloading.

Also make note that the *name* of the parameter is totally immaterial – only the data type is important. This means that the following methods have identical signatures:

```
Public Sub DoWork(ByVal X As Integer, ByVal Y As Integer)

Public Sub DoWork(ByVal Value1 As Integer, ByVal Value2 As Integer)
```

In both cases the signature is `DoWork(Integer, Integer)`.

Not only do the data types of the parameters define the method signature, but whether the parameters are passed `ByVal` or `ByRef` is also important. Changing a parameter from `ByVal` to `ByRef` will also change the method signature.

Combining Overloading and Optional Parameters

Overloading is more flexible than using optional parameters, but optional parameters have the advantage that they can be used to provide default values as well as making a parameter optional.

We can combine the two concepts – overloading a method with the `Overloads` keyword and also having one or more of those methods utilize optional parameters. Obviously, this sort of thing could get very confusing if overused, since we're employing two types of method "overloading" at the same time.

The `Optional` keyword causes a single method to effectively have two signatures. This means that a method declared as:

```
Public Sub DoWork(ByVal X As Integer, Optional ByVal Y As Integer = 0)
```

has two signatures at once: `DoWork(Integer, Integer)` and `DoWork(Integer)`.

Because of this, when we use overloading along with optional parameters, our other overloaded methods cannot match *either* of these two signatures. However, as long as our other methods don't match either signature, we can use the `Overloads` keyword as we discussed earlier. For instance, we could implement methods with the following different signatures:

```
Public Overloads Sub DoWork(ByVal X As Integer, _
    Optional ByVal Y As Integer = 0)
```

and

```
Public Overloads Sub DoWork(ByVal Data As String)
```

since there are no conflicting method signatures. In fact, with these two methods, we've really created three signatures:

❑   `DoWork(Integer, Integer)`

❑   `DoWork(Integer)`

❑   `DoWork(String)`

The IntelliSense built into the VS.NET IDE will show that we have two overloaded methods – one of which has an optional parameter. This is different from if we'd created three different overloaded methods to match these three signatures – in which case the IntelliSense would list three variations on the method from which we can choose.

Overloading the Constructor Method

We can combine the concept of a constructor method with method overloading to allow for different ways of creating instances of our class. This can be a very powerful combination, as it allows a great deal of flexibility in object creation.

We've already explored how to use optional parameters in the constructor. Now let's change our implementation in the `Person` class to make use of overloading instead. Change the existing `New` method as follows:

```
Public Overloads Sub New(ByVal Name As String, ByVal BirthDate As Date)
    mstrName = Name
    mdtBirthDate = BirthDate

    Phone("home") = "555-1234"
    Phone("work") = "555-5678"
End Sub
```

> The word Overloads here produces the following error with Beta 2: **A constructor cannot be declared with 'Overloads'.** This may be a bug with Beta 2 that could be changed in time for the final release.

With this change, we're returned to requiring the two parameter values be supplied, but we've also added the Overloads keyword to indicate that there will be at least one other implementation of the New method with a different method signature. Now add that second implementation as shown:

```
Public Overloads Sub New()
  Phone("home") = "555-1234"
  Phone("work") = "555-5678"
End Sub
```

> Again, the word Overloads here produces the following error with Beta 2: **A constructor cannot be declared with 'Overloads'.** If you are working with Beta 2, try deleting the Overloads word.

This second implementation accepts no parameters – meaning that we can now create Person objects in two different ways – either with no parameters or by passing the name and birth date:

```
Dim myPerson As New Person()
```

or:

```
Dim myPerson As New Person("Fred", "1/11/60")
```

This type of capability is very powerful, as it allows us to define the various ways in which applications can create our objects. In fact, the VS.NET IDE takes this into account so, when we are typing the code to create an object, the IntelliSense tool tip will display the overloaded variations on the method – providing a level of automatic documentation for our class.

Shared Methods and Variables

So far, all of the methods we've built or used have been **instance methods** – methods that require us to have an actual instance of the class before they can be called. These methods have used instance variables or member variables to do their work – meaning that they have been working with a set of data that is unique to each individual object.

VB.NET allows us to create variables and methods that belong to the *class* rather than to any specific *object*. Another way to say this is that these variables and methods belong to *all* objects of a given class and are shared across all the instances of the class.

We can use the Shared keyword to indicate which variables and methods belong to the class rather than to specific objects. For instance, we may be interested in knowing the total number of Person objects created as our application is running – kind of a statistical counter.

Shared Variables

Since regular variables are unique to each individual Person object, they don't allow us to easily track the total number of Person objects ever created. However, if we had a variable that had a common value *across* all instances of the Person class, we could use that as a counter. Add the following variable declaration to our Person class:

```
Public Class Person
   Implements IDisposable

   Private Shared sintCounter As Integer
```

By using the Shared keyword, we are indicating that this variable's value should be shared across all Person objects within our application. This means that if one Person object makes the value be 42, all other Person objects will see the value as 42 – it is a shared piece of data.

> *We are using the letter "s" as a prefix to this variable rather than "m". The letter "m" is commonly used for member variables (or module variables), but this variable is not a member variable – it is a shared variable. Using a different prefix can help distinguish between member and shared variables within our code.*

We can now use this variable within our code. For instance, we can add code to the constructor method, New, to increment the variable so it acts as a counter – adding 1 each time a new Person object is created. Change the New methods as shown:

```
Public Overloads Sub New()
   Phone("home") = "555-1234"
   Phone("work") = "555-5678"
   sintCounter += 1
End Sub

Public Overloads Sub New(ByVal Name As String, ByVal BirthDate As Date)
   mstrName = Name
   mdtBirthDate = BirthDate

   Phone("home") = "555-1234"
   Phone("work") = "555-5678"
   sintCounter += 1
End Sub
```

The sintCounter variable will now maintain a value indicating the total number of Person objects created during the life of our application. We may want to add a property routine to allow access to this value by writing the following code:

```
Public ReadOnly Property PersonCount() As Integer
   Get
      Return sintCounter
   End Get
End Property
```

Notice that we're creating a regular property that returns the value of a shared variable. This is perfectly acceptable. As we'll see shortly, we could also choose to create a shared property to return the value.

Now we could write code to use our class as follows:

```
Dim myPerson As Person

myPerson = New Person()
myPerson = New Person()
myPerson = New Person()

MsgBox(myPerson.PersonCount)
```

The resulting display would show 3 – since we've created three instances of the Person class.

Shared Methods

We cannot only share variables across all instances of our class, but we can also share methods. Where a regular method or property belongs to each specific object, a shared method or property is common across all instances of the class.

There are a couple of ramifications to this approach.

First off, since shared methods don't belong to any specific object, they can't access any instance variables from any objects. The only variables available for use within a shared method are shared variables, parameters passed into the method, or variables declared locally within the method itself. If we attempt to access an instance variable within a shared method, we'll get a compiler error.

Also, since shared methods are actually part of the *class* rather than any *object*, we can write code to call them directly from the class – without having to create an instance of the class first.

For instance, a regular instance method is invoked from an object:

```
Dim myPerson As New Person()

myPerson.Walk(42)
```

but a shared method can be invoked directly from the class itself:

```
Person.SharedMethod()
```

This saves the effort of creating an object just to invoke a method, and can be very appropriate for methods that act on shared variables, or methods that act only on values passed in via parameters. We can also invoke a shared method from an object just like a regular method. Shared methods are flexible in that they can be called with or without creating an instance of the class first.

To create a shared method we again use the Shared keyword. For instance, the PersonCount property we created earlier could easily be changed to be a shared method instead:

```
Public Shared ReadOnly Property PersonCount() As Integer
   Get
      Return sintCounter
   End Get
End Property
```

Since this property returns the value of a shared variable, it is perfectly acceptable for it to be implemented as a shared method. With this change, we can now find out how many `Person` objects have ever been created without having to actually create a `Person` object first:

```
MsgBox(Person.PersonCount)
```

As another example, in our `Person` class we could create a method that compares the ages of two people. Add a shared method with the following code:

```
Public Shared Function CompareAge(ByVal Person1 As Person, _
    ByVal Person2 As Person) As Boolean

  Return Person1.Age > Person2.Age

End Function
```

This method simply accepts two parameters – each a `Person` – and returns `True` if the first is older than the second. The use of the `Shared` keyword indicates that this method doesn't require a specific instance of the `Person` class for us to use it.

Within this code, we are invoking the `Age` property on two separate objects – the objects passed as parameters to the method. It is important to recognize that we're not *directly* using any instance variables within the method, but rather are accepting two objects as parameters and are invoking methods on those objects.

To use this method, we can call it directly from the class:

```
If Person.CompareAge(myPerson1, myPerson2) Then
```

Alternatively, we can also invoke it from any `Person` object:

```
Dim myPerson As New Person()

If myPerson.CompareAge(myPerson, myPerson2) Then
```

Either way, we're invoking the same shared method and we'll get the same behavior whether we call it from the class or a specific instance of the class.

Shared Properties

As with other types of method, we can also have shared property methods. Properties follow the same rules as regular methods – they can interact with shared variables, but not member variables, and they can invoke other shared methods or properties, but can't invoke instance methods without first creating an instance of the class.

We can add a shared property to our `Person` class with the following code:

```
Public Shared ReadOnly Property RetirementAge() As Integer
  Get
    Return 62
  End Get
End Property
```

This simply adds a property to our class that indicates the global retirement age for all people. To use this value, we can simply access it directly from the class:

```
MsgBox(Person.RetirementAge)
```

Alternatively, we can also access it from any `Person` object:

```
Dim myPerson As New Person()

MsgBox(myPerson.RetirementAge)
```

Either way, we're invoking the same shared property.

Delegates

There are times when it would be nice to be able to pass a procedure as a parameter to a method. The classic case is when building a generic sort routine, where we not only need to provide the data to be sorted, but we need to provide a comparison routine appropriate for the specific data.

It is easy enough to write a sort routine that sorts `Person` objects by name, or to write a sort routine that sorts `SalesOrder` objects by sales date. However, if we want to write a sort routine that can sort any type of object based on arbitrary sort criteria, that gets pretty difficult. At the same time, it would be nice to do, since some sort routines can get very complex and it would be nice to reuse that code without having to copy-and-paste it for each different sort scenario.

By using delegates, we can create such a generic routine for sorting – and in so doing we can see how delegates work and can be used to create many other types of generic routines.

The concept of a **delegate** formalizes the process of declaring a routine to be called and calling that routine.

> *The underlying mechanism used by the .NET environment for callback methods is the delegate.*
> *VB.NET uses delegates behind the scenes as it implements the* `Event`*,* `RaiseEvent`*,*
> `WithEvents`*, and* `Handles` *keywords.*

Declaring a Delegate

In our code, we can declare what a delegate procedure must look like from an interface standpoint. This is done using the `Delegate` keyword. To see how this can work, let's create a routine to sort any kind of data. Add a new module to our project by choosing the **Project | Add Module** menu option. Name the module `Sort.vb` and then add the following code:

```
Module Sort

    Public Delegate Function Compare(ByVal v1 As Object, ByVal v2 As Object) _
        As Boolean

End Module
```

This line of code does something interesting. It actually defines a method signature as a *data type*. This new data type is named `Compare` and it can be used within our code to declare variables or parameters that will be accepted by our methods. A variable or parameter declared using this data type can actually hold the address of a method that matches the defined method signature – and we can then invoke that method by using the variable.

Using the Delegate Data Type

We can write a routine that accepts this data type as a parameter – meaning that anyone calling our routine must pass us the address of a method that conforms to this interface. Add the following sort routine to the code module:

```
Public Sub DoSort(ByVal theData() As Object, ByVal GreaterThan As Compare)
   Dim outer As Integer
   Dim inner As Integer
   Dim temp As Object

   For outer = 0 To UBound(theData) - 1
     For inner = outer + 1 To UBound(theData) - 1
       If GreaterThan.Invoke(theData(outer), theData(inner)) Then
         temp = theData(outer)
         theData(outer) = theData(inner)
         theData(inner) = temp
       End If
     Next
   Next
End Sub
```

The `GreaterThan` parameter is a variable that holds the address of a method matching the method signature defined by our `Compare` delegate. The address of any method with a matching signature can be passed as a parameter to our `Sort` routine.

Note the use of the `Invoke` method, which is the way a delegate is called from our code. Also note that the routine deals entirely with the generic `System.Object` data type rather than with any specific type of data. The specific comparison of one object to another is left to the delegate routine that is passed in as a parameter.

Implementing a Delegate Method

All that remains is to actually create the implementation of the delegate routine and call our sort method. On a very basic level, all we need to do is create a method that has a matching method signature. For instance, we could create a method such as:

```
Public Function PersonCompare(ByVal Person1 As Object, _
    ByVal Person2 As Object) As Boolean

End Function
```

The method signature of this method exactly matches that which we defined by our delegate earlier:

```
Compare(Object, Object)
```

In both cases, we're defining two parameters of type `Object`.

Of course, there's more to it than simply creating the stub of a method. We know that the method needs to return a value of True if its first parameter is greater than the second parameter, but otherwise should be written to deal with some specific type of data.

The Delegate statement defines a data type based on a specific method interface. To call a routine that expects a parameter of this new data type, it must pass us the address of a method that conforms to the defined interface.

To conform to the interface, a method must have the same number of parameters with the same data types as we've defined in our Delegate statement. Additionally, the method must provide the same return type as defined. The actual name of the method doesn't matter – it is the number, order, and data types of the parameters and return value that count.

To find the address of a specific method, we can use the AddressOf operator. This operator returns the address of any procedure or method, allowing us to pass that value as a parameter to any routine that expects a delegate as a parameter.

Our Person class already has a shared method named CompareAge that generally does what we want. Unfortunately, it accepts parameters of type Person rather than of type Object as required by the Compare delegate. We can use method overloading to solve this problem. Change the existing CompareAge to be overloaded as follows:

```
Public Overloads Shared Function CompareAge(ByVal Person1 As Person, _
    ByVal Person2 As Person) As Boolean

  Return CType(Person1, Person).Age > CType(Person2, Person).Age

End Function
```

Then we can create a second implementation of CompareAge that accepts parameters of type Object as required by the delegate, rather than of type Person as we have in the existing implementation:

```
Public Overloads Shared Function CompareAge(ByVal Person1 As Object, _
    ByVal Person2 As Object) As Boolean

  Return CType(Person1, Person).Age > CType(Person2, Person).Age

End Function
```

This method simply returns True if the first Person object's age is greater than the second. The routine accepts two Object parameters rather than specific Person type parameters, so we have to use the CType() method to access those objects as type Person. We accept the parameters as type Object because that is what is defined by the Delegate statement. Since this method's parameter data types and return value match the delegate, we can use it when calling the sort routine. Place a button on the form and write the following code behind that button:

```
Private Sub button2_Click(ByVal sender As System.Object, _
    ByVal e As System.EventArgs) Handles button2.Click

  Dim myPeople(5) As Person

  myPeople(0) = New Person("Fred", #7/9/1960#)
```

```
   myPeople(1) = New Person("Mary", #1/21/1955#)
   myPeople(2) = New Person("Sarah", #2/1/1960#)
   myPeople(3) = New Person("George", #5/13/1970#)
   myPeople(4) = New Person("Andre", #10/1/1965#)

   DoSort(myPeople, AddressOf Person.CompareAge)
End Sub
```

This code creates an array of `Person` objects and populates them. It then calls the `DoSort` routine from our module, passing the array as the first parameter and the address of our shared `CompareAge` method as the second. To display the contents of the sorted array in the IDE's output window, we can add the following code:

```
Private Sub button2_Click(ByVal sender As System.Object, _
   ByVal e As System.EventArgs) Handles button2.Click

   Dim myPeople(5) As Person

   myPeople(0) = New Person("Fred", #7/9/1960#)
   myPeople(1) = New Person("Mary", #1/21/1955#)
   myPeople(2) = New Person("Sarah", #2/1/1960#)
   myPeople(3) = New Person("George", #5/13/1970#)
   myPeople(4) = New Person("Andre", #10/1/1965#)

   DoSort(myPeople, AddressOf Person.CompareAge)

   Dim myPerson As Person
   Dim intIndex As Integer

   For intIndex = 0 To UBound(myPeople) - 1
     myPerson = myPeople(intIndex)
     System.Diagnostics.Debug.WriteLine(myPerson.Name & " " & myPerson.Age)
   Next
End Sub
```

> Normally, we could use a **For Each** loop here, which would be easier. Unfortunately, there is a bug in Beta 2 when using **For Each** with arrays, and so we must use a numeric index variable instead.

When we run the application and click the button, the output window will display a list of the people, sorted by age:

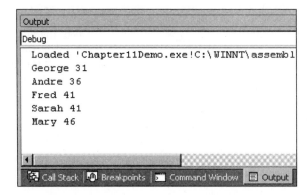

What makes this whole thing very powerful is that we can change the comparison routine without changing the sort mechanism. Simply add another comparison routine to the Person class:

```
Public Shared Function CompareName(ByVal Person1 As Object, _
    ByVal Person2 As Object) As Boolean

  Return CType(Person1, Person).Name > CType(Person2, Person).Name

End Function
```

and then change the code behind the button on the form to use that alternative comparison routine:

```
Private Sub button2_Click(ByVal sender As System.Object, _
    ByVal e As System.EventArgs) Handles button2.Click

  Dim myPeople(5) As Person

  myPeople(0) = New Person("Fred", #7/9/1960#)
  myPeople(1) = New Person("Mary", #1/21/1955#)
  myPeople(2) = New Person("Sarah", #2/1/1960#)
  myPeople(3) = New Person("George", #5/13/1970#)
  myPeople(4) = New Person("Andre", #10/1/1965#)

  DoSort(myPeople, AddressOf Person.CompareName)

  Dim myPerson As Person
  Dim intIndex As Integer

  For intIndex = 0 To UBound(myPeople) - 1
    myPerson = myPeople(intIndex)
    System.Diagnostics.Debug.WriteLine(myPerson.Name & " " & myPerson.Age)
  Next
End Sub
```

When we run this updated code, we'll find that our array contains a set of data sorted by name rather than by age:

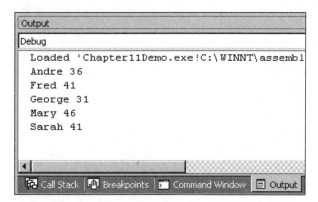

By simply creating a new compare routine and passing it as a parameter, we can entirely change the way that the data is sorted. Better still, this sort routine can operate on any type of object, as long as we provide an appropriate delegate method that knows how to compare that type of object.

Classes vs. Components

VB.NET has another concept that is very similar to a class – the component. In fact, we can pretty much use a component and a class interchangeably, though there are some differences that we'll discuss.

A component is really little more than a regular class, but it is one that supports a graphical designer within the VB.NET IDE. This means we can use drag-and-drop to provide the code in our component with access to items from the Server Explorer or from the Toolbox.

To add a component to a project, select the Project | Add Component menu option, give the component a name, and click Open in the Add New Item dialog:

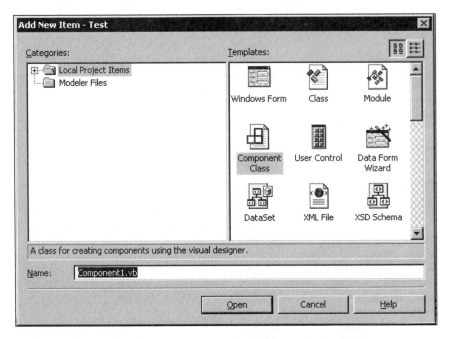

When we add a class to our project we are presented with the code window. When we add a *component* on the other hand, we are presented with a graphical designer surface, much like what we'd see when adding a Web Form to the project:

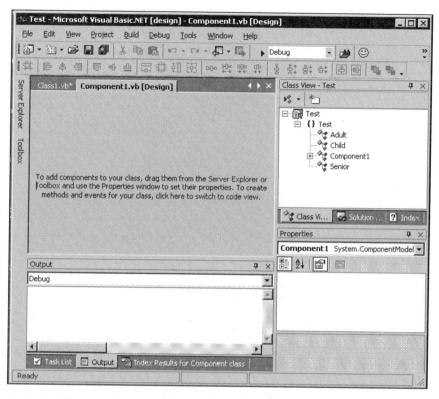

If we switch to the code view (by right-clicking in the designer and choosing View Code), we will see the code that is created for us automatically:

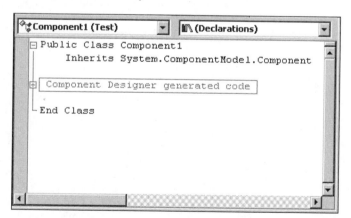

This isn't a lot more code than we'd see with a regular class, though there certainly are differences. First off, we see that this class inherits from System.ComponentModel.Component. While we'll discuss the concepts of inheritance in Chapters 12 and 13, it is important to note here that this Inherits line is what brings in all the support for the graphical designer we just saw.

There's also a collapsed region of code in a component. This region contains code generated by the graphical designer. Here's a quick look at what is included by default:

```vb
#Region " Component Designer generated code "

    Public Sub New(Container As System.ComponentModel.IContainer)
        MyClass.New()

        'Required for Windows.Forms Class Composition Designer support
        Container.Add(me)
    End Sub

    Public Sub New()
        MyBase.New()

        'This call is required by the Component Designer.
        InitializeComponent()

        'Add any initialization after the InitializeComponent() call

    End Sub

    'Required by the Component Designer
    Private components As System.ComponentModel.Container

    'NOTE: The following procedure is required by the Component Designer
    'It can be modified using the Component Designer.
    'Do not modify it using the code editor.
    <System.Diagnostics.DebuggerStepThrough()> Private Sub InitializeComponent()
        components = New System.ComponentModel.Container()
    End Sub

#End Region
```

As it stands, this code does very little beyond creating a single Container class object. However, if we switch the view back to the designer, we can drag-and-drop items onto our component. For instance, in the Toolbox there is a **Components** tab, which has entries for a variety of useful items such as a **MessageQueue**, a **DirectoryEntry**, and so forth. If we drag-and-drop a **Timer** (from the **Components** tab of the **Toolbox**) onto our component, it will be displayed in the designer:

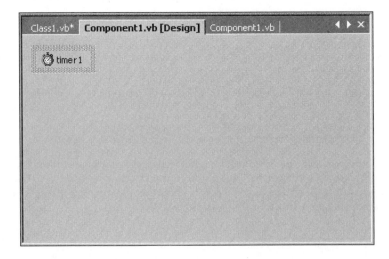

From here, we can set its properties using the standard **Properties** window in the IDE, just like we would for a control on a form. For instance, we can set its Name property to `theTimer`:

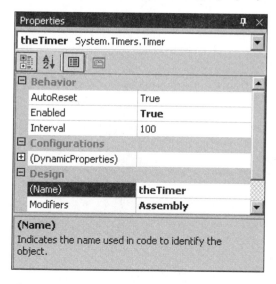

If we now return to the code window and look at the automatically generated code, we'll see that the region now includes code to declare, create, and initialize the `Timer` object:

```
#Region " Component Designer generated code "

    Public Sub New(Container As System.ComponentModel.IContainer)
        MyClass.New()

        'Required for Windows.Forms Class Composition Designer support
        Container.Add(me)
    End Sub
    Friend WithEvents theTimer As System.Timers.Timer

    Public Sub New()
        MyBase.New()

        'This call is required by the Component Designer.
        InitializeComponent()

        'Add any initialization after the InitializeComponent() call

    End Sub

    'Required by the Component Designer
    Private components As System.ComponentModel.Container

    'NOTE: The following procedure is required by the Component Designer
    'It can be modified using the Component Designer.
    'Do not modify it using the code editor.
    <System.Diagnostics.DebuggerStepThrough()> Private Sub InitializeComponent()
        Me.theTimer = New System.Timers.Timer()
        CType(Me.theTimer, _
            System.ComponentModel.ISupportInitialize).BeginInit()
        '
        'theTimer
        '
```

```
            Me.theTimer.Enabled = True
            CType(Me.theTimer, System.ComponentModel.ISupportInitialize).EndInit()

    End Sub

#End Region
```

Normally, we don't really care about the fact that this code was generated. Rather, what is important is that we now automatically, simply by dragging and dropping and setting some properties, have access to a Timer object named theTimer.

This means that we can write code within our component, just like we might in a class, to use this object:

```
    Public Sub Start()
      theTimer().Enabled = True
    End Sub

    Public Sub [Stop]()
      theTimer().Enabled = False
    End Sub

    Private Sub DoWork(ByVal sender As Object, ByVal e As EventArgs) _
        Handles theTimer.Tick
      ' do work
    End Sub
```

Here we can see that, with a simple drag-and-drop operation, we've gained access to a variable called theTimer referencing a Timer object, and we are able to create methods that interact with and use that object much like we would with a control dropped onto a form.

For the most part, we can use a component interchangeably with a basic class, but the use of a component incurs some extra overhead that a basic class does not, since it inherits all the functionality of System.ComponentModel.Component.

.NET Attributes

The .NET runtime environment can provide us with a great deal of power and capability. In many cases, we tap into this power through the use of a programming construct known as an **attribute**. An attribute is a tag that we can add to our code – to classes, methods, and variables – that instructs any code that interacts with our code how to behave.

Some attributes are instructions to the VB.NET compiler, some are instructions to the .NET runtime itself, others to the VS.NET IDE, and still others can be custom attributes that we might use for our own purposes. In this chapter, we'll stick to a discussion of attributes as they pertain to the .NET framework and typical VB development.

We specify an attribute on a class using the following syntax:

```
    <theAttribute()>  Public Class MyClass
```

For clarity, this is more often written using line continuation:

```
<theAttribute()> _
Public Class MyClass
```

This places the attribute or attributes on a separate line before the class declaration itself, increasing readability of the code.

Frequently, we'll want multiple attributes on a class. This is supported via the following syntax:

```
<theAttribute(), anotherAttribute()> _
Public Class MyClass
```

Each individual attribute is listed within the brackets, separated by commas.

Some attributes can also accept parameters. Take, for example, the Description attribute. This attribute is used to provide a text description for a class or method, and is supported by the VS.NET IDE. The result is that the description we provide via this attribute is automatically displayed as appropriate when people are working with our class. To use the Description attribute, add the following code to our Person class:

```
Imports System.ComponentModel

<Description("A simple person class")> _
Public Class Person
```

The Description attribute comes from the System.ComponentModel namespace and so we've added an Imports statement to bring that namespace into our class.

We can attach attributes to methods as well as to our class. Within the Person class, we can add a description to the PersonCount property for instance:

```
<Description("Returns the total number of Person objects")> _
Public ReadOnly Property PersonCount() As Integer
  Get
    Return sintCounter
  End Get
End Property
```

Often attributes accept named parameters, in which case we use the standard VB named parameter assignment of := in the call:

```
<anAttribute(SomeParam := theValue)> _
Public Class MyClass
```

Attributes are defined as a type of class. This means that they are syntax checked by the IDE and offer benefits such as IntelliSense. This also means that we can define our own attributes by creating an attribute class, and then we can use reflection to interrogate a class or object about its attributes – a powerful mechanism for building frameworks.

Attributes are an integral part of the .NET Framework. There are literally dozens of different attributes that are useful in various specific circumstances. Some attributes exist to support interaction with COM, others to support COM+ services, while still others are used within the .NET environment to support concepts such as Web Services.

What we've provided here should be enough information to understand how attributes work and how to use them within our code. We'll see examples of specific uses for attributes throughout the rest of the book.

Summary

VB.NET offers us a fully object-oriented language with all the capabilities we would expect. In this chapter, we've explored the basic concepts around classes and objects, as well as the separation of interface from implementation and data.

We've seen how to use the `Class` keyword to create classes, and how those classes can be instantiated into specific objects – each one an instance of the class. These objects have methods and properties that can be invoked by client code, and can act on data within the object stored in member or instance variables.

We also explored some more advanced concepts, including method overloading, shared or static variables and methods, and the use of delegates. Finally, we wrapped up with a brief discussion of attributes and how they can be used to affect the interaction of our class or our methods with the .NET environment.

In Chapter 12, we'll continue our discussion of object syntax as we explore the concept of inheritance and all the syntax that enables inheritance within VB.NET. We will also walk through the creation, implementation, and use of multiple interfaces – a powerful concept that allows our objects to be used in different ways depending on the interface chosen by the client application.

Then, in Chapter 13, we'll wrap up our discussion of objects and object-oriented programming by applying all of this syntax. We'll discuss the key object-oriented concepts of abstraction, encapsulation, polymorphism, and inheritance and see how they all tie together to provide a powerful way of designing and implementing applications.

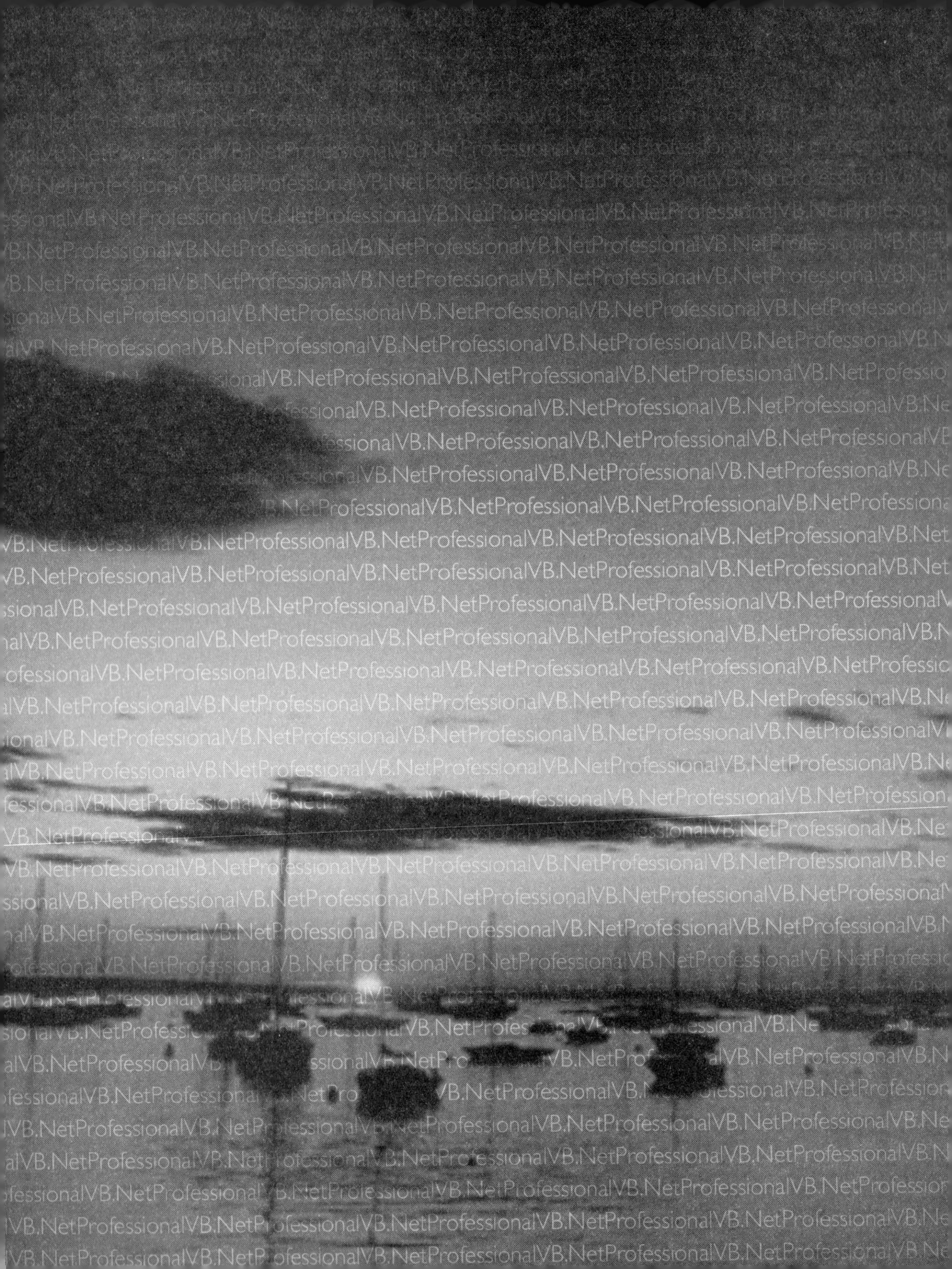
VB.NetProfessional

12

Inheritance and Interfaces

VB.NET is a fully object-oriented language. In Chapter 11 we covered the basics of creating classes and objects, including the creation of methods, properties, events, and instance variables.

We've seen the basic building blocks for abstraction, encapsulation, and polymorphism – concepts we'll discuss in more detail in Chapter 13. The final major techniques we need to cover are inheritance and the use of multiple interfaces.

Inheritance is the idea that we can create a class that reuses methods, properties, events, and variables from another class. We can create a class with some basic functionality, then use that class as a base from which to create other, more detailed, classes. All these classes will have the same common functionality from that base class, along with new, enhanced or even completely changed functionality.

In this chapter we'll cover the syntax that supports inheritance within VB.NET. This includes creating the base classes from which other classes can be derived, as well as creating those derived classes.

VB.NET also supports a related concept – multiple interfaces. We've already seen, in Chapter 11, that all objects have a native or default interface, which is defined by the Public methods, properties, and events declared in the class. In the .NET environment, an object can have other interfaces in addition to this native interface – in other words .NET objects can have multiple interfaces.

These secondary interfaces define alternative ways in which our object can be accessed by providing clearly defined sets of methods, properties, and events. Like the native interface, these secondary interfaces define how client code can interact with our object – essentially providing a "contract" that allows the client to know exactly what methods, properties, and events the object will provide. When we write code to interact with an object, we can choose which of the interfaces we want to use – basically we're choosing how we want to view or interact with that object.

In this chapter, we'll be using relatively basic code examples so we can focus right in on the technical and syntactic issues surrounding inheritance and multiple interfaces. In Chapter 13, we'll revisit these concepts using a more sophisticated set of code as we continue to explore object-oriented programming and how to apply inheritance and multiple interfaces in a practical manner.

Inheritance

Inheritance is the concept that a new class can be based on an existing class, inheriting its interface and functionality from the original class. In Chapter 11 we explored the relationship between a class and an object – where the class is essentially a template from which objects can be created:

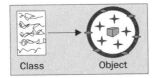

Class   Object

While this is very powerful, it doesn't provide all the capabilities we might like. In particular, there are many cases where a class only *partially* describes what we need for our object. We may have a class called Person, for instance, which has all the properties and methods that apply to all types of person – things like first name, last name and birth date. While useful, this class probably doesn't have everything we need to describe a *specific* type of person – such as an employee or a customer. An employee would have a hire date and a salary that are not included in the Person class, while a customer would have a credit rating – something neither the Person nor Employee classes would need.

Without inheritance, we'd probably end up replicating the code from the Person class into both the Employee and Customer classes so they'd have that same functionality as well as being able to add new functionality of their own.

Inheritance makes it very easy to create classes for Employee, Customer, and so forth. We don't have to recreate that code for an employee to be a person; it automatically gets any properties, methods, and events from the original Person class.

We can think of it this way. When we create an Employee class, which inherits from a Person class, we are effectively merging these two classes together. If we then create an object based on the Employee class, it not only has the interface (properties, methods, and events) and implementation from the Employee class, but it also has those from the Person class – automatically:

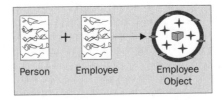

Person   Employee   Employee Object

This diagram shows how the Employee object was created from the Employee class – but that class essentially includes all the functionality and the interface from the Person class.

While an Employee object represents the merger between the Employee and Person classes, it is important to realize that the variables and code contained in each of those classes remains independent. There are two perspectives we need to understand.

From the *outside*, client code that interacts with the Employee object will see a single, unified object that represents the merger of the Employee and Person classes.

From the *inside*, the code in the Employee class and the code in the Person class aren't totally intermixed. Variables and methods that are `Private` are only available within the class where they were written. Variables and methods that are `Public` in one class can be called from the other class. Variables and methods that are declared as `Friend` are only available between classes if both classes are in the same VB.NET project. As we'll discuss later in the chapter there is also a `Protected` scope that is designed to work with inheritance – but again, this provides a controlled way for one class to interact with the variables and methods in the other class.

There is a standard notation called the universal modeling language (UML) that is typically used to diagram the relationships between classes, objects, and other object-oriented concepts. We can model the relationship between the Person, Employee, and Customer classes using UML:

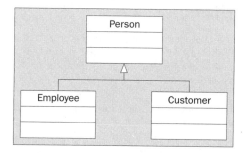

Each box in this diagram represents a class – in this case we have Person, Employee, and Customer classes. The line from Employee back up to Person, terminating in a triangle, indicates that Employee is derived from, or inherits from, Person. The same is true for the Customer class. We'll use UML through the rest of the chapter, as it is a standard diagramming notation for working with classes and objects.

> *If you'd like to learn more about UML,* Instant UML *by Pierre-Alain Muller (Wrox Press, 1861000871) is an excellent guide.*

We'll discuss when and how inheritance should be used in software design in more detail in Chapter 13. In this chapter, we'll cover the syntax and programming concepts necessary to implement inheritance. We'll create a base Person class, and then use that class to create both Employee and Customer classes that inherit behavior from Person.

Before we get into the implementation, however, we need to define some basic terms associated with inheritance. And there are a lot of terms – partly because there are often several ways to say the same thing, and the various terms are all used quite frequently and interchangeably.

> *Though we'll try to be consistent in our use of terminology in this book – it is important to note that in other books, articles, and online all these various terms are used in all their various permutations. This can make reading about and learning about object-oriented concepts difficult, but as we'll see, different terms for the same thing are often necessary to avoid radical misuse of English sentence structure.*

Inheritance, for instance, is also sometimes referred to as **generalization**. This is because the class from which we are inheriting our behavior is virtually always a more general form of our new class. A person is more general than an employee for instance.

The inheritance relationship is also referred to as an **"is-a" relationship**. When we create a Customer class that inherits from a Person class, that customer is a person. The Employee is a Person as well. Thus we have this "is-a" relationship. As we'll see later in this chapter, multiple interfaces can be used to implement something similar to the "is-a" relationship – the "act-as" relationship.

When we create a class using inheritance, we are inheriting behaviors and data from an existing class. That existing class is called the **base class**. It is also often referred to as a superclass or a parent class.

The class we create using inheritance is based on the parent class. It is called a **subclass**. Sometimes it is also called a child class or a derived class.

In fact, the process of inheriting from a base class to a subclass is often referred to as **deriving**. We are deriving a new class from the base class.

Implementing Inheritance

When we set out to implement a class using inheritance, we must first start with an existing class from which we will derive our new subclass. This existing class, or base class, may be part of the .NET system class library framework, it may be part of some other application or .NET assembly, or we may create it as part of our existing application.

Once we have a base class, we can then implement one or more subclasses based on that base class. Each of our subclasses will automatically have all of the methods, properties, and events of that base class – including the implementation behind each method, property, and event. Our subclass can add new methods, properties, and events of its own – extending the original interface with new functionality. Additionally, a subclass can replace the methods and properties of the base class with its own new implementation – effectively overriding the original behavior and replacing it with new behaviors.

Essentially inheritance is a way of merging functionality from an existing class into our new subclass. Inheritance also defines rules for how these methods, properties, and events can be merged – including control over how they can be changed or replaced, and how the subclass can add new methods, properties, and events of its own. This is what we'll explore as we go forward – what are these rules and what syntax do we use in VB.NET to make it all work.?

Creating a Base Class

Virtually any class we create can act as a base class from which other classes can be derived. In fact, unless we specifically indicate in the code that our class *cannot* be a base class, we can derive from it (we'll come back to this later in the chapter).

Create a new Windows Application project in VB.NET and name it Chapter12Demo. Then add a class to the project using the Project | Add Class menu option and name it Person.vb as shown in the following figure:

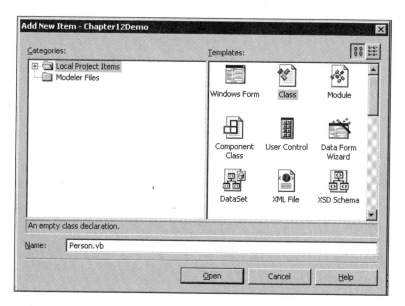

We start with the following code:

```
Public Class Person

End Class
```

At this point we technically have a base class, since it is possible to inherit from this class even though it doesn't do or contain anything.

We can now add methods, properties, and events to this class as we normally would – and all of those interface elements would be inherited by any class we might create based on Person. For instance, add the following code:

```
Public Class Person
  Private mstrName As String
  Private mdtBirthDate As String

  Public Property Name() As String
    Get
      Return mstrName
    End Get
    Set(ByVal Value As String)
      mstrName = Value
    End Set
  End Property

  Public Property BirthDate() As Date
    Get
      Return mdtBirthDate
    End Get
    Set(ByVal Value As Date)
      mdtBirthDate = Value
    End Set
  End Property
End Class
```

This gives us a simple method we can use to illustrate how basic inheritance works. This class can be represented by the following UML:

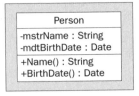

The overall box represents the Person class. In the top section we have the name of the class. In the middle section is a list of the instance variables, or attributes, of the class with their scope marked as Private due to the minus (–) symbol in front of each attribute. In the bottom section are the methods that make up the interface of the class – both marked as Public in scope due to the plus (+) symbol in front of each method.

Creating a Subclass

To implement inheritance we need to add a new class to our project. Use the Project I Add Class menu option and add a new class module named Employee.vb. We'll start with the following code:

```
Public Class Employee
   Private mdtHireDate As Date
   Private mdblSalary As Double

   Public Property HireDate() As Date
     Get
        Return mdtHireDate
     End Get
     Set(ByVal Value As Date)
        mdtHireDate = Value
     End Set
   End Property

   Public Property Salary() As Double
     Get
        Return mdblSalary
     End Get
     Set(ByVal Value As Double)
        mdblSalary = Value
     End Set
   End Property
End Class
```

This is a regular stand-alone class with no explicit inheritance. It can be represented by the following UML:

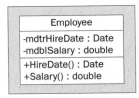

Again we can see the class name, its list of instance variables, and the methods it includes as part of its interface.

It turns out that, behind the scenes, this class inherits some capabilities from System.Object. *In fact every class in the entire .NET platform ultimately inherits from* System.Object *either implicitly or explicitly. This is why all .NET objects have a basic set of common functionality including* Equals, GetHashCode, GetType, ReferenceEquals, *and* ToString – *these all flow from the base* Object *type. We'll discuss this in detail later in the chapter.*

While having an employee object with a hire date and salary is useful – it should also have Name and BirthDate properties just like we implemented for our Person class. Without inheritance we'd probably just copy and paste the code from Person directly into the new Employee class, but with inheritance we can directly reuse the code from the Person class. Let's make our new class inherit from Person.

The Inherits Keyword

To make Employee a subclass of Person we just need to add a single line of code:

```
Public Class Employee
    Inherits Person
```

The Inherits keyword is used to indicate that a class should derive from an existing class – inheriting interface and behavior from that class. We can inherit from almost any class in our project, or from the .NET system class library or from other assemblies. It is possible to *prevent* inheritance – something we'll discuss later in the chapter. When using the Inherits keyword to inherit from classes outside our current project we need to either specify the namespace that contains that class or have an Imports statement at the top of the class to import that namespace for our use.

The fact that our Employee class is now a subclass of Person is illustrated by the following UML diagram:

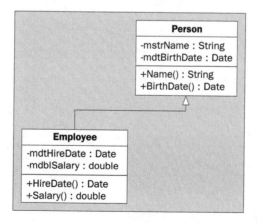

The line running from Employee back up to Person ends in an open triangle – which is the UML symbol for generalization – or inheritance. It is this line that indicates that the Employee class also includes all the functionality and the interface from Person.

This means that an object created based on the Employee class will not only have the methods HireDate and Salary, but will also have Name and BirthDate.

To test this, bring up the designer for `Form1` (which is automatically part of our project since we created a Windows Application project) and add the following TextBox controls along with a button to the form:

Control type	Name	Text value
TextBox	txtName	<blank>
TextBox	txtBirthDate	<blank>
TextBox	txtHireDate	<blank>
TextBox	txtSalary	<blank>
Button	btnOK	OK

We can also add some labels to make the form more readable. Our form designer should now look something like this:

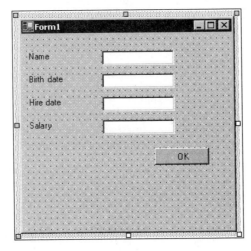

Double-click the button to bring up the code window and enter the following code:

```
Private Sub btnOK_Click(ByVal sender As System.Object, _
                        ByVal e As System.EventArgs) Handles btnOK.Click
    Dim objEmployee As New Employee()

    With objEmployee
        .Name = "Fred"
        .BirthDate = #1/1/1960#
        .HireDate = #1/1/1980#
        .Salary = 30000

        txtName.Text = .Name
        txtBirthDate.Text = Format(.BirthDate, "Short date")
        txtHireDate.Text = Format(.HireDate, "Short date")
        txtSalary.Text = Format(.Salary, "$0.00")
    End With
End Sub
```

Even though `Employee` doesn't directly implement `Name` or `BirthDate` methods, they are available for our use through inheritance. If we run this application and click on the button our controls will be populated with the values from the `Employee` object.

The following diagram shows how method calls from the form to our `Employee` object are actually serviced by the merger of the code from the `Employee` class and the `Person` class:

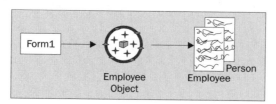

When the code in `Form1` invokes the `Name` property on our `Employee` object, the code from the `Person` class is executed, since the `Employee` class has no such method built-in. However, when the `HireDate` property is invoked on the `Employee` object, the code from the `Employee` class *is* executed since it does have that method as part of its code.

From the form's perspective it doesn't matter whether a method is implemented in the `Employee` class or the `Person` class – they are all simply methods of the `Employee` object. Also, since the code in these classes is merged together to create the `Employee` object, there is no performance difference between calling a method implemented by the `Employee` class or a method implemented by the `Person` class.

Overloading Methods

Though our `Employee` class automatically gained the `Name` and `BirthDate` methods through inheritance, it also has methods of its own – `HireDate` and `Salary`. This shows how we've extended the base `Person` interface by adding methods and properties to the `Employee` subclass.

We can add new properties, methods and events to the `Employee` class – and they will be part of any object created based on `Employee`. This has no impact on the `Person` class whatsoever, only on the `Employee` class and `Employee` objects.

We can even extend the functionality of the base class by adding methods to our subclass that have the same name as methods or properties in the base class – as long as those methods or properties have different parameter lists. We are effectively overloading the existing methods from the base class – essentially the same thing as overloading regular methods as we discussed in Chapter 11.

For example, our `Person` class is currently providing our implementation for the `Name` property. Employees may have other names we also want to store – perhaps an informal name and a very formal name in addition to their normal name.

One way to accommodate this requirement is to change the `Person` class itself to include an overloaded `Name` property that supports this new functionality. However, we're really only trying to enhance the `Employee` class, not the more general `Person` class, and so what we want is a way to add an overloaded method to the `Employee` class itself – even though we're overloading a method from its base class.

Overloading a method from a base class is done by using the `Overloads` keyword – just like we did when overloading a method in the same class in Chapter 11. The primary difference is that we *don't* need to go back and add the `Overloads` keyword to the base class itself – only the method in the subclass needs the `Overloads` keyword.

This is critical, since there's no guarantee that we even have access to the code for the base class. Since we can inherit from classes in the .NET system class library, or classes in assemblies available to us only as a DLL we must be able to overload methods without having the ability to see or change the code in the base class.

To overload the Name property, for instance, we can add a new property to the Employee class. First though, let's define an enumerated type using the Enum keyword. This Enum will list the different types of name we want to store. Add this Enum to the Employee.vb file – before the declaration of the class itself:

```
Public Enum NameTypes
   Informal = 1
   Formal = 2
End Enum

Public Class Employee
```

We can then add an overloaded Name property to the Employee class itself:

```
Public Class Employee
   Inherits Person

   Private mdtHireDate As Date
   Private mdblSalary As Double

   Private mcolNames As New Hashtable()

   Public Overloads Property Name(ByVal Type As NameTypes) As String
     Get
        Return mcolNames(Type)
     End Get
     Set(ByVal Value As String)
        mcolNames.Add(Type, Value)
     End Set
   End Property
```

This Name property is actually a property array – allowing us to store multiple values via the same property. In this case we're storing the values in a Hashtable object (similar to a Hashtable object), which is indexed by using the Enum value we just defined.

Technically the Overloads keyword is optional. If we don't use it our application will compile and run, but we'll get a warning message in the IDE indicating that we should be using the Overloads keyword.

Though this method has the same name as the method in the base class, the fact that it accepts a different parameter list allows us to use overloading to implement it here. The original Name property as implemented in the Person class remains intact and valid – but now we've added a new variation with this second Name property. This is illustrated by the following UML diagram:

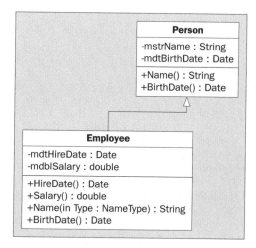

The diagram clearly indicates that the Name method in the Person class and the Name method in the Employee class both exist, and have different parameter lists.

It is also possible to *replace* the existing Name property from the Person class – that is called overriding and is something we'll discuss later in this chapter.

We can now change Form1 to make use of this new version of the Name property. First off, add a couple of new text box controls and associated labels. The text box controls should be named txtFormal and txtInformal and the form should now look like this:

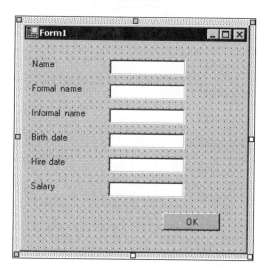

Now double-click on the button to bring up the code window and add code to work with the overloaded version of the Name property:

```
Private Sub btnOK_Click(ByVal sender As System.Object, _
    ByVal e As System.EventArgs) Handles btnOK.Click
  Dim objEmployee As New Employee()
```

```
With objEmployee
    .Name = "Fred"
    .Name (NameTypes.Formal) = "Mr. Frederick R. Jones, Sr."
    .Name (NameTypes.Informal) = "Freddy"
    .BirthDate = #1/1/1960#
    .HireDate = #1/1/1980#
    .Salary = 30000

    txtName.Text = .Name
    txtFormal.Text = .Name (NameTypes.Formal)
    txtInformal.Text = .Name (NameTypes.Informal)
    txtBirthDate.Text = Format(.BirthDate, "Short date")
    txtHireDate.Text = Format(.HireDate, "Short date")
    txtSalary.Text = Format(.Salary, "$0.00")
End With
End Sub
```

As we can see, the code still interacts with the original Name property as implemented in the Person class, but we are now also invoking the overloaded version of the property that is implemented in the Employee class.

Overriding Methods

So far we've seen how to implement a base class, then use it to create a subclass and finally we extended the interface by adding methods. We've also explored how to use overloading to add methods that have the same name as methods in the base class, but with different parameters.

However, there are times when we may want not only to extend the original functionality, but also to actually change or entirely replace the functionality from the base class. Instead of leaving the existing functionality and just adding new methods or overloaded versions of those methods, we might want to entirely **override** the existing functionality with our own.

We can do exactly this. If the base class allows it, we can substitute our own implementation of a method in the base class – meaning that our new implementation will be used instead of the original.

The Overridable Keyword

By default we can't override the behavior of methods on a base class. The base class must be coded specifically to allow this to occur by using the Overridable keyword. This is important, since we may not always want to allow a subclass to entirely change the behavior of the methods in our base class. However, if we do wish to allow the author of a subclass to replace our implementation, we can do so by adding the Overridable keyword to our method declaration.

Returning to our Employee example, we may not like the implementation of the BirthDate method as it stands in the Person class. In particular, we may not be able to employ anyone that is younger than 16 years of age, so any birth date value more recent than 16 years ago is invalid for an employee.

To implement this business rule, we need to change the way the BirthDate property is implemented. While we could make this change directly in the Person class, that would not be ideal. It is perfectly acceptable to have a *person* under age 16, just not an *employee*.

Open the code window for the Person class and change the BirthDate property to include the Overridable keyword:

```
Public Overridable Property BirthDate() As Date
  Get
    Return mdtBirthDate
  End Get
  Set(ByVal Value As Date)
    mdtBirthDate = Value
  End Set
End Property
```

This change allows any class that inherits from Person to entirely replace the implementation of the BirthDate property with a new implementation.

By adding the Overridable keyword to our method declaration we are indicating that we want to allow any subclass to override the behavior provided by this method. This means that we are giving permission for a subclass to totally ignore our implementation, or to extend our implementation by doing other work before or after our implementation is run.

If the subclass doesn't override this method, the method will work just like a regular method and will be automatically included as part of the subclass's interface. Putting the Overridable keyword on a method simply *allows* a subclass to override the method if we choose to do so.

The Overrides Keyword

In a subclass we override a method by implementing a method of the same name, and with the same parameter list as the base class and then using the Overrides keyword to indicate that we are overriding that method.

This is different from overloading, since when we *overload* a method we're adding a new method with the same name but a different parameter list. When we *override* a method we're actually replacing the original method with a new implementation.

Without the Overrides keyword we'll get a compilation error when we implement a method with the same name as one from the base class.

Open the code window for the Employee class and add a new BirthDate property:

```
Public Class Employee
  Inherits Person

  Private mdtHireDate As Date
  Private mdblSalary As Double
  Private mdtBirthDate As Date

  Private mcolNames As New Hashtable()

  Public Overrides Property BirthDate() As Date
    Get
      Return mdtBirthDate
    End Get
    Set(ByVal Value As Date)
      If DateDiff(DateInterval.Year, Value, Now()) >= 16 Then
        mdtBirthDate = Value
      Else
        Err().Raise(1001, "Employee", _
          "An employee must be at least 16 years old")
      End If
    End Set
  End Property
```

Since we're implementing our own version of the property, we have to declare a variable to store that value within the Employee class. This is not ideal, and there are a couple ways around this – including the MyBase keyword, which we'll discuss shortly and the Protected scope, which we'll discuss later in the chapter.

Notice also, that we've enhanced the functionality in the Set block so it now raises an error if the new birth date value would make the employee be less than 16 years of age. With this code we've now entirely replaced the original BirthDate implementation with a new one that enforces our business rule. This is illustrated by the following UML diagram:

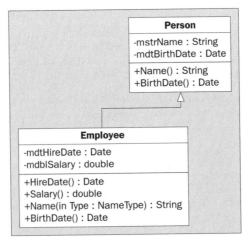

The diagram now includes a BirthDate method in the Employee class that has the same parameter list as the BirthDate method in the Person class. While perhaps not entirely intuitive, this is how UML indicates that we've overridden the method.

If we now run our application and click the button on the form everything should work as it did before. This is because the birth date we're supplying conforms to our new business rule. However, we can change the code in our form to use an invalid birth date:

```
With objEmployee
    .Name = "Fred"
    .Name(NameTypes.Formal) = "Mr. Frederick R. Jones, Sr."
    .Name(NameTypes.Informal) = "Freddy"
    .BirthDate = #1/1/2000#
```

When we click the button now we'll get an error indicating that the birth date is invalid – proving that we are now using the implementation of the BirthDate method from the Employee class rather than the one from the Person class.

Change the date value in the form back to a valid value so our application runs properly.

The MyBase Keyword

We've just seen how we can entirely replace the functionality of a method in the base class by overriding it in our subclass. However, this can be somewhat extreme – sometimes it would be preferable to override methods such that we *extend* the base functionality rather than *replacing* the functionality.

To do this we need to override the method using the `Overrides` keyword like we just did, but within our new implementation we can still invoke the *original* implementation of the method. This allows us to add our own code before or after the original implementation is invoked – meaning we can extend the behavior, while still leveraging the code in the base class.

To invoke methods directly from the base class we can use the `MyBase` keyword. This keyword is available within any class, and it exposes all the methods of the base class for our use.

> *Even a base class like `Person` is an implicit subclass of `System.Object`, and so it can use `MyBase` to interact with its base class as well.*

This means that within the `BirthDate` implementation in `Employee`, we can invoke the `BirthDate` implementation in the base `Person` class. This is ideal, since it means we can leverage any existing functionality provided by `Person`, while still enforcing our `Employee`-specific business rules.

To take advantage of this, we can enhance the code in the `Employee` implementation of `BirthDate`. First off, remove the declaration of `mdtBirthDate` from the `Employee` class. We won't need this variable any longer, since the `Person` implementation will keep track of the value on our behalf. Then change the `BirthDate` implementation in the `Employee` class as follows:

```
Public Overrides Property BirthDate() As Date
  Get
    Return MyBase.BirthDate
  End Get
  Set(ByVal Value As Date)
    If DateDiff(DateInterval.Year, Value, Now()) >= 16 Then
      MyBase.BirthDate = Value
    Else
      Err().Raise(1001, "Employee", _
        "An employee must be at least 16 years old")
    End If
  End Set
End Property
```

We can now run our application and we'll see that it works just fine even though the `Employee` class no longer contains any code to actually keep track of the birth date value. We've effectively merged the `BirthDate` implementation from `Person` right into our enhanced implementation in `Employee` – creating a hybrid version of the property.

We'll discuss the `MyBase` keyword in some more depth later in the chapter, but here we've seen how it can be used to allow us to enhance or extend the functionality of the base class by adding our own code in the subclass, but still invoking the base class method when appropriate.

Virtual Methods

The `BirthDate` method is an example of a **virtual method**. Virtual methods are those that can be overridden and replaced by subclasses.

Virtual methods are more complex to understand than regular non-virtual methods. With a non-virtual method there is only one implementation that matches any given method signature, so there's no ambiguity about which specific method implementation will be invoked. With virtual methods, however, there may be several implementations of the same method, with the same method signature, and so we need to understand the rules that govern which specific implementation of that method will be called.

When working with virtual methods we need to keep in mind that the data type of the *object* is used to determine the implementation of the method to call, rather than the type of the *variable* that refers to the object.

If we look at the code we've written in our form, we see that we're declaring an object variable of type Employee and we are then creating an Employee object that we can reference via that object:

```
Dim objEmployee As New Employee()
```

It is not surprising, then, that we are able to invoke any of the methods that are implemented as part of the Employee class – and through inheritance any of the methods implemented as part of the Person class:

```
With objEmployee
   .Name = "Fred"
   .Name(NameTypes.Formal) = "Mr. Frederick R. Jones, Sr."
   .Name(NameTypes.Informal) = "Freddy"
   .BirthDate = #1/1/1960#
   .HireDate = #1/1/1980#
   .Salary = 30000
```

When we call the BirthDate property we know that we're invoking the implementation contained in the Employee class – which makes sense since we know that we're using a variable of type Employee to refer to an object of type Employee.

However, because our methods are virtual methods, we experiment with some much more interesting scenarios. For instance, suppose that we change the code in our form to interact directly with an object of type Person instead of one of type Employee:

```
Private Sub btnOK_Click(ByVal sender As System.Object, _
     ByVal e As System.EventArgs) Handles btnOK.Click
   Dim objPerson As New Person()

   With objPerson
      .Name = "Fred"
      .BirthDate = #1/1/1960#

      txtName().Text = .Name
      txtBirthDate().Text = Format(.BirthDate, "Short date")
   End With
End Sub
```

Most obviously, we can no longer call the methods implemented by the Employee class, because they don't exist as part of a Person object – only as part of an Employee object. However, we can see that both the Name and BirthDate properties continue to function as we'd expect. When we run the application now it will work just fine. We can even change the birth date value to something that would be invalid for Employee:

```
.BirthDate = #1/1/2000#
```

The application will now accept it and work just fine, since the BirthDate method we're invoking is the original version from the Person class.

These are the two simple scenarios – where we have a variable and object of type `Employee` or a variable and object of type `Person`. However, since `Employee` is derived from `Person`, we can do something a bit more tricky. We can use a variable of type `Person` to hold a reference to an `Employee` object.

Because of this, we can change the code in `Form1` as follows:

```
Private Sub btnOK_Click(ByVal sender As System.Object, _
    ByVal e As System.EventArgs) Handles btnOK.Click
  Dim objPerson As Person
  objPerson = New Employee()

  With objPerson
    .Name = "Fred"
    .BirthDate = #1/1/2000#

    txtName().Text = .Name
    txtBirthDate().Text = Format(.BirthDate, "Short date")
  End With
End Sub
```

Notice that what we're doing now is declaring our variable to be of *type* `Person`, but the object itself is an instance of the `Employee` class. We've done something a bit complex here, since the data type of the variable is not the same as the data type of the object itself. The thing to remember is that a variable of a base class type can always hold a reference to an object of any subclass.

> *This is the reason that a variable of type `System.Object` can hold a reference to literally anything in .NET – because all classes are ultimately derived from `System.Object`.*

This technique is very useful when creating generic routines and makes use of an object-oriented concept called polymorphism that we'll discuss more thoroughly in Chapter 13. However, this technique allows us to create a more general routine that populates our form for any object of type `Person`. Add this code to the form:

```
Private Sub DisplayPerson(ByVal ThePerson As Person)
  With ThePerson
    txtName().Text = .Name
    txtBirthDate().Text = Format(.BirthDate, "Short date")
  End With
End Sub
```

Now we can change the code behind the button to make use of this generic routine:

```
Private Sub btnOK_Click(ByVal sender As System.Object, _
    ByVal e As System.EventArgs) Handles btnOK.Click
  Dim objPerson As Person
  objPerson = New Employee()

  With objPerson
    .Name = "Fred"
    .BirthDate = #1/1/2000#
  End With

  DisplayPerson(objPerson)
End Sub
```

The benefit here is that we can pass a `Person` object, or an `Employee` object to `DisplayPerson` and the routine will work the same either way.

When we run the application now things get interesting. We'll get an error when we attempt to set the `BirthDate` property because it breaks our 16 year old business rule – which is implemented in the *Employee class.* How can this be when our `objPerson` variable is of type `Person`?

This clearly demonstrates the concept of a virtual method. It is the data type of the object, in this case `Employee`, that is important. The data type of the *variable* is not the deciding factor when deciding which implementation of an overridden method is invoked

The following table illustrates which method is actually invoked based on the variable and object data types when working with virtual methods:

Variable	Object	Method invoked
Base	Base	Base
Base	Subclass	Subclass
Subclass	Subclass	Subclass

Virtual methods are very powerful and useful when we go to implement polymorphism using inheritance. A base class data type can hold a reference to any subclass object, but it is the type of that specific object that determines the implementation of the method. Because of this we can write generic routines that operate on many types of object as long as they derive from the same base class. We'll discuss this in more detail in Chapter 13.

Overriding Overloaded Methods

Earlier we wrote code in our `Employee` to overload the `Name` method in the base `Person` class. This allowed us to keep the original `Name` functionality, but also extend it by adding another `Name` method that accepted a different parameter list.

We've also overridden the `BirthDate` method. The implementation in the `Employee` class replaced the implementation in the `Person` class. Overriding is a related, but different, concept from overloading.

It is also possible to both overload and override a method at the same time.

In our earlier overloading example we added a new `Name` property to the `Employee` class, while retaining the functionality present in the base `Person` class. We may decide that we not only want to have our second overloaded implementation of the `Name` method, but that we also want to replace the existing one by overriding the existing method provided by the `Person` class.

In particular, we may want to do this so we can store the `Name` value in the `Hashtable` object along with our `Formal` and `Informal` names.

Before we can override the `Name` method we need to add the `Overridable` keyword to the base implementation in the `Person` class:

```
    Public Overridable Property Name() As String
      Get
        Return mstrName
      End Get
      Set(ByVal Value As String)
        mstrName = Value
      End Set
    End Property
```

With that done, the Name method can now be overridden by any derived classes. In the Employee class we can now override the Name method – replacing the functionality provided by the Person class. First, we'll add a Normal option to the Enum that controls the types of name value we can store:

```
Public Enum NameTypes
  Informal = 1
  Formal = 2
  Normal = 3
End Enum
```

Then we can add code to the Employee class to implement the replacement Name property:

```
    Public Overloads Overrides Property Name() As String
      Get
        Return Name (NameTypes.Normal)
      End Get
      Set(ByVal Value As String)
        Name (NameTypes.Normal) = Value
        MyBase.Name = Value
      End Set
    End Property
```

Notice that we're using both the Overrides keyword to indicate that we're overriding the Name method from the base class, and also the Overloads keyword to indicate that we're overloading this method in the subclass.

> *The Overloads keyword is optional, but we may see a compiler warning if we don't include it in our code.*

This new Name property not only contains code to store the value in the Hashtable object using the Normal index, but also maintains the value properly in the base class by using the MyBase keyword. To complete the linkage between this implementation of the Name property and the overloaded version that accepts a parameter we need to make one more change to that overloaded version:

```
    Public Overloads Property Name(ByVal Type As NameTypes) As String
      Get
        Return mcolNames(Type)
      End Get
      Set(ByVal Value As String)
        mcolNames.Add(Type, Value)
        If Type = NameTypes.Normal Then
          MyBase.Name = Value
        End If
      End Set
    End Property
```

This way, if the client code were to set the Name property by providing the Normal index, we are still updating the name in the base class as well as in the Hashtable object maintained by the Employee class.

Shadowing

Overloading allows us to add new versions of existing methods as long as their parameter lists are different. Overriding allows our subclass to entirely replace the implementation of a base class method with a new method that has the same method signature. As we've just seen, we can even combine these concepts to not only replace the implementation of a method from the base class, but also to simultaneously overload that method with other implementations that have different method signatures.

However, any time we override a method using the Overrides keyword, we are subject to the rules governing virtual methods – meaning that the data type of the *object* controls which implementation of the method is invoked. Sometimes we may want to be able to create a new implementation of a method in our subclass – replacing the implementation in the base class – but we don't want to follow the rules governing virtual methods. In particular, we may want to write client code that can use our object as though it were literally of the base class data type – totally being able to ignore the implementation in the subclass. This is a primary use for the Shadows keyword.

The Shadows keyword can also be used to entirely change the nature of a method or other interface element from the base class – though that is something that should be done with great care since it can seriously reduce the maintainability of our code. Normally, when we create an Employee object, we expect that it can only act as an Employee, but also as a Person since Employee is a subclass of Person. However, with the Shadows keyword we can radically alter the behavior of an Employee class so it *doesn't* act like a Person. This sort of radical deviation from what is normally expected invites bugs and makes code hard to understand and maintain.

We'll explore that in more detail later. First though, let's see how Shadows can be used to override non-virtual methods.

Overriding Non-Virtual Methods

Earlier in the chapter we discussed virtual methods and how they are automatically created in VB.NET when the Overrides keyword is employed. We can also implement **non-virtual methods** in VB.NET. Non-virtual methods are methods that cannot be overridden and replaced by subclasses, and so most methods we implement are non-virtual.

> **If we don't use the Overridable keyword when declaring a method, it is non-virtual.**

In the typical case, non-virtual methods are easy to understand. Since they can't be overridden and replaced, we know that there's only one method by that name, with that method signature and so when we invoke it there is no ambiguity about which specific implementation will be called. The reverse is true with virtual methods, where there may be more than one method of the same name, with the same method signature and so we need to understand the rules governing which implementation will be invoked.

Of course nothing is simple, and it turns out that we *can* override non-virtual methods by using the Shadows keyword. In fact, we can use the Shadows keyword to override methods regardless of whether or not they have the Overridable keyword in the declaration.

Obviously this can be *very* dangerous. The designer of a base class must use care when marking a method as `Overridable` – ensuring that the base class will continue to operate properly even when that method is replaced by other code in a subclass. Designers of base classes typically just assume that if they *don't* mark a method as `Overridable` that it *will* be called and not overridden. Thus, overriding a non-virtual method by using the `Shadows` keyword can have unexpected and potentially dangerous side effects since we are doing something that the base class designer assumed would never happen.

If that isn't enough complexity, it turns out that shadowed methods follow different rules than virtual methods when they are invoked. In other words, they don't act like regular overridden methods, but instead they follow a different set of rules to determine which specific implementation of the method will be invoked. In particular, when we call a non-virtual method, it is the data type of the *variable* that refers to the object that indicates which implementation of the method is called – not the data type of the *object* as with virtual methods.

To override a non-virtual method we can use the `Shadows` keyword instead of the `Overrides` keyword. To see how this works, let's add a new property to our base `Person` class:

```
Public ReadOnly Property Age() As Integer
  Get
    Return DateDiff(DateInterval.Year, Now(), BirthDate())
  End Get
End Property
```

We've added a new method to our base class – and thus automatically to our subclass – called `Age`.

This code has a bug – on purpose for illustration. The `DateDiff` parameters are in the wrong order, so we'll get negative age values from this routine. Why an intentional bug? Becomes sometimes there are bugs in base classes – sometimes in base classes we didn't write and can't fix because we don't have the source code. In this case we'll walk through the use of the `Shadows` keyword to help address a bug in our base class – acting under the assumption that for some reason we can't actually go fix the code in the `Person` class.

Notice that we're not using the `Overridable` keyword on this method, so any subclass is prevented from overriding the method by using the `Overrides` keyword. The obvious intent and expectation of this code is that all subclasses will use this implementation and will not override it with their own.

However, the base class cannot prevent a subclass from shadowing a method, and so it doesn't matter whether we use `Overridable` or not – either way works fine for shadowing.

Before we shadow the method, let's see how it works as a regular non-virtual method. First, we need to change our form to use this new value. Add a text box named `txtAge` and a related label to the form:

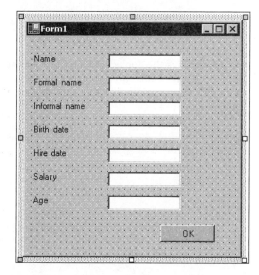

Next let's change the code behind the button to use the `Age` property. We'll also include the code to display the data on the form right here to keep things simple and clear:

```
Private Sub btnOK_Click(ByVal sender As System.Object, _
    ByVal e As System.EventArgs) Handles btnOK.Click
  Dim objPerson As Employee = New Employee()

  With objPerson
    .Name = "Fred"
    .BirthDate = #1/1/1960#

    txtName.Text = .Name
    txtBirthDate.Text = Format(.BirthDate, "Short date")
    txtAge.Text = .Age
  End With
End Sub
```

Also, don't forget to change the birth date value to something that will be valid for an `Employee`, since we don't want that to error out on us now.

At this point we can run the application and the age field should appear in our display as expected – though with a negative value due to the bug we introduced. There's no magic or complexity here – this is basic programming with objects and basic use of inheritance as we discussed at the beginning of this chapter.

Of course we don't want a bug in our code – but if we assume we don't have access to the `Person` class, and since the `Person` class doesn't allow us to override the `Age` method – what are we to do? The answer lies in the `Shadows` keyword – which allows us to override the method anyway.

Let's shadow the `Age` method within the `Employee` class – overriding and replacing the implementation in the `Person` class even though it is not marked as `Overridable`. Add the following code to `Employee`:

```
Public Shadows ReadOnly Property Age() As Integer
  Get
    Return DateDiff(DateInterval.Year, BirthDate(), Now())
  End Get
End Property
```

In many ways this looks very similar to what we've seen with the `Overrides` keyword, in that we're implementing a method in our subclass with the same name and parameter list as a method in the base class. In this case, however, we'll find some different behavior when we interact with the object in different ways.

Remember that our code in the form is currently declaring a variable of type `Employee` and is creating an instance of an `Employee` object:

```
Dim objPerson As Employee = New Employee()
```

This is the simple case, and not surprisingly when we run the application now we'll see that the value of the age field is correct – indicating that we just ran the implementation of the `Age` property from the `Employee` class. At this point we're seeing the same behavior that we got from overriding with the `Overrides` keyword.

Let's take a look at the other simple case – where we're working with a variable and object that are both of data type Person. Change the code in Form1 as follows:

```
Private Sub btnOK_Click(ByVal sender As System.Object, _
    ByVal e As System.EventArgs) Handles btnOK.Click
  Dim objPerson As Person = New Person()

  With objPerson
    .Name = "Fred"
    .BirthDate = #1/1/1960#

    txtName.Text = .Name
    txtBirthDate.Text = Format(.BirthDate, "Short date")
    txtAge.Text = .Age
  End With
End Sub
```

Now we have a variable of type Person and an object of that same type. We would expect that the implementation in the Person class would be invoked in this case, and that is exactly what happens – the age field will display the original negative value, indicating that we're invoking the buggy implementation of the method directly from the Person class. Again this is exactly the behavior we'd expect from a method overridden via the Overrides keyword.

This next one is where things get truly interesting. Change the code in Form1 as follows:

```
Private Sub btnOK_Click(ByVal sender As System.Object, _
    ByVal e As System.EventArgs) Handles btnOK.Click
  Dim objPerson As Person = New Employee()

  With objPerson
    .Name = "Fred"
    .BirthDate = #1/1/1960#

    txtName.Text = .Name
    txtBirthDate.Text = Format(.BirthDate, "Short date")
    txtAge.Text = .Age
  End With
End Sub
```

Now we are declaring the variable to be of type Person, but we are creating an object that is of data type Employee. We did this earlier in the chapter when exploring the Overrides keyword as well – and in that case we discovered that the version of the method that was invoked was based on the data type of the *object*. The BirthDate implementation in the Employee class was invoked.

If we run the application now we will find that the rules are different when the Shadows keyword is used. In this case, the implementation in the Person class is invoked – giving us the buggy negative value. The implementation in the Employee class is ignored – we get the exact opposite behavior to that with Overrides.

The following table summarizes which method implementation is invoked based on the variable and object data types when using shadowing or non-virtual methods:

Variable	Object	Method invoked
Base	Base	Base
Base	Subclass	Base
Subclass	Subclass	Subclass

In most cases the behavior we'll want for our methods is accomplished by the Overrides keyword and virtual methods. However, in those cases where the base class designer doesn't allow us to override a method and we want to do it anyway, the Shadows keyword provides us with the needed functionality.

Shadowing Arbitrary Elements

The Shadows keyword can be used not only to override non-virtual methods, but it can be used to totally replace and change the nature of a base class interface element. When we override a method we are providing a replacement implementation of that method with the same name and method signature. Using the Shadows keyword we can do more extreme things – like changing a method into an instance variable, or changing a Property into a Function.

However, this can be very dangerous, since any code written to use our objects will naturally assume that we implement all the same interface elements and behaviors as our base class – since that is the nature of inheritance.

> By totally changing the nature of an interface element, we can cause a great deal of confusion for programmers who will be interacting with our class in the future.

To see how we can replace an interface element from the base class, let's entirely change the nature of the Age property. In fact, let's change it from being a readonly property method to being a read-write property. We could get even more extreme – changing it to a Function or Sub.

To do this, remove the Age property from the Employee class and add the following code:

```
Public Shadows Property Age() As Integer
  Get
    Return DateDiff(DateInterval.Year, BirthDate(), Now())
  End Get
  Set(ByVal Value As Integer)
    BirthDate() = DateAdd(DateInterval.Year, -Value, Now())
  End Set
End Property
```

With this change, the very nature of the Age method has changed. It is no longer a simple read only property, now it is a read-write property that includes code to calculate an approximate birth date based on the age value supplied.

As it stands, our application will continue to run just fine. This is because we're only using the read-only functionality of the property in our form. We can change the form to make use of the new read-write functionality:

```
   Private Sub btnOK_Click(ByVal sender As System.Object, _
      ByVal e As System.EventArgs) Handles btnOK.Click
   Dim objPerson As Person = New Person()

   With objPerson
     .Name = "Fred"
     .BirthDate = #1/1/1960#
     .Age = 20

     txtName().Text = .Name
     txtBirthDate().Text = Format(.BirthDate, "Short date")
     txtAge().Text = .Age
   End With
End Sub
```

This will leave us with a syntax error, however.

The variable we're working with, objPerson, is of data type Person – and that data type does not provide a writable version of the Age property. This means that, in order to use our enhanced functionality, we must be using a variable and object of type Employee:

```
   Dim objPerson As Employee = New Employee()
```

If we now run the application and click the button we'll see that the Age is displayed as 20, and the birth date is now a value calculated based on that age value – indicating that we are now running the shadowed version of the Age method as implemented in the Employee class.

As if that wasn't odd enough, we can do some even more strange and dangerous things. We can change Age into a *variable* and we can even change its scope. For instance, we can comment out the Age property code in the Employee class and replace it with the following:

```
   Private Shadows Age As String
```

At this point we've changed everything. Age is now a String instead of an Integer. It is a variable instead of a Property or Function. It has Private scope instead of Public scope.

At this point our Employee object is totally incompatible with the Person data type – something that shouldn't occur normally when using inheritance.

This means that the code we wrote in Form1 will no longer work. The Age property is no longer accessible and can no longer be used and so our project will no longer compile. This directly illustrates the danger in shadowing a base class element such that its very nature or scope is changed by the subclass.

Since this change prevents our application from compiling, remove the line in the Employee class that shadows Age as a String variable – and uncomment the shadowed Property routine.

```
   Public Shadows Property Age() As Integer
     Get
       Return DateDiff(DateInterval.Year, BirthDate(), Now())
     End Get
     Set(ByVal Value As Integer)
       BirthDate() = DateAdd(DateInterval.Year, -Value, Now())
     End Set
   End Property
```

This will restore our application to a working state and we can move on.

Levels of Inheritance

So far we've created a single base class and a single subclass – thus demonstrating that we can implement inheritance that is a single level deep. However, we can create inheritance relationships that are many levels deep. These are sometimes referred to as chains of inheritance.

> *In reality we've been creating a two-level inheritance hierarchy so far because we know that our base class actually derived from* System.Object *– but for most purposes it is easiest to simply ignore that fact and treat only our classes as part of the inheritance hierarchy.*

Multiple Inheritance

Don't confuse multi-level inheritance with multiple inheritance, which is an entirely different concept that is not supported by either VB.NET or the .NET platform itself. The idea behind **multiple inheritance** is that we can have a single subclass that inherits from two base classes all at the same time.

For instance, we may have an application that has a class for Customer and another class for Vendor. It is quite possible that some customers are also vendors, so we might want to combine the functionality of these two classes into a CustomerVendor class. This new class would be a combination of both Customer and Vendor – so it would be nice to inherit from both of them at once – something like the following UML diagram might indicate:

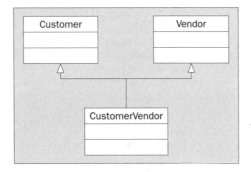

Here we see the line running from CustomerVendor back up into both Customer *and* Vendor and terminating in an open triangle in both cases. This indicates that CustomerVendor inherits from both of those classes.

While a useful concept, multiple inheritance is a complex and somewhat dangerous concept. Within the object-oriented community there is continual debate as to whether the advantages of code reuse outweigh the complexity that comes along for the ride.

Multiple inheritance is not supported by the .NET framework, and so it is likewise not supported by VB.NET. However, we can use multiple interfaces to achieve an effect similar to multiple inheritance – a topic we'll discuss later in the chapter when we discuss implementing multiple interfaces.

Multi-Level Inheritance

We've seen how a subclass derives from a base class with our `Person` and `Employee` classes:

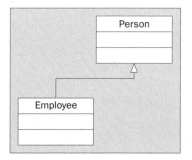

However, there's nothing to stop the `Employee` subclass from being the base class for yet another class – a sub subclass so to speak. This is not at all uncommon. In our example, we may find that we have different kinds of employees – some who work in the office, and others who travel.

To accommodate this, we may want to have OfficeEmployee and TravelingEmployee classes. Of course these are both examples of an employee – and should share the functionality already present in the Employee class. The `Employee` class already reuses the functionality from the `Person` class. The following UML illustrates how these classes are interrelated:

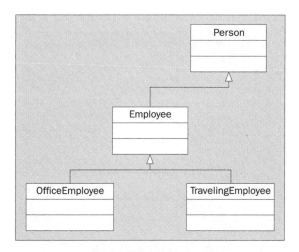

We can see that the `Employee` is a subclass of `Person` – and our two new classes are both subclasses of `Employee`. While both `OfficeEmployee` and `TravelingEmployee` are employees, and thus also people, they are each unique. An `OfficeEmployee` almost certainly has a cube or office number, while a `TravelingEmployee` will keep track of the number of miles traveled.

Add a new class to our project and name it `OfficeEmployee`. To make this class inherit from our existing `Employee` class, add the following code to the class:

```
Public Class OfficeEmployee
    Inherits Employee

End Class
```

With this change, the new class now has `Name`, `BirthDate`, `Age`, `HireDate`, and `Salary` methods. Notice that methods from both `Employee` and `Person` are inherited. A subclass always gains all the methods, properties, and events of its base class.

We can now extend the interface and behavior of `OfficeEmployee` by adding a property to indicate which cube or office number the employee occupies:

```
Public Class OfficeEmployee
   Inherits Employee

   Private mstrOffice As String

   Public Property OfficeNumber() As String
     Get
        Return mstrOffice
     End Get
     Set(ByVal Value As String)
        mstrOffice = Value
     End Set
   End Property
End Class
```

To see how this works, let's enhance our form to display this value. Add a new text box control named `txtOffice` and an associated label so our form looks as follows:

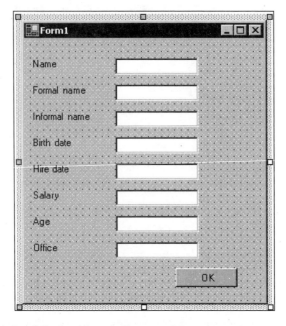

Now change the code behind the button to make use of the new property:

```
Private Sub btnOK_Click(ByVal sender As System.Object, _
     ByVal e As System.EventArgs) Handles btnOK.Click
   Dim objPerson As OfficeEmployee = New OfficeEmployee()
```

```
    With objPerson
      .Name = "Fred"
      .BirthDate = #1/1/1960#
      .Age = 20
      .OfficeNumber = "A42"

      txtName().Text = .Name
      txtBirthDate().Text = Format(.BirthDate, "Short date")
      txtAge().Text = .Age
      txtOffice().Text = .OfficeNumber
    End With
  End Sub
```

We've changed the routine to declare and create an object of type OfficeEmployee – thus allowing us to make use of the new property – as well as all existing properties and methods from Employee and Person since they've been "merged" into the OfficeEmployee class via inheritance.

If we now run the application we'll see that the name, birth date, age, and office values are displayed in the form.

Inheritance like this can go many levels deep with each level extending and changing the behaviors of the previous levels. In fact there is no specific technical limit to the number of levels of inheritance we can implement in VB.NET. Very deep inheritance chains are typically not recommended and are often viewed as a design flaw – something we'll discuss in more detail in Chapter 13.

Interacting with the Base Class, Our Class, and Our Object

We've already seen how we can use the MyBase keyword to call methods on the base class from within a subclass. The MyBase keyword is one of three special keywords that allow us to interact with important object and class representations:

❑   Me

❑   MyBase

❑   MyClass

Each of these keywords is very useful for different purposes.

The Me Keyword

The Me keyword provides us with a reference to our current object instance. Typically, we don't need to use the Me keyword, since any time we want to invoke a method within our current object we can just call that method directly.

To see clearly how this works, let's add a new method to the Person class that returns the data of the Person class in the form of a String. This will be a bit interesting in and of itself, since the base System.Object class defines the ToString method for this exact purpose. Remember that *all* classes in .NET ultimately derive from System.Object – even if we don't explicitly indicate it with an Inherits statement.

This means we can simply override the ToString method from the Object class within our Person class by adding the following code:

```
Public Overrides Function ToString() As String
   Return Name()
End Function
```

This implementation will return the person's Name property as a result when ToString is called.

> *By default, ToString returns the class name of the class. Up to now, if we had called the ToString method on a Person object we would have gotten a result of Chapter12Demo.Person.*

Notice that the ToString method is calling another method within our same class – in this case the Name method.

We could also write this routine using the Me keyword:

```
Public Overrides Function ToString() As String
   Return Me.Name()
End Function
```

This is redundant, however, since Me is the default for all method calls in a class. These two implementations are identical, and so typically the Me keyword is simply left off to avoid that extra typing.

To see how the ToString method now works, we can change our code in Form1 to use this value instead of the Name property:

```
Private Sub btnOK_Click(ByVal sender As System.Object, _
    ByVal e As System.EventArgs) Handles btnOK.Click
  Dim objPerson As OfficeEmployee = New OfficeEmployee()

  With objPerson
    .Name = "Fred"
    .BirthDate = #1/1/1960#
    .Age = 20
    .OfficeNumber = "A42"

    txtName.Text = .ToString
    txtBirthDate.Text = Format(.BirthDate, "Short date")
    txtAge.Text = .Age
    txtOffice.Text = .OfficeNumber
  End With
End Sub
```

When we run the application we'll see that the person's name is displayed appropriately – which makes sense since the ToString method is simply returning the result from the Name property.

Earlier we discussed virtual methods and how they work. Since either calling a method directly or calling it using the Me keyword invokes the method on the current *object* this means that the method calls conform to the same rules as an external method call. In other words, our ToString method may not actually end up calling the Name method in the Person class if that method was overridden by a class further down the inheritance chain such as the Employee or OfficeEmployee classes.

For example, we could override the Name property in our OfficeEmployee class such that it always returns the informal version of the person's name rather than the regular name. We can override the Name property by adding this method to the OfficeEmployee class:

```
Public Overloads Overrides Property Name() As String
  Get
    Return MyBase.Name(NameTypes.Informal)
  End Get
  Set(ByVal Value As String)
    MyBase.Name = Value
  End Set
End Property
```

This new version of the Name method relies on the base class to actually store the value – but instead of returning the normal name on request, we are now always returning the informal name:

```
Return MyBase.Name(NameTypes.Informal)
```

Before we can test this, we need to enhance the code in our form to actually provide a value for the informal name. Make the following change to that code:

```
Private Sub btnOK_Click(ByVal sender As System.Object, _
    ByVal e As System.EventArgs) Handles btnOK.Click
  Dim objPerson As OfficeEmployee = New OfficeEmployee()

  With objPerson
    .Name = "Fred"
    .Name(NameTypes.Informal) = "Freddy"
    .BirthDate = #1/1/1960#
    .Age = 20
    .OfficeNumber = "A42"

    txtName.Text = .ToString
    txtBirthDate.Text = Format(.BirthDate, "Short date")
    txtAge.Text = .Age
    txtOffice.Text = .OfficeNumber
  End With
End Sub
```

When we run the application we'll find that the name field displays the informal name. Even though the ToString method is implemented in the Person class, it is invoking the implementation of Name from the OfficeEmployee class. This is because method calls *within* a class follow the same rules for calling virtual methods as code *outside* a class – such as our code in the form.

We'll see this behavior with or without the Me keyword, since the default behavior for method calls is to implicitly call them via the current object.

While methods called from within a class follow the same rules for *virtual* methods, this is not the case for shadowed methods. Here we'll find that the rules for calling a shadowed method from *within* our class are different from those *outside* our class.

To see how this works, let's make the Name property in OfficeEmployee a shadowed method instead of an overridden method:

```
      Public Shadows Property Name() As String
        Get
          Return MyBase.Name(NameTypes.Informal)
        End Get
        Set(ByVal Value As String)
          MyBase.Name = Value
        End Set
      End Property
```

Before we can run our application we'll have to adjust some code in the form. Because we've overridden the `Name` property in `OfficeEmployee`, we'll find that the version of `Name` from `Employee` that acts as a property array is now invalid.

> **Shadowing a method replaces *all* implementations from higher in the inheritance chain – regardless of their method signature.**

To make our application operate we'll need to change the variable declaration and object creation to declare a variable of type `Employee` so we can access the property array – while still creating an instance of `OfficeEmployee`:

```
      Dim objPerson As Employee = New OfficeEmployee()
```

Since our variable is now of type `Employee`, we also need to comment out the lines that refer to the `OfficeName` property, since it is no longer available:

```
      With objPerson
        .Name = "Fred"
        .Name(NameTypes.Informal) = "Freddy"
        .BirthDate = #1/1/1960#
        .Age = 20
        '.OfficeNumber = "A42"

        txtName().Text = .ToString
        txtBirthDate().Text = Format(.BirthDate, "Short date")
        txtAge().Text = .Age
        'txtOffice().Text = .OfficeNumber
      End With
```

When we run the application now we'll find that it displays the name **Fred** rather than **Freddy** – meaning it is *not* calling the `Name` method from `OfficeEmployee`, but rather is calling the implementation provided by the `Employee` class. Remember that the code to make this call still resides in the `Person` class – but it now ignores the shadowed version of the `Name` method.

Shadowed implementations in subclasses are ignored when calling the method from *within* a class higher in the inheritance chain.

We'll get this same behavior with or without the `Me` keyword.

So the Me keyword, or calling methods directly, follows the same rules for overridden methods as any other method call. For shadowed methods, however, any shadowed implementations in subclasses are ignored and the method is called from the current level in the inheritance chain.

So why does the Me keyword exist? Primarily for clarity and to allow us to pass a reference to the current object as a parameter to other objects or methods. As we'll see when we look at the MyBase and MyClass keywords, things can get very confusing and there is value in using the Me keyword when working with MyBase and MyClass to ensure that it is always clear which particular implementation of a method we intended to invoke.

The MyBase Keyword

While the Me keyword allows us to call methods on the current object instance, there are times we might want to explicitly call into methods in our parent class. Earlier we saw an example of this when we called back into the base class from an overridden method in the subclass.

The MyBase keyword references only our immediate parent class, and it works like an object reference. This means we can call methods on MyBase, knowing that they are being called just like we had a reference to an object of our parent class's data type.

> There is no way to directly navigate up the inheritance chain beyond our immediate parent.

The MyBase keyword can be used to invoke or use any Public, Friend, or Protected element from the parent class. This includes all of those elements directly on the base class, and also any elements the base class inherited from other classes higher in the inheritance chain.

We've already used MyBase to call back into the base Person class as we implemented the overridden Name property in the Employee class.

> Any code within a subclass can call any method on the base class by using the MyBase keyword.

We can also use MyBase to call back into the base class implementation even if we've shadowed a method. Though we didn't remark on it at the time, we've already done this in our shadowed implementation of the Name property in the OfficeEmployee class. The highlighted lines indicate where we're calling into the base class from within a shadowed method:

```
Public Shadows Property Name() As String
  Get
    Return MyBase.Name(NameTypes.Informal)
  End Get
  Set(ByVal Value As String)
    MyBase.Name = Value
  End Set
End Property
```

The MyBase keyword allows us to merge the functionality of the base class into our subclass code as we see fit.

The MyClass Keyword

As we've seen, when we use the Me keyword or call a method directly our method call follows the rules for calling both virtual and non-virtual methods. In other words, as we discovered earlier with the Name property, a call to Name from our code in the Person class actually invoked the overridden version of Name located in the OfficeEmployee class.

While this behavior is useful in many cases, there are also cases where we'll want to ensure that we really are running the specific implementation from our class – where even *if* a subclass overrode our method we still want to ensure we're calling the version of the method that is directly in *our* class.

Maybe we decide that our ToString implementation in Person should *always* call the Name implementation that we write in the Person class – totally ignoring any overridden versions of Name in any subclasses.

This is where the MyClass keyword comes into play. This keyword is much like MyBase, in that it provides us with access to methods as though it were an object reference – in this case a reference to an instance of the class that contains the code we're writing when using the MyClass keyword. This is true even if the *instantiated* object is an instance of a class derived from our class.

We've seen that a call to ToString from within Person will actually invoke the implementation in Employee or OfficeEmployee if our object is an instance of either of those types. Let's restore the Name property in OfficeEmployee to be an overridden method rather than a shadowed method to see how this works:

```
Public Overloads Overrides Property Name() As String
  Get
    Return MyBase.Name(NameTypes.Informal)
  End Get
  Set(ByVal Value As String)
    MyBase.Name = Value
  End Set
End Property
```

With this change, and based on our earlier testing, we know that the ToString implementation in Person will automatically call this overridden version of the Name property, since the call to the Name method will follow the normal rules for virtual methods. In fact, if we run the application now we'll find that the name field on the form displays **Freddy** – the informal name of the person.

We can force the use of the implementation in our current class through the use of MyClass. Change the ToString method in Person as follows:

```
Public Overrides Function ToString() As String
  Return MyClass.Name()
End Function
```

We are now calling the Name method, but we're doing it using the MyClass keyword. When we run the application and click on the button we'll find that the name field in the form displays **Fred** rather than **Freddy** – proving that the implementation from Person was invoked even though the data type of the object itself is OfficeEmployee.

The `ToString` method is invoked from `Person`, since neither `Employee` nor `OfficeEmployee` provides an overridden implementation. Then, because we're using the `MyClass` keyword, the `Name` method is invoked directly from `Person` – explicitly defeating the default behavior we'd normally expect.

Constructors

As we discussed in Chapter 11, we can provide a special constructor method, named `New`, on a class and it will be the first code run when an object is instantiated. We can also receive parameters via the constructor method – allowing the code that creates our object to pass data into the object during the creation process.

Constructor methods are affected by inheritance differently from regular methods. A normal `Public` method, such as `BirthDate` on our `Person` class, is automatically inherited by any subclass. From there we can overload, override or shadow that method as we've discussed so far in this chapter.

Simple Constructors

Constructors don't quite follow the same rules. To explore the differences, let's implement a simple constructor method in our `Person` class:

```
Public Sub New()
   System.Diagnostics.Debug.WriteLine("Person constructor")
End Sub
```

If we now run the application we'll see the text displayed in the Output window in the IDE. This occurs even though the code in our form is creating an object of type `OfficeEmployee`:

```
Dim objPerson As Employee = New OfficeEmployee()
```

As we might expect, the `New` method from our base `Person` class is invoked as part of the construction process of the `OfficeEmployee` object – simple inheritance at work.

However, interesting things occur if we implement a `New` method in the `OfficeEmployee` class itself:

```
Public Sub New()
   System.Diagnostics.Debug.WriteLine("OfficeEmployee constructor")
End Sub
```

Notice that we are not using the `Overrides` keyword, nor did we mark the method in `Person` as `Overridable`. These keywords have no use in this context – and in fact will cause syntax errors if we attempt to use them on constructor methods.

When we run the application now we'd probably expect that only the implementation of `New` in `OfficeEmployee` would be invoked. Certainly that is what would occur with a normal overridden method. But of course `New` isn't overridden, and so when we run the application we'll find that *both* implementations are run:

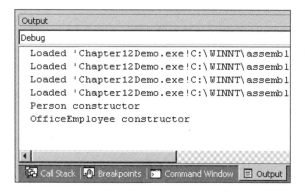

It is important to note that the implementation in the Person class ran *first*, followed by the implementation in the OfficeEmployee class.

This occurs because, as an object is created, *all* the constructors for the classes in the inheritance chain are invoked – starting with the base class and working out through all the subclasses one by one. In fact, if we implement a New method in the Employee class we can see that it too is invoked:

```
Public Sub New()
    System.Diagnostics.Debug.WriteLine("Employee constructor")
End Sub
```

When the application is run and the button clicked we'll see:

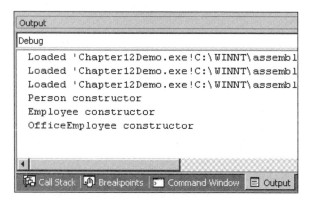

All three constructor methods were invoked – starting with the Person class and working down to the OfficeEmployee class.

Constructors in More Depth

The rules governing constructors without parameters are pretty straightforward. Things get a bit more interesting if we start requiring parameters on our constructors, however.

To understand what is going on, we need to get a slightly better understanding of how even our simple constructors are being invoked. While we *see* them as being invoked from the base class down through all subclasses to our final subclass, what is *really* happening is a bit different.

In particular, it is the subclass `New` method that is invoked first. However, VB.NET is automatically inserting a line of code into our routine at compile time. For instance, in our `OfficeEmployee` class we have a constructor:

```
Public Sub New()
   System.Diagnostics.Debug.WriteLine("OfficeEmployee constructor")
End Sub
```

VB.NET inserts what is effectively a call to constructor of our parent class on our behalf. We could do this manually by using the `MyBase` keyword with the following change:

```
Public Sub New()
   MyBase.New()
   System.Diagnostics.Debug.WriteLine("OfficeEmployee constructor")
End Sub
```

This call is required to be the first line in our constructor. If we put any other code before this line we'll get a syntax error indicating that our code is invalid. Since the call is always required, and since it always must be the first line in any constructor VB.NET simply inserts it for us automatically – behind the scenes.

It is also worth noting that if we don't explicitly provide a constructor on a class by implementing a `New` method, VB.NET creates one for us behind the scenes. The automatically created method simply has one line of code:

```
MyBase.New()
```

All classes have constructor methods, either created explicitly by us as we write a `New` method, or created implicitly by VB.NET as the class is compiled.

By always calling `Mybase.New()` as the first line in every constructor, we are guaranteed that it is the implementation of `New` in our top-level base class that will actually run first. Every subclass invokes the parent class implementation all the way up the inheritance chain until only the base class remains. Then its code runs, followed by each individual subclass as we've already seen.

Constructors with Parameters

This works great when our constructors don't require parameters. However, if our constructor *does* require a parameter, then it becomes impossible for VB.NET to automatically make that call on our behalf. After all, how would VB.NET know what values we want to pass as parameters?

To see how this works, let's change the `New` method in the `Person` class to require a `Name` parameter. We can use that parameter to initialize the object's `Name` property:

```
Public Sub New(ByVal Name As String)
   Me.Name = Name
   System.Diagnostics.Debug.WriteLine("Person constructor")
End Sub
```

Now our constructor requires a `String` parameter and uses it to initialize the `Name` property.

We are using the Me keyword to make our code easier to read. Interestingly enough, the compiler will actually understand and correctly compile the following:

```
Name = Name
```

But that is not at all clear to a developer reading the code. By prefixing the property name with the Me keyword we've made it clear that we're invoking a property on the object and providing it with the parameter value.

At this point we'll find that our application won't compile. This is because there is an error in the New method of our Employee class. In particular, VB.NET's attempt to automatically invoke the constructor on the Person class is no longer workable, since it has no idea what data value to pass for this new Name parameter.

There are three ways we can address this error. We can make the Name parameter Optional, we can overload the New method with another implementation that requires no parameter or we can manually provide the Name parameter value from within the Employee class.

If we make the Name parameter Optional, we're indicating that the New method can be called with or without a parameter. This means that one viable option is to call the method with no parameters – and so VB.NET's default of calling it with no parameters will work just fine.

If we overload the New method, we can implement a second New method that doesn't accept any parameters – again allowing VB.NET's default behavior to work as we've seen. Keep in mind that this solution would only invoke the overloaded version of New with no parameter – the version that requires a parameter would not be invoked.

The final way we can fix the error is by simply providing a parameter value ourselves from within the New method of the Employee class. To do this, change the Employee class:

```
Public Sub New()
    MyBase.New("George")
    System.Diagnostics.Debug.WriteLine("Employee constructor")
End Sub
```

By explicitly calling the New method of our parent class, we are able to provide it with the required parameter value. At this point our application will compile and run just fine.

Obviously we probably don't really want to hard-code a value in a constructor like this, so we may choose instead to change the Employee class to also accept a Name parameter:

```
Public Sub New(ByVal Name As String)
    MyBase.New(Name)
    System.Diagnostics.Debug.WriteLine("Employee constructor")
End Sub
```

Of course this just pushed the issue deeper – and now we'll find that the OfficeEmployee class has a compile error in its New method. Again we can fix it by having that method accept a parameter so it can provide it up the chain as required. Make the following change to OfficeEmployee:

```
    Public Sub New(ByVal Name As String)
       MyBase.New(Name)
       System.Diagnostics.Debug.WriteLine("OfficeEmployee constructor")
    End Sub
```

Now we find that the code in our form is no longer valid. We're attempting there to create an instance of OfficeEmployee without passing a parameter value. Let's update that code and then we can run the application:

```
    Private Sub btnOK_Click(ByVal sender As System.Object, _
        ByVal e As System.EventArgs) Handles btnOK.Click
      Dim objPerson As Employee = New OfficeEmployee("Mary")

      With objPerson
        '.Name = "Fred"
```

We're passing a name value to the constructor of OfficeEmployee. Also, we've commented out the line of code that sets the Name property directly – meaning that the value we've passed in the constructor will be displayed in our form.

The Protected Scope

We've seen how a subclass automatically gains all the Public methods and properties that comprise the interface of the base class. This is also true of Friend methods and properties – they are inherited as well, and are available only to other code in the same project as the subclass.

Private methods and properties are not exposed as part of the interface of the subclass – meaning that our code in the subclass cannot call those methods, nor can any code using our objects. These methods are only available to the code within the base class itself. This can get confusing, since the *implementation* contained in the Private methods are inherited and are used by any code in the base class, it is just that they aren't available to be called by any other code – including code in our subclass.

There are times when we want to create methods in our base class that *can* be called by a subclass as well as the base class, but not by code outside of those classes. Basically we want a hybrid between Public and Private – methods that are private to the classes in our inheritance chain, but are usable by any subclasses that might be created within the chain. This functionality is provided by the Protected scope.

Protected methods are very similar to Private methods, in that they are not available to any code that calls our objects. Instead, these methods are available to code within the base class – *and* to code within any subclass. The following table lists all the available scope options:

Scope	Description
Private	Available only to code within our class
Protected	Available only to classes that inherit from our class
Friend	Available only to code within our project/component

Table continued on following page

397

Scope	Description
Protected Friend	Available only to classes that inherit from our class (in any project) or to code within our project/component. This is a combination of Protected and Friend
Public	Available to code outside our class

The Protected scope can be applied to Sub, Function, and Property methods. To see how the Protected scope works, let's add an Identity field to the Person class:

```
Public Class Person
   Private mstrName As String
   Private mdtBirthDate As String
   Private mstrID As String

   Protected Property Identity() As String
     Get
       Return mstrID
     End Get
     Set(ByVal Value As String)
       mstrID = Value
     End Set
   End Property
```

This data field represents some arbitrary identification number or value assigned to a person. This might be a social security number, an employee number or whatever is appropriate.

The interesting thing about this value is that it is not currently accessible *outside* our inheritance chain. For instance, if we try to use it from our code in the form we'll discover that there is no Identity property on our Person, Employee, or OfficeEmployee objects.

However, there *is* an Identity property now available *inside* our inheritance chain. The Identity property is available to the code in the Person class just like any other method. The interesting thing is that even though Identity is not available to the code in our form, it is available to the code in the Employee and OfficeEmployee classes. This is because they are both subclasses of Person. Employee is directly a subclass, and OfficeEmployee is indirectly a subclass of Person because it is a subclass of Employee.

Thus, we can enhance our Employee class to implement an EmployeeNumber property by using the Identity property. To do this, add the following code to the Employee class:

```
Public Property EmployeeNumber() As Integer
   Get
     Return CInt(Identity)
   End Get
   Set(ByVal Value As Integer)
     Identity = CStr(Value)
   End Set
 End Property
```

This new property exposes a numeric identity value for the employee – but it uses the internal Identity property to manage that value.

We can override and shadow Protected elements just as we do with elements of any other scope.

Protected Variables

Up to this point we've focused on methods and properties and how they interact through inheritance. Inheritance, and in particular the `Protected` scope, also has an impact on instance variables and how we work with them.

Though it is not recommended, we can declare variables in a class using `Public` scope. This makes the variable directly available to code both within and outside of our class – allowing any code that interacts with our objects to directly read or alter the value of that variable.

Variables can also have `Friend` scope, which likewise allows any code in our class or anywhere within our project to read or alter the value directly. This is also generally not recommended as it breaks encapsulation.

> Rather than declaring variables with **Public** or **Friend** scope it is better to expose the value using a **Property** method so we can apply any of our business rules to control how the value is altered as appropriate.

Of course we know that variables can be of `Private` scope, and this is typically the case. This makes the variables accessible only to the code within our class and is the most restrictive scope.

As with methods, however, we can also use the `Protected` scope when declaring variables. This makes the variable accessible to the code in our class, and to the code in any class that derives from our class – all the way down the hierarchy chain.

There are times when this is useful, as it allows us to provide and accept data from subclasses, but act on that data from code in the base class. At the same time, exposing variables to subclasses is typically not ideal and we should use `Property` methods with `Protected` scope for this instead, since they allow our base class to enforce any business rules that are appropriate for the value, rather than just hoping that the author of the subclass only provides us with good values.

Events and Inheritance

So far we've discussed methods, properties, and variables in terms of inheritance – seeing how they can be added, overridden, extended, and shadowed. In VB.NET, events are also part of the interface of an object and they are impacted by inheritance as well.

Inheriting Events

In Chapter 11 we discussed how to declare, raise, and receive events from objects. We can add such an event to our `Person` class by declaring it at the top of the class:

```
Public Class Person
   Private mstrName As String
   Private mdtBirthDate As String
   Private mstrID As String

   Public Event NameChanged(ByVal NewName As String)
```

Then we can raise this event within the class any time the person's name is changed:

```
Public Overridable Property Name() As String
  Get
    Return mstrName
  End Get
  Set(ByVal Value As String)
    mstrName = Value
    RaiseEvent NameChanged(mstrName)
  End Set
End Property
```

At this point we can receive and handle this event within our form any time we're working with a Person object. The nice thing about this is that our events are inherited automatically by subclasses – meaning that our Employee and OfficeEmployee objects will also raise this event. Thus, we can change the code in our form to handle the event – even though we're working with an object of type OfficeEmployee.

First we can add a method to handle the event to Form1:

```
Private Sub OnNameChanged(ByVal NewName As String)
  MsgBox("New name: " & NewName)
End Sub
```

Note that we're not using the Handles clause here. In this case, for simplicity, we'll use the AddHandler method to dynamically link the event to this method. However, we could have also chosen to use the WithEvents and Handles keywords as described in Chapter 11 – either way works.

With the handler built, we can use the AddHandler method to link this method to the event on our object:

```
Private Sub btnOK_Click(ByVal sender As System.Object, _
    ByVal e As System.EventArgs) Handles btnOK.Click
  Dim objPerson As Employee = New OfficeEmployee("Mary")
  AddHandler objPerson.NameChanged, AddressOf OnNameChanged

  With objPerson
    .Name = "Fred"
```

Also note that we're uncommenting the line that changes the Name property. With this change, we know that the event should fire when the name is changed.

When we run the application now, we'll see a message box indicating that the name has changed – and proving that the NameChanged event really is exposed and available even though our object is of type OfficeEmployee rather than of type Person.

Raising Events from Subclasses

One caveat we need to keep in mind is that while a subclass exposes the events of its base class, the code in the subclass cannot *raise* the event.

In other words, we cannot use the RaiseEvent method in Employee or OfficeEmployee to raise the NameChanged event. Only code directly in the Person class can raise the event.

To see this in action, let's add another event to the Person class – an event that can indicate the change of other arbitrary data values:

400

```
Public Class Person
  Private mstrName As String
  Private mdtBirthDate As String
  Private mstrID As String

  Public Event NameChanged(ByVal NewName As String)
  Public Event DataChanged(ByVal Field As String, ByVal NewValue As Object)
```

We can then raise this event when the BirthDate is changed:

```
Public Overridable Property BirthDate() As Date
  Get
    Return mdtBirthDate
  End Get
  Set(ByVal Value As Date)
    mdtBirthDate = Value
    RaiseEvent DataChanged("BirthDate", Value)
  End Set
End Property
```

It would also be nice to raise this event from the Employee class when the Salary value is changed. Unfortunately we can't use the RaiseEvent method to raise the event from a base class, so the following code won't work (don't enter this code):

```
Public Property Salary() As Double
  Get
    Return mdblSalary
  End Get
  Set(ByVal Value As Double)
    mdblSalary = Value
    RaiseEvent DataChanged("Salary", Value)
  End Set
End Property
```

Fortunately there is a relatively easy way to get around this limitation. We can simply implement a Protected method in our base class that allows any derived class to raise the method. In the Person class we can add such a method:

```
Protected Sub RaiseDataChanged(ByVal Field As String, _
    ByVal NewValue As Object)
  RaiseEvent DataChanged(Field, NewValue)
End Sub
```

Then we can use this method from within the Employee class to indicate that Salary has changed:

```
Public Property Salary() As Double
  Get
    Return mdblSalary
  End Get
  Set(ByVal Value As Double)
    mdblSalary = Value
    RaiseDataChanged("Salary", Value)
  End Set
End Property
```

Notice that the code in `Employee` is *not* raising the event – it is simply calling a `Protected` method in `Person`. It is the code in the `Person` class that actually raises the event – meaning that all will work as we desire.

We can enhance the code in `Form1` to receive the event. First off, we need to create a method to handle the event:

```
Private Sub OnDataChanged(ByVal Field As String, ByVal NewValue As Object)
  MsgBox("New " & Field & ": " & NewValue)
End Sub
```

Then we can link this handler to the event using the `AddHandler` method:

```
Private Sub btnOK_Click(ByVal sender As System.Object, _
    ByVal e As System.EventArgs) Handles btnOK.Click
  Dim objPerson As Employee = New OfficeEmployee("Mary")
  AddHandler objPerson.NameChanged, AddressOf OnNameChanged
  AddHandler objPerson.DataChanged, AddressOf OnDataChanged
```

Finally we need to make sure we are changing and displaying the `Salary` property:

```
With objPerson
  .Name = "Fred"
  .Name(NameTypes.Informal) = "Freddy"
  .BirthDate = #1/1/1960#
  .Age = 20
  .Salary = 30000

  txtName.Text = .ToString
  txtBirthDate.Text = Format(.BirthDate, "Short date")
  txtAge.Text = .Age
  txtSalary.Text = Format(.Salary, "0.00")
End With
```

When we run the application and click the button now, we'll get message boxes displaying the changes to the `Name` property, the `BirthDate` property, and now the `Salary`.

Shared Methods

In Chapter 11 we explored shared methods and how they work – providing a set of methods that can be invoked directly from the class rather than requiring that we create an actual object.

Shared methods are inherited just like instance methods, and so are automatically available as methods on subclasses just as they are on the base class. If we implement a shared method in `BaseClass`, we can call that method using `SubClass` or any other class derived from `BaseClass`.

Like a regular method, shared methods can be overloaded and shadowed. They cannot, however, be overridden. If we attempt to use the `Overridable` keyword when declaring a `Shared` method we will get a syntax error.

For instance, we can implement a method in our `Person` class to compare two `Person` objects:

```
    Public Shared Function Compare(ByVal Person1 As Person, _
        ByVal Person2 As Person) As Boolean

      Return (Person1.Name = Person2.Name)

    End Function
```

To test this method, let's add another button to our form, name it btnCompare and set its Text value to Compare. Double-click on the button to bring up the code window and enter the following code:

```
    Private Sub btnCompare_Click(ByVal sender As System.Object, _
        ByVal e As System.EventArgs) Handles btnCompare.Click
      Dim emp1 As New Employee("Fred")
      Dim emp2 As New Employee("Mary")

      MsgBox(Employee.Compare(emp1, emp2))
    End Sub
```

This code simply creates two Employee objects and compares them. Note though, that the code uses the Employee class to invoke the Compare method – displaying the result in a message box. This establishes that the Compare method implemented in the Person class is inherited by the Employee class as we'd expect.

Overloading Shared Methods

Shared methods can be overloaded using the Overloads keyword in the same manner as we overload an instance method. This means our subclass can add new implementations of the shared method as long as the parameter list differs from the original implementation.

For example, we can add a new implementation of the Compare method to Employee:

```
    Public Overloads Shared Function Compare(ByVal Employee1 As Employee, _
        ByVal Employee2 As Employee) As Boolean

      Return (Employee1.EmployeeNumber = Employee2.EmployeeNumber)

    End Function
```

This new implementation compares two Employee objects rather than two Person objects – and in fact compares them based on employee number rather than by name.

We can enhance the code behind btnCompare in the form to set the EmployeeNumber properties:

```
    Private Sub btnCompare_Click(ByVal sender As System.Object, _
        ByVal e As System.EventArgs) Handles btnCompare.Click
      Dim emp1 As New Employee("Fred")
      Dim emp2 As New Employee("Mary")

      emp1.EmployeeNumber = 1
      emp2.EmployeeNumber = 1

      MsgBox(Employee.Compare(emp1, emp2))
    End Sub
```

While it might make little sense for these two objects to have the same EmployeeNumber value – it will prove a point. When we run the application now, even though the names values of the objects are different, our Compare routine will return True – proving that we're invoking the overloaded version of the method that expects two Employee objects as parameters.

The overloaded implementation is available on the Employee class or any classes derived from Employee such as OfficeEmployee. The overloaded implementation is not be available if called directly from Person, since that class only contains the original implementation.

Shadowing Shared Methods

Shared methods can also be shadowed by a subclass. This allows us to do some very interesting things – including converting a shared method into an instance method or visa versa. We can even leave the method as shared, but change the entire way it works and is declared. In short, just as with instance methods, we can use the Shadows keyword to entirely replace and change a shared method in a subclass.

To see how this works, we can use the Shadows keyword to change the nature of the Compare method in OfficeEmployee:

```
Public Shared Shadows Function Compare(ByVal Person1 As Person, _
    ByVal Person2 As Person) As Boolean

  Return (Person1.Age = Person2.Age)

End Function
```

Notice that this method has the same signature as the original Compare method we implemented in the Person class, but instead of comparing by name, here we're comparing by age. With a normal method we could have done this by overriding, but since Shared methods can't be overridden the only thing we can do is shadow it.

Of course the shadowed implementation is only available via the OfficeEmployee class. Neither the Person nor Employee classes, which are higher up the inheritance chain, are aware that this shadowed version of the method exists.

To use this from our Form1 code we can change the code for btnCompare as follows:

```
Private Sub btnCompare_Click(ByVal sender As System.Object, _
    ByVal e As System.EventArgs) Handles btnCompare.Click
  Dim emp1 As New Employee("Fred")
  Dim emp2 As New Employee("Mary")

  emp1.Age = 20
  emp2.Age = 25

  MsgBox(OfficeEmployee.Compare(emp1, emp2))
End Sub
```

Instead of setting the EmployeeNumber values, we're now setting the Age values on our objects. More importantly, notice that we're now calling the Compare method via the OfficeEmployee class rather than via Employee or Person. This causes the invocation of our new version of the method – and so the ages of the objects are compared.

Shared Events

As we discussed in Chapter 11, we can create shared events – events that can be raised by shared or instance methods in a class, whereas regular events can only be raised from within instance methods.

When we inherit from a class that defines a shared event, our new subclass automatically gains that event just like it does with regular events as we discussed earlier in this chapter.

As with instance events, a shared event cannot be raised by code within our subclass – it can only be raised using the RaiseEvent keyword from code in the class where the event is declared. If we want to be able to raise the event from methods in our subclass, we need to implement a Protected method on the base class that actually makes the call to RaiseEvent.

This is no different from what we discussed earlier in the chapter other than to note that with a shared event we can use a method with protected scope that is marked as shared to raise the event rather than using an instance method.

Creating an Abstract Base Class

So far, we've seen how to inherit from a class, how to overload and override methods, and how virtual methods work. In all of our examples so far, the parent classes have been useful in their own right and could be instantiated and do some meaningful work. Sometimes, however, we want to create a class such that it can only be used as a base class for inheritance.

MustInherit Keyword

Our current Person class is not only being used as a base class, but it can also be instantiated directly to create an object of type Person. Likewise, our Employee class is also being used as a base class for the OfficeEmployee class we created that derives from it.

If we want to make a class *only* act as a base class we can use the MustInherit keyword – thereby preventing anyone from creating objects based directly on the class and requiring them instead to create a subclass and then create objects based on that subclass.

This can be very useful when we are creating object models of real-world concepts and entities and is something we'll discuss in more detail in Chapter 13.

We can change Person to use the MustInherit keyword:

```
Public MustInherit Class Person
```

This has no effect on the code within Person or any of the classes that inherit from it. However, it does mean no code can instantiate objects directly from the Person class – instead we can only create objects based on Employee or OfficeEmployee.

Keep in mind that this doesn't prevent us from declaring variables of type Person – it merely prevents us from creating an object by using New Person(). We can also continue to make use of Shared methods from the Person class without any difficulty.

MustOverride Keyword

Another option we have is to create a method (Sub, Function, or Property) that must be overridden by a subclass. We might want to do this when we are creating a base class that provides some behaviors, but relies on subclasses to also provide some behaviors in order to function properly. This is accomplished by using the MustOverride keyword on a method declaration.

If a class contains any methods marked with MustOverride, the class itself must also be declared with the MustInhert keyword or we'll get a syntax error. This makes sense, since if we're requiring that a method be overridden in a subclass it only stands to reason that our class can't be directly instantiated but rather must be subclassed to be useful.

Let's see how this works by adding a LifeExpectancy method in Person such that it has no implementation but rather must be overridden by a subclass:

```
Public MustOverride Function LifeExpectancy() As Integer
```

Notice that there is no End Function or any other code associated with the method.

When using MustOverride, we *cannot* provide any implementation for the method in our class. Such a method is called an **abstract method** or **pure virtual function**, since it only defines the interface and no implementation.

Methods declared in this manner *must* be overridden in any subclass that inherits from our base class. If we don't override one of these methods, we'll generate a syntax error in the subclass and it won't compile.

This means we need to alter the Employee class to provide an implementation for this method:

```
Public Overrides Function LifeExpectancy() As Integer
   Return 90
End Function
```

Our application will compile at this point, since we are now overriding the LifeExpectancy method in Employee and so the required condition is met.

Abstract Base Classes

We can combine these two concepts – using both MustInherit and MustOverride – to create something called an **abstract base class**. Sometimes this is also referred to as a **virtual class**.

This is a class that provides no implementation, only the interface definitions from which a subclass can be created. An example might be as follows:

```
Public MustInherit Class AbstractBaseClass
   Public MustOverride Sub DoSomething()
   Public MustOverride Sub DoOtherStuff()
End Class
```

This technique can be very useful when creating frameworks or the high-level conceptual elements of a system. Any class that inherits AbstractBaseClass must implement both DoSomething and DoOtherStuff or a syntax error will result.

In some ways an abstract base class is very comparable to defining an interface using the Interface keyword. We'll discuss the Interface keyword in detail later in this chapter.

We could define the same interface as shown in this example with the following code:

```
Public Interface IAbstractBaseClass
   Sub DoSomething()
   Sub DoOtherStuff()
End Interface
```

Any class that implements the IAbstractBaseClass interface must implement both DoSomething and DoOtherStuff or a syntax error will result – and in that regard this technique is similar to an abstract base class.

There are differences, however. In particular, when we create a new class by subclassing the AbstractBase class, that class can in turn be subclassed. All classes derived from this base class will automatically have DoSomething and DoOtherStuff methods as part of their interface. The first non-abstract class in the inheritance chain (the first one not declared using MustInherits) will need to provide implementations for these methods. All subsequent subclasses will automatically get both the interface and implementation for the methods due to the nature of inheritance.

Contrast this with the interface approach, where each individual class must independently implement the IAbstractBase interface *and* provide its own implementation of the two methods. The implementation code in one class is never inherited by other classes that implement this interface. If we never intend to reuse the code that implements these methods as we create new classes then the interface approach is fine, but if we want code reuse within subclasses inheritance is the way to go.

Preventing Inheritance

If we want to prevent a class from being used as a base class we can use the NotInheritable keyword. For instance, we can change our SubSubClass as follows:

```
Public NotInheritable Class SubSubClass
```

At this point it is no longer possible to inherit from this class to create a new class.

Our SubSubClass is now **sealed** – meaning that it cannot be used as a base from which to create other classes.

If we attempt to inherit from SubSubClass we'll get a compile error indicating that it cannot be used as a base class. This has no effect on BaseClass or SubClass – we can continue to derive other classes from them.

Typically, we'll want to design our classes such that they can be subclassed, as that provides the greatest long-term flexibility in our overall design. There are times, however, when we will want to make sure that our class cannot be used as a base class and the NotInheritable keyword addresses that issue.

Multiple Interfaces

In VB.NET our objects can have one or more interfaces. All objects have a primary or native interface, which is composed of any methods, properties, events, or member variables declared using the Public keyword. Objects can also implement secondary interfaces in addition to their native interface by using the Implements keyword.

VB6 also had the concept of multiple interfaces, though the way we implemented them was not particularly intuitive or clear. The concept remains the same in VB.NET, but the syntax we use to define and implement interfaces is very clear and understandable.

Object Interfaces

The native interface on any class is composed of all the methods, properties, events, or even variables that are declared as anything other than `Private`. Though this is nothing new, let's quickly review what is included in the native interface to set the stage for discussing secondary interfaces.

To include a method as part of our interface we can simply declare a `Public` routine:

```
Public Sub AMethod()

End Sub
```

Notice that there is no code in this routine. Any code would be *implementation* and is not part of the interface. Only the declaration of the method is important when we're discussing interfaces. This can seem confusing at first, but it is an important distinction since separation of the interface from its implementation is at the very core of object-oriented programming and design.

Since this method is declared as `Public` it is available to any code outside our class – including other applications that may make use of our assembly.

If our method has a property we can declare it as part of our interface by using the `Property` keyword:

```
Public Property AProperty() As String

End Property
```

We can also declare events as part of our interface by using the `Event` keyword:

```
Public Event AnEvent()
```

Finally, we can include actual variables, or attributes, as part of our interface:

```
Public AnInteger As Integer
```

This is strongly discouraged, as it directly exposes our internal variables for use by code outside our class. Since the variable is directly accessible from other code, we give up any and all control over the way the value may be changed or by which code it may be accessed.

Rather than making any variable `Public`, it is far preferable to make use of a `Property` method to expose the value. In that way we can implement code to ensure that our internal variable is only set to valid values and that only appropriate code has access to the value based on our application's logic.

Using the Native Interface

In the end, the **native** (or primary) **interface** for any class is defined by looking at all the methods, properties, events, and variables that are declared as anything other than `Private` in scope. This includes any methods, properties, events or variables that are inherited from a base class.

We're used to interacting with the default interface on most objects, and so this will seem pretty straightforward.

Consider a simple class:

```
Public Class TheClass
  Public Sub DoSomething()

  End Sub

  Public Sub DoSomethingElse()

  End Sub
End Class
```

This defines a class, and by extension also defines the native interface that is exposed by any objects we instantiate based on this class. The native interface defines two methods, `DoSomething` and `DoSomethingElse`. To make use of these methods, we simply call them:

```
Dim myObject As New TheClass()

myObject.DoSomething()
myObject.DoSomethingElse()
```

This is the same thing we've been doing in Chapter 11 and so far in this chapter. However, let's take a look at creating and using secondary interfaces, as they are a bit different.

Secondary Interfaces

Sometimes it can be helpful for an object to have more than one interface – thus allowing us to interact with the object in different ways.

Inheritance allows us to create subclasses that *are* a specialized case of the base class. For example, our `Employee` *is-a* `Person`.

However, there are times when we have a group of objects that are *not* the same thing, but we want to be able to *treat* them as though they were the same. We want all these objects to *act-as* the same thing – even though they are all different.

For instance, we may have a series of different objects in an application – product, customer, invoice, and so forth. Each of these would have default interfaces appropriate to each individual object – and each of them *is-a* different class – there's no natural inheritance relationship implied between these classes. At the same time, we may need to be able to generate a printed document for each type of object. So we'd like to make them all *act-as* a printable object.

> *We'll discuss the* is-a *and* act-as *relationships in more detail in Chapter 13.*

To accomplish this we can define a generic interface that would enable generating such a printed document – we can call it `IPrintableObject`.

> *By convention, this type of interface is typically prefixed with a capital I to indicate that it is a formal interface.*

Each of our application objects can choose to implement the `IPrintableObject` interface. Every object that implements this interface must provide code to provide actual *implementation* of the interface – which is unlike inheritance, where the code from a base class is automatically reused.

By implementing this common interface, however, we are able to write a routine that accepts any object that implements the `IPrintableObject` interface and print it – totally oblivious to the "real" data type of the object or the methods its native interface might expose.

Before we see how to use an interface in this manner, let's walk through the process of actually defining an interface.

Defining the Interface

We define a formal interface using the `Interface` keyword. This can be done in any code module in our project, but a good place to put this type of definition is in a standard module. An interface defines a set of methods (`Sub`, `Function`, or `Property`) and events that must be exposed by any class that chooses to implement the interface.

Add a module to the project using **Project | Add Module** and name it `Interfaces.vb`. Then add the following code to the module – outside the `Module` code block itself:

```
Public Interface IPrintableObject

End Interface

Module Interfaces

End Module
```

A code module can contain a number of interface definitions, and these definitions must exist outside any other code block. Thus, they don't go within a `Class` or `Module` block – they are at a peer level to those constructs.

Interfaces must be declared using either `Public` or `Friend` scope. Declaring a `Private` or `Protected` interface will result in a syntax error.

Within the `Interface` block of code, we can define the methods, properties and events that will make up our particular interface. Since the scope of the interface is defined by the `Interface` declaration itself, we can't specify scopes for individual methods and events – they are all scoped the same as the interface itself.

For instance, add the following code:

```
Public Interface IPrintableObject
    Function Label(ByVal Index As Integer) As String
    Function Value(ByVal Index As Integer) As String
    ReadOnly Property Count() As Integer
End Interface
```

This defines a new data type – somewhat like creating a class or structure – that we can use when declaring variables.

For instance, we can now declare a variable of type `IPrintableObject`:

```
Private objPrintable As IPrintableObject
```

We can also have our classes implement this interface – which will require each class to provide implementation code for each of the three methods defined on the interface.

Before we implement the interface in a class, let's see how we can make use of the interface to write a generic routine that can print any object that does implement `IPrintableObject`.

Using the Interface

Interfaces define the methods and events (including parameters and data types), which an object is required to implement if they choose to support the interface. This means that, given just the interface definition, we can easily write code that can interact with *any* object that implements the interface – even though we don't know what the native data type of that objects will be.

To see how we can write such code, let's create a simple routine in our form that can display data to the Output window in the IDE from any object that implements `IPrintableObject`. Bring up the code window for our form and add the following routine:

```
Public Sub PrintObject(TheObject As IPrintableObject)
  Dim intIndex As Integer

  For intIndex = 1 To TheObject.Count
    System.Diagnostics.Debug.Write(TheObject.Label(intIndex) & ": ")
    System.Diagnostics.Debug.WriteLine(TheObject.Value(intIndex))
  Next
End Sub
```

Notice that we're accepting a parameter of type `IPrintableObject`. This is how secondary interfaces are used – by treating an object of one type as though it was actually of the *interface* type. As long as the object passed to this routine implements the `IPrintableObject` interface, our code will work fine.

Within the `PrintObject` routine we're assuming that the object will implement three elements – `Count`, `Label`, and `Value` – as part of the `IPrintableObject` interface. Secondary interfaces can include methods, properties, and events – much like a default interface – but the interface itself is defined and implemented using some special syntax.

Now that we have a generic printing routine, we need a way to call it. Bring up the designer for `Form1` and add a button and name it `btnPrint`. Double-click the button and put this code behind it:

```
Private Sub btnPrint_Click(ByVal sender As System.Object, _
    ByVal e As System.EventArgs) Handles btnPrint.Click
  Dim obj As New Employee("Andy")

  obj.EmployeeNumber = 123
  obj.BirthDate = #1/1/1980#
  obj.HireDate = #1/1/1996#

  PrintObject(obj)
End Sub
```

This code simply initializes an `Employee` object and calls the `PrintObject` routine.

Of course when we try to run this code we'll get a runtime error when trying to call `PrintObject`. `PrintObject` is expecting a parameter that implements `IPrintableObject` – and `Employee` implements no such interface.

If we use `Option Strict On` *this will show up as a compile-time error, allowing us to catch the problem earlier in the development cycle.*

Let's move on and implement that interface in `Employee` so we can see how it works.

Implementing the Interface

Any class (other than an abstract base class) can implement an interface by using the `Implements` keyword. For instance, we can implement our `IPrintableObject` interface in `Employee` by adding the following line:

```
Public Class Employee
    Inherits Person
    Implements IPrintableObject
```

This will cause the interface to be exposed by any object created as an instance of `Employee`. Of course this doesn't actually *implement* the interface, it just declares that we will implement it. In fact, we now have a compile error showing in the IDE, because we haven't implemented the methods and properties defined by the interface.

> To implement an interface, we must implement *all* the methods and properties defined by that interface.

Before we actually implement the interface, however, let's create an array to contain the labels for our data fields so we can return them via our `IPrintableObject` interface. Add the following code to the `Employee` class:

```
Public Class Employee
    Inherits Person
    Implements IPrintableObject

    Private marLabels() As String = {"ID", "Age", "HireDate"}
    Private mdtHireDate As Date
    Private mdblSalary As Double
```

To implement the interface we need to create methods and properties with the same parameter and return data types as those defined in the interface. The actual names of each method or property don't matter, because we'll be using the `Implements` keyword to link our internal method names to the external method names defined by the interface. As long as the method signatures match we are all set.

This applies to scope as well. Although the interface and its methods and properties are publicly available, we don't have to declare our actual methods and properties as `Public`. In many cases we may implement them as `Private` so they don't become part of our native interface and are only exposed via the secondary interface.

However, if we do have a `Public` method with a method signature we can use it to implement a method from the interface. This has the interesting side effect of having this method provide implementation for both a method on the object's native interface *and* on the secondary interface.

In this case we'll use a `Private` method so it is only providing implementation for the `IPrintableObject` interface. We can implement the `Label` method by adding the following code to `Employee`:

```
Private Function Label(ByVal Index As Integer) As String _
    Implements IPrintableObject.Label
  Return marLabels(Index - 1)
End Function
```

This is just a regular `Private` method that returns a `String` value. We're subtracting 1 from the `Index` value to make it appear as though our data set is 1-based rather than 0-based.

The interesting thing is that we've added the `Implements` clause to the method declaration.

```
Private Function Label(ByVal Index As Integer) As String _
    Implements IPrintableObject.Label
```

By using the `Implements` keyword in this fashion, we're indicating that this particular method is the implementation for the `Label` method on the `IPrintableObject` interface. The actual name of our private method could be anything – it is the use of the `Implements` clause that makes this work. The only requirement is that the parameter data types and the return value data type must match those defined by the `IPrintableObject` interface.

This is very similar to using the `Handles` clause to indicate which method should handle an event. In fact, like the `Handles` clause, the `Implements` clause allows us to have a comma-separated list of interface methods that should be implemented by this one function.

We can then move on to implement the other three elements defined by the `IPrintableObject` interface by adding this code to `Employee`:

```
Private Function Value(ByVal Index As Integer) As String _
    Implements IPrintableObject.Value
  Select Case Index
    Case 1
      Return EmployeeNumber()
    Case 2
      Return Age()
    Case 3
      Return Format(HireDate(), "Short date")
  End Select
End Function

Private ReadOnly Property Count() As Integer _
    Implements IPrintableObject.Count
  Get
    Return UBound(marLabels) + 1
  End Get
End Property
```

The `Value` method returns the value based on the `Index` value, while `Count` returns the number of data elements available – again adding 1 to make it appear that our data list is 1-based like a collection.

We can now run this application and click on the button. The Output window in the IDE will display our results – showing the ID, age, and hire date values as appropriate:

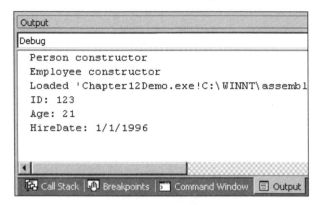

Any object could create a similar implementation behind the `IPrintableObject` interface, and the `PrintObject` routine in our form would continue to work – regardless of the native data type of the object itself.

Reusing Common Implementation

Secondary interfaces provide a guarantee that all objects implementing a given interface will have exactly the same methods and events – including the same parameters. However, as we've seen, we must manually implement the behaviors to within each individual class in order to make the interface actually do anything.

Where with inheritance we automatically gain the reuse of existing code from the base class, with secondary interfaces there is virtually no inherent reuse of code within our classes.

The `Implements` clause links our actual implementation to a specific method on an interface. For instance, our `Value` method is linked to `IPrintableObject.Label` using this clause:

```
Private Function Value(ByVal Index As Integer) As String _
    Implements IPrintableObject.Value
```

Sometimes our method might be able to serve as the implementation for more than one method – either on the same interface or on different interfaces.

Add the following interface definition to `Interfaces.vb`:

```
Public Interface IValues
    Function GetValue(ByVal Idx As Integer) As String
End Interface
```

This interface defines just one method, `GetValue`. Notice that it defines a single `Integer` parameter and a return type of `String` – the same as the `Value` method from `IPrintableObject`. Even though the method name and parameter variable name don't match, what counts here is that the parameter and return value data types *do* match.

Now bring up the code window for `Employee`. We'll have it implement this new interface in addition to the `IPrintableObject` interface:

```
Public Class Employee
  Inherits Person
  Implements IPrintableObject
  Implements IValues
```

We already have a method that returns values. Rather than re-implementing that method, it would be nice to just link this new `GetValues` method to our existing method. We can easily do this because the `Implements` clause allows us to provide a comma-separated list of method names:

```
Private Function Value(ByVal Index As Integer) As String _
    Implements IPrintableObject.Value, IValues.GetValue
  Select Case Index
    Case 1
      Return EmployeeNumber()
    Case 2
      Return Age()
    Case 3
      Return Format(HireDate(), "Short date")
  End Select
End Function
```

This is very similar to the use of the `Handles` keyword as we discussed in Chapter 11. A single method within our class, regardless of scope or name, can be used to implement any number of methods as defined by other interfaces as long as the data types of the parameters and return values all match.

Summary

As we've seen in Chapter 11 and now here in Chapter 12, VB.NET offers a full set of syntax for creating and working with classes and objects, providing the building blocks for abstraction, encapsulation, polymorphism, and inheritance.

In this chapter we've seen how to create both simple base classes as well as abstract base classes. We've also explored how we can define formal interfaces, a concept quite similar to an abstract base class in many ways.

We've also walked through the process of subclassing – creating a new class that derives both interface and implementation from a base class. The subclass can be extended by adding new methods or altering the behavior of existing methods on the base class.

VB.NET provides us with all the capabilities we need to build robust and sophisticated object-oriented applications. In Chapter 13 we'll pull this all together by discussing abstraction, encapsulation, polymorphism, and inheritance as they pertain to building practical software.

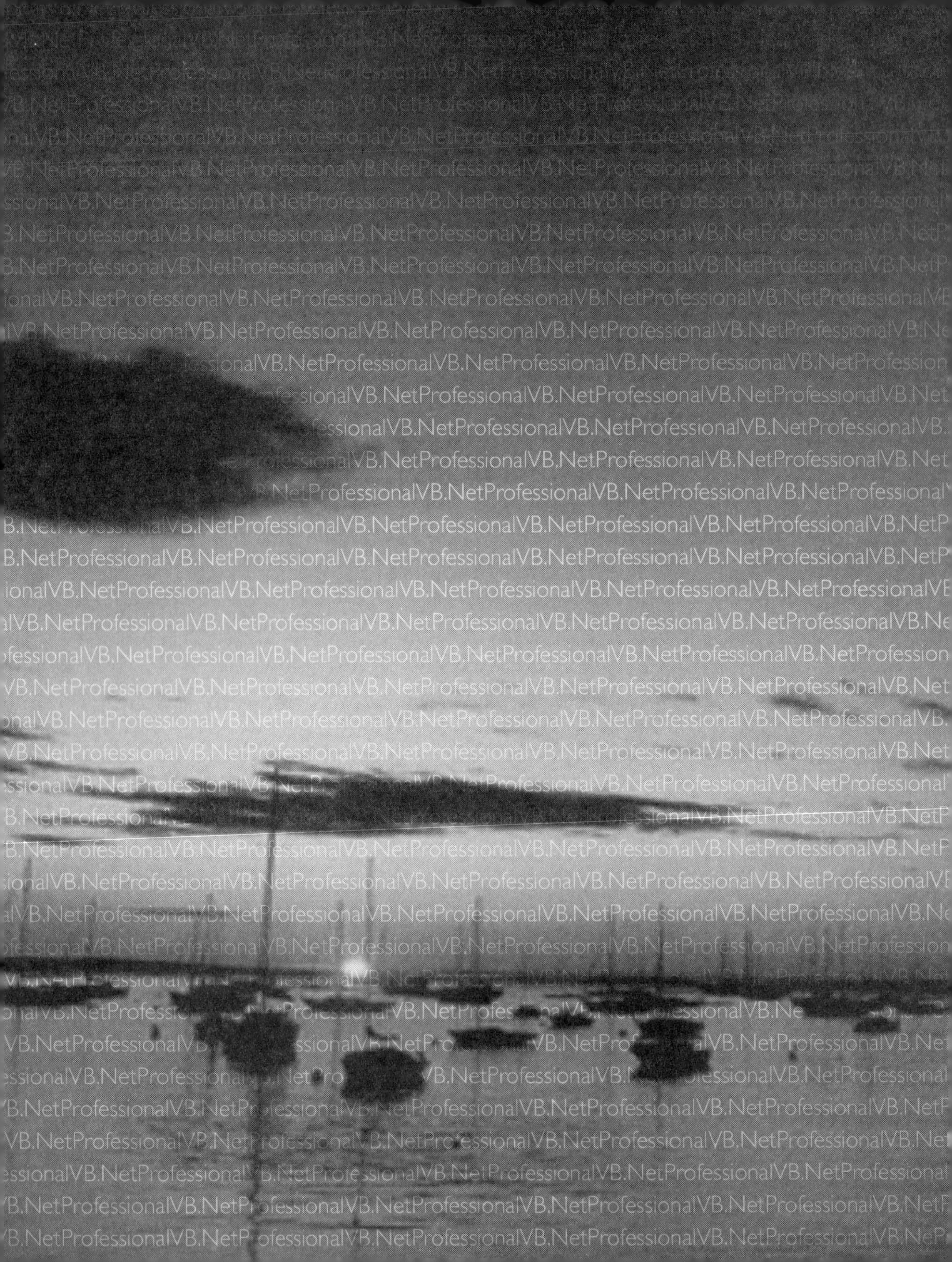
VB.NetProfessional

13

Applying Objects and Components

When Visual Basic 4.0 was released, it introduced a whole new era of programming for VB. Object-oriented programming was finally a possibility. Unfortunately, few object-oriented features were included in the VB language at that point. Most notably lacking were true implementation inheritance capabilities, one of the key defining criteria for any OO language. VB was also missing a large number of secondary features such as method overloading and overriding, and constructors.

With VB.NET, the VB language finally completes the transition to a fully OO language. We now have full inheritance, along with all of the associated features we'd expect.

While it certainly remains possible to create applications that require the programmer to have no more knowledge of objects in VB.NET than in VB3, these new capabilities are quite pervasive and so at least some basic understanding is required to take full advantage of VB.NET.

In Chapters 11 and 12, we explored the syntax provided by VB.NET for working with objects, creating classes, and implementing both inheritance and multiple interfaces. These are all powerful tools, providing us with the ability to create very maintainable and readable code – even for extremely complex applications.

However, just knowing the syntax and learning the tools is not enough to be successful. To successfully apply the object-oriented capabilities of Visual Basic to create applications requires an understanding of object-oriented programming, which is the applied theory behind object-oriented technology.

In this chapter we'll take the syntax we discussed in Chapters 11 and 12 and we'll see how it allows us to build object-oriented applications. We'll define and discuss the four major object-oriented concepts:

- ❑ Abstraction
- ❑ Encapsulation
- ❑ Polymorphism
- ❑ Inheritance

and how these concepts can be applied in our design and development to create effective object-oriented applications.

Abstraction

Abstraction is the process by which we can think about specific properties or behaviors without thinking about a particular object that has those properties or behaviors. Abstraction is merely the ability of a language to create "black box" code – to take a concept and create an abstract representation of that concept within a program.

A `Customer` object, for instance, is an abstract representation of a real-world customer. A `DataSet` object is an abstract representation of a set of data.

VB has supported abstraction since VB4.

Abstraction allows us to recognize how things are similar and ignore differences – to think in general terms, and not the specifics. A text box control is an abstraction, because we can place it on a form, and then tailor it to our needs by setting properties. Visual Basic allows us to define abstractions using class modules.

Any language that allows a developer to create a class from which objects can be instantiated meets this criteria, and Visual Basic is no exception. We can easily create a class to represent a customer, essentially providing an abstraction. We can then create instances of that class, where each object can have its own attributes such that it represents a specific customer.

In VB.NET we implement abstraction by creating a class using the `Class` keyword. Bring up VS.NET, create a new VB.NET Windows Application project, and name it `Chapter13Demo`.

Once the project is open, add a new class to the project using the **Project | Add Class** menu option. Name the new class `Customer`. Our class will start with the following simple code:

```
Public Class Customer

End Class
```

Now we can add some code to make this class represent a real-world customer in an abstract sense:

```
Public Class Customer
  Private mgID As Guid = Guid.NewGuid
  Private mstrName As String
  Private mstrPhone As String

  Public Property ID() As Guid
    Get
      Return mgID
    End Get
    Set(ByVal Value As Guid)
      mgID = Value
    End Set
  End Property

  Public Property Name() As String
    Get
      Return mstrName
    End Get
    Set(ByVal Value As String)
      mstrName = Value
    End Set
```

```
      End Property

      Public Property Phone() As String
        Get
            Return mstrPhone
        End Get
        Set(ByVal Value As String)
            mstrPhone = Value
        End Set
      End Property
   End Class
```

We know that a real customer is a lot more complex than an ID, name, and phone number. Yet at the same time, we know that in an abstract sense, our customers really do have names and phone numbers, and that we assign them unique ID numbers to keep track of them. Thus, given an ID, name, and phone number we know which customer we're dealing with and so we have a perfectly valid abstraction of a customer within our application.

We can then use this abstract representation of a customer from within our code. To do this, open the designer for `Form1` and add three text box controls to the form. Then add the following code to the form.

First off, we'll declare a variable and create a `Customer` object:

```
Public Class Form1
    Inherits System.Windows.Forms.Form
```

```
    Private mobjCustomer As New Customer()
```

Then, when the form is loaded we'll display the customer data in the text box controls:

```
    Private Sub Form1_Load(ByVal sender As System.Object, _
        ByVal e As System.EventArgs) Handles MyBase.Load

      TextBox1.DataBindings.Add("Text", mobjCustomer, "ID")
      TextBox2.DataBindings.Add("Text", mobjCustomer, "Name")
      TextBox3.DataBindings.Add("Text", mobjCustomer, "Phone")
```

```
    End Sub
```

We're using the ability of Windows Forms to data bind to a property on an object – in this case, we're binding our three text box controls' `Text` properties to the `ID`, `Name`, and `Phone` properties of our `mobjCustomer` object.

This code should work, but we will get a Null exception error when we run the application. This appears to be a bug in the beta version of VB.NET that causes instance variables not to be properly initialized prior to data binding. We can work around this error by initializing the values by hand – either in the form's `Load` event before we data bind, or within the classes themselves. Adding the code to the class will have the least overall impact, so let's do that. In the `Customer` class, where we declare the `mstrName` instance variable, change the code to initialize it as well:

```
    Private mstrName As String = ""
```

Also, in the `Customer` class where we declare the `mstrPhone` variable we'll need to initialize it:

```
    Private mstrPhone As String = ""
```

Now we have a simple UI that both displays and updates the data in our Customer object – with that object providing the UI developer with an abstract representation of the customer. When we run the application we'll see a display similar to the following:

Here we've displayed the pre-generated ID value, and have entered values for Name and Phone directly into the form.

Encapsulation

Perhaps the most important of the object-oriented concepts is that of **encapsulation**. Encapsulation is the concept that an object should totally separate its interface from its implementation. All the data and implementation code for an object should be entirely hidden behind its interface.

Another way to put this is that an object should be a "black box".

The idea is that we can create an interface (Public methods in a class) and, as long as that interface remains consistent, the application can interact with our objects. This remains true even if we entirely rewrite the code within a given method – thus the interface is independent of the implementation.

Encapsulation allows us to hide the internal implementation details of a class. For example, the algorithm we use to find prime numbers might be proprietary. We can expose a simple API to the end user, but we hide all of the logic used for our algorithm by encapsulating it within our class.

This means that an object should completely contain any data it requires, and that it should also contain all the code required to manipulate that data. Programs should interact with our object through an interface, using properties and methods. Client code should never work directly with the data owned by the object.

> *In object-speak, programs interact with objects by sending messages to the object indicating which method or property they'd like to have invoked. These messages are generated by other objects, or by external sources such as the user. The way the object reacts to these messages is through methods or properties.*

Visual Basic has provided full support for encapsulation through class modules since version 4.0. Using these modules, we can create classes that entirely hide their internal data and code, providing a well-established interface of properties and methods to the outside world.

For example, add a class to our project with the following code to define its native interface:

```
Public Class Encapsulation
   Public Function DistanceTo(ByVal X As Single, Y As Single) As Single

   End Function

   Public Property CurrentX() As Single
      Get

      End Get
      Set(ByVal Value As Single)

      End Set
   End Property

   Public Property CurrentY() As Single
      Get

      End Get
      Set(ByVal Value As Single)

      End Set
   End Property
End Class
```

This creates an interface for the class. At this point we can write client code to interact with the class, since from a client perspective all we care about is the interface. Bring up the designer for Form1 and add a button to the form, then write the following code behind the button:

```
Private Sub Button1_Click(ByVal sender As System.Object, _
      ByVal e As System.EventArgs) Handles button1.Click

   Dim obj As New Encapsulation()

   MsgBox(obj.DistanceTo(10, 10))
End Sub
```

Even though we have no actual code in our Encapsulation class, we can still write code to *use* that class because the interface is defined.

This is a powerful idea, since it means that we can rapidly create class interfaces against which other developers can create the UI or other parts of the application – while we are simultaneously creating the implementation behind the interface.

From here, we could do virtually anything in terms of implementing the class. For instance, we could use the values to calculate a direct distance:

```
Imports System.Math

Public Class Encapsulation
   Private msngX As Single
   Private msngY As Single
```

```
Public Function DistanceTo(ByVal X As Single, Y As Single) As Single
    Return Sqrt((X - msngX) ^ 2 + (Y - msngY) ^ 2)
End Function

Public Property CurrentX() As Single
    Get
        Return msngX
    End Get
    Set(ByVal Value As Single)
        msngX = Value
    End Set
End Property

Public Property CurrentY() As Single
    Get
        Return msngY
    End Get
    Set(ByVal Value As Single)
        msngY = Value
    End Set
End Property
End Class
```

Now when we run the application and click the button we'll get a meaningful value as a result:

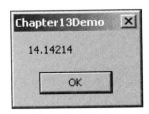

Where encapsulation comes into play however, is that we can change the *implementation* without changing the *interface*. For instance, we can change the distance calculation to find the distance between the points assuming no diagonal travel is allowed:

```
Public Function DistanceTo(ByVal X As Single, ByVal Y As Single) As Single
    Return Abs(X - msngX) + Abs(Y - msngY)
End Function
```

Which results in the following result being displayed if the program is run and we click the button:

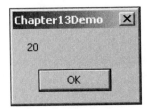

We haven't changed the interface of the class, and so our client program working has no idea if we have switched from one implementation to the other. A total change of behavior without any change to the client code at all. This is the essence of encapsulation.

Obviously, the user might have a problem if we made such a change to our object. If applications were developed expecting the first set of behaviors, and then we changed to the second, there could be some interesting side effects. However, the point here is that the client programs would continue to function, even if the results were quite different when we started.

Polymorphism

Polymorphism is often considered to be directly tied to inheritance (which we'll discuss next). In reality, however, it's independent to a large degree. Polymorphism means that we can have two classes with different implementations or code, but with a common set of methods or properties. We can then write a program that operates upon that interface and doesn't care about which type of object it operates at runtime.

Method Signatures

To really understand polymorphism we need to explore the concept of a **method signature**, also sometimes called a prototype. All methods have a signature, which is defined by the method's name and the data types of its parameters.

For instance, we might have code such as:

```
Public Function CalculateValue() As Integer

End Sub
```

In this example, the signature is:

   method()

If we add a parameter to the method the signature will change. For instance, we could change the method to accept a `Double`:

```
Public Function CalculateValue(Value As Double) As Integer
```

Then the signature of the method is:

   method(Double)

Polymorphism merely says that we should be able to write some client code that calls methods on an object – and as long as the object provides our methods with the method signatures we expect, we don't care which *class* the object was created from. Let's take a look at some examples of polymorphism as we explore the various ways we can implement it within VB.NET.

Implementing Polymorphism

We can use several techniques to achieve polymorphic behavior:

- ❑ Late binding
- ❑ Multiple interfaces
- ❑ .NET Reflection
- ❑ Inheritance

423

Late binding actually allows us to implement "pure" polymorphism at the cost of performance and ease of programming. Through multiple interfaces and inheritance we can also achieve polymorphism with much better performance and ease of programming. Reflection allows us to use either late binding or multiple interfaces, but against objects created in a very dynamic way – going even so far as to dynamically load a DLL into our application at runtime so we can use its classes.

We'll walk through each of these options to see how they are implemented and to explore their pros and cons.

Polymorphism through Late Binding

Typically when we interact with objects in VB.NET, we are interacting with them through strongly typed variables. For instance, in Form1 we interacted with the Encapsulation object with the following code:

```
Private Sub Button1_Click(ByVal sender As System.Object, _
    ByVal e As System.EventArgs) Handles button1.Click

  Dim obj As New Encapsulation()

  MsgBox(obj.DistanceTo(10, 10))
End Sub
```

The obj variable is declared using the type Encapsulation – meaning it is strongly typed, or **early bound**.

We can also interact with objects that are **late bound**. Late binding means that our object variable has no specific data type, but rather is of type Object. VB.NET treats the Object data type in a special way – allowing us to attempt arbitrary method calls against the object even though the Object data type doesn't implement those methods.

> *In VB.NET, the* Object *data type is very similar to the* Variant *data type found in previous versions of Visual Basic. It also includes the functionality found in the* Object *type from previous versions of Visual Basic.*

For instance, we could change the code in Form1 to be late bound as follows:

```
Private Sub Button1_Click(ByVal sender As System.Object, _
    ByVal e As System.EventArgs) Handles button1.Click

  Dim obj As Object = New Encapsulation()

  MsgBox(obj.DistanceTo(10, 10))
End Sub
```

When this code is run, we'll get the same result as we did before – even though the Object data type has no DistanceTo method as part of its interface. The late binding mechanism, behind the scenes, dynamically determines the real type of our object and invokes the appropriate method.

When we work with objects through late binding, neither the VB.NET IDE nor the compiler can tell if we are or are not calling a valid method. In this case, there is no way for the compiler to know that the object referenced by our obj variable actually has a DistanceTo method. It just assumes we know what we're talking about and compiles the code.

Then at *runtime*, when the code is actually invoked it will attempt to dynamically call the `DistanceTo` method. If that is a valid method our code will work, if it is not we'll get an error.

Obviously there is a level of danger when using late binding, since a simple typo can introduce errors that can only be discovered when the application is actually run. However, there is also a lot of flexibility, since code that makes use of late binding can talk to *any* object from *any* class as long as those objects implement the methods we require.

> *There is also a substantial performance penalty for using late binding. The existence of each method is discovered dynamically at runtime, and that discovery takes time. Additionally, the mechanism used to invoke a method through late binding is not nearly as efficient as the mechanism used to call a method that is known at compile-time.*

To make this more clear, we can change the code in `Form1` by adding a generic routine that displays the distance:

```
Private Sub Button1_Click(ByVal sender As System.Object, _
    ByVal e As System.EventArgs) Handles button1.Click

    Dim obj As New Encapsulation()

    ShowDistance(obj)
End Sub

Private Sub ShowDistance(ByVal obj As Object)
    MsgBox(obj.DistanceTo(10, 10))
End Sub
```

Notice that the new `ShowDistance` routine accepts a parameter using the generic `Object` data type – so we can pass it literally any value – `String`, `Integer`, or one of our objects. It will raise an error at runtime however, unless the object we pass into the routine has a `DistanceTo` method that matches the required method signature.

> This code requires `Option Strict Off` in the file containing the code that is calling the objects. This is the case by default, but is required when using late binding.

We know our `Encapsulation` object has a method matching that signature, so our code works fine. However, let's add another simple class to demonstrate polymorphism. Add a new class to the project and name it `Poly.vb`:

```
Public Class Poly
    Public Function DistanceTo(ByVal X As Single, ByVal Y As Single) As Single
        Return X + Y
    End Function
End Class
```

This class is about as simple as we can get. It exposes a `DistanceTo` method as part of its interface and provides a very basic implementation of that interface.

We can use this new class in place of the `Encapsulation` class *without changing the* `ShowDistance` *method* by using polymorphism. Return to the code in `Form1` and make the following change:

```
Private Sub Button1_Click(ByVal sender As System.Object, _
    ByVal e As System.EventArgs) Handles button1.Click

  Dim obj As New Poly()

  ShowDistance(obj)
End Sub
```

Even though we changed the class of object we're passing to ShowDistance to a radically different class, with a different overall interface and different implementation – since the method called within ShowDistance remains consistent our code will run.

Polymorphism with Multiple Interfaces

Late binding is nice, because it is flexible and easy. However, it is not ideal because it defeats the IDE and compiler type checking that allow us to fix bugs due to typos during the development process, and because it has negative impact on performance.

Fortunately, VB.NET not only provides this late binding ability, but also implements a stricter form of polymorphism through its support of multiple interfaces. We discussed multiple interfaces in Chapter 12, including the use of the Implements keyword and how to define interfaces.

With late binding we've seen how to treat all objects as equals by making them all appear using the Object data type. With multiple interfaces, we can treat all objects as equals by making them all implement a *common* data type, or interface.

This approach has the benefit that it is strongly typed – meaning that the IDE and compiler can help us find errors due to typos, since the name and data types of all methods and parameters are known at design-time. It is also fast in terms of performance; since the compiler knows all about the methods, it can use optimized mechanisms for calling them – especially as compared to the dynamic mechanisms used in late binding.

Let's return to the project and implement polymorphism with multiple interfaces. First off, add a module to the project using the **Project | Add Module** menu option and name it Interfaces.vb. Replace the Module code block with an Interface declaration:

```
Public Interface IShared
    Function CalculateDistance(ByVal X As Single, ByVal Y As Single) As Single
End Interface
```

Now we can make both the Encapsulation and Poly classes implement this interface. First, in the Encapsulation class add the following code:

```
Public Class Encapsulation
  Implements IShared

  Private msngX As Single
  Private msngY As Single

  Public Function DistanceTo(ByVal X As Single, ByVal Y As Single) As Single _
      Implements IShared.CalculateDistance

    Return Sqrt((X - msngX) ^ 2 + (Y - msngY) ^ 2)
  End Function
...
```

We can see that we're implementing the `IShared` interface, and since the `CalculateDistance` method's signature matches that of our existing `DistanceTo` method, we're simply indicating that it should act as the implementation for `CalculateDistance`.

We can make a similar change in the `Poly` class:

```
Public Class Poly
   Implements IShared

   Public Function DistanceTo(ByVal X As Single, ByVal Y As Single) As Single _
       Implements IShared.CalculateDistance

     Return X + Y
   End Function
End Class
```

Now this class also implements the `IShared` interface, and we're ready to see polymorphism implemented in our code.

Bring up the code window for `Form1` and change our `ShowDistance` method as follows:

```
Private Sub ShowDistance(ByVal obj As IShared)
   MsgBox(obj.CalculateDistance(10, 10))
End Sub
```

Notice that instead of accepting the parameter using the generic `Object` data type, we are now accepting an `IShared` parameter – a strong data type known by both the IDE and the compiler. Within the code itself, we are now calling the `CalculateDistance` method as defined by that interface.

This routine can now accept any object that implements `IShared` – regardless of what class that object was created from, or what other interfaces that object may implement. All we care about here is that it implements `IShared`.

Polymorphism through .NET Reflection

We've seen how to use late binding to invoke a method on any arbitrary object – as long as that object has a method matching the method signature we're trying to call. We've also walked through the use of multiple interfaces which allows us to achieve polymorphism through a faster, early bound technique. The challenge with these techniques is that late binding can be slow and hard to debug, and multiple interfaces can be somewhat rigid and inflexible.

We can use the concept of **reflection** within .NET to overcome some of these limitations. Reflection is a technology built into .NET that allows us to write code that interrogates a .NET assembly to dynamically determine the classes and data types it contains. We can then use reflection to load the assembly into our process, create instances of those classes and invoke their methods.

When we use late binding, VB.NET is making use of the .NET `System.Reflection` namespace behind the scenes on our behalf. We can choose to manually use reflection as well – which allows us even more flexibility in how we interact with objects.

For instance, suppose the class we want to call is located in some other assembly on disk – an assembly we didn't specifically reference from within our project when we compiled it. How can we dynamically find, load, and invoke such an assembly? Reflection allows us to do this – assuming that assembly is polymorphic. In other words, assuming it has either an interface we expect, or a set of methods we can invoke via late binding.

To see how reflection works with late binding, let's create a new class in a separate assembly (project) and use it from within our existing application.

Choose **File | Add Project | New Project** to add a new Class Library project to our solution. Name it `Chapter13Objects`. It will start with a single class module that we can use as a starting point. Change the code in that module as follows:

```
Public Class External
   Public Function DistanceTo(ByVal X As Single, ByVal Y As Single) As Single
      Return X * Y
   End Function
End Class
```

Now compile the assembly by choosing the **Build | Build Chapter13Objects** menu option.

Next, bring up the code window for `Form1`. Add an `Imports` statement at the top:

```
Imports System.Reflection
```

Then change the code behind the button to the following:

```
Private Sub Button1_Click(ByVal sender As System.Object, _
    ByVal e As System.EventArgs) Handles button1.Click

   Dim obj As Object
   Dim myDll As Reflection.Assembly

   myDll = System.Reflection.Assembly.LoadFrom( _
     "..\..\Chapter13Objects\bin\Chapter13Objects.dll")

   obj = myDll.CreateInstance("Chapter13Objects.External")
   MsgBox(obj.DistanceTo(10, 10))
 End Sub
```

There's a lot going on here, so let's walk through it a bit.

First off, notice that we're reverting to late binding – our `obj` variable is declared as type `Object`. We'll take a look at using reflection and multiple interfaces in a moment – but to start with we'll use late binding.

Next, we've declared a `myDll` variable as type `Reflection.Assembly`. This variable will contain a reference to the `Chapter13Objects` assembly that we'll be dynamically loading through our code. Note that we are *not* adding a reference to this assembly via **Project | Add References** – we'll get access to the assembly at runtime.

We then load the external assembly dynamically by using the `Assembly.LoadFrom` method:

```
myDll = System.Reflection.Assembly.LoadFrom( _
   "..\..\Chapter13Objects\bin\Chapter13Objects.dll")
```

This causes the reflection library to load our assembly from a file on disk at the location we specify. Once the assembly is loaded into our process, we can use the `myDll` variable to interact with it – including interrogating it to get a list of the classes it contains or to create instances of those classes.

We can also use the `Assembly.Load` *method, which will scan the directory where our application's EXE file is located (and the .NET global assembly cache) for any EXE or DLL containing the* `Chapter13Objects` *assembly. When it finds the assembly, it loads it into memory – making it available for our use.*

We can then use the `CreateInstance` method on the assembly itself to create objects based on any class in that assembly. In our case, we're creating an object based on the `External` class:

```
obj = myDll.CreateInstance("Chapter13Objects.External")
```

Now we have an actual object to work with – so we can use late binding to invoke its `DistanceTo` method. At this point our code is really no different than our earlier late binding example – other than that the assembly and object were created dynamically at runtime rather than being referenced directly by our project.

At this point we should be able to run the application and have it dynamically invoke the assembly at runtime.

Polymorphism through .NET Reflection and Multiple Interfaces

We can also use both reflection and multiple interfaces together. We've seen how multiple interfaces allows us to have objects from different classes implement the same interface and thus be treated identically. We've also seen how reflection allows us to load an assembly and class dynamically at runtime.

We can combine these concepts by using an interface that is common between our main application and our external assembly, and also using reflection to load that external assembly dynamically at runtime.

First off, we need to create this interface that will be shared across both application and assembly. To do this, add a new Class Library project to our solution named `Chapter13Interfaces`. Once it is created, drag-and-drop the `Interfaces.vb` module from our original application into the new project. This makes the `IShared` interface part of that project and no longer part of our base application.

Of course our base application still uses `IShared`, so we'll want to reference the `Chapter13Interfaces` project from our application to gain access to the interface. Do this by right-clicking on `Chapter13Demo` in the **Solution Explorer** window and selecting the **Add Reference** menu option. Then add the reference as shown in the following diagram:

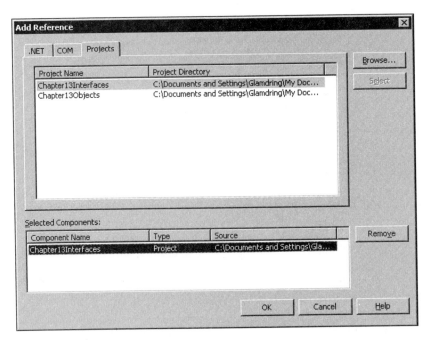

Since the IShared interface is now part of a separate assembly, we'll need to add an Imports statement to Form1, Encapsulation, and Poly so they are able to locate the IShared interface:

```
Imports Chapter13Interfaces
```

Make sure to add this to the top of all three code modules.

We also need to have the Chapter13Objects project reference Chapter13Interface, so right-click on Chapter13Objects in the **Solution Explorer** and choose **Add Reference** there as well. Add the reference to Chapter13Interfaces and click **OK**.

At this point both our original application and our external assembly have access to the IShared interface. We can now enhance the code in Chapter13Objects by changing the External class:

```
Imports Chapter13Interfaces

Public Class External
   Implements IShared

   Public Function DistanceTo(ByVal X As Single, ByVal Y As Single) As Single _
         Implements IShared.CalculateDistance

      Return X * Y
   End Function
End Class
```

With both the main application and external assembly using the same data type, we are now ready to implement the polymorphic behavior using reflection.

First off, build the solution by choosing Build | Build Solution from the menu. Then copy the Chapter13Objects.dll from the Chapter13Objects\bin directory to the Chapter13Demo\bin directory to make the new version of the DLL available for use by our application.

With that done, bring up the code window for Form1 and change the code behind the button to take advantage of the IShared interface:

```
Private Sub Button1_Click(ByVal sender As System.Object, _
    ByVal e As System.EventArgs) Handles button1.Click

  Dim myDll As Reflection.Assembly
  Dim obj As Object

  myDll = System.Reflection.Assembly.LoadFrom( _
    "..\..\Chapter13Objects\bin\Chapter13Objects.dll")
  obj = myDll.CreateInstance("Chapter13Objects.External")
  ShowDistance(obj)
End Sub
```

All we've done here is to change the code so we pass our dynamically created object to the ShowDistance method – which we know requires a parameter of type IShared. Since our class implements the same IShared interface (from Chapter13Interfaces) as is used by the main application this will work perfectly.

This technique is very nice, since the code in ShowDistance is strongly typed, providing all the performance and coding benefits, but the object itself is loaded dynamically – providing a great deal of flexibility to our application.

Polymorphism with Inheritance

Inheritance, which we discussed in Chapter 12, can also be used to enable polymorphism. The idea here is very similar to that of multiple interfaces, since a subclass can always be treated as though it were the data type of the parent class.

> *Many people consider the concepts of inheritance and polymorphism to be tightly intertwined. As we've seen, however, it is perfectly possible to use polymorphism without inheritance – a fact that VB developers have understood since Visual Basic 4.0.*

At the moment, both our Encapsulation and Poly classes are implementing a common interface named IShared. We are able to use polymorphism to interact with objects of either class via that common interface.

The same is true if these are child classes based on the same base class through inheritance. Let's see how this works.

In the Chapter13Demo project, add a new class named Parent. Insert the following code into that class:

```
Public MustInherit Class Parent
  Public MustOverride Function DistanceTo(ByVal X As Single, _
    ByVal Y As Single) As Single
End Class
```

As we discussed in Chapter 12, this is an abstract base class – a class with no implementation of its own. The purpose of an abstract base class is to provide a common base from which other classes can be derived.

To implement polymorphism using inheritance we do not need to use an abstract base class. Any base class that provides overridable methods (using either MustOverride or Overridable keywords) will work fine, since all its subclasses are guaranteed to have that same set of methods as part of their interface and yet the subclasses can provide custom implementation for those methods.

In this example we're simply defining the DistanceTo method as being a method that must be overridden and implemented by any subclass of Parent.

Now we can bring up the Encapsulation class and change it to be a subclass of Parent:

```
Public Class Encapsulation
   Inherits Parent
   Implements IShared
```

We don't need to quit implementing the IShared interface just because we're inheriting from Parent – inheritance and multiple interfaces coexist nicely. We do, however, have to override the DistanceTo method from the Parent class.

The Encapsulation class already has a DistanceTo method with the proper method signature, so we can simply add the Overrides keyword to indicate that this method will override the declaration in the Parent class:

```
Public Overrides Function DistanceTo(ByVal X As Single, _
   ByVal Y As Single) As Single Implements IShared.CalculateDistance
```

At this point our Encapsulation class not only implements the common IShared interface and its own native interface, but it also can be treated as though it were of type Parent since it is a subclass of Parent.

We can do the same thing to the Poly class:

```
Public Class Poly
   Inherits Parent
   Implements IShared

   Public Overrides Function DistanceTo(ByVal X As Single, _
      ByVal Y As Single) As Single Implements IShared.CalculateDistance

      Return X + Y
   End Function
End Class
```

Finally, we can see how the polymorphism works by altering the code in Form1 to take advantage of the fact that both classes can be treated as though they were of type Parent. First, we can change the ShowDistance method to accept its parameter as type Parent, and to call the DistanceTo method:

```
Private Sub ShowDistance(ByVal obj As Parent)
   MsgBox(obj.DistanceTo(10, 10))
End Sub
```

Then we can change the code behind our button to create an object of either type Encapsulation or Poly and pass it as a parameter to the method:

```
Private Sub Button1_Click(ByVal sender As System.Object, _
    ByVal e As System.EventArgs) Handles button1.Click

    ShowDistance(New Poly())
    ShowDistance(New Encapsulation())
End Sub
```

Polymorphism Summary

Polymorphism is a very important concept in object-oriented design and programming, and VB.NET provides us with ample techniques through which it can be implemented.

The following table summarizes the different techniques, their pros and cons and provides some high level guidelines about when to use each:

Technique	Pros	Cons	Guidelines
Late binding	Flexible, "pure" polymorphism	Slow, hard to debug, no IntelliSense	Use to call arbitrary methods on literally any object regardless of data type or interfaces. Useful when we can't control the interfaces that will be implemented by the authors of our classes.
Multiple interfaces	Fast, easy to debug, full IntelliSense	Not totally dynamic or flexible, requires class author to implement formal interface	Use when we are creating code that interacts with clearly defined methods that can be grouped together into a formal interface. Useful when we control the interfaces that will be implemented by the classes used by our application.
Reflection and late binding	Flexible, "pure" polymorphism, dynamically load arbitrary assemblies from disk	Slow, hard to debug, no IntelliSense	Use to call arbitrary methods on objects, where we don't know at design time which assemblies we will be using.

Table continued on following page

Technique	Pros	Cons	Guidelines
Reflection and multiple interfaces	Fast, easy to debug, full IntelliSense, dynamically load arbitrary assemblies from disk	Not totally dynamic or flexible, requires class author to implement formal interface	Use when we are creating code that interacts with clearly defined methods that can be grouped together into a formal interface, but where we don't know at design time which assemblies we will be using.
Inheritance	Fast, easy to debug, full IntelliSense, inherits behaviors from base class	Not totally dynamic or flexible, requires class author to inherit from common base class	Use when we are creating objects that have an *is-a* relationship, where we have subclasses that are naturally of the same data type as a base class. Polymorphism through inheritance should occur because inheritance makes sense, *not* because we are attempting to merely achieve polymorphism.

Inheritance

Inheritance is the concept that a new class can be based on an existing class, inheriting its interface and functionality from the original class. We discussed the mechanics and syntax of inheritance in Chapter 12, so we won't rehash them here. However, in Chapter 12 we really didn't discuss inheritance from a practical perspective, and that will be the focus of this section.

When to Use Inheritance

Inheritance is one of the most powerful object-oriented features a language can support. At the same time, inheritance is one of the most dangerous and misused object-oriented features.

Properly used, inheritance allows us to increase the maintainability, readability, and reusability of our application, by offering us a clear and concise way to reuse code – both via interface and implementation. Improperly used, inheritance allows us to create applications that are very fragile, where a change to a class can cause the entire application to break or require changes.

Inheritance allows us to implement an *is-a* relationship. In other words, it allows us to implement a new class that *is a* more specific type of its base class. This means that properly used, inheritance allows us to create child classes that *really are* the same as the base class.

Perhaps a quick example is in order. Take a duck. We know that a duck *is a* bird. However, a duck can also be food – though that is not its primary identity. Proper use of inheritance would allow us to create a Bird base class from which we can derive our Duck class. We would *not* create a Food class and subclass Duck from Food, since a duck isn't *really* just food – it merely acts as food sometimes.

This is the challenge. Inheritance is *not* just a mechanism for code reuse. It is a mechanism to create classes that flow naturally from some other class. If we use it anywhere we want code reuse, we'll end up with a real mess on our hands. If we use it anywhere we just want a common interface, but where the child class is not *really* the same as the base class then we should be using multiple interfaces – something we'll discuss shortly.

The question we must ask, when using inheritance, is whether the child class *is a* more specific version of the base class.

For instance, we might have different types of products in our organization. All of these products will have some common data and behaviors – they'll all have a product number and description, and they'll all have a price.

However, if we have an agricultural application we might have chemical products, seed products, fertilizer products, and retail products. These are all different – each having its own data and behaviors – and yet there is no doubt that each one of them really is a product. We can use inheritance to create this set of products as illustrated by the following UML diagram:

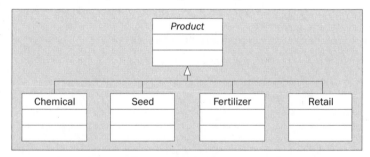

This diagram shows that we have an abstract base Product class, from which we derive the various types of product our system will actually use. This is an appropriate use of inheritance, because the child classes are obviously each a more specific form of the general Product class.

On the other hand, we might try to use inheritance just as a code sharing mechanism. For instance, we may look at our application, which has Customer, Product, and SalesOrder classes, and decide that all of them need to be designed so they can be printed to a printer. The code to handle the printing will all be somewhat similar, and so to reuse that printing code we create a base PrintableObject class. This would result in the following UML:

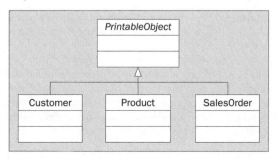

Intuitively we know that this doesn't represent an *is-a* relationship. While a Customer can be printed, and we are getting code reuse, a customer isn't really a specific case of a printable object. Implementing a system following this design will result in a fragile design and application. This is a case where multiple interfaces are a far more appropriate technology – as we'll discuss later.

To illustrate this point, we might later discover that we have other entities in our organization that are similar to a customer, but are not quite the same. Upon further analysis, we may determine that Employee, Customer, and Contact are all related because they are specific cases of a Person class. The Person class provides commonality in terms of data and behavior across all these other classes:

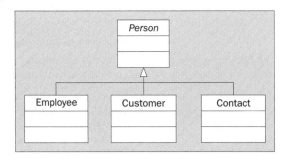

But now our Customer is in trouble – we've said it *is-a* PrintableObject, and we're now saying it *is-a* Person.

We *might* be able to just derive Person from PrintableObject:

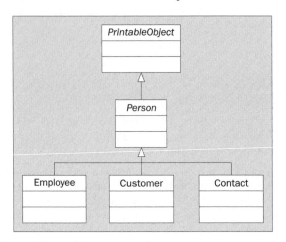

The problem with this is that now Employee and Contact are also of type PrintableObject – even if they *shouldn't be*. But we're stuck, since we unfortunately had decided early on to go against intuition and say that a Customer *is-a* PrintableObject.

This is a problem that could be solved by **multiple inheritance**, which would allow Customer to be a subclass of more than one base class – in this case of both Person and PrintableObject. However, the .NET platform and thus VB.NET don't support multiple inheritance in this way. Our alternative is to use inheritance for the *is-a* relationship with Person, and use multiple interfaces to allow the Customer object to *act as* a PrintableObject by implementing an IPrintableObject interface.

Application vs. Framework Inheritance

What we've just seen is how inheritance can accidentally cause reuse of code where no reuse was desired.

However, we can take a different view of this model by separating the concept of a framework from our actual application. The way we use inheritance in the design of a framework is somewhat different from how we use inheritance in the design of an actual application.

In this context, the word **framework** is being used to refer to a set of classes that provide base functionality that is not specific to our application, but rather may be used across a number of applications within our organization, or perhaps even beyond our organization. The .NET system class libraries are an example of a very broad framework we use when building our applications.

The PrintableObject class we discussed earlier, for instance, may have little to do with our specific application, but rather may be the type of thing that is used across many applications. If so, it is a natural candidate for being part of a framework, rather than being considered part of our actual application.

Framework classes exist at a "lower level" than application classes. For instance, the .NET system class library is a framework on which all .NET applications are built. We can layer our own framework on top of the .NET framework as well:

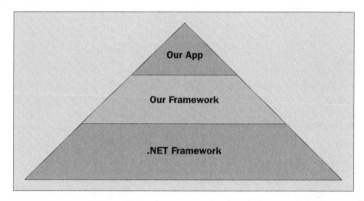

If we take this view, then the PrintableObject class wouldn't be part of our application at all, but rather would be part of a framework on which our application is built. In such a case, the fact that Customer is not a specific case of PrintableObject doesn't matter as much – since we're not saying it is such a thing, but rather we're saying it is leveraging that portion of the framework functionality.

To make this all work requires a lot of planning and forethought in the design of the framework itself. To see the dangers we face, consider that we might not only want to be able to print objects, but we might also want to be able to store them in a file. So we might not only have PrintableObject, but we might also have SavableObject as a base class.

The question then becomes – what do we do if Customer should be both printable *and* savable? If all printable objects are savable we might have:

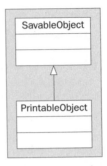

Or, if all savable objects are printable we might have:

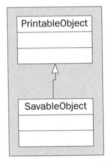

But really neither of these provides a decent solution, since the odds are that the concept of being printable and the concept of being savable are different and not interrelated in either of these ways.

When faced with this sort of issue, it is best to avoid using inheritance, and rather rely on multiple interfaces.

Inheritance and Multiple Interfaces

While inheritance is powerful, it is really geared around implementing the *is-a* relationship. Sometimes we will have objects that need to have a common interface, even though they *aren't* really a specific case of some base class that provides that interface. We've just been exploring that issue in our discussion of the PrintableObject, SavableObject, and Customer classes.

Sometimes multiple interfaces are a better alternative than inheritance. We discussed the syntax for creating and using secondary and multiple interfaces in Chapter 12.

Multiple interfaces can be viewed as another way of implementing the *is-a* relationship. It is often better, however, to view inheritance as an *is-a* relationship and to view multiple interfaces as a way of implementing an *act-as* relationship.

To think about this further, we can say that our PrintableObject concept could perhaps be better expressed as an interface – IPrintableObject.

When our class implements a secondary interface such as IPrintableObject, we're not really saying that our class *is a* printable object, we're saying that it can *act as* a printable object. A Customer *is-a* Person, but at the same time it can *act-as* a printable object. This is illustrated in UML as:

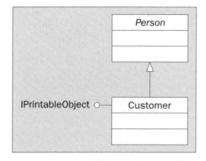

The drawback to this approach is that we get no inherited *implementation* when we implement
IPrintableObject. In Chapter 12 we discussed how to reuse common code as we implement an
interface across multiple classes. While not as automatic or easy as inheritance, it is possible to reuse
implementation code with a bit of extra work.

Applying Inheritance and Multiple Interfaces

We can see how this works in code by working with our Chapter13Demo project.

Creating the Person Base Class

We already have a simple Customer class in the project – so now let's add a Person base class. Choose
Project | Add Class and add a class named Person. Write the following code:

```
Public MustInherit Class Person
  Private mgID As Guid = Guid.NewGuid
  Private mstrName As String = ""

  Public Property ID() As Guid
    Get
      Return mgID
    End Get
    Set(ByVal Value As Guid)
      mgID = Value
    End Set
  End Property

  Public Property Name() As String
    Get
      Return mstrName
    End Get
    Set(ByVal Value As String)
      mstrName = Value
    End Set
  End Property
End Class
```

Subclassing Person

Now we can make the Customer class inherit from this base class, since it *is-a* Person. Also, since our
base class now implements both the ID and Name properties, we can simplify the code in Customer by
removing those properties and their related variables:

```
Public Class Customer
  Inherits Person
```

```
      Private mstrPhone As String = ""

   Public Property Phone() As String
      Get
         Return mstrPhone
      End Get
      Set(ByVal Value As String)
         mstrPhone = Value
      End Set
   End Property
End Class
```

This shows the benefit of subclassing `Customer` from `Person`, since we're now sharing the `ID` and Name code across all other types of `Person` as well.

Implementing IPrintableObject

However, we also know that a `Customer` should be able to *act-as* a printable object. To do this in a way such that the *implementation* is reusable requires a bit of thought.

First off though, we need to define the `IPrintableObject` interface.

We'll use the standard printing mechanism provided by .NET from the `System.Drawing` namespace – and so we'll need to add a reference to `System.Drawing.dll` to the `Chapter13Interfaces` project before we can define our new interface.

With that done, bring up the code window for `Interfaces.vb` in the `Chapter13Interfaces` project and add the following code:

```
Imports System.Drawing

Public Interface IPrintableObject
   Sub Print()
   Sub PrintPreview()
   Sub RenderPage(ByVal sender As Object, _
       ByVal ev As System.Drawing.Printing.PrintPageEventArgs)
End Interface
```

This interface ensures that any object implementing `IPrintableObject` will have `Print` and `PrintPreview` methods so we can invoke the appropriate type of printing. It also ensures the object will have a `RenderPage` method, which can be implemented by that object to render the object's data onto the printed page.

At this point we could simply implement all the code needed to handle printing directly within the `Customer` object. This isn't ideal, however, since some of the code will be common across any objects that want to implement `IPrintableObject` – and it would be nice to find a way to share that code.

To do this, let's create a new class – `ObjectPrinter`. This is a framework-style class, in that it has nothing to do with any particular application, but can be used across any application where `IPrintableObject` will be used.

Add a new class named `ObjectPrinter` to the `Chapter13Demo` project. This class will contain all the code common to printing any object. It makes use of the built-in printing support provided by the .NET system class library. To use this, we need to import a couple of namespaces, so add this code to the new class:

```
Imports System.Drawing
Imports System.Drawing.Printing
```

We can then define a `PrintDocument` variable, which will hold the reference to our printer output. We'll also declare a variable to hold a reference to the actual object we'll be printing. Notice that we're using the `IPrintableObject` interface data type for this variable:

```
Public Class ObjectPrinter
   Private WithEvents MyDoc As PrintDocument
   Private printObject As Chapter13Interfaces.IPrintableObject
```

Now we can create a routine to kick off the printing process for any object implementing `IPrintableObject`. This code is totally generic, so we'll write it here so it can be reused across any number of other classes:

```
Public Sub Print(ByVal obj As Chapter13Interfaces.IPrintableObject)
   printObject = obj

   MyDoc() = New PrintDocument()
   MyDoc().Print()
End Sub
```

Likewise, we can implement a method to show a print preview display of our object. Again, this code is totally generic, so we'll put it here for reuse:

```
Public Sub PrintPreview(ByVal obj As Chapter13Interfaces.IPrintableObject)
   Dim PPdlg As PrintPreviewDialog = New PrintPreviewDialog()

   printObject = obj

   MyDoc() = New PrintDocument()
   PPdlg.Document = MyDoc()
   PPdlg.ShowDialog()
End Sub
```

Finally, we need to catch the `PrintPage` event that is automatically raised by the .NET printing mechanism. This event is raised by the `PrintDocument` object whenever the document determines that it needs data rendered onto a page. Typically it is in this routine that we'd put the code to draw our text or graphics onto the page surface. However, since this is a generic framework class, we won't do that here, but rather we'll delegate the call back into the actual application object that we want to print:

```
Private Sub PrintPage(ByVal sender As Object, _
      ByVal ev As System.Drawing.Printing.PrintPageEventArgs) _
      Handles MyDoc.PrintPage

   printObject.RenderPage(sender, ev)
End Sub
End Class
```

This allows the application object itself to determine how its data should be rendered onto the output page.

Let's see how we can do that by implementing the `IPrintableObject` interface on our `Customer` class:

```
Imports Chapter13Interfaces

Public Class Customer
  Inherits Person
  Implements IPrintableObject
```

By adding this code, we're requiring that our `Customer` class implement the `Print`, `PrintPreview`, and `RenderPage` methods. To avoid wasting paper as we test, let's make both the `Print` and `PrintPreview` methods the same – and have them just do a print preview display:

```
Private Sub Print() _
    Implements IPrintableObject.Print, IPrintableObject.PrintPreview

  Dim p As New ObjectPrinter()
  p.PrintPreview(Me)
End Sub
```

Notice that we're using an `ObjectPrinter` object to handle the common details of doing a print preview. In fact, any class we ever create that implements `IPrintableObject` will have this exact same code to implement a print preview function – relying on our common `ObjectPrinter` to take care of the details.

We also need to implement the `RenderPage` method, which is where we actually put our object's data onto the printed page:

```
Private Sub RenderPage(ByVal sender As Object, _
    ByVal ev As System.Drawing.Printing.PrintPageEventArgs) _
    Implements IPrintableObject.RenderPage

  Dim PrintFont As New Font("Arial", 10)
  Dim LineHeight As Single = PrintFont.GetHeight(ev.Graphics)
  Dim LeftMargin As Single = ev.MarginBounds.Left
  Dim yPos As Single = ev.MarginBounds.Top

  ev.Graphics.DrawString("ID: " & ID().ToString, PrintFont, Brushes.Black, _
    LeftMargin, yPos, New StringFormat())

  yPos += LineHeight
  ev.Graphics.DrawString("Name: " & Name(), PrintFont, Brushes.Black, _
    LeftMargin, yPos, New StringFormat())

  ev.HasMorePages = False
End Sub
```

All of this code is unique to our object – which makes sense, since we're rendering our specific data to be printed. However, we don't need to worry about the details of whether we're doing printing to paper or print preview – that is handled by our `ObjectPrinter` class, which in turn uses the .NET framework. This allows us to just focus on generating the output to the page within our application class.

By generalizing the printing code in ObjectPrinter, we've achieved a level of reuse that we can tap into via the IPrintableObject interface. Any time we want to print a Customer object's data, we can have it *act-as* an IPrintableObject and call its Print or PrintPreview method. To see this work, let's change the code behind the button control on Form1:

```
Private Sub Button1_Click(ByVal sender As System.Object, _
    ByVal e As System.EventArgs) Handles button1.Click

    Dim obj As New Customer()
    obj.Name = "Douglas Adams"
    CType(obj, Chapter13Interfaces.IPrintableObject).Print()
End Sub
```

This code creates a new Customer object and sets its Name property. We then use the CType() method to access the object via its IPrintableObject interface to invoke the Print method.

When we run the application and click the button, we'll get a print preview display showing the object's data:

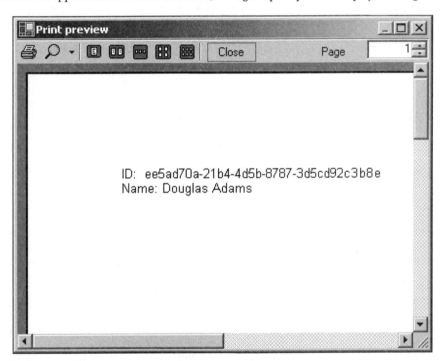

Our display will be similar to what is shown in the diagram.

How Deep to Go?

Most of the examples we've discussed so far in Chapter 12 and now in Chapter 13 have illustrated how we can create a child class based on a single parent class. That is called single-level inheritance. However, inheritance can be many levels deep. For instance, we might have a deep hierarchy such as:

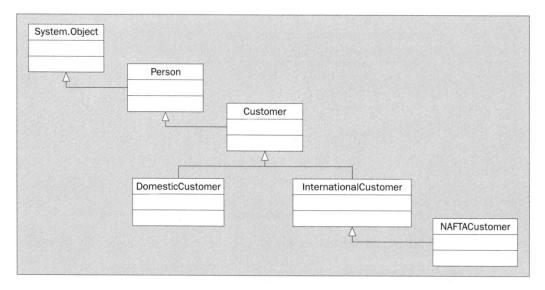

From the root of System.Object down to the NAFTACustomer we have four levels of inheritance. This can be described as a 4-level inheritance chain.

There is no hard and fast rule about how deep inheritance chains should go, but conventional wisdom and general experience with inheritance in other languages such as Smalltalk and C++ indicate that the deeper an inheritance chain becomes, the harder it is to maintain an application.

This happens for two reasons. First is the fragile base class or fragile superclass issue, which we'll discuss shortly. The second reason is that a deep inheritance hierarchy tends to seriously reduce readability of our code by scattering the code for an object across many different classes – all of which are combined together by the compiler to create our object.

One of the reasons for adopting object-oriented design and programming is to avoid so-called spaghetti code – where any bit of code we might look at does almost nothing useful, but instead calls various other procedures and routines in other parts of our application. To determine what is going on with spaghetti code, we must trace through many routines and mentally piece together what is going on.

Object-oriented programming *can* help us avoid this problem, but it is most definitely not a magic bullet. In fact, when we create deep inheritance hierarchies, we are often creating spaghetti code.

This is because each level in the hierarchy not only extends the previous level's interface, but almost always also adds functionality. Thus, when we look at our final NAFTACustomer class it may have very little code. In order to figure out what it does or how it behaves, we have to trace through the code in the previous four levels of classes – and we might not even *have* the code for some of those classes, since they may come from other applications or class libraries we've purchased.

On one hand we have the benefit that we're reusing code, but on the other hand we have the drawback that the code for one object is actually scattered through five different classes.

It is important to keep this in mind when designing systems with inheritance – use as few levels in the hierarchy as possible to provide the required functionality.

Fragile Base Class Issue

We've explored where it is and is not appropriate to use inheritance. We've also explored how we can use inheritance and multiple interfaces in conjunction to implement both *is-a* and *act-as* relationships simultaneously within our classes.

Earlier we noted that while inheritance is an incredibly powerful and useful concept, it can also be very dangerous if used improperly. We've seen some of this danger as we discussed the misapplication of the *is-a* relationship, and how we can use multiple interfaces to avoid those issues.

However, one of the most classic and common problems with inheritance is the **fragile base class** problem. This problem is exacerbated when we have very deep inheritance hierarchies, but exists even in a single-level inheritance chain.

> **The issue we face is that a change in the base class always affects all child classes derived from that base class.**

This is a double-edged sword. On one hand we get the benefit of being able to change code in one location and have that change automatically cascade out through all derived classes. On the other hand, a change in behavior can have unintended or unexpected consequences further down the inheritance chain – and that can make our application very fragile and hard to change or maintain.

Interface Changes

There are obvious changes we might make, that require immediate attention. For instance, we might change our `Person` class to have `FirstName` and `LastName` instead of simply `Name` as a property. Replace the `mstrName` variable declaration with:

```
Private mstrFirstName As String = ""
Private mstrLastName As String = ""
```

Notice that we are initializing these variables by hand. Normally this is not necessary, but by doing this we are working around the Beta 2 bug that would otherwise prevent data binding against our properties.

Now replace the `Name` property with the following:

```
Public Property FirstName() As String
  Get
    Return mstrFirstName
  End Get
  Set(ByVal Value As String)
    mstrFirstName = Value
  End Set
End Property

Public Property LastName() As String
  Get
    Return mstrLastName
  End Get
  Set(ByVal Value As String)
    mstrLastName = Value
  End Set
End Property
```

445

At this point, the Task List window in the IDE will show a list of locations where we need to change our code to compensate for the change. This is a graphic illustration of a base class change that causes cascading changes throughout our application. In this case we've changed the base class interface – thus changing the interface of all subclasses in the inheritance chain.

To avoid having to fix code throughout our application, we should always strive to keep as much consistency in our base class interface as possible. In this case, we can implement a read-only `Name` property that returns the full name of the `Person`:

```
Public ReadOnly Property Name() As String
  Get
     Return mstrFirstName & " " & mstrLastName
  End Get
.End Property
```

This resolves most of the items in the Task List window. We can fix any remaining issues by using the `FirstName` and `LastName` properties. For instance, in `Form1` we can change the code behind our button to:

```
Private Sub Button1_Click(ByVal sender As System.Object, _
    ByVal e As System.EventArgs) Handles button1.Click

  Dim obj As New Customer()
  obj.FirstName = "Douglas"
  obj.LastName = "Adams"
  CType(obj, Chapter13Interfaces.IPrintableObject).Print()
End Sub
```

Any change to a base class interface is likely to cause problems, so we must think carefully before making such a change.

Implementation Changes

Unfortunately there's another, more subtle type of change that can wreak more havoc on our application – and that is an implementation change. This is the core of the fragile base class problem.

In *theory* we can change the implementation of a class, and as long as we don't change its interface any client applications using objects based on that class will continue to operate without change. Of course reality is never as nice as theory, and more often than not a change to implementation will have some consequences in the behavior of a client application.

For instance, we might use a `SortedList` to sort and display some `Customer` objects. To do this, change the code behind our button on `Form1` as follows:

```
Private Sub Button1_Click(ByVal sender As System.Object, _
    ByVal e As System.EventArgs) Handles button1.Click

  Dim col As New SortedList()
  Dim obj As Customer

  obj = New Customer()
  obj.FirstName = "Douglas"
  obj.LastName = "Adams"
  col.Add(obj.Name, obj)
```

```
      obj = New Customer()
      obj.FirstName = "Andre"
      obj.LastName = "Norton"
      col.Add(obj.Name, obj)

      Dim i As DictionaryEntry
      For Each i In col
        obj = i.Value
        System.Diagnostics.Debug.WriteLine(obj.Name)
      Next
    End Sub
```

This code simply creates a couple of `Customer` objects, sets their `FirstName` and `LastName` properties and inserts them into a `SortedList` collection object from the `System.Collections` namespace.

Items in a `SortedList` are sorted based on their key value – and we are using the `Name` property to provide that key – meaning that our entries will be sorted by name. Since our `Name` property is implemented to return first name first, and last name second, our entries will be sorted by first name.

If we run the application, the Output window in the IDE will display the following:

```
Andre Norton
Douglas Adams
```

However, we can change the implementation of our `Person` class – not directly changing or impacting either the `Customer` class or our code in `Form1` – to return last name first and first name second:

```
Public ReadOnly Property Name() As String
  Get
    Return mstrLastName & ", " & mstrFirstName
  End Get
End Property
```

While no other code requires changing, and no syntax errors are flagged, the behavior of our application is changed. When we run it our output will now be:

```
Adams, Douglas
Norton, Andre
```

Maybe this change is inconsequential. Maybe it totally breaks the required behavior of our form. The developer making the change in the `Person` class might not even *know* that someone was using that property for sort criteria.

This illustrates how dangerous inheritance can be. Changes to implementation in a base class can cascade out to countless other classes in countless applications, having unforeseen side effects and consequences of which the base class developer is totally unaware.

Summary

Object-oriented programming flows from the four basic concepts of:

- ❑ Abstraction
- ❑ Encapsulation
- ❑ Polymorphism
- ❑ Inheritance

In this chapter we've provided some basic discussion of each concept and demonstrated how to implement them using VB.NET.

Properly applied, object-oriented design and programming can allow us to create very large and complex applications that remain maintainable and readable over time. However, OO is no magic bullet, and improperly applied these technologies and concepts can create the same hard to maintain code that we might create using procedural or modular design techniques.

It is not possible to fully cover all aspects of object-oriented programming in a single chapter. Before launching into a full-blown object-oriented project, we highly recommend going through other books specifically geared toward object-oriented design and programming.

VB.NetProfessionalVB.NetProfessionalVB.NetProfessionalVB.NetProfessionalVB.NetProfessional

14

Assemblies

In this very brief chapter we are going to focus on **assemblies**. The assembly is used by the CLR as the smallest unit for:

- ❑ Deployment
- ❑ Version control
- ❑ Security
- ❑ Type grouping
- ❑ Code reuse

As mentioned in previous chapters an assembly can be thought of as a "logical" DLL (assemblies can also be contained with an EXE file). It must contain a **manifest** (also referred to as the **assembly Meta Data**) and optionally any of the following three sections:

- ❑ Type Meta Data
- ❑ Microsoft Intermediate Language (MSIL) code
- ❑ Resources

An assembly can be comprised of one file:

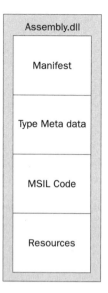

Or the structure can be split across multiple files as shown below (or any other combination that you would want):

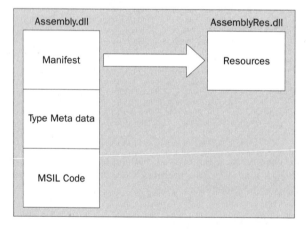

An assembly can only have one manifest section across all the files that make up the assembly. There is nothing stopping you, however, from having a resource section (or any of the other sections: Type Meta Data, MSIL Code) in each of the files that make up an assembly. The ability to split an assembly across multiple files can help with deployment and specifically on-demand downloading. The section of most interest to us in this chapter is the manifest.

The Manifest

The **manifest** is part of the mechanism by which an assembly is self-describing. So what's contained within the manifest? The manifest includes the following sections (which will be covered later in the chapter):

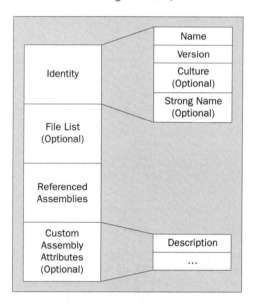

To look at what the manifest contains for a particular assembly we can use the **IL Disassembler** (Ildasm.exe) that is part of the .NET Framework SDK. When Ildasm.exe loads up, you can browse for an assembly to view by selecting **Open** from the **File** menu. Once an assembly has been loaded into Ildasm.exe it will disassemble the Meta Data contained within the assembly and present you with a treeview that you can use to navigate it:

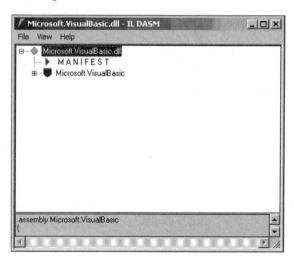

The full path of the assembly you are viewing will represent the root node. You will notice that the first node below the root is called M A N I F E S T and, as you probably have guessed, it contains all the information about the assembly's manifest. If you double-click on this node a new window will be displayed containing the information contained within the manifest:

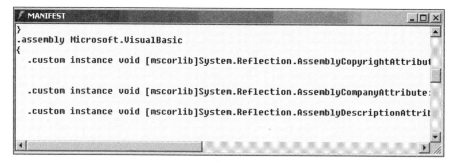

Your Manifest window will more than likely look different to that shown above. It's all very well knowing what sections are contained within the manifest and how to view them, but what are they used for?

The Identity Section

The **identity** section of the manifest is what is used to uniquely identify this particular assembly. The section can contain some optional information that may or may not be present. There are certain restrictions on the information that must appear in the identity section depending on the type of assembly. Assemblies come in two flavors so to speak: **application-private** and **shared**. We will cover the differences between the two later in this chapter. The identity section of an assembly can be found by looking for the .assembly (without a following extern) directive in the Manifest window of Ildasm.exe. In the above screenshot the line that denotes the beginning of the identity section is:

```
.assembly Microsoft.VisualBasic
```

From the diagram of the manifest we can see that the identity section can contain a number of subsections. Every assembly has a name that is declared as part of the .assembly directive, in the case of the above line we can see the assembly is called Microsoft.VisualBasic. The name of the assembly is very important, as this is what the CLR uses to locate the actual file that contains the assembly. The extension .dll is appended to the assembly name to give the name of the file that contains the assembly manifest.

The Version Number

The identity section must also contain an entry that describes what version of the assembly it is. A version number for an assembly is presented by the .ver directive in Ildasm.exe and in the above screenshot we can see that the Microsoft.VisualBasic assembly has a version number of 7:0:0:0 as indicated by the following entry in the .assembly section:

```
.ver 7:0:0:0
```

As you can see there are four parts to a version number:

Major : Minor : Build : Revision

Assemblies that have the same name but different version numbers are treated as completely different assemblies. If you have an assembly on your machine that has a version number of 1.5.2.3 and another version of the same assembly with a version number of 1.6.0.1 then the CLR will treat them as different assemblies. The version number of an assembly is part of what is used to define dependencies between assemblies. Later in this chapter we will look at versioning policies and how they relate to version numbers.

Strong Names

The identity section can also contain an optional **strong name**. The strong name is not a name as such but is in fact a public key that has been generated by the author of the assembly to uniquely identify it. A strong name is what is used to ensure that your assembly has a unique signature compared to other assemblies that may have the same name. Strong names were introduced to overcome the situation where you have created a component and another developer releases an assembly with exactly the same name that could be mistaken for being a new version of your component. Without strong names there is nothing you could do, the user would be unaware of this and blame you for any problems.

A strong name is based on public-private key encryption and will make the identity of your assembly unique. You can create a key pair that is used to create a strong name by using the **SN tool** included in the .NET Framework SDK. The public key is stored in the identity section of the manifest. A signature of the file containing the assembly's manifest is created and stored in the resulting PE file. The .NET framework uses these two signatures when resolving type references to ensure that the correct assembly is loaded at runtime. A strong name is indicated in the manifest by the `.publickey` directive in the `.assembly` section. From the screenshot above you can see that the `Microsoft.VisualBasic` assembly has a shared name.

The Culture

The final part of an assembly's identity is its **culture,** which is optional. Cultures are used to define what country/language the assembly is targeted for.

The combination of name, strong name, version number, and culture is used by the CLR to enforce version dependencies. So, you could create one version of your assembly targeted at English users, another for German users, and so on.

Cultures can be general in the case of English or more specific in the case of US-English. Cultures are represented by a string that can have two parts to it: primary and secondary (optional). The culture for English is `"en"` and the culture for US-English is `"en-us"`.

If a culture is not indicated for an assembly, it is assumed that the assembly can be used for any culture and is said to be **culture-neutral**.

A culture can be assigned to an assembly by including the attribute `AssemblyCulture` from the `System.Reflection` namespace in your assembly's code (usually within the `AssemblyInfo.vb` file):

```
<Assembly: AssemblyCulture("en")>
```

The culture of an assembly is represented in the manifest by the `.locale` directive in the `.assembly` section:

```
.locale = (65 00 6E 00 00 00 )                          // e.n...
```

Referenced Assemblies

The next section of the manifest that we are going to look at is the **referenced assemblies** section. As the name suggests, this section is where information is recorded about all the assemblies that are referenced by ours. An assembly reference is indicated in the manifest by the use of the .assembly extern directive:

```
MANIFEST                                                    _ |□| x|
.assembly extern mscorlib
{
    .publickeytoken = (B7 7A 5C 56 19 34 E0 89 )            // .z
    .ver 1:0:2411:0
}
```

You can see from the above figure that various pieces of information are stored about an assembly when it is referenced. The first piece of information stored is the name of the assembly. This is included as part of the .assembly extern directive. The screenshot above shows a reference to the mscorlib assembly. The name of the reference is used to determine the name of the file that contains the implementation of the assembly. The CLR takes the name of the assembly reference and appends .dll. So, in the example above, the CLR will look for a file called mscorlib.dll when it resolves the type references. The assembly mscorlib is a special assembly in .NET and contains all the definitions of the base types used in .NET and is in fact referenced by all assemblies. We will talk about the process that the CLR goes through to resolve a type reference later on in this chapter.

The .publickeytoken Directive

If the assembly being referenced contains a strong name, then a **hash** of the public key of the referenced assembly is stored as part of the record to the external reference. This hash is stored in the manifest using the .publickeytoken directive as part of the .assembly extern section. The assembly reference shown in the figure above contains a hash of the strong name of the mscorlib assembly. The stored hash of the strong name is compared at runtime to a hash of the strong name (.publickey) contained within the referenced assembly to help ensure that the correct assembly is loaded. The value of the .publickeytoken is computed by taking the low 8 bytes of a hash (SHA1) of the referenced assemblies strong name.

The .Ver Directive

The version of the assembly being referenced is stored in the manifest. This version information is used with the rest of the information stored about a reference to ensure the correct assembly is loaded, this will be discussed later in the chapter. If an application references version 1.1.0.0 of an assembly, it will not load version 2.1.0.0 of the assembly unless a version policy (discussed later in the chapter) exists to say otherwise. The version of the referenced assembly is stored in the manifest using the .ver directive as part of a .assembly extern section.

The .Locale Directive

If an assembly that is being referenced has a culture then the culture information will also be stored in the external assembly reference section using the .locale directive. As mentioned earlier it is the combination of name, strong name (if this exists), version number, and culture that makes up a unique version of an assembly.

Assemblies and Deployment

So we've looked at the structure of assemblies, in particular we've looked at the contents of the assembly manifest and how this is used to help provide a mechanism of self-description for the assembly. But how does the concept of assemblies help with deployment and the issues of versioning and DLL Hell? This section is focused on answering this question.

Application-Private Assemblies

To start answering the above question we need to look at the two types of assembly that can exist. The first is an **application-private assembly**. As the name implies this type of assembly is used by one application only and is not shared. This is the default style of assembly in .NET and is the main mechanism by which an application can be independent of changes to the system. The notion of private components was introduced with Microsoft Windows 2000 and the `.local` file. If a `.local` file is created in an application's directory and a component requested from the application, the search for the component would be started in the application's directory first. If the component is found in the application's directory then it is used. If the component could not be found locally then it would be searched for in the `system` path.

Application-private assemblies are deployed into the application's own directory. As application-private assemblies are not shared they do not need a strong name. Which means, at a minimum, they only need to have a name and version number in the identity section of the manifest. As the assemblies are private to the application, the application does not perform version checks on the assemblies as the application developer has control over the assemblies that are deployed to the application directory. If strong names exist, however, the CLR will check that the strong names match. If all the assemblies that an application uses are application-private and the CLR is already installed on the target machine, it is possible to simply copy the application's directory to the target machine, assuming there are no other dependencies that need to be created (for instance, databases, message queues, file associations, shortcuts). This can be accomplished due to the fact that assemblies are self-describing and contain all the information that is needed to resolve references. There is no need to copy and then register any components. The self-describing aspect of assemblies removes the dependency on the Registry, which means that applications can be backed up and copied more easily. This is a form of XCOPY deployment and cannot be used if an application uses shared assemblies (which are described below) or requires any other dependencies that cannot be simply copied.

Shared Assemblies

The second type of assembly is the **shared assembly** and as the name suggests this type of assembly can be shared amongst several applications. This type of assembly can be used in situations where it is not necessary to install a version of an assembly for each application that uses it. For instance it is not necessary to install the `System.Windows.Forms.dll` assembly for each application that uses it and it is far better to install a shared version of the assembly. The argument of the cost of hard disk space and how this relates to sharing components is slowly evaporating as the cost of disk space falls dramatically.

There are certain requirements that are placed upon shared assemblies. The assembly needs to have a globally unique name, which is not a requirement of application-private assemblies. As mentioned above strong names are used to create a globally unique name for an assembly. As the assembly is shared, all references to the shared assembly are checked to ensure the correct version is being used by an application. Shared assemblies are stored in the **Global Assembly Cache**, which is usually located in the `Assembly` folder in the `Windows` directory (for example, `C:\WINNT\Assembly`).

There need be no other changes to the code of the assembly to differentiate it from that of an application-private assembly. In fact, just because an assembly has a strong name does not mean it has to be deployed as a shared assembly; it could just as easily be deployed in the application directory as an application-private assembly.

You must have administrator rights to the machine you are installing a shared assembly on, which means that specific action must be taken ruling out the form of XCOPY deployment mentioned above. How is the strong name of an assembly used? It is first used when the shared assembly is placed into the GAC. A hash of the assembly is created using the public key stored as part of the Meta Data, which is then compared to the hash that was created when the component was compiled. If they differ, the component has been modified (since it was compiled) and it will not be installed. The second use of the strong name occurs when an application resolves a reference to an external assembly. It checks that the public key stored in the assembly is equal to the hash of the public key stored as part of the reference in the application. If the two do not match then the application knows that the external assembly has not been created by the original author of the assembly.

The Global Assembly Cache (GAC)

Each computer that has the .NET runtime installed has a Global Assembly Cache. You can view the assemblies that are contained within the GAC by navigating to the directory using the Windows Explorer:

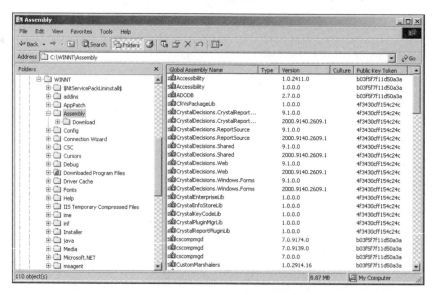

The gacutil.exe utility that ships with .NET is used to add and remove assemblies from the GAC. To add an assembly into the GAC using the gacutil.exe tool, use the following command line:

```
gacutil.exe /i myassembly.dll
```

To remove an assembly, use the /u option like this:

```
gacutil.exe /u myassembly.dll
```

The gacutil utility offers much the same functionality as shfusion.dll, which provides the user interface you see when you navigate to the GAC via Windows Explorer. We can remove this DLL to reveal the real contents of the GAC.

Follow these steps to view the GAC as you see it in the screenshot below:

1. Before you navigate to the GAC location, find `shfusion.dll` on your system and rename it

2. If it returns an "access denied", you will need to reboot and rename it as soon as it has rebooted

3. Once renamed, point Windows Explorer to the GAC location

4. *Warning: Do not tamper with the files and directories located here as it may have undesirable results*

Taking away the user interface of the GAC, you can see what is behind it better. When you register an assembly into the GAC, a directory is made, the assembly copied into it, and a brief description is recorded into a GAC file. This helps the user interface for the GAC to show the nicely formatted view you can normally see. When trying to locate an assembly, the CLR probes the GAC and the files that it contains to check if the matching assembly is stored within it.

Versioning Issues

Although COM was one of those landmark achievements in Windows programming history, it left much to be desired when it came to maintaining backward compatibility. COM used type libraries to describe its interfaces and each interface was represented by a GUID. Each interface ID was stored in the registry along with other related entries which made for a complex set of inter-related registry entries. The separation between the registry entries and the actual DLL on disk made it extremely easy for things to go wrong. A wrong registry entry or simply a mismatched GUID rendered the DLL useless. We were sometimes left with manual registry entry deletion or modification, which at its best was somewhat tedious.

The problem described here is that COM DLLs are not self-describing as they rely heavily on the registry having the correct entries. Another problem lies with the operating system not being able to best resolve differences between different DLL versions. Prior versions of Visual Basic rely on the `Server.coClass` and not the actual version of the DLL. Having the version information purely as information leaves nothing to decide what version differences there may be.

The frustrations caused by COM and its versioning policies have long plagued developers and administrators alike. In this section, we will attempt to give you some background into how the .NET Framework has attempted to resolve these issues and how we can utilize the methodology, tools, and policies that it provides.

Let's begin by looking at topics for a good solution to versioning issues of our .NET components. The itinerary is as follows:

❑ Application isolation

❑ Side-by-side execution

❑ Self-describing components

> In .NET, a version policy can be thought of as a set of rules that the CLR enforces that enable it to find, load, and execute your component. The CLR policy sets out to find if you have the authority to load an assembly, to find the correct version, and more. The CLR does not enforce its versioning policies onto application-private assemblies but only on the shared assembly.

Application Isolation

In order for an application to be *isolated* it should be self-contained and independent. This means that the application should rely on its own dependencies for ActiveX controls, components, or files, and not have those files shared with other Applications. The option of having **application isolation** is essential for a good solution to versioning problems.

If an application is isolated, components are owned, managed by, and used by the parent application alone. If a component is used by another application, even if it is the same version, it should have its very own copy. This ensures that each application can install and uninstall dependencies and not have it interfere with other applications.

> *Does this sound familiar? This is what most early Windows and DOS applications did until the emphasis was put into registering DLLs into the* system *directory. The wheel surely does turn! Also at that time, the registry started to replace our need for INI files, and now we will be moving back to the separate configuration file (which we will discuss later in this chapter) like the INI file, as it lends itself well to application isolation.*

The .NET Framework caters for application isolation by allowing us to create application-private assemblies that are for individual applications and are repeated physically on disk for each client. This means that each client is independent from the other. This non-sharing attitude works best for some scenarios.

Side-by-Side Execution

However, it is not always a good idea for an application to be completely isolated as sometimes code sharing is more beneficial and/or logical. If this is the case, the .NET Framework allows us to create and distribute shared assemblies. These assemblies must have versioning policies enforced as well as the ability to run side-by-side.

Side-by-side execution occurs when multiple versions of the same assembly can run at the same time. There are two types of side-by-side execution models and they are defined as being single machine execution in different processes and then more particularly within the same process.

The CLR is responsible for ensuring that assemblies are able to execute side-by-side. However side-by-side execution is not a CLR mechanism alone, as you can easily make unmanaged code execute side-by-side within the normal COM environment, which is known as **DLL/COM redirection**. Components that are to execute side-by-side must be installed within the application directory or a sub-directory of it. This ensures application isolation as was discussed previously.

Self-Describing

Many problems that we have had with COM components with regard to backward compatibility, resolving references, and versioning incompatibilities have largely been due to the way in which COM has traditionally stored information about the components it describes. Although the interfaces for a class are described together within a type library, the mechanism to find the owner of the class is left to registry entries. This means that, not uncommonly, the registry entries, being separate to the actual class, become misaligned. Therefore one of the most important "must haves" for good versioning policies is the fact that the component must describe itself completely. The assembly contains all the code (MSIL) and information the runtime requires to enforce a good versioning policy.

Version Policies

As mentioned above, a version number is comprised of four parts: major, minor, build, and revision. The version number is used as part of the identity of the assembly. The combination of the major and minor parts of a version number indicates if a version is compatible with a previous version or not. For example, an assembly with a version number of 1.0.0.0 is said to be incompatible with a version of 1.1.0.0 of the same assembly as the combination of the major and minor parts are different between the two. Conversely, an assembly with a version number of 1.0.0.0 is compatible with a version of 1.0.1.253 of the same assembly. When the version number of a component only changes by its build and revision parts, it is compatible. This is often referred to as **Quick Fix Engineering (QFE)**.

When an application comes across a type that is implemented in an external reference, the CLR has to determine what version of the referenced assembly to load. What steps does the CLR go through to ensure the correct version of an assembly is loaded? To answer this question, we need to look at version polices and how they affect what version of an assembly is loaded.

The Default Versioning Policy

We will start by looking at the **default versioning policy**. This policy is what is followed in the absence of any configuration files on the machine that modify the versioning policy. The default behavior of the runtime is to consult the manifest for the name of the referenced assembly and what version of the assembly to use.

If the referenced assembly does not contain a strong name it is assumed that the referenced assembly is application-private and is located in the application directory. The CLR takes the name of the referenced assembly and appends .dll to create the filename that contains the referenced assembly's manifest. The CLR then searches in the application's directory for the filename and, if found, it will use the version that was found even if the version number it different from the one specified in the manifest. Therefore, the version numbers of application-private assemblies are not checked as the application developer, in theory, has control over which assemblies are deployed to the applications directory. If the file could not be found the CLR raise a System.IO.FileNotFoundException.

Automatic Quick Fix Engineering Policy

If the referenced assembly contains a strong name, the process by which an assembly is loaded is different from that above and is detailed below:

1. The three different types of assembly configuration files (discussed later in the chapter) are consulted, if they exist, to see if they contain any settings that will modify which version of the assembly the CLR should load.

2. The CLR will then check to see if the assembly has been requested and loaded in a previous call. If it has it will use the loaded assembly.

3. If the assembly is not already loaded the GAC is queried for a match and if found this will be used by the application.

4. If any of the configuration files contain a codebase (discussed later) entry for the assembly, the assembly is looked for in the location specified. If the assembly cannot be found in the location specified in the codebase, a TypeLoadException is raised to the application.

5. If there are no configuration files or there are no codebase entries for the assembly the CLR then moves on to probe for the assembly starting in the application's base directory.

6. Finally, if the assembly still hasn't been found, the CLR will ask the Windows Installer service if it has the assembly in question. If it does the assembly is installed and the application uses this newly installed assembly. This is a feature called **on-demand installation**.

7. If the assembly hasn't been found by the end of this process a TypeLoadException will be raised.

Although a referenced assembly contains a strong name this does not mean it has to be deployed to the GAC. This allows application developers to install a version with the application that is known to work. The GAC is consulted to see if it contains a version of an assembly with a higher *build.revision* number to enable administrators to deploy an updated assembly without having to re-install or rebuild the application. This is known as **Automatic Quick Fix Engineering Policy**.

Configuration Files

The default versioning policy described above may not be the most appropriate policy for our requirements. Fortunately, we can modify this policy with the use of XML configuration files to meet our specific needs. There are three types of configuration files that can be created:

❑ The first is an **application configuration file** and is created in the application directory. As the name implies, this configuration file applies to one application only. We create an application configuration file by creating a file in the application directory with the same name as the application filename and appending `.config`. For example, suppose we have an application called `HelloWorld.exe` installed in the `C:\HelloWorld` directory. The application configuration file would be: `C:\HelloWorld\HelloWorld.exe.config`.

❑ The second type of configuration file is called the **machine configuration file**. It is named `machine.config` and can be found in the `<CLR INSTALL DIR>\Config` directory. The `machine.config` file overrides any other configuration files on a machine and can be thought of as containing global settings.

❑ The third type of configuration file is the **security configuration file** and contains information regarding code access security systems. The code access security system allows us to grant/deny access to resources by an assembly. This configuration file must be located within the `Windows` directory.

The main purpose of the configuration file is to provide binding-related information to the developer or administrator that wishes to override the default policy handling of the CLR.

Specifically, the configuration file, being XML based, has a root node named `<configuration>` and must have the end node of `</configuration>` present to be syntactically correct.

The configuration file is divided into specific types of nodes that represent different areas of control. These areas are:

❑ Startup

❑ Runtime

❑ Remoting

❑ Crypto

❑ Class API

❑ Security

Although all of these areas are important, for the purposes of this chapter we will look only at the first two nodes.

The settings that we are going to discuss can be added to the application configuration file. Some of the settings (these will be pointed out) can also be added to the machine configuration file. If a setting in the application configuration file conflicts with that of one in the machine configuration file then the setting in the machine configuration is used. When we talk about assembly references in the following discussion of configuration settings, we are talking about shared assemblies (in other words, assemblies that have a strong name).

Startup Settings

The `<startup>` node of the application and machine configuration files has a `<requiredRuntime>` node that specifies the runtime version required by the application. This is because different versions of the CLR can run on a machine side-by-side. The example below shows how we would specify the version of the .NET runtime inside the configuration file:

```
<configuration>
    <startup>
        <requiredRuntime version="1.0.0.0" safeMode="true"/>
    </startup>
</configuration>
```

Runtime Settings

The runtime node written as `<runtime>`, not to be confused with the `<requiredRuntime>` node above, specifies the settings managing how the CLR handles garbage collection and versions of assemblies. With these settings, we can specify which version of an assembly the application requires or redirect it to another version entirely.

Loading a Particular Version of an Assembly

The application and machine configuration files can be used to ensure that a particular version of an assembly is loaded. You can indicate whether this version should be loaded all the time or only to replace a specific version of the assembly. This functionality is supported through the use of the `<assemblyIdentity>` and `<bindingRedirect>` elements in the configuration file. For example:

```
<configuration>
    <runtime>
        <assemblyBinding xmlns="urn:schemas-microsoft-com:asm.v1">
            <dependentAssembly>
                <assemblyIdentity name="AssemblyName"
                                  publickeytoken="b77a5c561934e089"
                                  culture="en-us"/>
                <bindingRedirect  oldVersion="*"
                                  newVersion="2.0.50.0"/>
            </dependentAssembly>
        </assemblyBinding>
    </runtime>
</configuration>
```

The `<assemblyBinding>` node is used to declare settings for the locations of assemblies and redirections via the `<dependentAssembly>` node and also the `<probing>` node (which we will look at shortly).

In the example above, when the CLR resolves the reference to the assembly named `"AssemblyName"` it will load version 2.0.50.0 instead of the version that appears in the manifest. If you would like to only load version 2.0.50.0 of the assembly when a specific version is referenced then you can replace the value of the `oldVersion` attribute with the version number that you would like to replace (for example, 1.5.0.0). The `publickeytoken` attribute is used to store the hash of the strong name of the assembly to replace. This is used to ensure that correct assembly is identified. The same is true of the `culture` attribute.

Defining the Location of an Assembly

The location of an assembly can also be defined in both the application and machine configuration files. We can use the `<codeBase>` element to inform the CLR of the location of an assembly. This enables us to distribute an application and have the externally referenced assemblies downloaded the first time they are used. This is called on-demand downloading. For example:

```
<configuration>
    <runtime>
        <assemblyBinding xmlns="urn:schemas-microsoft-com:asm.v1">
            <dependentAssembly>
                <assemblyIdentity name="AssemblyName"
                                  publickeytoken="b77a5c561934e089"
                                  culture="en-us"/>
                <codeBase version="2.0.50.0"
                          href="http://www.wrox.com/AssemblyName.dll/>
            </dependentAssembly>
        </assemblyBinding>
    </runtime>
</configuration>
```

From the example above we can see that whenever a reference to version 2.0.50.0 of the assembly "AssemblyName" is resolved (and the assembly isn't already on the users computer), the CLR will try to load the assembly from the location defined in the href attribute. The location defined in the href attribute is a standard URL and can be used to locate a file across the Internet or locally.

If the assembly cannot be found or the details in the manifest of the assembly defined in the href attribute do not match those defined in the configuration file, the loading of the assembly will fail and you will receive a TypeLoadException. If the version of the assembly in the above example is actually 2.0.60.0 then the assembly will load, as the version number is only different by the *build.revision* parts.

Providing the Search Path

The final use of configuration files that we will look at is that of providing the search path for use when locating assemblies in the application's directory. This setting only applies to the application configuration file. By default the CLR will only search for an assembly in the application's base directory and it will not look in any sub-directories. We can modify this behavior by using the <probing> element in an application configuration file. For example:

```
<configuration>
    <runtime>
        <assemblyBinding xmlns="urn:schemas-microsoft-com:asm.v1">
            <probing privatePath="regional"/>
        </assemblyBinding>
    </runtime>
</configuration>
```

The privatePath attribute can contain a list of directories relative to the application's directory (separated by a semi-colon) that you would like the CLR to search in when trying to locate an assembly. The privatePath attribute cannot contain an absolute pathname.

As part of an assembly reference being resolved, the CLR will check in the application's base directory for it. If it cannot find it, it will look through in order all subdirectories specified in the privatePath variable, as well as looking for a sub-directory with the same name as the assembly. If the assembly being resolved is called "AssemblyName", the CLR will also check for the assembly in a sub-directory called "AssemblyName", if it exists.

This isn't the end of the story though. If the referenced assembly being resolved contains a culture, the CLR will also check for culture specific sub-directories in each of the directories it searches in. For example, if the CLR is trying to resolve a reference to an assembly named "AssemblyName" with a culture of en, a privatePath equal to that in the above example, and the application being run has a home directory of c:\ExampleApp, the CLR will look in the following directories to find the assembly (in the order they are shown):

- ❏   `C:\ExampleApp`
- ❏   `C:\ExampleApp\en`
- ❏   `C:\ExampleApp\en\AssemblyName`
- ❏   `C:\ExampleApp\regional\en`
- ❏   `C:\ExampleApp\regional\en\AssemblyName`

As you can see the CLR can potentially probe quite a number of directories to locate an assembly.

When an external assembly is resolved by the CLR it consults the configuration files first to see if it needs to modify the process by which it resolves an assembly. As you can see from the above discussion, the resolution process can be modified to suit your needs.

Summary

We started by looking at the structure of an assembly and how it contains Meta Data that enables it to describe itself. This mechanism of self-description will help us when we come to deploy our applications by removing dependencies on the registry, unlike COM components. If a machine has the CLR installed on it, it is more feasible that an application can be deployed to a machine simply by copying the files (although this does not apply if the application must install shared assemblies).

We also looked at how the identity of an assembly is used to allow multiple versions of an assembly to be installed on a machine and how this aids the side-by-side use of assemblies. We covered how an assembly is versioned and the process by which the CLR resolves an external assembly reference and how we can modify this process through the use of configuration files.

We also looked at how an assembly stores information such as version number, strong name, and culture about any external assemblies that it references. We also looked at how this information is checked at runtime to ensure that the correct version of the assembly is referenced and how we can use versioning policies to override this in the case of a buggy assembly. The assembly is the single biggest aid in reducing the errors that can occur due to DLL Hell and in helping with deployment, so we'll be returning to this subject later in the book.

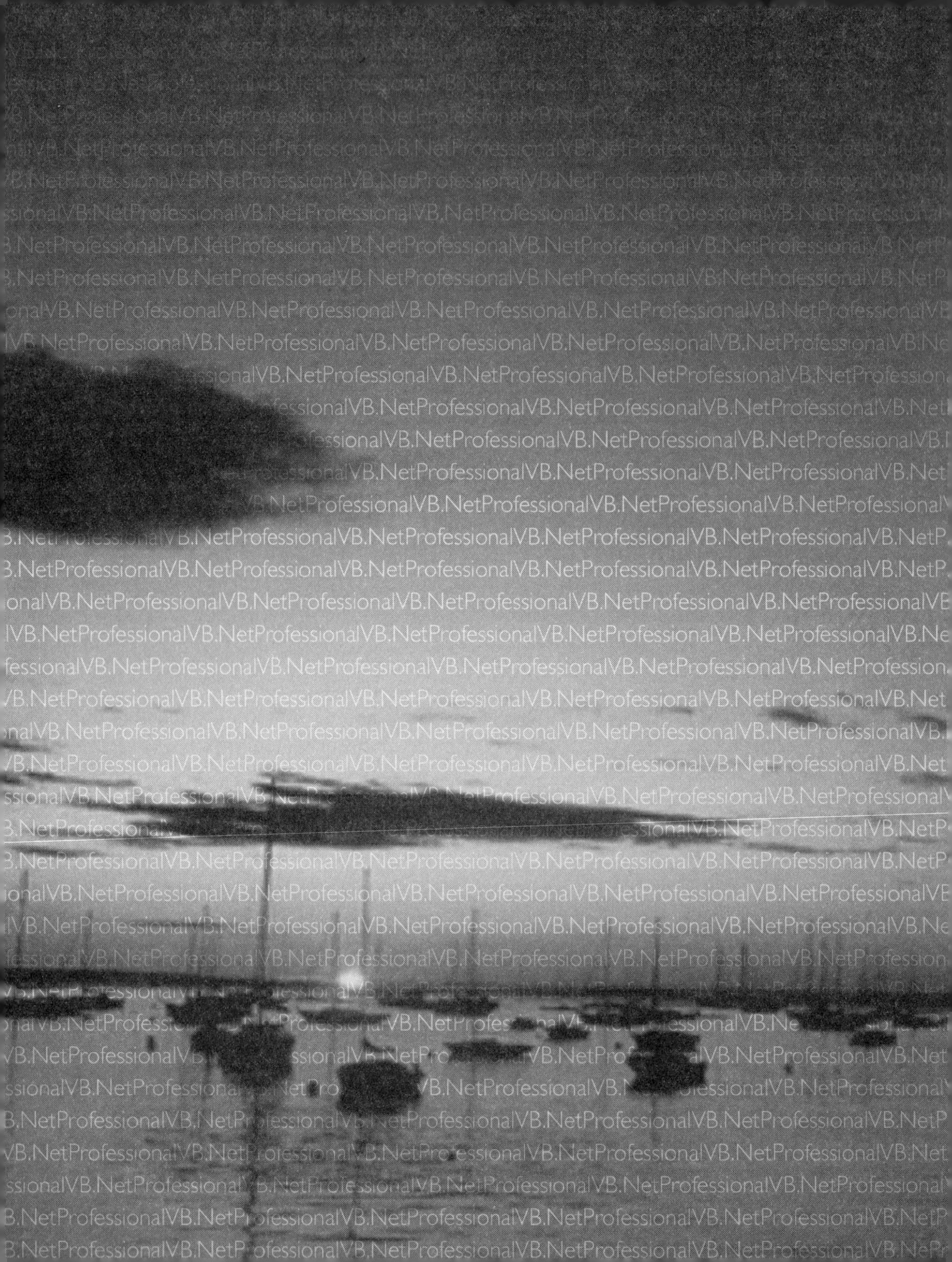

15
Threading

One of the things that the move from 16-bit to 32-bit computing gave us was the ability to write code that made use of threads. Although Visual C++ developers have been able to use threads for some time, Visual Basic developers haven't had a really reliable way to do so, until now. Previous techniques involved accessing the threading functionality available to Visual C++ developers. Although this worked, without adequate debugger support in the Visual Basic environment actually developing multithreaded code was nothing short of a nightmare.

This chapter will introduce the various objects in the .NET Framework that enable any consumer of the .NET Framework to develop multithreaded applications.

> **Please note at this point that in the remainder of this chapter, when we say Windows we're talking about Windows NT and the various flavors of Windows 2000.**

What is a Thread?

The principle of a thread is that it allows parts of your program to run independently of other parts. As you probably know, in Windows your program runs in a separate "process". This is an artificial division that gives your program isolation from other programs so that no problem can indirectly affect each other's operation. (We talk about this more later.) A thread is in effect an execution pointer, which allows Windows to keep track of which line of your program is running at any one time. This pointer starts at the top of the program and moves through each lines, branching and looping when it comes across decisions and loops and, at a time when the program is no longer needed, the pointer steps outside of the program code and the program is effectively stopped.

In threading, you have multiple execution pointers. This means that two or more parts of your code can run *simultaneously*. The classic example of multithreaded functionality is Microsoft Word's spell checker. When the program starts, the execution pointer starts at the top of the program and eventually gets itself into a position where you're able to start writing code. However, at some point Word will start another thread and create another execution pointer. As you type, this new thread examines the text as you type in the document and flags any spelling errors as you go, underlining them with a red wavy line:

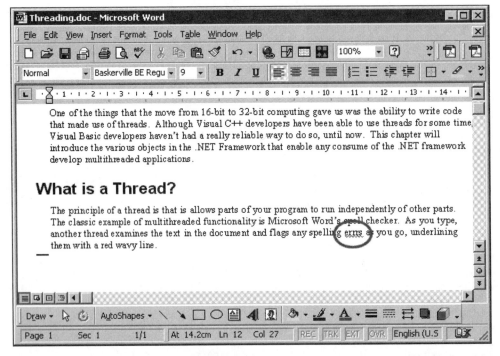

Every application has one primary thread. This thread serves as the main process thread through the application. Imagine you have an application that starts up, loads a file from disk, performs some processing on the data in the file, writes a new file and then quits. Functionally, it might look like this:

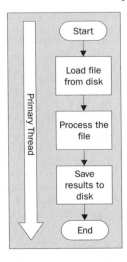

In this simple application, we only need to use a single thread. When the program is told to run, Windows creates a new process and also creates the "primary thread". To understand more about exactly what it is a thread does, we need to understand a little more about how your computer deals with different processes.

Processes vs. Threads

As you know, Windows is capable of keeping many programs in memory at once and allowing the user to switch between them. These programs manifest themselves as applications and services. The difference between applications and services is the user interface – services don't usually have a user interface that allows the user to interact with them, whereas applications do. (In this way Microsoft Word is an example of an application, whereas Internet Information Server is an example of a service.) The ability to run many programs at once is called "multitasking".

Each of these programs that your computer keeps in memory runs in a single "process". The process is started when the program starts and exists for as long as the program is running. As Windows is an operating system that supports multithreading, a program is able to create separate threads within its own process. However, we should note at this point that multitasking and multithreading are not necessarily the same thing. "Multitasking" means that the operating system can keep multiple programs in memory at once and give each of them an opportunity to run (more on this later), but "multithreading" specifically means this ability to create more than one thread inside a process.

To support a multitasking environment, both the operating system and the processor have to work together to divide up the available computing power between all of the executing processes. We're going to over simplify our description of how Windows divides up its processing time as the finer minutiae of this topic is beyond the scope of this discussion. However, let's take a broad look at how time-slicing works:

Imagine we have two processes running on Windows. In a given time period, Windows will give 50% of the processing power to the primary thread on the first process, and the remaining 50% to the primary thread on the second process:

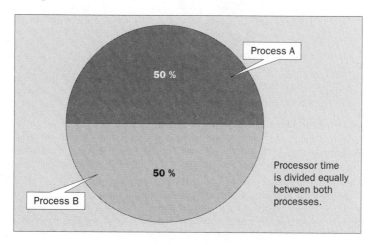

This division of processing power leads on to the concept of **process priority**. Briefly, setting priority on a process tells Windows to bias time-sharing towards a process of higher priority. This is useful in situations where you have a process that requires a lot of processor muscle, but it doesn't matter how long the process takes to do its work. A classic (and worthy) example of this is the Intel/United Devices Cancer Research Project. This project is based on having thousands of computers around the world running an algorithm that tries to match drug molecules with target proteins associated with the spread of cancer. This program runs continuously, but the actual calculations involve a great deal of math that tends to use a lot of processor power. However, this process runs at a very low priority, so if we need to use Word or Outlook or another application, Windows gives more processor time to the applications and less time to the research application. This means the computer can work smoothly when the user needs it to, letting the research application take up the slack.

> **You can learn more about the Intel/United Devices Cancer Research Project at** `http://www.ud.com/`.

Say we have **granularity** on our time slice of three seconds, in other words that, in a given time-slice divided between two processes, Process A is run for a second-and-a-half then Process B gets to run for a second-and-a-half. At the end of the period, Process A gets another chance to run for another second-and-a-half, then Process B gets to run. If another process is started, Processes A, B and C all get the opportunity to run for a single second. If Process B and Process C end, Process A gets all of the processor to itself, until another process is started. This is illustrated below:

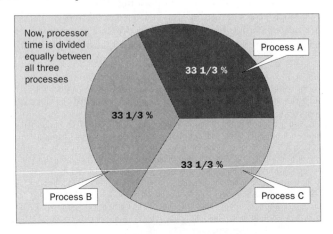

What's critical to understand about time slicing is that the processes don't have to actively participate in this process. If we have three processes running and a granularity of three seconds, at the end of the first section, Process A doesn't have to say to Windows "OK, my time is up, I'll wait". Instead, Windows just stops allocating time to the process and, effectively, it stops until it gets another opportunity to run. Windows instead starts processing Process B, until the end of the second two, when Windows stops allocating time to the process and starts Process C.

> **This is known as preemptive multitasking.**

As you might have guessed, this time slicing paradigm applies to threads as well. As you know, when a process is started it is given a primary thread. In the 33:33:33 time slice diagram we just saw, we had three threads, in other words one primary thread per process. As a thread runs, it has the opportunity to **spin up** other threads to do work. Imagine now that Process A and Process B both have a single thread, but the primary thread of Process C has started another thread and has a total of two threads:

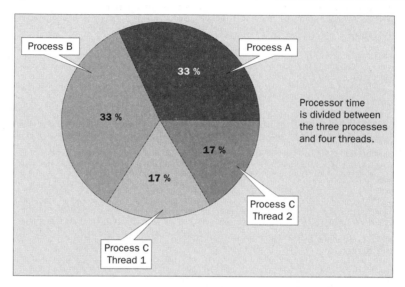

In this example, Process C is still getting one-third of the processing power per time slice. However, because Process C comprises two threads, the first thread is getting the first half of the one-third (17%) and the second thread is getting the second half of the one-third (again, 17%). So, at time "2 seconds", Windows stops executing Process B and starts executing the first thread of Process C. At time "2.5 seconds", Windows suspends the first thread of process C and moves onto the second thread. At time "3 seconds", the second thread of Process C is suspended and Process A is resumed. (Again, this is an oversimplification.) This is illustrated in the following figure:

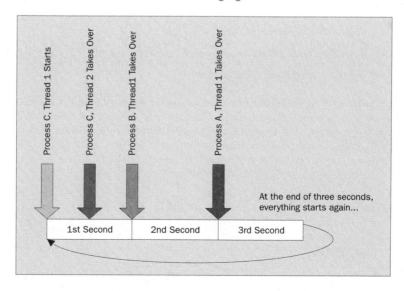

So why is all this important? Well, time slicing gets you to a point where all the processing power is shared equally. Without time slicing you can easily end up in a situation where you're at the mercy of badly behaving processes. If Windows wasn't capable of saying "OK, time to suspend this process and resume this different process" then it would have to say "I'll wait until you appear to be idle as being idle implies you've finished this bit of work, then I'll move on and start running this other process". If Windows relies on processes being well behaved, it's easy for a process to "hijack" the system and give an unfair priority to its own process. This can have a catastrophic effect if the process has gone into an endless loop, like this:

```
n = 2
Do While n = 2
Loop
```

If the operating system were waiting for this process to be idle before starting another process, no other running process would ever get a chance to finish. This would "hang" the entire machine. This scenario is described by **cooperative multitasking**. This was the multitasking paradigm used by 16-bit versions of Windows, Windows 3.1. It relied on the program giving the operating system the opportunity to run another program.

The other side to this is that the operating system runs more "smoothly". Since Windows is taking an active interest in how processes run, no process gets an unfair distribution of the processing power. Although this seems like a pretty nebulous concept, achieving this "smoothness" is one of the relevant reasons for using threads.

When to Use Threads

If we regard computer programs as being either application software or service software, we find there are different motivators for each one.

Application software uses threads primarily to deliver a better user experience. Common examples you may have experienced are:

- ❑ Microsoft Word – background spell checker
- ❑ Microsoft Word – background printing
- ❑ Microsoft Outlook – background sending and receiving of e-mail
- ❑ Microsoft Excel – background recalculation

You can see that in all of these cases, threads are used to do "something in the background". This provides a better user experience. For example, I can still edit a Word document while Word is spooling another to the printer. Or, I can still read e-mails while Outlook is sending my new e-mail. As an application developer, you should use threads to enhance the user experience. Below is a diagram showing the threads involved when the Word spell checker is utilized:

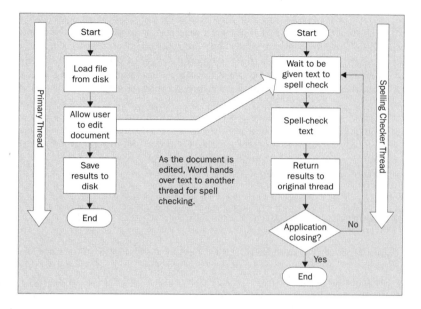

At some point during the application startup, code running in the primary thread would have spun up this other thread to be used for spell checking. As part of the "allow user to edit the document" process, we give the spell checker thread some words to check. This thread separation means that the user can continue to type, even though spell checking is still taking place.

Service software uses threads to deliver scalability and improve the service offered. For example, imagine I had a web server that receives six incoming connections simultaneously. That server needs to service each of the requests in parallel, otherwise the sixth thread would have to wait for me to finish threads one through five before it even got a look in. Here's how IIS might handle incoming requests:

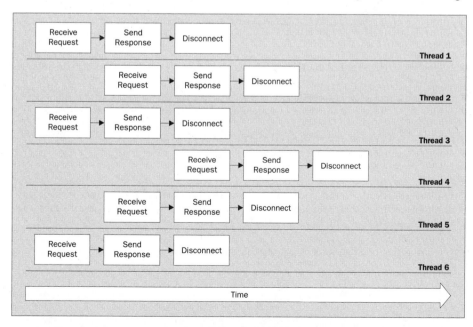

In this diagram, we've got six worker threads that exist only to help service requests from clients. Each request is handled by exactly one thread. This diagram doesn't show the other application threads that handle managing these threads. For example, the primary application thread will wait around for Windows to signal that the service needs to be stopped for various reasons. Another thread will listen to the incoming connection, and will either create a new thread, or find an existing thread that can service the requests. (Most server software uses thread pooling, a topic we discuss at the end of the chapter.)

ASP and ASP.NET development is a classic example of a situation where you don't care about threading, even though you're running in a multithreaded environment. Whenever your .asp or .aspx page is called you're only running in a pretty isolated fashion - you don't care what any of the other threads are doing. Even with ASP.NET, you're going to run in a very procedural way – in other words, start of the page to the bottom of the page.

A Threading Example

Creating a thread in.NET is extremely easy. All we have to do is create an instance of a System.Threading.Thread object and call the Start method. However, to do this we need a demonstration application. What we're going to do is build a simple application with a button and a text box. We'll start the thread when the button is clicked, and from within the button, we'll set the text on the text box.

Create a new Windows Application project and call it Thread Example. After the project has been created, the Form Designer will open to the default Form1 form. Lay out Form1 with a button called btnStartThread and a text box called txtResult:

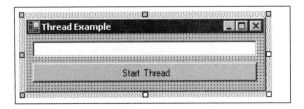

Double-click on the background of the form to create a new Load event handler. Add the following code:

```
Private Sub Form1_Load(ByVal sender As System.Object, _
        ByVal e As System.EventArgs) Handles MyBase.Load
    Me.Text &= " - Thread #" & _
        System.Threading.Thread.CurrentThread.GetHashCode
End Sub
```

The shared CurrentThread property can be used to access a Thread object that represents the currently executing thread. As this code will be running from within the primary thread, this Thread object will represent the primary thread. GetHashCode returns a unique identifier of the thread. When we run the code, the caption will, in effect, display the ID of the primary thread.

Once you've done that, we can look at getting the thread running.

Creating ThreadWorker

My preferred method for handling threads is to create a separate class for managing the starting and stopping of a thread. This class contains a private member called _thread that holds an instance of a System.Threading.Thread object. Instances of this "worker" class can then be instantiated by the main application and controlled exclusively through its methods. This encapsulates the threading functionality, meaning that the caller doesn't really have to worry about controlling the thread's "lifetime".

Create a new class called ThreadWorker and add this code:

```
Imports System.Threading

Public Class ThreadWorker

    ' members...
    Public TextBox As TextBox
    Private _thread As Thread

End Class
```

ThreadWorker will have a public method called SpinUp that will go ahead and start the thread. But, in order for a thread to start you need to provide an entry point by means of a delegate that references a method on our ThreadWorker class. The thread will call this delegate as soon as it's ready to start work. This is conceptually similar to the startup method that our Visual Basic projects have had up until now. In fact, the startup method is the entry point for the primary thread. As it's unlikely that any other threads will want to use the same entry point, we have to create a new one, hence our work here. Our delegate will be called Start (you are free to choose any name you like, I just like Start) and will be defined like this:

```
' Start - this method is the entry-point for the thread...
Private Sub Start()

    ' just set some text on the textbox...
        TextBox.Text = "Hello, world from thread #" & _
                Thread.CurrentThread.GetHashCode() & "!"
End Sub
```

Again, here we're using CurrentThread to get a Thread object that executes the currently executing thread. As this code should be running from within the new thread, the IDs should not match.

You can see that we don't have to do anything special from within Start to support the thread. Remember, you've already been writing code that runs in a thread - it's just that up until now you've only ever had a single thread.

Here's the code for the SpinUp method inside ThreadWorker that will start the thread:

```
' SpinUp - this method is called by the main application thread...
Public Sub SpinUp()

    ' create a thread start object that refers to our worker...
    Dim threadStart As ThreadStart
    threadStart = New ThreadStart(AddressOf Me.Start)
```

```
    ' now, create the thread object and start it...
    _thread = New Thread(threadStart)
    _thread.Start()

End Sub
```

That's it! To start the thread all we have to do is create a `System.Threading.ThreadStart` object, give it a delegate that references our entry point and pass it to a new `System.Threading.Thread` object. When we call `Thread.Start` the new thread will be created, and our `ThreadWorker.Start` delegated method will be called as the entry point.

Calling SpinUp

To call `SpinUp` we need to wire in some code behind the button. Add this code to `Thread Example`:

```
Private Sub cmdStartThread_Click(ByVal sender As System.Object, _
            ByVal e As System.EventArgs) Handles cmdStartThread.Click

    ' create a new worker...
    Dim worker As New ThreadWorker()
    worker.TextBox = txtResult()

    ' spin up the thread...
    worker.SpinUp()

End Sub
```

Since `txtResult` is a private member, we can't access it directly from the `ThreadWorker`. Instead, we use the `TextBox` property to pass a text box control to our instance of `ThreadWorker`. Code running inside of the thread can then set the `Text` property of this control to update the display.

To test the solution, run the project and click the **Start Thread** button. You should see something like this:

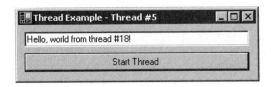

You can see that the IDs shown in the caption and in the textbox are different. This proves that the code to set the caption and the code to set the text in the textbox are indeed running on different threads.

That just about covers the basics of threading. The complete code snippet for `ThreadWorker` is listed below:

```
Imports System.Threading

Public Class ThreadWorker
    ' members...
```

```vbnet
Public TextBox As TextBox
Private _thread As Thread
' Start - this method is the entry-point for the thread...
Private Sub Start()

    ' just set some text on the textbox...
    TextBox.Text = "Hello, world!"
End Sub

' SpinUp - this method is called by the main application thread...
Public Sub SpinUp()

    ' create a thread start object that refers to our worker...
    Dim threadStart As ThreadStart
    threadStart = New ThreadStart(AddressOf Me.Start)

    ' now, create the thread object and start it...
    _thread = New Thread(threadStart)
    _thread.Start()

End Sub
End Class
```

Now we can look at why developing multithreaded applications requires more than a casual approach.

Synchronization

Windows provides isolation between different processes. What this means is that a process cannot directly affect another process, or rather, a process can only be affected in a controlled and well-understood manner.

For example, if I run up a process that crashes, in theory all the other processes should continue running. (As we know, there are rare situations where Windows just dies for some reason, in which case all the processes have been affected! This is especially true in situations where Windows is forced to display the "blue screen of death".) If I run up a process that tries to hog all of the processor for itself, other processes will continue running.

> *Again, a caveat. The way that Windows divides time is in reality more complex than the way that we've illustrated it here. Windows will in fact attempt to divide time based on the perceived need of the process. This means that if a process seems to need a lot of the processor and it's running at the same priority as other processes, Windows may not give processor share to the other applications. This leads to the apparent effect that no other processes can run.*

The most important aspect of process isolation, in relation to this discussion, is that of memory isolation. As a process, I am given my own block of memory. I cannot simply call into another process's allocated memory, either to read the memory or change it. This is great from both security and stability standpoints. Imagine an application that a user keys credit card numbers into. As a malicious programmer, I could theoretically start a process that continuously monitored the memory of the credit card application process. If I can watch the memory, I can extract the credit card information. Alternatively, my application might have a bug that inadvertently changes the memory of another process causing it to crash. Process isolation stops this from happening.

Changing memory in an uncontrolled manner can lead to catastrophic results. Most software is written with forward knowledge of how its memory should look, for example "I expect to see an object that provides a database connection at this address in memory". If I was another process and I was able to affect another process's memory, I could move or change that other process's memory causing it to crash.

When we're writing multithreaded code, the hardest issue is that of managing access to the memory allocated to the process. You don't, for example, want two threads writing to the same piece of memory at the same time. Equally, you don't want a group of threads reading memory that another thread is in the process of changing. This management of memory access is called **synchronization** and will take up the remainder of this discussion. It's properly managing synchronization that makes writing multithreaded code difficult.

Blocking, Wait States, and Signaling

Think back to our discussion about time slicing. Remember how we said that Windows automatically suspends and resumes our threads depending on its perceived processing needs, various priority settings and so on. Say we're running one process containing two threads. If we can somehow mark the second thread as "dormant" (in other words, tell Windows that it has nothing to do), there's no need for Windows to allocate time to it. Effectively, the first thread will receive 100% of the processor horsepower available to that process. When a thread is marked as dormant we say it's in a **wait state**.

Windows is particularly good at managing processes and threads. It's a core part of Windows' functionality and so the developers have spent a lot of time making sure that it's super-efficient and as bug free as software can be. This means that creating and spinning up threads is very easy to do and happens very quickly. Threads also only take up a small amount of system resources, but there is a caveat you should be aware of.

The activity of stopping one thread and starting another is called **context switching**. This switching happens relatively quickly, but only if you're relatively careful with the number of threads you create. If you spin up too many threads, the process will spend all of its time switching between different threads, perhaps even getting to a point where the code in the thread doesn't get a chance to run because as soon as you've started the thread it's time for it to stop again.

Creating thousands of threads is not the right solution. What you need to do is find a balance between the amount of threads that your application *needs* and the amount of threads that Windows can handle. There's no "magic number" or "right answer" to the question of "How many threads should I create?" Just be aware of context switching and experiment a little.

Take the Microsoft Word spell check example. The thread that performs the spell check is around all the time. Imagine you have a blank document containing no text. At this point, the spell check thread is in a wait state. Imagine you type a single word into the document and then pause. At this point, Microsoft will pass the word over to the thread and "signal" it to start working. The thread will use its own slice of the processor power to examine the word. If it finds something wrong with the word, it will tell the primary thread that a spelling problem was found and that the user needs to be alerted. At this point, the spell check thread drops back into a wait state until more text is entered into the document. Word doesn't spin up the thread whenever it needs to perform a check – rather the thread runs all the time but, if it has nothing to do, it drops into this efficient wait state. (We'll talk about how the thread starts again later.)

Again, we've oversimplified this. Word will "wake up" the thread at various times. However, the principle is sound – the thread is given work to do, it reports the results and then it starts waiting for the next chunk of work to do.

Principles of Blocking

When a thread is in a wait state, a "blocking" operation of some sort has usually put it there: in other words we run an operation and effectively say, "Do nothing until 'this' happens." Some system event will usually release the block, causing the thread to come out of the wait state and start doing something. When we say "event" we are *not* talking about a Visual Basic event. Although the naming convention is unfortunate, the principle is the same – something happens and we react to it.

Although blocking can be used to control the execution of threads, it's primarily used to control access to resources, including memory. This is the basic idea behind synchronization – if we need something, we block until we can access it

To understand how threads share memory, imagine we have this code:

```
Public Class Adder

    ' shared memory...
    Private Shared _value As Integer = 1

    ' method...
    Public Sub Increment()

        ' get the current value...
        Dim n As Integer = _value

        ' add one to it...
        n += 1

        ' set the value back...
        _value = n

    End Sub

End Class
```

We have a shared member called _value there. As you know, this means that all instances of Adder will use the same instance of _value. Therefore, if we have two instances of the class, the first of which changes _value to 27, all other instances of the class will also see _value as 27.

Now look at the Increment method. There's nothing complicated about this at all – we get the value from _value, store it locally in n, add one to it and then set _value to n.

But, with our multithreaded hat on, we can see that there's a problem with this. Imagine we have two instances of the class, each instance created in a separate thread. If we call Increment on both objects *simultaneously*, we won't get the results we want.

What we want to happen is that each time Increment is called we want 1 to be added to the shared _value. If we call the code like this:

```
Dim adder As New Adder
adder.Increment()
adder.Increment()
```

then we can guarantee that at the end, _value will be 3 (provided _value was initialized to a value of 1). However, if we have two threads acting on _value simultaneously, we can't guarantee this. If the calls are perfectly simultaneous, both threads will get 1 from _value when Increment is called. Both threads will add 1 to this value and both threads will set _value to 2. Even though we've called the method twice, we only feel the effect of having called it once.

In fact, the problem is much worse than this. We can't guarantee that calls are not made simultaneously across threads. We also can't guarantee that threads run at the same speed. Basically, unless we have absolute control over the synchronization, weird problems are going to occur.

Critical Sections

To get around this problem, we want to mark a block of code as accessible to only one thread at a time. This guarantees that each time we call Increment, the entire operation occurs. This way, we guarantee that each call to Increment will properly affect _value and, therefore, all the weird problems should go away.

This kind of block is called a **critical section**. To use it, a thread tries to enter the critical section. If no other thread is inside the critical section, the thread can go straight on and do its work. If another thread tries to get into the block while the first thread is inside it, that second thread will be "blocked" until the first thread leaves the critical section, as shown in the diagram below:

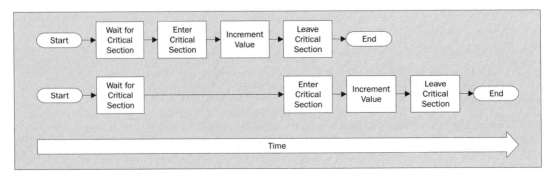

One problem with critical sections is that they create bottlenecks. Imagine we had 16 threads all trying to call Increment. Effectively, because only one thread can enter the critical section at a time, we have single-threaded code, and so get no advantage of multithreading. In fact, this thread will run slower than single-threaded code as we have the overhead of dealing with the extra threads and all of the context switching. What we need is a thread that understands more about what we want to do, something we'll look at now.

Reader/Writer Locks

If we were trying to access a file from a disk, we'd usually give Windows an indication of what we wanted to do with the file. This "mode" gives us certain permissions, but also enables sharing. For example, if we open a file for reading, there's no reason why another thread wanting to open the same file for *reading* cannot do so. In fact, ignoring operating system limitations, there's no limit to the number of times the file can be opened.

Compare this to *writing* the file. Only one thread should ever be able to write to the file, and this is on the proviso that no other thread is reading *or* writing to the file. If we're writing, we want exclusive access to the file. Although we've been talking about files, the same applies to memory. To summarize:

❑   There's no limit to the number of threads that can read from _value at any given moment

❑   Only one thread at a given moment can write to _value, providing that no other thread is reading from it or writing to it

The Framework provides a reader/writer lock that achieves this in the guise of an object called System.Threading.ReaderWriterLock. We'll see this in action in a moment.

Interestingly, a reader/writer lock won't actually help us reduce the bottleneck in the example we've seen so far. In all cases, this thread needs to write to _value, so we'll always need an exclusive lock that behaves in the same way as a critical section. However, in the majority of cases, using reader/writer locks is the most appropriate synchronization method and we'll look shortly at an example

On-Demand Blocking

We've examined the concept of blocking from the perspective of writing code that automatically blocks when attempting to access a lock of some kind, either a critical section lock or a reader/writer lock. Blocking is also used in an on-demand basis to pause and resume threads. Coming back to our Word spell checker example, we spin up the thread when the application starts then block until we need to check some words. We wait until we're signaled and, at that point, do the spell check. When we've finished, we block until we're signaled again, and so on.

This kind of block is achieved with a System.Threading.ManualResetEvent object. We'll see this in a moment, too.

Trying Synchronization

To illustrate what we've talked about so far, we're going to build a new Windows Application and build a very simple spell checker. Create a new Windows Application project now and call it Spell Checker.

We're going to use the default Form1 form to build our application. Add controls, as listed below, to the form until you get something that looks like this:

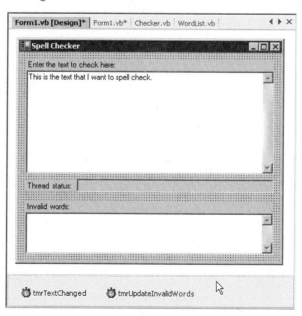

Here are the names of the controls that need to have their names changed:

❑ txtText – the textbox that contains the text that should be spell checked. Also, make sure you set the MultiLine property of this control to True

❑ txtThreadStatus – a read-only textbox that the thread will use to report back the time a spell check was performed

❑ txtInvalidWords – a textbox that displays the invalid words that were found by the spell checker

❑ tmrTextChanged – a timer that will be enabled whenever the text in txtText changes

❑ tmrUpdateInvalidWords – a timer that will be used to update the invalid word list

As you know, whenever Word finds a word that it thinks is spelled incorrectly, it underlines it with a red wavy line. To do this, Word has to have control over the various UI objects that actually render the page onto the screen. In our example, we don't have this fine level of control – we're using the standard System.Windows.Forms.TextBox control object, and without going through a considerable number of hoops, it's not easy for us to duplicate the "wavy line" functionality.

What Word does is maintain a list of the words that it thinks are invalid. (If the word is valid, Word doesn't care about it. It only needs to keep track of one list, and as the "invalid" word list is likely to be shorter, this is the one that it uses.) As text is typed into the document, Word adds the newly typed words into a queue that the spell checker thread periodically examines. The results of the spell check are then passed back to the main application thread as a list of invalid words. As Word renders each word, it checks to see if the word it's rendering appears in its invalid word list. If it does, it draws a red wavy line under the text.

To get a similar effect, we're going to use another textbox on our form to tell the user which words typed into the main edit area are invalid. As the text in txtText changes, we'll pass the whole lot over to a separate thread that will scan the words and create a list of invalid words. This list will then be passed back to Form1 through a delegate, whereupon a constantly running timer will take the list and add the contents to txtInvalidWords.

Creating WordList

The first object we're going to build is an object that contains a list of words. We're not going to call this "dictionary", as veteran ASP developers will already be familiar with another object called Dictionary, and new .NET developers will want to avoid name clashes.

WordList is simply going to hold a list of words in a System.Collections.ArrayList object. This object provides a very fast search facility called a "binary search", so we should be OK if we end up working with a very large dictionary. The caveat with using binary searches is that the list must be sorted alphabetically before we can search.

To populate WordList, we're going to read a file from disk. This file should contain a single word on each line, like this:

```
this
is
a
list
of
```

```
words
that
we
will
use
in
the
spell
checker
```

Create a list of words yourself, and save the file with the name `wordlist.txt` in the same build folder as your project, for example: `c:\My Projects\Spell Checker\bin\wordlist.txt`. Note that this will be a list of valid words, so any word that the user types that is not in this list will be returned by the spellchecker as "invalid".

> **If you want to use a more meaningful list of words, visit**
> `http://www.insidemedicine.com/words.html`.

Next, create a new class called `WordList` and add this code:

```
Imports System.IO

Public Class WordList
End Class
```

We'll be using the `System.IO` namespace to load the list of words into the word array. Now, add this code to define a new private member that will contain the collection, another to flag whether or not the list has been sorted and a method that can be used to add words to the collection:

```
Public Class WordList

    ' members...
    Private _wordList As New ArrayList()
    Private _isSorted As Boolean

    ' Add - add a word to the list...
    Public Sub Add(ByVal word As String)

        ' add it...
        word = word.ToLower
        If Not _wordList.Contains(word) Then _wordList.Add(word.ToLower)

        ' if we add a word, flag it as not sorted...
        _isSorted = False

    End Sub

End Class
```

To keep this example simple, we're going to ignore the problem of dealing with capitalization, by assuming that anything we ever work with will be lower-case. This is why we're using `ToLower` to convert the word to lower-case text, before adding it to the list. We also check to make sure that the word isn't already in the list when we add it.

Next we need to create the method to load the word list from disk. This method should be added to the `WordList` class. We'll start this with a `Try...Catch` block that will detect any problems with opening the file:

```
' Load - load a list of words from a file...
Public Sub Load(ByVal filename As String)

    ' try and open the file...
    Try

        ' open the file...
        Dim stream As New FileStream(filename, FileMode.Open)
        Dim reader As New StreamReader(stream)
```

As you know, the `System.IO.StreamReader` class contains a `ReadLine` method that will come in quite handy when we're loading up the file. Once we have the file, we can proceed to read in each word and add it to the list:

```
        ' clear the list...
        _wordList.Clear()

        ' go through the file...
        Do While True

            ' try and read a line...
            Dim buf As String = reader.ReadLine
            If buf = "" Then Exit Do

            ' add the word...
            _wordList.Add(buf)

        Loop
```

To make this code a little more efficient, we're not going to use the `Add` method we built earlier to add words to the list. If you recall, `Add` will transform the string into lower-case and scan the collection to make sure a word isn't already contained within it. What we want to do here is quickly populate the array. We'll assume that the words contained in `wordlist.txt` have already been qualified, and will always appear in lower-case with no words repeated.

Once we've worked through the file, we should close the reader and the stream. We'll also mark the list as not sorted:

```
        ' the resources must be closed...
        reader.Close()
        stream.Close()

        ' we'll assume the list is not sorted...
        _isSorted = False
```

Marking the list as "unsorted" wouldn't be 100% appropriate in a production system. Just as we're assuming that the list is properly qualified insofar as it contains all lower-case, non-repeated words, we should also assume that it's sorted. However, for this example it will be easier on you to assume the list is not sorted. That way, as you're experimenting with the data, you won't have to worry about inserting new values into the correct place in `wordlist.txt`.

Finally, we can close off the method:

```
    Catch

      ' report the error...
      MsgBox("The file '" & filename & _
              "' could not be loaded. (" & _
              Err().GetException.Message & ")")

    End Try

  End Sub
```

The last method we need on `WordList` is one that checks to see if a word is valid or not. We'll use the super-fast `BinarySearch` method on `ArrayList` to achieve this. What we'll do before we look for the word is sort the list if it's marked as "unsorted":

```
    ' Contains - is the word in the word list?
    Public Function Contains(ByVal word As String) As Boolean

      ' do we need to sort the list?
      If _isSorted = False Then
        _wordList.Sort()
        _isSorted = True
      End If

      ' do the search...
      Dim result As Integer = _wordList.BinarySearch(word)
      If result >= 0 Then
        Return True
      Else
        Return False
      End If

    End Function
```

Effectively, checking to see if the list is sorted at this point means that the first time `Contains` is called, the list will be sorted and `BinarySearch` will work in an optimal fashion. (`BinarySearch`, by the way, will return the index of the item in the list, or zero if the item is not in the list.) As it's unlikely that the list will be modified using `Add` before subsequent calls to `Contains`, the sort will only ever happen once.

Creating Checker

We're going to create our own self-contained class for handling the spell check process. `Checker` will also manage its own threading, meaning that aside from synchronization issues, we can pretty much rely on `Checker` properly starting and stopping its own thread.

Create a new class called `Checker` and add this code:

```
Imports System.Text
Imports System.Threading
Imports System.Collections.Specialized

Public Class Checker
End Class
```

To handle lists of words, we're going to be using a
`System.Collections.Specialized.StringCollection` object. This object makes it very easy to
work with lists of strings. Of course, we could use an `ArrayList` object as we did before, but our
primary motivation for using that was to obtain the binary search functionality.

Our object is going to need quite a number of members. First off, three members that will help us
handle the thread:

```
Public Class Checker
```

```
    ' members to handle the thread...
    Private _thread As Thread
    Private _isCancelled As Boolean
    Private _paused As New ManualResetEvent(False)
```

`Thread` (or `System.Threading.Thread`) you've already met, but you won't have met
`System.Threading.ManualResetEvent`. This object will provide a way for the application to tell
the thread to start spell checking. We'll see this in action later.

To do its work, we're going to give `Checker` a list of words to check. In this example, we're going to always
pass it the complete contents of `txtText.Text`, namely the entire document. In contrast, Word will only
pass new and changed words, not the entire document. We'll hold this list using these members:

```
    ' members to handle the list of words to check...
    Private _checkList As New StringCollection()
    Private _checkListLock As New ReaderWriterLock()
```

The `System.Threading.ReaderWriterLock` object provides the synchronization access that we've
been talking about. We'll use this to synchronize access to _checkList as we add words to it from the
main application thread and as we check words in it from the thread itself. There is no natural
relationship between these two objects. Rather, the code that we write will causes these two objects to
work together to get the synchronization effect that we want.

Finally, we'll need a set of member fields that will help us communicate with `Form1`:

```
    ' members to communicate with the user and caller...
    Public WordList As New WordList()
    Public OwnerForm As Form1
    Public OnCheckComplete As CheckComplete
```

Delegates

As you know, delegates can be used to create a free-form entry point into some piece of code in your
application. In this instance, we're going to use a delegate to tell `Form1` that the thread has finished
checking through the words, and also use it to pass through a `StringCollection` containing a list of
invalid words. To do this, we need to define the delegate. Add this code to `Checker`:

```
    ' need to create a callback delegate...
    Public Delegate Sub CheckComplete(ByVal_
            newInvalidWords As StringCollection)
```

Starting the Thread

The first method we need to add is `SpinUp`. This will tell the thread to start. In a short while, we're going to define the `Start` method, but for now just add this code to `Checker`:

```
' SpinUp - tells the thread to start...
Public Sub SpinUp()

    ' create a new ThreadStart...
    Dim start As New ThreadStart(AddressOf Me.Start)

    ' startup the thread...
    _thread = New Thread(start)
    _thread.Name = "Spell checker"
    _thread.Start()

End Sub
```

This is very similar to the example we saw earlier in the chapter.

One thing we need this thread to do is report back to us to tell us when it's running, and when it has run. This is quite important in helping us understand what's happening behind the scenes. Add this write-only property:

```
' ThreadStatus - set the status text for the thread...
Public WriteOnly Property ThreadStatus() As String
    Set(ByVal Value As String)
        OwnerForm.ThreadStatus = Now().ToString & ": " & Value
    End Set
End Property
```

We haven't built `Form1.ThreadStatus` yet, but when we do, it will simply change the `Text` property on `txtThreadStatus` to reflect whatever the thread wants to say.

Notice that we're ignoring synchronization problems with `ThreadStatus`, even though there is an argument that says we need to synchronize this block of code because the `Text` property can be accessed by more than one thread. For simplicity, we're going to ignore it and concentrate instead on resolving synchronization problems for the spell checking logic.

Add this code to kick off the `Checker.Start` method. Remember, this method will be called as the entry point for our new thread:

```
' Start - entry point for the thread...
Private Sub Start()

    ' set the status...
    ThreadStatus() = "Thread started"

    ' go into a loop...
    Do While True

        ThreadStatus() = "Waiting..."

        ' wait on the pause event...
        _paused.WaitOne()
```

As soon as we hit `WaitOne`, we'll drop into a super-efficient wait state again. When this happens, Windows will stop allocating time to the thread, effectively freeing up processing power for other threads in the process. _paused is a `System.Threading.ManualResetEvent` object, which means its purpose in life is to provide a way for threads to be dropped in and out of wait states by a process called **signaling**. When the object is **non-signaled**, we'll block. When the object is **signaled**, the thread will start running again by moving the execution pointer down to the next line. We'll see this in action in a moment.

When we signal _paused, we start running again by virtue of the fact that Windows starts allocating us time slices again. The first thing we do is see if we're canceled and, if we are, we drop out of the loop:

```
' are we cancelled?
If _isCanceled = True Then Exit Do
```

If we're not canceled, we have to check the words. To do this, we have to assume that the person who resumed us has used methods on the object that we haven't built yet to create a list of words to check in the _checkList string collection. We need to iterate through this collection, checking to see if any of the words are in our `WordList` object. If we find a word that's invalid, we'll add it to a collection called invalidWords:

```
' create somewhere to put the invalid words...
Dim invalidWords As New StringCollection()
```

However, before we can look at _checkList, we have to synchronize access to it and try to acquire a reader lock. This will mean that other threads can read the list, but no other threads can write it (in this instance, we're not going to have other threads reading the list at the same time, but we could well have something trying to write to it):

```
' lock the invalid word list for reading...
_checkListLock.AcquireReaderLock(-1)
```

That's all we have to do to acquire a lock on _checkListLock. The integer parameter that `AcquireReaderLock` takes is a timeout. Here, we've specified −1, which means that we want to wait for an infinite amount of time for the lock to become available. If we specified 1000, we'd wait for one second (1000 milliseconds) for the lock to become available. We might under other circumstances want to wait only, say, 30 seconds for the lock to become available. This brings up an important issue called **deadlocking** that we talk about at the end of this exercise.

Walking through the list of words is very easy:

```
' go through the words...
Dim word As String
For Each word In _checkList
  If Not WordList.Contains(word) Then invalidWords.Add(word)
Next
```

Once we've done that, we need to release the reader lock.

It is *critically* important that you release any lock that you acquire.

If we, for example, didn't unlock the reader at the end of this process, no one would ever be able to acquire a writer lock:

```
' release the lock...
_checkListLock.ReleaseReaderLock()
```

You are probably using exception handling in your applications. We've omitted it to keep things easier, but you must pay attention to the way you release your locks. Make sure that you release your locks in a Finally clause. As Finally is called irrespective of whether an exception was thrown or not, it's guaranteed to get called.

Once we've unlocked the list and done our work, we can pass the list of invalid words back to the primary application thread through the delegate we were given when we were configured:

```
' signal back to the caller that we're done...
OnCheckComplete.Invoke(invalidWords)
```

At the end of this process, we can loop back to the beginning of the thread handler code and wait for a new request to do some work. Before we do this, we need to reset the _paused ManualResetEvent object and put it back into a non-signaled state (we'll talk about this in a moment):

```
' pause the thread...
_paused.Reset()
```

Finally, we can finish the Start method:

```
Loop

' stop the thread...
ThreadStatus() = "Thread stopped"

End Sub
```

Resuming the Thread

When the thread first starts, we call _paused.WaitOne and the result of this is that the thread drops into a wait state. As we've said a few times now, _paused represents an instance of a ManualResetEvent object. This kind of object can either be signaled or non-signaled. When we created it, we created it with this line:

```
Private _paused As New ManualResetEvent(False)
```

The Boolean parameter on the constructor indicates the initial state of the object, and in this case we've said "Signaled = False".

Now that we've completed Start, we need to look at the method that instructs the thread to start checking the _checkList collection. Add this method to Checker:

```
' StartChecking - tell the thread to resume work...
Public Sub StartChecking()
  _paused.Set()
End Sub
```

By calling Set, as we are doing from StartChecking, we're signaling the object. By calling Reset, as we are doing from the end of the main thread loop implemented in Start, we're putting the object back into a non-signaled state. Set method always puts the object in a signaled state and Reset always puts it in a non-signaled state irrespective of the current state of the object.

If we call WaitOne on a non-signaled object, the thread will drop into a wait state until the thread is signaled again. As we create _paused in a non-signaled state, as soon as the thread starts, WaitOne will be called and the thread will drop into a wait state. When we call StartChecking from the primary application thread, _paused will be signaled, WaitOne will then return and the processing will start. After the processing is complete, we reset _paused, the loop jumps back up to the top and WaitOne is called again.

Together, this arrangement gives us a fine level of control over the execution of the thread.

Canceling and Stopping the Thread

When the application closes, we want to gracefully exit the thread. To do this, we need to get the infinite loop implemented in Start to drop out. If you recall, Start is actually called by the thread manager. As soon as Start returns, the thread is said to be dormant and is ready to be cleaned up.

Here's the code to cancel the thread. Add this method to Checker:

```
' Cancel - tell the thread to stop...
Public Sub Cancel()
    _isCancelled = True
    StartChecking()
End Sub
```

As soon as we call this method, it will return, irrespective of whether the thread has actually managed to quit the loop, and get to the end of the Start method. Ideally, we want to make sure that the thread has shut down properly. To do this, we need another method:

```
' StopThread - tells the thread to stop... we block until the thread
' does stop, so don't call this from the thread...
Public Sub SpinDown()

    ' tell the thread to cancel...
    Cancel()

    ' stop...
    _thread.Join()
    _thread = Nothing

End Sub
```

The Join method on _thread is a blocking call that drops the system into a wait state until the thread has finished executing and has got to a point where Windows has deleted it from its own internal threads subsystem. For this reason, SpinDown should not be called from the thread itself, but must be called from the primary application thread. As this call blocks, we're guaranteed that, by the time it returns, the thread has properly reached the end of Start and has finished its work.

Populating _checkList

All that remains now is to create some methods that update _checkList. These methods are pretty straightforward. First, let's look at the one that resets the list:

```
' ClearCheckList - resets the check list...
Public Sub ClearCheckList()

    ' lock and clear...
    _checkListLock.AcquireWriterLock(-1)
    _checkList.Clear()
    _checkListLock.ReleaseWriterLock()

End Sub
```

Notice how we're asking _checkListLock for a writer lock this time round. Also notice that we have to release the lock in the same way as we did for a reader lock.

Second, let's look at a method that adds a single word to the list. In this example, we're changing the word into all lower-case characters:

```
' AddWordToCheckList - adds a single word to the check list...
Public Sub AddWordToCheckList(ByVal word As String)

    word = word.ToLower

    ' lock, and add the single word...
    _checkListLock.AcquireWriterLock(-1)
    If Not _checkList.Contains(word) Then _checkList.Add(word)
    _checkListLock.ReleaseWriterLock()

End Sub
```

Lastly, we need a method that can take an entire block of text and strip out everything that's not an alphanumeric character. As this method comes across a word, the word will be added to the list through AddWordToCheckList. To use the spell checker, the primary thread will make life easy for itself and give us a block of text. We'll be expected to transform it into a list of words that the spell check algorithm can work through:

```
' AddToCheckList - add a sentence to the check list...
Public Sub AddToCheckList(ByVal buf As String)

    ' go through the string, removing everything that's not an alphanumeric...
    Dim safeBuf As New StringBuilder()
    Dim n As Integer
    For n = 0 To buf.Length - 1

        ' do we have an alpha?
        If Char.IsLetterOrDigit(buf, n) Then
            safeBuf.Append(buf, n, 1)
        Else
            safeBuf.Append(" ")
        End If
```

```
    Next

    ' split up the words...
    Dim words() As String = safeBuf.ToString.Split(" ".ToCharArray)

    ' go through each word and add it...
    Dim word As String
    For Each word In words

        ' trim the word and only add it if it's not blank...
        word = word.Trim
        If word <> "" Then
            AddWordToCheckList(word)
        End If

    Next

End Sub
```

That brings us to the end of the Checker object. Now we just need to wire it into the main application.

Using Checker

To use the Checker object, we need to hold an instance of it in the form, and we also need to have somewhere to store our list of invalid words. Remember, the way we're going to work this is handing over a list of words for Checker to take a look at, and when its finished we'll be passed a list of invalid words. Before we do that, we need to add some namespaces:

```
Imports System.IO
Imports System.Text
Imports System.Threading
Imports System.Collections.Specialized

Public Class Form1
    Inherits System.Windows.Forms.Form
```

Now, add these members to Form1:

```
Public Class Form1
    Inherits System.Windows.Forms.Form

    ' members...
    Private _checker As New Checker()
    Private _invalidWords As New StringCollection()
    Private _invalidWordsLock As New ReaderWriterLock()
```

As you know, Checker will use a delegate to call back into the primary thread (the thread that's running the form). We need to define a method on Form1 that has the same signature as this delegate, like this:

```
' OnCheckComplete - called when the spell checker has finished...
Public Sub OnCheckComplete(ByVal newInvalidWords As StringCollection)

    ' lock the invalid word list and update...
```

```
        _invalidWordsLock.AcquireWriterLock(-1)
        _invalidWords = newInvalidWords
        _invalidWordsLock.ReleaseLock()

    End Sub
```

When `OnCheckComplete` is called, it will be called from the spell checking thread, not the primary application thread. As we're now accessing the same data from different threads, we need to use the synchronization techniques we've already outlined to make sure everything stays in working order. Here, we're acquiring a writer lock, and keeping a reference to the string collection that the thread creates.

We now need to change the constructor of `Form1` to wire in the `Checker` object. You'll find the constructor hidden within the **Windows Form Designer generated code** region, so you may have to expand this out to find it. After the constructor has called `InitializeComponent`, we need to tell the `Checker` object who it belongs to:

```
    Public Sub New()
        MyBase.New()

        'This call is required by the Windows Form Designer.
        InitializeComponent()

        ' tell the spell checker who it belongs to...
        _checker.OwnerForm = Me
```

Then, we need to pass a reference to `OnCheckComplete` so that the delegate can be called:

```
        ' give the checker a delegate...
        _checker.OnCheckComplete = AddressOf Me.OnCheckComplete
```

Next, we need to load the word list. We're going to do this by using the `Application.ExecutablePath` property. We'll also use a `System.IO.FileInfo` object to help us extract the folder name from this path. You'll need to make sure that your `wordlist.txt` is stored in the same folder that the executable will be compiled into by Visual Studio. (By default, this will be the `bin` folder within the folder containing your project files).

```
        ' we'll need to get the dictionary from the application path
        Dim filename As String
        Dim fileInfo As New FileInfo(Application.ExecutablePath)
        filename = fileInfo.DirectoryName & "\wordlist.txt"
```

After we have the filename, we can tell `WordList` to load it:

```
        ' configure the checker's word list...
        _checker.WordList.Load(filename)
```

Finally, we can start the thread:

```
        ' start the spell check thread...
        _checker.SpinUp()
```

```
    End Sub
```

At this point, the thread will be running, but we have no way of telling it to check for words. For completeness, we also need to be able to stop the thread when the application window is closed. To do this we need to add the following code to `Form1`:

```
Protected Overrides Sub OnClosing(ByVal _
            e As System.ComponentModel.CancelEventArgs)

        ' we need to stop the spell check thread...
        _checker.SpinDown()

    End Sub
```

Reporting Status

Remember we created a property called `ThreadStatus` on the `Checker` object? Well, we need to create this property on `Form1` that supports `Checker`'s property:

```
Public Property ThreadStatus() As String
  Get
      Return txtThreadStatus().Text
  End Get
  Set(ByVal Value As String)
      txtThreadStatus().Text = Value
  End Set
End Property
```

Running the Spell Checker

To tell the spell checker to run, we need to use a combination of the `txtText.TextChanged` event, and the `tmrTextChanged` timer. When you create this timer, its `Enabled` property should be **False**, and its interval should be **500**.

Simply, when the text changes, we want to start the timer:

```
Private Sub txtText_TextChanged(ByVal sender As System.Object, _
            ByVal e As System.EventArgs) Handles _
                txtText.TextChanged
    tmrTextChanged().Enabled() = True
End Sub
```

This means that whenever we start typing text, half a second after that the timer will fire. When the timer fires, we need to stop the timer, populate the check list on `Checker` and then tell the thread to start running:

```
Private Sub tmrTextChanged_Tick(ByVal sender As System.Object, _
            ByVal e As System.EventArgs) Handles tmrTextChanged.Tick

    ' stop the timer...
    tmrTextChanged().Enabled = False

    ' clear the work list, and add all of our words...
    _checker.ClearCheckList()
    _checker.AddToCheckList(txtText().Text)
```

```
    ' tell the spell checker to start checking...
    _checker.StartChecking()

End Sub
```

Viewing the Results

As we said, we're not going to build a custom view of the text that's underlined with a red wavy line. Instead, we're going to set up another timer that constantly examines the _invalidWords collection and adds the contents to the txtInvalidWords textbox control.

> Note that the tmrUpdateInvalidWords timer control should be enabled, and have an interval of 100.

Add the following code to set up this timer:

```
Private Sub tmrUpdateInvalidWords_Tick(ByVal sender As System.Object, _
        ByVal e As System.EventArgs) Handles tmrUpdateInvalidWords.Tick

    ' get hold of a reader lock...
    _invalidWordsLock.AcquireReaderLock(-1)

    ' go through the string list and make a string builder...
    Dim builder As New StringBuilder(Now().ToString)
    builder.Append(" [")
    builder.Append(Environment.TickCount.ToString)
    builder.Append("]: ")

    ' loop...
    Dim word As String, isFirst As Boolean = True
    For Each word In _invalidWords
      If isFirst = True Then
        isFirst = False
      Else
        builder.Append(", ")
      End If
      builder.Append(word)
    Next

    ' update the text...
    txtInvalidWords().Text = builder.ToString

    ' release the lock...
    _invalidWordsLock.ReleaseReaderLock()

End Sub
```

The code is careful to put a reader lock around any access to _invalidWords. Checker will periodically update this value by calling OnCheckComplete, so we have to make sure that access is synchronized. Once we have confirmed that we can access it, we loop through it and update the display, effectively showing the user a list of invalid words.

Now that we've done that, we can try running the application. Here's what you'll see:

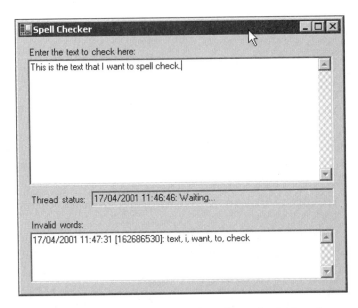

`Thread status` effectively shows the time that the thread last checked, and you can see that, by the way we have it set up, it runs as soon as the application starts because _paused is initially set as being signaled. `Invalid words` displays a list of the invalid words, so any word displayed here will *not* be in the `CheckWords` file. You'll also notice that this value is being constantly updated. The large integer value comes from the `Environment.TickCount` property, which gives the number of milliseconds that the computer has been running. Obviously, we're using `Now` to display the date and time.

That brings us to the end of this discussion on building a simple spell check application! Try it out, and see what you think. Remember to add words to `wordlist.txt` to vary the results.

Deadlocking

As a multithreaded developer, you should have considerable respect for two things: synchronization and deadlocking. I hope I've illustrated how synchronization can bite you, but let's look at deadlocking.

Both synchronization and deadlocking have the same effect on your development efforts – each can create bizarre bugs that are incredibly hard to track down. By getting synchronization wrong, you can get your program "out of step" and end up breaking or crashing the code several steps away from where you actually caused the problem. Deadlocking can result in your entire program freezing, again several steps away from where you caused the problem.

Deadlocking occurs when, for some reason, locks are not released. If you lock a reader/writer lock for writing and another thread wants to do the same, the second thread will stop executing until you release it. However, what happens if the second thread never gets access to the lock because the first lock never releases it? Simply, either the second thread will wait for an infinite amount of time for the lock to become available, or it will timeout. Either way, the second thread won't get access to the resource it needs to do its work, so something won't work properly. The other, more insidious deadlocking problem is where the first thread is waiting for a lock that the second thread has, but the second thread won't release that lock until it can obtain the lock on an object that the first thread has. In this case, neither thread can find a resolution to the problem and both threads stop completely.

> **Simply, make sure you unlock your locks when you're finished!**

Thread Pooling

We've seen how to create threads, and how to properly synchronize data access between threads. We've also seen a fairly complete implementation on using threads within a typical desktop application. What we haven't seen is how to use threads in a service.

Most service applications work by providing a thread that sits around waiting for an incoming connection of some kind. Once a connection is received, a new thread is created and that new thread is asked to service the new connection, as shown below:

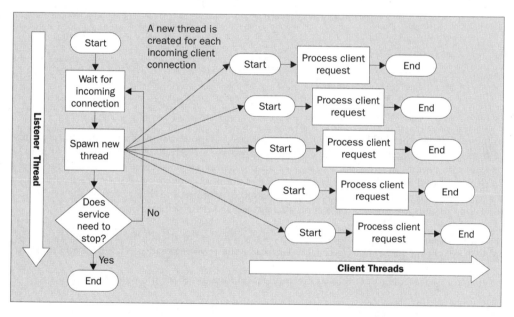

One way to streamline this process is to remove the overhead of creating a new thread each time a connection is created. This is done using a thread pool – a set of threads that sit around in memory waiting to be given some work, as illustrated in the following figure:

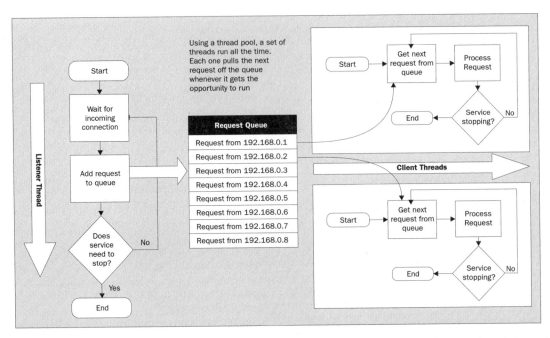

Under Windows with the .NET Framework, each process is automatically given a thread pool through the `System.Threading.ThreadPool` class. Each process can only have up to one thread pool, which can be shared between many different activities. In the classic service scenario that we're looking at, the thread pool may well be exclusively used to service incoming connections. However, the thread pool could also be used to run periodic activities, for example, examine the disk space on the server to make sure that it is not running low, check e-mail, etc., as well as service client connections.

Interestingly, thread pools make threading even easier than we've already seen. Obviously, we still need to deal with synchronization, but we don't need to actually create threads. .NET does all that for us.

In this exercise, we're going to create a new application that simulates the work of a server.

The Worker Object

To kick off, create a new Visual Basic Windows Application project called `Pooling`. Next, create a new class called `Worker`.

The `Worker` object is our conceptual object that is given some activity to do. In fact, we're not going to ask the object to do anything at all – rather we're going to ask it to sleep for a given period of time. In a server application, these objects would be created in response to an incoming connection, such as for a web server, but we'll create a new `Worker` object and give it a socket that it can use to pass data between itself and the client.

First of all, let's give the namespaces to the object, and also create some members:

```
Imports System.Threading

Public Class Worker
```

```
' members...
Public Id As Integer
Public SleepPeriod As Integer
Public Owner As Form1
Public OnWorkerStart As WorkerStart
Public OnWorkerEnd As WorkerEnd
Private _isCancelled As Boolean
```

Here's a breakdown of the members:

- ❑ Id – used to store a system unique ID for the worker. We'll use this when debugging to keep track of what's happening

- ❑ SleepPeriod – the period of time that the worker should "pretend" to work for

- ❑ Owner – the main application

- ❑ OnWorkerStart – a delegate provided by the owner that Worker will use to signal the start of work

- ❑ OnWorkerEnd – a delegate provided by the owner that Worker will use to signal the end of work

- ❑ _isCancelled – a Boolean that indicates whether the Worker has been canceled

Next, let's define the delegates that the owner will use to communicate with the worker:

```
' delegates...
Public Delegate Sub WorkerStart(ByVal workerObject As Worker, _
                    ByVal workerThread As Thread)
Public Delegate Sub WorkerEnd(ByVal workerObject As Worker, _
                    ByVal workerThread As Thread)
```

To add an item to the thread pool, all we have to do is provide a delegated method that matches the signature of System.Threading.WaitCallback. This is a delegate definition contained in the Framework that we need to use in order to work with the pool. We pass this method to the ThreadPool using a shared method, like this:

```
' Go - tell the object to start working...
Public Sub Go()

    ' queue me...
    ThreadPool.QueueUserWorkItem(AddressOf Me.Start)

End Sub
```

Notice that when we're using the ThreadPool, we don't have to manage the lifetime of the thread. We only need to provide an entry point and the Framework itself does everything else for us.

After we've called Go and subsequently called QueueUserWorkItem, the thread pool manager will wait for an opportunity for us to start running. If the thread pool is empty, or the pool determines that another thread will be created, a new thread will be spun up. Alternatively, if a thread is in the pool but isn't working through a work item, this existing thread will be used. It's this use of existing threads that makes using the thread pool efficient as we don't have the overhead of creating threads *every* time. When this happens, our delegate will be called. We can't actually control when this will happen – all we know is that it will happen at some point in the future.

We now need to implement `Start`. All this method needs to do is call an `AddToLog` function that we'll build in a moment, and call the delegates. We also pretend to do work by using the `Thread.Sleep` method:

```
' Start - called when the thread pool wants us to do something...
Public Sub Start(ByVal state As Object)

    ' start...
    AddToLog("Started")
    If Not OnWorkerStart Is Nothing Then _
                OnWorkerStart.Invoke(Me, Thread.CurrentThread)

    ' if we're cancelled, don't do anything...
    If _isCancelled = False Then

        ' sleep for a while and simulate some work...
        thread.Sleep(SleepPeriod)

    End If

    ' stop...
    If Not OnWorkerEnd Is Nothing Then _
                OnWorkerEnd.Invoke(Me, Thread.CurrentThread)
    AddToLog("Stop")

End Sub
```

This method will only be called when a thread becomes available in the pool. That's why we have to use `Thread.CurrentThread` to get hold of a thread object – it's the only way we can determine which thread we're running in.

Notice how we're using `If` statements to see if a delegate has been provided. This means that the developer doesn't have to provide delegates if she doesn't want to, for example the developer might not need to know when a worker has started. This is quite a neat technique to use that may well help developers down the line use the object more easily.

We're going to use the `txtStatus` control on the application's form to let the worker provide status information to the user. Add this method:

```
' AddToLog - call into us...
Public Sub AddToLog(ByVal buf As String)
    Owner.AddToLog("[id:" & Id.ToString & ", thread:" & _
        Thread.CurrentThread.GetHashCode.ToString & "] " & buf)
End Sub
```

`Thread.GetHashCode` is a useful method that will give you a unique identifier for the thread. This will let us keep track of how many threads are running during debugging, but in practical day-to-day use is typically of little use. We'll see this working when we run the application.

Finally, we need to create a method that can cancel the worker:

```
' Cancel - cancel the worker when it starts...
Public Sub Cancel()
    _isCancelled = True
End Sub
```

The reason why we need this ability to cancel the worker is because if the application closes before the worker has started running, we need to be able to "short circuit" the code that actually does the activity that, by virtue of the fact the application is not running, no longer needs to be performed.

Creating Worker Objects

I've made this part of the exercise a little more complicated than it should be, simply to make it easier to understand what's happening inside the pool.

First of all, this is the layout of the form:

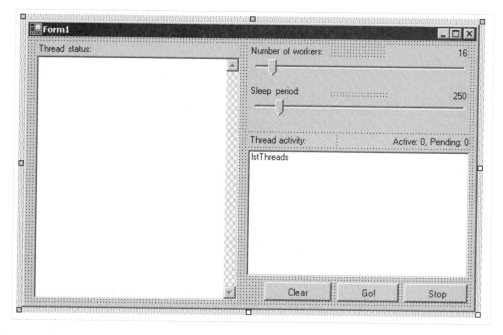

Here are the controls:

❑ txtStatus – a textbox control that the workers use to report their progress

❑ trkNumWorkers – a TrackBar control that varies the number of workers. Set Minimum to 1, Maximum to 256, and Value to16

❑ lblNumWorkers – a label that reports the number of workers selected on the TrackBar control

❑ trkSleepPeriod – a TrackBar control that varies the number of milliseconds passed to Thread.Sleep by the worker. Set the Minimum to 0 and the Maximum to 2500. Set the Value to 250

❑ lblSleepPeriod – a label that reports the number of milliseconds selected on the TrackBar control

❑ lblNumActive – a label control used to report the number of active threads and the number of pending workers

- ❏ lstThreads – a list box control used to report the number of running threads

- ❏ cmdClear – a button control used to clear txtStatus

- ❏ cmdGo – a button control used to create Worker objects

- ❏ cmdStop – a button control used to cancel all of the pending workers

Now that the form has been designed, we can go ahead and define a few members. You also need to include the namespace import directive in the top of the code listing:

```
Imports System.Threading

Public Class Form1
    Inherits System.Windows.Forms.Form

    ' members...
    Private _workerId As Integer
    Private _statusLock As New ReaderWriterLock()
    Private _threadList As New Hashtable()
    Private _completeWorkerList As New ArrayList()
    Private _activeWorkerList As New ArrayList()
    Private _threadListLock As New ReaderWriterLock()
```

Here's what they will do:

- ❏ _workerId – provides an area to store the system unique worker ID

- ❏ _statusLock – used to synchronize access to txtStatus.Text

- ❏ _threadList – used to store a list of the threads that are being used and have ever been used

- ❏ _completeWorkerList – used to store a list of the workers that are being processed or that need to be processed

- ❏ _activeWorkerList – used to store a list of the workers that are currently being processed

- ❏ _threadListLock – used to synchronize access to _threadList, _completeWorkerList, and _activeWorkerList

We need a few methods that provide simple UI updates. Add these methods and event handlers to your code:

```
Public Sub AddToLog(ByVal buf As String)
    _statusLock.AcquireWriterLock(-1)
    txtStatus().Text &= Now().ToString & ": " & buf & Chr(13) & Chr(10)
    _statusLock.ReleaseWriterLock()
End Sub


Private Sub trkNumWorkers_Scroll(ByVal sender As System.Object, _
            ByVal e As System.EventArgs) Handles trkNumWorkers.Scroll
    lblNumWorkers().Text = trkNumWorkers().Value.ToString
End Sub


Private Sub trkSleepPeriod_Scroll(ByVal sender As System.Object, _
            ByVal e As System.EventArgs) Handles trkSleepPeriod.Scroll
```

```
        lblSleepPeriod().Text = trkSleepPeriod().Value.ToString
End Sub


Private Sub cmdClear_Click(ByVal sender As System.Object, _
            ByVal e As System.EventArgs) Handles cmdClear.Click
    txtStatus().Text = ""
    lstThreads.Items.Clear()
End Sub
```

Creating the Workers

One thing that it's important to understand is that we're not creating "threads" when we use the thread pool. We're creating "workers" by creating instances of objects from the Worker class, and we're then asking those objects to ask the thread pool to allocate time in the pool for us some time in the future. This is an important distinction – everything we've done so far we've had a fine degree of control over when the thread will actually be created, (in other words we've created a new Thread object and called Start). When using a thread pool we're saying "run me when you can", and when we get executed will depend on server load. We also don't have control over how big the pool gets, so we might queue 10,000 worker objects, but the pool may only create four threads.

Here's the start of the handle for cmdGo that will go on to create the workers:

```
Private Sub cmdGo_Click(ByVal sender As System.Object, _
            ByVal e As System.EventArgs) Handles cmdGo.Click

    ' get the number of threads and "speed" from the sliders...
    Dim numWorkers As Integer = trkNumWorkers().Value
    Dim sleepPeriod As Integer = trkSleepPeriod().Value
```

To create the workers, we just have to use a simple loop. We provide an ID, the period of time each worker should sleep for when it's running and references to our delegated methods:

```
    ' create the workers...
    Dim n As Integer
    For n = 1 To numWorkers

        ' create a worker...
        Dim worker As New Worker()
        worker.Id = _workerId
        _workerId += 1
        worker.SleepPeriod = sleepPeriod
        worker.Owner = Me
        worker.OnWorkerStart = AddressOf Me.WorkerStart
        worker.OnWorkerEnd = AddressOf Me.WorkerEnd
```

We want to keep a list of workers that have been created and are either running, or are waiting to start:

```
    ' add it to the definitive list of workers...
    _threadListLock.AcquireWriterLock(-1)
    _completeWorkerList.Add(worker)
    _threadListLock.ReleaseWriterLock()
```

Finally, we can tell the worker to start working and close off the event handler:

```
    ' tell the worker to start...
    worker.Go()

  Next

End Sub
```

Now we've done that, we can create the delegates that manage the list of working threads.

Creating the Delegates

As a user of a thread pool, you might not actually care what threads are running or what workers are currently being processed. However, for this example we want to try and illustrate what's going on behind the scenes so we're going to use our `WorkerStart` and `WorkerEnd` delegates to provide notification of what's happening in the threads so we can report back to the user.

We're going to maintain a list of the threads in `_threadList` (in fact, we're going to hold on to the integer ID of the thread, not a `Thread` object as you might expect). We're going to use this list to keep track of all the threads that we've ever seen. We can't tell when Windows has removed a thread from its own internal threading subsystem, so threads that actually no longer exist may well appear as "idle". Don't forget, this exercise has been designed to show you how the thread pool works – some of the functionality we include in this application will rarely be used in the real world. This will give us an idea of how big the thread pool is growing in response to our usage. We also keep a list of the workers that are being processed in `_activeWorkerList`. Here's the code for `WorkerStart`:

```
  ' WorkerStart - called when a worker has started...
  Public Sub WorkerStart(ByVal workerObject As Worker, ByVal workerThread As Thread)

    ' update the list...
    _threadListLock.AcquireWriterLock(-1)
    Try
      _threadList.Add(workerThread.GetHashCode, workerObject.Id)
    Catch
      _threadList.Item(workerThread.GetHashCode) = workerObject.Id
    End Try

    ' add this to the worker list...
    _activeWorkerList.Add(workerObject)

    ' update the list...
    UpdateThreadView()

    ' release the lock
    _threadListLock.ReleaseWriterLock()

  End Sub
```

We use a `Try...Catch` block to make it easier to update the list. If we try and add an item to the list and that item is already in there, an exception will be thrown in which case we can perform an update. We haven't seen `UpdateThreadView` yet, but we'll build it in a moment.

You can see that we're using a `Hashtable` object to keep track of the threads. We index this table against the thread object itself, and against each thread we store the ID of the thread that we're working with. Notice that we're careful to maintain locking against these lists so that everything is properly synchronized.

Here's the code for `WorkerEnd`:

```
' WorkerEnd - called when a worker has finished...
Public Sub WorkerEnd(ByVal workerObject As Worker, ByVal workerThread As Thread)

   ' update the list...
   _threadListLock.AcquireWriterLock(-1)
   _threadList(workerThread.GetHashCode) = 0

   ' remove this from the worker list...
   _completeWorkerList.Remove(workerObject)
   _activeWorkerList.Remove (workerObject)

   ' update the list...
   UpdateThreadView()

   ' release the lock...
   _threadListLock.ReleaseWriterLock()

End Sub
```

You can see that this method removes the worker from both the complete and active list. Notice as well how rather than removing the thread from _threadList we set the ID of its worker to zero. This allows us to keep track of the threads that aren't actually doing anything at a given moment in time, but as we said we actually can't determine whether or not a thread still exists.

To report back on the status of the threads, we need to add this method:

```
' UpdateThreadView- update the list...
Public Sub UpdateThreadView()

   ' lock the list for reading...
   _threadListLock.AcquireReaderLock(-1)

   ' change the list...
   lstThreads().Items.Clear()

   ' go through the items...
   Dim item As Object
   For Each item In _threadList.Keys

     ' create the string...
     Dim buf As String = "Thread " & item.ToString
     If CType(_threadList(item), Integer) <> 0 Then
       buf &= " working with Worker " & _threadList(item).ToString
     Else
       buf &= " is idle"
     End If

     ' add that...
```

```
        lstThreads().Items.Add(buf)

    Next

    ' tell it how many are active...
    lblNumActive().Text() = "Active: " & _activeWorkerList.Count.ToString & _
                 ", Pending: " & _completeWorkerList.Count.ToString

    ' release the lock...
    _threadListLock.ReleaseReaderLock()

End Sub
```

With all that in place, we can test it.

Testing the Solution

To try it the first time, keep the number of threads set to 16 and keep the sleep period at 250 milliseconds. Click Go. This will create sixteen `Worker` objects and each worker object will pause for a quarter-of-a-second when it runs:

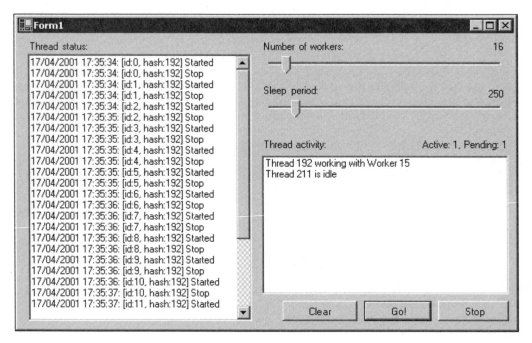

You'll see that the thread pool runs all of the workers in a single thread, up until the last few workers are executed. Windows uses a heuristic routine to determine how many threads should be in the pool, and how many threads should be running concurrently. In this example, it will create the second thread when demand for the first thread reaches a certain point.

> Due to the various factors that affect the thread pool, you may find it tricky to exactly duplicate the results as seen here. Play with the sliders until you see the effect you want. If you're running a highly specified multiprocessor machine, you may not get the same effect that you can see here. Windows may well decide it can afford to kick off more threads initially because you have more than one process and no amount of fiddling with the sliders will get this effect.

What's really important to understand when talking about the thread pool is that although we're only running at most two workers at a time, all sixteen are queued almost immediately and that the first thread starts sometime after our loop has finished. (This is because our loop is very quick to run. If our loop takes longer to execute, or we wait for inbound connections, we may well find that the first thread starts before the last worker is queued.) In effect, the sixteenth worker has to wait quite a long time to get a chance to execute.

Now, without quitting, change the number of workers to 32 and set the sleep period to 1000 and try again. You'll see something like this:

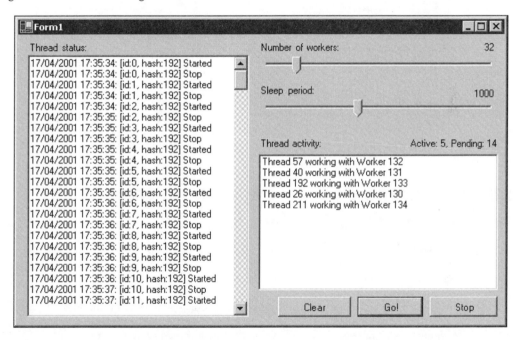

You'll see that immediately we start using two threads. That's because the second time round we already have two threads in the pool ready to go. Since we've told each thread to take a longer period of time to do the processing, there's more demand on the pool so we end up with more threads. You'll see this effect if you click Go for a third time. This time, however, all five threads allocated to the pool will start working.

Now that you've seen how to use the thread pool to make handling multiple asynchronous operations easier to handle, let's look at how the thread pool can improve on our spell checker example.

Canceling Pending Workers

One of the issues with the thread pool is that once a work item has been queued, it cannot be un-queued. If you decide at some point that you don't want your work item to be processed, you need to flag it as "cancelled". This is likely to happen if you decide to close down your application or the work that the worker was asked to do is no longer required or relevant.

We maintain a list of pending and active workers in _completeWorkerList for just this reason. Should we need to cancel all or some of the workers, we can iterate through this list and call Cancel for each one. Here's the code for the cmdStop.Click handler:

```
Private Sub cmdStop_Click(ByVal sender As System.Object, _
            ByVal e As System.EventArgs) Handles cmdStop.Click

  ' go through our worker list and tell every worker object to cancel...
  _threadListLock.AcquireReaderLock(-1)
  Dim worker As Worker
  For Each worker In _completeWorkerList
    worker.Cancel()
  Next

  ' release the lock...
  _threadListLock.ReleaseReaderLock()

End Sub
```

As each work item is asked to work, we already check to see if _isCancelled is set to True, (in other words that at some point someone has called Cancel). If this has happened, we drop out of the end of the work item. Notice how we still continue to call OnWorkerStart and OnWorkerEnd. This lets our caller keep track of the list of workers and threads in the normal manner.

Using the Thread Pool to Improve on the ManualResetEvent.WaitOne Scenario

You'll recall that with our spell checker we created a separate thread that sat around waiting for a ManualResetEvent object to be signaled. In reality, that thread didn't actually spend much of its lifetime working and so was in a wait state for the majority of its life.

Although there's no serious problem with this approach, it's not as efficient as it might be. Rather, we could use the thread pool to allocate a thread to us whenever we needed to go away and run a spell checker. This would mean that we were, effectively, creating a thread on demand.

But there's a wrinkle here – although the thread pool object is around all the time by virtue of a shared function, the thread pool contains no threads until the first work item is queued at which time a thread is created and calls into a delegate to start the work. That gives us no advantage over our previous approach, save for the fact that the thread pool will close down threads that have been idle for a period of time, restarting them should they be needed later on.

If you have a number of threads that behave in the same way as the spell checker thread, you may well find it advantageous to use the thread pool. Again, there are no hard and fast rules about how many threads you need to get the advantage – experimentation is key.

Another Demonstration

As we're nearing the end of the discussion, we're going to look at a fairly simple example of how to use the thread pool to handle a scenario where we have 64 workers that periodically need to run in a thread. Create a new Visual Basic Windows Application project and call it `Register Example`.

We're going to create another class called `RegisterWorker` to handle our worker objects. This will be fairly similar to the one we just worked with. Create the new class now and add this code:

```
Imports System.Threading

Public Class RegisterWorker

    ' members...
    Public Id As Integer
    Private _event As New ManualResetEvent(False)
    Public OnWorkerStart As WorkerStart
    Public OnWorkerEnd As WorkerEnd

    ' delegates...
    Public Delegate Sub WorkerStart(ByVal workerObject As RegisterWorker, _
                        ByVal workerThread As Thread)
    Public Delegate Sub WorkerEnd(ByVal workerObject As RegisterWorker, _
                        ByVal workerThread As Thread)

End Class
```

To register the worker, we have to use the `ThreadPool.RegisterWaitForSingleObject` method. This method can be configured to fire whenever an object is signaled, or when a given period of time elapses. This timeout feature is particularly useful. Imagine you have a thread that needs to check for e-mail every five minutes, but you also might want to tell the thread to check for e-mail on demand. This technique is perfect for this – create a new `ManualResetEvent` object, register it with the thread pool, but give it a timeout of five minutes. (This timeout period is the time between you registering the object with the thread pool and it being automatically started.) You can then either signal the `ManualResetEvent` object by using its `Set` method, or you can wait for it to timeout and start running.

Just like we've seen throughout these examples, we need to register a delegate that will be used to kick off the work. Add this code to `RegisterWorker`:

```
' Register - register the object...
Public Sub Register()

    ' make sure that we're reset...
    _event.Reset()

    ' register the object with the thread pool...
    Dim callback As WaitOrTimerCallback = AddressOf Me.Start
    threadpool.RegisterWaitForSingleObject(_event, callback, Nothing, -1, True)

End Sub
```

Taking the parameters in order for `RegisterWaitForSingleObject`: firstly, we need to give it the `ManualResetEvent` object. This object must be non-signaled for this to work, so we call `Reset` to make sure that it is. Otherwise, the worker would be registered with the pool immediately. Secondly, we give it the delegate we want to call into. Thirdly, we give it a state object. We don't need to use this, so we'll use `Nothing`. Next, we supply a timeout value of −1, meaning that we want to wait forever. Finally we indicate if we want to receive only one notification during the lifetime of the object. We've set this to `True`, meaning that when we signal the event our delegate will only ever be called once. If we don't do this, our delegate will get called constantly, which is not what we want. What we have to do is tell it to call us once and then re-register the event after we've done our work. The "timeout" is a once only occurrence, so as soon as it's fired once, it will never be fired again. That's why we have to register it again. We'll see this in a moment.

Next, we need a method that will kick off the worker. When we added _event to the thread pool, it was non-signaled. This signals the object, so the thread pool will recognize it, find a thread to run it in, and use the `Start` method as the entry point.

```
' Go - called when we need the thread to start running...
Public Sub Go()
  _event.Set()
End Sub
```

Finally, we need to do some work. This is pretty similar to the way we did it before:

```
' Start - delegate called when the event is signalled...
Private Sub Start(ByVal state As Object, ByVal wasSignalled As Boolean)

  ' tell the caller we've started...
  If Not OnWorkerStart Is Nothing Then _
          OnWorkerStart.Invoke(Me, thread.CurrentThread)

  ' here's where we'd do some work!
  Thread.Sleep(1000)

  ' tell the caller we've finished...
  If Not OnWorkerEnd Is Nothing Then _
          OnWorkerEnd.Invoke(Me, thread.CurrentThread)

  ' tell the worker to start waiting again...
  Register()

End Sub
```

Notice how we're calling `Register` again at the end of the method. This will allow us to re-signal the worker at a later time if we need it to do something else. Notice how we reset _event at the beginning of `Register`. This keeps everything in order for the next time we want to run.

Creating the UI

For this example, we're going to create 64 workers. To simulate these workers being started, we're going to create 64 buttons on a form. Since VB.NET no longer supports control arrays, the best way to create our 64 buttons is to do it programmatically from within the form's constructor. Before we build the button, we need to add a textbox called `txtStatus` to the form:

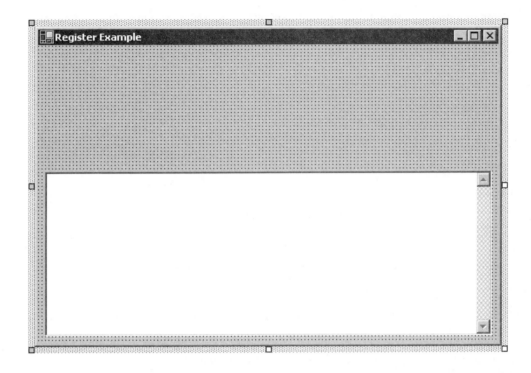

We also need to create a new version of the button control that it's tied into a specific worker and can automatically call Worker.Go whenever the button is pressed. Create a new class called WorkerButton and add this code:

```
Imports System.Windows.Forms

Public Class WorkerButton
  Inherits Button

  Private _worker As RegisterWorker

  ' Constructor...
  Public Sub New(ByVal worker As RegisterWorker)
    _worker = worker
    Text() = _worker.Id.ToString
  End Sub

  ' OnClick - called when the button is clicked...
  Protected Overrides Sub OnClick(ByVal e As EventArgs)

    ' tell the worker to do something...
    _worker.Go()

  End Sub

End Class
```

Add these members to `Form1`, along with the following namespace declaration at the top of the code listing:

```
Imports System.Threading

Public Class Form1
    Inherits System.Windows.Forms.Form

    ' members...
    Const NumWorkers As Integer = 64
    Private _workers(NumWorkers) As RegisterWorker
    Private _workerButtons(NumWorkers) As Button
    Private _statusLock As New ReaderWriterLock()
```

To use this button, we need to modify the form's constructor. Find the **New** method and add this code:

```
Public Sub New()
    MyBase.New()

    'This call is required by the Windows Form Designer.
    InitializeComponent()

    ' set our caption so we know what thread we are...
    Me.Text &= " - Main Application Thread: " & thread.CurrentThread.GetHashCode
```

The first thing we've done is to modify the form's caption to report the ID of the current thread. As New is called from the primary thread in the process, the caption will always display the ID of the primary thread. This will assure us that the workers are indeed running in their own threads.

Next, we need to define some metrics about how we'll be laying out the controls:

```
    ' we're going to dynamically create controls, so keep track of x, y, etc...
    Dim spacing As Integer = 10
    Dim x As Integer = spacing
    Dim y As Integer = spacing
    Dim width As Integer = 30
    Dim height As Integer = 20
```

Now we can start creating the workers:

```
    ' create the workers...
    Dim n As Integer
    For n = 0 To NumWorkers - 1

        ' create a worker object...
        _workers(n) = New Worker()
        _workers(n).OnWorkerStart = AddressOf Me.WorkerStart
        _workers(n).OnWorkerEnd = AddressOf Me.WorkerEnd
        _workers(n).Id = n
```

After we've created the worker, we can register it:

```
        ' tell the worker to wait...
        _workers(n).Register()
```

Now we can create a new instance of our button control, position it on the form and add it to the form's control array:

```
    ' create the new button...
    _workerButtons(n) = New WorkerButton(_workers(n))
    _workerButtons(n).Left = x
    _workerButtons(n).Top = y
    _workerButtons(n).Width = width
    _workerButtons(n).Height = height

    ' add the button to our list of controls...
    Controls().Add(_workerButtons(n))
```

After positioning the control, we can move to the next position and repeat the loop. At the end of each line, we move down to the left-most position of the next line.

```
    ' move to the next position...
    x += (width + spacing)
    If x > Me.Width - (width + spacing) Then
      x = spacing
      y += (height + spacing)
    End If

  Next
```

Finally, we need to adjust the position of txtStatus so that it occupies the remaining space on the screen:

```
    ' finally, adjust txtstatus...
    txtStatus().Top = y + (height + spacing)
    txtStatus().Height = Me.Height - txtStatus().Top - (3 * spacing)

  End Sub
```

We need to provide code for the delegated methods, and also build a helper to add log messages to txtStatus:

```
Public Sub WorkerStart(ByVal workerObject As RegisterWorker, _
                      ByVal workerThread As Thread)
  AddToLog("Worker " & workerObject.Id.ToString & _
          " started in thread " & workerThread.GetHashCode)
End Sub

Public Sub WorkerEnd(ByVal workerObject As RegisterWorker, _
                    ByVal workerThread As Thread)
  AddToLog("Worker " & workerObject.Id.ToString & " finished")
End Sub

Public Sub AddToLog(ByVal buf As String)
  _statusLock.AcquireWriterLock(-1)
  txtStatus().Text &= Now().ToString & ": " & buf & Chr(13) & Chr(10)
  _statusLock.ReleaseWriterLock()
End Sub
```

Testing the Solution

That's all we need to do to get this solution started. Run it up, click on one or two of the buttons and you'll see something like this:

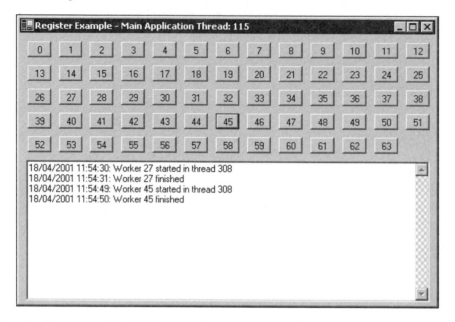

You'll see that because we signaled the two objects consecutively we ended up with the same thread being reused. If you try clicking lots of different buttons quickly, you'll see that at some point another thread or two will be added to the pool to service the requests.

Summary

In this chapter, we took a fairly involved look at the subject of threading in .NET and how VB.NET developers now have access to a rich set of threading functionality. We started off by looking at how threads can be created, how they relate to processes and then briefly touched on the differences between multitasking and multithreading. We then worked through a sample application to illustrate threading in operation.

Our focus then moved on to the rather tricky subject of thread synchronization, in order to manage multithreaded code effectively, with details regarding the associated topics of blocking, wait state and signaling. To illustrate these principles we then developed a Spell Checker sample application.

In the final part of the chapter we looked at the nature of thread pools in relation to service applications, considering both how thread pools can be used to make the job of managing multiple asynchronous threads easier, and how the same pool can be used to look after multiple blocking event objects.

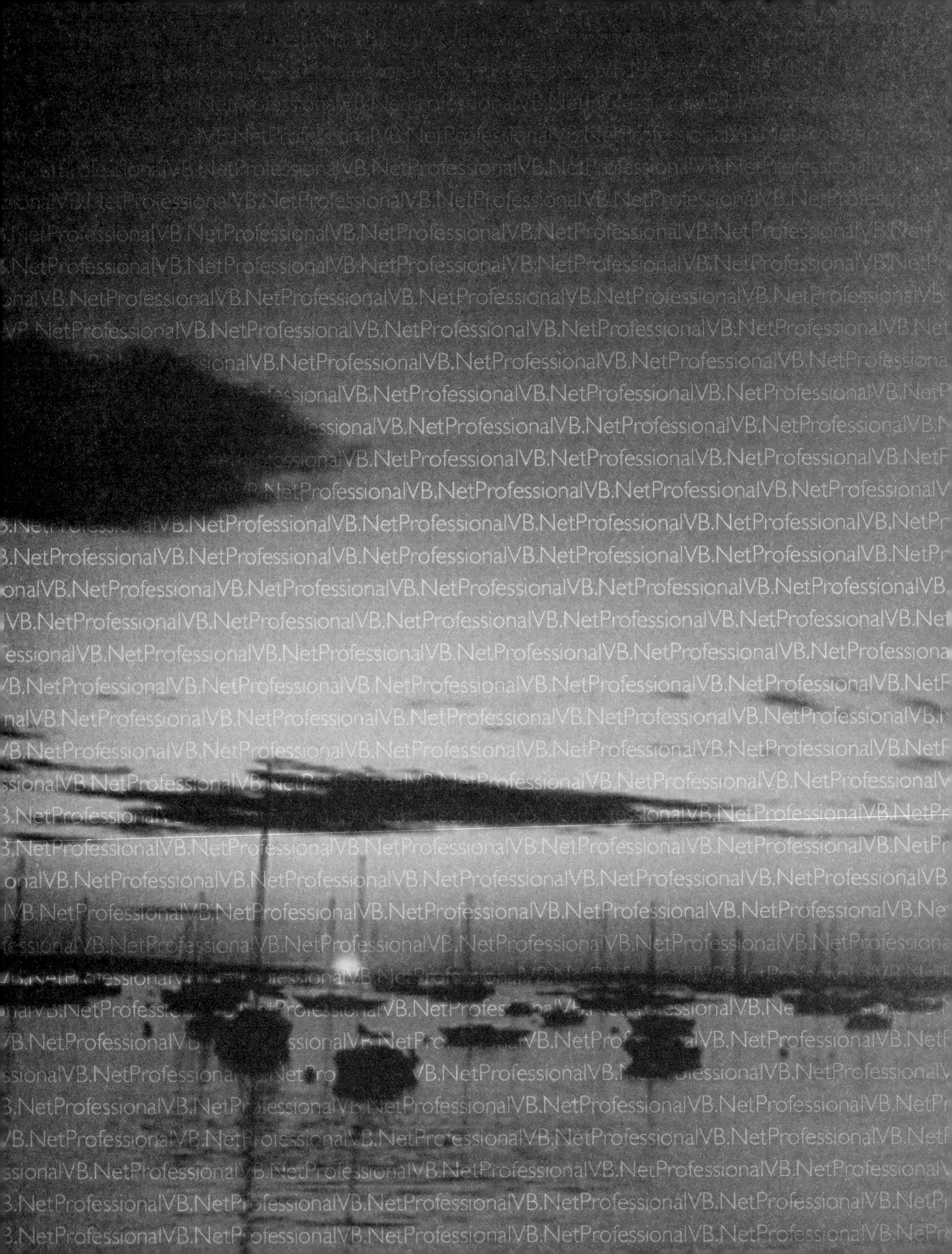

16

Working with Classic COM and Interfaces

When we all gathered together to plan this book (in the most virtual sense, of course), we all agreed on one thing: this was to be a book about VB.NET. It wasn't about introducing .NET, or migrating from VB6. No, the emphasis was to be firmly on developing new stuff using new tools. We're all .NET programmers now. We've moved on.

This, however, is the point at which the real world breaks in. There is one legacy in the Microsoft world that we can't ignore (OK, two, if you count DOS boxes). However, much as we try, we just can't ignore the vast body of technology surrounding Microsoft's **Component Object Model**, or **COM**. This model has been the cornerstone of so much Microsoft-related development over the last few years that we have to take a long, hard look at how we are going to integrate all that stuff into the new world. This time around, we won't have Y2K available to us as an excuse for just getting rid of it all.

In this chapter, then, we're going to start by taking a brief backward glance at COM. We're then going to compare it with how components interact in .NET, and see what tools Microsoft have provided us with to help link the two together. Having looked at the theory, we'll then try it out by building a few example applications. Firstly, we'll take a legacy basic COM object and run it from a VB.NET program. Then we'll repeat the trick with a full-blown ActiveX control. Finally, we'll turn things around and try running some VB.NET code in the guise of a COM object.

As we do all this, try to remember one thing: COM is, to a large extent, where .NET came from. In evolutionary terms, COM's kind of like Lucy, the *Australopithecus* from ancient Ethiopia. So, if it seems a little clunky at times, let's not to be too hard on it. In fact, let's not refer to it as "Nasty, tired, clunky old COM" at all. Let's simply call it "Classic COM".

A Five-Minute Tour of COM

Before we look into COM –.NET interoperability, we should make sure that we are aware of the main points about COM itself. We won't attempt to do anything more than skim the surface here, however. Whilst the basic concepts are fundamentally simple, the underlying technology is anything but. Some of the most impenetrable books on software that have ever been written have COM as their subject, and there is no wish on the part of the authors to add to the word count.

COM was pretty well Microsoft's first attempt at creating a language-independent standard for programming. The idea was that interfaces between components would be defined according to a binary standard. This would mean that you could, for the first time, invoke a VB component from a VC++ application, and vice versa. It would also be possible to invoke a component in another process or even on another machine, via Distributed COM, or DCOM. We won't be looking at out-of-process servers here, however, as the vast majority of components developed to date are in-process. To a large extent, DCOM was fatally compromised by bandwidth, deployment, and firewall problems and never achieved a high level of acceptance.

A COM component implements one or more **interfaces**, some of which are standard ones provided by the system and some of which are custom interfaces defined by the component developer. An interface defines the various methods that an application may invoke. Once specified, an interface definition is supposed to be inviolate so that, even if the underlying code changes, applications that use the interface don't need to be rebuilt. If the component developers find that they have left something out, they should define a new interface containing the extra functionality in addition to that in the original interface. This has in fact happened with a number of standard Microsoft interfaces. For example, the IClassFactory2 interface extends the IClassFactory interface by adding features for managing the creation of licensed objects.

The key to getting applications and components to work together is **binding**. COM offers two forms of binding: early and late.

In **early-binding**, the application uses something called a **type library** at compile time to work out how to link in to the methods in the component's interfaces. A type library can either come as a separate file, with extension .tlb, or as part of the DLL containing the component code.

In **late-binding**, no connection is made between the application and its components at compile time. Instead, the COM runtime searches through the component for the location of the required method when the application is actually run. This has two main disadvantages: first of all, it's slower and, secondly, it's unreliable. If a programming error is made (for example, the wrong method is called, or the right method with the wrong number of arguments), it doesn't get caught at compile time.

If a type library is not explicitly referred to, there are two ways in which to identify a COM component: by **class ID**, which is a GUID, and by **ProgID**, which is a string and looks like "MyProject.MyComponent". These are all cross-referenced in the registry. In fact, COM makes extensive use of the registry to maintain links between applications, their components, and their interfaces. All experienced COM programmers know their way around the registry blindfold.

VB6 has a lot of COM features embedded into it, to the extent that many VB6 programmers aren't even aware that they are developing COM components; for instance, if you create a DLL containing an instance of a VB6 class, you will in fact have created a COM object without even asking for one. We'll see how easy this is during the course of this chapter.

There are clearly similarities between COM and .NET. So, all we've got to do to make them work together is put a wrapper around a COM object to make it into an assembly, and vice versa – isn't it? Well, it turns out that that isn't far away from the truth…

COM and .NET in Practice

It's time to get serious and see if all this seamless integration really works. In order to do this, we're going to have to simulate a legacy situation. Let's imagine that our enterprise depends on a particular COM object that was written for us a long time ago by a wayward genius, who subsequently abandoned software development and has gone to live in a monastery in Tibet. Anyway, all we know is that the code works perfectly and we need it for our .NET application.

We have one, or possibly two, options here. If we have the source (which is not necessarily the case) and we have sufficient time (or, to put it another way, money), we can upgrade the object to .NET and continue to maintain it under VS.NET. For the purist, this is the ideal solution for going forward, and there are some tips on how to do this at the end of this chapter. However, maintaining the source as it is under VS.NET isn't really a viable option; VS.NET does offer an upgrade path, but it doesn't cope well with COM objects using interfaces specified as abstract classes.

If upgrading to .NET isn't an option, all we can do is simply take the DLL for our COM object, register it on our .NET machine, and use the .NET interoperability tools. This is the path that we're going to take in this section.

So what we need is a genuine legacy COM object, and what we're going to have to use is genuine legacy VB6. For the next section, then, we're going to be using VB6. If you've already disposed of VB6, or never had it in the first place, feel free to skip this section. The DLL is available as part of the download, in any case.

A Legacy Component

For our legacy component, we're going to imagine that we have some kind of analytics engine that requires a number of calculations. Because of the highly complex nature of these calculations, their development has been given to specialists, while the user interface for the application has been given to UI specialists. A COM interface has been specified that all calculations must conform to. This interface has the name `IMegaCalc` and has the following methods:

Method	Description
`Sub AddInput (InputValue as Double)`	Add input value to calculation
`Sub DoCalculation ()`	Do calculation
`Function GetOutput () as Double`	Get output from calculation
`Sub Reset ()`	Reset calculation for next time

Step 1: Defining the Interface

The first thing we have to do is define our interface. In VB6, the way to do this is to create an abstract class, that is, one without any implementation. So, let's create an ActiveX DLL project called `MegaCalculator`. Within this, we'll create a class called `IMegaCalc`. This is what the code looks like:

```
Option Explicit

Public Sub AddInput(InputValue As Double)

End Sub

Public Sub DoCalculation()

End Sub

Public Function GetOutput() As Double

End Function

Public Sub Reset()

End Sub
```

From the main menu, select File | Make MegaCalculator.dll and we've got our interface defined and registered.

Step 2: Implementing Our Component

For the purposes of this demonstration, the actual calculation that we're going to perform is going to be fairly mundane: in fact, we're going to calculate the mean of a series of numbers. So let's create another ActiveX DLL project, called MeanCalculator this time. We need to add a reference to the type library for the interface that we're going to implement, so select the **MegaCalculator** DLL via the References dialog that appears when you select Project | References.

Having done that, we can go ahead and write the code for the mean calculation. We do this in a class called MeanCalc:

```
Option Explicit

Implements IMegaCalc

Dim mintValue As Integer
Dim mdblValues() As Double
Dim mdblMean As Double

Private Sub Class_Initialize()
    IMegaCalc_Reset
End Sub

Private Sub IMegaCalc_AddInput(InputValue As Double)
    mintValue = mintValue + 1
    ReDim Preserve mdblValues(mintValue)
    mdblValues(mintValue) = InputValue
End Sub

Private Sub IMegaCalc_DoCalculation()
Dim iValue As Integer

    mdblMean = 0#

    If (mintValue = 0) Then Exit Sub

    For iValue = 1 To mintValue
```

```
        mdblMean = mdblMean + mdblValues(iValue)
    Next iValue

    mdblMean = mdblMean / mintValue

End Sub

Private Function IMegaCalc_GetOutput() As Double
    IMegaCalc_GetOutput = mdblMean
End Function

Private Sub IMegaCalc_Reset()
    mintValue = 0
End Sub
```

As before, we select File | Make MeanCalculator.dll, and we've got our component built and registered. It has a default interface called MeanCalc (which contains no methods, and is thus invisible to the naked eye), plus an implementation of IMegaCalc. Notice that, if you leave out any of the methods that are required to implement the IMegaCalc interface, you will get a compile error when you attempt to make the DLL; the implementation must be complete.

Our first VB6 interlude is over.

Step 3: Registering Our Legacy Component

We now have our legacy component. If we're developing our new .NET application on the same machine, we don't need to do anything more, because our component will already have been registered by the build process. However, if we're working on an entirely new machine, we'll need to register it there. The easiest way to do this is to open up a command box, and register it, like this:

And we should see this result:

Because MeanCalculator implements an interface from MegaCalculator, we'll also have to repeat the trick with that DLL. We're now ready to use our component from a .NET application.

The .NET Application

For our .NET application, all we're going to do is instantiate a `MeanCalc` object, and get it to work out a mean for us. So let's create a Windows Application project in VB.NET called `CalcApp`. This is what the form looks like:

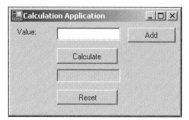

The two textboxes are called `txtInput` and `txtOutput` respectively; the second one is not enabled for user input. The three command buttons are `btnAdd`, `btnCalculate`, and `btnReset` respectively.

Referencing the Legacy Component

Before we dive into writing the code behind those buttons, we need to make our new application aware of the `MeanCalculator` component. So we have to add a reference to it, via the **Project | Add Reference** menu item. This brings up a dialog with three tabs: .NET, COM, and Projects. Select **MeanCalculator** and **MegaCalculator** from the **COM** tab:

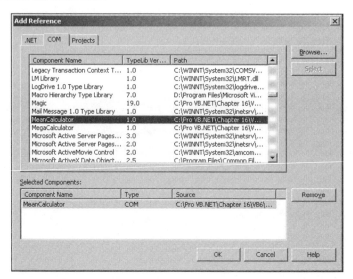

Now hit the **OK** button:

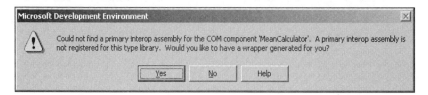

Whoops! What's that all about? Actually, this is good news, because what it means is that VS.NET is actually doing some of the hard work for us. What it's doing is automatically creating a **primary interop assembly**. This is a .NET assembly that effectively wraps the COM DLL and re-presents it for use by .NET applications. So you should click on the Yes button to confirm that you want this to happen.

Notice that, in the list of references in the Solution Explorer, we can now see both MeanCalculator and MegaCalculator:

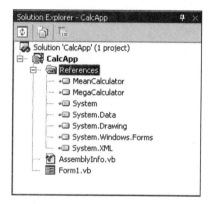

Inside the .NET Application

Now that we've successfully got our component referenced, we can go ahead and finish coding up our application. First of all, we add a global variable (mobjMean) to hold a reference to an instance of the mean calculation component:

```
Public Class Form1
    Inherits System.Windows.Forms.Form

    Dim mobjMean As MeanCalculator.MeanCalc
```

Next, we need to open up the section labeled Windows Form Designer generated code, and add the following instruction to New:

```
Public Sub New()
    MyBase.New()

    'This call is required by the Windows Form Designer.
InitializeComponent()

    'Add any initialization after the InitializeComponent() call

    mobjMean = New MeanCalculator.MeanCalc()

End Sub
```

This is where we actually create the component that we're going to use.

Finally, we need to add the code behind the buttons. First of all, the Add button:

```
Private Sub btnAdd_Click(ByVal sender As Object, _
        ByVal e As System.EventArgs) _
```

525

```
              Handles btnAdd.Click
        mobjMean.AddInput(CDbl(txtInput.Text))
    End Sub
```

All we're doing here is adding whatever's in the input textbox into the list of numbers for the calculation. Next, here's the code behind the `Calculate` button:

```
Private Sub btnCalculate_Click(ByVal sender As Object, _
            ByVal e As System.EventArgs) Handles btnCalculate.Click
    mobjMean.DoCalculation()
    txtOutput.Text = mobjMean.GetOutput()
End Sub
```

This performs the calculation, retrieves the answer, and puts it into the output textbox. Finally, the code behind the `Reset` button simply resets the calculation:

```
Private Sub btnReset_Click(ByVal sender As Object, _
            ByVal e As System.EventArgs) Handles btnReset.Click
    mobjMean.Reset()
End Sub
```

Trying It All Out

Of course, the proof of the pudding is in the eating, so let's see what happens when we run it. First of all, let's put one value in, say 2, and click on **Add**. Now enter another value, say 3, and click on **Add** once more. When you click on **Calculate**, you'll get the mean of the two values (2.5 in this case):

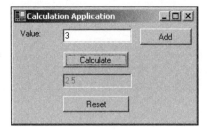

Using TlbImp Directly

Some of you may have found that slightly unsatisfactory. Are we really going to go through that process of creating a default interop assembly every time we add a reference to `MeanCalculator`? Wouldn't it be better if we did it just once and for all? The answer is that we can do just that.

The process that creates the default interop assembly on behalf of VS.NET is called `TlbImp.exe`. The name stands for **Type Library Import**, and that's pretty much what it does. It comes as part of the .NET Framework SDK, and you might find it convenient to extend the `PATH` environment variable to include the `\bin` directory of the .NET Framework SDK.

`TlbImp` takes a COM DLL as its input and generates a .NET assembly DLL as its output. By default, the .NET assembly has the same name as the type library, which will – in the case of VB6 components – always be the same as the COM DLL. This means that we'll have to explicitly specify a different output file. We do this by using the `/out:` switch. So that we can see what's going on at each step in the process, we'll also specify `/verbose`:

```
tlbimp MeanCalculator.dll /out:MeanCalculatorNet.dll /verbose
```

Let's see what happens:

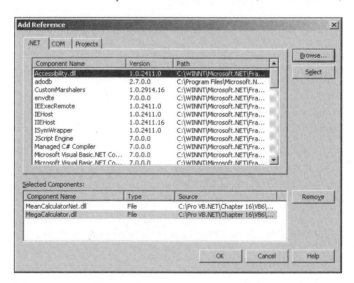

Notice that `Tlbimp` has encountered a reference to another COM type library, `MegaCalculator`, and it has very kindly imported that one as well. Note that the imported DLL retains the name `MegaCalculator.dll`. This means that if you happen to be storing both DLLs in the same place, `Tlbimp` is going to find itself attempting to overwrite the COM version of `MegaCalculator.dll` with the .NET one (it won't actually do this, by the way, and the import will fail). The way around this is to explicitly run `Tlbimp` on `MegaCalculator` first, specifying `MegaCalculatorNet.dll` as your output.

Referencing Imported DLLs

Having converted our COM DLLs into .NET assemblies, let's see what happens when we reference them in an application. Instead of selecting the COM tab from the Add Reference dialog, we select the .NET tab. We then need to browse to find the assembly DLLs in the usual manner, and select them, thus:

Notice that this time around, we had to add references to *both* components.

This is what we add to the code for our form this time:

```
Public Class Form1
    Inherits System.Windows.Forms.Form

    Dim mobjMean As MeanCalculatorNet.MeanCalc
```

And this is how we instantiate it:

```
Public Sub New()
    MyBase.New()

    'This call is required by the Windows Form Designer.
    InitializeComponent()

    'Add any initialization after the InitializeComponent() call

    mobjMean = New MeanCalculatorNet.MeanCalc()

End Sub
```

The only difference from the previous version of the code is that we're explicitly referencing the .NET wrapper that we've created using `TlbImp`, rather than referencing the COM object.

Late-Binding

We've seen that we can successfully do early-binding on COM components within a .NET application. But what if we want to do late-binding? What if we don't have access to a type library at application development time? Can we still make use of the COM components? Does the .NET equivalent of late-binding even exist?

The answer is that, yes, it does, but, no, it's nothing like as transparent as with VB6. The extent of the understatement in that last sentence will soon become clear.

Let's take a look at what we used to do in VB6. If we wanted to do early-binding, what we would do is this:

```
Dim myObj As MyObj
Set myObj = New MyObj ' or Set myObj = CreateObject (•MyLibrary.MyObject•)

MyObj.MyMethod (...)
```

For late-binding, it would look like this instead:

```
Dim myObj as Object
Set myObj = new MyObj ' or Set myObj = CreateObject (•MyLibrary.MyObject•)

MyObj.MyMethod (...)
```

There's actually an enormous amount of stuff going on under the covers here; if you're interested in looking into this further, try *VB COM: Visual Basic 6 Programmer's Introduction to COM* (Wrox Press, ISBN 1861002130).

An Example for Late-Binding

For our sample, let's extend the calculator to a more generic framework that can feed inputs into a number of different calculation modules rather than just the fixed one. We'll keep a table in memory of calculation ProgIDs and present the user with a combo box to select the right one.

The Sample COM Object

The first problem we encounter with late-binding is that you can only late-bind to the default interface, which in our case is `MeanCalculator.MeanCalc`, not `MeanCalculator.IMegaCalc`. So we're going to have to re-develop our COM object as a stand-alone library, with no references to other interfaces.

As before, we'll build a DLL under VB6, copy it over to our .NET environment and re-register it there. We'll call this VB6 DLL `MeanCalculator2.dll`, and the code in the class (called `MeanCalc`) should look like this:

```
Option Explicit

Dim mintValue As Integer
Dim mdblValues() As Double
Dim mdblMean As Double

Private Sub Class_Initialize()
    Reset
End Sub

Public Sub AddInput(InputValue As Double)
mintValue = mintValue + 1
    ReDim Preserve mdblValues(mintValue)
    mdblValues(mintValue) = InputValue
End Sub

Public Sub DoCalculation()
Dim iValue As Integer

    mdblMean = 0#

    If (mintValue = 0) Then Exit Sub

    For iValue = 1 To mintValue
        mdblMean = mdblMean + mdblValues(iValue)
    Next iValue

    mdblMean = mdblMean / mintValue

End Sub

Public Function GetOutput() As Double
    GetOutput = mdblMean
End Function

Public Sub Reset()
    mintValue = 0
End Sub
```

As before, we'll need to move this across to our .NET machine and register it using `RegSvr32`.

The Calculation Framework

For our generic calculation framework, we'll create a new application in VB.NET called `CalcFrame`. We'll basically use the same dialog as last time, but with an extra combo box at the top:

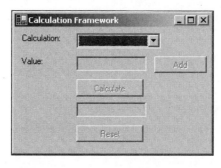

The new combo box is called `cmbCalculation`. We've also disabled the controls `txtInput`, `btnAdd`, `btnCalculate`, and `btnReset`, until we know if the selected calculation is valid.
We'll start off by importing the `Reflection` namespace; we'll need this for handing all the late-binding:

```
Imports System.Reflection
```

Then we add a few member variables:

```
Public Class Form1
    Inherits System.Windows.Forms.Form

        Private mstrObjects() As String
        Private mnObject As Integer
        Private mtypCalc As Type
        Private mobjCalc As Object
```

Next, we need to add a few lines to New:

```
Public Sub New()
    MyBase.New()

    'This call is required by the Windows Form Designer.
    InitializeComponent()

    'Add any initialization after the InitializeComponent() call

    mnObject = 0
    AddObject("Mean", "MeanCalculator2.MeanCalc")
    AddObject("StdDev", "StddevCalculator.StddevCalc")

    If (mnObject > 0) Then
        cmbCalculation.SelectedIndex = 0
    End If

End Sub
```

What we're doing here is building up a list of calculations. Once we've finished, we select the first one in the list. Let's just take a look at that subroutine `AddObject`:

```
Private Sub AddObject(ByVal strName As String, ByVal strObject As String)
    cmbCalculation.Items.Add(strName)
    mnObject = mnObject + 1
    ReDim Preserve mstrObjects(mnObject)
    mstrObjects(mnObject - 1) = strObject
End Sub
```

Here, we're adding the calculation name to the combo box and its ProgID to an array of strings. Neither of these is sorted, so we get a one-to-one mapping between them.

Let's see what happens when we select a calculation via the combo box:

```
Private Sub cmbCalculation_SelectedIndexChanged(ByVal sender As Object, _
        ByVal e As System.EventArgs) _
```

```
            Handles cmbCalculation.SelectedIndexChanged
    Dim intIndex As Integer
        Dim bEnabled As Boolean

        intIndex = cmbCalculation.SelectedIndex
        mtypCalc = Type.GetTypeFromProgID(mstrObjects(intIndex))

        If (mtypCalc Is Nothing) Then
            mobjCalc = Nothing
            bEnabled = False
        Else
            mobjCalc = Activator.CreateInstance(mtypCalc)
            bEnabled = True
        End If

        txtInput.Enabled = bEnabled
        btnAdd.Enabled = bEnabled
        btnCalculate.Enabled = bEnabled
        btnReset.Enabled = bEnabled

    End Sub
```

There are two key calls here. The first is to `Type.GetTypeFromProgID`. This takes the incoming ProgID string and converts it to a `Type` object. This may either succeed or fail; if it fails, we disable all controls and let the user try again. If it succeeds, however, we go on to create an instance of the object described by the type. We do this in the call to the static method `Activator.CreateInstance`.

So let's assume that our user has selected a calculation that we can successfully instantiate. What next? The next thing is that the user enters a number and clicks on the **Add** button. This is what happens:

```
    Private Sub btnAdd_Click(ByVal sender As Object, _
            ByVal e As System.EventArgs) Handles btnAdd.Click
        Dim objArgs() As Object
        objArgs = New Object(0) {CDbl(txtInput.Text)}
        mtypCalc.InvokeMember("AddInput", BindingFlags.InvokeMethod, _
                        Nothing, mobjCalc, objArgs)
    End Sub
```

The important call here is to `InvokeMember`. Let's take a closer look. There are five parameters here:

❑   The first parameter is the name of the method that we want to call: `AddInput` in this case. So instead of going directly to the location of the routine in memory, we ask the .NET run-time to find it for us.

❑   The value from the `BindingFlags` enumeration tells it that we want it to invoke a method for us.

❑   The next parameter is to provide language-specific binding information, which isn't needed in this case.

❑   The fourth parameter is a reference to the COM object itself (the one that we instantiated using `Activator.CreateInstance` above).

❑   Finally, the fifth parameter is an array of objects representing the arguments for the method. In this case, there's only one argument: the input value.

Something very similar to this is going on underneath VB6 late-binding, except that here it's exposed to us in all its horror. In some ways, that's no bad thing, because it should bring it home to you that late-binding is something to avoid if at all possible. Anyway, let's carry on and complete the program. Here are the remaining event handlers:

```
Private Sub btnCalculate_Click(ByVal sender As Object, _
           ByVal e As System.EventArgs) Handles btnCalculate.Click
    Dim objResult As Object
    mtypCalc.InvokeMember("DoCalculation", BindingFlags.InvokeMethod, _
                     Nothing, mobjCalc, Nothing)
    objResult = mtypCalc.InvokeMember("GetOutput", _
             BindingFlags.InvokeMethod, Nothing, mobjCalc, Nothing)
    txtOutput.Text = objResult
End Sub

Private Sub btnReset_Click(ByVal sender As Object, _
           ByVal e As System.EventArgs) Handles btnReset.Click
    mtypCalc.InvokeMember("Reset", BindingFlags.InvokeMethod, _
                     Nothing, mobjCalc, Nothing)
End Sub
```

Running the Calculation Framework

OK, let's quickly complete the job by running the application. Here's what happens when we select the non-existent calculation StdDev:

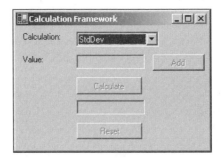

And here's what happens when we repeat our earlier calculation using **Mean**:

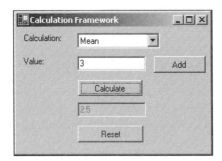

One final word about late-binding. We took care to ensure that we checked to see that the object was successfully instantiated. In a real-life application, we would also need to take care that the method invocations were successful, ensuring that all exceptions were caught. We don't have the luxury of having the compiler find our bugs for us!

ActiveX Controls

Let's move on from basic COM objects to ActiveX controls. These are still COM objects, with the crucial extension that they have to implement a whole further set of interfaces relating to user interface characteristics. We're going to do pretty much the same as we did with the basic COM component (apart from late-binding, which has no relevance to ActiveX controls) – build a legacy control using VB6 and then import it into a VB.NET project.

A Legacy ActiveX Control

For our legacy control, we're going to build a simple button-like object that is capable of interpreting a mouse click and can be one of two colors according to its state. We do this by taking a second foray into VB6; once again, if you don't have VB6 handy, feel free to skip the next section, download the OCX file, and pick it up when we start developing our .NET application.

Step 1: Create the Control

This time, we need to create an ActiveX Control project. We'll call the project Magic, and the control class MagicButton, so as to give a proper impression of its remarkable powers. From the toolbox, we select a Shape control and place it on the UserControl form that VB6 provides us with. Rename the shape to shpButton, and change its properties as follows:

Property	Value
FillStyle	0 – Solid
Shape	4 – Rounded Rectangle
FillColor	Gray (&H008F8F8F&)

Add a label on top of the shape control and rename this to lblText. Change its properties as follows:

Property	Value
BackStyle	0 – Transparent
Alignment	2 – Center

Switch to the code view of MagicButton.

Now we need to add two properties called Caption and State, and an event called Click, as well as code to handle the initialization of the properties and persisting them, to ensure that the shape resizes correctly and that the label is centered. We also need to handle mouse clicks. The code in MagicButton should look like this:

```
Option Explicit

Public Event Click()

Dim mintState As Integer

Public Property Get Caption() As String
    Caption = lblText.Caption
End Property
```

```
Public Property Let Caption(ByVal vNewValue As String)
    lblText.Caption = vNewValue
    PropertyChanged ("Caption")
End Property

Public Property Get State() As Integer
    State = mintState
End Property

Public Property Let State(ByVal vNewValue As Integer)
    mintState = vNewValue
    PropertyChanged ("State")

    If (State = 0) Then
        shpButton.FillColor = &HFFFFFF&
    Else
        shpButton.FillColor = &H8F8F8F&
    End If
End Property

Private Sub UserControl_InitProperties()
    Caption = Extender.Name
    State = 1
End Sub

Private Sub UserControl_ReadProperties(PropBag As PropertyBag)
    Caption = PropBag.ReadProperty("Caption", Extender.Name)
    State = PropBag.ReadProperty("State", 1)
End Sub

Private Sub UserControl_WriteProperties(PropBag As PropertyBag)
    PropBag.WriteProperty "Caption", lblText.Caption
    PropBag.WriteProperty "State", mintState
End Sub

Private Sub UserControl_Resize()
    shpButton.Move 0, 0, ScaleWidth, ScaleHeight
    lblText.Move 0, (ScaleHeight - lblText.Height) / 2, ScaleWidth
End Sub

Private Sub lblText_Click()
    RaiseEvent Click
End Sub

Private Sub UserControl_MouseUp(Button As Integer, Shift As Integer, _
                                X As Single, Y As Single)
    RaiseEvent Click
End Sub
```

If we build this, we'll get an ActiveX control called `Magic.ocx`.

Step 2: Registering Our Legacy Control

We now have our legacy control. As before, if we're developing our new .NET application on the same machine, we don't need to do anything more, because our control will already have been registered by the build process. However, if we're working on an entirely new machine, we'll need to register it there. As before, we need to open up a command box and register it, like this:

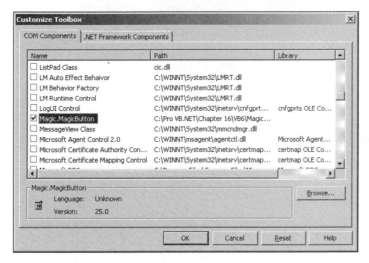

Having done that, we're ready to build our .NET application.

A .NET Application, Again

This .NET application is going to be even more straightforward than the last one. All we're going to do this time is show a button that will change color whenever the user clicks on it. Let's create a Windows Application project in VB.NET called ButtonApp. Before we start to develop it, however, we need to extend the toolbox to incorporate our new control. We do this via the Tools | Customize Toolbox menu item:

When we click on the OK button, we can see that our magic button class is now available to us in the toolbox. Let's add one to our form:

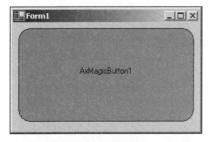

Notice that references to AxMagic and Magic have just been added to the project, in the Solution Explorer window. All we need to do now is initialize the Caption property to ON, change the Text of the form to Button Application, and code up a handler for the mouse click event:

```
Private Sub AxMagicButton1_Click(ByVal sender As System.Object, _
        ByVal e As System.EventArgs) Handles AxMagicButton1.ClickEvent
```

```
        AxMagicButton1.State = 1 - AxMagicButton1.State
        If (AxMagicButton1.State = 0) Then
            AxMagicButton1.Caption = "OFF"
        Else
            AxMagicButton1.Caption = "ON"
        End If
    End Sub
```

Trying It All Out, Again

So what happens when we run this one? First of all we see this:

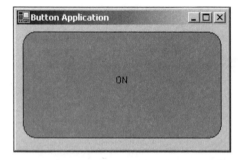

And if we click on the control, it changes to this:

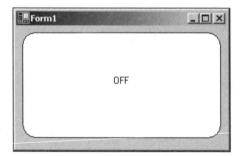

Using .NET Components in the COM World

So, we've established beyond all doubt that we can use our COM legacy components in the brave new .NET world. We don't have to throw everything out *quite* yet. It's now time to consider the opposite question: can we run .NET components in the COM world?

Actually, the question we should first be asking is probably this one: why on earth should we want to run .NET components in the COM world? It's not immediately obvious, in fact, because migration to .NET would almost certainly be application-led in most cases, rather than component-led. However, it's possible (just) to imagine a situation where a particularly large application remains unmigrated while component development moves over to .NET. Well, let's pretend that that's the case for the next section. The technology's quite cool, anyway.

A .NET Component

Let's take a look at our definitely non-legacy component. We'll implement an exact copy of the functionality that we did earlier with MegaCalculator and MeanCalculator, except using VB.NET rather than VB6. If it gets boring, you can amuse yourselves by playing "spot the difference".

Start off by creating a Class Library project called MegaCalculator2. This is the entire code of the class library:

```
Public Interface IMegaCalc

    Sub AddInput(ByVal InputValue As Double)

    Sub DoCalculation()

    Function GetResult() As Double

    Sub Reset()

End Interface
```

As we saw in Chapter 12, this is how we declare our interfaces in VB.NET.

Next, we create another Class Library project, called MeanCalculator3. This will contain a class called MeanCalc that is going to implement the IMegaCalc interface, in a precise analogue of the MeanCalc in our original VB6 MeanCalculator project. As before, we'll need to add a reference to MegaCalculator2 first.

This is what the code looks like:

```
Public Class MeanCalc
    Implements MegaCalculator2.IMegaCalc

    Dim mintValue As Integer
    Dim mdblValues() As Double
    Dim mdblMean As Double

    Public Sub AddInput(ByVal InputValue As Double) _
            Implements MegaCalculator2.IMegaCalc.AddInput
        mintValue = mintValue + 1
        ReDim Preserve mdblValues(mintValue)
        mdblValues(mintValue - 1) = InputValue
    End Sub

    Public Sub DoCalculation() Implements _
            MegaCalculator2.IMegaCalc.DoCalculation
        Dim iValue As Integer

        mdblMean = 0

        If (mintValue = 0) Then Exit Sub

        For iValue = 0 To mintValue - 1 Step 1
            mdblMean = mdblMean + mdblValues(iValue)
        Next iValue

        mdblMean = mdblMean / iValue

    End Sub
```

```
      Public Function GetResult() As Double Implements _
                      MegaCalculator2.IMegaCalc.GetResult
          GetResult = mdblMean
      End Function

      Public Sub Reset() Implements MegaCalculator2.IMegaCalc.Reset
          mintValue = 0
      End Sub

      Public Sub New()
          Reset()
      End Sub

  End Class
```

This is all quite similar to the VB6 version, apart from the way in which `Implements` is used. Let's build the assembly.

Now we come to the interesting part: how do we register the resulting assembly so that a COM-enabled application can make use of it?

RegAsm

The tool provided with the .NET Framework SDK to register assemblies for use by COM is called `RegAsm`. You'll need to check with your documentation to find out where it's located and change your path accordingly, as it's not in the same place as the other three tools. Perhaps they don't get on.

`RegAsm` is very simple to use. If all you're interested in is late-binding, then you simply run it like this:

However, there's probably even less reason for late-binding to an exported .NET component than there is for early-binding, so we'll move on to look at early-binding. For this, we need a type library, so we need to add another parameter:

If we now take a look in our target directory, we see that not only do we have the original MeanCalculator3.dll, but we've also acquired a copy of the MegaCalculator2.dll and two type libraries: MeanCalculator3.tlb and MegaCalculator2.tlb. We'll need both of these, so it was good of RegAsm to provide them for us. We need the MegaCalculator2 type library for the same reason as .NET needed the MegaCalculator assembly: because it contains the definition of the IMegaCalc interface that MeanCalculator is using.

Testing with a VB6 Application

Turning the tables again, we need to build a VB6 application to see if this is really going to work. Let's copy the type libraries over to our pre-.NET machine (if that's where VB6 is running) and create a Standard EXE project in VB6. We'll call this CalcApp2. We'll need to create references to our two new type libraries, so we go to the References dialog and select them:

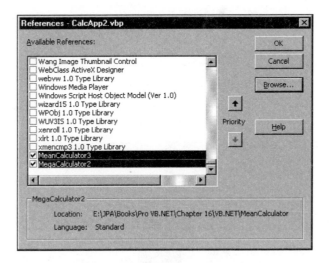

Now we've got all we need to create our application. Let's create the same form that we did for the VB.NET CalcApp:

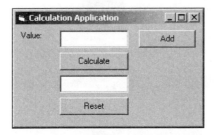

As before, the text boxes are txtInput and txtOutput, respectively, and the command buttons are btnAdd, btnCalculate, and btnReset.

And here's the code behind it:

```
Option Explicit

Dim mobjCalc As MeanCalculator3.MeanCalc
Dim mobjMega As MegaCalculator2.ImegaCalc
```

```
Private Sub btnAdd_Click()
mobjMega.AddInput (txtInput.Text)
End Sub

Private Sub btnCalculate_Click()
    mobjMega.DoCalculation
    txtOutput.Text = mobjMega.GetResult
End Sub

Private Sub btnReset_Click()
    mobjMega.Reset
End Sub

Private Sub Form_Load()
    Set mobjCalc = New MeanCalculator3.MeanCalc
    Set mobjMega = mobjCalc
End Sub
```

Notice that, this time, we have to explicitly get hold of a reference to the interface `IMegaCalc`. The default interface of the component, `MeanCalc`, is entirely empty.

We make the executable via the File | Make CalcApp2.exe menu item, and then we can move it back to our .NET machine (unless, of course, we're already there). Let's run it up and see what happens:

Well, that's not *quite* what we expected. What's happened here?

In COM, the location of the DLL containing the component is available via the registry. In .NET, the assembly always has to be either in the current directory or the global assembly. All the registry is doing for us here is converting a COM reference to a .NET one; it's not finding the .NET one for us.

But it's easy to sort out. All we have to do to resolve matters is move the two assemblies, for `MegaCalculator` and `MeanCalculator`, to our current directory, and try again:

That's better.

So we've established that – in the unlikely event of having to run .NET from a COM-oriented application – Microsoft has provided us with the tools.

TlbExp

In fact, Microsoft has provided us with not one, but *two* alternative tools. The other one is TlbExp, which – as its name suggests – is the counterpart of TlbImp. This is how we can use TlbExp to achieve the same result as RegAsm in the previous section:

```
C:\WINNT\System32\cmd.exe                                              _ □ ×
C:\>TlbExp "Pro VB.NET\Chapter 16\VB.NET\MeanCalculator3\bin\MeanCalculator3.dll
" /out:MeanCalculator3.tlb
TlbExp - .NET Assembly to Type Library Converter Version 1.0.2914.16
Copyright (C) Microsoft Corp. 2001.  All rights reserved.

Assembly exported to C:\MeanCalculator3.tlb

C:\>
```

Well, nearly the same. The only difference is where the type library ends up.

Summary

COM isn't going to go away for quite some time yet, so .NET applications have to interoperate with COM, and they have to do it well. In this chapter, we have looked at how all this works in practice.

- ❑ We managed to make a .NET application early-bind to a COM component, using the import features available in VB.NET.

- ❑ We looked at the underlying tool, Tlbimp.

- ❑ We managed to make it late-bind as well, although it wasn't a pleasant experience.

- ❑ We incorporated an ActiveX control into a .NET user interface, again using the features of VB.NET.

- ❑ We looked at using Regasm and TlbExp to export type libraries from .NET assemblies, so as to enable VB6 applications to use .NET assemblies as if they were COM components.

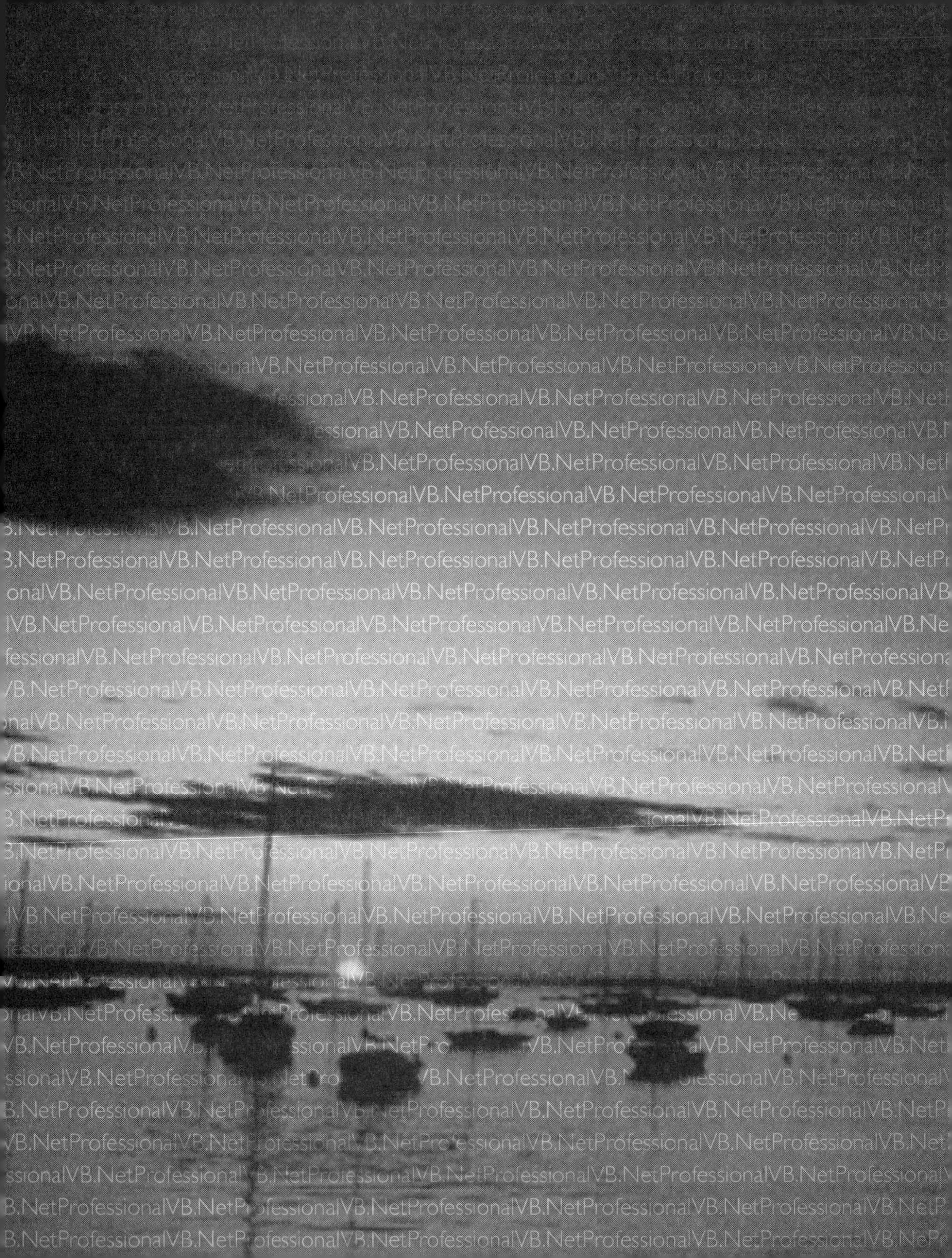
VB.NetProfessional

17

Component Services

In the previous chapter, we explored the vast hinterland of legacy software known as COM. We're now going to look at "What COM Did Next" and how that fits into the world of .NET, in the shape of **.NET Component Services**. You could be forgiven for thinking that Component Services is yet another version of legacy software, except that much of it hasn't been around for long enough to be considered as legacy. However, there is more to it than that. The end result is something of a compromise between the old COM world and .NET.

To understand Component Services, we need to go back in time to around 1997. Microsoft had, by this time, become by far the dominant supplier to the PC market, and was looking for something else to do. The obvious thing was to move into the enterprise server market, and a number of initiatives began to emerge from Redmond during this time. Among these, in no particular order, were **Microsoft Transaction Server** (codenamed Viper), **Microsoft Message Queue** (codenamed Falcon), and **Microsoft Clustering Services** (codenamed Wolfpack). The aim of every single one of these developments was to bring something that had previously been esoteric, specialized, and generally mainframe-based within the scope of standard PC technology. Indeed, MTS is now part of every single Windows 2000 installation, while MSMQ is an optional extra that comes free with the installation kit. The point was made strongly that transactions are, indeed, a part of everyday life, even when we hadn't previously seen them.

Handling transactions involved a considerable extension to the NT/COM runtime, for one thing. It also involved the introduction of several new standard COM interfaces: some to be used or implemented by transactional components, and some to be used or implemented by the underlying resource managers, such as SQL Server. These additions, along with some other innovations relating to areas like asynchronous COM, came to be known as **COM+**.

When .NET came along, there must have been considerable debate as to whether this vast infrastructure should be completely re-implemented within .NET or whether it should be tacked onto the side. In the event, Redmond pragmatism seems to have won the day because, under .NET, the **Component Services** (as they have been renamed) sit slightly uneasily between pure .NET and the kind of legacy COM stuff that we saw in the previous chapter. The end result is perfectly acceptable from an operational point of view, but it's a moot point as to how elegant all this really is.

In this chapter, then, we're going to explore the .NET Component Services. In particular, we're going to look at transaction processing and queued components. We should perhaps point out that this is an enormous subject, and one that could easily fill a whole book by itself. In this chapter, we will only be able to scratch the surface of it. However, by the end of the chapter, you should have a reasonable understanding at least of how all the various pieces fit together. Let's start by looking at what transactions are, and how they fit into VB.NET.

Transactions

A transaction is one or more linked units of processing placed together as a single unit of work, which either succeeds or fails. If the unit of work succeeds, the work is then committed. However, if the unit fails, then every item of processing is rolled back and the process is placed back to its original state. The standard example taken from the world of commerce usually involves transferring money from account A to account B. The money must either end up in account B (and nowhere else), or – if something goes wrong – stay in account A (and go nowhere else). Here are a few more examples that help to explain how transactions work:

❑ Software change control. Each new version of a software package potentially involves changes to several of the underlying source files. The new version is only defined when every single one of the changes has been successfully made.

❑ Arranging a doubles tennis match. A time must be agreed when all four players can be there. If only three can turn up, it won't be much of a game. The actual transaction may fail many times before a mutually convenient time is agreed.

❑ Almost any military maneuver involving more than one unit.

❑ Taking off in an airplane. This involves an enormous number of elements. For example, all the fuel must be on board, all the doors must be closed, air traffic control must have granted clearance, all the baggage must be on, and so on.

Most electronic transactions are, inevitably, to do with commerce, and basically involve ensuring electronically that transfers of money, foreign exchange deals, and so on, do happen in a controlled manner with the minimum risk of something going wrong.

The ACID Test

Transaction theory starts with **ACID**. According to the ACID theory, all transactions should have the following properties:

❑ **Atomicity**: A transaction is **atomic**. However many different components the transaction involves, and however many different method calls on those components, the system treats it as *one single operation* which either entirely succeeds or entirely fails. If it fails, the system is left in the state as if the transaction had never happened.

- ❑ **Consistency**: All changes are done in a consistent manner. The system goes from one valid state to another.

- ❑ **Isolation**: Transactions that are going on at the same time are isolated from each other. If transaction A changes the system from state 1 to state 2, transaction B will see the system in *either* state 1 *or* 2, but *not* some half-baked state in between the two.

- ❑ **Durability**: If a transaction has been committed, the effect will be permanent, even if the system fails.

Let's illustrate this by a concrete example. We'll imagine that, having spent a happy afternoon browsing in your favorite bookstore, you decide to shell out some of your hard-earned dollars for a copy of – yes – *Professional VB.NET* (wise choice). You take the copy to the checkout, and you ask if they happen to have a less dog-eared one. A transaction is going on here: you pay money, and the store provides you with a book.

There are only two reasonable outcomes. Either you get the book and the store gets their money, or you don't get the book and the store don't get their money. If, for example, there is insufficient credit on your card, you'll walk out of the shop without the book. If, on the other hand, there are no more copies of the book in the stockroom, you don't hand over your card at all. In either case, the transaction doesn't happen at all. The only way for the transaction to complete is for you to get the book and the store to get their money. This is the principle of atomicity.

If, on the other hand, the store decides to provide you with a copy of, say, Neal Stephenson's *Cryptonomicon* instead, you might reasonably feel that you have ended up with an outcome that wasn't originally on the agenda. This would be a violation of the principle of consistency. (Actually, if I were you, I'd go for *Cryptonomicon*, but ask them to knock a dollar or two off the price.)

Let's now imagine that there is one copy of the book in the storeroom. However, another potential buyer has gone up to the till next to you. As far as the person at the next till is concerned, your respective transactions are isolated from each other (even though you are competing for the same resource). Either your transaction succeeds or the other person's does. What very definitely *doesn't* happen is that the bookstore decides to exert the wisdom of Solomon and give you half each.

Once you have taken the book home, let's imagine that the bookstore calls you up and asks you if they could have the book back. Apparently, someone important (well, far more important than you, anyway) needs a copy. You would feel that this was a tad unreasonable, and a violation of the principle of durability. Even if you were to go bankrupt the very next day after you left the store, they would have no claim on you.

At this point, it's worth considering what implications all this is likely to have on the underlying components. How on Earth can you ensure that all of the changes in the system can be unwound if the transaction is aborted at some point? Think about it – you're in the middle of updating heaven knows how many database files, and something goes wrong.

There are three aspects to rescuing this situation with transactions. First of all, we have to know that something has gone wrong. Secondly, we need to know how to perform the recovery. Thirdly, we need to co-ordinate the process of recovery. The middle part of the process is handled by the resource managers themselves – the likes of SQL Server and Oracle are fully equipped to deal with two-phase commit and rollback (even if the resource manager in question is re-started part-way through a transaction), and we don't need to worry about any of that. The last part of the process, co-ordination, is handled by the .NET runtime (or at least the Component Services part of it). The first part, knowing that something is wrong, is shared between the components themselves and the .NET runtime. This isn't at all unusual: sometimes a component can detect that something has gone wrong itself and signal that recovery is necessary while, on other occasions, it may not be able to do so, because it has crashed.

We'll see how all this works as we build our first transactional application. However, before we do that, we need to look at how transactions are implemented within .NET component services.

Transactional Components

But what actually are the components that are managed by Component Services? What purpose do they serve? To answer that, we need to consider what a typical real-world n-tier application looks like. The bottom tier is the persistent data store – typically an industry-standard database such as SQL Server or Oracle. The software here is concerned with maintaining the integrity of the application's data and providing rapid and efficient access to it. The top tier is the user interface. This is a completely different specialization, and the software here is concerned with presenting a smooth, easy to follow front-end to the end-user. This layer shouldn't actually do any data manipulation at all, apart from whatever formatting is necessary to meet each user's presentational needs. The interesting stuff is in the tiers in-between – in particular, the business logic. In the .NET/COM+ transactional model, the software elements that implement this are components running under the control of the Component Services runtime.

Typically, these components are called into being to perform some sort of transaction and then – to all intents and purposes – disappear again. For example, a component might be called into play to transfer information from one database to another in such a way that the information was either in one database or the other, but not both. This component might have a number of different methods, each of which did a different kind of transfer. However, each method call would carry out a complete transfer:

```
Public Sub TransferSomething()
    TakeSomethingFromA
    AddSomethingToB
End Sub
```

Crucially, this means that most transaction components have no concept of **state**: there are no properties that hold values between method calls. Persistence is left to the outside tiers in this model. This takes a little bit of getting used to at first, because it runs counter to everything that we learned in first grade object-orientation classes, so let's take a minute or two to consider what we're actually gaining from this. The business logic is the area of the system that requires all the transactional management. Anything that happens here needs to be monitored and controlled to ensure that all the ACID requirements are met. The neatest way to do this in a component-oriented framework is to develop the business logic as components that are required to implement a standard interface. The transaction management framework can then use this interface to monitor and control how the logic is implemented from a transactional point of view. The transaction interface is a means for the business logic elements to talk to the transaction framework and for the transaction framework to talk back to the logic elements.

So what's all this about not having state? Well, if we maintain state inside our components, then we've immediately got ourselves a scaling problem. The middle tiers of our application are now seriously resource-hungry. If you want an analogy from another area of software, consider why the Internet scales so well. The reason that it does is because HTTP is a stateless protocol. Every HTTP request stands in isolation, so no resources are tied up in maintaining any form of session. It's the same with transactional components.

This is not to say that you can't ever maintain state inside your transactional components, if you really, really want to. You can. However, it's not recommended, and we certainly won't be doing it in the examples in this chapter.

Before we move on into some practical examples, there's one other thing we need to talk about. We said earlier that transactional components are called into being, do their thing and then disappear again. This isn't the most efficient way of doing things, as instantiating a component takes a fair amount of effort. It would be better if we had a whole pool of components sitting there waiting to be used, and in fact it turns out that we can do just this. We'll see how it works in practice later on in the chapter.

It's about time for our first example!

Transactions: An Example

For our transaction example, we're going to build a simple business logic component that transfers data from one bank account (Wrox's in fact) to another one (mine, of course). Wrox's bank account will be represented by a row in one database (BankOfWrox), whilst mine will be represented by a row in another one (BankOfJon – it's kind of a sideline).

There's one important point that we should make right from the start. You can't have transactions without any resource managers. It's very tempting to think that you can experiment with transactional component services without actually involving, say, a database, because (as we shall see) none of the methods in the transactional classes makes any explicit references to one. However, if you do try to do this, you will find that your transactions don't actually trouble the system's statistics. Fortunately, you don't need to go out and lay out your hard-earned cash for a copy of SQL Server (nice though that is), because Visual Studio.NET comes with a stripped-down (but fully functional) copy of SQL Server, which goes under the name of **Microsoft Database Engine**, or **MSDE**.

Creating Our Databases

> **At the time of press, Enterprise Edition of VS.NET is needed in order to create the databases within VS.NET. If you do not have this edition, you will need to create the databases using SQL Server Enterprise Manager and then continue with the rest of the example.**

The first thing we have to do, then, is set up our databases. Move your cursor over the Server Explorer window, and see the start of a tree of servers. Your computer should be in there; open up this node, and you should see SQL Servers. Open this up, and you should see something like MYCOMPUTER\NETSDK. OK, you've found your SQL Server:

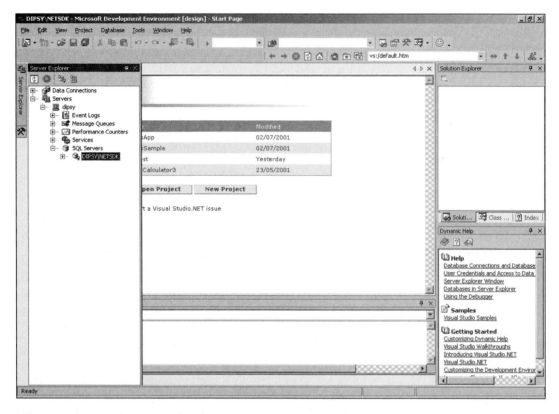

The next thing to do is right-click on this, and select New Database from the menu. You should see a dialog box like this appear:

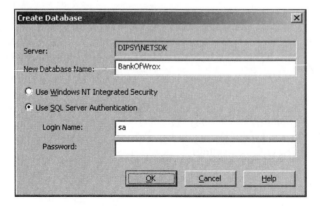

We enter our database name (BankOfWrox), and elect to use SQL Server Authentication (the login name provided with MSDE is sa, with no password).

You should now see BankOfWrox in the tree below MYCOMPUTER\NETSDK. The next thing to do is set up the database. If you open up the new node, you should see a number of other nodes, including Tables. Right-click on this, and select New Table from the menu. You should now see a dialog something like this:

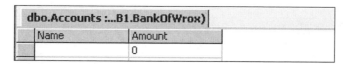

Create two columns, Name and Amount, as shown. Make sure that Amount is set up to be the primary key. When you click on the close box, you'll see a dialog like this:

As suggested, use the name Accounts for the table. You should now see a child node called Accounts below Tables in the tree.

OK, that's BankOfWrox created. We now repeat the whole process for BankOfJon. The structure is exactly the same, although it doesn't need to be for the purposes of this example.

Populating Our Databases

The next thing we need to do is populate our databases. If we right-click over Accounts, and select Retrieve Data from Table from the menu, we will see a grid which will enable us to add rows and initialize the values of their columns:

As will be seen, we have entered two accounts in BankOfWrox, Pro VB.NET and Pro XML 2e, and allocated $5000 to each. We repeat the process for BankOfJon, setting up one account, Jon, with $0 in it. (So Jon is either (a) broke or (b) wise enough not to leave any cash lying around in this sort of account. Go figure.)

The Business Logic

The next step is to create our transactional component to support our business logic. Create a new Class Library project called `TransSample`. Then add a reference to the `System.EnterpriseServices` namespace, thus:

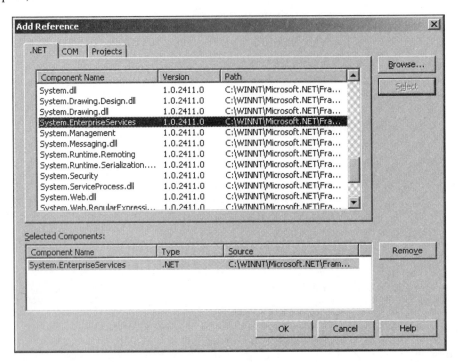

We're going to need this reference because, in order to come under the control of the Component Services runtime, our component needs to inherit from the `System.EnterpriseServices.ServicedComponent` class.

The Main Function

Here's the main function in our component, `TransferMoney`:

```
Imports System.EnterpriseServices

Public Class TransSample
    Inherits ServicedComponent

    Public Function TransferMoney(ByVal intDollars As Integer) As Boolean
        If TakeFromWrox(intDollars) = True Then
            If AddToJon(intDollars) = True Then
                ContextUtil.SetComplete()
                TransferMoney = True
            Else
                ContextUtil.SetAbort()
                TransferMoney = False
            End If
        Else
```

```
                ContextUtil.SetAbort()
                TransferMoney = False
           End If
    End Function
```

Let's take a look at that more closely. First of all, notice the `Imports` statement; that's ensuring that we have access to the `System.EnterpriseServices.ServicedComponent` class. Now, ignoring, for the moment, the references to `ContextUtil`, we can see that we have effectively divided up the logic into two halves: the half that takes money from the Wrox account (represented by the private function `TakeFromWrox`), and the half that adds it to Jon's account (represented by the private function `AddToJon`). For the function to complete successfully, each of the two halves must complete successfully as well.

So what does `ContextUtil` do? The `ContextUtil` class represents the context of the transaction. Within that context, there are basically two bits that control the behavior of the transaction from the point of view of each participant: the **consistent** bit and the **done** bit. The done bit determines whether or not the transaction is finished, so that resources can be re-used (we'll have more to say on this later, when we talk about Just-In-Time Activation and Object Pooling). The consistent bit determines whether or not the transaction was successful from the point of view of the participant. This is established during the first phase of the two-phase commit process. In complex distributed transactions involving more than one participant, the overall consistency and completeness are voted on, so that a transaction is only consistent or done when everyone agrees that it is. If a transaction completes in an inconsistent state, it is not allowed to proceed to the second phase of the commit.

In this case, we only have a single participant, but the principal remains the same: we can determine the overall outcome by setting these two bits, and we do this via `SetComplete` and `SetAbort`, which are static methods in the `ContextUtil` class. Both of these set the done bit to `True`. `SetComplete` also sets the consistent bit to `True`, whereas `SetAbort` sets the consistent bit to `False`. In our example, `SetComplete` is only set if both halves of the transaction are successful.

The First Half of the Transaction

Now let's see what's going on in the two halves of the transaction itself. First of all, here's the function that takes the money out of the Wrox account:

```
    Private Function TakeFromWrox(ByVal intDollars As Integer) As Boolean
        Dim strConn As String
        Dim strCmd As String

        Dim objConn As SqlClient.SqlConnection
        Dim objAdapter As SqlClient.SqlDataAdapter
        Dim objBuilder As SqlClient.SqlCommandBuilder

        Dim objDataset As DataSet
        Dim objTable As DataTable
        Dim objRow As DataRow


        Dim intBalance As Integer
```

We start off by establishing a connection to our database, and extracting the entire table from it. Note that you'll need to change your server name (unless it happens to be `DIPSY`, that is):

```
    strConn = "DATABASE=BankOfWrox;SERVER=DIPSY\NETSDK;UID=sa;PWD=;"
    strCmd = "Select * From Accounts"

    objConn = New SqlClient.SqlConnection(strConn)
    objAdapter = New SqlClient.SqlDataAdapter(strCmd, objConn)
    objBuilder = New SqlClient.SqlCommandBuilder(objAdapter)
```

The call to `SqlCommandBuilder` sets up the default SQL commands that will be used when we update the database. Next, we extract the row for Pro VB.NET into a `DataRow` object:

```
    objDataset = New DataSet()
    objAdapter.Fill(objDataset)

    objTable = objDataset.Tables(0)
    objRow = objTable.Rows(0)
```

We get the current balance, and see if we can afford to transfer the amount that we've asked for. If not, we set the result of the function to `False`:

```
    intBalance = CInt(objRow("Amount"))

    If intDollars > intBalance Then
        TakeFromWrox = False
```

Otherwise, we subtract the amount, and update the table accordingly, setting the result to `True`:

```
    Else
        intBalance = intBalance - intDollars

        objRow("Amount") = intBalance
        objAdapter.Update(objTable)

        TakeFromWrox = True
    End If
```

Finally, we close the database:

```
    objConn.Close()
End Function
```

The Second Half of the Transaction

The second half of the transaction is similar, except that the failure conditions are slightly different. First of all, Jon has stipulated that he doesn't want fiddly bits of loose change from Wrox, and so won't accept any transfer of less than $500. Secondly, we've inserted a bug such that an attempt to transfer a negative amount will cause a divide by zero. We'll see why we did this rather bizarre act of sabotage in a little while.

Here's the code:

```
    Private Function AddToJon(ByVal intDollars As Integer) As Boolean
        Dim strConn As String
        Dim strCmd As String

        Dim objConn As SqlClient.SqlConnection
        Dim objAdapter As SqlClient.SqlDataAdapter
        Dim objBuilder As SqlClient.SqlCommandBuilder

        Dim objDataset As DataSet
        Dim objTable As DataTable
        Dim objRow As DataRow

        Dim intBalance As Integer

        If intDollars < 0 Then
            intDollars = intDollars / 0
        ElseIf intDollars < 500 Then
            AddToJon = False
        Else
            strConn = "DATABASE=BankOfJon;SERVER=DIPSY\NETSDK;UID=sa;PWD=;"
            strCmd = "Select * From Accounts"
            objConn = New SqlClient.SqlConnection(strConn)
            objAdapter = New SqlClient.SqlDataAdapter(strCmd, objConn)
            objBuilder = New SqlClient.SqlCommandBuilder(objAdapter)

            objDataset = New DataSet()
            objAdapter.Fill(objDataset)

            objTable = objDataset.Tables(0)
            objRow = objTable.Rows(0)

            intBalance = CInt(objRow("Amount"))

            intBalance = intBalance + intDollars

            objRow("Amount") = intBalance
            objAdapter.Update(objTable)

            objConn.Close()

            AddToJon = True
        End If
    End Function
End Function
```

Our business logic component is complete. Let's see how we bring it under the control of Component Services. First of all, of course, we need to build our DLL in VS.NET by selecting Build | Build. When it is finished, we should receive a message in our Output window stating that we had successfully built one process.

The RegSvcs Tool

Because the Component Services infrastructure is COM-oriented, we need to use a tool that does two things: it needs to expose the .NET component as a COM component, and it then needs to register that COM component with Component Services. Component Services handles all transaction coordination. In other words, you only have to declare your required scripts and components, and then Component Services tracks any changes and restores data should the transaction fail. The tool to do this is called RegSvcs. It's part of the .NET Framework, like the other tools (such as RegAsm) that we encountered in the previous chapter. There are a number of different options associated with the RegSvcs tool and they are outlined in the table overleaf:

Option	Description
/appname:(name)	Specifies the name of the COM+ 1.0 for the target application.
/c	Creates the target application or gives an error message if it already exists.
/componly	Configures components only, without methods or interfaces.
/exapp	Expects an existing application.
/extlb	Uses an existing type library.
/fc	Finds or creates the target application (default).
/help or /?	Displays a usage message containing tool options and command syntax.
/nologo	Suppresses the Microsoft logo output.
/noreconfig	Doesn't reconfigure the existing target application.
/parname:(name)	Specifies the name or ID of the target partition.
/quiet	Specifies quiet mode; suppresses the logo and success output.
/reconfig	Reconfigures an existing target application (default).
/tlb:(typelibraryfile)	Specifies the filename for the type library to install.
/u	Uninstalls the target application.

Before we run RegSvcs, you might find it convenient to extend the PATH environment variable to include the directory where RegSvcs is located. This is given by %windir%\Microsoft.NET\Framework\v1.0.xxxx, where xxxx is the number of the .NET Framework build.

This is what happens when we run it:

```
C:\>RegSvcs "C:\Pro VB.NET\Chapter 17\TransSample\bin\TransSample.dll"
RegSvcs - .NET Services Installation Utility Version 1.0.2914.16
Copyright (C) Microsoft Corp. 2000-2001.  All rights reserved.

The following installation error occurred:
1: The assembly 'C:\Pro VB.NET\Chapter 17\TransSample\bin\TransSample.dll' does
not have a strong name.

C:\>
```

Actually, that wasn't really what we wanted to see. RegSvcs is telling us that our DLL doesn't have a strong name, which we discussed in Chapter 14. The problem that we are facing is that the assembly that we've just created is a private assembly. In order to make it available to the transaction framework, we need to turn it into a shared assembly. To do this, we need to give the assembly a **cryptographically strong name**, generally referred to as its **shared name**.

What does cryptographically strong mean, then? What it means is that the name has been signed with the private key of a dual key pair. This isn't the place to go into a long discussion on dual key cryptography, but the essence of this is as follows:

- ❑ A pair of keys are generated, one public and one private.
- ❑ If something is encrypted using the private key, it can only be decrypted using the public key from that pair.

This means that it is an excellent tool for preventing tampering with information. If, for example, the name of an assembly were to be encrypted using the private key of a pair, then the recipient of a new version of that assembly could verify the origin of that new version, and be confident that it was not a rogue version from some other source. This is because only the original creator of the assembly retains access to its private key.

This is slightly scary stuff, because we don't usually expect to get involved in cryptography unless we're either (a) paranoid or (b) routinely working in the field of security. However, it's not a big deal in .NET, because Microsoft has helpfully provided us with a tool to generate key pairs. The tool is called sn, where sn stands for strong name.

The sn Tool

sn is another of those command line tools that come as part of the .NET package. This one is located in the \bin subdirectory from the .NET Framework SDK path. It's a very simple tool to use if all we want to do is generate a key pair. We use the -k command line option, plus the name of the key file that we want to create, thus:

```
sn -k "C:\Pro VB.NET\Chapter 17\TransSample\sgKey.snk"
```

Let's run it and see what happens:

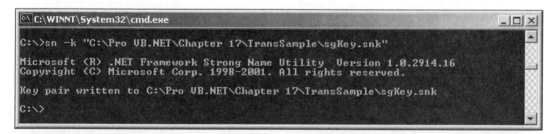

Giving the Assembly a Strong Name

We now have to make sure that our assembly uses the strong name. Let's go back to our Visual Studio project, and take a look at the AssemblyInfo.vb file that was automatically created for us. Here's what we need to do to the assembly code:

```
Imports System.Reflection
Imports System.Runtime.InteropServices


' General Information about an assembly is controlled through the following
' set of attributes. Change these attribute values to modify the information
' associated with an assembly.
```

```
' Review the values of the assembly attributes

<Assembly: AssemblyTitle("")>
<Assembly: AssemblyDescription("")>
<Assembly: AssemblyCompany("")>
<Assembly: AssemblyProduct("")>
<Assembly: AssemblyCopyright("")>
<Assembly: AssemblyTrademarkAttribute("")>
<Assembly: AssemblyKeyFileAttribute _
          ("C:\Pro VB.NET\Chapter 17\TransSample\sgKey.snk")>

' Version information for an assembly consists of the following four values:
'
'       Major Version
'       Minor Version
'       Build Number
'       Revision
'
' You can specify all the values or you can default the Build and Revision Numbers
' by using the '*' as shown below:

<Assembly: AssemblyVersion("1.0.*")>

<Assembly: CLSCompliant(True)>
```

This new line is telling .NET where to find the file containing the strong name that the assembly should be signed with.

Registering with Component Services

Once we've built the DLL again, we can run RegSvcs once more. This is what we see this time:

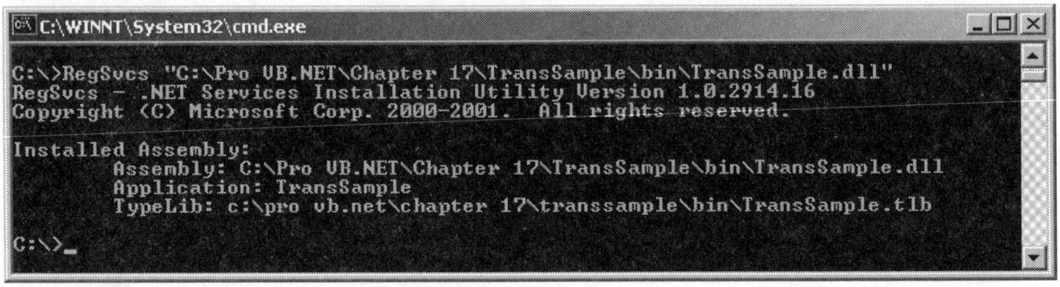

```
C:\WINNT\System32\cmd.exe                                          _ □ ×

C:\>RegSvcs "C:\Pro VB.NET\Chapter 17\TransSample\bin\TransSample.dll"
RegSvcs - .NET Services Installation Utility Version 1.0.2914.16
Copyright (C) Microsoft Corp. 2000-2001.  All rights reserved.

Installed Assembly:
        Assembly: C:\Pro VB.NET\Chapter 17\TransSample\bin\TransSample.dll
        Application: TransSample
        TypeLib: c:\pro vb.net\chapter 17\transsample\bin\TransSample.tlb

C:\>_
```

This is better. Note that we could have given it a different application name by passing it into the command line, thus:

```
RegSvcs "C:\Pro VB.NET\Chapter 17\TransSample\bin\TransSample.dll" TransSampleApp
```

We could also have changed the name of the type library that it generated as well by passing this as the third parameter. The type library, of course, is only there because Component Services talks COM, and not native .NET.

The Component Services Console

The **Component Services Console** is the control interface for Component Services. This is an MMC snap-in, which you can find (on Windows 2000) by selecting Control Panel | Administrative Tools | Component Services. If you open it up, you'll see something like this:

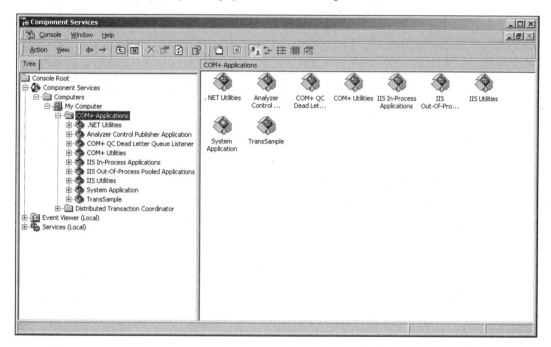

Hey! That's the name of our sample, under COM+ Applications! A COM+ application is a set of related COM+ components that have been packaged together. RegSvcs creates a new application for every component that it registers. If you want to bundle together a series of components from separate DLLs, you can do this, but you can only do it by creating a new application via the Component Services Console; try right-clicking on COM+ Applications and then selecting New. We'll explore the console a little more as we go on.

That's all very nice, but we're missing a couple of things. First of all, we need a test application. Secondly, and more importantly, we need to tell Component Services that we're interested in transactions.

A Test Application

Let's deal with the first problem straight away. We'll create a Windows Application project called TransApp and make a very simple form, like so:

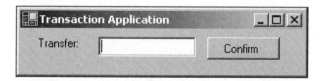

The text field is called `txtDollars` and the command button is called `btnConfirm`.

In order to access our transactional component, we need to add references to a couple of DLLs. First of all, we need to add a reference to the transactional component DLL itself. We'll need to browse for this, as it isn't currently in the global assembly cache (even though we've registered it with COM+ services by means of `RegSvcs`). Here's what we find:

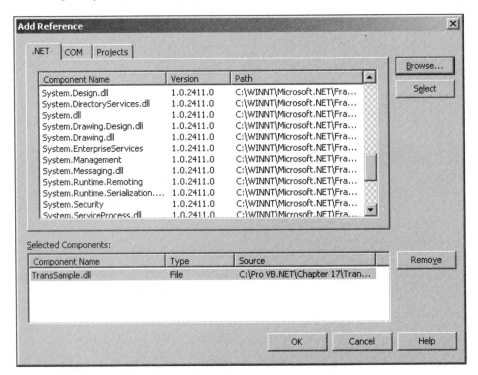

Secondly, in order to access the objects in this DLL, we'll also need to make our application aware of the `System.EnterpriseServices` assembly, so we'll need to add a reference to that as well.

Having done that, we need to import `TransSample` into our application:

```
Imports TransSample.TransSample

Public Class Form1
    Inherits System.Windows.Forms.Form
```

Here's the code behind our `Confirm` button:

```
Private Sub btnConfirm_Click(ByVal sender As System.Object, _
            ByVal e As System.EventArgs) Handles btnConfirm.Click
    Dim objTrans As TransSample.TransSample
    objTrans = New TransSample.TransSample()

    If objTrans.TransferMoney(CInt(txtDollars.Text)) = True Then
        MsgBox ("Transfer complete")
```

```
        Else
            MsgBox ("Transfer failed")
        Endif

        objTrans = Nothing
    End Sub
```

The Transaction Attribute

We now need to tell Component Services how we wish our component to enter a transaction. There are two ways of doing this. Firstly, we can do it via the Component Services Console. First of all, we need to open up the explorer tree to locate the TransSample component, thus:

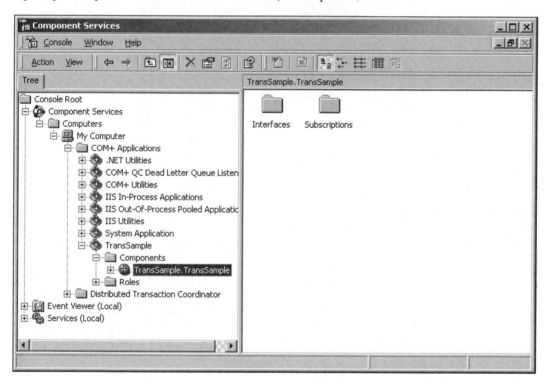

Next, we right click over this, and select Properties from the menu, then the Transactions tab:

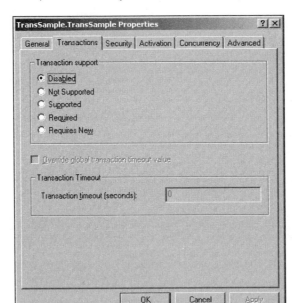

We can then select one of the available options; we'll discuss what these all mean in a little while.

However, it's a little tiresome to require our system manager to do this every time, especially if we already know that our component is always going to have the same transaction characteristics. So there's an alternative mechanism available to us: we can explicitly set up an attribute in the code for our component.

Attributes are items of declarative information that can be attached to elements of code, such as classes, methods, data members, and properties. Anything that uses these can query their values at runtime. One such attribute is called TransactionAttribute, and – unsurprisingly – this is used for specifying the transaction characteristics of a component class. The value of this attribute is taken from an enumeration called TransactionOption. Both TransactionAttribute and TransactionOption are within the System.EnterpriseServices namespace, by the way. Let's take a look at that enumeration. It can take the following values:

Value	Description
Disabled	Ignore any transaction in the current context; this is the default.
NotSupported	Create the component in a context with no governing transaction.
Required	Share a transaction if one exists; create a new transaction if necessary.
RequiresNew	Create the component with a new transaction, regardless of the state of the current context.
Supported	Share a transaction if one exists. If it doesn't, create the component in a transaction-free context.

Notice that the available values are exactly the same as the ones shown in the Transaction tab! In our case, we've got a stand-alone transaction, so either RequiresNew or Required is equally valid.

Let's go back to our TransSample project, make the change, rebuild, and re-register the component:

```
Imports System.EnterpriseServices
```

```
<TransactionAttribute(TransactionOption.RequiresNew)> Public Class TransSample
    Inherits ServicedComponent
```

```
Public Function TransferMoney(ByVal intDollars As Integer) As Boolean
```

Before we start running our application, open up the section of the explorer tree in the Component Services Console labeled Distributed Transaction Coordinator, and select Transaction Statistics. You should see something like this:

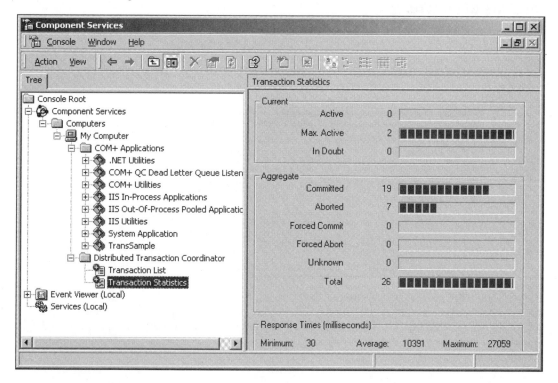

Now run the application.

Enter 1000 and hit the Confirm button. You should see the number of current active transactions briefly go from none to one, followed by the number of committed transactions and the total both going up by one. Great! We've implemented our first transaction! And if we check the two databases, we can see that the amount in BankOfWrox's Pro VB.NET account has been reduced to $4000, whereas Jon's account in BankOfJon has been increased by $1000. (Because I'm worth it, says Jon.)

Invalid Data

So what happens if we enter a value that we know to be invalid? There are two options here: either we try to transfer more money than there is in the Pro VB.NET account, or we try to transfer less than Jon will accept. Let's run the application again and try to transfer $10000. As expected, the transaction will fail, and no changes will be made to the accounts. Pro VB.NET still has $4000, and Jon still has $1000. This isn't too much of a big deal, because the invalid condition is spotted before any database manipulation is carried out. If we look at the transaction statistics, we can see that the number of *aborted* transactions has been incremented this time.

However, let's try to transfer $100. This time around, the first part of the transaction is successful, but the *second* part fails. Again, the number of aborted transactions is incremented. But what's happened to the database? Well, fortunately for everyone concerned, we see that there is still $4000 in the Pro VB.NET account, and still $1000 in Jon's. The *entire transaction* has failed.

Something Goes Wrong

Remember that bit of mindless vandalism that we did to the AddToJon function, so that it would divide by zero if we entered a negative value? Here's where we get to try it out.

Let's run the application again, and try to transfer $-1. This time we get a rather unpleasant response:

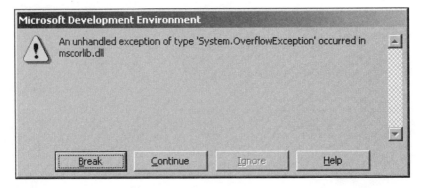

But we were halfway through a transaction! Never mind, because if we look at the transaction statistics, we see that the aborted count has gone up by one. More importantly, if we check the databases, we see that Pro VB.NET *still* has $4000, and Jon still has $1000. So we're protected against software failures as well.

Other Aspects of Transactions

There are a number of other things that we can do with transactions that we should briefly cover here. We will first of all discuss how manual transactions differ from automatic ones, and then look at Just In Time activation and object pooling.

Manual Transactions

So far in this chapter, we have in fact been talking about **automatic transactions**. That is, transactions where Component Services determines when a transaction is about to start, according to the transaction attributes of the components taking part. In most cases, this is the sort of transaction that we'd be using by choice. However, there are also **manual transactions**, which are transactions that are started whenever we want them to. For example, within ADO.NET, you can use the `BeginTransaction` method on the `Connection` object to start a manual transaction. This returns a reference to a `Transaction` object, and you can use the `Commit` or `Rollback` methods on this to determine its outcome.

Just In Time

Creating and deleting components takes time. So, instead of discarding the component when we've finished with it, why not keep it around in case another instance is required? The mechanism by which we do this is called **Just In Time (JIT) activation**, and it's set by default for all automatic transactional components (it's unset by default for all other COM+ components, however).

We know by now that all good transactional components are entirely stateless. However, real life dictates differently, because – for example – we might want to maintain a link to our database, one that would be expensive to set up every time. The JIT mechanism provides us with a couple of methods that we can override in the `ServicedComponent` class in this case.

The method that gets invoked when a JIT component gets activated is called `Activate`, and the component that gets invoked when it is deactivated is called – unsurprisingly – `Deactivate`. In `Activate/Deactivate` you should put the things that you would normally put in your constructor/deconstructor. In addition JIT can be activated by adding the `JustInTimeActivation` attribute to any class within `ServicedComponent`.

Object Pooling

We can, if we want, take this a stage further and maintain a pool of objects already constructed and prepared to be activated whenever required. When the object is no longer required or deactivated, it is returned to the pool until the next time it is required. By retaining objects, we do not have to continually create them from new, which in turns reduces the performance costs of our application. We can use the `ObjectPoolingAttribute` attribute within our class to determine how the pool is to operate:

```
<TransactionAttribute(TransactionOption.RequiresNew), _
ObjectPoolingAttribute (MinPoolSize=5, MaxPoolSize=20, CreationTimeOut=30)> _
Public Class TransSample
```

Holding Things Up

A JIT-activated component will be deactivated whenever the current method call returns, unless we tell it otherwise. The way that we control this is by means of methods in the `ContextUtil` class. The `ContextUtil` is the favored method to obtain information about the context of the COM+ 1.0 object.

If we invoke `ContextUtil.DisableCommit`, we are effectively telling Component Services that we are not finished yet; in other words, we're setting the consistency and done bits of the transaction to `False`. The transaction is in an indeterminate state for the time being. Once we are happy that everything is complete, we can call `ContextUtil.EnableCommit`, setting the consistency to `True` and the done bit to `False`. This says that we are happy for the component to be deactivated at the end of the current method call. However, it doesn't say whether or not the transaction is complete or not. It's up to us to invoke either `SetComplete`, setting both the consistency and done parts to true, or `SetAbort`, which sets the consistency to false and done to true or in other words, aborting the call.

As has been shown, `ContextUtil` allows us to control the activity of the object and retrieve any information about its context.

Queued Components

The traditional component programming model is very much a **synchronous** one. Put simply, you invoke a method and you get a result. Job done! However, a little thought reveals the unfortunate fact that an awful lot of real-world problems are inherently **asynchronous**. You can't always wait for a response to your request before moving on to the next task. So if we are to be able to tackle everything that the real world throws at us, we need to introduce an asynchronous component model.

Actually, it's a little more complicated than that. The synchronous model is quite simple to manage, because the three possible outcomes of a request are quite straightforward to handle. First of all, the request can be successful. Secondly, the software can crash. Finally, the software can simply not respond at all; in which case, we will have to time it out. However, if we are dealing with asynchronous requests, we have to handle all manner of unusual conditions. For example, the target system may not currently be operational, so we will have to take a decision on how long to wait before it comes back up again. Each outstanding request will take up system resources, so we will have to manage these resources carefully. We need to be able to know when the response comes back. And so on.

We are in fact dealing with a whole new infrastructure here, an infrastructure to handle **reliable messaging**. Microsoft's product to tackle this type of problem is MSMQ, or Microsoft Message Queue.

The idea behind reliable messaging is that once you have sent a message to a given target, you can effectively forget about it. The system will handle storing and forwarding of messages to their target, and handle retries and timeouts for you, eventually giving up and returning messages to your dead letter queue if all else fails. MSMQ is in fact a whole technology in itself, and we're not going to cover it in any great detail here. However, we are going to look at where it impinges on .NET Component Services. Welcome to **queued components**.

The principle behind queued components is quite simple. With standard component technology, every method call is entirely synchronous. You invoke the method and you wait for the response. If something fails along the way, you may have to wait a long time, but the system will eventually time you out. This is – generally speaking – all well and good if we are dealing with a single, self-contained system. However, once we get out into the big wide distributed computing world, things get a little messier. We have to consider the possibility that it isn't sensible to wait for a response before moving on to the next task. This is where queued components come in. The idea is that you literally do just invoke the method and then continue processing.

Naturally, this places some restrictions on the kind of component that we can use for this kind of thing. For example, we can't have any output arguments, and we can't have any return value. However, there are some cool things that we can do, and we're going to explore them in the next section.

> In order to run the Queued Components examples, MSMQ is needed, which comes with Windows 2000 Server and Windows 2000 Professional.

Queued Components: An Example

The Queued Component

We're going to write a very simple logging component that takes a string as its input, and writes it out to a sequential file, as well as outputting it in a message box. For the purposes of a simple example, the client and the server will be on the same machine; however, in real life they would be separate. So let's create a class library project called Reporter. As usual with component services, we need to add a reference to the System.EnterpriseServices namespace. This is how our class starts:

```
Imports System.IO
Imports System.EnterpriseServices

Namespace Reporter

    <InterfaceQueuing()> Public Interface IQReporter
        Sub Log(ByVal strText As String)
    End Interface
```

The first thing we do is define an interface. We need to separate out the interface from the implementation because the implementation, residing on the server, is going to be sitting on another machine somewhere. The client isn't the slightest bit interested in the details of this; all it needs to know is how to interface to it. Notice the <InterfaceQueuing()> attribute; that's indicating to the component services runtime that this is a queueable interface.

Let's take a look at the actual implementation. As with our transactional component, we inherit from ServicedComponent, and we also implement the interface that we have just defined:

```
Public Class ImplReporter
    Inherits ServicedComponent
    Implements IQReporter
```

In the logging method, all we do is output a message box, open up a StreamWriter component to append to our log file, and then close it again.

```
Sub Log(ByVal strText As String) Implements IQReporter.Log

    MsgBox(strText)
```

```
            Dim objStream As StreamWriter
            objStream = New StreamWriter("C:\account.log", True)

            objStream.WriteLine(strText)
            objStream.Close()

        End Sub

    End Class

End Namespace
```

And that's it for the code for the component. Let's take a look at what we have to do to the assembly definition:

```
Imports System.Reflection
Imports System.Runtime.InteropServices
Imports System.EnterpriseServices

' General Information about an assembly is controlled through the following

...

<Assembly: AssemblyTitle("")>
<Assembly: AssemblyDescription("")>
<Assembly: AssemblyCompany("")>
<Assembly: AssemblyProduct("")>
<Assembly: AssemblyCopyright("")>
<Assembly: AssemblyTrademark("")>
<Assembly: AssemblyKeyFile("C:\Pro VB.NET\Chapter 17\Reporter\sgKey.snk")>
<Assembly: ApplicationQueuing(Enabled:=True, QueueListenerEnabled:=True)>
<Assembly: ApplicationAccessControl _
            (Value:=False, Authentication:=AuthenticationOption.None)>
<Assembly: ApplicationActivation(ActivationOption.Server)>
<Assembly: CLSCompliant(True)>
```

The first addition is a reference to the EnterpriseServices namespace. In the actual assembly code, the first reference we need to make is to our old friend, the strong name key file. Next, we ensure that queuing is correctly enabled for this component. The next line is a special line to enable message queuing to work correctly in a workgroup environment, by switching off authentication. If we didn't do this, we would need to set up an entire domain structure. In real life, that's exactly what we would use, so you would need to remove this line. Finally, we ensure that the component runs as a server, rather than as a library. This was optional in the case of transactional components, but it's mandatory for queued components. We'll see why soon.

Consoles Again

We're ready to build our component. As before, we register it using RegSvcs. Let's take a look at the Component Services Console to see how we're doing:

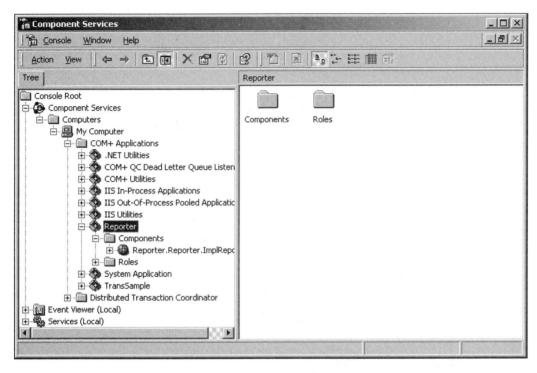

That looks fine, but there's one other console that we should be looking at right now. This is the **Computer Management Console**. You can get to this either from the system console, or by right-clicking on the My Computer icon, and selecting Manage from the menu. This is what it looks like:

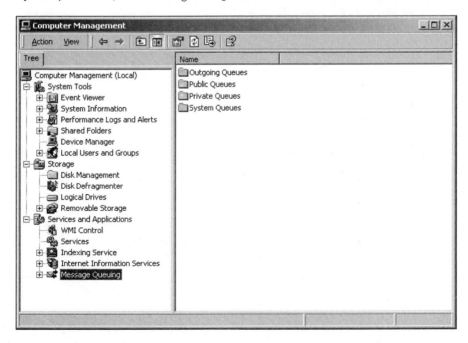

Tucked away, right at the bottom, is the part we're interested in. You'll actually need to open up Services and Applications to find it. Let's take a closer look:

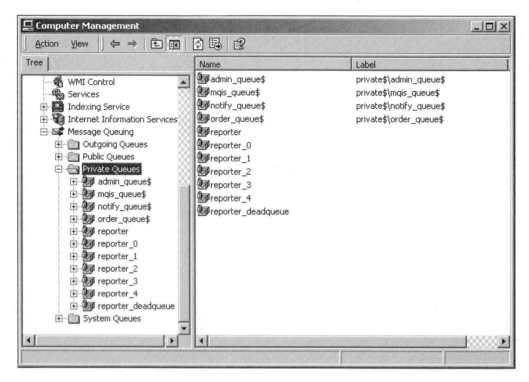

Cool! Component Services has set up some queues for us. There are five queues feeding into the main one, so we've got our infrastructure ready. Remember, by the way, that all this would be running on the server machine in real life, not the client.

The Client

Let's build our client now. This is where it gets unexpectedly messy, so hang on to your hats. The problem is that all of this is built on top of the MSMQ infrastructure, which is – inevitably – a COM infrastructure. Worse, the kind of things that we are going to do involve **marshaling** COM objects into a stream suitable for inserting into a queued message. Did I say marshaling? For the purposes of this discussion, we can think of marshaling as basically intelligently serializing the contents of a method invocation on an interface. We do this in such a way that they can then be deserialized at the other end and turned into a successful invocation of the same method in a remote implementation of the interface. We get COM to do this for us by constructing a **moniker**, which is basically an intelligent name.

In that last paragraph, we have skated at high speed over around 100 pages or so of the average COM treatise. If you're interested in pursuing all this further, there are many books in the Wrox catalog that discuss it in more detail. If, however, you're of a more pragmatic nature, well ... let's just do it, eh?

We'll start by creating a Windows application project called QueuedApp. We need to add a reference to our Reporter component, in the usual manner. Here's the form:

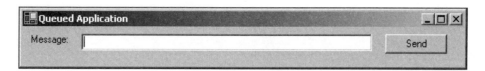

The text box is called `txtMessage`, and the button is called `btnSend`.

Here's the code:

```
Imports System.Runtime.InteropServices
Imports Reporter

Public Class Form1
  Inherits System.Windows.Forms.Form

  Private Sub btnSend_Click(ByVal sender As System.Object, _
              ByVal e As System.EventArgs) Handles btnSend.Click
```

Here's the crucial line. The important things to note are the references to our interface and its implementation. Everything else remains the same:

```
Dim iQReporter As Reporter.Reporter.IQReporter
iQReporter = _
  CType(Marshal.BindToMoniker("queue:/new:Reporter.Reporter.ImplReporter"), _
  Reporter.Reporter.IQReporter)
```

Here's the queued call:

```
iQReporter.Log(txtmessage.text)
```

Finally, we have to release the reference to the underlying COM object:

```
Marshal.ReleasecComobject(iQReporter)
  End Sub
End Class
```

Like I said, it's not pretty, but you only have to do it once to be able to do it many times over.

Queuing Invocations

Let's try running it, shall we, and enter a suitable message:

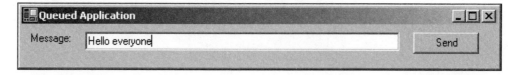

We click on the Send button and ... nothing happens. Let's take a look at our message queue:

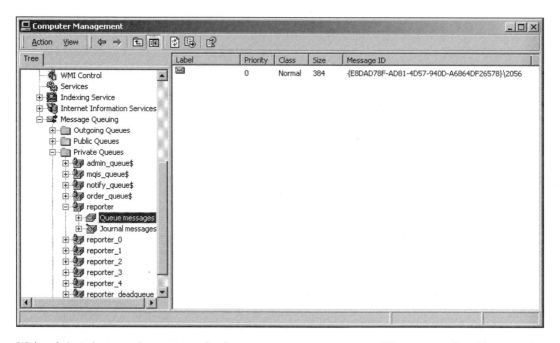

We've definitely created a message. So that represents our invocation. If we were to be able to read it, we would see "Hello everyone" embedded somewhere in it. (Unfortunately, the console only allows us to inspect the start of the message, but if we do so, we can see the name of our component in there.)

But why hasn't it been actioned? The answer is that we haven't actually started our server. Remember that we said that our component had to run as a server? This is why. The server has to sit there all the time, serving the incoming queue. So let's go to the Component Services Console, right-click on Reporter, select Start from the menu, and we're off. Lo and behold, there's our message box:

And if we look in the file, we've updated that too:

And if we run our application again, we'll see the message boxes popping up straight away now.

Transactions with Queued Components

Now why did we call that file account.log? The thing is that MSMQ is, like SQL Server, a resource manager, and it can take part in transactions. At first, this is a little counter-intuitive, because how on earth can anything so asynchronous as MSMQ have anything to do with transactions? The point is that it is *reliable*. If we take the transaction to go up to the point at which a message is securely in the queue, we have definitely got something that can participate. What happens at the other end of the queue is an entirely separate transaction. Of course, if something goes wrong there, we may need to look at setting up a compensating transaction coming back the other way to trigger some kind of rollback.

For our final example, then, we're going to take our original transactional component, and add in a queued element, so that not only does the transfer of money take place, but the fact also gets logged to a remote file. We'll use exactly the same queued component as last time. And that's why we called the file account.log.

We start off by making a clone of TransSample, called TransSample2. We need to add a reference to Reporter and a couple more imports:

```
Imports System.EnterpriseServices
Imports System.Runtime.InteropServices
Imports Reporter
```

We also need a new private subroutine:

```
Private Sub ReportTransfer(ByVal intDollars As Integer)
  Dim iQReporter As Reporter.Reporter.IQReporter
  iQReporter = _
    CType(Marshal.BindToMoniker("queue:/new:Reporter.Reporter.ImplReporter"), _
    Reporter.Reporter.IQReporter)

  iQReporter.Log("Transferring $" + CStr(intDollars))

  Marshal.ReleaseComobject(iQReporter)
End Sub
```

This may look kind of familiar from the previous queued component example application. Finally, we add a call to this:

```
Public Function TransferMoney(ByVal intDollars As Integer) As Boolean
    ReportTransfer(intDollars)

  If TakeFromWrox(intDollars) = True Then
      If AddToJon(intDollars) = True Then
```

So we're including a queued component in our transaction. It's been deliberately placed at the start to see if it genuinely takes part in the two-phase committal. If the transaction fails, we shouldn't see any messages come through.

Here's what happens if we transfer $1000:

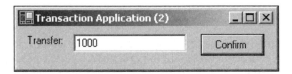

We eventually see the message box from our queued component:

So we know it's OK for valid transfers. What happens if we try to transfer $100? As we know from the earlier example, this will fail.

Summary

In this chapter, we have looked at the .NET Component Services, those parts of .NET that address issues required for serious enterprise computing. To begin with, we looked at transactions, what they are, and the ACID (Atomicity, Consistency, Isolation, Durability) theory describing their properties. This was followed by an example showing how transactions are controlled and monitored via the Component Services Console. Included here, we introduced and described the RegSvcs application used to register components with Component Services.

After we had finished our transactional components example, we then went on to look at some of the other activities that could be carried out with transactions including manual transactions, just in time attributes, object pooling, and the ContextUtil class.

We also looked at how the two-phase commit is organized so that the failure of a single participant in the transaction causes the entire transaction to be abandoned. Then we looked at queued components, and how these can be used for asynchronous method invocations. Finally, we looked at how these could be combined with transactions.

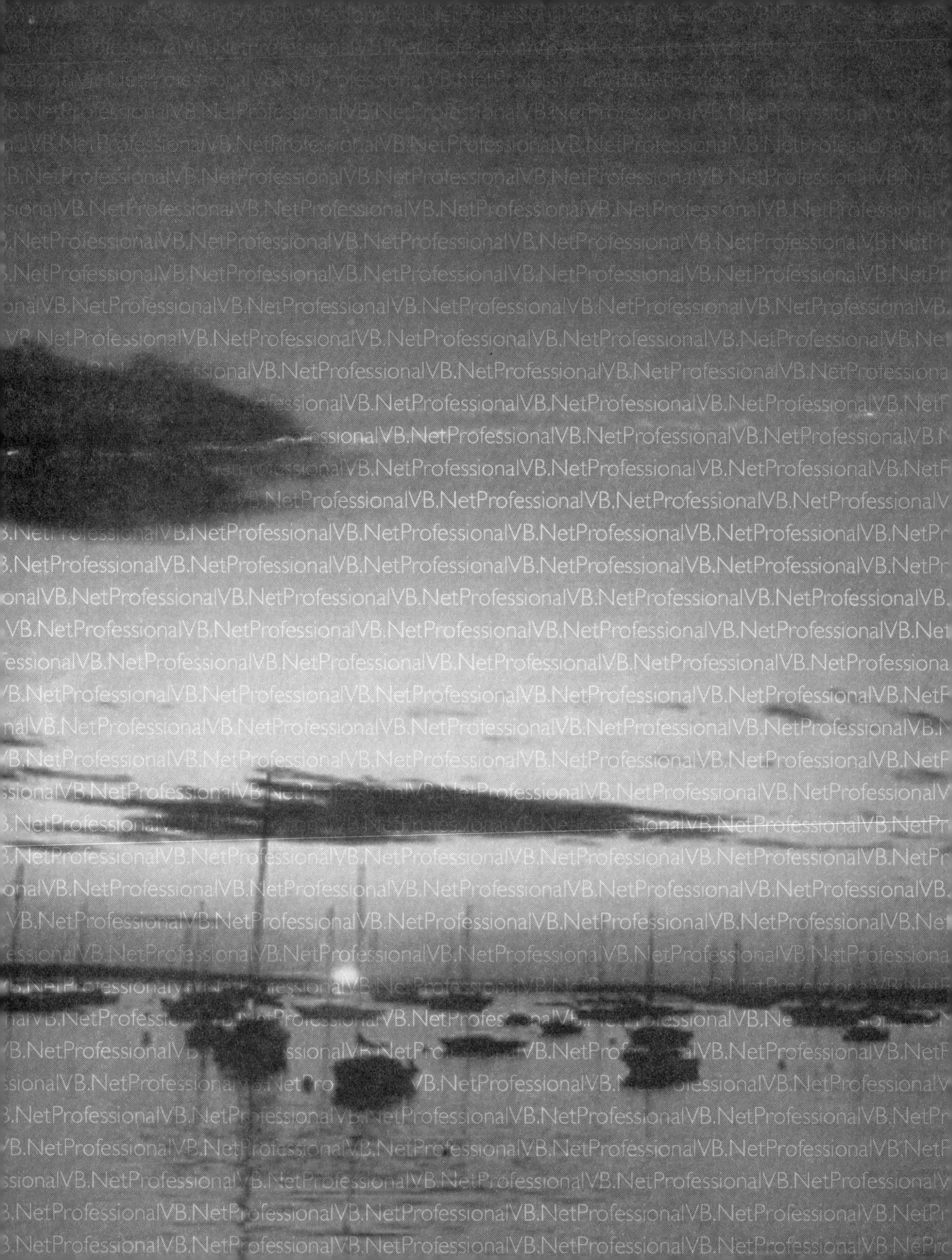

18

Data Access with ADO.NET

ADO.NET is the successor to ActiveX Data Objects 2.6 (ADO). Really, it is more of an evolution, just as the .NET Framework in general is an evolution of COM+. The main goal of ADO.NET is to allow you to easily create distributed, data sharing applications in the .NET Framework. ADO.NET is built upon industry standards such as XML, and, like ADO, provides a data access interface to communicate with OLE DB-compliant data sources, such as SQL Server and Oracle. Data-utilizing consumer applications can use ADO.NET to connect to these data sources and retrieve, manipulate, and update data.

In solutions requiring disconnected or remote access to data, ADO.NET uses XML to exchange data between programs or with web pages. Any component that can read XML can make use of ADO.NET components. A receiving component does not even have to be an ADO.NET component if a transmitting ADO.NET component packages and delivers a data set in an XML file. Transmitting information in XML-formatted data sets enables programmers to easily separate the data processing and user interface components of a data-sharing application onto separate servers. This can greatly improve both performance and maintainability for systems supporting many users. This will be covered in more detail when `DataSets` are looked at.

For distributed applications, the use of XML data sets in ADO.NET provides performance advantages relative to the COM marshaling used to transmit disconnected data sets in ADO. Since transmission of data sets occurs through XML streams in a simple text-based standard accepted throughout the industry, receiving components have none of the architectural restrictions required by COM. XML data sets used in ADO.NET also avoid the processing cost of converting values in a `Recordset`'s `Fields` collection to data types recognized by COM. Virtually any two components from different systems can share XML data sets provided that they both use the same XML schema for formatting the data set. We will cover this in more detail later in the chapter when we talk about `DataSet` objects.

ADO.NET also supports the scalability required by web-based data-sharing applications. Web applications must serve tens, hundreds, or even thousands of users. By default, ADO.NET does not retain lengthy database locks or active connections that monopolize limited resources. This allows the number of users to grow with only a small increase in the demands made on the resources of a system. Although it was possible to have the same functionality in ADO 2.6, it was not a default setting for a `Recordset` object to be disconnected, which got several programmers in trouble.

As you will see later in this chapter, ADO.NET is a very extensive and flexible API for accessing many types of data. Also, it is similar enough to ADO that you will be able to leverage a lot of the knowledge that you already have to pick up the ADO.NET object model fairly quickly. It should be noted here, however, that to get the most out of this chapter you need a good understanding of ADO.

In this chapter, we are going to give you an understanding of what you need to know about the ADO.NET object model in order to be able to build flexible, fast, and scalable data access objects and applications. Specifically, we will focus on the following topics:

❑   ADO.NET architecture

❑   Differences between ADO and ADO.NET

❑   Working with Managed Providers

❑   Building a data access component

❑   Using `DataSet` objects to bind to DataGrids

❑   `DataSet` object XML schema

Why Do We Need ADO.NET?

You have already learned ADO, so why should you have to learn a new data access object model when the old one works OK? Well, you can use ADO in the .NET Framework if you really want to, but you will pay the price for going through the COM layer (for more details on this see Chapter 16). Also, the .NET Framework does not support the COM `Variant` data type, which is what ADO uses for the values of Field objects in a Recordset object. This means that if you used an ADO Recordset object in .NET, the .NET CLR would have to constantly perform type-conversions for every field in order to be able to access the data. These type-conversions can become quite costly if you have to do them all of the time. But the most significant reason for embracing ADO.NET is that you get a truly disconnected data architecture, tight integration with XML, a common data representation (utilizing .NET data types) with the ability to combine data from multiple and varied data sources, and optimized facilities for interacting with a database. Also, ADO.NET is obviously very tightly integrated with the rest of the .NET Framework, and makes use of all of the .NET Framework object hierarchy and design patterns. For example, all classes in the .NET Framework inherit from the `Object` class, which has some very useful methods and properties, such as the `ToString()` and `GetType` methods (see Chapter 6 for more details about the `Object` class). Since all of the classes in ADO.NET are part of the .NET Framework, they too ultimately inherit from the `Object` class. Also, another nice benefit of using ADO.NET is that it is very tied to the .NET XML class framework (see Chapter 19).

As you can see, ADO.NET clearly builds upon the foundation that was laid down by ADO, as well as offering us a few new tools for our data access toolset. Let's investigate the ADO.NET architecture more closely to see what we get when we use ADO.NET.

ADO.NET Architecture

The main design goals of ADO.NET are to:

- ❑ Leverage Current ADO Knowledge
- ❑ Support the N-Tier Programming Model
- ❑ Provide XML Support

In distributed applications, the concept of working with disconnected data has become very common. A disconnected model means that once you have retrieved the data that you need, the connection to the data source is dropped, and you are working with the data locally. The reason why this model has become so popular is that it frees up precious database server resources, and this leads to highly scalable applications. The ADO.NET solution for disconnected data is the DataSet object.

ADO.NET Components

In order to better support the disconnected model, the ADO.NET components separate data access from data manipulation. This is accomplished via two main components: the DataSet and the .NET Data Provider. The diagram below illustrates the concept of separating data access from data manipulation:

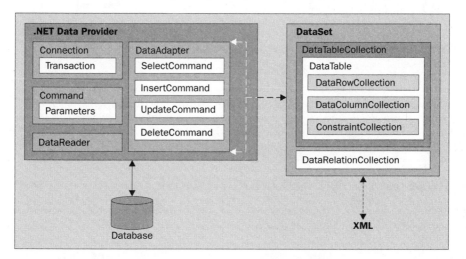

The DataSet is the core component of the disconnected architecture of ADO.NET and is basically what the Recordset object was to ADO. The DataSet is explicitly designed for data access independent of any data source. As a result it can be used with multiple and differing data sources, XML data, or indeed to manage data local to an application, such as an in-memory data cache. The DataSet contains a collection of one or more DataTable objects made up of rows and columns of data, as well as primary key, foreign key, constraint and relation information about the data in the DataTable objects. It is basically an in-memory database, but the cool thing is that it does not care whether its data is obtained from a database, an XML file, a combination of the two, or elsewhere.

The other core element of the ADO.NET architecture is the .NET Data Provider, whose components are designed for data manipulation (as opposed to data access with the DataSet) as listed in the table over leaf:

Object	Activity
`Connection`	Provides connectivity to a data source.
`Command`	Enables access to database commands to return and modify data, run stored procedures, and send or retrieve parameter information.
`DataReader`	Provides a high-performance stream of data from the data source.
`DataAdapter`	Provides the bridge between the `DataSet` object and the data source.

The `DataAdapter` uses `Command` objects to execute SQL commands at the data source to both load the `DataSet` with data, and also to reconcile changes made to the data in the `DataSet` back to the data source. We will take a closer look at this later when we cover the `DataAdapter` object in more detail.

> *It should be noted here that .NET Data Providers can be written for any data source, though this is beyond the scope of the present book.*

The .NET Framework ships with two .NET Data Providers: The SQL Server .NET Data Provider and the OLE DB .NET Data Provider.

> **NOTE: Please do not confuse the OLE DB .NET Data Provider with generic OLE DB providers.**

The general rule of thumb is to use the SQL Server provider when accessing SQL Server, and .NET OLE DB Provider when connecting to any other data source. The .NET OLE DB Provider is used to access any data source that is exposed through OLE DB, such as the OLE DB provider for Oracle, ODBC, etc. We will be looking at these more closely later in this chapter.

Differences Between ADO and ADO.NET

As we mentioned earlier, ADO.NET is an evolution of ADO. The following table lists several data access features and how each feature differs between ADO and ADO.NET:

Feature	ADO	ADO.NET
Memory-resident data representation	Uses the `Recordset` object, which holds single rows of data, much like a database table.	Uses the `DataSet` object, which can contain one or more tables represented by `DataTable` objects.
Relationships between multiple tables	Requires the JOIN query to assemble data from multiple database tables in a single result table. Also offers hierarchical recordsets, but they are hard to use.	Supports the `DataRelation` object to associate rows in one `DataTable` object with rows in another `DataTable` object.

Feature	ADO	ADO.NET
Data visitation	Traverses rows in a `Recordset` sequentially, by using the `.MoveNext` method.	The `DataSet` uses a navigation paradigm for non-sequential access to rows in a table. Accessing the data is more like accessing data in a collection or array. This is possible because of the `Rows` collection of the `DataTable`; it allows you to access rows by index. Follows relationships to navigate from rows in one table to corresponding rows in another table.
Disconnected access	Provided by the `Recordset` but it has to be explicitly coded for. The default for a `Recordset` object is to be connected via the `ActiveConnection` property. You communicate to a database with calls to an OLE DB provider.	Communicates to a database with standardized calls to the `DataAdapter` object, which communicates to an OLE DB data provider, or directly to a SQL Server data provider.
Programmability	All `Recordset` field data types are COM Variant data types, and usually correspond to field names in a database table.	Uses the strongly typed programming characteristic of XML. Data is self-describing because names for code items correspond to the "real world" problem solved by the code. Data in `DataSet` and `DataReader` objects can be strongly typed, thus making code easier to read and to write.
Sharing disconnected data between tiers or components	Uses COM marshaling to transmit a disconnected recordset. This supports only those data types defined by the COM standard. Requires type conversions, which demand system resources.	Transmits a `DataSet` as XML. The XML format places no restrictions on data types and requires no type conversions.
Transmitting data through firewalls	Problematic, because firewalls are typically configured to prevent system-level requests such as COM marshaling.	Supported, because ADO.NET `DataSet` objects use XML, which can pass through firewalls.

Table continued on following page

Feature	ADO	ADO.NET
Scalability	Since the defaults in ADO are to use connected `Recordset` objects, database locks and active database connections for long durations contend for limited database resources.	Disconnected access to database data without retaining database locks or active database connections for lengthy periods limits contention for limited database resources.

In order to make things clearer, let's look at some code to see the differences and similarities between ADO and ADO.NET. First, we will look at some familiar ADO code that grabs a `Recordset` of the `authors` table in the `pubs` database and traverses through it, outputting each author name as it goes:

```vb
'VB 6 Code
'References ADO 2.6
Private Sub TraverseRecordset()

   Dim strSQL As String
   Dim strConn As String
   Dim objRS As ADODB.Recordset
   Dim strResult As String

   'Build the SQL and Connection strings
   strConn = "Provider=SQLOLEDB;Initial Catalog=pubs;" _
       & "Data Source=(local);User ID=sa;password=;"
   strSQL = "SELECT * FROM authors"

   'Create an instance of the Recordset
   Set objRS = New ADODB.Recordset

   With objRS

      'Make the Recordset client-side with a static cursor
      .CursorLocation = adUseClient
      .CursorType = adOpenStatic

      'Open the Recordset
      .Open strSQL, strConn

      'Disconnect the Recordset
      Set .ActiveConnection = Nothing

      'Loop through the records and print the values
      Do Until .EOF
        strResult = .Fields("au_fname").Value _
        & " " & .Fields("au_lname").Value
        Debug.Print strResult
        .MoveNext
      Loop

   End With

   'Clean up
   Set objRS = Nothing

End Sub
```

As you can see in the code above, we have to explicitly tell the ADO recordset object that we want it to be a client-side, disconnected recordset. Note how we also have to clean up the memory when we are done with the object.

Now, we will look at a few ways of doing this same operation in ADO.NET. First, we will see how it is done with the DataSet component. Here is the code for traversing through a DataSet:

```
'VB.NET code
'References:   (1)System, (2)System.Data, (3)System.XML

Private Sub TraverseDataSet()

  Dim strSQL As String
  Dim strConn As String
  Dim objDA As SqlClient.SqlDataAdapter
  Dim objDS As New Data.DataSet()
  Dim intCounter As Integer
  Dim strResult As String

  'Build the SQL and Connection strings
  strConn = "Initial Catalog=pubs;Data Source=(local);" _
       & "User ID=sa;password=;"
  strSQL = "SELECT * FROM authors"

  'Initialize the SqlDataAdapter with the SQL
  'and Connection strings, and then use the
  'SqlDataAdapter to fill the DataSet with data
  objDA = New SqlClient.SqlDataAdapter(strSQL, strConn)
  objDA.Fill(objDS)

  With objDS.Tables(0)

    'Loop through the records and print the values
    For intCounter = 0 To .Rows.Count - 1
      strResult = .Rows(intCounter).Item("au_fname").ToString _
      & " " & .Rows(intCounter).Item("au_lname").ToString
      Console.WriteLine(strResult)
    Next

  End With

End Sub
```

In this code snippet, we start out the same way as before by building our SQL and connection strings. Instead of passing them directly to the DataSet object (like we do with the ADO Recordset), we pass them to a SqlDataAdapter object. This object abstracts the data access location from the DataSet object. After calling the SqlDataAdapter's constructor, we then call its Fill method to populate our DataSet object. Note how the same operation with a DataSet object contains fewer lines of code. This is mostly due to the fact that the DataSet object is already disconnected, so we do not have to write that plumbing. Also notice how there is no need to call a MoveNext method. There are sure to be a number of readers who have forgotten to call MoveNext in ADO, and then seen their computer's CPU usage skyrocket.

We will cover the details of the SqlCommand, SQLDataReader, SqlDataAdapter and the DataSet objects in the next section of this chapter.

.NET Data Providers

.NET Data Providers are used for connecting to a database, executing commands, and retrieving results. Those results are either processed directly (via a `DataReader`), or placed in an ADO.NET `DataSet` (via a `DataAdapter`) in order to be exposed to the user in an *ad hoc* manner, either combined with data from multiple sources, or to be passed around between tiers. The .NET Data Provider is designed to be lightweight, creating a minimal layer between the data source and the .NET programmer's code, increasing performance while not sacrificing functionality. Currently, the .NET Framework supports two data providers: the SQL Server .NET Data Provider (for Microsoft SQL Server 7.0 or later), and the OLE DB .NET Data Provider.

Let's now take a look at the four objects that the .NET Data Provider consists of, as outlined previously.

Connection Object

To connect to a specific data source, we use a data `Connection` object. To connect to Microsoft SQL Server 7.0 or later, we need to use the `SqlConnection` object of the SQL Server .NET Data Provider. To connect to an OLE DB data source, or Microsoft SQL Server versions before 7.0 using the OLE DB Provider for SQL Server (SQLOLEDB), then we need to use the `OleDbConnection` object of the OLE DB .NET Data Provider.

Connection String Format – OleDbConnection

For the OLE DB .NET Data Provider, the connection string format is identical to the connection string format used in ADO with the following exceptions:

❑ The `Provider` keyword is required

❑ The `URL`, `Remote Provider`, and `Remote Server` keywords are not supported

Here is an example `OleDbConnection` connection string connecting to an Oracle database:

```
Provider=msdaora;Data Source=MyOracleDB;User Id=myUsername;Password=myPassword;
```

Connection String Format – SqlConnection

The SQL Server .NET Data Provider supports a connection string format that is similar to the OLE DB (ADO) connection string format. The only thing that you need to leave off, obviously, is the `Provider` name-value pair, since we are using the SQL Server .NET provider. Here is an example of a `SqlConnection` connection string:

```
Initial Catalog=pubs;Data Source=(local);User ID=sa;password=;
```

Command Object

After establishing a connection, you can execute commands and return results from a data source (such as SQL Server) using a `Command` object. A `Command` object can be created using the `Command` constructor, or by calling the `CreateCommand` method of the `Connection` object. When creating a `Command` object using the `Command` constructor, you need to specify a SQL statement to execute at the data source, and a `Connection` object. The `Command` object's SQL statement can be queried and modified using the `CommandText` property. See the following code snippet as an example of executing a `SELECT` command and returning a `DataReader` object:

```
'Build the SQL and Connection strings
strConn = "Initial Catalog=pubs;Data Source=(local);User ID=sa;password=;"
strSQL = "SELECT * FROM authors"

'Initialize the SqlDataReader with the SQL
'and Connection strings, and then use the
'SqlDataAdapter to fill the DataSet with data
objCommand = New SqlClient.SqlCommand(strSQL, New
SqlClient.SqlConnection(strConn))

'Open the connection
objCommand.Connection.Open()

'Execute the query, return a SQLDataReader object.
'CommandBehavior.CloseConnection flags the
'DataReader to automatically close the db connection
'when it is closed.
objDR = objCommand.ExecuteReader(CommandBehavior.CloseConnection)
```

Like ADO's Command object, the CommandText property of the Command object will execute all SQL statements in addition to the standard SELECT, UPDATE, INSERT, and DELETE statements. For example, you could create tables, foreign keys, primary keys, etc. by executing the applicable SQL from the Command object.

The Command object exposes several Execute methods to perform the intended action. When returning results as a stream of data, ExecuteReader is used to return a DataReader object. ExecuteScalar is used to return a singleton value. ExecuteNonQuery is used to execute commands that do not return rows, which usually includes stored procedures that output parameters and/or return values.

When using the Command object with a Stored Procedure, you may set the Command object's CommandType property to StoredProcedure. The other possible values are TableDirect and Text. The TableDirect value indicates that you want the whole table returned, while Text allows you to enter any SQL statement that you wish. With a command type of StoredProcedure, you may use the Parameters property of the Command to access input and output parameters and return values. Command parameters can be accessed regardless of the Execute method called. However, when calling ExecuteReader, return values and output parameters are not accessible until the DataReader is closed. This is due to the fact that while the DataReader is in use, the associated connection is busy serving the DataReader. While in this state, no other operations can be performed on the connection other than closing it. Parameters are indicated either with a placeholder (a question mark) or with a named parameter variable. Parameters for queries involving OleDbCommand objects use question marks; queries that use SqlCommand objects use named parameters.

When using a DataAdapter with a DataSet, Command objects are used to return and modify data at the data source through the DataAdapter object's SelectCommand, InsertCommand, UpdateCommand and DeleteCommand properties.

> **Note that the DataAdapter object's SelectCommand property must be set before the Fill method is called.**

The `InsertCommand`, `UpdateCommand`, and `DeleteCommand` properties must be set before the `Update` method is called. We will take a closer look at this later in this chapter when we look at the `DataAdapter` object.

DataReader Object

You can use the `DataReader` to retrieve a read only, forward-only stream of data from the database. Using the `DataReader` can increase application performance and reduce system overhead because only one buffered row at a time is ever in memory. With the `DataReader` object, you are getting as close to the raw data as possible in ADO.NET; you do not have to go through the overhead of populating a `DataSet` object, which sometimes may be expensive if the `DataSet` contains a lot of data. The disadvantage of using a `DataReader` object is that it requires an open database connection and increases network activity.

After creating an instance of the `Command` object, a `DataReader` is created by calling `Command.ExecuteReader` to retrieve rows from a data source. Here is an example of creating a `DataReader` and iterating through it:

```
'References:   (1)System, (2)System.Data, (3)System.XML

Private Sub TraverseDataReader()

  Dim strSQL As String
  Dim strConn As String
  Dim objCommand As SqlClient.SqlCommand
  Dim objDR As SqlClient.SqlDataReader
  Dim strResult As String

  'Build the SQL and Connection strings
  strConn = "Initial Catalog=pubs;Data Source=(local);User ID=sa;password=;"
  strSQL = "SELECT * FROM authors"

  'Initialize the SqlDataReader with the SQL
  'and Connection strings, and then use the
  'SqlDataAdapter to fill the DataSet with data
  objCommand = New SqlClient.SqlCommand(strSQL, _
        New SqlClient.SqlConnection(strConn))

  'Open the connection
  objCommand.Connection.Open()

  'Execute the query, return a SqlDataReader object.
  'CommandBehavior.CloseConnection flags the
  'DataReader to automatically close the db connection
  'when it is closed.
  objDR = objCommand.ExecuteReader(CommandBehavior.CloseConnection)

  With objDR

    'Loop through the records and print the values
    Do While .Read = True
      strResult = .GetString(1) & " " & .GetString(2)
      Console.WriteLine(strResult)
    Loop
```

```
                  'Close the DataReader (and its db connection)
                  .Close()

            End With

      End Sub
```

In this code snippet, we use the `SqlCommand` object to execute our query via the `ExecuteReader` method. This method returns a populated `SqlDataReader` object to us, and then we loop through it and print out the author names. The main difference with this code compared to the previous `TraverseDataSet()` example is that we have to stay connected while we loop through the data in the `DataReader` object; this is due to the fact that `DataReader` reads in only a small stream of data at a time in order to conserve memory space.

> **At this point an obvious design question is whether to use the `DataReader` or the `DataSet`. The answer to this question really depends upon performance. If you want high-performance, and you are only going to access the data that you are retrieving once, then the `DataReader` is the way to go. If you need access to the same data multiple times, or if you need to model a complex relationship in memory, then the `DataSet` is the way to go. As always, test each option out thoroughly before deciding which is best.**

The `Read` method of the `DataReader` object is used to obtain a row from the results of the query. Each column of the returned row may be accessed by passing the name or ordinal reference of the column to the `DataReader`, or, for best performance, the `DataReader` provides a series of methods that allow you to access column values in their native data types (`GetDateTime`, `GetDouble`, `GetGuid`, `GetInt32`, etc.). Using the typed accessor methods when the underlying data type is known will reduce the amount of type conversion required (converting from type `Object`) when retrieving the column value.

The `DataReader` provides a non-buffered stream of data that allows procedural logic to efficiently process results from a data source sequentially. The `DataReader` is a good choice when retrieving large amounts of data since not all of the data is cached in memory, just one row at a time. You should always call the `Close` method when you are through using the `DataReader` object, as well as closing the `DataReader` object's database connection, because the Garbage Collector will do it only when it gets around to it. Relying purely on the Garbage Collector means that you may have an open database connection lying around unused and not being put back into the connection pool right away. Note how we used the `CommandBehavior.CloseConnection` enumeration value on the `SqlDataReader.ExecuteReader` method. This tells the `SqlCommand` object to automatically close the database connection when the `SqlDataReader.Close` method is called.

> **NOTE: If your `Command` contains output parameters or return values, they will not be available until the `DataReader` is closed.**

DataAdapter Object

Each .NET Data Provider included with the .NET Framework has a `DataAdapter` object: the OLE DB .NET Data Provider includes an `OleDbDataAdapter` object, and the SQL Server .NET Data Provider includes a `SqlDataAdapter` object. A `DataAdapter` is used to retrieve data from a data source and populate `DataTables` and constraints within a `DataSet`. The `DataAdapter` also resolves changes made to the `DataSet` back to the data source. The `DataAdapter` uses the `Connection` object of the .NET Data Provider to connect to a data source, and `Command` objects to retrieve data from, and resolve changes to, the data source from a `DataSet` object. This differs from the `DataReader`, in that the `DataReader` uses the `Connection` to access the data directly, without having to use a `DataAdapter`. The `DataAdapter` essentially decouples the `DataSet` object from the actual source of the data, whereas the `DataReader` is tightly bound to the data in a read only fashion.

The `SelectCommand` property of the `DataAdapter` is a `Command` object that retrieves data from the data source. The `InsertCommand`, `UpdateCommand`, and `DeleteCommand` properties of the `DataAdapter` are `Command` objects that manage updates to the data in the data source according to modifications made to the data in the `DataSet`. The `Fill` method of the `DataAdapter` is used to populate a `DataSet` with the results of the `SelectCommand` of the `DataAdapter`. It also adds or refreshes rows in the `DataSet` to match those in the data source. Below we look again at our example from the `TraverseDataSet()` method used previously that shows how to fill a `DataSet` object with information from the `authors` table in the `pubs` database:

```
'References:   (1)System, (2)System.Data, (3)System.XML

Dim strSQL As String
Dim strConn As String
Dim objDA As SqlClient.SqlDataAdapter
Dim objDS As New Data.DataSet()

'Build the SQL and Connection strings
strConn = "Initial Catalog=pubs;Data Source=(local);User ID=sa;password=;"
strSQL = "SELECT * FROM authors"

'Initialize the SqlDataAdapter with the SQL
'and Connection strings, and then use the
'SqlDataAdapter to fill the DataSet with data
objDA = New SqlClient.SqlDataAdapter(strSQL, strConn)

objDA.Fill(objDS)

With objDS.Tables(0)

    'Loop through the records and print the values
    For intCounter = 0 To .Rows.Count - 1
      strResult = .Rows(intCounter).Item("au_fname").ToString _
      & " " & .Rows(intCounter).Item("au_lname").ToString
      Console.WriteLine(strResult)
    Next

End With
```

Note how we use the `SqlDataAdapter`'s constructor to pass in and set the `SelectCommand`, as well as passing in the connection string in lieu of a `SqlCommand` object that already has an initialized `Connection` property. We then just call the `SqlDataAdapter` object's `Fill` method and pass in an initialized `DataSet` object. If the `DataSet` object is not initialized, the `Fill` method will raise an exception (`System.ArgumentNullException`). Now, let's take a look at some code in which we use a `DataSet` to insert data from the `DataSet` data to the `pubs` database:

```
'References:   (1)System, (2)System.Data, (3)System.XML

Private Sub UpdateDataSet()

    Dim strSQL As String
Dim strConn As String
```

```
Dim objDA As SqlClient.SqlDataAdapter
Dim objDS As New Data.DataSet()
Dim objCB As SqlClient.SqlCommandBuilder
Dim objRow As Data.DataRow
Dim intCounter As Integer
Dim strResult As String

'Build the SQL and Connection strings
strConn = "Initial Catalog=pubs;Data Source=(local);User ID=sa;password=;"
strSQL = "SELECT * FROM authors"

'Initialize the SqlDataAdapter with the SQL
'and Connection strings
objDA = New SqlClient.SqlDataAdapter(strSQL, strConn)

'Initialize the SQLCommandBuilder by passing in
'our DataAdapter.  This will build the INSERT, UPDATE,
'and DELETE commands for the DataAdapter object.
objCB = New SqlClient.SqlCommandBuilder(objDA)

'Use the SqlDataAdapter to fill the DataSet with
'the authors table
objDA.Fill(objDS, "Authors")

'Add a new author to the local table in memory
objRow = objDS.Tables("Authors").NewRow
objRow("au_id") = "335-22-0707"
objRow("au_fname") = "Tim"
objRow("au_lname") = "McCarthy"
objRow("phone") = "760-930-0075"
objRow("contract") = 0
objDS.Tables("Authors").Rows.Add(objRow)

'Write the update back to the server
objDA.Update(objDS, "Authors")

'Indicate success
Console.WriteLine("New author added!")
Console.ReadLine()

    With objDS.Tables(0)

        'Loop through the records and print the values
        For intCounter = 0 To .Rows.Count - 1
            strResult = .Rows(intCounter).Item("au_fname").ToString _
            & " " & .Rows(intCounter).Item("au_lname").ToString
            Console.WriteLine(strResult)
        Next
        Console.ReadLine()

    End With

End Sub
```

This code starts out exactly the same as the TraverseDataSet method did. It starts to differ when we use a CommandBuilder object. This is a helper object which will internally build the INSERT, UPDATE, and DELETE commands for our DataAdapter object for us. The only caveat is that we have to make sure that our SELECT command has the primary key of the table that we are working on, in this case the au_id field. To use the CommandBuilder object, simply pass in the initialized DataAdapter object to the CommandBuilder's constructor. We then call the Fill method of the DataAdapter, and specify that we are filling the Authors DataTable (we will cover this in more detail later).

Now comes the interesting part. In order to add the new row to the `Authors` table, we use the `DataTable's` `NewRow` method to return an initialized `DataRow` object. We then reference the fields in the `DataRow` object by the column name, and set their respective values. Once we have finished setting the fields, we then have to add the new `DataRow` to the `Authors` `DataTable`. This is done by calling the `Add` method of the `DataTable's` `Rows` property. So far everything we have done in this update has been offline; nothing has been written to the database. In order to write the changes to the database, we simply call the `Update` method of our `DataAdapter` object, and pass in the `DataSet` and the name of the `DataTable` (`Authors`) to update. By doing this, the `DataAdapter` will implicitly invoke the `INSERT` command that was built for us by the `CommandBuilder` object. The next part of the code is the same as the `TraverseDataSet` method; it simply writes out the names of the authors to the screen.

SQL Server .NET Data Provider

The SQL Server .NET Data Provider uses Tabular Data Stream (TDS) to communicate with SQL Server. This offers a great performance increase, since TDS is SQL Server's native communication protocol. As an example of how much of an increase you can expect, when we ran some simple tests accessing the `authors` table of the `pubs` database we saw the SQL Server .NET Data Provider perform about 70% faster than the OLE DB .NET Data Provider! The SQL Server .NET Data Provider is lightweight and it performs very well, mainly thanks to not having to go through the OLE DB or ODBC layer.

> **This is very important, since going through the OLE DB or ODBC layers means that the CLR has to marshal (convert) all of the COM data types to .NET CLR data types each time data is accessed from a data source. By using the SQL Server .NET Data Provider, everything runs within the .NET CLR, and the TDS protocol is faster than the other network protocols previously used for SQL Server.**

To use this provider, you need to include the `System.Data.SqlClient` namespace in your application. Also, it will only work for SQL Server 7.0 and above. I highly recommend using SQL Server .NET Data Provider any time you are connecting to a SQL Server 7.0 and above database server. The SQL Server .NET Data Provider requires the installation of MDAC 2.6 or later.

OLE DB .NET Data Provider

The OLE DB .NET Data Provider uses native OLE DB through COM Interop (see Chapter 16 for more details) to enable data access. The OLE DB .NET Data Provider supports both manual and automatic transactions. For automatic transactions, the OLE DB .NET Data rovider automatically enlists in a transaction and obtains transaction details from Windows 2000 Component Services. The OLE DB .NET Data Provider does not support OLE DB 2.5 interfaces. OLE DB providers that require support for OLE DB 2.5 interfaces will not function properly with the OLE DB .NET Data Provider. This includes the Microsoft OLE DB Provider for Exchange and the Microsoft OLE DB Provider for Internet Publishing. The OLE DB .NET Data Provider requires the installation of MDAC 2.6 or later. To use this provider, you need to include the `System.Data.OleDb` namespace in your application.

The DataSet Component

The `DataSet` object is central to supporting disconnected, distributed data scenarios with ADO.NET. The `DataSet` is a memory-resident representation of data that provides a consistent relational programming model regardless of the data source. The `DataSet` represents a complete set of data including related tables, constraints, and relationships among the tables, basically like having a small relational database residing in memory.

> **Note: Since the `DataSet` contains a lot of Meta Data in it, you need to be careful about how much data you try to stuff into it, since it will be consuming memory.**

The methods and objects in a `DataSet` are consistent with those in the relational database model. The `DataSet` can also persist and reload its contents as XML and its schema as XSD. It is completely disconnected from any database connections; therefore, it is totally up to you to fill it with whatever data you need in memory.

DataTableCollection

An ADO.NET `DataSet` contains a collection of zero or more tables represented by `DataTable` objects. The `DataTableCollection` contains all of the `DataTable` objects in a `DataSet`.

A `DataTable` is defined in the `System.Data` namespace and represents a single table of memory-resident data. It contains a collection of columns represented by the `DataColumnCollection`, which defines the schema and rows of the table. It also contains a collection of rows represented by the `DataRowCollection`, which contains the data in the table. Along with the current state, a `DataRow` retains its original state and tracks changes that occur to the data.

DataRelationCollection

A `DataSet` contains relationships in its `DataRelationCollection` object. A relationship (represented by the `DataRelation` object) associates rows in one `DataTable` with rows in another `DataTable`. The relationships in the `DataSet` can have constraints, which are represented by `UniqueConstraint` and `ForeignKeyConstraint` objects. It is analogous to a `JOIN` path that might exist between primary and foreign-key columns in a relational database. A `DataRelation` identifies matching columns in two tables of a `DataSet`.

Relationships enable you to see what links information within one table to another. The essential elements of a `DataRelation` are the name of the relationship, the two tables being related, and the related columns in each table. Relationships can be built with more than one column per table, with an array of `DataColumn` objects for the key columns. When a relationship is added to the `DataRelationCollection`, it may optionally add `ForeignKeyConstraints` that disallow any changes that would invalidate the relationship.

ExtendedProperties

The `DataSet` (and the `DataTable` and `DataColumn`) has an `ExtendedProperties` property. `ExtendedProperties` is a `PropertyCollection` where a user can place customized information, such as the `SELECT` statement that was used to generate the resultset, or a date/time stamp of when the data was generated. Since the `ExtendedProperties` contains customized information, this is a good place to store extra, user-defined data about the `DataSet` (or `DataTable` or `DataColumn`), such as a time when the data

589

should be refreshed. The `ExtendedProperties` collection is persisted with the schema information for the `DataSet` (as well as `DataTable` and `DataColumn`). Below is an example of adding an expiration property to a `DataSet`:

```
Private Sub DataSetExtended()

    Dim strSQL As String
    Dim strConn As String
    Dim objDA As SqlClient.SqlDataAdapter
    Dim objDS As New Data.DataSet()

    'Build the SQL and Connection strings
    strConn = "Initial Catalog=pubs;Data Source=(local);User ID=sa;password=;"
    strSQL = "SELECT * FROM authors"

    'Initialize the SqlDataAdapter with the SQL
    'and Connection strings, and then use the
    'SqlDataAdapter to fill the DataSet with data
    objDA = New SqlClient.SqlDataAdapter(strSQL, strConn)
    objDA.Fill(objDS)

    'Add an extended property called "expiration"
    'Set its value to the current date/time + 1 hour
    objDS.ExtendedProperties.Add("expiration", DateAdd(DateInterval.Hour, 1, Now))
    Console.Write(objDS.ExtendedProperties("expiration").ToString)
    Console.ReadLine()

End Sub
```

This code starts out by filling a `DataSet` with the `authors` table from the `pubs` database. We then add a new extended property, called `expiration`, and set its value to the current date and time plus one hour. We then simply read it back. As you can see, it is very easy to add extended properties to `DataSet` objects. The same pattern also applies to `DataTable` and `DataColumn` objects.

Creating and Using DataSet Objects

The ADO.NET `DataSet` is a memory-resident representation of data that provides a consistent relational programming model regardless of the source of the data it contains. A `DataSet` represents a complete set of data including the tables that contain, order, and constrain the data, as well as the relationships between the tables. The advantage to using a `DataSet` over using an ADO 2.6 recordset object is that the data in a `DataSet` can come from multiple sources, and it is fairly easy to get the data from multiple sources into the data set. Also, you can define your own constraints between the data tables in a `DataSet`. With ADO `Recordset` objects, it was possible to have data from multiple sources, but it did require a lot more work. Also, constraints were not supported in ADO `Recordset` objects, which made it harder to model data from a database when you were disconnected from the data source.

There are several methods of working with a `DataSet`, which can be applied independently or in combination. You can:

❑ Programmatically create `DataTables`, `DataRelations`, and `Constraints` within the `DataSet` and populate them with data.

❑ Populate the `DataSet` from an existing relational database management system using a `DataAdapter`.

❑ Load and persist the `DataSet` using XML.

Here is a typical usage scenario for a `DataSet` object:

1. A client makes a request to a Web Service.

2. Based on this request, the Web Service populates a `DataSet` from a database using a `DataAdapter` and returns the `DataSet` to the client.

3. The client can then view the data and make modifications.

4. When finished viewing and modifying the data, the client passes the modified `DataSet` back to the Web Service, which again uses a `DataAdapter` to reconcile the changes in the returned `DataSet` with the original data in the database.

5. The Web Service may then return a `DataSet` that reflects the current values in the database.

6. (Optional) The client can then use the `DataSet` class's `Merge` method to merge the returned `DataSet` with the client's existing copy of the `DataSet`; the `Merge` method will accept successful changes and mark with an error any changes that failed.

The design of the ADO.NET `DataSet` makes this scenario fairly easy to implement. Since the `DataSet` is stateless, it can be safely passed between the server and the client without tying up server resources such as database connections. Although the `DataSet` is transmitted as XML, Web Services and ADO.NET automatically transform the XML representation of the data to and from a `DataSet`, creating a rich, yet simplified, programming model. Additionally, because the `DataSet` is transmitted as an XML stream, non-ADO.NET clients can consume the same Web Service as that consumed by ADO.NET clients. Similarly, ADO.NET clients can interact easily with non-ADO.NET Web Services by sending any client `DataSet` to a Web Service as XML and by consuming any XML returned as a `DataSet` from the Web Service. One thing to be careful of is the size of the data; if there are a large number of rows in the tables of your `DataSet`, then it will eat up a lot of bandwidth.

Programmatically Creating DataSet Objects

Just like with the ADO Recordset object, you can programmatically create a `DataSet` object to use as a data structure in your programs. This could be quite useful if you have complex data that needs to be passed around to another object's method. For example, when creating a new customer, instead of passing 20 arguments about the new customer to a method, you could just pass the programmatically created `DataSet` object with all of the customer information to the object's method. In comparison to the ADO Recordset, it is a little bit different in ADO.NET when you want to create new instances of `DataSet` objects that contain complex data. In ADO, you could programmatically create hierarchically `Recordset` objects using the `Shape` syntax, but most people did not like dealing with the complexity of this syntax. The `DataSet` object offers a much richer, and easier to use model for building complex data representations. Let's take a look at some sample code to programmatically build a shaped `Recordset` in ADO, and then we will contrast the code with how we build the same type in ADO.NET.

Here is some ADO code to programmatically build a shaped `Recordset` of data containing customer order information. This sample will build a `DataSet` containing customer order information for one customer and one order, and it will output the data to the screen as XML:

```
'VB 6 Code

Sub ADOShapeSyntax()
Dim cnShape As ADODB.Connection
```

```
    Dim rstCustomers As ADODB.Recordset
    Dim rstCustomerOrders As ADODB.Recordset
    Dim stmXML As ADODB.Stream
    Dim strRSShape As String
    Dim strXML As String

    'Initialize ADO objects
    Set cnShape = New ADODB.Connection
    Set rstCustomers = New ADODB.Recordset
    Set stmXML = New ADODB.Stream

    strRSShape = "SHAPE APPEND NEW adInteger AS CustomerID," _
        & " NEW adVarChar(100) AS FirstName," _
        & " NEW adVarChar(100) AS LastName," _
        & " NEW adVarChar(100) AS Phone," _
        & " NEW adVarChar(255) AS Email," _
        & " ((SHAPE APPEND NEW adInteger AS CustomerID," & _
            " NEW adInteger AS OrderID," & _
            " NEW adCurrency AS OrderAmount, " & _
            " NEW adDate AS OrderDate)" & _
        " AS rstCustomerOrders RELATE CustomerID TO CustomerID) "

    cnShape.Open "Provider=MSDataShape;Data Provider=NONE;"
    rstCustomers.Open strRSShape, cnShape, adOpenStatic, adLockOptimistic

    With rstCustomers
      .AddNew
      .Fields("CustomerID").Value = 1
      .Fields("FirstName").Value = "Miriam"
      .Fields("LastName").Value = "McCarthy"
      .Fields("Phone").Value = "555-1212"
      .Fields("Email").Value = "tweety@hotmail.com"
      Set rstCustomerOrders = .Fields("rstCustomerOrders").Value
      rstCustomerOrders.AddNew
      rstCustomerOrders.Fields("CustomerID").Value = 1
      rstCustomerOrders.Fields("OrderID").Value = "12345"
      rstCustomerOrders.Fields("OrderAmount").Value = 22.22
      rstCustomerOrders.Fields("OrderDate").Value = #11/10/2001#
      rstCustomerOrders.Update
      .Save stmXML, adPersistXML
    End With

    'Get the XML string
    With stmXML
      .Type = adTypeText
      .Charset = "ascii"
      strXML = .ReadText
      Debug.Print strXML
    End With

    'Clean up
    Set cnShape = Nothing
    Set rstCustomers = Nothing
    Set rstCustomerOrders = Nothing
    Set stmXML = Nothing

End Sub
```

Notice how relatively complex the shaped provider syntax code is. Here is the code for accomplishing the exact same thing using an ADO.NET `DataSet` object:

```
'References (1) System, (2) System.Data, (3) System.XML

Private Sub BuildDataSet()

    Dim objDS As New Data.DataSet("CustomerOrders")
    Dim dtCustomers As Data.DataTable = objDS.Tables.Add("Customers")
    Dim dtOrders As Data.DataTable = objDS.Tables.Add("Orders")
    Dim objDR As Data.DataRow

    With dtCustomers
      .Columns.Add("CustomerID", Type.GetType("System.Int32"))
      .Columns.Add("FirstName", Type.GetType("System.String"))
      .Columns.Add("LastName", Type.GetType("System.String"))
      .Columns.Add("Phone", Type.GetType("System.String"))
      .Columns.Add("Email", Type.GetType("System.String"))
    End With

    With dtOrders
      .Columns.Add("CustomerID", Type.GetType("System.Int32"))
      .Columns.Add("OrderID", Type.GetType("System.Int32"))
      .Columns.Add("OrderAmount", Type.GetType("System.Double"))
      .Columns.Add("OrderDate", Type.GetType("System.DateTime"))
    End With

    objDS.Relations.Add("r_Customers_Orders", _
      objDS.Tables("Customers").Columns("CustomerID"), _
      objDS.Tables("Orders").Columns("CustomerID"))

    objDR = dtCustomers.NewRow()
    objDR("CustomerID") = 1
    objDR("FirstName") = "Miriam"
    objDR("LastName") = "McCarthy"
    objDR("Phone") = "555-1212"
    objDR("Email") = "tweety@hotmail.com"
    dtCustomers.Rows.Add(objDR)

    objDR = dtOrders.NewRow()
    objDR("CustomerID") = 1
    objDR("OrderID") = 22
    objDR("OrderAmount") = 0
    objDR("OrderDate") = #11/10/1997#
    dtOrders.Rows.Add(objDR)

    Console.WriteLine(objDS.GetXml())

  End Sub
```

Here is what the resulting XML of the `DataSet` looks like:

```
<CustomerOrders>
 <Customers>
  <CustomerID>1</CustomerID>
  <FirstName>Miriam</FirstName>
```

```
    <LastName>McCarthy</LastName>
    <Phone>555-1212</Phone>
    <Email>tweety@hotmail.com</Email>
  </Customers>
  <Orders>
    <CustomerID>1</CustomerID>
    <OrderID>22</OrderID>
    <OrderAmount>0</OrderAmount>
    <OrderDate>1997-11-10T00:00:00.0000</OrderDate>
  </Orders>
</CustomerOrders>
```

Notice how the code is much easier to read and more logical. We start out by first defining a `DataSet` object (`objDS`) named `CustomerOrders`. We then create two tables, one for Customers (`dtCustomers`), and one for Orders (`dtOrders`), and we then define the columns of the tables. Notice how we call the Add method of the `DataSet`'s Tables collection. We then define the columns of each of the tables, and create a relation in the `DataSet` between the `Customers` table and the `Orders` table on the `CustomerID` column. Finally, we create instances of Rows for the tables, add the data, and then append the Rows to the Rows collection of the `DataTable` objects. This operation contained fewer lines of code than the ADO example, was much more object-oriented, and as a result, is much easier to follow. This will usually result in code that is faster to write, easier to read, and less bug-prone.

> **Note: If you create a `DataSet` object with no name, it will be given the default name of `NewDataSet`.**

Typed DataSet Objects

Along with late bound access to values through weakly typed variables, the `DataSet` provides access to data through a strongly typed metaphor. Tables and columns that are part of the `DataSet` can be accessed using user-friendly names and strongly typed variables.

A typed `DataSet` is a class that derives from a `DataSet`. As such, it inherits all of the methods, events, and properties of a `DataSet`. Additionally, a typed `DataSet` provides strongly typed methods, events and properties. In practice, this means you can access tables and columns by name, instead of using collection-based methods. Aside from the improved readability of the code, a typed `DataSet` also allows the compiler to automatically complete lines as you type. For example, we have been loading the authors table into a `DataTable` in a `DataSet` in most of our examples. When we want to reference the au_lname field in the first row of the authors table, we can write the following code:

```
strLastName = objDS.Tables("Authors").Rows(0).Item("au_lname").ToString()
```

But, if we were using a strongly typed `DataSet`, we could just write the following line of code:

```
strLastName = objDS.Authors.Rows(0).LastName
```

In the code above, we are actually getting a `String` data type at compile-time instead of at runtime, since the strongly typed `DataSet` provides access to values as the correct strongly typed value at compile-time. With a strongly typed dataset, type mismatch errors are caught when the code is compiled rather than at runtime. The disadvantage is that it is less flexible, since you need to know all of the datatypes at compile-time instead of just at runtime. After we cover DataSets and XML in the next section, we will build a strongly typed `DataSet` object.

DataSet Objects and XML

The ADO.NET `DataSet` can easily be written as XML and a `DataSet` object's schema can be easily written as XML Schema Definition (XSD) language schema. A `DataSet` can also be easily generated from an XML stream that may or may not provide a schema. XML and XSD provide a convenient format for transferring the contents of a `DataSet` to remote clients and back, or just to a file on the file system for longer-term storage. Here is what the XML looks like for the `Authors DataSet` object that we created previously in the `TraverseDataSet` method:

```
<NewDataSet>
  <Table>
    <au_id>172-32-1176</au_id>
    <au_lname>White</au_lname>
    <au_fname>Johnson</au_fname>
    <phone>408 496-7223</phone>
    <address>10932 Bigge Rd.</address>
    <city>Menlo Park</city>
    <state>CA</state>
    <zip>94025</zip>
    <contract>true</contract>
  </Table>
  .................
  <Table>
    <au_id>998-72-3567</au_id>
    <au_lname>Ringer</au_lname>
    <au_fname>Albert</au_fname>
    <phone>801 826-0752</phone>
    <address>67 Seventh Av.</address>
    <city>Salt Lake City</city>
    <state>UT</state>
    <zip>84152</zip>
    <contract>true</contract>
  </Table>
</NewDataSet>
```

Here is what the XSD schema for the `Authors DataSet` object looks like:

```
<xsd:schema id="NewDataSet" targetNamespace="" xmlns=""
 xmlns:xsd="http://www.w3.org/2001/XMLSchema"
 xmlns:msdata="urn:schemas-microsoft-com:xml-msdata">
  <xsd:element name="NewDataSet" msdata:IsDataSet="true">
    <xsd:complexType>
      <xsd:choice maxOccurs="unbounded">
        <xsd:element name="Table">
          <xsd:complexType>
            <xsd:sequence>
              <xsd:element name="au_id" msdata:DefaultValue="NULL"
                type="xsd:string" minOccurs="0" msdata:Ordinal="0" />
              <xsd:element name="au_lname" msdata:DefaultValue="NULL"
                type="xsd:string" minOccurs="0" msdata:Ordinal="1" />
              <xsd:element name="au_fname" msdata:DefaultValue="NULL"
                type="xsd:string" minOccurs="0" msdata:Ordinal="2" />
              <xsd:element name="phone" msdata:DefaultValue="NULL"
                type="xsd:string" minOccurs="0" msdata:Ordinal="3" />
```

```
                <xsd:element name="address" msdata:DefaultValue="NULL"
                  type="xsd:string" minOccurs="0" msdata:Ordinal="4" />
                <xsd:element name="city" msdata:DefaultValue="NULL"
                  type="xsd:string" minOccurs="0" msdata:Ordinal="5" />
                <xsd:element name="state" msdata:DefaultValue="NULL"
                  type="xsd:string" minOccurs="0" msdata:Ordinal="6" />
                <xsd:element name="zip" msdata:DefaultValue="NULL"
                  type="xsd:string" minOccurs="0" msdata:Ordinal="7" />
                <xsd:element name="contract" msdata:DefaultValue="NULL"
                  type="xsd:boolean" minOccurs="0" msdata:Ordinal="8" />
              </xsd:sequence>
            </xsd:complexType>
          </xsd:element>
        </xsd:choice>
      </xsd:complexType>
    </xsd:element>
  </xsd:schema>
```

Now, in order to make the XSD a little more useful, we have decided to change some of the names, like the `DataSet` name and the `Table` name to make them more readable. Here is the new XSD file:

```
<xsd:schema id="AuthorsDS" targetNamespace="" xmlns=""
  xmlns:xsd="http://www.w3.org/2001/XMLSchema"
  xmlns:msdata="urn:schemas-microsoft-com:xml-msdata">
  <xsd:element name="AuthorsDS" msdata:IsDataSet="true">
    <xsd:complexType>
      <xsd:choice maxOccurs="unbounded">
        <xsd:element name="Authors">
          <xsd:complexType>
            <xsd:sequence>
              <xsd:element name="au_id" msdata:DefaultValue="NULL"
                type="xsd:string" minOccurs="0" msdata:Ordinal="0" />
              <xsd:element name="au_lname" msdata:DefaultValue="NULL"
                type="xsd:string" minOccurs="0" msdata:Ordinal="1" />
              <xsd:element name="au_fname" msdata:DefaultValue="NULL"
                type="xsd:string" minOccurs="0" msdata:Ordinal="2" />
              <xsd:element name="phone" msdata:DefaultValue="NULL"
                type="xsd:string" minOccurs="0" msdata:Ordinal="3" />
              <xsd:element name="address" msdata:DefaultValue="NULL"
                type="xsd:string" minOccurs="0" msdata:Ordinal="4" />
              <xsd:element name="city" msdata:DefaultValue="NULL"
                type="xsd:string" minOccurs="0" msdata:Ordinal="5" />
              <xsd:element name="state" msdata:DefaultValue="NULL"
                type="xsd:string" minOccurs="0" msdata:Ordinal="6" />
              <xsd:element name="zip" msdata:DefaultValue="NULL"
                type="xsd:string" minOccurs="0" msdata:Ordinal="7" />
              <xsd:element name="contract" msdata:DefaultValue="NULL"
                type="xsd:boolean" minOccurs="0" msdata:Ordinal="8" />
            </xsd:sequence>
          </xsd:complexType>
        </xsd:element>
      </xsd:choice>
    </xsd:complexType>
  </xsd:element>
</xsd:schema>
```

Take this XSD Schema, and save it to a file called `authors.xsd`, and make sure it is in the same directory as your other code files for this chapter. Now that you have the XSD schema for the `authors DataSet`, you can create a strongly typed `DataSet`. To create the strongly typed `DataSet`, you can use the `XSD.EXE` tool that is in the .NET Framework SDK (located in `\Program Files\Microsoft.NET\FrameworkSDK\Bin`). At the command line, type the following:

```
xsd.exe /d /l:VB authors.xsd /n:AuthorsDS
```

The above line will execute the `XSD.EXE` tool and will use the `authors.xsd` file to generate a VB component class with a namespace of `AuthorsDS`. Next, just include the file that was generated from the tool, `authors.vb`, into your project (or you can compile that file as a `dll` and reference it in your project), and you now have a strongly typed `DataSet` for the `authors` table to program against.

Here is the code for iterating through the new strongly typed `Authors DataSet`:

```
Private Sub TraverseTypedDataSet()

    Dim strSQL As String
    Dim strConn As String
    Dim objDA As SqlClient.SqlDataAdapter
    Dim objDS As New AuthorsDS.AuthorsDS()
    Dim objAuthorsRow As AuthorsDS.AuthorsDS.AuthorsRow
    Dim strResult As String

    'Build the SQL and Connection strings
    strConn = "Initial Catalog=pubs;Data Source=(local);User ID=sa;password=;"
    strSQL = "SELECT * FROM authors"

    'Initialize the SqlDataAdapter with the SQL
    'and Connection strings, and then use the
    'SqlDataAdapter to fill the DataSet with data
    objDA = New SqlClient.SqlDataAdapter(strSQL, strConn)
    objDA.Fill(objDS, "Authors")

    'Loop through the records and print the values
    For Each objAuthorsRow In objDS.Authors
        strResult = objAuthorsRow.au_fname & " " & objAuthorsRow.au_lname
          Console.WriteLine(strResult)
    Next
    Console.ReadLine()

End Sub
```

Notice how everything looks pretty much the same as the `TraverseDataSet` method from before, but this time we use our strongly typed `DataSet` instead of a generic `DataSet` object.

It's pretty nice that we get all of this for free in ADO.NET! This is much better than the `Rowset` Schema in previous versions of ADO.

ADO.NET DataTable Objects

A `DataSet` is made up of a collection of tables, relationships, and constraints. In ADO.NET, `DataTable` objects are used to represent the tables in a `DataSet`. A `DataTable` represents one table of in-memory relational data. The data is local to the .NET application in which it resides, but can be populated from a data source such as SQL Server using a `DataAdapter`.

The `DataTable` class is a member of the `System.Data` namespace within the .NET Framework Class Library. You can create and use a `DataTable` independently or as a member of a `DataSet`, and `DataTable` objects can also be used by other .NET Framework objects including the `DataView`. You access the collection of tables in a `DataSet` through the `DataSet` object's `Tables` property.

The schema, or structure, of a table is represented by columns and constraints. You define the schema of a `DataTable` using `DataColumn` objects as well as `ForeignKeyConstraint` and `UniqueConstraint` objects. The columns in a table can map to columns in a data source, contain calculated values from expressions, automatically increment their values, or contain primary key values.

> *More information on this topic can be found within the section of the .NET Framework SDK Documentation titled "Defining the Schema of a DataTable".*

If you populate a `DataTable` from a database, it will inherit the constraints from the database so you do not have to do all of that work manually.

A `DataTable` must also have rows in which to contain and order the data. The `DataRow` class represents the actual data contained in the table. You use the `DataRow` and its properties and methods to retrieve, evaluate, and manipulate the data in a table. As you access and change the data within a row, the `DataRow` object maintains both its current and original state.

You can create parent/child relationships between tables within a database, like SQL Server, using one or more related columns in the tables. You create a relationship between `DataTable` objects using a DataRelation. DataRelations can then be used to return a row's related child or parent rows.

> *Please refer to the "Programmatically Creating DataSet Objects" section in this chapter for an example of using DataRelation objects.*

Connection Pooling in ADO.NET

Pooling connections can significantly enhance the performance and scalability of your application. Connection pooling is a great story in ADO.NET; it comes for free! Both the SQL Client .NET Data Provider and the OLE DB .NET Data Provider automatically pool connections using Windows 2000 Component Services and OLE DB Session Pooling, respectively. The only requirement is that you must use the exact same connection string each time if you want to get a pooled connection.

Universal Data Link (UDL) files can be used to supply OLE DB connection information to the OLE DB Provider.

NOTE: UDL files are analogous to a DSN file for ODBC connections.

However, since UDL files can be modified externally to any ADO.NET client program, connections that use UDL files are not pooled. This is because the connection information can change without the ADO.NET client being aware of the change. As a result, for connection strings that contain UDL files, ADO.NET will parse the connection information found in a UDL file every time a connection is opened. Therefore, it is strongly suggested that you use a static connection string instead of a UDL file when using the OLE DB .NET Data Provider.

The SQL Client .NET Data Provider relies on Windows 2000 Component Services to provide connection pooling using an implicit pooling model by default.

Building a Data Access Component

In order to better demonstrate what we have learned so far about ADO.NET, we are going to build a data access component. This component is designed to abstract the processing of stored procedures. The component we are building will be targeted at SQL Server, and it is assumed that all data access to the database will be through stored procedures. The idea of only using stored procedures to access data in a database has a number of advantages, such as scalability, performance, flexibility, security, etc. The only disadvantage is that you have to use stored procedures, and not SQL strings. Through the process of building this component we will see how stored procedures are implemented in ADO.NET. We will also be building on the knowledge that we have gained from the previous chapters.

This component's main job is to abstract stored procedure calls to SQL Server, and one of the ways we do this is by passing in all of our stored procedure parameter Meta Data as XML. We will look at this XML later in this section. The other job of the component is to demonstrate the use of some of the new objects in ADO.NET.

> **The code for this project is quite extensive and we will only examine the key parts of it in this chapter. The full source is available for download from www.wrox.com.**

Let's start with the beginning of the component. The first thing we do is declare our namespace, our class, and the private members of the class:

```
Option Explicit On
Option Strict On

Imports System.Data.SqlClient
Imports System.Xml

Namespace IK.Data

  Public NotInheritable Class SQLServer

    Inherits System.ComponentModel.Component

    'Private members
    Private mobjConnection As SqlConnection
    Private mstrSPConfigXML As String
    Private mstrSPConfigXMLFile As String
    Private mstrModuleName As String
    Private mblnDisposed As Boolean = False

    Private Const EXCEPTION_MSG As String = "There was an error in " _
    & "the method. Please see the Application Log for details."
```

We start out with our `Option` statements. Note that we are using the `Option Strict` statement. This helps prevent logic errors and data loss that can occur when you work between variables of different types. Next, we import the namespaces that we need for our component. In this case, most of our dependencies are on `System.Data.SqlClient`. We declare a namespace here, `IK.Data`, but you can use any unique namespace that you wish. We then proceed to declare our class and derive it from `System.ComponentModel.Container`, and it is this inheritance that makes our class a component. We will call our class `SQLServer`, to indicate that it wraps data access calls to SQL Server. Next, we declare our private data members. We use the `EXCEPTION_MSG` constant to indicate a generic error message for any exceptions that we throw.

Constructors

Now we get to declare our constructors for the SQLServer class. This is where we can really take advantage of function overloading, and it gives us a way to pass data to our class upon instantiation. First, we declare a default constructor:

```
Public Sub New()

  MyBase.New()

  'Initialize private members
  mstrSPConfigXML = ""
  mstrSPConfigXMLFile = ""
  mstrModuleName = Me.GetType.ToString

End Sub
```

In this constructor, as well as all constructors in VB, we call MyBase.New() the default constructor of our base class. Next, we initialize our private members' data. Notice how we use the GetType() method of Object so we know at runtime what the name of our class is.

The next constructor we create allows for a database connection string to be passed in. By abstracting the database connection string out of this component, we give users of our component more flexibility in how they decide to store and retrieve their database connection strings. Here is the code for the constructor:

```
Public Sub New(ByVal ConnectionString As String)

        'Call the base class constructor
        MyBase.New()

        'Initialize private members
        mobjConnection = New SqlConnection(ConnectionString)
        mstrSPConfigXML = ""
        mstrSPConfigXMLFile = ""
        mstrModuleName = Me.GetType.ToString

    End Sub
```

The only difference between this constructor and the default constructor is that we are passing in a database connection string and assigning it to the constructor of our mobjConnection (SqlConnection) object.

In the last constructor, we pass in both a database connection string and a string of XML representing the stored procedure parameters for the stored procedure we want to call. Here is the code for the constructor:

```
Public Sub New(ByVal ConnectionString As String, ByVal SPConfigXML As String)

        'Call the base class constructor
        MyBase.New()

        'Initialize private members
        mobjConnection = New SqlConnection(ConnectionString)
        mstrSPConfigXML = SPConfigXML
```

```
            mstrSPConfigXMLFile = ""
            mstrModuleName = Me.GetType.ToString

    End Sub
```

This constructor simply sets the database connection and stored procedure parameter configuration for private members.

Properties

Now, let's look at the properties of our object. Our object contains the following properties: DBConnection, SPConfigXML, and SPConfigXMLFile. The DBConnection and SPConfigXML properties are added in case the user of our object did not want to supply them via a constructor call. The DBConnection property creates a new SqlConnection instance and returns the underlying connection string of the SqlConnection object (mobjConnection). The SPConfigXMLFile property allows the user of the object to pass in a valid file name containing the XML representing the stored procedure parameter Meta Data. All of the properties are read-write.

Here is the code for the DBConnection property:

```
    Public Property DBConnection() As String

        Set(ByVal Value As String)
            mobjConnection = New SqlConnection(Value)
        End Set
        Get
            Try
                Return mobjConnection.ConnectionString
            Catch
                Return ""
            End Try
        End Get

    End Property
```

Stored Procedure XML Structure

Rather than having the user of our object be responsible for populating the Parameters collection of a Command object, in this case we will abstract it out into an XML structure. The structure is very simple; it basically allows you to store the Meta Data for one or more stored procedures at a time. This has a huge advantage in the fact that you can change all of the parameters on a stored procedure without having to recompile this object. Below is what the XML structure for the Meta Data looks like:

```
<StoredProcedures>
 <StoredProcedure name>
  <Parameters>
   <Parameter name size datatype direction isNullable value />
  </Parameters>
 </StoredProcedure>
</StoredProcedures>
```

Here is what some sample data for the XML structure looks like:

```xml
<?xml version="1.0"?>
<StoredProcedures>
 <StoredProcedure name="usp_Get_Authors_By_States">
  <Parameters>
   <Parameter name="@states" size="100" datatype="VarChar"
    direction="spParamInput" isNullable="True" />
   <Parameter name="@state_delimiter" size="1" datatype="Char"
    direction="spParamInput" isNullable="True" />
  </Parameters>
 </StoredProcedure>
</StoredProcedures>
```

The valid values for the `direction` attribute are: `spParamInput`, `spParamOutput`, `spParamReturnValue`, and `spParamInputOutput`. The valid values for the `datatype` attribute are: `BigInt`, `Binary`, `Bit`, `Char`, `DateTime`, `Decimal`, `Float`, `Image`, `Int`, `Money`, `NChar`, `NText`, `NVarChar`, `Real`, `SmallDateTime`, `SmallInt`, `SmallMoney`, `Text`, `Timestamp`, `TinyInt`, `UniqueIdentifier`, `VarBinary`, `VarChar`, and `Variant`. These values map directly to the SQL data types in SQL Server 2000. We will call this file `PubsStoredProcedures.xsd` and save it in the root directory of our project.

Methods

ExecSPReturnDS

This public function executes a stored procedure and returns a `DataSet` object. It takes a stored procedure name (`String`) and an optional list of parameter values (`ArrayList`). Here is the code for `ExecSPReturnDS`:

```vb
Public Function ExecSPReturnDS(ByVal SPName As String, Optional ByVal _
                    ParamValues As ArrayList = Nothing) As DataSet

        Dim objCommand As SqlCommand
        Dim objDA As SqlDataAdapter
        Dim objDS As New DataSet()

        Try

            'Make sure that the object has not been disposed yet
            If mblnDisposed = True Then
                Throw New ObjectDisposedException(mstrModuleName, _
                "This object has already been disposed.")
            End If

            'Make sure we are getting a valid stored procedure name.
            ValidateSPName(SPName)

            'Initialize the SQLCommand object
            objCommand = New SqlCommand(SPName, mobjConnection)
            objCommand.CommandType = CommandType.StoredProcedure

            'Build the parameters, if any
```

```
              BuildParameters(objCommand, ParamValues)

              'Initialize the SQLDataAdapter with the
              'SQLCommand object
              objDA = New SqlDataAdapter(objCommand)

              'Fill the DataSet
              objDA.Fill(objDS)

              'Return the value
              Return objDS

          Catch objException As Exception

              LogError(objException)
              Throw New Exception(EXCEPTION_MSG, objException)

          Finally

              'Close the connection and return the value
              objCommand.Connection.Close()

          End Try

      End Function
```

This function uses three objects to accomplish its mission: the `SqlCommand`, `SqlDataAdapter`, and `DataSet` objects. We first wrap everything in a `Try-Catch-Finally` block to make sure that we trap any exceptions that are thrown. The first thing we do is to make sure our object did not have its `Dispose` method called on it yet. Here is the code for the `Dispose` method:

```
      Public Overloads Sub Dispose()

          If mblnDisposed = False Then

              Try

                  'Free up the database connection resource by
                  'calling its Dispose method
                  mobjConnection.Dispose()

              Finally

                  'Call the base type's Dispose() method.
                  MyBase.Dispose()

                  'Because this Dispose method has done the necessary
                  'cleanup, prevent the Finalize method from being called.
                  GC.SuppressFinalize(Me)

                  'Let our class know that Dispose() has been called
                  mblnDisposed = True

              End Try

          End If

      End Sub
```

We do this by checking the mblnDisposed private variable. If it is True, then we throw an exception. The Dispose method closes the current connection (mobjConnection) if it is open by calling the base type's Dispose method, and then prevents the Finalize method from being called. Finally, we set the mblnDisposed private member to the value of True.

The next thing we do in ExecSPReturnDS is to make sure that the stored procedure name that we receive is a valid stored procedure name. We do this by calling the ValidateSPName private method. Here is the code for ValidateSPName:

```
Private Sub ValidateSPName(ByRef SPName As String)

    'The name must be between 1 and 128 characters long.
    If Len(SPName) < 1 Or Len(SPName) > 128 Then
      Throw New Exception("A valid stored procedure name must " _
                & "be provided.")
    End If

End Sub
```

This method just performs a check to make sure that the stored procedure name is between 1 and 128 characters long, in accordance with the SQL Server object naming conventions. If it is not, then we throw an exception. Looking back at the code for ExecSPReturnDS, we then call the SqlCommand object's constructor and pass in the stored procedure name, and then set its Connection and CommandType properties.

```
'Initialize the SQLCommand object
          objCommand = New SqlCommand(SPName, mobjConnection)
          objCommand.CommandType = CommandType.StoredProcedure
```

We make sure that we pass in the CommandType.StoredProcedure enumeration value, since we are executing a stored procedure. Once the SqlCommand object is properly initialized, we pass it by reference to the BuildParameters method. We will take a look at this method in more detail later.

```
'Build the parameters, if any
BuildParameters(objCommand, ParamValues)
```

After the parameters have been added to the SqlCommand object, the next step is to pass the SqlCommand object to the SqlDataAdapter's constructor:

```
'Initialize the SQLDataAdapter with the
'SQLCommand object
objDA = New SqlDataAdapter(objCommand)
```

After doing this, we then call the Fill method of the SqlDataAdapter to fill our DataSet object:

```
'Fill the DataSet
objDA.Fill(objDS)
```

We then return the DataSet object back to the caller:

```
'Return the value
Return objDS
```

If there was an exception caught, then we log the exception data to the Application Log via the `LogError` private method, and then throw a new exception with our generic exception message. We nest the original exception inside of the new exception via the `innerException` constructor parameter:

```
Catch objException As Exception

    LogError(objException)
    Throw New Exception(EXCEPTION_MSG, objException)
```

In the `Finally` block, we close the `SqlCommand` object's `connection` property.

```
Finally

    'Close the connection and return the value
    objCommand.Connection.Close()
```

BuildParameters

This private method is the heart of this object, and does the most work. It is responsible for parsing the stored procedure parameter XML and mapping all of the parameter properties into the `Parameters` property of the `SqlCommand` object. Here is the signature of the method:

```
Private Sub BuildParameters(ByRef Command As SqlCommand, _
            ByRef ParamValues As ArrayList)
```

You will notice that both of its arguments, `SqlCommand` and `ArrayList`, are passed in by reference. Since it is a private method, there is no need to copy the state of these objects, so we just pass them `ByRef`. The `ParamValues` argument is an `ArrayList` of the values for each of the parameters, and these values must be in the same order as their corresponding parameters in the XML. The first thing we do in this method is to see if in fact there is any XML being passed in or not. Here is the code that checks for the XML:

```
'See if there is an XML string or XML file of
'parameters() for the stored procedure
If Len(mstrSPConfigXML) = 0 And Len(mstrSPConfigXMLFile) = 0 Then

    'No parameters to add, so exit
    Exit Sub

End If
```

The code above simply checks if there is an XML string or an XML file name in the object's private variables. If it cannot find either one, then we exit the method. It is entirely possible that users of this object may have stored procedures with no parameters at all.

After we pass this test, we then try to load whatever XML we have into an `XmlDocument` object. We have chosen an `XmlDocument` object (`objDOM`) to parse the XML as loading all of the stored procedure XML into memory will not hurt performance; it is a small amount of data. As an alternative, we could have used an `XmlReader` object to load in only what we needed into memory at runtime. Here is the code to load the XML:

```
'See if there is an XML string of parameters
'for the stored procedure
If Len(mstrSPConfigXML) > 0 Then
```

```
        'Try to load the XML into a DOM
        Try
            objDOM.LoadXml(mstrSPConfigXML)

        Catch objXMLException As XmlException

            'Throw an exception if the load failed
            Throw objXMLException

        End Try

    End If

    'See if there is an XML file of parameters
    'for the stored procedure
    If Len(mstrSPConfigXML) = 0 And Len(mstrSPConfigXMLFile) > 0 Then

        'Try to load the XML into a DOM
        Try
            objDOM.Load(mstrSPConfigXMLFile)

        Catch objXMLException As XmlException

            'Throw an exception if the load failed
            Throw objXMLException

        End Try

    End If
```

First we try to load the XML string, and then we try to load the XML file. If any of these operations fail, we throw an XmlException object.

The next step is to get the name of the stored procedure and clear the SqlCommand object's Parameters collection:

```
    'Now we have a DOM Document in memory

    'Get the name of the stored procedure
    strSPName = Command.CommandText

    'Clear the parameters collection for the SQLCommand
    Command.Parameters.Clear()
```

We then use the name of the stored procedure as the key in our xpath query of the XML, and then execute the xpath query:

```
    'Get the node list of <Parameter>'s for the stored procedure
    strXPathQuery = "/StoredProcedures/StoredProcedure[@name='" _
        & strSPName & "']/Parameters/Parameter"
    objParameterNodes = objDOM.SelectNodes(strXPathQuery)
```

This query is executed off the `XmlDocument` object and returns an `XmlNodeList` object. We then start the loop through the `Parameter` elements in the XML and retrieve all of the mandatory `Parameter` attributes:

```
'Loop through the stored procedure <Parameter> elements
For Each objNode In objParameterNodes

  'Get the attribute values for the <Parameter> element.

  'name
  Try
    strParameterName = objNode.Attributes.GetNamedItem("name").Value
  Catch
    Throw New Exception("Error getting the 'name' attribute " _
             & "for the <Parameter> element.")
  End Try

  'size
  Try
    intParameterSize = CInt(objNode.Attributes.GetNamedItem("size").Value)
  Catch
    Throw New Exception("Error getting the 'size' attribute " _
             & "for the <Parameter> element.")
  End Try

  'datatype
  Try
    intSQLDataType = GetSQLDataType _
             & (objNode.Attributes.GetNamedItem("datatype").Value)
  Catch
    Throw New Exception("Error getting the 'datatype' attribute " _
             & "for the <Parameter> element.")
  End Try

  'direction
  Try
    intParameterDirection = GetParamDirection _
             & (objNode.Attributes.GetNamedItem("direction").Value)
  Catch
    Throw New Exception("Error getting the 'direction' attribute " _
             & "for the <Parameter> element.")
  End Try
```

Since these attributes are mandatory, if any of them are missing, we throw an exception. Notice the two helper functions being called, `GetSQLDataType` and `GetParamDirection`. These functions simply convert the string value from the XML into the proper enumeration value.

Next, we get the optional attributes:

```
'Get the optional attribute values for the <Parameter> element

  'isNullable
  Try
    blnIsNullable = CBool(objNode.Attributes.GetNamedItem("isNullable").Value)
  Catch
    blnIsNullable = False
```

```
      End Try

      'precision
      Try
        bytPrecision = CByte(objNode.Attributes.GetNamedItem("precision").Value)
      Catch
        bytPrecision = 0
      End Try

      'scale
      Try
        bytScale = CByte(objNode.Attributes.GetNamedItem("scale").Value)
      Catch
        bytScale = 0
      End Try
```

These attributes are optional mainly because of their data types. Since they are Boolean and Byte data types, we just go ahead and convert them to False and 0 if they are missing.

Now that we have the Parameter attributes, the next step is to get the corresponding value for the Parameter:

```
      'Get the value of the parameter. This could be passed in from
      'one of the public methods, or it could be an attribute value
      'in the XML <Parameter> element.
      Try
        'Check the XML first
        objParameterValue = objNode.Attributes.GetNamedItem("value").Value
      Catch
        'Now check the ParamValues ArrayList
        Try
          objParameterValue = ParamValues.Item(intParamCounter)
        Catch
          Throw New Exception("Error getting the corresponding value for " _
                  & "the '" & strParameterName _
                  & "' <Parameter> element.")
        End Try
      End Try
```

We first check to see if the value was passed in along with the XML via the value attribute. If it was not, then we check to see if there is a corresponding value in the ArrayList of values. If we still do not get a Parameter value, then we throw an exception.

Now we are ready to create the SqlParameter object and set its Direction property. We do so with the following code:

```
      'Create the parameter object. Pass in the name, datatype,
      'and size to the constructor.
      objParameter = New SqlParameter(strParameterName, intSQLDataType, _
                  intParameterSize)

      'Set the direction of the parameter.
      objParameter.Direction = intParameterDirection
```

We then set the optional property values of the `SqlParameter` object:

```
'If the optional attributes have values, then set them.
If bytPrecision > 0 Then
  objParameter.Precision = bytPrecision
End If
If bytScale > 0 Then
  objParameter.Scale = bytScale
End If
```

Finally, we set the `Value` property of the `SqlParameter` object, add the `SqlParameter` object to the `SqlCommand` object's `Parameters` collection, increment our counter, complete our loop, and finish the method:

```
'Set the value of the parameter
objParameter.Value = objParameterValue

'Add the parameter to the SqlCommand's parameter collection
Command.Parameters.Add(objParameter)

'Increment the counter
intParamCounter = intParamCounter + 1

Next 'Each objNode In objParameterNodes

End Sub
```

Next we are going to look at `ExecSPReturnDR`. This function is almost identical to `ExecSPReturnDS`, except that it returns a `SqlDataReader` object instead of a `DataSet` object

ExecSPReturnDR

As in the previous function, this public function executes a stored procedure and returns a `SqlDataReader` object. Also, it takes a stored procedure name (`String`) and an optional list of parameter values (`ArrayList`). Here are the code snippets for `ExecSPReturnDR` which differ from `ExecSPReturnDS`:

```
Public Function ExecSPReturnDR(ByVal SPName As String, _
Optional ByVal ParamValues As ArrayList = Nothing) As SqlDataReader

  Dim objCommand As SqlCommand
  Dim objReader As SqlDataReader

  Try

...

    'Build the parameters, if any
    BuildParameters(objCommand, ParamValues)

    'Open the connection (required for the ExecuteReader method).
    mobjConnection.Open()

    'Execute the sp and get the SqlDataReader.
    objReader = objCommand.ExecuteReader
```

```
        'Return the value
        Return objReader

    Catch objException As Exception

...

    End Function
```

This function uses two objects to accomplish its mission: the `SqlCommand` and `SqlDataReader` objects. The only part where this function differs from `ExecSPReturnDS` is right after we call the `BuildParameters` private method. In this case, we have to make sure that the `SqlCommand` object's `SqlConnection` is opened. This is because the `SqlDataReader` requires an open connection. We then call the `ExecuteReader` method of the `SqlCommand` object to get our `SqlDataReader` object. Since this method returns a `SqlDataReader` object, which requires an open database connection, we do not close the connection in this method. It is up to the caller to close the `SqlDataReader` and the connection when finished. This can be accomplished via the `Dispose` method on our object. Otherwise, the connection will be closed when the last reference to `SqlConnection` falls out of scope and is collected by the Garbage Collector.

The next function we are going to look at, `ExecSPReturnXML`, is almost identical to the last two functions, except that it returns a string of XML instead of a `DataSet` or a `DataReader`.

ExecSPReturnXML

This public function executes a stored procedure and returns a string of XML. This function requires that the stored procedure contains a FOR XML clause in its SQL statement. Once again, it takes a stored procedure name (`String`) and an optional list of parameter values (`ArrayList`). The code that differs from the previous examples is:

```
Public Function ExecSPReturnXML(ByVal SPName As String, _
        Optional ByVal ParamValues As ArrayList = Nothing) As String

    Dim objCommand As SqlCommand = Nothing
    Dim objXMLReader As XmlReader = Nothing
    Dim strXML As String

    Try

...

        'Build the parameters for the SqlCommand object.
        BuildParameters(objCommand, ParamValues)

    'Open the connection (required for the ExecuteXmlReader method).
                mobjConnection.Open()

                'Execute the sp and get the XmlReader.
                objXMLReader = objCommand.ExecuteXmlReader()

                'Build the string of XML.
                Do Until objXMLReader.Read = False
                    strXML += objXMLReader.ReadOuterXml
                Loop
```

```
                        'Return the XML.
                        Return strXML

          Catch objException As Exception

          . . .

          End Function
```

This time the two objects used to accomplish this function are the `SqlCommand` and `XmlReader` objects. In this case, the only part where this function differs is right after we call the `BuildParameters` private method. In this case, we have to make sure that the `SqlCommand` object's `SqlConnection` is opened, as the `XmlReader` requires an open connection. We then call the `ExecuteXmlReader` method of the `SqlCommand` object to get our `XmlReader`. Next, we loop through the `XmlReader`'s data to build a string of XML that we return. Finally, we close the `XmlReader` and the `SqlConnection` objects.

Next we turn to `ExecSP` which only needs the `SqlCommand` object to get its work done, to execute stored procedures that do not return result sets.

ExecSP

This public method executes a stored procedure and does not return a value. It takes a stored procedure name (`String`) and an optional list of parameter values (`ArrayList`) for its arguments. Here is the code for `ExecSP`:

```
     Public Sub ExecSP(ByVal SPName As String, _
              Optional ByVal ParamValues As ArrayList = Nothing)

        Dim objCommand As SqlCommand = Nothing

        Try

        . . .

           'Build the parameters for the SqlCommand object.
           BuildParameters(objCommand, ParamValues)

           'Execute the stored procedure, and do not return any rows
           objCommand.ExecuteNonQuery()

        Catch objException As Exception

        . . .

        End Sub
```

It is almost identical to the other `Exec*` functions, except for when it executes the stored procedure. It uses the `SqlCommand` object's `ExecuteNonQuery` method. This ensures that the `SqlCommand` does not return any type of `DataReader` object to read the results. This method will be mostly used to execute `INSERT`, `UPDATE`, and `DELETE` queries that do not return any results.

Finally, the last public function we are going to create is `ExecSPOutputValues`.

ExecSPOutputValues

This last public function in our component executes a stored procedure and returns an `ArrayList` object that contains output parameter values. It is not meant for stored procedures that return resultsets. As with the previous examples, this function takes a stored procedure name (`String`) and an optional list of parameter values (`ArrayList`) for its arguments. Here is the code for `ExecSPOutputValues`:

```
Public Function ExecSPOutputValues(ByVal SPName As String, _
        Optional ByVal ParamValues As ArrayList = Nothing) As ArrayList

    Dim objCommand As SqlCommand = Nothing
    Dim arlParameters As New ArrayList()
    Dim objParameter As SqlParameter = Nothing

    Try

    ...

        'Execute the stored procedure, and do not return any rows
        objCommand.ExecuteNonQuery()

        'Build the ArrayList of output values
        For Each objParameter In objCommand.Parameters
          If objParameter.Direction = ParameterDirection.Output Then
            arlParameters.Add(objParameter.Value)
          End If
        Next

        'Return the output values
        Return arlParameters

    Catch objException As Exception

    ...

    End Function
```

This function is almost identical to `ExecSP`, except after `objCommand.ExecuteNonQuery` is called. Then, we iterate through the `SqlCommand` object's `Parameters` collection and look for all of the parameters that are output parameters. Next, we take the values of the output parameters and add them to the `ArrayList` object that we return.

Using DataSet Objects to Bind to DataGrids

Now that we have built our data access component, it is time to test it.

> Be sure to run the **UDF.sql** file – available with the code download – in your SQL Server's Query Analyzer before testing the data access component. This will create the necessary stored procedure and function in the pubs database.

A nice way to test it is to call the `ExecSPReturnDS` function, take the `DataSet` object that was created, and then bind the `DataSet` to a `DataGrid`. We also get to see how easily the `DataSet` object and the `DataGrid` control integrate together. To do this, create a new Visual Basic Windows Application solution, and add references to `IK.Data`, `System`, `System.Data`, `System.Drawing`, `System.Windows.Forms`, and `System.XML`. Now import `IK.Data`, add a `Button` (named `btnTest`) and a `DataGrid` (named `DgdAuthors`) to your form, and bind the `DataGrid` to the `DataSet` object. Here is what your form should look like:

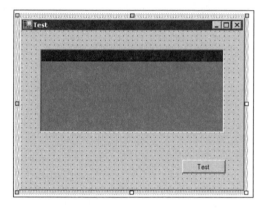

Here is what your references should look like:

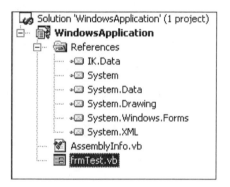

Lastly, here is the code for the test application:

```
Imports IK.Data

Public Class frmTest

    Inherits System.Windows.Forms.Form

Windows Form Designer generated code

    Private Sub btnTest_Click(ByVal sender As System.Object, _
               ByVal e As System.EventArgs) _
               Handles btnTest.Click

      Dim strConn As String
      Dim objDS As DataSet
```

```
      Dim objSQL As SQLServer
   Dim objArrayList As New ArrayList()

      Try

         'Set the SQL Managed Provider connection string
         strConn = "Initial Catalog=pubs;Data Source=(local); " _
             & "User ID=sa;password=;"

         'Call the SQLServer component constructor and
         'pass the db connection string
         objSQL = New SQLServer(strConn)

         'Set the XML file property
         objSQL.SPConfigXMLFile = Application.StartupPath _
                      & "\PubsStoredProcedures.xml"

         'Add the two parameter values
         objArrayList.Add("CA")
         objArrayList.Add("^")

         'Execute the sp, and get the DataSet object back
         objDS = objSQL.ExecSPReturnDS("usp_Get_Authors_By_States", _
                      objArrayList)

         'Bind the DataGrid to the DataSet object
         dgdAuthors.SetDataBinding(objDS.Tables(0), Nothing)

      Catch objException As Exception

         'Display the exception message,
         'along with the nested exception message
         MsgBox(objException.Message & objException.InnerException.Message)

      End Try

   End Sub

   End Class
```

We start out the code by supplying a database connection string to the SQLServer object constructor. We then set the XML file property of the SQLServer object by placing our XML file (PubsStoredProcedures.xml) in the path of the assembly. After that, we add two parameter values to the ArrayList object; these values are in the same order that the parameters are in the XML file. Next, the ExecSPReturnDS method of the SQLServer object is called so that a populated DataSet object is returned based upon a stored procedure that returns rows. Once we have the DataSet object, we simply call the SetDataBinding method of our DataGrid object. The SetDataBinding method takes two arguments, a data source (Object), and a data member (String). In this case, we do not have a data member, so we pass in Nothing. If you try to pass in an empty string, an exception will be thrown.

Finally, the results should look like:

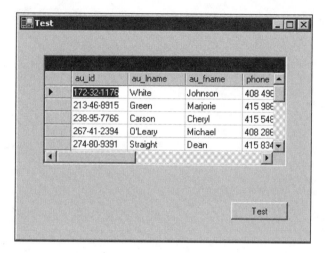

Summary

In this chapter, we have taken a look at how ADO has evolved into ADO.NET. We have seen and used the main objects in ADO.NET that you need to quickly get up and running in order to build data access into your .NET applications. We took a fairly in-depth look at the `DataSet` object, since this is the core object of ADO.NET, and we also compared and contrasted ADO and ADO.NET so you could actually see the easier programming model. Finally, we built our own custom data access component. The intent of our data access component was to make it easy to separate data access code from the rest of business logic code in .NET applications.

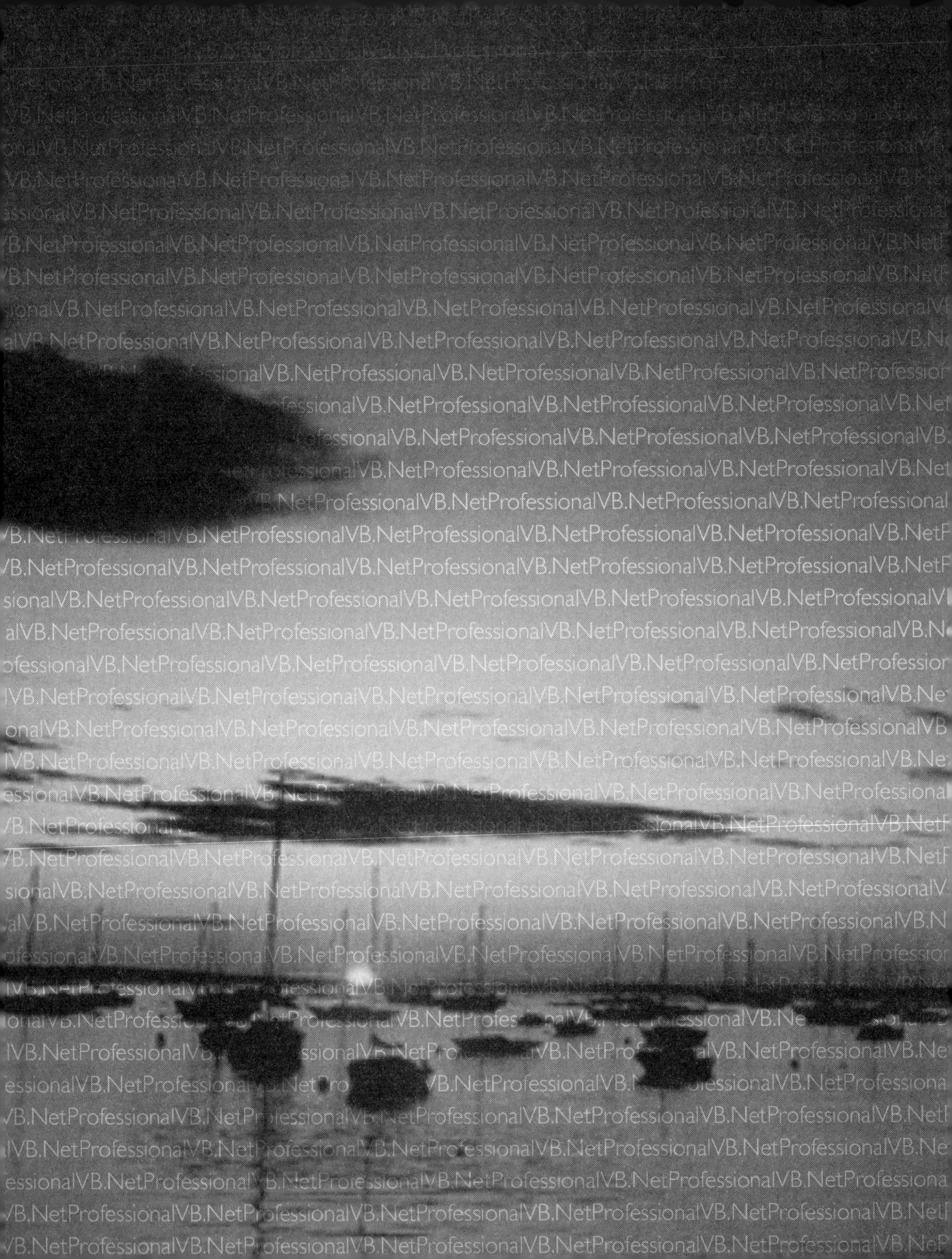
VB.NetProfessional

Using XML in VB.NET

This chapter presents the features of the .NET Framework that facilitate the generation and manipulation of XML. As a technology, XML can be categorized as vast. To put the scope and importance of XML in perspective consider the fact that the .NET Framework exposes five XML specific namespaces that contain over one hundred fifty different classes. Adding to this complexity are the dozens of classes that support and implement XML related technologies such as ADO, ADO.NET, SQL Server 2000 and BizTalk. This chapter attempts to make sense of this barrage of knowledge by introducing some basic XML concepts and demonstrating how VB.NET in conjunction with the .NET Framework can make use of XML. An excellent starting point for any developer looking to hone their XML skills is, *Professional XML, Second Edition* from Wrox Press, ISBN 1861005059.

This chapter presents a brief tutorial on XML introducing the rationale for this technology and making some salient observations. This chapter will then describe the .NET Framework's XML related namespaces including `System.Xml`, `System.Xml.Serialization`, and `System.Xml.Xsl`. A subset of the classes exposed by these namespaces will be examined in detail. This chapter will also touch on a set of technologies that utilize XML, specifically ADO.NET and SQL Server. After reading this chapter, developers will be able to generate, manipulate, and transform XML.

VB.NET relies on the classes exposed in XML-related namespaces in order to transform, intricately manipulate, and stream XML documents. The .NET namespaces specific to this aspect of XML development include:

- ❑ `System.Xml` – this namespace provides core support for a variety of XML standards (DTD, namespace, DOM, XDR, XPath, XSLT, and SOAP).

- ❑ `System.Xml.Serialization` – provides the objects used to transform objects to/from XML documents or streams using serialization.

❑ `System.Xml.Serialization.Schema` – provides a set of objects that allow schema to be loaded, created, and streamed. This support is achieved using a suite of objects that support the in-memory manipulation of the entities that compose an XML schema.

❑ `System.Xml.XPath` – provides a parser and evaluation engine for the XML Path Language (XPath).

❑ `System.Xml.Xsl` – provides the objects necessary when working with, XSL, **eXtensible Stylesheet Language** transforms (**XSLT**).

The XML-related technologies utilized by VB.NET include other technologies that generate XML documents and allow XML documents to be managed as a data source. The technologies that facilitate this type of interaction with XML documents include:

❑ ADO – the legacy COM objects provided by ADO have the ability to generate XML documents in stream or file form. ADO can also retrieve a previously persisted XML document and manipulate it. Within this chapter, ADO will not be present. ADO and other legacy COM APIs can be accessed seamlessly from VB.Net so when porting a legacy application to VB.Net one possible alternative would be to use the original database access technology (ADO).

❑ ADO.NET – the data access technology of .NET, ADO.NET, uses XML as its underlying data representation. The manifestation of this is that the in-memory data representation of ADO.NET's `DataSet` object is XML. The results of data queries are represented as an XML document, XML can be imported into a `DataSet` and exported from a `DataSet`.

❑ SQL Server 2000 – XML specific features were added to SQL Server 2000 (`FOR XML` queries to retrieve XML documents and `OPENXML` in order to represent an XML document as a rowset). VB.NET can use ADO.NET in order to access SQL Server's XML-specific features. The documents generated by and consumed by SQL Server can be manipulated programmatically using the XML-specific class exposed by the .NET Framework.

This list of technologies that can generate XML is by no means complete. The .NET Server BizTalk can be used to generate XML or XML can be generated programmatically. VB developers used to developing with the Jet database will find this data engine does not have nearly the support for XML as SQL Server 2000. With the release of Microsoft's free, lightweight version of SQL Server (MSDE), Jet has received less focus from Microsoft.

Introduction to XML

XML is the standard for sharing data between applications. This standard means that bank-to-bank transactions can share a common data representation. A consumer's transactions with their bank can share a common representation. When TV commercials are inserted into a stream of video, the data describing the add insertion is passed using XML. Sports scores and statistics can be rapidly disseminated in a common format using XML. The number of uses for a common data representation standard such as XML is limitless.

XML is a tagged data representation similar in format to HTML. As a technology, XML leverages one of the most useful features of HTML, readability. XML differs from HTML in that XML represents data while HTML is a mechanism for displaying data. In fact, the tags in XML describe the data. An example of an XML document is as follows:

```
<?xml version="1.0" encoding="utf-8"?>
<prescriptions>
  <WXClientPrescription dentistName="Dr. Jam" medicationID="1"
                        quantity="21">
  </WXClientPrescription>
  <WXClientPrescription dentistName="Dr. Jam" medicationID="2"
                        quantity="22">
  </WXClientPrescription>
</prescriptions>
```

The previous XML document is used to represent a set of medical prescriptions written by a dentist. The standard used to represent a prescription would be useful to dentists, doctors, insurance companies, government run medical systems, and pharmacies. This information can be shared using XML because:

❑   The data (tags) in XML are self describing (tag dentistName is the name of the dentist)

❑   XML is an open standard

XML supports the parsing of data by applications not familiar with the contents of the XML document. XML documents can also be associated with a description (a schema) that informs an application as to the form of the data within the XML document.

At this stage, XML looks simple. It is just a human readable way to exchange data that is universally accepted as the standard with which to exchange data. The APIs for manipulating XML have been standardized. The parsers for verifying and manipulating XML have been standardized. The W3C consortium (www.w3c.org) controls the XML standard rather than having a single corporation dictate what is XML. In support of XML, standards have evolved for specifying schemas, transforming XML, retrieving XML from databases, linking and query documents, and displaying documents. It should be clear why one thousand page plus tomes such as *Professional XML, Second Edition* exists for this technology.

The basics of XML are as follows:

❑   XML data is contained in a document.

❑   A document is well formed if it adheres to the standard.

❑   Tags are used to specify the contents of a document (for example, <WXClientPrescription> and dentistName).

❑   Documents contain XML elements that can be thought of as the objects within a document.

❑   Elements are the basic building block of the document. Each element contains a start (for example, <WXClientPrescription>) and end tag (</WXClientPrescription>). A tag can be both a start and an end tag such as <WXClientPrescription/>. Data can be contained in the element (element content) or within attributes contained in the element. For example, <WXClientPrescription>is an XML element.

❑   Within the document, the objects (XML elements) are described using attributes. Our example XML document contained attributes such as dentistName and medicationID. The values of these attributes are what specifically describe the element (dentistName has a value of "Dr. Jam" and medicationID has a value of "1").

❑   XML is hierarchical. One document can contain multiple elements. Elements can contain children. Children can contain children. In our example, <prescriptions> contained child elements of type <WXClientPrescription>.

The XML document hierarchy is basically a tree containing nodes. Our document has a root node, <prescriptions>. The branches of this node were elements of type <WXClientPrescription>. The leaves of the XML element, <WXClientPrescription>, were its attributes (dentistName, quantity, and medicationID).

Jargon aside; the practical manipulation of XML entails taking the prescription in the document whose root is <prescriptions> and displaying for the staff of the dental clinic, transforming the prescriptions so a pharmacy can fill the prescription, saving the contents of these prescriptions to VB.NET objects, and persisting these prescriptions of a file or database. These practical aspects of XML manipulation make up the most common style of tasks performed by applications that leverage XML.

XML Serialization

The simplest way to demonstrate VB.NET's support for XML is not with a complicated technology such as SQL Server, BizTalk or ADO.NET. Instead, we will demonstrate XML by serializing a class. The serialization of an object (an instance of a class) takes the said object and writes it out to a stream such as a file or a socket. Think of this as *dehydrating* a class. Once serialized, any class can be re-hydrated again (de-serialized) by reading it back from a stream such as a socket or a file. The type of serialization we are discussing is XML serialization where XML is used to represent a class in serialized form.

In order to understand XML serialization, let's examine class, WXClientPrescription. This class is implemented in VB.NET and is used by a dentist in order to write a prescription for medication. This class could be instantiated on a dentist's PDA, laptop, or even mobile phone provided the .NET Framework was installed. An instance of class, WXClientPrescription, corresponding to each prescription could be serialized to XML and sent over a socket using the PDA's cellular modem. If the dentist's PDA did not have a cellular modem, the instance of class, WXClientPrescription, could be serialized to a file. The prescription would be processed when the PDA was dropped into a docking cradle and synced. This might take place when the dentist returned to the office after treating a patient. What we are really talking about is data in a proprietary form (an instance of class, WXClientPrescription) needing to be converted into a generic representation (XML).

Namespace, System.Xml.Serialization, supports the serialization of objects to XML and deserialization of objects from XML. Objects are serialized to either documents or streams using class, XmlSerializer. The basics of using this object are simple:

❑   Define an object that implements a default constructor (Public Sub New()). For example, consider object, WXClientPrescription, found in application, VBNetXML03, which can downloaded from the Wrox web site:

```
Public Class WXClientPrescription

    ' These are Public because we have yet to implement
    ' properties to provide program access

    Public dentistName As String
    Public medicationID As Integer
    Public quantity As Integer

    Public Sub New()
    End Sub

    Public Sub New(ByVal dentistName As String, _
```

```
            ByVal medicationID As Integer, _
            ByVal quantity As Integer)
    Me.dentistName = dentistName
    Me.medicationID = medicationID
    Me.quantity = quantity
 End Sub

End Class
```

❑ Call `XmlSerializer`'s constructor specifying the object to serialize and its type (see call below to function, `GetType`):

```
Dim serialize As XmlSerializer = _
    New XmlSerializer(GetType(WXClientPrescription))
```

❑ Create an instance of the same type as was passed as parameter to the constructor of `XmlSerializer`:

```
Dim prescription As WXClientPrescription = _
    New WXClientPrescription("Dr. Jam", 101, 10)
```

❑ Call the `Serialize` method of the `XmlSerializer` instance and specify the stream to which the serialized object is written (parameter one, `Console.Out`) and the object to be serialized (parameter two, `prescription`):

```
serialize.Serialize(Console.Out, prescription)
Console.Out.WriteLine()
```

The output generated by the previous code, found as part of `WXClientDentist` in `VBNetXML03`, snippet is as follows:

```
<?xml version="1.0" encoding="IBM437"?>
<WXClientPrescription xmlns:xsi="http://www.w3.org/2001/XMLSchema-instance"
xmlns:xsd="http://www.w3.org/2001/XMLSchema">
  <dentistName>Dr. Jam</dentistName>
  <medicationID>0</medicationID>
  <quantity>10</quantity>
</WXClientPrescription>
```

This output demonstrates the default behavior of how the `Serialize` method serializes an object. Each object serialized is represented as an element named, "classname". Our object of type, `WXClientPrescription`, is contained in an XML element named, `<WXClientPrescription>`. The individual data members of the class serialized are contained in elements named for each data member. For class, `WXClientPrescription`, the data members are (`dentistName`, `medicationID`, and `quantity`) and subsequently the XML elements are `<dentistName>`, `<medicationID>`, and `<quantity>`. Also part of the XML document generated is the specific version of XML generated (1.0), the encoding used (IBM437), and schemas used to describe our serialized object (http://www.w3.org/2001/XMLSchema-instance and http://www.w3.org/2001/XMLSchema).

Database developers are familiar with the concept of a schema – a schema describes the data (name, type, scale, precision, length, etc.). XML schemas are similar. A schema can be associated with an XML document. Either the actual schema or a reference to where the schema resides can be contained in the XML document. In either case, an XML schema is a standard representation that can be used by all applications that case consume XML. Each application can therefore validate the contents of the XML document generated by the `Serialize` method of class, `XmlSerializer`. This validation can be performed using the supplied schema.

Our code snippet that demonstrated the `Serialize` method of class, `XmlSerializer`, displayed the XML generated to `Console.Out`. Clearly, we do not expect an application to use `Console.Out` when it would like to access a `WXClientPrescription` object in XML form. The basic idea shown was serialization in two lines of code (one call to a constructor and one call to method, `Serialize`). The entire section of code responsible for serializing the instance of class, `WXClientPrescription`, is as follows:

```
Try
    Dim serialize As XmlSerializer = _
                New XmlSerializer(GetType(WXClientPrescription))
    Dim prescription As WXClientPrescription = _
            New WXClientPrescription("Dr. Jam", 101, 10)

    serialize.Serialize(Console.Out, prescription)
    Console.Out.WriteLine()
Catch ex As Exception
    Console.Error.WriteLine(ex.ToString())
End Try
```

The `Serialize` method's first parameter is overridden so that it can serialize XML to a file (filename as type, `String`), a `Stream`, `TextWriter`, or `XmlWriter`. When serializing to `Stream`, `TextWriter`, or `XmlWriter` a third parameter to the `Serialize` method is permissible. This third parameter is of type, `XmlSerializerNamespaces`, and is used to specify a list of namespaces that qualify the names in the XML generated document. The permissible overrides of the `Serialize` method are defined as follows:

```
Public Sub Serialize(Stream, Object)
Public Sub Serialize(TextWriter, Object)
Public Sub Serialize(XmlWriter, Object)
Public Sub Serialize(Stream, Object, XmlSerializerNamespaces)
Public Sub Serialize(TextWriter, Object, XmlSerializerNamespaces)
Public Sub Serialize(XmlWriter, Object, XmlSerializerNamespaces)
```

An object is reconstituted using the `XmlSerializer` object's `Deserialize` method. This method is overridden and can therefore de-serialize XML presented as a `Stream`, `TextReader`, or `XmlReader`. The overloads for method, `Deserialize`, are as follows:

```
Public Function Deserialize(Stream) As Object
Public Function Deserialize(TextReader) As Object
Public Function Deserialize(XmlReader) As Object
```

Before demonstrating the `Deserialize` method, we will introduce a new class, `WXClientMultiPrescription`. This class contains an array of prescriptions (an array of class, `WXClientPrescription`). Class, `WXClientMultiPrescription`, is defined as follows:

```
Public Class WXClientMultiPrescription

    Public prescriptions() As WXClientPrescription

    Public Sub New()
    End Sub

    Public Sub New(ByVal prescriptions() As WXClientPrescription)
        Me.prescriptions = prescriptions
    End Sub
End Class
```

The WXClientMultiPrescription class contains a fairly complicated object, an array of WXClientPrescription objects. Serialization and de-serialization of this class is more complicated than a single instance of a class that contains several simple types. The act of serializing and de-serializing such a composite class might be more complicated but the programming effort involved is just as simple as was previously demonstrated. The following code snippet from application, VBNetXML03, demonstrates an object of type, WXClientMultiPrescription, being rehydrated using file, justaddwater.xml. This object is de-serialized using this file in conjunction with the XmlSerializer object's Deserialize method:

```
' Open file, ..\justaddwater.xml
Dim dehydrated As FileStream = _
    New FileStream("..\justaddwater.xml", FileMode.Open)

' Create an XmlSerializer instance to handle deserializing,
' WXClientMultiPrescription
Dim serialize As XmlSerializer = _
        New XmlSerializer(GetType(WXClientMultiPrescription))

' Create an object to contain the deserialized instance of the object
Dim prescriptions As WXClientMultiPrescription = _
      New WXClientMultiPrescription()

' Deserialize object
prescriptions = serialize.Deserialize(dehydrated)
```

Once deserialized, the array of prescriptions can be displayed:

```
Dim prescription As WXClientPrescription

For Each prescription In prescriptions.prescriptions
    Console.Out.WriteLine("{0}, {1}, {2}", _
                          prescription.dentistName, _
                          prescription.medicationID, _
                          prescription.quantity)
Next
```

The file, justaddwater.xml, was created using code found in, VBNetXML03, that is not shown here. It is just code that serializes an instance of type, WXClientMultiPrescription. The output generated by displaying our de-serialized object containing an array of prescriptions is as follows:

Dr. Jam, 1, 11
Dr. Jam, 2, 12
Dr. Jam, 3, 13
Dr. Jam, 4, 14

Class, XmlSerializer, also implements the CanDeserialize method. The prototype for this method is as follows:

```
Overridable Public Function CanDeserialize(ByVal xmlReader As XmlReader) _
                As Boolean
```

If CanDeserialize returns True, then the XML document specified by the xmlReader parameter can be de-serialized. If the return value of this method is False, then the XML specified cannot be de-serialized.

623

The FromTypes method of class, XmlSerializer, facilitates the creation of arrays containing XmlSerializer objects. This array of XmlSerializer objects can be used in turn to process arrays of the type to be serialized. The prototype for method, FromTypes, is as follows:

```
Public Shared Function FromTypes(ByVal types() As Type) As XmlSerializer()
```

Before further exploring the dark recesses of namespace, System.Xml.Serialization, let us consider the overloaded term, attribute.

SourceCode Style Attributes

Thus far we have seen attribute applied to a specific portion of an XML document. Visual Basic has its own flavor of attribute as does C# and each of the other .NET languages. This other type of attribute will henceforth be called **SourceCode Style** attributes. Attributes in the purely sourcecode sense refer to annotations to sourcecode (class, data member, method, etc.) that specify information that can be used other applications accessing the original code.

In the context of namespace, System.Xml.Serialization, SourceCode Style attributes can be used to change the names of the elements generated for a class's data members; in addition, to generate XML attributes instead of XML elements for a class's data members. In order to demonstrate this we will use class, WXLaClientLaPrescription, which contains data members: dentistName, medicationID, and quantity. It just so happens that the default XML generated when serializing this class is not in a form that can be readily consumed by our external application. A French development team has written this external application and hence the XML element and attribute names are in French rather than in English.

In order to rename the XML generated for data member, dentistName, a Sourcecode Style attribute will be used. This Sourcecode Style attribute would specify that when class, WXLaClientLaPrescription, is serialized the dentistName data member would be represented as an XML element, <LaDentistLaName>. The actual Sourcecode Style attribute that specifies this is as follows:

```
<XmlElementAttribute("LaDentistLaName")> Public dentistName As String
```

Class, WXLaClientLaPrescription, contains other Sourcecode Style attributes:

- <XmlAttributeAttribute("LaMedicationLaID")> specifies that data member, medicationID, is to be serialized as an XML attribute named, LaMedicationLaID.

- <XmlAttributeAttribute("LaHowLaMuch")> specifies that data member, quantity, is to be serialized as an XML attribute named, LaHowLaMuch.

It is worth mentioning that the author of the chapter is an American and takes full responsibility for the accuracy of the French translation.

Class, WXLaClientLaPrescription found as part of VBNetXML03, in its entirety is defined as follows:

```
Public Class WXLaClientLaPrescription

    ' These are Public because we have yet to implement
    ' properties to provide program access
    <XmlElementAttribute("LaDentistLaName")> Public dentistName As String
```

```
        <XmlAttributeAttribute("LaMedicationLaID")> _
            Public medicationID As Integer
        <XmlAttributeAttribute("LaHowLaMuch")> Public quantity As Integer

        Public Sub New()
        End Sub

        Public Sub New(ByVal dentistName As String, _
                        ByVal medicationID As Integer, _
                        ByVal quantity As Integer)
            Me.dentistName = dentistName
            Me.medicationID = medicationID
            Me.quantity = quantity
        End Sub
    End Class
```

Class, `WXLaClientLaPrescription`, can be serialized as follows:

```
    Dim serialize As XmlSerializer = _
        New XmlSerializer(GetType(WXLaClientLaPrescription))
    Dim prescription As WXLaClientLaPrescription = _
        New WXLaClientLaPrescription("Dr. Jam", 101, 10)

    serialize.Serialize(Console.Out, prescription)
```

The output generated by the previous code snippet reflects the Sourcecode Style attributes associated with class, `WXLaClientLaPrescription`:

```
<?xml version="1.0" encoding="IBM437"?>
<WXLaClientLaPrescription xmlns:xsi="http://www.w3.org/2001/XMLSchema-instance"
                          xmlns:xsd="http://www.w3.org/2001/XMLSchema"
    LaMedicationLaID="101" LaHowLaMuch="10">
  <LaDentistLaName>Dr. Jam</LaDentistLaName>
</WXLaClientLaPrescription>
```

In the previous example output, notice that the value of `medicationID` is contained in XML attribute, `LaMedicationLaID`, and that the value of `quantity` is contained in XML attribute, `LaHowLaMuch`. The value of `dentistName` is contained in XML element, `LaDentistLaName`.

The saga of the Sourcecode Style attributes does not end here. Our example only demonstrated the Sourcecode Style attributes exposed by the `XmlAttributeAttribute` and `XmlElementAttribute` classes contained in the `System.Xml.Serialization` namespace. A variety of other Sourcecode Style attributes exist in this namespace that also control the form of XML generated by serialization. The classes associated with such Sourcecode Style attributes include but are not limited to: `XmlTypeAttribute`, `XmlTextAttribute`, `XmlRootAttribute`, `XmlIncludeAttribute`, `XmlIngoreAttribute`, and `XmlEnumAttribute`.

System.Xml Document Support

The `System.Xml` namespace implements a variety of objects that support standards-based XML processing. The XML-specific standards facilitated by this namespace include: XML 1.0, Document Type Definition (DTD) Support, XML Namespaces, XML schemas, XPath, XSL/T, DOM Level 2 (Core implementation) and SOAP 1.1, and SOAP Contract Language and SOAP Discovery. Namespace, `System.Xml`, exposes over thirty separate classes in order to facilitate this level of XML standard's compliance.

With respect to generating and navigating XML documents, there are two styles of access:

❑ Stream-based – System.Xml exposes a variety of classes that read XML from and write XML to a stream. This approach tends to be a fast way to consume or generate an XML document because it represents a set of serial reads or writes. The limitation with this approach is that it does not view the XML data as a document composed of tangible entities such as nodes, elements, and attributes. An example of where a stream could be used would be when receiving an XML document from a socket or a file.

❑ Document Object Model (DOM)-based – System.Xml exposes a set of objects that access XML documents as data. The data is accessed using entities from the XML document tree (nodes, elements, and attributes). This style of XML generation and navigation is flexible but may not yield the same performance as stream-based XML generation and navigation. DOM is excellent technology for editing and manipulating documents. For example, the functionality exposed by DOM might make merging your checking, savings, and brokerage accounts simpler.

XML Stream-Style Parsers

When demonstrating XML serialization we alluded to XML stream-style parsers. After all, when an instance of an object was serialized to XML it had to be written to a stream and when de-serialized it was read from a stream. When an XML document is parsed using a stream parser, the parser always points to the current node in the document. The basic architecture of the stream parsers is as follows:

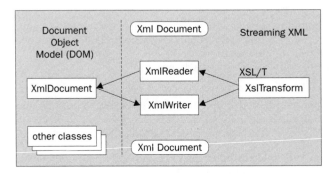

The classes that access a stream of XML (read XML) and generate a stream of XML (write XML) are contained in the System.Xml namespace and are as follows:

❑ XmlWriter – this abstract class specifies a non-cached, forward-only stream that writes an XML document (data and schema).

❑ XmlReader – this abstract class specifies a non-cached, forward-only stream that reads an XML document (data and schema).

Our diagram of the classes associated with the XML stream-style parser referred to one other class, XslTransform. This class found in the System.Xml.Xsl namespace is not an XML stream-style parser but is used in conjunction with XmlWriter, and XmlReader. This class will be reviewed in detail in the section covering namespace, System.Xml.Xsl.

Namespace, System.Xml, exposes a plethora of additional XML manipulation classes in addition to those shown in the architecture diagram. Classes shown in the diagram include:

❏ XmlResolver – this abstract class resolves an external XML resource using a URI Class. XmlUrlResolver, is an implementation of an XmlResolver.

❏ XmlNameTable – this abstract class provides a fast means by which an XML parser can access element or attribute names.

These additional classes discussed still do not fully represent the broad suite of classes exposed by System.Xml.

Writing an XML Stream

An XML document can be created programmatically. One way to perform this task is by writing the individual components of an XML document (schema, attributes, elements, etc.) to an XML stream. Using a unidirectional write-stream means that each element and its attributes must be written in order. The idea is that data is always written at the head of the stream. In order to accomplish this we would use a writable XML stream class (a class derived from XmlWriter). Such a class insures that the XML document we generate correctly implements the XML standard: W3C Extensible Markup Language (XML) 1.0 specification and the Namespaces in XML specification.

But why would this be necessary since we have XML serialization? We need to be very careful here to separate interface (XML) from implementation. XML serialization worked for a specific class, WXLaClientLaPrescription. The class is a proprietary implementation and not the format in which data is exchanged. For this one specific case the XML document generated when WXLaClientLaPrescription is serialized just so happens to be the XML format used when generating a prescription. Class, WXLaClientLaPrescription, was given a little help from Sourcecode Style attributes in order to conform to a standard XML representation of a prescription.

In a different application, if the software used to manage the entire dental practice wants to generate prescriptions, it will have to generate a document of the appropriate form. Our dental practice management software will achieve this by using an XML stream writer, XmlTextWriter. This class is derived from our XML stream writing class, XmlWriter, as follows:

```
Object
    XmlWriter
        XmlTextWriter
```

Before reviewing the subtleties of class, XmlTextWriter, it is important to note that this class exposes over forty methods and properties. The example presented in this section will provide an overview that touches on a subset of these methods and properties. This subset of XmlTextWriter's implementation allows an XML document to be generated corresponding to a medical prescription.

The code that generates an XML document corresponding to a medical prescription is found in, application, VBNetXML02, which can also be downloaded from the Wrox website. Ultimately our instance of the XmlTextWriter class, prescriptionTextWriter, is a file on a disk. This means that the XML document generated is streamed to this file. Since variable, prescriptionTextWriter, represents a file it must:

❏ Be created – the instance of the XmlTextWriter class, prescriptionTextWriter, is created using New.

❑ Be opened – the file the XML is streamed to, `PrescriptionsProgrammatic.XML`, is opened by passing the filename to the constructor associated with `XmlTextWriter`.

❑ Generate the XML document – this process is described in detail at the end of this section.

❑ Be closed – the file (the XML stream) is closed using `XmlTextWriter`'s `Close` method.

The basic infrastructure for managing the file (the XML text stream) is as follows:

```
Dim xmlTextWriter As XmlTextWriter = Nothing

prescriptionTextWriter = _
    New XmlTextWriter("..\PrescriptionsProgrammatic.XML", Nothing)


' ***********************************************************************
' Generate XML document here using the methods/properties of XmlTextWriter
' ***********************************************************************



prescriptionTextWriter.Close()
```

Before writing the actual elements and attributes of our XML document, certain properties of `XmlTextWriter` will be specified in order to make our document esthetically pleasing. Specifically we will set the `Formatting` property to `Formatting.Indent`. This setting allows child elements of the XML document to be indented. We will also set `IndentChar` to the space character and the value of property `Indentation` to 4. These settings respectively mean that the character used in child element indentation is the space character and the number of spaces indented is four. The code responsible for configuring our XML text stream in this manner is as follows:

```
prescriptionTextWriter.Formatting = Formatting.Indented
prescriptionTextWriter.Indentation = 4
prescriptionTextWriter.IndentChar = " "
```

With the preliminaries completed (file created and formatting configured), the process of writing the actual attributes and elements of our XML document can begin. The sequences of steps used to generate our XML document is as follows:

❑ Call method, `WriteStartDocument`, in order to write the XML declaration and specify version 1.0. The XML generated by this method is as follows:

`<?xml version="1.0" standalone="no"?>`

❑ Write an XML comment using method, `WriteComment`. This comment describes from whence the concept for this XML document originated and generates the following:

`<!--Same as generated by serializing, WXClientPrescription -->`

❑ Begin writing XML element, `<WXLaClientLaPrescription>`, by calling method, `WriteStartElement`. We can only begin writing this element because its attributes and child elements must be written before the element can be ended with a corresponding, `</WXLaClientLaPrescription>`. The XML generated by the `WriteStartElement` method is as follows:

`<WXLaClientLaPrescription>`

- ❏ Write the attributes associated with element, `<WXLaClientLaPrescription>`, by calling the `WriteAttributeString` method twice. The XML generated by calling method, `WriteAttributeString`, twice adds to our `WXLaClientLaPrescription` XML element currently written to:

  `<WXLaClientLaPrescription LaMedicationLaID="101" LaHowLaMuch="10">`

- ❏ Using method `WriteElementString`, write the child XML element, `<LaDentistLaName>`, contained in XML element, `<WXLaClientLaPrescription>`. The XML generated by calling this method is as follows:

  `<LaDentistLaName>Dr. Jam</LaDentistLaName>`

- ❏ Complete writing the `<WXLaClientLaPrescription>`parent XML element by call method, `WriteEndElement`. The XML generated by calling this method is as follows:

  `</WXLaClientLaPrescription>`

The sourcecode associated with application, `VBNetXML02`, uses the various methods and properties of variable, `prescriptionTextWriter`, again and again rather monotonously. This variable is of type, `XmlTextWriter`. In order to simplify coding, VB's `With` keyword is used (`With prescriptionTextWriter`). The sourcecode associated with application, `VBNetXML02`, is as follows:

```
Dim prescriptionTextWriter As XmlTextWriter = Nothing

prescriptionTextWriter = _
    New XmlTextWriter("..\PrescriptionsProgrammatic.XML", Nothing)

With prescriptionTextWriter
    .Formatting = Formatting.Indented
    .Indentation = 4
    .IndentChar = " "
    .WriteStartDocument(False)
    .WriteComment( _
        "Same as generated by serializing, WXLaClientLaPrescription")
    .WriteStartElement("WXLaClientLaPrescription")
    .WriteAttributeString("LaMedicationLaID", "101")
    .WriteAttributeString("LaHowLaMuch", "10")
    .WriteElementString("LaDentistLaName", "Dr. Jam")
    .WriteEndElement() ' End WXLaClientLaPrescription

    .Close()
End With
```

The XML document generated is persisted to file, `PrescriptionsProgrammatic.XML`. The contents of this file are as follows:

```
<?xml version="1.0" standalone="no"?>
<!--Same as generated by serializing, WXClientPrescription -->
<WXLaClientLaPrescription LaMedicationLaID="101" LaHowLaMuch="10">
    <LaDentistLaName>Dr. Jam</LaDentistLaName>
</WXLaClientLaPrescription>
```

The previous XML document is the same in form as the XML document generated by serializing the `WXLaClientLaPrescription` class. Notice in the previous XML document that element, `<LaDentistLaName>`, is indented four characters. This was achieved using the `Formatting`, `Indentation`, and `IndentChar` properties of the `XmlTextWriter` class.

Our sample application, VBNetXML02, covered only twenty-five percent of the methods and properties exposed by the XML stream writing class, XmlTextWriter. Other methods implemented by this class include methods that manipulate the underlying file such as the Flush method. XML text can be written directly to the stream using the WriteRaw method. The XmlTextWriter class also exposes a variety of methods that write a specific type of XML data to the stream. These methods include WriteBinHex, WriteCData, WriteString, and WriteWhiteSpace.

So at this stage of our investigation into VB.NET and XML we can generate the same document two different ways. Two different applications took two different approaches to generate a document that represents a standardized medical prescription. Trust us, there are even more ways to generated XML depending on circumstance. For example, we could receive a prescription from a patient's doctor and this prescription would have to be transformed from the XML format used by the doctor's office to our own prescription format.

Reading an XML Stream

XML documents can be read from a stream. The way a readable stream works is that data is traversed in the stream in order (first XML element, second XML element, etc.). This traversal is very quick because the data is processed in one direction and features such as write and move backwards in the traversal are not supported. At any given instance, only data at the current position in the stream can be accessed.

Before exploring how an XML stream can be read we should explain why it should be read. To answer this pressing question let's return to our dental office. Imagine the application that manages the dental practice can generate a variety of XML documents corresponding to prescriptions, appointments, and laboratory work such as making crowns and dentures. All the documents (prescription, appointment, and laboratory work) can be extracted in stream form and processed by a report generating application. This application prints up the schedule of appointments for a given day, the prescriptions that are outstanding for the scheduled patients, and the laboratory work required to treat the patients scheduled. The report generating application processes the data by reading in a stream of XML and parsing the said stream.

One class that can be used to read and parse such an XML stream is XmlTextReader. This class is derived from XmlReader. When constructed an XmlTextReader can read XML from a file (specified by a string corresponding to the file's name), a Stream, or an XmlReader. For demonstration purposes, XmlTextReader will be used in order to read an XML document contained in a file. The application that will demonstrate this is, VBNetXML01. Reading XML from a file and writing it to a file is not the norm when it comes to XML processing. For the sake of our examples, a file is the simplest way to access XML data. This simplified access allows us to focus more intimately on XML specific issues.

The first step in accessing a stream of XML data is to create an instance of the object that will open the stream (the readOfficeInfo variable of type XmlTextReader) and to open the stream itself. Application, VBNetXML01, performs this as follows (where DentalManage.xml is the name of the file containing the XML document):

```
Dim readOfficeInfo As XmlTextReader

readOfficeInfo = New XmlTextReader("..\DentalManage.xml")
```

The basic mechanism for traversing each stream is to traverse from node-to-node using the Read method. Node types in XML include "element" and "whitespace". Numerous other node types are defined (see enumeration, XmlNodeType) but for the sake of our example we will focus on traversing streams XML elements and the whitespace that is used to make the elements more readable (carriage returns, linefeeds, and indentation spaces). Once the stream is positioned at a node, the MoveToNextAttribute method can be called to read each attribute contained in an element. The MoveToNextAttribute method will only traverse attributes for nodes that contain attributes (nodes of type element). An example of an instance of type, XmlTextReader, traversing each node and then traversing the attributes of each node is as follows:

```
While readOfficeInfo.Read()
    ' Process node here
    While readOfficeInfo.MoveToNextAttribute()
        ' Process attribute here
    End While
End While
```

The previous code snippet that reads the contents of the XML stream does not utilize any knowledge of the stream's contents. A great many applications know exactly what the stream they are going to traverse looks like. Such applications can use XmlReadText in a more deliberate manner and not simply traverse the stream without foreknowledge.

Once our example stream has been read, it can be closed using the Close method:

```
readOfficeInfo.Close()
```

The code that traverses an XML document is found in subroutine, WXReadXML. This subroutine takes the filename containing the XML to read as a parameter (ByVal fileName). The code for subroutine, WXReadXML, is as follows and is basically the code we just outlined:

```
Private Sub WXReadXML(ByVal fileName As String)
    Dim readOfficeInfo As XmlTextReader

    readOfficeInfo = New XmlTextReader(fileName)
    While readOfficeInfo.Read()
        WXShowXMLNode(readOfficeInfo)
        While readOfficeInfo.MoveToNextAttribute()
            WXShowXMLNode(readOfficeInfo)
        End While
    End While
    readOfficeInfo.Close()
End Sub
```

For each node encountered after a call to the Read method, WXReadXML, calls the WXShowXMLNode subroutine. Similarly for each attribute traversed, the WXShowXMLNode subroutine is called. This subroutine breakdown each node into its sub-entities:

❑ Depth – the XmlTextReader's Depth property determines the level at which a node resides in the XML document tree. To understand depth consider the following XML document composed solely of elements: <A><B></B><C><D></D></C></A>. Element <A> is the root element and when parsed would return a Depth of 0. Elements <B> and <C> are contained in <A> and are hence a Depth value of 1. Element <D> is contained in <C>. The Depth property value associated with <D> (depth of 2) should therefore be one more than the Depth property associated with <C> (depth of 1).

❑ Type – the type of each node is determined using `XmlTextReader`'s `NodeType` property. The node returned is of enumeration type, `XmlNodeType`. Permissible node types include the basics: `Attribute`, `Element`, and `Whitespace`. Numerous other node types can also be returned including: `CDATA`, `Comment`, `Document`, `Entity`, and `DocumentType`.

❑ Name – the type of each node is retrieved using the `Name` property of `XmlTextReader`. The name of the node could be an element name such as, `<WXLaClientLaPrescription>`, or an attribute name such as, `LaMedicationLaID`.

❑ Attribute Count – the number of attributes associated with a node is retrieved using the `AttributeCount` property of `XmlTextReader`'s `NodeType`.

❑ Value – the value of a node is retrieved using the `Value` property of `XmlTextReader`. For example the element node named, `<LaDentistLaName>`, contains a value of, `Dr. Jam`.

Subroutine `WXShowXMLNode` is implemented as follows:

```
Private Sub WXShowXMLNode(ByVal reader As XmlReader)
    Dim depthCount As Integer

    If reader.Depth > 0 Then
        For depthCount = 1 To reader.Depth
            Console.Write("  ")
        Next
    End If

    If reader.NodeType = XmlNodeType.Whitespace Then
        Console.Out.WriteLine("Type: {0} ", reader.NodeType)
    ElseIf reader.NodeType = XmlNodeType.Text Then
        Console.Out.WriteLine("Type: {0}, Value: {1} ", _
                            reader.NodeType, _
                            reader.Value)
    Else
        Console.Out.WriteLine("Name: {0}, Type: {1}, " & _
                            "AttributeCount: {2}, Value: {3} ", _
                            reader.Name, _
                            reader.NodeType, _
                            reader.AttributeCount, _
                            reader.Value)
    End If
End Sub
```

Within the `WXShowXMLNode` subroutine, each level of node depth adds two spaces to the output generated:

```
If reader.Depth > 0 Then
    For depthCount = 1 To reader.Depth
        Console.Write("  ")
    Next
End If
```

The reason for this is to make the output generated human readable (so a human can tell the depth of each node displayed). For each type of node, subroutine, `WXShowXMLNode`, displays the value of the `NodeType` property. The `WXShowXMLNode` subroutine makes a distinction between nodes of type, `Whitespace`, and other types of nodes. The reason for this is simple. A node of type, `Whitespace`, does not contain a name or attribute count. The value of such a node is any combination of whitespace characters (space, tab, carriage return, etc.). It does not make sense to display the properties if the

NodeType is `XmlNodeType.WhiteSpace`. Nodes of type `Text` have no name associated with them so for this type subroutine `WXShowXMLNode` only displays the properties, `NodeType`, and `Value`. For all other node types, the `Name`, `AttributeCount`, `Value`, and `NodeType` properties are displayed.

A portion of the output generated by subroutine `WXReadXML`, being called and using subroutine `WXShowXMLNode` is as follows:

```
Name: DentalManageDump, Type: Element, AttributeCount: 0, Value:
 Type: Whitespace
 Name: WXClientMultiPrescription, Type: Element, AttributeCount: 0, Value
  Type: Whitespace
  Name: prescriptions, Type: Element, AttributeCount: 0, Value:
   Type: Whitespace
   Name: WXClientPrescription, Type: Element, AttributeCount: 0, Value:
    Type: Whitespace
    Name: dentistName, Type: Element, AttributeCount: 0, Value:
     Type: Text, Value: Dr. Jam
```

This example managed to use three methods and five properties of `XmlTextReader`. The output generated was informative but far from practical. As a class, `XmlTextReader` exposes over fifty methods and properties so we have just scratched the surface of this highly versatile class. The remainder of this section will introduce a more realistic use of `XmlTextReader` and demonstrate how the classes of `System.Xml` handle errors.

Example: Traversing XML Using XmlTextReader

An application can easily use `XmlTextReader` in order to traverse a document that is received in a known format. The document could thus be traversed in a deliberate manner. Recall earlier that a class was implemented that serialized arrays of prescriptions. Our next example (found in application, VBNetXML01) will take an XML document containing multiple such XML documents and traverse them. Each prescription will be forwarded to the pharmacy by sending a fax. The document will be traversed as follows:

```
Read root element:  <DentalManageDump>
    Process each <WXClientMultiPrescription> element
        Read <prescriptions> element
            Process each <WXClientPrescription>
                Send fax for each prescription here
```

The basic outline for our program's implementation is to open a file containing the XML document to parse (variable, `readOfficeInfo`) and to traverse from element-to-element within this document:

```
Dim readOfficeInfo As XmlTextReader
Dim drName, medication, quantity As String

readOfficeInfo = New XmlTextReader(fileName)
readOfficeInfo.Read()
readOfficeInfo.ReadStartElement("DentalManageDump")
Do While (True)
    '*******************************************************
    ' * Process WXClientMultiPrescription elements here *
    '*******************************************************
Loop
readOfficeInfo.ReadEndElement() ' </DentalManageDump>
readOfficeInfo.Close()
```

The previous code snippet opened the file using the constructor to the XmlTextReader object and closed the file using the Close method of this class. The previous code snippet also introduced two methods of the XmlTextReaderClass:

❑ ReadStartElement(String) – verifies that the current node in the stream is an element and that the element's name matches the string passed to method, ReadStartElement. If the verification is successful, the stream is advanced to the next element.

❑ ReadEndElement() – verifies that the current element is an end tab and if the verification is successful the stream is advanced to the next element.

The application knows that an element name, <DentalManageDump>, will be found at a specific point in the document. The ReadStartElement method verifies this foreknowledge of the document format. Once all the elements contained in element, <DentalManageDump>, have been traversed the stream should point to the end tag, </DentalManageDump>. The ReadEndElement method verifies this.

The code that traverses each element of type, <WXClientMultiPrescription>, similarly uses the ReadStartElement and ReadEndElement methods to indicate the start and end of <WXClientMultiPrescription> and <prescriptions> elements. The code that ultimately parses the list of prescription and faxes the pharmacy (using subroutine, WXFranticallyFaxThePharmacy) is as follows:

```
Dim readOfficeInfo As XmlTextReader
Dim drName, medication, quantity As String

readOfficeInfo = New XmlTextReader(fileName)
readOfficeInfo.Read()
readOfficeInfo.ReadStartElement("DentalManageDump")
Do While (True)
    readOfficeInfo.ReadStartElement("WXClientMultiPrescription")
    readOfficeInfo.ReadStartElement("prescriptions")
    Do While (True)
        readOfficeInfo.ReadStartElement("WXClientPrescription")
        drName = readOfficeInfo.ReadElementString()
        medication = readOfficeInfo.ReadElementString()
        quantity = readOfficeInfo.ReadElementString()
        readOfficeInfo.ReadEndElement() ' clear </WXClientPrescription>
        WXFranticallyFaxThePharmacy(drName, medication, quantity)
        ' Should read next WXClientPrescription node
        ' else we quit
        readOfficeInfo.Read()
        If ("WXClientPrescription" <> readOfficeInfo.Name) Then
            Exit Do
        End If
    Loop

    readOfficeInfo.ReadEndElement() ' clear </prescriptions>
    readOfficeInfo.ReadEndElement() ' clear </WXClientMultiPrescription>
    ' Should read next WXClientMultiPrescription node
    ' else we quit
    readOfficeInfo.Read() ' clear </DentalManageDump>
    If ("WXClientMultiPrescription" <> readOfficeInfo.Name) Then
        Exit Do
    End If
Loop
readOfficeInfo.ReadEndElement() ' </DentalManageDump>
readOfficeInfo.Close()
```

Three lines within the previous code could contain a call to the `ReadElementString` method. The lines of code are:

```
drName = readOfficeInfo.ReadElementString()
medication = readOfficeInfo.ReadElementString()
quantity = readOfficeInfo.ReadElementString()
```

While parsing the stream, it was known that an element existed named, `<dentistName>`, and this element contained the name of the dentist. Rather than parsing the start tag, getting the value, and parsing the end tag, it was easier just to get the data using method, `ReadElementString`. This method retrieves the data string associated with an element and advances the stream to the next element. The `ReadElementString` method was also used to retrieve the data associated with XML elements, `<medicationID>` and `<quantity>`.

The output of this example was a fax that we will refrain from showing. The emphasis of this example was to show that it is simpler to traverse a document when its form is known. The format of the document is still verified by `XmlTextReader` as it is parsed.

The `XmlTextReader` class also exposes properties that give more insight into the data contained in the XML document and the state of parsing: `IsEmptyElement`, `EOF`, and `IsStartElement`. This class also allows data in a variety of forms to be retrieved using methods such as `ReadBase64`, `ReadHex`, and `ReadChars`. The raw XML associated with the document can also be retrieved using `ReadInnerXml` and `ReadOuterXml`. Once again, we have scratched the surface of a class, `XmlTextReader`, rich in functionality.

Handling Exceptions

XML is text and could easily be read using mundane methods such as `Read` and `ReadLine`. A key feature of each class that reads and traverses XML is inherent support for error detection and handling. To demonstrate this consider the following malformed XML document found in file, `malformed.XML`:

```
<?xml version="1.0" encoding="IBM437"?>
<WXLaClientLaPrescription LaMedicationLaID="101", LaHowLaMuch="10">
  <LaDentistLaName>Dr. Jam</LaDentistLaName>
<WXLaClientLaPrescription>
```

Given a cursory look, the previous XML document does not appear to be malformed. By wrapping a call to the method we developed, `WXReadXML`, we can see what type of exception is raised when the `XmlTextReader` detects that malformed XML within this document:

```
Try
    WXReadXML("..\Malformed.xml")
Catch xmlEx As XmlException
    Console.Error.WriteLine("XML Error: " + xmlEx.ToString())
Catch ex As Exception
    Console.Error.WriteLine("Some other error: " + ex.ToString())
End Try
```

The methods and properties exposed by the `XmlTextReader` class raise exceptions of type, `XmlException`. Every class in the `System.Xml` namespace raises exceptions of type `XmlException`. Not surprisingly, the `XmlException` class is found in namespace, `System.Xml`. Although this discussion of errors used an instance of type `XmlTextReader` the concepts reviewed apply to all errors generated by classes found in the `System.Xml` namespace.

The properties exposed by XmlException include:

❑   LineNumber – line within XML document where error occurred.

❑   LinePosition – position within line specified by Line where error occurred.

❑   Message – error message corresponding to the error that occurred. This error took place at the line in the XML document specified by LineNumber and within the line at the position specified by LinePosition.

The error displayed when subroutine, WXReadXML, is run thus processing malformed.xml is as follows:

XML Error: System.Xml.XmlException: The ',' character, hexadecimal value 0x2C, cannot begin a name. Line 2, position 49.

We know precisely where the error detect took place, Line 2, position 49. Looking closely at our document there is a comma separating the attributes in element, <WXLaClientLaPrescription> (LaMedicationLaID="101", LaHowLaMuch="10"). This comma is invalid. Removing the comma and running the code again (exercising the parser, XmlTextReader) reveals the following output:

XML Error: System.Xml.XmlException: This is an unexpected token. Expected 'EndElement'. Line 4, position 27.

Once again, we recognize the precise error. In line 4, we do not have an end element, </WXLaClientLaPrescription>, but have a begin element, <WXLaClientLaPrescription>. Adding the missing slash in line 4 and the code executes without error.

The properties provided by the XmlException class (LineNumer, LinePosition, and Message) provide a useful level of precision when tracking down errors. The XmlTextReader class also exposes a level of precision with respect to the parsing of the XML document. This precision is exposed by the XmlTextReader through properties such as LineNumber and LinePosition.

Document Object Model (DOM)

The classes of namespace, System.Xml, that support the Document Object Model (DOM) interact as follows:

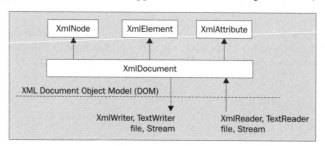

Within the previous diagram, an XML document is contained in a class named, XmlDocument. Each node within this document is accessible and managed using XmlNode. Nodes can also be accessed and managed using a class specifically designed to process a specific node's type (XmlElement, XmlAttribute, etc.). XML documents are extracted from the XmlDocument using a variety of mechanisms exposed through such classes as XmlWriter, TextWriter, Stream, and file (specified by filename of type String). XML documents are consumed by an XmlDocument using a variety of load mechanisms exposed through such classes as XmlReader, TextReader, Stream, and file (specified by filename of type String).

Where a DOM-style parser differs from a stream-style parser is with respect to movement. Using DOM, the nodes can be traversed forwards and backwards. Nodes can be added to the document, removed from the document, and updated. This flexibility comes at a cost, performance. It is faster to read or write XML using a stream-style parser.

The DOM-specific classes exposed by `System.Xml` include:

❑   `XmlDocument` – class corresponds to an entire XML document. A document is loaded using the `Load` method. XML documents are loaded from a file (filename specified as type `String`), `TextReader` or `XmlReader`. A document can be loaded using `LoadXml` in conjunction with a string containing the XML document. In order to `Save` XML documents, the `Save` method is used to save formats file (filename specified as type `String`), `TextWriter` and `XmlWriter`. The methods exposed by `XmlDocument` reflect the intricate manipulation of an XML document. For example, the following self-documenting creation methods are implemented by this class: `CreateAttribute`, `CreateCDataSection`, `CreateComment`, `CreateDocumentFragment`, `CreateDocumentType`, `CreateElement`, `CreateEntityReference`, `CreateNode`, `CreateProcessingInstruction`, `CreateSignificantWhitespace`, `CreateTextNode`, `CreateWhitespace`, and `CreateXmlDeclaration`. The elements contained in the document can be retrieved. Other methods support the retrieving, importing, cloning, loading, and writing of nodes.

❑   `XmlNode` – class corresponds to a node within the DOM tree. This class supports data types, namespaces, and DTDs. A robust set of methods and properties are provided to create, delete, and replace nodes: `AppendChild`, `CloneNode`, `InsertAfter`, `InsertBefore`, `PrependChild`, `RemoveAll`, `RemoveChild`, and `ReplaceChild`. The contents of a node can similarly be traversed in a variety of ways: `FirstChild`, `LastChild`, `NextSibling`, `ParentNode`, and `PreviousSibling`. The methods and properties presented represent just a portion of `XmlNode`'s functionality.

❑   `XmlElement` – class corresponds to an element within the DOM tree. The functionality exposed by this class contains a variety of methods used to manipulate an element's attributes: `GetAttribute`, `GetAttributeNode`, `RemoveAllAttributes`, `RemoveAttributeAt`, `RemoveAttributeNode`, `SetAttribute`, and `SetAttributeNode`. These methods are a subset of the element-specific manipulation supported by `XmlElement`.

❑   `XmlAttribute` – class corresponds to an attribute of an element (`XmlElement`) within the DOM tree. An attribute contains data and lists of subordinate data. For this reason it is a less complicated object than an `XmlNode` or an `XmlElement`. An `XmlAttribute` retrieves its owner document (property, `OwnerDocument`), retrieves its owner element (property, `OwnerElement`), retrieves its parent node (property, `ParentNode`), retrieves its name (property, `Name`). The value of an `XmlAttribute` is a read/write property, `Value`. Class, `XmlAttribute`, also implements a variety of other methods and properties.

Given the diverse number of methods and properties exposed by `XmlDocument`, `XmlNode`, `XmlElement`, and `XmlAttribute` it should be clear that any XML 1.0 compliant document can be generated and manipulated using these classes. To further clarify, these classes expose a great deal of functionality when it comes to the generation and manipulation of XML documents. We have already discussed that these classes compared to their XML-stream counterparts afford more flexible movement within the XML document and more flexible editing.

A similar comparison could be made between DOM and data serialized and de-serialized using XML. Using serialization the type of node (for example, attribute or element) and the node name is specified at compile time. There is no on-the-fly modification of the XML generated by the serialization process.

637

Other technologies that generate and consume XML are not as flexible as DOM. This includes technologies such as ADO.NET and ADO, which generate XML of a particular form. SQL Server does expose a certain flexibility when it comes to the generation (FOR XML queries) and consumption of XML (OPENXML). The choice between using classes within DOM and using SQL Server is a choice between using a language such as VB.NET to manipulate objects or to require SQL Server be installed and perform most XML manipulation in the SQL language.

Even though a variety of DOM-related classes were presented from namespace, System.Xml, a great many more classes were not discussed in this chapter. Exploring the remaining caverns (classes) of namespace, System.Xml, is an exercise left to the reader.

Example: DOM Traversing Raw XML Elements

Our first DOM example will load an XML document into an XmlDocument object using a string that contains the actual XML document. This scenario is typical of an application that uses ADO.NET to generate XML but then uses the objects of DOM to traverse and manipulate this XML. ADO.NET's DataSet object contains the results of ADO.NET data access operations (as reviewed in a previous chapter). The DataSet class exposes method, GetXml. This method retrieves the underlying XML associated with the DataSet. The following code snippet, which can be found in the application VBNetXML06, is a typical usage where the contents of the DataSet (method, GetXml) are loaded into the XmlDocument (method, LoadXml):

```
Dim xmlDoc As New XmlDocument()
Dim ds As New DataSet()

' set up ADO.Net DataSet() here
xmlDoc.LoadXml(ds.GetXml())
```

This example will simply traverse each XML element (XmlNode) in the document (XmlDocument) and display the data accordingly. The data associated with this example will not be retrieved from a DataSet but will instead be contained in a string, rawData. This string is initialized as follows:

```
Dim rawData As String = _
    "<prescriptions>" & _
    "   <WXClientPrescription>" & _
    "      <dentistName>Dr. Jam</dentistName>" & _
    "      <medicationID>1</medicationID>" & _
    "      <quantity>11</quantity>" & _
    "   </WXClientPrescription>" & _
    "   <WXClientPrescription>" & _
    "      <dentistName>Dr. Jam</dentistName>" & _
    "      <medicationID>2</medicationID>" & _
    "      <quantity>22</quantity>" & _
    "   </WXClientPrescription>" & _
    "</prescriptions>"
```

The XML document in string instance, rawData, is a portion of the XML hierarchy associated with a prescription written at our dental office. The basic idea in processing this data is to traverse each <WXClientPrescription> XML element in order to display the data it contains. Each node corresponding to a <WXClientPrescription> XML element can be retrieved from our XmlDocument using the GetElementsByTagName method and specifying a tag name of "WXClientPrescription". The GetElementsByTagName method returns a list of XmlNode objects in the form of a collection of type XmlNodeList. Using VB.NET's For Each construct this list, XmlNodeList (clientPrescriptionNodes), can be traversed as individual XmlNode elements (clientPrescriptionNode). The code for handling this is as follows:

```
Dim xmlDoc As New XmlDocument()
Dim clientPrescriptionNodes As XmlNodeList
Dim clientPrescriptionNode As XmlNode

xmlDoc.LoadXml(rawData)
' Traverse each <WXClientPrescription>
clientPrescriptionNodes = _
    xmlDoc.GetElementsByTagName("WXClientPrescription")
For Each clientPrescriptionNode In clientPrescriptionNodes
    '***********************************************************
    ' Process <dentistName>, <medicationID> and <quantity> here
    '***********************************************************
Next
```

Each XmlNode can then have its contents displayed by traversing the children of this node using the ChildNodes method. This method returns an XmlNodeList (baseDataNodes) that can be traversed one XmlNode list element at a time (For Each baseDataNode in the collection). The code for performing this traversal of elements <dentistName>, <medicationID>, and <quantity> is as follows:

```
Dim baseDataNodes As XmlNodeList
Dim baseDataNode As XmlNode
Dim bFirstInRow As Boolean

baseDataNodes = clientPrescriptionNode.ChildNodes
bFirstInRow = True
For Each baseDataNode In baseDataNodes
    If (bFirstInRow) Then
        bFirstInRow = False
    Else
        Console.Out.Write(", ")
    End If
    Console.Out.Write(baseDataNode.Name & ": " & baseDataNode.InnerText)
Next
Console.Out.WriteLine()
```

The bulk of the previous code retrieves the name of the node using the Name property and the InnerText property of the node. The InnerText property of each XmlNode retrieved respectively contains the data associated with the XML elements (nodes) <dentistName>, <medicationID>, and <quantity>. Our example displays the contents the XML elements to Console.Out. Our XML document is displayed as follows:

dentistName: Dr. Jam, medicationID: 1, quantity: 11
dentistName: Dr. Jam, medicationID: 2, quantity: 22

Numerous more practical methods for using this data could have been implemented. These include:

❑ The contents could have been directed to an ASP.Net Response object. The data retrieved could have been used to create an HTML table (<TABLE> table, <TR> row, and <TD> data) that would be written to the Response object.

❑ The data traversed could have been directed to a ListBox or ComboBox Windows Forms control. This would allow the data returned to be selected as part of a GUI application.

❑ The data could have been edited as part of our application's business rules. For example, we could have used the traversal to verify that the <medicationID> matched the <quantity>. For example if a medication must be taken three times a day then the quantity prescribed must be 3, 6, 9, etc.

Our example in its entirety is as follows:

```
Dim rawData As String = _
 ' XML data not shown for reason of brevity
Dim xmlDoc As New XmlDocument()
Dim clientPrescriptionNodes As XmlNodeList
Dim clientPrescriptionNode As XmlNode
Dim baseDataNodes As XmlNodeList
Dim baseDataNode As XmlNode
Dim bFirstInRow As Boolean

xmlDoc.LoadXml(rawData)
 ' Traverse each <WXClientPrescription>
clientPrescriptionNodes = xmlDoc.GetElementsByTagName("WXClientPrescription")
For Each clientPrescriptionNode In clientPrescriptionNodes
    baseDataNodes = clientPrescriptionNode.ChildNodes
    bFirstInRow = True
    For Each baseDataNode In baseDataNodes
        If (bFirstInRow) Then
            bFirstInRow = False
        Else
            Console.Out.Write(", ")
        End If
        Console.Out.Write(baseDataNode.Name & ": " & baseDataNode.InnerText)
    Next
    Console.Out.WriteLine()
Next
```

Example: DOM Traversing XML Attributes

This next example will demonstrate traversing data contained in attributes and updating these attributes based on a set of business rules In this example the XmlDocument object is populated by retrieving an XML document from a file. After the business rules edit the object, it will be persisted back to the file from whence it was retrieved. The code for handling this is as follows where the Load method is used to retrieve an XML document from a file and the Save method is used to persist the edited document back to a file:

```
Dim xmlDoc As New XmlDocument()

xmlDoc.Load("..\DentalOfficeReadyPrescriptionsV2.xml")
'*********************************************
' Business rules process document here
'*********************************************
xmlDoc.Save("..\DentalOfficeReadyPrescriptionsV2.xml")
```

The data contained in the file, DentalOfficeReadyPrescriptionsV2.xml, is a variation of the infamous dental prescription. We have altered our rigid standard (for the sake of example) so that the data associated with individual prescriptions is contained in XML attributes instead of XML elements. An example of this prescription data is as follows:

```
<WXClientPrescription dentistName="Dr. Jam" medicationID="1" quantity="11">
```

We have demonstrated already how to traverse the XML elements associated with a document. For brevity's sake assume we have successfully retrieved the XmlNode associated with XML element, <WXClientPrescription>. The code to traverse an XmlNode with Name property of <WXClientPrescription>is as follows:

640

```
        Dim attributes As XmlAttributeCollection
        Dim attribute As XmlAttribute
        Dim medicationID As Integer
        Dim quantity As Integer

        attributes = node.Attributes()
        For Each attribute In attributes
            If 0 = String.Compare(attribute.Name, "medicationID") Then
                medicationID = attribute.InnerXml
            ElseIf 0 = String.Compare(attribute.Name, "quantity") Then
                quantity = attribute.InnerXml
            End If
        Next
```

The previous code snippet traverses the attribute of an XmlNode by retrieving a list of attributes using the XmlNode's Attributes method. The value of this method is used to set the attributes object (data type, XmlAttributeCollection). The individual XmlAttribute objects (variable, attribute) contained in attributes are traversed using For Each. Within the For loop the contents of the medicationID and the quantity attribute are saved for processing by our business rules.

Our business rules execute an elaborate algorithm that insures that the medication in the prescription is provided in the correct quantity. This rule is the medication associated with MedicationID=1 must be dispensed 21 tablets at a time (quantity of 21). In the event of an invalid quantity, the code for enforcing this business rule uses the ItemOf property to look up the XmlAttribute object associated with the quantity attribute. The Value property of the XmlAttribute object is used to set the correct value of the medication's quantity. The code performing this business rule is as follows:

```
    If medicationID = 1 Then
        ' medication must be taken 3 times a day for a week (21 times)
        If quantity <> 21 Then
            attributes.ItemOf("quantity").Value = "21"
        End If
    End If
```

What is truly elegant about this example is that the list of attributes was traversed using For Each. After this ItemOf was used to look up a specific attribute that had already been traversed. This would not have been possible if reading an XML stream with an object derived from the XML stream reader class, XmlReader.

This example is found in project VBNetXML06. The sourcecode for this application is as follows:

```
    Sub WXTraverseAttributes(ByRef node As XmlNode)
        Dim attributes As XmlAttributeCollection
        Dim attribute As XmlAttribute
        Dim medicationID As Integer
        Dim quantity As Integer

        attributes = node.Attributes()
        For Each attribute In attributes
            If 0 = String.Compare(attribute.Name, "medicationID") Then
                medicationID = attribute.InnerXml
            ElseIf 0 = String.Compare(attribute.Name, "quantity") Then
                quantity = attribute.InnerXml
```

```
                End If
        Next

        If medicationID = 1 Then
            ' medication must be taken 3 times a day for a week (21 times)
            If quantity <> 21 Then
                attributes.ItemOf("quantity").Value = "21"
            End If
        End If
    End Sub

    Sub WXReadDentalDOM()
        Dim xmlDoc As New XmlDocument()
        Dim clientPrescriptionNodes As XmlNodeList
        Dim clientPrescriptionNode As XmlNode

        xmlDoc.Load("..\DentalOfficeReadyPrescriptionsV2.xml")
        ' Traverse each <WXClientPrescription>
        clientPrescriptionNodes = _
            xmlDoc.GetElementsByTagName("WXClientPrescription")
        For Each clientPrescriptionNode In clientPrescriptionNodes
            WXTraverseAttributes(clientPrescriptionNode)
        Next

        xmlDoc.Save("..\DentalOfficeReadyPrescriptionsV2.xml")

    End Sub
```

XSLT Transforms

It should come as no surprise that XML is associated with yet another acronym, XSLT (extensible style sheet transforms). XSLT is a language that is used to transform XML documents. We have performed a similar task before. Recall that when working with XML serialization we rewrote the WXClientPrescription class. This class was used to serialize a prescription object to XML using nodes that contained English-language names. The rewritten version of this class, WXLaClientLaPrescription, serialized XML nodes containing French names. Sourcecode Style attributes were used in conjunction with the XmlSerializer class in order to accomplish this transformation. Two words in this paragraph should have sent chills down the spine of any experienced developer: "rewrote" and "rewritten". The point of an XSL Transform is to use an alternative language (XSLT) to transform the XML rather than rewriting the sourcecode, SQL commands, or other mechanism used to generated SQL.

Conceptually XSLT is straightforward. A file containing an *.xslt extension is written. This file describes the changes (transformations) that will be applied to a particular genre of XML file. Once this is completed an XSLT processor is run specifying the source XML file and the XSLT file. The System.Xml.Xsl namespace and its class, XslTransform, expose an example of such an XSLT processor.

The XSLT file is actually an XML document. Certain elements within this document are XSLT specific commands. There are dozens of XSLT commands that can be used in writing an XSLT file. In our first example, we will explore the following XSLT elements (commands):

- ❏ `stylesheet` – indicates the start of the style-sheet (XSL) in the XSLT file.

- ❏ `template` – this element denotes a reuseable template used to produce specific output. This output is generated using a specific node type within the source document under a specific context. For example the text, `<xsl: template match="/">`, selects all root nodes ("/") for the specific transform template.

- ❏ `for-each` – this element applies the same template to each node in the specified set. Recall that we demonstrated a class (`WXClientMultiPrescription`) that could be serialized. This class contained an array of prescriptions. Given the XML document generated when a `WXClientMultiPrescription` is serialized, each prescription serialized could be processed using, `<xsl:for-each select = "WXClientMultiPrescription/prescriptions/WXClientPrescription">`.

- ❏ `value-of` – retrieves the value of the speicified node and inserts it into the document in text form. For example the following, `<xsl:value-of select="dentistName" />`, would take the value of XML element, `<dentistName>`, and insert it into the transformed document.

The `WXClientMultiPrescription` class when serialized generates XML such as (where ... indicates where additional `<WXClientPrescription>` elements may reside):

```
<?xml version="1.0" encoding="us-ascii" ?>
<WXClientMultiPrescription>
  <prescriptions>
    <WXClientPrescription>
      <dentistName>Dr. Jam</dentistName>
      <medicationID>1</medicationID>
      <quantity>11</quantity>
    </WXClientPrescription>

    ...
  </prescriptions>
</WXClientMultiPrescription>
```

The previous XML document is used to generate a report that is viewed by the dental practice's managing doctor. This report is in HTML form so it can be viewed via the Web. The XSLT elements we previously reviewed (`stylesheet`, `template`, and `for-each`) are all the XSLT elements required to transform our XML document (how data is stored) into an HTML file (how data is displayed). XSLT file, `WXDisplayThatPuppy.xslt`, contains the following text that is used to transform a serialized version of class, `WXClientMultiPrescription`:

```
<?xml version="1.0" encoding="UTF-8" ?>
<xsl:stylesheet xmlns:xsl="http://www.w3.org/1999/XSL/Transform"
    version="1.0">
  <xsl:template match="/">
    <HTML>
      <TITLE>Who's prescribing what</TITLE>
      <BODY>
          <TABLE BORDER="1">
            <TR>
              <TD><B>Dentist</B></TD>
              <TD><B>Medication ID</B></TD>
              <TD><B>Quantity</B></TD>
            </TR>
            <xsl:for-each select=
              "WXClientMultiPrescription/prescriptions/WXClientPrescription">
```

```
            <TR>
                <TD><xsl:value-of select="dentistName" /></TD>
                <TD><xsl:value-of select="quantity" /></TD>
                <TD><xsl:value-of select="medicationID" /></TD>
            </TR>
            </xsl:for-each>
        </TABLE>
      </BODY>
    </HTML>
  </xsl:template>
</xsl:stylesheet>
```

In the previous XSLT file, the XSLT elements are marked in boldface. These elements perform operations on the source XML file containing a serialized WXClientMultiPrescription object and generate the appropriate HTML file. For those not familiar with HTML our file contains a table (marked by the table tag, <TABLE>) that contains a set of rows (each row marked by a table row tag, <TR>). The columns of the table are contained in table data tags, <TD>. The previous XSLT file contains the header row for the table:

```
<TR>
    <TD><B>Dentist</B></TD>
    <TD><B>Medication ID</B></TD>
    <TD><B>Quantity</B></TD>
</TR>
```

Each row containing data (an individual prescription from the serialized object, WXClientMultiPrescription) is generated using the XSLT element, for-each, to traverse each <WXClientPrescription> element within the source XML document:

```
<xsl:for-each select=
    "WXClientMultiPrescription/prescriptions/WXClientPrescription">
```

The individual columns of data are generated using XSLT element, value-of to query the elements contained each <WXClientPrescription> element (<dentistName>, <quantity>, and <medicationID>):

```
<TR>
    <TD><xsl:value-of select="dentistName" /></TD>
    <TD><xsl:value-of select="quantity" /></TD>
    <TD><xsl:value-of select="medicationID" /></TD>
</TR>
```

The code to create a displayable XML file using the System.Xml.Xsl namespace is as follows (console application, VBNetXML04):

```
Dim myXslTransform As XslTransform = New XslTransform()
Dim destFileName As String = "..\ShowIt.html"

myXslTransform.Load("..\WXDisplayThatPuppy.xslt")
myXslTransform.Transform("..\OneWXClientMultiPrescriptions.xml", _
                         destFileName)
System.Diagnostics.Process.Start(destFileName)
```

This consists of only five lines of code with the bulk of the coding taking place in the XSLT file. Our previous code snippet created an instance of an `XslTransform` object named, `myXslTransform`. Class, `XslTransform`, is found in the `System.Xml.Xsl` namepace. The `Load` method of this class is used to load the XSLT file we previously reviewed, `WXDisplayThatPuppy.xslt`. The `Transform` method takes a source XML file as the first parameter which in our case was a file containing a serialized `WXClientMultiPrescription` object. The second parameter is the destination file that will be created by the transform (filename, `..\ShowIt.html`). The `Start` method of the `Process` class is used to display the `*.html` file. The `Start` method launches a process that is most suitable for displaying the file provided. Basically, the extension of the file dictates which application will be used to display the file. On a typical Windows machine, the program used to display this file is Internet Explorer, which displays the following:

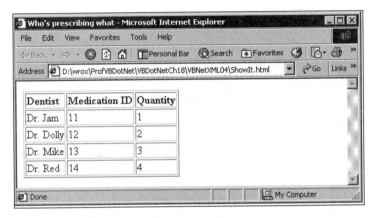

Do not confuse displaying this HTML file with ASP.NET. Displaying an HTML file in this manner takes place on a single machine without the involvement of web server. ASP.NET is more complex than displaying an HTML page in the default browser.

As was demonstrated the backbone of the `System.Xml.Xsl` namespace is the `XslTransform` class. This classes uses XSLT files transform XML documents. Class, `XslTransform`, exposes the following methods and properties:

❑ `XmlResolver` – this get/set property is used to specify a class (abstract base class, `XmlResolver`) that is used to handle external references (import and include elements within the style sheet). These external references are encountered when a document is transformed (method, `Transform`, is executed). Namespace, `System.Xml`, contains a class `XmlUrlResolver`, which is derived from `XmlResolver`. The `XmlUrlResolver` class resolves external resource based on **Uniform Resource Identifier** (URI).

❑ `Load` – this method loads an XSLT style sheet to be used in transforming XML documents. This method is overloaded multiple times. It is permissible to specify the XSLT style sheet as a parameter of type: `IXPathNavigator`, filename of XSLT file (specified as parameter type, `String`), `XmlReader`, and `XPathNavigator`. For each type of XSLT supported an overloaded member is provided that allows an `XmlResolver` to also be specified. For example is possible to call `Load(String, XmlResolver)` where `String` corresponds to a filename and `XmlResolver` is an object that handles references in the style sheet of type `xsl:import` and `xsl:include`. It would be permissible to pass in a value of `Nothing` for the second parameter of the `Load` method (no `XmlResolver` specified).

❑   `Transform` – this method transforms a specified XML document using the previously specified XSLT style sheet and optional `XmlResolver`. The location where the transformed XML is to be output is specified as a parameter to this method. This method is overloaded multiple times. The first parameter of each overloaded method is the XML document to be transformed. This parameter can be represented as an `IXPathNavigable`, XML filename (specified as parameter type, `String`), and `XPathNavigator`.

The most straightforward variant of the `Transform` method is `Transform(String, String)`. In this case, a file containing an XML document is specified as the first parameter (data type, `String`) and a filename that receives the transformed XML document is specified as the second parameter (data type, `String`). This is exactly how the first XSLT example utilized the `Transform` method:

```
myXslTransform.Transform("..\OneWXClientMultiPrescriptions.xml", _
                          destFileName)
```

The first parameter to the `Transform` method can also be specified as an `IXPathNavigable` or `XPathNavigator`. Either of these parameter types allows the XML output to be sent to an object of type `Stream`, `TextWriter` or `XmlWriter`. When these two flavors of input are specified, a parameter containing an object of type `XsltArgumentList` can be specified. An `XsltArgumentList` object contains a list of arguments that are used as input to the transform.

XSLT Transforming between XML Standards

Our first example used four XSLT elements in order to transform an XML file into an HTML file. Such an example has merit but it does not demonstrate an important use of XSLT. Another major application of XSLT is to transform XML from one standard into another standard. This may involve renaming elements/attributes, excluding elements/attributes, changing data types, altering the node hierarchy, and representing elements as attributes and vice-versa.

A case of differing XML standards could easily happen to our software that automates dental offices. The software including its XML representation of a medical prescription is so successful that we sell 100,000 copies. Just as we celebrate, a consortium of the largest pharmacies announces that they will 1) no longer be accepting faxed prescriptions and 2) they are introducing their own standard for the exchange of prescriptions between medical/dental offices and pharmacies.

Rather than panic, we simply ship an upgrade that comes complete with an XSLT file. This upgrade (a bit of extra code plus the XSLT file) transforms our XML representation of a prescription into the XML representation dictated by the consortium of pharmacies. By using an XSLT file, we can ship the upgrade immediately. If the consortium of pharmacies revises their XML representation, we are not obliged to change our sourcecode. Instead, we can simply ship and upgraded XSLT file that will insure each dental office is compliant.

Our example of transforming between XML standards is contained in VB console application, `VBNetXML04`. The specific sourcecode that executes the transform is as follows:

```
Dim myXslTransform As XslTransform = New XslTransform()

myXslTransform.Load("..\ConvertLegacyToNewStandard.xslt")
myXslTransform.Transform("..\DentalOfficeReadyPrescriptions.xml", _
                         "..\PharmacyReadyPrescriptions.xml")
```

The three lines of code simply:

1. Create an `XslTransform` object

2. Use the `Load` method to load an XSLT file (`ConvertLegacyToNewStandard.xslt`)

3. Use the `Transform` method to transform a source XML file (`DentalOfficeReadyPrescriptions.xml`) into a destination XML file (`PharmacyReadyPrescriptions.xml`)

Recall that the input XML document (`DentalOfficeReadyPrescriptions.xml`) does not match the format required by our consortium of pharmacies. The contents of this source XML file look as follows:

```
<?xml version="1.0" encoding="utf-8" ?>
<DentalManageDump>
    <WXClientMultiPrescription>
        <prescriptions>
            <WXClientPrescription>
                <dentistName>Dr. Jam</dentistName>
                <medicationID>1</medicationID>
                <quantity>11</quantity>
            </WXClientPrescription>
            <!-- additional <WXClientPrescription>'s specified here -->
        </prescriptions>
    </WXClientMultiPrescription>
    <!-- additional </WXClientMultiPrescription>'s specified here -->
</DentalManageDump>
```

Notice in the previous XML document that two XML comments are included (as specified by `<! comment >`). The comments indicate where more `<WXClientPrescription>` elements can be placed in the document (`<!-- additional <WXClientPrescription>'s specified here -->`) and where more `<WXClientMultiPrescription>` elements can be placed in the document (`<!-- additional </WXClientMultiPrescription>'s specified here -->`).

The format exhibited in the previous XML document does not match the format of the consortium of pharmacies. To be assimilated by the collective of pharmacies we must transform the document as follows:

❑ Rename element `<DentalManageDump>` to `<Root>`.

❑ Remove element `<WXClientMultiPrescription>`.

❑ Remove element `<prescriptions>`.

❑ Rename element `<WXClientPrescription>` to `<PharmacyPrescription>`.

❑ Remove element `<dentistName>` (doctor's name is not to be contained in the document).

❑ Rename element `<quantity>` to `HowMuch` and make `HowMuch` an attribute of `<PharmacyPrescription>`.

❑ Rename element `<medicationID>` to `MedValue` and make `MedValue` an attribute of `<PharmacyPrescription>`.

❑ Display attribute, `HowMuch`, before attribute, `MedValue`.

A great many of the steps performed by the transform could have been achieved using an alternative technology. For example, we could have used **Sourcecode Style** attributes with our serialization to generate the correct XML attribute and XML element name. Sure if we'd known in advance that a consortium of pharmacies was going to develop a standard, we could have written our classes to be serialized based on the standard. The point was we didn't know and now one standard (our legacy standard) has to be converted into a newly adopted standard of the pharmacy consortium. The worst thing we could do would be to change our working code and then force all users working with the application to upgrade. It is vastly simpler to add an extra transformation step to address the new standard.

The XSLT file that facilitates the transform is, `ConvertLegacyToNewStandard.xslt`. A portion of this file is implemented as follows:

```
<xsl:template match="WXClientPrescription">
    <!-- rename <WXClientPrescription> to <PharmacyPrescription> -->
    <xsl:element name="PharmacyPrescription">
        <!-- Make element 'quantity' attribute HowMuch
            Notice attribute HowMuch comes before attribute MedValue -->
        <xsl:attribute name="HowMuch">
            <xsl:value-of select='quantity'></xsl:value-of>
        </xsl:attribute>
        <!-- Make element medicationID attribute MedValue  -->
        <xsl:attribute name="MedValue">
            <xsl:value-of select='medicationID'></xsl:value-of>
        </xsl:attribute>
    </xsl:element>
    <!-- end of PharmacyPrescription element -->
</xsl:template>
```

In the previous snippet of XSLT, the following XSLT elements were used to facilitate transformation:

❑ `<xsl:template match="WXClientPrescription">` -- all operations in this `template` XSLT element will take place on the original document's `WXClientPrescription` node.

❑ `<xsl:element name="PharmacyPrescription">` -- the element corresponding to the source document's `WXClientPrescription` element will be called, `PharmacyPrescription`, in the destination document.

❑ `<xsl:attribute name="HowMuch">` -- an attribute name, `HowMuch`, will be contained in the previously specified element. The previously specified elemen is `<PharmacyPrescription>`. This XSLT element, `attribute`, for `HowMuch` comes before the XSLT element, `attribute`, for `MedValue`. This order was specified as part of our transform to adhere to the new standard.

❑ `<xsl:value-of select='quantity'>` -- retrieve the value of the source document's `<quantity>` element and place it in the destination document. This instance of XSLT element, value-of, provides the value associated with attribute, `HowMuch`.

Those keeping score may have noticed two new XSLT elements have crept into our vocabulary, `element` and `attribute`. Both of these XSLT elements live up to their names. Specifying the XSLT element named, `element`, places an element in the destination XML document. Specifying the XSLT element named, `attribute`, places an attribute in the destination XML document. The XSLT transform found in file, `ConvertLegacyToNewStandard.xslt`, is too long to review completely. When reading this file in its entirety, remember that this XSLT file contains documentation to specify precisely what aspect of the transformation is being performed at which location in the XSLT document. For example the following comments let it be known what XSLT element, `attribute`, is about to do:

```
<!-- Make element 'quantity' attribute HowMuch
     Notice attribute HowMuch comes before attribute MedValue -->
<xsl:attribute name="HowMuch">
    <xsl:value-of select='quantity'></xsl:value-of>
</xsl:attribute>
```

The previous example spanned several pages and contained a miniscule three lines of code. One of the lessons to be learned with XML is that there is more to it than learning VB.NET and the .NET Framework. The XML language is important as is XSLT and a half-dozen or so other acronyms (DTD, XML-Schema, XPATH, and XOPEN).

Other System.Xml.Xsl Classes and Interfaces

The other classes and interfaces exposed by namespace, System.Xml.Xsl, include:

- ❑ IXsltContextFunction – this interface accesses at runtime a given function defined in the XSLT style sheet.

- ❑ IXsltContextVariable – this interface accesses at runtime a given variable defined in the XSLT style sheet.

- ❑ XsltArgumentList – this class contains a list of arguments. These arguments are of type XSLT parameter or XSLT extension objects. Recall that the XsltArgumentList object is used in conjunction with the Transform method of class, XslTransform.

- ❑ XsltContext – this class contains the state of the XSLT processor. This context information allows XPath expressions to have their various components resolved (functions, parameters, and namespaces).

- ❑ XsltException, XsltCompileException – these classes contain the information pertaining to an exception raised while transforming data. XsltCompilationException is derived from XsltException.

ADO.NET

ADO.NET has already been covered within this text. It should be recognized that ADO.NET enables VB.NET applications to generate XML documents and to use such documents to update persisted data. ADO.NET natively represents its DataSet's underlying data store in XML. ADO.NET also allows SQL Server specific XML support to be accessed. When we examine ADO.NET and XML our focus will not be each nifty feature of ADO.NET but will instead focus only on the features that allow the XML generated and consumed to be customized.

The DataSet properties and methods that are pertinent to XML include Namespace, Prefix, GetXml, GetXmlSchema, InferXmlSchema, ReadXml, ReadXmlSchema, WriteXml, and WriteXmlSchema. An example code snippet, from VBNetXML05, that uses the GetXml method is as follows:

```
Dim adapter As New _
    SqlDataAdapter("SELECT ShipperID, CompanyName, Phone " & _
                   "FROM Shippers", _
```

```
                        "SERVER=localhost;UID=sa;PWD=sa;Database=Northwind;")
Dim ds As New DataSet()

adapter.Fill(ds)
Console.Out.WriteLine(ds.GetXml())
```

The previous code used the Northwind database and retrieved all rows from the Shippers table. This table was selected because it contains only three rows of data. The XML returned by GetXml is as follows where ... signifies where <Table> elements were removed for the sake of brevity:

```
<NewDataSet>
 <Table>
  <ShipperID>1</ShipperID>
  <CompanyName>Speedy Express</CompanyName>
  <Phone>(503) 555-9831</Phone>
 </Table>
  ...
</NewDataSet>
```

What we are trying to determine from the previous XML document is how to customize the XML generated. The more customization we can perform at the ADO.NET level the less need there will be later. With this in mind, we notice that the root element is <NewDataSet> and that each row of the DataSet is returned as an XML element, <Table>. The data returned is contained in an XML element named for the column in which the data resides (<ShipperID>, <CompanyName>, and <Phone> respectively).

The root element, <NewDataSet>, is just the default name of the DataSet. This name could have been changed when the DataSet was constructed by specifying the data set name as a parameter to the constructor:

```
Dim ds As New DataSet("WeNameTheDataSet")
```

If the previous version of the constructor was executed then the <NewDataSet> element would be renamed, <WeNameTheDataSet>. After the DataSet has been constructed, we can still set property, DataSetName, thus changing element, <NewDataSet> to a name such as, <WeNameTheDataSetAgain>:

```
ds.DataSetName = "WeNameTheDataSetAgain"
```

The <Table> element is actually the name of a table in the DataSet's Tables property. Programmatically we can change <Table> to <WeNameTheTable> as follows:

```
ds.Tables("Table").TableName = "WeNameTheTable"
```

We can customize the names of the data columns returned by modifying the SQL to use alias names. For example, we could retrieve the same data but generate different elements using the following SQL:

```
SELECT ShipperID As TheID, CompanyName As CName, Phone As TelephoneNumber
FROM Shippers
```

Using the previous SQL statement the `<ShipperID>` element would become the `<TheID>` element. The `<CompanyName>` element would become `<CName>` and `<Phone>` would become `<TelephoneNumber>`. The column names can also be changed programmatically by using the `Columns` property associated with the table in which the column resides. An example of this is as follows where the XML element, `<TheID>`, is changed to `<AnotherNewName>`.

```
ds.Tables("WeNameTheTable").Columns("TheID").ColumnName = _
    "AnotherNewName"
```

The emphasis on this chapter is not to dissect ADO.NET and the XML it generates. The reader should be cognizant that ADO.NET generates XML. This XML could be transformed using `System.Xml.Xsl`. This XML could be read as a stream (`XmlTextReader`) or written as a stream (`XmlTextWriter`). The XML returned by ADO.NET could even be de-serialized and used to create an object or objects using `XmlSerializer`. What is important is to recognize what ADO.NET generated XML looks like. If you know its format, then you can make it into whatever you like.

ADO.Net and SQL Server XML Features

Those interested in fully exploring the XML-specific features of SQL Server should take a look at *Professional SQL Server 2000 XML* from Wrox Press, ISBN 1861005466. The subject matter of that text is SQL Server and is not .NET-specific. In recognition of this, an example will be provided that bridges between *Professional SQL Server 2000 XML* and the current .NET Framework.

Two of the major XML-related features exposed by SQL Server are:

❑   FOR XML – the FOR XML clause of a SQL SELECT statement allows a rowset to be returned as an XML document. The XML document generated by a FOR XML clause is highly customizable with respect to the document hierarchy generated, by column data transforms, representation of binary data, XML schema generated and a variety of other XML nuances.

❑   OPENXML – the, OPENXML, extension to Transact-SQL allows a stored procedure call to manipulate an XML document as a rowset. Subsequently this rowset can be used to perform a variety of tasks such as SELECT, INSERT INTO, DELETE, and UPDATE.

SQL Server's support for OPENXML is a matter of calling a stored procedure. A developer who can execute a stored procedure call using VB.NET in conjunction with ADO.NET can take full advantage of SQL Server's support for OPENXML. FOR XML queries have a certain caveat when it comes to ADO.NET. To understand this caveat, consider the following FOR XML query:

```
SELECT ShipperID, CompanyName, Phone FROM Shippers FOR XML RAW
```

Using SQL Server's Query Analyzer, this FOR XML RAW query generated the following XML:

```
<row ShipperID="1" CompanyName="Speedy Express" Phone="(503) 555-9831"/>
<row ShipperID="2" CompanyName="United Package" Phone="(503) 555-3199"/>
<row ShipperID="3" CompanyName="Federal Shipping" Phone="(503) 555-9931"/>
```

The same `FOR XML RAW` query can be executed from ADO.Net as follows:

```
Dim adapter As New _
    SqlDataAdapter("SELECT ShipperID, CompanyName, Phone " & _
                      "FROM Shippers FOR XML RAW", _
  "SERVER=localhost;UID=sa;PWD=sa;Database=Northwind;")
Dim ds As New DataSet()

adapter.Fill(ds)
Console.Out.WriteLine(ds.GetXml())
```

The caveat with respect to a `FOR XML` query is that all data (the XML text) is returned via a resultset containing a single row and a single column named, `XML_F52E2B61-18A1-11d1-B105-00805F49916B`. The output from the previous code snippet demonstrates this caveat where ... represents similar data not show for reasons of brevity:

```
<NewDataSet>
 <Table>
  <XML_F52E2B61-18A1-11d1-B105-00805F49916B>
   &lt;row ShipperID="1" CompanyName= "Speedy Express" Phone="(503) 555-9831"/&gt;
   ...
  </XML_F52E2B61-18A1-11d1-B105-00805F49916B>
 </Table>
</NewDataSet>
```

The value of our single row and single column turned contains what looks to be XML but contains `/&lt;` instead of the less-than character and `/&gt;` instead of the greater-than character. The symbols "<" and ">" cannot appear inside XML data. For this reason they must be entity encoded (represented as `/&gt;` and `/&lt;`). The data returned in element, `<XML_F52E2B61-18A1-11d1-B105-00805F49916B>` is not XML but is data contained in an XML document.

In order to fully utilize `FOR XML` queries the data must be accessible as XML. The solution to this quandary is the `ExecuteXmlReader` method of the `SQLCommand` class. When this method is called, a `SQLCommand` object assumes it has executed a `FOR XML` query and returns the results of this query as an `XmlReader` object. An example of this is as follows, again found in VBNetXML05:

```
Dim connection As New _
    SqlConnection("SERVER=localhost;UID=sa;PWD=sa;Database=Northwind;")
Dim command As New _
    SqlCommand("SELECT ShipperID, CompanyName, Phone " & _
                  "FROM Shippers FOR XML RAW")
Dim memStream As MemoryStream = New MemoryStream()
Dim xmlReader As New XmlTextReader(memStream)

connection.Open()
command.Connection = connection
xmlReader = command.ExecuteXmlReader()
' Extract results from XMLReader
```

The XmlReader created in the previous code snippet is of type XmlTextReader that is derived from class, XmlReader. The XmlTextReader is backed by a MemoryStream, hence it is an in-memory stream of XML that can be traversed using the methods and propertiese exposed by the XmlTextReader class. We will not discuss how to use the XmlTextReader class in order to access XML. Streaming XML generation and retrieval was already discussed in detail in a previous section of this chapter.

Using the ExecuteXmlReader method of the SQLCommand class it is possible to retrieve the result of FOR XML queries. For those of you who haven't read Wrox's *Professional SQL Server 2000 XML*, it is worthwhile to review why FOR XML is so important. The theme to XML is configurability. If data is stored in the database in one form a mechanism is needed to retrieve this data as XML. This mechanism is the FOR XML query. What makes FOR XML style of queries so powerful is that it can configure the data retrieved. The three types of FOR XML query support the following forms of XML customization:

❑   FOR XML RAW – returns each row of a resultset inside an XML element named, <row>. The data retrieved is contained as attributes of element, <row>. The attributes are named for the column name or column alias in the FOR XML RAW query.

❑   FOR XML AUTO – by default returns each row of a resultset inside an XML element named, for the table or table alias contained in the FOR XML AUTO query. The data retrieved is contained as attributes of this element. The attributes are named for the column name or column alias in the FOR XML AUTO query. By specifying FOR XML AUTO, ELEMENTS it is possible to retrieve all data inside elements rather than inside attributes. All data retrieved must be in attribute or element form. There is no mix-and-match capability.

❑   FOR XML EXPLICIT – this form of FOR XML query allows the precise XML type of each column returned to be specified. The data associated with a column can be returned as an attribute or an element. Specific XML types such as CDATA and ID can be associated with a column returned. Even the level in the XML hierarchy in which data resides can be specified using a FOR XML EXPLICIT query. This style of query is fairly complicated to implement.

FOR XML queries are flexible. Using FOR XML EXPLICIT and the dental database, it would be possible to generate any form of XML medical prescription standard. The decision that needs to be made is where XML configuration takes place. Programmatically using VB.NET a developer could use XmlTextReader and XmlTextWriter to create any style of XML document. Using the XSLT language and an XSLT file, the same level of configurability could be achieved. SQL Server and in particular FOR XML EXPLICIT would allow the same level of XML customization but this customization would take place at the SQL level and may even be configured to stored procedure calls.

Summary

This one chapter presented an overview of a subject area that merits an entire book. The XML facilities available to a VB.NET application are vast. With respect to the generation of XML technologies such as XML serialization, ADO.NET and FOR XML SQL were investigated. ADO.NET can also consume XML that was not explored directly just as SQL Server supports OPENXML in order to modify data using XML. The facility to consume XML was not as important as the facilities used to massage XML documents into a form that could be consumed by ADO.NET, SQL Server, or every important third-party application (the famous pharmacies consortium and their XML representation of a medical prescription).

A subset of the classes of namespace, System.Xml, was reviewed. These classes included those that supported document-style XML access (XMmlDocument, XmlNode, XmlElement, and XmlAttribute). The System.Xml also supports stream-style XML access (XmlReader and XmlWriter). XML streams are also useful for retrieving SQL Server FOR XML queries using ADO.NET.

VB was shown utilizing XSLT style sheets to transform XML data. The classes supporting this functionality are found in System.Xml.Xsl. Transformation data using XSLT was demonstrated and with this approach the programming impetus was on the XSLT language rather than on the VB.NET language.

Namespace, System.Xml.Serialization, and its class, XmlSerializer, facilitated this functionality. Sourcecode Style attributes were introduced in conjunction with serialization. This style of attributes allows the customization of the XML serialized to be extended to the sourcecode associated with a class. What is important to remember about serialization classes directly is that a required change in the XML format becomes a change in the underlying sourcecode. Developers should resist the temptation to rewrite the serialized classes in order to conform to some new XML data standard (such as the prescription format endorsed by our consortium of pharmacies). Technologies such as XSLT exposed via the System.Xml.Xsl namespace should be examined first as alternatives.

Given the breadth of the XML-related features exposed by Visual Basic .NET and the .NET Framework, you could say that XML is quite an important technology. Ultimately this technology could be the underpinnings of all electronic commerce, banking transactions, and data exchange of almost every conceivable kind. The beauty of XML is that it isolates data representation from data display. Technologies such as HTML contain data that is tightly bound to its display format. XML does not suffer this limitation yet at the same time has the readability of HTML.

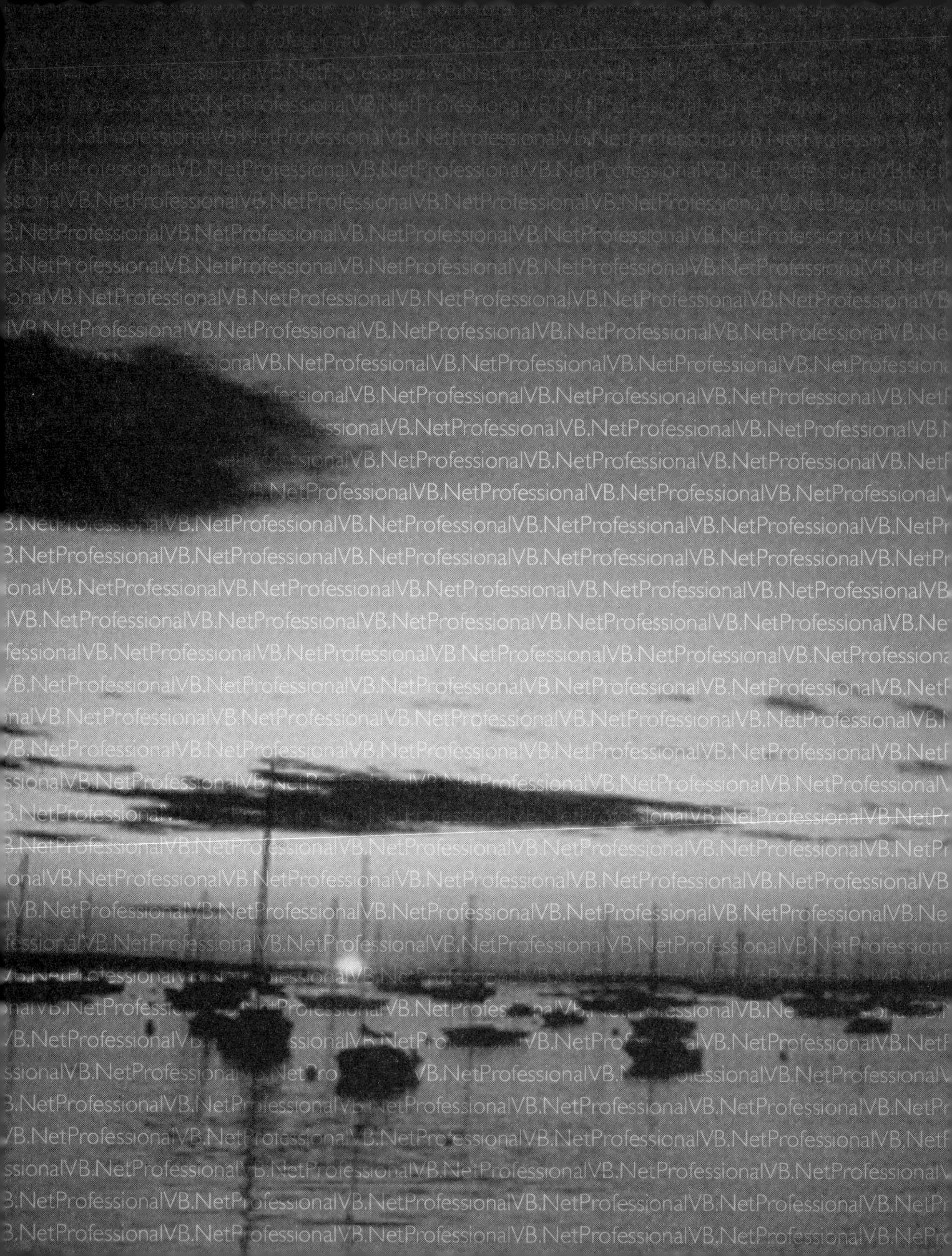
VB.NetProfessional

20

Web Forms

As Visual Basic developers, chances are that you are developing more and more applications that deal with the World Wide Web. Visual Basic programmers have gravitated naturally to Microsoft's Active Server Pages (ASP) technology as a means to develop web applications. This is because of the similarity between programming VB and VBScript. Unfortunately, ASP did not have a visual metaphor for creating web interfaces like the VB form; Visual InterDev was, at best, a poor first attempt by Microsoft. With VB.NET, Microsoft has bridged that gap by merging Visual InterDev within Visual Basic and has provided VB programmers with a visual ability for generating web interfaces, using what is called a Web Form.

This chapter explores Web Forms and how you can benefit from their use. This chapter is meant to whet your appetite for developing Web Forms and, if you want to learn more, you can refer to *Professional ASP.NET* (Wrox Press, ISBN 1861004885).

Web Forms are part of the new ASP.NET technology. They allow a programmer to use one of several different languages to quickly create web pages that combine visual HTML forms with server-side code. In a manner very similar to a VB Windows Form – which has a visual element (the form and its controls) and the code behind it – a Web Form also has an HTML form, that is visible within a browser, as well as server-side code encapsulated within a code class (`.cs`) file.

A Web Form in Action

The easiest way to learn about Web Forms is to see them in action, and then take them apart to see how they are constructed. Let's look at a very simple Web Form – the quintessential Hello World example.

Setting Up the Environment

Before you begin creating Web Forms, make sure you compare your environment with the checklist below. Normally, if you installed Visual Studio.NET on a Windows 2000 machine and chose a typical install, you should be all set. However, in case your situation is different, please ensure the following:

❑ Visual Studio.NET's system requirements specify that you need to be running Microsoft Windows 2000 Server or Professional, Microsoft Windows XP Professional Beta 2, or Microsoft Windows NT 4.0 Server.

❑ If you are creating Web Forms pages (rather than just HTML, or HTML and ASP pages), the server computer should also have the .NET Framework installed. If you have installed VS.NET, you should be ready to go. However, if you are developing on one computer and expect it to be deployed on a separate server, the server needs to have the .NET Framework installed too.

❑ According to Microsoft, it is highly recommended that the server computer be formatted with NTFS (NT File System) rather than FAT (File Allocation Table). This results in better performance and substantially greater security, as well as offering additional options for sourcecode control.

The HelloWorld Web Form

Create a new ASP.NET Web Application project in VS.NET. Name the project HelloWorld and make sure that you select the default http://localhost/ as your location for the project:

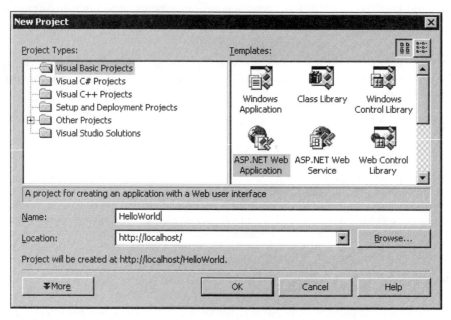

Click OK and you will be presented with a new solution. By default, VS.NET has created a new Web Form for you, called WebForm1.aspx. Notice the new extension for ASP.NET files.

When you clicked OK, a few things happened. Apart from creating a new folder in your Visual Studio Projects directory, VS.NET also established a web application on the target web server (in this case, the local web server, localhost). On the web server, VS.NET:

❑ Creates a duplicate physical folder under the \inetpub\wwwroot directory, named after your project

❑ Marks the folder as an IIS application, allowing script to be executed

❑ Creates a FrontPage Web if you have FrontPage Server Extensions installed, allowing you to author the web application via FrontPage also

You can treat the Web Form in front of you as a normal VB form, dropping controls onto it by dragging them from the toolbox. For now, drag a Label control from the toolbox and drop it onto the top left of the form. Use the Properties windows to set its caption (its Text property) to "Hello World". Your screen will look like this:

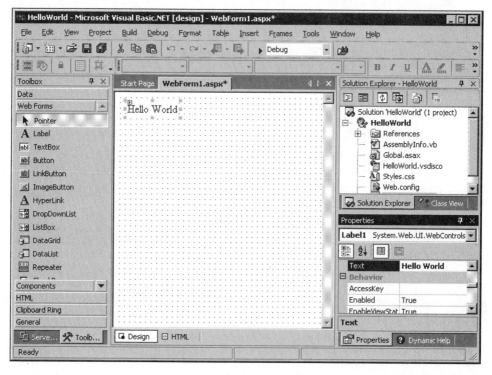

For this example, that's all we need to do. We shall now execute our application. Normally, Visual Studio.NET executes applications in a special "debug" mode that allows you to monitor the progress of your application. For now, we simply want to execute our application in "release" mode, or production mode. Change the Solution Configurations drop-down menu on your toolbar from Debug to Release. Click on the Start icon on the toolbar, or select Debug | Start from the menu. If all goes well, your browser will open the WebForm1.aspx file and you should see the text "Hello World" within the browser window:

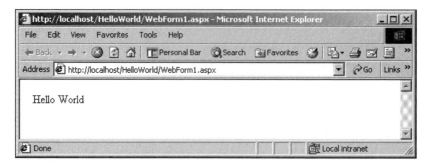

Right-click on the browser and select View Source to see what the output produced by our solution looks like. You will see that it is pure HTML, generated at runtime by our aspx file.

```
<!DOCTYPE HTML PUBLIC "-//W3C//DTD HTML 4.0 Transitional//EN">
<HTML>
  <HEAD>
    <title></title>
    <meta name="GENERATOR" content="Microsoft Visual Studio.NET 7.0">
    <meta name="CODE_LANGUAGE" content="Visual Basic 7.0">
    <meta name=vs_defaultClientScript content="JavaScript">
    <meta name=vs_targetSchema
    content="http://schemas.microsoft.com/intellisense/ie5">
  </HEAD>
  <body MS_POSITIONING="GridLayout">

    <form name="Form1" method="post" action="webform1.aspx" id="Form1">
    <input type="hidden" name="__VIEWSTATE" value="dDwtMTU3ODAzNTQ4MDs7Pg==" />

    <span id="Label1" style="Z-INDEX: 101; LEFT: 19px; POSITION: absolute; TOP:
    16px">Hello World</span>

    </form>

  </body>
</HTML>
```

Notice that there is an HTML form within our page, even though we did not ask for one. We'll look at this more closely later on in this chapter. Our label is included within the span tag:

```
<span id="Label1" style="Z-INDEX: 101; LEFT: 19px; POSITION: absolute; TOP:
16px">Hello World</span>
```

The span tag acts as a container to hold our label and its style attribute defines its location and size. Let us return to our VS.NET solution to see what makes this Web Form tick. Web Forms are very similar to Windows Forms, and we'll see how much alike they are with this next example.

Within our HelloWorld application, we have a single Web Form, WebForm1.aspx. Let's create a new one with a little more to it.

From the menu, select Project | Add Web Form. In the Add New Item dialog box that pops up, make sure you have selected Web Form and that its name is WebForm2.aspx:

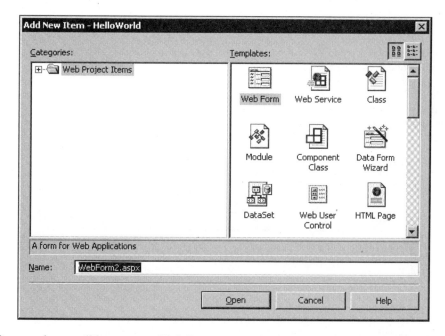

Click **Open** and you will have a new Web Form in your Solution. Double-click on **WebForm2.aspx** in the **Solution Explorer** window to make sure that you are working with the new form you have just added. Then repeat the earlier process of adding a `Label` to the form. In addition, also add a `Button` control to the form underneath the `Label`. Widen the width of the label by clicking on it and dragging its resizing handles.

From the **Properties** window, set the `ID` property of the `Label` (which defines its name) to be `lblText`. Leave its `Text` property as `Label`.

Then click on the `Button` and set its `ID` property to `btnSubmit`. Click once on the button and press the *Enter* key, or right-click on the button and select **View Code**. You will be taken to the code behind the form. Wait a minute, though! This is not a Windows Form, yet buttons can have code behind them!

In ASP.NET, controls *do* have code behind them. As you can see, we have a subroutine called `btnSubmit_Click` that will be executed when the button is clicked. This code is executed on the *server*, not the client browser, whenever the form is submitted and sent back to the server. We'll see more details later on. For now, enter the following as the code for the click event:

```
    Private Sub btnSubmit_Click(ByVal sender As System.Object, ByVal e As
System.EventArgs) Handles btnSubmit.Click
        lblText.Text = "Hello World"
    End Sub
```

You will notice that IntelliSense works when you type in this line. ASP programmers had this functionality with InterDev, but VS.NET's IntelliSense provides more HTML elements for use in your code.

Close the code window and return back to the design mode for the form. Change the `Text` property of the button to `Submit`. Finally, we are ready to view this form in action.

If you try to use the Start button to run the project, it will open up WebForm1.aspx since that is the starting form for the project. In order to view the second Web Form, you can set it to be the starting form by right-clicking on its name in the Solution Explorer and selecting Set As Start Page from the popup menu. Then press the Start button.

The new Web Form – WebForm2.aspx – opens up in the browser, displaying a label and a button. The label has the default caption of Label. Click on the Submit button and the text Hello World appears within the label. When you clicked on the submit button, the code behind the button was executed. Just like a Windows Form.

The Anatomy of a Web Form

Web Forms bridge the gap between VB programming and traditional ASP programming. By offering a visual technique to drag and drop controls onto a page, and code for events behind the controls, Web Forms bring a very familiar metaphor to web development.

A Web Form is made up of two components – the visual elements that you can see in the design view, and the code behind the controls and the page. The visual elements form the template for the presentation of the web page in the end user's browser. The code is executed on the server when the page loads and in response to other events that you have coded for. If you try to create a Web Form by hand, using a text editor, you will probably end up creating both these components within the same physical file. And that is fine as long as it has an .aspx extension. With VS.NET, however, the visual elements are defined in the .aspx file, while the code elements are defined in the .vb file that accompanies the Web Form.

The following figure shows the two components that make up our WebForm2.aspx Web Form within our HelloWorld web application:

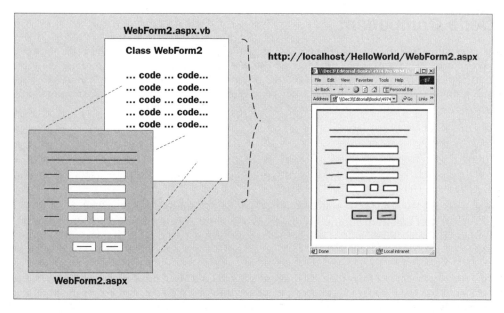

By dividing the components into separate files and, therefore, within the VS.NET environment, into separate "views", Web Forms provide a very familiar environment for the VB programmer. With traditional VB, you first "paint" the form by dragging and dropping controls, and then write code for the events that the controls expose. When developing Web Forms, you first create the look of your web page by dragging and dropping controls onto the page, and then you write code for the events exposed by the controls.

The Template for Presentation

The .aspx file forms the User Interface component of the Web Form and serves as a template for its presentation in the browser. This .aspx file is the "Page", as referred to in ASP.NET terms, and it contains HTML markup and Web Forms specific elements. You can drag and drop several types of controls onto a Web Form. These include:

- ❑ HTML controls
- ❑ Web Form controls
- ❑ Validation controls
- ❑ Data related controls
- ❑ COM and .NET components registered on your machine
- ❑ Items from your clipboard

We shall take a look at these different kinds of controls later on in this chapter.

The Code Component

If you code with VS.NET, the `.vb` file that accompanies the `.aspx` file forms the code component of your Web Form. To view this file, click on the **Show All Files** icon in the toolbar along the top of the Solution Explorer. Then expand the **WebForm2.aspx** node, to reveal **WebForm2.aspx.vb**. This `.vb` file contains a single `Public Class` named after your Web Form. In the `WebForm2.aspx` example, the `WebForm2.aspx.vb` code component has the following initial structure:

```
Public Class WebForm2
    Inherits System.Web.UI.Page
    Protected WithEvents lblText As System.Web.UI.WebControls.Label
    Protected WithEvents btnSubmit As System.Web.UI.WebControls.Button
```

If you expand the **References** section within the **Solution Explorer**, you will find that all of the objects within your project inherit their functionality from a number of base classes available within the .NET Framework. These include the `System` classes responsible for `Data`, `Drawing`, `Web`, `Web Services`, and `XML`.

In addition, as you can see from the code fragment above, our `WebForm2` class itself inherits from the `System.Web.UI.Page` class. This allows the code within our Web Form to access the built-in `Request`, `Response`, `Session`, `Application`, and `Server` objects.

Every control that you place on the form and, consequently, in the `.aspx` file, is represented within the `.vb` file as an event code if it exposes an event that can be handled via server-side code. This is very much reminiscent of the way that VB code-behind forms work.

In our case, we have the `Click` event of our `btnSubmit` button represented by this fragment of code:

```
    Private Sub btnSubmit_Click(ByVal sender As System.Object, ByVal e As
System.EventArgs) Handles btnSubmit.Click
        lblText.Text = "Hello World"
    End Sub
```

Before going on to look at the processing flow of ASP.NET pages, let's take a look at another example that will drive home the point that Web Forms make web development uncannily like VB development.

A More Complex Example

Suppose that we wish to display a calendar for the current month in a web page. Generating a dynamic calendar for a traditional ASP page involves writing at least 50 to 100 lines of code. You have to create a table to host the calendar, figure out the month and the year, and output the days of the week header. Then you need to figure out what day the current month begins with and how many days there are in the month. Finally, you can output the days of the month starting with 1 and going on till the end of the month. When you output the days, you need to make sure that you are placing each week horizontally in one row (a <TR> tag) of a table. When you reach the end of one week, you need to close the row (a </TR> tag) and begin a new one. Finally, when you are done with the days of the month, you probably need to output a few blank days to make the table appear even and look good on the screen. All this takes up a lot of ASP code, especially if you want the calendar to be generated dynamically.

There was an alternative before Web Forms. You could simply use a client-side ActiveX control – a Calendar control in your web page. However, this had its own problems. ActiveX controls are not supported by all browsers – only IE really supports them. The Calendar control may not exist on your user's computer, so you have to worry about distributing it. Also, an ActiveX control will only work on the Windows platform, so your web site users on Macs, for example, will not be able to view the page properly.

Web Forms bring the ease of development with an ActiveX control to the world of ASP and web development and, yet, at the same time, they output standard HTML on demand.

In our HelloWorld project, add a new Web Form. By default, this form will be called WebForm3.aspx; accept the default name. Then, open up the Web Form in design view. From your toolbox, look for the Calendar control under the Web Forms group. Double-click or drag it onto the form. That's it! You now have a fully functional calendar in your web page – albeit a very plain looking one.

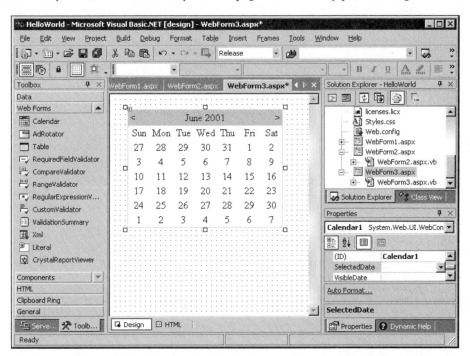

Before we run this Web Form, let's make it look a little better. Using the Properties window, set the following properties like so:

Property	Setting
ID	myCal
BackColor	A light yellow (#FFFFC0)
BorderColor	Black
BorderStyle	Solid

Table continued on following page

Property	Setting
BorderWidth	1px
DayHeaderStyle, BackColor	Light orange (#FFC080)
DayHeaderStyle, BorderColor	Dark red (#C00000)
DayHeaderStyle, BorderStyle	Inset
DayHeaderStyle, BorderWidth	1px
DayHeaderStyle, Font, Bold	True
DayNameFormat	Short
Font, Name	Verdana
Font, Size	X-Small
NextPrevFormat	ShortMonth
OtherMonthDayStyle, ForeColor	Silver
SelectedDayStyle, BackColor	Dark blue (#0000C0)
SelectedDayStyle, ForeColor	White

Alternatively, you can select one of the predetermined formats available for the calendar. Click on the Calendar control and, under the **Properties** window, click on the link marked **AutoFormat**. Select an option from the **AutoFormat** window to inherit the same look for your Calendar control.

When you are done, repeat the process we did earlier – set this page to be the startup page and then run the project.

All you did was drag and drop a calendar control onto a web page in your design environment and set a few properties to make it look different. In your browser, you should have a web page that looks like this:

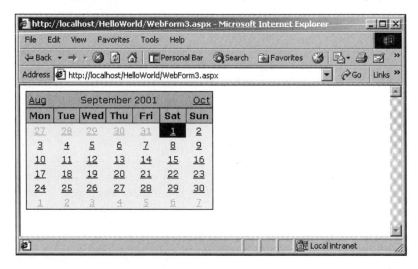

Take a look at the code generated behind this page. It's hundreds of lines long! Not only that, this is not a static calendar painted on the browser. It is fully interactive. Click on any day and it becomes highlighted in blue. Click on another day and the selection changes. Click on the other months listed at the top of the calendar and the month view automatically changes.

Our Web Form contains the `Calendar` control that is being executed at runtime. The `Calendar` control is a Web Form server control that is outputting plain HTML to be viewed in the browser (IE and Netscape version 4.0 or above). And we developed it using VB.NET, just like developing and deploying a VB.NET Windows Form.

The Processing Flow of ASP.NET Web Forms

Traditional web development, especially ASP development, has always involved generating an HTML page and adding script code to it. An ASP page in traditional ASP (ASP versions prior to ASP.NET) was therefore a plain text file separated into blocks of ASP code and HTML code. When a browser requested an ASP page from the web server, the ASP engine kicked in and parsed the page, before its output was sent back to the browser. At runtime, the ASP engine would interpret the ASP code one line at a time. It would execute each line that contained ASP script code, and would output unchanged every line that contained plain HTML text. The traditional ASP web development model was therefore one of HTML pages with code added to them.

The diagram below shows a simplistic view of how the processing flow takes place in traditional ASP:

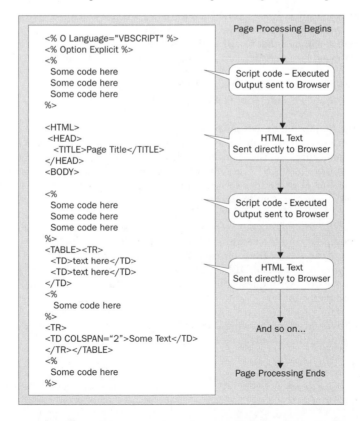

For more information on "traditional" ASP, see Professional Active Server Pages 3.0 *(Wrox Press, ISBN 1861002610).*

Web Forms turn this paradigm of web development upside down. With Web Forms, every page is actually an executable program that is "executed". The page's execution results in HTML text being outputted. You can therefore focus on developing with controls and code elements that output HTML, instead of worrying about interspersing code around HTML text.

What exactly is a Web Form? A VB.NET Web Form *is* an ASP.NET page. As we've already seen, Web Forms (or ASP.NET pages) are text files with an .aspx extension. On a .NET server (any IIS server where the .NET Framework has been installed), when a browser requests an .aspx file, the ASP.NET runtime parses and compiles the page. This process is similar to the way that the ASP engine in ASP 3.0 and below parsed the page. The main difference is that the ASP.NET runtime compiles the page into a .NET Framework class file. The code is compiled and not interpreted line by line each time the page is executed using a script engine. This results in improved runtime performance since the web page code is compiled and stored in cache for reuse.

A typical Web Application project (a project that contains Web Forms) developed in VB will have at least one .aspx file. If you incorporate controls and code on the form, the code itself is placed in the .vb file. That is, if your Web Form is called WebForm1, you will end up with WebForm1.aspx and WebForm1.aspx.vb. The .aspx file corresponds to the traditional ASP .asp file and contains primarily HTML code that defines your web page. The .aspx.vb file contains the "code-behind-the-web page" VB code.

In addition, a Web Application project usually has a Global.asax and a Web.config file. The Global.asax file is the .NET counterpart of the Global.asa file used in ASP web applications. It contains code for event handlers that fire when the Application and the Session begin and end. A complete description of this file and its uses is available in *Professional ASP.NET* (Wrox Press, ISBN 1861004885).

The Web.config file is new to .NET. It is an XML formatted file that stores the configuration settings for your web application. This includes features such as debug mode, compiling options, etc.

These files are actually located in two separate places. The files need to be executed on the web server and, therefore, their primary location is the web server. However, VS.NET also keeps a copy in its local cache. VS.NET synchronizes the files between its local cache and the server. When you work with a file in VS.NET and then save it, VS.NET automatically updates both the local cache as well as the file on the web server. Some local cache files serve a temporary purpose (they may be intermediary files, for example), and these are not written to the server.

When you use VS.NET to deploy your web application, it uses the standard model for VB applications – your project is compiled and the resulting files are deployed. In the case of a web application, all of the code files (but not the .aspx files) for each Web Form are compiled into a DLL along with all other executable files in your project. The DLL is then deployed to the web server as a single unit, without the sourcecode. When the browser requests the .aspx file, the DLL file and the .aspx file are compiled into a new class and then run.

Let's take our HelloWorld example, where we added the second Web Form to our application and ran it. We have the following files in our project:

❑   WebForm2.aspx
❑   WebForm2.aspx.vb

❏   `Global.asax`

❏   `Global.asax.vb`

❏   `Web.config`

Remember, we did not write any code for the `Global.asax` file and its code file `Global.asax.vb`. VS.NET automatically creates them for us with placeholders for code.

When we deploy this project, by pressing the Start button, the following files are copied to the web server with no change or compilation:

❏   `WebForm2.aspx`

❏   `Global.asax`

When we deploy this project, the following files are compiled into a single DLL called `HelloWorld.dll`:

❏   `WebForm2.asax.vb`

❏   `Global.asax.vb`

At this time, our web server contains the following three files for this web application:

❏   `WebForm2.aspx`

❏   `Global.asax`

❏   `HelloWorld.dll`

When we request the `.aspx` file in our browser, ASP.NET dynamically generates a temporary `.cls` class file out of the contents of the `.aspx` file. This temporary `.cls` file is then compiled into a temporary `.dll` file. This temporary `.dll` file inherits from the `HelloWorld.dll` file and, therefore, has access to all of the code within `HelloWorld.dll`. The temporary `.dll` file finally invokes the `HelloWorld.dll` file that contains the compiled code from the `WebForm2.vb` file. This results in HTML being rendered onto the browser.

Remember, the .NET Framework exposes a number of classes from which .NET applications derive functionality and definitions. The root class includes the `System` class that provides system level functionality. Web Forms derive their "look and feel" functionality, or UI elements, from the `System.Web.UI` class. Each `.aspx` file represents one web page in a web application. When a browser requests an `.aspx` file for the very first time, ASP.NET generates the temporary `.cls` class file dynamically for the page by inheriting from the `System.Web.UI.Page` namespace. This class exposes the `Request`, `Response`, `Server`, `Application`, and `Session` objects, properties, and methods that ASP programmers are familiar with.

The above steps may seem like a lot of work. However, these steps are performed only once for each page. When the class is dynamically generated, it is also cached in a special directory so that subsequent requests for the same page are executed much faster. Once a page has been compiled into a class, it is cached until the next time that you make a change to the page. Therefore, as long as a page's code does not change, the page executes using the class file.

The diagram below shows how the processing flow takes place in ASP.NET for a Web Form.

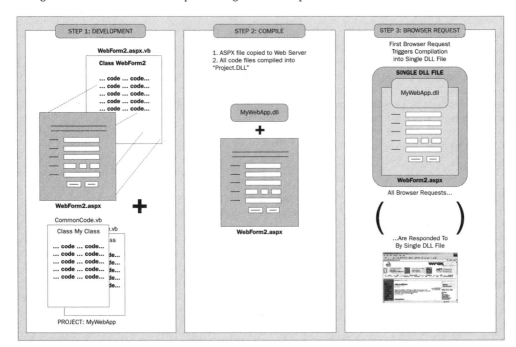

The Controls Available in Web Forms

Web Form controls are different to controls used in VB.NET Windows Forms. This is because Web Form controls operate within the ASP.NET page framework. There are four kinds of controls for use in Web Forms:

- ❑ HTML Server Controls
- ❑ ASP.NET Server Controls
- ❑ Validation Controls
- ❑ User Controls

Before we take a look at these types, let's examine the idea behind server-side controls.

The Concept of Server-Side Controls

Like in traditional ASP, you can use the <% and the %> tags to separate ASP code from plain HTML code. However, if you rely on these tags to delimit ASP code, you will be responsible for maintaining state when the page is submitted back to the server. This means that, if you want to create an interactive web application, you will be responsible for obtaining the data from the Request object, passing it back to the browser when the page returns, and keeping track of it. This task – maintaining state – has been a big worry for ASP programmers up till now.

For example, consider the case where you have a form with a single text box and a button that submits the form:

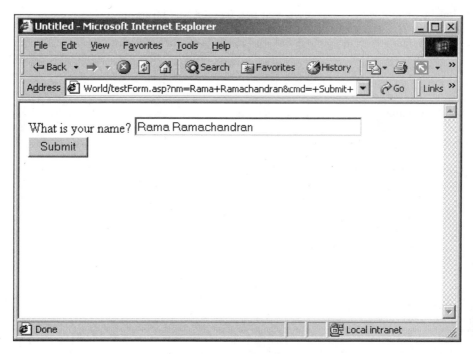

When the form is submitted, assume that it returns back with the value of the textbox intact. To be able to do this, you will need to code a form in this manner:

```
<!DOCTYPE HTML PUBLIC "-//W3C//DTD HTML 4.0 Transitional//EN">

<html>
<head>
    <title>Untitled</title>
</head>

<body>
<FORM ACTION="testForm.asp">
What is your name?
<INPUT TYPE="text" NAME="nm"
VALUE="<%= Request("nm") %>" SIZE="40"
MAXLENGTH="40"><BR>
<INPUT TYPE="submit" NAME="cmd" VALUE=" Submit ">
</FORM>

</body>
</html>
```

Remember, you cannot name the textbox "name", since that is a reserved keyword in client-side scripting and this will cause problems. Hence, we call our textbox "nm". As you can see, you – the programmer – are responsible for maintaining the value of the text entered in the text box and returning it back to the browser:

```
VALUE="<%= Request("nm") %>" SIZE="40"
```

You do this by obtaining the value of the text box (named "nm") from the Request object, and using that value as the VALUE attribute of the text box. The first time around, since the Request object does not have a value named nm, it will be blank and so the user will see a blank text box. When the user enters a value and presses the submit button, the same form is returned back but, this time, with the value of the text box filled in.

With Web Forms, Microsoft has introduced a new concept that takes care of managing state automatically without having to write any incremental code. Web Forms allow you to indicate that a particular form control needs to automatically maintain state when submitted by the user. You do this by using the runat="server" attribute for the form controls as well as the form.

This one line change makes your form controls behave like **server-side controls** rather than just client-side controls. To take our example from above, if we change the code to the following:

```
<!DOCTYPE HTML PUBLIC "-//W3C//DTD HTML 4.0 Transitional//EN">

<html>
<head>
   <title>Untitled</title>
</head>

<body>
<FORM ACTION="testForm.aspx" runat="server">
What is your name?
<asp:textbox NAME="nm"
VALUE="" SIZE="40"
MAXLENGTH="40" runat="server"/><BR>
<INPUT TYPE="submit" NAME="cmd" VALUE=" Submit ">
</FORM>

</body>
</html>
```

and save the file with an .aspx extension (to make sure that the ASP.NET runtime handles its processing), we will get automatic state maintenance without writing any further code. Notice the differences. First, it is an .aspx file. Second, the FORM tag itself has an indication runat="server":

```
<FORM ACTION="testForm.aspx" runat="server">
```

This causes the ASP.NET runtime to create additional code to handle the state. This is done via a hidden form field that is appended to your form. If you chose to view the source of your file in the browser, this is what you would see in place of the FORM tag code:

```
<form name="ctrl1" method="post" action="testForm.aspx" id="ctrl1">
<input type="hidden" name="__VIEWSTATE" value="YTB6MTU3MTczMTA4Nl9fX3g=351fc6c3" />
```

As you can see, the ASP.NET runtime has added additional code, including a form NAME and an ID, as well as a hidden field called __VIEWSTATE. ASP.NET uses this hidden field to transfer state information between the browser and the web server. It compresses the information needed into a cryptic field value. All controls on the web page that need their state information maintained are automatically tagged within this single hidden field value.

Notice too that, instead of using a simple INPUT tag for our textbox, we used the special asp:textbox tag. This is required to make sure that the textbox behaves like a server-side control.

HTML Server Controls

HTML Server Controls are HTML elements exposed to the server by using the runat="server" attribute. In VS.NET, HTML Server Controls are included within the **Web Forms** group of the **Toolbox**. The regular HTML Form Controls (TextBox, CheckBox, Listbox, etc.) are available within the **HTML** group. HTML Server Controls are identical to regular HTML Form controls in look, feel, and behavior, except that the presence of the runat="server" enables you to program them within the Web Forms page framework.

HTML Server Controls are available for the HTML elements most commonly used on a web page to make it interactive – such as the FORM tag, the HTML <INPUT> elements (TextBox, CheckBox, Submit button), ListBox (SELECT), Table, and Image. These pre-defined HTML Server Controls share the basic properties of the generic controls and, in addition, each control typically provides its own set of properties and its own event.

In the VS.NET environment, you can create a regular HTML control by clicking on the **HTML** group within your toolbox and then dragging a **Text Field** control onto the Web Form. Then give it the name txtFirst_Name by changing its ID property. This will result in a regular HTML control with the following code:

```
<INPUT
style="Z-INDEX: 102; LEFT: 24px; POSITION: absolute; TOP: 72px"
type=text id=txtFirst_Name >
```

Actually, the values within the style attribute will be different in your case, depending on where on the web page you actually placed your control.

To convert a regular HTML control to an HTML Server Control (and vice versa), simply right-click on the control in the design mode and select (or uncheck) the menu option **Run As Server Control**. If you select it, you will see the following:

```
<INPUT
style="Z-INDEX: 102; LEFT: 24px; POSITION: absolute; TOP: 72px"
type=text id=txtFirst_Name runat="server">
```

Notice the difference – the final attribute that denotes that this is a server control.

HTML controls are created from classes in the .NET Framework class library's System.Web.UI.HtmlControls namespace. Regular HTML controls are parsed and rendered simply as HTML elements. For example, a regular Text Field HTML control will be parsed and rendered as an HTML text box.

By converting HTML controls to HTML Server Controls, you gain the ability to:

❑   Write code for events generated on the control that are executed on the server-side, rather than on the client-side. For example, you can respond with server-side code to the Click event of a Button.

❑ Write code for events in client script. Since they are displayed as standard HTML form controls, they retain the ability to handle client-side script as always.

❑ Automatically maintain the values of the control on a round-trip when the browser submits the page to the server.

❑ Bind the value of the control to a field, property, method, or expression in your server-side code.

HTML Server Controls are included for backward compatibility with existing ASP applications. They make it easier to convert traditional ASP applications to ASP.NET (Web Forms) applications. However, everything that can be done with HTML Server Controls can be done – with more programmatic control – by using the new ASP.NET Server Controls.

ASP.NET Server Controls

HTML controls are just wrappers around regular HTML tags and do not offer any programmatic advantage in terms of controlling their look and feel. ASP.NET Server Controls, on the other hand, do not necessarily map to a single HTML element and provide a much richer UI output. We have already seen this with our Calendar ASP.NET Server Control.

VB.NET ships with over twenty ASP.NET Server Controls, ranging from simple controls like TextBoxes, Buttons, and Labels, to more complex Server Controls such as the AdRotator, Calendar, and DataGrid.

When you drag and drop each of these controls onto your Web Form, they display their own distinctive UI. For example, a TextBox may simply be visible as a text box, but the Calendar control or the DataGrid control will appear as a tabular construct.

Behind the scenes, these controls are prefixed with the asp: tag. For example, in WebForm1.aspx, when we placed a Label on the page and set its Text property to Hello World, our Label uses the following code to define it:

```
<asp:Label id=Label1 style="Z-INDEX: 101; LEFT: 19px; POSITION: absolute; TOP:
16px" runat="server">Hello World</asp:Label>
```

You can view the HTML source of any control by right-clicking anywhere on the page and selecting View HTML Source from the context menu. Similarly, when we dragged a Button onto the form, instead of obtaining the normal HTML INPUT TYPE="SUBMIT" text, we get the following:

```
<asp:Button id=cmdSubmit runat="server" Text="Button"></asp:Button>
```

Notice that the code does not represent a regular HTML control, but rather an ASP.NET control. The attributes refer to the ASP.NET control's properties. At runtime, the ASP.NET control is rendered on the web page by using plain HTML, which depends on the browser type as well as the settings on the control. For example, the button above may be rendered on the target browser either as an INPUT TYPE="SUBMIT" HTML element, or as a <BUTTON> tag, depending on the browser type.

The following ASP Server Controls ship with VB.NET and are available for use in a Web Form, and are found in the Web Forms section of the Toolbox:

Control	Purpose
Label	Displays non-editable text.
TextBox	Displays editable text in a box.
Button	Displays a button, usually used to carry out an action.
LinkButton	Behaves like a button, but appears like a hyperlink.
ImageButton	Displays a button with an image rather than with text.
HyperLink	Creates a hyperlink for navigation.
DropDownList	Presents a list in a drop-down combo box.
ListBox	Presents a list of items in a scrollable box.
DataGrid	Displays information (usually from a database) in a tabular format with rows and columns.
DataList	Displays information from a database, very similar to the Repeater control.
Repeater	Displays information from a database using HTML elements that you specify, repeating the display once for each record.
CheckBox	Displays a single check box allowing users to check on or off.
CheckBoxList	Displays a set of check boxes as a group; useful when you want to bind it to data from a database.
RadioButton	Displays a single radio button.
RadioButtonList	Displays a group of radio buttons where only one radio button from the group can be selected.
Image	Displays an image.
Panel	Creates a bounding box on the Web Form that acts as a container for other controls.
Calendar	Displays an interactive calendar.
AdRotator	Displays a sequence of images, either in pre-determined or random order.
Table	Creates a table.

Validation Controls

Validation Controls are different from HTML or ASP.NET Server Controls in that they do not possess a "visual" identity. Their purpose is to provide easy client-side or server-side validation for other controls. For example, you may have a textbox that you need the user to fill in, and you may need to only accept certain entries. For example, it could be a textbox that requires a date in a certain format, like DD/MM/YY. Validation Controls allow you to generate validation scripts (client- or server-side) with a few clicks.

To use Validation Controls, you first attach the Validation Control to an input control and then set its parameters, so as to test for things like:

❑   Data entry in a required field

❑   Specific values or patterns of characters

❑   Entries between ranges

VB.NET ships with the following Validation Controls, also in the Web Forms section of the Toolbox:

Control	Purpose
RequiredFieldValidator	Ensures that the user does not leave a field blank.
CompareValidator	Compares the user's entry against another value – a constant, the property of another control, or even a database value.
RangeValidator	Makes sure that the user's entry is between the lower and upper boundary values specified.
RegularExpressionValidator	Checks to make sure that the entry matches a pattern defined by the developer.
CustomValidator	Checks the user's entry against validation logic you code yourself.

The easiest way to understand the power and capability of Validation Controls is to see them in action.

Add a new Web Form to your HelloWorld solution (by default, it will be called WebForm4.aspx; accept the default values). Drag a TextBox control on to the Web Form and change its ID property to txtName.

Then drag a RequiredFieldValidator control from your toolbox onto the Web Form, right next to the TextBox.

Next, add a Button control onto the form, below the TextBox, and set its Text property to Submit.

Now, let's set the properties for the Validation Control. Change its ID to rfvTxtName, to signify to ourselves that it is going to be bound to the TextBox we just created. Then click on the ControlToValidate property and select the txtName TextBox from the drop-down list that appears. By doing so, we have bound the Validation Control to the txtName TextBox ASP.NET Server Control. Finally, change the ErrorMessage property to the text that we want to display if the user is in error: "Required Field. Please enter your name."

When you are done, your screen should look like:

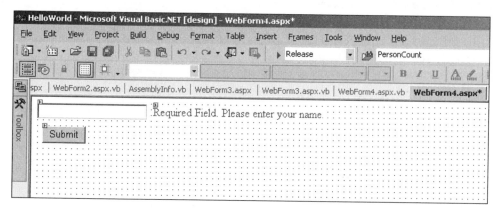

Set the WebForm4.aspx as the startup page and run the project. You should see the page in the browser with just a textbox and a button visible. Do not type anything into the textbox and just click the button to simulate a user submitting the form without entering a required field. Voila! Our form submission is not accepted. We get a red error message saying that the field is required:

If you decide to check the code behind this page, you will find that the Validation Controls write a lot of client-side JavaScript code to handle the data validation. As a developer, you did not have to worry about it. You just dragged and dropped the Validation Control that you needed. The other Validation Controls also work in the same way – drop a Validation Control, attach it to a Server Control, and set the validation parameters.

User Controls

The final set of controls available is the User Controls. Similar to traditional VB User Controls, these are Web Forms that you create and then use within other Web Forms. This allows you to build "visual components" for your Web Forms – useful when creating toolbars, template UI elements, etc.

User controls are covered in great detail in the next chapter in this book.

Events in Web Forms

Events in the world of Windows Forms are triggered by one of three different circumstances. An event can occur when the user makes an action – moves the mouse, uses the keyboard, etc. An event can occur when the system makes an action – loads a page, reacts to another process or application, etc. Finally, an event can occur without the engagement of either users or system, simply being caused by the passage of time.

In the world of the Web, however, the very stateless nature of the HTTP protocol forces web pages to have different event handling strategies. Consider the following:

❑   A browser requests a web page.

❑   The web server serves the page by processing its code in a linear fashion.

❑   The output of the server processing is sent back to the browser as HTML.

❑   The browser renders the page on the screen based on the HTML output.

❑   At this point, the page no longer exists on the server.

❑   The user takes some action on the web page.

❑   If the server has to react to this action, the page has to be posted back to the web server before the web server can react to the action.

❑   This process continues over and over…

Web Forms expose events to the web developer, allowing you to write code for the events. This code is different from client-side script. The code for the event is evaluated and executed on the server.

If a Web Form can trigger an event for the mouse activity on a button, for instance, in such a way that the server can take action on the event, then the form will need to be posted every time the user moves the mouse. This is not practical. Because of this, Web Forms expose very limited events for different controls (usually only the Click event).

The Web Form's Life Cycle

VB developers trying to create Web Forms face a few shocks, the first of which is the concept of a Web Form's life cycle. Imagine developing a traditional VB form that goes through the following event code each time you display it on screen:

1. Form_Initialize: No problem.

2. Form_Load: No problem.

3. Form_QueryUnload: Huh?

4. Form_Unload: What?

5. Form_Terminate: No kidding?

This is the VB6 form's equivalent of the ASP.NET Web Form's cycle. This would be nonsensical for a VB6 form because it would load itself and then unload immediately afterwards!

In the case of Web Forms, when a browser requests a page, the Web Form is first loaded, then its events are handled, and finally it is discarded or unloaded from memory before the HTML output is sent to the browser. So, a Web Form goes through the cycle of load and unload each time that a browser makes a request for it.

Let's take a look at the stages in the life of a Web Form on the web server before its output is sent to the browser:

❑ Configuration – This is very similar to the `Form_Initalize` and the `Form_Load` stages of a VB6 form. This is the first stage of a Web Form's life cycle on the web server. During this stage, the page and control state is restored and then the page's `Page_Load` event is raised.

❑ The `Page_Load` event is built into every page. Since it occurs in the first stage of a Web Form's processing, this event is a useful tool for the web developer. The `Page_Load` event can be used to modify control properties, set up data binding or database access, and restore information from previously saved values before the page is visible on the browser.

❑ Event handling – If this is the first time that the browser has requested the page, no further events need to be handled. However, if this page is called in response to a form event, then the corresponding event handler in the page is called during this stage. Code within the event handler is then executed.

❑ Cleanup – This is the final stage in the page's life cycle. It is the equivalent of the `Form_Unload` and `Form_Terminate` events of traditional VB. Remember, in the case of a Web Form, at the end of its processing, the page is discarded. The cleanup stage handles the destruction by closing files, database connections, by invoking the `Page_Unload` event. Like the Page_Load event, the Page_Unload event is built into every page. It can be used to clean up – delete variables and arrays from memory, remove objects from memory, close database connections, etc.

Event Categories

Events in Web Forms can be classified into different categories:

❑ Intrinsic events

❑ Client-side events versus server-side events

❑ Postback versus non-postback events

❑ Bubbled events

❑ Application and session events

Intrinsic Events

Most Web Form controls support a click-type event. This is necessitated by the fact that, in order for an event to be processed, the Web Form needs to be posted back to the server. Some Web Form controls also support an `OnChange` event that is raised when the control's value changes.

Client-Side Versus Server-Side Events

ASP.NET Server Controls only support server-side events. However, the HTML elements that are outputted by these Server Controls support client-side events themselves. For example, the MouseOver event is used to change the source of an Image control and display a different image when the user rolls the mouse over the control. If you decide to use the ASP.NET ImageButton Server Control, you will be able to write code for the ImageButton's Click event, which will be processed on the server. However, you can also write client-side code for the MouseOver event of the ImageButton to handle the rollover. If you write code for both – the client- and server-side event – only the server-side event will be processed.

Postback Versus Non-Postback Events

As mentioned earlier, server-side event processing happens when the form is posted back to the server. By default, these click-type events are postback events. The OnChange event is raised when a control's value changes. For example, if you write code for the OnChange event of a TextBox, when the user changes its value, the event is not fired immediately. Instead, these changes are cached by the control until the next time that a post occurs. When the Web Form is posted back to the server, all the pending events are raised and processed. On the server-side, all of the OnChange events – that were cached and raised *before* the Click event that posted the form – are processed before the posting Click event.

Client-side events are automatically processed in the client browser without making a round trip to the browser. So, for example, validation client-side scripts do not need a postback to the server.

Bubbled Events

ASP.NET server controls such as the Repeater, DataList, and DataGrid controls can contain child controls that themselves raise events. For example, each row in a DataGrid control can contain one or more buttons. Events from the nested controls are **bubbled**, that is, they're sent to the container. The container in turn raises a generic event called ItemCommand with parameters that allow you to discover which individual control raised the original event. By responding to this single event, you can avoid having to write individual event handlers for child controls.

Application and Session Events

Continuing the tradition of ASP application and session events, VB.NET Web Forms support the same high-level events. These events are not specific to a single page but, rather, work at the user and/or web application level. These events include the ApplicationStart and ApplicationEnd events for the application level scope, and the SessionStart and SessionEnd events for the session (individual user) level scope. You can write code for these special events within the Global.asax file.

Web Forms Versus ASP

It is very easy to think of Web Forms (ASP.NET) as the next version of ASP – that Microsoft has released a new version of ASP and is just calling it ASP.NET to equate it to the other .NET initiatives. ASP 3.0, for instance, was basically the previous version (ASP 2.0) souped up with new functionality, performance improvements, and one new object. So, ASP.NET has to be on the same level – right? This is not entirely true.

While Web Forms *are* the next version of ASP (ASP ceases to exist as a separate offering from Microsoft with the introduction of ASP.NET, though it will continue to be supported), it is not just a souped up version. It is vastly different.

Let us see what these differences are:

1. ASP was an interpreted application. This leads to poor performance, as compared to executable Windows desktop applications.

Web Forms are compiled into class `.dll` files and are invoked as "applications" on the web server. This leads to vastly improved performance. The performance drop you see when you test your application for the very first time is, in fact, indicative of this change. ASP.NET checks to see if the sourcecode for the page has changed in any way. If it has (like in your testing mode), it recompiles the page and saves the compiled output for all subsequent requests.

2. In ASP, you are entirely responsible for managing view state and control state via code. If you want a form control to display the value entered by the user before the form is posted, you have to obtain the value from the `Request` object and use it as part of the `VALUE` attribute of the control. The onus is entirely on the web developer.

Web Forms provide automatic maintenance of view state and control state. By simply using server-side controls, you automatically obtain the ability to retain state for the control during server round trips.

3. With ASP, you can only write code with script languages such as VBScript and JScript. These languages do not support typed variables or early binding on objects.

Web Forms support VB code as well as C# code. You can use a coding language that supports typed variables (`Dim x As Integer`) as well as early binding on objects (`Dim objRS As ADODB.Recordset`). This results in additional benefits, like IntelliSense making it easier to assign property values and invoke methods on objects.

4. With ASP, you are responsible for generating client-side validation code. When you have forms with large numbers of controls that need validation, this can be a cumbersome task – even if you have created custom routines that can simply be "copy and pasted". You still need to write the code yourself to invoke these routines. Web Forms provide a very robust, drag and drop, validation control feature. Not only can you drag and drop your way to setting up validation parameters – required fields, types of accepted input, range of accepted input, etc. – Web Forms also write the client-side validation routines for you.

If you have used COM components with ASP applications, you know that, every time you need to change and update the COM component on the web server, you need to release the component from the web server (or COM+) before you can overwrite it with the new component. ASP programmers are used to bringing down the web server or stopping and starting the COM+ services to allow such changes.

With Web Forms, because of just-in-time compiling to native code, components can be updated without having to stop and start the web services.

5. ASP configuration settings are stored in the metabase (meta information database) of the IIS web server. This makes it difficult to port the ASP application from one server to another. The metabase configuration settings have to be set up individually on the new web server each time you move the ASP application.

With Web Forms, all configuration settings are stored in an XML-formatted text file that can be easily moved from one web application directory to another. The XML-formatted `Config.web` file allows you to create portable configuration settings.

6. Debugging of ASP applications has always been a daunting task. The only surefire way to debug ASP applications running on a web server is to pepper the ASP page with `response.write` statements, to output the values of variables in your code. This is similar to peppering a VB form with `Debug.Print` statements.

Web Forms provide an automatic tracing capability. When you set the `Trace` and the `TraceMode` properties of a Web Form, ASP.NET automatically maintains a log of actions performed, and their timestamp. When the page is rendered on the browser, ASP.NET automatically appends an HTML table listing all of the trace activity. You can also write your own tracing code to be appended to this log.

Transferring Control Among Web Forms

Earlier in this chapter, we mentioned that VB developers will get a shock when they try to create Web Forms because the familiar metaphor of VB development is turned upside down in the world of Web Form development. Well, get ready for shock number two!

In a traditional VB application, suppose you have two forms, `Form1` and `Form2`. If you want the application to transfer control from `Form1` (which is currently open on the screen) to `Form2`, all it takes is this code:

```
Load Form2
Form2.show
```

Of the two lines above, the first line is optional. You can use the first line if you plan to set some properties for `Form2`'s controls, or invoke a subroutine within `Form2` before showing it.

How do you do the same with a Web Form? Can you "show" `WebForm2` from `WebForm1`? The answer will surprise you. No, you can't. Not in the way that you can with traditional VB.

There are two ways to transfer control from one Web Form to another:

❑ HyperLink: In `WebForm1`, you can create a hyperlink to allow the user to navigate to `WebForm2` by using a `Hyperlink` HTML tag (`<A>`). If you wish, you can pass additional arguments to the second form when navigating to it, by using the `Query String` – the portion of the URL that appears after the question mark in a browser's address bar. This technique of transferring control is very fast, since it transfers control to the second page directly without having to post the first page and process its events/contents.

❑ Redirecting: The second technique is to use the server-side `Response.Redirect` method to transfer control to a second page. The `Response.Redirect` issues an `Object Moved` command to the browser, forcing the browser to request the second page via a client-side request. Another similar technique is to use the `Server.Transfer` method to transfer control to a second page. The `Server.Transfer` method directly transfers control and session state to the second page without making a client round trip.

A Final Example

This chapter has given you a short overview of Web Forms and their capabilities. Hopefully, your appetite for using VB.NET to build Web Forms has been whetted.

We will wrap up this chapter by showing you how to build a small Web Form application. Our application is a "Loan Slicer" application. Consider the scenario – you have a current home mortgage loan and you pay a certain sum of money as your monthly payment towards the loan. However, by simply making one additional payment per year towards the principal repayment, you can drastically reduce the life of the loan and repay it off faster. This is "loan slicing". We want to build a Web Form application that will allow an end user to not only figure out what the monthly payment for a mortgage loan will be (that would be a wimpy little application), but also to see how the loan gets "sliced" off if the user wishes to pay an additional sum each month towards the principal.

We begin by asking the user to enter the principal loan amount, the interest rate per annum, and the number of years for which the loan will be taken. We then calculate the monthly payment due for the loan, and display a table of how the payments slowly eat their way through the loan till the loan is fully paid off. If the user wishes to view the "loan slicing" effect, he can specify a new monthly payment value higher than the original amount, and see how quickly the loan gets paid off.

So, let's begin. Start VB.NET and select New Project. Select the project type to be ASP.NET Web Application and give it the name LoanSlicer. Ensure that the target server is localhost (your own computer).

VS.NET creates a default Web Form, WebForm1.aspx. Before we start adding controls to the form, right-click on the Web Form and select Properties to view the DOCUMENT Property Pages window. Then change the Page Layout to FlowLayout:

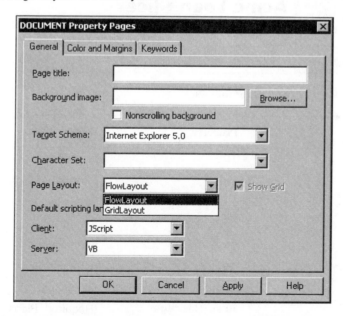

Now click OK. FlowLayout enables you to treat the Web Form as if it were a word processing document. You can insert text and paragraph marks, and the result is translated into HTML. Controls are placed where the cursor currently is in the text.

Drag a `Label` control onto this form and position it at the top left (you can move it around by inserting or deleting paragraph marks, just as you would move an inserted object in a Microsoft Word file). Set its:

❏   `ID` property to be `lblTitle`

❏   `Text` property to be `"Acme Loan Slicer"`

❏   `Font, Size` property to `Large`

❏   `Font, Bold` property to `True`

❏   `Font, Name` property to `Verdana`.

We are building this loan slicer using the US mortgage loan formula, as opposed to that of other countries where it is different.

Press *Enter* to the right of the `Label` to create a new paragraph. Then – in sequence – insert a `Label` control, a `TextBox` control, and a `RequiredFieldValidator` control. Your Web Form should look like this:

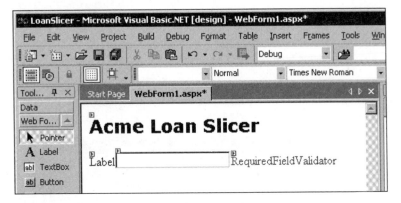

Set the properties for these controls as follows:

Control	Property	Value
Label	ID	Leave this unchanged.
	Text	Principal Amount ($):
	Font, Bold	True
	Font, Name	Verdana
TextBox	ID	txtPrincipal
RequiredFieldValidator	ID	rfvPrincipal
	ControlToValidate	txtPrincipal
	ErrorMessage	(Required. Please try again.)

Insert two more rows of `Label` and `TextBox` and `RequiredFieldValidator` controls, placing each set underneath the one above. To move to the next line without creating a new paragraph, use *Shift+Enter* to create a soft return (
 tag).

Set the properties for the second row of controls as follows:

Control	Property	Value
Label	ID	Leave this unchanged.
	Text	Interest Rate (%):
	Font, Bold	True
	Font, Name	Verdana
TextBox	ID	txtInterest
RequiredFieldValidator	ID	rfvInterest
	ControlToValidate	txtInterest
	ErrorMessage	(Required. Please try again.)

Set the properties for the third row of controls like so:

Control	Property	Value
Label	ID	Leave this unchanged.
	Text	Period (Years):
	Font, Bold	True
	Font, Name	Verdana
TextBox	ID	txtYears
RequiredFieldValidator	ID	rfvYears
	ControlToValidate	txtYears
	ErrorMessage	(Required. Please try again.)

Underneath these three sets of controls, place another row with a Label and a TextBox control, with these properties:

Control	Property	Value
Label	ID	Leave this unchanged.
	Text	Loan Slicer Monthly Amount ($):
	Font, Bold	True
	Font, Name	Verdana
TextBox	ID	txtSlicerAmount

Underneath these four rows of controls, place a Button with these properties:

Control	Property	Value
Button	ID	btnCalculate
	Text	Calculate

Next, place a Label control beneath the Button and set its properties:

Control	Property	Value
Label	ID	lblMonthlyPayment
	Text	Monthly Payment:
	Font, Bold	True
	Font, Name	Verdana
	BackColor	Light blue (#C0FFFF)

And, finally, underneath the label, place a DataGrid control. For the DataGrid control, first set the following minimal but very important properties:

Control	Property	Value
DataGrid	ID	dgValues
	Visible	False

To set the appearance of the DataGrid control, instead of setting individual properties, click the AutoFormat link at the bottom of the Properties window. From the list, experiment with the look you want. The screenshot below shows "Professional 1":

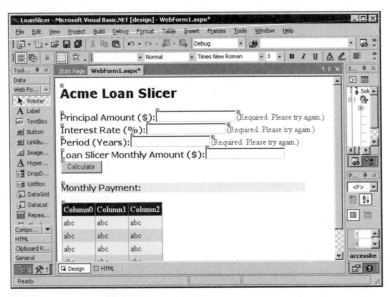

Before we go any further, let's test out this Web Form. We have not placed any code in it and so it shouldn't do much, but at least we can make sure that it looks fine. Before you proceed, make sure that you select **Release** from the **Solution Configurations** drop-down box on your toolbar. This will ensure that you run in final release mode, rather than in **Debug** mode.

Click the **Start** button to run the project. You should get the Web Form displayed in a browser. The `DataGrid` and the `RequiredFieldValidators` should be invisible. Go ahead and click on the `Calculate` button without entering any values in any of the text boxes. You should instantly get the red error messages next to each text box, as shown here:

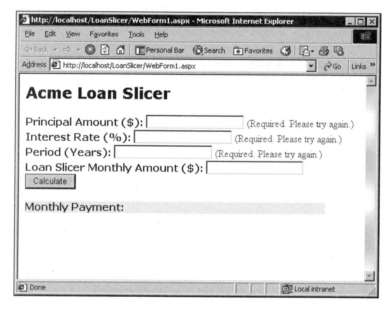

We are all set. Now let's proceed to write code for the form.

Calculating the monthly payment for a mortgage loan is a little convoluted to explain, but very simple to code. Here is the formula:

$$MP = P * (MI / 1 - (1 + MI)^{(-N)})$$

assuming the following:

Variable Name	Represents
MP	Monthly payment
P	Principal loan amount (the amount borrowed)
MI	Monthly interest rate in decimals (that is, the annual interest rate divided by 1200)
N	Number of months in the loan

and that * is multiply, / is divide, and ^ is "raise to the power of".

687

This is the formula that we will be using for calculating our monthly payment. Once we calculate the monthly payment, it is simple to construct a grid containing the following information:

A	B	C	D	E	F	G	H	I
Month / Year	Loan Amount	Original Payment	Interest Paid	Principal Paid	Balance Loan	New Payment	New Principal Paid	New Balance Loan

Let us begin by adding code to our `Calculate` button. Double-click on the button to add a call to a subroutine we will be building as part of the next step:

```
Private Sub btnCalculate_Click(ByVal sender As System.Object, ByVal e As
System.EventArgs) Handles btnCalculate.Click
        CalculateValues()
    End Sub
```

At the bottom of the `WebForm1` class, before the `End Class` statement, add this `CalculateValues` subroutine:

```
Private Sub CalculateValues()
        Dim dblPrincipal As Double
        Dim dblInterest As Double
        Dim lngYears As Long
        Dim dblMonthlyPayment As Double
        Dim dblMonthlyInterest As Double
        Dim lngN As Long

        ' -- Get our values from the text boxes
        dblPrincipal = Me.txtPrincipal.Text
        dblInterest = Me.txtInterest.Text
        lngyears = Me.txtYears.Text
        ' -- Calculated intermediary values
        dblMonthlyInterest = (dblInterest / (12 * 100))
        lngN = lngYears * 12
        ' -- Monthly Payment calculation:
        dblMonthlyPayment = (dblPrincipal * (dblMonthlyInterest / (1 - (1 + _
            dblMonthlyInterest) ^ (-lngN))))

        ' -- Assign the value to the Blue label
        Me.lblMonthlyPayment.Text = "Monthly Payment: " & _
            format(dblMonthlyPayment, "$#,##0.00")

    End Sub
```

As you can see from the code, after declaring all the variables we will be using, we first obtain our values from the textboxes on the form:

```
' -- Get our values from the text boxes
dblPrincipal = Me.txtPrincipal.Text
dblInterest = Me.txtInterest.Text
lngyears = Me.txtYears.Text
```

We then calculate the intermediary variable values:

```
' -- Calculated intermediary values
dblMonthlyInterest = (dblInterest / (12 * 100))
lngN = lngYears * 12
```

Finally, we are ready to calculate the monthly payment:

```
' -- Monthly Payment calculation:
dblMonthlyPayment = (dblPrincipal * (dblMonthlyInterest / (1 - (1 + _
    dblMonthlyInterest) ^ (-lngN))))
```

which we store in the variable dblMonthlyPayment. We output this value as the Text property of the blue label on the screen, performing some formatting so that it is presented as a dollar amount:

```
' -- Assign the value to the Blue label
Me.lblMonthlyPayment.Text = "Monthly Payment: " & _
    format(dblMonthlyPayment, "$#,##0.00")
```

That was the easy part. Let's test it again by running our application. Enter the following values: Principal = 100000, Interest Rate = 6.75, Years = 10. You should get the output shown in the figure below:

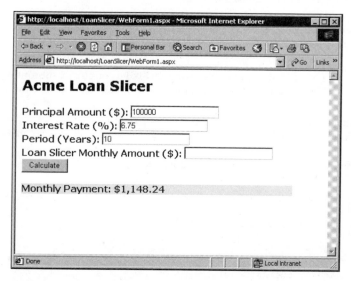

Now comes the difficult part – populating the DataGrid with our values.

Before we look at the code, let us understand what we are trying to do. We need to display a DataGrid full of rows and columns that represent our loan payouts. We want to display the current loan amount, the monthly payment, the interest paid, the principal paid, and the balance loan amount for every month of every year in the loan period.

In addition, if the user has entered a Loan Slicer Monthly Amount – an amount that he/she is willing to pay that is larger than the monthly payment due – we need to also figure out how the new monthly payment will pay off the loan faster – and therefore "slice" it.

Normally, a `DataGrid` is bound to a database. We don't have a database in this scenario. We could dump the values into a database and have the `DataGrid` then read the database. But that would be very inefficient. A better way would be to create our own "database" on the fly. We can do that by creating a `DataTable` object and populating it with values. Our `DataGrid` can be bound to a `DataView` object at runtime. To do so, we need to write code as follows:

```
OurDataGridObject.DataSource = OurDataViewObject
```

A `DataView` object can be created and initialized by an existing `DataTable` object. Therefore, we can create a `DataView` object by using a `DataTable` object, as follows:

```
OurDataViewObject = New DataView(OurDataTableObject)
```

A `DataTable` object in turn consists of rows and columns, or rather `DataRow` objects and `DataColumn` objects. To create a row for a table, we use a `DataRow` object as follows:

```
OurDataTable.Rows.Add OurDataRow
```

The `DataColumn` objects can also be created at runtime by using the following code:

```
OurDataTable.Columns.Add OurDataColumn
```

And finally, we can create a `DataColumn` object by passing the `Column` definition as follows:

```
OurDataColumn = New DataColumn(strColumnName, ColumnDataType)
```

We can put all of this code together in the following `BuildPayoutGrid` subroutine. Add the following code to the bottom of the `CalculateValues` subroutine, immediately before the `End Sub`:

```
' -- Proceed to build our Monthly Payment Grid
BuildPayoutGrid(dblPrincipal, dblMonthlyInterest, dblMonthlyPayment)
```

Then add the code for the `BuildPayOutGrid` subroutine itself:

```
Private Sub BuildPayoutGrid(ByVal dblP As Double, ByVal dblMI As Double, _
    ByVal dblM As Double)
    ' -- Variables to hold our output data
    Dim dtPayout As DataTable
    Dim drPayout As DataRow
    Dim datMonthYear As Date
    Dim dblSlicerAmount As Double
    Dim dblNewBalance As Double
    Dim dblMonthlyInterestPaid As Double


    ' -- Make sure we have the new "Loan Slicer" monthly amount
    dblSlicerAmount = Me.txtSlicerAmount.Text
    ' -- if the user has not entered one, add one additional payment
    ' -- per year as the new slicer amount
    If dblSlicerAmount = 0 Then
        dblSlicerAmount = dblM + (dblM / 12)
    End If
```

```
        Me.txtSlicerAmount.Text = dblSlicerAmount
        ' -- Create a new DataTable
        dtPayout = New DataTable()
        ' -- Create nine string columns
        dtPayout.Columns.Add(New DataColumn("Month/Year", GetType(String)))
        dtPayout.Columns.Add(New DataColumn("Loan Amount", GetType(String)))
        dtPayout.Columns.Add(New DataColumn("Original Payment", _
            GetType(String)))
        dtPayout.Columns.Add(New DataColumn("Interest Paid", GetType(String)))
        dtPayout.Columns.Add(New DataColumn("Principal Paid", GetType(String)))
        dtPayout.Columns.Add(New DataColumn("Balance Amount", GetType(String)))

        dtPayout.Columns.Add(New DataColumn("New Payment", GetType(String)))
        dtPayout.Columns.Add(New DataColumn("New Principal Paid", _
            GetType(String)))
        dtPayout.Columns.Add(New DataColumn("New Balance Amount", _
            GetType(String)))

        dblNewBalance = dblP
        ' -- Populate it with values
        ' -- Start with current Month/Year
        datMonthYear = Now()
        Do While dblP > 0
            ' -- Create a new row for our table
            drPayout = dtPayout.NewRow()

            drPayout(0) = MonthName(Month(datMonthYear)) & ", " & _
                Year(datMonthYear)
            drPayout(1) = Format(dblP, "$#,##0.00")
            drPayout(2) = Format(dblM, "$#,##0.00")

            dblMonthlyInterestPaid = (dblP * dblMI)

            drPayout(3) = Format(dblMonthlyInterestPaid, "$#,##0.00")
            drPayout(4) = Format(dblM - dblMonthlyInterestPaid, "$#,##0.00")
            drPayout(5) = Format(dblP - (dblM - dblMonthlyInterestPaid), _
                "$#,##0.00")
            ' -- new values
            If dblNewBalance >= 0 Then
                drPayout(6) = Format(dblSlicerAmount, "$#,##0.00")
                drPayout(7) = Format(dblSlicerAmount - dblMonthlyInterestPaid, _
                    "$#,##0.00")
                drPayout(8) = Format(dblNewBalance - (dblSlicerAmount - _
                    dblMonthlyInterestPaid), "$#,##0.00")
            Else
                drPayout(6) = "PAID"
                drPayout(7) = "IN"
                drPayout(8) = "FULL"
            End If
            ' -- Add the row to the table
            dtPayout.Rows.Add(drPayout)
            ' -- Next month
            datMonthYear = DateAdd(DateInterval.Month, 1, datMonthYear)
            ' -- Starting Loan Amount is previous month's Ending balance
            dblP = (dblP - (dblM - dblMonthlyInterestPaid))
```

```
            dblNewBalance = (dblNewBalance - (dblSlicerAmount - _
                dblMonthlyInterestPaid))

        Loop
        ' -- Create a new DataView and bind it to the DataGrid
        With dgValues
            .Visible = True
            .DataSource = New DataView(dtPayout)
            .DataBind()
        End With
    End Sub
```

Let's examine this code piece by piece.

We begin by declaring the variables we will need:

```
        ' -- Variables to hold our output data
        Dim dtPayout As DataTable
        Dim drPayout As DataRow
        Dim datMonthYear As Date
        Dim dblSlicerAmount As Double
        Dim dblNewBalance As Double
        Dim dblMonthlyInterestPaid As Double
```

We first make sure that we have a "Loan Slicer" amount in the textbox on the screen. If not, we simply add one additional monthly payment per year to calculate a new, larger monthly payment. We then update the textbox with the new "slicer" amount:

```
        ' -- Make sure we have the new "Loan Slicer" monthly amount
        dblSlicerAmount = Me.txtSlicerAmount.Text
        ' -- if the user has not entered one, add one additional payment
        ' -- per year as the new slicer amount
        If dblSlicerAmount = 0 Then
            dblSlicerAmount = dblM + (dblM / 12)
        End If
        Me.txtSlicerAmount.Text = dblSlicerAmount
```

We then create a blank `DataTable`:

```
        ' -- Create a new DataTable
        dtPayout = New DataTable()
```

We make sure that our `DataTable` has the columns we need. We add `DataColumns` to the `DataTable`. These `DataColumns` are created on the fly by passing column definition arguments to the `DataColumn` that we create:

```
        ' -- Create nine string columns
        dtPayout.Columns.Add(New DataColumn("Month/Year", GetType(String)))
        dtPayout.Columns.Add(New DataColumn("Loan Amount", GetType(String)))
        dtPayout.Columns.Add(New DataColumn("Original Payment", _
            GetType(String)))
        dtPayout.Columns.Add(New DataColumn("Interest Paid", GetType(String)))
```

```
dtPayout.Columns.Add(New DataColumn("Principal Paid", GetType(String)))
dtPayout.Columns.Add(New DataColumn("Balance Amount", GetType(String)))

dtPayout.Columns.Add(New DataColumn("New Payment", GetType(String)))
dtPayout.Columns.Add(New DataColumn("New Principal Paid", _
    GetType(String)))
dtPayout.Columns.Add(New DataColumn("New Balance Amount", _
    GetType(String)))
```

We store the loan amount in a new variable to calculate the effect of the new "slicer" amount also:

```
dblNewBalance = dblP
```

We are now ready to populate the `DataTable` columns with values, and the `DataTable` with rows. To do so, we begin with the current month:

```
' -- Populate it with values
' -- Start with current Month/Year
datMonthYear = Now()
```

We need to dump the output as long as there is an outstanding balance on the loan. Therefore, we use a `Do...While...Loop` till our loan amount reduces to zero:

```
Do While dblP > 0
```

We begin the process of creating our "database on the fly" by creating a new row for our `DataTable`. This new row will automatically have nine columns addressed by the column numbers 0 to 8:

```
' -- Create a new row for our table
drPayout = dtPayout.NewRow()
```

We set the values for each column in the current row. This is relatively simple. We know the initial loan amount and the monthly payment. We calculate the monthly interest on the outstanding loan amount and, from that, we can figure out how much of our monthly payment is interest and how much is the payoff of the principal itself. The balance is the amount of the loan left:

```
drPayout(0) = MonthName(Month(datMonthYear)) & ", " & _
    Year(datMonthYear)
drPayout(1) = Format(dblP, "$#,##0.00")
drPayout(2) = Format(dblM, "$#,##0.00")

dblMonthlyInterestPaid = (dblP * dblMI)

drPayout(3) = Format(dblMonthlyInterestPaid, "$#,##0.00")
drPayout(4) = Format(dblM - dblMonthlyInterestPaid, "$#,##0.00")
drPayout(5) = Format(dblP - (dblM - dblMonthlyInterestPaid), _
    "$#,##0.00")
```

We calculate the last three columns of figures based on our new "slicer" amount using the same logic as the original amount. What this means is that the first six columns will show the loan being paid out month after month, based on the bank's monthly payment figure, while the last three columns will show the loan getting sliced and paid off much faster because of the larger monthly payment. Since we know that the loan will get sliced, we also add logic to display a text "PAID IN FULL", instead of negative numbers when the loan balance reaches zero.

```
' -- new values
If dblNewBalance >= 0 Then
    drPayout(6) = Format(dblSlicerAmount,  "$#,##0.00")
    drPayout(7) = Format(dblSlicerAmount - dblMonthlyInterestPaid, _
        "$#,##0.00")
    drPayout(8) = Format(dblNewBalance - (dblSlicerAmount - _
        dblMonthlyInterestPaid), "$#,##0.00")
Else
    drPayout(6) = "PAID"
    drPayout(7) = "IN"
    drPayout(8) = "FULL"
End If
```

Once we have filled nine columns with figures, we are ready to add the row to the `DataTable`:

```
' -- Add the row to the table
dtPayout.Rows.Add(drPayout)
```

Since we are in a loop, we need to get our data ready for the next pass. We increment the date by one month and update the value of our loan amount to the balance amount remaining. We do the same for the new sliced loan balance. We then complete the loop:

```
' -- Next month
datMonthYear = DateAdd(DateInterval.Month, 1, datMonthYear)
' -- Starting Loan Amount is previous month's Ending balance
dblP = (dblP - (dblM - dblMonthlyInterestPaid))
dblNewBalance = (dblNewBalance - (dblSlicerAmount - _
    dblMonthlyInterestPaid))
```

```
Loop
```

When we finish processing the loop, we have a `DataTable` filled with values. We create a `DataView` based on the `DataTable` and assign it to the `DataSource` property of the `DataGrid`, all in one swoop. We also make sure that the `DataGrid` is visible (remember, in design mode, we had set it to be invisible). Finally, we invoke the `Bind` method to actually bind the `DataGrid` to the `DataView` created on the fly:

```
    ' -- Create a new DataView and bind it to the DataGrid
With dgValues
    .Visible = True
    .DataSource = New DataView(dtPayout)
    .DataBind()
End With
```

That's it! We get a neat HTML table filled with rows and columns of output from our `DataGrid`. Run the application and enter a **Principal Amount** of 100000, an **Interest Rate** of 6.75, a **Period** value of 10 and a **Loan Slicer Amount** value of 1500. You should see:

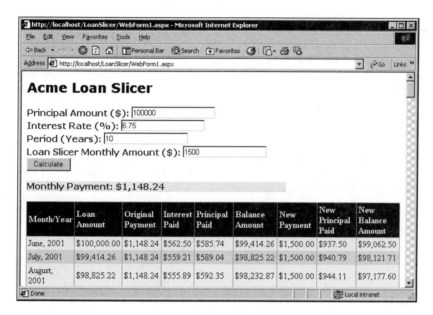

If we scroll down the page, we can see that our calculations are on the mark. At the end of 10 years, we have completely paid off our loan amount. However, because of our Loan Slicing feature, we see that, by simply paying an additional $350 per month, we can cut down our loan from 10 years to around 7.5 years. Our DataGrid ends when the principal loan amount reduces to zero. Long before that, our Loan Slicer indicates that we have PAID IN FULL our loan:

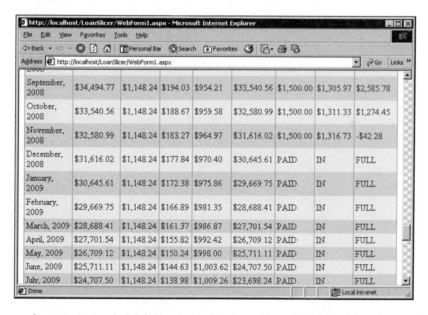

And there you have it. A simple Web Forms application with a slight twist. You also saw how to bind a DataGrid to a non-database source that you are calculating on the fly.

Summary

This chapter gave you an overview of what you can accomplish with Web Forms in VB.NET. Web Forms provide you the power of Rapid Application Development for developing web applications. They are to web applications what Visual Basic was to windows applications when it was first released.

Web Forms are built on the Common Language Runtime and provide all the benefits of those technologies, including a managed execution environment, type safety, inheritance, and dynamic compilation for improved performance. Web Forms provide a familiar "code behind forms" design metaphor for Visual Basic programmers. They automatically manage state and values for controls when a web page is posted back to the server. Additionally, Web Forms can generate an enormous amount of HTML code and client-side JavaScript code for data validation with a few clicks of your mouse.

Web Forms are the future for web development in the Microsoft .NET Framework.

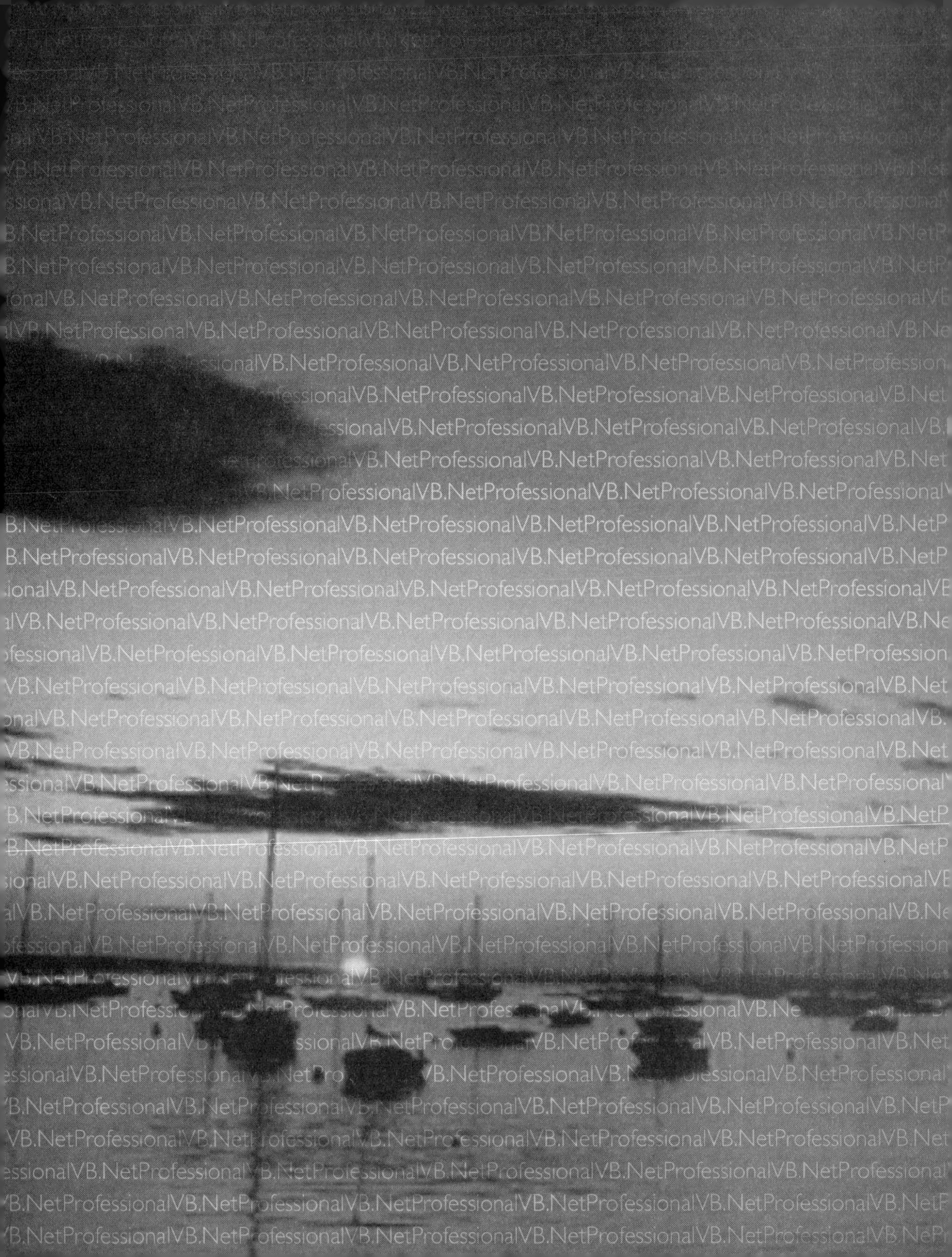
VB.NetProfessional

Creating Web Controls

It's probably only fair to warn you that this topic could easily be the subject of its own book, as it encompasses an entirely new form of Visual Basic control development. Custom web controls are likely to become one of the biggest arenas for third-party control development, as various vendors vie to fill the large gap in functionality left by the controls in the basic HTML specifications. This isn't meant as a slight to the controls that Microsoft has provided, by the way, but rather to point out the contrast between the rich functionality available in the Win32 controls and the basic functionality supported by the W3C's native HTML controls. Microsoft has actually done an excellent job of wrapping up the basic functionality of the standard HTML controls and extending the most practical into server controls for .NET. They've also added some impressive new controls (such as the web calendar control) that take ASP web development into areas of functionality and sophistication typically reserved for desktop applications.

As we'll see in the next section, though, there are times when we will want to go beyond what the W3C and Microsoft have provided for us.

Why Create Your Own Controls?

In each new web project, we come across problems that require novel solutions – problems that range from maintaining state in an essentially stateless environment to rolling out a consistent, robust site with unprecedented alacrity. As we saw in the previous chapter, .NET has responded to the first problem by providing us with state mechanisms that are built right into the platform. .NET has responded to the second problem by providing us with an extensible set of classes to help us build reusable web controls and components for our web sites.

Imagine a day when web site developers can stop worrying about which browser the client is using and which OS that browser is running on. A day, for instance, when a web site developer can drag a menu control onto a web form and let the control determine whether the client's browser is capable of rendering a DHTML menu or whether the menu should be output as a list of text-based hyperlinks. That's the philosophy of custom web controls in .NET. Smart controls that abstract the vagaries of HTML (or WML or WAP or...) and allow web developers to focus on providing the best possible user experience, benefiting both the developer and the end user.

There are other benefits to creating custom web controls as well. We can create controls that meet our requirements, encapsulate our code, and re-use it. For instance, many of us have developed a login form at one time or another and quite a few of us have also experienced the hassle of having to redevelop that login form for successive web sites. With .NET, we are now able to turn the login form into a class and take advantage of all of the benefits of object-oriented design, including inheritance and encapsulation.

So the benefits of creating custom web controls are fairly obvious in that they are centered around three of the four tenets of object oriented design: abstraction, encapsulation, and inheritance.

> *Custom web controls also take advantage of polymorphism, especially when participating in ASP page control management.*

When to Create Your Own Controls

According to Microsoft, there are four basic scenarios where we might want to create our own custom web control:

1. We have an ASP.NET page (or a portion of one) that provides a user interface (UI) or some functionality that we would like to reuse.

2. We have an existing Web Forms control that meets most of our requirements. We want to customize it by adding, altering, or removing functionality until it meets all of our requirements.

3. We need a control that combines the functionality of two or more existing Web Forms controls.

4. We need a web control with functionality that can't be found in an existing Web Form control or even in a combination of existing Web Form controls.

We should also add a fifth scenario to Microsoft's list – one that is likely to come into play in larger team development environments:

5. We want to use the functionality of a control written in one language on an ASP.NET page that uses a different language.

Types Of Custom Web Controls

.NET offers us four different types of custom web controls that we can use to address these scenarios:

❑ Web User Controls

❑ Sub-classed controls

❑ Composite controls

❑ Templated controls

Let's take a look at each type in turn and discuss where they might fit into the development scenarios.

Web User Controls

Web User Controls (WUCs) in the web environment are different from Windows Forms User Controls. WUCs are portions of a web page that typically combine HTML and server-side script. They have almost all of the characteristics of the ASPX page class in that they support design time HTML, Codebehind, and dynamic compilation. In fact, they are so close to ASPX pages that Microsoft originally called them **Pagelets**! In contrast, Windows Forms User Controls are strictly class-based and, while they make use of the Windows Forms Designer, they do not allow for separation of code and content like WUCs do.

WUCs are extremely easy to create. You can build one from scratch by adding a Web User Control item to a web project and working with it exactly the same way as you would an ASPX page. More frequently, though, you'll take a portion of UI and/or functionality from one of your existing ASP.NET pages, place it into a separate file with an .ascx extension and – voila! – you've created a WUC! Yes, it is really that simple to create an abstracted, encapsulated, and reusable component!

> *A WUC may require some tweaking if you've copied certain directives (any of the @ Page directives or the @ OutputCache directive) or if you've included <HTML> or <BODY> tags – we'll discuss the necessary modifications later on.*

Of course, like most things we've seen in .NET, the ease with which we can create WUCs doesn't take away from the power and flexibility that they can offer. It's just that WUCs – and everything else in the .NET framework – have been designed from the ground up to be simple yet extensible!

In previous versions of ASP, you might have used a Server-Side Include (SSI) to achieve the same effect as a WUC. In fact, in ASP.NET you could still use an SSI to encapsulate common functionality or UI elements, but WUCs provide much greater flexibility and extensibility. They offer several advantages over SSIs:

❑ WUCs provide their own namespace behind the scenes. This means that variables, methods, events, and constituent controls in the WUC will not conflict with identically named counterparts on the hosting page or within other instances of the same WUC.

❑ WUCs can be parameterized, which means that other developers can set properties for the control by specifying attributes in the element that inserts the WUC on the hosting page.

❑ WUCs can be written in any .NET compliant programming language, even if it's not the same server-side language used by the page that hosts it (see scenario #5 above).

Once we've created our WUC, we can then choose to create or expose properties, methods, and events to the page that hosts the control – or not! A WUC can be a black box that reveals nothing of its inner workings or it can fully expose its contents. The choice is up to us.

Sub-Classed Controls

Sub-classed controls represent the most basic form of custom web control development. They are created as classes and create their HTML output directly through methods of the HtmlTextWriter class, a utility class provided by the hosting page for writing to the HTML response stream. A fairly typical example of a sub-classed control would be the ImageButton control, which inherits most of its functionality from the Image control and then adds support for a click event and a command event with associated command properties.

Don't let the phrase the most basic form of custom web control development mislead you, though. Controls of this type can be very complex and detailed. Basic merely refers to the fact that sub-classed controls do not use complex techniques like **class composition** or **templating** in rendering themselves. We'll discuss class composition and templating in the next two sections.

Typically, sub-classed controls are created by inheriting from one of the following base classes in the System.Web.UI namespace, or from one of their derivatives:

❑ System.Web.UI.WebControls.WebControl – for controls with a UI

❑ System.Web.UI.Control – for controls without a UI

> We might also choose to inherit from the
> **System.Web.UI.HTMLControls.HTMLControl** class to create a server control for
> an HTML tag that Microsoft didn't include in the **HtmlControls** namespace, but
> there is not much point in doing this. .NET has the **HTMLGenericControl** class if we
> want to create a server control for an HTML tag that isn't already represented in the
> **System.Web.UI.HTMLControls** namespace. The **HTMLGenericControl** class has
> a **TagName** property to determine which tag it renders, which gives us the ability to
> create a server control for any HTML tag that we'd like.

By inheriting from these classes, sub-classed controls get all of the plumbing necessary to interact with the Page class, as well as the abilities to maintain state, to data bind, and to participate in server-side events.

Composite Controls

A composite control is a **container control** for other controls created by **class composition**. Class composition means that a composite control creates its child controls programmatically as classes, rather than as nested HTML or XML (the way that WUCs do) or as parameters within its element tag (the way that templated controls do). Composite controls are more or less equivalent to WUCs with the exception that they are compiled solely from a class file and persisted as part of an assembly, whereas WUCs are compiled on demand from an ASCX file (and, optionally, a Codebehind class file) and are not persisted in an assembly. Being a container control means that composite controls act as a host control for other controls. A typical example of a container class would be a Panel web control.

Composite controls are created through the standard class mechanisms in .NET. They can be created either by inheriting from the controls in the `System.Web.UI` namespace or by implementing one or more of the interfaces in the `System.Web.UI` namespace.

While implementing interfaces is an option for creating custom web controls, it is far too complex a subject to deal with here.

Composite controls typically start by inheriting from the `System.Web.UI.Control` class (although you could certainly use one of its derivatives). The `Control` class provides the `Controls` collection to store child controls in and it also provides methods for rendering the child controls. All that is required of us when we develop a composite control is that we override the base class's `CreateChildControls` method to create instances of the child control classes and add them to the `Controls` collection. Once the child controls have been added to the `Controls` collection, the built-in functionality of the `Control` class will handle rendering them for us.

For more information on composite controls, see Professional ASP.NET *(Wrox Press, ISBN 1861004885).*

Templated Controls

The last of the four types, templated controls, are types of container control also referred to in the Microsoft documentation as **lookless controls**. These are controls that separate their UI from their behavior, allowing the page author to customize the appearance of their constituent controls without the use of code. Some examples of templated controls in the `System.Web.UI.WebControls` namespace are the `Repeater` and `Datalist` classes.

The requirements for a templated control are that it implements the `INamingContainer` interface and that it exposes one or more properties of type `System.Web.UI.ITemplate`. The name of each of these **template properties** can then be mapped to the tag name of a **template element** nested inside the templated control. Then, within the template element, the page author can specify whatever they would like for the appearance of that portion of the templated control, from literal text right on up to complex combinations of nested elements!

It might seem like the first sentence of the previous paragraph is a mistake. A property whose type is an interface? What's going on here? Let's take a look at the listing for a page with a `Repeater` control on it, and the output that it produces, and see if we can't make a little more sense of this:

```vb
<%@ Page Language="vb" %>
<HTML>
  <HEAD>
    <script runat="server">
      Private Sub Page_Load(ByVal sender As System.Object, _
          ByVal e As System.EventArgs) Handles MyBase.Load
        Dim strCastArray() As String = {"Dorothy", _
                                        "The Wizard", _
                                        "Toto", _
                                        "etc."}
        Repeater1.DataSource = strCastArray
        Repeater1.DataBind()
      End Sub
    </script>
```

```
      </HEAD>
      <body>
        <asp:Repeater id="Repeater1" runat="server">
          <HeaderTemplate>
            <h3>
              The Cast<hr>
            </h3>
          </HeaderTemplate>
          <ItemTemplate>
            <div>
              <%# Container.DataItem %>
            </div>
          </ItemTemplate>
          <AlternatingItemTemplate>
            <div style="BACKGROUND-COLOR: silver">
              <%# Container.DataItem %>
            </div>
          </AlternatingItemTemplate>
        </asp:Repeater>
      </body>
    </HTML>
```

This generates the following HTML source code:

```
<HTML>
  <HEAD>

  </HEAD>
  <body>

        <h3>
          The Cast<hr>
        </h3>

        <div>
          Dorothy
        </div>

        <div style="BACKGROUND-COLOR: silver">
          The Wizard
        </div>

        <div>
          Toto
        </div>

        <div style="BACKGROUND-COLOR: silver">
          etc.
        </div>

  </body>
</HTML>
```

which looks like this in Internet Explorer 6.0:

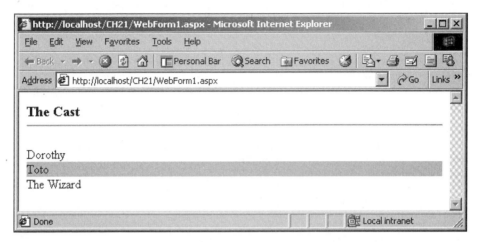

Notice that the `Repeater` control has `HeaderTemplate`, `ItemTemplate`, and `AlternatingItemTemplate` elements, none of which actually exists as either a server object or a client element. The reason for this is that, when the control parser for the page comes across unknown elements nested within a control that implements the `INamingContainer` interface, it checks the container control for a property with the same tag name as the unknown element. If the parser finds a matching property name, it then makes use of **reflection** (a technique for inspecting the structure of an object) to determine whether the property is of type `ITemplate`.

The parser then creates the unknown element as a special template builder control, either of type `CompiledTemplateBuilder` or `TemplateBuilder`, both of which implement `ITemplate`. It associates the nested content with the template builder control and passes the template builder control into the templated control as the value for the template property.

So what's happening here is that we have a specialized control that implements the interface being created behind the scenes, and then gets passed into our templated control. This is how we come to have properties of an interface type. It is a bit of an odd concept to wrap one's head around, but essentially this is what allows us to map specific data elements of our templated control to elements or element attributes provided by the user of our control.

> *For thorough coverage of templated controls, see* Professional ASP.NET *(Wrox Press, ISBN 1861004885).*

Now that we've covered the basic types of custom web controls, let's discuss where each type might fit into the development cycle.

When To Use Custom Web Controls

The easiest path to follow when creating custom web controls is to develop standard ASP.NET pages and, when we determine that we have something that can be re-used, separate it off into a WUC.

You could stop at this point, already having taken advantage of the abstraction and encapsulation provided by the WUC control. But if we want to use our control in multiple sites and still have a single set of source code for our control, we'll want to look at re-writing the control as one of the class-based custom web control types. This is because we can deploy the compiled code for a class-based control to multiple sites or to the GAC for a given web server. If we change the source code, it is a simple thing to manage versions and to re-deploy the updated assembly. WUCs, on the other hand, require that their ASCX files exist locally within each web application that uses them. This means that we'd need to copy any changes to the ASCX file manually to each web site that uses the control and, hopefully, not accidentally overwrite any other changed versions.

> **The best part of this is that the same code that you write for your ASP.NET page or your WUC will still work with minor modifications when you port it over to a sub-classed, composite, or templated control!**

Aside from migrating a WUC, we could also look at developing a class-based control when we want greater control over the HTML elements that comprise a control and the behavior of those elements (as well as the behavior of the control as a whole). Sub-classed controls make sense when we are building single element output, enhancing the functionality of an existing control, or generating unstructured or loosely structured output. Composite controls are excellent when we want to combine multiple controls or when we are looking at building complex or repeated combinations of other controls. Templated controls offer us a way of giving the consumer of our control a structured method for altering its appearance. Remember too that class-based custom web controls also take advantage of much of the same framework used to create custom Windows Forms controls, so you can leverage the skills that you gain in both areas. In fact, it is one of Microsoft's stated design goals to make web control development accessible even to developers who do not have a great deal of familiarity with HTML!

We will concentrate on web user controls and sub-classed controls for the rest of this chapter.

Creating a Web User Control

If you take a look around the Web for any length of time you'll come across a whole host of standard UI functionality that would make for great custom web controls. Some examples would be things like:

❑ Login forms

❑ Menus

❑ Search widgets

❑ Headers, footers, and copyright notices

❑ Tables of contents

❑ Site navigation elements

Let's take an example from the Wrox web site and see if we can wrap it up into a WUC. If you navigate your browser to www.wrox.com, you'll probably see a vertical navigation bar something like the one opposite:

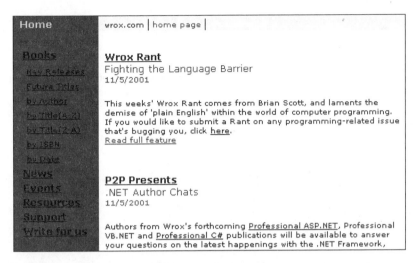

What we have here is a vertical list of hyperlinks nested in a table with a red background. If you happen to be on a page that matches one of the hyperlink addresses from the list, then the corresponding element becomes rendered with white text with no text decoration (i.e. no underline).

For the purposes of our example, we're going to alter the Wrox navigation bar's functionality a bit. We'll make our example into a navigation bar that lists the rest of the examples that we're going to build in this chapter. We'll reduce the number of entries in the bar and we'll take advantage of some of the ASP.NET Hyperlink server control's behaviors to simplify our implementation.

For convenience sake, from this point forward in this chapter, you can presume that any reference to a server control is a reference to an ASP.NET server control, and not an HTML server control unless it specifically says otherwise.

When we're finished, we'll have a page that looks like this:

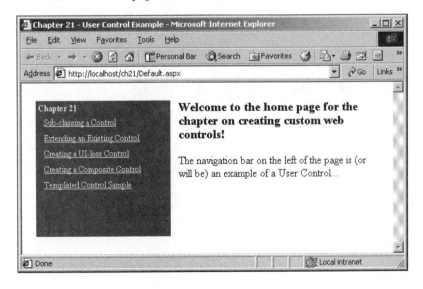

We'll need a web application to work from, so open up Visual Studio and create a new **Web Application** project called **CH21**. Let's start with an existing web page and work our way through creating a WUC from it.

Download the code samples from the Wrox Press site at www.wrox.com. Then add the file named `OriginalPage.aspx`, which you'll find in the directory for this chapter, as an existing item to the **CH21** project (via the **Project | Add Existing Item** menu).

Visual Studio will inform you that the class file for this web form isn't in the project and will offer to create one for you:

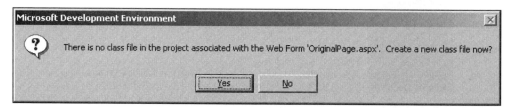

You can decline the offer, as this particular page doesn't actually use a **Codebehind** page. This probably won't be typical of the pages you write in ASP.NET, but we're going to work without Codebehind for this section.

Rename the file from `OriginalPage.aspx` to `Default.aspx` in order for the code to work properly, and then double-click on `Default.aspx` to open it up in the **Design View**. Select **View | HTML Source** so that we can look at the code listing:

```
<%@ Page Language="vb" AutoEventWireup="true" %>
<%@ Import Namespace="System.Drawing" %>
<html>
<head>
  <title>Chapter 21 - User Control Example</title>
  <script runat="server" ID="Script1">

    Sub Page_Load(Source As Object, E As EventArgs)
      Dim strPath As String = Request.Path.ToLower
      SetCurrentLink(strPath, hypHome)
      SetCurrentLink(strPath, hypExample1)
      SetCurrentLink(strPath, hypExample2)
      SetCurrentLink(strPath, hypExample3)
      SetCurrentLink(strPath, hypExample4)
      SetCurrentLink(strPath, hypExample5)
    End Sub

    Private Sub SetCurrentLink(ByVal strPath As String, _
                ByRef hypToTest As HyperLink)
      With hypToTest
        If .NavigateUrl.ToLower().IndexOf(strPath) > -1 Then
          .NavigateUrl = String.Empty
          .ForeColor = Color.Yellow
        End If
      End With
    End Sub
```

```
      </script>
  </head>
  <body>
    <form id="Form1" method="post" runat="server">
      <table cellspacing="10" width="99%" border="0" height="100%">
        <tr>
          <td width="200" valign="top">
            <table id="tblNavBar" bgcolor="#cc0033"
                width="100%" height="100%">
              <tr>
                <td colspan="2">
                  <asp:HyperLink runat="server" ID="hypHome"
                      navigateurl="/CH21/Default.aspx"
                      font-bold="True" forecolor="Black">
                    Chapter 21
                  </asp:HyperLink>
                </td>
              </tr>
              <tr>
                <td width="5px">
                   
                </td>
                <td>
                  <asp:HyperLink runat="server" ID="hypExample1"
                      navigateurl="/CH21/SubClassingAControl.aspx"
                      forecolor="Black">
                    Sub-classing a Control
                  </asp:HyperLink>
                </td>
              </tr>
              <tr>
                <td>
                   
                </td>
                <td>
                  <asp:HyperLink runat="server" ID="hypExample2"
                      navigateurl="/CH21/ExtendingAControl.aspx"
                      forecolor="Black">
                    Extending an Existing Control
                  </asp:HyperLink>
                </td>
              </tr>
              <tr>
                <td>
                   
                </td>
                <td>
                  <asp:HyperLink runat="server" ID="hypExample3"
                      navigateurl="/CH21/Clock.aspx"
                      forecolor="Black">
                    Creating a UI-less Control
                  </asp:HyperLink>
                </td>
              </tr>
              <tr>
```

```
              <td>
                 
              </td>
              <td>
                <asp:HyperLink runat="server" ID="hypExample4"
                     navigateurl="/CH21/CompositeControl.aspx"
                     forecolor="Black">
                   Creating a Composite Control
                </asp:HyperLink>
              </td>
            </tr>
            <tr>
              <td>
                 
              </td>
              <td>
                <asp:HyperLink runat="server" ID="hypExample5"
                     navigateurl="/CH21/TemplatedControl.aspx"
                     forecolor="Black">
                   Templated Control Sample
                </asp:HyperLink>
              </td>
            </tr>
            <tr>
              <td colspan="2" height="100%">
                <!-- This row takes up any slack space at the
                      end of this table -->
                 
              </td>
            </tr>
          </table>
        </td>
        <td valign="top">
          <h3>
            Welcome to the home page for the chapter
            on creating custom web controls!
          </h3>
          <p>
            The navigation bar on the left of the page
            is (or will be) an example of a User Control...
          </p>
        </td>
      </tr>
    </table>
  </form>
</body>
</html>
```

The code in this example is intentionally simplified so that we can concentrate on the specifics of creating a WUC. All the same, let's take a quick tour of the highlights.

Let's walk through the code.

Since we are not using a Codebehind window, we need to set the `AutoEventWireup` attribute of the `@ Page` directive to `True` to tell ASP.NET to use the `Page_Load` method to handle the firing of the `Page_Load` event.

> *You can also manually add the `Handles MyBase.EventName` statement after each event that you want to wire up, but setting the `AutoEventWireup` attribute of the `@ Page` directive to `True` instructs the page to do this for you behind the scenes for any procedures named in the `Object_EventName` style.*
>
> *If you intend to use the `Handles` statement you must specifically set the `AutoEventWireup` attribute to `False`. If you set it to `True` or omit it, your `Object_EventName` event handler will be called twice.*
>
> *For readability and troubleshooting purposes, you should probably choose one technique or the other and stick with it. Bear in mind that, if you foresee moving event handling procedures out of an ASPX page and into a Codebehind page, you should probably use the `Handles` statement. That way your procedures will not require editing in order to be wired up in the Codebehind class.*

We also set the default language for the page, and import the `System.Drawing` namespace so that we don't have to fully qualify references to its members in our code:

```
<%@ Page Language="vb" AutoEventWireup="true" %>
<%@ Import Namespace="System.Drawing" %>
```

The code works by comparing the path of the currently displayed page to the URLs specified for the `Hyperlink` server controls in our navigation bar. It does this during the `Page_Load` event by calling a helper procedure named `SetCurrentLink` and passing it the path of the currently requested page along with a reference to the hyperlink object that we want to check it against:

```
Sub Page_Load(Source As Object, E As EventArgs)
   Dim strPath As String = Request.Path.ToLower
   SetCurrentLink(strPath, hypHome)
   SetCurrentLink(strPath, hypExample1)
   SetCurrentLink(strPath, hypExample2)
   SetCurrentLink(strPath, hypExample3)
   SetCurrentLink(strPath, hypExample4)
   SetCurrentLink(strPath, hypExample5)
End Sub
```

`SetCurrentLink` does its comparison by using the `String` object's built-in `IndexOf` method. We can write it this way because the `NavigateUrl` property is of type `String` and therefore naturally has all of the methods and properties of any other string object:

```
Private Sub SetCurrentLink(ByVal strPath As String, _
            ByRef hypToTest As HyperLink)
   With hypToTest
     If .NavigateUrl.ToLower().IndexOf(strPath) > -1
        .NavigateUrl = String.Empty
        .ForeColor = Color.Yellow
     End If
   End With
End Sub
```

We could have used the `InStr()` function to do the same thing but this is more in keeping with Visual Basic.NET's stronger focus on object-oriented programming. We had to use the `ToLower` method because the `IndexOf` method does not have an overloaded version that supports case-insensitive comparisons. We also used `ToLower` when we assigned the request path to `strUrl` so that we would be comparing one lowercase string with another lowercase string.

If the code finds a `Hyperlink` control with a matching path, it causes the control to be rendered as an anchor instead of as a hyperlink. It does this by resetting the `Hyperlink` control's `NavigateUrl` property to an empty string.

> *This can be a little confusing if you aren't familiar with the history of HTML. In SGML, the precursor to HTML, the "A" in an <A> tag stood for Anchor and the tag was used as a placeholder in a document (like a bookmark in Microsoft Word). When the tag was defined in HTML, it was assigned two duties: you could assign an anchor tag a name and use that name to refer to a given spot in a document (called an anchor), or you could specify a hyperlink reference for the tag and then click on the tag to navigate to another page (in which case it's called a hyperlink). In order to differentiate between the two tasks that the <A> tag can perform, browsers typically underline hyperlinks and they leave an anchor tag's formatting alone.*

This is a prime example of how server controls can simplify web page development!

When the `Hyperlink` server control goes to render itself it takes into account that, if its `NavigateUrl` property is an empty string, then it shouldn't add the `href` attribute to the `<A>` tag. This causes the client's browser to render the tag as an anchor instead of as a hyperlink.

If we tried to do the same thing with basic HTML, we'd have to insert an inline conditional clause in the middle of our HTML to determine whether or not to include the `href` attribute, for example:

```
<% If Len(thisUrl) = 0 Then %>
<a id="hypHome">Chapter 21</a>
<% Else %>
<a id="hypHome" href="/CH21/Default.aspx">Chapter 21</a>
<% End If %>
```

> *This also means that we don't need to specifically turn off the text decoration for the anchor tag, as the browser will automatically turn off the underline for us.*

We also want to give another visual signal that this link represents our current location in the hierarchy by setting its `ForeColor` to the `System.Drawing.Color` collection constant `Yellow`:

```
.NavigateUrl = String.Empty
.ForeColor = Color.Yellow
```

> *Note that we didn't have to fully qualify the reference to the `Color` collection, thanks to the `@ Import` directive that we put at the top of the page.*

That's pretty much it! It's a simple example but it gives us plenty of room for enhancements later on as we look deeper into the features available in WUCs.

Now it's probably a good idea to make sure that our page works before we go through with converting it to a WUC. We could just open a browser and navigate to http://localhost/CH21/default.aspx, but let's get our project set up for debugging first. Right-click on `Default.aspx` in the Solutions Explorer window and select the **Set As Start Page** option.

Now, when we click the **Start** button, Visual Studio will compile the web project, launch a browser window, start our web application, and display `Default.aspx`. The page should look something like this:

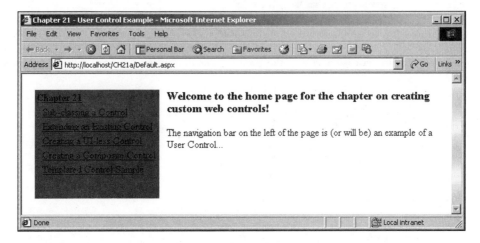

Adding a Web User Control Item to the Project

Hopefully, everything has worked up to now so we can go ahead and create our WUC. The first step is to add a file for the WUC to the project.

Right-click on the **CH21** project in the **Solution Explorer** and choose **Add | Add New Item** from the context menu. Click on the **Web User Control** item in the **Templates** panel. Change the name from `WebUserControl1.ascx` to `NavBar.ascx`. Then click **Open**.

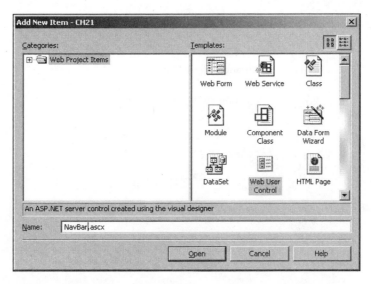

The WUC file should now be open in the **Design View**. Switch to the **HTML View**.

Next we'll want to cut the HTML and code from `Default.aspx` that makes our WUC tick and paste it into our newly created ascx file. Delete the existing text in `NavBar.ascx` and move the following sections over from `Default.aspx`:

```
<%@ Page Language="vb" AutoEventWireup="true" %>
<%@ Import Namespace="System.Drawing" %>
```

We're taking the above section because we still want to set the default language for our control, we still want to have ASP.NET associate our event code with the events that it is supposed to handle, and because we still want to get easy access to the `Color` collection in the `System.Drawing` namespace.

We'll also need the script block that does all of the setup work:

```
<script runat="server" ID="Script1">

  Sub Page_Load(Source As Object, E As EventArgs)
    Dim strPath As String = Request.Path.ToLower
    SetCurrentLink(strPath, hypHome)
    SetCurrentLink(strPath, hypExample1)
    SetCurrentLink(strPath, hypExample2)
    SetCurrentLink(strPath, hypExample3)
    SetCurrentLink(strPath, hypExample4)
    SetCurrentLink(strPath, hypExample5)
  End Sub


  Private Sub SetCurrentLink(ByVal strPath As String, _
              ByRef hypToTest As HyperLink)
    With hypToTest
    If .NavigateUrl.ToLower().IndexOf(strPath) > -1 Then
      .NavigateUrl = String.Empty
      .ForeColor = Color.Yellow
    End If
    End With
  End Sub

</script>
```

and the inner table that holds our navigation elements:

```
<table id="tblNavBar" bgcolor="#cc0033"
    width="100%" height="100%">
  <tr>
    <td colspan="2">
      <asp:HyperLink runat="server" ID="hypHome"
          navigateurl="/CH21/Default.aspx"
          font-bold="True" forecolor="Black">
        Chapter 21
      </asp:HyperLink>
    </td>
  </tr>
  <tr>
```

```
      <td width="5px">
         
      </td>
      <td>
        <asp:HyperLink runat="server" ID="hypExample1"
            navigateurl="/CH21/SubClassingAControl.aspx"
            forecolor="Black">
          Sub-classing a Control
        </asp:HyperLink>
      </td>
    </tr>
    <tr>
      <td>
         
      </td>
      <td>
        <asp:HyperLink runat="server" ID="hypExample2"
            navigateurl="/CH21/ExtendingAControl.aspx"
            forecolor="Black">
          Extending an Existing Control
        </asp:HyperLink>
      </td>
    </tr>
    <tr>
      <td>
         
      </td>
      <td>
        <asp:HyperLink runat="server" ID="hypExample3"
            navigateurl="/CH21/Clock.aspx"
            forecolor="Black">
          Creating a UI-less Control
        </asp:HyperLink>
      </td>
    </tr>
    <tr>
      <td>
         
      </td>
      <td>
        <asp:HyperLink runat="server" ID="hypExample4"
            navigateurl="/CH21/CompositeControl.aspx"
            forecolor="Black">
          Creating a Composite Control
        </asp:HyperLink>
      </td>
    </tr>
    <tr>
      <td>
         
      </td>
      <td>
        <asp:HyperLink runat="server" ID="hypExample5"
            navigateurl="/CH21/TemplatedControl.aspx"
            forecolor="Black">
```

```
        Templated Control Sample
      </asp:HyperLink>
    </td>
  </tr>
  <tr>
    <td colspan="2" height="100%">
      <!-- This row takes up any slack space at the
           end of this table -->
       
    </td>
  </tr>
</table>
```

All that should be left in the `Default.aspx` page are the `HTML`, `Head`, and `Body` tags, and the outer table.

Modifying Pre-existing Code for Use in a Web User Control

We only need to make a few modifications to get code from an ASP.NET web form to work in a WUC. The differences between the two are:

❑ WUCs don't allow a couple of directives aimed specifically at pages. The directives that are not allowed are @ `Page` and @ `OutputCache`.

❑ It isn't recommended to include `<html>`, `<head>`, or `<body>` elements in a WUC. It isn't forbidden either, but it will make your WUC unfriendly to any page that already contains these elements.

❑ It is also recommended not to put `<form>` tags in a WUC. The reason for this is that your WUC could not then be placed inside a form on the hosting page (ASP.NET doesn't allow for nested server forms).

❑ You may optionally change any page event handlers from `Page_EventName` to `Control_EventName`. The WUC will still work whether you change this or not though.

You may wish to ignore the third recommendation if you are creating a login form or a self-contained search form, you know that you won't be nesting it in another form, and you want the action and other attributes of the form to remain consistent throughout every instance of the control. You might want to note that, since we didn't include any of the `<html>`, `<head>`, `<body>` or `<form>` elements, the only real change we need to make in `NavBar.ascx` is to change the @ `Page` directive to an @ `Control` directive:

```
<%@ Control Language="vb" AutoEventWireup="true" %>
```

For consistency, though, we'll change the `Page_Load` procedure name to `Control_Load`:

```
Sub Control_Load(Source As Object, E As EventArgs)
```

> This isn't wired up automatically outside of the Codebehind window in Beta 2, but that should be corrected in the final release. If you are working with Beta 2, you will want to leave the procedure named as **Page_Load** for this demo or add the **Handles MyBase.Load** statement to the end of the procedure declaration.

The @ Control Directive

The @ Control directive supports all of the same attributes that the @ Page directive does, with the exception of the AspCompat attribute and the tracing attributes (trace and traceMode). ASP compatibility and tracing can only be set at the page or web site level. We haven't included either of these attributes in our navigation bar example so we don't need to make any other modifications to the @ Control directive.

As a point of interest, ASP.NET will actually interpret any <%@ %> directive that does not specify the directive name as an @ Page or an @ Control, based on whether it is in an ASPX or an ASCX file, respectively. So, the following statement would work in both file types without modification:

```
<%@ Language="vb" AutoEventWireup="true" %>
```

The question, of course, is whether this will continue to be supported in future versions of ASP.NET!

That's it! You've created your first WUC and, yes, they can really be that easy! Let's head back to the Default.aspx page and add our new WUC to it.

Web User Controls and the @ Register Directive

We'll need to register our new control with the page before we'll be able to add it to the page. Place the following line at the top of Default.aspx:

```
<%@ Register TagPrefix="ch21uc" TagName="NavBar" src="NavBar.ascx"%>
```

The @ Register directive tells the compiler how to identify the element tags for our custom controls and where to locate their code. The TagPrefix and TagName attributes tell the compiler the syntax we'll use when we create elements for our WUC. The src attribute identifies the file that contains the code for the WUC and can be either a relative or absolute reference. So the page now knows that it should create any tag of the form <tagprefix:tagname runat="server"> as an instance of the WUC found at the location specified in src.

In the left cell of the two cell table that we used to contain our original navigation bar elements, type in the following XML-style element declaration:

```
<body>
  <form id="Form1" method="post" runat="server">
    <table cellspacing="10" width="99%" border="0" height="100%">
      <tr>
        <td width="200" valign="top">
          <ch21uc:navbar id="MyNavBar" runat="server" />
        </td>
        <td valign="top">
          <h3>
            Welcome to the home page for the chapter
            on creating custom web controls!
          </h3>
          <p>
            The navigation bar on the left of the page
            is (or will be) an example of a User Control...
```

```
              </p>
           </td>
        </tr>
      </table>
   </form>
```

You could alternatively write the highlighted line as:

```
<ch21uc:navbar id="MyNavBar" runat="server"></ch21uc:navbar>
```

The page will accept either empty tags or tag pairs but, since the control that we've created isn't meant to contain nested text or HTML elements, the former is more appropriate. It's a strong indicator to anyone else who looks at our page that they aren't expected to include any additional content within our element.

> *Empty tags are tags like <img>, <br>, and <hr> which do not have closing tags. They are called empty tags because they do not allow for nested content in the way that a tag pair element like a paragraph tag does (e.g. <p>some nested text</p>).*

> *You might be wondering why the first version of these two highlighted lines has the extra '/' before the closing chevron of the tag. It's a part of the XML and XHTML specifications that all empty elements be identified as such by including a closing slash before the end of the tag.*

As we've seen above, WUCs are very simple to create. Creating one doesn't even require writing any additional code! They don't have to remain simple, though. In the following sections, we'll take a look at some of the more advanced techniques that we can use when creating WUCs.

Reaching Into a Web User Control

The way our WUC stands now, it is pretty much a black box as far as our page is concerned. Well, that's not entirely true. By virtue of being a WUC, it inherits the standard methods, properties, and events of the `System.Web.UI.UserControl` class, but there is no direct way to access the controls or the code it contains. It could contain nothing but the literal text "Hello World!" or it could contain a highly complex collection of elements and script but, without exposing any custom properties, methods, or events, the hosting page would never know!

> *You can actually access the contained controls through the WUC's `Controls` collection and `FindControl` method. This looks like a security loophole since the controls should be of `Protected` scope by default.*

So how do we expose custom properties, methods, and events, you ask? Pretty much the same way as you would for any other class! Any members of a WUC marked as `Public` will be available to the hosting page. That means that we can expose any variables, property statements, functions, procedures, and events we choose in a manner consistent with the rest of the Visual Basic.NET architecture!

Exposing a Variable as a Custom Property

As an example, let's expose a custom property on our WUC that sets the background color of our navigation bar's table. We'll call it BackColor to keep it consistent with the rest of the ASP.NET server controls. Because this property doesn't affect the behavior of our control and because it doesn't require us to perform any action when the value changes, we'll create this property as a public variable. In .NET parlance, you'll frequently hear a variable-based property referred to as a **field**. Add the following line at the beginning of the script block in NavBar.ascx:

```
<script runat="server">
    Public BackColor As Color = ColorTranslator.FromHtml("#cc0033")
```

What we've done is to create a public variable of type System.Drawing.Color and initialize it with the Wrox Press red background color. Why not just create a variable of type string, though? By using the Color type, we're allowing our user to specify any of the named colors known to .NET, an RGB (Red-Green-Blue) value, a hex value, or an ARGB (Alpha-RGB) value. The Color class will also ensure that only *valid* named colors and color values can be assigned to our property. For instance, trying to assign either "PurpleHaze" or "#gg0000" to BackColor will generate run-time exceptions because they don't represent valid colors.

When we go to initialize the BackColor property, or to make use of it in an HTML tag, we run into a bit of a wrinkle, though. The Color class is based on 32-bit ARGB values while HTML uses 24-bit RGB or named colors. Now, if we were using BackColor to set the color on an ASP.NET server control, this wouldn't be a problem at all! The server controls automatically render any property that uses the Color type in an HTML friendly fashion, as either a hex value or a known color name. The HTML controls are another matter though – in order to have them render correctly, we need to convert from the ARGB values of the Color class to HTML friendly values manually.

To do this we can use the System.Drawing.ColorTranslator class like so:

```
<table id=tblNavBar bgcolor="<%=ColorTranslator.ToHtml (BackColor)%>"
    width="100%" height="100%">
```

The ToHtml method takes the BackColor value and checks to see if it represents a known color name. If it does, then it writes out the name of the color; if it doesn't, it strips off the Alpha channel value and returns a hexadecimal value representing the remaining RGB channels – prefaced with a hash sign (#) of course!

Conversely, we use the FromHTML method to convert from a web color to an ARGB value, which is what we did earlier when we initialized the BackColor property:

```
Public BackColor As Color = ColorTranslator.FromHtml("#cc0033")
```

To set the BackColor property in our hosting page, we specify it as an attribute in the element for the control:

```
<ch21uc:navbar id="MyNavBar" runat="server"
    backcolor="Chartreuse" />
```

Go ahead and add this backcolor attribute to the MyNavBar element and check it out in your browser. On second thought, let's stick with Wrox red, shall we!

Exposing a Custom Property

So we've seen the way to set up a variable-based or unmanaged property. Why don't we see what it looks like when we want to control what happens when the user accesses a custom property? It shouldn't surprise you by now to learn that we use the exact same syntax as we would if we were creating a custom property in any other Visual Basic.NET class.

Let's set up a property that will allow the consumer of our control to specify the current link directly. We'll add a little spice to the example by exposing the property complete with an enumeration of the available controls. Then we'll finish it up by modifying our existing code to make use of the new property. We'll start right under our public variable property example, by putting in a couple of private, module-level variables to help us maintain and control the use of the new property:

```
Public BackColor As Color = ColorTranslator.FromHtml("#cc0033")

    Private mblnLinksHaveBeenChecked As Boolean
    Private mlclCurrentLink As LinkControlList = LinkControlList.Default
```

Note we've declared `mlclCurrentLink` as a variable of type `LinkControlList` and initialized it to one of `LinkControlList`'s members. `LinkControlList` is the enumeration type representing the `Hyperlink` controls in the WUC that we're going to create next:

```
    Public Enum LinkControlList
        [Default] = -1
        Home
        Example1
        Example2
        Example3
        Example4
        Example5
    End Enum
```

If you aren't familiar with it already then the code for the enumeration type will probably seem pretty strange. The square brackets around the name of the first member of the enumeration (`Default`) allow us to take advantage of VB.NET's ability to allow us to use **keywords** and **reserved** words for the names of properties, procedures, and variables. That's probably not the most bizarre looking portion of the enumeration though!

You've probably noticed that the only member that we've specifically assigned a value to is `Default`. That's because any enumeration member that is not specifically set *automatically* takes on a value of one plus the previous member's value. So `Home` is one plus the value of `Default` (or 1+(−1)=0), `Example1` is one plus the value of `Home` (or 1+0=1), and so on. This behavior comes in extremely handy when we go to add a new member to the list, as we don't have to waste time manually renumbering the members that come afterwards!

> **If we were willing to start the enumeration list at zero, we wouldn't even have to assign a value to the first member.**

Now on to the property definition:

```
    Public Property CurrentLink() As LinkControlList
      Get
        Return mlclCurrentLink
      End Get
      Set(ByVal Value As LinkControlList)
        If mblnLinksHaveBeenChecked Then
          Throw New Exception("The current link has already been rendered.")
        ElseIf Not System.Enum.IsDefined(mlclCurrentLink.GetType(), Value) Then
          Throw New ArgumentOutOfRangeException("CurrentLink", _
            Value, "Not a valid CurrentLink value! " & _
            "Please select a member from the LinkControlIndex enumeration.")
        Else
          mlclCurrentLink = Value
        End If
      End Set
    End Property
```

As you can see, it's a standard public read/write property definition. We've set the property type to match our enumeration type but that's about the only major variation. The `Get` section simply returns the value of the corresponding internal variable although it does use the new `Return` syntax instead of the VB6 style `propertyname = somevar` syntax. Which style you use is mostly a matter of personal preference, but the `Return` syntax offers a few benefits over the traditional syntax:

❏   It offers greater clarity and readability. It differentiates the statement that returns the value from other variable assignments.

❏   It is easier to maintain. If we want to change the name of the property we only need to change the property declaration statement, instead of having to also find and change one or more property assignment statements.

❏   It is less prone to logic errors when Option Explicit is off. The other style leaves us with an extra opportunity for a typo to accidentally create a new variable instead of returning the correct value.

In the `Set` portion of the property declaration, we do a little exception checking before setting the internal variable to the new property value:

```
    If mblnLinksHaveBeenChecked Then
      Throw New Exception("The current link has already been rendered.")
```

The first section of the `If` statement is checking to see if our control has already called the `SetCurrentLink` method or not. If it has, then we throw an exception to alert the consumer of our control that it is too late in the control's lifecycle to set the current link.

In the next section, the `ElseIf` statement checks to make sure that the value that has been passed in to us is actually a member of the `LinkControlIndex` enumeration:

```
    ElseIf Not System.Enum.IsDefined(mlclCurrentLink.GetType(), Value) Then
      Throw New ArgumentOutOfRangeException("CurrentLink", _
        Value, "Not a valid CurrentLink value! " & _
        "Please select a member from the LinkControlIndex enumeration.")
```

> Even though the `System` namespace has been imported by default, we still have to qualify the reference to `System.Enum` class to distinguish it from the `Enum` keyword.

If the hosting page has tried to set the index to an unacceptable value, say 5, then this will cause our property to throw one of the standard system exception types. We use one of the constructor methods of the `ArgumentOutOfRangeException` class to expose as much information about the exception as possible.

This constructor takes three arguments. The first is the name of the argument that caused the exception, which we'll use to pass back the name of the property. The second passes in a reference to the invalid argument itself and exposes it through the `ActualValue` property of the exception. The third argument is a custom message that we'll use to give back an exception message that's slightly more informative than the default one.

And finally, if the new value makes it past our validation code, we set our internal variable equal to it:

```
Else
   mlclCurrentLink = Value
End If
```

At this point, the public property is available to the hosting page but it doesn't do much yet. We'll need to make some changes to the rest of the code to implement it and, while we're at it, we might as well make a few optimizations. We can start by switching from using the `Load` event to making use of the `PreRender` event instead. Just like with an ASPX `Page` object, the `PreRender` event happens well after the `Load` event and just before the controls on the WUC are actually written to the HTML output stream. Note that `PreRender` and `Load` have the same event signature so all we have to do is change the procedure name:

```
Sub Control_PreRender(ByVal sender As Object, ByVal e As System.EventArgs)
   Dim strPath As String
```

> As mentioned before, if you are using Beta 2 you will want to write this as
> `Page_PreRender`.

By doing this, we delay the calls to `SetCurrentLink` until as late as possible, giving script in the host container as much opportunity as possible to set the `CurrentLink` property.

It's time to implement the functionality behind the property. We're going to be replacing most of the existing code in the `PreRender` event procedure:

```
Sub Control_PreRender(ByVal sender As Object, ByVal e As System.EventArgs)
   Dim strPath As String
   Dim i As Integer
   Dim mLinkControls() As HyperLink = {hypHome, _
                     hypExample1, _
                     hypExample2, _
                     hypExample3, _
                     hypExample4, _
```

```
                    hypExample5}

   If mlclCurrentLink = LinkControlList.Default Then
    strPath = Request.Path.ToLower
    For i = 0 To mLinkControls.GetUpperBound(0)
     If SetCurrentLink(strPath, mLinkControls(i)) Then
      mlclCurrentLink = CType(i, LinkControlList)
      Exit For
     End If
    Next
   Else
    strPath = mLinkControls(mlclCurrentLink).NavigateUrl.ToLower
    SetCurrentLink(strPath, mLinkControls(mlclCurrentLink))
   End If
   mblnLinksHaveBeenChecked = True
  End Sub
```

Note that the `If` *statement expects a return value from the* `SetCurrentLink` *procedure. We'll be converting* `SetCurrentLink` *to a function shortly.*

The first major change is that we need to be able to access our `Hyperlink` controls via the indices created in the `LinkControlList` enumeration. To do that we create the `mLinkControls()` array of type `Hyperlink` and initialize it with references to our `Hyperlink` server controls:

```
Dim mLinkControls() As HyperLink = {hypHome, _
                  hypExample1, _
                  hypExample2, _
                  hypExample3, _
                  hypExample4, _
                  hypExample5}
```

The next step is to check and see if the `CurrentLink` property has been set, by comparing it to the `LinkControlList.Default` member. If it hasn't been set, then we loop through the array calling `SetCurrentLink` for each of the hyperlink objects, until we find one whose `NavigateURL` property matches the request path:

```
If mlclCurrentLink = LinkControlList.Default Then
 strPath = Request.Path.ToLower
 For i = 0 To mLinkControls.GetUpperBound(0)
  If SetCurrentLink(strPath, mLinkControls(i)) Then
   mlclCurrentLink = CType(i, LinkControlList)
   Exit For
  End If
 Next
```

This differs from the original code that we had because we are now using a `For Loop` to walk an array of controls, where previously we had hard coded the calls for each control. This is obviously more flexible than the previous technique as all we need to do to add a new control to the list is to add it to the array and add a corresponding entry in the `LinkControlList` enumeration. This automatically includes the new control in the `For Loop`. It also allows us to make an easy optimization by giving us a simple way to stop checking the rest of the hyperlink objects once a matching path has been found.

We'll do one more thing once we've found the current link and that is to set the internal variable for the `CurrentLink` property. Now if code in the container cares to inquire as to which link was actually set, it will be able to get the value back out.

If it turns out that the `CurrentLink` property has been set, we'll skip looping through the controls and call `SetCurrentLink` directly for the indicated control:

```
Else
 strPath = mLinkControls(mlclCurrentLink).NavigateUrl.ToLower
 SetCurrentLink(strPath, mLinkControls(mlclCurrentLink))
End If
```

We needed to force the path comparison to be equal in `SetCurrentLink`, so we set the `strPath` variable equal to the path of the control that we are passing in. It's a bit of a hack, but it keeps the example simple.

Finally, we have to set the `mblnLinksHaveBeenChecked` flag so that we can prevent any attempts to set the current link after this code has finished:

```
mblnLinksHaveBeenChecked = True
```

We do need to go back and change one more thing before we can test our new code. We've added an `If` statement up above that looks for a return value from `SetCurrentLink` to determine whether the item being tested is actually the current link. Since `SetCurrentLink` is defined as a sub procedure and not a function, we need to change its declaration and modify it so that it returns a value of `True` when it finds the current link:

```
Private Function SetCurrentLink(ByVal strPath As String, _
             ByRef hypToTest As HyperLink) As Boolean
  With hypToTest
   If .NavigateUrl.ToLower().IndexOf(strPath) > -1 Then
    .NavigateUrl = String.Empty
    .ForeColor = Color.Yellow
    Return True
   End If
  End With
End Function
```

To test our changes, add the following server-side script block to the `Default.aspx` page:

```
<html><head>

<script runat=server language="vb">

 Sub Page_Load(ByVal Sender As System.Object, ByVal e As System.EventArgs)
  MyNavBar.CurrentLink = MyNavBar.LinkControlList.Example3
 End Sub

</script>

<title>Chapter 21 - Web User Control Example</title>

</head>
```

When you run the project, the current link will be set to Example3 and you should get a page that looks like this:

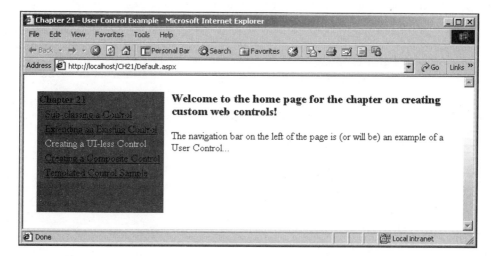

Exposing a Custom Method

Exposing a custom method is again a matter of taking a private sub or function and marking it as available to other objects outside of the current class. Let's try it out by creating a sub procedure that sets the style of all of the `Hyperlink` controls in our WUC. Here is the code for the procedure:

```
Public Sub SetLinkStyle(ByRef MasterStyle As Style, _
            Optional ByVal Merge As Boolean = True)
  Dim objControl As Control
  For Each objControl In Me.Controls
   If TypeOf objControl Is HyperLink Then
     If Merge Then
       CType(objControl, Hyperlink).MergeStyle(MasterStyle)
     Else
       CType(objControl, Hyperlink).ApplyStyle(MasterStyle)
     End If
   End If
  Next
End Sub
```

The goal of an example is to illustrate the topic at hand clearly, and not necessarily to write examples that are fully optimized for performance. Considering how important efficient code is to web application scalability, though, the author would like to point out that, while having the If statement in the For loop is easier to read, it is not very efficient. In production grade code, this should be written with a top level If statement that determines whether to branch off and run a loop that merges the style or to run a loop that applies the style.

The important part for us right now is declaring the sub procedure as `Public`. After that, we've exposed the method and the rest is just implementation details!

The way that the procedure works is by taking in two parameters. The first is a
`System.Web.UI.WebControls.Style` object that has been set up with all of the attributes that we
want to apply. The second parameter is used to indicate how to combine the attributes of the `Style`
object that has been passed in with the `Style` object of each of our `Hyperlink` controls. If we want to
keep all of the non-blank style attributes of each `Hyperlink` control and only add attributes from the
passed in `Style` object, we'll set the `Merge` parameter to `True`. If, instead, we want to copy all of the
non-blank attributes of the `NewStyle` object over to each `Hyperlink`, overwriting any
matching attributes, then we'll want to set the `Merge` parameter to `False`.

The procedure itself cycles through all of the server controls in our WUC looking for ones of the
Hyperlink type. When it finds one, it casts the generic Control type to the Hyperlink type so that it can
get access to the appropriate `MergeStyle` or `ApplyStyle` method. Test our new method by adding
this to the script block in `Default.aspx`:

```
Sub Page_PreRender(ByVal sender As Object, ByVal e As System.EventArgs)
  MyNavBar.CurrentLink = MyNavBar.LinkControlList.Example3

  Dim objStyle As New Style()
  With objStyle
    .ForeColor = System.Drawing.Color.AntiqueWhite
    .Font.Underline = False
    .Font.Size = FontUnit.Point(9)
  End With
  MyNavBar.SetLinkStyle(objStyle, False)
End Sub
```

The resulting form should look like this:

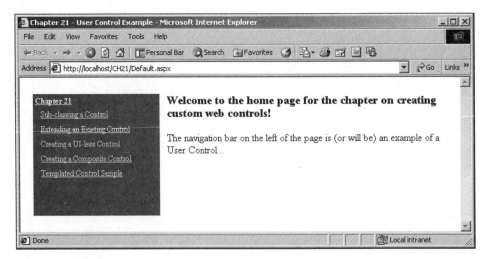

Creating an Event

At its most basic, creating a new event in a WUC is a fairly simple task. All it takes is a declaration of the
event and then you raise the event from somewhere in the code.

> Although not strictly a requirement for creating an event, it is a strongly encouraged convention to provide a protected overridable **OnEventName** method, that is called internally to raise the event rather than raising it directly. This convention makes our control easier to work with when it is inherited from, by allowing other developers to modify the event raising logic (that is, adding their own code or events that run before, after, or instead of our event).

Add the following in the declarations section of NavBar.ascx:

```
Public BackColor As Color = ColorTranslator.FromHtml("#cc0033")

Public Event CurrentLinkProcessed(ByVal Sender As System.Object, _
             ByVal e As System.EventArgs)

Private mblnLinksHaveBeenChecked As Boolean
```

This declares a new event called CurrentLinkProcessed, which we'll raise at the end of the Control_PreRender code. It's a good idea to keep the event signature (the parameter declarations) consistent with the ASP.NET standard for web control events. That standard is to pass the object that triggered the event and an instance of a class that gives information about the event itself to the event handler. Typically, that class is the EventArgs class or a class that derives from it. You may use any class you like, but it really is the best practice to at least inherit from the EventArgs class.

Now let's add the event raising method mentioned in the note above:

```
Protected Overridable Sub OnCurrentLinkProcessed( _
    ByVal e As System.EventArgs)
  RaiseEvent CurrentLinkProcessed(Me, e)
End Sub
```

Remember that, by marking the method as Protected, we are making this method available only to code within our class and to classes that inherit from it. By marking it as Overridable, we are allowing any classes that derive from this to sink, modify, or replace the event.

We use the RaiseEvent syntax to differentiate this from a call to an ordinary procedure. Having declared the event, we still need to call our event raising method from somewhere in our code. Add this line at the end of the Control_PreRender event:

```
mblnLinksHaveBeenChecked = True

Call OnCurrentLinkProcessed(EventArgs.Empty)

End Sub
```

Here we pass in an EventArgs object and we let the OnCurrentLinkProcessed method pass along the reference to the current instance of our WUC. Since we don't have any additional information about the event that we want to include, we use the shared Empty field (a.k.a. public variable) of the EventArgs object to return an EventArgs object with its ExtendedInfo property set to Nothing.

So now that we've created the CurrentLinkProcessed event, let's see what it takes for the hosting container to respond to it!

Handling Web User Controls' Events

When we work with controls that have been created via tags in an ASPX page, creating event handlers is an exceptionally simple process. If we create a control programmatically, the process is a bit more involved but still reasonably simple. The good news with custom web controls and WUCs is that nothing is different with event handling. We can use the exact same techniques!

So, for our example, we only need to write the procedure that we want to use to respond to the event:

```
Public Sub MyNavBar_CurrentLinkProcessed(ByVal Sender As System.Object, _
                    ByVal e As System.EventArgs)
  Dim strMessage as String _
    = "CurrentLink is: " & CStr(Sender.CurrentLink)& "<BR>"
  Response.Write(strMessage)
End Sub
```

Then wire it up by specifying it in an OnEventName attribute of the given element:

```
<ch21uc:navbar id="MyNavBar" runat="server"
  onCurrentLinkProcessed="MyNavBar_CurrentLinkProcessed" />
```

The UserControl class that our control is inherited from takes care of delegating the event handler for us and all we need to do is sit back and watch!

> If you are used to the way that Internet Explorer wires up client-side events for us, it might surprise you to discover that you can't just create a procedure for a server event called **MyNavBar_OnCurrentLinkProcessed** and have it wired up automatically.
>
> While you can call the procedure whatever you want, if you're *not* using Codebehind, you will always need to specify the name of the handling function in the **OnEventName** attribute of the element tag. If you *are* using a Codebehind class, then you can keep with the .NET standard and use the **Handles** statement.

We've essentially finished our WUC demo now and all that remains is to test it out. View the Default.aspx page in your browser and you should get results like the following:

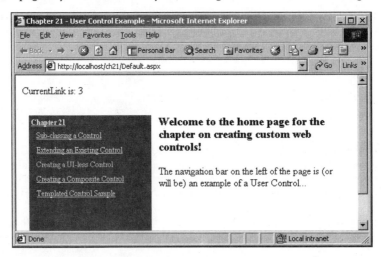

If you look at the top of the page, you'll see the `Response.Write` output indicating that the `CurrentLinkProcessed` event has fired. Since we've specifically set the current link to `Example3`, the index value for the `CurrentLink` property is 3, of course.

Comment out the line in the `Control_PreRender` event that sets the current link, so that the NavBar control will go back to determining the link based on the current location:

```
'MyNavBar.CurrentLink = MyNavBar.LinkControlList.Example3
```

Now view the page and you should get this output instead:

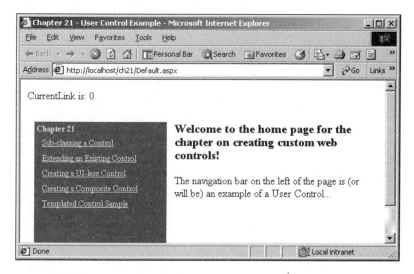

As expected, the `CurrentLinkProcessed` event fires whether we manually set the current link or not. Here we get the index value 0 indicating that `hypHome` is the current link.

> If you've used previous versions of ASP, you may be wondering why the
> `Response.Write` output is at the top of the page. This happens because the
> `CurrentLinkProcessed` event is firing before any HTML has actually been written
> to the output stream.

If you want more control over where this output goes on your page, you can replace the `Response.Write` call with a statement that adds a `LiteralControl` to the `Controls` collection of either the page or one of the server controls on it. In this case, try rewriting the `CurrentLinkProcessed` event handler like so:

```
Public Sub MyNavBar_CurrentLinkProcessed(ByVal Sender As System.Object, _
                       ByVal e As System.EventArgs)
   Dim strMessage as String _
     = "CurrentLink is: " & CStr(Sender.CurrentLink) & "<BR>"
   Form1.Controls.Add(New LiteralControl(strMessage))
End Sub
```

This places the message just before the closing tag of the Form1 server control.

> *ASP.NET provides the* PlaceHolder *control for positioning dynamically added controls. The* PlaceHolder *control has no UI of its own but serves only as a lightweight container control for other server controls.*

> *To use a* PlaceHolder *control, add the control from the Toolbox to the Design View of an ASPX page. Position the control where you want your dynamically added controls to go. Then, in code, call the* Add *or* AddAt *methods of the* PlaceHolder.Controls *collection.*

The next couple of sections cover some additional topics that should be of interest to you as you continue to work with WUCs, before we move on to discuss sub-classed custom web controls.

Reaching Out of a Web User Control

This can be a fairly simple process if all you are looking for is the standard members of the hosting page or parent control (if our custom control is nested inside of other server controls). The UserControl class that our control inherits from exposes a Page field and a Parent field, respectively, for accessing the container hierarchy above us. So, if you want to know what the value of the hosting page's IsValid property is, refer to it with the following syntax:

```
If Me.Page.IsValid Then
  'Code to use if the host page passed validation
  ...
Else
  'Code to use if the host page did not pass validation
  ...
End If
```

Similarly, if you want access to one or more of the controls on a host container (maybe you're looking for other instances of your WUC), remember that you have access to the container's FindControl method and the Controls collection.

Casting to the Hosting Container's Type at Runtime

Be forewarned that, if you want to access a variable, property, or method that you've added to a page or a hosting container, you'll need to cast it ("it" meaning the object returned by the Page or Parent fields) to the appropriate type first. In other words, the Page and Parent fields return objects of the base class Page and Control types. Any custom members of the specific instance of the page or control in question are not directly available through these objects. If you want to get access to, say, a public variable on the hosting page called strTestVar, you can't just use the following:

```
Response.Write(Me.Page.strTestVar)
```

If you do, you'll get a compiler error telling you that, "The name 'strTestVar' is not a member of 'System.Web.UI.Page'." So, in order to get to strTestVar, we need to get a reference to the class of the ASP.NET page itself instead of the reference to its base class, System.Web.UI.Page. We can't use the Ctype() function to convert between the two because we would need the type name from the current ASP page. Since that type name changes whenever our control is hosted by another page, we need a method to convert one object to another type – one that works even if we don't know the type until runtime. The shared method ChangeType(), from the System.Convert class, can do this for us:

```
Dim objPageInstance as Object _
        = System.Convert.ChangeType(Me.Page, Me.Page.GetType)
```

`ChangeType` takes two arguments – the object you want to convert and the type that you want to convert it to. In this case we get the object from `Me.Page` and we use the same object's `GetType` method to get at the type that the object was originally instanced from. Now we have access to *all* of the public members of the hosting page. We can rewrite our `Response.Write` statement as:

```
Response.Write(objPageInstance.strTestVar)
```

As long as the hosting page actually has an `strTestVar` string field or property, we'll get the value back instead of an error!

Other Web User Control Features

WUCs offer a wealth of features and functionality; more, really, than we could expect to cover even in an entire chapter dedicated solely to their use and development. So, to give the other control types their fair share of discussion we'll close off this section with a brief overview of some of the more salient topics.

Web User Control Namespaces

In the section that introduced WUCs, it was mentioned that they provide their own namespace. This means that we'll never have a naming conflict with any of the child controls created in a WUC. If you take a look at the sourcecode from the example we've been working with, you'll find that each named element from our custom control has been given a new ID, one that is unique throughout the hosting page. This is accomplished by concatenating the unique ID of our WUC with the ID of the constituent element, creating a new unique ID!

To illustrate this, take a look at this portion of the sourcecode that our WUC sample generates:

```
<a id="MyNavBar_hypHome" href="/CH21/Default.aspx"
    style="color:AntiqueWhite;font-size:9pt;font-weight:bold;">
  Chapter 21
</a>
```

Notice that the client-side ID generated for this element is the ID of the WUC, an underscore, and the ID of the hyperlink server control from within the WUC. This combination should guarantee us a unique ID on the client side for each of the server controls in the WUC, no matter how many instances of the WUC are added to the page.

This happens because the base `UserControl` class implements the `INamingContainer` interface, a tagging interface that instructs the hosting container to create a separate naming scope for each instance of a WUC. This interface will also come in handy later as we develop other types of container controls, since its use is not limited to WUCs.

Adding Web User Controls Programmatically

WUCs can also be added programmatically. Because they don't reside in class files there is a special method used to load them, though. The method is called `LoadControl` and it is available in every page and container control. The `LoadControl` syntax is:

```
HostingContainer.LoadControl("SomePath/MyUserControl.ascx")
```

where `HostingContainer` is the page or other container object that we want to add the WUC to, and where `SomePath/MyUserControl.ascx` is the virtual path to the file where the WUC is saved.

The important thing to keep in mind as you read the remainder of the chapter is that WUCs share almost all of the features and functionality of the class-based forms of custom web control development. So, if you see something cool in the remaining portion of this chapter, chances are it applies to WUCs as well!

Creating a Sub-Classed Control

There are actually a couple of variations on basic sub-classed controls that we can create. We can roll our own by inheriting from the `System.Web.UI.WebControl` class (custom web controls), we can inherit from one of the controls in the `System.Web.UI.Webcontrols` or `System.Web.UI.HTMLcontrols` (extending an existing control), or we can inherit from the `System.Web.UI.Control` class (creating a control without a UI). We'll discuss them all in this section but, for now, let's cover a little bit of setup first.

See the previous chapter for a discussion of the available server controls.

Setting up a Test Bed Project

Let's start off our class-based examples by setting up our web control library and adding a test bed project to it. The following are the basic steps that you can follow whenever you work with Web Control Libraries or Web Custom Control items:

1. Create a new Web Control Library project (or add a Web Custom Control item to an existing project).

2. If you want to use a root namespace that is different from the name of the project you must go into the project properties dialog and change the value in the Root Namespace field. Unlike C#, defining the namespace in a VB class file (using a `Namespace...End Namespace` block) actually creates a new namespace within the root namespace.

3. To create a test bed for the controls, you'll want to add a Web Project to the solution where you'll be developing your control(s). It doesn't matter whether you create a new project or use an existing one. The only recommendation here is the commonsense one: don't use a production server for a test bed site!

We're going to use a single project and a single namespace for the rest of the examples in this chapter. We'll also use the CH21 web application that we created in the WUC example as our test bed. Use the following steps as a guideline, making allowances for the server name in your test environment:

4. So start by creating a new project titled "CH21Controls". Be sure to select the Close Solution option before continuing.

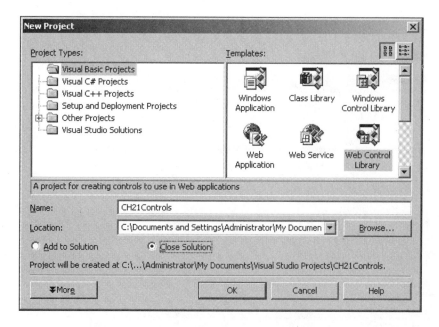

5. If you are asked to save changes to the CH21 web application solution and its files, choose **Yes**.

6. We're going to use the default namespace (which is the same as the project name) so we don't need to change any of the project settings. If you wanted to change the namespace though, you could right-click on the project in the **Solution Explorer** and select **Properties**. In the **General** properties section of the **CH21Controls Property Pages** dialog box is the text box for the **Root Namespace** of the project.

7. Select **File | Add Project | Existing Project From Web** from the menu bar.

8. Enter the URL of the server that is currently hosting the CH21 web application (although the dialog box only says to enter the URL of the server, you can type in the full address of the application if you prefer).

9. Open the `CH21.vbproj` file when the **Add Existing Project** dialog box displays.

10. Once the web application project has loaded, right-click on the **CH21** project in the **Solution Explorer** window and select **Set as Startup Project**. We need to do this so that we'll have an executable project when we click the **Start** button.

11. Right-click on the CH21 project again, this time selecting the Add Reference menu option. In the Add Reference dialog box, go to the Projects tab. CH21Controls should already be displayed in the list box:

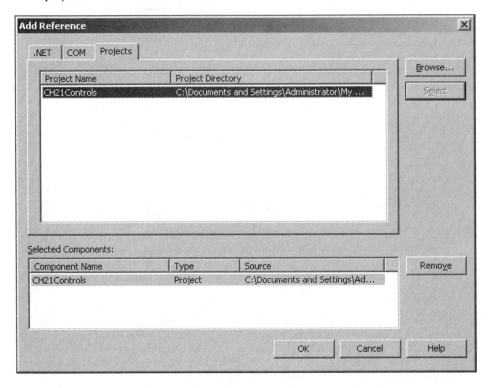

12. Double-click on the CH21Controls project to add it to the Selected Components list box and then click OK. We've now made it so that the two projects will be built together when the project is run and that the CH21Controls.dll will be copied to the CH21 web application's Bin folder.

Now that we've set up our test bed project let's move into the next section and start authoring our first sub-classed control.

Sub-Classed Controls and the Web Custom Control Template

To become familiar with the basics of class-based custom web control development in VB.NET, let's start off by examining the custom web control template provided with .NET.

First, change the name of the class file that was created for us to SubClassedControl.vb. If the file isn't open already, double-click on it to open it up in the code editor window. Now do a search for WebCustomControl1 and replace each occurrence with SubClassedControl.

Now let's take a look at the code that has been created for us:

```
Imports System.ComponentModel
Imports System.Web.UI

<DefaultProperty("Text"), _
 ToolboxData( _
   "<{0}:SubClassedControl runat=server></{0}:SubClassedControl>")> _
Public Class SubClassedControl

    Inherits System.Web.UI.WebControls.WebControl

    Dim _text As String

    <Bindable(True), Category("Appearance"), DefaultValue("")> _
    Property [Text]() As String
     Get
       Return _text
     End Get

     Set(ByVal Value As String)
       _text = Value
     End Set
    End Property

    Protected Overrides Sub Render(ByVal output As _
       System.Web.UI.HtmlTextWriter)
       output.Write([Text])
    End Sub

End Class
```

Believe it or not, this is all the code we need to build a custom web control! We could compile this code right now and it would work just fine. It might be a bit boring, but it would work!

Important Assemblies in Custom Web Control Development

Let's take a closer look at what Visual Studio has done for us:

```
Imports System.ComponentModel
Imports System.Web.UI
```

These first two lines import some namespaces that will be of value to us as we develop our custom web control:

❑ System.ComponentModel – contains classes for implementing and licensing components, including the MemberAttribute class that allows us to describe properties of our class like the default property and the how our class should appear in the design environment. While it is possible to write a custom web control that doesn't draw on this namespace, it would seriously hamper its use in development environments like Visual Studio.

❑ System.Web.UI – contains the ASP.NET classes, including the state management classes, enumerations for attributes, styles, tags, output caching, and persistence, and the text writer classes that we'll be using to write our control's output to the response stream.

Common Toolbox Attributes

The next line declares our class and defines some attributes that tell the design environment how to represent our control:

```
<DefaultProperty("Text"), _
 ToolboxData( _
 "<{0}:SubClassedControl runat=server></{0}:SubClassedControl>")> _
Public Class SubClassedControl
```

Let's review these attributes:

❑   `DefaultProperty` – tells the design environment which property to highlight in the property window when a control based on our class is selected.

This shouldn't be confused with the meaning of a default class property from VB6!

In VB6 we could go through an arcane process to identify the default property of a class. This would then become the property that we would access if we typed the name of an instance of our class without any additional qualifiers. For example if the default property of `MyClass` *in VB6 was the* `Text` *property, then, typing:*

```
Dim myInstance as New MyClass
myInstance = "Hello world!"
```

was equivalent to typing:

```
Dim myInstance as New MyClass
myInstance.Text = "Hello world!"
```

This no longer works in Visual Basic.NET.

The `DefaultProperty` *attribute referred to here is intended for an entirely different purpose. It is meant as an instruction to the design environment, not the compiler!*

❑   `ToolboxData` – this attribute gives the design environment a template for inserting the element tags of our control when it is added to an ASP.NET page from the toolbox. If we are writing a control that is intended as an empty tag – like the <br> or <img> tags – then we would change this attribute to something like `ToolboxData("<{0}:SubClassedControl runat=server/>")>`.

Changing the `ToolboxData` *attribute to insert a self-closing tag does not change the output that is rendered for the client. If you need to override your control's closing tag characteristics, you should create a new control builder class for your control. For more information see* Professional ASP.NET *(Wrox Press, ISBN 1861004885) or the* Control Builder Overview *topic in the* .NET Framework Developer's Guide.

Following our class declaration is the instruction to inherit from the base class `WebControl`:

```
Inherits System.Web.UI.WebControls.WebControl
```

This one line gives us access to all of the properties, methods, and events that will facilitate the creation of the UI for our control, and it provides all of the plumbing necessary for the control to be hosted by an ASP.NET page.

Next comes a block of code to define a custom property for our control, its attributes, and the internal variable to store the property value in. It could just as easily have been called the `Message` property, but `Text` is more consistent with the naming conventions for control properties.

```
Dim _text As String

<Bindable(True), Category("Appearance"), DefaultValue("")> _
Property [Text]() As String
   Get
      Return _text
   End Get

   Set
      _text = Value
   End Set
End Property
```

> **The naming convention that Microsoft is using in .NET for internal variables that map to a property is `_propertyname` where `propertyname` is the lowercase version of the property name (e.g. `_caption` for the `Caption` property). We'll use this convention for the rest of the chapter.**

The first portions of the property declaration are again attributes (or Meta Data) to help with the proper use of our control:

❑　`Bindable` – the `Bindable` property is used by the compiler to determine whether or not this property can participate in data binding.

❑　`Category` – the `Category` property is intended for the design environment and tells it how to group the property in the Properties window.

❑　`DefaultValue` – the `DefaultValue` property is Meta Data that identifies what the default value of the property is supposed to be. It is typically used by the design environment to identify when the value of the property has been changed.

> **`DefaultValue` does *not* set the value of the property! It only describes what that value should be.**

Naming Class Members with Reserved Words

Note the square brackets around the `[Text]` property name. Remember that we mentioned earlier that this allows us to use keywords and reserved words as property, method, or event names. However, when we refer to these members in code, they must be wrapped in square brackets (which you can see in the `Render` method). This is to remove any ambiguity as to whether we are referring to the keyword or to our custom member. The only exception to this is when the name is preceded by an object reference. When that happens the reference is fully qualified and the square brackets are no longer necessary to distinguish the custom member from the identically named keyword or reserved word.

The Render Method

The interesting part is what happens when we override the `Render` method. The hosting container calls the `Render` method of our control when it is ready to insert our control into the **output stream**. The output stream is a buffer for holding the characters that will form our HTML response to the client browser. The page passes the `Render` method an `HtmlTextWriter` object in its `output` argument, which we use as the mechanism for writing to the output buffer (we'll come back to the `HtmlTextWriter` class in a moment).

Generally, you'll end up overriding one or more of the base class's rendering methods (`Render`, `RenderBeginTag`, `RenderContents`, `RenderChildren`, or `RenderEndTag`) in most of the sub-classed controls that you create. Overriding the control's rendering methods gives us the opportunity to create our own custom content; otherwise we'd end up with the base control's rendering of the control. In the template, the version of the `Render` method supplied overrides the base `Render` method to write literal text output. By doing so it prevents the `WebControl` from rendering the tags that it normally produces, and prevents any of the attributes that would normally be added to that tag from being rendered as well:

```
Protected Overrides Sub Render( _
    ByVal output As System.Web.UI.HtmlTextWriter)
  output.Write([Text])
End Sub
```

So now we have a control that writes its `Text` property directly to the output stream without adornment or modification.

> **This is not a recommended practice!** Although you'll frequently see examples and demos that write directly to the output stream like this, it is a gross simplification! In real-world code development, you should only use this technique for outputting literal text; for any other output, especially outputting beginning and ending tags, use the specialized writing and rendering methods of the **HtmlTextWriter** class.

The point above can't be stressed enough. Writing a control where all of the output is done through the `HtmlTextWriter.Write()` method will either prevent or seriously hamper your control from enjoying the benefits of the ASP.NET framework. Specifically:

❑ The control would require its own attribute writing and style handling logic.

❑ It would require its own client-side naming and namespace handling conventions.

❑ It could introduce non-standard behavior when working with other controls or ASP.NET pages.

❑ It could even prevent the control from being properly rendered in browsers that support upcoming versions of the HTML standard.

The temptation always exists to resort to using `HtmlTextWriter.Write` when outputting a simple set of tags or text. After all, if all you want to do is write a simple <br> or <hr> tag, it's easier to type in:

```
output.Write("<br>")
```

than it is to type in:

```
output.RenderBeginTag(HtmlTextWriterTag.Hr)
output.RenderEndTag()
```

It's a false economy, though. Aside from the fact that the utility methods of `HtmlTextWriter` can take care of so much of the coding, if you use them you can count on having controls that will render correctly in browsers that are compliant with new HTML standards.

ASP.NET Delivers Different Code for Different Standards

So how does ASP.NET do it? We've already seen in the previous chapter that ASP.NET server controls change how they are rendered based on the version of HTML supported by the client's browser. The `Page` class manages this automatic process with assistance from classes that derive from `HtmlTextWriter`. When a request comes in from a client, the ASP.NET page determines the type of browser that the client has and uses that to decide which type of `HtmlTextWriter` object to create. Currently, if the client is considered to be **downlevel**, then the page creates an `Html32TextWriter` object to render HTML 3.2 compliant markup. Otherwise, it creates an `HtmlTextWriter` object that will render HTML 4.01 compliant output.

So, as browsers come out with support for new standards, Microsoft (or third party vendors) will supply new HTML text writers that override the utility methods and shared constants of the `HtmlTextWriter` base class to comply with those standards. Once the `Page` class has been updated to be aware of new sub-classes of `HtmlTextWriter`, a control created with the utility methods will, in most cases, automatically render output that is compliant with the new standard!

For more information on the W3C guidelines for HTML to XHTML compatibility, check out http://www.w3.org/TR/xhtml1/#guidelines. For information on the HTML 4.01 recommendations for use of the OBJECT element as a replacement for the APPLET, IMG, and IFRAME elements, see http://www.w3.org/TR/html401/struct/objects.html.

The Rendering Methods Subset

When we look at examples illustrating custom web control development, frequently the only output method of a control that gets customized is the `Render` method. While this technique works for keeping demonstrations simple, it can leave something to be desired when we want to start developing professional quality controls. To create a sub-classed control that takes better advantage of the controls in the `WebControls` namespace, we need to examine the subset of rendering methods that the base class provides.

The web control architecture is designed to allow fine-grained control of how we want to inherit rendering behavior; it's designed so that we can choose exactly the parts of the rendering process that we want to customize. The way that the web control architecture works is that the base `WebControl` class (and all of the controls derived from it) provides five separate methods that correspond to the various stages of control rendering. In order of execution they are:

❑ `RenderBeginTag` – responsible for outputting the opening character of the tag and the tag name, this method also calls `AddAttributesToRender`. It uses the read-only `TagName` property of the control to determine which tag to output and uses it in a call to the `HtmlTextWriter`'s `RenderBeginTag` method.

❑ AddAttributesToRender – this method adds the identification, style, and standard tag attributes to the HtmlTextWriter's internal attribute collections by repeatedly calling the HtmlTextWriter's AddAttribute and AddStyleAttribute methods. Note that none of the AddAttributesToRender, AddAttribute, or AddStyleAttribute methods actually produces output; instead they prepare the attributes for later rendering, by the HtmlTextWriter.RenderBeginTag method, by adding items to the HtmlTextWriter's internal collections.

❑ RenderContents – produces the content after the beginning tag and before the ending tag. If the tag contains nested server controls then this method will instead call the RenderChildren method and let it handle creating the inner content. It will not call RenderChildren if the tag does not support nested controls (for example, controls like the Image control).

❑ RenderChildren – handles creating the child control content, by cycling through this control's Controls collection and calling each Render method of each child control in the collection.

❑ RenderEndTag – outputs the closing tag if necessary through a call to the HtmlTextWriter.RenderEndTag method. Typically, whether the control requires a closing tag or not is determined by the HtmlTextWriter and the control builder class associated with the control. Whether your control requires a closing tag or not, it should either implement the RenderEndTag behavior or inherit it from its base class.

> The control's rendering methods are only responsible for invoking the associated methods of the **HtmlTextWriter** object. In all of the control's rendering methods, it is only the **HtmlTextWriter** object that actually adds to the output stream.

All of the methods in the rendering subset take the HtmlTextWriter instance for the control as their only argument. With the exception of RenderChildren, they each make use of public constants from the HtmlTextWriter class to determine how their tag is written (that is, HtmlTextWriter.TagLeftChar for the opening chevron of the opening and closing tags, HtmlTextWriter.SelfClosingTagEnd for the forward slash and closing chevron of a self-closing element, etc.).

As for the Render method itself, it acts as a wrapper for the other five methods. Its main purpose is typically not to produce the control's output but, instead, to invoke the RenderBeginTag, RenderContents, and RenderEndTag methods (with RenderBeginTag and RenderContents calling AddAttributesToRender and RenderChildren in turn).

Developing Sub-Classed Controls from System.Web.UI.WebControl (An Example)

We've been working with the Web Custom Control template so far but, now that we've examined the rendering methods in greater detail, why don't we redevelop the template to take advantage of them?

By overriding the Render method directly and not invoking the rest of the web control rendering method subset members, or calling the HtmlTextWriter's rendering methods directly, the template creates a literal text control (for example, the Text property without any surrounding tags). If we want to create a label control, we need to modify the template's code to have it create tags and attributes, as well as output the contents of the Text property. The best way to do this is to override the RenderContents method and move the output write statement there. So remove the Render method override from the SubClassedControl class and replace it with the following:

```
Protected Overrides Sub RenderContents( _
       ByVal writer As System.Web.UI.HtmlTextWriter)
   writer.Write([Text])
End Sub
```

For some reason, Beta 2 uses the argument name **output** for the **HtmlTextWriter** argument for the **Render** method supplied in the web custom control template, even though the rendering methods use the name **writer** for the same argument.

With this one change, we go from a literal text control to a control that outputs a complete tag – including support for the full set of tag and style attributes! To see which tag we get from the default WebControl implementation, let's add a host page to our project and check out the results.

Creating a Hosting Page

Right-click on the CH21 project and select Add | Add Web Form from the context menu. Call the new web form SubClassingAControl.aspx. Then right-click on SubClassingAControl.aspx in the Solution Explorer and select Set As Start Page.

To keep from adding a whole bunch of positioning attributes to our control when we add it to the design surface, right-click on the design surface and select Properties. Now change the page layout property to FlowLayout.

Now we're ready to add our control.

Adding a Custom Web Control to the Toolbox

Our control's class declaration includes Meta Data that tells the Toolbox how to write the control's element tags to the page. It would be nice to see that in action so let's add our control to the Toolbox.

We can only add compiled components to the Toolbox, so we need to build CH21Controls into a DLL before we can add the SubClassedControl. Right-click on the CH21Controls project and select Build.

In the Toolbox, select the tab that you want to display the control on. Since it should still be relatively uncluttered, let's choose the General tab. Right-click anywhere on the General tab's surface and pick Customize Toolbox from the context menu.

In the Customize Toolbox dialog box, select the .NET Framework Components tab. Click on the Browse button and locate CH21Controls.dll in the CH21Controls\Bin folder. Check its box, then press OK:

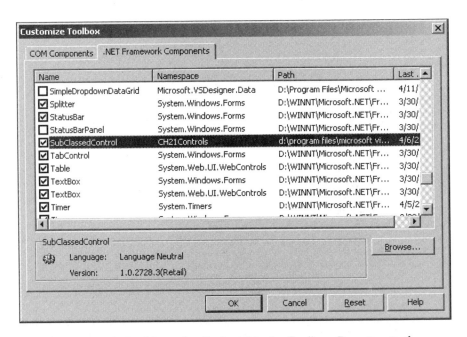

The `SubClassedControl` should now be displayed in the Toolbox. Drag it onto the `SubClassingAControl.aspx` page. The control should now appear on the page, looking as though we have added an empty literal text server control:

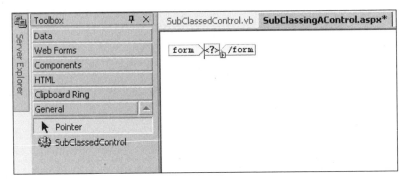

It is useful to keep the Show details for non-visible elements setting turned on so that you can be sure that your server controls are within the form tags. If you want to turn this setting on or off in your copy of Visual Studio, you can find it under the Display settings in the HTML Designer folder, reached via Tools | Options.

Let's switch to the HTML view mode and we'll take a look at the code that the Toolbox has added for us. You should find a set of element tags like the following in the body of the page:

```
<form id="Form1" method="post" runat="server">
  <cc1:SubClassedControl id=SubClassedControl1 runat="server">
  </cc1:SubClassedControl>
</form>
```

The element tag is based on the template provided in the `ToolboxData` attribute for the class. It looks essentially the same as the template except that Visual Studio has substituted a tag prefix for the `{0}` placeholder and has assigned a unique ID to the element.

Of course, if you dragged the control onto the page and the page is set up for grid layout, you'll also have a bunch of positioning attributes.

> The **Toolbox** does not get updated with the latest value of your control's `ToolboxData` attribute when you rebuild your solution. If you change the `ToolboxData` attribute between builds, you'll need to remove the control from the **Toolbox** and then re-add it before you'll see your changes.

Custom Controls and the @ Register Directive

Just below the @ `Page` directive at the top of the file, you'll also find an @ `Register` directive like the following:

```
<%@ Register TagPrefix="cc1" Namespace="CH21Controls"
        Assembly="CH21Controls" %>
```

This version of the @ `Register` directive is a little different from the one that we saw in the WUCs section. For one thing, it doesn't have an `src` attribute – it has an `Assembly` attribute instead. The `src` and `Assembly` attributes serve the same purpose, though, and that is to identify the location of the controls in the namespace to the compiler and to the design environment. In the case of a WUC, that location was a file but, in the case of our sub-classed control, the location is an assembly containing the compiled code for our control.

Earlier, we discussed why the compiler needs to know the location of our control, but why does the design environment need to know it? When we first open the page, Visual Studio puts us into a graphical design mode. Now, when we add a custom control to the page, Visual Studio wants to be able to provide a graphical representation of our control in the Design view. So, when we first enter Design view, Visual Studio actually instantiates our control and asks it to render itself – which is why the design environment also needs to know where to find our control!

The second reason that we need the @ `Register` directive is to define a tag prefix so that we can uniquely identify the controls that belong to any given namespace in an assembly. Visual Studio has picked a tag prefix for us, although it's not very informative. Let's use the tag prefix `ch21cwc`, which stands for Chapter 21 Custom Web Controls, instead.

We'll need to change it in two places. First, in the @ `Register` directive:

```
<%@ Register TagPrefix="ch21cwc" Namespace="CH21Controls" Assembly="CH21Controls"
%>
```

And also in the element tags:

```
<ch21cwc:subclassedcontrol id=SubClassedControl1 runat="server">
</ch21cwc:subclassedcontrol>
```

Don't forget to make the tag prefix change in both the opening *and* closing tags.

Specifying a Default TagPrefix for the Assembly

If you don't like the default tag prefix that the design environment provides, we can instruct it to use a default `TagPrefix` value. We can assign a default tag prefix for each namespace in our assembly through the use of the `TagPrefix` attribute. The `TagPrefix` attribute can be added to the `AssemblyInfo.vb` file and it uses the syntax:

```
<Assembly: System.Web.UI.TagPrefix("NamespaceName", "TagPrefix")>
```

So, in our case, we would add the following to the `AssemblyInfo.vb` file for the `CH21Controls` project:

```
<Assembly: System.Web.UI.TagPrefix("CH21Controls", "ch21cwc")>
```

> *If you don't want to have to fully qualify TagPrefix, you can add a statement to import System.Web.UI at the top of the AssemblyInfo.vb file.*

Save the file, close it, and compile the project. The next time that a control from `CH21Controls` is added to a new page from the **Toolbox**, it will also add an `@ Register` directive with its `TagPrefix` attribute set to `ch21cwc`!

Show Me!

All right, so we've written our control, we've put it on a hosting page, and now all that is left is to give it some text to display. In the opening tag of our control, add some content in the `Text` attribute (feel free to type in "Hello world" if you're a traditionalist!):

```
<ch21cwc:subclassedcontrol id=SubClassedControl1 runat="server"
 text="Sub-classed control with attribute text!">
</ch21cwc:subclassedcontrol>
```

Now start the application and see what we get in the browser! Your page should look very similar to this:

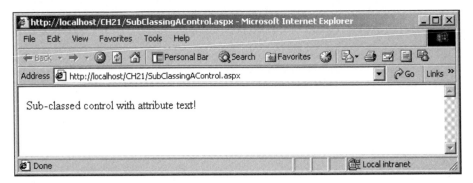

Now let's see what kind of tag the `WebControl` base class created for us. Right-click on the page and select **View Source**. You shouldn't need to look too far to find our control's output. When you do, it should look something like this:

```
<span id="SubClassedControl1">
 Sub-classed control with attribute text!
</span>
```

So <span> is the default tag name for the WebControl class, but what if we had wanted our control to use a <div> or an <h1> tag instead? If we were sub-classing from any other control, we would want to override the RenderBeginTag method and call the HtmlTextWriter's RenderBeginTag method with the appropriate tag name. Since we are inheriting directly from the WebControl class, we can take advantage of the extra constructors that WebControl has to offer.

The WebControl Constructors

WebControl offers two additional constructors over and above the basic constructor. They are:

❑ New(ByVal tag As HtmlTextWriterTag) – this constructor takes a member from the HtmlTextWriterTag enumeration and uses that value to initialize the read-only TagKey and TagName properties.

❑ New(ByVal tag As String) – this constructor takes in the tag name as a string and uses that value to initialize the read-only TagKey and TagName properties.

So, if we want to render a control that inherits directly from WebControl as any tag other than a <span>, we should override the default class constructor and supply the appropriate tag to the constructor of our base class. To have our control rendered as a <div>, we'll supply the following constructor:

```
Public Sub New()
 MyBase.New(HtmlTextWriterTag.Div)
End Sub
```

We call the base class's tag key constructor instead of its tag name constructor because using a tag key offers the greatest extensibility. Should our control be hosted in any other form of output stream, we can supply it with a customized HtmlTextWriter class that maps any unsupported tag keys to an equivalent tag name. With a tag name, what we supply is always what we'll get!

Start the application again and let's see if we get the results that we want. The screen output should look pretty much the same but, when we view the source, we should see that the control has now been output as a <div> element:

```
<div id="SubClassedControl1">
 Sub-classed control with attribute text!
</div>
```

So far, so good! Earlier, when we set the display text for our new control, we used the text attribute to pass in the value to our control. Take a moment and change the control tags so that the text is now nested between them instead:

```
<ch21cwc:subclassedcontrol id=SubClassedControl1 runat="server">
 Sub-classed control with nested text!
</ch21cwc:subclassedcontrol>
```

Now try running the application. You should get a parser error:

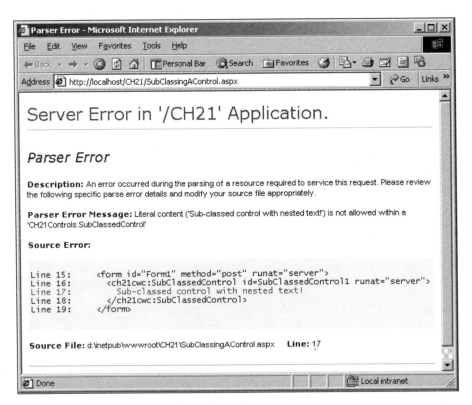

This is because Microsoft has disallowed nesting in the base `WebControl` class by default. It seems to be a bit of an odd choice, considering that most people who are familiar with HTML will expect to be able to nest content within our tags, rather than specifying content through attributes. Since we'd probably like to give them the choice to use either technique, let's see how we can change the default behavior of our control in this regard.

Allowing/Disallowing Nested Controls

If we want to allow controls or literal text to be nested within our control, there is an attribute that can be added to the class declaration. The attribute that we want is the `ParseChildren` attribute. If we add it to the class declaration like so:

```
<DefaultProperty("Text"), _
  ToolboxData( _
   "<{0}:SubClassedControl runat=server></{0}:SubClassedControl>"), _
  ParseChildren(False)> _
Public Class SubClassedControl
```

we are telling the compiler to add the attribute to the Meta Data for the class so that the page parser can determine at runtime whether the control is allowed to have nested (child) controls or not. Now, by default the `WebControl` class has its `ParseChildren` attribute set to `True`, which means it does not allow nested elements unless they correspond to properties of the control (typically this setting would be used in a databound control like the `Repeater` control).

> If you are using Beta 2, it is a good idea to specify the `ParseChildren` attribute on all of your custom controls, even if you are using the same setting as the `WebControl` class. That way, if the base class attribute is modified for the release version, your control will not behave unpredictably.

By setting it to `False` in our class, we are instructing the parser to convert any nested text into `LiteralText` controls, to instantiate any nested server controls, and to add everything to a collection of child controls for our control. After that, it is up to us as control developers to determine whether to render some, none, or all of the child controls in the collection.

> Any nested tags that are not marked with the `runat="server"` attribute will be treated as literal text and will not be instantiated as HTML server controls. In other words, the elements will still be output on the client-side, but we won't have access to them in server-side script.

For more information, including additional parameter variations, see the Using ParseChildren Attribute *topic of the* .NET Framework Developer's Guide.

Special Cases in Rendering Content

So now, by adding the `ParseChildren(False)` attribute to our class definition, nested content will no longer cause a parser error. Since we've overridden the method in the base control that would call the `RenderChildren` method, we still need to add code to our method to *actually* render that content! We need to go back to the `RenderContents` method and make use of some of the collections and state properties that we have inherited from the `System.Web.UI.Control` class.

The `Control` class, which `WebControl` inherits from, includes a collection to contain child controls, as well as two properties that indicate special states for that collection. The collection is (not surprisingly) called `Controls` and the two properties are `HasControls` and `IsLiteralContent`. The purpose of the `Controls` collection has already been discussed above, so we'll just take a look at the two properties here. `HasControls` and `IsLiteralContent` are essentially shortcuts that avoid the overhead associated with having to call upon the `Controls` collection directly. `HasControls` indicates whether we have any nested controls and it is equivalent to:

```
Controls.Count > 0
```

`IsLiteralContent` checks for the special case where we have nested content, but where none of that content defines server controls. In other words, we have either plain text or client-side HTML (which server-side code treats as though it were literal text) between the beginning and ending tags of our control. To give us access to the content on the server-side, ASP.NET stores it all in a single `LiteralControl` and adds that control to our `Controls` collection. So `IsLiteralControl` is shorthand for:

```
Controls.Count = 1 And TypeOf Controls(0) Is LiteralControl
```

It's more efficient to call `HasControls` *and* `IsLiteralContent` *because they have already been evaluated during the parsing stage.*

So, to decide what to do with nested elements in our control, we'll add the following to our overridden RenderContents method:

```
Protected Overrides Sub RenderContents( _
        ByVal writer As System.Web.UI.HtmlTextWriter)
  If Not HasControls Then
   writer.Write([Text])
  ElseIf IsLiteralContent Then
   writer.Write(CType(Controls(0), LiteralControl).Text)
  Else
   MyBase.RenderChildren(writer)
  End If
End Sub
```

The conditional statements above first check to see if we have any nested content. If we don't then, as before, we output the value of the Text property. If we *do* have nested content, then we check for the special case where the content doesn't have any nested server controls and output the Text property of the LiteralText control directly. Finally, if we have more than one control in the collection or we have one control but it isn't a LiteralText control, then we call on the RenderChildren method of our base control to walk through our Controls collection and render each child control in turn.

> *In case you're wondering why we haven't chosen to output the Text attribute when we have nested content, it's because that is the way that the .NET server controls with a Text property generally behave.*

When the only nested content that we have is literal text or client-side HTML, it's good practice to expose that content on the server-side by setting the Text property equal to the nested content. So we'll go back to the Text property procedures and modify them to make them aware of the IsLiteralText special case:

```
<Bindable(True), Category("Appearance"), DefaultValue("")> _
Property [Text]() As String
  Get
    If IsLiteralContent Then
     Return CType(Controls(0), LiteralControl).Text
    Else
     Return _text
    End If
  End Get

  Set(ByVal Value As String)
    If IsLiteralContent Then
     CType(Controls(0), LiteralControl).Text() = Value
    Else
     _text = Value
    End If
  End Set
End Property
```

This way, if code in the hosting container retrieves or changes the Text property, they will get access to the text that will actually be displayed on the page.

Summary

In this chapter, we've taken a long look at the various forms of custom web control development that are available in the .NET Framework. We've seen how the web development process has been designed, from the ground up, to leverage existing skill sets and to take full advantage of the powerful new object-oriented features in Visual Basic.NET.

We've examined the basic structure of web user and sub-classed controls, and covered some best practices for control design. We also took a brief look at composite and templated controls.

Hopefully, this chapter will act as a good starting point for your exploration of the wealth of web control development options that .NET has to offer!

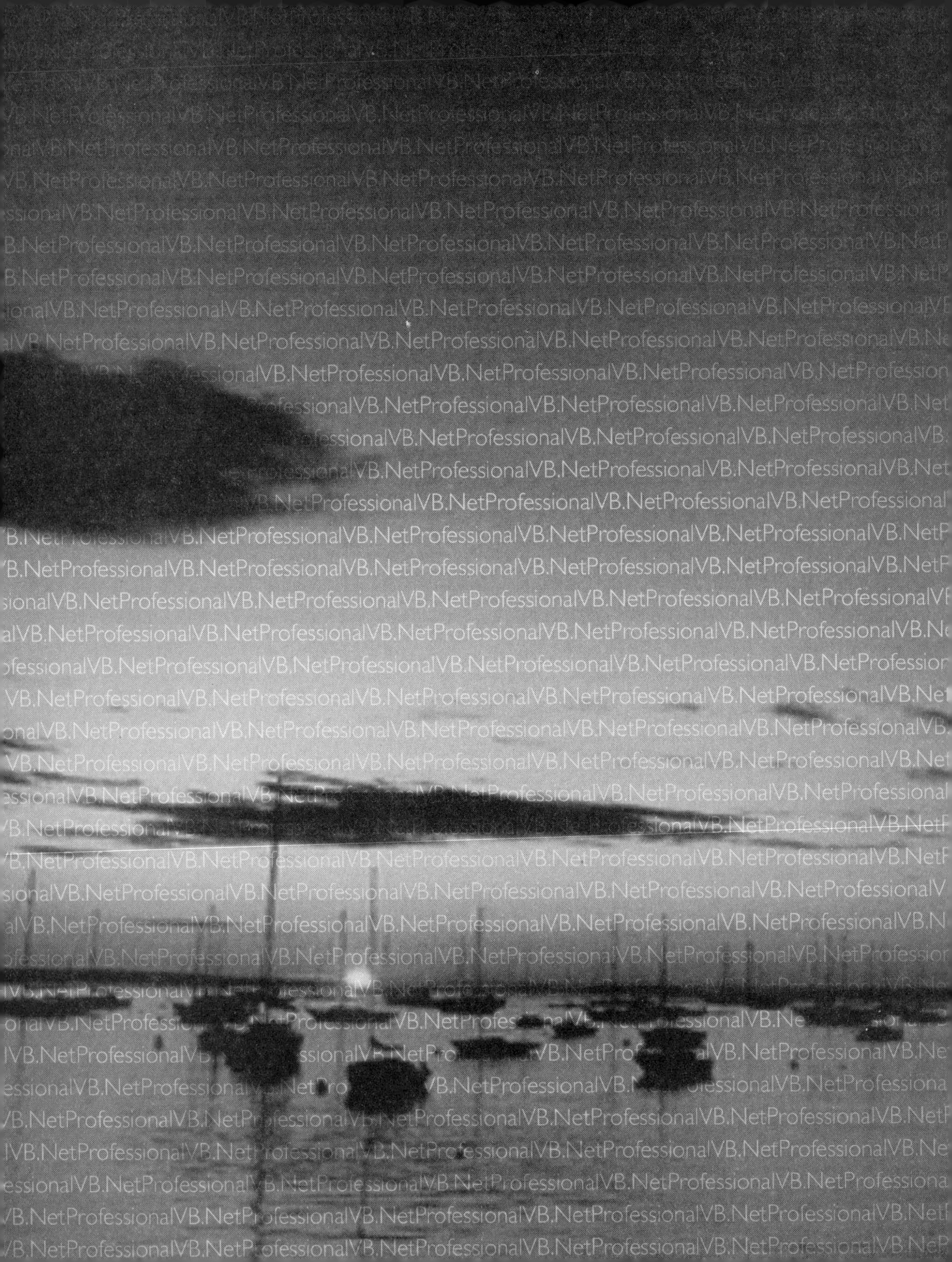
VB.NetProfessional

22

Web Services in VB.NET

In this chapter, we'll divert a bit from the structured Visual Basic discussion to dive into a short history of multi-tier architecture and network operating systems. We'll discuss the early days of the network-as-the-computer, and some of the future.

We'll then take a look at a sample Web Service, making it accessible to the Internet, and accessing it from a client application – both with the VS.NET IDE and using the command line tools. From there we'll move on to a key feature of Web Services – the **Service Repository**, **discovery**, and **UDDI** (**Universal Description, Discovery, and Integration**) – features which allow remote programmers to correctly access your service.

We'll get into more in-depth topics when we discuss the four namespaces found in the CLR (`System.Web.Services`, `System.Web.Description`, `System.Web.Services.Discovery`, and `System.Web.Services.Protocols`), and how to access them with Visual Basic.NET. Then we will move to a discussion of the serious topics, such as security, transactions, and the downsides of any distributed architecture (including Web Services). Finally, we'll wrap up with a short discussion of where we go from here, and how we get there.

Introduction to Web Services

A **Web Service** is a group of functions, packaged together for use in a common framework throughout a network. This is shown in the diagram below, where Web Services provide access to information through standard Internet Protocols via a WSDL contract – an XML description of the service. This simple concept provides for a very wide variety of potential uses by developers of Internet and Enterprise applications alike:

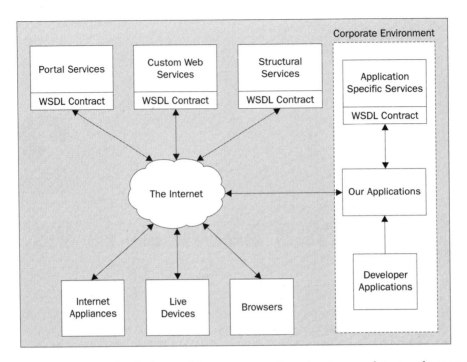

Web Services are going to be the heart of the next generation of systems architecture because they are:

❑ Architecture neutral. Web Services don't depend on a proprietary wire format, schema description, or discovery standard.

❑ Ubiquitous. Any service that supports the standards can support the service.

❑ Simple. Creating Web Services is easy, quick, and can be free. The data schema is human readable. Any language can participate.

❑ Interoperable. Since the Web Services all speak the same standards, they can all speak to one another.

Is a Web Service All Those Things?

In basic terms, a Web Service is an object with an XML document describing all of the methods, properties, and events sitting between the code and the caller. Any body of code written in just about any language can be described with this XML document, and then anything that speaks SOAP can access the object. That's because the parameters you'd type after the function name are passed via XML to the Web Service.

Microsoft has put a wrapper around all of the XML schemas that support Web Services (including Simple Object Access Protocol and Web Services Description Language) so that they look like .NET or COM objects. We'll talk about how the world views a Web Service, then how Microsoft views Web Services.

Early Architectural Designs

It is important to know the past, since it points the way to the future. An understanding of the history of the search for a decent **remote method invocation** (**RMI**) protocol is imperative to our understanding of why Web Services are so important. Each of the RMI systems created before Web Services solved a particular set of problems, and we will see how Web Services crosses platform boundaries to solve them all.

The Network Angle

Throughout the history of computing, the networking operations were largely handled by the operating system. UNIX, the networking host of early computing, featured a body of shell operations that gave remarkable user control over the operations of the network. Personal computing was slower to catch up, with the popular Microsoft and Apple software not supporting networking protocols inherently until the mid-90s. Third party add-ons by Novell and Banyan were available earlier, but still were only adjunct to the operating system. The concept of the network being the computer did not infiltrate the development community until the explosion of the World Wide Web.

Application Development

Let's break from networking for a minute and look at how application development progressed through this time. Early Time Sharing Operation systems allowed several people to use the same application with its built-in data. These single tier systems didn't allow for growth in the system size, and data redundancy became the standard, with nightly batch jobs synchronizing the data becoming a standard through the 70s and early 80s.

Eventually, the opportunity presented by networks became the overriding factor in systems development, and enterprise network developers began offering the loosely termed **Object Request Brokers** (**ORBs**) on their systems: Microsoft's MTS, **CORBA** (**Common Object Request Broker Architecture**), and the like. These ORBs allowed for the separation of the user interface from the business logic using tightly coupled method pooling. This three-tier architecture brings us to the present in development terms, so let's step back for a second and let networking catch up.

Merging the Two with the Web

In a now famous meeting in August of 1990 at CERN, Tim Berners-Lee and Robert Cailliau presented a paper suggesting an implementation of SGML they thought would be useful for "document registration, online help, and project documentation." The HTTP protocol was born. There had been several other information delivery protocols before, like Gopher; what made HTTP different was the extensibility of the related language, HTML, and the flexibility of the transport layer, TCP/IP. Suddenly movement of many formats of data was possible in a stateless, distributed way. Software-as-a-service was on its way.

Meanwhile, the PC world was stretching its network wings. Low-level protocols supported by network systems and the Internet became a staple in applications, with SMTP and FTP providing file and information transfer among distributed servers. **Remote procedure calls** (**RPC**) took things to the next level, but were platform specific, with UNIX implementations in CORBA and Microsoft's **Distributed COM** (**DCOM**) leading the pack. Slowly, the Internet and PC merged, and slick examples of the mix between software-as-a-service and RPC make it difficult to figure who is sending what to where, either via PCs or the Internet.

Enterprise development took a clue from the emerging technologies in WAN networking and personal computing, and development for these large-scale business systems began to mature. As usage of networks grew, developers began to solve problems like scalability, reliability, and adaptability, with the traditional flat-format programming model. Multi-tier development began to spread the data, processing, and user interface of applications over several machines connected by local area networks. This made applications more scalable and reliable by allowing for growth and providing redundancy. Gradually, vendor compliance and the Java programming language provided adaptability, allowing the applications to run in a variety of circumstances on a variety of platforms.

As fast as things are moving ahead, however, there was a dichotomy between the capabilities of the network and the features of the programming environment. Specifically, after the introduction of XML there still existed no "killer app" using its power. XML is a subset of Standard Generalized Markup Language (SGML), an international standard that describes the relationship between a document's content and its structure. It allows developers to create their own tags for hierarchical data transport in an HTML-like format. With HTTP as a transport and SOAP as a protocol, there still needed to be an interoperable, ubiquitous, simple, broadly supported system for the execution of business logic throughout the world of Internet Application development.

The Foundations of Web Services

The hunt began with a look at existing protocols. As has been the case for years, the Microsoft versus Sun Alliance debate was heating up among RPC programmers. CORBA versus DCOM was, is, and continues to be, a source of continuing argument for developers using those platforms for distributed object development. After Sun added Remote Method Invocation to Java with Java-RMI, we had three distributed object protocols that fit none of the above requirements.

First, let's focus on DCOM and RMI, because they are manufacturer specific. CORBA is centrally managed by the Object Management Group, so it is a special case and should be considered separately.

RMI and DCOM do the same thing for different platforms. Both provide distributed object invocation for their respective platforms, extremely important in this era of distributed networks. Both allow for the enterprise-wide reuse of existing functionality, dramatically reducing cost and time-to-market. Both provide encapsulated object methodology, preventing changes to one set of business logic from affecting another. Finally, similarly to ORB-managed objects, maintenance and client weight are reduced by the simple fact that applications using distributed objects are by nature multitier.

DCOM

DCOM's best feature is the fact that it is based on COM – surely the most prevalent desktop object model in use today. COM components are shielded from one another, and calls between them are so well-defined by the OS specific languages that there is practically no overhead to the methods. Each COM object is instantiated in its own space, with the necessary security and protocol providers. If an object in one process needs to call an object in another process, COM handles the exchange by intercepting the call and forwarding it through one of the network protocols.

When you use DCOM, all you are doing is making the wire a bit longer. In NT4.0 Microsoft added the TCP/IP protocol to the COM network architecture and essentially made DCOM Internet savvy. Aside from the setup on the client and server, the inter-object calls are transparent to the client, and even to the programmer.

Any Microsoft programmer can tell you, though, that DCOM has its problems. First, there is a customer wire transport function, so most firewalls will not allow DCOM calls to get through – even though they are by nature quite benign. There is no way to query DCOM as to the methods and properties available unless you have the opportunity to get the sourcecode or request the remote component locally. And there is no standard data transfer protocol – though that is less of a problem since DCOM is mostly for Microsoft networks.

Remote Method Invocation in Java

RMI is Sun's answer to DCOM. Java relies on a really neat but very proprietary protocol called Java Object Serialization, which protects objects marshaled as a stream. The client and server both need to be constructed in Java for this to work, but it simplifies remote method invocation even more, as Java doesn't care if the serialization takes place on one machine or across 1500 miles. Similarly to DCOM, RMI allows the object developer to define an interface for remote access to certain methods.

CORBA

CORBA uses Internet Inter-ORB Protocol to provide remote method invocation. It is remarkably similar to Java Object Serialization in this regard. Since it is only a specification, though, it is supported by a number of languages on diverse operating systems. With CORBA, the ORB does all the work, such as finding the pointer to the parent, instantiating it so that it can receive remote requests, carrying messages back and forth, dispute arbitration and trash collection. The CORBA objects use specially designed sub-ORB objects balled Basic or Portable Object Adapters to communication with remote ORBs, allowing developers more leeway in code reuse.

At first blush, it seems CORBA is our ace in the whole. Only one problem – it doesn't really work that way. CORBA suffered from the same thing the Web Browsers do – poor implementations of the standards, causing lack of interoperability between Object Request Brokers. With IE and Netscape, a little differential in the way the pages display is written off as cosmetic, or worst case you have to rewrite some code for the two browsers. If there is a problem with the CORBA standard though, it is a *real* problem. Not just looks are affected, but network interactions too, as if there were 15 different implementations of HTTP.

The Problems

The principal problem of the DCOM/CORBA/RMI methods is the complexity of the implementation. The transfer protocol of each of these is based on manufacturer standards, generally preventing interoperability. In essence, the left hand has to know what the right hand is doing. This prevents a company using DCOM from communicating with a company using CORBA, emphasizing platform as a reason for doing business with one another.

First, we have the problem of wire format. Each of these three methods use an OS-specific wire format that encompasses information only supplied by the operating system in question. The problem with this is that two diverse machines cannot usually share information. The benefit is security. Since the client and server can make assumptions about the availability of functionality, data security can be managed with API calls to the operating system

Second is the number of issues concerned with describing the format of the protocol. Aside from the actual transport layer we have to have a schema or layout for the data that moves back-and-forth. Each of the three contemporary protocols makes great assumptions between the client and server. DCOM, for instance, provides ADO/RDS for data transport, where RMI has JDBC. While we can endlessly argue the benefits of one over the other, we'll agree on the fact that they don't play well together.

Third is the problem of knowing where to find broadly available services, even within your own network. We've all faced the problem of having to call up the COM+ MMC panel so we could remember how to spell this component or that method. When the method is resident on a server ten buildings leave and we don't have access to the MMC console, the next step is digging through the text documentation – if there is any.

The Other Players

On a path to providing these services we stumble across a few other technologies. While **Java Applets** and Microsoft's **client-side ActiveX** aren't technically distributed object invocation, they do provide distributed computing and provide important lessons. Fortunately, we can describe both in the same section since they are largely the same, with different operating systems as their backbone.

Applets and client-side ActiveX are both attempts to use the HTTP protocol to send thick clients to the end user. In a circumstance where a user can provide a platform previously prepared to maintain a thicker-than-HTML client base to a precompiled binary, the ActiveX and Applet protocols pass small applications to the end user, usually running a web browser. These applications are still managed by their servers, at least loosely, and usually provide custom data transmission, utilizing the power of the client to manage the information distributed, as well as display it.

This concept was taken to the extreme with **Distributed Applet-based Massively Parallel Processing**, a strategy that used the power of the Internet to complete processor-intense tasks like 3D rendering or massive economic models with a small application installed on the user's computer. If you view the Internet as a massive collection of parallel processors – sitting mostly unused – you have the right idea. An example of this type of processing is the Search for ExtraTerrestrial Intelligence at Home (SETI) project.

What we learned here is that HTTP can provide distributed computing. The problem we discovered is that the tightly coupled connection between the client and server had to go, given the nature of today's large enterprises. The HTTP angle did show developers that using an industry recognized transport did solve problem number one of the Distributed Object Invocation crowd – wire format. Using HTTP meant that no matter what the network, the object could communicate. The client still had to know a lot about the service being sent, but the network didn't.

The goal is "Distributed Object Invocation Meets The World Wide Web". The problems that face us are wire format, protocol, and discovery. The solution, a standards-based, loosely-coupled method invocation protocol with a *big* catalog. Microsoft, IBM, and Ariba set out in 1999 to create just that, and generated the Request For Comments for Web Services.

What All the Foundations Missed

You may notice that in showing the majority of the above services we have not mentioned much about language – because it was a problem overlooked by the foundations. Even RMI didn't see reality – you can't make everyone use the same language, even if it is a great language. No matter how it is sliced, what the cutting board is made of or what knife you use, different languages are better for different things.

HTTP – A Language Independent Protocol

What we *really* need is a language independent protocol that allows for a standard wire transfer, protocol language, and catalog service. Java and Remote Scripting and ActiveX taught us that HTTP is the wire transfer of choice.

Why is this? What does HTTP do that is so great? First, it is simple. The header added to a communication by HTTP is straightforward enough that a power user could type it at a command prompt if he had to. Second, it doesn't require a special data protocol – it just uses ASCII text. Finally, it is extensible. Additional headers can be added to the HTTP header for application specific needs, and intermediary software just ignores it.

XML – Cross-Language Data Markup

Now that we have the standard wire transfer protocol that we know works, we need a language and a transport mechanism. Existing languages don't really have data description functions, aside from the data management object models like ADO. XML fits the bill because it is self-describing. There's no need for the left hand to know what the right hand is doing. An XML file transported over HTTP doesn't need to know the answering system's network protocol or its data description language. The concepts behind XML are so light and open; everyone can agree to support them. In fact, almost everyone has. XML has become the ASCII of the Web, with nods to Tim Bray.

XML is important to Web Services because it provides a universal format for information to be passed from system to system. We knew that, but Web Services actually uses XML as the object invocation layer, changing the input and output to tightly formatted XML so as to be platform and language independent.

SOAP – The Transfer We Need

Enter **Simple Object Access Protocol** (**SOAP**), which uses HTTP to package essentially one-way messages from service to service in such a way that business logic can interpolate a request/response pair. In order for your web page to get the above listing, for instance, a SOAP request would look something like this:

```
POST /Directory HTTP/1.1
Host: Ldap.companyname.com
Content-Type: text/xml;
charset="utf-8"
Content-Length: 33
SOAPAction: "Some-URI"

<SOAP-ENV:Envelope
 xmlns:SOAP-ENV="http://schemas.xmlsoap.org/soap/envelope/"
 SOAP-ENV:encodingStyle="http://schemas.xmlsoap.org/soap/encoding/">
  <SOAP-ENV:Body>
    <m:FindPerson xmlns:m="Some-URI">
      <NAME>sempf</NAME>
    </m: FindPerson>
  </SOAP-ENV:Body>
</SOAP-ENV:Envelope>
```

This is an HTTP page request, just like you'd see for an HTML page except the Content-Type specifies XML and there is the addition of the SOAPAction header. SOAP has made use of the two most powerful parts of HTTP – content neutrality and extensibility. Here is the response statement from the server:

```
HTTP/1.1 200 OK
Content-Type: text/xml;
charset="utf-8"
Content-Length: 66

<SOAP-ENV:Envelope
 xmlns:SOAP-ENV="http://schemas.xmlsoap.org/soap/envelope/"
```

```
       SOAP-ENV:encodingStyle="http://schemas.xmlsoap.org/soap/encoding/"/>
        <SOAP-ENV:Body>
          <m:FindPersonResponse xmlns:m="Some-URI">
            <DIRECTORY>Employees
            <PERSON>
                <NAME>Bill Sempf</NAME>
                <FUNCTION>Architect
                    <TYPE>Web Services</TYPE>
                </FUNCTION>
                <CONTACT>
                    <PHONE TYPE=CELL>123-456-7890</PHONE>
                    <PHONE TYPE=HOME>555-111-2222</PHONE>
                </CONTACT>
            </PERSON>
            </DIRECTORY>
          </m: FindPersonResponse >
        </SOAP-ENV:Body>
      </SOAP-ENV:Envelope>
```

SOAP allows us to send the XML files back-and-forth among remote methods. It is tightly similar to XML-RPC, a protocol developed by Dave Winer in parallel with the SOAP protocol. Both protocols provide similar structures, but it is the official SOAP protocol that is used by VB.NET.

SOAP isn't specific to VB.NET, either. The **SOAP Toolkit** is a set of tools that Microsoft's Web Services Team provides free of charge. It contains a wonderful WSDL editor, retrofit objects for Windows 2000 and NT4 boxes, and more. You can find it at http://msdn.microsoft.com/webservices.

Web Services Description Language

A **Web Services Description Language** (**WSDL**) document is a set of definitions. Six elements are defined and used by the SOAP protocol: types, message, portType, binding, port, and service. Essentially adding another layer of abstraction, the purpose of WSDL is to isolate remote method invocations from their wire transport and data definition language. Once again, it is a specification, not a language, so it is much easier to get companies to agree to its use.

As WSDL is just a set of descriptions in XML, it has not so much a protocol as a grammar. Below you'll find the sample service contract for the UpdateRemote Web Service we'll be building later in the chapter. You will be able to see this file by surfing to http://localhost/WebService1/Service1.asmx?WSDL after you install the samples:

```
<?xml version="1.0" encoding="utf-8" ?>
<definitions xmlns:s="http://www.w3.org/2001/XMLSchema"
  xmlns:http="http://schemas.xmlsoap.org/wsdl/http/"
  xmlns:mime="http://schemas.xmlsoap.org/wsdl/mime/"
  xmlns:tm="http://microsoft.com/wsdl/mime/textMatching/"
  xmlns:soap="http://schemas.xmlsoap.org/wsdl/soap/"
  xmlns:soapenc="http://schemas.xmlsoap.org/soap/encoding/"
  xmlns:s0="http://Localhost/WebService1"
  targetNamespace="http://Localhost/WebService1"
  xmlns="http://schemas.xmlsoap.org/wsdl/">
<types>
 <s:schema attributeFormDefault="qualified" elementFormDefault="qualified"
    targetNamespace="http://Localhost/WebService1">
  <s:import namespace="http://www.w3.org/2001/XMLSchema" />
```

```xml
    <s:element name="AcceptUpdate">
     <s:complexType>
      <s:sequence>
       <s:element minOccurs="1" maxOccurs="1" name="dsDataSet" nillable="true">
        <s:complexType>
         <s:sequence>
        <s:element ref="s:schema" />
        <s:any />
       </s:sequence>
      </s:complexType>
     </s:element>
    </s:sequence>
   </s:complexType>
  </s:element>
  <s:element name="AcceptUpdateResponse">
   <s:complexType>
    <s:sequence>
     <s:element minOccurs="1" maxOccurs="1" name="AcceptUpdateResult"
       type="s:boolean" />
    </s:sequence>
   </s:complexType>
  </s:element>
</s:schema>
   </types>
<message name="AcceptUpdateSoapIn">
 <part name="parameters" element="s0:AcceptUpdate" />
</message>
<message name="AcceptUpdateSoapOut">
 <part name="parameters" element="s0:AcceptUpdateResponse" />
</message>
<portType name="Service1Soap">
 <operation name="AcceptUpdate">
  <input message="s0:AcceptUpdateSoapIn" />
  <output message="s0:AcceptUpdateSoapOut" />
 </operation>
</portType>
<portType name="Service1HttpGet" />
 <portType name="Service1HttpPost" />
  <binding name="Service1Soap" type="s0:Service1Soap">
   <soap:binding transport="http://schemas.xmlsoap.org/soap/http"
     style="document" />
   <operation name="AcceptUpdate">
   <soap:operation soapAction="http://Localhost/WebService1/AcceptUpdate"
     style="document" />
  <input>
   <soap:body use="literal" />
  </input>
  <output>
   <soap:body use="literal" />
  </output>
 </operation>
</binding>
<binding name="Service1HttpGet" type="s0:Service1HttpGet">
 <http:binding verb="GET" />
  </binding>
<binding name="Service1HttpPost" type="s0:Service1HttpPost">
```

```
    <http:binding verb="POST" />
  </binding>
  <service name="Service1">
   <port name="Service1Soap" binding="s0:Service1Soap">
    <soap:address location="http://localhost/WebService1/Service1.asmx" />
   </port>
   <port name="Service1HttpGet" binding="s0:Service1HttpGet">
    <http:address location="http://localhost/WebService1/Service1.asmx" />
   </port>
   <port name="Service1HttpPost" binding="s0:Service1HttpPost">
    <http:address location="http://localhost/WebService1/Service1.asmx" />
   </port>
  </service>
</definitions>
```

This is what makes it all work. You'll notice that each of the inputs and outputs of the
`AcceptUpdateResponse` function are defined as elements in the schema. .NET uses this to build library
files that understand how best to format the outgoing requests – so no matter what operating system develops
the WSDL, as long as it is well formed, a Windows application can consume it with SOAP and .NET.

In fact, IIS with the .NET framework is set up to use the WSDL to provide a great user interface for
developers and consumers to check out and test Web Services. If you remove the `?wsdl` from the above
URL you'll see a very nicely formatted documentation screen for the service. Click on the function
name and you'll get the screen shown below. This is all dynamically generated from the WSDL
document, which is dynamically generated from ASP.NET code. Abstraction makes it all work.

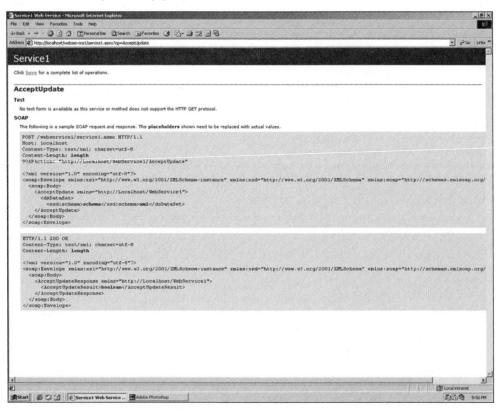

The benefit to knowing how WSDL works is being able to define your own descriptions. More documentation would be available on the listing of functions screen before this one, had we added it to the WSDL. Also, we could manually define HTTP Post and Get schemas – though it wouldn't do much good since the sole function of this particular service is to pass a Microsoft-specific DataSet.

Example Web Service

We'll take our first look at Web Services by creating a remote procedure call that updates MyCompany's web site from the data in the intranet. For the sake of example, we'll imagine that a third party provider hosts the site. Our SQL Server and the hosting company's SQL Server are behind firewalls, and the Internet Information Server is in a De-Militarized Zone – a safe though exposed network position.

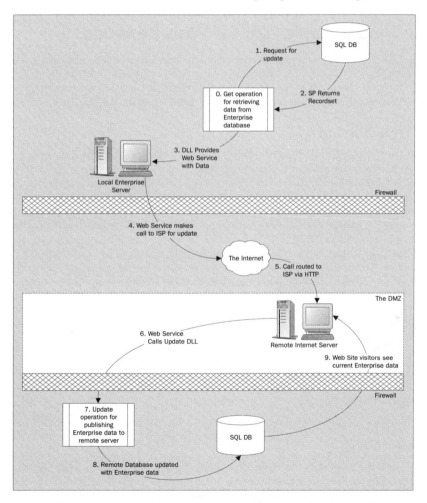

In order to get the data from our site to the remote site, we'll call a Web Service on the remote web server from our intranet. Since the SOAP envelope is sent via HTTP, our firewall will allow it through, and ADO.NET on the IIS box will handle the actual database manipulation. The remote firewall will allow database calls only from the IIS box, and our data will be updated safely through the security.

In real life, the class file UpdateRemote would be local to our intranet server, and the database file would be a SQL Server on a second PC. Across the Internet, as shown in the diagram, the Web Service would be on an IIS box sitting outside the network firewall. The DLL that actually provides the data functions would be on an application server inside the firewall and the database would again be on a separate machine.

For our application, though, we'll have two SQL Server databases (called ItemsLocal and ItemsRemote) on the same server. Both databases will have a single table, Items. This will have a few fields like ItemId, Description, and Quantity. Open the ItemsLocal file and add a few sample items.

Finally, you are going to have to have IIS installed on your development machine. Visual Studio will warn you on install if you don't, that you won't be able to make web applications. To install IIS on a Windows 2000 PC, reinsert your install CD and select the option to install Windows 2000 Add-ons. Internet services is one of the options.

Using the Visual Basic IDE for Web Services

The VB.NET IDE shows a marked improvement from the add-ins provided for Visual Studio 6 in the SOAP Toolkit. For instance, Web Services are shown as references on a project, rather than in a separate dialog. The discovery process, discussed later, is used to its fullest, providing much more information to the developer. In short, it is nearly as easy to consume a Web Service with VB.NET as it is to use DLLs.

Creating a New Service

When you launch VB.NET, you'll see the familiar New Project dialog. The fifth option is ASP.NET Web Service, which acts just like the New Web Project option in Visual InterDev 6.0. You're expected to enter a URL for the creation of the service – this can be the http://localhost/ drive on your development machine, or a remote server that supports .NET and Front Page Server Extensions. We'll use the localhost for this example.

After providing a URL, VB.NET creates five new files, including a blank .asmx file called Service1.asmx, a Global.asax file, a Web.config file, and a discovery file called WebService1.vsdisco. Quite a bit of the code you need has been pre-entered for you. For instance, the .disco file will be preset for dynamic discovery based on the known protected directories of your server:

```
<?xml version="1.0" encoding="utf-8" ?>
<dynamicDiscovery xmlns="urn:schemas-dynamicdiscovery:disco.2000-03-17">
<exclude path="_vti_cnf" />
<exclude path="_vti_pvt" />
<exclude path="_vti_log" />
<exclude path="_vti_script" />
<exclude path="_vti_txt" />
<exclude path="Web References" />
</dynamicDiscovery>
```

Make a DataSet

For simplicity we'll use the DataSet Designer feature of VS.NET. The DataSet Designer will allow us to quickly and easily create the data access we need, without having to dig through tons of ADO.NET code.

Right-click on the WebService1 project in the Solution Explorer and select Add | Add New Item. One of the options is a new DataSet – accept the default name of Dataset1.xsd. This creates a new DataSet schema on the fly, and it's already strongly typed for us.

In the Server Explorer window, right-click on **Data Connections** and select **Add Connection**. Make sure you select the **Microsoft OLE DB Provider for SQL Server** from the first tab, and your server's name and login information in the **Connection** tab. Select **ItemsRemote** as the database to which we want to connect and click on **OK**.

If not already open; double-click on the **Dataset1.xsd** file in the Solution Explorer. Then, go back to the Server Explorer, expand the data connection we just made and drag the `Items` table onto the designer surface of `Dataset1.xsd`. The layout of our table appears in the schema file, and we have access to the data we need. This database should be empty of data, since we didn't put anything in it, but we'll change that when we consume the service.

Build the Service

Click on the **View Code** button in the Solution Explorer to view the ASP.NET code behind `Service1.asmx`. Microsoft has thoughtfully provided us with some starter code, which we'll uncomment and use:

```
<WebMethod()> Public Function HelloWorld() As String
    HelloWorld = "Hello World"
End Function
```

We'll make a few changes to this sample. First, rename this function to `AcceptUpdate` and have it take a `DataSet` as a parameter. Add a namespace parameter so that our function can be distinguished from other services on the Web. Then we simply add code to merge the DataSet in the class file, which we just added, to the DataSet passed to the method. The block of IDE code in the `#Region` segment remains unchanged.

```
Imports System.Web.Services

<WebService(Namespace:="http://Localhost/WebService1")> _
Public Class Service1 : Inherits WebService

#Region " Web Services Designer Generated Code "

    Public Sub New()
        MyBase.New()

        InitializeComponent()

    End Sub

    Private components As System.ComponentModel.Container

    <System.Diagnostics.DebuggerStepThrough()> _
    Private Sub InitializeComponent()
        components = New System.ComponentModel.Container()
    End Sub

    Protected Overloads Overrides Sub Dispose(ByVal disposing As Boolean)
    End Sub

#End Region

    <WebMethod()> Public Function AcceptUpdate( _
            ByVal dsDataSet As DataSet) As Boolean
```

```
        Dim dsRemoteDataset As New Dataset1()
        dsRemoteDataset.Merge(dsDataSet)
        dsRemoteDataset.AcceptChanges()
        dsRemoteDataset = Nothing

    End Function

    End Class
```

Right-click on the Service1.asmx file in the Solution Explorer and select **Build and Browse**. If there are no errors, you'll see a simple screen listing `AcceptUpdate` as the sole method of the service. Click on **AcceptUpdate** and you'll get a screen like that earlier shown in the *WSDL* section of this chapter. No HTTP form is provided because our service doesn't support HTTP post or get. Complex objects are only served by SOAP.

Consuming the Service

For our consuming application, we will provide a class file called `UpdateRemote` – so create a new Class Library project and the class within it both with that name. For now, we'll have a single function called `sendData`. This time we'll code the DataSet by hand, since we need to use the `DataAdapter` to fill it with data from the local database.

Add a Web Reference

The only bit of magic here is the adding of a web reference with the VS.NET IDE. As we'll see below, we are really creating a proxy DLL with the WSDL file of the service and referencing it in the project, but the IDE makes it very easy.

Right-click on the **UpdateRemote** project in the Solution Explorer and select **Add Web Reference**. You'll see a simple form that advertises Microsoft UDDI services. Enter the URL of our service in the **Address** bar – this would be at the ISP in our real life scenario, but if you've been following along it'll be http://localhost/webservice1/service1.asmx:

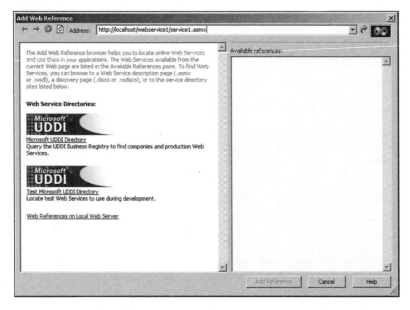

The service description page we've just seen when we built our service appears in the left-pane, with .NET specific information in the right. Click on the **Add Reference** button at the bottom of the window to add this to the project. The service appears in a new folder in the Solution Explorer, **Web References**:

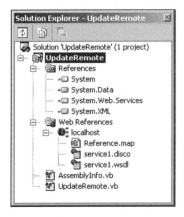

One Line of Code

The COM architecture continually promised "one line of code" to generate great results. Web Services live up to the promise, minus the declarations. We now need only call the referenced Web Service and pass the generated DataSet, and we are done. Compared to the scores of lines of XML we would have to write to pass the DataSet in the existing Microsoft technologies, this is a breeze.

Add the `sendData` function to the `UpdateRemote` class:

```
Public Class UpdateRemote

    Function sendData() As Boolean


        Dim wsRemoteUpdate As New localhost.Service1()
        Dim dsLocalData As DataSet = New DataSet()

        Dim strSQL As String
        Dim strConn As String
        Dim objDA As SqlClient.SqlDataAdapter

        strConn = "Data Source=(local);User ID=sa;password=;" & _
                  "Initial Catalog=ItemsLocal"
        strSQL = "SELECT * FROM Items"


        objDA = New SqlClient.SqlDataAdapter(strSQL, strConn)
        objDA.Fill(dsLocalData, "Items")

        'Call the Web Service, passing the DataSet
        wsRemoteUpdate.AcceptUpdate(dsLocalData)

    End Function

End Class
```

Right-click on the UpdateRemote project and select Build. If there are no errors, generate a test container and the UpdateRemote.dll. Call the sendData() method, and look at the ItemsRemote database, the data from ItemsLocal will now be in the once empty Items table. Here's the code you should use:

```
Public Class Form1
    Inherits System.Windows.Forms.Form

    Private Sub Form1_Load( _
            ByVal sender As System.Object, _
            ByVal e As System.EventArgs) Handles MyBase.Load

        Dim objRemote As New UpdateRemote.UpdateRemote()

        objRemote.sendData()


    End Sub
End Class
```

VB.NET and System.Web.Services

Now that we have seen the protocols and looked at a sample, we get to look at the interesting part – how Microsoft has objectified all of these tools in the CLR.

The SOAP toolkit provided a number of wizards to accomplish most of the obstacle course required to set up a Web Service, but the CLR provides the abstract classes. The System.Web.Services namespace provides five classes and three other namespaces that allow programmatic exposure of methods to the Web.

System.Web.Services Namespace

The System.Web.Services namespace includes these component classes:

- ❑ WebService
- ❑ WebServiceAttribute
- ❑ WebMethodAttribute
- ❑ WebServicesConfiguration
- ❑ WebServicesConfigurationSectionHandler

The WebService class is the base class from which all the ASP.NET services are derived, and includes access to the public properties for Application, Context, Server, Session, Site, and User. ASP programmers will recognize these objects from the ASP namespace. Web Services can access the IIS object model from the WebService class, such as application-level variables:

```
<%@ WebService Language="VB" Class="Util"%>
    Imports System.Web.Services

Public Class Util : Inherits WebService

WebMethod(_
```

```
        Description = "Application Hit Counter",
        EnableSession = "False")

    Public Function <WebMethod()> HitCounter() As String

        If (Application("HitCounter") = null) Then
            Application("HitCounter") = 1
        Else
            Application("HitCounter") = Application("HitCounter") + 1
        End If
        HitCounter = Application("HitCounter")

    End Function

End Class
```

WebService is an optional base class. If you don't need ASP services, you don't have to use it. The WebMethodAttribute class, however, is a necessity if you want your class to be available over the Web. From above:

```
    Dim oWebMethod as WebMethod
        oWebMethod.Description = "Application Hit Counter"
        oWebMethod.EnableSession = "False"
```

The WebService class is similar to the WebMethodAttribute class in that it allows you to add the description string to an entire class, rather than method by method. We'd add it before the class declaration above:

```
    [ WebService(Description="Common Server Variables")]
    public class ServerVariables: WebService
```

Instead of using WSDL in the contract to describe these services, the System.Web.Services namespace provides programmatic access to these properties. IIS Service Discovery will use these descriptions when queried. This way we have removed the necessity to struggle with the myriad of protocols surrounding Service Contract Language and SOAP.

The next three classes associated with System.Web.Services support three major features of Web Services: Description, Discovery, and Protocol.

System.Web.Services.Description Namespace

The Description namespace provides a host of classes that provide total management of the WSDL Descriptions for your Web Service. This object manages every element in the WSDL schema as a class property. There are no less than 60 classes, and it probably will have grown by the time this is published. You may only use one of them a year, but it pays to know they exist.

Let's look at an example. In our discussion above on the benefits of WSDL description, we mentioned the benefits of being able to query a Web Service about methods and parameters of it. The Description namespace provides methods for the discovery of methods and parameters, gathering the information from the service contract and providing it to the object model in our VB code.

If we are working on the HTTP-GET protocol (as opposed to SOAP, for instance), the `HttpGetRequestResponseInfo` class provides access to the information we can find in the contract in the `requestResponse` element. In the `serviceDescription` element, we find all parameter info for all three protocols, including HTTP-GET.

```
<httpget xmlns="urn:schemas-xmlsoap-org:get-sdl-2000-01-25">
  <service>
    <requestResponse name="IsValidEmail" href="http://aspx.securedomains.com
            /sempf/validate.asmx/IsValidEmail">
    <request>
     <param name="sEmail"/>
    </request>
    <response>
     <mimeXml ref="s0:boolean"/>
    </response>
    </requestResponse>
  </service>
</httpget>
```

The parameter, `sEmail`, is shown in the schema as a request element. This is available to us in our VB.NET code through the `Request` property of the `HttpGetRequestResponseInfo` object:

```
Imports System.Web.Services.Description

ReadOnly Property ExpectedParameters() As String
  Get
    ExpectedParameters = HttpGetRequestResponseInfo.Request
  End Get
End Property
```

System.Web.Services.Discovery Namespace

The `Discovery` namespace provides access to all of the wonderful features of the `.disco` files on a dynamic basis. Since Microsoft is currently trying to integrate Web Services as a remoting protocol and not pushing the public service side as much, we don't see the use of `.disco` files as often in the Microsoft side of things. Your business partner might be using them, though, so this namespace proves useful. For instance, you can access the `DiscoveryDocument` using the `Discovery` class:

```
Imports System.Web.Services.Discovery

ReadOnly Property DiscoveryDocument(strURL As String) As DiscoveryDocument
  Get
    DiscoveryDocument = DiscoveryClientProtocol.Discover(strURL)
  End Get
End Property
```

Like the `Description` namespace, the `Discovery` namespace provides many tools to build a `.disco` document on the fly. For instance, the Dynamic Discovery document has a class with methods available to set exclude paths and write the document back down, inherited from `Object`.

System.Web.Services.Protocols Namespace

All of the wire service problems we solved above with HTTP and SOAP are handled here in the `Protocols` namespace. Handling references to classes also referenced in other Web Services namespaces, the `Protocols` namespace will prove to be a handy tool. The objects referenced by the `Protocols` namespace include:

- ❏   Cookies per RFC 2019

- ❏   HTML forms

- ❏   HTTP request and response

- ❏   MIME

- ❏   Server

- ❏   SOAP, including SOAPException, our only error handling mechanism

- ❏   URI and URLs

- ❏   XML

… among others.

The `Protocols` namespace is particularly handy for managing the connection type by a client. A consumer of a Web Service can use HTTP GET or HTTP POST to call a service, as well as HTTP SOAP. Microsoft's .NET initiative focuses on SOAP. The `Protocols::SoapMethodAttribute` class allows the developer to set special attributes of a public method for when a client calls it using SOAP:

```
<%@ WebService Language="VB" class="MyUser" %>
imports System;
imports System.Web.Services;
imports System.Web.Services.Protocols;

public class MyUser : Inherits WebService

   SoapMethod(Action="http://MySoapmethod.org/Sample",
     RequestNamespace="http://MyNameSpace.org/Request",
     RequestElementName="GetUserNameRequest",
     ResponseNamespace="http://MyNameSpace.org/Response",
     ResponseElementName="GetUserNameResponse")
   WebMethod(Description="Obtains the User Name")
     public function GetUserName()
        [...]
     end function
end class
```

Architecting with Web Services

Web Services will impart two remarkable benefits to users – one more obvious, another less so. First, they will replace common binary RPC formats, such as DCOM, CORBA and RMI. Since these use a proprietary communication protocol, they are significantly less architecturally flexible than Web Services. In the future days of Internet appliances utilizing more and more of the Internet, platform neutrality will be a boon.

Less obvious but more impacting, Web Services will be used to transfer structured business communication in a secure manner – potentially ending the 15-year hold Sterling has had on the EDI market. HTTPS with 128 bit SSL can provide the security necessary for intra-company information transfer.

Why Web Services?

So why Web Services? First, they are remarkably easy to deploy with VB.NET. The key to remoting with Web Services is the SDL contract – written in the dense WSDL protocol we looked at earlier. IIS 5.0 does that for you in conjunction with the .NET Framework, analyzing your VB code and dynamically generating the WSDL code for the contract.

Also, they are inherently cross-platform, even if created with Microsoft products. Yes, we've heard this before, but so far this seems to be true. Since the standard XML schemas are centrally managed, and IBM mostly built the WSDL specification, Microsoft seems to have toed the line on this one.

Finally, they best represent where the Internet is going – toward an architecturally neutral collection of appliances, rather than millions of PCs surfing the World Wide Web. Encapsulating code so that you can simply and easily allow cell phones to use your logic is a major boon to developers – even if they don't know it yet.

How This All Fits Together

It is important to note that Web Services are not a feature of the .NET Framework per se. In fact, Web Services run fine on Windows NT4 SP6, with SOAP Toolkit installed. You can do most anything we are doing here with VB6 and IIS 4.0.

The .NET Framework encapsulates the Web Services protocol into objects, however. It is now an integrated part of the strategy, rather than an add-on. If you are currently working in a VB6 environment, take a look at the SOAP toolkit, and understand that the services you build are available not only to different flavors of Windows, but to IBM and Sun platforms as well.

The goal of Web Services is to provide a loosely coupled, ubiquitous, universal information exchange format. Toward that end, SOAP is not the only mechanism for communicating with Web Services. HTTP-GET and HTTP-POST are also supported by .NET, passing the parameters via `querystring` or `stdin`. Response is via HTTP response, just like normal RPCs with SOAP. This allows legacy Web applications to make use of Web Services without the benefit of the .NET Framework.

Web Service Proxies

Visual Studio.NET generates proxies invisibly, just like the creation of DLL files for normal COM+ projects. In fact, the Web Proxies are even DLL files, because you are generating a library for use by the application. Since .NET no longer requires the registration of DLL files, though, we can toss them around like popcorn.

In the previous two examples, we invoked the `proxy` flag of the `WebServiceUtil` command to generate a DLL file our consumer used to refer to the remote Web Service. The library was generated using the SDL contract, and can even change providers midstream. The proxy functionality is the core of the mesh between .NET and the universal Web Services protocols. The command as we used it looks something like this:

```
Webserviceutil
  /c:proxy /pa:yourfile.sdl /l:language /protocol: protocol
  /namespace:myNameSpace /out:location /imports:AdditionalNamespaces
  /xsd:MySchema.xsd
```

Enemies of the State

State refers to the status of any object at a given time. Stateful application persist the existence of their objects so as to provide access to properties or watch for events. While methods can use state, they don't need to. A good example is a connection to a database, which can be maintained in situ to reduce the overhead of opening and closing. If you maintain the database connection, you don't need to re-lookup the cursors each and every time the user accesses data – because they start where they left off.

Maintaining state makes it easier on the programmer but *much* harder on the operating system. Each persisted object package takes up a thread, which has its own overhead. If you suddenly go from 100 users to 1000 users with a stateful system, you may need to significantly increase RAM, because each user maintains a lock on a portion of memory.

Stateless objects are more difficult to design, but they provide one of the four key needs of today's applications – scalability. With our above example, the growth from 100 to 1000 users will increase the strain on the system, but since each object is closed moments after the application is done with it there is little expansion of memory use. Object pooling takes things to the next step, providing an artful "waiting period" for objects to be reused before being closed.

Now – step from the world of VB to the world of the Web. Bad enough for a corporate intranet to have persisted objects hanging around tying up memory and network resources, but if Web Services use state, then we'll have persisted objects tying up Internet resources! Stateful objects send messages between the client and server to maintain their store of information – be it on the same machine, over the LAN, or over the Internet. In short – methods only for the Web Services, please.

Using DNS as a Model

How does any computer know where to find a web page? Every machine doesn't know every location of every page, right? Of course not! There is a big catalog called **DNS** that is replicated by most Internet Service Providers, which translates domain names (like yahoo.com) into IP numbers (like 204.71.200.74).

The benefit of the DNS system is that it offers a further level of abstraction between the marketing and the wires. We all remember yahoo.com, but probably not 204.71.200.74. The DNS has provided an important mnemonic for us poor humans. With Web Services, it becomes even more important, as there is not only the function name, but the parameters that we must remember.

Three things make up the **Web Service Repository**: a standard format, a language, and a database. We have already discovered the language, WSDL. This can be used to layout the discovery information we need to publicize about our Web Services. The format of choice is called **DISCO** (short for DISCOvery of all things). Finally, and most exciting – the Web Services answer to DNS – **UDDI** (**Universal Description, Discovery, and Integration**). Let's talk about DISCO first.

DISCO

One way to enable a repository is to have applications that look for services. In order to implement this, we drop a DISCO document into the Web Service directory – a file that an application can look for that enables the discovery of the Web Services present in that directory, or on that machine. Alternatively, we can mark each particular service we would like to enable.

Web Service discovery is the process of locating and interrogating Web Service descriptions, which is a preliminary step for accessing a Web Service. It is through the discovery process that Web Service clients learn that a Web Service exists, what its capabilities are, and how to properly interact with it.

771

Dynamic Discovery with IIS

Admittedly not as fun as it sounds, **dynamic discovery** is Web Services's answer to the `robots.txt` file. Dynamic discovery automatically exposes Web Services beneath a given URL on a web site. By placing this document at the root of your service's directories you give a prospective consumer the opportunity to obtain information about all services contained in that directory or subdirectories.

To enable dynamic discovery for your Web Services, you'll create a `<filename>.disco` document at the root of your Web Services directory. This XML file contains the *excluded* directories within the hierarchy, so that the dynamic discovery process knows where not to go to gather information about the Web Services present:

```xml
<?xml version="1.0" ?>
<dynamicDiscovery xmlns="urn:schemas-dynamicdiscovery:disco.2000-03-17">
<exclude path="_vti_cnf"/>
<exclude path="_vti_pvt"/>
<exclude path="_vti_log"/>
<exclude path="_vti_script"/>
<exclude path="_vti_txt"/>
</dynamicDiscovery>
```

In order for the dynamic discovery to be noticed by visiting consumers, you should refer to it in the `<HEAD>` of your default HTML or ASP document:

```html
<HEAD>
<link type='text/xml' rel='alternate' href='Default.disco'/>
<TITLE></TITLE>
</HEAD>
```

Or, if you have an XML page as your default:

```xml
<?xml-stylesheet type="text/xml" alternate="yes" href="default.disco" ?>
```

Not-so-Dynamic Discovery with IIS

We've got to say that dynamic discovery is the way to go with IIS. The discovery process is very well tuned. If you work with another web server, though, or are a hands-on sort, you can roll-your-own discovery documents for each Web Service.

A **discovery document** is just an XML file with references listed in the `discovery` hierarchy. Within the hierarchy, you can add as many service contracts as you have services, and references to other DISCO documents throughout the server:

```xml
<?xml version="1.0" ?>
<disco:discovery xmlns:disco="http://schemas.xmlsoap.org/disco"
    xmlns:scl="http://schemas.xmlsoap.org/disco/scl">
  <scl:contractRef ref="http://ServerName/ServiceName.asmx?SDL"/>
  <scl:contractRef ref="http://ServerName/AnotherName.asmx?SDL"/>
  <scl:contractRef ref="http://ServerName/ThirdName.asmx?SDL"/>
  <disco:discoveryRef ref="Folder1/default.disco"/>
  <disco:discoveryRef ref="Folder2/default.disco"/>
  <disco:discoveryRef ref="Folder3/default.disco"/>
</disco:discovery>
```

This is essentially what IIS will do for you using Dynamic Discovery.

The DISCO concept depends on the client knowing where to start. If you don't know that a business offers a particular Web Service, you won't know where to look for a DISCO document. UDDI is all about changing that.

The UDDI Project

It seems to COM programmers that Web Service discovery is a simple thing. If you need the documentation to a DCOM method, you just pick up the phone and call the manager of the code. Business to business communications work like that, right? The assumption we are making is that everything is working like planned. Rarely, though, does the documentation actually exist as assumed. Employees leave. Services are forgotten. Fact is, if your developers have to sit around answering the phone every day, fielding questions about distributed services, they won't get anything done anyway.

A better way to solve this problem is using a Web Services description file on each company's web site. That is the purpose of the DISCO format. This will allow crawlers to index Web Services just like they index web sites. The `robots.txt` approach, however, is dependent on the ability for a crawler to locate each web site and the location of the service description file on that web site. The current system relies upon the interlocking nature of web sites to crawl from site to site, and there is no such visible connection between Web Services. This leaves the programmer having to know where to begin looking for a Web Service before he starts.

UDDI takes an approach that relies upon a distributed registry of businesses and their service descriptions implemented in a common XML format. You can learn all about UDDI at http://www.uddi.org, but we'll give you an intro to it here and talk about how it relates to Microsoft in general, and VB.NET in particular.

UDDI is basically a group of web-based registries similar to DNS servers, where businesses provide descriptions of their web services in terms of an XML file with "white", "yellow", and "green" pages. The white pages include how and where to find the service. The yellow pages include ontological classifications and binding information, and the green pages include the technical specification of the service.

In the XML schema for UDDI, this breaks into four elements: `businessEntity`, `businessService`, `bindingElements`, and meta data, or `tModels`. The `tModels` provide additional important technical information that falls outside the `bindingElements` element, but that is necessary for the consumption of the service once bound.

The XML schema for this is so long that Wrox wouldn't let us put it in the book. You can go see it at http://www.uddi.org/schema/uddi_1.xsd if you'd like, but you don't have to do that because UDDI provided an API that is built into CLR, as we'll see in the next section. Generally, though, each API function represents a publicly accessible SOAP message used to get or place information about a registry entry. For instance, the `findService` SOAP message lists available services based on the conditions specified in the arguments:

```
<find_service businessKey="uuid_key" generic="1.0" [ maxRows="nn" ]
              xmlns="urn:uddi-org:api" >
   [<findQualifiers/>]
   <name/> | <categoryBag/> | <tModelBag/>
</find_service>
```

The parameters it accepts include `maxRows`, `businessKey`, `findQualifiers`, `name`, `categoryBag`, and `tModelBag`. On success, it returns a `serviceList` as a SOAP response object. On the whole, it's not that much different from what we are used to in the COM world, except it is entirely an open standard.

Using UDDI

The best thing about UDDI is how easy it is to use. Many of us who started early in the Internet field remember filling out the InterNIC's domain add/change forms, and having our own representative at the 'NIC to help us when we were stuck. Now, though, the Web handles registration of services – you only need to really have a grasp of the discovery schema if you are going to build a registration site.

In fact, Microsoft has a UDDI mirror of its own at http://uddi.microsoft.com/ where you can register your Web Services, just like adding them to DNS or a search engine. Of course, you'll have to have a Microsoft Passport (another UDDI registered Web Service) to do it, but it is rather a simple task. After registering against your Passport, you enter business and contact information that is stored in your UDDI registry. Then you can add your Services.

Where UDDI is Headed

UDDI is the invisible fourth layer in the stack of protocols that represent Web Services. Like DNS is to the HTTP protocol, UDDI provides a needed interface between the SOAP messaging and the ubiquity of the service that is so important, but difficult to achieve.

Going forward, UDDI as an organization sees itself being a global provider of discovery services for the business-to-business Web Services market, hosted throughout the world. For instance, software companies can build applications that customize themselves based on services information in the UDDI registry on installation. Online marketplaces can back their marketsites with UDDI technology; to better serve the growing needs of B2B value added services.

Future services planned by UDDI include extension of the technology far beyond the specifications in the Open Draft. Eventually, regional and hierarchical searches will be accomplished through simple, effective conventions. Their goal is much farther reaching than InterNIC's was at the beginning – truly using the lessons learned in the past to shape the future.

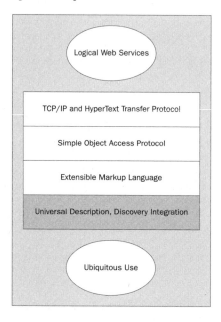

Security in Web Services

When you open up a procedure call to remoting, you have the potential to fall prey to accidents, poor end-user implementation, and crackers. Any application design needs to include some level of security. Web Services demand inclusion of security.

Security problems with Web Services fall into two categories – that of interception, and that of unauthorized use. SOAP messages intercepted by crackers potentially exposes private information like account numbers and passwords to the public. Unauthorized use at least costs money, and at most wreaks havoc within a system.

Very few of the concepts we are discussing here are things we would like to see in the hands of those wearing the black hats. Even the simple validation service handles e-mail addresses – a valuable commodity in this world of "opt in" spamming. If you add Social Security or account numbers to the service, is becomes even more of a concern. Fortunately, the wire transport of choice provides a 128-bit solution to our problem: HTTPS.

The Secure Sockets Layer

The Secure Sockets Layer, or SSL, is a protocol consumed by HTTP in the transfer of Internet data from web server to browser. On the Web, the process works like this:

1. The user calls a secure web document, and a unique public key is generated for the client browser, using the server's root certificate

2. A message, encrypted with the server's public key, is sent from the browser

3. The server can decrypt the message using its private key

The protocol in the URI represents HTTP; if it were changed to HTTPS:

```
<address uri="https://aspx.securedomains.com/sempf/Validate.asmx" />
```

then the service would make an SSL call to the server. Remember that SSL is significantly slower than HTTP, so you will suffer a performance hit. Given the sensitivity of much of the information passing over Web Services, it is probably worth the slowdown.

Directory Level Security

A developer also has the option to code security into his application. This solves different problems than SSL, and in fact you may wish to combine the two services for a complete security solution.

Unauthorized access is a potential problem for any remote system, but for Web Services it is more so. The open architecture of the system provides crackers with all the information they need to plan an attack. Fortunately, simplicity often is the best defense. Use of the NT security options already on your server is your best bet to defend against unauthorized users.

In order to use NTFS with Web Services, you'll need to do three things.

1. Make a new user in the Users group, let's say WSuser, with a password of WSpass.

2. Set the NTFS permissions for the folder containing your Web Service files by right clicking on the folder and clicking the Security tab. Remove Everyone from the Users group and add WSuser.

3. Turn on NTFS permissions in the web server by opening IIS in MMC and right-clicking on the Web Services folder we just modified. Select the Directory Security property sheet and uncheck everything except Basic Security.

If you try your Web Service now, you will get an Access Denied error. To amend this, we'll have to make dynamic adjustments to the WSDL file in order to accept a username and password. Fortunately, the System.Web.Service.Protocols namespace has just the thing for that – the ClientProtocol class.

The ClientProtocol class is the base class for all Web Service clients. For HTTP, the HTTPClientProtocol class inherits its properties. For SOAP, we have the SOAPClientProtocol class. They both support the UserName and Password properties once found in the ROPE constructor of SOAP 1.0. The simplest way to modify the consumer to use the directory level security is to hard code the username and password into the ASP.NET:

```
<script language="VB" runat="server">
Function CheckValid (Src as Object, E as EventArgs)

    Imports System.Web.Service.

    Dim clsProtocol as New SoapClientProtocol
    clsProtocol.Username = "WSuser"
    clsProtocol.Password = "WSpass"

    Dim clsValidate as New Validate
    Dim blnValid as clsValidate.IsEmail(sEmail.Text)

    lblValid = blnValid

End Function
</script>
```

You could obviously request the values from the user, get the form global attributes of the project, or get them from a database.

Working Together

Though this is a fine way to prevent unauthorized access, you are sending the Username and Password in clear text over the Internet, with cool <USERNAME> and <PASSWORD> tags to really help the black-hats find them. The real security of this is using both SSL and directory level security together. Though slow and at times inconvenient, it is a small price to pay for the heightened level of security. Though this is different from the traditional role-based COM+ security, it is still very effective for running this information across the wire.

Other Types of Security

The Windows platform in general provides for other forms of security. For instance, the CryptoAPI supplies access to most of the commonly used encryption algorithms – outside from the protocols used in Secure Sockets Layer. Digital Certificates (sort of a personal form of SSL ServerCertificates) is now rapidly becoming a powerful force in security. This chapter isn't a treatise on security, so we'll have to refer you elsewhere for details. Start at the web sites of Verisign and Microsoft.

The Down Side

There is a down side to any distributed architecture. We've covered most of them in this chapter thus far and suggested workarounds – security, state, speed, and connectivity. Let's go over them once more to help make sure that Web Services are the way to go.

Security

Obviously, sending credit cards numbers over the Internet has been a clear problem with commerce since the very start. After six years, architects of the Internet and the Big Marketing Machine have convinced consumers that the little gold key in the corner means that even a truck full of crackers couldn't crack their credit card transaction this side of forever. But now, there is no little key. People using Internet appliances will probably not have the same visual clues that the transaction is secure, and we'll have a row about this in the press.

The solution there is management of client expectations. If we build services securely to begin with, there will be no instances to draw concern or scrutiny. Consider the security of everything you write. It's fairly easy, and the payoff is great.

State

State is less of a problem because in Windows DNA, Microsoft has been saying for years that n-tier statefulness has to go. Most of us are used to it. Those who aren't need to get on the boat with the rest of us. Don't use properties. Don't watch for events. Architect your solutions to be loosely coupled. That's what Web Services are made to do. You can do other things with Web Services, but you shouldn't. Best to toe the company line on this one.

Transactions

Web Services are not made for transactional systems. If our web server at MyCompany.com were to access a database at UPS for example, and the connection dropped in the middle, the lock on the database would remain without giving the network system at UPS a chance to solve the problem. Web Services are by nature loosely coupled. They are not designed for tight transactional integration.

A common use of Web Services, communication between differing systems, prompted a number of technology architects to design a number of XML transaction protocols like 2PC. These packages provide for a code of understanding between two systems that can assume that the network link will remain stable.

Speed and Connectivity

Speed and connectivity are going to be continuing problems until we have the ubiquitous bandwidth George Gilder talks about in Telecosm. Right now, the majority of Internet devices that could really benefit from Web Services – cell phones, PDAs – are stuck at the paltry 14,000 bits per second currently supported by most wireless providers. That is just those with Internet access, too, which is not the majority.

For application development, this is a concern because when the router goes down, the application goes down. Right now, our intranets continue to function when our ISP drops the ISDN. With Web Services running the links to our customers and suppliers, that ISDN line becomes the company lifeline. Redundancy of connections and a firm partnership with your service provider are the only solution.

Where We Go from Here

The cell phone is a listening device. It listens for a call to its network address from the cell network. When it receives one, it follows some logic to handle the call. Sound familiar? This works just like the RPC architecture, and will be the format for a new host of devices that listen for our Web Services calls over the G3 wireless network.

The first lines of the W3C XML group's charter say:

> **"Today, the principal use of the World Wide Web is for interactive access to documents and applications. In almost all cases, such access is by human users, typically working through Web browsers, audio players, or other interactive front-end systems. The Web can grow significantly in power and scope if it is extended to support communication between applications, from one program to another."**

Right now, the principle use for Web Services is business-to-business services. Both RPC and document delivery will bring Web Services to the forefront within 18 months because of ease-of-use and architecture neutrality. New business communication will be via XML and Web Services, rather than EDI and VANs. Micropayment may actually become a reality. There are scores of promises that the Internet made since its inception that can be fulfilled with Web Services and XML.

It won't stop there though. The power of listening devices will bring Web Services development into user-to-user markets from business-to-business. Did you all see Steve Ballimer's address at the .NET launch? This kid is wandering around the zoo with the map and tour information on his cell phone. A friend of the family is also at the zoo that day, and the two phones collaborate to help them find a place to meet for lunch. Later that day, they have a picture taken and stored on their remote storage location, to be picked up by the grandparents and stored on a digital picture frame.

It sounds far-fetched, we know, but we hope you can see how the power of Web Services on .NET could make it possible. SOAP isn't just about replacing the RPC architecture already out there. It is a fundamentally different way to think about the network as the platform.

Summary

In this chapter, we've looked at the need for an architecturally neutral, ubiquitous, easy-to-use, and interoperable system to replace DCOM, RMI, and CORBA. We've discussed how Web Services fill the gaps successfully because HTTP is used as the language independent protocol, XML is its language (in WSDL) and transport mechanism, and SOAP allows us to package up messages for sending over HTTP.

Then we moved on to look at how to create and consume our Web Services programmatically using VB.NET.

We then discussed the abstract classes provided by the CLR to set up and work with Web Services. In particular, we looked at the `WebService`, `WebServiceAttribute`, `WebMethodAttribute`, `WebServicesConfiguration`, and `WebServicesConfigurationSectionHandler` component classes of the `System.Web.Services` namespace, in addition to the `System.Web.Services.Description` namespace, the `System.Web.Services.Discovery` namespace, and the `System.Web.Services.Protocols` namespace.

Next, we took a high-level look at some of the technologies supporting Web Services – namely DISCO and UDDI – before briefly covering security in Web Services.

Finally, we talked about some of the downsides to using any distributed architecture (Web Services included) and where Web Services might take us in the future.

VB.NetProfessionalVB.NetProfessionalVB.NetProfessional

23

Windows Services

There are times when we need to run an application in the background without any interaction or user logged into the server machine. In the Windows environment, this is typically done by the use of Windows NT or Windows 2000 services.

> **A service is a program that can automatically start when the operating system is booted and does not rely on the user being logged into the system.**

You can think of a service as a twenty-four hour store or supermarket. Some are open from dawn to dusk to facilitate your needs and others are not. While you're sleeping at night, the store owners do everything they can to keep the store running. A service acts in the same way. If you set up a service application and ensure that a person or, in this case, an NT account is there to manage it, then the service will be available to run day and night. The application is there to provide you with a service. The service is constantly running in the background and making itself available anytime you need it, just as the store does.

Windows Service Examples

There are many types of services that are continually running on your computer. Programs such as SQL Server, Exchange Server, and Internet Information Server (IIS) use Windows Services to continually monitor for events and perform tasks on your computer. Other programs such as antivirus applications use services as well. These applications log into your system when your computer starts up and monitor for viruses that come into your system through the use of other programs. Only a background service could do something like this.

Imagine that we are running an FTP server and want to monitor and process files within a certain directory from our customers. With services, we can do this. We could extract the information from these files to process orders, update address or billing information, or even upload sample code from our users on to our web site. We could also write an application that monitors a list of Internet addresses to ensure that those web servers are up and running. The service is there working in the background for us. It can also help to provide automation in our businesses or work place and help with our daily routines. Most of us prefer not to be awake twenty-four hours a day doing work. Therefore, we create services to do this for us.

Now consider a stock price reporting system. We could build a system that pulls stock prices from a web site and extracts the information from those web pages, and then e-mails the information on the latest prices either to us or to a group of users. We could set thresholds to only send out an e-mail if the stock price reaches a certain price. This could be automated to pull information every ten minutes or every ten seconds. We really have a lot of flexibility on the types of applications that we can create and are only limited by our imagination.

As a last example of a service program, think about Microsoft Transaction Server (MTS). MTS is an object broker that manages instances of components and is used regularly by professional developers worldwide. This service is constantly running in the background to manage your components for you as soon as your computer is booted, just like IIS or Exchange Server. With MTS you are able to choose which account your components will run under. You are able to specify a local account or a user account to tell how you want the particular component to interact with the system. Every process that runs on NT or 2000 must use some type of security account, which makes it important that these services support some type of security feature that facilitates NT user accounts.

You can view the many services that are used on your computer by opening the Services Control Manager in the **Control Panel's Administrative Tools**. All of these services are able to automatically log into your system by way of a user or system account. The user account is a regular NT account that allows the program to interact with the system. In essence, the service will impersonate a user and log into the system. Many programs, during installation, will prompt you for a user ID and password of an existing user account. This account is used for the sole purpose of getting into your system. With Visual Studio.NET, we are able to facilitate all of the features required to run a service and are able to do so easily. Instead of focusing on how we can get a service application installed, we can now focus on the application itself because installation is so easy.

Creating a Windows Service

Using VS.NET, we can easily create Windows Services by creating an application that is installed as a service. For example, suppose we want to monitor for files in a directory and react to the data in those files. We could write a Windows Service application that waits for those files, extracts the information, and then starts another process to use that data.

When we build a service application, we are basically defining the code within it that controls what happens when the service is started and stopped, what commands can be sent to the service, and what actions should be taken when those commands are received. This is done by placing code in the events of the service, for example: OnStop and OnStart.

When we place code in the OnStart event, we are telling the application that we want to perform these tasks when the application starts. This is just like the Main procedure in a console application; it's our startup code. Therefore, anything we want to have happen once when the service starts will be placed here.

The OnStop event works in the same way. When a user stops the service, we can place code in the OnStop event to perform the tasks that we want. Based on the decision the user has made, we can decide what action we want to take. We can log an event or send out an administrative alert; it really depends on your requirements.

We can also specify if the user is allowed to stop or pause the service. We may only want a service to be running or stopped because of live or critical applications – we wouldn't want people to be able to pause a service that controls a pump extracting toxic fumes out of a chemical plant. There's always one person out there who is curious about what the red button does. We want to take control out of the hands of the user in this case. This might be a bit of an extreme example, but it makes the point clear. The more we have the ability to control the behavior of our applications, or the more flexible we can make them, the safer they can be.

After we have created and built the application, we use the command prompt to install it by running the command line utility InstallUtil.exe, passing the path to the service executable. We can then use the Services Control Manager to start, stop, pause, resume, and configure the service. We can also accomplish many of these same tasks in the Services node in the VS.NET Server Explorer or by using the ServiceController class. We will go through these methods by creating a sample service project.

The Windows Service Project

We will learn about service applications by creating a file monitoring service. This application will monitor for files in a particular directory. When a file is found, our service will notify a particular user by sending an e-mail message along with a file attachment. The message that we send will include the first few lines of text of the file that was found and the attachment will be the file itself.

With VB.NET, we are able to create a Windows Service from one of the built-in templates:

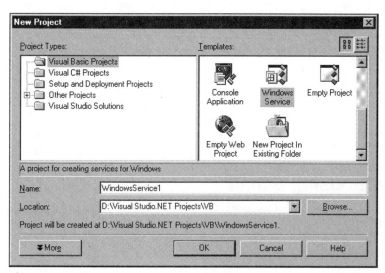

Start by creating a new project and selecting the Windows Service template. Name this project WindowsService1 and click on OK. This will create a new service class called Service1.vb. Right-click on the design surface, select Properties, and set the ServiceName property to VBTestService.

Next well examine some of the areas of code that we will be using.

View `Service1.vb`'s code. Notice that our project uses the `System.ServiceProcess` namespace. This namespace is used to install and run a Windows service:

```
Imports System.ServiceProcess
```

The `Service1` class that was generated is derived from the `ServiceBase` class. Using this class, we can define specific behavior for start, stop, pause, and continue commands, as well as behavior when the system shuts down. This base class is called when the service first starts and triggers the `OnStart` event. Other events such as `OnStop`, `OnPause`, and `OnContinue` are triggered through this class as well:

```
Inherits System.ServiceProcess.ServiceBase
```

This base class provides us with some methods for overriding the start and stop processes. We will use these later to do some work:

```
Protected Overrides Sub OnStart(ByVal args() As String)
    ' Add code here to start your service. This method should set things
    ' in motion so your service can do its work.
End Sub

Protected Overrides Sub OnStop()
    ' Add code here to perform any tear-down necessary to stop your service.
End Sub
```

> When using **OnContinue** and **OnPause**, be sure that the **ServiceBase**
> **CanPauseAndContinue** property is set to **True** when the service is initialized.

We can also override other methods such as `OnContinue`, `OnPause`, and `OnShutdown` if so desired. We might want to override these methods to keep track of when a service is interrupted. If we wanted to know when someone paused the service, we could place some code in the `OnPause` event to log the event. In addition, when the service continues after being paused, we could place code in the `OnContinue` event to log this event as well. Exposure of these events allows for better monitoring of the service.

Writing Events Using E-mail

One of the methods that we will use to verify that our service is working properly will be e-mail. Virtually everyone has some type of e-mail service on their computer and this provides a good mechanism to communicate events or alerts to the user. To accomplish this we will use the e-mail services in .NET, in particular the `MailMessage`, `MailAttathment`, and `SmtpMail` class objects:

- ❑ The `MailMessage` class is used to build an e-mail message. It defines to whom we will send our message, the subject, the priority, and any attachments to send along with the message.

- ❑ The `MailAttachment` class defines a list of attachments that will be sent with our message.

- ❑ The `SmtpMail` class provides the actual mechanism to send the message. It uses the `Send` method and takes a `MailMessage` object as a parameter.

To use the e-mail services of .NET, an SMTP (Simple Mail Transfer Protocol) mail service must be installed and configured on your computer. SMTP is a common protocol used for sending e-mail messages over the Internet.

Our e-mail service uses the `System.Web.Mail` namespace, so be sure to add `System.Web.dll` to your project references when using any e-mail services in .NET. Now add the following line of code in the `Service1` class:

```
Imports System.ServiceProcess
Imports System.Web.Mail
```

Creating a SendMail Procedure

We will begin by creating a procedure called `SendMail` that will be used to e-mail our messages to the user. Insert the following code in `Service1.vb` after the `Component Designer generated code` region:

```
Private Sub SendMail(ByVal Subject As String, _
                     ByVal SendTo As String, _
                     ByVal Message As String, _
                     Optional ByVal FileName As String = "")

    Dim Mail As New MailMessage()

    ' Add a file attachment if specified
    If FileName <> "" Then
        Mail.Attachments.Add(New MailAttachment(FileName))
    End If

    ' Setup some e-mail information
    With Mail
        .From = "support@mydomain.com"
        .To = SendTo
        .Subject = Subject
        .Body = Message
        .Priority = MailPriority.High
    End With

    ' Send the e-mail message
    Dim SendMail As New SmtpMail()
    SendMail.Send(Mail)
End Sub
```

Here, we have specified the subject, e-mail address, message, and file attachment properties as parameters to the `SendMail` procedure.

Let's now look at some of the properties that we have set:

❑ The `From` property contains the name or e-mail address of the person sending the e-mail. This property does not validate the data placed in it. In other words, we could place any e-mail address here and it will appear that the message came from this address. You can lookup the properties of who an e-mail actually came from, but this feature can cause you to think that the message came from another user. This could be misleading if used incorrectly.

❑ The `To` property is set to the e-mail address of the person we want to send our message to, for example, myname@mydomain.com.

❑   The `Priority` property is the priority that we want to set on the message and includes `High`, `Low`, and `Normal`. In this case, we will set it to `High` to help our e-mail messages stand out a little better when we read them. Most, if not all e-mail readers are able to show a priority flag and what level it's at – `High` being of greatest importance and `Low` being of least importance.

Once we have set our `MailMessage` properties, we need to create an `SmtpMail` object and call its `Send` method, passing in the `MailMessage` object as a parameter.

Coding the OnStart and OnStop Events

In the `OnStart` and `OnStop` events, we will send an e-mail to notify the user of when the service starts and stops.

In the `OnStart` event, we'll add some code to call to the `SendMail` procedure and specify a subject, message, and a valid e-mail address to send to:

```
Protected Overrides Sub OnStart(ByVal args() As String)
    ' E-mail when the service starts
    SendMail("VBTestService - Started", "webmaster@mydomain.com", _
            "Starting VB Service")
End Sub
```

In the `OnStop` event, add some code to call the `SendMail` procedure. This time we are sending a message to the user letting them know that the service has stopped:

```
Protected Overrides Sub OnStop()
    ' E-mail when the service stops
    SendMail("VBTestService - Stopped", "webmaster@mydomain.com", _
            "Stopping VB Service")
End Sub
```

The AutoLog Property

By default, the `ServiceBase` class writes events to the application log in the Event Viewer, by way of the `ServiceBase.AutoLog` property. The `AutoLog` property instructs the service to use the application event log to report command failures, as well as information for `OnStart`, `OnStop`, `OnPause`, and `OnContinue` events on the service. This can be used as additional information to verify that the service has started. What is actually logged to the event log is an entry saying **Service started successfully** and **Service stopped successfully**, and any errors that might have occurred.

We can turn off the event log reporting by setting the `AutoLog` property to `False`. This is done by right-clicking on the design surface of `Service1` and selecting **Properties**. If we also want to disable or enable the ability to pause, continue, stop, or shutdown the service, we can set the properties here as well:

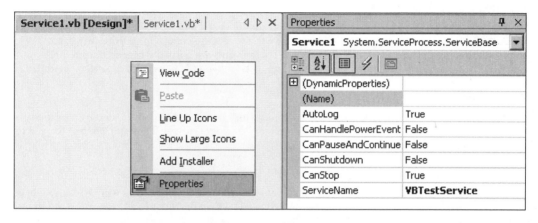

In the next section, we will implement a file monitoring control into our project.

Creating a File Monitor

For performance reasons, we should do all of our work on a separate thread to our main application thread. We want to leave our main application free to accept any requests from the user or operating system. We can do this by using some of the different components that create their own threads when they are launched. The Timer component and the FileSystemWatcher component are two examples. When the Timer component fires its Elapsed event, a thread is spawned and any code placed within that event will work on that newly created thread.

By creating a process on separate threads, we are able to perform more tasks. You can think of this as like standing in line at a grocery store. The more cash registers a store has open, the more people the store owners are able to push through the lines. In turn, the grocery store is able to do more business in a day and is more productive compared to only having one cash register.

The FileSystemWatcher Component

The main application runs on a specific thread ID. We can create another thread easily by using the FileSystemWatcher component, which is under the **Components** tab in the **Toolbox**, or we can use the System.IO class to create this object manually. In either case, the FileSystemWatcher uses its own thread when executing its Created, Changed, Deleted, or Renamed events. This object will manage threads as it sees fit. Therefore, we can place any work within the events to run off a separate thread from our main application, which means better performance.

The FileSystemWatcher component is used to monitor for files in a particular directory. Events will fire if a file is created, changed, deleted, or renamed within a specified directory. It can be used to automatically move files from one system to another, or to read and process files.

Let's now implement the component. Drag-and-drop a FileSystemWatcher control from the **Toolbox** onto the designer surface of Service1.vb. This control will automatically be called FileSystemWatcher1.

The EnableRaisingEvents Property

We don't want the service to send out any notifications until we tell it to, so set the `FileSystemWatcher`'s `EnableRaisingEvents` property to `False`. This will prevent the control from firing any events. We will enable it during the `OnStart` event in the service. These events are normally triggered from the `NotifyFilter` property. Events will fire depending on whether a file is created, copied, or modified.

The Path Property

Next, the path that we want monitoring is the `Temp` directory on the `C` drive, so set the `Path` property to `C:\TEMP` (be sure to check that there is a `TEMP` directory on your C drive). This path can be changed to monitor any directory depending on your system.

The NotifyFilter Property

We only want to watch for when the last modified value of a file has changed. This will be when a file is copied or created in the specified `Path` property. To do this we set the `NotifyFilter` property to `LastWrite`. We could also watch for other changes such as attributes, security, file name, size, and directory name changes as well, just by changing `NotifyFilter` property. We can also specify multiple changes to watch for by using the `Or` operator.

The Filter Property

The types of files that we will look for are text files. This is done by setting the `Filter` property to `*.txt`.

The IncludeSubdirectories Property

If we wanted to watch subdirectories, we would set the `IncludeSubdirectories` property to `True`. In this sample, we're leaving it as `False`, which is the default value.

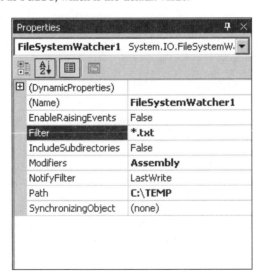

Adding FileSystemWatcher Code to OnStart and OnStop

Now that we have some properties set, let's add some more code to the `OnStart` event. To ensure that we are running on separate threads, we will log the thread ID of the main application in the service's `OnStart` event using the `AppDomain.GetCurrentThreadID` function.

We also need to start the `FileSystemWatcher1` component so it will start triggering events when files are created or copied into the directory we're monitoring, so we set the `EnableRaisingEvents` property to `True`:

```
Protected Overrides Sub OnStart(ByVal args() As String)

    ' E-mail when the service starts
    SendMail("VBTestService - Started", "webmaster@mydomain.com", _
        "Starting VB Service on thread: " & AppDomain.GetCurrentThreadID())

    ' Start monitoring for files
    FileSystemWatcher1.EnableRaisingEvents = True
End Sub
```

Once our file monitoring properties are initialized, we are ready to start the monitoring.

When the service stops we need to stop the file monitoring process. Since `FileSystemWatcher1` has spawned a new thread, we want to ensure that the thread stops. By disabling the events, we stop the thread. Add this code to your `OnStop` event:

```
Protected Overrides Sub OnStop()
    ' Stop monitoring for files
    FileSystemWatcher1.EnableRaisingEvents = False

    ' E-mail when the service stops
    SendMail("VBTestService - Stopped", "webmaster@mydomain.com", _
            "Stopping VB Service")
End Sub
```

The Created Event

Next, we will do some work in the `Created` event of our `FileSystemWatcher` component. Select **FileSystemWatcher1** from the **Class Name** drop-down and select **Created** from the **Method Name** drop-down, and the `Created` event will be added to your code.

This event will fire when a file has been placed or created in the directory that we are monitoring. This event fires because the last modified information on the file has changed. When we copy a file over, a new file is actually created in the system. This event is where our new thread gets created.

Add code to the `Created` event as follows:

```
Public Sub FileSystemWatcher1_Created(ByVal sender As Object, _
        ByVal e As System.IO.FileSystemEventArgs) _
        Handles FileSystemWatcher1.Created

    ' Read the file that was created in the directory we are monitoring

    Dim streamFile As StreamReader
    Dim lineData As String
Dim someData As String
    Dim linesRead As Integer

    Try
        ' Open the file that was created
        streamFile = New StreamReader(e.FullPath())
```

```
        While linesRead < 5
            ' track how many lines we read
            linesRead += 1
            ' read one line at a time
            lineData = streamFile.ReadLine
            ' if lineData is nothing then we reached end of file
            if lineData = Nothing then linesRead = 5
            ' store the data being read
            someData = someData & lineData
        End While

    Catch eof As IO.EndOfStreamException
        ' The end of the file has been reached.

    Catch eIOExcep As IO.IOException
        ' Some kind of error occurred, e-mail the error
        SendMail("VBTestService - File Read Error", _
                "webmaster@mydomain.com", _
                "File: " & e.FullPath() & _
                " Error: " & eIOExcep.Message)
    Finally
        ' Close the file
        streamFile.Close()
    End Try

    ' E-mail the name of the file that is present as well as the file itself
    SendMail("VBTestService - File Present", _
            "webmaster@mydomain.com", "File found: " & e.FullPath() & _
            ", Thread ID: " & AppDomain.GetCurrentThreadID() & _
            Chr(13) & Chr(13) & somedata, e.FullPath())
End Sub
```

Since we are using the `StreamReader` class, be sure to include the `System.IO` namespace at the top of the `Service1` class:

```
Imports System.ServiceProcess
Imports System.Web.Mail
Imports System.IO
```

Let's walk through the code. First, we determine which file has shown up in our monitored directory using the `FullPath` property to discover its full file path:

```
streamFile = New StreamReader(e.FullPath())
```

This path is returned from the `System.IO.FileSystemEventsArgs` class parameter.

We next open the file using the `StreamReader` class. This class uses the `System.IO` namespace and is used mainly for reading files. The `StreamReader` is a good class for reading one line of data at a time within a text file. Once the file is opened, we grab the first few lines of text within it, as we'll be using them later as part of the e-mail message:

```
While linesRead < 5
    ' track how many lines we read
    linesRead += 1
    ' read one line at a time
    lineData = streamFile.ReadLine
    ' if lineData is nothing then we reached end of file
```

```
            if lineData = Nothing then linesRead = 5
            ' store the data being read
            someData = someData & lineData
      End While
```

In the final step, we e-mail the file that was found, use the lines of text that we grabbed as the message, and log the thread ID:

```
      SendMail("VBTestService - File Present", _
             "webmaster@mydomain.com", "File found: " & e.FullPath() & _
             ", Thread ID: " & AppDomain.GetCurrentThreadID() & _
             Chr(13) & Chr(13) & somedata, e.FullPath())
```

If an error occurs while reading the file, we send an e-mail to the user indicating which error message was generated:

```
      Catch eIOExcep As IO.IOException
          ' Some kind of error occurred, e-mail the error
          SendMail("VBTestService - File Read Error", _
                 "webmaster@mydomain.com", _
                 "File: " & e.FullPath() & _
                 " Error: " & eIOExcep.Message)
```

We are using this particular example to monitor for files and notify users. We can modify our code to do any other work required by our application in this event, such as paging a user or logging to the event log. We could also parse the information and log it into a database, which would be useful if our data contained customer or order information. It can also be used to perform tasks based on the information contained within these files. We could also handle our files differently here; instead of reading the files, we could convert them to a different format like an Acrobat PDF file or Excel file using some conversion tools.

We need to add an `Installer` class to this project to install and run the application, which we will talk about later in this chapter. Before that, however, we will go through another example – how we can use a Windows service with remoting services.

Creating a Remoting Service

This next example we're creating will be used as a **remoting service**. This will allow client applications to connect to a remote object, in a way similar to Web services. This connection can be either local or across the network. With remoting, we can specify the communication protocol as either an HTTP channel or a TCP channel. Using HTTP, the data that is sent across the network is in an XML-based format. Using the TCP channels, we can gain better performance since a binary format is used.

There will be situations when you may not have IIS available to be used as a host for your remoting objects. So by creating a Windows service application, we can activate the remoting service and have it listen for any clients attempting to connect to its objects. In this example, we call the `Northwind` sample SQL Server database and retrieve a list of employee records as a DataSet. We will call a SQL command to select all employees from the employee table and populate a DataGrid on a client application.

This assumes that you have SQL Server 7.0 or 2000 on your computer or another computer that you have access to.

To build this sample, we will need to do three things:

1. Build a class that returns a `DataSet` object filled with employee information

2. Build a service or host server to listen for clients

3. Build a test client application to test the service

Building a Test Object

We will start by creating an object that will be hosted in our service. The purpose of our object will be to return a `DataSet` object.

Add a new **Class Library** project to your existing solution and call it `RemoteTestObject`:

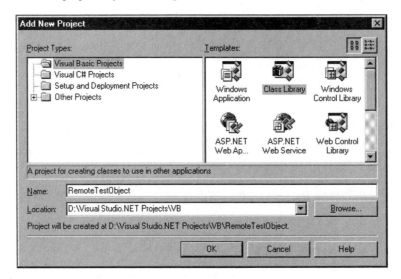

Rename `Class1.vb` as `TestObject.vb`, and rename the class itself, `Class1`, as `TestObject`. Add the following code:

```
Imports System.Data.SqlClient

Public Class TestObject

    Inherits MarshalByRefObject

    Public Function GetEmployeeList() As DataSet

        ' Declare a new DataSet object
        Dim myDataSet As New DataSet()

        ' Create the ConnectionString and create a SqlConnection.
```

```
      Dim connectString As String = _
          "User ID=sa;Password=;Initial Catalog=Northwind;" & _
          "Data Source=localhost;"

      Dim myConnection As SqlConnection = New SqlConnection(connectString)

      Dim myCommand As SqlCommand = New SqlCommand( _
          "SELECT LastName, FirstName, Title, Address, City, PostalCode" & _
          " FROM Employees", myConnection)

      ' Set the command type
      myCommand.CommandType = CommandType.Text

      ' Open the connection
      myConnection.Open()

      ' Create a SqlDataAdapter for the Suppliers table.
      Dim myDataAdapter As SqlDataAdapter = New SqlDataAdapter(myCommand)

      ' Fill the DataSet object
      Try
          myDataAdapter.Fill(myDataSet)
      Catch
          Return Nothing
      End Try

      myConnection.Close()

      Return myDataSet

    End Function

  End Class
```

We will be working with the SQLClient namespace to communicate with our database, so we start with a System.Data.SqlClient import statement above the class:

```
Imports System.Data.SqlClient
```

Next, inside the TestObject class, we add a public function called GetEmployeeList that returns a DataSet object. We need to declare a new DataSet object that will be used to return the object.

Next, we declare a connection string to the database that includes a User ID, Password, Initial Catalog (which is just the database name), and the Data Source (which is the server name – in this case we're using the SQL Server on the local machine so we have used localhost as the server name). We then create a new SqlConnection object by passing the connection string that we just created.

```
      Dim connectString As String = _
          "User ID=sa;Password=;Initial Catalog=Northwind;" & _
          "Data Source=localhost;"

      Dim myConnection As SqlConnection = New SqlConnection(connectString)
```

Next, we create a `SqlCommand` object that uses a SQL statement and the `SqlConnection` object as its parameters:

```
Dim myCommand As SqlCommand = New SqlCommand( _
    "SELECT LastName, FirstName, Title, Address, City, PostalCode" & _
    " FROM Employees", myConnection)

' Set the command type
myCommand.CommandType = CommandType.Text
```

Notice that we specify the command type as `CommandType.Text`. Specifying this type is more efficient since the object doesn't have to look up what type the command is.

Having set up our `SqlCommand` object, we open the database connection, and use the `Fill` method of a `SqlDataAdapter` object to fill our `DataSet` object up with data. To create a `SqlDataAdapter` object, we must use a `Command` object as a parameter:

```
Dim myDataAdapter As SqlDataAdapter = New SqlDataAdapter(myCommand)

' Fill the DataSet object
Try
    myDataAdapter.Fill(myDataSet)
Catch
    Return Nothing
End Try
```

Note that, to access this test object across networks using remoting, we must inherit our class from `MarshalByRefObject`. This class is used to create objects for use across the network:

```
Inherits MarshalByRefObject
```

We have now completed this `RemoteTestObject` application. Compile the code into an assembly to be used in our service application. We will now go back to the `WindowsService1` application to add some code to host the `RemoteTestObject` assembly.

Hosting the Test Object

In `WindowsService1`, we need to add a project reference to the `RemoteTestObject` project that we've just created. We can also just add a .NET reference and browse for the `RemoteTestObject.dll` instead, if we want:

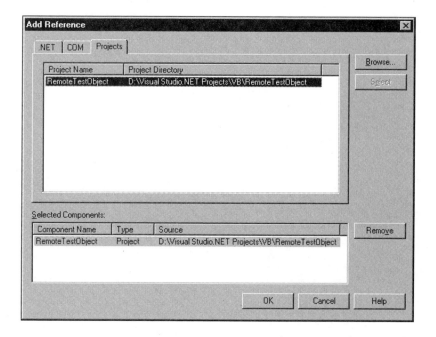

Additionally, be sure to include a reference to the `System.Runtime.Remoting.dll` in any remoting project that you build.

We also need to add some more import statements to reference the Remoting namespace at the top of our Service1 class:

```
Imports System.ServiceProcess
Imports System.Web.Mail
Imports System.IO
Imports System.Runtime.Remoting
Imports System.Runtime.Remoting.Channels
Imports System.Runtime.Remoting.Channels.Tcp
```

The first import statement allows us to use Remoting, along with the System.Runtime.Remoting.dll we have referenced. The Remoting.Channels namespace allows us to work with channels services such as HTTP or TCP. The Channels.Tcp statement allows us to work specifically with the TCP protocol when communicating with our objects.

To activate our service and start listening for clients, we will add some code to the OnStart event in our Service1 class:

```
Protected Overrides Sub OnStart(ByVal args() As String)

    Dim chan As TcpChannel
    chan = New TcpChannel(52000)
    ChannelServices.RegisterChannel(chan)
```

```
    RemotingConfiguration.RegisterWellKnownServiceType( _
        Type.GetType("RemoteTestObject.TestObject, RemoteTestObject"), _
        "EmployeeService", WellKnownObjectMode.Singleton)

    ' E-mail when the service starts
    SendMail("VBTestService - Started", "webmaster@mydomain.com", _
        "Starting VB Service on thread: " & _
        AppDomain.GetCurrentThreadId())

    ' Start monitoring for files
    FileSystemWatcher1.EnableRaisingEvents = True
End Sub
```

We create a new `TcpChannel` connection by calling the `RegisterChannel` method of the `TcpChannel` object, where the channel is set to 52000:

```
    Dim chan As TcpChannel
    chan = New TcpChannel(52000)
    ChannelServices.RegisterChannel(chan)
```

Note that if we had assigned a port that is already in use, we would get an exception error.

We then register our service by calling the `RemotingConfiguration.RegisterWellKnownServiceType` method. In this method, we are registering our assembly, our service name or universal resource identifier (URI), and how our object will be activated each time that the object is called by a client:

```
    RemotingConfiguration.RegisterWellKnownServiceType( _
        Type.GetType("RemoteTestObject.TestObject, RemoteTestObject"), _
        "EmployeeService", WellKnownObjectMode.Singleton)
```

Using the Configure Method with a Configuration File

We've used code here to set our remote values but we could have used the `RemotingConfiguration.Configure` method with a configuration file instead. Using a configuration file allows us to change the remote object names, channels, and transport types without re-compiling our sourcecode. We also have this option when building the client.

Here is a sample configuration file, which is always in an XML-based format:

```
    <configuration>
      <system.runtime.remoting>
        <application name="RemotingHello">
          <service>
            <wellknown mode="SingleCall"
                    type="RemoteTestObject.TestObject, RemoteTestObject"
                    objectUri="EmployeeService" />
          </service>
          <channels>
            <channel port="52000"
                    type="System.Runtime.Remoting.Channels.Tcp.TcpChannel,
                        System.Runtime.Remoting" />
```

```
            </channels>
          </application>
        </system.runtime.remoting>
      </configuration>
```

Creating a Test Client Application

Once we have our service application and object built, we need to create a test client application. Our test application will call the remote object we've created.

Add a new Windows Application to your existing solution and call it RemoteTestClient:

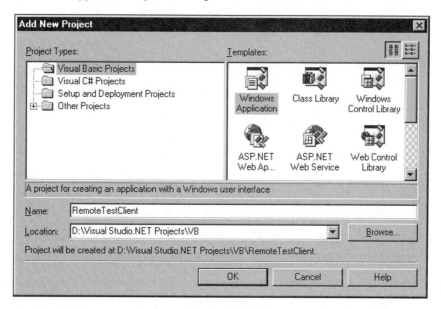

We need to add a project reference to the RemoteTestObject assembly again. Therefore, both our Windows Service and the client application will reference the RemoteTestObject assembly. We are referencing the object libraries directly in our project so we can compile. The libraries act as a placeholder until we can actually get a reference to the remote object.

Once again, be sure to add the System.Runtime.Remoting.dll to your project references.

We also need to include some remoting namespaces as we did in our Windows service application. Add these import statements to the top of the Form1 class:

```
Imports System.Runtime.Remoting
Imports System.Runtime.Remoting.Channels
Imports System.Runtime.Remoting.Channels.TCP
```

Add a DataGrid control to Form1. We will use this DataGrid to show information from the DataSet object that we get from the remote object.

Next, double-click on `Form1` and add the following code to the `Form_Load` event:

```
Public Class Form1

    Inherits System.Windows.Forms.Form

Private Sub Form1_Load(ByVal sender As System.Object, _
                   ByVal e As System.EventArgs) Handles MyBase.Load
```

```
    Dim chan As TcpChannel
    chan = New TcpChannel()
    ChannelServices.RegisterChannel(chan)

    Dim obj As RemoteTestObject.TestObject

    Try
        obj = _
        CType(Activator.GetObject(Type.GetType("RemoteTestObject.TestObject, " & _
        "RemoteTestObject"), "tcp://localhost:52000/EmployeeService"), _
        RemoteTestObject.TestObject)

        If obj Is Nothing Then
            MessageBox.Show("Could not locate server")
        Else
            DataGrid1.DataSource=obj.GetEmployeeList
        End If
    Catch
        MessageBox.Show("Could not connect to remote object")
    End Try
End Sub
```

Here, we are registering a new `TcpChannel`, declaring the `RemoteTestObject.TestObject`, creating a new instance of our object using `Activator.GetObject`, and then displaying the result from our object.

We call the `GetEmployeeList` method on our remote object to return a `DataSet` object and fill the DataGrid:

```
        DataGrid1.DataSource=obj.GetEmployeeList
```

After we add our code to the client application, we can compile it. To test our remote service, we need to install and run our service first, and then connect to our service using the client. In the next section, we will discuss how to install our services.

Installing the Service

Service applications won't run from within the IDE or from the command line – they must be installed into the Windows environment so they can be controlled. To install the service, we can use an installation program or we can use the `InstallUtil.exe` command line utility.

In order to install the service properly, we must set up an `Installer` class in our `WindowsService1` application. This class will set up all of the behavior needed for our service.

There are two methods of setting up an `Installer` class. We will use the first method for our sample project.

Method 1 – With the Mouse

By pointing and clicking, we can add an installer to our project. Right-click on the design surface of `Service1` in our `WindowsService1` application and select **Add Installer**.

A new class called `ProjectInstaller` will automatically be added to your project. Two components will be added to the `ProjectInstaller` class – `ServiceProcessInstaller1` and `ServiceInstaller1`. These two components will be used to specify a service name, an account to run under, and the way that the service will start:

Set the `Account` property of `ServiceProcessInstaller1` to `LocalSystem`.

Next, we need to modify the properties of the `ServiceInstaller1` component. Select `ServiceInstaller1` and, from the Properties window, set the `ServiceName` to `VBTestService`. Make sure that the `StartType` is set to `Manual`. This tells the service not to start until someone actually starts it.

Method 2 – Writing Our Own Code

The second method is to create an `Installer` class manually. We just need to code the essential pieces of the installer. The reason we would want to use a pre-built class is for re-usability. We can set up this class like a template and just drop it into our service applications when needed. It's easy enough just to point and click to add an installer class and then set a few properties on the controls, but using a template helps enforce standards. We also have control of our objects with no black box or hidden code in generated code regions.

> For code re-usability, develop an **Installer** class template and use it with all your service applications. Just change the service name for each application.

Add a new class and insert the code shown below to set up a re-usable installer class:

```
Imports System.Configuration.Install
Imports System.ServiceProcess
Imports System.ComponentModel


' This class enables us to install the application.
' Use it as a template for all your service applications.

' InstallUtil.exe only comes with .NET SDK

' To install run InstallUtil WindowsService1.exe
' To un-install run InstallUtil WindowsService1.exe /u

' To start the service type NET START VBTestService
```

```
' To stop the service type NET STOP VBTestService

<RunInstaller(True)> Public Class ProjectInstaller
    Inherits Installer

    ' Define the service name
    Const SERVICE_SERVICENAME As String = "VBTestService"

    Private objServiceInstaller As ServiceInstaller
    Private objProcessInstaller As ServiceProcessInstaller

    Public Sub New()
        MyBase.New() ' create an instance of our base class

        ' Installs an executable containing classes that extend ServiceBase
        objProcessInstaller = New ServiceProcessInstaller()

        ' Installs a class that extends ServiceBase to implement a service
        objServiceInstaller = New ServiceInstaller()

        ' Set the service to run under the system account
        objProcessInstaller.Account = ServiceAccount.LocalSystem

        ' Un-comment this code to set the service to run under a specific
        ' account
        'objProcessInstaller.Account = ServiceAccount.User
        'objProcessInstaller.Username = "Administrator"
        'objProcessInstaller.Password = "XXXXXX"

        ' Set the service start type to manual
        objServiceInstaller.StartType = ServiceStartMode.Manual

        ' Set the name of the service
        objServiceInstaller.ServiceName = SERVICE_SERVICENAME

        ' Installs the service by writing service application information
        ' to the registry
        Installers.Add(objServiceInstaller)
        Installers.Add(objProcessInstaller)
    End Sub
End Class
```

> Include `System.Configuration.Install.dll` in your project references when using the `Installer` class.

Let's examine the code in this custom installer class. The class is derived from the `Installer` class, which helps us install applications on to our computers. The `Imports System.ComponentModel` statement is used here so that we can define the `RunInstaller` attribute with our `ProjectInstaller` class. This invokes the installer during the installation of the assembly. Since our class is inherited from an `Installer` class, we must specify `RunInstaller()` with a `True` parameter to actually invoke the installer:

```
<RunInstaller(True)> Public Class ProjectInstaller
    Inherits Installer
```

We declare the constant `SERVICE_SERVICENAME` to hold the actual service name, allowing us to change the value for each project that we create:

```
Const SERVICE_SERVICENAME As String = "VBTestService"
```

We declare two private objects, a `ServiceInstaller` and `ServiceProcessInstaller` class. These are the same two classes that were automatically placed on the `Service1` class in method 1. In this situation, we're dealing strictly with the objects, not the visual components. We then create a new instance to these objects:

```
Private objServiceInstaller As ServiceInstaller
Private objProcessInstaller As ServiceProcessInstaller

' Installs an executable containing classes that extend ServiceBase
    objProcessInstaller = New ServiceProcessInstaller()

    ' Installs a class that extends ServiceBase to implement a service
    objServiceInstaller = New ServiceInstaller()
```

We specify an account in which the service will run. In this case, we set the `Account` property to `LocalSystem`, indicating that the service will run under the System account on the machine:

```
objProcessInstaller.Account = ServiceAccount.LocalSystem
```

The System account allows the service to run independently of the access privileges of the user currently logged in. This will allow the service to start automatically when the machine reboots and when no user is logged in as long as the `StartType` is set to `Automatic`. The System account does not require a password. Running under the System account rather than a specified user account avoids the problems that can occur if a user account lacks a permission that the service requires.

If we need to use a user account, we can specify an account on the local machine or an account in another domain, assuming that that account has privileges on the box we're running the service from. If we set the `Account` property to `User` and don't specify a username and password, the installer will present a login dialog box at install time asking for a username and password:

We can prevent this dialog box from prompting us if we set the `Username` and `Password` properties in our code.

The InstallUtil.exe Utility

The service information is stored in the Registry in subkeys located in the following path:

```
HKEY_LOCAL_MACHINE\SYSTEM\CurrentControlSet\Services\<Service name>
```

After you have coded your `Installer` class, build your solution. Once our project is built, we can install the service using the `Installutil.exe` utility. This utility is normally installed in the `\WINNT\Microsoft.NET\Framework\vX.X.XXX` directory corresponding to whichever version you're using. Make sure that the PATH system variable in your **Environment Variables** (behind **Control Panel | System | Advanced**) includes this path. The service is installed from the command line window, so in the `WindowsService1` project's bin directory, run the following command:

```
Installutil WindowsService1.exe
```

To uninstall the service use the `/u` switch:

```
Installutil WindowsService1.exe /u
```

Running the Service

We can now start the service from the command line window:

```
NET START VBTestService
```

To stop the service use the NET STOP command from the command line window:

```
NET STOP VBTestService
```

Alternatively, we can use the Server Explorer in VS.NET to start and stop the service. Under **Servers**, choose your server and then select **Services** to find **VBTestService**. You can right-click on it to start or stop the service:

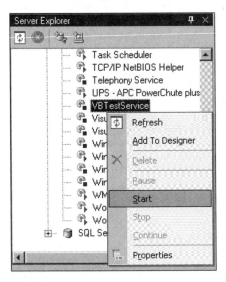

In Windows 2000, we can also use Control Panel I Administrative Tools I Services to start and stop the service. Once the service is installed, it will show up as VBTestService and by right-clicking on it we can choose to start or stop it. We also have the stop and play buttons at the top of the window to use as well:

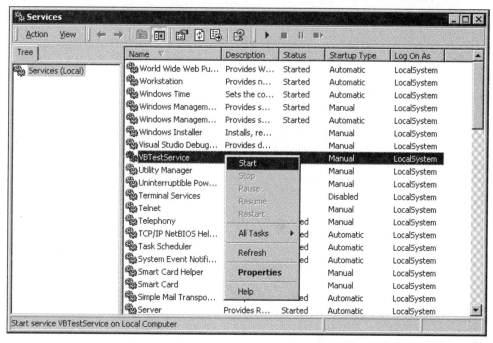

Upon successful compilation of our solution, we will get an e-mail for any file that we copy or create in the monitored directory. So, after dropping some sample text files into our monitored directory, we should receive e-mails at the e-mail address specified in the code (webmaster@mydomain.com was the example address used above). Each of the created e-mail messages contains information from each file. To view the e-mails sent by the service, open up the user's e-mail program. As you can see in the next screenshot, we have received our e-mail messages with the red exclamation mark next to them indicating that they are high priority. Notice also that we have a file attached to the messages as well:

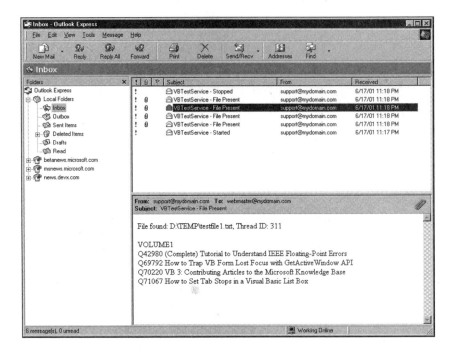

Let's look next at how we would go about debugging the service application.

Debugging the Service

Because a service must be run from within the context of the Services Control Manager rather than from within VS.NET, debugging a service is not as straightforward as debugging other Visual Studio.NET application types. To debug a service, you must start the service and then attach a debugger to the process in which it is running. You can then debug your application using all of the standard debugging functionality of Visual Studio.NET.

> You should not attach to a process unless you know what the process is and understand the consequences of attaching to and possibly killing that process.

The only time you can debug a service is when it's running. When you attach the debugger to the service, you are interrupting the service. The service is suspended for a short period while you attach to it. The service will also be interrupted when you place breakpoints and step through you code.

Attaching to the service's process allows you to debug most, but not all, of the service's code. For instance, because the service has already been started, you cannot debug the code in the service's OnStart method this way, or the code in the Main method that is used to load the service. To debug the OnStart event or any code under the Component Designer generated code region, you have to add a dummy service and start that service first. In the dummy service, you would create an instance of the service that you want to debug. You can place some code in a Timer object and create the new instance of the object that you want to debug after thirty seconds or so. You want to allow yourself enough time to attach to the debugger before the new instance is created. Meanwhile, you can place breakpoints in your startup code to debug those events.

To Debug a Service

1. Install your service.

2. Start your service, either from the Services Control Manager, Server Explorer, or from code.

3. In VS.NET, select Processes from the Debug menu. The Processes dialog box appears:

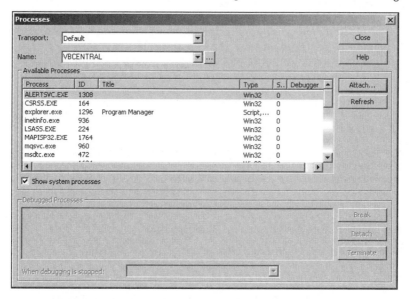

4. Click on the Show system processes option.

5. In the Available Processes section, click on the WindowsService1.exe process, and then the Attach button. The Attach to Process dialog box appears:

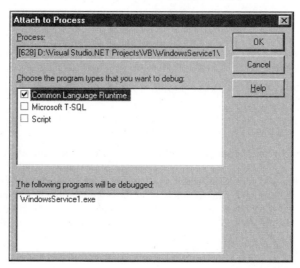

6. Make sure that just the **Common Language Runtime** option is selected and then click **OK**. You will return to the **Processes** dialog. Before you close the **Processes** dialog, you have the option to select either **Detach from this process** or **Terminate this process**, once debugging is finished. If you select the first option, your service will still run once you stop debugging. In this case, select **Terminate this process** and select **Close**. You can now debug your process.

7. Place a break point in the `FileSystemWatcher1.Created` event and, after a second, the application should break into your code. Using this method, you can place various breakpoints throughout your application to debug your code. When finished, select **Stop Debugging** from the **Debug** menu. You can also select **Processes** from the **Debug** menu, click on your debugged process, and then click **Detach** or **Terminate**.

Summary

In this chapter, we created a file monitoring service that e-mails a user any time a file is created or placed in our directory. We also looked at a way to host a remote object using the remoting technology. There are many other applications that a service can be used for, such as:

❑ Automatically moving statistical files from a database server to a web server

❑ Pushing general files across computers and platforms

❑ A watchdog timer to ensure that a connection is always available

❑ An application to move and process FTP files

The possibilities are endless and with VB.NET these solutions can be created easily.

The general steps that we take to create a service application are as follows:

❑ Create a new Windows service application using the **Windows Service** template

❑ Drag and drop components onto the designer surface of service class that is generated, namely `Service1`

❑ Override the service's `OnStart` and `OnStop` events and log information to ensure that the service is running

❑ Place code in the component events to do work

❑ Create an `Installer` class

❑ Use `Installutil.exe` to install the service

❑ Use the Server Explorer, Services Control Manager, or the command line to start and stop the service

We've learned that creating Windows services is very simple to do in VB.NET. We're able to create applications as services without worrying so much about how we're going to implement the service, thanks to the use of the `Installer` class. We've also learned that, once we've attached our service process to the debugger, we're able to debug our application like any other application. We can now take this knowledge and apply it towards any service application that we desire.

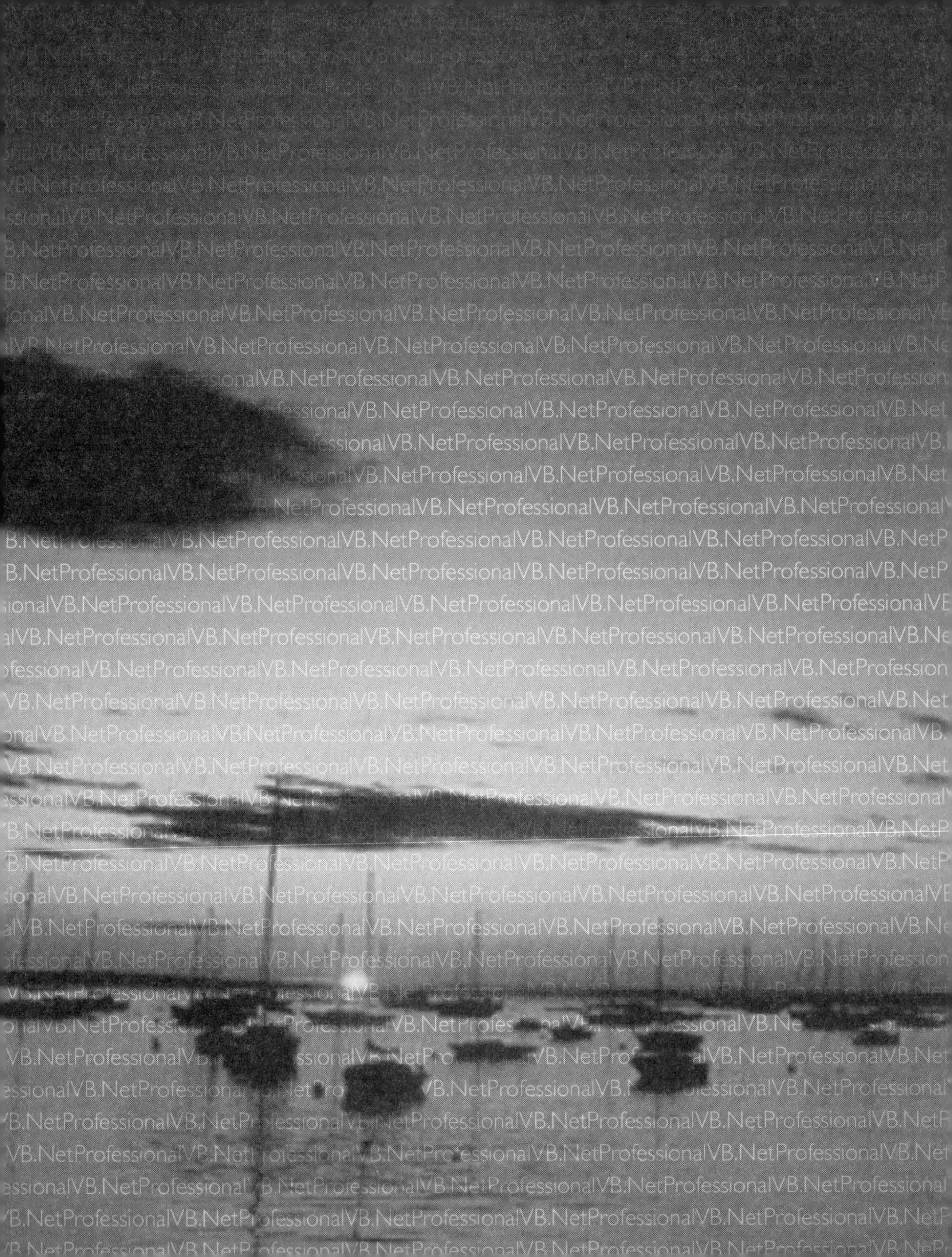
VB.NetProfessional

24

Deployment in .NET

Assuming you haven't thrown this book away in horror after reading the title of this chapter, we are going to move on to the topic of application deployment. All sorts of errors seem to occur when we try to run the application we just created (which worked perfectly on our machine) on another machine. Even more infuriating is that problems tend to occur months later when a user has installed another piece of software that is totally unrelated to ours. You will be pleased to hear that there are many new features in Visual Studio.NET and the CLR that will make application deployment easier.

This chapter is going to look at what Visual Studio.NET and the CLR have to offer us in the way of deployment. For many years application deployment wasn't treated as an integral part of the development lifecycle of an application. It was often treated as an afterthought – not considered until the application had been finished. With the increasing componentization of products this has led to a number of problems that can be downright annoying to the end user. This is not to say that it is the developer's fault that these problems occur, it could be attributed to a form of growing pains as we move towards a more component-based software architecture.

We are going to start this chapter by discussing the problems that occur when we deploy applications and a number of terms that are used when talking about application deployment. We will then move to look at what the CLR contains that helps us alleviate some of the deployment issues discussed previously. The remainder of the chapter will then focus on the practical aspects of creating deployment projects in Visual Studio.NET, which will include a number of walkthroughs.

Deployment in .NET is a huge topic and we couldn't hope to cover every aspect in the pages that we have for this chapter. What this chapter should give you is the understanding, basic knowledge, and desire to learn more about the options available to you.

Application Deployment

We are going to start this section by discussing the main issues associated with application deployment and defining a few common terms that are used. We will then move on to discuss the deployment options available prior to .NET. Hopefully, this will give you an understanding of the issues to be overcome when considering deployment in .NET.

But what do we mean by the term "application deployment". In the context of this chapter, it means the process of taking an application, packaging it up, and installing it on another machine. This includes installing the application new, re-installing it or upgrading it. It applies to: traditional Windows-based applications, Web-based applications that will need to be installed within the confines of another web server, and any of the other Visual Basic project templates.

DLL Hell

The two small words "DLL" and "Hell" describe what is in fact a very large problem for application developers today. If you are aware of the problems that **DLL Hell** encompasses then please feel free to skip this section.

What does DLL Hell mean? The term is actually used to describe a number of problems that can arise when multiple applications share a common component. The common component is usually a .dll or a COM component. The problems usually arise for one of three reasons, which will be discussed below:

❑　The first common cause of DLL Hell is when you install a new application that overwrites a shared component with a version that is not compatible with the version that already resides on the computer. Any applications that relied on the previous version of the component could well be rendered unusable. This is often caused when you install an application that overwrites a system file (for example MFC42.dll) with an older version. Any application that relied on the functionality of the newer version will stop working. When installing the application on the computer the installer should check that it is not overwriting a newer version of the component. However, not all installations do this check.

❑　The second cause occurs when a new version of a shared component is installed that is binary compatible (the public interface matches exactly) with the previous version, but in updating the functionality, a new bug has been introduced into the component which could cause any application that depends on the component to misbehave or stop working. This type of error can be very hard to diagnose.

❑　The third common cause occurs when an application uses a feature of a common component that is actually an undocumented and unexpected behavior of the component: a side effect. When this shared component is updated with a newer version the side effect may well have disappeared, breaking any applications that depended on it. There are many undocumented API calls available in DLLs, the problem is that because they are undocumented they may well disappear in a subsequent version without warning.

As the above discussion indicates, DLL Hell can be caused by a variety of reasons and the effects can be wide ranging. Applications may stop working but worse still it could introduce subtle bugs that may lie undetected for some time. It may be some time before you realize an application has stopped working, which can make it significantly harder to detect the cause of the problem.

Microsoft has tried to address some of these issues with the release of Windows 2000 (and to a lesser extent Windows ME) by introducing Windows File Protection and Private DLLs:

❑ As the name suggests Windows File Protection is a mechanism by which the OS protects a list of system DLLs from being overwritten with a different version. Normally only service packs and other OS updates can update the DLLs that are protected, although this can be overridden by changing some registry keys. This should reduce some of the causes of DLL Hell that are caused by the overwriting of system DLLs.

❑ The second feature introduced is that of private DLLs. Private DLLs are used by one particular application only and are not shared amongst different applications. If an application relies on a specific version of a .dll or COM component then it can be installed in the application directory and a .local file created in the directory to inform that OS to look for private DLLs first and then move on to look for shared DLLs.

You will be pleased to hear that Microsoft has incorporated new features into the CLR and the .NET framework that will help to overcome DLL Hell and make deployment easier. These new features will be discussed throughout the course of this chapter.

XCOPY Deployment

The term **XCOPY deployment** was coined to describe an ideal deployment scenario. Its name derives from the DOS xcopy command that is used to copy an entire directory structure from one location to another. XCOPY deployment relates to a scenario where all you have to do to deploy an application is to copy the directory (including all child directories) to the computer that you would like to run the program.

Why can't we use XCOPY deployment at present? The main reason is that the process of installing an application currently is a multi-step process. For example, any application that uses a COM component will require a number of steps to install it on another computer. First, the component needs to be copied to the machine, and then the component must be registered on the machine, creating a dependency between the component and the registry. The application requires the entry in the registry to activate the component. Because of this coupling between the component and the registry it is not possible to install the component by simply copying it from one machine to another.

All but the simplest of applications also require other dependencies (such as databases, message queues, document extensions) to be created on the new computer. The CLR tries to overcome the problem of the coupling between the registry and components but at present it cannot help with the dependencies that are required by more advanced applications. We are closer to XCOPY deployment with .NET and in some cases we may actually be able to achieve a form of it.

The issue of what runtime files need to be on a computer to run an application needs to be addressed. For a .NET application to run on a computer it needs to have the necessary core CLR files installed, as well as any files required by the application. Some people argue that if you need to install a runtime prior to installing an application then this can never be classed as true XCOPY deployment. To start with the CLR will be distributed as a downloadable installation routine (or distributed as part of an applications setup routine), but we can expect it to be included in future service packs and natively included as part of the operating system in future versions of Microsoft Windows. Once the CLR has been installed it will not need to be installed again, so perhaps we can define a requirement of an application to be that a particular version of the CLR be installed.

Deployment Options Prior to .NET

Prior to Visual Studio.NET there were a number of deployment options available to the developer, some supplied by Microsoft and others supplied by third party companies, each trying to ease the pain of deploying applications. In this section, we will take a brief look at some of these options.

Manual Installation

As the name suggests, the **manual installation** method involves copying all the files manually into the correct place and then completing any other steps that are required to complete the installation of the software, for example registering any COM components and adding any other registry entries. It could also mean setting up database connections, etc. There is no automation in this deployment method and the steps have to be repeated on every computer that the application needs to be installed on. This installation method is time consuming and is not feasible for most applications, as it often requires advanced knowledge that perhaps the typical user of the application cannot be expected to have or learn. This is the installation method most used when components are installed onto a server, especially when they use COM+.

Custom Installer

The second deployment method we will look at is the use of a **custom installation program**. We can use the installation program to define the steps and actions that are required to install the application on a computer. The program then packages up all the required files including the instructions into an application the users can use to install the application on their machines.

The **Package and Deployment Wizard**, which was provided with VB6, is an example of such an application. You run the wizard, selecting the files that need to be copied and to where they need to be copied. The wizard then creates an installation that can be run on another computer.

Another variant often used to create an installation program is script based (for example InstallShield). It basically packages up any files that need to be copied and allows us to write a script to define what needs to be done when the installer is run. The script-based approach is very flexible in that we can easily incorporate any additional processing that needs to be done when installing an application (for example creating a new database).

There are many other variants on this theme of creating an installation program. As you can see there is no consistency between the installation programs, and each program can offer different functionality (or lack of). Microsoft acknowledged this inconsistency and tried to come up with a solution, which will be discussed next.

Windows Installer

Microsoft introduced the **Windows Installer** service as part of Windows 2000 as the solution to the shortcomings of the existing installation programs. Although the Windows Installer service was released as part of Windows 2000, it can also be installed on previous version of Windows and is automatically installed with several Microsoft applications (for example Office 2000). The Windows Installer service is what Microsoft calls an **operating system component**. The service implements all the required rules that a setup needs, for instance: do not overwrite a system file with an older version.

Instead of creating an executable that contains all the rules to install the application, you create a file, called a **Windows Installer package file** (.msi), which describes what needs to be done to install your application. An application is described in the resulting Windows Installer package as being made up of three parts: components, features, and products. Each part is made up of any number of the previous parts. For example a product is made up of several features, and a feature may contain one or more components. The component is the smallest part of the installation and contains a group of files and other resources that all need to be installed together. We will not be going into the underlying details of the Windows Installer architecture. If you are interested then you should take a look at the Windows Installer SDK documentation in MSDN.

The files that make up a product can be packaged externally in a number of cabinet files or the files can be packaged up into the resultant `.msi` file. As you will see later, there are a number of options within the deployment project templates that allow us to specify how the products files are packaged. When the user requests that a particular application needs to be installed they can just double-click the `.msi` file (assuming the Windows Installer service is installed). If the Windows Installer service is not installed there is usually a `Setup.exe` file that will install the Windows Installer service first and then go on to run the `.msi` file. The service will read the file and determine what needs to be done (for example what files need to be copied and where they need to be copied to) to install the application. All the installation rules are implemented centrally by the service and do not need to be distributed as part of a setup executable. The Windows Installer package file contains a list of actions (for example copy file mfc40.dll to the windows system folder) and what rules need to be applied to these actions. It does not contain the implementation of the rules

The Windows Installer service also provides a rich API that developers can use to include features such as on-demand installing into their applications. One of the biggest complaints about previous installers is that if the installation fails, the user's computer is often left in an unstable state. The Windows Installer service overcomes this by providing a rollback method. If the installation fails for some reason, the Windows Installer service will rollback the computer to its original state. So we could say that the installation is transactional.

You can create a Windows Installer package file manually using the Windows Installer SDK tools. This is not very user-friendly so Microsoft released the **Visual Studio Installer** (**VSI**) as an add-on for Visual Studio 6. The VSI integrated into the development environment and made the development of the Windows Installer package files easier. Three out of the four actual deployment/setup templates in Visual Studio.NET use Windows Installer technology. We will look at these in more detail later in the chapter.

Application Deployment in Visual Studio.NET

The first part of this chapter focused on some background issues relating to application deployment and some of the deployment options that have been previously available to developers. We're now going to turn our attention to looking at how the CLR and the .NET framework can help with deployment and resolve the issue of DLL Hell. Finally, we will take a look at the deployment project templates that are available within Visual Studio.NET.

Visual Studio.NET Deployment Projects

So you have decided that you need to package your application in some way so that it can be installed on other machines. The option of just zipping up the application directory is not satisfactory or not possible. What can you do? You will be pleased to hear that Visual Studio.NET provides a set of project templates that can be used to help package your application and deploy it. The remainder of this chapter will focus on these project templates. We will start by taking a look at the different templates and what they should be used for, after which we will take a practical look at the creation of three of these project templates.

Project Templates

Visual Studio.NET includes five project templates that can be used for setup and deployment in .NET. Before we discuss the project templates we need to define the difference between setup and deployment. A **setup** is an application/process that you create that packages your application up and provides an easy mechanism by which it can be installed on another machine. **Deployment** is the process of taking an application and installing it on another machine, usually by the use of a setup application/process.

The five project templates available within Visual Studio.NET can be created by the same means as any other project in Visual Studio.NET, by using the New Project dialog box:

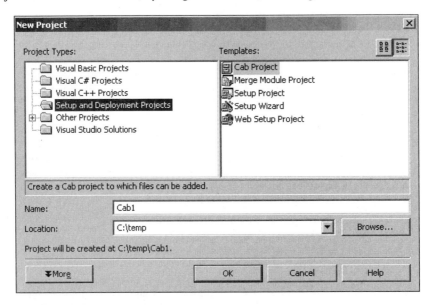

As you can see from the figure above you need to select the Setup and Deployment Projects node from the treeview of project types to the left of the dialog box. Out of the five available project templates there are four actual project templates:

❑   Cab Project

❑   Merge Module Project

❑   Setup Project

❑   Web Setup Project

And one wizard that can be used to help create one of the four project templates listed above:

❑   Setup Wizard

Let's now consider each of the project types in turn.

The Cab Project Template

As its name implies, the Cab Project template is used to create a **cabinet file**. A cabinet file (.cab) can contain any number of files. It is usually used to package components into a single file that can then be placed on a web server so that the cab file can be downloaded by a web browser.

Controls hosted within Internet Explorer are often packaged into a cabinet file and a reference added to the file in the web page that uses the control. When Internet Explorer encounters this reference it will check that the control isn't already installed on the user's computer, at which point it will download the cabinet file, extract the control, and install it to a protected part of the user's computer.

Cabinet files can be compressed to reduce their size and consequently the time it takes to download them.

The Merge Module Project Template

The Merge Module Project template is used to create a **merge module**, which is similar to a cabinet file in that it can be used to package a group of files. The difference is that a merge module file (.msm) cannot be used by itself to install the files that it contains. The merge module file created by this project template can be used within another setup project.

Merge modules were introduced as part of the Microsoft Windows Installer technology to enable a set of files to be packaged up into an easy to use file that could be re-used and shared between Windows Installer-based setup programs. The idea is to package up all the files and any other resources (for example, registry entries, bitmaps, etc.) that are dependent on each other into the merge module.

This type of project can be very useful for packaging a component and all its dependencies, and using the resulting merge file in the setup program of each application that uses the component.

Microsoft suggests that a merge module should not be modified once it has been distributed, which means a new one should be created. The notion of packaging everything up into a single re-distributable file can help alleviate the issues of DLL Hell as the package contains all dependencies.

The Setup Project Template

The Setup Project template is used to create a standard Windows Installer setup for an application. This type of project will probably be the most familiar to developers who have used the Visual Studio Installer add-on for Visual Studio 6. The Setup Project template can be used to create a setup package for a standard Windows application, which is normally installed in the Program Files directory of a user's computer.

The Web Setup Project Template

The Web Setup Project template is used to create a Windows Installer setup program that can be used to install a project into a virtual directory of a web server. It is intended to be used to create a setup program for a web application.

The Setup Wizard

The Setup Wizard can be used to help guide you through the creation of one of the above four setup and deployment project templates. The steps that the wizard displays to you depend on whether the wizard was started to add a project to an existing solution or started to create a totally new project.

Creating a Deployment Project

A deployment project can be created in exactly the same way as any other project in Visual Studio.NET by using the New | Project option from the File menu or by using the New Project button on the Visual Studio start page.

You can also add a deployment project to an existing solution by using the Add Project item from the File menu. You will then be presented with the Add New Project dialog box where you can select the deployment template of choice.

Walkthroughs

Now that we have looked at how we can create a deployment project, the next two sections are going to contain practical walkthroughs of the creation of two deployment projects. The two walkthroughs are going to cover different scenarios:

❑   Desktop application

❑   Web application

Each of the above scenarios will detail a different deployment project template. They have been chosen to try and demonstrate the two most common deployment scenarios. Hopefully, you will be able to use the walkthroughs and apply or modify them to your own needs. We will not use the wizard to create the deployment projects in the walkthroughs. This decision has been taken so that you will be able to understand what is required to create a deployment project. The wizard can be used to help guide you through the creation of a deployment project and therefore hide from you some of the steps that we will be taking in the walkthroughs. However, the wizard can be very useful in providing the base for a deployment project.

Desktop Application

The first deployment scenario that we are going to look at is that of a desktop application where a user installs and runs an application on his machine. The application will be Windows-based and we will need to ensure that everything it needs is distributed with the application executable. This type of deployment scenario is one of the most typical that you will come across.

In this deployment scenario, the package needs to be created in such a way that it will guide the user through the process of installing the application on his or her machine. The best deployment template for this scenario is the Setup Project and this is what we will be using throughout this section.

1. Before we start getting into the specifics of this project type we need to create an application that will serve as our desktop application that we want to deploy. For this example we are going to use the Windows Application project type. Create a new project and choose Windows Application from the list of available Visual Basic project templates. We will not add any code to the project and will use it as the new project wizard created it. At the moment we have a solution with one project contained within it.

2. Add a new project to the solution and choose Setup Project from the list of available Setup and Deployment Project templates. You will now have a solution containing two projects:

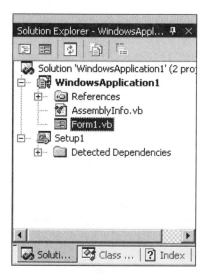

3. The deployment project does not contain any files at present, just a folder called Detected Dependencies, which we will discuss later. Notice also the buttons that appear along the top of the Solution Explorer. These are used to access the editors of this deployment project template and will be discussed later in this chapter.

4. Next, we need to add files to the setup project and in particular we need to look at how we can add the file created by the windows application project. We can add files to the setup deployment project in two ways. The first is to make sure the setup project is the active project and then choose the Add item from the Project menu. The second method is to right-click the setup project file in the solution explorer and choose Add from the popup menu.

5. Both these methods enable you to choose from one of four options.

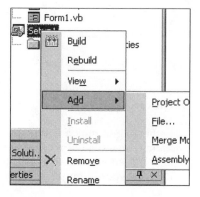

If you select File from the submenu, you will be presented with a dialog box that will allow you to browse for and select a particular file to add to the setup project. This method is sufficient if the file you are adding is not the output from another project within the solution. This option is very useful in web setup projects as it allows you to include external business components (if they are used) etc.

The Merge Module option allows us to include a merge module in the deployment project. If you select this option, you will be presented with a dialog box that you can use to browse for and select a merge module to include in your project. Third party vendors can supply merge modules or we can create our own with Visual Studio.NET.

The Assembly option can be used to select a .NET component (assembly) to be included in the deployment project. If you select this option you will be presented with a window that you can use to select an assembly to include from those that are installed on your machine.

If the deployment project is part of a solution (as in this walkthrough) you can use the Project Output submenu item. As the name implies, this allows you to add the output from any of the projects in the solution to the setup project. We want to add the output of the windows application project to the setup project. So we need to select the Project Output menu item to bring up the dialog box that will enable us to accomplish this task:

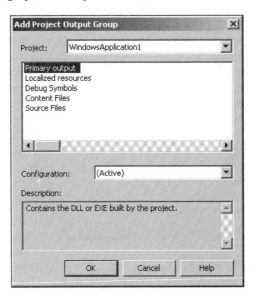

6. The Add Project Output Group dialog box is split into several parts.

The combo box at the top contains a list of the names of all the non-deployment projects in the current solution. In our case there is only one project – WindowsApplication1.

Below the combo box is a listbox containing a list of all the possible outputs from the selected project. If you click on a possible output a description appears in the Description box at the bottom. The type of output we are interested in is the Primary output so make sure this is selected. The different types of output are summarized in the table at the end of this step.

Below the list of possible outputs is a combo box that allows us to select the Configuration to use for the selected project. We will use the (Active) option as this will use whatever configuration is in effect when the project is built. The combo box will also contain all the possible build configurations for the selected project.

Click OK to return to the solution.

Project Output	Description
Primary output	The primary output of a project is the resulting DLL or EXE that is produced by building the particular project.
Localized resources	The localized resource of a project is a dll that contains only resources. The resources within the dll are specific to a culture or locale. This is often called a satellite dll.
Debug Symbols	When the particular project in question is compiled a special file is created that contains special debugging information about the project. These are called debug symbols. The debug symbols for a project have the same name as the primary output but with an extension of PDB. The debug symbols provide information to a debugger when an application is being run through it.
Content Files	This project output is used only with ASP.NET Web Applications. The content files of a web application are the html, graphic files etc. that form the 'content' of the web site.
Source Files	This will include all the source files for the selected project including the project file. The solution file is NOT included.

7. Now, not only has the output from the Windows application been added to the Setup1 project but the Detected Dependencies folder contains quite a few entries.

Whenever you add a .NET component to this deployment project its dependencies are added to this folder. The dependencies of the dependencies will also be added and so on until all the required files have been added. This functionality has been included to help ensure that all the dependencies of an application are deployed along with the application. The files listed in the Detected Dependencies folder will be included in the resulting setup and, by default, will be installed into the application's directory as application-private assemblies. This default behavior helps to reduce the possible effects of DLL Hell by making the application use its own copies of dependent files.

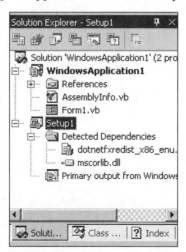

8. If you do not want a particular dependency file to be included in the resulting setup you can exclude it by right-clicking on the particular entry under Detected Dependencies and selecting Exclude from the popup menu. The dependency will now have a little stop sign before its name to indicate that it has been excluded:

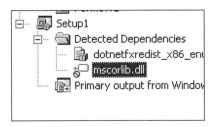

Dependencies can also be excluded by selecting the particular dependency and using the Properties window to set the Exclude property to True. The listed dependencies will be refreshed whenever a .NET file is added to or removed from the setup project taking into account any files that have already been excluded.

You may decide that you want to exclude a detected dependency from the setup of an application because you know that the dependency is already installed on the target computer. This is fine if you have tight control over what is installed on a users machine. If, however, you don't and you deploy the application with the missing dependency, your application could well be rendered unusable. In the above screenshot you can see that there are two entries in the folder. The first `dotnetfxredist_x86_enu.msm` is a merge module dependency. As mentioned previously a merge module is used to package a group of files that are dependent on each other. This merge module contains a re-distributable version of the CLR and will be installed on the users computer when the installation is run. The second entry `mscorlib.dll` is a special assembly in .NET and contains all the definitions of the base types used in .NET and is in fact referenced by all assemblies.

9. We can select an item in the setup project in the Solution Explorer and that particular item's properties will be displayed in the Properties window. For example, if we select the root node of the setup project (Setup1) the Properties window will change to show us the details of the setup project:

> As with any other project in Visual Studio.NET there are a set of project properties that can also be modified. The project properties are accessed by right-clicking the project file and choosing Properties from the popup menu. These properties will be covered later in the chapter.

We are not going to include a discussion of every single property of all the different project items as we could probably fill a whole book on the subject. Instead, we will take a look at the properties from the root setup node and each of the two different project items. We are going to start with the root setup node (Setup1). Before we start our discussion, make sure that the node is selected and take some time to browse the list of available properties. The root setup node represents the resulting output from this deployment project type: Windows Installer package (.msi). Therefore, the Properties window contains properties that will affect the resulting .msi that is produced.

Properties of the Root Setup Node

The first property we are going to look at is `ProductName`. This property, as the name tells us, is used to set the textual name of the product that this Windows Installer package is installing. By default it is set to the name of the setup project (in our case `Setup1`). The value of this property is used throughout the steps of the resulting setup. For instance, it is used for the text of the title bar when the resulting .msi file is run. The property is used along with the `Manufacturer` property to construct the default installation directory:

```
C:\Program Files\<Manufacturer>\<ProductName>
```

The `ProductName` property is also used by the Add/Remove Programs control panel applet, to show that the application is installed:

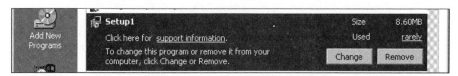

From the screenshot above you can see there is a link that you can click on to get support information about the selected application:

A number of the properties of the setup project can be used to customize the support information that is shown. The following table contains details of the how the properties relate to the support information that is shown:

Support Information	Related Property(s)	Description
Publisher	Manufacturer	The Manufacturer property is used to help create the default installation directory for the project and provide a textual display of the manufacturer of the application contained within the Windows Installer package.
	ManufacturerUrl	This property is used in conjunction with the Manufacturer property to make a hyperlink for the **Publisher** part of the support information. If a value is entered, the name of the **Publisher** will be underlined, which can then be clicked to allow you to visit the publisher's web site. If a value is not included the publishers name does not act as a hyperlink.
Version	Version	This is the version number of the Windows Installer package. It can be changed to match the version number of the application that the package installs. But this has to be done manually.
Contact	Author	This property is used to hold the name of the company/person that created the Windows Installer package. By default this has the same value as the Manufacturer property.
Support Information	SupportPhone	This property can be used to provide a support telephone number for the application.
	SupportUrl	This property can be used to provide a URL for the product's support web site. The value of this property will be represented as a hyperlink in the support information window.
Comments	Description	This property can be used to include any information that you would like to appear in the support information window. For instance, it could be used to detail the opening hours of your support department.

The next property that we are going to look at for the root setup node is called AddRemoveProgramsIcon. As you can probably guess, this property allows us to set the icon that appears in the Add/Remove Programs control panel applet for the application contained within this Windows Installer package. We can select (None) from the drop-down list, which means that we do not want to change the icon and the default icon will be used. Alternatively, we have the option to (Browse...) for an icon, which brings up a window that allows us to find and select the particular icon we would like to use. We do not have to use a standalone icon file; we can use an icon from an executable or DLL that is contained within the project.

The remainder of the properties for the root setup node are summarized in the table below:

Property	Description
DetectNewerInstalledVersion	If this property is set to True and a newer version of the application is found on the machine then the installation will not continue. If the property is set to False then this check will not occur and the application will install even if there is a newer version on the computer already.
Keywords	This property enables you to set a number of keywords that can be used to locate this installer.
Localization	This property is used to set which locale this installer has been designed to run in. The values of this property will affect what string resources are used within the installation.
PackageCode	This property is a GUID that is used to uniquely identify this installer. This property is used to link the installer with a specific version of the application that it installs.
ProductCode	This property is a GUID that is used to uniquely identify the particular version of the application contained within it.
RemovePreviousVersion	If this property is set to True and an older version of the application is found on the machine then the installation will remove the old version and continue on with the installation. If the property is set to False then this check is not done.
SearchPath	This property is used to specify a search path that Visual Studio uses when it builds the setup project and needs to find the detected dependencies.
Subject	This property is used to provide an additional text string of what the installation is used for.
Title	This property is used to set the textual title of the application that is installed. By default this property will have the same name as the setup project.
Upgrade Code	This property is a GUID and is used to uniquely identify a product. This property should stay the same for all versions of the same application. The ProductCode and PackageCode properties changes depending on the specific version of the product.

Properties of the Primary Output Project Item

We are now going to move on and take a quick look at the properties of the primary output project item. We are going to look at a few of the properties in depth and then summarize all the properties in a table at the end of the section.

The first property we are going to look at is Folder, which is used to set where the selected file (in our case the primary output from the WindowsApplication1 project) is installed when the Windows Installer package is run on a user computer. The default installation folder for the file is the Application Folder. You can change the folder by using the Select Folder window that is shown when you click on the ellipsis button for this property:

To change the installation folder for the selected file all we need to do is select the required folder from the above window.

The list of available folders can be changed using the File System editor, which will be covered later in the chapter.

By default the setup project has a number of folders already defined for our use. The are summarized in the table below:

Folder	Description
Application Folder	The application folder is where traditional windows based applications are installed. The application folder by default is: `<Program Files>\<Manufacturer>\<ProductName>`
Global Assembly Cache Folder	This is a special folder where shared assemblies are installed. It is usually in a directory called Assembly in the windows directory.
User's Desktop	This folder relates to the user's desktop. We can use this folder to add a shortcut to the user's desktop.
User's Programs Menu	This folder relates to the user's programs menu (accessed from the start button). This folder is especially useful as it is where most applications are accessed from (via shortcuts).

If you choose to have a file installed to a particular folder and that folder does not exist on the users computer then the folder will be automatically created by the installer. If the user installing the application does not have access to the folder then an error will be reported back to the user. This is especially true if you try to install a shared assembly to the `Global Assembly Cache Folder` and you are not part of the Administrators of the computer.

The rest of the properties of the project output item are summarized in the table below:

Property	Description
Condition	This enables you to enter a condition that will be evaluated when the installation is run. If the condition evaluates to `True` then the file will be installed, likewise if the condition evaluates to `False` then the file won't be installed. Suppose we only wanted a particular file to be installed if the installation was being run on Microsoft Windows 2000, we could enter the following for the condition: `VersionNT >= 5`
Dependencies	Selecting this property will display a window that shows all the dependencies of the selected project output.
Exclude	You can use this property to indicate whether you want the project output to be excluded from the resulting Windows Installer package.
ExcludeFilter	This property enables you to exclude files from the project output using wildcards. For example, if you enter a wildcard of `*.txt`, then all files that are part of the project output that have an extension of .txt will be excluded from the resulting Windows Installer package. Selecting this property will display a window that will allow you to enter any number of wildcards.
Folder	As mentioned previously this property allows you to select the target folder for the project outputs.
Hidden	This property allows you to install the files that make up the project output as hidden files. This property basically toggles on/off the hidden attribute of the files.
KeyOutput	This property expands to provide information about the main file that makes up the project output. In our case it will show information of the WindowsApplication1.exe file.
Outputs	Selecting this property will display a window that lists all the files that are part of the project output and where these files are located on the development machine.
PackageAs	This property can be used to indicate whether the project output should be packaged according to what is defined in the project properties (`vsdpaDefault`) or externally (`vsdpaLoose`) to the resulting Windows Installer package. The default is to use the project properties setting.
Permanent	This property is used to indicate whether the files that make up the project output should be removed when the application is uninstalled (`False`) or left behind (`True`). It is advisable that all the files that are installed by an application be removed when the application is uninstalled. Therefore this property should be set to `False`, which it is by default.

Table continued on following page

Property	Description
ReadOnly	This property is used to set the read only file attribute of all the files that make up the project output. As the name suggests this makes the file readonly on the target machine.
Register	This property allows you to instruct the Windows Installer to register the files contained within the project output as COM objects. This only really applies to projects (for example Class Library project template) that have been compiled with the **Register for COM Interop** project property set.
SharedLegacy	This property indicates whether the files that make up the project output are to be reference counted once installed. This really only applies to files that are going to be shared across multiple applications. When the installation is removed the files will only be uninstalled if the reference count is equal to zero.
System	This property indicates that the files contained within the project output are to be treated as system files and protected by windows file protection.
Transitive	This property indicates whether the condition specified in the condition property is re-evaluated when the installation is re-run on the computer at a later date. If the value is True then the condition is checked on each additional run of the installation. Whereas a value of False will cause the condition only to be run the first time the installation is run on the computer. The default value is False.
Vital	This property is used to indicate that the files contained within the project output are vital to the installation. Meaning that if the installation of these files fails then the installation as a whole should fail. The default value is True.

Properties of the Detected Dependency Items

We are now going to take a brief look at the properties of the two different items that are contained within the Detected Dependencies folder. The first item named dotnetfxredist_x86_enu.msm is a merge module dependency and the second is an assembly dependency. We will only cover the properties that are different to those of the project output item (discussed above). Most of the additional properties are readonly and cannot be changed. They are used purely to provide information to the developer. Let's start by taking a look at the additional properties of the assembly dependency item (mscorlib.dll):

Property	Description
DisplayName	It contains the filename of the selected assembly. Readonly.
Files	Selecting this property will display a window that will list all the files that make up the selected assembly. Readonly.
HashAlgorithm	This property shows what hash algorithm was used by the manifest in hashing the files contents (to stop tampering). Readonly.
Language	This property will show what language this assembly is targeted at. This property relates to the culture of an assembly. If the property is empty then assembly is culture (language) independent. Readonly.

Property	Description
PublicKey PublicKeyToken	These two properties are used to show information about the strong name of the selected assembly. If an assembly has a strong name then either of these two properties will contain a value (other than all 0s). One or the other of these properties are used and not normally both. Readonly.
SourcePath	This property contains the location of where the selected assembly can be found on the development computer. Readonly.
TargetName	This property contains the filename of the assembly, as it will appear on the target machine. ReadOnly.
Version	This property shows you the version number of the selected assembly. Readonly.

All of the additional properties of the assembly dependency are readonly and are there to provide information to the developer. We will now summarize the additional properties of the merge module dependency (dotnetfxredist_x86_enu.msm) in the table below:

Property	Description
MergeModuleProperties	A merge module can contain a number of custom configurable properties. If the selected merge module contains any they will appear here. In the case of our example there are no custom properties.
Author	This property stores the name of the author of the merge module. Readonly.
Description	This property is used to store a textual description of the merge module. Readonly.
LanguageIds	This property is used to indicate what language the selected merge module is targeted at. Readonly.
ModuleDependencies	Selecting this property will show a window that lists all the dependencies of the selected merge module. Readonly.
ModuleSignature	This property will display the unique signature of the merge module. Readonly.
Subject	This property is used to display additional information about the merge module. Readonly.
Title	This property is used to simply state the title of the merge module. Readonly.
Version	This property is used to store the version number of the selected merge module. The version number of the merge module usually changes as the version number of the files it contains changes. Readonly.

This has been a brief look at the Setup Project template. It uses all the project defaults and provides a standard set of steps to the user when they run the Windows Installer package. More often than not this simple approach of including a single application file and its dependencies is not good enough. Fortunately, the setup project can be customized extensively to meet our needs. We can create shortcuts, directories, registry entries, etc. These customizations and more can be accomplished using the set of built-in editors, which will be covered after the next walkthrough.

Web Application

The other deployment scenario we are going to look at is that of a web application that has been created using the Web Application project template. We are assuming that the web application is being developed on a development web server and that we will need to create a deployment project to transfer the finished application to the production web server. Although the previous deployment scenario is one of the most typical, this scenario has to come a very close second.

From the simple requirements defined above we can see that the best deployment template to use is the Web Setup Project template. There is one major difference between this template and the previous Setup Project template, in that the Web Setup Project will by default deploy the application to a virtual directory of the web server on which the setup is run, whereas a Setup Project will deploy the application to the Program Files folder on the target machine by default. There are obviously some properties that differ between the two project templates, but other than that they are pretty similar. They both produce a Windows Installer package and have the same set of project properties discussed later in the chapter.

1. As with the other walkthroughs, we need to create an application that we can use to deploy. Start a new project and make sure you select ASP.NET Web Application from the list of available Visual Basic project templates. We are not going to add any code to the project that we just created, as it is being used purely as a base for the deployment project. Now add a Web Setup Project template. Our solution contains two projects.

As with the previous walkthroughs the deployment project does not contain any files at present. There is also a folder called Detected Dependencies in the solution explorer that acts in exactly the same way as in the previous walkthrough:

2. The next step that we need to look at is adding the output of the web application to the deployment project. This is accomplished in pretty much the same way as the previous walkthrough. So to start with, add the Primary output from the web application to the deployment project using the method described in the previous walkthroughs.

3. If we built the solution now and tried to deploy the application onto the production web server it would not work. When adding the Primary output from a web application, only the compiled code of the web application including its detected dependencies are added to the deployment project. All the other files that make up a web application (html files, style sheets, etc.) are not included as part of the Primary output of the project.

To include these files in the deployment project we need to add another project output to the deployment project. This time we need to include the Content Files of the web application. The resulting project should look pretty similar to the screenshot below:

4. Now if we build the solution, the resulting Windows Installer package will include the compiled code of the web application along with its dependencies, as well as the other files that make up a web application, ASP.NET files, style sheets, etc.

Most of the topics discussed in the last walkthrough apply to this walkthrough. As mentioned earlier the Setup Project and Web Setup projects are very similar and are only really different in where they install the application by default.

Modifying the Deployment Project

In the last two walkthroughs we created the default Windows Installer package for the particular project template. We didn't customize the steps or actions that were performed when the package was run. What if we had wanted to add a step into the installation process that displayed a readme file to the user? Or what if we needed to create registry entries on the installation computer? The walkthroughs did not cover how to customize the installation to our needs, which is what this section is going to focus on. There are six editors that we can use to customize a Windows Installer-based deployment project:

- ❑ File System editor
- ❑ Registry editor
- ❑ File Types editor
- ❑ User Interface editor
- ❑ Custom Actions editor
- ❑ Launch Conditions editor

The editors are accessible through the View | Editor menu option or by using the corresponding buttons at the top of the Solution Explorer.

We can also modify the resulting Windows Installer package through the project properties window. In this section we are going to take a brief look at each of the six editors and the project properties, and how they can be used to modify the resulting Windows Installer package. We will only be able to cover the basics of each of the editors, enough to get you going. We will use the project created in the desktop application walkthrough in this section.

Project Properties

The first step we can take in customizing the Windows Installer package is to use the project properties. The project properties dialog box is accessed by right-clicking the root of the setup project and selecting Properties from the popup menu or by selecting the Properties item from the Project menu when the setup project is the active project. Both of these methods will bring up the project properties dialog box:

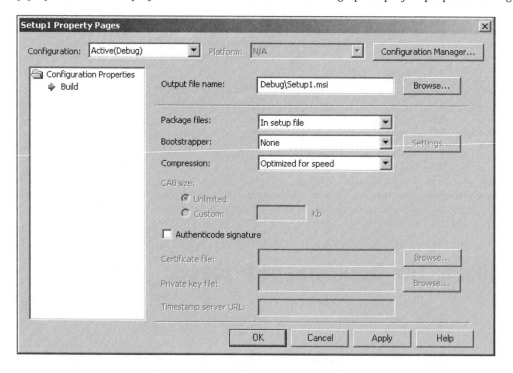

As you can see from the previous screenshot there is only one page that we can use to set the properties of the project: Build.

The Build Page

We will now take a look at the `Build` page and how the options can be used to affect how the resulting Windows Installer package is built.

Build Configurations

The first thing to notice is that like most other projects in Visual Studio.NET we can create different build configurations. We can modify the properties of a project for the currently active build configuration or we can modify the properties for all the build configurations. We use the Configuration combo box to change what build configuration we want to change the properties for. In the previous screenshot, notice that we are modifying the properties for the currently active build configuration: Debug. The button labeled Configuration Manager allows us to add, remove, and edit the build configurations for this project.

Moving on we can see an option called Output file name, which can be used to modify where the resulting Windows Installer package (.msi) file will be created. We can modify the filename and path directly or we can press the Browse button.

Package Files

By using the next setting, Package files, we can specify how the files that make up the installation are packaged up. The table below describes the possible settings:

Package:	Description
As loose uncompressed files	When we build the project, the files that are to be included as part of the installation are copied to the same directory as the resulting Windows Installer package (.msi) file. As mentioned above, this directory can be set using the Output file name setting.
In setup file	When the project is built, the files that are to be included as part of the installation are packaged up in the resulting Windows Installer package (.msi) file. By using this method we only have one file to distribute. This is the default setting.
In cabinet file(s)	With this option, when the project is built, the files that are to be included as part of the installation are packaged up into a number of cabinet files. The size of the resulting cabinet files can be restricted by the use of a number of options, which will be discussed later in this section. This option can be very useful if you want to distribute the installation program on a set of floppy disks.

What happens if we try to install the resulting Windows Installer package on a machine that does not have the Windows Installer services running on it? Not a great deal! Luckily, there is a project option that will help us overcome this problem: Bootstrapper. There are three options available from the combo-box:

❑   None

❑   Windows Installer Bootstrapper

❑   Web bootstrapper

If None is selected then only the Windows Installer package file will be produced when the setup project is built. If you select Windows Installer Bootstrapper then some additional files will be placed in the output directory when the setup project is built. These additional files will install the Windows Installer services on the machine that it is run on. With this option selected, four additional files will be added to the directory that contains the resulting Windows Installer package file. The table below details the additional files:

File	Description
Setup.exe	If a user does not have the Windows Installer service installed on his machine he can use this file to install the application. When running this file the Windows Installer services will be installed onto the machine (if it is not already installed) and then the .msi file will be run and the installation will continue as normal.
Setup.ini	This is a configuration file that is used by Setup.exe after it has installed the Windows Installer services (if needed) and contains one setting – the name of the .msi file to run.
InstMsiA.exe	This file is the installation for the Windows Installer services for a Windows 95 or 98-based machine.
InstMsiW.exe	This file is the installation for the Windows Installer services for a Windows NT or 2000.

The final option is Web Bootstrapper. This option allows you to produce a number of additional files that can be used to allow the application to be installed over the Internet. When you select this option a window will be presented to you:

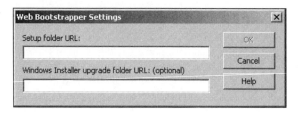

This window is used to set two options of the web bootstrapper:

❑   The **Setup folder URL** setting is used to define the location of where the Windows Installer package file produced will be located when deployed. This setting needs to be the URL of a folder.

❑   The **Windows Installer upgrade folder URL** setting is where you can optionally set the location of where the two Windows Installer service installer files (InstMsiA.exe and InstMsiW.exe) are located. This setting (if used) needs to be the URL of a folder. If this setting is not used, it is assumed that two file are located at the URL specified by the Setup folder URL setting.

When we build the setup project with this option, three additional files are created in the output directory: `Setup.exe`, `InstMsiA.exe` and `InstMsiW.exe`. The only file that has a different function from that discussed previously is the `Setup.exe` file, which we will discuss later in this section. The Windows Installer package (.msi) file that was created by the build needs to be copied to the web server so that it is available via the URL specified in the `Setup folder URL` setting. The `InstMsiA.exe` and `InstMsiW.exe` files need to be copied to the web server so they are accessible via the URL specified in the `Windows Installer upgrade folder URL` setting. If no value was specified for this property then they need to be copied to the same location as the Windows Installer package file. The `Setup.exe` file can then be distributed to anyone who wants to install your application.

When the user executes the `Setup.exe` file, it first checks that the correct version of the Windows Installer service is installed. If it is not, then the required setup (`InstMsiA.exe` or `InstMsiW.exe`) file is downloaded from the URL specified in the above settings and then installed. Once the correct version of the Windows Installer service is installed, the `Setup.exe` file then downloads the package file (.msi) from the location specified. Once the package has been downloaded, the installation continues as normal by executing this Windows Installer package. If the package file cannot be downloaded then you will receive an error informing you that it could not be downloaded. The installation will then end.

The advantage of using this technique is that you do not have to deploy the Windows Installer setup files to each of the clients, they are available centrally from one location over the web. Several installers can share the same download location. The Windows Installer package file that contains your application is also not distributed to each client. They download it from a central location. This allows you to change the package and have clients pick up this change automatically when they install the application. The disadvantage to this approach is that anyone who installs your application will need to have an Internet connection and if the files are large, it could take a long time to download them

Compression

We also have the option to modify the compression used when packaging up the files that are to be contained within the installation program. The three options (Optimized for speed, Optimized for size, and None) are pretty self-explanatory and will not be covered in this book. The default, however, is Optimized for speed.

Setting the Cabinet File Size

If we want to package the files in cabinet files then we have the option to specify the size of those resulting cabinet file(s):

❑ The first option we have is to let the resulting cabinet file be of an unlimited size. What this effectively means is that all the files will be packaged into one big cabinet file. The resulting size of the cabinet file will also be dependent on the compression method selected.

❑ If, however, creating one large cabinet file is not practical, especially if you want to distribute your application on floppy disks (1440Kb of space per floppy), you can use the second option to specify the maximum size of the resulting cabinet file(s). If you select this option you need to fill in the maximum size that a cabinet file can be. This figure is in Kb. If all the files that need to be contained within this installation exceed this size then multiple cabinet files will be created.

Using the Solution Signing Options

The final set of options are concerned with signing the resulting Windows Installer package using Authenticode. To enable Authenticode signing you must make sure the checkbox is checked. This will enable you to set the three settings that are required to sign the package file:

Setting	Description
Certificate file	This setting is used to define where the Authenticode certificate file can be found. This file is used to sign the package.
Private key file	This setting is used to define where the private key file is. This file contains what we call an encryption key that is used to sign the package.
Timestamp server URL	This setting allows you to optionally specify the URL of a timestamp server. The timestamp server will be used to get the time of when the package was signed.

We will not be covering Authenticode signing in this chapter. If you are interested in this option you should consult the MSDN documentation.

The File System Editor

Now that we have taken a look at the project properties we are going to move on to look at the editors that are available for us to use to customize the resulting Windows Installer package. You will need to make sure that the current active project is the setup project.

We are going to start by taking a look at the File System editor, so start it via the View | Editor menu option. The File System editor is used to manage all the file system aspects of the installation including:

❑ Creating folders on the user's machine

❑ Adding files to the folders defined

❑ Creating shortcuts

Basically, this is the editor we use to define what files need to be installed and where they are installed on the user's machine.

The File System editor is split into two panes:

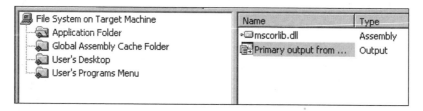

The left-hand pane shows a list of the folders that have been created automatically for the project (discussed earlier in the chapter). When you select a folder in the left-pane, two things happen: firstly, the right-hand pane of the editor displays a list of the files that are to be installed into the selected folder, and secondly, the Properties windows will change to show you the properties of the currently selected folder.

Adding Items to a Folder

To add an item that needs to be installed to a folder, we can either right-click on the folder in the left-hand pane and choose Add from the popup menu, or we can select the required folder and right-click in the right-hand pane and again choose Add from the popup menu. You will be presented with four options, three of which have been discussed earlier in the walkthroughs:

- ❏   Project Output
- ❏   File
- ❏   Assembly

The fourth option (Folder) allows us to add a sub folder to the currently selected folder. This sub folder then becomes a standard folder that can be used to add files. If we add any .NET components or executables, the dependencies of these components will also be added to the installation automatically.

Adding Special Folders

When we create a new deployment project, a set of standard folders will be created for us (listed in the desktop application section). What if the folders created do not match our requirements? Well, we can also use the File System editor to add special folders. To add a special folder, right-click anywhere in the left-hand pane (other than on a folder) and you will be presented with a popup menu that has one item: Add Special Folder. This menu item expands to show you a list of folders that you can add to the installation (folders already added to the project will be grayed out):

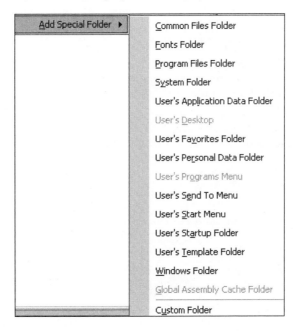

As you can see from the screenshot there are a number of system folders that we can choose from. They are summarized in the following table:

Name	Description	Windows Installer property
Common Files Folder	Files (non-system) that are shared by multiple applications are usually installed to this folder.	[CommonFilesFolder]
Fonts Folder	This folder is used to contain all the fonts that are installed on the computer. If your application used a specific font you want to install it into this folder.	[FontsFolder]
Program Files Folder	Most applications are installed in a directory below the program files folder. This acts as root directory for installed applications.	[ProgramFilesFolder]
System Folder	This folder is used to store shared system files. The folder typically holds files that are part of the OS.	[SystemFolder]
User's Application Data Folder	This folder is used to store data on a per-application basis that is specific to a user.	[CommonAppDataFolder]
User's Desktop	This folder represents the user desktop. This folder could be used to create and display a shortcut to your application that a user could use to start your application.	[DesktopFolder]
User's Favorite Folder	This folder is used as a central place to store links to the user's favorite web sites, documents, folders, etc.	[FavoritesFolder]
User's Personal Data Folder	This folder is where a user will store their important files. It is normally referred to as 'My Documents'.	[PersonalFolder]
User's Programs Menu	This folder is where shortcuts etc. are created to applications that appear on the user's program menu. This would be an ideal place to create a shortcut to your application.	[ProgramMenuFolder]
User's Send To Menu	This folder stores all the users send to shortcuts. A send to shortcut is displayed when you right-click a file in the Windows Explorer and choose Send To. The send to shortcut usually invokes an application passing in the pathname of the files it was invoked from.	[SendToFolder]
User's Start Menu	This folder can be used to add items to the user's start menu. This is not often used.	[StartMenuFolder]
User's Startup Folder	This folder is used to start applications whenever the user logs into the computer. If you would like your application to start every time the user logs in, then you could add a shortcut to your application in this folder.	[StartupFolder]

Name	Description	Windows Installer property
User's Template Folder	This folder contains templates specific to the logged in user. Templates are usually used by applications like Microsoft Office 2000.	[TemplateFolder]
Windows Folder	This folder is the Windows root folder. This is where the OS is installed.	[WindowsFolder]
Global Assembly Cache Folder	This folder is used to store all the shared assemblies on the user's computer.	

If none of the built-in folders matches your requirements, you can even use the item at the bottom of the list to create you own custom folder. This is where the Windows Installer property column of the above table comes. Suppose we wanted to create a new directory in the user's favorites folder called Wrox Press. We could accomplish this by adding the correct special folder and then adding a sub folder to it. Another way to accomplish this is to create a custom folder, the process of which we will include below:

1. Right-click in the left-hand pane of the file editor and choose Custom Folder from the popup menu.

2. The new folder will be created in the left-hand pane of the editor. The name of the folder will be edit mode, so enter the text Wrox Press. And press *enter*.

3. The folder will now be selected and the Properties window will have changed to show the properties of the new folder. The properties of a folder are summarized in the table below:

Property	Description
(Name)	This is the name of the selected folder. The name property is used within the setup project as the means by which you select a folder.
AlwaysCreate	This property is used to indicate whether this folder should be created on installation even if it's empty (True). If the value is False and there are no files to be installed into the folder, then the folder will not be created. The default is False.
Condition	This enables you to enter a condition that will be evaluated when the installation is run. If the condition evaluates to True then the folder will be created, likewise if the condition evaluates to False then the folder won't be created.
DefaultLocation	This is where we define where the folder is going to be created on the target machine. We can enter a literal folder name (for example C:\Temp), or we can use a Windows Installer property, or a combination of the two. A Windows Installer property contains information that is filled in when the installer is run. In the above table of special folders there was a column called Windows Installer property. The property defined in this table would be filled in with the actual location of the special folder at runtime. Therefore, if we entered [WindowsFolder] as the text for this property, the folder created would represent the Windows special folder.

Table continued on following page

Property	Description
Property	This property is used to define a Windows Installer property that can be used to override the `DefaultLocation` property of the folder when the installation is run.
Transitive	This property indicates whether the condition specified in the condition property is re-evaluated on subsequent (re-)installs. If the value is `True` then the condition is checked on each additional run of the installation. Whereas a value of `False` will cause the condition only to be run the first time the installation is run on the computer. The default value is `False`.

4. Set the DefaultLocation property to `[FavoritesFolder]\Wrox Press`.

5. We could now add some shortcuts to this folder using the technique described below.

6. When the installation is run, a new folder will be added to the user's favorite folder called Wrox Press.

Creating Shortcuts

The final aspect of the File System editor that we are going to look at is that of creating shortcuts.

The first step in creating a shortcut is to locate the file that is to be the target of the shortcut. Select the target file and right-click on it. The popup menu that appears will include an option to create a shortcut to the selected file, which will be created in the same folder. Select this option.

To add the shortcut to the user's desktop we need to move this shortcut to the folder that represents the user's desktop. Likewise we could move this shortcut to the folder that represents the user's programs menu. Cut and paste the new shortcut to the User's Desktop folder in the left-hand pane of the editor. The shortcut will now be added to the user's desktop when the installation is run. You will probably want to rename the shortcut, which can be accomplished easily via the Rename option of the popup menu.

We have only taken a brief look at the File System editor. You are encouraged to explore what can be accomplished by using the editor.

The Registry Editor

The next editor that we are going to look at is the Registry editor, which is used to:

❏ Create registry keys

❏ Create values for registry keys

❏ Import a registry file

Like the File System editor, the Registry Editor is split into two panes:

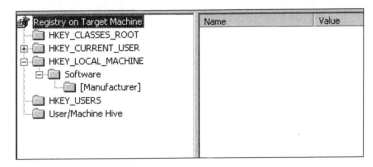

The left-hand pane of the editor represents the registry keys on the target computer. When you select a registry key, two things happen: firstly, the right-hand pane of the editor will be updated to show the values that are to be created under the selected registry key, and secondly, if the registry key selected is not a root key in the left-hand pane, the Properties window will be updated with a set of properties for this registry key.

When you create a new deployment project a set of registry keys will be created for you that correspond to the standard base registry keys of Windows. Notice in the screenshot that there is a key defined with a name of [Manufacturer]. When the installation is run, this will be replaced with the value of the Manufacturer property that we discussed earlier in the chapter. [Manufacturer] is a property of the installation and can be used elsewhere within the installation. There are a number of these properties defined that can be used in much the same way (consult the 'Property Reference' topic in the MSDN documentation for a full list).

Adding a Value to a Registry Key

So what do we need to do to add a value to a registry key? We must first select the required registry key (or create it) that is going to hold the registry values and then there are a number of ways that we can add the registry value:

- ❑ We can right-click on the registry key and use the resulting popup menu
- ❑ We can right-click in the right-hand pane and use the resulting popup menu
- ❑ We can use the Action menu

The menu items contained within the Action menu will depend on where the current focus is. For illustrational purposes here, select one of the Software registry keys. The Action menu will contain one item, New, which contains a number of menu items:

- ❑ Key
- ❑ String Value
- ❑ Environment String Value
- ❑ Binary Value
- ❑ DWORD Value

Using this menu we can create a new registry key below the currently selected key (via Key), or we can create a value for the currently selected registry key using one of the four Value types: String, Environment String, Binary, and DWORD.

So let's take a look at how we can create a registry entry that informs the application whether or not to run in debug mode. The registry value must be applicable to a particular user, called Debug, and contain the text True or False.

1. The first step that needs to be completed is to select the following registry key in the left-hand pane of the editor:

    HKEY_CURRENT_USER\Software\[Manufacturer]

    The registry key HKEY_CURRENT_USER is used to store registry settings that apply to the currently logged in user.

2. Now, we want to create a value so that it is applicable to only this application and not all applications created by us. What we need to do is create a new registry key below the HKEY_CURRENT_USER\Software\[Manufacturer] key that is specific to this product, so select the Action | New | Key menu item.

3. When the key is created, the key name will be editable, so give it a name of [ProductName] and press *Enter*. This will create a key that is given the name of the product contained within this Windows Installer package. The ProductName property of the setup was discussed earlier in this chapter.

4. Now that we have created the correct registry key, we need to create the actual registry value. Making sure that our new registry key is selected, choose String Value from the Action | New menu and give the new value a name of Debug.

5. Once the value has been created we can set a default value for it, in our case False. Make sure that the new value is selected, the Properties window will have changed to show you the details for this value. Notice that there is a property called Value, which we will use to set the initial value. Enter False as the value for the Value property and that's it:

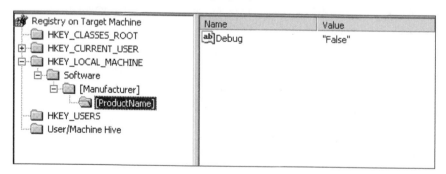

When the Windows Installer package is run the Debug registry value will be created. As you can see Registry manipulation is fairly straightforward.

We can move most keys and values in the Registry editor around by using cut-and-paste or simply by dragging and dropping the required item.

It is important to note that if a value already exists in the registry, the Windows Installer package will overwrite the existing value with that defined in the Registry editor.

Importing Registry Files

If you already have a registry file that contains the registry settings that you would like to be created, you can import the file into the Registry editor, which saves having you manually enter the information. To import a registry file you need to make sure the root node (Registry on Target Machine) is selected in the left-hand pane of the editor. You can then use the Import item of the Action menu to select the registry file to import.

> **Registry manipulation should be used with extreme caution. Windows relies heavily on the registry and as a result of this you can cause yourself a great number of problems if you delete/overwrite/change registry values and keys without knowing the full consequences of the action.**

If you want to create the registry entries that are required to create file associations you can use the editor covered next.

The File Types Editor

The File Types editor can be used to create the required registry entries to establish a **file association** for the application being installed, where a file association is simply a link between a particular file extension and a particular application. For example, the file extension .doc is normally associated with Microsoft WordPad unless Microsoft Word is installed.

When we create a file association, not only do we create a link between the file extension and the application, we also define a set of actions that can be performed from the context menu of the file with the associated extension. Looking at our Microsoft Word example, if we right-click on a document with an extension of .doc, we get a context menu that can contain any number of actions, for example, Open and Print. The action in bold (Open by default) is the default action to be called when we double-click on the file, so in our example double-clicking a Word document will start Microsoft Word and load the selected document.

This editor takes the pain out of creating a file extension.

Creating File Extensions

So how do we create a file extension using the editor? We will answer this question by walking through the creation of a file extension for our application. Let's say that our application uses a file extension of .set and that the file is to be opened in the application when we double-click on the file. To accomplish this we need to start the File Types editor, which unlike the last two editors, only has one pane to its interface:

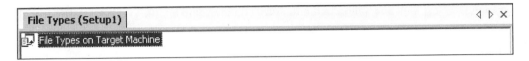

1. To add a new file type we need to make sure the root element (File Types on Target Machine) is selected in the editor. We can then choose Add File Type from the Action menu.

2. Give the new file type the following name: Example File Type.

3. Before we continue we must set the extension and application that this file type uses. These are both accomplished using the Properties window.

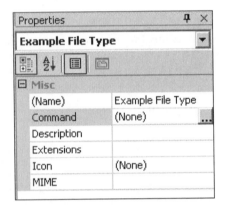

Enter .set as the value for the Extensions property.

To associate an application with this file type we need to use the Command property. The ellipsis button for this property presents us with a dialog box where we can select an executable file contained within any of the folders defined in the File System editor. In our case select WindowsApplication1.exe from the Application Folder as the value for Command.

4. When we created the new file type, a default action was added for us called &Open – select it. Now take a look at the Properties window again. Notice the Arguments property, we can use this to add command line arguments to the application defined in the last step. In the case of the default action that has been added for us, the arguments are "%1", where the value %1 will be replaced by the filename that invoked the action. We can add our own hard-coded arguments (for example /d). An action is set to be the default by right-clicking on it and selecting Set as Default from the popup menu.

That concludes our brief look at the File Types editor.

The User Interface Editor

The User Interface editor is used to manage the interface that the user uses to proceed through the installation of the application. The editor allows us to define the dialog boxes that are displayed to the user and in what order they are shown. The User Interface editor looks like this:

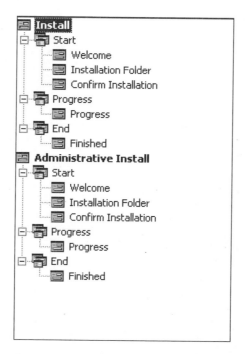

The editor uses a treeview with two root nodes: Install and Admin. Below each of these nodes there are three nodes that represent the stages of installation: Start, Progress, and End. Each of the three stages can contain a number of dialog boxes that will be displayed to the user when the resulting Windows Installer package is run. A default set of dialog boxes is predefined when we create the deployment project. The default dialog boxes that are present depend on the type of deployment project: Setup Project or Web Setup Project. The above screenshot shows the dialog boxes that are added by default to a Setup Project. If, however, you are creating a Web Setup Project the Installation Folder dialog will be replaced by an Installation Address dialog. Using the above screenshot we will discuss the two modes that installer can be run in and what the three stages of the installation are.

Installation Modes

We'll start by taking a look at the two modes that the installation runs it: Install and Admin. These basically distinguish between an end user installing the application and a system administrator performing a network setup.

> To use the **Admin** mode of the resulting Windows Installer package you can use `msiexec.exe` with the `/a` command line parameter:
>
> `msiexec.exe /a <PACKAGE>.msi`

The Install mode will be the one that is most used and is what we will use in this discussion. As mentioned earlier the steps the installation goes through can be split into three stages and are represented as sub nodes of the parent installation mode.

The Start Stage

The Start stage is the first stage of the installation and contains the dialog boxes that need to be displayed to the user before the actual installation of the files etc. begins. The Start stage should be used to gather any information from the user that may affect what is installed and where it is installed. This stage is commonly used to ask the user to select the base installation folder for the application and to ask the user what parts of the system he would like to install. Another very common task of this stage is to ask the user what their name is and what organization they work for. At the end of this stage the Windows Installer service will determine how much disk space is required on the target machine and check that this amount of space is available. If the space is not available, the user will receive an error and the installation will not continue.

The Progress Stage

The Progress stage is the second stage of the Installer and is where the actual installation of the files occurs. There isn't usually any user interaction in this stage of installation. There is normally one dialog box that indicates the current progress of the installation. The current progress of the installation is calculated automatically.

The End Stage

Once the actual installation of the files etc. has finished the Installer moves into the End stage. The most common use of this stage is to inform the user that the installation has completed successfully. It is often used to provide the option of running the application straight away or to view any release notes.

Customizing the Order of Dialog Boxes

The order in which the dialog boxes appear within the treeview determines the order in which they are presented to the user when the resulting Windows Installer package is run. Dialog boxes cannot be moved between the different stages.

The order of the dialog boxes can be changed by dragging the respective dialog boxes to the position in which we want them to appear. We can also move a particular dialog box up or down in the order in which it is shown by right-clicking on the dialog box and selecting either Move Up or Move Down.

Adding Dialog Boxes

A set of pre-defined dialog boxes have been added to the project for us, but what happens if these do not match our requirements? As well as being able to modify the order in which the dialog boxes appear, we can also add or remove dialog boxes from any of the stages.

When adding a dialog box we have the choice of using a built-in dialog box or importing one.

To illustrate how to add a dialog box, we will look at an example of adding a dialog box to display a ReadMe file to the user of Windows Installer package. The ReadMe file will need to be displayed before the actual installation of the files etc. occurs.

1. The first step is to determine the mode in which the dialog box is to be shown: Install or Admin. In our case we are not interested in the Admin mode so we will use the Install mode.

2. The next step is to determine the stage in which the dialog box is to be shown. In our example, we want to display the ReadMe file to the user before the actual installation of the files occurs, which means we will have to show the ReadMe file in the Start stage. Make sure the Start node is selected below the Install parent node.

3. We are now ready to add the dialog box. Using the Action menu again, select the Add Dialog menu item, which will display a dialog box where you can choose from the built-in dialog boxes:

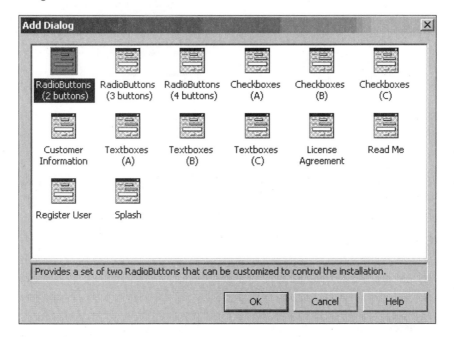

4. As you can see from the screenshot there are a number of built-in dialog boxes to choose from. Each dialog box has a short description that appears at the bottom of the window to inform you of its intended purpose. In the case of our example, we want to use the Read Me dialog box, so select it and click on OK.

5. New dialog boxes are always added as the last dialog box in the stage that they are added to, so now we need to move it into the correct position. In our case we want the Read Me dialog box to be shown immediately after the Welcome dialog box, so drag and drop it into position.

Properties of the Dialog Boxes

Like most other project items in Visual Studio.NET, dialog boxes have a set of properties that we can change to suit our needs using the Properties window. If you make sure a dialog box is selected, you will notice that the Properties window changes to show the properties of the selected dialog box. The properties that appear depend on the dialog box selected. Details of all the properties of the built in dialog boxes can be found by looking at the 'Properties of the User Interface Editor' topic in the MSDN documentation.

The Custom Actions Editor

The Custom Actions editor is used for fairly advanced installations and allows us to define actions that are to be performed due to one of the following installation events: Install, Commit, Rollback, and Uninstall. For example, we can use this editor to define an action that creates a new database when the installation commits.

The custom actions that are added using this editor can be windows script-based or compiled executables or DLLs.

Before we continue with our discussion of this editor make sure that it is loaded. Once loaded you will notice that it uses a treeview to represent the information, pretty much like the User Interface editor. There are four nodes that represent each of the four installation events that you can add custom actions to:

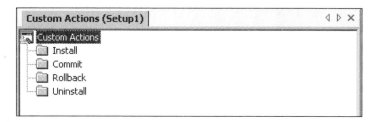

As with the User Interface editor, the order in which the actions appear determines the order in which they are run and this can be modified by simply dragging and dropping the actions, or by using the context menus of the actions to move them up or down.

Adding a Custom Action

To add a custom action we must select the node of the event into which we want to install the action. You can then use the Action menu to select the executable, DLL or script that implements the custom action. The four actions that are defined in the editor are defined in the following table:

Event	Description
Install	The actions defined for this event will be run when the installation of the files etc. has finished but before the installation has committed.
Commit	The actions defined for this event will be run when the installation has been committed and has therefore been successful.
Rollback	The actions defined for this event will be run when the installation fails and rolls back the machine to the same state as before the install was started.
Uninstall	The actions defined for this event will be run when the application is being uninstalled from the machine.

Suppose we wanted to start our application up as soon as the installation had been completed successfully. We could use the following process to accomplish this:

1. First we need to decide when the action must occur. Using the above table we can see that the Commit event will be run when the installation has been successful. Make sure this node is selected in the editor.

2. We are now ready to add the actual action we would like to happen when the commit event is called. Using the Action menu again, select the Add Custom Action menu item, which will display a dialog box that we can use to navigate for and select a file (exe, dll or windows script) from any that are included in the File System Editor. In the case of our example select Primary output from WindowsApplication (Active), which is contained within the Application Folder.

3. As with most items in the editors that we are discussing, the new custom action has a number of properties that we can use. These properties are summarized in the table below:

Property	Description
(Name)	This is the name given to the custom action selected.
Arguments	This property allows you to pass command line arguments into the executable that makes up the custom action. This only applies to custom actions that are implemented in executable files (.exe). By default the first argument passed in can be used to distinguish what event caused the action to run. The first argument can have the following values: /Install /Commit /Rollback /Uninstall
Condition	This enables you to enter a condition that will be evaluated before the custom action is run. If the condition evaluates to True then the custom action will run, likewise if the condition evaluates to False then the custom action will not run.
CustomActionData	This property allows you to pass additional information to the custom action.
EntryPoint	This property is used to define the entry point in the dll that implements the custom action. This only applies to custom actions that are implemented in dynamic linked libraries (.dll). If no value is entered then the installer will look for an entry point in the selected dll with the same name as the event that caused the action to run (Install, Commit, Rollback, Uninstall).
InstallerClass	If the custom action is implemented by an Installer class (consult the MSDN documentation for more information) in the selected component then this property must be set to True. If not it must be set to False.
SourcePath	This property will show the path to the actual file on the developer's machine that implements the custom action.

Set the InstallClass property to equal False as our application does not contain an installer class.

4. That's it. When we run the Windows Installer package and the installation is successful, our application will automatically start.

The custom action that we implemented above is very simple, however, custom actions can be used to accomplish any customized installation actions that you could want. I suggest that you take some time to play around with what can be accomplished using custom actions.

The Launch Conditions Editor

The Launch Conditions editor can be used to define a number of conditions for the target machine that must be met before the installation will run. For example, if your application relies on the fact that the user must have Microsoft Word 2000 installed on their machine to run your application, you can define a launch condition that will check this.

You can define a number of searches that can be performed to help create launch conditions:

❏ File search

❏ Registry search

❏ Windows Installer search

As with the Custom Actions editor, the Launch Conditions editor uses a treeview to display the information contained within it:

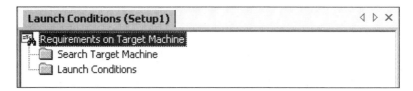

There are two root nodes: the first (Search Target Machine) is used to display the searches that have been defined, the second (Launch Conditions) contains a list of the conditions that will be evaluated when the Windows Installer package is run on the target machine.

As with many of the other editors, the order in which the items appear below these two nodes determines the order in which the searches are run and the order in which the conditions are evaluated. If we wish, we can modify the order of the items in the same manner as previous editors.

> **The searches are run and then the conditions are evaluated as soon as the Windows Installer package is run, before any dialog boxes are shown to the user.**

We are now going to look at an example of adding a file search and launch condition to a setup project. For argument's sake, let's say that we want to make sure that our users have Microsoft Word 2000 installed on their machine before they are allowed to run the installation for our application.

Adding a File Search

We begin by searching for the Microsoft Word 2000 executable:

1. Making sure the Search Target Machine node is currently selected in the editor, add a new file search by selecting the Add File Search item from the Action menu.

2. The new item will need to be given a meaningful name, so enter Word2KSearch.

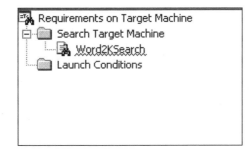

Modifying the File Search Properties

Like most items contained within the editors mentioned in this chapter, the new file search item has a set of properties that we can modify using the Properties window. The properties of the file search item determine the criteria that will be used when searching for the file. Most of the properties are self-explanatory and have been covered in previous sections and will not be covered in this chapter.

In our example here, we need to search for the Microsoft Word 2000 executable, which means that a number of these properties will need to be modified to match our own search criteria.

1. The first property that we need to modify is FileName, which is used to define the name of the file that the search will look for. In our case we need to search for Microsoft Word 2000 executable, so enter winword.exe as the value for this property. Previous versions of Microsoft Word used the same filename.

2. There is no need for us to search for the file from the root of the hard drive. The Folder property can be used to define the starting folder for the search. By default, the value is [SystemFolder], which indicates that the search will start from the Windows system folder. There are a number of these built-in values that we can use, if you are interested then you can look up what these folders correspond to in the 'Adding Special folders' previously in this chapter.

In our example, we do not want to search the Windows system folder as Microsoft Word is usually installed in the Program Files folder, so set the value of the Folder property to [ProgramFilesFolder] to indicate that this should be our starting folder.

3. When the search starts it will only search the folder specified in the Folder property as indicated by the default value (0) of the Depth property. The Depth property is used to specify how many levels of subfolders the search will look in from the starting folder specified above for the file in question. There are performance issues relating to the Depth property. If a search is performed for a file that is very deep in the file system hierarchy, it can take a long time to find the file. Therefore it is advisable that wherever possible you should use a combination of the Folder and Depth properties to decrease the possible search range. The file that we are searching for in our example will probably be at a depth of greater than 1, so change the value to 3.

4. There may be different versions of the file that we are searching for on a user's machine. We can use the remaining properties to specify a set of requirements for the file that must be met for it to be found, for example, minimum version number, minimum file size.

5. We are searching for the existence of Microsoft Word 2000, this means that we will need to define the minimum version of the file that we want to find. To search for the correct version of `winword.exe` we need to enter `9.0.0.0` as the value for the `MinVersion` property. This will ensure that the user has Microsoft Word 2000 or later installed and not an earlier version.

6. The result of the file search will need to be assigned to a Windows Installer property so that we can use it to create a launch condition later. This is going to be a bit of a tongue-twister. We need to define the name of the Windows Installer property that is used to store the result of the file search using the `Property` property. Enter `WORDEXISTS` as the value for the `Property` property. If the file search is successful, the full path to the found file will be assigned to this Windows Installer property, otherwise it will be left blank.

Creating a Launch Condition

A file search alone is pretty useless. Which takes us on to the second step of the process of ensuring the user has Microsoft Word 2000 installed, creating a launch condition. We can use the results of the file search described above to create a launch condition.

1. Make sure the Launch Conditions node is selected in the editor and add a new launch condition to the project by selecting Add Launch Condition from the Action menu.

2. We need to give this new item a meaningful name and in the case of our example we will give it a name of `Word2KExists`.

3. This new item has a number of properties that we will need to modify. The first property we will change is called `Message` and is used to set the text of the message box that will appear if this condition is not met. Enter any meaningful description that describes why the installation cannot continue.

4. The next property that we will need to change is called `Condition` and is used to define a valid deployment condition that is to be evaluated when the installation runs. The deployment condition entered must evaluate to `True` or `False`. When the installer is run, the condition will be evaluated, if the result of the condition is `False` then the message defined will be displayed to the user and the installation will stop.

For our example, we need to enter a condition that takes into account if the `winword.exe` file was found. We can use the Windows Installer property defined above (`WORDEXISTS`) as part of the condition. As the property is empty if the file was not found and non-empty if the file was found, we can perform a simple test on whether the property is empty to create the condition. Enter `WORDEXISTS <> " "` as the value for the `Condition` property.

Hopefully, from the above discussion of this search you will be able to apply the knowledge gained, to understand how to use the other searches and create your own launch conditions.

We have now finished our brief discussion of the editors that we can use to modify the resulting Windows Installer package to our needs. We have only looked briefly at the functionality of the editors and you are advised to spend some time playing around with them, as they are extremely powerful.

Building

The final section of this chapter is concerned with how to build the deployment or setup project you have created. There is basically no difference between how you build a VB.NET application and deployment/setup project. If the project is the only project contained within the solution then you can just use the Build item from the Build menu, which will cause the project to be built. As with the other projects you will be informed of what is happening during the build through the Output window.

The deployment/setup project can also be built as part of a multi-project solution. If the Build Solution item is chosen from the Build menu, all the projects in the solution will be built. Any deployment or setup projects will be built last. This is to ensure that if they contain the output from another project in the solution that they pick up the latest build of that project.

As with most other project templates in Visual Studio.NET, you can set the current build configuration to be used when building the project. This will not be covered in this chapter as it has been covered previously in the book. As you can see building a setup/deployment project is basically the same as building any other project template.

Summary

We are now at the end of our brief tour on the huge subject of deployment in .NET. We could not hope to cover everything on the subject in one chapter. Hopefully you will have gained enough knowledge to help you explore the subject fully. We have covered a number of topics in this chapter including:

- ❑ How assemblies are used as the foundations of deployment in .NET

- ❑ How assemblies are structured to help reduce the problems of deployment, known as DLL Hell

- ❑ How assemblies move us towards the goal of true XCOPY deployment

- ❑ Visual Studio.NET setup and deployment project types

- ❑ Setup/Deployment project editors

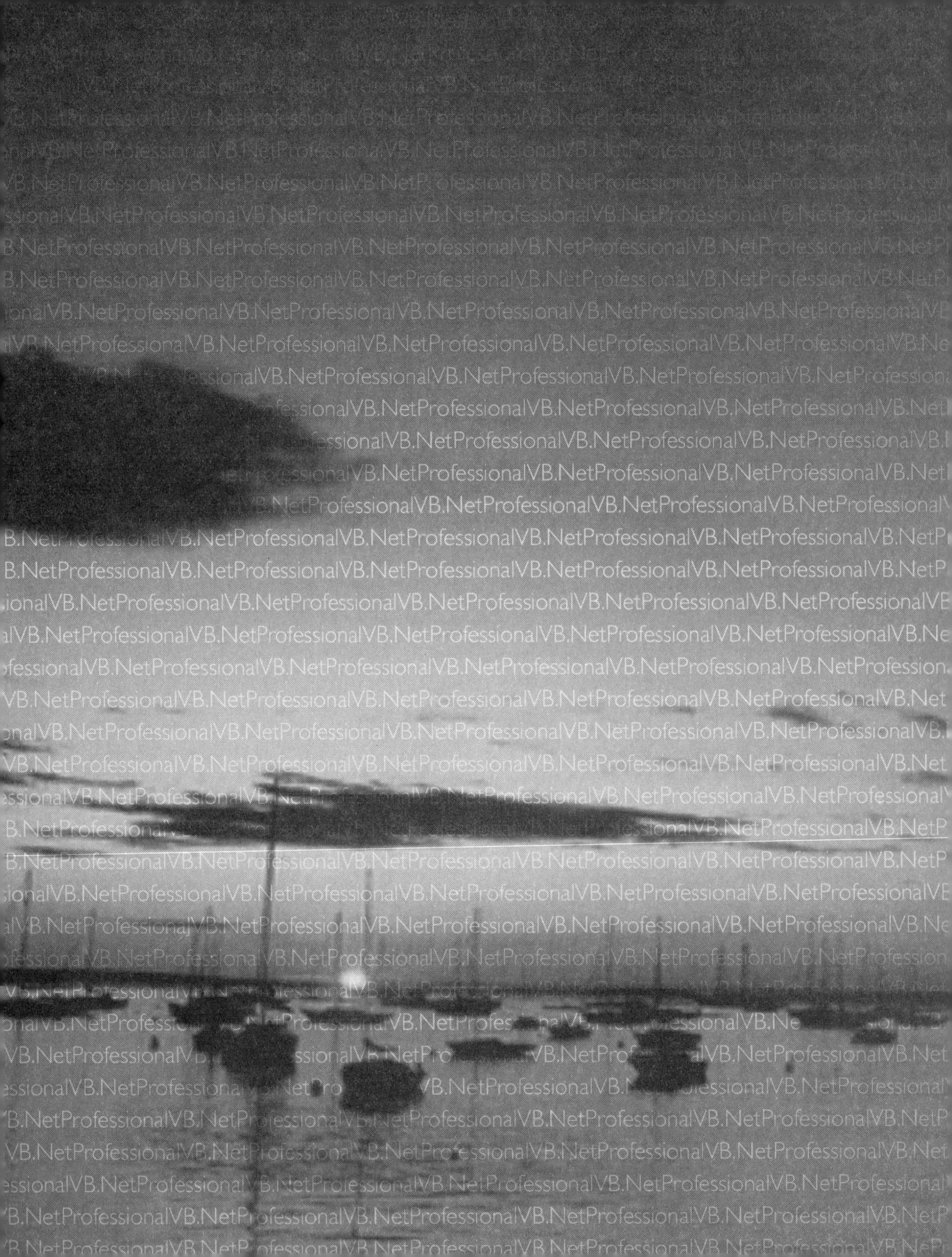
VB.NetProfessional

Security in the .NET Framework

The .NET Framework has provided us with additional tools and functionality with regard to security. We now have the `System.Security.Permissions` namespace, which allows us to control code access permissions along with role based and identity permissions. Through our code we can control access to objects programmatically, as well as receive information on the current permissions of objects. This security framework will assist us in finding out if we have permissions to run our code, instead of getting half way through and having to deal with permission-based exceptions. In this chapter we will cover:

- ❑   Concepts and definitions
- ❑   Permissions
- ❑   Roles
- ❑   Principals
- ❑   Code Access Permissions
- ❑   Role Based Permissions
- ❑   Identity Permissions
- ❑   Managing Permissions
- ❑   Managing Policies
- ❑   Cryptography

We also have two utilities that we will discuss, `Caspol.Exe` and `Permview.exe`, which assist us in establishing and maintaining our security policies and determining who can access our assembly objects. This chapter will go into each of these features of the .NET Framework in addition to looking at the use of certificates in signing code within the WinForms environment.

Security Concepts and Definitions

Before going on, let's also detail the different types of security that we will be illustrating in this chapter and how they can relate to real scenarios:

Security Type	Related concept in `Security.Permissions` namespace or Utility	Purpose
NTFS	None	Lock down specific files on any given machine.
Security Policies	`Caspol` Utility, `PermView` Utility	Set up overall security policy for a machine or user from an operating system level.
Cryptographic	Strong Name and Assembly, generation, `SignCode` Utility	Use of Public-Key infrastructure and Certificates.
Programmatic	Groups and Permission Sets	For use in pieces of code that are being called into. Provides extra security to prevent users of calling code from violating security measures implemented by the program that are not provided for on a machine level.

There are many approaches to providing security on our machines where our shared code is hosted. If multiple shared code applications are on one machine, each piece of shared code can get called from many front-end applications. Each piece of shared code will have its own security requirements for accessing environment variables – such as the registry, the file system, and other items – on the machine that it is running on. From an NTFS perspective, the administrator of our server can only lock down those items on the machine that are not required to be accessed from *any* piece of shared code running on it. Therefore, some applications will want to have additional security built in to prevent any calling code from doing things it is not supposed to do. The machine administrator can further assist the programmers by using the utilities provided with .NET to establish additional machine and/or user policies that programs can implement. As a further step along this line, the .NET environment has given us programmatic security through **Code Access** security, **Role Based** security, and **Identity** security. As a final security measure, we can use the cryptographic methods provided to require the use of certificates in order to execute our code.

Security in the .NET infrastructure has some basic concepts that we will discuss here. Code security is managed and accessed in the .NET environment through the use of security policies. Security policies have a relationship that is fundamentally tied to either the machine that code is running on, or to particular users under whose context the code is running. To this end, any modifications to the policy are done either at the machine or user level.

We establish the security policy on a given set of code by associating it with an entity called a **group**. A group is created and managed within each of the machine and user based policies. These group classifications are set up so that we can place code into categories. We would want to establish new code groups when we are ready to categorize the pieces of code that would run on a machine, and assign the permissions that users will have to access the code. For instance, if we wanted to group all Internet applications and then group all non-Internet applications together, we would establish two groups and associate each of our applications with its respective group. We could then associate those groups with different permissions. As another example, if we wanted to limit our Internet applications' access to the local file system, we could create a permission set that limits that access and associates the Internet application group with the new permission set. By default, the .NET environment gives us one code group named `All Code` that is associated with the `FullTrust` permission set.

Permission sets are unique combinations of security configurations that determine what each user with access to a machine can do on that machine. Each set determines what a user has access to – for instance, whether they can read environment variables, the file system, or execute other portions of code. Permission sets are maintained at the machine and user levels through the utility Caspol.Exe. Through this utility, we can create our own permission sets, though there are seven permission sets that ship with the .NET infrastructure that are also useful, as shown in this table:

Permission Set	Explanation
FullTrust	Allows full access to all resources – adds assembly to a special list that has FullTrust access.
Everything	Allows full access to everything covered by default named permission sets, only differs from FullTrust in that the group does not get added to the FullTrust Assembly List.
Nothing	Denies all access including Execution.
Execution	Allows execution only access.
SkipVerification	Allows object to bypass all security verification.
Internet	Grants default rights that are normal for Internet Applications.
LocalInternet	Grants rights that are not as restricted as Internet, but not full trust.

Security that is used within the programming environment also makes use of permission sets. Through code, we can control access to files in a file system, environment variables, file dialogs, isolated storage, reflections, registry, sockets, and UI. Isolated Storage and Virtual file systems are new operating system level storage locations that can be used by programs and are governed by the machine security policies. These file systems keep a machine safe from file system intrusion by designating a regulated area for file storage. The main access to these items is controlled through Code Access Permissions.

Although many methods that we use in VB.NET give an identifiable return value, the only return value that we will get from security methods is if the method fails. If a security method succeeds, it will not give a return value. If it fails, it will return an exception object reflecting the specific error that occurred.

Permissions in the System.Security.Permissions Namespace

The System.Security.Permissions namespace is the namespace that we will use in our code to establish and use permissions to access many things such as the file system, environment variables, and the registry within our programs. The namespace controls access to both operating system level objects as well as code objects. In order to use the namespace in our project we need to include the Imports System.Security.Permissions line with any of our other Import statements in our project. Using this namespace gives us access to using the CodeAccessPermission, and PrincipalPermission classes for using Role-Based permissions and also utilizing information supplied by Identity permissions. CodeAccessPermission is the main class that we will use as it controls access to the operating system level objects our code needs in order to function. Role Based permissions and Identity permissions grant access to objects based on the identity that the user of the program that is running carries with them.

In the table below, those classes that end with the word Attribute, such as
EnvironmentPermissionAttribute, are the classes that allow us to modify the security level at which
our code is allowed to interact with each respective object. The attributes that we can specify reflect either
Assert, Deny, or PermitOnly permissions. If permissions are asserted we have full access to the object,
while if we have specified Deny permissions we are not allowed to access the object through our code. If we
have PermitOnly access only objects within our program's already determined scope can be accessed, and
we cannot add any more resources beyond that scope. In our table we also deal with security with regard to
Software Publishers. A Software Publisher is a specific entity that is using a digital signature to identify itself
in a web-based application. Below is a table of the namespace members that apply to Windows Forms
programming with an explanation of each:

Class	Description
CodeAccessSecurityAttribute	Specifies security access to objects such as the registry and file system
EnvironmentPermission	Controls ability to see and modify system and user environment variables
EnvironmentPermissionAttribute	Allows security actions for environment variables to be added via code
FileDialogPermission	Controls ability to open files via a file dialog
FileDialogPermissionAttribute	Allows security actions to be added for File Dialogs via code
FileIOPermission	Controls ability to read and write files in the file system
FileIOPermissionAttribute	Allows security actions to be added for file access attempts via code
IsolatedStorageFilePermission	Controls ability to access a virtual file system within the isolated storage area of an application
IsolatedStorageFilePermissionAttribute	Allows security actions to be added for virtual file systems via code
IsolatedStoragePermission	Controls ability to access the isolated storage area of an application
IsolatedStoragePermissionAttribute	Allows security actions to be added for the isolated storage area of an application
PermissionSetAttribute	Allows security actions to be added for a permission set
PrincipalPermissionAttribute	Allows for checking against a specific user. Security principals are a user and role combination used to establish security identity
PublisherIdentityPermission	Allows for ability to access based on the identity of a software publisher

Class	Description
PublisherIdentityPermissionAttribute	Allows security actions to be added for a software publisher
ReflectionPermission	This controls the ability to access non-public members of a given type
ReflectionPermissionAttribute	Allows for security actions to be added for public and non-public members of a given type
RegistryPermission	Controls the ability to access registry keys and values
RegistryPermissionAttribute	Allows security actions to be added for registry keys and values
SecurityAttribute	Controls which security attributes are representing code, used to control the security when creating an assembly
SecurityPermission	The set of security permission flags for use by .NET. This collection is used when we want to specify a permission flag in our code
SecurityPermissionAttribute	Allows security actions for the security permission flags
UIPermission	Controls ability to access user interfaces and use the Windows clipboard
UIPermissionAttribute	Allows security actions to be added for UI Interfaces and the use of the clipboard

Code Access Permissions

Code access permissions are controlled through the CodeAccessPermission class within the System.Security.Permissions namespace, and its members make up the majority of the permissions we'll use in our attempt to secure our code and operating environment. Below is a table of the class methods and an explanation of their use:

Method	Description
RevertAll	Reverses all previous assert, deny or permit only methods
RevertAssert	Reverses all previous assert methods
RevertDeny	Reverses all previous deny methods
RevertPermitOnly	Reverses all previous permit only methods
Assert	Sets the permission to full access so that the specific resource can be accessed even if the caller hasn't been granted permission to access the resource

Table continued on following page

Method	Description
CheckDemand	Checks the current permissions to determine if the resource can be accessed in a specific manner
Copy	Copies a permission object
Demand	Returns whether or not all callers in the call chain have been granted the permission to access the resource in a given manner
DemandImmediate	Returns whether the immediate caller has been granted the permission to access the resource in a given manner
Deny	Denies all callers access to the resource
Equals	Determines if a given object is the same instance of the current object. Parameters are two objects
FromXML	Establishes a permission set given a specific XML encoding. This parameter is an XML encoding
GetHashCode	Returns a hash code associated with a given object
GetType	Returns the type of a given object
Intersect	Returns the permissions two permission objects have in common
IsSubsetOf	Returns result of whether the current permission object is a subset of a specified permission
PermitOnly	Determines that only those resources within this permission object can be accessed even if code has been granted permission to other objects
ToString	Returns a string representation of the current permission object
ToXML	Creates an XML representation of the current permission object
Union	Creates a permission that is the union of two permission objects

Role-Based Permissions

Role-based permissions are permissions granted based on the user and role that code is being called with. Users are generally authenticated within the operating system platform and hold a Security Identifier (SID) that is associated within a security context. The SID can further be associated with a role, or a group membership that is established within a security context. The .NET role functionality supports those users and roles associated within a security context and also that have support for generic and custom users and roles through the concept of principals. A principal is an object that holds the current caller credentials, which is termed the identity of the user. Principals come in two types - **Windows** principals and **non-Windows** principals. Windows-based Principal objects are objects that store the Windows SID information regarding the current user context associated with the code that is calling into the module where we are using Role-based permissions. Non-Windows Principals are principal objects that are created programmatically via a custom login methodology and which are made available to the current thread.

Role-based permissions are not set against objects within our environment like code access permissions. They are instead a permission that is checked within the context of the current user and role that a user is part of. Within the `System.Security.Permissions` namespace, the concept of the principals and the `PrincipalPermission` class of objects are used to establish and check permissions. If a programmer passes the user and role information during a call as captured from a custom login, the `PrincipalPermission` class can be used to verify this information as well. During the verification, if the user and role information is `Null` then permission is granted regardless of user and role. The `PrincipalPermission` class does not grant access to objects, but has methods that determine if a caller has been given permissions according to the current permission object through the demand method. If a security exception is generated then user does not have sufficient permission.

Below is the table of the methods in the `PrincipalPermission` class and a description of each:

Method	Description
Copy	Copies a permission object
Demand	Returns whether or not all callers in the call chain have been granted the permission to access the resource in a given manner
DemandImmediate	Returns whether the immediate caller has been granted the permission to access the resource in a given manner
Deny	Denies all callers access to the resource
Equals	Determines if a given object is the same instance of the current object. Parameters are two objects
FromXML	Establishes a permission set given a specific XML encoding. Parameter is an XML encoding
GetHashCode	Returns a hash code associated with a given object
GetType	Returns the type of a given object
Intersect	Returns the permissions two permission objects have in common
IsSubsetOf	Returns result of whether the current permission object is a subset of a specified permission
IsUnrestricted	Returns result of whether the current permission object is Unrestricted
ToString	Returns a string representation of the current permission object
ToXML	Creates an XML representation of the current permission object
Union	Creates a permission that is the union of two permission objects

As an example of how we might use these, here is a code snippet which captures the current Windows principal information and displays it to the screen in the form of a message box output. Each element of the principal information could be used in a program to validate against, and thus restrict code execution based on the values in the principal information. In our example we have inserted an `Imports System.Security.Principal` line at the top of our module so we could use the identity and principal objects:

```
Imports System.Security.Principal
Imports System.Security.Permissions
```

```
. . .

Private Sub btnRoleBasedPermissions_Click _
    (ByVal sender As System.Object, ByVal e As System.EventArgs)

  Dim objIdentity As WindowsIdentity = WindowsIdentity.GetCurrent
  Dim objPrincipal As New WindowsPrincipal(objIdentity)

  MessageBox.Show(Str(objPrincipal.Identity.IsAuthenticated))
  MessageBox.Show(Str(objIdentity.IsGuest))
  MessageBox.Show(objIdentity.ToString)

  objIdentity = Nothing
  objPrincipal = Nothing

End Sub
```

In the code above we have illustrated a few of the properties that could be used to validate against when a caller wants to run our code. Sometimes we want to make sure that the caller is an authenticated user, and not someone who bypassed the security of our machine with custom login information. This is achieved through the following line of code:

```
MessageBox.Show(Str(objPrincipal.Identity.IsAuthenticated))
```

and will output in the MessageBox as either True or False.

Another piece of information to ensure that our caller is not bypassing system security would be to check and see if the account is operating as a guest. We do this by this line of code:

```
MessageBox.Show(Str(objIdentity.IsGuest))
```

Once again, the IsGuest returns either True or False, based on whether the caller is authenticated as a guest.

Our final MessageBox in our example displays the ToString value for the identity object. This is a value that tells us what type of identity it is, either a Windows identity or non-Windows identity. The line of code that executes is:

```
MessageBox.Show(objIdentity.ToString)
```

The output from our code is shown in the screenshot below:

Again, the principal and identity objects are used in verifying the identity or aspects of the identity of the caller that is attempting to execute our code. Based on this information we can lock down or release certain system resources. We will show how to lock down and release system resources through our code access permissions examples coming up.

Identity Permissions

Identity permissions are pieces of information, also called **evidence**, by which a piece of code can be identified. Examples of the evidence would be the strong name of the assembly or the digital signature associated with the assembly.

> *A strong name is a combination of the name of a program, its version number, and its associated cryptographic key and digital signature files.*

Identity permissions are granted by the runtime based on information received from the trusted host, or someone who has permission to provide the information. Therefore, they are permissions that we don't specifically request. Identity permissions provide additional information to be used by the runtime when we configure items in the Caspol utility. The additional information that the trusted host can supply includes the digital signature, the application directory, or the strong name of the assembly.

Managing Code Access Permissions

In this section we'll be looking at the most common type of permissions, that of programmatic access permissions, and how they are used. As our example we created a Windows Form and place three buttons on it. Behind each button are the individual code snippets from below. This WinForm will be used to illustrate the concept we previously mentioned, namely that, if a method fails, an exception object is generated which contains our feedback. Note at this point, that in the case of a real-world example we would be setting up permissions for a calling application. In many instances we don't want a calling application to be able to access the registry, or we want a calling application to be able to read memory variables, but not change them. However, in order to demonstrate the syntax of our commands, in our examples below we have placed the attempts against the objects we have secured in the same module. In our examples, we first set up the permission that we want and grant the code the appropriate access level we wish it to be able to utilize. Then we use code that accesses our security object to illustrate the effect our permissions have on the code that accesses the objects. We'll also be tying together many of the concepts discussed so far by way of these examples.

To begin with, let's look at an example of trying to access a file in the file system, which will illustrate the use of the FileIOPermission class in our Permissions namespace. In the first example, the file C:\testsecurity\testing.txt has been secured at the operating system level so that no one can access it. In order to do this, the system administrator would set the operating system security on the file to no access. Now run this code:

```
Imports System.Security.Principal
Imports System.Security.Permissions
Imports System.IO

...

Private Sub btnFileIO_Click(ByVal sender As System.Object, _
                            ByVal e As System.EventArgs)
Dim oFp As FileIOPermission = New _
  FileIOPermission(FileIOPermissionAccess.Write, "C:\testsecurity\testing.txt")

oFp.Assert()
Try
    Dim objWriter As New IO.StreamWriter _
```

```
        (File.Open("C:\testsecurity\testing.txt", IO.FileMode.Open))
    objWriter.WriteLine("HI There")
    objWriter.Flush()
    objWriter.Close()
    objWriter = Nothing
Catch objA As System.Exception
    MessageBox.Show(objA.Message)
End Try

End Sub
```

Let's walk through the code. In this example, we are going to attempt to open a file in the
C:\testsecurity directory called testing.txt. We set the file access permissions within our code so
that the method, irrespective of who called it, should be able to get to it with the following lines:

```
Dim oFp As FileIOPermission = New _
    FileIOPermission(FileIOPermissionAccess.Write, "C:\testsecurity\testing.txt")

oFp.Assert()
```

We used the Assert method, which declares that the resource should be accessible even if the caller has not
been granted permission to access the resource. However, in this case, since the file is secured at the operating
system level (by the system administrator), we get the following error that was caught in our exception handling:

Now, let's look at that example again with full operating system rights, but the code permissions set to Deny:

```
Protected Sub btnFileIO_Click(ByVal sender As
Object, ByVal e As System.EventArgs)

Dim oFp As FileIOPermission = New
FileIOPermission(FileIOPermissionAccess.Write,
"C:\testsecurity\testing.txt")
oFp.Deny()

Try

Dim objWriter As New IO.StreamWriter
(File.Open("C:\testsecurity\testing.txt",
IO.FileMode.Open))
        objwriter.WriteLine("HI There")
objWriter.Flush()
objWriter.Close()
        objWriter = Nothing

Catch objA As System.Exception
        messagebox.Show(objA.Message)

End Try
End Sub
```

We virtually have the same piece of code above, but the `CodeAccessPermission` method we used is the `Deny` method, which denies all callers access to the object regardless of whether the operating system granted them permission. With the `Deny` method, we catch the following error in our exception handler:

As you can see, this error differs from the first by reflecting a Security.Permissions.FileIOPermission failure as opposed to an operating system level exception.

Now let's look at an example of how we would use the `EnvironmentPermission` class of the namespace to look at `EnvironmentVariables`.

```
Protected Sub btnTestEnvironmentPermissions_Click _
  (ByVal sender As Object, ByVal e As System.EventArgs)

  Dim oEp As EnvironmentPermission = New EnvironmentPermission _
    (environmentpermissionaccess.read, "Temp")

  Dim sEv As String
  oEp.assert()

  Try
      sEv = environment.GetEnvironmentVariable("Temp")
      console.WriteLine("Assert was a success")

  Catch objA As System.Exception
      console.WriteLine("Assert failed")

  End Try

  oep.revertassert()
  oep.Deny()

  Try
      sEv = environment.GetEnvironmentVariable("Temp")
      console.WriteLine("Deny was a success")

  Catch objA As System.Exception
      console.WriteLine("Deny failed")

  End Try

  console.WriteLine(oep.ToString)

End Sub
```

There is a lot going on in this example, so let's look at it carefully. We first establish an environment variable permission and use the `assert` method to ensure access to the code which follows:

```
Dim oEp As EnvironmentPermission = New EnvironmentPermission _
  (environmentpermissionaccess.read, "Temp")

Dim sEv As String
oEp.assert()
```

We then try to read the environment variable into a string. If the string read succeeds we write a line to the console to reflect the success. If the read fails we write a line to the console reflecting the failure:

```
Try
    sEv = environment.GetEnvironmentVariable("Temp")
    console.WriteLine("Assert was a success")

Catch objA As System.Exception
    console.WriteLine("Assert failed")

End Try
```

Next, we revoke the assert we previously issued by using the `RevertAssert` method and establish `Deny` permissions:

```
oep.RevertAssert()
oep.Deny()
```

We then try again to read the variable, and write the appropriate result to the console:

```
Try
    sEv = environment.GetEnvironmentVariable("Temp")
    console.WriteLine("Deny failed")
Catch objA As System.Exception
    console.WriteLine("Deny was a success")
End Try
```

We finally write the `ToString` of the method to the console. Below is the output on the console as a result from running our subroutine. The first two lines of our console output below give us the feedback from our `Assert` and `Deny` code, followed by the output of our `ToString` method:

```
Assert was a success
Deny failed
<Permission class="System.Security.Permissions.EnvironmentPermission, mscorlib,
Ver=1.0.2204.21, Loc=", SN=03689116d3a4ae33" version="1">
  <Read>Temp</Read>
</Permission>
```

As you can see, the `ToString` method is an XML representation of the permission object that is currently in effect. The first and second lines in the output are the system information of the version of the VB.NET security environment that was running at the time the button was clicked. The third line is the environment variable name surrounded by the Read tags, which was the permission in effect at the time the `ToString` method was executed.

Let's look at one more example of where the permissions would affect us in our program functionality, that of accessing the registry. We would generally access the registry on the computer that was the central server for a component in our Windows Forms Application.

When we use the `EventLog` methods to create entries in the machine event logs we access the registry. To illustrate this concept, in the following code example we'll deny permissions to the registry and see the result:

```
Protected Sub btnTestRegistryPermissions_Click(ByVal _
    sender As Object, ByVal e As System.EventArgs)

Dim oRp As New _
    RegistryPermission(Security.Permissions.PermissionState.Unrestricted)
oRp.Deny()

Dim objLog As New EventLog()
Dim objLogEntryType As EventLogEntryType

Try
    Throw (New EntryPointNotFoundException())
    Catch objA As System.EntryPointNotFoundException
    Try
      If Not objLog.SourceExists("Example") Then
        objLog.CreateEventSource("Example", "System")
      End If
      objLog.Source = "Example"
      objLog.Log = "System"
      objLogEntryType = EventLogEntryType.Information
      objLog.WriteEntry("Error: " & objA.message, objLogEntryType)
    Catch objB As System.Exception
        Messagebox.Show(objB.Message)
    End Try
End Try

End Sub
```

As we walk through our code, we start with setting up registry permission and setting it to Deny access:

```
Dim oRp As New _
    RegistryPermission(Security.Permissions.PermissionState.Unrestricted)
oRp.Deny()
```

Next we set up to Throw an exception on purpose in order to set up writing to an event log:

```
    Throw (New EntryPointNotFoundException())
```

When the exception is caught, it checks the registry to make sure a specific type of registry entry source is already in existence:

```
        If Not objLog.SourceExists("Example") Then
          objLog.CreateEventSource("Example", "System")
        End If
```

And at this point our code fails with the error message shown below:

Request for permission of type 'System.Security.Permissions.RegistryPermission' failed.

These examples can serve as a good basis for use in developing classes that access the other objects within the scope of the `Permissions` namespace, such as reflections and UI permissions.

Managing Security Policy

As we stated in the introduction to the chapter, we have two new command line utilities that help us configure and view security policy at both machine and user levels. When we manage security policy at this level we are doing so as an administrator of machine or user policy for a machine that is hosting code that will be called from other front-end applications. `Caspol.Exe` is a command line utility that has many options to give us the ability to configure our security policies (`Caspol` standing for Code Access Security Policy). As mentioned in the concepts section, user and machine policy are associated with groups and permission sets. There is one group that is provided for us, that being the `AllCode` Group.

The `Caspol` utility has two categories of commands for us to review. The first category listed in the table below is the set of commands that give us feedback on what the current security policy is.

Command	Short Command	Parameters	Effect
-List	-l	None	This lists the combination of the following three options
-ListGroups	-lg	None	This will list only groups
-ListPset	-lp	None	This will list only permission sets
-ListFulltrust	-lf	None	This will list only assemblies which have full trust privileges
-Reset	-rs	None	This will reset the machine and user policies to the default for .NET. This is handy if a policy creates a condition that is not recoverable. Use this command carefully as you will lose all changes made to the current policies
-ResolveGroup	-rsg	Assembly File	This will list what groups are associated with a given assembly file
-ResolvePerm	-rsp	Assembly File	This will list what permission sets are associated with a given assembly file

If we wanted to list the groups active on our local machine at the DOS prompt we would type:

```
Caspol -Machine -ListGroups
```

The output will look similar to the following (though will differ slightly depending upon the machine you are working on):

Let's talk about the above screen, so that we know some of the other things that are listed besides what we specifically requested. On the third line we see that code access security checking is on. On the following line we see that the machine is not checking for the user's right to execute the Caspol utility, since Execution checking is off. The Policy change prompt is on, so if the user executes a Caspol command that will change system policy there will be a "Are You Sure?" style prompt which appears to confirm that this is really intentional. The level is also listed on our screen prior to our requested output, which is detailed at the bottom listing the groups present on the machine. There are two levels that the policies pertain to, those being the machine and the user. When changing policy, if the user is not an administrator, the user policy is affected unless the user specifically applies the policy to the machine through use of the -machine switch as illustrated in our screenshot. If the user is an administrator the machine policy is affected unless the user specifically applies the policy to the user level through the use of the -user switch.

Let's now look at another request result example. This time we will ask for a listing of all of the permission sets on our machine. At the command prompt we would type:

```
Caspol -machine -listpset
```

And we would see the output similar to the following. The output overleaf has been shortened for space considerations, but the output would contain a listing of all of the code explicitly set to execute against the seven permission sets that we mentioned in our definitions section. Also note that the output is an XML representation of a permission object. The listing details the named permission sets and what each one has as active rights. For instance the first permission set is named LocalInternet, while the next lines detail the Permission class being an environment permission with read access to the three environment variables – UserName, Temp and Tmp. The next class detail is regarding FileDialogpermissions, and it lists those as being unrestricted. The screenshot then goes on to detail the effective settings for IsolatedStorage and others:

Let's now look at the second category of commands that go with the Caspol utility as shown in the table below. These commands are those we will use to actually modify policy:

Command	Short Command	Parameters	Effect
-AddFullTrust	-af	Assembly File Name	Adds a given Assembly file to the full trust permission set
-AddGroup	-ag	Parent Label, Membership, Permission Set Name	Adds a code group to the code group hierarchy
-AddPSet	-ap	Permission Set Path, Permission Set Name	Adds a new named permission set to the policy; the permission set should be an XML file
-ChgGroup	-cg	Membership, Permission Set Name	Changes a code group's information
-ChgPset	-cp	File Name, Permission Set Name	Changes a named permission set's information
-Force	-f		This option is not recommended. It forces Caspol to accept policy changes even if the change could cause Caspol itself not to be able to be executed

Command	Short Command	Parameters	Effect
-Recover	-r		Recovers policy information from a backup file that is controlled by the Utility
-RemFullTrust	-rf	Assembly File Name	Removes a given Assembly file from the full trust permission set
-RemGroup	-rg	Label	Removes a code group
-RemPSet	-rp	Permission set name	Removes a permission set. The seven default sets cannot be removed

Let's begin our discussion of these commands with a few more definitions that will help us understand the parameters that go with our commands. An **assembly file** is created within VB.NET each time we do a build where our version is a release version. An assembly needs to have a strong name associated with it in order to be used in our permissions groupings. An assembly gets a **strong name** from being associated with a digital signature uniquely identifying the assembly. We carry out this association in addition to providing other pieces of evidence to be used with the strong name within the property pages of our application.

Open the SecurityApp application from the source code for this chapter. Below is the screenshot of the project's property page that pertains to building the assembly with a strong name:

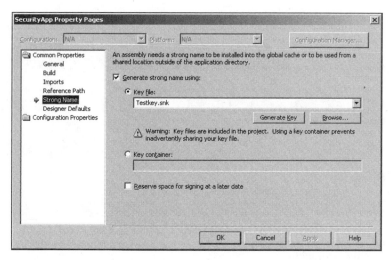

The strong name configuration screen is where we associate our assembly with an existing originating key file in order for VB to generate a strong name during the build process. During the build, VB generates the strong name, and then we can add our assembly to our security configuration. Place the executable, SecurityApp.exe, which was created from our build, into the C:\testsecurity directory on the local machine for use with our policy method illustrations.

If we wanted to add our assembly to the fulltrust permission set we would type:

```
Caspol -addfulltrust C:\testsecurity\SecurityApp.exe
```

Below is a screenshot of the outcome of our command:

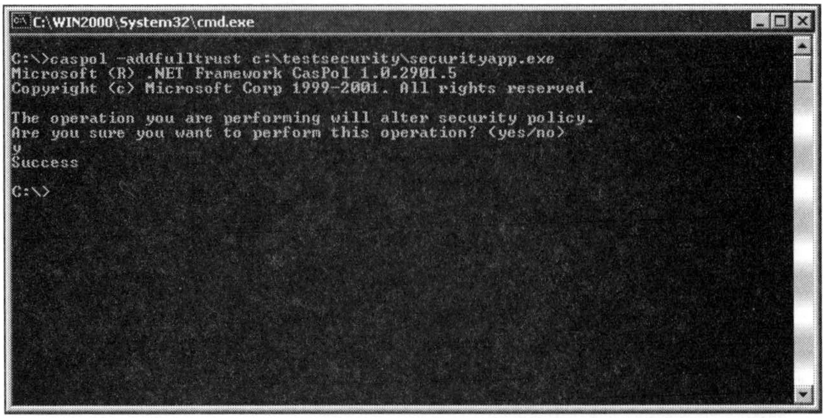

As we can see, we were prompted before our command altered our security policy, and then our new application was added to the `fulltrust` assembly list. We can confirm it was added by issuing the following command:

```
Caspol -listfulltrust
```

The excerpt of output from our command that includes our new assembly would look like:

In the screenshot, we can see our application name, version, and key information that was associated with our `.exe` file when we did our build.

Now, let's look at the creation and addition of a permission set to our permission sets in our security policy. Permission sets can be created by hand, in any text editor, in an XML format and saved as an `.XML` file. Below is a listing from one such file that was created for this example:

```
<PermissionSet class="System.Security.NamedPermissionSet" version="1">
<Permission class="System.Security.Permissions.FileIOPermission, mscorlib,
SN=03689116d3a4ae33" version="1">
```

```
      <Read> C:\TestSecurity </Read>
  </Permission>
  <Permission class="System.Security.Permissions.EnvironmentPermission, mscorlib,
  SN=03689116d3a4ae33" version="1">
      <Read> [TEMP] </Read>
  </Permission>
      <Name>SecurityExample</Name>
      <Description>Gives Full File Access</Description>
  </PermissionSet>
```

The listing has multiple permissions within the permission set. The listing sets up read file permissions within one set of tags as shown below:

```
<Permission class="System.Security.Permissions.FileIOPermission, mscorlib,
SN=03689116d3a4ae33" version="1">
    <Read> C:\TestSecurity </Read>
</Permission>
```

We then set up read access to our Temp environment variable in the second set of permission tags:

```
<Permission class="System.Security.Permissions.EnvironmentPermission, mscorlib,
SN=03689116d3a4ae33" version="1">
    <Read> [TEMP] </Read>
</Permission>
```

The listing also gives our custom permission set the name of SecurityExample with a description:

```
<Name>SecurityExample</Name>
<Description>Gives Full File Access</Description>
```

When we want to add our permission set to our policy, we would type:

```
Caspol -addpset C:\testsecurity\securityexample.xml securityexample
```

In the above command, we are issuing the -addpset flag to indicate that we want to add a permission set, followed by the XML file containing our permission set, followed finally by the name of our permission set. The outcome of our command looks like the following screenshot:

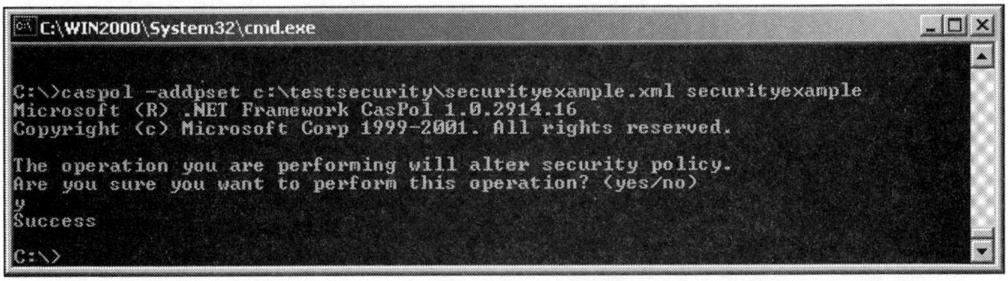

We can then list our security permission sets by typing `Caspol -listpset`. Here is the excerpt that shows our new security permission set:

As you can see, typing `Caspol -listpset` gives a listing of just the permission sets within our policy. Our named permission set `SecurityExample` shows up under the `Named Permission Sets` heading, and its description is listed just after its name.

Now that we have a permission set, we can add a group that our assembly object fits into and which enforces our new permission set. We add this group by using the `AddGroup` switch in `Caspol`. The `AddGroup` switch has a couple of parameters that need more explanation. The first parameter is `parent_label`. When we look at the group screenshot below, we can see our `All` code group has a `1.` before it. The labels within code groups have a hierarchy that gets established when we add groups, and so we need to specify what our parent label would be. In our case since the only one that exists is `1.`, that is what we'll be designating. Since we designate 1, the new group will become a child of 1. The second parameter is `membership`. The `membership` parameter has a certain list of options that we can put in based on the table below. Each option designates a piece of information we are providing about the pieces of code that we will add to our group. For instance we would state that we will only be adding code that had a specific signature with the `-Pub` option, or add only code in a certain application directory with the `-AppDir` option:

Option	Description
-All	All Code
-Pub	Code that has a specific signature on a certificate file
-Strong	Code that has a specific strong name, as designated by a file name, code name, and version
-Zone	Code that fits into the following zones: MyComputer, Intranet, Trusted, Internet, or Untrusted

Option	Description
-Site	Originating on a web site
-Hash	Code that has a specific assembly hash
-AppDir	A specific application directory
-SkipVerif	Code that requests the skipverification permission
-URL	Originating at a specific URL

The third parameter to the AddGroup command is the permission set name that we want associated with our group. Our group that we will create will be under parent label 1, and we will designate the -Zone parameter as being MyComputer since our code lives on a local drive. We will also associate the new group with our SecurityExample permission set by typing the following command:

```
Caspol -addgroup 1. -Zone MyComputer SecurityExample
```

We can see that our output from the command was successful in the figure below:

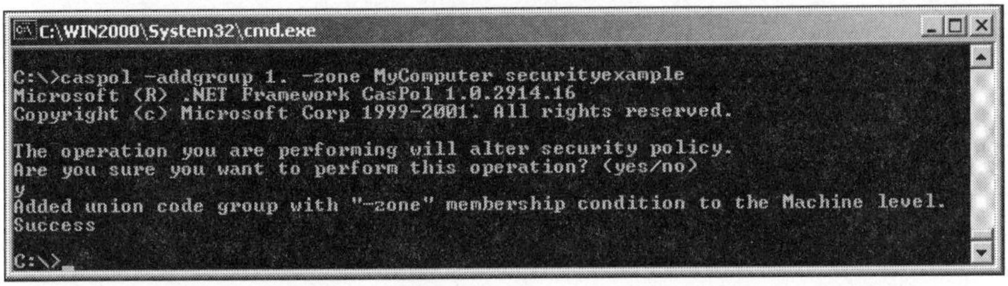

In our screenshot that follows, we use the -listgroups command to list our new group:

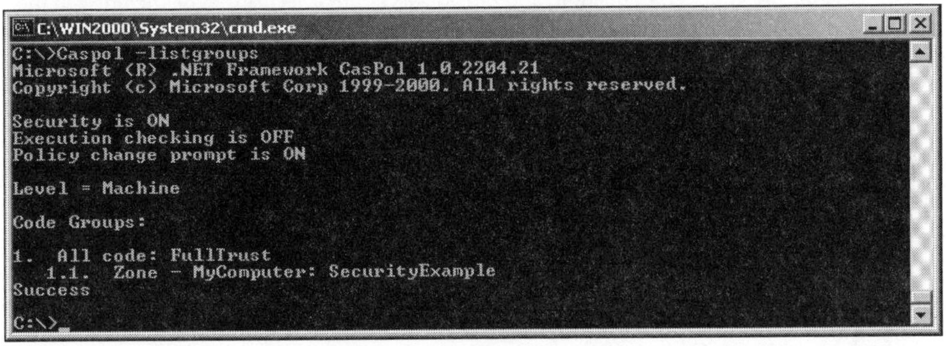

In the screenshot we can see that a 1.1 level was added with our SecurityExample permission set attached to all code that fits into the MyComputer Zone. Now let's verify that our assembly object fits into the MyComputer Zone by using our resolveperm command:

```
C:\WIN2000\System32\cmd.exe                                    _ |□| x|
C:\>caspol -resolveperm c:\testsecurity\securityapp.exe
Microsoft (R) .NET Framework CasPol 1.0.2901.5
Copyright (c) Microsoft Corp 1999-2001. All rights reserved.

Resolving permissions for level = Enterprise
Resolving permissions for level = Machine
Resolving permissions for level = User

Grant =
<PermissionSet class="System.Security.PermissionSet"
               version="1"
               Unrestricted="true">
   <IPermission class="System.Security.Permissions.StrongNameIdentityPermission,
 mscorlib, Version=1.0.2411.0, Culture=neutral, PublicKeyToken=b77a5c561934e089"

               version="1"
               PublicKeyBlob="0024000004800000940000000602000000240000525341310
0040000010001000100CF9DAF9C91EE2BAF19FDBAFB45BE6F1C5AC11D7E2156E960A1BF6D700BB8D4428
C30B45971A355453E543116462B24F3FCF1CBAE6CCD83E87B9C97E176CC8359EFE1A43BFF84A881
48D5799269B9CBB9AFB4C73B0AF6F76E9B680D47A1075435EA59D4463D0F87580D25E9FD824DBC7A
C52EF23E3F629E74A482BBCCB0BDEAB"
               Name="SecurityApp"
               AssemblyVersion="0.0.0.0"/>
   <IPermission class="System.Security.Permissions.UrlIdentityPermission, mscorl
ib, Version=1.0.2411.0, Culture=neutral, PublicKeyToken=b77a5c561934e089"
               version="1"
               Url="file:///C:/testsecurity/securityapp.exe"/>
   <IPermission class="System.Security.Permissions.ZoneIdentityPermission, mscor
lib, Version=1.0.2411.0, Culture=neutral, PublicKeyToken=b77a5c561934e089"
               version="1"
               Zone="MyComputer"/>
</PermissionSet>

Success
```

As we can see at the bottom of the screenshot it lists which ZoneIdentityPermission the assembly object has been associated with, that being MyComputer. In addition each assembly will get a URLIdentityPermission specifying the location of the executable.

Not only do we have the utility that helps us with managing security permission sets and groups, but we also have a utility that views the security information regarding an assembly called permview.exe. (Permview stands for Permissions Viewer.) Permview is not as complex as Caspol because its main purpose is to give a certain type of feedback regarding the security requests of assemblies. In fact, the Permview utility only has two switches, one for the output location, and one for declarative security to be included in the output. In order to specify an output location the switch is /Output and then a file path is appended to the command line after the switch. The Permview utility brings up another concept we have yet to cover – that of declarative security. Declarative security is displayed in the Permview utility with the /Decl switch, and is security that a piece of code requests at an assembly level. Since it is at the assembly level, the line which requests the security is at the top of the VB module, even before our Import statements. We can request one of three levels of security as shown in the table below:

Level	Description
RequestMinimum	Permissions the code must have in order to run
RequestOptional	Permissions that code may use, but could run without
RequestRefused	Permissions that you want to ensure are never granted to the code

Requesting permissions at the assembly level will help ensure that the code will be able to run, and not get permission based security exceptions. Since we have users calling our code, the declarative security ensures the callers have proper security to do all that our code requires, otherwise a security exception will be thrown. Below is an example of the syntax of how we would request minimum permissions, and the code would be placed at the top of our procedure. This example also illustrates syntax as described in the table at the beginning of our chapter regarding permissions in the `Security.Permissions` namespace. It also illustrates the use of a security constant, `SecurityAction.RequestMinimum` for the type of security we are requesting.

```
<Assembly: SecurityPermissionAttribute(SecurityAction.RequestMinimum)>
```

Once this line is added to our assembly, `Permview` will report on what the assembly requested by listing minimal, optional, and refused permission sets – including our security permission set under the minimal set listing.

Cryptography Under .NET

Cryptography is a very deep subject in the .NET environment, as Microsoft has given us a wide set of tools to assist in many of the cryptography needs that we encounter when we are trying to encode and decode data, creating hashing algorithms, generating random numbers, authenticating messages, and formulating digital signatures. If we wish to require the use certificates for applications that access our code, we need to use a digital signature to do so. In this section we'll be concentrating on how we will use digital signatures to sign our code, but we'll do an overview of some of the definitions and utilities that help us in our cryptography needs.

Digital signatures use what is known as a public-key method of encoding and decoding data. Each entity that will access data needs to maintain a pair of related keys, one of which is a public-key, the other of which is termed a private-key, both being unique to the assembly for which the keys were generated. The public-key and private-key form a key pair that is used in communications between the caller of a program and the host of a program. The public-key can be made available to anyone wishing to use the assembly because it is used to encode the data that is sent to receivers. The private portion of the key is kept private by the receiver and is used to decode the data received. Digital signatures use the public-key method to authenticate an identity and protect the integrity of data. The digital signature is a means by which people can identify a piece of code, rather than an encrypt/decrypt mechanism. Hash functions, random number generation, and message authentication codes are means to encrypt and decrypt information. Once the functions, numbers or codes are generated programmers can use them in custom cryptography algorithms.

There are many command line tools in the .NET Framework, including `Caspol` and `Permview`, which help us with the security of our system. Below is a table with the utilities and a description of what they do:

Tool	Description
Al	Assembly Generation Utility, takes files and creates a Portable Execution File
Caspol	Security management utility
Cert2Spc	Creates a Software Publisher's Certificate
CertMgr	Manages Certificates and Trust Lists
ChkTrust	Checks the Validity of a signed file
MakeCert	Generates a test-only certificate
Permview	Requested Permission Viewing utility
Peverify	Determines type-safety of an assembly

Table continued on following page

Tool	Description
Secutil	Obtains a X509 Certificate or strong name in a manner easily integrated in source files
SetReg	Changes registry settings for certificates and digital signatures
Signcode	Digitally signs an assembly
Sn	Strong Name Tool - Key manager and signature verification for strong names
StoreAdm	Manages isolated storage – lists or removes existing stores for specific user

We will concentrate here on the Signcode utility, which allows us to digitally sign an assembly. The Signcode utility has the ability to sign an assembly so that it is easier to see the details regarding security restrictions to be placed on the assembly. The utility signs an assembly file, or in other words associates an assembly file with a certificate file. Although the Signcode utility has many options, the only required arguments are the option we want to use to sign with and either assembly file to sign. While there are certificate providers to obtain real certificates from, such as Verisign, we can also make test certificates for our testing purposes. Below is an example using the makecert command to make a test certificate for our sample application in this chapter, as well as an example of using signcode to sign our test application with our test certificate:

Below is a table of all of the options from the Signcode utility with a description of each option:

Option	Description
-$ authority	Digital signing authority
-a algorithm	Hashing algorithm for signing (Sha1 or Md5 which is default)
-c file	Software publishing certificate file
-cn name	Common Name of Certificate
-I info	Place to go for additional info (URL)
-j dllname	Name of DLL that contains and returns attributes for signing files
-jp parameter	Parameter to be passed with -j option. Parameter is specific to invividual DLL listed in -j parameter
-k keyname	Key container name
-ky keytype	Key type

Option	Description
-n name	Text name representing content of file to be signed
-p provider	Name of the cryptographic provider on the system
-r location	Location of the certificate store in the registry – default is current user
-s store	Certificate store containing signing certificates
-sha1 thumbprint	If using Sha1 algorithm, this is the hash of the certificate
-sp policy	Add all certificates to a chain or just to the Spc store
-spc file	File for containing certificates
-t URL	Timestamp when signing
-tr number	The number of timestamp attempts until success
-tw number	The delay between each timestamp
-v pvkfile	File containing private key
-x	Do not sign file, timestamp only
-y type	Cryptographic provider type to use
-?	Displays help

Once an assembly is signed, the certificate information is available as evidence for use in security policy decisions.

Along with digital signatures and the utilities we have outlined so far we also have the System.Security.Cryptography namespace which provides many of the Cryptographic services in the .NET environment including hashing, random number generation, and formation of digital signatures. The Cryptographic services in .NET implement what is known as **Symmetric** and **Asymmetric** algorithms. What we have been talking about so far, the Public-Key and Private-Key pair combinations is an example of an Asymmetric algorithm. The Cryptography namespace can help to generate and verify key pair combinations. Symmetric algorithms only require a single key for encryption and decryption, and the Cryptography namespace can help generate and verify the Symmetric algorithms as well. In addition to these algorithms, the Cryptography namespace can assist in using hash functions and random number generation to generate unique values to assign to our assemblies to assist in generating unique encrypted keys.

Summary

In this chapter, we discussed many aspects of security in relation to our code. Let's recap over what we reviewed:

- ❏ We said that it is important to identify and request any permissions that our code needs to have at various levels, in order for our code to run in an optimal way and not to generate unnecessary exceptions.

- ❏ We looked at the `System.Security.Permissions` namespace and how it relates to managing permissions within our code.

- ❏ We reviewed three types of security – role, based, code access, based, and identity, based – and how these types relate and can be used in the permissions processing sections of our code.

- ❏ We looked at some examples of working with code access permissions against the file system, registry, and environment variable classes within the `Permissions` namespace.

- ❏ We generated an assembly object, which included a strong name, and discussed how this comes into play when using the security command line utilities.

- ❏ We reviewed the two command line utilities for security management, `Caspol` and `Permview`.

- ❏ We discussed cryptography and how we can use the `Signcode` utility to sign our assemblies.

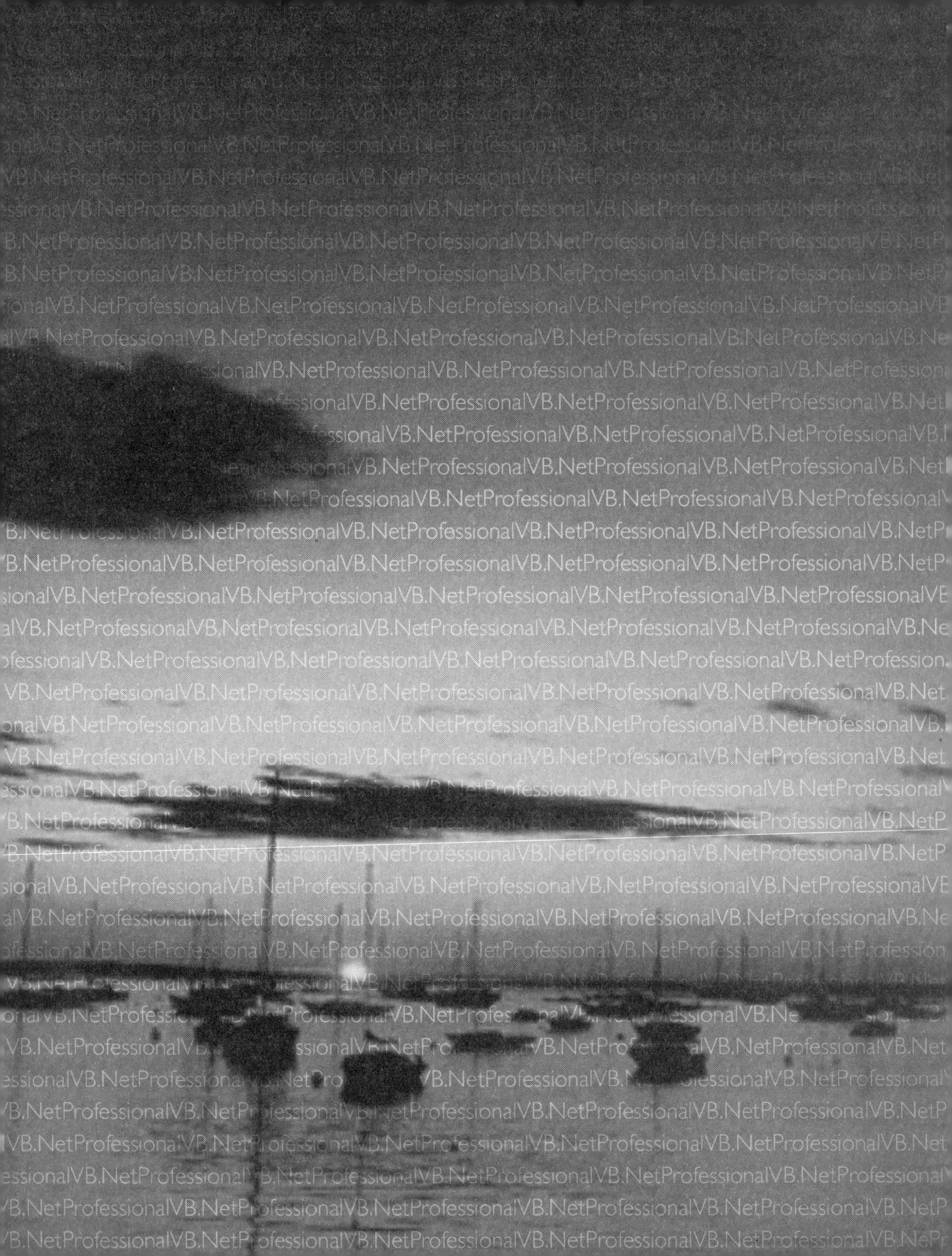

Using the Visual Basic Compatibility Library

The Visual Basic Compatibility Library is provided in the .NET environment in order to assist in the conversion of existing code, as well as providing backward compatibility and support for developers who are transitioning to the new version. There has been much said about the newest version of VB, and how we should handle our legacy code. Many are saying that anything new should be started in the latest version, and anything old should be rewritten from ground up instead of run through a conversion. Regardless of which way we choose to handle our VB6 code, the compatibility library will come in handy along the way. While the compatibility library is a very nice tool, please keep in mind as we go through this chapter that our main goal should be to use it as a temporary solution to the learning curve presented by new software revisions. Please also keep in mind that the compatibility library is not all-inclusive and therefore may not assist in all instances when a programmer is undergoing the task of converting code to VB.NET.

What is the Compatibility Library?

The compatibility library is a library made up of the VB6 functions that have been replaced in VB.NET due to reorganization into different libraries, syntax changes or just that they weren't deemed necessary anymore. At the end of the chapter is a complete list, including information about what each function was replaced by. The library is used by the conversion tools and can also be used by adding a reference to it within a VB.NET project.

When the Library is used by the Conversion Tools

The compatibility library is referenced automatically in any project that has run through the conversion tool. During the conversion, if a function is no longer supported, it has a note by it and the VB6 compatibility library equivalent is used. The notes that appear in the code are comments right by the line of code where the issue is. For instance, when the conversion tool was run on the VB6 version of the VBBank DLL the conversion tool placed the following note in the Account class module due to a change in support of the GetObjectContext.SetAbort statement:

'UPGRADE_ISSUE: COM expression not supported: Module methods of COM objects. Click for more: ms-help://MS.MSDNVS/vbcon/html/vbup1060.htm

It is important to review code that is noted and replace it with the newer code syntax since the older code will not be as efficient.

A couple of examples of when the library has been used by the conversion tools follow. The examples are taken from running the VBBank sample through the conversion utility and comparing that to the new sample in the VB.NET samples library.

In the VB6 version of the VBBank there are a few things we can look at that have changed, encompassing the topics of default properties and object creation.

First of all, the default properties for fields in ADO recordsets have changed. In VB6 the code that was getting the Balance field from a recordset looked like:

```
lngBalance = adoRS.Fields("Balance").Value
```

When run through the conversion utility it changed to:

```
lngBalance = VB6.GetDefaultProperty &_
(adoRS.Fields("Balance").Value)
```

In the VB.NET version this same code is written as:

```
IntBalance = cint(adoRS.Fields("Balance").Value)
```

As you can see there are two important changes in the line of code written in VB.NET. Not only is there a change in where our default data type changes are reflected, but also the VB6.DefaultProperty does not need to be designated. The default property changes as they relate to recordsets are primarily for making code easy to read. For instance using the same VB.NET structure above, the default property is Item for the Fields object, so we didn't need to specify it as:

```
IntBalance = cint(adoRS.Fields.Item("Balance").Value)
```

(Although it should be noted that the Item designator would work). In contrast, we can no longer take as many shortcuts as we used to. For instance below is an example that would not work, since, at the very least, the Fields collection must be designated now:

```
IntBalance = cint(adoRS("Balance").Value)
```

With respect to the changes in the way we create objects, the conversion utility incorporates the use of the compatibility library in the following way:

```
objCreateTable = VB6.CreateObject("VB6Bank.CreateTable")
```

The VB.NET code for this same type of instruction is as follows, illustrating the use of the new keyword in object creation:

```
Dim ct as New CreateTable
```

The main point to the object creation changes is to simplify the code used. As illustrated above, where we declared the object then set the variable equal to the created object, we now can use the new keyword in one line to accomplish the same task.

When to use the Library in projects

The compatibility library is primarily for transitioning to the new environment. As you will see outlined in the table at the end of the chapter, there are a *few* major changes to the language which drive *most* of the changes in syntax with regards to the functions. As mentioned before, the conversion tools automatically put the reference into a converted project, but we want to clean up our projects and remove the reference for stability and speed.

Referencing the Compatibility Library

The compatibility library can be added as a reference, and is located under the .NET Framework tab of the Add Reference dialog. It is listed as Microsoft.VisualBasic.Compatibility, as illustrated in the following screen shot:

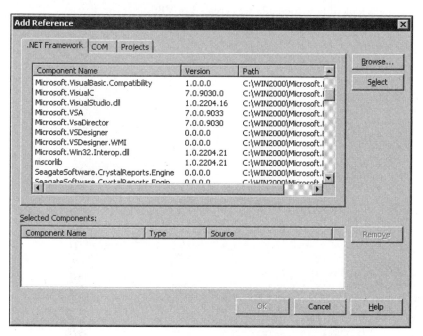

Once the reference is added to the project you will want to add the following imports line to your code:

```
Imports Microsoft.VisualBasic.Compatibility
```

Compatibility Library Examples

Let's start with looking at `FileIO` operation changes, which make up a good deal of our compatibility library. We open files differently, write and read from files a little differently, and close files differently now. We'll use a small sample executable project to illustrate how `FileIO` has changed. The code below our screenshot is taken from the `Click` event of the button:

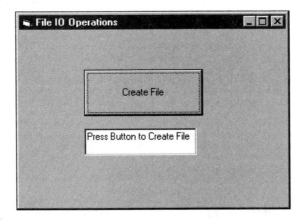

Our code simply opens a file, writes two lines to it, and closes the file, populating a textbox with status while working. Let's look at how the code was created in VB6:

```
'This is VB6 code
Private Sub cmdCreateFile_Click()
    Dim Handle As Integer
    Handle = FreeFile
Open "c:\Testing.txt" For Output As Handle
    txtCreate = "Writing File"
Write #Handle, "This is line 1"
Write #Handle, "This is line 2"
Close #Handle
    txtCreate = "File Written"
End Sub
```

Now, let's look at what the conversion tool did with our code:

```
Private Sub cmdCreateFile_Click(ByVal eventSender As System.Object, ByVal
eventArgs As System.EventArgs) Handles cmdCreateFile.Click
    Dim Handle As Short
    Handle = FreeFile()
    FileOpen(Handle, "c:\Testing.txt",OpenMode.Output)
    txtCreate.Text = "Writing File"
    WriteLine(Handle, "This is line 1")
```

```
      WriteLine(Handle, "This is line 2")
      FileClose(Handle)
      txtCreate.Text = "File Written"
   End Sub
```

There are a few alterations to our code that should interest us here. The conversion tool changed how our variable was dimensioned to Short instead of Integer due to the changes in data type definition.

In addition we can see how our Open and Write functions have changed to FileOpen and WriteLine. In VB6 we opened a file with:

```
Open "c:\Testing.txt" For Output As Handle
```

The conversion utility changed it to the syntax of the updated FileOpen function as:

```
FileOpen(Handle, "c:\Testing.txt",OpenMode.Output)
```

As you can see, there is just a syntactical difference between the two lines, changing to a function that has the OpenMode parameter within it. In addition, while in VB6 we write a line to the file using the following syntax:

```
Write #Handle, "This is line 1"
```

In VB.NET the function now looks like:

```
WriteLine(Handle, "This is line 1")
```

Along with those functions, the conversion tool has forced us to use property assignment with our textbox because the default properties of Object are dealt with differently now, as illustrated by the following code:

```
txtCreate.Text = "Writing File"
```

Now let's look at one approach we could use to do the same thing in VB.NET:

```
Private Sub cmdCreateFile_Click(ByVal sender As System.Object, ByVal e As
System.EventArgs) Handles

cmdCreateFile.Click
Dim objWriter As New IO.StreamWriter(File.Open&_
   ("c:\Testing.txt",FileMode.OpenOrCreate))
txtcreate.Text = "Writing File"
objWriter.Write("This is Line 1")
objwriter.Write("This is Line 2")
objWriter.Flush()
objWriter.Close()
txtCreate.Text = "File Written"
objWriter = Nothing
End Sub
```

When working with the `StreamWriter` object and other associated file functions, we need to keep in mind that they have moved to the `System.IO` namespace. The major differences in how we do things include, using stream writers to create, read, and write files as well as having the open and close functions directly related to the stream writer interface instead of directly opening the file through a file handle.

The other major revision area that you will note from our reference table is the way we handle forms. Let's look specifically at how the constants and default properties have changed in comparison to VB6. The example shown below is the `Click` event of the button shown on the screen shot:

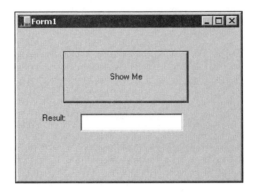

First, let's look at the code as it was in VB6. You will see we use VB constants which determines our message box style and the comparison in our `if` statement:

```
'This is VB6 code
    Private Sub cmdGoForIt_Click()
    Dim bRes As String
bRes = MsgBox("Click OK for testing", vbOKCancel,&_
 "Testing")
    If bRes = vbOK Then
        txtResult = bRes
    Else
        txtResult = "You should have hit OK"
    End If
    End Sub
```

Below is the code after running through the conversion utility. You will see that we have the `MsgBoxResult.OK` evaluation as well as the `MsgBoxStyle.OKCancel` method replacing `vbOKCancel`:

```
'Conversion tool code
Private Sub cmdGoForIt_Click (ByVal eventSender  & _
As System.Object, ByVal eventArgs As System.EventArgs)
    Dim bRes As String
    bRes = CStr(MsgBox("Click OK for testing", MsgBoxStyle.OKCancel, "Testing"))
If bRes = CStr(MsgBoxResult.OK) Then
        txtResult.Text = bRes
    Else
        txtResult.Text = "You should have hit OK"
    End If
End Sub
```

Now let's look at how we would do it in VB.NET:

```
'VB.NET code
Private Sub cmdGoForIt_Click(ByVal sender &_
As Object, ByVal e As System.EventArgs)
    Dim bRes As Integer
bres = (MessageBox.Show("Click OK for testing", &_
"Testing", MessageBox.OKCancel))
    If bRes = DialogResult.OK Then
        txtResult.Text = str(bres)
    Else
        txtResult.Text = "You should have hit OK"
    End If
End Sub
```

When we look at our lines that evaluate the results of our messagebox we can see how our code has been changed. Our VB6 code such as:

```
If bRes = vbOK Then
```

has been altered by the conversion utility so as to read as:

```
        If bRes = CStr(MsgBoxResult.OK) Then
```

and has changed to be more specific to the functions that relate to the object the program is dealing with in VB.NET:

```
        If bRes = DialogResult.OK Then
```

In summary, as you can see from the examples, the major areas which have changed have done so dramatically. As a result, it is important to choose wisely between code conversion and rewriting code completely, although the conversion utility can be nice to use as a source of information regarding what will need to be changed in our existing code. We have a nice tool in the compatibility library to help us through the change, but as always, learning the new coding styles will be the most efficient way to tackle projects in the future.

The following pages have a complete listing of the compatibility library and the reasons and replacements for the functions that are included.

Compatibility Library Reference Listing

This section provides a complete list of the compatibility functions and what they are replaced by in the .NET environment. As mentioned before, the .NET replacements fall into several categories. The categories we will reference here include Declaration syntax changes, Elements replaced by Methods, Data type change, Boolean Operator changes, and Class and Interface Changes.

Declaration Syntax Changes

Declaration Syntax changes mainly encompass declaring multiple variables on one line. For instance, where in VB6 the following statement would evaluate to both variables being an integer:

```
Dim A as Integer, B as Integer
```

in VB.NET we can do the same thing without repeating the As Integer keywords:

```
Dim A, B as Integer
```

Elements Replaced by Methods

Method, Element	Changed Reason	New Method, Element, Namespace
CopyArray	Moved to Copy method of Array class	Copy method of Array class
FontChangeBold	Moved to Font class of System.Drawing namespace	Bold property of Font class relative to an object that the Font class is being applied to
FontChangeItalic	Moved to Font class of System.Drawing namespace	Italic property of Font class relative to an object that the Font class is being applied to
FontChangeName	Moved to Font class of System.Drawing namespace	Name property of Font class relative to an object that the Font class is being applied to
FontChangeSize	Moved to Font class of System.Drawing namespace	Size property of Font class relative to an object that the Font class is being applied to
FontChangeStrikeOut	Moved to Font class of System.Drawing namespace	StrikeOut property of Font class relative to an object that the Font class is being applied to
FontChangeUnderline	Moved to Font class of System.Drawing namespace	Underline property of Font class relative to an object that the Font class is being applied to
FontChangeWeight	Moved to Font class of System.Drawing namespace	Size property of Font class relative to an object that the Font class is being applied to
Math	Moved to Math class in System	
Oct	Moved to Math class	
PixelstoTwipsX	Moved to System.Drawing namespace	See Point Converter class
PixelstoTwipsY	Moved to System.Drawing namespace	See Point Converter class

Data Type Changes

The data type changes that affect us most in the VB.NET environment surround the date and time functions, integer data type changes, and universal data type changes. The changes to date and time functionality are mainly data type changes to 8 byte formats. The Integer data types have been expanded and changed. What used to be an Integer in VB6 was a 16 bit size, and is now a 32 bit size. The 16 bit size has been changed to the Short data type. The previous Long data type was a 32 bit size, and is now a 64 bit size. Constant usage and support for the standard VB constants has changed as well. Constants from VB6, such as the familiar VBOK we used for messagebox feedback has changed to be supported within the objects they relate to. For instance, as we illustrated in our previous examples, what we used to see as a plain VBOK return from a messagebox is now declared as a DialogResult.OK.

Method, Element	Changed Reason	New Method, Element, Namespace
FixedLengthString	Data type change	Strings are no longer fixed length
ZorderConstants	Support changed for constants	

Boolean Operator Changes

In VB6 the And, Or, Not were used for Bitwise and Boolean operations. In the new version of VB they have added specific Bitwise operators so that our regular And, Or, Not, and Xor are Boolean as contrasted with BitAnd, BitOr, BitNot, and BitXOr being Bitwise.

Method, Element	Changed Reason	New Method, Element, Namespace
And	Bitwise operation changes – expanded to have new Bitwise elements	And as well as BitAnd
Imp	Replaced by = operator	
EQV	Replaced by = operator	
Or	Bitwise operation changes – expanded to have new Bitwise elements	Or as well as BitOr
Not	Bitwise operation changes – expanded to have new Bitwise elements	Not as well as BitNot
Xor	Bitwise operation changes – expanded to have new Bitwise elements	Xor as well as BitXOr

Class and Interface Changes

There are a couple of new classes which encompass the majority of our changes from generic VB6 functions to class-based functions in VB.NET. The `System.Windows.Forms` namespace holds all of the classes that make up the objects that we place on our forms and their properties. Also, the `System.IO` namespace has been added to encompass the file access functionality. The first table below relates to the `System.Windows.Forms` namespace, and the second table is an alphabetic listing of other namespaces that are affected:

Method, Element	Changed Reason	New Method, Element, Namespace
ButtonArray	Replaced by `Button` class in new `System.Windows.Forms`	
ComboBoxArray	Moved to `CheckBox` class in `System.Windows.Forms`	
CheckBoxArray	Moved to `CheckBox` class in `System.Windows.Forms`	
CheckedListBox Array	Moved to `CheckBox` class in `System.Windows.Forms`	
DirDrive	Moved to `System.Windows.Forms`	Use `OpenFileDialog` and `SaveFileDialog` methods
DirListBox	Moved to `System.Windows.Forms`	Use `OpenFileDialog` and `SaveFileDialog` methods
DirListBox Array	Moved to `System.Windows.Forms`	Use `OpenFileDialog` and `SaveFileDialog` methods
DriveListBox	Moved to `System.Windows.Forms`	Use `OpenFileDialog` and `SaveFileDialog` methods
DriveListBox Array	Moved to `System.Windows.Forms`	Use `OpenFileDialog` and `SaveFileDialog` methods
FileListBox	Moved to `System.Windows.Forms`	Use `OpenFileDialog` and `SaveFileDialog` methods
FileListBox Array	Moved to `System.Windows.Forms`	Use `OpenFileDialog` and `SaveFileDialog` methods
GetCancel	Moved to `System.Windows.Forms`	`CancelButton` property of `Form`
GetDefault	Moved to `System.Windows.Forms`	Default button has moved to be the `Accept` button property
GetFile Description	Moved to `System.Windows.Forms`	`FileVersionInfo.` `FileDescription` property
GetItemData	Moved to `System.Windows.Forms`	Use `ItemData` property of object
GetItemString	Moved to `System.Windows.Forms`	Use `GetItemText` method

Method, Element	Changed Reason	New Method, Element, Namespace
GroupBoxArray	Moved to System.Windows.Forms	Group Box Collection of GroupBox class
LabelArray	Moved to System.Windows.Forms	
ListBoxArray	Moved to System.Windows.Forms	
ListBoxItem	Moved to System.Windows.Forms	
MenuItemArray	Moved to System.Windows.Forms	
PanelArray	Moved to System.Windows.Forms	
PictureBox Array	Moved to System.Windows.Forms	
ShowForm	Moved to System.Windows.Forms	Changed to Form.Show
Support	Moved to System.Windows.Forms	
TabControl Array	Moved to System.Windows.Forms	
TabLayout	Moved to System.Windows.Forms	TabBase class
TextBoxArray	Moved to System.Windows.Forms	
TimerArray	Moved to System.Windows.Forms	
WhatsThisMode	Moved to System.Windows.Forms	
Zorder	Moved to System.Windows.Forms	

Method, Element	Changed Reason	New Method, Element, Namespace
BaseControl Array	Replaced by BaseControlBuilder Class	BaseControlBuilder with Array as type
BaseOCXArray	Replaced by BaseControlBuilder Class	BaseControlBuilder with OCX as type
BOF	Moved to File class in System.IO namespace	

Table continued on following page

Method, Element	Changed Reason	New Method, Element, Namespace
Close	Replaced by `System.IO` namespace file operations	
Constants	Collection of `Constants` is related with object relationships	
CreateObject	`New` keyword instantiates objects	Replace with usage of `New`
EOF	Moved to `File` class in `System.IO` namespace	
FileAttr	Moved to `File` class in `System.IO` namespace	`Attributes` property
FileGet	Moved to `File` class in `System.IO` namespace	
FileGetObject	Moved to `File` class in `System.IO` namespace	
FilePut	Moved to `File` class in `System.IO` namespace	
FilePutObject	Moved to `File` class in `System.IO` namespace	
FileSystem	Replaced by `System.IO` namespace functionality	Use overloaded `Open` methods
Format	Moved to `Format` method members of `System` namespace	Use individual methods of `System` namespace, such as `Decimal.format`
GetActive Control	Moved into `ContainerControl` class	`ActiveControl` property
GetEXEName	Moved to `System.Reflection` namespace	Use `GetExecutingAssembly` method
GetHInstance	Moved to `System.Runtime.Interopser vices` namespace	
GetPath	Moved to `System.IO` namespace	
HscrollBar Array	Replaced by `HscrollBar` class	
LineInput	Moved to `System.IO` namespace	
Open	Moved to `System.IO` namespace	

Method, Element	Changed Reason	New Method, Element, Namespace
OpenAccess	Moved to System.IO namespace	
OpenforAppend	Moved to System.IO namespace	
OpenforInput	Moved to System.IO namespace	
OpenforOutput	Moved to System.IO namespace	
OpenMode	Moved to System.IO namespace	
OpenShare	Moved to System.IO namespace	
SendKeys	Moved to System.IO namespace	SendKeys class
SetAppearance	Moved to System.IO namespace	Choose appropriate appearance property of object being worked with
SetBorderStyle	Moved to System.IO namespace	Use appropriate BorderStyle property for object
SetCancel	Moved to System.IO namespace	CancelButton property of Form
SetDefault	Moved to System.IO namespace	Default button has moved to be the Accept button property
SetDefault Property	Moved to System.IO namespace	DefaultPropertyattribute of field object
SetItemData	Moved to System.IO namespace	Use ItemDate property of object
SetItemString	Moved to System.IO namespace	Use SetItemText method
SetListBoxColumns	Moved to System.IO namespace	Columns property of listbox class
SetResource BaseName	Moved to System.IO namespace	
Tag	Tag property of field no longer supported	
TwipsPerPixelX	Moved to System.Drawing namespace	See Point Converter class

Table continued on following page

Method, Element	Changed Reason	New Method, Element, Namespace
`TwipsPerPixelY`	Moved to `System.Drawing` namespace	See `Point Converter` class
`TwipsToPixelsX`	Moved to `System.Drawing` namespace	See `Point Converter` class
`TwipsToPixelsY`	Moved to `System.Drawing` namespace	See `Point Converter` class
`VScrollBar Array`	Replaced by `VscrollBar` class	
`Write`	Moved to `System.IO` namespace	
`WriteLine`	Moved to `System.IO` namespace	

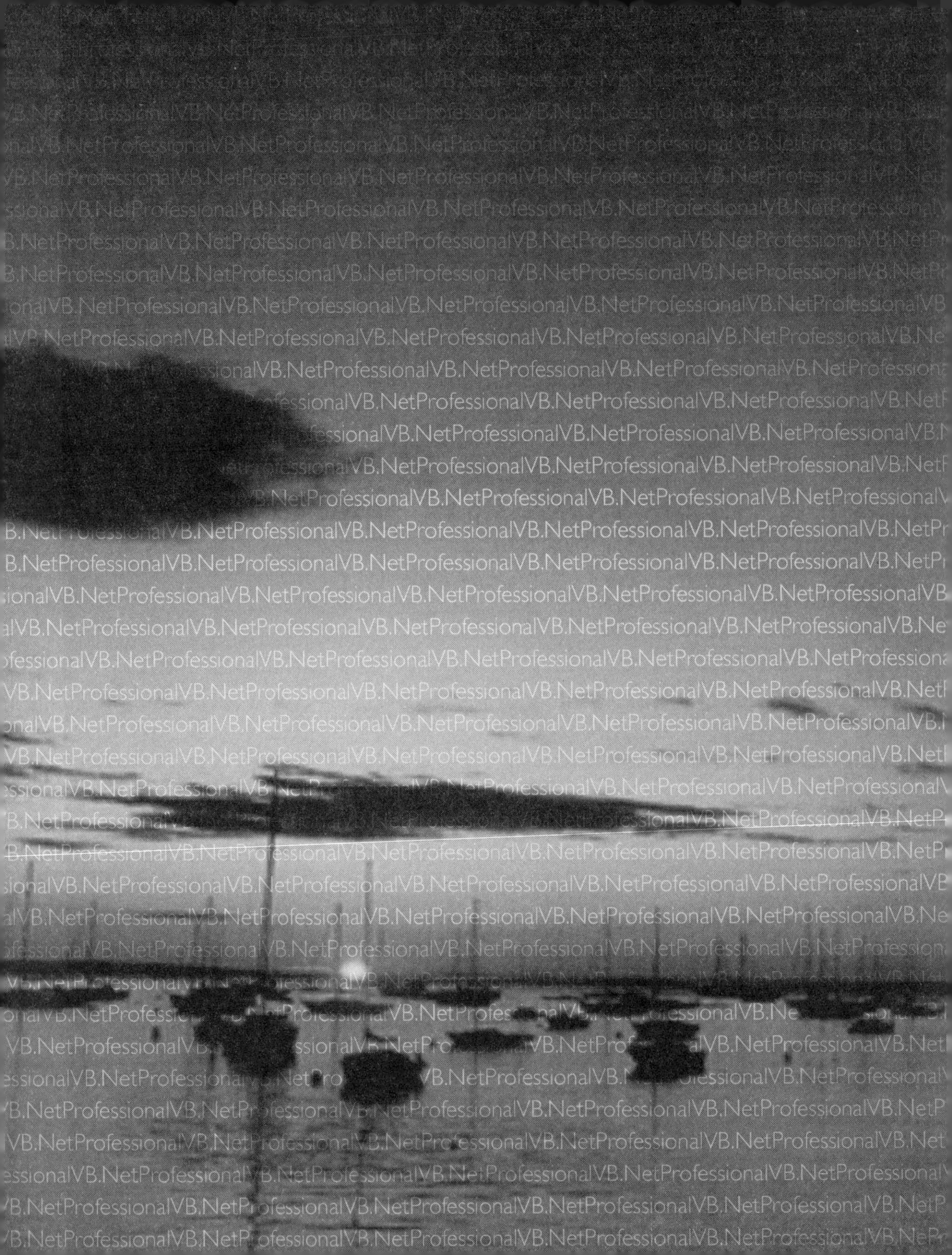

Index

A Guide to the Index

The index is arranged hierarchically, in alphabetical order, with symbols preceding the letter A. Most second-level entries and many third-level entries also occur as first-level entries. This is to ensure that users will find the information they require however they choose to search for it.

909

G

O

S

Effective Data Presentation using ASP.NET Server Control

Introduction

Effective data presentation is not simply a case of presenting the data effectively, but also of efficient retrieval of the data; and to achieve maximum efficiency during paging, we have to take only the data required for display. Here we see two different methods for doing this. While using datagrid's in-built paging functionality, the control displays the navigation buttons (either Next and Previous buttons or numeric page numbers). However every time a user clicks these links, the data source is recreated and re-bound to the DataGrid. The entire data source, not just the page being displayed, is returned. If the table we are paging through has thousands of records in it, all the records are queried, transported to the Web Form, and then a selected few (the current page) are displayed. This results in a serious resource issue on the database.

So by customizing the paging we can control the number of records returned from the database. In this series of two articles I will be demonstrating two methods of implementing a custom paging solution using the ASP.NET and server controls with SQL Server. The page, which we will create, renders ten records per page from the Orders table in the Northwind database. There are two types of page-navigation links:

❑   A VCR-style navigation panel, which contains buttons, that allows the user to move to first, last, previous, or next page.

❑   Jumps to a specific page type navigation.

Record paging:

Paging through records becomes an essential part of many Web applications, when the application handles large amount of data and all of the data has to be displayed to the user. One of ASP's greatest features is the ease with which an ASP page can access, retrieve, or modify the database information. To achieve this we intermix the HTML and Server-Side Script to present the data effectively. ASP.NET though, the next generation of ASP, offers new means of retrieving data with ADO+ or ADO.Net, along with its full set of complex controls including embedded controls (such as the **Repeater, DataList,** and **DataGrid ASP.NET** controls) with flexible means of binding controls to information in a data store. This approach allows us to bind any control property to information in almost any kind of data store, from the simplest to the most sophisticated, and gives virtually complete control over the data movement, from the data store to the page and back.

DataGrid Web Control:

As the name specifies the DataGrid control presents the data in a tabular manner. The DataGrid ASP.NET server control is a multi-column, data-bound grid, which allows us to define various types of columns, both to layout the contents of the grid and also to add a specific functionality. Such functionality includes selecting, editing or sorting, and can also specify the paging behavior, either by automatically setting the DataGrid paging property to true, or by setting the paging property as desired by customizing the datagrid control programmatically. By manually setting the paging property we can provide our own paging controls, and set the page to display. This option allows us to move to any number of pages at a time, jump to a specific page, and so on. **See Figure 1.**

Why Manual Paging?

The DataGrid server control enables easy paging through data. You can set the DataGrid to use paging, and specify a page size (number of records to display). Each time the page is loaded the Datagrid will recreate the entire data set and automatically move to the appropriate place in the data set. It then displays enough rows to make up one page of the grid.

When we are working with a large dataset, recreating the entire dataset each time is a large waste of resources. In such a case, we should retrieve just the records needed for the page at that time. To allow this, we turn off the automatic paging feature of the grid so that it doesn't assume it is working with the entire data set. We then take responsibility in our own code for retrieving only the data for a single page. So manually setting the paging is effective when large amounts of data have to be displayed.

Customizing the Paging with DataGrid:

The Task of getting the correct ten records lies in a Store Procedure that in turn takes a smart query as its input parameter. The query will be dynamically built each time depending upon the data requested.

Procedure for Paging

```
CREATE PROCEDURE [Sp_Paging]
@ParmQuery Varchar (3000),
@ParmTotalRecs Int output
AS
EXEC(@ParmQuery)
SELECT @ParmTotalRecs = COUNT(*) FROM Orders
```

This stored procedure takes the entire query as an input parameter (@ParmQuery). In addition to this it returns the total number of records from the Orders table as an output parameter (@ParmTotalRecs).

Building Smart Query

```
Select Top 10 OrderId,CustomerId,OrderDate,ShippedDate from Orders where OrderId
in (select top 20 OrderId from Orders Order By OrderId ASC) Order by OrderId Desc
```

The above query is built dynamically, and is passed as an input parameter to the stored procedure Sp_paging. Now lets see the way in which this query works:

Assume that the user needs records between 11 and 20 (the second 10 records), to achieve this a sub-query is used. In the sub-query the top 20 records are selected in ascending order and the bottom 10 records are selected in the main query. Basically the subquery gets the 20 records with the highest quantity, it is then the main query, which selects the TOP 10 records, and reverses the sort order so that it returns the bottom 10 records.

Note: The TOP clause limits the number of rows returned in the result set. This works only with SQL Server. For Oracle database we can use ROWNUM pseudocolumn to get exact records. **See query given below:**

```
SELECT * FROM(SELECT ROWNUM R, A.* FROM(select
OrderId,CustomerId,OrderDate,ShippedDate from Orders) A )WHERE R BETWEEN 11 and 20
```

Designing and Creating Web Forms

```
<%@ Import Namespace="System.Data" %>
<%@ Import Namespace="System.Data.SqlClient" %>
<Html>
<head><Title>Custome Paging</Title>
</head>
<body>
<form runat="server" method="post">
<table border=0 width=742 BgColor=#000000><tr align=center><td align=center>
<table border=0 width=740 BgColor=#ffffff><tr align=center><td align=center>
 <asp:DataGrid runat="server" id="DGpaging"
  Width="740"
  Cellpadding="4"
  Cellspacing="0"
  Gridlines="Horizontal"
  HorizontalAlign="Center"
  HeaderStyle-CssClass="tableHeader"
  ItemStyle-CssClass="tableItem"
  AlternatingItemStyle-BackColor="#00bfff"
  AllowPaging="True"
  AllowCustomPaging="True"
  PageSize="10"
  PagerStyle-Visible="False"
 />
 </td></tr>
 <tr align=center><td align=center>
 <b>Page
    <asp:Label id="CurrentPage" CssClass="pageLinks" runat="server" />
    of
    <asp:Label id="TotalPages" CssClass="pageLinks" runat="server" />
 </td></tr>
 <tr align=center><td align=center>
  <asp:LinkButton runat="server" CssClass="pageLinks"
    id="FirstPage" Text="[First Page]"
    OnCommand=" VCRTypeNavigation_OnClick " CommandName="First" />
   <asp:LinkButton runat="server" CssClass="pageLinks"
    id="PreviousPage" Text="[Previous Page]"
    OnCommand=" VCRTypeNavigation_OnClick" CommandName="Prev" />
   <asp:LinkButton runat="server" CssClass="pageLinks"
    id="NextPage" Text="[Next Page]"
```

```
        OnCommand=" VCRTypeNavigation_OnClick" CommandName="Next" />
    <asp:LinkButton runat="server" CssClass="pageLinks"
    id="LastPage" Text="[Last Page]"
    OnCommand=" VCRTypeNavigation_OnClick" CommandName="Last" />
</td></tr>
<tr align=center bgcolor="#00008b"><td>
<asp:label id="PageLabel" runat="server" Font-Name="verdana" Font-Color="#FFFFFF"
Font-size="10pt" />
<asp:TextBox id="PageNumber" runat="server" maxlength ="2" Text="1" />
<asp:button id="gotopage" runat="server"  Text="Go" OnClick = "
GoTopageNavigation_onClick " />
</td>
</tr>
</table>
</td></tr></table>
<Input type="hidden" runat="server" id="TxtReminder">
<Input type="hidden" runat="server" id="TxtPageNo">
</form>
</body>
</html>
```

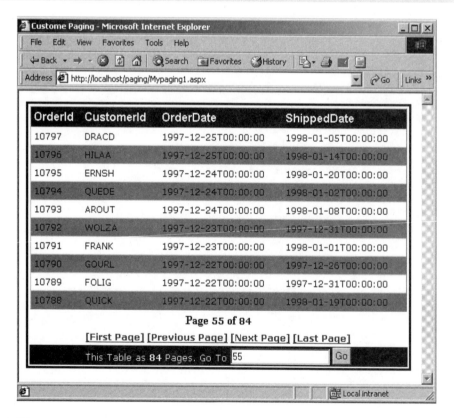

Figure1: The above image shows you the web form design

We place a DataGrid on the web form. Setting the property **allowpaging(default is True)** of the DataGrid to false disables the inbuilt paging property of the DataGrid, but the `PageSize` property is set to the number of pages, here 10, that should be displayed in each page. Since we use our own way of paging through records, we set the `PagerStyle-visible` property to False, which hides the Navigation Links.

Under the DataGrid there are two Label controls. These are used to indicate the current position e.g. page 55 of 84. Below these are the LinkButton controls, which are used to navigate through the data. Each LinkButton specifies an event handled, namely `VCRTypeNavigation_OnClick()`, as its `OnCommand` event handler. The same event handler is used for all the four LinkButtons. Their CommandName property is used to determine the navigation through the pages.

Just under the LinkButton are the Label Control, Textbox Control and a Button Control. The button Control specifies an eventhandler namely `GoToPageNavigation_OnClick()` as its `EventArgs`. This helps in Jumping to the page specified in the textbox control. There are two hidden textboxes, which pass the values between pages to build the query dynamically.

Programmatic Part for Paging:

There are three-event handlers and one method. The event handlers are `Page_Load()`, `VCRTypeNavigation_OnClick()`, `GoToPageNavigation_OnClick()` and the method is `BindData()`. The `Page_Load()` event handler is used to set values only during the initial loading of the page. This is as a click on a Button will trigger a `PostBack` event, which is handled by the `VCRTypeNavigation_OnClick()` and `GoToPageNavigation_OnClick()` event handles. The `BindData()` method is the core of the entire code. This is where a call to the stored procedure is made and returns only the data needed.

The page-level variables are `CurrentPageNo`, `StaringPage`, `EndPage` and `Reminder`. These variables either set the values for building a query, or get the values to build a query, and are used in all the events and methods.

BindData() Method

```
Sub BindData()
 Dim myDataSet              As New DataSet()
 Dim myDataSetCommand       As SQLDataSetCommand
 Dim param                  As SQLParameter
 Dim ConString              As String
 Dim StrSql                 As String
StrSql="Select top " & StartingPage &" OrderId,CustomerId,OrderDate,ShippedDate
from orders where orderid in (select top " & Endpage & " orderid from orders order
by orderid asc) order by orderid desc "

ConString = "server=localhost;database=Northwind;uid=sa;pwd=;"
myDataSetCommand = New SQLDataSetCommand("sp_Paging", ConString)
With myDataSetCommand.SelectCommand
  .CommandType = CommandType.StoredProcedure
  .Parameters.Add(New SQLParameter("@ParmQuery", SqlDBType.VarChar,3000))
  .Parameters.Add(New SQLParameter("@ParmTotalRecs", SqlDBType.Int))
  .Parameters("@ParmTotalRecs").Direction = ParameterDirection.Output
  .Parameters("@ParmQuery").Value =  StrSql
 End With
```

```
myDataSetCommand.FillSet(myDataSet, "orders")
DGPaging.DataSource = myDataSet.Tables("orders").DefaultView
DGPaging.DataBind()
Reminder= myDataSetCommand.SelectCommand.Parameters("@ParmTotalRecs").Value Mod
DGPaging.PageSize
TxtReminder.Value=Reminder
CurrentPageNumber=TxtPageNo.value.CInt(Expression)
CurrentPage.Text=TxtPageNo.value
If Not Page.IsPostBack Then
  TotalPages.Text =
System.Math.Ceiling(myDataSetCommand.SelectCommand.Parameters("@ParmTotalRecs").Va
lue/DGPaging.PageSize)
End If
PageLabel.Text="<font color=#FFFFFF> This Table as <b> " & TotalPages.Text & "</b>
Pages.    Go To </font>"
PageNumber.Text=CurrentPage.Text
Select Case CurrentPageNumber
  Case 1
    PreviousPage.Enabled = "False"
    NextPage.Enabled="True"
  Case TotalPages.Text.CInt(Expression)
    NextPage.Enabled="False"
    PreviousPage.Enabled="True"
  Case Else
    PreviousPage.Enabled="True"
    NextPage.Enabled="True"
End Select
End Sub
```

The BindData() method is used to show the DGPaging (DataGrid control), which displays the records by calling the Stored Procedure SP_Paging. The BindData method uses a DataSet and SQLDataSetCommand to get the data from the database. A dynamically built query is passed as an input parameter (@ParmQuery) to the Procedure. This query is built by setting the Startingpage and Endpage variables to the pages requested. The hidden fields are used to maintain the state of the page. The @ParmTotalRecs parameter is an output parameter, which returns the total number of records in a table, and sets the Reminder variable to calculate the total number of page.

Using Select Case evaluator, we either enable or disable the "Previous Page" and "Next Page" Link Buttons based on the CurrentPageNumber value. We certainly do not want a "Previous Page" link if the user is looking at the first page. The Enable property of the Link Button determines whether the Text property renders with an HREF attribute or not. Either way the text is still displayed.

Page_Load() Event Handler

```
<Script runat="server" language="vb" >
Protected CurrentPageNumber As Integer
Protected StartingPage      As Integer
Protected Reminder          As Integer
Protected Endpage           As Integer

Sub Page_Load(Source As Object, E As EventArgs)
```

```
If  Not Page.IsPostBack Then
   StartingPage=DGpaging.Pagesize
   EndPage=DGpaging.Pagesize
   TxtPageNo.value=1
   BindData()
End If
End Sub
```

A `Page_load()` event is triggered every time a page gets loaded. If the page is not a post back, the `page_load()` event handler calls the method `BindData()` and sets the default values to hidden fields `HiddenStartNo` and `HiddenEndNo` to build the Query. These values are set to show the first ten records in the grid. All other subsequent post backed requests are handled either by `GoTopageNavigation_onClick()` or `VCRTypeNavigation_onClick()` event handlers.

GoTopageNavigation_onClick() Event Handler

```
Sub GoTopageNavigation_onClick(Source As Object, E As EventArgs)
Dim PageNo AS Integer
Reminder=TxtReminder.Value.CInt(Expression)
TxtPageNo.value=PageNumber.Text.CInt(Expression)
PageNo=PageNumber.Text.CInt(Expression)
If PageNo=>TotalPages.Text.CInt(Expression) Then
    If Reminder=0 then
        Startingpage=DGPaging.Pagesize
    Else
        StartingPage=Reminder
  End If
  EndPage=TotalPages.Text.CInt(Expression) * 10
  TxtPageNo.Value=TotalPages.Text.CInt(Expression)
Else
  Startingpage=DGPaging.Pagesize
  EndPage=PageNo * 10
End if
BindData()
End Sub
```

`GoToPageNavigation_onClick()` event handler is triggered whenever the user clicks on the **Go** submit button, after setting the value in the Textbox `pageNumber`. This event handler checks whether the requested page is the last one, if so it checks for the number of records available in the last page by checking the value in the `TXTReminder` hidden field. If value in `TxtReminder` is greater than zero then that value is set to the `Startingpage` variable. If the requested page is not the last one then the requested page value with the multiple of 10 will be assigned to the `EndPage` variable. The `BindData()` method is called, after setting the values for `StartingPage` and `EndPage`.

VCRTypeNavigation_onClick Event Handler

```
Sub VCRTypeNavigation_OnClick(Source As Object, E As CommandEventArgs)
 Reminder=TxtReminder.Value.CInt(Expression)
 Select Case e.CommandName
 Case "First"
  StartingPage=DGPaging.Pagesize
```

```
      CurrentPageNumber = 1
      TxtPageNo.value=CurrentPageNumber
      EndPage=CurrentpageNumber * 10
Case "Last"
   if Reminder=0 then
        Startingpage=DGPaging.Pagesize
   Else
        StartingPage=Reminder
   End If
   CurrentPageNumber = TotalPages.Text.CInt(Expression)
   TxtPageNo.value=CurrentPageNumber
   EndPage=CurrentpageNumber * 10
Case "Next"
   if CurrentPage.Text.CInt(Expression)+1=TotalPages.Text.CInt(Expression) then
        StartingPage=Reminder
   Else
        StartingPage=DGPaging.Pagesize
   End if
   CurrentPageNumber = CurrentPage.Text.CInt(Expression) +1
   TxtPageNo.value=CurrentPageNumber
   EndPage=CurrentpageNumber * 10
Case "Prev"
   StartingPage=DGPaging.Pagesize
   CurrentPageNumber = CurrentPage.Text.CInt(Expression) -1
   TxtPageNo.value=CurrentPageNumber
   EndPage=CurrentpageNumber * 10
End Select
BindData()
End Sub
```

`NavigationLink_OnClick()`VCRTypeNavigation_OnClick() event handler is triggered whenever the user clicks on any of the four Link Buttons namely **'First'**, **'Last'**, 'Next' or 'Prev'. Here we simply reset the values for the `CurrentPageNumber`, `StartingPage` and `EndPage` variables depending on the link clicked. In the Last and Next Select Case evaluator we first check whether the requested page is similar to the `GoToPageTypeNagigater_onClick()` Event Handler. The `BindData()` method is called after the values are set.

Summary

In this article we have seen the way of customizing the paging behavior using the ASP.Net's DataGrid, and have also seen two different styles of paging. These paging techniques can also be used in other ASP.Net server controls and also in our classic ASP applications.

In my next article on Effective Data Presentation using ASP.Net Server controls I would like to discuss another paging method. This time using SQL Server 2000's user-defined function, and DataList control, with a simple example of a shopping cart application.

http://msdn.microsoft.com/library/periodic/period00/ASPPlus.htm
http://msdn.microsoft.com/library/periodic/period00/adoplus.htm
http://www.asptoday.com/articles/20000925.htm
http://www.asptoday.com/articles/20000926.htm

p2p.wrox.com
The programmer's resource centre

A unique free service from Wrox Press
with the aim of helping programmers to help each other

Wrox Press aims to provide timely and practical information to today's programmer. P2P is a list server offering a host of targeted mailing lists where you can share knowledge with your fellow programmers and find solutions to your problems. Whatever the level of your programming knowledge, and whatever technology you use, P2P can provide you with the information you need.

ASP — Support for beginners and professionals, including a resource page with hundreds of links, and a popular ASP+ mailing list.

DATABASES — For database programmers, offering support on SQL Server, mySQL, and Oracle.

MOBILE — Software development for the mobile market is growing rapidly. We provide lists for the several current standards, including WAP, WindowsCE, and Symbian.

JAVA — A complete set of Java lists, covering beginners, professionals,and server-side programmers (including JSP, servlets and EJBs)

.NET — Microsoft's new OS platform, covering topics such as ASP+, C#, and general .Net discussion.

VISUAL BASIC — Covers all aspects of VB programming, from programming Office macros to creating components for the .Net platform.

WEB DESIGN — As web page requirements become more complex, programmer sare taking a more important role in creating web sites. For these programmers, we offer lists covering technologies such as Flash, Coldfusion, and JavaScript.

XML — Covering all aspects of XML, including XSLT and schemas.

OPEN SOURCE — Many Open Source topics covered including PHP, Apache, Perl, Linux, Python and more.

FOREIGN LANGUAGE — Several lists dedicated to Spanish and German speaking programmers, categories include .Net, Java, XML, PHP and XML.

How To Subscribe

Simply visit the P2P site, at **http://p2p.wrox.com/**

Select the 'FAQ' option on the side menu bar for more information about the subscription process and our service.

wrox

Programmer to Programmer™

Wrox writes books for you. Any suggestions, or ideas about how you want information given in your ideal book will be studied by our team.
Your comments are always valued at Wrox.

Free phone in USA 800-USE-WROX
Fax (312) 893 8001

UK Tel.: (0121) 687 4100   Fax: (0121) 687 4101

Professional VB.NET – Registration Card

Name _____

Address _____

_____

_____

City _____ State/Region_____

Country _____ Postcode/Zip_____

E-Mail _____

Occupation _____

How did you hear about this book?

☐ Book review (name) _____

☐ Advertisement (name) _____

☐ Recommendation _____

☐ Catalog _____

☐ Other _____

Where did you buy this book?

☐ Bookstore (name) _____ City_____

☐ Computer store (name) _____

☐ Mail order_____

☐ Other _____

What influenced you in the purchase of this book?

☐ Cover Design ☐ Contents ☐ Other (please specify):

How did you rate the overall content of this book?

☐ Excellent ☐ Good ☐ Average ☐ Poor

What did you find most useful about this book? _____

_____

_____

What did you find least useful about this book? _____

_____

_____

Please add any additional comments. _____

_____

What other subjects will you buy a computer book on soon?

_____

What is the best computer book you have used this year?

_____

Note: This information will only be used to keep you updated about new Wrox Press titles and will not be used for any other purpose or passed to any other third party.

wrox

Programmer to Programmer™

Note: If you post the bounce back card below in the UK, please send it to:

Wrox Press Limited, Arden House, 1102 Warwick Road,
Acocks Green, Birmingham B27 6HB. UK.

Computer Book Publishers